PENNSYLVANIA GERMAN PIONEERS

IN TWO VOLUMES

Volume I

1727–1775

Map of the Palatinate during the Eighteenth Century
(From J. B. Homann's Atlas, Nurenberg, 1716)

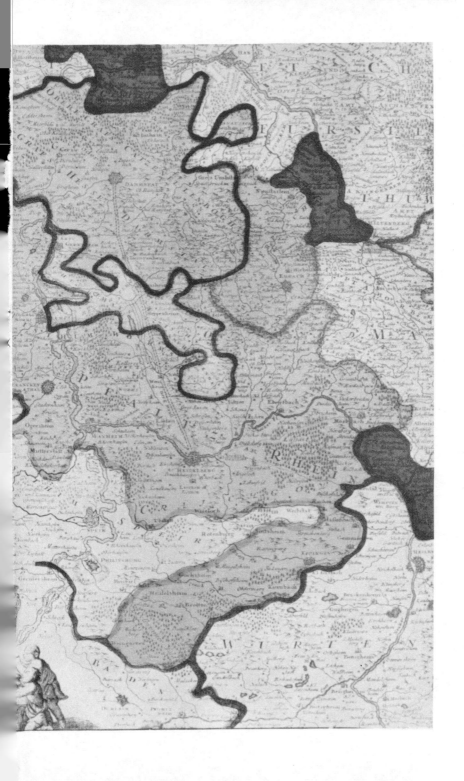

PENNSYLVANIA GERMAN PIONEERS

A Publication of the Original Lists of Arrivals
In the Port of Philadelphia
From 1727 to 1808

By

RALPH BEAVER STRASSBURGER, LL.D.

President of the Pennsylvania German Society

Edited by

WILLIAM JOHN HINKE, PH.D., D.D

Second Printing

IN TWO VOLUMES

VOLUME I
1727 - 1775

Baltimore

GENEALOGICAL PUBLISHING CO., INC.

1980

Originally Published: Norristown, Pennsylvania, 1934
Reprinted, with the permission of the
Pennsylvania German Society,
by Genealogical Publishing Co., Inc.
Baltimore, 1966, 1975, 1980
Publisher's Preface © 1966
by Genealogical Publishing Co., Inc.
Baltimore, Maryland
All Rights Reserved
Library of Congress Catalogue Card Number 66-23871
International Standard Book Number: Volume I: 0-8063-0323-9
Set Number: 0-8063-0882-6
Made in the United States of America

Publisher's Preface

The publisher wishes to acknowledge his gratitude to the Pennsylvania German Society for their kindness in extending permission to reprint this invaluable record of the early German immigrants to Pennsylvania. The lists therein, containing more than 38,000 names of persons who arrived in the port of Philadelphia between the years 1727 and 1808, form the basis of the ancestry of hundreds of thousands of Americans, enabling them to determine with certainty the time of their ancestors' arrivals in Pennsylvania and the place from whence they came.

The present printing in two volumes contains all the genealogical and historical data in the original three volume edition published in 1934. Volume II of the original edition, consisting entirely of signatures in facsimile, was not considered of sufficient genealogical value to warrant the additional cost of reproduction and, hence, has been omitted from the present printing in order to make available a modestly priced reprint.

Except for this deliberate omission, the omission of other illustrations not of importance, and the reduction of the size of the margins to further lower the cost, our reprint is an exact reproduction of the original edition, which is listed as Number 146 in the recently revised and e n l a r g e d edition of Harold Lancour's BIBLIOGRAPHY OF SHIP PASSENGER LISTS, 1538-1825 (1963).

GENEALOGICAL PUBLISHING CO.

Baltimore, Maryland
1966

THIS WORK IS DEDICATED
TO THE

PENNSYLVANIA GERMAN PIONEERS AND
THEIR DESCENDANTS,

who have spread throughout the United States
and whose industry, patriotism and achievements
have played an important part in the up-building
of our nation

R. B. Strassburger

FOREWORD

Pennsylvania German migration and its part in the settlement and development of America form an epic tale of faith and zeal, of sacrifice and achievement. The story has been told and the Pennsylvania German pioneers have come into their rightful place as builders of our nation. But the task of giving a complete list of the passengers, their signatures and the names of the ships that brought them to Philadelphia has remained unfinished. The purpose of this publication is to furnish these lists, which are the most exhaustive of their kind. They meet a need keenly felt for many years. Their historical value to posterity is further enhanced by the fact that of all the American colonies, in Pennsylvania alone were such lists made, although uncounted thousands came to this country from the old world through other ports in the East and South.

The land of what subsequently came to be known as Pennsylvania was granted, as is well known, by King Charles II of England to William Penn in 1681, in liquidation of a debt of 16,000 pounds which the British crown owed to Penn's father. It was the largest tract ever granted in America to a single individual. Penn was made the proprietary of the province, invested with the privilege of creating a political government. He had fee simple title to more than 40,000 square miles of territory. Under his charter Penn was also governor of the province, which he and his sons held as proprietaries, with the exception of about two years under William III, until the revolution of 1776. Thus, in a strict sense, Pennsylvania was not the colony of any foreign power. But as a British subject Penn owed allegiance to the Crown, and while the government of Pennsylvania was proprietary in form, it was English in substance and non-British subjects were known as foreigners.

In order to procure settlers for his land, Penn visited the Rhine provinces, whose once peaceful valleys, thriving fields and vine-clad hills had become the hunting ground of political and religious fanatics. Personally and through agents Penn dis-

seminated the news of his acquisition and invited the Rhine-
landers, the suffering Palatines, to help him found a State in
which religious and civil liberty would prevail. Beginning with
the Germantown settlement in 1683, under the leadership of
Pastorius, up to the revolution and the dawn of the nineteenth
century a large-scale immigration followed, which spread not
only through Pennsylvania but into the South and the new
West, influencing every phase of American life. It is this immigration with which the present volumes deal.

When the pioneers arrived, the government of Pennsylvania
was in the hands of British subjects. Penn's agents were
Englishmen; the English language was used; English common
law was in force. It early became a matter of concern to these
Englishmen that so large a body of continentals, speaking another language and accustomed to another form of government, should be admitted to the land, even though they came
at the invitation of Penn himself. Therefore, in 1727, the
Provincial Council, at the recommendation of Governor Patrick Gordon, passed a law, suggested ten years before by
Governor William Keith, requiring all continentals who arrived
at Philadelphia to take oaths of allegiance to the British crown.
Two years later the continental immigrants were required also
to take oaths of abjuration and fidelity to the proprietor and
the laws of the province. The oaths were administered and
subscribed to before public officials.

The original lists, with the pioneers' signatures, are still in
the possession of the State of Pennsylvania, and these lists
form the basis of the genealogical antecedents of the hundreds
of thousands of Americans who have descended from the first
arrivals. As will be seen in the following pages, there were
three lists: those kept by the captains of ships, the lists of the
signers of the oath of allegiance and of the signers of the oath
of abjuration.

In violation of the Provincial Council's instructions, the captains' lists were prepared carelessly and without regard to
uniformity. Few gave complete lists of names, and the occupations of the passengers and the places of their origin were ig-
nored. The lists were handled indifferently and many were
lost. The oath of allegiance lists were incomplete, in that they
contained only the signatures of the adult males who did not

happen to be ill on the day they had to sign their names.

But the lists of the signers of the oath of abjuration were preserved in bound books and in their complete state these lists are printed in the present work for the first time. The allegiance lists were incorporated in the Provincial Council minutes from 1727 until 1736 and were published by the State of Pennsylvania in 1852 under the title of "Colonial Records."

This publication may have inspired I. Daniel Rupp to publish, four years later, a book entitled "A Collection of Thirty Thousand Names of German, Swiss, Dutch, French, Portuguese and Other Immigrants in Pennsylvania—Chronologically Arranged from 1727 to 1776." Rupp strove to arrange the names of the ships in chronological form, but the names of the passengers were not printed in the order in which they appeared on the official lists. The names were generally written in the German script, and many required translation. It should be stated, in justice to Rupp, that he worked in the face of great difficulties in publishing his book, together with other editions, including the names of children and of adults, covering a period of twenty years.

Forty years ago the Commonwealth of Pennsylvania printed the lists in the "Archives," using Rupp's work as the basis, and adding to it the captains' lists made after the revolution and until 1808, when the listing was discontinued. It should be mentioned that during the revolution, when immigration temporarily ceased, a "test oath" of allegiance was required of Continental immigrants settling in Pennsylvania.

Many errors in translation and transcription occur in the lists as published in the "Archives." It is also to be noted that there was no index of names in Rupp's publication and that the index in the "Archives" is confusing. Nor do the "Archives" contain all the lists. Forty hitherto unpublished ship lists were discovered in the preparation of the present work and they are included in these pages.

Interest in the study of Pennsylvania German pioneers is most marked. About three hundred family associations, tracing their ancestry to these pioneers, meet annually in Pennsylvania. It will be a great satisfaction to their members to be able to fix precisely the spelling of the names of their ancestors, the ships carrying them across the sea and the date of their arrival in the port of Philadelphia. The opportunity is thus presented for the re-translation, re-transcription and re-indexing of the names in the original records, such as is given in this work. There may be, however, a difference of opinion as to the spelling of the signatures, and in order to afford immediate access to the form in which the original signatures appear, it has been thought expedient to prepare and print facsimiles of the original lists, which are presented in Volume II. Such a collection of facsimiles has never been published before.

These ancestors of ours were more than mere immigrants, in the everyday sense of the word. They were even more than refugees from a beloved and despoiled homeland. They were pioneers in that they came not to a ready-made republic of opportunity but to a virgin land inhabited by savages. They blazed the trail that helped to transform that land into the America of today, built our institutions and moulded American character. Many were men of eminence in the fatherland; others came up from the penury and virtual slavery of the redemptioner system. Together they worked and won, together they fought America's battles and led in public service, industry, science, education, invention and in that art of agriculture which is the very foundation of our national wealth and of human progress. As publisher of this work, we cheerfully accept full responsibility for its title.

It is a pleasure to acknowledge the generous co-operation of the Pennsylvania State Library, through its director, Captain Frederic A. Godcharles, in making accessible the official lists in the archives of the Commonwealth to be photographed and photostated for this publication. We are fortunate in having had the invaluable services of Professor William J. Hinke, widely known as an authority in Pennsylvania German historical and literary research, in editing the lists, and we wish to give full credit to him for making these pages possible. The Pennsylvania German Society, under whose auspices these volumes are published, particularly the members of its administrative committee, Henry S. Borneman, and Frederick S. Fox, were of great help in solving the problems which inevitably arise in the preparation of a work of such magnitude.

It is a work which has waited long to be done and we are happy to be its sponsor. We are confident that the years of earnest effort involved in its compilation will be abundantly rewarded with the approval of the descendants of the Pennsylvania German pioneers to whom it is dedicated.

RALPH BEAVER STRASSBURGER

Normandy Farm,
Gwynedd Valley, Pa.

INTRODUCTION

The lists of early arrivals in Pennsylvania, which are printed in this volume, are of such importance for the history of Pennsylvania Germans in this country, that it seems worth while to present at some length the history of their origin. This is all the more desirable, because the existence of these lists is a unique phenomenon, which merits explanation. In none of the other ports of the American colonies, through which German settlers entered, were such lists prepared or preserved. Thousands of Germans came to America through the ports of Boston, New York, Baltimore, Charleston and Savannah. Thus, for example, all the early German Reformed missionaries, sent to Pennsylvania by the Church of Holland, came by way of New York. The same is true of the Lutheran missionaries, who were sent from Halle, Germany. But whatever settlers came through these other ports, their names are lost, at least in the large majority of cases, because no record was kept of them at the time of their arrival. In Philadelphia alone did the authorities insist on the preparation of careful and detailed lists of arrivals. We naturally ask, what reasons induced them to have these lists prepared with so much care? In order to answer this question fully we must go back to the beginning of German immigration into Pennsylvania.

EARLY GERMAN IMMIGRATION

One of the best surveys of the early German immigration into Pennsylvania is given by the Rev. Henry Melchior Muehlenberg, the patriarch of the Lutheran Church, who himself came to Pennsylvania in 1742, and evidently gave a good deal of attention to this question of immigration. In his report to Halle, dated July 9, 1754, he writes:

"Shortly before and at the opening of this century some Germans made the beginning by crossing the great Atlantic ocean and settling in this land of the West. They settled here and made use of the freedom which we enjoy here undisturbed

xiii

in matters of religion, according to the fundamental laws of the First Proprietary of this Province of Pennsylvania, William Penn.

"In the first period, namely from 1680 to 1708, some came by chance, among whom was one Henry Frey, whose wife is said to be still living. He came about the year 1680. About the same time some Low Germans from Cleve sailed across the ocean, whose descendants are still to be found here, some of whom were baptized by us, others still live as Quakers.

"In the second period, in the years 1708, 1709, 1710, to 1720, when the great exodus from the Palatinate to England took place, and a large number of people were sent by Queen Anne to the Province of New York, not a few of them came to Pennsylvania. These got along with some devotional books, sermon books, Arndt's *True Christianity* and hymn books, with which they had been provided through the unwearied interest of the Rev. Anthony William Boehm, at that time court preacher at St. James. Even at that time some reached here, who, although some of them may have had good intentions, had separated from our fellowship in Europe, for reasons unknown to us. They kept separate here and lived by themselves. These had no concern for the preservation of the pure doctrine or the building of the necessary churches and the erection of good schools, much less did they attempt to purchase lands for such buildings in the interest of their descendants, although they could have bought one hundred acres for a price which we have now to pay for half an acre. They allowed their children and grandchildren to grow up without the necessary instruction, omitting also the use of the means of grace, the Word of God and the sacraments. . . . Most of them went over to the Quakers, whose religion, as is well known, is here in the ascendant, or with later arrivals they joined other churches which have sprung up here, or they did not want to have anything to do with religion. At the end of this period a large number of High Germans arrived, who were real Separatists. They brought along a deep-seated hatred of or disinclination to the doctrine and constitution of our Church, or they were Baptists (Dunkers, as they are called here), Mennonites, Schwenkfelders, or similar kinds, whose full recital would lead us too far astray. . . .

"In the following third period, from about the year 1720 to 1730, the number of High German Evangelical Christians, from the German Empire, the Palatinate, Württemberg, Darmstadt and other places increased largely. Also many families from the State of New York came over here, whc had been sent there by Queen Anne. These have spread and settled in all parts of this province. . . .

"Some of those who arrived in the middle of this period brought preachers along or secured them accidentally, such as Messrs. Henckel, Falckner, Stoever, etc., some of whom died early, others were unable to cope with the work. Our brethren, living in New York State and New Jersey, turned to Hamburg and Holland and from there secured bye and bye some preachers, such as Messrs. Kochendahler, Justus Falckner, Berkemeyer, Knoll, Wolf and Hartwich, some of whom died long ago, others, because of quarrels arising among them, have not been able to build up Zion. They also received books and assistance for schools and churches from Holland.

"At the end of this and the beginning of the next period a still larger number of Germans came to this country. These brought some schoolmasters along with them or took up with some who came with them. These read at first sermons, but soon imagined they were able to officiate as ministers and dispense the sacraments, although they took poor care of the children. Thus the province has been peopled more and more with Englishmen, Scotch and Irish, as well as with German Lutherans and Reformed people." [1]

We are now in a position to fill in this excellent outline of Muehlenberg with some interesting details.

The first ship, of which a record has survived bringing a larger number of Germans to Philadelphia, was the ship "America," Captain Joseph Wasey, which landed at Philadelphia on August 20, 1683. It brought Francis Daniel Pastorius, the leader of a colony of German Mennonites, who came in two sections. The smaller number came in this first ship, in the company of Pastorius. They were: Jacob Schumacher, George Wertmüller, Isaac Dilbeck, his wife Mariette and two boys, Abraham and Jacob, Thomas Gasper, Conrad Bacher (alias

---

[1] See *Hallesche Nachrichten*, new ed., Vol. II, pp. 194–196.

Rutter) and an English maid Frances Simpson. They had left
Rotterdam May 4th and Gravesend June 6, 1683.[2]

The main body of Mennonites followed shortly afterwards.
They came with Captain Jeffries, on the ship "Concord," a
ship of 500 tons, 130 feet long and 32 feet wide. It had left
Gravesend on July 24, 1683, with thirteen Mennonite families,
consisting of thirty-three persons. They came from Crefeld, in
the County of Cleves. The heads of these families were: Dirck,
Herman and Abraham Isaac Opp den Graeff (three brothers)
Lenert Arets, Tunnes Kunders, Reinert Tisen, Wilhelm
Strepers, Jan Leusen, Peter Keurlis, Jan Simens, Johan Bleick-
ers, Abraham Tünes and Jan Lücken. They reached Philadelphia on October 6, 1683. Shortly afterwards, on October 24th
of the same year, Pastorius founded Germantown for them,
where forty-two people settled in twelve homes. Most of them
were weavers, the rest were farmers and tradesmen. These
were the German "Pilgrim Fathers," who sought and found
freedom of worship in Pennsylvania.

The next group of Germans to arrive in Philadelphia were
the "Mystics of the Wissahickon," as they have been called.
They arrived on the ship "Sarah Maria Hopewell," Captain
Tanner, on June 23, 1694. The leader of the party was John
Kelpius. Among the members were Henry Bernhard Koester,
a former Lutheran minister, Daniel Falckner, who in 1703 became the first Lutheran pastor ordained in the province, John
Selig and Conrad Matthaei, the last a Swiss from the Canton
of Berne. They selected as their place of settlement a tract,
known as the Ridge, near the place where the Wissahickon
Creek rushes through a narrow ravine and joins the Schuylkill.[3]

In the second period, mentioned by Mr. Muehlenberg, from
1710 to 1720, there were three German colonies that deserve
special mention.

The first was a colony of ten families of Swiss Mennonites,

---

[2] A letter of Pastorius, describing his journey to America, and his settlement at Germantown, was discovered by the writer years ago, in the City
Library of Zurich, Switzerland. It was published by former Governor Penny-
packer in his *Settlement of Germantown*, pp. 133–151 (Proceedings of the
Pennsylvania German Society, vol. IX).

[3] For the history of this colony see Sachse, *German Pietists of Pennsylvania,
1694–1708*, Philadelphia, 1895.

who settled after their arrival on 10,000 acres of land "near the head of the Pequea Creek," in Lancaster County. They came on the ship "Mary Hope," Captain John Annis. They left Gravesend on June 29, 1710, and landed in Philadelphia on September 23, 1710. On the same ship came also the Rev. Samuel Guldin, and his family, a Swiss pietist, who had been deposed by the ecclesiastical authorities of Berne, because of his pietistic inclinations. He wrote an interesting letter [4] to his friends in Switzerland, describing at length his journey across the ocean as well as the conditions which he found on his arrival in Pennsylvania.

Another noteworthy group of Germans arrived in the year 1717. It was a group of Lutherans, headed by the Rev. Anthony Jacob Henckel and his son-in-law, Valentine Geiger. They arrived on one of three vessels which reached Philadelphia in September, 1717. On September 19, 1717, "Capt. Richmond, Capt. Tower & Capt. Eyers, waited upon the [Provincial] Board with a List of Palatines they had imported here from London; by which list it appeared that Capt. Richmond had imported one hundred & sixty-four, Capt. Tower ninety-one, and Capt. Eyers one hundred and eight." [5] In 1718, Anthony Jacob Henckel acquired a tract of 250 acres in Hanover township, where as Muehlenberg testifies, he "ministered for a number of years to the first settlers of that region." [6]

ORIGIN OF THE SHIP LISTS

It was through the arrival of these three ships of 1717, with their 363 Palatines, that the attention of the provincial authorities was first directed, with serious concern, to these newcomers. On September 17, 1717, Governor William Keith:

"Observed to the Council, that great numbers of foreigners, from Germany, strangers to our language and Constitution, having lately been imported into this Province, daily dispersed themselves immediately after Landing, without producing any Certificates, from whence they came or what they were; & as they seemed to have first landed in Britain, &

---

[4] This letter of Guldin was translated and published by the writer in the *Journal of the Presbyterian Historical Society*, Vol. XIV, (1930) pp. 28–41; 46–73.

[5] See *Colonial Records*, Vol. III, p. 29.

[6] *Hallesche Nachrichten*, new ed., Vol. II, p. 353.

afterwards to have left it without any License from the Government, or so much as their knowledge, so in the same manner they behaved here, without making the least application to himself or to any of the Magistrates; That as this Practice might be of very dangerous Consequences, since by the same method any number of foreigners from any nation whatever, as well Enemys as friends, might throw themselves upon us; The Governor, therefore, thought it requisite that this matter should be considered by the Board, & accordingly it was considered, & 'tis Ordered thereupon, that all masters of vessels who have lately imported any of these foreigners be summoned to appear at this Board, to render an Account of the Number and character of their Passengers respectively from Britain; That all those who are already Landed be required by a Proclamation, to be issued for that purpose, to Repair within the space of one month to some Magistrate, particularly to the Recorder of this City, to take such Oaths appointed by Law as are Necessary to give assurances of their being well affected to his Majesty and his government; But because some of these foreigners are said to be Mennonists, who cannot for Conscience sake take such Oaths, that those persons be admitted upon their giving any Equivalent assurances in their own way and manner, & that the Naval Officer of this Port be required not to admit any inward bound vessel to an Entry, until the Master shall first give an exact list of all their passengers imported by them." [7]

In response to this order of the Council the captains of the three ships that had just arrived appeared before the Council two days later and handed in lists of the Palatines whom they had imported. After this one action, however, the order of the Council was apparently forgotten or failed to be enforced. At least there are no more references in the minutes of the Council to this subject, which implies that during the next ten years no other captains were required to submit lists. Neither is there any evidence that the proclamation of the Governor was issued or that the subject of immigration excited any more discussion.

This, however, does not mean that no more Germans arrived, for we find that they continued to come in constantly in-

[7] *Colonial Records,* Vol. III, p. 29.

creasing numbers. In 1719, Jonathan Dickinson, one of the members of the Provincial Council, wrote, "we are daily expecting ships from London which bring over Palatines, in number six or seven thousand. We had a parcel that came about five years ago, who purchased land about sixty miles west of Philadelphia, and proved quiet and industrious." [8] The last sentence refers undoubtedly to one of the later colonies of Swiss Mennonites that settled in Lancaster County.

In the year 1720, the American Weekly Mercury, printed in Philadelphia, contained the first notice of a ship bringing Palatines to Pennsylvania. On September 1, 1720, the Mercury states: "On the 30th [of August arrived] the ship Laurel, John Coppel, [captain] from Liverpool and Cork with 240 odd Palatine Passengers come here to settle." [9] It was most likely this ship which brought the Rev. John Philip Boehm to Pennsylvania, the founder of the Reformed Church in Pennsylvania.

How many Germans arrived during the first three periods, which we have been considering, from 1680 to 1730, is difficult to determine. Various, widely divergent, opinions have been expressed, even by contemporary writers, during the eighteenth century.

One estimate was made in 1730, by the Rev. John Wilhelmius, the friend of the Palatines in Rotterdam, where he came personally in contact with them. He reported to the Synod of South Holland, that there were "already 15,000 Reformed confessors of the Palatinate in Pennsylvania." [10] When that statement was sent to Pennsylvania, the Rev. John Bartholomew Rieger, who was at that time pastor in Philadelphia, replied on November 22, 1731:

"It is to be regretted that the estimate of the number of [Reformed] confessors is not correct. The number would, indeed, be considerable, but, as there were no regular pastors,

---

[8] Rupp's *Thirty Thousand Names*, p. 10.

[9] This extract from the Mercury, together with many other extracts from contemporary newspapers, made by the writer and handed by him to his friend, Mr. Frank R. Dieffenderffer, was published by him in his *German Immigration into Pennsylvania*, p. 202. (Vol. X of the Proceedings of the Pennsylvania German Society).

[10] From the minutes of the Synod of South Holland, held at Breda, July 4–14, 1730.

for so long a time, most of the people have gone over to the
sects or have entirely separated themselves from all church
connections. The rest of the truly Reformed people is, therefore, rather small and perhaps not more than three thousand
can be counted in the whole land." [11]

In a later letter of March 4, 1733, Rieger supplemented
the above estimate with the following statement:

"As regards the number of the members of the Reformed
Church in Pennsylvania, we make answer that we think that
there must be altogether about 15,000 Germans, but these people live scattered over more than 300 or 400 miles and have no
churches in the rural sections. We had thus far two regularly-
called ministers, who cannot possibly be everywhere. Hence it
is impossible to ascertain the actual number of members." [12]

In view of these statements we must conclude that the total
number of Germans in the province by the year 1730 must
have been considerable. But they did not attract special attention nor call forth special comment until a new governor, Patrick Gordon, took office in 1726. In the next year, on September 14, 1727:

"The Governor acquainted the board, that he had called
them together at this time to inform them that there is lately
arrived from Holland, a Ship with four hundred Palatines, as
'tis said, and that he has information they will soon be followed by a much greater Number, who design to settle in the
back parts of this province; & as they transport themselves
without any leave obtained from the Crown of Great Britain,
and settle themselves upon the Proprietors untaken up Lands
without any application to the Proprietor or his Commissioners of property, or to the Government in general, it would be
highly necessary to concert proper measures for the peace
and security of the province, which may be endangered by such
numbers of strangers daily poured in, who being ignorant of
our Language & Laws, & settling in a body together, make, as
it were, a distinct people from his Majesties Subjects.

"The Board taking the case into their serious Consideration, observe, that as these People pretended at first that they

---

[11] The original letter of Rieger is in the Synodical Archives at The Hague,
No. 74. I. 10.

[12] Letter in the Archives at The Hague, No. 74. I. 15.

fly hither on the Score of their Religious Liberties, and come under the Protection of his Majesty, It's requisite that in the first Place they should take the Oath of Allegiance, or some equivalent to it to his Majesty, and promise Fidelity to the Proprietor & obedience to our Established Constitution: And therefore, until some proper Remedy can be had from Home, to prevent the Importation of such Numbers of Strangers into this and others of his Majesties Colonies,

" 'Tis ORDERED, that the Masters of Vessells importing them shall be examined whether they have any Leave granted them by the Court of Great Britain for the Importation of these Foreigners, and that a List shall be taken of the Names of all these People, their several Occupations, and the Places from whence they come, and shall be further examined touching their Intentions in coming hither; And further, that a Writing be drawn up for them to sign declaring their Allegiance & Subjection to the King of Great Britain & Fidelity to the Proprietary of this Province, & that they will demean themselves peaceably towards all his Majesties Subjects & strictly observe and conform to the laws of England and of this Government." [13]

In compliance with this order of Council, a paper was submitted to the Council, at its next meeting, on September 21, 1727, which contained an oath of allegiance to George the Second, King of England and a declaration of fidelity to the Proprietor of the province together with a promise to obey the laws of the province. A signed list of the new arrivals was laid before the Board, containing the names of one hundred and nine male adults. The captain of the ship William and Sarah, William Hill, was then questioned, if he had any license for bringing in these people. He replied that he had no other license than the clearance papers which he had received from the port authorities at Dover, England. With this answer the Board had to be satisfied. The Palatines who were well were then called in and fifty-one of them signed the oath of allegiance, headed by the Rev. G. M. Weis, who had been their leader on the journey to Pennsylvania.

These quotations from the minutes of the Provincial Coun-

---

[13] *Colonial Records*, Vol. III, pp. 282–283. For the oath of allegiance see below, pp. 2–4.

cil make it perfectly plain that the passenger lists and the lists of signatures to the oath of allegiance were called forth by a government scare. The governor and Council were afraid that the peace and security of the province were menaced by "such large numbers of strangers pouring in daily into the province," as the Clerk of Council expresses it. In their eagerness to re- move this terrible danger they cast about for a remedy. The remedy which they selected was twofold: First, the captains of ships importing these strangers were ordered to submit lists of all the people they imported, and, secondly, the male pas- sengers of sixteen years and upwards were ordered to sign the oath of allegiance to the English king. Fortunately the danger which they foresaw was altogether imaginary, or else their remedy would have been ineffective. But, though their fear was uncalled-for and their remedy ineffective, we are reaping today the benefits of their folly. For this government scare has preserved for us tens of thousands of names, which delight the historian and the genealogist. Besides, later governors of Pennsylvania did not hesitate to give the newcomers their un- qualified approval. In 1738, for example, Governor George Thomas, in a message to the Provincial Assembly, declared:

"This Province has been for some years the asylum of the distressed Protestants of the Palatinate, and other parts of Germany; and I believe it may with truth be said that the present flourishing condition of it is in great Measure owing to the Industry of those people; and should any discourage- ment divert them from coming hither, it may well be appre- hended that the value of your Lands will fall, and your Ad- vances to wealth be much slower; for it is not altogether the goodness of the soil, but the Number and Industry of the People that make a flourishing Country." [14]

CONTENTS OF THE SHIP LISTS

Just as remarkable as the manner in which the lists came into existence is their contents. A careful analysis of the lists brings to light many interesting facts. We are, of course, eager to find out how the detailed orders of the Council were actually carried out.

The order relating to the duty of the captains had three

[14] *Colonial Records,* Vol. IV, p. 315.

points. First, they were to make a list of all the people they imported. Secondly, they were to give their several occupations, and thirdly, they were to give the places from which the passengers had come. What a boon it would have been for genealogists, if the captains had strictly complied with these orders! How much trouble and research they could have saved the present-day historians. But alas, none of the captains paid the slightest attention to the last two points of the order of Council. Neither the occupations nor the places of domicile in Europe were ever recorded by them.

Not even the first point, that they should hand in lists of the names of the people they imported, was interpreted alike by all the captains. Most of them thought that to give the names of the male adults was all that was required. Only twenty-five captains have given complete lists of all the men, women and children. Three captains have given the names of the men and women, but omitted the children, while sixty-four captains atoned somewhat for their remissness in carrying out the orders by giving the ages of the passengers, an item that they had not been asked to give, but which we are glad to insert, wherever they are found. Sometimes the captains give the total number of freights, children being counted as "half freights." In two instances (Nos. 1–2) the totals in each family are given. Looking at the captains' lists as a whole, we must say, that they are of all sorts and descriptions. Each one made his list to suit himself, without any reference to the orders of the Council. At first, when the signatures were made in the presence of the Provincial Council, the captains were required to attest the correctness of the list by an affidavit. This custom prevailed from 1727 to 1740, or down to list No. 80. After that attestations by captains are no longer found on the lists.

But what proved in course of time the most serious fact regarding the captains' lists remains to be mentioned. Each captain wrote his list on a large, loose sheet of paper, which he handed to the magistrate at Philadelphia, sitting as a Court. Sometimes it was the Governor, sometimes the Mayor of the City, sometimes a city magistrate, before whom the captains appeared. The first forty-three lists, down to October 19, 1736, were signed before the Provincial Council. As a result, the Clerk of Council incorporated the names of the signers of the oath of allegiance into the minutes of the Council. But after 1736 this was no longer done.

What became of the lists of the captains, handed in on loose sheets of paper? Sad to relate, most of them were lost. Of the 324 ships arriving between 1727 and 1775, we have the captains' lists of only 138 ships.

In addition to the captains' lists we have the lists of the signers of the oath of allegiance. On these lists we naturally expect to find the signatures of all the male adults on the ships. But here we meet with another disappointment. What we actually find, at least on the first seventy lists, are the names of all the male adults who were well on the day of signing and were able to appear at the Court House. If any of the male passengers were sick, they were not required to sign later. Beginning in August 1739, we find that the Clerk of Council signed the names of the absent passengers. But, in the earlier lists, there is often a serious discrepancy between the male adults that were on board and those that actually signed. Thus, for example, on the very first captain's list there are 109 names, but only 51 persons actually appeared in the Court House and signed the oath. The others, who are reported as sick, "never came to be qualified."

The names of these signers of the oath of allegiance were also written on large, loose sheets of paper. The result was the same as noted in the case of the captains' lists. Most of them were lost. Only 138 of these lists of signatures of the oath of allegiance have survived to the present day. But they are not all of the same ships as the captains' lists.

But, strange to say, there is a third set of lists. Rupp, in his *Collection of Thirty Thousand Names,* informs us, p. 40, that this set of lists, which he calls C, is an autograph duplicate of B, the list of signers of the oath of allegiance, and that this list is preserved in book form. The fact is, that Rupp has entirely misjudged the character of these lists, although his statement has been faithfully copied by later historians, as if it were the Gospel truth. On the face of it, it is absurd to suppose that the passengers signed the oath of allegiance twice. What would have been the purpose of such a strange procedure?

Evidently neither Rupp nor any of the later historians took the trouble to examine the third set of signatures carefully enough to discover their true purpose. A careful scrutiny of these lists brings to light the following, rather surprising, facts:

First of all, the lists are not found in one book, as we might have inferred from the statement of Rupp, but in a series of six large folio volumes, of which we give the following, detailed description:

1. EXHIBIT A.

A paper-bound volume, 7 x 12 inches in size, containing 79 numbered pages, of which pp. 10, 77 and 78 are blank. Like all the succeeding volumes it opens with a set of oaths (about which more presently) to which the passengers attached their signatures. The volume includes lists 9–44, from August 19, 1729, to August 30, 1737.

2. EXHIBIT B.

A paper-bound volume, 8 x 12 inches in size. Beginning with two pages of oaths, it has 63 numbered pages, and contains lists Nos. 45–77, from September 10, 1737, to September 30, 1740.

3. EXHIBIT C.

A paper-bound volume, 8 x 12 inches in size. It has 89 numbered pages, of which pp. 25 and 41 are blank. It contains lists Nos. 78–120, from November 25, 1740, to September 15, 1748.

4. EXHIBIT D.

A paper-bound volume, 8 x 13 inches in size. It contains 96 numbered pages, of which p. 17 is counted twice; p. 51 is omitted in the count; and pp. 94–95 are blank; pp. 1–6 are found in the rear of the book. The lists in the book include Nos. 121–153, September 15, 1748, to August 28, 1750.

5. EXHIBIT E.

A paper-bound volume, 9 x 14 inches in size. It has 63 numbered pages, of which pp. 2, 3, 18, 28, 29, 38, 60 and 61 are blank; pp. 11–12 are omitted in the count, while the first two pages are marked 0 and 00. The lists contained in the volume are Nos. 154–176, August 28, 1750, to October 16, 1751.

6. EXHIBIT F.

It is a large leather-bound volume, 11 x 17 inches in size. It has 263 numbered pages, of which pp. 21–22 are omitted in the count; p. 24 is counted twice, marked 24A and 24B. The following pages are blank: pp. 2, 132, 133, 135–138, 144, 158, 162, 180, 187, 188; p. 167 was missed in the count; p. 168 was counted twice; pp. 183–186 have been cut out, but the stubs of the leaves show that they once existed; p. 257 was also counted twice. At the end of the volume are many unnumbered, blank pages. The lists in the book are Nos. 177–324, September 15, 1752, to October 9, 1775.

A second remarkable fact about these six volumes is, that each volume opens with an oath or, to be more exact, there are two oaths, which are not identical with the oath of allegiance, but entirely new oaths, whose real significance has apparently been missed by earlier investigators, for none of them has drawn attention to them.[15]

The first of these oaths reads:

"I A B do solemnly & sincerely promise & declare that I will be true & faithful to King George the Second and do sincerely and truly Profess Testifie & Declare that I do from my heart abhor, detest & renounce as impious & heretical that wicked Doctrine & Position that Princes Excommunicated or deprived by the Pope or any Authority of the See of Rome may be deposed or murthered by their Subjects or any other whatsoever. And I do declare that no Foreign Prince Person Prelate State or Potentate hath or ought to have any Power Jurisdiction Superiority Preeminence or Authority Ecclesiastical or Spiritual within the Realm of Great Britain or Dominions thereunto belonging."

The second oath, slightly abbreviated, reads:

"I A B. do solemnly, sincerely and truly acknowledge, profess testify & declare that King George the Second is lawful & rightful King of the Realm of Great Britain & all others his Dominions & countries thereunto belonging, and I do solemnly & sincerely declare that I believe the Person pretending to be Prince of Wales during the Life of the late King James and since his Decease pretending to be and Taking upon himself the Style and Title of King of England by the Name of James the Third . . . has any Right & Title whatsoever to the Crown of the Realm of Great Britain. And I do renounce & refuse any allegiance & obedience to him, etc."

In the minutes of the Council these oaths are called "the

[15] This statement ought to be qualified somewhat. The oaths were printed in the *Pennsylvania Archives,* 2nd series, Vol. XVII, pp. 3–4, but it was not stated that these oaths had anything to do with the C lists.

Declaration of Fidelity and Abjuration." They were adopted by an act of the Legislature of Pennsylvania, passed May 10, 1729, of which the first two sections read as follows:

(Section I.) Be it enacted by the Honorable Patrick Gordon, Esquire, Lieutenant-Governor of the Province of Pennsylvania, &c., by and with the advice and consent of the freemen of the said Province in General Assembly met, and by the authority of the same, That all persons being aliens born out of the allegiance of the King of Great Britain and being of the age of sixteen years or upwards shall within the space of forty-eight hours after their being imported or coming into this province, by land or water, go before some judge or justice of the peace of the said province or before the mayor or recorder of the city of Philadelphia for the time being and there take the oaths appointed to be taken instead of the oath of allegiance and supremacy and shall also take the oath of abjuration, for which each person shall pay to the person administering the said oaths the sum of twelve pence and no more. And if any such alien (being of age aforesaid) shall refuse or neglect to take the oaths aforesaid, it shall and may be lawful to and for any judge, justice of the peace or other magistrate of this government forthwith to cause such person or persons to be brought before them and oblige them to give security for their good behavior and appearance at the next court of general quarter-sessions of the peace to be held for the city or county where such Magistrate resides.

And for the more effectual discouraging the practice of importing such persons as may affect the peace of and become chargeable to the inhabitants of this province from foreign states and kingdoms and from parts beyond the seas:

(Section II.) Be it enacted by the authority aforesaid, That every person being an alien born out of the allegiance of the King of Great Britain and being imported or coming into this province by land or water shall pay the duty of forty shillings for the uses in this act hereafter mentioned.

And that all masters of vessels, merchants or others who shall import or bring into any port or place within this province any Irish servant or passenger upon redemption, or on condition of paying for his or her passage upon or after their arrival in the plantations, shall pay for every such Irish servant or passenger upon redemption as aforesaid the sum of twenty shillings.[16]

[16] *Statutes at Large of Pennsylvania,* Vol. IV, 1724–1744, pp. 135–140.

These and later sections of this law were so severe that they would have seriously interfered with all immigration. Hence they were soon rescinded by a new law, passed February 14, 1730.[17] But the section demanding a signature to the oath of abjuration remained in force and it explains satisfactorily the third set of lists. This oath of abjuration, aimed against Catholics, was one of the results of the great upheaval in England, which led to the overthrow of the Catholic house of the Stuarts and the establishment of the Protestant princes of the house of Hanover, as kings of England, in 1689.

It was indeed a fortunate circumstance for us that this oath of abjuration was prescribed in 1729. It caused the names of the signers to be entered into bound books, which have escaped the fate of the other two lists. Beginning with the ninth list, on August 17, 1729, these lists run continuously, with but two omissions,[18] down to the 324th list, on October 9, 1775. It is, therefore, this third set of signatures which is alone complete. Instead of being merely a copy of the other list it is really the backbone of the whole series of lists, and the most important set, from which we derive most of our information regarding the ships and their passengers.

Internal evidence shows that the two lists of signatures (lists B and C) were made before different clerks, seated probably at different desks. This can be inferred from the fact that when the passengers were unable to write and the clerk wrote the name for them, the same name is often spelled in two different ways on the two lists. Besides, the chirography of the clerks differs on the two lists. These facts show that there were two clerks, each superintending the making of one list.

The ordinary, and for many years the only, place for signing the oaths was the Court House at Philadelphia on High (now Market) Street, between 2nd and 3rd, of which we present an old drawing. But as early as 1741, three lists were signed at Passayunk and Wicacoa (Nos. 83, 84, 85). After 1766, it was a common occurrence to have the passengers sign the lists at some other place. Such was the house or the office of the Mayor (Nos. 260, 263, 265, 267, 268, 270, 272, 274,

---

[17] L. c., Vol. IV, p. 170.

[18] The omissions are List 229 A and 233 A, of which only the captains' lists are in existence.

275), or the office of Isaac Jones (Nos. 278, 279) or Robert Ritchie's store (No. 309) or Joshua Fisher & Son's store (No. 307) or Messrs. Willing & Morris's store (Nos. 277, 300, 306) or even Dowers and Yorkes Rigging Loft (No. 311) or John Appowen's Sail Loft (No. 312). But even during the last years the oaths were occasionally signed at the Court House (Nos. 283, 288, 292, 299, 301, 304, 322, 324).

STATISTICS OF THE SHIP LISTS

As all the lists are now published with all the information which the lists contain, it is possible to give more definite information about the number of ships, the number of subscribers to the oaths and the total number of German pioneers that arrived from 1727 to 1775, than was ever possible before. And besides, a large number of conflicting statements can now be definitely dismissed as unhistorical.

The following is the number of ships bringing German pioneers to the port of Philadelphia, between the years 1727 to 1775.

YEAR	NO.	YEAR	NO.	YEAR	NO.
1727	5	1743	9	1760	none
1728	3	1744	9	1761	1
1729	2	1745	none	1762	none
1730	3	1746	2	1763	4
1731	4	1747	5	1764	11
1732	11	1748	7	1765	5
1733	7	1749	22	1766	5
1734	2	1750	15	1767	7
1735	3	1751	16	1768	4
1736	3	1752	19	1769	4
1737	7	1753	19	1770	7
1738	16	1754	19	1771	9
1739	8	1755	2	1772	8
1740	6	1756	1	1773	15
1741	10	1757	none	1774	6
1742	5	1758	none	1775	2
		1759	none		

This is a total of 324 ships, five more than in Rupp's *Thirty Thousand Names* and two more than in Vol. XVII of the second series of the *Pennsylvania Archives*. There were 43 ships in the first ten years, 68 in the second decade, 125 in the third decade, 26 in the fourth decade, and 62 in the last nine years.

The largest number of ships in a single year were the twenty-two ships in the year 1749.

What curious information has been in circulation about these ships is well illustrated by a quotation from the ancient, but well-known historian, Robert Proud. In his *History of Pennsylvania,* he states: [19]

"In the summer of 1749 twenty-five sail of large ships arrived with German passengers alone; which brought about twelve thousand souls, some of the ships about six hundred each; and in several other years nearly the same number of these people arrived annually; and in some years as many from Ireland. By an exact account of all the ships and passengers annually which have arrived at Philadelphia, with Germans alone, nearly from the first settlement of the Province till about the year 1776, when their importation ceased, the number of the latter appears to be about thirty-nine thousand; and their internal increase has been very great."

Now, the curious thing about this statement, frequently quoted, is, as we are able to prove, that nearly every item mentioned is wrong. First, there were no twenty-five ships in 1749; second, they did not bring twelve thousand souls; third, the ships did not carry about six hundred Germans each, and lastly, the total was not about thirty-nine thousand. Let us present the evidence for these statements. According to the lists, as printed in this volume, the ships arriving with German passengers in 1749 were as follows:

ARRIVALS IN THE YEAR 1749

NAME OF SHIP	DATE	PASSENGERS
Elliot	Aug. 24	240
Crown	" 30	476
Chesterfield	Sep. 2	255
Albany	" 2	285
St. Andrew	" 9	400
Priscilla	" 11	293
Christian	" 13	300
Two Brothers	" 14	312
Edinburgh	" 15	360
Phoenix	" 15	550
Patience	" 19	270
Speedwell	" 25	215
Ranier	" 26	277
Dragon	" 26	503
Isaac	" 27	206

[19] Proud, *History of Pennsylvania,* Vol. II, pp. 273–274.

NAME OF SHIP	DATE	PASSENGERS
Ann	" 28	242
Jacob	Oct. 2	249
Leslie	" 7	400
Lydia	" 17	[450] [20]
Dragon	" 17	244
Fane	" 17	184
Good Intent	Nov. 9	76

This list shows that only twenty-two ships arrived at Philadelphia in 1749, that the largest number carried on any one ship was 550, but that the average number was 308, and that the total number of passengers on all the twenty-two ships was only 6,787, which is a little more than half of what Proud claimed it to have been.

Regarding the total number of passengers down to 1776, we shall submit our figures presently. Unfortunately, the lists themselves do not give definite figures as to the total number, but we can approximate it fairly closely. What is known definitely is as follows:

(1) The number of persons signing the C lists, including also the first eight B lists, which are missing in the C set, is 26,016.

(2) The number of names on the Captains' lists is 13,760. The names of the signers on the corresponding C lists is 10,018. Hence there are 3,742 names on the captains' lists, which are in excess of the names on the corresponding lists of signatures. This makes a total of 29,758 different names on the lists.[21]

(3) The total number of passengers is known of 178 ships. The number on these ships was 36,129. The total number of signers on these 178 ships was 14,423. Hence

$$\frac{36,129}{14,423} = \frac{2.50495}{1} \quad \text{or approximately} \quad 2.5 = 2\frac{1}{2} = \frac{5}{2}$$

The ratio of passengers to signers was therefore approximately 5 to 2. On the basis of these figures the total number of passengers was approximately 65,040. This proves conclusively that all previous estimates have been far from the correct figures.

A total of 324 ships is listed in this volume, covering the

[20] This total is not given on the list. It is an estimate.

[21] To these should be added 129 names which are found on a new list of ship No. 30, which has just come to light and which we print in an appendix. The grand total of all names is, therefore, 29,887.

years 1727 to 1775. Of these there must have been at least 170
different ships. We cannot be sure of the exact number, as
there were different ships bearing the same name. There were
at least two ships named Dragon, one arriving September 26,
1749, Captain George Spencer, the other on October 17, 1749,
Captain Daniel Nicholas; two ships named Edinburgh, arriving but a few days apart, September 14, 1753, and October 2,
1753, respectively. Also two Neptunes, arriving September 30,
1754, and December 13, 1754. There were two Sallys, one arriving October 5, 1767, the other November 10, 1767. When
ships with the same name arrive twenty years apart, the pre-
sumption is that they are different ships. Thus, the ship Adventure is listed October 2, 1727, and again September 23, 1732.
Then there is another Adventure entering the harbor of Philadelphia on September 25, 1754. Can they be the same ship?
Many of the ships, 112 in number, made the journey only once,
but others made the trip frequently. The ship St. Andrew is
listed nine times, the Two Brothers eight times, the Edinburgh
seven times, the Minerva, Lydia, Friendship and Crawford
six times, the ships Samuel, Patience, Robert & Alice, Mary,
Loyal Judith, Chance and Brothers, each five times. Five ships
arrived four times, thirteen ships three times and twenty-four
ships twice.

A number of different names were applied to these ships or
sailing vessels. Most of them are merely called ships. But
twenty-five are called snows, fourteen brigantines, four brigs
(which according to the dictionaries are to be distinguished
from the brigantines) four are called pinks, eleven galleys, and
six billenders or billinders. All these names have long passed
out of common use, along with the sailing vessels themselves.

The record which the captains made was similar to that of
the ships. The 324 ships were commanded by 193 captains. Of
these 146 made the trip to Philadelphia only once, but 47 made
frequent trips. One of them, Thomas Arnot, with a record of
twenty-four years of service, from 1747 to 1771, crossed the
Atlantic thirteen times, Charles Smith, 1763–1773, crossed the
ocean eleven times, John Mason, 1742–1753, crossed eight
times, James Russel, 1748–1754, crossed seven times, so did
John Osmond, 1765–1774, and Thomas Coatam, 1741–1754.
Four crossed six times, Hugh Percy, 1731–1754, William
Muir, 1749–1754, John Steadman, 1731–1738, and James

Abercrombie, 1743–1754. Three captains crossed five times, two captains four times, thirteen captains three times and twenty twice.

Some of these captains were reputed to be cruel and inhuman masters. Governor Gordon refers in one of his letters to the "horrid barbarity, with which the passengers were treated," by one captain, while the passengers themselves called him "a wicked murderer of souls." [22] But others were known as kind and considerate. Christopher Schultze, who came on the ship Saint Andrew, landing at Philadelphia, September 12, 1734, wrote of the captain, John Steadman: "We had a very good captain, who kept strictly to his contract, and very able sailors, who had very much patience with us." [23]

JOURNEY TO PENNSYLVANIA

The journey to Pennsylvania fell naturally into three parts. The first part, and by no means the easiest, was the journey down the Rhine to Rotterdam or some other port. Gottlieb Mittelberger in his *Journey to Pennsylvania in the year 1750*, writes: [24]

"This journey lasts from the beginning of May to the end of October, fully half a year, amid such hardships as no one is able to describe adequately with their misery. The cause is because the Rhine boats from Heilbronn to Holland have to pass by 26 custom houses, at all of which the ships are examined, which is done when it suits the convenience of the customhouse officials. In the meantime the ships with the people are detained long, so that the passengers have to spend much money. The trip down the Rhine lasts therefore four, five and even six weeks. When the ships come to Holland, they are detained there likewise five to six weeks. Because things are very dear there, the poor people have to spend nearly all they have during that time."

The second stage of the journey was from Rotterdam to one of the English ports. Most of the ships called at Cowes, on

[22] Diffenderffer, *German Immigration*, p. 64.

[23] Brecht, *Genealogical Record of Schwenkfelder Families*, p. 49.

[24] *Gottlieb Mittelberger's Journey to Pennsylvania in the year 1750 and return to Germany in the year 1754. Translated from the German by Carl Theo. Eben*, Philadelphia, John Jos. McVey, 1888, p. 18. Gottlieb Mittelberger arrived in Philadelphia on September 29, 1750, with the ship Osgood, Capt. William Wilkie. See below list No. 157C, p. 445.

the Isle of Wight. This was the favorite stopping place, as 142 ships are recorded as having sailed from Rotterdam to Cowes. Other ships touched at one of seven other channel ports. Taking them from east to west they were: Deal, where twenty-two ships stopped, Dover, with eleven ships, Portsmouth thirty-two ships, Gosport, near Portsmouth, two ships, Porte in Dorsetshire, one ship (No. 109), Plymouth two ships, Falmouth, in Cornwall, four ships. One ship (No. 297) went from Rotterdam to London, one ship (No. 263) from Rotterdam to Berwick upon Tweed, on the east coast of England, near the Scotch border, five ships from Rotterdam to Leith in Scotland, two ships from Rotterdam to the Orkney islands (Nos. 110, 163) and one ship from Rotterdam to St. Christopher, one of the West India islands.

Another harbor in Holland, which was frequently used as a starting point for the ocean journey was Amsterdam. From there two ships went to Dover, two to Portsmouth, two to Gosport, three to Cowes, one to Tingmouth (now Teignmouth) in Devonshire, one to Shields, on the east coast of England and one to Aberdeen.

Beginning with the year 1752, nine ships started in various years from Hamburg, Germany, and from there went either to Cowes or to Plymouth. No less than thirty-one ships came directly from London to Philadelphia. From 1766 to 1775, ten ships started from Lisbon, Portugal, while two ships are listed as coming from Boston and one from South Carolina to Philadelphia.

In England there was another delay of one to two weeks, when the ships were waiting either to be passed through the custom house or waiting for favorable winds. When the ships had for the last time weighed their anchors at Cowes or some other port in England, then, writes Mittelberger, "the real misery begins with the long voyage. For from there the ships, unless they have good wind, must often sail eight, nine, ten to twelve weeks before they reach Philadelphia. But even with the best wind the voyage lasts seven weeks."

The third stage of the journey, or the ocean voyage proper, was marked by much suffering and hardship. The passengers being packed densely, like herrings, as Mittelberger describes it, without proper food and water, were soon subject to all sorts of diseases, such as dysentery, scurvy, typhoid and smallpox. Children were the first to be attacked and died in large numbers. Mittelberger reports the deaths of thirty-two children on his ship. Of the heartless cruelty practised he gives the following example: "One day, just as we had a heavy gale, a woman in our ship, who was to give birth and could not under the circumstances of the storm, was pushed through the port-hole and dropped into the sea, because she was far in the rear of the ship and could not be brought forward."

The terrors of disease, brought about to a large extent by poor food and lack of good drinking water, were much aggra-vated by frequent storms through which ships and passengers had to pass. "The misery reaches the climax when a gale rages for two or three nights and days, so that every one believes that the ship will go to the bottom with all human beings on board. In such a visitation the people cry and pray most pit-eously. When in such a gale the sea rages and surges, so that the waves rise often like mountains one above the other, and often tumble over the ship, so that one fears to go down with the ship; when the ship is constantly tossed from side to side by the storm and waves, so that no one can either walk, or sit, or lie, and the closely packed people in the berths are thereby tumbled over each other, both the sick and the well—it will be readily understood that many of these people, none of whom had been prepared for hardships, suffer so terribly from them that they do not survive." [25]

When at last the Delaware River was reached and the City of Brotherly Love hove in sight, where all their miseries were to end, another delay occurred. A health officer visited the ship and, if any persons with infectious diseases were discovered on the ship, it was ordered to remove one mile from the city. As early as 1718, Dr. Thomas Graeme was appointed to visit and report on all incoming vessels. But no reports from him are on record until the year 1738. On September 14, 1738, Governor George Thomas laid before the Board the reports of Dr. Graeme, "setting forth the condition of four ships lately arrived here from Rotterdam and Amsterdam; And it being observed from one of the said reports that were the Passengers on Board the ships Nancy and Friendship allowed to be immediately landed, it might prove dangerous to the

[25] L. c. p. 21.

health of the Inhabitants of this Province and City, It is Ordered that the Masters of the said Ships be taken into Custody for their Contempt of the Governour's Order, signified to them by Thos. Glenworth, pursuant to a Law of this Province, to remove to the Distance of one Mile from this City, and that they shall remain in Custody till they shall give security in the sum of Five Hundred Pounds each, to obey the said Order, and not to land any of their passengers Baggage, or Goods, till the Passengers shall have been viewed and Examined, and untill they shall receive a Licence from the Governor for so doing." [26]

The Governor urged at this time that a hospital be erected for sick passengers, but the Assembly refused to act until an epidemic broke out in the city of Philadelphia. Then the Assembly voted to buy Fisher Island, at the junction of the Schuylkill with the Delaware. The island was bought in 1743. On February 3, 1743, Governor Thomas approved a bill,[27] passed by the Assembly, for the purchase of this island of three hundred and forty-two acres, with the buildings on it, to be used for a hospital. The name of the island was changed to Province Island, and as such it appears on the map of Philadelphia, which we present. The erection of an adequate hospital was, however, delayed until the year 1750.

How serious conditions were and how many of the sick passengers died, after being brought to Province Island, appears from a statement of Jacob Shoemaker, an undertaker, which he handed in to the Council on November 14, 1754:

> "An Accompt of the Palatines buried this Year.
> For Alexander Stedman 62
> For Henry Cepley 39
> For Benjamin Shoemaker 57
> For Daniel Benesett 87
> For Michael Hilligass 8
> —————
> 253

Jacob Shoemaker upon his affirmation saith the above acc^t of Burials since 14 Sept. last is exact & read from his Book & the Acc^t of Coffins except those from Michael Hilligass which he thinks may be 6 or 8 more.

Jacob Shoemaker.

Affirmed before me,
Chas. Willing.   Nov. 14, 1754.[28]

[26] *Colonial Records,* vol. IV, p. 306f.

[27] L. c., Vol. IV, p. 638.

[28] Preserved with the ship-lists of the year 1754. The persons for whom the passengers were buried were the Philadelphia merchants, to whom they were consigned.

A vivid account of the arrival of these passenger ships in the harbor of Philadelphia, is given by the Rev. Henry M. Muehlenberg, in a report, which he sent to Halle in the year 1769. He writes: [29]

"After much delay one ship after another arrives in the harbor of Philadelphia, when the rough and severe winter is before the door. One or more merchants receive the lists of the freights and the agreement which the emigrants have signed with their own hand in Holland, together with the bills for their travel down the Rhine and the advances of the 'new-landers' for provisions, which they received on the ships on account. Formerly the freight for a single person was six to ten louis d'ors, but now it amounts to fourteen to seventeen louis d'ors.[30] Before the ship is allowed to cast anchor at the harbor front, the passengers are all examined, according to the law in force, by a physician, as to whether any contagious disease exists among them. Then the new arrivals are led in procession to the City Hall and there they must render the oath of allegiance to the king of Great Britain. After that they are brought back to the ship. Then announcements are printed in the newspapers, stating how many of the new arrivals are to be sold. Those who have money are released. Whoever has well-to-do friends seeks a loan from them to pay the passage, but there are only a few who succeed. The ship becomes the market-place. The buyers make their choice among the arrivals and bargain with them for a certain number of years and days. They then take them to the merchant, pay their passage and their other debts and receive from the government authorities a written document, which makes the newcomers their property for a definite period."

When we examine the dates of arrival of the ships, we note that the large majority of them arrived in the fall. In August twenty-nine, in September one hundred and thirty-eight, in October eighty-six, in November thirty-three and in December fourteen. In none of the other months did the totals exceed five ships for each month. Muehlenberg was, therefore, entirely correct when he stated that most of the ships reached

[29] *Hallesche Nachrichten,* new ed., Vol. II, pp. 460–461.

[30] The equivalent of the louis d'or is about $4.50, though its purchasing power at that time was much greater.

Philadelphia when the hardships of winter were staring the newcomers in the face.

But, in spite of all difficulties and hardships, new settlers continued to come. The wonder is not that so many succumbed, but that so many faced all hardships uncomplainingly and after a few years of service emerged from all difficulties as successful farmers, who made the country blossom as a rose. It only shows of what sturdy stuff these pioneers were made. Modern historians describing their hardships do, no doubt, more complaining than they themselves ever did.

Among the interesting documents, brought to Pennsylvania by the German pioneers, two deserve special mention.

The first was a passport, with which all the emigrants coming from Germany and Switzerland were supposed to be provided. One of these passports, of which we present a facsimile, reads as follows:

"We, the Burgomaster and Council of the city of Chur [Choire] in the Canton of the Grisons, confess herewith that, through the grace of God, we enjoy at present in our city and neighboring places, a good, healthy and pure air and that no dangerous plague or infectious disease prevails.

"In testimony whereof the bearer of this, Mr. Andrew Loretz, a citizen here, and single, who intends to travel to Amsterdam, for purposes of business, has been given this certificate, provided with the seal of our chancery, so that he may pass and repass at all places, freely and unimpeded.

"Given the 8th of September 1784.

$$\left\{ \text{Seal} \right\} \quad \begin{array}{l} \text{Certified} \\[1em] \text{Chancery of Chur.''} \end{array}$$

The second document, which was taken along on the journey to America, was a letter of recommendation, issued by the pastor of the church to the members of his flock, when they left their homes. One of these letters of recommendation, which has survived, and of which we present also a facsimile, reads as follows:

"The bearer of this letter, John Michael Paulus,[31] hitherto a member of our congregation at Essenheim and Catharine,

[31] The present descendants of the Paulus family are still members of the Reformed Church, in the Creutz Creek congregation in York County.

his lawful wife, both members of our Church, Reformed according to the Word of God, are willing and have the intention, in the name of God, to undertake the journey to the American Colonies, belonging to England, that they may find there a more abundant livelihood. They are herewith commended, upon their difficult and dangerous journey, to the protection of the Almighty, the love of our faithful Savior Jesus Christ and the communion of the Holy Spirit, to keep them in body and soul. I recommend them faithfully to all ecclesiastical and secular authorities, as well as to the Christian and charitable consideration of every person.

"Given at Essenheim in the Electoral Palatinate, near the city of Mayence, May 2, 1742.

"J. Radernher, pastor of the Reformed Church here."

What makes this certificate of special interest is the fact that Mr. Paulus was one of the fellow-passengers of John Andrew Strassburger, when he came to Pennsylvania on the ship Loyal Judith, which landed at Philadelphia September 3, 1742.

PUBLICATION OF THE SHIP LISTS

There is still one more question to be discussed—the relation of this publication to the earlier editions of these lists. What is it that justifies the present publication?

Reference has already been made to the fact that the oath of allegiance as well as the oath of abjuration were signed in the Court House at Philadelphia. Hence, the Clerk of Council copied the signatures to the oath of allegiance into the minutes of the Council. In this way the first forty-three lists, from September 18, 1727, to October 19, 1736, found their way into the minutes of the Council. They were published by the State of Pennsylvania in 1852, under the title *Colonial Records*. The lists appear in Vols. III–IV of these records.

It was most likely this publication in the *Colonial Records* that drew the attention of I. Daniel Rupp, the well-known historian of Pennsylvania to the lists. At any rate, in 1856, he published a book, entitled *A Collection of Thirty Thousand Names of German, Swiss, Dutch, French and Other Immigrants in Pennsylvania from 1727 to 1776*, etc. It contained the names of all the males of sixteen years and upwards, in the body of the book, the children's names being given in an appendix. In 1875 and later, other editions appeared, which Rupp calls "carefully revised and much improved." The improvement consisted in the fact that the names of the children under sixteen years were inserted, in the case of each ship, with which children are given, immediately under the names of the adults. Rupp also added sixteen appendices and an "Interpretation of the Baptismal Names."

There are two main criticisms to be made of the publication of Rupp. In the first place, he was too arbitrary in his treatment of the lists. In not one case did he reproduce the lists exactly as he found them in the originals, but he radically changed the lists in everything that allowed of change. He changed the headings, he changed the arrangement of the names and he changed the spelling of the names. Secondly, he misread hundreds of names.

The headings were made up by Rupp from the *Colonial Records,* or condensed from the actual headings as found on the lists. In this attempt to condense many slips were made, only a few of which need to be mentioned, by way of example. Occasionally he omitted the name of the ship. Thus in No. 43, he states that 110 persons were imported in the brigantine Perthamboy, which should be, in the brigantine John, of Perthamboy. In list 141, he omits both the name of the ship as well as the captain, the ship was Lydia and the captain John Randolph (See our No. 142).

More frequently he misreads the names of the ships. Richmond and Elizabeth (No. 33) should be Richard and Elizabeth. Virginus Grace (No. 46) should be Virtuous Grace. The name of ship No. 58 should not be Nancy and Friendship, but Friendship; while the name Nancy belongs to No. 59. The ship Bawley, No. 188, should be the ship Rawley, see our list, No. 191. Robert and Oliver (No. 55) should be Robert and Alice. Instead of Morton Star (No. 296) we should read Morning Star (see our list, No. 301).

A number of captains' names are also misread and misprinted. Thomas Arnt should be Thomas Arnot, William McNair should read William Muir, Captain Lickey should be changed to Captain Lickley.

The dates of the ships are frequently misprinted: October 25, 1748 (No. 123) should be August 24, 1749 (see our No. 124). September 17, 1750 (No. 156) should be October 17, 1750 (our No. 158). For Jan. 23, 1767 (No. 258) read Jan.

13, 1767 (our No. 263). October 30, 1770 (List 277) should be October 3, 1770 (our No. 282). Instead of June 21, 1774 (No. 314) read Sept. 29, 1774 (our No. 319).

Even worse than this is the fact that Rupp dropped occasionally the whole of the heading and thereby merged two passenger lists into one. Thus list 148 (our list 149), dated August 15, 1750, giving the passengers of the ship Royal Union, extends in Rupp's book to the second column of p. 230.[32] With the name Jacob Crebler a new list, our list 150 C, begins, which contains the passengers of the ship St. Andrew. They arrived on the same date, August 15, 1750.

In Rupp's list, No. 159, dated August 26, 1751, two lists have been merged, by dropping out several pages of manuscript. What Rupp prints is the first part of the passengers of the ship Anderson, and on p. 247, beginning with Michael Barle, the last part of the passengers of the ship Elizabeth (see our No. 162 C). He also overlooked our list, No. 84, although it is found in three forms (No. 84 A, B and C), and he omitted two later lists, No. 229 A and 233 A, as printed in our edition.

Another objectionable feature of Rupp's lists is that he rearranged the names in all the lists. Instead of following the order of the names as given on the originals, he rearranged them, apparently without any order and plan. In some of the lists, as for example on pp. 188–189, he printed the short names first, and placed the long names, consisting of three elements, at the end. As a result, it is difficult to identify his lists, when we compare them with the originals.

The order of the names was often of great significance and importance. In many cases the Palatines came over in colonies, with their leader at the head of the list. This is the case in the very first list, headed by the Rev. G. M. Weis, a German Reformed minister. We know definitely from his ordination certificate that he was the leader of this colony of Palatines.[33] The two important Lutheran ministers, John Caspar Stoever, father and son, head the eighth list, dated September 11, 1728. Rupp puts their names near the end of the list. The tenth list, dated September 11, 1729, is headed by Alexander Mack, Sr.,

[32] We are quoting the second edition, first published in 1875.
[33] This certificate is printed in the writer's *History of the Goshenhoppen Charge*, p. 36f.

the leader of this Dunker colony. Rupp puts his name in 14th place. The sixteenth list, dated September 21, 1731, is headed in the original by the Rev. John Bartholomew Rieger. We have definite proof that he came to Pennsylvania at the head of a colony. Rupp gives his name the 36th place in his list. The Lutheran minister, Rev. John Christian Schultz, heads list No. 24. Rupp apparently thought this of no importance, for he puts his name in the 17th place. The sum total of all his re-arrangements is, that he has obscured many important historical facts, which lie buried in his lists.

The most serious criticism of Rupp's book, is however, that in literally hundreds of cases he failed to decipher the names correctly. It is, of course, true that in some cases no man living can decipher with certainty the awful scribbles of some of the writers. But, when there are several lists of a ship, we can secure much better results by a comparative study of the lists, which Rupp entirely neglected. He has not even copied the baptismal names as he found them in the originals, but substituted in most cases the modern spelling. Moreover, his placing of the sick people at the end of the lists is arbitrary. In the originals they are scattered through the lists.

This careful analysis shows how sadly defective and imperfect is the edition of Rupp. No wonder the State of Pennsylvania felt that these lists should be published in a more complete and perfect form. They were issued in 1890, under the editorship of Dr. William H. Egle, as Vol. XVII of the second series of the *Pennsylvania Archives*. This publication excelled the book of Rupp in completeness. First of all, it added the captains' lists. It is true, not all of them were printed, for out of the 138 captains' lists, which have survived, only 97 appeared in print. Besides, in some cases, as in lists Nos. 1, 58, 60, 61 and 84, the captains' lists were substituted in place of the other lists, although this is not stated by the editor. Thus, the very first list in Vol. XVII of the *Archives* is the captain's list, while the actual signatures were omitted, much to the mystification of the student, who wonders what has become of the list which Rupp gives as his first list.

Another evidence of the more complete form, in which the lists are found in this edition, is the fact that the later lists, from 1786 to 1808, were included. This has added thousands of names to those of Rupp. But not all of the later lists were printed. For some reason which is not apparent all the lists of the years 1785, 1791 and 1792 were overlooked, so that our edition contains about forty new lists, from 1785 to 1808, which are not found in the *Archives*.

Unfortunately Dr. Egle, who was a good historian but no German scholar, was compelled to take over the names as printed by Rupp, with all their mistakes, except that he corrected most of the headings. In view of these facts, which can easily be verified by any one, qualified to read the originals, we must conclude that the former publications of these lists contain many grave defects, which seriously impair their usefulness. There has been, therefore, a long and persistent demand for a more accurate publication. This demand the present publication seeks to meet.

This new edition has two main objectives. First of all, it aims to present all the lists that arc now in existence in full, without any change or abbreviation. There are at present, from 1727 to 1775 three hundred and twenty-four lists in the archives of the State of Pennsylvania. From 1785 to 1808, the number is one hundred and eighty-two. In the first period there are three kinds of lists, as we have seen. These have been distinguished as follows:

1. The captains' lists, marked **A.**
2. The signers of the oath of allegiance, marked **B.**
3. The signers of the oath of abjuration, marked **C.**

In order to present all the evidence now available regarding these lists, extracts from the minutes of the Provincial Council have been added, in the case of the first forty-three lists. In addition, the reports of the health officers on the condition of the health of the passengers are now given for the first time. There are thirty-one such health-certificates, two in 1741 and twenty-nine from 1753 to 1755. Finally, in the notes, the editor has identified quite a number of the passengers. As his studies have been confined principally to the history of the Reformed and Lutheran churches in Pennsylvania, these notes mention only Reformed and Lutheran leaders. There are hundreds of other names that can easily be identified. But that task has been left to later investigators.

In the second place, this new edition aims to justify its existence by greater accuracy in reproducing the lists. This we aim to do by printing the names in the exact order as found in the originals. The printed book is meant to offer as exact a transcript of the lists as can be made, with the exception of some details, as will appear in the following rules, which have been observed in editing the text:

1. The lists have been numbered by the editor, the numbers being placed in square brackets.

2. Most of the lists have headings in the originals. But when no heading was given, the editor has added a heading, enclosed in square brackets.

3. The headings of the lists are unpunctuated in the originals. Punctuation marks have been added by the editor.

4. In many of the captains' lists, the names are numbered. These numbers have been omitted.

5. Unusual arrangements of the names in the captains' lists have been disregarded. The names have been printed in the usual arrangement.

6. Capital letters have been substituted for all small letters used to begin Christian names as well as surnames.

7. The surnames have always been spelled as in the originals. Only in a few cases has the correct spelling been added by the editor in square brackets.

8. Names that are spelled wrong have not been corrected, even though the error appeared plainly through the other lists.

9. The phrase "Sick on board" is always given in the correct English spelling, instead of the many varying spellings that occur on the originals. They can be seen on the facsimiles.

10. Other phrases, as "der Alt" or "der Jung," have been changed to the corresponding English "Senior" and "Junior."

11. Initials and marks of persons who could not write have been enclosed in round brackets ( ), to distinguish them from the signature made by the clerk.

12. The phrase "his mark" which often accompanies the mark made by the signer, has always been omitted, as its insertion between the lines would have disfigured the text.

13. Many of the curious and strange marks of the signers have not been imitated, but ordinary marks have been substituted. The original marks can be seen on the facsimiles.

14. The line, placed by many signers above their "m" or "n" to indicate that they are to be doubled, has not been inserted, but instead the letters have been doubled.

The main emphasis of the editor has been laid throughout upon the proper decipherment of the names of the passengers. Wherever there was more than one list of a ship, the names on the different lists have been carefully compared. From this comparative study of the lists, many new and better readings have been obtained. There are, however, many names which defy all pain and patience to read them correctly. In these cases a question mark, enclosed in square brackets, indicates the uncertainty in the reading.

But the chief distinction of the present edition is the fact that all the lists of signatures are reproduced in facsimiles in Vol. II. These facsimiles comprise all the signatures on the B and the C lists. The captains' lists have been omitted, as they are written in English characters. These facsimiles will enable the student who can read the German script to test the accuracy of the decipherment. It is this feature of the new edition, which will give it permanent value and importance.

This fine result could not have been secured without the whole-hearted co-operation of the authorities of the Pennsylvania State Library and Archives, Captain Frederic A. Godcharles, the Director of the State Library and Dr. Hiram H. Shenk, the State Archivist, who supplied most cheerfully photostats for all the lists and information, whenever it was needed. The editor wishes to thank them heartily for all their valued assistance, without which the lists could not have been printed.

Other persons who gave assistance in this work were Mr. H. S. Borneman, the Secretary of the Society, who gave his wholehearted support to the work, Mr. H. W. Kriebel of Pennsburg, Pa., who prepared the first copies of the lists, Mr. Frederick S. Fox, who acted as representative of Mr. Strassburger, and finally Mr. Strassburger himself, who has shouldered the large, financial burden, to make this edition a reality.

WILLIAM J. HINKE.

Auburn Theological Seminary,
Auburn, New York.

TABLE OF CONTENTS

xlvii

PAGE

Table of Contents

liii

PAGE

PENNSYLVANIA GERMAN PIONEERS

OFFICIAL LISTS OF PERSONS
ARRIVING IN THE PORT OF PHILADELPHIA

PRESERVED IN THE ARCHIVES OF THE
COMMONWEALTH OF PENNSYLVANIA AND
NOW PUBLISHED FOR THE FIRST TIME IN
THEIR ENTIRETY

Volume I

Colonial Period

1727–1775

OATHS OF ALLEGIANCE AND ABJURATION

On September 14, 1727, Patrick Gordon, the Lieutenant Governor of the Province of Pennsylvania, called together the Provincial Council, and "acquainted the board, that he had called them together at this time to inform them that there is lately arrived from Holland, a Ship with four hundred Palatines, as 'tis said, and that he has information they will be very soon followed by a much greater Number, who design to settle in the back parts of this province; & as they transport themselves without any leave obtained from the Crown of Great Britain, and settle themselves upon the Proprietors untaken up Lands without any application to the Proprietor or his Commissioners of property, or to the Government in general, it would be highly necessary to concert proper measures for the peace and security of the province, which may be endangered by such numbers of Strangers daily poured in, who being ignorant of our Language & Laws, & settling in a body together, make, as it were, a distinct people from his Majesties Subjects.

"The Board taking the same into their serious consideration, observe, that as these People pretended at first that they fly hither on the Score of their religious Liberties, and come under the Protection of His Majesty, it's requisite that in the first Place they should take the Oath of Allegiance, or some equivalent to it to His Majesty, and promise Fidelity to the Proprietor & obedience to our Established Constitution; And therefore, until some proper Remedy can be had from Home, to prevent the Importation of such Numbers of Strangers into this or others of His Majesties Colonies.

" 'TIS ORDERED, that the Masters of the Vessells importing them shall be examined whether they have any Leave granted them by the Court of Britain for the Importation of these Foreigners, and that a List shall be taken of the Names of all these People, their several Occupations, and the Places from whence they come, and shall be further examined touch-

3

ing their Intentions in coming hither; And further, that a Writing be drawn up for them to sign declaring their Allegiance & Subjection to the King of Great Britain & Fidelity to the Proprietary of this Province, & that they will demean themselves peaceably towards all his Majesties Subjects, & strictly observe, and conform to the Laws of England and of this Government.

"At a Council held at the Courthouse of Philadelphia, September 21st, 1727,   Present:

"The Honble Patrick Gordon, Esqr, Lieut. Governor.

James Logan,   William Fishbourn, } Esq'rs.
Richard Hill,

"A Paper being drawn up to be signed by those Palatines, who should come into this Province with an Intention to settle therein, pursuant to the order of this Board, was this day presented, read & approved, & is in these Words:

"We Subscribers, Natives and Late Inhabitants of the Palatinate upon the Rhine & Places adjacent, having transported ourselves and Families into this Province of Pensilvania, a Colony subject to the Crown of Great Britain, in hopes and Expectation of finding a Retreat & peaceable Settlement therein, Do Solemnly promise & Engage, that We will be faithful & bear true Allegiance to his present MAJESTY KING GEORGE THE SECOND, and his Successors, Kings of Great Britain, and will be faithful to the Proprietor of this Province; And that we will demean ourselves peaceably to all His said Majesties Subjects, and strictly observe & conform to the Laws of England and of this Province, to the utmost of our Power and best of our understanding." [1]

This declaration of allegiance is found at the head of all the papers, bearing the signatures of immigrants, marked B in the following pages. Beginning with August 19, 1729, the immigrants were required to sign two additional declarations, which were entered in a bound book. The latter in course of time became a series of bound books, to each of which these two declarations were prefixed. The signatures to these declarations are marked C in the following pages.

The two additional declarations, to which the immigrants affixed their signatures in the bound books, were as follows:

"I A B do solemnly & sincerely promise & declare that I

---

[1] See *Colonial Records of Pennsylvania*, Vol. III, p. 282 f.

will be true & faithful to King George the Second and do solemnly sincerely and truly Profess Testifie & Declare that I do from my Heart abhor, detest & renounce as impious & heretical that wicked Doctrine & Position that Princes Excommunicated or deprived by the Pope or any Authority of the See of Rome may be deposed or murthered by their Subjects or any other whatsoever. And I do declare that no Forreign Prince Person Prelate State or Potentate hath or ought to have any Power Jurisdiction Superiority Preeminence or Authority Ecclesiastical or Spiritual within the Realm of Great Britain or the Dominions thereunto belonging.

"I A B do solemnly sincerely and truly acknowledge profess testify & declare that King George the Second is lawful & rightful King of the Realm of Great Britain & of all others his Dominions & Countries thereunto belonging, And I do solemnly & sincerely declare that I do believe the Person pretending to be Prince of Wales during the Life of the late King James, and since his Decease pretending to be & taking upon himself the Stile & Title of King of England by the Name of James the third, or of Scotland by the Name of James the Eighth or the Stile & Title of King of Great Britain hath not any Right or Title whatsoever to the Crown of the Realm of Great Britain, nor any other the Dominions thereunto belonging. And I do renounce & refuse any Allegiance or obedience to him & do solemnly promise that I will be true and faithful, & bear true allegiance to King George the Second & to him will be faithful against all traiterous Conspiracies & attempts whatsoever which shall be made against his Person Crown & Dignity & I will do my best Endeavours to disclose & make known to King George the Second & his Successors all Treasons and traiterous Conspiracies which I shall Know to be made against him or any of them. And I will be true & faithful to the Succession of the Crown against him the said James & all other Persons whatsoever as the same is & stands settled by An Act Entituled An Act declaring the Rights & Liberties of the Subject & settling the Succession of the Crown to the late Queen Anne & the Heirs of her Body being Protestants, and as the same by one other Act Entituled An Act for the further Limitation of the Crown & better securing the Rights & Liberties of the subject is & stands settled & entailed after the Decease of the said late

Queen, & for Default of Issue of the said late Queen, to the late Princess Sophia Electoress & Dutchess Dowager of Hannover & the Heirs of her Body being Protestants; and all these things I do plainly & sincerely acknowledge promise & declare according to these express Words by me spoken & according to the plain & common Sense and understanding of the same Words, without any Equivocation mental Evasion or secret Reservation whatsoever. And I do make this Recognition Acknowledgement Renunciation & Promise heartily willingly & truly."

LISTS OF PENNSYLVANIA GERMAN PIONEERS
1727–1775

[List 1 A] A List of ye Palatine Passengers, Imported on ye Ship William & Sarah, Willm Hill, Ma^r from Rotterdam. Philad^a ye 18th Sept. 1727.

PERSONS NAMES	NO. PERSONS	PERSONS NAMES	NO. PERSONS
Hans Jerrick Swaep	6	Willm Jurgens	1
Hans Mart^n Leristeyn	2	Johan Wester, sick	1
Benedice Strome	2	Willm Heer	1
Jan Hend^k Scaub	3½	Hans Adam Milder	2
Hans Jerrick Shoomaker	6½	Anspel Anspag	2½
Abraham Beni	5	Henrick Meyer	4
Hans Martain Shoomak^r	1	Adam Henrich	2
Frederick Heiligas	4½	Jacob Gons	2
Hans Mich^l Pagman	1	Ulrich Steere	3
Sebastian Creef	4	Sebastian Vink	2
Johan^s Habaraker	2½	Tonicus Meyer	5
Alex^r Diebenderf	2	Jacob Swicker, sick	1
Hieronemus Milder, D.	2	Hans Jer. Herzels	4
Johan Willm Mey	2	Jan Bernard Wolf	6
Henericus Bell	1	Steven Frederick	3½
Caspar Springler	4	Ann Floren	1½
Hans Heri^k Siegler	3	Philip Fernser	1
Michael Peitley	4½	Hans Jacob Ekman	2
Hans Mich^l Tiell	3½	Hans Fill Heysinger	1
Jan Barne^d Lerinstey	1	Hendrick Wittser	1
Jacob Jost	2	Hans Jerrick Hoy, sick	1
Johannes Hoet	3½	Jacob Pause	2½
Daniel Levan, Con.	8	Andr^w Saltsgerrer, Conn.*	1
Hans Mich^l Weider, Con.	2	Hans Jerrick Wolf	2½
And^w Simmerman	8	Jacob Milder, dead	3½
Leonart Seltenrich, dead	2	Hans Jerrick Bowman	1
Hans Jerrick Wigler	2	Johannes Wester	1

* The word "Conn." was probably intended for Conestoga.

PERSONS NAMES	NO. PERSONS	PERSONS NAMES	NO. PERSONS
Johannes Storm's boy	1	Conrad Miller, sick	5
Hans Jerig Anspag	2½	Christopher Walter	4
Phillip Swyger	2	Ulrick Hertsell, Skipach	2
Christoᵣ Milder, dead	2	Hans Adam Stoll, Conn.	3
Elias Meyer	3½	Hans Jerick Guyger, Conn.	4½
Petter Spingler	1	Hans Martin Wilder	2½
Martin Prill	3	Hans Jerig Viegle	
Johˢ Tobˢ Serveas	1	Hans Jerig Arldnold, dead	6½
Peter Seyts	4½	Hans Jerig Cramer	3
Johanes Ekman	4	Hans Jerig Reter	2½
Johanes Hendᵏ Gyger, sick	2	Albert Swoap	1
Christoᵣ Labengyger	2	Hendrick Gouger, sick	3½
Johanes Berret	4	Diederich Roede	1
Andrew Holtspan	4	Hans Jerig Roedebas, Skipach	2
Jacob Swarts	4	Hans Adam Beinder	4½
Hans Jerick Schaub, Conn.	3	Christopher Wittmer	1
Hans Michˡ Phauts, Skibach	5	Hendrick Hartman	3
Christian Snyder, Germt.	2	Clement Eirn	2
Bastian Smith	2	Philip Jacob Reylender	5
Johanes Barteleme	1	Johanes Michˡ Peekell	1
Tobias Frye	4	Ernest Roede	1
Johannes Tiebenderf, Conn.	4	Philip Seigler	5½
Jacob Mast, Skipach	4	Philip Roedeull	2
Joseph Aelbragt	3½	Rudolph Wilkes	3
Nicholas Adams	2	Hans Jerig Milder	1
Jacob Meyer	2	Abraham Farn	4
Johanes Leyb	4	Uldrich Staffon	3
Johanes Balt, Germt.	4		

[Endorsed:]

This is a true List of Passengers, imported in the Ship William & Sarah, Willᵐ Hill, Mastᵣ from Rotterdam, among whom are no convicts.

Given upon oath,

by Tho. Tober.

"At a Council held at the courthouse of Philadelphia, September 21st, 1727, . . . A signed list was laid before the Board, of the Names of one hundred & nine Palatines, who with their families, making in all about four hundred Persons, were imported into this Province in the Ship William and Sarah, William Hill, Master, from Rotterdam, but last from Dover, as by Clearance from the Officers of his Majesties Customs there; And the said Master being asked, if he had any license from the Court of Great Britain for transporting those People, & what their Intentions were in coming hither, said that he had no other License or Allowance for their Transportation than the above Clearance, and that he believed they designed to settle in this Province. They were then called in, and the several Persons whose names were subjoyned did repeat & subscribe the foregoing Declaration."

From the Minutes of the Provincial Council, printed in *Colonial Records,* vol. III, p. 283.

[List 1 B] Palatines imported in the ship Willm & Sarah, Willm Hill, Comm^r from Rotterdam, who hereunto sett their hands the 21st of Sepr 1727, in the presence of the Govr & Council.

G. M. Weis, V.D.M.*	Hans Mart. (W) Weller
Johann Geörg Schwab	Hans Jerg Vögelle
Hans Bernhart Wolff	Willem Herr
Joh. Friederich Hilligass	Johannes Barth
Rudolff Beyl	Hans Caspar Spengler
Hans Michel Diel	Hans Görg Crcmmer
Sebästian Gräff	Hanns Martin Mill
Johannes Huth	Andres (A) Holsbacher
Philibs Jacob Rheinlender	Jacob Bausel
Philip (X) Zigler	Hans Adam (/) Miller
Tobias Frey	Johan Jacob Cuntz
Hans Jerch Anspacher	Hans Jörg Wolff
Johann Peter Seitz	Philib Rutschly
Joseph Albrecht	Hans Ernst Rudi
Johannes Eckman	Elias Meyer
Jerich Schuhmacher	Hans Michael Zimmerman
Jacob Jost	Hans Görg Welcker
Michel Böttle	Hans Phillip Schweikhardt
Rutolff Wellecker	Allexand. Dübendörfer
Jeorg Petter	Hans Martin Liebenstein

* For the history of this colony, led by the Reformed minister, George Michael Weiss, see *History of the Goshenhoppen Charge,* pp. 19–45.

Johan Tiderich Rudi
Hans Jerg Hertzel
Johannes Leib
Joh. Henrich Hartman
Hans Georg Ziegler
Johanes Haberacker

Henrich Meyer
Jacob Meyer
Christoph Walter
Henry (H) Sippen
Hans Michel Pfautz

[List 2 A] A List of Palatyns, Imported In yᵉ Ship James Goodwill, David Crockatt, Master, from Rotterdam, Sept 27, 1727.*

	Men to be sworn	Number in family		Men to be sworn	Number in family
Michael Sigrist	1	6	Hans Michael Fiedler	1	3
Michael Tanner	1	2	Philip Schaberger	1	5
Joseph Schurgh	1	3	Hendrich Wolfe	1	2
Hans Haggy	1	4	Jurgh Steiniger	1	7
Jurgen Miller	1	5	Joseph Clap		
Hans Leaman	1	5	Johan Adam Philple		
Hans Langneker	1	2	Jurg Clap		
Hendrich Aberlee	1	5	Ludowigh Clap	6	14
Raynard Jung	1	3	Christian Miller		
Jacob Wygart ⎫			Jurg Coch		
Wm. Wygart ⎭	2	2	Jacob Walter, Senʳ ⎫		
Tewalt Leatherman	1	6	Jacob Walter, Junʳ ⎭	2	6
Hans Michal Kunts ⎫			Christopher Kirchofe	1	5
Jurg Michael Kunts ⎭	2	4	Jacob Siegel	1	6
Ulrich Stoupher	1	6	Jacob Gass, Senʳ, sick ⎫		
Ulrich Zug	1	4	Jacob Gass, Junʳ ⎬	3	6
Peter Zug	1	4	Fredrich Gass ⎭		
Barthol. Sigrist	1	4	John Miller ⎫		
Abraham Aberholt	1	4	Joseph Miller ⎬	3	9
Jacob Fritz	1	3	Hans Miller ⎭		
Adam Kiener ⎫			Jacob Arnet	1	3
Wm. Kiener ⎬	3	9	Paul Hein ⎫		
Hans Kiener ⎭			Hans Hein ⎭	2	6
Christian Webber	1	4	Bastian Merree	1	1
Margaret Heislern		4	Michael Lybert	1	3

* Date entered by different hand.

	Men to be sworn	Number in family		Men to be sworn	Number in family
Jurg Zengh	1	2	Hendrich Schultz	1	1
Jacob Gangwyer	1	1	Hans Foster	1	1
				53	166

[Endorsed:]

Names of the Palatines who subscribed the Declaration. 27ᵗʰ Sepʳ 1727.

Da. Crockat, 53 P[ersons].

"At a Council held in the Courthouse of Philadia, Septemʳ 27ᵗʰ 1727, . . . A List was presented to the Board of the names of Fifty-three Palatines, who with their Families making in all about two hundred Persons were imported into this Province in the Ship James Goodwill, David Crocket, Mr., from Rotterdam, but last from Falmouth, as by the Masters Affidavit signed by the Officers of the Customs there, it appeared upon Enquiry that the Master had no particular License for their Transportation."

From the Minutes of the Provincial Council, printed in *Colonial Records,* Vol. III, p. 284.

[List 2 B] Palatines imported in the Ship James Goodwill, David Crockat, Mʳ from Rottʳ, who hereunto sett their hands, 27ᵗʰ Sepʳ 1727, in the presence of the Governʳ & Council.

Michael Sygrist	Uhly Staufer
Michel Daner	Ulrich Zug
Joseph (IOS) Schurgh	Peter Zug
Ha[n]s Häge	Bartholomeus Sigrist
Yerg Miller [?]	Abrahm Ebersohl
Hannes (L) Leman	Jacob (F) Fritz
Hans (H) Langneker	Adam Kinner
Heinrich Eberle	Ulrich Kiner
Reinhardt Jung	Hanes Kiner
Jacob Wiggerdt	Christian Weber
Johann Wilhelm Wigardt	Hans Michael (H) Fiedler
Hans Depelt Lederman	Philip (OO) Schafberger
Hans Michell Kuntz	Henrich Wolff
Jerg Michel Kuntz	Jerg Steinieger

Joseph (K) Clap
Johann Adam Völpel
Jörg Valentin Klap
Johann Ludwig Klap
Hans Georg Koch
Johan Jacob Waldter
Jacob Walder
Christoph Kirchhoff
Jacob Siegel
Friderich Gass
Hans Jacob Gass

Johannes Miller
Hans Miller
Joseph Miller
Jacob Arnet
Paul (PH) Hein
Bastian Müri
Michael Leiberth
Jerg Zeng
Jacob (X) Gangwyer
Hendrich (O) Schultz
Hans Mich. [?] Forster

[List 3 A] A List of the Palatine men on Bord ye Ship Molley, Above ye Age of 16 yeares, as p. thar owne List. [Qualified Sept. 30, 1727.]

Hans Erick Ouer
Frances Stoupe
Hanse Stuber
Hans Jacob Bender
Michael Spowner, sick
Hans Erick Keelb
Hans Erick Herriger
Luterich Detterey
Hans Ouer Parrent
Luterich Peetter
Hans Adam Soulder
Hanse Michell Smith
Johannes Snider
Andres Elick
Porchas Hoffman
Felix Good
Johannes Crouse
Weyan Teale
Michale Sebasten
Hans Ubruk Shamaker, dead
Augusten Weder
Hans Lenord Hoffman
Hans Teyger
Marten Hosuer
Henrick Penhort

Henrick Fults, sick
Hans Erick Tetner
Merix Foux
Stephannus Raper
Erick Lutwich Zell
Samuell Bare
Hans Rinck
Hans Erick Shillingberg
David Marten
Jacob Marten
Henerick Hoffman
Jost Moser, sick
Christane Moser, sick
Ulrick Schillingbergen
Michell Shenck
Christane Walltone
Hanse Moser
Hans Yow
Jacob Shir
Hans Erick Crable
Henerck Meyer
Michell Crable
Samuell Owerhoulster
Fellone Younge
Jacob Roust

Hans Cooble
Jacob Baer
Hans Funck, sick
Michell Frances
Petter Good
Christane Solderman, sick
Jacob Horrester, dead
Samuell Good
Jacob Houer
Rodulf Landish
Rodulf Baine

Martine Kindige
Jacob Wanner
Orick Leep
Christane Willand
James Miller
Martine Kearstuter
Johannes Mattes Eyger
Johannes Pealer
Hans Miller, sick
Hans Michell
Hans Erick Feilter

[Endorsed:]
Names of the Palatines imported in the Molly, Jnº Hodgson, from Deal. 30ᵗʰ Sepʳ 1727, signed the Declaration. 72 P[ersons.]

"At a Council held at the courthouse of Philadelphia, Septʳ 30th, 1727, . . . A List was presented to the Board of the Names of Seventy Palatines, who with their Families, making in all about Three hundred Persons, were imported in the Ship Molley, Jno. Hodgeson, Master, from Rotterdam, but last from Deal as by Clearance from Officers of the Customs there."

From the Minutes of the Provincial Council, printed in *Colonial Records,* Vol. III, p. 287.

[List 3 B] Palatines Imported in the Ship Molly, John Hodgeson, Mʳ, from London, who hereunto sett their hands, 30ᵗʰ Sepʳ 1727, in the presence of the Govʳ & Council.

Hans Jerg Huber
Frantz Stupp
Hans Jacob Benter
Hans Jerige (X) Kelb
Hanns Jerg Horger
Johann Ludwig Dederer
Andries (X) Baerns
Ludwig Borz
Michel Schmidt
Andreas Illig
Burckhardt Hoffman
Felix Guth

Johannes Kraus
Wyan (W) Diell
Michel (S) Sebastiyan
Augustyn (A) Weder
Hans (X) Leenerd Hofman
Hanns Steger
Hans Michel Guth
Hans Michel Guth [?]
Martin Hauser
Hans Heinrich Bernhardt
Hans Jerg Dieter
Marx Fuchs

Stevus Reppert
Jerg Ludwig Gesell
Samuel Behr
Johannes Ring
Hans Jergh (×) Schellenberg
Davidt Mardtin
Jacob Marttin
Heinrich Kaufman
Ulrigh (O) Schellenberg
Michel (O) Schenck
Christian Velte
Hans Moser
Jacob Scherer
Henrich (×) Kryebiel
Henrich (HM) Mayer
Michael Krebiel
Samuel (O) Oberholts
Felden Gehr
Hans Jacob Rudt

Hans Kobel
Jacob Bähr
Michel Frantz
Peder Gut
Samuel Gut
Jacob Huber
Rudolf (RL) Landes
Rudolf (B) Been
Mardtin (MK) Kindigh
Jacob (×) Wanner
Ulrich Leib
Christyan (×) Miller
Hans (H) Hoogstadt
Joh. Mathys (J) Egener
Johannes Büller
Hans Jer. (×) Folcks
Dobias Schorch
Christian Wenger

[List 4 A] A List of Palatine Passengers imported in the Adventure Galley, John Mirion, Commander, from Rotterdam. Arrived at Philad[a] in October 1727. [Qualified Oct. 2, 1727.]

Mich[l] Miller
Ulrich Pitcha
Jasper Mingale
Jan Badler
Johannes Layman
Jasper Neye
Christo. Miller
Jacob Lydie
Jaqus Symone
Mich[l] Ikart
Johannes Ulrick
Hans Adam Oser
Peter Shilling
Jacob Meyer
Mathias Risling
Jacob Powman

Peter Rule
Jacob Smith
Mich[l] Kern
John Seyham
Christo. Exell
Derrick Romshower
Frans Baster Frans
Joannes Cortes
Peter Wiser
Jn[o] Sower
Nich[o] Corn
Hans Martator
Adam Pister
Joost Coope
Palzer Lyme
Jacob Willhelmus

Jacob Hoghman

Jacob Fisher

Ulrick Riser

Katherine Rowland

Leonard Rodennill

Carolo Horlogh

Hendrick Horlogh

Jacob Riser

Alexd^r Fritley

Anna Barbara Fiseling

Peter Boorlinger

Christian Frier

Benetick Nuel

Hans Peter Hus

Scipilo Hoffmaning

Jacob Filler

Hans Holdeman

Christo. Ulrick

Hans Hisley

Evan Fosterhave

Christian Piger

Joanes Yirk Heriger

Henery Smith

In all 55, given upon Oath.

"At a Council held at Philadelphia, October 2d, 1727, . . . A List was presented to the Board of Fifty three Palatines, who with their Families, making in all about one hundred and forty Persons, were imported in the Ship Adventure, Jno. Davies, Master, from Rotterdam, but last from Plymouth, as by Clearance from the Officers of Customs there." From the Minutes of the Provincial Council, printed in *Colonial Records,* Vol. III, p. 288.

[List 4 B] Palatines Imported in the Ship Adventure, Jno Davis, M^r, from Rott^r, who hereunto sett their hands Octob^r 2^d 1727.

Michel Müller

Johannes Beydeler

Johannes Lemahn

Casber Ney

Christopher (CM) Miller

Jacob Leidy

Jacque Simoult

Michael Eichert

Johannes Ullerich

Hans Adam (W) Osser

Peeter (+) Shilling

Mathias (X) Rysling

Jacob Bauman

Peeter (P) Rool

John (H) Seyham

Frans Baltzar (F) Frans

Johannes Kurtz

Johann Peter Weisner

Nicklos Chron

Balsar Leine

Jacob (IWH) Wihelmus

Ulrich Rieser

Joh. Carl (IKH) Horlacher

Nicolas (H) Keyser

Jean Dieter Borleman

Johann Petter Hess

Christopher (CH) Ulrik

Christian (CB) Bikler

Johann Jacob Stutzman

Daniel Borman

Georg Christoff Oechslen

[List 5 A] In the Friendship of Bristoll, Jnᵒ Davis, Mʳ, from Rotterdam, wiᵗʰ Sundry Palatine passengers as under [Oct. 16, 1727.]

Peter Hackman	Adam Lepert
Jnᵒ Forrer	Hillis Castle
Andrew Urmi, dead	Jnᵒ Overholsor, dead
Michal Eberam, sick	Abraham Miller
Andrew Swarts	Albert Bowman
Joseph Eberam, sick	Hans Jeri Miller
Henry Strickler	Nicholas Bogert
Jacob Trycler, dead	Matthias Andreas, dead
Jacob Histant	Hans Jeri Hofman
Jnᵒ Histant	Nicholas Chresman
Abrᵐ Swarts	Matthew Swizer
Christian Mayer	Peter Welde
Jnᵒ Feyseg	Jacob Sneppely
Peter Puckslear	Phillip Remer
Jacob Snyder, dead	Peter Folock, sick
Peter Hansberger, sick	Christian Fide, sick
Hans Reser	Phillip Reed
Peter Leman	Phalatine Gratz
Jeremiah Lowman	Henry Sneppley
Christian Crybile	Vinsent Mayer
Nicholas Chasrood, sick	Henry Schenholts
Henry Croo, dead	Uldrich Leemer, sick
Ulrich Scheren, sick	Johannes Castle
Martin Scheleren	Peter Fennima, sick
Henry Leer	Falkert Adest, dead
Jnᵒ Crybile, sick	Lodowick Bente

[Endorsed:]

Names of the Palatines, Imported in the Friendship, John Davis, from Rottʳ. Signed the Declaration of their Fidelity, the 16ᵗʰ Octʳ 1727.

"At a Council held at the Courthouse of Philadelphia, Octʳ 16th, 1727, . . . A List was presented to the Board of the Names of Forty six Palatines, who with their Families, making in all about Two hundred Persons, were imported here in the Ship Friendship of Bristol, John Davies, Mr., from Rotterdam, but last from Cows, as by Clearance from the Officers of the

Customs there." From the Minutes of the Provincial Council, printed in *Colonial Records,* Vol. III, p. 290.

[List 5 B] Palatines imported in the Ship Friendship of Bristol, John Davies, M^r, from Rotterdam, who hereunto sett their hands, the 16th day of Octr 1727, In presence of the Govr & Council.

Petter Hagmann	Albreght (A) Bauman
Johannes Forrer	Johann Georg Müller
Andreas Schwartz	Niclaus Bucher
Henrich Strickeller	Johann Jörg Hoffman
Jacob Hiestandt	Niklos Crössman
Johannes Hiestandt	Mathes Schweitzer
Abraham Schwartz	Peter (P) Welde
Christian Meyer	Jacob (J) Sneppelen
Johanes Bense	Philip (X) Reemer
Peter (X) Pixseler	Vallentin Kratz
Hans Riess	Henrich Schnebli
Peter (O) Leeman	Johann Vincens Meyer
Hans (H) Jerig Lauman	Johannes Schönholtzer
Christiyan (X) Krayebiel	Johannes Kassel
Martyn (X) Schaffener	Jacob Eberhartt
Yer[g] Henrich Lahr	Michel Eberhartt
Adam Libhart	Johann Philb Ried *
Yilles Kassel	Nicolas (X) Piere [Biery]
Jeremya (X) Miller	Michel (X) Miller

[List 6 A] A List of Palatine Passengers, Imported in the Ship Mortonhouse, John Coultas, Commander, from Rotterdam, but last from Deal, arrived ye 23^d of August 1728.

Dirck Begtoll	Valten Keuler
Jacob Brulasher	Hans Meyer
Philip Snolt	Hans Facts
Xtopher Benker	Xtian Newswange
Peter Middelcalf	Johan Herer
Xtophel Meng	Velde Grae
Abraham Wolf	Mich^l Keiler

* For the descendants of John Philip Ried see *History and Genealogy of the Reed Family,* by Dr. W. H. Reed, Norristown, 1929.

Johannes Wilhelm
Johannes Bair
Frans Latshow
Hans Berlie
Jacob Witsell
Jacob Heytshoe
Johannes Coopman
Werhelm Dillinger
Hans Wolf Dillinger
Baltes Gering
Rodolp Heller
Andries Evie
Hend^k Raan
Bernerd Hensell
Hend^k Ishelman
Michiel Seybell
Johannes Tracktehengst
Johannes Morgestern
Johannes Frankhuyse
Stephen Haltsbielder
Philip Engert
Johannes Root
Johannes Naycommet
Christopher Sullenger
Jacob Kegenhower
Hans Ulrick Doddere
Johannes Kets Miller
Hans Martin Miller
Hans Jacob Miller
Hans Leendert Miller
Coenraad Keer
Dirck Oordt
Jacob Hoogh
Hans Dirk Haak
Hans Dirk Root

Jonas Keeler
Mich^l Detemer
Martin Shoup
Jacob Storm
Jacob Brunner
Mich^l Ranck
Pieter Loets
John Lagerom
Fredrick Leder
Casper Heydering
Johan Edesman
Johan Stock
Uldrick Shurk
Uldrick Shurk
Johan Shurk
Dirk Smith
Jacob Joost
Clements Tonkelberg
Clements Tonkelberg
Peiter Tonckelberg
Fredrick Tonkelberg
Johan Joost Smit
Johan Pieter Melch
Vincent Stougher
Mich^l Honest
Godfrey Henk
Johannes Christ
Johan Elbreat Keeler
Martin Vogelhove
Johan Mathys Peiter
Johannes Roar
69 Women
56 Children
80 [Men]
_____
205 [Total]

[Endorsed:]

List of the Names of the Palatines, imported in the Ship Mortonhouse, Jn° Coultas, Commander.

Qualified 24th Augt 1728.

"At a Council held at the Courthouse of Philadelphia,

August 24th, 1728, . . . A List was presented to the Board of the Names of Eighty Palatines, who with their Families, making in all about Two hundred Persons, were imported in the Ship Mortonhouse, John Coultas, Master, from Rotterdam, but last from Deal, as by Clearance from the Officers of the Customs there, bearing Date the fifteenth day of June, 1728." From Minutes of Provincial Council, printed in *Colonial Records,* Vol. III, p. 327.

[List 6 B] Palatines imported in the Ship Mortonhouse, John Coultas, M^r, from Rotterdam, but last from Deal, as by clearance thence, bearing date 15th June 1728. Subscribed the above declaration 24th Augt 1728.

Jörg Bechtell
Philip Noldt
Christof Benders
Peter Mittelkauff
Johan Christoph Meng
Abraham Wolff
Felde (O) Kille
Han Seyt
Hans Fritz
Christ. (X) Nuswanger
Johannes Huber
Hans (W) Weldgrau
Michel Kehler
Johannis (X) Baer
Johannis (X) Baer
Johannes Bölle
Jacob (+) Wissel
Jacob Heidschuh
Hanes Kauff[man]
Henry (X) Wilhelm Dielinger
Hans (X) Wolf Dielinger
Baltus (X) Gerringer
Rudolf Heeller
Andres Ewig
John Henry (X) Raens
Barnet (O) Henssel
Henrich Eschelmann

Michel (X) Saipell
Johannes Wildhengst
Johannes Morgenstern
Staffen (O) Hattsebieller
Hans (+) Philip
Johannes Roth
Johannes Neykomet
Jacob (X) Coger
Johan Georg Doderer
Johannes (HKM) Kitsmiller
    the above likewise signs for
Conrad Ridt
Johann Georg Roth
John Jacob Hock
Jonas Köhler
Hans Michell Dettmer
Mardin Schaub
Jacob Storm
Jacob Brunner
Johann Michael Ranck
Johannes (X) Leegerhoen
Frederick (X) Leeder
Kasper (X) Heydricks
Johannes (O) Edisma
John Er [?]
Uli Schürch
Udry Schürch

Johannes (✕) Schorck
Georg Schmitt
Jacob Jost
Clemens Dunkelberg
Peter Denk (✕) Bergh
Frederick D (✕) Bergh
Johann Jost Schmidt
Johann Peter Mölich

Finchent (✕) Plauser
Gottfrit Henke
Johannes (✕) Krist
Johann Albrecht Köhler
Martin Voglhutter
Johannes (✕) Roer
Johannes Franckhauser
J. Marius Jordannus

[List 7 A] Palatines imported in the Ship Albany, Capt Oxman. Sworn 4th Septr 1728.

Mr. Strickem
Mr. Chaplin
Daniel Bengel
Simon Shaller
Philip Thoman
Philip Glaser
Hans Adam Mire, sick
Larance Belits
Henry Stelfelt
Caspar Oot
Friederich Egelberger
Conraat Teboy
Jacob Danbach
Jacob Beigel
Hans Jerik Beigel
Michel Keim

Kasper Keshit
Elexander Zaartman
Jacob Weis
Johanes Schenefelt
Jerik Boog
Jerik Moots
Jerik Gertner
Andrew Ablen
Hans Miller
John Bloom
Hens Jerick Riger
Martin Caleb
Johan Carle Keil
Jerig Frederick Bergenslott
    Van Hokmel (in Germantown)

The above is a true list of the masters of the Palatine Familys, imported in the ship Albany, from Rotterdam to Philadelphia.

Given in on Oath ye 4th day of September 1728.

p. Laz^s Oxman.

Sworn before Chas Read.

"At a Council in the courthouse of Philadelphia, Sept. 4th, 1728, . . . A List was presented of the Names of Thirty Palatines, who with their Families, making in all about One Hundred Persons, were imported here in the Ship Albany, Lazarus Oxman, Master, from Rotterdam, but last from Portsmouth, as by Clearance from the Officers of the Customs

there, bearing date the 22d of June, 1728." From the Minutes
of the Provincial Council, printed in *Colonial Records,* Vol.
III, p. 328 f.

[List 7 B] Palatines imported in the Albany, Captain Lazarus Oxman, M^r, from Rotterdam, but last from [Portsmouth]
as by clearance date. . . . Subscribed the foregoing Declaration 4th Sepr. 1728.

Georg Friedrich v. Berbisdorff
Friederich Christoph van Strys-
   skap
Matthias Koplin
Johan Daniel Bengel
Simon Schaller
Philip (D) Thoman
Johann Philip Glaser
Lorentz Belitz
Henrich Stellfelt
Casper (O) Hoot
Friederich Eichelberger
Conrad Dupoy
Hans Jacob Donbach
Hans Jacob Biehel

Gurg Wendel Biehel
Michel (O) Keim
Casper Riedt
Allexander Zarttmann
Jacob (W) Weis
Johannes Schönefelldt
Hans Gerg Buch
Hans Gerg Motz
Georg Gerthner
Andreas (A) Ablin
Hans (H) Miller
Jaen Bloemen
Hans Jerich (O) Riger
Martin (M) Calb
Johan Carl Keil

[List 8 A] List of the Mens Names above 16 years old
aboard ye James Goodwill, Mr David Crokatt, Commander,
from Rotterdam to Philadelphia in Pennsylvania, arrived the
11th Septemb^r 1728.

Ullerig Engelar
Andries Krafft
George Graff
Jan Leend^r Holstiender
Michael Neff
Jacob Fucks
Matthias Firrumsler
Egidius Grim
Johannes Gurts
Johan Leend^t Keller
Isaac Crison
Jacob Herman

Thomas Koppenheffer
Christoff Graff
Martin Valk
Hans Mich^l Ruiter
Martin Moeser
Henderik Phillip Seller
Frederik Sholl
Jacob Beyer
Mich^l Korr
Adam Engeler, sick
Loerens Durr
Sebastian Durr

Bartel Eberle	Teobald Mekeling
Sebastian Eberle	Hans George Seyler
Hans Adam Moesser	Jacob Sinc
George Shoemaker	Hans Veery Bants
Jacob Kun	Andries Stickeler
Leond[r] Hicker	Hans Jacob Slauss
Johan Casp[r] Steffer, Sen[r]	Johannes Ruspag
Johan Casper Steffer, Jun[r]	Hans George Mettler
Jacob Mekeling	Adam Summer

Thirty seven families produces Forty Two persons above 16 years.

Dav[d] Crokatt.

"At a Council held in the Courthouse of Philadelphia, Septem[r] 11th, 1728. . . . A List was presented of the Names of Forty two Palatines, who with their Families, making in all about Ninety persons, were imported here in the Ship James Goodwill, David Crockat, Master from Rotterdam, but last from Deal, as by Clearance from the officers of the Customs there, bearing Date the Fifteenth day of June, 1728." From the Minutes of the Provincial Council, printed in *Colonial Records,* Vol. III, p. 331.

[List 8 B] Palatines imported in the Ship James Goodwill, David Crockatt, M[r], from Rott[r], but last from [Deal] as by clearance dated. . . . Subscribed the forgoing declaration 11th Sepr 1728.

Johann Caspar Stöver, Miss.*	Madtheus Fernssler
Johann Caspar Stöver,	Johann Egidius Grimm
Ss. Theol. Stud.	Joannes (O) Gurts
Ulrich Englert	Johann Leonhart Keller
Andres Krafft	Isac Crison [?]
Gorg Graff	Jacob (✕) Herman
Johannes Leonhart Holsteiner	Thomas (✕) Kopenhaver
Michel Neff	Johann Christoph Groff
Jacob (O) Fucks	Hans Martin Valck

* These two Stoevers are famous Lutheran ministers. Stoever, Sr., the father, labored in Virginia; Stoever, Jr., the son, in Pennsylvania.

Hans Mich. (×) Rider
Martin Moser
Philips Henrich Söller
Friedrich Scholl
Jacob (×) Bayer
Michel Kur
Laurence (O) Dur
Sebastian Dörr
Bartell [Eberle]
Bastian Eb[erle]
Johan Adam Moser
Jerg Schuhmacher

Jacob Kuhn
Leon^d (O) Hicker
Jacob Mec[kling]
Theobald (D) Mechling
Hans Jerik (O) Seyler
Jacob Zenck
Hans Virech (O) Bontz
Andreas Strickel
Hans Jacob Schlauch
Johannes (O) Ruspag
Hans Jerg Mettler
Adam Sommer

[List 9 A] A List of Palatinate Passengers, Imported into Philadelphia in the Ship Mortonhouse, James Coultas, Commander, from Rotterdam. Aug.^st 17th 1729.

Dirick Truer
Juliana Truer
John Philip Ranck
Anna Barbara Rank
Jno Miller
Marg^t Miller
Eliz^a Erynstein
Connard Werness
Katherine Werness
Casper Dorest
Dilman Colb
Judith Colb
Michael Urelick
Anna Maria Urelick
Mich^l Boarst
John Haake
Rudolph Moor
Hance Jacob Roatslice
Uldery Roat
Lucy Roat
Nich^o Peffel
Barbara Peffel
Hendrick Doabs

Ultiner Snebler
Hendrick Plim
Hance Hendrick Ubera
Alce Ubera
Christopher Brown
John Furra
Jno Christ^n Croll
Mary Cunningham
Hendrick Warner
Sarah Warner
Gerrard Miller
Eliz^a Miller
Anna Maria Massin
Andrew Mayes
Hance Mich^l Hyder
Katherine Hyder
Jacob Creeple
Peter Weegar
Hendrick Sligloff
Anna Christian Sligloff
Analis Sligloff
Hendrick Sootera
Hance Uldrick Fry

Christopher Fry
Medelin Reymene
Jacob Bowman
Anna Bowman
Betsila Bowman
Anna Bowman, Junr
Apalone Sneeveler
Jno Casper Inkleree
John Miller
Jacob Over
Anna Marye Over
David Montandon
Jacob Reeif, formerly in Pa.
Jno Danl Worley
Valentine Fickus
Jno Adam Moor
Freenick Reeif, who is wife to
    Jacob Reif, inhabitant in Penn-
    sylvania.
John Rice
Katherine Rice
John Steven Regensberger
Dirick Adam Weedle
Ulderick Croll
Adam Shamback
Anna Dorothy Shamback
Coonrod Killinor
Johannes Binkler
Moret Creetor
Jacob Reyser
Eliz^a Reyser
Jacob Fetter
Richd Fetter
Anna Margarett Fetter
Philip Jacob Back
George Danl Back
Mich^l Wever
Phillis Wever
Wendel Wyant
Andrew Bastian
Adam Bastian

Martin Alstadt
Anna Judith Alstadt
Rudolph Walder
Hannah Barbary Walder
Hendrick Killhaver
Simon Reel
Eliz^a Seller
Jacob Seller, Junr, formerly in
    Pensyl^a.
Nicholas Carver
Jacob Eshelman
Welder Keyser
Agnis Keyser
Abraham Kensinger
Anna Barbara Kensinger
Frenee Kensinger
Richard Halder
Baltzar Roer
Katherine Ramerin
Christopher Bumgarner
Ursley Bumgarner
Anna Marya Abezant
Johannes Orde
Johanna Beagleson
Johannes Dirick Greesman
Frederick Marsh
Christian Longinacre
Dirick Greesman
Marya Greesman
Corol Arant Mooselback
Anna Barbary Longinacre
Mary Eliz^a Mooselback
Anna Margarett Mooselback
Peter Moll
Eliz^a Shamback
Johannes Middle
Hendrick Sneevler
    (Sworn Before in Capt. Davis's
    Comp^y)
Jacob Sellser (Sworn formerly)
    122 persons.

Sworn Before the Governour in Council, 19th August 1729.
Cleared from Deal in Great Britain. James Coultas.

R^t Charles

"At the Courthouse of Philadelphia, August 19th, 1729,
. . . A List was presented of the Names of Seventy five Palatines, who with their families, making in all about One hundred
& Eighty persons, were imported here in the Ship Mortonhouse,
James Coultas, Mr., from Rotterdam, but last from Deal, as
by Clearance thence dated 21st of June last." From Minutes of
the Provincial Council, printed in *Colonial Records,* Vol. III,
p. 367.

[List 9 B] Palatines imported in the ship Mortonhouse, Ja^s
Coultas, M^r, from Rotterdam, but last from Deal p. Clearance
thence, dated 21st June 1729. Subscribed this Declaration 19th
Augt. 1729.

Carl Ernst Musselbach	Jakob Crebil
Georg Threhr [Dreher]	Henrich Schlengeluf
Johan Philip Ranck	Henrich Gunter
Hans Müller	Hans Uldric (H) Vry
Kunradt Wörntz	Christ (O) Vry
Casper (X) Dorest	Jacob (O) Bowman
Dielman Kolb	Johan Nicolas Prietschler
Hans Michel Frölich	Johannes Müller
Michael Borst	Jacob (O) Obere
Johannes Hoock	David Montandon
Roedolp (X) Moor	Peter Weger
Hans Jacob (O) Roodlys	Valentine (/) Ficus
Uldric (X) Root	Adam Orth
Nicolaas (O) Peffell	Hanns Michel Heider
Heinrich Dubs	Johannes Reis
Mr. (X) Meli [?]	Johann Stephen Rumer
Henrich Blim	Görg Adam Wedel
Hans Ullrich Hüber	Ulrich (/) Croll
Christ (B) Baown	Adolph Schombach
Christ (C) Kroll	Conrad (O) Kilner
Hendk. (H) Werner	Johannes (/) Binkler
Gerhard Müller	Michel Weber
Andres Mys	Rudolff Walder

Hendrick (O) Killhaver
Simon Rohl
Nicolas (X) Carver
Jacob Eschelmann
Velten Keiser
Abraham (A) Keynsinger
Reynard (O) Halder
Baltsar (O) Roer

Christ (X) Bumgarner
Johannes (O) Orde
Johan Georg Crössman
Friederich Marsteller
Georg Crössman
Johann Peter Moll
Christian (/) Longenacre
Johannes (H) Middle

[List 9 C] Palatines imported in the ship Mortonhouse, James Coultas, Mr, From Rottr, but last from Deal.

Carl Ernst Musselbach
Georg Threhr
Johan Philip Ranck
Hans Muller
Konradt Wörntz
Casper (X) Dorest
Dielman Kolb
Hans Michel Frölich
Michael Borst
Johannes Hoock
Rudolph (X) Moore
Hans Jac. (O) Roatshlie
Uldry (X) Roat
Nicolas (O) Peffell
Heinrig Dubs
Ultimer (X) Snebler
Henrick Blim
Hans Ulrich [Huber]
Christop (B) Brown
Jno Christ. (C) Croll
Hendrick (H) Warner
Gerhard Miller
Andres Mös
Jakob Crebil
Henrich Schlengeuff
Henrich Gunter
Hans Ulrich (H) Fry

Christoph (O) Fry
Jacob (O) Bowman
Johan Nicolas Prietschler
Johannes Müller
Jacob (O) Over
David Montandon
Peter Weger
Valentyn (/) Vykus
Adam Orth
Hans Michel Heider
Johannes Reis
Johann Stephan Rümer
Georg Adam Wedel *
Uldrich (O) Kroll
Atolph Schombach
Conraad (O) Kilmer
Johannes (/) Benkelker
Michel Weber
Hans Merten Alltstatt
Hendk. (8) Kelhever
Simon Rohl
Nicolaas (X) Kerver
Jacob Eschelmann
Velten Keiser
Abraham (A) Kinsinger
Rheinhardt Attler
Baltes (O) Oord

* The original has been repaired at this place, obliterating the name, but traces of its presence remain.

Christ (X) Boomgardner
Johannes (O) Oord
Johan Georg Crössman
Friederich Marsteller

Georg Crössman
Johann Peter Moll
Christ (O) Langen Ekker
Johannes (X) Middel

Philad^a Aug. 19th 1729.

The foregoing qualifications were taken & subscribed by the several Palatines whose names are contained in this & preceding Page.

[List 10 A] A List of Passengers Imported in the Ship Allen from Rotterdam, James Craiges, Master, Septem^r 11th, 1729.

Alixander Mack
Johannes Mack
Felte Mack
Alixander Mack, Junr
John Hendrick Kalklieser
Jacob Kalklieser
Emanuell Kalklieser
Andrus Ponne
William Knipper
Hisbert Benter
Peter Lisley
Hance Contee
Jacob Possart
Jacob Wise
Christian Snyder
Jacob Snyder
Johannes Flickinger
Felte Beecher
Jacob Lisley
Christopher Matten
Paul Lipekipp
Christopher Kalklieser
Christian Cropp
Andries Cropp
Jacob Cropp, sick
Christian Cropp, Junr.
Hance Slaughter

Johannis Pettickhover
Johannis Kipping
Hance Erick Cogh
John Michael Amwigh
Hance Urick Kissle
John Jacob Kissle, sick
Ulderick Eley
Rinehart Hammer
Samuell Galler
Conrat Iller
Hance Gasper Kulp
John Martin Crist
John Jacob Hopback
Johannes M^cinterfeer
Christian Kitsintander
Linhart Amwigh
Mathias Snyder
Joseph Prunder
Johannes Prunder, sick
Mathias Ulland
Jorick Hoffart
Johannes Perger
Johannes Weightman
Phillip Michael Fiersler
Valentine Perhart Hisle
Hance Jorick Klauser
Hendrick Holstein, Germ^t.

Feltin Rafer
Jorick Fetter
John Jacob Knight
Alixander Till
Henderick Peter Middledorf
Mathew Bradford ⎱
Nicholas Bayly ⎰ English
David Lisley
Jacob Possart
Daniell Cropp, sick

THESE FOLLOWING ARE UNDER
THE AGE OF FIFTEEN.

Johannes Possart
Christopher Gotlip Matter
John Henderick Prundar
Johannes Ulland
Christian Hoffart

THESE FOLLOWING ARE FE-
MALE PASSENGERS.

Christina Margaret Kessell
Anna Barbara Kessell
Eve Tabaek Elee
Susan Hammer
Dorothia Galler
Margaret Iller
Elizabeth Iller
Maria Iller
Anna Phillis Kulp
Anna Catrina Crist
Magdelina Hopback
Phronick Mickinturfer
Anna Barbara Kitsintander
Magdelina Amwigh
Magdelin Snyder
Caterina Lisbet Prunder
Anna Maria Latrine
Catrina Ulland

Anna Margaret Hoffart
Anna Margaret Hoffart, Jun[r]
Anna Ursella Perger
Maria Phillis Whitman
Maria Catrina Fiersler
Susannah Catrina Hissle
Anna Maria Klauser
Maria Magdelina Campbin
Anna Maria Barbara Rafer
Agnis Kalklieser
Joanna Margaret Ponne
Ferina Knipper
Anna Margaret Mack
Caterina Benter
Anna Caterina Lisley
Marylis Lisley
Susanah Possart
Marilis Possart
Susanah Snyder
Stinkee Becker
Elizabeth Lisley
Maria Agnis Matten
Christina Lipkipp
Maria Kalklieser
Anna Marg[t] Mackin
Phillipina Mackin
Rosina Cropp
Caterina Slaughter
Anna Lisbet Pettickhofer
Maeta Lina [Pettickhofer]
Ketruid [Pettickhofer]
Anna Kipping
Sivilla Kipping
Anna Catrina Cogh
Anna Maria Ackhorden
Magdelina Ackhorden
Christina Lisley
Eve Possart
Johanna Kipping
Caterina Iller
  James Craigie [Captain]

In Council, 15th Septem^r 1729.

The Govr present w^t Messrs Laurence & Asheton, James Craigs made Oath to the above List.

James Craigie

Robt. Charles.

N.B. the Ship cleared from Cows in the Isle of Wight.

"At the Courthouse of Philadelphia, September 15th, 1729, . . . A List was presented of the names of Fifty nine Palatines, who with their Families, making in all about One hundred & twenty six Persons, were imported in the Ship Allen, James Craigie, Master, from Rotterdam, but last from Cows, as by Clearance thence dated 7th of July last." From the Minutes of the Provincial Council, printed in *Colonial Records,* Vol. III, p. 368.

[List 10 B] Palatines imported in the ship Allen, James Craigs, Master, from Rotterdam, but last from Cowes as by Clearance thence, dated 7th July 1729. Subscribed this Declaration 15th Septem^r 1729.

Allexander Mack
Johannes Mak
Velten Mak
Allexander Mack, Junr
Johan Hendrick Kalckgleser
Jacob Kalcklöser
Andres Bony
Wilhelmens Knepper
Hisbert (O) Benter
Pieter Lesle
Hans Gunde
Jacob Bosserdt
Jacob Wiss
Christian Schneider
Jacob Heider
Johannes Flückiger
Jacob Lesle
Velten Becker
Paul (X) Lipkip
Christ Marte
Christoffel Kalckglöser
Andreas Kropf

Kriste Kropf
Christen Kropf
Hance (X) Slaughter
Johannes Pettenkoffer
Johannes Kipping
Hans Jorg Koch
Hans Jacob Kiessel
Uldrich Oellen
Rinhart (X) Hammer
Saml (O) Galler
Cunrad Oell[en]
Hans Caspar Kolb
Johann Mardin Kross
Jno Jacob (X) Hopback
Johannes (X) M^cinterfeer
Christian (X) Kitsenlander
Leonhart Amweg
Mattdes Schneider
Joseph Bruner
Mattheus (MVL) Ulland
Jorick (X) Hoffart
Johannes (B) Perger

Johannes (H) Wightman   Jorg Dieter
Philip (X) Fiersler   Johan Jacob Knecht
Valentin Perhart (X) Hirsle Alexanter Dihell
Hans Jorick (HIK) Klauser   Henrich Peter Middeldorf
Felten (V) Rafer

[List 10 C] Palatines imported in the ship Allen, James Craigs, M^r, from Rotterdam, but last from Cows as by clearance thence.

Allexander Mack *   Hans Georg Koch
Johannes Mak   Hans Jörg Kiesel
Velten Mak   Hans Ulrich Oelen
Allexander Mack, Junr Rinhart (X) Hammer
Johann Hendrick Kalckgleser   Saml (O) Galler
Jacob Kalcklöser   Cunrath Oellen
Andres Boni   Hans Kaspar Kolb
Wilhelmens Knepper   Johann Mardin Kress
Hisbert (B) Benter   John Jacob (X) Hopback
Pieter Lesle   Johannes (X) M^{c}interfeer
Hans Gunde   Christian (X) Kilsenlander
Jacob Bosserdt   Leonhart Amweg
Jacob Wiss   Matdes Schneider
Christian Schneder   Joseph Bruner
Johannes Flickiger   Matheus (MVL) Ulland
Jacob Sneider   Jorick (X) Hoffer
Velten Becker   Johannes (B) Perge
Jacob Lesle   John (H) Wightman
Christ Marte   Philip (X) Fiersler
Paul (X) Lipkip   Valentine Perhart (X) Hisle
Christophel Kalckgloser   Hans Joreck (HIK) Klauser
Christ. Kropf   Felten (A) Rafer
Andreas Kropf   Jorg Dieter
Hanes (X) Slaughter   Johan Jacob Knecht
Kristen Kropf   Alexanter Dihell
Johanes Pettenkoffer   Henrich Peter Middeldorff
Johannes Kipping

* For the history of Alexander Mack and his colony of German Baptist Brethren or Dunkers, see G. N. Falkenstein, *The German Baptist Brethren or Dunkers* (Proceedings of Pennsylvania German Society, Vol. X), pp. 58–76.

Philadelphia, Septr. 15th 1729.

The foregoing qualifications were taken & subscribed by the several Palatines whose names are contained in this & the preceding Page.

[List 11 A] Palatines imported in the Thistle of Glasgow, Colin Dunlop, M^r, from Rott^r, but last from Dover p. Clearance June 19th. [Qualified Aug. 29, 1730.]

Loudwick Has	Casper Bittner
Bernard Sighmond	Paulus Titenhaver
Hans Jacob Teil	Joannes Sherer
Joannes Dunkell	Justice Sherer
Christopher Bader	Nickel Kinser
Peter Oler	George Hofman
Leonard Grau	Joannes Hofman
Jerrimias Hess	Philip Hauts
Velde Grisimer	Laurence Post
Christian Leman	Abraham Transu
Casper Feman	Casper Hartman
Steven Reiner	Thos. Hammon
Rudolph Draugh	Cristian Shram
Johannes Kun	Jacob Sterfell
Willem Heim	Rudolph Andreas
Loudwick Ditman	Fredrick Peifer
Johan Hendrick Smith	Leonard Caplinger
Gerard Zin	Joannes Caplinger
Cristoph Angubrant	Wolfer Sperger
Hendrick Fortne	Velde Bydleman
Michel Thomas, sick	Titrick Bydleman
Hans Minigh	Ellias Bydleman
Mathias Thais	Jacob Ammon
Peter Biswanger	Ullwrick Styner
Frik Reimer	Thos. Hess
Nickell Fiser	Hendrick Hess
Jacob Nagoll	Johan Ekel Lukenbill
Jan Casper Smith	James Morce
Geo. Sumger	Hendrik Lukenbill
Ulrick Sherer	Hendrik Gutt
Philip Groscost	Casper Criger

Peter Travinger
Loudwick Moler
Bernard Ren
Titrick Cover
Loudwick Hurtzell
Geo. Hurtzell
Peter Federolph
Leonard Hooginunk

Peter Moller
Fredrick Lenkenberger
Valantine Michell
Christoph Hendrick
Geo. Undertenerd
Christian Thomas
Colin Dunlop.

Phil^a Augt 29th 1730.

Sworn to before The Honble Govr & several of the City Magistrates.

R. Charles, Cl. Con.

In all 260 men W. & Children.

"At the Courthouse at Philadelphia, Augt 29th, 1730, . . . A List was presented with the names of Seventy Seven Palatines, who with their families, making in all about Two hundred & sixty Persons, were imported here in the Ship Thistle of Glasgow, Colin Dunlap, Mr., from Rotterdam, but last from Dover, as by Clearance from that Port." From the Minutes of the Provincial Council, printed in *Colonial Records,* Vol. III, p. 385.

[List 11 B] Palatines imported in the ship Thistle of Glasgow, Colin Dunlop, M^r. Qualified Augt 29th 1730.*

Johan Jörch
Lutwig Has
Bernhardt Sigmund
Hans Jacob Diehl
Johannes Dunkel
Christoph Batter
Johan Petter Ohller
Löhnhart Grau
Jeremias (X) Hes
Christian (K) Leman
Velde (O) Grisimer
Caspar (K) Fiehman
Steven (R) Reiner
Rudolph (X) Draugh
Johannes (X) Kun

Loudwick (X) Ditman
Johan Henrich Schmitt
Gerhart Zinn
Christoph Ankenbrantt
Jean Henri (X) Fortinaux
Hans (X) Minigh
Peter (B) Biswanger
Friedrich Reiner
Nickel (X) Fiser
Jacob Nagel
Johan Casper Schmidt
Johan Zwinger
Ulrich Scherer
Philip (O) Groscost
Casper (K) Bittner

* The endorsement on the back of the list is here used as the heading.

Johan Paulus Düttenhöffer

Johannes Scherrer

Johan Augustus Scherrer

Nickel Cuntzer

Hans Gorg Hoffman

Joannes (X) Hoffman

Philip (X) Hauts

Abraham Transu

Lorentz Hoff

Casper (H) Hartman

Thomas Hamman

Christian (K) Shram

Jacob Stiffel

Rudolf Andres

Fredrick (PF) Peifer

Leonhart Köpplinger

Johanes Keplinger

Wolfer (A) Sperger

Felden Meidelman

Elias Meidelmann

Dettrich Beitelman

Ulrick (X) Steyner

Jacob (H) Ammon

Dhommes Hess

Henrich Hess

Joan Ekel (X) Lukenbourg

Henrich Luckenbill

Hans Simon Mey

Hendrick (X) Gutt

Peter Trawiener

Caspar Krieger

Bernhard Renn

Dieterich Kober

Lutwig Mahler

Jerg Hertzel

Ludwig Hertzel

Länhart Hochgenug

Peter Federolf

Peter Müller *

Friederich Lünberger

Carle Vallenthien Michaels

Johann Matheus Theiss

Christofer Henerich

Michel Thommas

[List 11 C] Palatines imported in the ship Thistle, Colin Dunlop, M^r, from Rott^r, but last from Dover.

Johannes Jörch

Ludwig Has

Bernhardt Sigmundt

Valtein Griesemer

Hans Jacob Diehl

Johann Petter Ohler

Christof Batter

Johannes Dunkel

Lönhard Grau

Cristian Leman

Jeremias (X) Hess

Casper (X) Feman

Stefen (R) Reiner

Rudolph (X) Draug

Joannes (X) Kun

Willem (W) Heim

Loudwick (X) Dittman

Johan Henrich Schmitt

Gerhart Zinn

Christoph Ankenbrantt

Jean Hanri Fortinaux

Hans (X) Minnig

Friederich Reiner

Peter (B) Biswanger

* This is the famous Peter Miller, later for many years the leading spirit of the Seventh Day Dunkers at Ephrata. For his ministry in the Reformed churches of Pennsylvania see *History of the Goshenhoppen Charge*, pp. 72–95.

Nickel (X) Fiser
Johan Casper Schmidt
Johan Zwinger
Jacob Nagel
Ulrich Scherer
Philip (X) Groscost
Casper (K) Bittner
Johan Paulus Dittenhöffer
Nickel Cuntzer
Johan Augustus Scherer
Hans Geo. (X) Hofman
Joannes (H) Houf[man]
Philip (X) Hauts
Lorentz Hoff
Abraham Transu
Casper (H) Hartman
Thomas Hamman
Christian (X) Shram
Jacob Stiffel
Rudolf Andres
Frederick (F) Peifer
Leonhart Köpplinger
Johannes Kepplinger
Wolfer (A) Sperger
Feld. Meidelmann

Dettrich Beydelmann
Elias Beidelman
Jacob (H) Ammon
Ulrick (X) Steyner
Dommes Hess
Henrich Hess
Johan (X) Ekel Lukenbill
Hans Simon Mey
Henrich Lückenbill
Hendrick (X) Gutt
Caspar Krieger
Peter Trawiener
Bernhard Renn
Dieterich Kober
Lutwig Mohler
Ludwig Hertzel
Yorg Hertzel
Peter Federolf
Länhartt Hochgenug
Peter Müller
Friederich Lienenberger
Carle Vallenthien Michaels
Christofer Henerich
Johann Mattheis Theiss

Philad^{ia} Augt. 29th 1730.

The foregoing qualifications were taken & subscribed by the several Palatines whose names are contained in this & preceding Page, before the Honble the Govern^r & several of the Magistrates.

Robt. Charles, Cl. Con.

NB. The qualifica^{ns} of the Palat^s imported in the ship Alex^r & Anne, Wm Clymer, M^r, are on a Paper apart, I being at N. York w. our Govern^r when that vessel arrived. R. Charles. [See p. 36 f.]

[List 12 A] Ship Alexander and Anne, William Clymer, Master.   Septr. 5, 1730.

Antony Miller
Daniel Cristman

Adam Fillipott
Hans Lensenns

Johan Frederick Lanseness	Bernhard Myler
Johannes Herler	Hans Michel Burger
Johan Adam Atler	Jacob Myler
Martin Muller	Martin Burger
Johan Peter Wuller	Hans Jacob Oberholts
Frans Plum	Johan Fredrick Waller
Jacob Miller	Henrick Marte
Martin Creiner	George Mich¹ Brinsins
Waldes Langhaer	Johan Philip Curnert
Martin Yonger	Leopold Hilligas
Michael Blesser	Henrick Clemer
Peter Tilman	Johannes Cleyner
Adam Shuler	Mathias Seltzer
Johannes Vitner	Hans Jerich Ham
David Sussoltz	Johan Nicol Brecher
Michael Harkman	Johanes Woldman
Rudolph Mastersundts	Christian Princeland
Conrad Yongman	Johan Sebastian Graft
Fredrick Meyer	Hans Michael Verdus
Charles Kallar	Hans Bartel Hemberger
Hans Ulrich Crinston	Johan Carl Hornberger

"At the Courthouse of Philadelphia, Sepᵣ 5th, 1730, . . . A list was presented of the Names of Forty six Palatines, who with their families, making in all about one hundred and thirty persons, were imported here in the Ship Alexr. & Ann, William Clymer, Master, from Rotterdam, but last from Deal." From the Minutes of the Provincial Council, printed in *Colonial Records,* Vol. III, p. 386.

[List 12 B] [Palatines imported in the Ship Alexander & Anne, William Clymer, Master, from Rotterdam, but last from Deal. Qualified Sept. 5th, 1730.]

Anthony Miller	Marthin Müller
Daniel (✕) Christman	Johan Peter Walber
Adam (O) Hillipott	Frantz Blum
Hantz Lansiscus	Jacob Müller
Johan Henrich Lansiscus	Martin (M) Creiner
Johans Herbel	Baltes Lanckhaer
Johann Adam Stadler	Martin Jerger

Michel Belsch[er]

Peter (O) Edelmann

Adam Schuler

Johannes Widner

David Süsholtz

Michel Ackermann

Rudolff Messerschmidt

Conrad Stamm

Friedrich Meyer

Carl Keller

Hans Veltin Brenneisen

Eberhardt Meyer

Hans Michel Bürger

Jacob Meyer

Martin Bucher

Hans Jacob (H) Overholtz

Johan Henrich Weber

Henerich (H) Marte

Jerg Michel Brenneisen

Johann Philipp Emmert

Leopold Hilligas

Henerich (HK) Clemer

Johan Andres Klemmer

Mattheus Seltzer

Hans Gerg Ham [?]

Johann Michael Beyerle

Johannes Volckmann

Christof Steinlein [?]

Johann Sebastian Graff

Hans Michel (X) Wiedner

Hans Bardel Horrnberger

John Carl Hornberger

[List 12 C] We do swear or solemnly declare, that we deny all obedience to the Pope of Rome; and further swear or solemnly declare that no Prince or Person whatsoever hath any Right or Title to the Crown of Great Britain but his Majesty George the Second and his lawful Issue.

Anthony Miller

Daniel (X) Christman

Adam (O) Hilpott

Hantz Lansiscus

Johan Henrich Lansiscus

Johans Herbel

Johan Adam Stadler

Martin Müller

Johan Peter Walber

Frantz Blum

Jacob Müller

Martin (M) Creiner

Balser Lankhaer

Martin Jarger

Michel Belscher

Piter (O) Edelman

Adam Schuler

Johannes Widner

David Süssholtz

Meichel Ackermann

Rudolff Messerschmidt

Conrad Stamm

Friedrich Meyer

Carl Keller

Hans Veltin Brenneisen

Eberhardt Meyer

Hans Michel Bürger

Jacob Meyer

Martin Bucher

Hans Jacob (H) Overholtz

Johan Henrich Weber

Hennrich (H) Marte

Jerg Michel Brenneisen

Johann Philipp Emmert

Leopold Hilligas

Hennrich (HK) Clemer

Johan Andres Klemmer	Christoff Steinlein [?]
Mattheus Seltzer	Johann Sebastian Graff
Hans Geor. Ham [?]	Hans Michel (✕) Widner
Johann Michael Beyerle	Hans Bardel Hornberger
Johannes Volckmann	Johan Carl Hornberger

Septr 5th 1730. The Persons whose names are above written took & subscribed the Qualification by Law directed before His Majestys Justices of the Peace for the City & County of Philad^ia.

[List 13 A] A List of Passengers on board ye Ship Joyce, William Ford, Comd^r, from Boston. [Qualified Nov. 30th. 1730.]

	YEARS		YEARS
Christian Miller	60	Hans Michell Fisher	30
Mickell Shever	50	Henry Kilon	30
Hans Leonard Shever	12	Hans Overback	30
Nicholas Swort	38	Zeck. Parte	15
Daniel Swort	31	Godfrey Shoall^s.	24
Hans Whickel	25	Christian Swort	11
Lodwick Whickel	27	Jacob Swort	10
Joseph Tom	35	Jacob Swort	8
John Bear	40	Hans Swort	7
Hans Jacob Bear	17	Lewis Whickel	3
Andrew Miller	13	Hendrick Bear	6
Leonard Coale	32		
Frederick Elversite	24	WOMEN	
Henry Shever	24	Anna Maria Shever	45
Egram Hall	24	Barbra Shever	15
Jacob Hall *	20	Maudlin Shever	10
Johanes Coones	24	Bevel Swort	1
Mark Minger	24	Margret Whickel	26
John Hoaf	27	Margret Whickel	1
Mathew Moyal	13	Anna Barbra Tom	34
Lareunce Moyal	12	Christina Tom	2
Andrew Hofman	22	Anna Maria Bear	43
Hans Jedrick Moyal	27	Anna Margret Miller	50
Leonard Fodry	22	Anlis Miller	18

* Name crossed out.

	YEARS		YEARS
Anna Barbra Miller	11	Elizabeth Aplin	26
Maria Barbra Bear	16	Kathrine Shernock	4
Anna Coal	33	Barbra Moyal	37
Margret Elversite	23	Margret Holston	37
Anna Margret Shever	26	Maria Brabra	21
Sophia Hall	30		

Swore to November 30th 1730, before the Govr, Mr. Brooke, Mr Griffits, Mr Hamilton, Mr Hasel, & Mr Claypole. William Ford.
24 Qualified. 52 in ye Whole.
"At the Courthouse of Philadelphia, Novr 30th, 1730. . . . A List was presented of the names of Twenty four Palatines, who with their Families, making in all about fifty two Persons, were imported here in the Ship Joyce, William Ford, Master, from Boston." From Minutes of Provincial Council, printed in *Colonial Records,* Vol. III, p. 389.

[List 13 B] Palatines imported in the Ship Joyce, William Ford, Master, from Boston. This Declaran signed & Underwrin. Persons qualified Novr. 30th 1730.

Christian Miller
Michael (S) Shaver
Nicolas (N) Swort
Daniel (X) Swort
Hans (W) Wichel
Johann Ludwig Heintz
Joseph Dommi
John (O) Bear
Hans Jacob (X) Bear
Leonhart Kolb
Friederich Eberscheidt
Henry (X) Shever
Egram (O) Hall
Johannes Cuntz
Marx Nitzen
Johann Atam Hoff
Andreas Hoffmann
Hans Ulrich (X) Mayer
Leonhardt Pfuder
Johan Michael Fischer
Henrich Kilian
Johannes Oberbäck
Zacharias Barth
A. G. Schultze

[List 13 C] Palatines imported in the Ship Joyce, William Ford, Master, from Boston.

Christian Müller
Michael (O) Shaever
Nicolas (N) Swort
Daniel (X) Swort

Hans (W) Wichel
Johann Ludwig Heintz
Joseph Dommi
John (O) Bear
Hans Jacob (X) Bear
Leonhart Kolb
Friederich Eberscheidt
Henry (X) Shever
Egram (O) Hall
Johannes Cuntz

Marx Nitzen
Johan Atam Hoff
Andreas Hoffman
Hans Ulrich (X) Mayer
Leonhardt Pfuder
Johan Michael Fischer
Henrich Kilian
Johannes Oberbäck
Zacharias Barth
A. G. Schultze

Philad^{ia} Nov. 30th 1731 [read 1730].
Present: The Hon^{bl} P. Gordon, Esqr Lt Govr.

Henry Brooke ⎫
Saml Hasel ⎬ Esq^{rs}, Counsellors,

Tho. Griffits, Esqr, Mayor,

And. Hamilton, Esqr, Record^r ⎫ of the
Geo. Claypole, Alderm^n ⎬ city
⎭ Phila.

The foregoing qualifications were taken & subscribed by the several Foreigners whose names are above written.

Robt Charles, Cl. Con.

[List 14 A] A List of Passengers. Names on board the Ship Samuel, Hugh Percy, Comm^r, from Rotterdam. Arrived August ye 16th Anno 1731.

MENS NAMES OF SIXTEEN
YEARS OF AGE & UPWARDS

George Crisner
John Fisher
Michiel Clime
Engelberd Shroud
Henry Knop
Phillip Knop
Casper Haulhausen
Conrad Kerdt
Jacob Groust
Jacob Scheive
Joan Hendrick Hermel

Fred^k Babemeyer
Ludewig Faun
Johanis Midsker
Joest Wenst
Christopher Rink
Conrad Muller
Ludwig Goodbrod
Christopher Ritter
George Tebald Madinger
George Bender
Johanis Diderick
George Loreman
Phillip Vogel
Andries Erlewyn

Johanis Milburger
Hans Retter
Ludwig Heck
Christopher Bour
Ludwig Sourmilg
Johanis Kauns
Johanis Phingler
Hans Adam Wartman
Johan George Kaugh
Jurgeck Hendricks
Barent Tysen
George Wenst
George Loreman
Hans George Fleger

WOMENS NAMES OF SIXTEEN
YEARS OF AGE & UPWARDS

Ann Crisner
Ann Fisher
Barbary Melburger
Susean Clime
Hannah Shroud
Katrena Knop
Ann Knop
Dorothy Breling
Barbary Oven
Elizabeth Babemeyer
Ann Sourmilg
Barbary Hans
Ann Wenst
Motley Muller
Ann Diderick
Elizabeth Wartman
Magreta Madinger
Elizabeth Merdinger
Magreta Camping
Barbary Fredrakin
Elizabeth Hofmining
Mary Heck
Elizabeth Loreman
Elizabeth Loreman

Barbary Loreman
Eve Bender
Catrena Vogell
Ann Erlewyn
Mary Ritter
Eve Fleger
Easter Milburger
Barbary Goodbrod
Mary Smithing

NAMES OF THE CHILDREN

Mertin Crisner
Elizabeth Crisner
Barbary Crisner
Fleny Fisher
Elizabeth Clime
John Shroud
George Knop
Peter Knop
Menea Knop
Mary Sourmilg
Catrena Sourmilg
Neals Sourmilg
George Hans
Michiel Hans
Hanis Hans
Charlis Muller
Elizabeth Muller
John Dedarick
Abraham Wartman
Mary Wartman
Jacob Hofmining
Katrena Hofmining
Elizabeth Heck
Katrena Loreman
Mary Loreman
Paser Vogell
Crates Ritter
Motley Ritter
Hans Ritter
Mary Fleager

Katrena Fleager
Hendrick Mulberger
John Mealbury
Gorge Goodbrod
Ann Mealbury

George Goodbroad
Anthony Smithing
[Total] 107.
A True List.
Hugh Percy.

Augt 17th 1731.
Present: His Hon^r ye Lt Govr, S. Hasel, Esqr, Thos Griffits, Esqr, Mayor.
Oath was made to the foregoing List by Hugh Percy, Master of the Ship Samuel.

Robt Charles, Cl. Con.

"At the Courthouse of Philadelphia, Aug. 17th, 1731, · · · A List was presented of the Names of Thirty nine Palatines, who with their Families, making in all One hundred & seven Persons, were imported here in the Ship Samuel, Hugh Peircy, Master, from Rotterdam, but last from Cowes, as by Clearance from that Port." From Minutes of the Provincial Council, printed in *Colonial Records,* Vol. III, p. 410.

[List 14 B] Palatines imported in the Ship Samuel, Hugh Percy, M^r, from Rott^r, but last from Cowes in G. Britain. Qualified Augt 17th 1731.

Johann Görg Kirschner
John (+) Fisher
Johann Michael Gleim
Engelberd Schraidt
Johan Henrich Knopp
Villips Knopp
Caspar Holtzhausen
Conratt Eckert
Johann Jacob Krauss
Johann Jacob Scheibe
Johan [Hen]rich Hammel
Friedrich (X) Babemeyer
Ludwig Han
Johannes Metzger
Joest (X) Wenst
Christ (+) Rink
Conrad Möller

Lodw. (X) Goodbrood
Christ. (O) Ritter
Geo. Sebald (O) Madinger
Hans Gorg Bender
Johannes Diterichs
Hans Jerg Lohrman
Filibs Friedrich Vogel
Andreas (X) Erlewyn
Johannes Milbürger
Hans Ritter
Lodwick (H) Heck
Johann Christoffel Bauer
Ludwig Sauermilch
Johann Kuntz
Johannes Spengler
Hans Adam Warthmann
Johan Georg Koch

Jürgen Hendrich   Hanns Jerg Lohrman
Barent (✕) Tisen   Hans Georg Pflueger
Jörg Balser Wentz

[List 14 C] Palatines imported in the Ship Samuel, Hugh Percy, Ma^r, from Rotterdam, but last from Cowes in England, by clearance thence. Qualified Augt 17th 1731.

Joahnn Görg Kirschner   Hans Gorg Bender
Joannes (+) Fisher   Johannes Diterichs
Johann Michael Gleim   Hans Jerg Lohrman
Engelberd Schraidt   Villibs Vogel
Johan Henrich Knopp   Andreas (+) Erlewyne
Villips Knopp   Johanes Ulberger
Caspar Holtzhausen   Hans Ritter
Conratt Eckert   Lodwick (H) Heck
Johann Jacob Krauss   Johann Christoffel Bauer
Johann Jacob Scheibe   Ludwig Sauermilch
Johan Henrich Hammel   Johannes Kuntz
Fredrick (✕) Babemeyer   Johannes Spengler
Ludwig Han   Hans Adam Warthmann
Johannes Metzger   Johan Georg Koch
Joest (✕) Wenst   Jürgen Hendrich
Christ (+) Rink   Barent (+) Tisen
Conrad Möller   Jörg Balser Wentz
Lodwich (✕) Goodbrood   Hans Jerg Lohrman
Christ. (O) Riter   Hans Georg Pflueger
Geo. Sebald (M) Madinger

Philad^ia Augt 17th 1731. Present: The Honble Patrick Gordon, Esqr, Samuel Hasell, Esqr, a member of Council, Thomas Griffits, Esqr, Mayor of Phila. The foregoing qualifications were taken & subscribed by the several Foreigners whose names are contained in this & the preceding Page.

Robt Charles, Cl. Con.

[List 15 A] Account of Palatine Passengers on board of ye Pensilvania Merchant, John Stedman, Commander, from Rotterdam, at the day of their arrival at Philadelphia, September ye 10th 1731.

MEN ABOVE SIXTEEN

Michail Gybert
Michail Feter
Michail Moll
Adam Kremer
Fredrick Wilsheyt
Hartman Huntseker
Bartel Kooker
Jacob Lanius
Pieter Smit
Abraham Saler
Nicholas Reymel
Martin Bogher
Gerich Hendrick
Christian Smit
Hans Jerick Kelyenar
Jacob Steenar
Christian Wiyser
Johannes Diel
Abraham Freeman
Frederick Gybert
Frederick Stroubel
Christian Smit
Gerich Meyer
Gerich Bergstraser
Johan Hendrick Smit
Barent Arent
Christophel Moll
Valentine Shults
Frans Kryke
Jacob Kryke
Hendrick Kremer
Balser Seler
John Nicholas Steymutch
John Adam Egling
Christophel Beyer
Jacob Tilsover
Johan Schinkel
Valentine Snyder
Philip Beyer

Conrad Suyvert
Hans Martin Schults
Roolof Kusman
Johannes Reymert
Nicholas Fuys
Laurence Rod
Conrad Koogh
Jacob Mumma
Melchier Wilsteyts
Adam Sower
Michael Giger
Johannes Shaak
Engelbert Lak
Johannes Gerich Smith
Hans Michael Horloger
Borket Kilmiere
Johannes Bischof
Andreas Meyer

WOMEN ABOVE 16 YEARS OF AGE

Anna Maria Rygen
Barbel Bischof
Barbel Selern
Margarite Shilling
Margarite Smit
Anna Smit
Clove Stroublen
Julian Laamsen
Creeto Car
Catherina Kar
Lucretia Wildheydt
Magdalena Wildheydt
Barbara Wildheydt
Barbara Egling
Anganias Reymert
Margaret Kusman
Barbara Snyder
Katrina Kooker
Eliz. Kreemer
Eliz. Kreemer

Anlias Sybert
Marilis Sybert
Sabina Gybert
Catrina Gybert
Eliz. Gybart
Eliz. Rod
Eliz. Lak
Katrina Vilsover
Charlote Stadleven
Katrina Feter
Helena Feter
Katrina Feter
Crete Kelgenna
Eliz. Porkholderen
Maria Kortson
Maria Arent
Anna Smit
Anna Huntseker
Frena Huntseker
Eliz. Huntseker
Frenech Horloger
Annabaert Hoog
Margarite Beyer
Cathrine Shultsone
Eliz. Shultsone
Katarina Smit
Magdalina Eselman
Maria Fobsingaren
Catharina Steynmutch
Rosina Moll
Margarite Moll
Anlyas Moll
Maria Beyeren
Magdalena Stouden
Catherina Stouden
Leona Islewood
Joanna Fetter

CHILDREN UNDER THE AGE
OF 16

Hendrick Beyer

Jerick Beyer
Catrina Beyer
Johannes Steynmutch
Lenard Steynmutch
Jacob Schults
Catrina Beyer
Johannes Koog
Julian Koog
Maria Horloger
Maria Milderen
Anna Huntseker
Ursul Huntseker
Meyer Huntseker
Hannes Huntseker
Abraham Arent
Frederick Kelgenar
Michael Feter
Katrina Feter
Conraed Moll
Margarite Moll
Maria Stadleren
Catrina Stadleren
Anna Velsover
Magdalena Lak
Magdalena Fuys
Catarine Rood
Margarite Rood
Julian Gybert
Barnet Gybert
Sabina Gybert
Mathias Gybert
Godlieb Gybert
Cathrina Sybert
Gerich Sybert
Eve Kreemer
Christian Kreemer
Adam Kreemer
Maria Kreemer
Laurence Kooker
Christian Kooker
Heinrich Kar

Christian Kar
Gerich Hendrich Kar
Eliz. Wiltheydt
Frederich Wiltheydt
Jacob Mumma
Margaret Mumma
Frederich Mumma
Rosina Smit
Johanna Zeelie

Margarite Zeelie
Jacob Arent
Catrina Arent
David Arent
Maria Fuys
Anlies Sybert
Christina Kreemer
In Number of Men, Women and
Children 175.

Philad^ia Sep^t 11th 1731.

In Presence of the Honble ye Lt. Govr, S. Griffits Esqr, May^r, W. Allen Esqr.

The above List was sworn to by the Master.

John Stedman.
Robt Charles, Cl. Con.

"At the Courthouse at Philadelphia, Septr 11th, 1731, · · · A List was presented of the Names of Fifty seven Palatines, who with their Families, making in all One hundred & seventy five Persons, were imported here in the Ship Pennsylvania Merchant, Jno. Stedman, Master, from Rotterdam, but last from Dover, as by Clearance from that Port." From Minutes of the Provincial Council, printed in *Colonial Records,* Vol. III, p. 413.

[List 15 B] Palatines imported in the Ship Pensylvania Merch^t, Jno Stedman, M^r, from Rott^r, but last from Dover. Qualified Septr 11th 1731.

Michael Geberth
Michal Feder
Johan Michel Moll
Hans Adam Kremer
Friedrich Wulheit
Hartman (X) Hunsecker
Johan Bahrtel Gucker
Jacob Lanius
Peter (PS) Smit
Abraham Sahler
Johann Nicklaus Rei[mel]
Martin Boger

Jerg Henrich
Christian Schmid
Hans Gorg Kelchner
Jacob (J) Steiner
Christian Weisser
Johannes Diehl
Abraham (+) Freeman
Friedrich Geberth
Friedrich Strubel
Christian Schmidt
Johann Georg Mayer
Johann Görg Bergstrosser

Johann Hennrich Schmidt
Johann Berndt Arndt *
Christoffel Moll
Valentine (+) Shults
Frantz Krück
Johan Jacob Krück
Henrich Krämer
Baltzer Seyler
Johann Nicklaus Steinmetz
Hans Adam Eychelen
Christoff Beier
Johann Jakob Woltzhoffer
Johannes Sch[en]kel
Vallentin Schneider
Johann Philip Beyer
Conrad (S) Sybert
Hans Martin Schultz

Ruluf (RC) Casman
Joannes (X) Rymert
Nicklas Fuss
Laurence (+) Roodt
Conrad (CK) Koogh
Jacob Mumma
Melcher Wistholtz
Adam Sauer
Michael (X) Gyger
Joannes (++) Shaak
Johann Engelbertt Lack
Johann Georg Schmidt
Hans Michael Horlacher
Burkhart Kullmer
Johannes Bischoff
Andreas Beyer

[List 15 C] Palatines Imported in the Ship Pensylv^a Merch^t, Jn° Stedman, M^r, from Rott^r, but last from Dover.

Michael Geberth
Michel Feder
Johan Michel Moll
Hans Adam Kremer
Fridrich Wuheit
Martin (X) Hunsecker
Johan Bahrtel Gucker
Jacob Lanius
Peter (PS) Smit
Abraham Sahler
Johan Weis
Martin Boger
Jerg Heinrich
Christian Smid
Hans Georg Kelchner
Jacob (X) Steiner
Christian Weisser
Johannes Diehl

Abr^a (+) Freeman
Friedrich Geberth
Friedrich Strubel
Christian Schmidt
Johann Geörg Mayer
Johann Gorg Bergströsser
Johann Hennrich Schmidt
Johan Berndt Arndt
Christoffel Moll
Valentine (O) Shults
Frantz Krück
Johan Jacob Krück
Henrich Krämer
Baltzer Seyler
Johann Nicklaus Steinmetz
Hans Adam Eychelen
Christopf Beier
Jacob Wöltzhoffer

* For the descendants of John Bernhard Arndt see *The Story of the Arndts*, by John Stover Arndt, Philadelphia, 1922.

Johannes Schenkel
Vallentin Schneider
Johann Phipp Beyer
Conrad (S) Sybert
Hans Martin Schultz
Ruluf (RC) Casman
Joannes (×) Rybert
Nicklas Fus
Laurence (+) Roodt
Conrad (CK) Koogh
Jacob Mumma

Melcher Wistholtz
Adam Sauer
Mich¹ (×) Geyger
Joannes (++) Shaak
Johann Engelbertt Lack
Johan Georg Schmidt
Burckhart Kullmer
Hans Michael Horlacher
Johanes Büschof
Andreas Beyer

Philadelphia, Septr 11th 1731.

Present The Honble Patrick Gordon, Esqr, Lt Govr, Thomas Griffits, Esqr, Mayor of Philadia, William Allen, Esqr, one of His Matys Justices of the Peace for ye sd City & County of Phila. The foregoing Qualifications were taken & subscribed by the several Foreigners whose names are contained in this & the preceding Page.

Robt Charles, Cl. Con.

[List 16 A] A List of Passengers Names Brought from Rotterdam to Philadelphia In the B[ritannia], Capt Michael Francklin, Comender, Viz.

MENS NAMES OF SIXTEEN YEARS OF AGE & UPWARDS	AGES		AGES
		Johanes Albert	33
		Abraham Althaus	24
		Henrick Bahn	23
Johanas Bathelomus Rieger	..	Michel Bladner	23
Louis Timothée	..	Veith Bruninger	35
Giles Gilesz	50	Johan Jacob Beyer	33
Gysbert Boers	22	Hans Adam Beyer	30
Johanis Boars	20	Hanrich Blicher	26
Jacob Savelkoel	18	Leonard Bock	33
Henrick Geber, Senr	50	Hans Boshung	39
Hendrick Geber, Junr	18	Hans Georg Ebert	30
Johannis Geber	20	Hans Michel Ebert	35
Jacob Rish	32	Johan Eshelman	19
Lucka Vetter	55	Johan Eigenter	33
David Vetter	21	Johanis Frey	30

	AGES		AGES
Hans Michel Debelbesin	22	Jacob Meyer	28
Hans Debelbesin	18	Michel Moths	24
Hans Georg Debelbesin	16	Johan Casper Muntz	16
Hans Michel Wilhelm	22	Christian Muller	60
Joseph Beyer	19	Herman Muller	25
Hans Georg Freidle	25	Mathias Nehs, Senr	58
Hans Georg Gunt	40	Johan Nehs	26
Jacob Gunt	16	Dewald Nehs	24
Hans Peter Gaetner	26	Hans Georg Nehs	21
Hans Michel Henninger	32	Matthias Nehs, Junr	27
Rudolph Holsinger	44	Georg Passage	20
Hans Leonard Holtsapfel	47	Gabriel Rosher	29
Erazamus Holtzapfel	20	Johan Roht	44
Henrick Herberts	40	Jacob Rohr	28
Jacob Hachman	20	Johan Adam Rupert	25
Johan Heistand	19	Johan Leonard Steininger	35
Michel Horsh	18	Mathias Smeisser	16
Daniel Hubert	20	Hans Georg Muller	25
Christian Hubert	20	Leonard Beylmeyer	25
Jacob Karoll	35	Johan Martin Sakreiter	20
Vrich Keyser	70	Johan Michel Shaetner	36
Henrich Kram	34	Michel Stoker	31
Nicholaus Kennel	42	Georg Wilhelm Schwarts	23
Jacob Kobel	29	Henrich Ludwig Schwarts	42
Abraham Kern	28	Johan Adam Shrother	39
Georg Dietrich Kehl	46	Valentine Sigmund	22
Johan Kerkner	25	Jacob Shumaker	22
Gottfried Kraft	63	Johanis Smidt	24
Valentine Klein	20	Christoph Teuber	30
Wilhelm Kerkes	28	Hans Vogler	32
Georg William Lautermilch	27	Leonard Vieror	24
Christoph Lehman	42	Ohswald Wald	41
Philip Lutz	24	Hans Martin Wetzell	31
Hans Peter	18	Georg Wanamaker	30
Michel Meyer	29	Johan Jacob Wynand	19
Jacob Mautz	24	Casper Wys	33
Jacob Meyer	26	Jacob Wirtz	26
Stoffel Meyer	23	Mich^l Nehs	30
Thomas Meyer	23	Jacob Nehs	31
Hans Hendrik Martin	30		

AGES

WOMENS NAMES OF SIXTEEN
YEARS OF AGE & UPWARDS

	AGES		AGES
		Feronica Keyser	66
		Magdelena Keyser	28
Elizabeth Timothee	..	Anna Melia Keyser	19
Gertrowte Gilesz	40	Clara Kram	32
Helena Gilesz	20	Katherina Elizabeth Kenel	50
Elizabeth Gilesz	17	Maria Kobel	30
Katherina Geber	48	Katherina Kern	22
Sarah Geber	16	Elizabeth Kern	55
Margerita Vetter	18	Maria Ursela Kehl	40
Johaneva Frey	33	Katherina Margerita Kehl	16
Katharina Albert	30	Maria Epha Krafft	43
Katherina Rish	33	Christina Kerkes	28
Maria Katherina Blatner	27	Magdelena Lautermilch	22
Barbara Bruninger	40	Feronica Leyman	25
Katherina Bladner	36	Katherina Meyer	28
Anna Rosina Beyer	20	Sophia Meyer	25
Anna Maria Bladner	20	Katherina Meyer	21
Katherina Birkin	23	Anna Martin	32
Elizabeth Buck	36	Anna Maria Moths	22
Barbera Bushung	37	Katherina Muller	50
Magdelena Debelbesin	18	Margerita Muller	22
Elizabeth Margerita	18	Veronica Martin	23
Margerita Eigenter	..	Maria Barbara Nehs	60
Solomia Fridley	24	Anna Katherina Nehs	28
Anna Maria Gunt	40	Dorothea Neahs	27
Margerita Gartner	26	Maria Magdelena Oberkuhn	28
Anna Maria Henniger	26	Susanna Margerita Kohler	33
Anna Meyering	60	Maria Margerita Roht	43
Elizabeth Meyering	30	Anna Barbara Rupert	24
Magdalena Holsinger	26	Anna Barbara Heininger	32
Anna Barbara Holtsapel	57	Barbara Smeisser	50
Anna Barbara Katermena	23	Margerita Smeisser	20
Barbara Horsh	40	Hester Margerita Shaetner	30
Maria Magdelina Karol	35	Margerite Stocker	24
Vaita Hirt	45	Maria Elizabeth Schwartz	36
Maria Elizabeth Hirt	from 28	Anna Katherina Slauch	20
Anna Maria Hirt	to	Anna Maria Shrother	47
Anna Barbara Hirt	20	Katherina Smidt	30
		Maria Katherine Teuber	29
		Katherin Fogeler	28

	AGES		AGES
Anna Barbara Waldt	34	Anna Barbara }	6
Maria Barbara Wetzell	33	Christina	3
Margerite Wanamacher	30	David Brecht	13
Sicilia Wys	26	Casper Debelbesin	10
Maria Barbara Wetzeler	19	Katherina }	12
		Anna Kreta	5
CHILDRENS NAMES BEING		Henriks } Eigenter	10
UNDER SIXTEEN YEARS		Ludwig	3
		Magdelena	2
Peter }		Dorothia	6
Louis }		Lawrence } Freidle	2
Charles } Timothee, from 6 to 1		Hans Georg }	15 d.
Mary }		Hans Georg }	12
Katherina Geber	13	Johanis } Gunt	8
Maria Geber	9	Maria Elizabeth }	6
Daniel Geber	3	Joseph Horsh	8
Sophia Vetter	13	Peter Horsh	2
Magdelena }		Elizabeth } Karroll	7
Peter } Rish, from 6 to 3		Conrad }	2½
Henrick }		Gertrowte } Kearn	8
Nicholaus Frey	6	Johannes }	3
Christina Barbara Albert	9	Philip Christoph } Kohl	11
Anna Katherin Albert	5	Hans Georg }	7
Sophia Katherin Albert	3	Barbara }	10
Georg Michel Blatner	2	Katherina } Lehman	3
Hans Adam Bruninger	5	Johanis }	1
Hans Adam Bruninger	1	Elizabeth }	6
Anna Melia Bruninger	7	Angau [?] }	3½
Hans Adam Beyer's children:		Rudolf } Martin	7
Dorothea }	12	Barbara }	2
Elizabeth } Beyer	10	Magdelena }	7
Jacob }	8	Hans Jacob }	5
Christ. Selmᵃ. }	5	Katherina } Nehs	2
Maria Katherina }	10	Michel }	1
Maria Sabina }	8	Elizabeth Margerite Rosher	5w.
Leonard } Bock	5	Anna Margerite Roht	13
Maria Elizabeth }	2½	Hans Jacob }	11
Hans Michel }	1	Maria Margerite } Roht	6
Magdelena }	11	Anna Catherina }	..
Hans Philip } Bushung	9	Georg Smeisser	9

AGES		AGES
Justus Rupertus Schwartz 11	Hans Martin ⎤	6
Johannes Schwartz 8	Nicholaus ⎬ Wetzell	4
Johan Michel ⎤ Shrother 12	Katherina ⎦	3
Hans Georg ⎦ 10	Johannes Moll	15
Roselva ⎤ Waldt 6	Conrat Henninger	9
Hans Henrich ⎦ 4	A true List
Mich¹ Francklin.

Philad^ia Septr 21st 1731.

Michael Franklin, Master of the Ship Brittannia, made Oath to the foregoing List in presence of the Honble Pat. Gordon, Esqr, Lieu^t. Govr., Thomas Laurence, Esq., Derick Jansen, Esq., C. Plumsted, Esq.

Robt Charles.

"At the Courthouse of Philadelphia, Septr 21st, 1731, · · · A List was presented of the Names of One hundred & six Palatines, who with their families, making in all Two hundred & sixty nine Persons, were imported here in the Ship Britannia, of London, Michael Franklyn, Mr., from Rotterdam, but last from Cowes, as by Clearance from that Port." From the Minutes of the Provincial Council, printed in *Colonial Records,* Vol. III, p. 414.

[List 16 B] Palatines imported in the Ship Britannia of London, Michael Franklyn, M^r, from Rott^r, but last from Cowes p. clearance thence. Qualified at Philad^ia Sept. 21st 1731.

Johannes Bartholomay Rieger
   Hochteutscher Prediger
Louis Timothée
Geles Gelesen
Gisbertus Boors
Johannes Bars
Jacob (+) Sevenkoel
Henrich Geber
Johannes Geber
Johenrich Geber
Jacob Räsch
Lucas Vetter
David Vetter

Johannes Albert
Abram (X) Halshaus
Johan Henrich Bahn
Hans Michael Blattner
Veith (O) Bruningher
Johan Jacob (H1B) Beyer
Johan Adam Beyer
Hendrick (+) Blicher
Leonard (LBOK) Bock
Hans Boschung
Hans Jerg Ebert
Hans Mich¹ (X) Ebert
Johannes (X) Eshelman

Johannes Ageder
Johannes (O) Frey
Hans Mich¹ (H) Debilbissen
Hans George (HI) Deibelbesin
Hans Michel Willhelm
Joseph (+) Beyer
Hans Georg (H) Gunt
Hans Georg (H) Friedle
Jacob (H) Gunt
Hans Petter Garner
Hans Michel Hemminger
Rudolph (H) Holsinger
Hans Lenhart Holtzapfell
Erasmus (H) Holstaffle
Hendrich Horberts
Jacob (+) Hachman
Johan (H) Hiestand
Michel (+) Horsch
Daniel (X) Hubert
Christian (X) Hubert
Jacob Carl
Ulrich (O) Keyser
Henrich (HK) Kram
Nicklaus Kunel
Jacob (IK) Kobel
Abraham (O) Kern
Görg Dierich Köhl
Johannes Kirchner
Gottfried (O) Krafft
Vallentin Klein
Wilhelm (+) Kerkes
Wendel (+) Lautermilch
Christoph (H) Lehman
Johann Philipp Lutz
Hans Peter Lederman
Mich¹ (X) Meyer
Hans Jacob Mautz
Jacob Meyer
Christoffel Meyer
Johan Thomas Meyer

Hans Henrich (O) Martin
Jacob Meir
Michel (M) Moths
Johann Caspar Müntz
Christian (O) Muller
Herman (O) Muller
Mattdes Nöss
Johan (H) Nehs
Dewald (H) Nehs
Hans Jerg Nöss
Matthes (H) Nehs, junior
Georg (J) Passage
Gabriel (X) Röscher
Johannes Rath
Jacob (IR) Rohr
Johann Adam Ruppert
Leonhart Steininger
Hans Görg Möller
Johann Leonhart Bihlmeier
Johann Christian Sackreider
Johan Michel (H) Schrotner
Michel (M) Stocker
Görg Willhelm Schwartz
Henrig Lutwig Schwartz
Johann Adam Schröter
Valentin (O) Siegmund
Jacob Schumacher
Johannes Schmitt
Christoffel Deuber
Hans Vogler
Lenhart Firohr
Oswald (O) Wald
Hans Martin (HMW) Wetzel
Jörg Wanmacher
Johann Jacob Weynand
Casper Weis
Jacob (X) Wirtz
Michael Ness
Jacob (H) Nehs

[List 16 C] Palatines Imported in the Ship Britannia of London, Michael Franklyn, Master, from Rotterdam, but last from Cowes.

Johannes Bartholomay Rieger *
  Hochteutscher Prediger
Louis Timothée
Geles Gelesen
Gisbertus Boors
Johannys Bars
Jacob (X) Savenkoell
Henrich Geber
Johannes Geber
Johenrich Geber
Jacob Räch
Lucas Vetter
David Vetter
Johan Albert
Abraham (X) Halshaus
Johan Henrich Bahn
Hans Michael Blattner
Veith (O) Brunningher
Johan Jacob (HIB) Beyer
Johann Adam Beyer
Hendrick (X) Blicher
Leonard (LBOK) Bock
Hans Boschung
Hans Jerg Ebert
Hans Mich^l (+) Ebert
Johannes (+) Eschelman
Johannes Ageder
Johannes (X) Frey
Hans Mich. (H) Debelbissen
Hans George (HI) Debelbissen
Hans Michel Willhelm
Joseph (+) Beyer
Hans George (H) Friedle
Hans Geo. (H) Gunt

Jacob (H) Gunt
Hans Pedder Gartner
Hans Michel Hemminger
Rudolph (H) Holsinger
Hans Lenhart Holtzapfell
Erasmus (H) Holtsaffle
Hendrich Herbertz
Jacob (X) Hachman
Johan (H) Heistand
Mich^l (+) Horsh
Danl (+) Hubert
Christian (X) Hubert
Jacob Carl
Ulrich (O) Keyser
Henrich (H) Klam
Niclaus Kunel
Jacob (IK) Kobel
Abraham (O) Kerne
Görg Dierich Köhl
Johannes Kirchner
Gottsmitt (O) Kraft
Vallentin Klein
Wilhelm (+) Kerkes
William (+) Lauthermilch
Christ. (HI) Lehman
Johann Philipp Lutz
Hans Petter Ledermann
Mich. (X) Meyer
Hans Jacob Mautz
Jacob Meier
Christoffel Meyer
Johan Thomas Meyer
Hans Henrich (X) Martin
Jacob Meier

* This is the well-known Reformed minister, John Bartholomew Rieger, who arrived in Philadelphia at the head of a colony.

Mich. (M) Mothes
Johan Caspar Müntz
Christian (C) Miller
Herman (O) Miller
Mattdes Ness
Johan (H) Nehs
Dewald (H) Nehs
Hans Jerg Nöss
Matthias (H) Nehs
George (J) Passage
Gab. (X) Rosher
Johannes Roth
Jacob (IR) Roth
Johann Adam Ruppert
Leonhart Steininger *
Hans Görg Möller
Johann Leonhardt Bihlmeier
Johann Christian Sackreider
Johan Mich¹ (H) Shroatner

Mich. (M) Stocker
Görg Willem Schwartz
Henrich Lutwig Schwartz
Johann Adam Schröter
Valentin (S) Sigmund
Jacob Schumacher
Johannes Schmitt
Christoffel Deuber
Hans Vogler
Lenhart Firohr
Ostwald (O) Wald
Hans Martin (MW) Wetzell
Jörg Wanmacher
Johann Jacob Weynandt
Casper Weis
Jacob (X) Wurts
Michael Ness
Jacob (N) Nehs

Philad^ia Sepr 21st 1731.

Present The Honble Patrick Gordon, Lt Govr,

Clement Plumsted, Esqr ⎫
Samuel Hasell, Esqr ⎬ Members of Council
            ⎭

Derick Jansen Esqr, one of His Majestys Justices of Peace for the City of Philad^ia.

The foregoing qualifications were taken & subscribed by the several Foreigners whose Names are contained in both of the preceding Leaf & on the last Page of this Book where by mistake these Persons subscribed them.

Robt Charles, Cl. Con.

[List 17 A] A List of the Names of Passengers Imported in the Snow Lowther, Joseph Fisher, M^r, from Rotterdam, to Philadelphia. [Qualified Oct. 14, 1731.]

Christian Leman
Jno Christian Leman
Jacob Michael
Jacob Kerzey
John Vendal Kersey

Jacob Brooner
Henrick Bowman
Jno. Matthias Kramer
John Yerke Hamricke
Philip Peter Visanant

* This name and those that follow are found on the last page of Exhibit A.

Jnᵒ Peter Visanant
Henrick Howervass
Philip Eckord
Ulrick Michael
Jacob Holtsinger
Christolf Homborn
Melcher Heydon
Philip Kitchin
Dort Hoste
Johannes Reech
Anthony Bankaulf
Nicholas Smith
Johannes Ulrick
Johannes Conrad Frank
Jacob Snevely
Christopher Neubert
Philip Ulrick
Christopher Knowen
Christian Ernst Hagenmiller
Grosper Bowman
Casper Peter
George Shoults
Daniel Vessinger
John Godfrey Leman
Margret Michael
Anna Barbara Kerzey
David Vincent Kerzey
Conrad Kerzey
Ulrick Kerzey
Catharina Kerzey
Sophia Brooner
Jeremiah Brooner
Jeremiah Michael Brooner
Wolf Henrick Brooner
Appollona Brooner

Margaret Brooner
Margreeden Brooner
Elizabeth Sherren
John Albright
Margaretta Kramer
Isabella Agnes Kramer
Amaryllis Eliza Hamrick
Paul Hamrick
Margaretta Hamrick
Clara Hamrick
Maria Katharina Merchant
Jnᵒ Yerke Merchant
Jnᵒ Ludwick Merchant
Allena Visanant
Jnᵒ. Adam Visanant
Anna Maria Spotson
Margaretta Howervass
Margaretta Howervass, Junʳ
Philippena Howervass
Anna Barba Howervass
Margaretta Eckord
Susanna Eckord
Maria Elizᵃ Forrain
Johannes Swoap
Maria Mattelina Fingareen
Maria Margaretta Michael
Catharina Michael
Philip Lawrence Michael
Barbara Holtsinger
Jacob Holtsinger
Barbara Holtsinger, Junʳ.
Two Infants not Baptized
45 [women and children]
33 [men]
In all 78 Persons.

Oct 14ᵗʰ 1731.
The Honᵇˡ Pat. Gordon, Esqʳ. Lᵗ. Govʳ.
Clemᵗ Plumsted,
T. Griffits, } Esqʳˢ
R. Asheton,

The foregoing List was sworn to by Joseph Fisher, Ma[r], of y[e] said Snow Lowther.

Joseph Fisher.
Rob[t] Charles, Cl. Con.

"At the Courthouse of Philadelphia, October 14th, 1731, . . . A list was presented of the Names of Thirty three Palatines, who with their Families, making in all Seventy eight Persons, were imported in the Snow Louther, Joseph Fisher, Master, form Rotterdam, but last from Dover, as by Clearance from that Port." From the Minutes of the Provincial Council, printed in *Colonial Records,* Vol. III, p. 416 f.

[List 17 B] Palatines imported in the Snow Lowther, Joseph Fisher, M[r], from Rotterdam, but last from Dover. This declaration signed & underwritten. Palatines qualified Oct. 14[th] 1731.

Gottfried Lehmann	Philip Kinss
Johann Christian Lehmann	Dorst (H) Hooste
Jacob Michgel	Hannes Rösch
Jacob (O) Keesey	Anton Bannkauf
Johan Wen[d]el Giss[e]	Johan Nickel Schmid
Hans Jacob Brunner	Johans Ullrich
Henrich Bruner	Johann Conradt Franck
Johann Matthias Cramer	Jacob (S) Snevely
Hans Jerg Hamerich	Christ[o] (N) Newbert
Philip Peter (F) Visanant	Hans Philip Ullerich
John Peter Fissnand	Joh. Christoph Knauer
Henrich Havervass	Christian Ernst Hagenmüller
Philip (O) Eckford	Casper Bauman
Ulrich Michell	Caspar Betschen
Jacob Holtzinger	George Scholz
Christoffel Amborn	Daniel Weisiger
Melchor (H) Hoyden	

[List 17 C] Palatines in the Snow Lowther of Whitehaven, Joseph Fisher, M[r].

Gottfried Lehmann	Johan Wendel Giss[e]
Johann Christian Lehmann	Hans Jacob Brunner
Jacob Michgel	Henrich Bruner
Jacob (O) Keesey	Johann Matthias Cramer

Hans Jerg Hamerich
Philip Peter (F) Visanant
Johan Peter Fissnand
Henrich Haverwass
Philip (O) Eckord
Ulrich Michell
Jacob Holtzinger
Christoffel Amborn
Melchor (H) Hoyden
Philip Kinss
Dorst (H) Hoste
Hanns Rösch
Anton Bannkauf

Johan Nickel Schmid
Johans Ullrich
Johann Conradt Franck
Jacob (S) Snevely
Christo (N) Newber[t]
Hans Philip Ullerich
Joh. Christoph Knauer
Christian Ernst Hagenmüller
Casper Bauman
Caspar Betschen
George Scholtz
Daniel Weisiger

Philad^ia Octr 14th 1731.
Present The Honble Patrick Gordon, Esqr. L^t. Govr.
Clem. Plumsted Esqr ⎱ Members of
Ralph Asheton Esqr ⎰ Council
Thos. Griffits, Esqr May^r of Philad^ia.
The foregoing qualifications were taken and subscribed by
the sev^l Foreigners, whose names are above written.
                            Robt Charles, Cl. Con.

[List 18 B] Palatines imported in the Ship Norris, Thomas
Loyd, M^r, from Boston. This Declaration signed May 15th,
1732.*

Kasper Schirch
Marthin Gassner
Mathias (X) Weber
Johann Philip Weber
Johann Jacob Manncher [?]
Johann Michael Sigmund
Johann Ditrich Jungmann

Johannes (O) Behn
Christian (X) Reninger
Johannes (H) Herman
Valentine (X) Westheber
Johann Georg Liebenstein
Michael Anderrass

"At the Courthouse of Philadelphia, May 15th, 1732, . . .
Thirteen Palatines, who with their Families, making in all

* These immigrants were the unfortunate survivors of the ill-fated ship Love
and Unity, which landed at Martha's Vineyard, near Boston, after over one hundred of its one hundred and fifty passengers had died on board ship. See Diffenderffer, *The German Immigration into Pennsylvania*, Lancaster, 1900, pp.
63–68.

—— Persons, were imported here in the Ship Norris, Thomas Lloyd, Ma^r, from Boston, did this day take & subscribe the Effect of the Oaths of Allegiance, Supremacy & Abjuration; and likewise did repeat and Sign the Declaration inserted in the Minute of the 21st September, 1727." From the Minutes of the Provincial Council, printed in *Colonial Records,* Vol. III, p. 428 f.

[List 18 C] Palatines fr. the Ship Norris, Thomas Loyd, Master, from Boston.

Casper Schirch	Johannes (O) Behn
Marthin Gasner	Christian (X) Reninger
Mathias (X) Weber	Johannes (H) Herman
Johann Philib Weber	Valentine (X) Westheber
Johann Jacob Manncher [?]	Johan Georg Liebenstein
Johann Michael Sigmund	Michael Anderras
Johann Ditrich Jungmann *	

Philad^ia May 15th 1732.

Present The Honble The Govern^r, with several Magistrates. The foregoing Qualifications were taken & subscribed by the sev^l Foreigners, whose Names are above written.

Robt Charles, Cl. Con.

* John George Jungmann, a son of John Ditrich, has left the following description of this journey in his autobiography: "Supplied with provisions for twelve weeks, we sailed to Falmouth, England, where we stayed three weeks and where we loaded up many necessary things. Twelve days after our departure from this place, the captain assured us that we had covered half of our journey, which revived our courage. After that we had a calm, followed by a severe storm, which raged exceedingly. After having traveled eight weeks, water and bread were curtailed, and during the last six weeks we received no bread and nothing else from the captain than daily a pint of water for myself, my father and my sister. From this one can infer how we lived. Every sensitive heart will shudder when I say that rats and mice and the above-mentioned water were our only food. A rat was sold for 1½s. and a mouse for 6d. The captain thought that all the passengers had many valuables with them. Hence he did not want to land us, but left us to starve to death, in which he had a large measure of success, for of the 156 souls only 48 reached the American shore, and hardly a single person would have survived, if the remaining passengers had not revolted and seized the captain. Whereupon after three days, in the week before Christmas, we landed not far from Rhode Island, after having spent 25 weeks on this journey. . . . I was in such a miserable condition that I could not stand erect, but almost crawled on hands and feet." See Trexler, *Skizzen aus dem Lecha Thale,* p. 37; and Diffenderffer, *The German Immigration into Pennsylvania,* pp. 64–68.

[List 19 A] A List of Passengers Names and Ages on board the Ship Samuel, Hugh Percy, Com^r, From Rotterdam. [Qualified August 11, 1732.]

MENS NAMES OF SIXTEEN YEARS OF AGE AND UPWARDS	AGES		AGES
		John Brechbiel	19
		Jacob Stauffer	19
Merdin Gerhard	27	Nicolas Strass	19
John Bendler	24	Georg Goedake	24
Johan George Nungeser	25	Leonhard Keffer	27
Nicholas Cörber	22	Merdin Weiggell	24
George Philib Windermuth	25	Friderick Mulschlegel	30
Lorents Knochel	46	Michiel Kreiter	20
Hans Jacob Bockly	46	John Miller	21
Christopher Bockly	20	Christian Bendler	24
Mathias Bockly	17	Henrich Ramsaur	30
Ullrich Bockly	19	Adam Neidig	29
Samuel Brand	24	Juilis Door	33
John Heneberger	19	Georg Glassbrenner	21
Michiel Dierstein	20	Sebaldt Kramer	32
Henrick Ebby	30	Wendell Breckbiel	24
Jacob Beelerth	24	Georg Kleinhans	22
Gottfrit Staal	30	Wendell Heell	34
Hans George Klingman	24	Wihlm Bergheimer	20
Michiel Georg	60	Cristian Biry	20
Jacob Oberholtser	28	Andreas Miller	22
John Mosiman	23	Andreas Stautsenberger	25
Petter Wettstein	26	John Ulerich	20
Adam Andras	16	Petter Hailman	20
Christian Frants, Senr	47	Chretian Geeman	24
Christian Frants, Junr	26	Benedigt Geeman	20
Friderick Keffer	49	Leonhard Ziegler	21
Jacob Crist	22	Friderick Shits	22
Samuel Scheer	21	John Shits	21
Jacob Hesser	23	Petter Baltsbach	23
Lionhard Deebler	43	Jacob Knöchell	28
George Deebler	21	Mardin Geller	22
Oswald Hosteetter	30	Jacob Erdman	19
George Bender	33	Georg Hornig	20
John Lents	24	Jacob Kiffer	27

	AGES	WOMENS NAMES OF SIXTEEN	
Caspar Wardman	26	YEARS OF AGE AND UPWARDS	
Georg Klingman	27		AGES
Jacob Guth	20	Kathrina Gerhart	45
Ulerich Burckholter	22	Mergreed Gerhart	30
Paullus Boger	40	Barbara Bockly	42
Philip Boger	18	Rossina Brand	20
Carl Balmer	20	Elizabet Ewy	28
Christian Balmer	24	Maria Belerth	19
Frederick Aldorffer	25	Katrina Staal	32
Annastasius Uller	23	Veronica Ebberlin	17
Johanes Zieger	41	Thorodea Georgin *	45
Georg Stegger	30	Christina Georgin	20
Georg Heyl	31	Thoredea Klingman	25
Petter Stey	30	Anna Mosiman	20
Wendel Berndheisell	22	Elisabeth Wettstein	23
John Berndheisell	20	Margreth Augen	30
Michiel Baumgertner	21	Elisabeth Augen	32
John Baumgertner	21	Kathrina Tielen	23
Jacob Albrecht	37	Anna Frantsin	37
Friderick Hartman	33	Barbara Frantsin	20
Wendell Gerlach	22	Eva Frantsin	19
John Helfurt	33	Magdalena Frantsin	15
Ullerich Fischer	28	Maria Kifferin	46
Jacob Weiss	45	Elisabeth Kifferin	18
Henrich Beerett	34	Frents Tiliwahessin	23
Petter Schellenburger	33	Anna Christin	49
Jacob Gochnauer	20	Veronica Sheer	46
Christian Gochnauer	17	Gretha Fiesterin	20
Petter Frith	18	Maria Hostettin	28
Andreas Shittler	29	Sibila Nortin	22
Georg Quickell	30	Kathrina Benderin	32
Carl Seyb	27	Maria Creasmanin	20
Wendell Werbell	33	Gretha Merstelen	19
Philip Werbell	34	Gretha Wirbelin	18
Augustinus Wendell	16	Maria Lentsin	25
Petter Schneider	27	Christina Lentsin	49
Elias Meyer	42	Maria Kifferin	23
Adam Helligass	24	Torothea Weiggell	20

* The ending *"in"* ought to be dropped, as it is the *feminine* ending in German.

AGES		AGES
Susanna Bendlerin	23	Magratha Kresmenin 30
Elisabeth Bendlerin	22	Kathrina Seyb 29
Ann Ramsaurin	32	Sara Werberlin 35
Margreth Neidigin	28	Kathrina Meyerin 37
Anna Brechbielin	20	Susanna Meyerin 16
Thoredea Klinhasin	19	
Barbara Hellin	38	**CHILDRENS NAMES AND AGES**
Salome Berghermerin	25	Maria Gerhart 3
Gertrauth Birin	22	Henrick Berkly 12
Anna Millerin	20	Barbara Bockly 11
Silige Stautsenbergerin	24	Kathrina Bockly 8
Anna Gemanin	23	Lisbetha Evy 8
Maria Kifferin	25	Kathrina Evy 6
Greda Wardmanin	24	John Evy 4
Kathrina Klingman	24	Mergretha Evy 3
Susanna Guth	20	Georg Staal 12
Ester Burckhalter	20	Barbara Eberly 12
Eva Bogerin	35	Henrick Eberly 17
Christina Ziegerin	40	Elisabeth Oberholtster 6
Margretha Ziegerin	16	Sam¹ Oberholtster 3
Kathrina Steggerin	28	Magratha Wettstein 6
Barbara Heylin	30	Judith Frantsin 12
Margretha Steyin	25	John Frants 7
Katrina Stellin	24	Michiel Frants 6
Magdalena Albrecht	35	Veronica Frants 8
Rossina Hartmanin	27	Elizabeth Frants 3
Maria Helfertin	30	Babara Hosstetin 10
Susanna Bergheimerin	18	John Hostetin 10
Maria Fisherin	28	Anna Hostetin 6
Torethea Weissin	40	Veronica Hostetin 3
Barbara Weissin	19	Maria Benderin 8
Anna Berethin	28	Katrina Benderin 3
Maria Shellenbergerin	30	Valendine Hunceker 12
Anganea Frith	17	John Lents 3
Kathrina Gochnouerin	18	Abrah. Wulshleg 8
Margretha Kremerin	27	Christian Wulshleg 5
Sofia Kremerin	16	John Ramsaur 9
Magretha Shehittlern	27	Ann Neiginin 7
Maria Quickelin	27	Philip Neidig 6

	AGES		AGES
Barbara Hellin	12	Kathrana Fisherin	4
Anna Hellin	11	Rosina Weissin	13
Gottlib Hell	9	Kathrina Weissin	8
Kathrina Hellin	5	Kiliana Weissin	10
Maria Hellin	4	John Bereth	8
Rosina Hellin	3	Henry Bereth	6
Leonerd Bergh	8	Casper Bereth	3
Veltin Bergh	6	Georg Shellenberger	9
Maria Milerin	4	Magdlina Shellenberger	10
Solome Goutsen	6	Barbara Lutsin	11
Jacob Keffer	8	Susanna Lutsin	5
Lena Keferin	4	Maria Schittlerin	5
Petter Klingman	8	George Kramer	12
Kathrina Wertsin	9	Friderith Kramer	9
Mathias Boger	13	Gottfrith Kramer	7
Michiel Boger	12	Maria Quickerlin	8
Justina Bogerin	5	Christian Beller	8
Jacob Zeiger	12	Johanes Werbell	13
Susanna Zeigerin	9	Kathrina Schneidern	7
Georg Beerger	12	Elisabeth Schneider	5
Eva Steggerin	9	Michiel Mayer	12
Mergretha Steyin	5	Adam Meyer	6
Eva Stayin	3	Kathrina Meyerlin	8
Michiel Albreth	13	106 men	
Eva Albrethin	9	89 women	
Maria Albrethin	3	84 children	
Cristina Albrethin	3		
Georg Harman	8	279 Total	
Margrath Helfurtin	10		

Philad^{ia} Augt 11th 1732.

At the Courth^e before the Govr, S. Hassel, Esqr, May^r,
T. Griffits, Esqr, this List was sworn to by the Master.
A true List.

Hugh Percy.

Robt Charles, Cl. Con.

"At the Courthouse of Philadelphia, Aug. 11th, 1732. . . .
A List was Presented of the Names of One Hundred and Six
Palatines, who with their Families, making in all about Two
hundred and Seventy nine Persons, were imported here in the

Ship Samuel, of London, Hugh Percy, Master, from Rotterdam, but last from Cowes, as by Clearance of the Officers of the Customs there." From the Minutes of the Provincial Council, printed in *Colonial Records,* Vol. III, p. 431.

[List 19 B] Palatines imported in the Ship Samuel, of London, Hugh Piercy, Master, from Rotterdam, but last from Cowes in Gr. Britain p. Clearance thence. Qualified August 11th 1732.

Martin (X) Gerhard
Jn⁰ (X) Bindler
Johann Gorg Nungesser
Niklas Körper
Georg Philip Windemuth
Laurents (X) Knochel
Hans Jacob Becklin
Christoph Böckle
Matteus Böckle
Ullrich Bäckhle
Samuel Brand
Jn⁰ (X) Heneberger
Michel Dirstein
Henrich (H) Ebby
Johan Jacob Behlerdt
Gottfried Stahl
Hans Georg Klingemann
Michel Görg
Jacob Oberholtzer
Hans Muselman
Peter Wetzstein
Johann Adam Andres
Christian (C) Frants, Senʳ
Christian (O) Frants, Jnʳ
Friedrich Kieffer
Jacob (H) Crist
Samuel Scherer
Jacob (X) Fleiser
Leonhart Döbler
Jorg Döbler
Oswald (O) Hostetter

Jerg Benter
Johannes Lentz
Johannes Brechbil
Jacob Stauffer
Johann Nicol Strass
Hans Georg Goedeke
Johann Leonhardt Kieffer
Mardin Weigell
Frederick (F) Mulchslager
Michel Kreiderer
Johnes Miller
Christian Bendler
Henrich Ramsauer
Hans Adam Nei[di]g
Jelles Dohr
Johann Görg Glassbrenner
Johann Sebalt Kremer
Wendell Brechbühll
Johann Görg Kleinhans
Hans Wendel Höll
Wilhelm (X) Bergheimer
Christian (O) Bury
Andreas Müller
Andreas Stäutzeberger
Johannes Uhrig
Johann Peter Heylmann
Christian Geman
Bendich Geman
Johan Leonhardt Ziegler
Johann Friedrich Schütz
Johann Philip Schütz

Peter Balschbach
Jacob (X) Knechell
Martin Geller
Johann Jacob Erdmann
Georg Ludwig Hornung
Jacob Kieffer
Caspar (X) Wartman
Jorich (X) Klingman
Jacob Gut
Ullrich Burkalter
Hans Paulus (HPB) Boger
Johan Fil. Boger
Carl Diedrich [?] Balmer
Christian Balmer
Frederick (X) Aldorffer
Anastasius Uhler
Johan Ziger
Hans Jerig (X) Steger
Jorg Heyl
Peter (O) Stey
Wendel (X) Berndheisell
John (X) Berndheisell

Hans Michel Baumgertner
John (X) Bumgardner
Jacob (X) Albrecht
J. F. Hartman
Wendel Gerlach
John (X) Helford
Henrich Ulrich Fischer
Jacob (H) Weyes
Henrich (HB) Berret
Peter (X) Schellenberger
Jacob Gohnauer
Christian (X) Goehnaur
Peter Frit
Andreas (X) Shetler
Hans Gorg Quichel
Carl (KS) Seyb
Wendel Wörbel
Philip Wendel
Augustinus (X) Wendell
Peter (X) Schneider
Elisaus Maayer
Adam Hillegas

[List 19 C] Palatines imported in the Ship Samuel of London, Hugh Percy, M^r., from Rott^r, but last from Cowes.

Martin (X) Gerhard
John (X) Bendler
Johann Georg Nungesser
Niklas Kerper
Georg Philip Windemuth
Laurents (X) Knochel
Hans Jacob [Böckle]
Christoph Bäckle
Matteus Böckle
Ullrich Beckhle
Samuel Brand
Jno (X) Heneberger
Michel Dirstein
Henrich (H) Ebby
Johan Jacob Behlerdt

Gottfried Stahl
Hans Georg Klingmann
Michel Görg
Jacob Oberholtzer
Hans Mosieman
Peter Wetzstein
Johann Adam Andres
Christ. (X) Frants, Senr
Christ^n (O) Frants, Jn^r
Friedrich Kiefer
Jacob (H) Crist
Samuel Scherer
Jacob (X) Fleiser
Leonhart Döbler
Jerg Döbler

Oswald (X) Hostetter

Jerg Bender

Johannes Lentz

Johannes Brechbil

Jacob Staufer

Johann Nicol. Strass

Hans Georg Goedeke

Johan Leonhardt Kieffer

Mardin Weigell

Frederick (F) Mulchslager

Michel Keiderer

Johnes Miller

Christian Beudler

Henrich Ramsauer

Hans Adam Nei[di]g

Jelles Dehr

Johan Görg Glassbrenner

Johan Sebalt Kremer [?]

Wendell Brechbühll

Johann Görg Kleinhans

Hans Wendel Höll

Wilhelm (X) Bergheimer

Christian (X) Bury

Andreas Müller

Andreas Stäutzeberger

Johannes Uhrig

Johann Peter Heylmann

Christian Geman

Bendich Geman

Johan Leonhardt Zigler

Johann Friedrich Schütz

Johan Philip Schütz

Petter Balschbach

Jacob (X) Knechell

Martin Giller

Johann Jacob Erdmann

Georg Ludwig Hornung

Jacob Kieffer

Caspar (X) Wartman

Jorich (X) Klingman

Jacob Gut

Ullrich Burghalter

Paulus (H) Boger

Johan Filib Boger

Carl Diedrich [?] Balmer

Christian Balmer

Frederick (X) Aldorffer

Anastasius Uhler

Johnes Ziger

Hans Jerig (X) Steger

Jerg Heyl

Peter (X) Stey

Wendel (O) Berndheisel

John (O) Berndhersel

Hans Michel Baum[gardner]

John (O) Bumgardner

Jacob (X) Albrecht

J. F. Hartmann

Wendel Gerlach

John (X) Helford

Henrich Ulrich Fisher

Jacob (H) Weyes

Henrich (HB) Berret

Peter (X) Shellenberger

Jacob Gohnauer

Christian (X) Goehnaur

Peter Frit

Andreas (X) Shetler

Hans Georg Quickel

Carl (KS) Seyb

Wendel Wörbel

Philip Wendel

Augustinus (X) **Wendel**

Peter (X) Schneider

Eliseus Maeyer

Adam Hillegas

Philad^ia August 11th 1732.

Present The Honble Patrick Gordon, Esqr, Lt Govr, Saml

Hasell, Esqr, Mayor, with others of the City Magistrates. The foregoing Qualifications were taken & subscribed by the several foreigners whose Names are contained in the above & two preceding Pages.

Robt Charles, Cl. Con.

[List 20 A] A List of Palatine Passengers on Board the Ship Pensilvania Merchant, John Stedman, Commander, from Rotterdam. [Qualified Sept. 11, 1732.]

MENS NAMES

Cuspurd Wooldrich
Mathias Zulkover
Jacob Gysen
Conrad Frick
Michael Reyn
Hendrick Christen
Jan Jacob Buss
Michael Will
Johan Celeberger
Philip Frank
Michael Emeldt
Leonard Emeldt
Hans Graff
Jerick Michael Holsteyner
Hans Jerich Smit
Jacob Roodt
Hans Jerich Conce
Hans Coun
Christophel Stedler
Hans Jerich Couger
Simeon Carlee
Mathias Heyser
Adam Louer
Hartman Lower
Stephven Hook
Simon Pieter Holsteyner
Jacob Hans
Hans Michael Moog
Vendael Fiseir

Nicholas Miller
Jan Pieter Strack
Benedick Eselman
Michael Witmer
Jerich Michael Swynhart
Hans Michael Cromeryn
Philip Cavel
Cornelius Kraem
Hans Rudler
Woolf Copenhaver
Michael Copenhaver
Johannes Weaver
Mathias Minegen
Conrad Shenigh
Jeriam Ein
Daniel Miller
Johannes Hottel
Christian Steinback
Woolf Cankloots
Palus Lyntsenbelger
Hans Jacob Meyer
Paul Ruyter
Hendrick Ruyter
Jerich Beats
William Creusumer
Jerich Mirts
Michael Slinagur
Pieter Gauf
Barent Wolfinger
Adam Bouer
Bastian Wageneir

Joannis Faase
Jerich Palsgrave
Jacob Shaad
Michael Caap
Fridrich Caap
Gabriel Konigh
Leonard Conraed
Carle Olinar
Vindael Wynheymer
Adam Zeyler
Jerich Mynhard
Mathias Shaup
Fridrich Ernigh

WOMEN AND CHILDREN

Eva Oldrich
Margaret Linamens
Philip Oldrich
Pieter Oldrich
Susanna Oldrich
Anna Barbel
Margaret Sweren
Lena Brown
Gertrouy Frick
Benedick Bartholomus
Maria Reyn
Anna Christen
Margaret Christen
Magdalen Christen
Jerick Christen
Hendrick Christen
Eva Christen
Catharine Christen
Salme Christen
Maria Christen
Anna Puss
Cathrina Puss
Anna Frank
Catharina Conce
Hans Conce
Eva Conce

Catharine Conce
Margaret Strickler
Maria Barbel
Elisabeth Lower
Elizabeth Lower
Esra Houk
Maria Holsteyner
Sophia Engelhart
Susanna Fisar
Magdalena Swynhart
Eva Swynhart
Andreas Swynhart
Barbara Swynhart
Johan Swynhart
Barbara Mack
Anna Mack
Maria Cavel
Barbara Cabal
Elizabeth Cram
Maria Lotsharing
Cathrina Lotsharing
Maria Lotsharing
Maria Capehaver
Barbara Copehaver
Rosina Copehaver
Catharina Copehaver
Maria Mincham
Catharina Eier
Christian Miller
Michael Miller
Margaret Hottel
Anna Hottel
Curla Hottel
Jerich Hottel
Hendrich Hottel
Johannes Hottel
Dorothy Stenback
Barbara Meyer
Margaret Meyer
Susanna Meyer
Hanickel Myer

Casparus Meyer	Bustnip Woolfinger
Elizabeth Ruyter	Pieter Woofinger
Martin Ruyter	Johannes Woolfinger
Anna Ruyter	Elizabeth Kerkener
Paul Ruyter	Barbara Isack
Caspart Ruyter	Jacob Isack
Barbel Ruyter	Fredrick Isack
Maria Beats	Barbara Bower
Adam Beats	Maria Ernich
Magdalena Beats	Frederich Ernich
Cathrina Beats	Anna Ernich
Margaret Marts	A true List.
Dorothy Marts	John Stedman.
Elizabeth Marts	73 Men
Susan Beyeren	98 Women & Children
Maria Slynegar	
Michael Slinegar	171 [Total]
Margaret Gouf	3 dead
Pieter Gouf	168 [Persons]
Odels Woolfinger	

Philad^ia Sept^emr 11th 1732.

Present: The Honble Pat. Gordon, Esqr, Lt Govr, S. Hassell, Esqr, May^r, A. Hamilton, Esqr, Recorder.

The foregoing List was upon Oath declared by John Stedman to be a true & exact one.

Robt Charles, Cl. Con.

"At the Courthouse of Philadelphia, Septr 11th, 1732. . . . A List was presented of the Names of Seventy Palatines, who with their families, making in all One hundred & sixty eight Persons, were imported here in the Ship Pensylva. Merchant, John Stedman, Master, from Rotterdam, but last from Plymouth, as by Clearance thence." From the Minutes of the Provincial Council, printed in the *Colonial Records,* Vol. III, p. 452.

[List 20 B] Palatines imported in the Ship Pensylvania Merch^t, of London, Jno Stedman, M^r, from Rott^r, but last from Plymouth, p Clearance thence. Qualified Septem^r 11th 1732.

Joseph Casparing [?]

Matthias Zollikoffer, von
   Alten Klingen *

Jacob Giss

Conrad (✗) Frick

Michel Rein

Hendrich (H) Christian

Joan Jacob (✗) Buss

Michel Wüll

Johan (S) Seleberger

Philip (O) Frank

Michael Immel

Leonhard Immel

Hans Georg Graff

Georg Michael Hohlsteiner

Hans Jerig (✗) Smit

Jacob Rod

Hans Görg Cuntz

Christofel (✗) Stedler

Johann Georg Gauger

Simon Carle

Maddes Hauser

Adam (L) Louer

Hartmann (✗) Lauer

Simon Peter Holsteiner

Jacob (H) Hans

Hans Michel Much

Wendel Fizeer [?]

Johann Klas Müller

Johann Peter Strack

Benedict (|) Eiselman

Michael (O) Witman

Georg Michael Schweinhart

Hans Michael Krumrein

Filbs Keblle

Cornelius Kram

Hans (O) Rootelee

Wolff (W) Copenhaver

Michael (H) Copenhaver

Johannes (O) Weber

Matthes Menchen

Conradt Schönig

Johann Georg Amend

Dangel Müller

Johannes (O) Hoorle

Christian (H) Steinback

Albrecht Wolff Kongetz [?]

Paulus (L) Linsenbigler

Hans Jacob Meyer

Paul (PR) Reyter

Johann Görg Bätz

Wm. (O) Chriesmerg

Georg Mertz

Michael (✗) Slinager

Ditrich Gauff

Bernhart Wolffinger

Bastian Wagner

Johannes Faass

Jörg Paltzgraff

Jacob (✗) Shaad

Michael Capp

Georg Fridrich Capp

Gabriel (O) Konigh

Hans Leon^d (H) Conraad

Carl Ohliger

Wendel Weinheimer

Adam (+) Zeyler

Hans Jorig (+) Mindhard

Mathias (+) Shaaup

Friederich Erny

[List 20 C] Palatines imported in the Ship Pensylv^a Merch^t, Jn° Stedman, M^r.

---

* This is a place name in Switzerland. It was read V. D. M. by Rupp.

Caspar Ullrich
Matthias Zollikoffer
    von Alten Klingen
Jacob Giss
Conrad (X) Frick
Michel Rein
Hendrich (H) Christian
Joh. Jacob (X) Buss
Michael Wüll
Johan (Sch) Seleberger
Philip (O) Frank
Michael Immel
Leonhard Immel
Hans Georg Graff
Georg Michael Hohlsteiner
Hans Jerig (X) Smit
Jacob Rod
Hans Görg Cuntz
Christofel (X) Stedler
Johann Georg Gauger
Simon Carle
Maddes Hauser
Adam (O) Louer
Hartman (X) Louer
Simon Peter Holsteiner
Jacob (H) Hans
Hans Michel Much
Wendel Fizeer [?]
Johan Klaus Müller
Johann Peter Strack
Bendict (|) Eiseleman
Michael (O) Witman
Georg Michael Schweinhart
Hans Michael Krumrein
Filbs Kebell
Cornelius Kram

Hans (O) Rootelie
Wolf (W) Copenhaver
Michael (H) Copenhaver
Johannes (O) Weaver
Matthes Menchen
Konradt Schönig
Johann Georg Amend
Dangel Mullell
Johannes (O) Hoorle
Christian (H) Steinbach
Albrecht Wolffgang
Paulus (L) Linsenbegler
Hans Jacob Meyer
Paulus (PR) Ryter
Henrich (HR) Ryter
Johann Görg Bätz
Wm. (O) Chriesmerg
Georg Mertz
Michael (X) Slinager
Ditrich Gauff
Bernhardt Wolffinger
Bastian Wagner
Johannes Faas
Jorg Paltzgraff
Jacob (X) Shaad
Michael Capp
Georg Friedrich Capp
Gabriel (O) Konigh
Hans Leon^d (H) Conraad
Carl Ohliger
Wendel Weinheimer
Adam (|) Zeyler
Hans Jerig (X) Mynhard
Mathias (X) Shaaup
Friederich Erny

Philad^ia Sepr 11th 1732.

At the Courth° in presence of the Govr, the Mayor and Recorder of the City, the foregoing Qualifications were taken &

subscribed by the several foreigners whose Names are contained on this Leaf.

Robt Charles, Cl. Con.

[List 21 A] A List of Palentines arrived in the Port of Philadelphia on board of the Johnson Galley of London, David Crockatt, Com^r, Septr 18th O.S., 1732.

MEN ABOVE 16 YEARS *

Johannes Steyman
Johannes Yerrick Steyman
Lowrence Hartman
Johannes Harwick
Paul Wegerline
Jacob Miller
Johannes Jorig Miller
Valentine Bayer
Henrick Saen
Coneradt Behen
Jacob Miller
Johannes Mich^el Lochtner
Johannes Yegener
Tomas Matern
Andreas Overbeck
Jacob Cruiz
Jacob Rouse
Valentine Renner
Daniel Schwe
Johannes Schell
Isau Cushwa
Johannes Messinger
Bernard Piffer
Mathias Brown Wart
Jacob Rower
Christopher Ernhardt
Conradt Bowlong
Andreas Lower

Lawrence Webern
Tobias Hagle
Jacob Konts
Christopher Rise
Frederick Rise
Willim Kellie
Adam Hemler
Andreas Hembler
Conradt Schymer
Martin Bulinger
Martin Bulinger
Philip Timmerman
Michael Dieder
Johannes Dieder
Nicolas Ewick
Johannes Ewick, sick
Paul Wynhamer
Johannes Bastian
Lawrence Bastian
Johannes Bastian, Junr
Henry Bowman
Lodawick Fridele
Anthony Gilbert
Johan Balser Bott
Philip Yerick
Valentine Vield
Nicollas Vield
Frederick Miller
Adam Humele
Thomas Souder

* This list has such a peculiar arrangement, that it was deemed best to disregard it.

Hans Adam Verner
Valentine Umstadt
Johannes Sufrance
Bartholomay Moorhead
Lawrence Konce
Lodawick Leeman
Joh[s] Yerick Paulse
Nicolas Evelandt
Martin Bower
Johannes Everman
Johannes Albright
Henrick Young
Conradt Sadler
Adam Lochbergher
Christopher Englandt
Christopher Bayer
Leonardt Momma
Henry Oswaldt
Leonardt Wayer
Johannes Smith
Lawrence Bawder
Rudolph Bonner
Henry Aple
Frederick Boomgardner
Henrick Miller
Peter Derber
Peter Seyler
Peter Gabele
Philip Smith
Johan Peter Smith
Jacob Neythelzer
Conradt Seyver
Hans Yerich Tray
Jacob Tray
Johan Shullmyer
Michele Shullmyer
Johannes Tray
Johannes Hammer
Johan Henerick Messersmitt
Martin Caplinger
Tomas Cryle

Hans Wilhelm Brant
Christian Sneyder
Conradt Sneyder
Johan Leon[d] Hermer
Pieter Kynter
Johan Frans Rouse
Paulus Leyderer
Fredrich Meyer
Hans Jorig Gump
Hans Jorig Samm
Johan Adam Cryle
Thomas Crydle, Sen[r]
Johan Jerig Overcogler

WOMEN ABOVE 14

Elizabeth Steyman
Agnes Steyman
Katharine Hartman
Barbara Steyman
Katharine Steyman
Elizabeth Steyman
Anna Maria Harwick
Otilia Wegerline
Margaritta Miller
Elizabeth Miller
Katharine Bayer
Katharine Saen
Marie Hartman
Katharine Behen
Charlotta Miller
Maria Lochtner
Katharina Yegener
Margereta Matern
Susanna Feghtern
Elizabeth Overbeck
Rosina Cruiz
Clara Rouse
Margaretta Renner
Maria Schwe
Elizabeth Messinger
Julian Piffer

Barbara Piffer
Anna Cockabeteren
Julian Brown Waart
Margeretta Rower
Katharina Ernhardt
Elizabeth Bowlong
Christianna Lower
Gerdrudt Webern
Apolonia Hagle
Maria Konts
Maria Katharina Rice
Elizabeth Rise
Margeritta Kellie
Barbara Hembler
Maria Schymer
Elizabeth Bulinger
Barbara Timmerman
Elizabeth Dieder
Catharine Dieder
Susana Dieder
Catherine Wynhamer
Maria Bastian
Matelina Bastian
Anna Bastian
Elizabeth Bastian
Julian Shelling
Anna Maria Friddele
Ursilla Bott
Margeritta Yerich
Anna Millia Frankin
Luisa Francisca Knapping
Elizabeth Vield
Marg^t Vield
Chrystien Snyder
Margaretta Souder
Katharina Verner
Maria Sufrance
Maria Konce
Eva Leeman
Katharine Paulse
Regina Evelandt

Susanna Bower
Elizabeth Everman
Anna Albright
Elizabeth Young
Matelina Sadler
Maria Loobacker
Barbara Lochbergher
Maria Englandt
Anna Bayer
Julian Momma
Marg^t Wayer
Marg^t Miller
Engele Derber
Mateline Seyler
Maria Gabele
Seville Nythelzer
Matelina Seyver
Elizabeth Seyver
Susanna Tray
Katharine Shullmyer
Margaretta Tray
Elizabeth Henerick Messersmitt

BOYS UNDER 16

Paulus Harwick
Jacob Harwick
Nicollus Harwick
Jacob Wegerline
Johan Jacob Miller
Johannes Overbeck
Philips Overbeck
Lodawick Schwe
Michale Messinger
Paule Messinger
Jacob Messinger
Johannis Rower
Johannes Lower
Johannes Herman Lower
Henrick Webern
Adam Hagle
Johannes Konts

Martin Rise
Hans Jureg Ewick
Adam Ewick
Philip Wynhamer
Henrick Wynhammer
Jacob Wynhamer
Herman Bastian
Jacob Friddele
Henrick Bott
Paul Vield
Adam Verner
Jacob Umstadt
Conradt Stock
Martin Evelandt
Jacob Evelandt
Johannes Everman
Jacob Albright
Lodawick Albright
Johan Young
Alex^r Sadler
Henerick Sadler
Johannes Sadler
Anthony Momma
David Momma
Christian Momma
Michael Seyler
Valentine Seyler
Lawrence Seyver
Conradt Seyver
Johan Conradt Tray

GIRLS UNDER 14

Katharine Wegerline
Otilia Wegerline
Anna Clara Wegerline
Maria Miller
Anna Miller
Katharine Miller
Anna Bayer
Anna Saen
Elizabeth Hartman

Maria Christiana Behen
Barbara Miller
Elizabeth Matern
Matelina Overbeck
Katharina Renner
Margeretta Schwe
Maria Messinger
Margeretta Piffer
Anna Brown Waart
Maria Ernhardt
Anna Bowlong
Elizabeth Lower
Elizabeth Hagle
Anna Hagle
Barbara Konts
Margeritta Rise
Anna Schymer
Elizabeth Bulinger
Juliana Timmerman
Maria Timmerman
Elizabeth Bastian
Maria Friddele
Maria Franciscos Friddele
Elizabeth Vield
Margaretta Souder
Katharina Verner
Gertrudt Konce
Marg^t Konce
Maria Konce
Maria Leighman
Margeretta Mosen
Maria Evelandt
Helena Bower
Maria Everman
Matelina Albright
Barbara Albright
Christiana Albright
Anna Young
Catharina Sadler
Katharina Sadler
Julian Momma

Katharina Momma

Anna Wayer

Elizb^t Wayer

Elizabeth Miller

Matelina Seyler

Martha Seyler

Maria Susanna Nythelzer

Marg^t Nythelzer

112 men, 98 women, 120 boys
and girls, 330 persons.

A true List.

Dav^d Crokatt.

Philad^{ia} Septr 19th 1732.
At the Courth° Present:
The Honble Lt Govr; Saml Hasell, Esqr, Mayor.
"At the Courthouse aforesaid, Septr 19th, 1732. One hundred & twelve Palatines, who with their families, making in all Three hundred & thirty Persons, were imported in the Ship Johnson of London, David Crockat, Mr., from Rotterdam, but last from Deal, as by Clearance thence." From the Minutes of the Provincial Council, printed in *Colonial Records*, Vol. III, p. 453.

[List 21 B] Palatines imported in the Pink Johnson of London, David Crockatt, M^r, from Rotterdam, but last from Deal, p. Clearance thence. Qualified Septem^r 19th 1732.

Johans Steinman

Johann Jörg Steinmann

Laurence (X) Hartman

Joh^s (X) Harwick

Paulus Wegerlein

Hans Jacob Müller

Joh^s Jorig (|) Miller

Faldin Bey[er]

Henrich Sim

Conrad (C) Behn

Jacob Müller

Joh^s Mich^l (O) Lochtner

Hans Henrich Jegner

Tomas (|) Matern

Andreas (O) Overbeck

Jacob (|) Cruis

Jacob (|) Rouse

Valentine (|) Renner

Danl (D) Schew

Johann Martin Schilling

Isua (|) Cushwa

Johannes Mösinger

Bernhardt Peffer

Mathias (MB) Brownwaart

Jacob (R) Rowers

Christof Ehrenhart

Conrath Bollon

Antreas Lohr

Lorens Weber

Tobias Hegelle

Johan Jacob Kuntz

Christof Riess

Fridrich Riss

Joh. Wilh. Köllin

Adam Heiler

Andreas (O) Heinler

Johann Conrad Scheimer

Hans Martin (B) Bulinger

Johann Martin Bullinger
Hans Filb Zimmerman
Johann Michel Dieter
Johannes Dieter
Nicolas (I) Ewick
Paulus Weinheimer
Johannes Bastian
Lorentz Bastian
Johannes Bastian
Johenrich Baum
Lutwig Friedle
Anthoni Gilbert
Johann Balthasar Bott
Johan Philipp Görig
Valentine (X) Vield
Nicolas (O) Wield
Adam (O) Hummel
Frederick (X) Miller
Thomas Sauder
Hans Adam (O) Werner
Johan Velten Umstatt
Johanes Söffrens
Bartholomeus Morth
Lorentz Kuntz
Lutwick (O) Leeman
Johann Görg Baltz
Nicolas (O) Evelandt
Johann Martin Bauer
Johannes Ebermann
Johannes Albrecht
Johan Henrich Jung
Conraad (O) Sadler
Johann Adam Leberger
Christoff Englend
Johann Christoph Beyer
Lenhart Mumma
Henry (HOW) Oswalt

Leonart (W) Weyer
Johannes Schmitt
Laurence (O) Bawder
Rudolph (X) Bonner
Henrich Appel
Johan Fridrich Baumgärdtner
Johan Henrich Miller
Pieter (O) Derber
Peter (O) Gabele
Peter Seyler
Philip (O) Smit
Johan Peder Schmitt
Johan Jacob Neuzehöltzer
Conrath Siebers
Hans Jerig (O) Tray
Jacob (O) Tray
Michael (X) Shallmayer
Johs (O) Sullmayer
Johannes Frey
Johs (O) Hammar
Johannes Heinrich Messerschmidt
Martin (X) Caplinger
Tomas (O) Cryle
Hans Wilhelm (X) Brant
Christian (C) Sneyder
Conradt Schneidter
Johann Leonhart Herman
Johannes Petter Gunther
Johan Frantz Russ
Johann Paullus Lederer
Frederick (X) Mayer
Johann Georg Gumpp
Johann Görg Sehm
Johann Adam Kreil
Thomas Kreul
Johann Georg Oberkogler

[Endorsed:]
Palatines imported in the Pink Johnson, of London, Dav.
Crockatt, Mr. Qualified Septr 19th 1732.

[List 21 C] Palatines imported in The Pink Johnson of London, David Crockatt, M^r., from Rott^r. Qualified Sepr. 19th 1732.

Johans Steinman
Johann Jörg Steimann
Laurens (X) Hartmann
Johannes (X) Erwig
Paulus Wegerlein
Hans Jacob Müller
Johann (O) Georg Müller
Faldin Bey [er]
Henrich Sim
Conrad (O) Bohm
Jacob Müller
Michel (O) Lochner
Hans Henrich Jegner
Thomas (I) Mottern
Andreas (O) Overbeck
Hans Jacob (I) Krauss
Jacob (I) Rausch
Hans Valentine (I) Renner
Daniel (D) Schuhl
Johann Martin Schilling
Isai (I) Cuschwah
Johannes Mösinger
Bernhardt Pfeffer
Matthes (MB) Brounwart
Johan Jacob (R) Rohr
Christoff Ehrenhart
Conrath Bollon
Antreas Lohr
Lorens Weber
Tobias Hegelle
Johan Jacob Kuntz
Christof Riss
Fridrich Riss
Joh. Wilhelm Köllin
Adam Heiler
Andreas (O) Hitner
Johann Conradt Scheimer
Hans Martin (O) Bullinger

Johann Martin Bullinger
Hans Filb Zimmerman
Johann Michel Dieter
Johannes Dieter
Nicolaus (I) Ewig
Paulus Weinheimer
Johannes Bastian
Lorentz Bastian
Johannes Bastian
Johenrich Bauman
Ludwig Friedle
Anthoni Gilbert
Johan Balthasar Bott
Johan Philipp Görich
Valentin (X) Wild
Nicolaus (O) Wild
Johann Adam (O) Hummel
Friederich (X) Müller
Thomas Sauder
Hans Adam (O) Werner
Johan Valten Umstatt
Johanes Söffrens
Bartholomes Morti
Lorentz Kuntz
Ludwig (O) Lehmann
Johann Görg Baltz
Nicolaus (O) Eveland
Johann Martin Bauer
Johannes Ebermann
Johann Albrecht
Johan Henrich Jung
Conrad (CS) Sattler
Johann Adam Leberger
Christoff England
Johann Christoph Beyer
Lenhart Mumma
Henrich (HOW) Ostwald
Leonhard (W) Weyer

Johannes Schmitt
Laurenz (O) Bader
Rudolph (X) Bonner
Henrich Appel
Johan Fridrich Baumgärdtner
Johan Henrich Mill [er]
Pieter (O) Darbeer
Peter (O) Gabel
Peter Seyler
Philip (O) Shmid
Johann Peder Schmitt
Johann Jacob Neuzehölzer
Conrath Sieber
Hans Georg (O) Trey
Johan Jacob (O) Trey
Gerhard (O) Michel Scholmeyer
Johan (O) Scholmeyer
Johannes Frey

Johannes (O) Hanauer
Johanns Henrich Messerschmidt
Hans Martin (K) Keplinger
Thomas (|) Kreyl
Hans Wilhelm (O) Brand
Christian (S) Schneider
Conradt Schneider
Johann Leonhardt Herman
Johann Peter Günther
Johan Frantz Russ
Johann Paulus Lederer
Friederich (|) Meyer
Johann Georg Gumpp
Johann Georg Sehm
Johann Adam Kreil
Thomas Kreul
Johan Georg Oberkogler

Philadelphia, Septem^r 19th 1732.

At the Courth° before the Govr, Mayor & others of the Magistrates the foregoing Qualifications were taken & subscribed by the sev^l foreigners, whose Names are contained in the foregoing Leaf & this Page.

Robt Charles, Cl. Con.

[List 22A] [List of the Palatines imported in the Pink Plaisance, John Parrett, M^r, from Rott^r, but last from Cowes. Qualified Sepr 21st, 1732.]

MENS NAMES	AGES		AGES
		Hans Zimberman	30
John Fillip Muller	38	Saml Myear	50
Johanes Muller	36	Martin Myear	37
Jurig Bast	46	Jacob Schere	65
Johanis Cline	44	Pallus Hartsligh	50
Conrad Shirf	34	Jurrig Wagner	50
Daniel Stiffer	24	Hans Huber	54
Basston Rudey	24	Jurig Peter Knight	31
Christ^n Huffer	34	Christ^n Martin	63
Melker Feeler	43	Jacob Bessaker	46

	AGES		AGES
Felix Fisler	50	Ulrigg Boucher	45
Rudolf Richard	46	Henrick Hartsligh	50
Mathias Muller	26	Nicholis Teni	23
Joan Jacob Kook	32	Andris Woolf	26
Johans Hunsinar	23	Nicholas Carn	39
Johanis Frans Foox	25	Hans Melker Werfle	20
Tobias Pekluff	43	Jacob Stofar	20
Johanis Fulker	58	Johanis Landis	20
Carl Wagonar	52	Hans Kessel	17
Bollser Schonbarger	42	Villrigg Waginar	20
Jacob Roots	58	Hendrix Hartsligh	40
Stepen Long	47	Hendrix Hartsligh, Junr.	17
Christian Strom	26	Johan Jacob Felker, sick	17
Rudolph Christon	45	Lenard Hartsell	24
Peter Biker	32	Urigg Hartsell, sick	18
Hans Stemphley	47	Elias Wagner	19
Ulrich Stelley	32	Fillip Utt	40
Hans Leight	60	Andris Cramer	20
Hans Jacob Kyser	24	Hans Woolf Barlet	25
Paulus Keyser	27		
Velley Danler, sick	23	WOMENS NAMES	
Hans Danler	21	Anna Eve Conaten	34
Mathias Cramer	40	Catarrina Hartsell	51
Nicklos Zimberman	50	Magdilen Carnin	45
Ulrich Zimberman	27	Anna Fellar	50
Saml Harnis	28	Eliza^t Bush	75
Jacob Bloom	20	Salome Zimarman	34
Hans Shear	27	Barbarey Bogarey	35
Henry Kern *	27	Hester Rigard	43
Johanis Gross, sick	36	Eliza Pectlof	32
Andris Flockinger	20	Anna Barlit	24
Jacob Swisser	44	Mari Marlin Wagner	60
Chris Albrit Long	32	Annis Drowtwine	30
John Wm Stope	44	Barbr. Hartsell	50
Jurrig Banhart Man	31	Anna Rosin Clin	40
Nicklos Ish, sick	21	Anna Margrit Man	27
Fran^cs Stedel	32	Susan Kiser	29
Philip Kisner	32	Catrin Man	27
Adam Zimberman	23	Maria Crissta	36

* Name partially erased.

AGES

	AGES
Maria Collar	19
Anna Dority Woolf	30
Frany Augmon	20
Anna Selek	22
Anna Stapan	18
Anna Maree Basst	44
Katharina Roots	58
Anna Maree Shunburg	27
Anna Margreth Fux	22
Aploney Shapen	69
Catarin Light	50
Sharlot Stedel	33
Christian Muller	35
Anna Mare Muller	26
Eliz^b. Kucken	30
Barvil Fisler	48
Franick Miear	39
Orsell Wagner	48
Madelen Bear	20
Frena Bear	18
Frena Bulgren	22
Eliz. Cramir	62
Anna Mire Miar	32
Barba Staphen	20
Catarin Scrivers	30
Maria Catrin Swisar	50
Matlina Stamplin	43
Christan Bricker	29
Anna Harnis	28
Hestar Brollar	57
Ossel Long	42
Ells Marty	60
Anna Cratsar	20
Barbil Zimarman	27
Anna Stalley	27
Anna Mare Bissacor	20
Eliz. Zimarman	30
Eliza Bezengreen	24
Matelin Sharin	20
Fravin Martin	16

	AGES
Anna Light	19
Barbary Hufarin	18
Franey Hufar	20
Marey Grist	80
Christan Hartsel	27
Eliz. Burn	18
Maria Crisst	18
Maria Gotliven Ricarten	17
Orrla Feslarin	20
Magdelin Sheren	26

CHILDREN

Hans Zimberman
Christian Zimberman
Bastian Zimberman
Johanas Bast
Jacob Man
Hans Martin Hubar
Jacob Hubar
Jacob Burn
Jacob Miar
Martin Miar
Christon Miar
Hans Pickleather
Hans Peter Steley
Martin Marta
John Manvell Brallion
Kongur Pactoll
Bastion Roots
Andaris Steedel
Ronyard Richards
Urik Willm Karn
Jacob Feglear
Christopher Muler
Hans Urig Muler
Filip Muler
Jacob Bizanor
John Barnats Strop
Mathias Cline
Hendrick Cline

Ulrich Reyser
Michael Share
Maria Zimberman
Magritt Kisaron
Margrett Wagener
Anna Miar
Anna Barba Bickrer
Eliz. Brickerin
Anna Barbra Stelin
Maria Zimberman

Fronik Martin
Soffia Catarina Picktlen
Jacob Benia Hatslin
Margrit Bugarin
Margaret Karn
Margarett Kerharten
Eliz^th Hezelarin
A true List.
Jn° Parett.

Philad^ia Septr 21st 1732.

At the Courth° Present: The Honble the Govr, S. Hasell, Esqr, May^r.

The foregoing List was sworn to by the Master.

R. Charles, Cl. Con.

"At the Courthouse aforesaid, Septr. 21st 1732. Seventy two Palatines, who with their families, making in all One hundred eighty eight Persons, were imported in the Pink Plaisance, John Paret, Mr., from Rotterdam, but last from Cowes as by Clearance thence." From the Minutes of the Provincial Council, printed in the *Colonial Records,* Vol. III, p. 454.

[List 22 B] Palatines imported in the Pink Plaisance, John Parrett, M^r, from Rotterdam, but last from Cowes, p. Clearance thence. Qualified Septr. 21st 1732.

Johann Philip Müller
Johanes Müller
Gerg Bast
Joh^s (✕) Cline
Conrath Scharff
Danl (O) Stouffer
Melcher Feler
Bastian Rudi
Christian Huber
Hans Zimmerman
Saml (O) Meyer
Marte Mayer
Jacob (✕) Schere
Paulus Hertzel

Hans Görg Wagner
Hans Huber
Georg Peter Knecht
Christian (O) Martin
Jacob Besiker
Felix Fissler
Rudolff Reichert
Matthes Müller
Johann Jacob Koch
Johannes Hunsicer
Johann Frantz Fuchs
Tobias (O) Peckluf
Joh^s (O) Fulker
Carl Wagner

Balthaser Schönberger
Jacob Rutz
Stephen (X) Long
Christian (O) Strom
Rudolff Christen
Peter (PB) Biker
Hans Stömfly
Ulrich (O) Stalley
Hans Lichtin
Hans Jacob Geyser
Paulus (O) Keyser
Hans (X) Danler
Mathias (O) Cramer
Nicolas (X) Zimmerman
Ulrich (O) Zimmerman
Samuel Harnisch
Jacob (O) Bloom
Hans Scherrer
Andres Flickiger
Jacob (X) Swisser
Christoff Albrecht Lang
Johann Wilhelm Straub *

Jerg Bernhart Mohn
Francis (O) Stedel
Johann Philip Kistner
John Ad^m (X) Zimmerman
Hans Ulrich Bucher
Henrich Hertzell
Nicklas Somi
Anttres Wolff
Nicolas (O) Carn
Hans Melchior Werffel
Jacob Stauffer
Joh^s (O) Landis
Hans (O) Gesell
Jann Ulrich Wagner
Hendrich (O) Hartslegh
Hans Leonhart Hertzel
Elias Wagner
Philip Ott
Andreas (O) Cramer
Johan Wolff Berlett
Ulrich (O) Reyser
Michel Schärrer

[List 22 C] Palatines imported in the Pink Plaisance, John Parrett, M^r., from Rott^r., but last from Cowes. Qualified Sepr. 21st 1732.

Johann Philip Müller
Johannes Müller
Gerg Bast
Johannes (X) Klein
Conrath Scharff
Daniel (O) Stauffer
Melcher Feler
Bastian Rudi
Christian Huber
Hans Zimmerman
Samuel (O) Meyer
Marte Mayer

Jacob (X) Scheerer
Paulus Hertzel
Hans Görg Wagner
Hans Huber
Georg Peter Knecht
Christian (X) Martin
Jacob Besiker
Felix Fissler
Rudolff Reichert
Matthes Müller
Johann Jacob Koch
Johannes Huisiner

* For this Reformed schoolmaster and preacher, see *Life of John Philip Boehm*, p. 54.

Johann Frantz Fuchs
Tobias (O) Bechtluf
Johann (V) Velker
Carl Wagner
Baltheser Schönberger
Jacob Rutz
Stephen (✕) Lang
Christian (S) Strohm
Rudolff Christen
Peter (PB) Bricker
Hans Stemfly
Ulrich (O) Steily
Hans Lichtin
Hans Jacob Geyser
Paulus (O) Keyser
Hans (✕) Danler
Matthias (O) Kramer
Nicolaus (✕) Zimmerman
Ulrich (O) Zimmerman
Samuel Harnisch
Jacob (O) Bloom
Hans Scherrer
Andres Flickiger
Jacob (O) Schweitzer

Christoff Albrecht Lang
Johann Wilhelm Straub
Jerg Bernhart Mohn
Frantz (O) Steedel
Johann Philip Kistner
John Adam (O) Zimmerman
Hans Ulrich Bucher
Henrich Hertzell
Nicklas Somm [?]
Antres Wolff
Nicolaus (✕) Kern
Hans Melchior Werffel
Jacob Stauffer
Johan (O) Landis
Hans (O) Gesell
Hans Ulrich Wagner
Henrich (✕) Hertzel
Hans Leonhart Hertzell
Elias Wagner
Philip Ott
Andreas (O) Krämer
Johan Wolff Berlett
Ulrich (O) Resser
Michel Schärrer

Septem^r 21st 1732.

At the Courthouse before the Govr, Mayor & other Magistrates, the foregoing Qualifications were taken & subscribed by the sev^l foreigners whose Names are contained in this & the preceding Page.

Robt Charles, Cl. Con.

[List 23 A] A List of ye names of all ye men & ages on board ye Adventure [Robt. Curson, M^r., from Rotterdam. Qualified Sepr. 23, 1732.]

	AGES		AGES
Michell Millier	30	Friderick Tendellpek	30
Michell Brand	22	Hans Jerig Able	25
Mich^l. Groce	18	Martine Ronger	18
Georg Briner	20	Paul Songsinger	20

	AGES		AGES
David Ollseller	45	Tobies Mosser	30
Jnº Arts	35	Andreas Schaup	
George Moser	48	Leonart Moser	
Baltzar Stever	33	Paulus Moser	
Andreuss Killiaen	30	Hans Jorig Lichtner	
Jerimy Glance	29	Hans Melcher Stecher	
Andreuss Horne	32	Hans Michal Haagh	
Matt. Wallder	25	Hans Michal Meik	
David Fessher	40	Hans Pieter Styger	
Mich¹. Mossher	38	Leonard Aam, sick	
Sim¹ Mieire	40		
Lawrence Swiner	45	WOMENS NAMES AND AGES	
Yerack Onru	30	Even Millier	30
Conratt Long	38	Anna Margrett Branden	28
Mich¹. Pots	40	Ossell Trumpin	40
Pauley Porterner	34	Marrea Medl. Glance	30
Hans Linnard Nidy	28	Hannah Combin	30
Jnº Habling	32	Marrea Kinn	23
Do. Shoull	48	Dº. Barber	30
Do. Wincleplank	36	Dº. Margrett	35
Hendrick Steiger	52	Appalona Ollseller	41
Mathias Richall	23	Margeratt Walton	25
Jacob Canter	38	Dº. Ollseller	57
Hendrich Lips	25	Even Mosser	40
Dan¹ Collmere	25	Even Barber Mosser	16
Matt. Wagner	23	Christian Ditto	24
Oellrig Houy	26	Mattlena Ditto	28
Bernaerd Shirtle	23	Even Christian Stigen	23
Mich¹. Kogh	23	Marrea Barbʳ. Stiver	30
Sim¹ Gillanger	20	Eve Crispin Dº.	48
Jnº. Baker	23	Anna Marrea Fissher	25
Paule Lissen	44	Susanah Barber Mosser	40
Jnº Lissen	46	Evens Medlelen	52
Andrews Wise	22	Marrea Lagener	32
George Regalle	24	Dº. Mirene	38
Fellting Shyp	22	Hanah Stiger	46
Nick¹. Bocker	23	Credle Ditto	17
Jnº Graufeus	19	Margret Potts	22
Conrod Clever	23	Dittº Orona	21
Nick Bortle	24	Hannah Boble Long	28

	AGES		AGES
Ditto Unruine	26	Hanna Margrett Ditto	12
Appolona Afferline	35	Hannah Boble D°.	10
Alizabeath Winkleplankin	36	Even Ditto D°.	8
Mattelena Colemerrine	36	Hanna Margrett Mosser	12
Welly Hannah Lipesine	24	Anna Marea D°.	10
Marreas Rigline	23	Anna Margreatte D°.	8
Katterene Shoulen	31	Allenna Marger Ollseller	11
Margeratte Olever	44	Marrea Boble	9
Katterrena Kanteren	38	Anna Margreate Glance	9
Merreles Porterren	37	Susanna Ossell Trumpt	12
Margreate Nyden	25	Anna Barberer Ditto	8
Katterena Paulteren	25		
Luiss Lissen	36	BOYS NAMES & AGES	
Susannah Orttsine	39	Hance Adam Trumpt	10
Credlelass Bennech	18	D°. Micalle Glance	4
		Hance Peter Ollseller	13
GERRELLS NAMS & AGES		Basion Mosser	6
Merreless Bennech	7	Simon D°.	11
Johanna Luiss Lissine	13	Hance Jerack D°.	8
Marrea Katterrine D°.	9	D°. Miere	9
Johan Maria Lissene D°.	11	Hance Lennord D°.	6
Marrea Martine Kanten	4	Jerack Adam Stiger	9
Hanna Mcla Porterren	8	Hance Micall Peter	11
Hanna Mirea Shoulen	6	Hance Felter Haverlene	8
Katterrena Ditto	4	Passions Sheule	9
Credleless Winkleplanken	12	Hance Felter Winkleplanken	10
Hanna Boble Ditto	7	Larrance Lessen	6
Margerate Pottsen	5	Jn° Jacob Cahler	13
Ditto Stigeren		Jn° Jerack D°.	9
Appalona Mirenen	11	Jacob Portterner	10
Katterrena Fisher	13	Simon Bennites	13
Handless Ditt°	11	Johanas Artes	5
Hanna Mela Cripsizer	14		

"At the Courthouse aforesaid, Sepr 23^d, 1732. Fifty seven Palatines, who with their Families, making in all One hundred & forty five Persons, were imported here in the Ship Adventure, Robert Curson, Mr., from Rotterdam, but last from Cowes, as by Clearance thence." From the Minutes of the Provincial Council, printed in *Colonial Records,* Vol. III, p. 455.

[List 23 B] Palatines imported in the Ship Adventure, Robert Curson, M^r, from Rotterdam, but last from Cowes, p. clearance thence. Qualified Septr 23^d 1732.

Ha[n]s Michal Miller
Michael Brandt
Michael Gross
Johann Gorg Präuner
Frederick (O) Tendelspech
Hans Jerig (O) Able
Hans Martin Ranger
Hans Paulus Zantzinger
David Holtzeder
Joh^s (✕) Aarts
Jorich Mosser
Balthas Stüber
Andreas Kilian
Hieronymus Glantz
Andreas (O) Horne
Mathias (✕) Walder
David Fischer
Michel Moser
Simon Meyer
Lorenz Zwirner
Jerg Unruh
Conrath Long
Mich^l (M) Potts
Balser Bortner
Hans Leon^d (✕) Nydy
Johannes Heberling
Johann Scholl
Joh^s (✕) Wingleplech
Henrich Steger

Madteis Riegel
Henrich Lips
Hans Jacob Kander
Daniel Kolmer
Mathias (✕) Wagner
Hans Ulerich Hui
Bernhard (✕) Shertle
Mich^l (O) Koogh
Simon (O) Gillinger
Johannes (O) Becker
Paul Le Cene
Jean Le Cene
Andreas (O) Wise
Jerg Rigel
Fallendin Scheib
Nickel Bogert
Johannes Grawius
Conrad Clewer
Nicolas (✕) Bortle
Dowid Moser
Andreas (✕) Schaup
Leonart (O) Moser
Paulus Mos[e]r
Ha[n]s Jerig Lechner
Hans Melcher Stecher
Hanns Michael Haag
Georg Michael Mack
Hans Peter (O) Steyger
Jerich Leohart Gam

[List 23 C] Palatines imported in the Ship Adventure, Robt Curson, M^r from Rott^r. Qualified Sepr 23^d 1732.

Ha[n]s Michel Miller
Michael Brandt
Michael Gross
Johann Gorg Präuner

Friedrich (O) Dintelsbeck
Hans Georg (O) Abel
Hans Martin Ranger
Hans Paulus Zantzinger

David Holtzeder
Johannes (X) Artz
Jorich Mosser
Balthas Stüber
Andreas Kilian
Hieronymus Glantz
Andreas (O) Horn
Matthias (X) Walter
David Fischer
Michel Moser
Simon Meyer
Lorenz Zwirner
Jerg Unruh
Conrath Long
Michel (X) Putz
Balser Bortner
Hans Leonhard (X) Kneide
Johannes Heberling
Johans Scholl
Johannes (X) Winckelplech
Henrich Steger
Madteis Riegel
Henrich Lips
Hans Jacob Kander
Daniel Kolmer

Matthes (O) Wagner
Hans Ullerrich Hui
Bernhard (X) Scheertel
Michel (O) Koch
Simon (O) Gellinger
Johannes (O) Becker
Paul Le Cene
Jean Le Cene
Andreas (O) Weys
Jerg Rigel
Fallendin Scheib
Nickel Bogert
Johannes Grawius
Conrad Clewer
Nicolaus (X) Bartel
Dowid Moser
Andreas (X) Kap
Leonhard (X) Moser
Paulus Mos[e]r
Hans Jerig Lehner
Hanns Melcher Stecher
Hanns Michael Haag
Georg Michael Mack
Hans Peter (O) Steyger

September 23ᵈ 1732.

At the Courthouse before the Governor & sundry Magistrates the foregoing Qualifications were taken & subscribed by the several foreigners whose Names are contained in this & the preceding Page.

Robᵗ Charles, Cl. Con.

[List 24 A] [Palatines imported in the Ship Loyal Judith, of London, Robᵗ Turpin, Mʳ. Qualified Sepʳ 25ᵗʰ 1732.]

MENS NAMES	AGES		AGES
Andreas Chars	47	John Adam Able	44
Adam Char	20	Hans Jacob Able	16
Jnᵒ Michell Emort	39	Matthew Barstayn	39
Jacob Stealy	25	Roland Brown	30

	AGES		AGES
Mathias Smith	40	John Jurgh Rick	32
Hendrick Papts	35	Hants Mickell Kragin	31
John Jurigh Smith	21	Jurigh Ritter, sick	37
John Jurigh Brothell	32	Wm Bearne	36
Phillip Spinchire	45	Jurgh Hants Kunts	55
Jacob Spinchire	48	Hants Jurgh Kunts	19
Pieter Scheaver	24	John David Lince	20
Christian Reap	24	Baulus Miller	53
Piter Kitter	45	Cronomus Miller	23
Jacob Miller	52	Hants Wattlee	50
Hendrick Gaabell	65	Petter Sowder	48
Johanns Oterpack	27	Hants Philipp Sowder	17
Jurgh Burghart	56	Samuell Griffe	45
John Jurgh Noll	36	Johanes Jerig Houfman	45
Petter Rouch	35	Martien Heylman	23
Fredrick Killer	30	Johannes Heylman	16
John Jurge Waganer	52	Martin Waybrick	43
Mickell Pents	27	Jurigh Harkman	28
John Jacob Kinssell	36	Hants Jurig Obremiler	24
John Jurgh Pelman	40	Christopher Lay	37
John Mickell Rayer	45	Johan Jurig Fredrik	30
Hants Carll Reayer	22	Hants Jurigh Honick	20
Hants Martin Rayer	16	John Feyt Jurigher	42
Christien Ely	49	Andreas Shank	23
Hants David Elly	20	Mickell Smith	25
Jacob Lishire, dead	37	Jacob Billmayer	18
Jacob Lishire	30	Michell Emert	42
Lodwick Happell	36	Phillip Gripper	29
Mathews Shitz	34	John Mickell Houpacker	32
Coneard Fry [?]	52	Petter Shultes	20
Phillip Lendea Ceavy	26	Petter Cooker	20
Hans Jurge Reser	52	Jurigh Mickel Rey	22
Jurgh Adam Reser	22	John Cristian Shults, V.D.M.	30
Phillip Roup	51	John Jurgh Hotreman	32
Michell Roup	22	Jacob Stambagh	28
Lenord Kegill	48	John Fridrick Hayster	25
Barnard Walter	58	Hants Jurgh Able	63
Conrad Millear	17	Jacob Krech	22
Hendrick Acker	32	John Fradrick Burghart	30
Phillip Jacob Acker	36	Johanes Vogall	32

	AGES		AGES
Johannes Pens	23	Hans Martin Power	30
Hants Andreas Cochenderfer	..	Jurigh Miller	23
Hants Adam Gasser	32	Hants Jurgh Strian	21
Johan Hendrick Eckler	21	Johannes Smeltzer	26
Jones Wolf	40	Johannnes Repman	19
Lenard Losts	25	Johann Michell Albert	20
Marcus Yong	23	Christian Kym	32
Mathew Yong	21	Fredrick Sheaver	19
Hendrick Laybagger	46	Hans Martin Waybright	17
Johan Nicolas Reymer	30	Johannes Reep	..
Joseph Baker	25	Casper Creamer	..
Baltser Conkell	20	Conrad Walther	..
Valentayn Roepert, sick	28	John Jorig Fredrich Emert	..
Jnº. Jurgh Furkill	28	Jacob Rats	..
Hants Bintneagle	31	119 Men.	
Hants Jurgh Roup	27		
Hans Shooman	32	A true List.	
Johanes Ester	25	Rob. Turpin.	

Philad^{ia} Septr 25th 1732.

At the Courth^o in presence of the Honble the Govr & Sam. Hasell, Esqr, May^r, the within List was swore to by Rob. Turpin, Master of Pink Loyal Judith.

Robt Charles, Cl. Con.

"At the Courthouse aforesaid, Sepr 25th 1732. One hundred and fifteen Palatines, who with their Families, making in all . . . Persons, were imported here in the Ship Loyal Judith, of London, Robert Turpin, Master, from Rotterdam, but last from Cowes, as by Clearance thence." From the Minutes of the Provincial Council, printed in *Colonial Records,* Vol. III, p. 456.

[List 24 B] Palatines imported in the Ship Loyall Judith, of London, Robt. Turpin, M^r., from Rotterdam, but last from Cowes, p. Clearance thence. Qualified Sepr. 25th 1732.

Johannes Christian Schultz, Minister.*	Johan Adam Gaar
Andreas Gaar	Johann Michael Ebert
	Jacob Steli

* This is a well-known Lutheran minister.

Hans Adam Abel
Johann Jacob Abel
Mathias (O) Paarsteyn
Rudolph (X) Brown
Mathias (X) Smit
Hendrich (O) Papst
Johann Georg Schmidt
Hans Filipp Spanseuller
Jacob Spansailer
Hans Peter Schäfer
Christian (X) Reepp
Peter Keiter
Johannes Keiter
Jacob (J) Miller
Henrich Gobell
Joh[s] (X) Outerbach
Han[n]s Jerch Burk[art]
Hans Jerig (X) Noll
Peter Rauch
Friedrich Köhler
Hans Jerg Wagner
Mich[l] (X) Pents
Jacob Küntzel
Joh[s] Jerig (O) Pelman
Jn[o] Mich[l] (X) Rayer
Johann Carl Reyer
Johann Martin Roir
Christians Ehley
Hans David (O) Ely
Jacob (O) Lischire
Ludwig Happel
Mathäus Schütz
Conrad Fry
Filip Lutwi[g] Güfi
Hans Jerg Riser
Gorg Adam Riser
Philip Raup
Mich[l] (X) Roup
Lenhart Kegell
Bernard (X) Walter
Hendrick (H) Acker

Phil. Jacob (H) Acker
Johann Georg Rücke
Hans Mich. (X) Criger
Wilhelm (X) Berne
Hans Gerg Kuntz
Hans Gerg Kuntz
Joh[s] David (X) Lince
Baulus Müller
Cronomus (X) Miller
Hans Wadtli
Pedter Saudter
Johann Filb Sauter
Samuel (O) Griffe
Johann Georg Hoffmann
Marthin Heilmann
Johannes Heilman
Marthin Weybrecht
Johann Georg Obermüller
Georg Christoph Lay
Johann Georg Friderich
Johann Georg Honnig
Johann Veit Jorger
Andreas (X) Shank
Georg Michael Schmidt
Jacob Bühlmayer
Michael Emmert
Philipp Ernst Grüber
Johann Michael Hoffacker
Georg Peter Schultes
Johann Peter Kucher
Jerig Mich[l] (O) Rey
Johan Georg Nadderman
Hans Jacob Stambach
Johann Friderich Hesser
Hans Jerig (O) Able
Jno Fred. (JFB) Burghart
Johannes Vogel
Johannes Benz
Andreas Kochendorff
Hans Atam Gasser
Johann Henrich Eckler

Jonas (X) Woolf
Lenhart Lotz
Marcus Jung
Matheus Jung
Henrich Leibacher
Johan Nicklaus Römer
Johan Becker
Baltzar (X) Conkell
Johs Jerig (O) Furkell
Johs (X) Pintnagle
Hans Jerg Raub
Johan Summann
Johannes Hüster
Hans Martin Bau[er]

George Müller
Hans Jerig (X) Traan
Johs (X) Smeltzer
Johannes Rebmann
Johann Michel Albert
Christian Gum
Friedrich Schäfer
Hans Martin Weybrecht
Johs (O) Reep
Hans Jerig (X) Birstler
Casper Krämer
Conrad Walther
Johann Gorg Fredrig Emmert
Jacob Protz

[List 24 C] Palatines imported in the Ship Loyall Judith, of London, Robt. Turpin, Mr. Qualifd. Sepr. 25th 1732.

Johannes Christian Schultz,
    Minister.
Andreas Gaar
Johan Adam Gaar
Johann Michael Ebert
Jacob Steli
Hans Adam Abel
Johann Jacob Abel
Matthes (O) Barestein
Rudolph (X) Brown
Matthes (O) Schmidt
Henrich (O) Pabst
Johann Georg Schmidt
Hans Fielips Spanseuller
Jacob Spansailer
Hans Peter Schäfer
Christian (X) Rape
Peter Keiter
Johannes Keiter
Jacob (X) Müller
Henrich Gobell
Johannes (X) Otterbach
Hans Jerch Burkart

Hans Georg (X) Noll
Peter Rauch
Friedrich Köhller
Hans Jerg Wagner
Michael (X) Pens
Jacob Küntzel
Hans Georg (O) Bellmann
Hans Michael (X) Reyer
Johann Carl Reyer
Johann Martin Roir
Christians Ehley
Hans David (O) Ehly
Jacob (O) Lischer
Ludwig Happel
Mathäus Schütz
Conrad Fry
Philip Lutwi[g] Güfi
Hans Jerg Riser
Gorg Adam Riser
Philip Raupp
Michael (X) Raub
Lenhart Kegell
Bernhard (X) Walter

Henrich (H) Acker
Philip Jacob (X) Acker
Johann Gorg Rück
Hans Michael (X) Krieger
Wilhelm (O) Berne
Hans Jerg Kuntz
Hans Jerg Kuntz
Hans David (X) Lentz
Baulus Müller
Hieronimus (M) Muller
Hans Wadtli
Pedter Saudter
Johann Filb Sauter
Samuel (X) Griffi
Johann Georg Hoffmann
Marthin Heilman
Johannes Heilmann
Marthin Weybrecht
Johann Georg Obermüller
Georg Christoph Lay
Johann Georg Friederich
Johann Georg Honnig
Johann Veit Jorger
Andreas (X) Schenck
Georg Michael Schmidt
Jacob Bühlmayer
Michael Emmert
Philipp Ernst Grüber
Johann Michael Hoffacker
Georg Peter Schultes
Johann Peter Kucher
Georg Michael (X) Rey
Johan Gorg Nadderman
Hans Jacob Stambach
Johann Friderich Hesser
Hans Georg (O) Abel

Johann Friderich (X) Burck-
hart
Johannes Vogel
Johannes Benz
Andreas Cochenderff
Hans Atam Gasser
Johann Henrich Eckler
Jonas (X) Wolff
Lenhart Lotz
Marcus Jung
Mattheus Jung
Heinrich Leibacher
Johan Nicklaus Römer
Joseph Herman Becker
Balthasar (O) Gunkel
Johann Georg (O) Vorkel
Johannes (X) Pintnagel
Hans Jerg Raub
Johan Schauman
Johannes Hüster
Hans Martin Baur
George Müller
Hans Georg (X) Thran
Johannes (O) Schmeltzer
Johannes Rebmann
Johan Michel Albert
Christian Güm
Friedrich Schäffer
Hans Martin Weybrecht
Johannes (O) Reep
Hans Georg (X) Börstler
Casper Krämer
Conrad Walther
Johann Friedrich Emmert
Jacob Protz

Septr 25th 1732.

At the Courthouse before the Govr, attended by some of the
Magistrates, the foregoing Qualifications were taken & sub-

scribed by the sev¹ foreigners whose Names are contained on this Leaf & the preceding Page.

Robᵗ Charles, Cl. Con.

[List 25 A] [Passengers imported in the Ship Mary, John Gray, Master. Qualified Sept. 26, 1732.]

MENS NAMES ON BORD THE MARY	AGES		AGES
		Hance Jacob Chissler	22
		Jerick Chissler	18
Nicolas Taller	45	Henery Chissler	16
Hance Froshorn	32	John Frederick Rousenburg	19
Michal Abreman	56	Jacob Walter	48
Jacob Abreman	19	Jacob Walter	19
Arnold Treetershan	42	Herman Sim	25
Conerat Miller	40	Simon Miller	25
Table Kees	20	Wennell Kettle	43
Christian Clinger	26	Rhineholt Ysel	32
Jacob Stemple	40	Albright Hawse	33
Nicolas Stemple	70	Erreck Mens Emler	27
Johans Loudmilck	28	Carle Lissey	20
Hansad. Miller	23	Michal Mans	33
Jacob Hoak	25	Hans Erick Cling	16
Christopher Kizer	36	Jacob Hasman	40
Cornelus Teele	25	Johanes Went	27
Jerick Philp Pear	27	Michal Dane	37
Daniel Peliger	30	Hans Jericke Deane, dead	16
Albright Strows	20	Christan Mineer	28
Jacob Triolpare	22	Hance Jerck Mineer	26
Conrade Abraman	23	Henrick Teaney	19
Anders Moser	24	Hance Adam Roberts	48
Casper Maire	20	John Lew De Avasong	18
Hance Jerack Ebener	34	Perce Flewies	38
Hance Halwalop	25	Leonhart Sable, dead	40
Hance Jacob Wartt	56	Hance Jereck Cole	26
Hance Jacob Wartt	17	Hance Martin Errenst	26
Staffa Kenama	60	Hance Jergenbright	45
Jacob Kenama	16	Johanes Hoover	57
Johannes Mizer	23	Hance Peter Verly	27
Henery Chissler	52	Hance Errick Smith, dead	44

	AGES		AGES
Canesh Ever	50	Johan Philip Pickle	16
Jerricks Felder Pickle	32	Men	69
Jeneck Hennick Right	17	Women & child.	122
Nicolas Kents	58		
Baldos Click, dead	33	[Total:]	191
Christopher Pickle	48	A true List	
		John Gray.	

"At the Courthouse aforesaid, Sep[r] 26th, 1732.
Sixty one Palatines, who with their Families, making in all one hundred ninety one Persons, were imported in the Ship Mary, of London, John Gray, Master, from Rotterdam, but last from Cowes, as by Clearance thence." From the Minutes of the Provincial Council, printed in *Colonial Records,* Vol. III, p. 457.

[List 25 B] Palatines Imported in the Ship Mary, of London, John Gray, Master, from Rotterdam, but last from Cowes by Clearance thence. Qualified September 26th 1732.

Nicolas (O) Staller
Hans Jerg Froschauer
Michael (O) Ebermann
Hans Jacob Eberman
Arnolt Riettershan
Conrath Miller
Dewald (O) Kase
Christian (O) Cling
Jacob Stempel
Nicholas (O) Stemple
Johan (+) Loudermilch
Hans Adam Miller
Jacob (X) Hauk
Christoff (CK) Kiser
Rynholl (O) Ezle
Cornelius (O) Teele
Georg Philip Pier
Daniel Billiger
Albrecht Strauss
Jacob Dreibelbiss
Conrade (O) Abermann

Andreas (M) Moser
Casper (O) Miere
Hance Jerick (HE) Ebenno
Hans Michel Walck
Hans Jacob Würth
Jacob Würth
Staffen (SY) Kennemar
Johannes Meyer
Henry (X) Cheasler
Hance Jacob (H) Chessler
Jerg Schüssler
Henry (H) Chessler
Johan Friederich Rauschenberger
Jacob (WA) Walther
Jacob Walder
Hermans (O) Sin
Simon Müller
Winnale (L) Cettler
Albrecht Haas
Jak. Marcus Imler
Cale (O) Lisa

Georg Kling
Johannes Worth
Michell Dörr
Christian (X) Miner
Hance Jerreck (X) Miner
Hance Henrick (X) Tany
Hance Adam (S) Robetes
Jean Louis D'anion
Pierre Fleury
Joh. Georg Kohl

Mardin Ernst
Hance (HIE) Jergenbright
Hance Peter (O) Verly
Jerrick Felder (O) Pickle
Nicolas (+) Kent
Hans Michel Ments
Johannes Schaffner [?]
Johans Huber
Christoph Bickel

[List 25 C] Palatines imported in the Ship Mary of London, Jnº Gray, Master. Qualified Sepr 26th 1732.

Nicolaus (O) Stahler
Hans Jerig Froschauer
Michael (O) Ebermann
Hans Jacob Eberman
Arnolt Riettershan
Conrath Miller
Dewald (O) Kase
Christian (O) Kling
Jacob Stempel
Nicolaus (O) Stempel
Johann (X) Lautermilch
Hans Adam Miller
Jacob (X) Hauk
Christoph (CK) Keiser
Reinhold (O) Esel
Cornelius (O) Teele
Georg Philip Pier
Daniel Billiger
Albrecht Strauss
Johann Jacob Dreibelbis
Conrad (X) Ebermann
Andreas (M) Moser
Caspar (X) Meyer
Hans Georg (HE) Ebener
Hans Michel Walck
Hans Jacob Würth
Jacob Würth
Stephen (SY) Kennemar

Johannes Mayer
Henrich (O) Schüsler
Hans Jacob (H) Schüsler
Jerg Schüsler
Henrich (O) Schüsler
Johann Friedrich Rauschenberger
Jacob (WA) Walter
Jacob Walder
Hermann (O) Sim
Simon Müller
Wendel (L) Ketterle
Albrecht Haas
Isack Marcus Imler
Carel (O) Eisen
Georg Kling
Johannes Werth
Michell Dörr
Christian (X) Minier
Hans Georg (X) Minier
Hans Henrich (X) Teany
Hans Adam (X) Robertus
Jean Louis Danion
Pierre Fleury
Joh. Georg Kohl
Mardin Ernst
Hans Georg (HIE) Erchen-
brecht
Hans Peter (O) Verly

Georg Felte (O) Pickel
Nicolaus (X) Kent
Hans Michel Mantz

Johannes Schaffner
Johannes Huber
Christoph Bickel

Septem^r 26th 1732.

At the Courthouse before the Governor & several of the City Magistrates, the foregoing Qualifications were taken & subscribed by the several foreigners whose Names are contained in this Leaf.

Robt Charles, Cl. Con.

[List 26 A] A True List of all the Passengers on board the Dragon, Commander Charles Hargrave, from Rotterdam. [Qualified Sepr. 30th 1732.]

MENS NAMES

Andreas Beetel
Peter Matern
Georg Dirr
Michael Dirr
Martin Wytknecht
Christoph Hoffman
Jacob Lypersberger
Georg Adam Bender
Wendel Laaber
Georg Roodt
Adam Romich
Frederich Romich
Leonhard Schlosser
Leonhard Muller
William Franck
Peter Rowdenbosh
Henry Rowdenbosh
Jacob Shark
Henrich Groober
Peter Wolff
Johannes Hearburger
Johan Wittman
Jacob Klein
Henrich Klein

Johann Kyjer
Wilhelm Kyjer, sick
Hans Georg Kroner
Dietrich Kraner
Peter Schlosser
William Tsiegler
Johannes Shryok
Nicolaus Muller
Christian Hoober
Daniel Steinmetz, sick
Philip Hoffman
John Hayea, sick
Jacob Hayea, sick
Georg Hayea
Simon Peltzner
Philip Shlowch
Andreas Shlowch
Michael Rysner
Rudolph Illick
Martin Kopler
Henrich Baasler
Ludwig Schitz
Leonhard Pence
Michael Graaf
Tobias Paul
Georg Fawntz

Georg Tsober, sick
Jacob Byerle
Christoph Basserer
Simon Basserer, dumb
Ulrich Bare
Georg Bare, sick
Georg Hayl
Georg Adam Hayl
Georg Syp
Ludwich Syp
Frans Syp
Henrich Zowck, sick
Laurence Bechtle, sick

Felix Bronner
Michael Nusloch, sick
Dietrich Boocher, sick
Jacob Tups, sick
Wolfgang Birle, sick
Hans Georg Soldner
Friederich Engelhart Uhlmann,
   sick

Men	70
Women	53
Children	62
[Total]	185

A True List of Passengers entered from on Bord yᵉ Ship Dragon.

pr. Charles Hargrave.

"At the Courthouse aforesaid, Sepʳ 30th, 1732.

Fifty five Palatines, who with their families, making in all One hundred & seventy Persons, were imported here in the Ship Dragon, Charles Hargrave, Master, from Rotterdam, but last from Plymouth, as by Clearance thence." From the Minutes of the Provincial Council, printed in *Colonial Records,* Vol. III, p. 458.

[List 26 B] Palatines imported in the Ship Dragon, Chas. Hargrave, Mʳ, from Rotterdam, but last from Plymouth p. Clearance thence. Qualified Septʳ 30ᵗʰ 1732.

Peter (O) Matern
Hans George (O) Dirr
Michˡ Dirr
Martin Weidknecht
Christian (O) Hofman
Jacob (✕) Lypersburger
Hansh (O) Laabour
Hans Adam Bender
Earick (O) Road
Johann Adam Romich
Johann Friedrich Romich
Leonard (O) Slosser

Leonard (O) Miller
Johan Wilhelm Franck
Peter Raudenbusch
Heinrich Raudenbusch
Hans Jacob Schörck
Henrich Gruber
Hans Peter Wolff
Johannes Heerburger
Johannes Witmann
Jacob Klein
Henrich Klein
Johannes Geiger

Johann Georg Gruner
Johann Dietrich Gruner
Peter Schlosser
Hans Wilhelm Ziegler
Johannes Schreyiackh
Johan Nicklaus Müller
Christian Huber
Johann Pett[er] Hofman
Hans Jergi Hegi
Sio. Belser [?]
Johann Philipp Schlauch
Andreas Schlauch
Hans Michell Reisner
Hans Rudolff Illig
Hans Martin Kappler
Henrich Bosller

Jerg Ludwig Schütz
Lenhart Bentz
Michael Graaff
[Tobias] Ball
Gerg Fantz
Johann Jacob Beyerle
Christoff Beser
Hans Ulrich Beer
Hans Jerg Heill
George (X) Hoyle
Georg Seib
Ludwick (O) Sipe
Frantz Seib
Felix Brunner
Hans Gerg Soldner

[List 26 C] Palatines imported in the Ship Dragon, Chas.
Hargrave, M[r]. Qualif[d] Sep[r]. 30th 1732.

Peter (O) Matern
Hans Georg (O) Dirr
Michel (X) Dirr
Martin Weidknecht
Christoph (O) Hoffman
Hans Georg (X) Leipersberger
Hans Wendel (O) Lahber
Hans Adam Bender
Hans Georg (O) Road
Johann Adam Romich
Johann Friedrich Romich
Leonhard (O) Schlosser
Leonhard (X) Müller
Johann Wilhelm Franck
Peter Raudenbusch
Heinrich Raudenbusch
Hans Jacob Schörck
Henrich Gruber
Hans Peter Wolff
Johannes Heerburger
Johannes Widtmann

Jacob Klein
Heinrich Klein
Johannes Geiger
Johann Georg Gruner
Johann Dietrich Gruner
Peter Schlosser
Hans Wilhelm Ziegler
Johannes Schreyiackh
Johan Nicklaus Müller
Christian Huber
Johann Pett[er] Hofmann
Hans Jergi Hegi
Simon Belsner
Johann Philip Schlauch
Andreas Schlauch
Hans Michell Reisner
Hans Rudolf Illig
Hans Martin Kappler
Henrich Bosler
Jerg Ludwig Schütz
Lenhart Bentz

Michael Graff

Tobias Ball

Gerg Fantz

Johann Jacob Beyerle

Christoff Beser

Hans Ulrich Beer

Hans Gerg Heill

Georg (X) Hayl

Georg Seib

Ludwig (O) Sype

Frantz Seib

Felix Brunner

Hans Gerg Soldner

September 30th 1732.

At the Courthouse before the Govr & sevl of the Magistrates the foregoing Qualifications were taken & subscribed by those foreigners whose Names are contained on this Leaf.

Robt Charles, Cl. Con.

[List 27 A] [Passengers imported in the Ship Pleasant, James Morris, Master. Qualified Oct. 11th 1732.]

MENS NAMES	AGES		AGES
		Phillip Shillin	30
Balster Spingler	24	Connard Colp	34
Henrey Spingler	26	Connard Clasparner	30
Johannes Keller	32	Connard Ralfure, sick	29
Jarrick Senck	25	Peter Ralfure, sick	25
Jarrick Bare	21	Jacob Hornbarger	33
Lennard Lutes, sick	24	Hance Petter Sigmount	22
Jarrick Pasler *	23	Barnet Counts	35
Ulrey Betterman	25	Felicks Meller	40
Ulrich Petters	24	Connard Hellebran, sick	34
Jarrick Henrich Petters	19	Philip Crasler	20
Jerrich Spingler	31	Marthies Ambrose	37
Jarrich Keller	20	Johannas Cambord	32
Jacob Fridrich Clim	17	Fridrick Nots	32
Henrey Roch	26	David Menner, sick	20
Jacob Podom	18	Adam Shillin	24
Johannes Jacob Timmanes	20	Micharl Cock, sick	33
Isich Rouddebus	27	Johannes Moke	34
Marthiy Jargon	30	Andrew Swiser, sick	33
Henrey Akers	40	Jacob Froch, sick	40
Jarrick Follick	30	Fridrich Pasler	27
Jerrick Pisell, sick	23	Olrey Pasler	36

* Name crossed out.

	AGES		AGES
Michael Favon, sick	30	Johannes Tablemier	23
Gasper Winterout	28	Christofour Spraher, sick	33
Jarrick Phillip Snatherly	28	Connar Roupe	33
Jarrick Carne, sick	25	Jarrick Mich^r Favon	23
Hance Michael Snatherly	25	David Meneir, sick	
Jarrick Mess	50	J. George Passage, sick	
Vallentine Miller	32	A true List.	
Hance Michr^l Hofman	34	Ja. Morris, Master.	

Philad^{ia} Octr 11th 1732.
At the Courth° Present:
   The Honble Lt Govr, Henry Brooke, Esqr, Chas. Read, Esqr.
The foregoing List was declared by the Master upon Oath
to be a true one.

Robt Charles, Cl. Con.
"At the Courthouse of Philadelphia, Octr 11th, 1732.
   Forty two Palatines, who with their families, making in all
. . . Persons, were imported in the Ship Pleasant, James Morris, Master, from Rotterdam, but last from Deal, as by Clearance thence." From the Minutes of the Provincial Council,
printed in *Colonial Records,* Vol. III, p. 465.

[List 27 B] Palatines imported in the Ship Pleasant, James
Morris, M^r, from Rotterdam, but last from Deal, p. Clearance
thence. Qualified Octr 11th 1732.

Balzer Spengler	Johan Jacob Timanus
Henrich Spengler	Isaac (✗) Raudebusch
Johannes Keller	Matthias (MI) Jurian
Johann Geörg Senck	Henrich (O) Eckert
George (O) Bear	Hans Görg Falck
Friedrich (O) Baasler	Philip (O) Schellig
Ulrich Bodmer	Conrath Kolb
Ulrich (✗) Peters	Conrat Glasbrenner
Jerg Henri Ped[ers]	Jacob (O) Hornberger
Jerg Spengler	Hans Peter (O) Sigmund
Jerg Keller	Hans Bern (O) Kuntzer
Jacob Friderich Klem	Felix Miller
Henrich Roth	Hans Philip (O) Kresler
Jacob Podum	Matheis Ambrosi

Johannes Gamber
Friederich Notz
Hans Adam (O) Schilling
Johannes (O) Moak
Ulrich (O) Baasler
Johan Casper Wenterott
Jerg Filp Schnatterly

Hans Michel Schnatterly
Georg (O) Mess
Valtin Müller
Hans Michel (O) Hoffman
Johannes Taffelmeyer
Conrad (O) Rowp
Georg Michel (O) Favian

[List 27 C] Palatines imported in the Ship Pleasant, James Morris, Master. Qualified Oct. 11th 1732.

Balzer Spengler
Henrich Spengler
Johannes Keller
Johann Georg Senck
Jarig (O) Bare
Frederick (O) Pasler
Ulrich Bodmer
Ulrich (X) Peters
Jerg Henri Ped[ers]
Jorg Spengler
Jerg Keller
Jacob Friderich Klem
Henrich Roth
Jacob Podum
Johan Jacob Timanus
Isaac (O) Roudenbush
Mathias (MI) Jergon
Henry (O) Akers
Hans Görg Falck
Philip (O) Shillin
Conrath Kolb

Conrat Glasbrenner
Jacob (O) Hornbarger
Hans Pieter (O) Sigmont
Barnard (O) Konts
Felix Miller
Philip (O) Crasler
Matheis Ambrosi
Johannes Gamber
Friederich Notz
Hans Adam (O) Shillin
Johannes (X) Moke
Ulrick (O) Pasler
Johan Casper Wenterott
Jerg Filib Schnatterly
Hans Michel Schnatterly
Jerig (O) Mess
Valtin Müller
Hans Michl (O) Hofman
Johanes Tafelmeyer
Conrad (O) Roup
Jerig Michl (O) Favon

Octr 11th 1732.

At the Courthouse before the Govr & sevl Magistrates the foregoing Qualifications were taken & subscribed by the several foreigners whose Names are on the other side of this Leaf.

Robt Charles, Cl. Con.

[List 28 A] A List of Palatine Passengers on Board the Ship John and William, Constable Tymperton, Commander, from Rotterdam. [Qualified October 17, 1732.]

Hans Earhart Vosselman
Pieter Harbyn, sick
Hans Emich
Helflick Shedeicher
Laurence Rosier, sick
Johannes Deynen
Stephen Matts
Fridrich Cooler, sick
Pieter Huvigh
Michael Wysel
Fridrich Wisel
Laurence Keiyfer
Philip Melchionar, sick
Ludwick Melchionar
Johannes Yege
Bartel Moll
Philip Reynhart
Hans Pieter Britbill
Benedick Britbill
Jacob Britbill
Hans Britbill
Johan Vintenhelver, sick
Hans Jerick Spreaker
Johannes Nagel
Pieter Smidt
Johannes Hunsam
Johan Michael Hufman
Nicholas Paushon
Bernard Weymer
Balsar Gerloch
Christian Low
Conraed Low
Ludwick Hugel
Jacob Weyber
Morris Lorrence
Johannes Shook
Hans Jacob Reyl
Jerig Adam Stis
Philip Jacob Proops, sick
Michael Miller, sick
Abraham Dubo

Philip Dubo, sick
Hans Jerick Roerbach
Johan Michael Smit
Adam Wilt
Gerich Albrecht
Antonius Albrecht
Hans Woolf Doopel, sick
Joseph Houbly, sick
Hans Philip Glais
Conrad Gets
Nicholaus Kooger
Jacob Kooger
Mathias Menser
Bastian Trookmiller
Giedon Huffer
Hans Reyl
Johan Martin Shoppfield
Hans Jerich Martin
Casperrias Vielard
Paul Derst
Hendrick Gek
Mathias Rubichon
Johannes Vigelie
Jacob Hendrick
Philip Melchior Meyer
Johan Jerich Vansettel
Pieter Apfel
Jerich Vybert
Jacob Sheare
Michael Proops, sick

WOMEN AND CHILDREN

Elisabetha Margareta
Margaret Harbyn
Dorothy Emich
Nicholas Emich
Johannes Emich
Jacob Emich
Marilas Shyndech
Cathrina Matts
Dorothy Rosar

Dorothy Kooler
Elisabeth Kooler
Barbara Hyvigh
Susanna Wysel
Ablonia Wysel
Barbara Wysel
Barbara Kuyser
Maris Savina [Kuyser]
Johan David [Kuyser]
Luodwick Melchionar
Anna Drogo
Maria Katrina
Paulina Yege
Katrina Moll
Maria Britbill
Anna Britbill
Maria Helferen
Christophel Helferen
Cathrina Spreakering
Maria Nagelin
Cathrena Shabel
Maria Smit
Maria Hausman
Eva Hausman
Magdalena Panchson
Andreas Panchson
Hendrich Panchson
Maria Panchson
Eve Panchson
Barbara Veymert
Johannes Veymert
Maria Gerloch
Anna Gluf Lowein
Philip Lowein
Christian Lowein
Barbara Lowein
Margaret Lowein
Anna Hugel Reyn
Christina Bever
Jacob Bever
Dorothy Bever

Barbara Lorrence
Maria Shooken
Hans Shooken
Maria Shooken
Cathrina Shooken
Jacob Lorrence
Eve Reylen
Jerick Reylen
Jacob Vry
Catharin Spis
Susanna Spis
Michael Proops
Felder Proops
Cathrina Miller
Cathrina Miller
Philiphbena Miller
Caspar Miller
Hans Miller
Michael Miller
Cathrina Proops
Anna Dubo
Anna Smit
Barbara Albrecht
Peter Albrecht
Hans Albrecht
Susan Husselich
Bernard Husselich
Michael Husselich
Maria Glassen
Maria Getson
Cathrina Trookmiller
Cathrina Reyl
Michael Reyl
Maria Reyl
Anna Martin
Maria Martin
Michael Martin
Magdalena Vielard
Charl. De Meyeren
Cathrina Vansettel
Johan Revenooch

Apalonia Apel
Sophia Rynhart
Anna Kootson
Anna Wyberton
Gertruy Smiden

Maria Vyberton
Susan Vyberton
[71 men, 98 women & children].
A true List.
Constable Tymperton.

Philad^{ia} Octr 17th 1732.
At the Courthouse Present:
The Honble, the Lt Govr, S. Hasell, Esqr, May^r, Charles Read, Esqr.
The foregoing List was by the Master af^d declared to be a full & true one.

Robt Charles, Cl. Con.

"At the Courthouse of Philadelphia, October 17th, 1732.
Sixty one Palatines, who with their families, making in all One hundred and sixty nine persons, were imported in the Pink John & William of Sunderland, Constable Tymperton, Master, from Rotterdam, but last from Dover, as by Clearance thence." From the Minutes of the Provincial Council, printed in *Colonial Records,* Vol. III, p. 466.

[List 28 B] Palatines imported in the Pink John & William, of Sunderland, Constable Tymperton, M^r., from Rotterdam, but last from Dover p. Clearance thence. Qualified October 17th 1732.

Bernhard (X) Weymer
C. Wilgar
Moritz (O) Lorentz
Jerig (O) Albright
Lorentz (O) Keefer
Jacob (JB) Brakebill
Stephen (O) Mattes
Bartel Maul
Hans Gorg Marttin
Hans Erhart Vosselman
Hans (O) Emich
Feltich (O) Sheydecker
Joh^s (O) Deynen
Pieter (O) Haywigh
Michael Weissel

Fredrick (O) Wysell
Ludwig Johann Herr
Johann Jägi
Johann Philippus Reinhart
Hans Pieter (O) Brechbill
Benedict (O) Brechbill
Hans (O) Brechbill
Hans Jerig (O) Spreicker
Johannes (O) Nagel
Pieter (O) Smidt
Johannes (O) Housam
Johann Michael Hoffman
Johann Nicklaus Boschung
Balser Gerlach
Christman Low

Conraad (O) Low
Lodwig (O) Hugel
Jacob Weber
Johannes (O) Shook
Hans Jacob Reyel
Hans Adam (O) Stis
Abraham (O) Dubo
Hans Jerig (O) Roarback
Johann Nicklaus Schmidt
Adam (O) Wilt
Antoni Albrecht
Hans Philip (O) Glais
Conraad (O) Getts
Nick. Koger
Jacob Koger

Mattheus Manser
Bastian (O) Trookmiller
Gideon (O) Huffer
Hans Rihl
Johan Martin Schöpfer
Johann Paul Derst
Henrich Geck
Mathias (O) Rubichon
Johannes Vögle
Jacob Henrich
Philip Melchior Meyer
Johan Jörg Wahnsidel
Johann Peter Apfel
Jerig (O) Vypert
Jan Jacob Scherr

[List 28 C] Palatines imported in the Pink John & William, Constable Tymperton, Master. Qualified Octr 17th 1732.

Bernhard (X) Wymer
C. Wilgar
Moritz (X) Laurenz
Georg (O) Albrecht
Laurenz (O) Kieffer
Jacob (JB) Brechbiel
Stephen (O) Matthes
Bartel Maul
Hans Gorg Marttin
Hans Erhart Vosselmann
Johannes (O) Emich
Felten (O) Scheadecker
Johannes (O) Deynen
Pieter (O) Haywigh
Michael Weissel
Frederick (O) Wyssel
Ludwig Johan Ernst Herr
Johanns Jägi
Johann Phillippus Reinhart
Hans Peter (O) Brechbill
Benedic (O) Brechbill
Hans (O) Brechbill

Hans Georg (O) Sprecher
Johannes (O) Nagel
Peter (O) Smidt
Johannes (O) Housam
Johan Michael Hoffman
Johann Nicklaus Boschung
Balser Gerlach
Christman Lau
Conrad (O) Law
Ludwig (O) Hoogel
Jacob Weber
Johannes (O) Schook
Hans Jacob Reyel
Georg Adam (O) Stiess
Abraham (O) Dubo
Hans Georg (O) Rohrbach
Johann Nicklaus Schmid
Adam (O) Wilt
Antoni Albrecht
Hans Philips (O) Kleas
Conrad (O) Götz
Nicklaus Koger

Jacob Koger
Jacob Mattheus Manser
Sebastian (O) Trockenmiller
Gideon (O) Hoffer
Hans Rihl
Johan Martin Schöpfele
Johann Paul Derst
Henrich Geck

Matthias (O) Rubichon
Johannes Vögle
Jacob Henrich
Philip Melchior Meyer
Philip Jörg Wahnsidel
Johann Peter Apfel
Georg (O) Wypert
Jan Jacob Scherr

October 17th 1732.

At the Courthouse before the Governor and several Magistrates the foregoing Qualifications were taken & subscribed by the several foreigners whose Names are contained on this Leaf.

Robt Charles, Cl. Con.

[List 29 A] [Passengers imported in the Ship Samuel, Hugh Percy, Master, from Rotterdam. Qualified August 17, 1733.]

	AGES		AGES
Hans Peter Fry	44	Matthew Ley	28
Listen Walter	33	Peter Pysell	44
Hans Jerick Strohaver	33	Michal Stersebagh	42
Casper Elias Tayler	37	Meliker Freys	32
Abraham Koon	50	Hans Wervell	54
Frederick Koon	22	Hans Jerick Wervell	18
Hans Jacob Symmer	24	Martin Jibe	47
Jacob Rusher	52	Bernard Wolf	29
Christian Krapts	33	Gasper Joust	21
Hendrick Bishop	20	Salomon Miller	22
Jerick Rouk, Senr.	48	Hans Wolf Iseman	22
Jerick Rouk. Junr.	24	Hans Jacob Hoff	33
Hans Jacob Rouk	17	Jacob Matthews	29
Peter Coonts	47	Leonard Wise	29
Hans Jacob Reed	45	Johannes Cresiner	23
Leonard Lightner	36	Philip Hettser	18
Hans Jerick Peck	30	Gillian Smith	40
Hans Jacob Tamooroon, sick	36	Christian Lafell	22
Andrews Fry	35	Gasper Iseman	53
Frederick Leyday	38	Meliker Wagner	48
Frederick Alterfer	18	Augustus Wagner	19
Michall Smith	34	Jacob Kimmerling	24

	AGES		AGES
Hans Adam Long	30	Bernard Trossell	38
Michal Propts	54	Hendrick Meder	52
Johan Michal Propts	21	Christian Tanner	21
Jerick Soller	52	Gasper Martin	20
Gasper Kervell	40	Hans Peter Mock	25
Hendrick Fisher	38	Valentine Snyder	22
Andrews Wegener	45		
Hans Koofman	43	WOMENS NAMES & AGES	
Hendrick Adam	28	Barbella Fry	37
William Fisher	26	Barbara Walter	24
Gasper Millhouse	28	Maria Crete Myring	26
Andrews Welts	44	Maria Catharina Strohaver	30
Gasper Brander	44	Anna Barbara Tayler	30
Jacob Fegley	32	Eve Koon	59
Johanes Lerick	26	Catharina Koon	24
Johannes Snapp	37	Anna Maria Rusher	42
Lawrence Snapp	21	Catharina Rusher	17
Martin Wonner	36	Christina Rusher	15
Hendrick Peter	26	Christina Krapts	24
Peter Hansminger	39	Catharina Rouk	46
Conrad Kempf	48	Maria Barbella Coonts	45
Christian Kempf	18	Maria Barbella Coonts	19
Gilbert Kempf	16	Anna Maria Reed	55
Hendrick Roodt	45	Sabina Lightner	45
Peter Cornelius	48	Anna Barbara Tamoroon	37
Jacob Kerkehouser	29	Catharina Barbara Fry	30
Nicholas Kaun	41	Appellonia Fry	58
Leonard Tyminger	39	Maris Salma Fry	14
Marks Clyne	45	Maria Mettlina Leyday	37
Peter Knoble	43	Anna Ursula Smith	31
Elias Hesly	35	Anna Maria Ley	24
Hendrick Holler	44	Susannah Pysell	33
Peter Holler	18	Crete Stersebagh	24
Gasper Schoffner	21	Ursula Snyding	25
Jacob Creder	21	Maria Lydia Wervell	52
Peter Troksell	42	Maria Lydia Wervell	26
Olerick Flyckinner	26	Elizabeth Wervell	17
Hans Adam Fokerall	48	Anna Catharina Jibe	44
Hendrick Feseler	50	Anna Maria Jibe	16
Lawrence Siber	53	Anna Barbara Hoff	33

	AGES		AGES
Maria Crete Wise	38	Catharina Holler	40
Catharina Smith	46	Christina Holler	16
Maria Crete Smith	14	Elizabeth Kollren	50
Maria Crete Iseman	53	Catharina Troksell	30
Maria Crete Iseman	24	Laodicea Flykinner	25
Catharina Long	33	Juliana Fokerall	43
Maria Crete Matthews	24	Maria Fokerall	16
Martha Wagner	38	Maria Feseler	48
Barbara Bropts	53	Maria Crete Feseler	22
Anna Kervell	39	Catharina Wagner	19
Maria Kervell	19	Maria Crete Siber	53
Anna Eve Kervell	15	Maria Crete Siber	14
Anna Lydia Fisher	36	Anna Maria Trossel	32
Catharina Adam	26	Anna Gertroud Meder	32
Catharina Faugen	34	Catherine Meder	13
Maria Crete Fry	17		
Anna Maria Welts	27	CHILDRENS NAMES AND AGES	
Appellonia Brander	42	Valentine Fry	12
Eve Maria Fegely	27	Eve Fry	10
Anna Maria Lerick	28	Anna Maria Fry	8
Barbara Snapp	34	Hans Peter Fry	4
Elizabeth Wonner	33	Christian Fry	2
Catharina Peter	32	Barbara Strohaver	8
Catharina Hansminger	33	Cathrina Strohaver	4
Catharina Trootmenyn	62	Hans Peter Strohaver	1
Anna Maria Kempf	38	Philip Adam Tayler	10
Catharina Roed	40	Hans Martin Tayler	8
Anna Eve Roed	13	Rosina Tayler	4
Elizabeth Cornelius	47	Christina Tayler	2
Elizabeth Cornelius	20	Hans Jerick Koon	15
Susanah Kerkehouser	28	Anna Crete Koon	11
Maria Crete Kerkehouser	50	Anna Crete Rusher	10
Catharina Kaun	40	Anna Barball Rusher	8
Maria Crete Tyminger	40	Metelina Rusher	7
Elizabeth Clyne	42	Maria Psalma Rusher	5
Juliana Clyne	13	Maria Crete Krapts	4
Ursula Knoble	43	Anna Percy Krapts	½
Anna Maria Knoble	16	Michael Rouk	10
Susanah Hesly	31	Maria Eve Rouk	8
Elizabeth Rittern	20	Michall Coonts	13

	AGES		AGES
Hans Jerick Coonts	9	Barbara Brander	8
Maria Crete Coonts	7	Charlotte Brander	1
Maria Catharina Coonts	5	Christina Fegely	4
Jerick Reed	15	Jacob Fegely	1
Anna Lydia Reed	11	Hans Jerick Lerick	3
Maria Dorothea Reed	8	Johannes Snapp	12
Hans Jacob Reed	4	Lawrence Snapp	10
Hans Jerick Lightner	8	Barbara Snapp	3
Hans Michall Tamooroon	3	Maria Crete Wonner	10
Elizabeth Fry	9	Anna Maria Wonner	6
Mettelina Fry	3	Christian Wonner	1
Christopher Fry	8	Henry Peter	1
Jacob Leyday	13	Hendrick Hansminger	10
Michall Leyday	10	Catharina Hansminger	8
Wolrick Leyday	4	Hans Philip Hansminger	6
Catharina Leyday	1	Nicolas Hansminger	1
Hans Peter Pysell	8	Frederick Kempf	8
Hans Jacob Pysell	3	Hans Peter Kempf	6
Barbella Pysell	1	Catharina Kempf	2
Leonard Wervell	8	William Roed	12
Catharina Jibe	10	Catharina Roed	9
Martin Jibe	14	Lawrence Cornelius	11
Hans Jacob Jibe	7	Vronicke Cornelius	8
Hans Jerick Jibe	4	Mattelina Kerkehouser	1
Christina Hoff	2	Michal Kaun	12
Anna Maria Smith	11	Hendrick Kaun	8
Agnes Smith	4	Johannes Kaun	3
Cathrina Iseman	11	Dorothea Kaun	½
Barbella Iseman	9	Hans Adam Tyminger	11
Christian Long	6	Barbara Tyminger	..
Appellonia Long	4	Catharina Tyminger	..
Ursula Long	1	Eliz. Clyne	1
Barbara Bropts	8	Catharina Clyne	10
Barbara Kervell	10	Dorothea Clyne	8
Elizabeth Kervell	6	Marks Clyne	4
Eve Kervell	4	Erasmus Hesly	8
Anna Maria Fisher	11	Maria Crete Hesly	1
Susanah Fisher	3	Hendrich Holler	13
Hans Jacob Fisher	2	Catharina Holler	7
Catharina Adam	2	Dorothea Holler	3

	AGES		AGES
Philip Fokerall	15	Benedict Siber	11
Eleanor Fokerall	9	Catharine Rossel	10
Jerick Fokerall	7	Jerick Rossel	4
Jacob Fokerall	3	Maria Crete Rossel	2
Godfrey Fokerall	1	George Meder	8
Peter Troksell	9	A true List.	
Daniel Troksell	7	Hugh Percy.	

Sworn to the 17th of Augt 1733, before the Govr & other Magistrates.

Robt Charles.

"At the Courthouse of Philadelphia, August 17th, 1733.
Ninety Palatines, who with their Families, making in all Two hundred & ninety one Persons, were imported here in the Ship Samuel of London, Hugh Percy, Master, from Rotterdam, but last from Deal, as by Clearance thence." From the Minutes of the Provincial Council, printed in *Colonial Records,* Vol. III, p. 515.

[List 29 B] Palatines imported in the Ship Samuel, of London, Hugh Percy, Master, from Rotterdam, but last from Deal, as p. clearance thence. Qualified Augt. 17th 1733.

Hans Peter (X) Frey	Andreas Frey
Johann Lichtenwallner	Friedrich Leiby
Hans Jerg Strohauer	Friederich Alldörfer
Elias (E) Taylor	Michael Schmidt
Abraham (AK) Koen	Mattes Ley
Friederich Kuhn	Hans Peter Beissel
Johan Jacob Zimmer	Michael (X) Sturtzebach
Jacob (H) Rausher	Hans M. (X) Fries
Christen Kröbs	Hans (H) Wevel
Henrich (X) Bishof	Hans Jurig (J) Wervel
Hen Seire (HR) Rook	Martin Seib
Hanns Gerg Ruch	Hans Bernhart Wolff
Hans Jacob (O) Ruch	Hans Casper (O) Joost
Peter (X) Koentz	Solomon (S) Miller
Hans Jacob Ridt	Hans Wolf (E) Eiseman
Hans Jerig (O) Peck	Hans Jacob (H) Hoff
Hans Leonhartt Lehner	Hans Jacob Matisis

Johann Leonharth Weiss
Johann Jacob Griesinger
Johan Fili Hötzer
Kilian Schmid
Christian Löffel
Hans Kasper Eyseman
Malcker (H) Wagner
Jusdus Simonus Wager
Hans Jacob (K) Kaemmerlin
Hans Adam Lang
Michael (P) Probst
Johann Michall Probst
Hanns Jerg Zoller
Johan Caspar Körber
Johan Henrich Fischer
Andres Wigner
Johan Kaufman
Johann Henrich Adam
Johan Wilhelm Fischer
Caspar (CM) Millhouse
Anderes Weltz
Hans Casper (B) Brenner
Joh. Jacob Wenger
Johan (O) Lorig
Johannes (SH) Shnap
Lorentz Schnepp
Martten Wanner
Henrich Beter

Pedter Ensminger
Johann Conradt Kämpff
Christian Kämpff
Gilbert Kämpff
Henrich Roht
Peter Cornelius
Jacob Gerckenhauser
Nicholas (N) Kan
Hans Lenard Einiger
Marx Klein
Johan Peter Knobell
Alies (X) Hasele
Heinrich Haller
Petter Haller
Johan Caspar (X) Schaffner
Jacob (J) Krater
Petter Drachsel
Ulrich (O) Flickrer
Hans Adam Fuckroth
Henrich (F) Fesseler
Lorentz Seybert
Hans Bernhardt Trossell
Henry (O) Meder
Christian (X) Danner
Caspar (O) Martin
Hans Peter (H) Mock
Valentin (S) Sneider

[List 29 C] At the Courth° of Philadelphia, Aug. 17th 1733.
Present The Honble Patrick Gordon, Esqr, Lt Governor,

Ralph Asheton
Saml Hassell, Esqr, Mayr } Counsellors
Charles Read, Esqr

The Palatines whose Names are underwritten, being imported in the Ship Samuel, Hugh Percy, Master, from Rotterdam, but last from Deal, did this day take and subscribe the Oaths to the Government, viz.

Hans Peter (X) Fry
Johann Lichtenwallner

Hans Jerg Strohauer
Elias (E) Tayler

Abraham (AK) Koen
Friderich Kuhn
Johan Jacob Zimmer
Jacob (H) Rausher
Christian Kröbs
Henrich (X) Bishof
Hans Jurg (H) Ruck
Hans Gerg Ruch
Hans Jacob (O) Ruch
Peter (X) Koentz
Hans Jacob Ridt
Hans Leonhartt Lehner
Hans Jurg (O) Peck
Andreas Frey
Friderich Leiby
Friederich Alldörfer
Michael Schmiedt
Matt. Ley
Hans Peter Beissel
Michael (X) Sturzebach
Hans Melchior (O) Fries
Hans (H) Wervel
Hans Jurg (J) Wervel
Martin Scheib
Hans Bernhart Wolff
Hans Caspar (O) Joost
Salomon (S) Miller
Hans Wolff (E) Eiseman
Hans Jacob (H) Hoff
Hans Jacob Mathes
Johann Leonharth Weiss
Johann Jacob Griesinger
Johan Fili Hetzer
Kilian Schmid
Christian Löffel
Hans Kaspar Eyseman
Melcker (H) Wagner
Jusdus Simonius Wager
Hans Jacob (K) Kümmerlin
Hans Adam Lang

Michael (P) Probst
Johann Michall Probst
Hans Jerg Zoller
Johan Caspar Körber
Johan Henrich Fischer
Andreas Wigner
Johan Kaufmann
Johann Henrich Adam
Johan Wilhelm Fischer
Caspar (M) Mühlhaus
Anderes Weltz
Hans Caspar (B) Brenner
Jacob Wenger
Johan (X) Lorig
Johannes (S) Shnap
Lorentz Schnepp
Martin Wanner
Heinrich Beter
Pedter Ensminger
Johann Conradt Kämpff
Christian Kämpff
Gilbert Kämpff
Henrich Roht
Petter Cornelius
Jacob Gerckenhauser
Nicolaus (X) Kan
Hans Lehnard Einiger
Marx Klein
Johan Peter Knobel
Elias (X) Hasele
Heinrich Haller
Petter Haller
Johan Caspar (S) Schaffner
Jacob (J) Krater
Petter Drachsel
Ulrich (V) Flickeer
Hans Adam Fuckeroth
Henrich (F) Fesseler
Lorentz Seybert
Hans Bernhardt Trossell

Henry (O) Meder   Hans Peter (H) Mock
Christian (X) Danner   Valentin (S) Sneider
Caspar (O) Martin

[List 30 A] Account of the Mens Names of 16 years and upwards, Brought from Rotterdam in the Elizabeth, Capt. Edward Lee. [Qualified Aug. 27, 1733].*

MENS NAMES	AGES		AGES
		Stephen Lowman	31
Johannes Kernoser	40	Jacob Bonnett	32
Philip Sover	23	Wolfcon Miller	41
Johannes Moon	33	Jacob Miller	17
Mich¹ Crowell	32	Simon Shearman	49
Johan Joseph Faller, sick	23	Jurigh Ditto	17
Johan Jurgh Peitry	27	Johanes Noll	29
John Hendrick Shetty	22	Jacob Houbler	30
Conrad Shott	50	France Wice	27
Philip Foust	30	Taball Troud	27
Mich¹ Rutt	56	Hans Martin Troud	56
Johan Hendrick Tinick	33	Hans Jurigh Ley, sick	28
Coblin Hetrick	40	Jurigh Ore	51
Hendrick Stence	39	Johannes Ore	19
Hans Peter Houfman	28	Jacob Server	56
Johannes Long	20	Jacob Server, Junʳ	36
Johan Peter Foust	44	Rodolph Server	21
Philip Foust	20	Jacob Houswett	34
Jacob Eibe	34	Jacob Hendrich	28
Ulrich Shue	48	Johan Hendrich Tabas	28
John Jacob Shue	20	Nicholas Sly, sick	24
Johannes Lotz	35	Jacob Shittle	22
Mathias Whiteman	56	Philip Smith	33
Mathew Whiteman, sick	34	Hans Jurigh Nort	45
Henrich Still	60	Jacob Tilliner	33
Simon Lindar	53	Andreas Clipsadle	22
Simon Lindar, Junʳ	16	Jurigh Hendrick March	20
Fredrick Onselt	24	Johan Ulrich Cool	30
Michael Fabar	35	Johan Fagley	28
Andreas Pogner	34	Henry Stricker	29

* The complete list, just found, is given in the appendix.

	AGES		AGES
Mich¹ Rainard	23	Hans Jacob Mixt	20
Malster Mixt	54	Edward Lee [Captain]	

"At the Courthouse aforesaid, August 27th, 1733.

Fifty eight Palatines, who with their Families, making in all one hundred & seventy two Persons, were imported here in the Ship Eliza, of London, Edward Lee, Master, from Rotterdam, but last from Dover, as by Clearance thence, were qualified as before." From the Minutes of the Provincial Council, printed in *Colonial Records,* Vol. III, p. 516.

[List 30 B] Palatines imported in the Ship Elizabeth, of London, Edward Lee, Master, from Rotterdam, but last from Dover, pt. Clearance thence. Qualified Aug. 27ᵗʰ 1733.

Johannes Kirschner
Johann Uhland Daner
Johannes Mohn
Johann Michael Grauel
Johann Georg Petry
Johann Henrich Schötte
Conrad (×) Shodt
Johann Fillibs Faust
Michel Ruht
Johan Henrich Dänig
Coral (×) Hetrech
Henrich Stentz
Hans Beter Hoffman
Johannes (×) Young
Johan Petter Faust
Johann Lebs Faust
Jacob Michel Eyb
Ulrech (S) Shoe
Jacob Schuh
Johannes (×) Loats
Matheis Weidtman
Hendrich (O) Still
Simon Linder
Simon (×) Linder
Georg Friederich Unseldt
Michael (×) Faber

Aron (×) Doganer
Steffan Lauman
Hans Yerech (×) Perger
Jaques Bonet
Wolffgang Miller
Jacob Müller
Simon Schirman
Jörg Schirman
Johannes (×) Knoll
Jacob (H) Koobler
Frantz Weiss
Johan Debalt Trautt
Jurich (HO) Ore
Johannes Herrgeröder
Jacob (×) Server
Jacob Surber
Rudolff Sorber
Jacob (HW) Housewart
Jacob Hänrich
Johan Henrich Dewess
Jacob Zettel
Johann Philippus Schmitt
Hans Jerg Nordt
Jacob Dellinger
Andreas Klebsattel
Georg Henrich Mertz

Johann Ulrich Gaull
Johannes Vögelin
Henrich (✕) Stricker

Michael (✕) Ranhard
Balser (BM) Mets
Hans Jacob (M) Mets

[List 30 C] At the Courthouse of Philadelphia, August 27th 1733. Present The Honble Pat. Gordon, Esqr., Lt Governor, Samuel Hassell, Esqr., Mayr. Charles Read, Esqr.
The Palatines whose Names are underwritten, imported in the Ship Elisabeth of London, Edward Lee, Master, from Rotterdam, but last from Dover, did this day take & subscribe the Oaths to ye Government.

Johannes Kirschner
Johan Uhland Danner
Johannes Mohn
Johann Michael Grauel
Johann Georg Petry
Johann Henrich Schötte
Conrad (✕) Shoot
Johan Fillibs Faust
Michel Ruht
Johan Henrich Dänig
Coral (O) Herrech
Henrich Stentz
Hans Beter Hoffman
Johannes (O) Young
Johan Petter Faust
Johan Lebs Faust
Jacob Michel Eyb
Ulrech (S) Shoe
Jacob Schuh
Johanes (✕) Loats
Matheus Weidtman
Henrich (O) Still
Simon Linder
Simon (✕) Linder
Georg Friederich Unselt
Michiel (✕) Faber
Aran (✕) Dogener
Steffan Lauman
Han Yerech (✕) Perger

Jaques Bonet
Wolfgang Müller
Jacob Müller
Simon Schirman
Jörg Schirman
Johann (✕) Knoll
Jacob (H) Koobler
Frantz Weiss
Johan Debalt Trautt
Jurich (HO) Ore
Johannes Herrgeröder
Jacob (O) Server
Jacob Sorber
Rudolff Sorber
Jacob (HW) Housewort
Jacob Hänrich
Johan Henrich Dewess'
Jacob Zettel
Johann Philippus Schmitt
Hans Jerg Nordt
Jacob Dellinger
Andreas Klebsattel
Georg Henrich Mertz
Johann Ulrich Gaull
Johanns Vögelin
Henrich (✕) Stricker
Michiel (✕) Ranhard
Balser (BM) Mets
Hans Jacob (M) Mets

[List 31 A] [Passengers imported in the Ship Hope, Daniel Reid, Master, from Rotterdam. Qualified August 28, 1733.]

MENS NAMES

Name	AGES	Name	AGES
		Henrick Smit	31
Ulrig Wisler	36	Pitter Arnt	21
Ulrig Rayenhart	29	Andrias Luck	45
Hans Crombacker	26	Harman Arnt	50
Hans Steman	49	Daniel Root	30
Petter Steman	26	Hanis Henrick	20
Hans Steman	21	Adam Rayfel	24
Cristian Stoder	45	Hans Jurig Ayslburg	29
Hans Rood	22	Hans Lenar Stein	21
Hans Timerman	63	Hans Jurick Koller	23
Hans Timerman	16	Michel Buss	36
Cristian Timerman	14	Hans Jurick Hofnar	22
Josaph Floriey	51	Pitter Smook	20
Josaph Floriey	19	Daffid Esler	20
Johanes Floriey	15	John Jackop Mikle	22
Cristian Keer	27	Karl Gramp	30
Migiel Witman	65	Bastian Scyster	23
Ulrige Witman	31	Henrick Humberg	45
Pitter Witman	21	Hans Lenart Humberg	18
Hans Witman	20	Micgel Humberger, sick	15
Pitter Eslman	50	Pitter Selar	31
Cristian Eslman	19	Cristian Jonliey	20
Olrige Langneker	69	Andrias Besenar	24
Olrig Langnecker	22	Jurick Kraysman	32
Jackop Langnecker	19	Migel Drayter	20
Jackop Benke	35	Hans Jerick Gobl	40
Hans Snebliey	37	Jacobes Kerwar	40
Cristian Blanck	34	Cristoffel Kown	48
Jerick Wiednar	41	Adam Simon Kown	19
Hans Jurig Brimer	27	Francys Kestelipsger	32
Fredrick Becker	48	Abraham Millar	22
Jackop Lughboom	34	Jacobes Bart	26
Rudolph Brack	47	Henrick Feess	24
Cristian Riblet	27	Benedick Weess	36
Barnard Kelder	37	Martin Spitelmayer	54
Conrad Rauff	40	Hans Adam Spitelmayer	18
Jerick Rigtar	47	Migeel Ibeliey	45

	AGES		AGES
Jacobes Rolleman	35	Catrina Reben	35
William Grous	27	Madlena Lederman	26
Hans Henrick Foglie	50	Barbra Eslman	16
Matayias Figelie	23	Anna Blasinin	71
Hans Lennart Figle	21	Anna Menckel	23
Migel Stenbrand	37	Anna Figliey	33
Stifan Lunneker	33	Madlena Figliey	26
Jacobes Linck, sick	50	Madlena Rubelie	70
Abraham Grutson	19	Barbra Rittes	28
Hans Jackop Skruhgefier	34	Anna Katrina Rittes	35
Daniel Hislar	29	Anna Klara Rittes	50
Rulloff Snebliey	25	Anna Barbel Bek	23
Hans Jarick Scrayack	31	Anna Katrina Bek	17
Hans Scrayack	28	Cristina Lugtbom	33
Jackop Scrayack	19	Anna Brack	36
		Catrina Keldrien	48
WOMENS NAMES		Margrita Kelerin	16
		Madlena Ruff	34
Anna Ester	25	Anna Rigter	49
Barbra Bengtel	29	Anna Rigter	15
Margret Copfirsin	65	Anna Smit	32
Barbra Raynhart	23	Agnis Smiten	27
Anna Bergtold	26	Sibela Stenbrander	37
Maria Scutesen	29	Ana Madlena Linck	40
Anna Scutesen	20	Ana Katrina Arnt	27
Madelen Steman	18	Slutik Luck	37
Anna Stofer	19	Ana Margrit Arnt	48
Anna Gerebel	48	Margrita Root	30
Elisbat Snebliey	44	Ana Scraybrin	30
Anna Rood	19	Barbra Snebliey	24
Anna Gislerin	22	Barbra Scrayack	28
Barbra Timerman	20	Sabina Rayfel	26
Anna Timerman	18	Barbra Rayfel	20
Anna Bonghart	55	Julian Ayselberger	29
Anna Maria Bugh	40	Maria Kolirin	24
Maria Floriey	21	Maria Marieng	24
Hanliey Floriey	17	Eieffa Busing	36
Anna Lederman	24	Orstel Hoffnar	29
Elisabet Bergtold	50	Julian Humberger	47
Anna Bergtold	26	Eva Seckering	20
Anna Witman	16		

	AGES		AGES
Froneck Junliey	40	Hanes Snebliey	11
Elisbat Junliey	19	Kasper Snebliey	9
Catrina Krayseman	38	Katrina Snebliey	6
Barbra Gobel	38	Anna Katrina Snebliey	12
Maria Barbra Kerwar	30	Anna Barbra Snebliey	10
Margrita Kon	43	Anna Bekrin	12
Rosina Klipsegel	34	Migler Becker	10
Maria Madlena Millar	26	Anna Lugetbom	10
Barbra Weesen	36	Fridrick Brack	14
Maria Spitelmayer	50	Cristina Brack	11
Anna Maria Spitelmayer	24	Madlena Brack	8
Anna Madlena Spitelmayer	21	Barbra Keldrin	10
Elizabet Ibliey	30	Catrina Ruff	13
Aplon Rollman	36	Elisbat Ruffin	12
Madlena Grows	29	Hans Ruffin	10
Anna Maria Figlien	46	Hans Ruffin	7
Catrina Figlien	19	Henrick Smit	8
Anna Maria Figlien	16	Janes Smit	4
		Jurig Adam Bueys	13
CHILDRENS NAMES		Lodwick Buss	11
Maria Greta Wees	5½	Maria Margrita Buss	9
Maria Pitter Ibliey	12	Janis Buss	7
Hans Adam Ibliey	11	Julian Humberger	12
Resina Ibliey	8	Jans Humberger	10
Hans Migel Ibliey	6	Lisbat Humberger	8
Hans Jan Rollman	9	Anna Selirieg	8
Maria Rollman	7	Johanes Junliey	14
Maria Figlien	12	Hans Raynart Junliey	9
Hans Jurick Figliey	7	Jerick Hunslman	11
Barbra Stenbrander	8	Margrita Hunslman	13
Sibila Stenbrander	6	Antoniey Gobel	12
Hans Adam Linck	11	Anna Maria Gobel	10
Resina Linck	7	Madlena Gabel	8
Migerl Arnt	13	Jurig Adam Gabel	5
Anna Maria Arnt	8	Hans Jurig Gabel	3½
Susana Scrayack	7	Jacobs Kerwar	10
Cristian Stoden	9	Hans Jerick Kerwar	9
Jackup Eslman	11	Jan Kerwar	7
Pitter Eslman	9	Efa Barbra Kan	13

AGES

Anna Maria Kan	9	A true List
Migel Klipsegel	9	Daniel Ried.
Hans Jerick Klipsegel	7	

[Endorsed:]
A List of the Passengers on Bord of the Hope Geeley [Galley] 1733.
"At the Courthouse aforesaid, August 28th, 1733.

Eighty four Palatines, who with their families, making in all Two hundred & twenty six persons, were imported here in the Ship Hope, of London, Daniel Reid, Master, from Rotterdam, but last from Cowes, as by Clearance thence, were qualified as before." From the Minutes of the Provincial Council, printed in *Colonial Records,* Vol. III, p. 517.

[List 31 B] Palatines imported in the Ship Hope, of London, Daniel Reid, M^r, from Rotterdam, but last from Cowes, p. Clearance thence. Qualified Augt 28th 1733.

Ulrich Wissler	Jacob (X) Loninacre
Ulrich Reinhardt	Jacob Bürcki
Hans Grumbacher	Hans (HS) Snabley
Hans (H) Stayman	Christian (CB) Blank
Peter Steiman	Hanns Georg Wittner
Hans Stiman	Hanns Georg Brimmer
Christian (Christ) Stouder	Frederick (O) Becker
Hans Rat	Jacob Lochbaum
Nicholas (NZ) Timberman	Rudolph (RB) Brock
Hans (O) Timberman	Christian (O) Reblet
Joseph (J) Flure	Barnard (BK) Keller
Joseph (J) Flure	Conrad (IK) Rouf
Johannes (J) Flure	Jourge (R) Righter
Christian Kerr	Henrich Schmidt
Michl. (W) Whitmer	Peter (O) Arent
Ulrick (V) Whitmer	Daniell Rott
Peter (W) Whitmer	Hans Jerg Schreyeck
Better Eschelman	Frantz Klebsattel
Christian (C) Esleman	Andreas Lauck
Ulrich (I) Loninacre	Herman (H) Arand
Ulrich (X) Loninacre, Junr.	Johannes Hindrig von Rath

Johan Adam Reiffel	Johann Adam Simon Cumm
Hans Jerg Eichelberger	Abraham Miller
Johann Leonhart Stein	Jacob (X) Bart
Hanns Jerg Kohler	Henrich (T) Tace
Johan Michael Busch	Benedict (P) Wise
Hanns Jerg Höffner	Marti Spitlenmayer
Peter Schmuck	Hans Adam (X) Spittlemire
Johan David Deschler	Michael (X) Abley
Johann Jacob Mückli	Jacob Rulman
Johann Carl Gromp	Wilhelm Krauss
Bastian (TB) Tryster	Henrich (+) Figley
Henrich Umberiger	Mathis (/) Fegley
Hans Leonhart Umberger	Barnard (F) Fegley
Peter Sayler	Hans Michel Strumber [?]
Christian (X) Yoniley	Stephen (X) Slunaker
Andreas Besinger	Abraham Kreutter
Gerg Kreissman	Hans Jacob Schreiber
Georg Michael Treitter	Daniel (X) Hueselman
Hans Jerg Gobel	Rudolf Schnebli
Hans Jacob Gerber	Hans Michael Schreyack
Johan Christoph Cumm	Jacob Schreyack

[List 31 C] At the Courthouse of Philad^ia, August 28th 1733. Present The Honble Patrick Gordon, Esqr, L^t. Govr., Charles Read, Ralph Asheton, Esq^rs.

The Palatines whose Names are underwritten, being imported in the Ship Hope, of London, Daniel Reid, M^r, from Rotterdam, but last from Cowes, did this day take & subscribe the Oaths to the Government.

Ulrich Wissler	Joseph (J) Fleure
Ulrich Reinhardt	Johanes (F) Fleure
Hans Grumbacher	Christian Ker
Hans (H) Stayman	Michiel (W) Whitmer
Peter Steiman	Ulrich (U) Whitmer
Hans Steinman	Peter (BW) Whitmer
Christian (CH) Stouder	Better Eschelman
Hans Rat	Christian (I) Eselman
Nicholas (NZ) Timberman	Ulrich (I) Loninacre
Hans (X) Timberman	Ulrich (X) Loninacre, Junr.
Joseph (J) Fleure	Jacob (X) Loninacre

Jacob Bürcki

Hans (HS) Snabley

Christian (CB) Blank

Hanns Georg Weittner

Hanns Gorg Brimmer

Frederick (O) Becker

Jacob Lochbaum

Rudolf (RB) Brock

Christian (O) Reblet

Barnard (O) Keller

Conrad (K) Rouf

Jourge (R) Righter

Heinrich Schmidt

Peter (H) Arant

Daniell Ratt

Hans Jerg Schreyeck

Frantz Klebsattel

Andreas Lauck

Herman (H) Arand

Johannes Hindrig Von Rath

Johan Adam Reiffel

Hans Jerg Eichelberger

Johann Leonhart Stein

Hanns Jerg Kohler

Johann Michael Busch

Hanns Jerg Höffner

Peter Schmuck

Johann David Deschler

Johann Jacob Mückli

Johann Carl Grop

Bastian (B) Tryster

Henrich Umberiger

Hans Leonhardt Umberger

Peter Sayler

Christian (+) Yonily

Andreas Besinger

Jerg Kreissemann

Georg Michael Treitter

Hans Jerg Gobel

Hans Jacob Gerber

Johan Christoff Cumm

Johann Adam Simon Cumm

Abraham (X) Miller

Jacob (X) Bart

Henrich (X) Tace

Benidick (P) Wise

Marti Spitelmayer

Hans Adam (X) Spitlemire

Michiel (X) Abley

Jacob Rulman

Wilhelm Krauss

Henrich (F) Fegley

Mathis (F) Fegley

Barnard (B) Fegley

Hans Michel Strumber [?]

Steven (X) Slunacker

Abraham Kreuntter

Hans Jacob Schreiber

Daniel (X) Hueselman

Rudolff Schnebli

Hans Michael Schreyack

Jacob Schreyack

[List 32 A] A List of Palatine Passengers Come on Board the Ship Pensilvania Merchant, John Stedman, Commander, from Roterdam In Holland. [Qualified September 18, 1733.]

MENS NAMES

Johan Kleym

Goetloop Kleym

Jerick Shults

David Shults

Andreas Mosman

Christian Mosman

Hans Borkhard

David Borkhard

Johan Shoenvelett
Melchior Grousaam,* sick
Johannes Naase
Pieter Marrot
Hendrick Riet, sick
Andreas Kleyn
Hans Jerick Klyn
Jerick Sheytt
Johannes Rigel
Johannes Rigel, Junr.
Daniel Rigel
Andreas Oulenbacher
Valentine Presel
Michael Walter
Carolus Borkhard
Johan Wynant
Paulus Borkhard
Jacob Knoop
Jacob Oat
Michael Oat
Ludwick Evaldt
Michael Ludwick
Daniel Ludwick
Philip Smeyer
Alexander Casser
Pieter Roodt
Christian Louer
Mathias Kish
Johan Michael Stout
Johan Jost Olwyn
Philip Angleberger
Michael Seydebender
Daniel Endt
Valentine Endt
Pieter Saling
Adam Folmer
Jerick Vinter
Hans Martin Souter
Fredrick Gets

Johannes Miem
Pieter Smit
Hendrick Smit
Jacob Unger, sick
Adam Beyer
Christophel Yslsbach
Michael Keylechner
Jerick Bartel Shever
Paulus Shever
Andreus Vry
Barent Maus
Johan Ludovick Seys
Andreas Boier
Hans Jerick Houk
Pieter Straub
Jacob Kaars
Christian Hook
Hans Jerick Grondt
Jerick Adam Bouk
Fredrick Claus
Johannes Cordinar
Mathias Beighler
Justus Osteroodt
Hans Jerick Grim
Erata Excepted in all 71 Men

WOMENS NAMES

Magdalena Klymen
Elisabeth Shoenvelden
Anna Shultsen
Maria Jacobin
Anna Krausam
Susanna Krausam
Maria Krausam
Anna Krausam
Margaret Naze
Elizabeth Naze
Marian Marrot
Ann Judit Marrot

---

* Balthaser Krauss is omitted. He appears in the Schwenkfelder lists. See Brecht, *Genealogical Record of the Schwenkfelder Families*, N. Y., 1923, p. 34.

Fraunek Kleynen
Anlies Sleydt
Julian Sheyett
Gertrouy Rigel
Sarah Rigel
Anlies Oulabachren
Dorothy Vullerin
Margaret Spany
Anna Borkhard
Cathrina Borkhard
Anna Knop
Gertrouy Oat
Agnes Evaldt
Maria Smyeren
Magdalena Casern
Sophia Roodt
Endick Endt
Catharina Endt
Christina Bartholemew
Maria Saling
Margaret Speting
Anna Stoloyn
Christina Kets
Margaret Smit
Elisabeth Smit
Sarah Islsbach
Anna Shever
Anlias Shever
Elizabeth Shever
Susan Fry
Cathrina Maus
Maria Bourin
Cathrina Bourin
Caritas Vishering
Maria Straub
Margaret Caars
Barbara Hougen
Hanna Grondt
Eva Claasing
Margarit Coulerin
Maria Hooghen

Maria Cordinar
Maria Bigler
Anna Bigler
In all 56 Women

CHILDRENS NAMES

Hendrick Souchvridt
Philip Marrot
Guiliam Marrot
Jean Marrot
Benjamin Marrot
Daniel Marrot
Marian Marrot
Susan Marrot
Sarah Marrot
Hans Jerick Riet
Hendrick Kleym
Caspar Kleym
Maria Oulbachren
Abraham Rigel
Elizabeth Borkhard
Johannes Evaldt
Maria Evaldt
Johan Smyer
Elizabeth Smyer
Johan Cassar
Mathias Cassar
Anna Casseren
Magdalena Casser
Johan Roodt
Jacob Roodt
Christina Roodt
Pieter Roodt
Catrina Saling
Elizabeth Saling
Jerick Vinter
Hans Vinter
Andreas Stoloyn
Marilis Stoloyn
Johan Stoloyn
Jacob Shultsen

Johan Kets	Elizabeth Vishering
Elizabeth Kets	Jacob Straub
Bernard Kets	Pieter Straub
Johan Ruyter	Jerick Houk
Pieter Ingold	Maria Claasin
Jacob Frick	Rosina Clasing
Paulus Shever	Anna Cornar
Jerich Shever	Salumi Cornar
Jerich Strebeck	Paulus Cornar
Christian Strebeck	Elizabeth Bigler
Johan Shever	Anna Bigler
Margaret Shever	Andreas Bigler
Christophel Fry	In all 64 Children.
Margaret Bourin	
Anna Bourin	A true List.
Sophia Vishering	Philad^{ia} Septr 18th 1733.
Christian Vishering	John Stedman.

"At the Courthouse aforesaid, September 18th, 1733.

Sixty seven Palatines, who with their families, making in all One hundred eighty seven persons, were imported here in the Briganteen Pennsylvania Merchant, of London, John Stedman, Mr., from Rotterdam, but last from Plymouth, as by Clearance thence, were qualified as before." From the Minutes of the Provincial Council, printed in *Colonial Records*, Vol. III, p. 518.

[List 32 B] Palatines imported in the Ship Pennsylvania Merchant, John Stedman, M^r, from Rotterdam, but last from Plymouth. Qualified Septr 18th 1733.

Johann Klemm	Hans (H) Burkhard
Gottlob Klemm	David (X) Burkhard
Georg Scholtz	Johan Schönfeldt
David Scholtz *	Johannes Naass
Andreas Mosemann	Pierre Marot
Christians Mosiman	Andreas (X) Kleym

* Thirteen of these passengers, including George Scholtz, his wife, Anna, and son, David, Melchior Krauss, his wife, Anna, his sons, Balthasar and Melchior, and his daughters, Maria, Anna and Susanna, formed a colony of Schwenkfelders. David Scholtz has left an interesting description of this journey, see Brecht, *Genealogical Record of the Schwenkfelder Families*, p. 35.

Jerg Klein
Jerch Schoit
Johannes Riegel
Johannes Riegel
Daniel Rigell
Andreas Aullenbacher
Johann Vallentin Pressel
Michael (O) Walter
Carolus (X) Burckhard
Johann Philipp Weynand
Jacop Knop
Jacob Ott
Johan Michel Ott
Ludwig Ewalt
Michael (M) Ludwig
Daniel (O) Ludwig
Philip Schmyer
Alexander (C) Cassar
Peter (P) Roodt
Christ Lauer
Mattes Gisch
Johann Michel Staudt
John Just Ohlwein
Philipp Angelberger
Michael Seydenbender
Johan Daniel Endt
Johan Vallentin Endt
Johan Peter Saling

Adam Vollmer
Hanns Jerg Winter
Hans Martin (X) Sauter
Frederick (F) Gotz
Johannes Mihm
Peter (P) Smidt
Johann Adam Beyer
Johann Christopfel Igelsbach
Michael Kelchner
Jörg Barthel Schäffer
Paulus Schäffer
Andreas (A) Fry
Bernhart Mauss
Johann Ludwig (X) Seess
Andreas Bauer
Hans Jereck (X) Hauk
Petter Straub
Johann Jacob Karst
Christian (X) Hook
Hans Jerick (H) Grondt
Jerick Adam (B) Kock
Friedrich Glass
Johannes (IG) Gardner
Mattheus Büchler
Justes Osterroth
Johann Jerg Grimm
Hendrich Schmitt

[List 32 C] At the Courthouse of Philadelphia, September 18, 1733. Present the Honble Patrick Gordon, Esqr, Lt Govern^r, Saml Hassell, Ralph Asheton, Charles Read.

The Palatines whose Names are underwritten, imported in the Brigantine Pennsylvania Merchant, of London, John Stedman, Master, from Rotterdam, but last from Plymouth, did this day take and subscribe the Oaths to the Government.

Johann Klemm
Gottlob Klemm
Gorg Scholtz
David Scholtz

Andreas Mosemann
Christian Mosiman
Hans (H) Burkhard
David (X) Burkhard

Johan Schönfeldt	Johan Vallentin Endt
Johannes Naass	Johan Peter Saling
Pierre Marot	Adam Vollmer
Andreas (X) Kleym	Hanns Jerg Winter
Georg Klein	Hans Martin (X) Sauter
Jerch Schoit	Frederich (F) Gotz
Johannes Riegel	Johannes Mihm
Johannes Riegel	Peter (P) Smit
Danniel Rigell	Johann Adam Beyer
Andreas Aullenbacher	Johann Christoffel Igelsbach
Johann Vallentin Pressel	Michael Kelchner
Michael (O) Walter	Jörg Barthel Schäffer
Carolus (X) Burckhard	Paulus Schäffer
Johann Philipp Weynand	Andreas (A) Vry
Jacob Knop	Bernhart Mauss
Jacob Ott	John Ludwig (X) Seess
Johan Michel Ott	Andreas Bauer
Ludwig Ewalt	Hans Jerg (X) Hauk
Michel (M) Ludwig	Petter Straub
Daniel (O) Ludwig	Johan Jacob Karst
Phillip Schmyer	Christian (X) Hook
Alexander (O) Casser	Hans Jerg (H) Grondt
Peter (P) Roodt	Jerg Adam (B) Koch
Christ Lauer	Friederich Glass
Mattes Gisch	Johannes (IG) Gordner
Johan Michel Staudt	Mattheus Büchler
Johan Just Ohlwein	Justus Osteroth
Philipp Angelberger	Johann Jerg Grimm
Michael Seydenbender	Hendrich Schmitt
Johan Daniel Endt	

[List 33 A] A List of the Passengers imported in the Brigantine Richard and Elizabeth, Captain Christopher Clymer, Sept 28, 1733.

MENS NAMES	AGES		AGES
Francis Schuler	44	Johan Conrad Leap	20
Jacob Gripe	21	Philip Jacob Edelman	25
David Mertz	44	Matthes Bouser	63
Johan Nicholas Mertz	18	Matthes Bewser	22
George Leap	56	Christian Bewser	18

	AGES		AGES
Philip Mire	36	Margaretha Edelman	26
David Edelman	49	Esther Bouser	49
Adam Spoon	34	Anna Margaretha Mire	40
Jacob Hainel	20	Anna Barbara Stammin	26
Ludwig Rigerd, sick	28	Anna Maria Edelman	54
Michael Wise	29	Anna Elisabeth Bewser	20
George Shuffard	44	Anna Margaretha Spoon	23
Yoost Heck	35	Gertrud Shuffard	32
Jacob Hunsinger	30	Sophia Glass	28
Hance Jacob Liebegood	39	Eva Maria Heck	35
Jacob Harmon	40	Margaretha Liebegood	40
Hans Jacob Uts	27	Catherina Harmon	33
Hans Georg Uts	50	Maria Catherina Uts	24
Hance Peter Sowmy	59	Barbara Holler	77
Hance Jacob Sowmy	22	Maria Magdalena	58
Hance Peter Sowmy	20	Maria Shoemacher	24
Otto Frederick Sowmy	15	Barbara Burghalter	34
Joseph Shumaker	25	Anna Barbara Sager	28
Ulrich Burghalter	40	Margaretha Schenemansgruber	28
Johan Nicholas Sager	39	Engelina Peck	37
Georg Schenemansgruber	35	Anna Margaretha Wollet	24
Matthes Peck	39	Maria Magdalena Winterberger	24
Johannes Wollet	38		
Henry Winterberger	26	Maria Magdalena Sherer	22
Hans Sherer	30	Magdalena Christ	44
Jacob Christ	54	Eva Catherina ——	31
Marcus Christ	17	Maria Barbara Tadigsman	35
George Angsted	37	Anna Maria Tadigsman	25
Marcus Beegler	28	Margaretha Weaver	17
Philip Tadigman	36	Anna Margaretha Wootring	32
Johannes Weaver	22	Magdalena Wisen	25
Johannes Rosensteel	19	Barbara Kossely	25
Abraham Wootring	33		
Matthias Rehsh	29	**BOYS**	
		Johan Peter Mertz	13¾
WOMEN		Baltasar Edelman	4
Maria Schuler	47	Daniel Bewser	11½
Veronica Mertz	40	Jacob Bewser	9½
Catherina Leap	50	Johan Henrich Spoon	4
Anna Christina Leap	24	Johannes Shuffard	10

	AGES		AGES
Johan Jacob Heck	6	Anna Catherina Heck	10
Johan Jacob Liebegood	10	Anna Gretha Liebegood	10
Dewald Harmon	13	Anna Catherina Liebegood	3½
Jacob Harmon	6	Catherina Harmon	11
Hance Harmon	3½	Barbara Harmon	8
Hance Peter Harmon	9 m.	Catherine Barbara ——	6 m.
Hance Michael Sowmy	10	Anna Barbara Haltin	50
Johannes Sowmy	5	Maria Magdalena Swomy	24
Hance Peter Burghalter	1¼	Elisabeth Burghalter	14
Johan Henrich Sager	8	Anna Catherina Burghalter	12
Samuel Sager	6	Anna Magdalena ——	8
Johan Christian Sager	2	Anna Barbara Burghalter	4
Antony Peck	12	Margaretha Burghalter	2½
Johan Henrich Peck	7	Anna Maria Sager	12½
George Angsted	6	Anna Barbara Sager	10
Johannes Angsted	1	Maria Louisa ——	3½
Philip Tarrisman	6	Christina Barbara Sager	6 m.
Hance Peter Wootring	9	Anna Catherina Peck	10
		Veronica Sherer	4 m.
GIRLS		Eva Catherina ——	4
Christina Mertz	3¾	Maria Catherina Tadigsman	9
Anna Maria Leap	14	Anna Maria Tadigsman	3¼
Anna Margaretha Leap	12	Maria Barbara Tadigsman	½
Maria Esther ——	14	Anna Margaretha Wootring	7
Magdalena Bewser	7½	Maria Magdalena Wootring	4½
Anna Maria ——	4	Anna Louisa Wootring	2
Anna Catherina ——	1½		
Anna Elisabetha ——	7	A true List.	
Anna Maria ——	17 w.	Chris^r Clymer.	

"At the Courthouse aforesaid, September 28th, 1733:

Forty three Palatines, who with their families, making in all One hundred thirty seven Persons, were imported here in the Briganteen Richard & Elizabeth, of Philadelphia, Christopher Clymer, Master, from Rotterdam, but last from Plymouth, as by Clearance thence, were qualified as before." From the Minutes of the Provincial Council, printed in *Colonial Records,* Vol. III, p. 519.

[List 33 B] Palatines Imported in the Brig^n Rich^d & Elizabeth, Christopher Clymer, Master, from Rotterdam, but last from Plymouth, p. Clearance thence. Qualified Septr 28th 1733.

Frantz Schuller
Jacob Greib
David (M) Mertz
Hans Nickel Mertz
George (H) Leap
Johan Conrad (H) Leap
Filb Jacob Edelmann
Matheus Bausser
Matheus (O) Bausser
Christian Bausser
Philip (M) Mire
David (X) Edelman
Adam Spahn
Jacob Hennel
Michael (X) Wise
Johan Georg Schufferd
Johann Jost Heck
Jacob Huntzicker
Hans Jacob (X) Leebegood
Jacob (X) Herman
Hans Jacob (X) Uts
Hans Jurk (X) Uts

Hans Peter (O) Somey
Hans Jacob (O) Somey
Hans Peter (O) Somey
Otto Frederick (O) Somey
Joseph Schumacher
Ulrich (X) Burghalter
Johan Nickel Seeger
Georg Schönmansgruber
Matdes Beck
Hannes Wollett
Henry (+) Winterberger
Hans Schürer
Jacob (X) Krist
Marcus (X) Krist
Görg Angstet
Marx Bigler
Filbs Dedigman
Johannes Weber
Johannes (II) Rosensteel
Abraham Wotring
Maddis Resch

[List 33 C] At the Courthouse of Philadelphia Sept^r, 28th, 1733. Present The Honble Patrick Gordon, Esqr, Lieu^t Governor, Saml Hasell, Esqr, Edward Roberts, George Fitzwater.

The Palatines whose Names are underwritten, imported in the Brigantine Rich^d & Elizabeth, of Philadelphia, Christ. Clymer, Master, from Rotterdam, but last from Plymouth, did this day take & Subscribe the Oaths to the Government.

Frantz Schuller
Jacob Greib
David (M) Mertz
Hans Nickel Mertz
George (H) Leap

Hans Conrad (H) Leap
Filb Jacob Edelman
Matheus Bausser
Mathis (O) Beasler
Christian Bausser

Philip (M) Mire
David (+) Edelman
Adam Spahn
Jacob Hennel
Michael (O) Wise
Johan Jerg Schufferd
Johan Jost Heck
Jacob Huntzicker
Hans Jacob (X) Lebegood
Jacob (X) Herman
Hans Jacob (X) Uts
Hans Jurk (+) Uts
Hans Peter (X) Somey
Hans Jacob (O) Somey
Hans Peter (O) Somey
Otto Frederick (O) Somey
Joseph Schumacher

Ulrich (X) Bughlater * [!]
Johan Nickel Seeger
Georg Schönmansgruber
Matdes Beck
Johannes Wollett
Henry (X) Winterberger
Hans Schürer
Jacob (X) Krist
Marcus (X) Krist
Görg Anngstet
Marx Bigler
Filbs Dedigman
Johannes Weber
Johannes (H) Rosensteel
Abraham Wotring
Maddies Resch

[List 34 A] List of the Men passengers imported in the
Ship Mary, Captain James Benn, Sept. 29, 1733.

David Karker
Johannes Holtz, sick
Hance Jurk Hurlocher
Godfrey Reich
Johannes Yorde
Andreas Dries
Cornelius Dries
Peter Dries
Johan Adam Dries
Jacob Spingler
Peter Hite
Elias Stricker
Johannes Stricker
Michael Noll
Philip Thomas Trump
Henry Sower
Johannes Wingerman
Christian Blaser

Johannes Deitsher
Peter Deitsher
Hans Jurk Ribble
Jacob Franck
Arnold Billig
Frederik Funk
Michael Friedly
Johannes Reichenbach
Nicholas Sowter
Hans Martin Brown
Andreas Nay
Philip Jacob Rootrock
Johannes Rootrock
Christian Sooter
Hans Michael Hammer
Michael Tiel
Jurk Pappenberger
Jurk Pappenberger, Junr

* This name should have been "Burghalter," as given in lists A and B.

Jurk Derey
Christian Retelsberger
Jacob Hoffman
Frederick Durflinger
Asimus Rambach
Hans Michael Keller
Jacob Berkley
Hans Jacob Berkly
Nicholas Mauritz
Walter Breuninger
Hans Adam Werner
Frederik Kehler
Peter Apple
John Peter Kettel
Jacob Gehtel
Johannes Lap
Johannes Slabach
John Henry Slabach
Jacob Leser

This is a true List of all the
Men passengers above 14 years.
Philadelphia,

Sept. 29, 1733.
James Benn.

WOMENS NAMES

Abel Korker
Susanna Yorden
Anna Maria Reich
Anna Maria Dries
Maria Elisabeth Spingler
Anna Christina Hite
Maria Catharina Stricker
Catherina Barbara Sower
Anna Barbara Blasin
Catherina Wingerman
Anna Gertruda Blaser
Anna Barbara Deitsher
Anna Eva Ribble
Maria Sophia Frank
Barbara Friedly

Catherina Reichenbach
Anna Barbara Souter
Maria Elisabeth Brown
Maria Elisabeth Nay
Maria Eleonora Sower
Christina Souter
Catherina Hammer
Catherina Pappenberger
Eva Catherina Hoffman
Margaretha Durflinger
Maria Catherina Rambach
Anna Maria Koller
Dorothea Berkley
Anna Barbara Berkley
Margaretha Breuninger
Barbara Werner
Elisabeth Kehler
Clara Apple
Sarah Kettle
Hanna Christina Lap
Maria Elisabeth Slabach
Catherina Löscher

BOYS	AGES
David Korker	12
Hans George Yorden	12
Johannes Yorden	9
Baltasar Reich	3
Stophel Spengler	13
Philip Stricker	9
Adam Stricker	7
Henry Stricker	$4\frac{1}{2}$
Johan Philip Wengerman	13
Johan Adam Blaser	$13\frac{1}{2}$
Hans Matz Blaser	$6\frac{1}{2}$
Nicolaus Blaser	$3\frac{1}{2}$
Christophel Deitscher	4
Jacob Deitscher	2
One boy, Funk, not yet bapt[t].	7 w.
Hans Henry Souter	7

	AGES		AGES
John Jacob Brown	1	Johanna Barbara Deitscher	8½
Hans Michel Nay	3½	Maria Barbara Ribble	1
Adam Pappenberger	4	One Girl, Funk, not yet bap^t.	7 w.
David Hoffman	8	Elisabeth Friedly	14½
David Rambach	8	Catherina Reichenbach	8½
Hans Jacob Rambach	2	Maria Barbara Reichenbach	5
Hans Michel Koller	2½	Anna Maria Reichenbach	2
Hans Jacob Berkley	9 m.	Anna Margaretha Souter	3
Hans Jacob Breuninger	13½	Maria Christina Brown	14
Peter Kettle	10	Anna Margaretha Brown	11
Rudolph Lap	11	Catherina Brown	3¾
Tewald Slabach	13	Anna Barbara Nay	7
Henry Slabach	16	Maria Margaretha Souter	6
Hans Georg Loscher	14	Christina Pappenberger	9
		Elisabeth Pappenberger	11
GIRLS		Anna Maria Hoffman	11
Anna Catherina Korker	14	Maria Magdalena Hoffman	4
Anna Elisabeth Yordin	5	Barbara Durflinger	13½
Maria Dorothea Reich	3	Anna Elisabeth Rambach	10
Maria Barbara Dries	13	Sibylla Rambach	4
Barbara Elisabeth Dries	24	Maria Magdalena Berkley	16
Anna Maria Dries	11	Catherina Berkley	6½
Maria Elisabeth Spengler	16	Barbara Berkley	3
Anna Elisabeth Hite	3	Anna Maria Breuninger	9
Elisabeth Sower	3½	Margaretha Kettle	19
Maria Magdalena Winger-		Christina Kettle	13
man	11	Johanna Margaretha Kettle	4
Hanna Felicia Wingerman	8	Anna Maria Lap	9
Anna Margaretha Winger-		Anna Catherina Lap	8
man	3½	Dorothea Slabach	5
Catherina Blaser	11½	Catherina Loscher	17½
Maria Magdalena Blaser	9½	Barbara Loscher	16
Anna Margaretha Blaser	2	Margaretha Loscher	9
Susanna Elizabeth Deitscher	11½		

"At the Courthouse aforesaid, September 29th, 1733.

Thirty four Palatines, who with their families, making in all One hundred & Seventy Persons, were imported here in the Pink Mary of Dublin, James Benn, Master, from Rotterdam, but last from Plymouth, as by Clearance thence, were qualified as before." From the Minutes of the Provincial Council, printed in *Colonial Records,* Vol. III, p. 519.

[List 34 B] Palatines Imported in the Pink Mary, of Dublin, James Benn, Master, from Rotterdam, but last from Plymouth, p. clearance thence. Qualified Septr 29th 1733.

Davidt Karcher
Hans Georg Horlacher
Gottfried Reich
Johannes (O) Yorde
Andreas (X) Dries
Cornelius (X) Dries
Peter (X) Dries
Johan Adam (X) Dries
Jacob (X) Spingler
Peter (O) Hite
Elias (O) Strickler
Johannes Stricker
Johan Michel Noll
Philip Thomas (+) Trump
Henrich Sauer
Johannes Wingertmann
Christian (O) Blaser
Johannes (+) Teutscher
Johann Peter Theuscher
Johan Jeorg Riebell
Jacob (F) Frank
Johann Arnold Büllig
Fritrich Funk
Michael (M) Friedly
Johannes (J) Reichenbach
Nicklaus Soder
Johann Martin Braun

Andtreas Ney
Philips Jacob Rothrock
Johannes Rothrock
Christian (CS) Sooter
Hans Michael (HM) Hammer
Johan Michel Dill
Georg Pfaffenberger
Jurk (JP) Pfaffenberger
Jerch Düry
Christian (CR) Retelsberger
Jacob (JH) Hoffman
Friedrich Dörfflinger
Asinus Rambach
Hans Michael (K) Keller
Jacob (O) Berkel
Hans Jacob Birkel
Nicklaus Moretz
Baltzer Breuinger
Johann Adam Wörner
Jörg Friederich Köhler
Peter (PA) Apple
Johan Peter Gettell
Johan Jacob Göttell
Johannes (L) Lap
Johannes (H) Slabach
Johan Henry (H) Slabach
Jacob Löscher

[List 34 C] At the Courthouse of Philadelphia, Septr 29, 1733. Present The Honble Patrick Gordon, Esqr, Lieu^t Governor, Samuel Hasell, Esqr, Charles Reed, Esqr.

The Palatines whose Names are underwritten, imported in the Pink Mary of Dublin, James Benn, Master, from Rotter-

dam, but last from Plymouth, did this day take & subscribe the
Oaths to ye Goverm^t.

David Karcher
Hans Georg Horlacher
Gottfried Reich
Johannes (O) Yorde
Andreas (✕) Dries
Cornelius (✕) Dries
Peter (✕) Dries
Jno Adam (✕) Dries
Jacob (✕) Spingler
Peter (O) Hite
Alias (O) Strickler
Johannes Stricker
Johan Michel Noll
Philip Thomas (+) Trump
Henrich Sauer
Johannes Wingertmann
Christian (O) Blaser
Johannes (IT) Teuttscher
Johann Peter Theuscher
Johann Georg Riebell
Jacob (F) Frank
Johann Arnold Büllig
Fritrich Funk
Michael (M) Friendly
Johannes (J) Reichenbach
Nicklaus Soder
Johann Martin Braun

Andtreas Ney
Philips Jacob Rothrock
Johannes Rothrock
Christian (CS) Sooter
Hans Michael (HM) Hammer
Johan Michel Dill
Georg Pfaffenberger
Jurk (JP) Pfaffenberger
Jorg Düry
Christian (CR) Retelsberger
Jacob (JH) Hoffman
Fridrich Dörfflinger
Asinus Rambach
Hans Michael (K) Keller
Jacob (B) Berkel
Hans Jacob Birkel
Nicklaus Moretz
Baltzer Breuinger
Johann Adam Wörner
Jörg Friedrich Köhler
Peter (PA) Apple
Johan Peter Gettel
Johann Jacob Göttel
Johannes (L) Lap
Johannes (H) Slabach
Jno Henry (H) Slabach
Jacob Löscher

[List 35 A] List of all the Passengers imported in the ship
Charming Betty, Capt John Ball, Philadelphia, October 11,
1733.

MEN	YEARS		YEARS
Johan Katner	40	Ulrich Leebegoot	45
George Katner	18	Johan Pieter Leebegoot	16
Henry Meakle	34	Adam Spag	60
Peter Gruber	34	Nicholas Burger	20
Samuel Loody	18	Wilhelm Imler, sick	55
Christian Andereck	28	Peter Stocker	53

	YEARS		YEARS
Johan Vogt	53	Andreas Vogt	12
Johan Long	45	Caspar Vogt	8
Johan Long, Junr	15	Johan Georg Long	1
Nicolas Heltsell		Christoffel Heltsel	$4\frac{1}{2}$
		Hans Jacob Heltsel	$1\frac{1}{2}$

WOMEN

GIRLS

	YEARS		YEARS
Feronica Katner	34	Maria Katner	11
Susanna Meckle	35	Maria Meckle	$3\frac{1}{2}$
Anna Gruber	24	Catherina Meckle	$\frac{1}{2}$
Maria Loody	46	Dorothea Loody	9
Susanna Leebegoot	36	Elisabeth Loody	9
Margaretha Burger	50	Maria Loody	$3\frac{1}{2}$
Anna Burger	25	Anna Lebegoot	5
Anna Imler	20	Maria Leebegoot	5
Anna Stocker	51	Margaretha Burger	10
Maria Vogt	46	Margaretha Burger	$\frac{1}{2}$
Anna Long	36	Catherina Imler	20
Maria Dorothea Heltzel	30	Sabina Imler	18
		Maria Stocker	17

BOYS

	YEARS		YEARS
		Barbara Stocker	13
Johan Henrich Katner	9	Catherina Vogt	18
Henrich Adam Katner	8	Maria Vogt	16
Martin Gruber	$1\frac{1}{2}$	Maria Long	10
Adam Leebegoot	13	Catherina Long	8
Jacob Leebegoot	10	Barbara Long	4
Adam Spag	12	Eva Catherina Heltsel	12
Philip Burger	12		
George Breitengross	13	October 12th 1733.	
Ludwig Imler	11	A true List.	
Johan Imler	7	John Ball.	

"At the Courthouse of Philadelphia, Oct. 12th, 1733.

Fifteen Palatines, who with their Families, making in all Sixty two Persons, were imported here in the Ship Charming Betty, John Ball, Master, from London, were this day qualified as usual." From the Minutes of the Provincial Council, printed in *Colonial Records*, Vol. III, p. 524.

[List 35 B] Palatines imported in the Ship Charming Betty, John Ball, Master, from London, p. clearance thence. Qualified October 12th 1733.

Johannes Kettner
Georg Michel Kettner
Heinrich Möckli
Peter (X) Gruber
Samuel Ludi
Christian Anderich [?]
Ulrich (X) Leebegood
Johan (X) Leebegood

Adam (SA) Spag
Nicholas (X) Burger
Peter (O) Stocker
Johan Paul Vogt
Johans Lang
Johan (X) Lang, Junr
Nicholas (NH) Heltzel

[List 35 C] At the Courthouse of Philadelphia October 12th, 1733. Present The Honble Patrick Gordon, Esqr, Lieu^t Governor, Thomas Griffits, Esqr, Mayor.

The Palatines whose Names are underwritten, imported in the Ship Charming Betty, Jn° Ball, Master, from London, did this day take and subscribe the Oaths to the Government.

Johann Kettner
Georg Michel Kettner
Heinrich Möckli
Hans Peter (X) Gruber
Samuel Ludi .
Christian Anderich [?]
Ulrich (U) Leebegoot
Johan (X) Leebegoot

Adam (SA) Spag
Nicholas (X) Burger
Peter (O) Stocker
Johan Paul Vogt
Johans Lang
Johan (+) Lang, Junr
Nicholas (NH) Heltzel

[List 36 A] A List of the Names of the passengers of the Ship S^t. Andrew Galley, Capt. John Stedman, from Rotterdam. [Qualified September 12th 1734.] *

Christopher Wigner
Melchior Hiebner
Georg Hiebner
Christopher Krieble, sick
Georg Krieble
David Hiebner, sick
Balsher Jackle
Georg Jackle
Christopher Shubart
Melchior Krieble, Senr

Caspar Krieble
Jurge Anderas
Balsher Hoveman
Melchior Krieble, Junr
Abraham Jackle
Georg Hoveman
Balthasar Hoveman
Georg Reynald, sick
Georg Reynald, Junr
Hans Weigner

* The originals of lists 36A and 36B are preserved in the Schwenkfelder Historical Library at Pennsburg, Pa.

Georg Weigner, Senr

Melchior Weigner

David Jackle, sick

Balthasar Jackle

Caspar Jackle

Jeremias Jackle

Christopher Jackle

Gregorius Meyster

Christopher Reynald

Hans Jackle

Georg Mentzel

Melchior Mentzel

Melchior Neiman

Tobias Hatranf

Georg Weys

Caspar Heydrick

Balthasar Heydrick

Christopher Neiman

Matias Jackle

Georg Sholtze

Christopher Weigner

Christopher Jackle

Georg Anders

David Seibt

Christopher Seibt

Georg Heydrick

Gregorius Sholtze

David Meyster

Georg Dresher

Christopher Dresher

Melchior Meyster

Balthser Anders

George Sholtze

Melchior Sholtze

Christopher Sholtze

Caspar John

Frederick Scheps

Andreas Warmer, sick

Fred^k Lodw^k Urdans

Bernard Stenback

Georg Boemsh

Christopher Paus

Johannes Hiebner

David Shubart

Wilhelm Pott

Degenhart Pott

Wilhelmus Witten

Johannes Van Dobgen

Peter Shoemaker

Hendrick Riegher

Georg Roots

Valentine Humief

Jacob Romfiel

Nicholas Deck

Nicholas Winder

Johannes Woolfang

Jacob Willhelm

Uldrich Spies

Peter Yeager

Hans Martin Treyster, sick

Caspar Stanner

Hans Georg Meyer

Peter Freytle

Johannes Singer

Conradt Fray

Matias Margar

Valentine Tiel

Abraham Tiel

Hendrick Romfield

WOMEN AND CHILDREN

Susannah Winer

Rosina Winer

Maria Hiebner

Maria Krieble

Susannah Krieble

Anna Krieble

Christopher Krieble

Maria Krieble

Rosina Krieble

Maria Hiebner

Rosina Krieble

Christopher Hiebner
Regina Jackle
Anna Jackle
Susannah Jackle
Maria Jackle
Rosina Jackle
Barbara Shubart
David Shubart
Anna Maria Shubart
Susannah Shubart
Maria Krieble
Susannah Krieble
Georg Krieble
Maria Anders
Urcilla Hoveman
Anna Hoveman
Rosina Hoveman
Christopher Hoveman
Anna Krieble
Urcilla Hoveman
Maria Jackle
Susannah Jackle
Rosina Jackle
Barbara Hoveman
Susannah Hoveman
Barbara Reynald
Susannah Reynald
Christopher Reynald
Anna Weigner
Melchior Weigner
Maria Weigner
Rosina Weigner
Susannah Jackle
Maria Meyster
Christopher Meyster
Anna Meyster
Maria Meyster
Susannah Reynald
Barbara Reynald
Susannah Jackle

Balthasar Jackle
Urcilla Mentzle
Barbara Mentzle
Anna Mentzel
Barbara Mentzel
Maria Neyman
Anna Warner
Barbara Hatranf
Maria Hatranf
Georg Hatranf
Abraham Hatranf
Melchior Hatranf
Rosina Hatranf
Anna Weys
Eva Heydrick
Rosina Heydrick
Christopher Heydrick
Susanna Neiman
David Neiman
Rosina Jackle
Maria Jackle
Regina Jackle
Susannah Sholtze
Anna Sholtze
Susannah Sholtze
Maria Sholtze
Barbara Sholtze
Susannah Weigner
Susannah Weigner
Maria Weigner
Abraham Weigner
Georg Weigner
Rosina Weigner
Regina Jackle
Anna Anders
Urcilla Anders
Judith Seibt
Caspar Seibt
Abraham Heydrick
Rosina Sholtze

Susannah Sholtze
Rosina Sholtze
Eva Meyster
Anna Meyster
Maria Dresher
Rosina Dresher
Maria Dresher
Regina Paynter
Anna Anders
Georg Anders
Maria Hiebner
Anna Hiebner
Hans Hiebner
Melchior Hiebner
Susannah Shubart
David Shubart
Cartrout Pott
Peter Loobach
Johann Willhelm Pott
Catrina Gadrout Pott
Johannes Pott
Georg Hend^k Roots
Maria Catrina Humief
Veronica Shoepin
Catrina Romfiel
Barbara Freeman
Jacob Freeman
Catrina Freeman
Margaret Theeman
Catrin^a Marg^t Romfiel
Anna Deck
Johan Hend^k Deck
Johannes Deck
Anna Barbara Deck
Maria Ferey
Anna Maria Winder
Andreas Winder
Anna Margaret Winder
Marilis Winder
Maria Catrina Winder

Elizabeth Woolfang
Georg Mich. Woolfang
Johannes Woolfang
Anna Catrina Willhelm
Jacob Willhelm
Valantine Willhelm
Maria Catrina Hunrof
—— Willhelm
Maria Dorothea Spies
Fredrick Treyster
Maria Barbara Spies
Hans Jacob Spies
Maria Elizabeth Spies
Catrina Stanner
Johan Nicholas Stanner
Johan Jacob Stanner
Maria Magdalena Stanner
Maria Urcella Meyer
Maria Ann Meyer
Anna Veronica Frytle
Maria Ingle Frytle
Philip Frytle
Catrina Singer
Catrina Singer
Maria Catrina Prining
Maria Elizabet^a Prining
Anna Barbara Felkerin
Hans Georg Felkerin
Maria Eva Felkerin
Maria Sarah Felkerin
Maria Kellering
Marilis Martin
Catrina Hildebrand
  alias Timberman
Catrina Hildebrand
Johan Jacob Hildebrand
John Elizabet Hildebrand
Dorothea Beitler
Odoren Dupee
Flora Dupee

Margaret ——   A true List.
Clement Dupark   John Stedman.

September 12th 1734.

"At the Courthouse of Philadelphia, September 12th, 1734. Eighty nine Palatines, who with their Families, making in all two hundred sixty one Persons, were imported here in the Ship Saint Andrew, John Stedman, Master, from Rotterdam, but last from Plymouth, as by Clearance thence, this day took and subscribed the Effect of the Government Oaths, and also the Declaration prescribed by the Order of Council of the 21st of September, 1727." From the Minutes of the Provincial Council, printed in *Colonial Records,* Vol. III, p. 568.

[List 36 B] Palatines imported in the Ship St Andrew, John Stedman, Master, from Rotterdam, but last from Plymouth, as p. Clearance thence. Qualified Sept. 12th 1734.

Christoph Wiegner	Jeremias Jäckel
Melcher Hübner	Christian (X) Jakele
George Hübner	Gregorius (X) Meisther
George Kribel	Christoph Reinwalt
Baltzer Jäckel	Hans Heinrich Jäckel
George Jäckel	George (O) Mentzell
Christoph Shoebart	Melcher (M) Mentzell
Melchior Kribel	Melcher (M) Newman
Casper Kribel	Tobias Harttranfft *
George Ander	George Weiss
Balthasar Hoffmann	Caspar Heydrich
Melchior Kribel, Junr	Baldthasar Heidrich
Abraham Jäckel	Christoph Nevman
Jörge Hoffman, Senr	Matthias Jäkel
Balser Hoffman, Junr	George Scholtze
George Reinwald	Christophel (W) Wiegner
Hans (W) Wiegner	Christoph Jäckel
George (W) Wiegner	George Anders
Melchior Wiegner	David Seibb
Baltzer Jäckel	Christoph Seibb
Casper Jäckel	George Heydrich

* This is the ancestor of John Frederick Hartranft, from 1873–1879 Governor of Pennsylvania.

Gregorius Scholtze
David Meschter
George Drescher
Christoph Drescher, Junr
Melcher (O) Meishter
Baltzer Anders
George Scholtze
Melchior Scholtze
Christoph Scholtze *
Caspar John
Friedrich Schöps
H. L. Urckhaus
Bernhardt Steinbach
Christoph Paus
George (×) Bausch
Hans (×) Hübner
David (×) Shoebart
Wilhelmus Pott
Degenhart Pott
Wilhelmus Widten
Johannes van Dubke

Peter (×) Shoemaker
Jacob Friedrich Rieger
Johann Jörg Ruitz
Valentin Unruch
Jacob Rumpfellt
Nicholas (×) Dek
Nicholas (×) Winder
Johannes (×) Wildfang
Jacob Wilhemi
Ullrich (×) Spies
Peter (×) Jäger
Caspar (K) Störller
Georg Meyer
Petter Freidel
Johanes Senger
Conradt Frey
Matthias (+) Marker
Valentin (+) Dihl
Abraham (×) Dihl
Henrich Rumpfeld

[List 36 C] At the Courthouse of Philadelphia Septr 12th, 1734. Present The Honourable Patrick Gordon, Esqr, Governor, Thomas Griffitts, Esqr, Mayor, Thomas Lawrence, Esqr, Charles Read, Esqr.

The Palatines whose Names are underwritten, imported in the Ship S^t. Andrew, John Stedman, Ma^r from Rotterdam, but last from Plymouth, did this day take and subscribe the Oaths to the Government.

Christoph Wiegner
Melchior Hübner
George Hübner
George Kribel
Baltzer Jäckel
George Jäckel
Christoff Schubert
Melchior Kribel
Casper Kribel

George Anders
Balthasar Hoffmann
Melchior Kribel, Junior
Abraham Jäckel
Görge Hoffman, Senior
Balthsar Hoffman, Junior
George Reinwald
Hans (×) Wigner
George (W) Wiegner

* For the diary of Christopher Schultz, regarding this journey, see Brecht, *Genealogical Record of the Schwenkfelder Families*, pp. 45–50.

Melchior Wiegner
Baltzer Jäckel
Casper Jäckel
Jeremias Jäckel
Christoff Jäckel
Gregorius (X) Mester
Christoph Reinwalt
Hans Hänrich Jäckel
George (O) Mentzel
Melchior (M) Mentzel
Melchior (M) Neuman
Tobias Hertteranfft
George Weiss
Caspar Heydrich
Baldthasar He[idrich]
Christoph Neuman
Matthus Jäckel
George Scholtze
Christoffer (CW) Wigner
Christoph Jäckel
George Anders
David Seibt *
Christoph Seibt
George Heydrich
Gregorius Scholtze
David Meschter
George Drescher
Christoph Drescher, Junior
Melchior (O) Masters
Baltzer Anders
George Scholtze
Melchior Scholtz
Christoph Scholtz

Caspar John
Friedrich Schöps
Hendrich Ludewig Urckhaus
Bernhardt Steinbach
Christoff Pauss
George (X) Bänsche
Hans (X) Hübener
David (DS) Schubert
Wilhelmus Pott
Degenhart Pott
Wilhelmus Widten
Johannes van Dubke
Peter (X) Schumacher
Jacob Friederich Rieger
Johann Jörg Ruitz
Valetin Unruch
Jacob Rumpfellt
Nicklaus (X) Deck
Nicklas (X) Wender
Johanes (X) Wildfang
Jacob Wilhelmi
Uhlerich (X) Spies
Peter (X) Jäger
Johan Caspar (K) Störller
Georg Mayer
Petter Freidel
Johanes Senger
Conrad Frey
Mattisias (+) Marcker
Vallentin (X) Thiel
Abraham (X) Dihl
Henrich Rumpfeld

[List 37 A] A List of the Passengers on Board the Ship Hope Galley, Daniel Riedt, Comand[r]. [Qualified Sep[r] 23[d] 1734.]

MENS NAMES	AGES		AGES
Jacobus Bowman	28	Fredrick Kufer	63
Bernhartus Richard	29	Jacob Koser	23

* For a letter of David Seibt, describing this journey, see *The Pennsylvania German*, Vol. IX (1908), pp. 367-370.

	AGES		AGES
Hans Hendrick Hofman	22	Joahin Andreas Miller	21
Hans Jacob Fishbach	30	Anthony Noble	53
John Wilhelm Kras	48	Anthony Noble, Junr	18
Michal Gerber	27	Johan Alberts Longerfield	30
Christian Houser	50	Godtfrid Sheerwagen	49
Peter Gortner	30	Christian Otto Schultz	22
Michal Fikle	25	Carl Fulker	23
Ulrich Buler	29	John Robeson, Brit.	30
Joanis Richter	26	Wilhelm Haer	54
Phillip Esping	28	Cornelius Paraed	23
Christian Farnie	27	Francis Dasons	21
Joanis Keyser	50	John Delmer	23
Jurgen Heynsman	45	Patrick Camell	20
Joanis Heynsman	16	Darbie Silvin	24
Johan Adam Shroof	25	John Gamel	20
Johan Peter Groose	30	Daniel Cammeron	21
Johan Hendrick Klaknor	45	William Pursell	30
Peter Stam	20	Oyn Doniwand	26
August Henrich Kuntsman	22	Bernhard Camell	27
Johan Henrich Heinsman	30	Mark Fey	20
Christopher Rabie	27	Bernhard Megie	26
Johan Phillip Duldt	19	Dorbie Carie	21
Henrich Steldts	31	Nathaniel Morrin	30
Zacharias Ohlbach	36	John Nouland	24
Zacharias Flomerfield	21	Joseph Lameer	24
Johan Wilhelm Ohlbach	28	Barnabie Franchie	22
Johanis Jung	40	John Grun	40
Jost Smith	46	John Camerson	40
Peter Smith	17	William Carter	23
Johanis Nohe	40	Patrick Heney	21
Johan Henrich Otterbach	30		
Johan Herbert Weber	22	WOMENS NAMES	
George Lubcken	25	Anna Margret Hofman	20
Joanis Peter Apgard	20	Cathrina Fishbach	28
Simon Kierbach	23	Sophia Margret Kraz	36
Johan Arent Riesh	28	Eliza Cathrine Jongen	32
Siemonis Beuell	16	Anna Cathrine Jongen	20
Johan Henrich Weshbach	24	Eliz^a Maria Holdinghousen	30
Johan Henrich Otterbach	21	Anna Gerber	22
Johan Jurg Anthony Miller	25	Maria Leshrin	17

	AGES	CHILDRENS NAMES	AGES
Barbera Heglerin	52		
Anna Housrin	50	Johan Casper Krazs	11
Johanna Housrin	16	Johan Phillip Krazs	$3\frac{1}{2}$
Anna Margritta Clundin	20	Anna Gerber	$\frac{1}{2}$
Anna Magdelena Bechtlerin	26	Bastian Lesher	11
Anna Eliz[a] Farnie	23	Niclaus Houser	11
Cathrine Farnie	29	Hans Michal Keysor	8
Maria Cathrine Keyserin	48	Juliana Keysor	4
Johanna Keysrin	20	Anthony Heinsman	11
Anna Maria Beuler	33	Maria Magdelena Heinsman	9
Cathrine Heynsman	45	Margreta Susanna Shroof	2
Susanna Heynsman	20	Johan Henry Groos	2
Maria Cathrine Shroof	23	Freyja Cathrine Groos	4
Anna Cathrine Grootz	26	Joanis Gerard Klakner	4
Clara Klacknerin	37	Maria Eliz[a] Klakner	11
Anna Dumat Ohlbach	37	Cathrina Klakner	7
Anna Cathrine Fock	20	Magdelina Klakner	3
Gerderuth Flomerfield	21	Joanis Wilhelm Ohlbach	11
Anna Eliz[a] Ohlbach	26	Joanis Gerard Ohlbach	6
Anna Maria Jongen	32	Anna Margret Ohlbach	8
Eliz[a] Bechtlerin	57	Gerderuth Margreta Ohlbach	2
Maria Barbara Bechtlerin	18	Joanis Peter Ohlbach	2
Anna Maria Bechtlerin	20	Harmon Jung	4
Anna Christina Smith	45	Maria Gerderuth Jung	5
Eliz[a] Magdelen Smith	20	Eliz[a] Jung	1
Maria Clara Nohe	40	John Jacob Nohe	$2\frac{1}{2}$
Gerderuth Nohe	16	Maria Clara Nohe	$5\frac{1}{2}$
Anna Maria Kierbach	26	Cathrine Noble	5
Freyja Cathrine Kierbach	21	Joanis Lesher	15
Maria Riesh	28	Joseph Heinsman	15
Maria Margret Weshbach	19	Henrich Willhelm Riesh	15
Anna Maria Beust	17	Anna Cathrine Nohe	10
Maria Eliz[a] Bomerin	18		
Catharine Noble	42	Phil[a] Sept[r] 23[d] 1734.	
Christ. Eliz[a] Longerfield	36	The above is a true List of the Pala-	
Regina Barbera Spedin	40	tines imported by me.	
Susanna Zimmerman	20	Daniel Reed.	

"At the Courthouse of Philadelphia, September 23d, 1734.
Forty nine Palatines, who with their Families, making in all

One hundred twenty seven Persons, were imported in the Ship Hope, Daniel Reid, Master, from Rotterdam, but last from Cowes, as by Clearance thence, were this day qualified as usual." From the Minutes of the Provincial Council, printed in *Colonial Records*, Vol. III, p. 570.

[List 37 B] Palatines Imported in the Ship Hope, Daniel Ried, Master, from Rotterdam, but last from Cowes, as by clearance thence. Qualified Septr 23^d 1734.

Jacob Bauman	Zachrias Ahlbach
Barnhard (X) Richer	Zach. (X) Flammersfield
Jacob Koffer	Johan Wilhelm Ahlbach
Hans Henrich Hoffman	Johannes Jung
Hans Jacob Fischbach	Josht (X) Shmidt
Johann Wilhelm Gross	Johann Peter Schmitt
Michael Gerber	Johannes Näh
Christen Huser	Johan Hennerich Otterpach
Michael Fickel	Johan Herberd Weber
[Ulrich] (O) Puler	George Lübcken
Johannes Richter	Johannes Antger
Philip Esping	Simon (X) Kirbach
Christian Farnie	Johann Arnolt Reisch
Johannes Keiser	Simo Beiel
Jerg Heinsman	Johan Henrich Weschenbach
Johan (X) Hinnsman	Johan Henrich Otter[bach]
Johann Adam Schroff	Johann Georg Antony Müller
Johann Petter Gross	Johann Andreas Müller
Johan Henrich Klöckner	Antony Nobel
Petter Stamm	Antony Nobel, Junior
August Heinrich Kunstmann	Johann Albert Langerfeldt
Johann Heinrich Heisman	Gottfriedt Schierwagen
Christoff Rabe	Christian Otto Schultz
Joh. Philips Doldt	Cornelis Paraet
Henerich Stoltz	

[List 37 C] At the Courthouse of Philadelphia, Septr 23^d, 1734. Present The Honble Patrick Gordon, Esqr, Lieu^t Governor, Thomas Griffits, Esqr, Mayor, Charles Read, Esqr.

The Palatines whose Names are underwritten, imported in the Ship Hope, Daniel Reed, Master, from Rotterdam, but last from Cowes, did this day take and subscribe the Oaths to the Government.

Jacob Bauman
Ber[n]hart (X) Richer
Jacob Koffer
Hans Henrich Hoffman
Hans Jacob Fischbach
Johann Wilhelm Gross
Michel Gerber
Christen Huser
Michael Fickel
Ulrich (O) Buler
Johannes Richter
Philip Esping
Christian Farnin
Johannes Keiser
Jerg Heinsman
Johanes (X) Hinnsman
Johann Adam Schroff
Johann Petter Gross
Johan Henrich Klöckner
Petter Stamm
August Heinrich Kunstman
Johann Heinrich Heisman
Christoff Rabe
Joh. Philip Doldt
Henrich Stoltz

Zachrias Ahlbach
Zacharias (X) Flamerfeld
Johan Wilhelm Ahlbach
Johannes Jung
Jost (X) Shmith
Johann Peter Schmitt
Johannes Näh
Johan Henerich Otterpach
Johan Herberd Weber
George Lübcken
Johannes (X) Antger
Simon (X) Kirbach
Johann Arnolt Roisch
Simo Beuel
Johan Henrich Weschenbach
Johan Henrich Otter[bach]
Johan Georg Antony Müller
Johann Andreas Müller
Antony Nobel
Antony Nobel, Junior
Johann Albert Langerfeldt
Godtfried Schierwagen
Christian Otto Schultz
Corneelis Paraet

[List 38 A] Liste Van de Schwitzers Soo op Schiep genant de Mercurius, Van d'Heer Capitain William Wilson, in Philadelphia arriveert.* [Qualified May 29, 1735.]

MEN	AGES	MEN	AGES
Henrdryk Götschy, absent	17	Jacob Bossart	40
Conrad Wuertz	26	Jacob Schenkel	27
Abraham Weidman	25	Hendryk Huber	30
Rodolph Weidman	26	Jacob Naf	39
Jacob Rathgep	24	Jacob Dentzler	40

* This Dutch heading of the list reads in English: "List of Switzers who arrived in Philadelphia on the ship called Mercury, Captain William Wilson."

MEN	AGES	MEN	AGES
Hs. Ulric Aner	42	Jacob Schmid	32
Johannes Weys	43	Jacob Schmid, absent	15
Balthasar Bossart	30	Conrad Meyer	51
Hendryk Merck	19	Melchior Meyer, absent	15
Killian Merck, sick	16	Jacob Naf	24
Johannes Meyer	39	Caspar Gut	19
Caspar Notzly	45	Caspar Bleiler	47
Caspar Schweitzer	20	Jacob Matzinger	37
Hendryk Oswald	20	Abraham Wackerly	30
Jacob Frey	50	Conrad Rutschy	27
Jacob Homberger, sick	16	Christian Erhard Neumeister	..
Jacob Meyer	39	Johannes Moelig	40
Jacob Bertschinger	19	Phillipp Willem Kleyn	23
Hendryk Brunner	17	Hendryk Forst	19
Hans Kubler	43		
Jacob Weidman	40	**WOMEN**	
Conrad Keller	36	Esther Götschy	44
Conrad Naf	22	Barbara Götschy	18
Jacob Bucher, sick	39	Esther Götschy	16
Jacob Metler	17	Anna Götschy	24
Hs. Muller	23	Magdalena Steininger	30
Hendryk Muller, sick	21	Marie Weber	30
Johannes Ott	19	Barbara Haller	23
Johannes Heid	24	Cleovea Schenckel	30
Hendryk Schreyber	22	Elizabeth Possart	17
Martin Schellenberg	20	Ursula Grendelmeyer	27
Conrad Zuppinger, sick	36	Anna Naf	19
Jacob Maurer	40	Magdalena Phister	37
Johan Hend. Maurer	19	Verena Krebser	30
Hendryk Scheuchzer, ab.	43	Verena Kern	30
Jacob Schellenberg	45	Verena Eberhard	27
Hendryk Muschque	23	Elizabeth Winckler	31
Hendryk Surber	50	Barbara Weys	18
Hendryk Surber, absent	15	Elisabeth Weys	16
Ulric Amman	24	Susanna Bindschedler	30
Rodolph Aberly	22	Elisabeth Wettstein	39
Jacob Wiest	24	Elisabeth Peter	21
Rodolph Egg	19	Regula Appell	39
Rodolph Walder	39	Barbara Weidman	36
Conrad Naf	52	Anna Isler	43

WOMEN	AGES		AGES
Barbara Meyer	39	Jacob Dentzler	9
Barbara Eberhard	30	Rodolph Dentzler	5
Regula Stolz	37	Abraham Dentzler	3
Barbara Glaur	31	Margareth Dentzler	4
Catherine Isler	34	Abraham Dubendorffer	9
Barbara Albrecht	40	Anna Brunner	11
Regula Maurer	23	Hs. Ulric Brunner	6
Catherine Ruegg	20	Verena Aner	9
Verena Bentz	19	Felix Aner	7
Ursula Schelleberg	17	Hs. Ulric Aner	5
Regula Eberhard	19	Margareth Aner	4
Marguerit Zupinger	19	Catherine Weys	9
Margueret Maurer	42	Susanna Weys	3
Elisabeth Maurer	19	Anna Weys	6
Anna Stuz	30	Caspar Possart	10
Barbara Dappeller	52	Hendryk Possart	3
Magdelen Krebser	49	Rodolph Possart	2
Barbara Schmid	15	Hans Merck	6
Magdalene Weidmann	49	Hs. Conrad Merck	5
Elisabeth Haller	20	Leonard Meyer	14
Anna Naf	19	Jacob Meyer	9
Magdel. Mantz	29	Barbara Meyer	4
Catherin Meyly	29	Anna Barbara Frey	10
Barbara Lips	30	Elisabeth Frey	8
Juliane Catherine Bartin	..	Hendryk Frey	6
Marie Cather. Kirberger	39	Hs. Jacob Meyer	8
Marguerit Kentzing	29	Magdalena Meyer	6
		Jacob Kubler	5
CHILDREN		Elisabeth Kubler	5
Rodolph Götschy	12	Rodolph Dubendorffer	8
Mauritz Götschy	10	Anna Dubendorffer	6
Beat Götschy	8	Jacob Weidmann	5
Magdalena Götschy	6	Mathias Keller	1
Judith Weidman	2	Jacob Bucher	10
Barbara Weidmann	3m.	Hendryk Bucher	8
Rodolph Possart	10	Marie Muller	5
Anna Possart	6	Anna Cleophe Schreik	2
Rodolph Hueber	6	Hs. Ulric Zupinger	12
Lisabeth Hueber	3m.	Hendryk Zuppinger	6
Elisabeth Naf	4	Anna Marg. Mauer	7

CHILDREN	AGES	CHILDREN	AGES
Verena Surber	5	Jacob Rutschy	10
Jacob Walder	4	Hendryk Rutschy	7
Hans Jacob Naf	9	Hs. Jacob Rutschy	2w.
Jacob Naf	7	Ennreich Moelig	7
Felix Schmid	12	Veronica Gertrut Moelig	15
Barb. Schmid	5	Andreas Moelig	4
Hs. Hend. Bleuler	13	Marie Cath. Moelig	1½
Catherine Bleuler	9	Gottfried Moelig	10
Hs. Jacob Bleuler	8		
Felix Matzinger	8	A true List.	
Verena Wackerly	2	Wm. Wilson.	

"At the Courthouse of Philad[ia], May 29th, 1735.

Fifty four Palatines, and Switzers, who with their Families, making in all one hundred seventy six Persons, were imported here in the Ship Mercury, of London, William Wilson, Master, from Rotterdam, but last from Cowes, as by Clearance from thence, were this day qualified as usual." From the Minutes of the Provincial Council, printed in *Colonial Records,* Vol. III, p. 593.

[List 38 B] Palatines and Switzers, Imported in the Ship Mercury, of London, William Wilson, Master, from Rotterdam, but last from Cowes, by clearance thence. Qualified May 29th, 1735.

Conrad Wuertz *	Jacob (×) Tanzler
Abraham Weidman	Johan Ulrick (×) Ahaner
Rutolff Weidman	H. Hansen Weyss
Hans Jacob Radtgäb	Balsahar (×) Bosserd
Jacob Boshaar	Henry (×) Merck
Jacob (JS) Schenker	Hans Weimer
Heinrich Huber	Caspar (×) Netzlji
Jacob (×) Naff	Caspar (×) Schweitzer

* Regarding the history of this colony see *History of the Goshenhoppen Reformed Charge,* pp. 96–130. The leader of the colony was the Rev. Maurice Goetschy, who died on his arrival in Philadelphia. His place was taken by his son, John Henry Goetschy. The business manager of the colony was John Conrad Wirtz (Wuertz), the brother-in-law of John Henry Goetschy. Wirtz was at first a schoolteacher, but from 1742–1763 officiated, in numerous German and Dutch Reformed churches, as pastor.

Henry (O) Oswald
Jacob Frey
Jacob Meyer
Jacob (O) Perdschenger
Henry (O) Bruner
Hans Küber
Jacob Weidman
Hans Cunrath Käller
Conrad (X) Naffe
Jacob (XX) Madler
Hans Müller
Hans Odt
Johanes Heit
Heinrich Schriber
Martin (O) Shelberger
Jacob (O) Muumer
Hendri Scheuchzer
Jacob (O) Scheuchser
Henry (X) Mosock

Henry (H) Surber
Hans Ulrich (H) Amon
Rudolph (H R) Aberly
Jacob (X) Wüst
Rud[ol]ff Eyg
Rudolph (X) Walter
Jacob Conrad (X) Naffe
Jacob (X) Schmit
Conrad (X) Meyer
Jacob Näff
Kaspr Gut
Caspar (X) Plauler
Jacob Matz[inger]
Abraham (X) Weckerly
Cunrath Rütschi
Christoph Neumeister
Johannes Mölich
Philibs Klein
Hennrich Forst

[List 38 C] At the Courth° of Phil[a], May 29[th], 1735. Present, The Honble Patrick Gordon, Esqr, Lt Govr, Thomas Lawrence, Charles Read, Esq[rs].

The Palatines whose Names are underwritten, imported in the Ship Mercury, of London, William Wilson, Master, from Rotterdam, but last from Cowes, did this day take & subscribe the Oaths to the Government.

Conrad Wuertz
Abraham Weidman
Rutolff Weidman
Hans Jacob Radtgäb
Jacob Boshaar
Jacob (S) Schenckel
Heinrich Huber
Jacob (X) Naff
Jacob (X) Tantzler
Johan Uhlrich (X) Ahaner
H. Hansen Weyss
Balsatzar (X) Bossert
Henry (X) Merck

Hans Weimer
Caspar (X) Netzly
Caspar (K) Schweitzer
Henry (O) Oswald
Jacob Frey
Jacob Meyer
Jacob (X) Pertschinger
Henry (X) Bruner
Hans Küber
Jacob Weidman
Hans Cunrath Käller
Conrad (X) Naffe
Jacob (XX) Mädler

Hans Müller
Hans Odt
Johanes Heit
Henrich Schriber
Martin (O) Shellberg
Jacob (M) Maurer
Hendri Scheuchzer
Jacob (O) Shelleberg
Henry (X) Mosoke
Henry (H) Surber
Hans Uhlrig (H) Amman
Rudolph (HR) Aberly
Jacob (X) Wyst
Rud[ol]ff Eyg

Rudolph (X) Walter
Jacob Conrad (X) Naffe
Jacob (X) Schmit
Conrad (X) Meyer
Jacob Näff
Kaspr Gut
Caspar (X) Pleuler
Jacob Winger
Abraham Wekerly
Cunrath Rütschi
Christoph Neumeister
Johannes Mölich
Philips Klein
Hennrich Forst

[List 39 A] A List of Palatine Passengers from on Board the Mary, [James Marshall, Master, from Liverpool. Qualified June 28, 1735.]

MENS NAMES

Melchior Shults
Zachrias Fredrick
Hyndrick Possart
Pieter Swab
Andreas Brinker
Nicholas Botikofer
Heyndrick Woerman
Johannes Woerman
Jacob Widmer
Andreas Widmer
Willem Gessel
Solomon Ruckstoll
Solomon Ruckstoll
   In All 13 Men

WOMEN & CHILDREN

Anna Possart
Caspar Possart
Hyndrick Possart
Regula Brinker
Hyndrick Brinker

Conrad Brinker
Hans Brinker
Jacob Brinker
Magdalena Woerman
Rede Woerman
Barbara Woerman
Orsula Woerman
Hyndrick Woerman
Elizabeth Woerman
Anna Woerman
Elizabeth Woerman
Marget Widmer
Jacob Widmer
Marget Widmer
Anna Widmer
Susannah Widmer
Elisabeth Widmer
Barbara Rookstool
Olive Rookstool
Barbara Rookstool
Hyndrick Rookstool
39 in all.

"At the Courthouse of Philad^{ia}, June 28th, 1735.

Thirteen Palatines, who with their Families, making in all thirty nine persons, were imported here in the Brig Mary, of Philadelphia, James Marshall, Master, from London, were this day qualified as usual." From the Minutes of the Provincial Council, printed in *Colonial Records,* Vol. III, p. 597.

[List 39 B] Palatines imported in the Brigantine Mary of Philadelphia, James Marshall, Master, from London. Qualified June 28th 1735.

Melchior Scholtze	Johnis Wuhrman
Zacharias Frie[dri]ch	Jacob (×) Widmar
Heinrich Boschart	Wilhelm (×) Gesel
Peter Schwaab	Sallamon Rückstul
Andreas (×) Brinker	Solomon (×) Ruckstool, Junr
Nicklaus Bütekofer	Andreas Widmer
Heinrich Weuhrman	

[List 39 C] At the Courth^o of Philadel^a June ye 28th 1735. Present The Honble Patrick Gordon, Esqr, Lt Govr, Henry Brooke, Charles Read, Esq^{rs}.

The Palatines whose names are underwritten, imported in the Brigantine Mary, of Philadelphia, James Marshall, Master, from London, did this day take and subscribe the Oaths to the Government.

Melchior Scholtze	Johanns Wurhman
Zacharias Friederich	Jacob (×) Wiedmer
Heinrich Boschart	Wilhelm (×) Gesel
Peter Schwaab	Sallamon Ruckstul
Andreas (×) Brinker	Solomon (×) Ruckstool, Junr
Nicklaus Bütekofer	Andreas Widmer
Heinrich Weuhrman	

[List 40 A] [Passengers in the Ship Oliver, Samuel Merchant, Master, from South Carolina. Qualified August 26, 1735.]

MENS NAMES	AGES		AGES
Hans Booker	54	Lazerus Winger	19
John Booker	20	Hans Koller	40

AGES			AGES
Christan Brenholts	39	Lizarberth Lyinburger	20
Hans Pinkley	23	Barberry Lyinburger	14
Christan Swaller	24	Lizarberth Mesler	25
Hans Lyinburger	50	Ann Wewer	25
Hans Lyinburger	25	Ann Wewer	20
Abram Meeseley	43	Barbry Yelin	25
Hans Martey	44	Barbry Yelin	45
Uldrick Mesler	30	Christan Yelin	20
Jacob Starley	20	Mardling Spring	23
Christan Wewer	28	Margat Otlersin	40
Uldrick Yelin	27	Apploney Greeno	60
Johannes Atterley	40	Marry Naws	38
William Naws	39		
Peter Hankler	21	CHILDRENS NAMES & AGES	
		Benjeaman Booker	13
WOMENS NAMES		Christan Booker	10
		Jacob Coller	9
Christana Booker	35	Peter Lyinburger	8
Ann Winger	56	Hannah Lyinburger	3
Ann Winger	18	Ann Mesler	13
Susannah Koller	35	Hans Wewer	7
Anna Brenholts	40	Christan Wewer	3
Lizarberth Lyinburger	45		

"At the Courthouse of Philad^ia, August 26th, 1735.

Eighteen Switzers, who, with their Families, making in all forty five Persons, were imported here in the Billinder Oliver, Samuel Merchant, Master, from South Carolina, were this day qualified as usual." From the Minutes of the Provincial Council, printed in *Colonial Records,* Vol. III, p. 607.

[List 40 B] Switzers imported in the Billender Oliver, Samuel Merchant, Master, from South Carolina. Qualified August the 26th 1735.

Hans Bucher	Hans Lüwenbörg
Lazarus Wengen	Abraham Mäuslin
Hans (H K) Koller	Johannes Marti
Christian (CBR) Brenholts	Ullrich Mischler
Hans Mich^l (H) Pingley	Jacob (X) Stelly
Christen Zwallen	Christian (W) Weber

Ulrich (W) Yilia	Pietter Henckels
Johannes Etter	Hans (HL) Leyenburger
Jacob Wilhelm Naass	Hans Bucher.*

[List 40 C] At Philadelphia August 26ᵗʰ 1735. Present The Honᵇˡᵉ Patrick Gordon, Esqʳ, .Lᵗ Governor, Charles Read, Esqʳ.

The Foreigners whose names are underwritten, late Inhabitants of the Canton of Bern in Switzerland, imported in the Billender Oliver, Samuel Merchant, Master, from South Carlonia, did this day take & subscribe the Oaths to the Government.

Hans Bucher	Ullrich Mischler
Lazarus Wenger	Jacob (X) Stelly
Hans (HK) Kolle	Christian (W) Weber
Christian (OBR) Brenholtz	Uhlrech (U) Willerich
Hans Michel (H) Bingley	Johannes Etter
Christen Zwallen	Jacob Wilhelm Naass
Hans Loüwenbörg	Pietter Henckels
Abraham Mäuslin	Hans (HL) Leyenburger
Johannes Marti	Hans Bucher

[List 41 A] [Palatines imported in the Ship Harle, Ralph Harle, Master, from Rotterdam. Qualified September 1, 1736.] †

NAMES	AGES	NAMES	AGES
Frantz Hecker	34	Abraham Deckart	48
Johannes von Latsen	50	Johannes Hannewald	23
J. Peter von Latsen	25	Johannes Lorents	40
Christian von Latsen	18	Jacob Gemling	23
Johannes Krick	29	Valentin Vogt	33
J. Philip Wick	25	Daniel Brun	16
Philip Wagemann	23	Michel Kraul	53

* This Bernese colony has been discussed at length by Mr. G. Kurtz, the State archivist of Bern, in *Lists of Swiss Emigrants in the Eighteenth Century to the American Colonies,* edited by Prof. A. B. Faust, Vol. II, Washington, 1925, pp. 20-24.

† There is a duplicate Captain's list, with the names anglicized, which we omit as of no special importance. The list which we present is written in fine German script.

NAMES	AGES	NAMES	AGES
Hs Nickel Zeisloff	33	Dieterich Marte	27
Balthasar Zeisloff	29	Jacob Weil	39
Georg Zeisloff	27	J. Wilhelm Speck	23
Wilhelm Hetterling	27	Peter Stutenbecker	38
Daniel Nargang	20	Johannes Wilms	48
Peter Nargang	33	Henrich Stutenbecker	29
Nickolaus Treber	44	Henrich Gerhardt	48
Christoph Treber	17	Andreas Krim	18
Michel Jochim	33	Jacob Daubenspeck	22
Andreas Jochim	40	Andreas Heylmann	29
Carl Kern	30	Matheis Brug	23
Nicolaus Rebel	23	J. Peter Vögeli	18
J. Georg Schacke	36	J. Georg Mein	16
Jacob Amandus	30	Johannes Rothrock	50
Leonhardt Cronbach	29	Jacob Barth	50
Vincents Schacke	34	Jacob Seydemann	17
Jacob Hochstettler	32	Nickel Post	17
Jacob Eysen	54	Hendrich Dups	28
Johannes Rupel	35	Andreas Kratz	22
Friederich Beckel	21	Jacob Lippert	26
Jacob Eysen	21	Valentin Neu	24
Jacob Jeyser	23	Johannes Schneider	28
Arndt Corts	29	Johannes Zachrias	26
Friederich Mennardt	29	Nicolaus Melcher	28
Rudolf Hackman	20	Balthasar Stubanus	40
Jacob Vellmann	55	Ludwig Weicker	19
Jacob Sontag	32	J. Henrich Brunner	24
Cornelius Weygand	22	Eberhardt Abeler	20
Abraham Saaler	30	J. Georg Basel	20
Adam Seyder	38	J. Ludwig Kammerer	21
Nickel Lang	34	Michel Weickel	44
Adam Bohn	27	Lyborius Meerschroot	18
Ludtwig Ley	25	Christian Schreyack	18
Christian Erb	46	Conradt Franckenberger	20
Peter Rensch	37	Johannes Businger	25
Hans Melchior Beyer	21	Daniel Meyer	25
Andreas Narrgang	37	Johannes Risemann	27
Johannes Bittler	30	Johannes Hess	46
Clemens Stuttenbecker	36	J. Christophel Windemuth	60
Matheis Speck	53	Paulus Brunner	28

NAMES	AGES	NAMES	AGES
Joh. Georg Wambold	23	Philip Mens	38
Conradt Krim	20	Henrich Weidebach	49
J. Georg Scheydeler	22	Caspar Koperschmitt	50
Christian Landes	26	Johannes Franckeberger	18
Andreas Gross	25	Andreas Franck	19
Leonhardt Jäger	26	Johannes Fuchs	19
Adam Schaus	32	Christoph Rudolf	19
Zachrias Sitzler	45	Peter Masteller	30
Valentin Scherer	19	Peter Hyronimus	29
Peter Rup	30	Thomas Hummel	25
Michel Noll	17	A^n Elisabetha Abelin *	23
Isaac Leopoldus	25	Cathrina Von Latsin	46
Jacob Christler	42	M^{ar} Margreth Heckerin	32
Johannes Meyer	48	Julianna Wackin	26
Nickel Anger	47	Catharina Rheinin	19
Caspar Meyer	32	A^n Elisabeth Hannewaldin	27
Joseph Linck	25	Catharina Margreth Vögelin	46
Ludwig Maurerer	21	A^n Margreth Deckartin	43
Christian Steckel	25	Sibila Elisabeth Kraulin	30
Caspar Stolling	38	A^n Catharina Zeisloffin	22
Jacob Nuss	20	Susanna Hetterlingin	33
Ewald Beyer	21	A^n Maria Nargangin	23
Conradt Paap	27	M^{ar} Anna Treberin	21
Johannes Brandt	16	Catharina Treberin	20
Matheis Deck	37	M^{ar} Engel Treberin	19
Henrich Wohlgemuth	29	Anna Maria Jochimin	30
Abraham Wohlgemuth	22	Margreth Jochimin	34
Joseph Wolgemuth	20	M^{ar} Christina Schackin	28
Geo. Adam Warner	26	M^{ar} Catharina Hochstettlerin	42
Christian Suder	23	A^n Margreth Vincentsin	30
Johannes Gerber	32	Mª Eva Hochstettlern	28
Jonathan Hager	22	A^n Margreth Eysin	21
Matheis Reser	28	Susana Maria Eysin	18
Jacob Kuntz	23	Mª Anna Treberin	34
Jacob Hollinger	30	A^n Catharina Rupelin	29
Jacob Ledermann	21	J^a Judith Schmittin	20
Jacob Cochenauer	21	A^n Margreth Schmittin	53
Herman Drutt	32	Anna Beckelin	23

* To get the correct German name, the ending *"in"* ought to be dropped in every case, as it is the *feminine* ending in German.

NAMES	AGES	NAMES	AGES
A^n Elisabeth Kortsin	23	A^n Catharina Barthin	38
A^n Catharina Weylin	32	A^n Catharina Vögelin	50
A^n Barbara Vollmanin	41	A^n Elisabeth Meinin	20
Maria Langin	33	Catharina Wamboldin	20
Margreth Renschin	34	A^n Maria Wamboldin	21
Catharina Jotherin	38	A^n Eva Meyerin	22
Catharina Nargangin	40	Elisabeth Meyerin	18
A^n Cath. Stutenbeckerin	28	A^n Elisabeth Hochschildin	25
Christinà Speckin	56	A^n Catharina Herwardin	30
A^n Margreth Stutenbeckerin	38	Catharina Elis. Schneiderin	21
A^n Margreth Wilmsin	36	A^n Catharina Pausin	19
Maria Catharina Gerhardin	38	A^n Catharina Mastellerin	28
Maria Elisabeth Heylmanin	28	A^n Catharina Angnesin	38
Anna Meemardin	22	A^n Maria Ambrosin	25
Elisabeth Hackmanin	25	Catharina Elisabeth Seylerin	18
Anna Maria Lippertin	29		
A^n Catharina Neuin	25	[A duplicate list has this signa-	
A^n Elisabeth Weygelin	38	ture:]	
Eva Elisabeth Segelin	22	With women & children making	
A^n Margreth Rothrockin	19	in all Three hundred eighty	
A^n Elisabeth Hessin	40	eight Persons. Ralph Harle.	
Luwis Lossing	19	September 1, 1736.	

"At the Courthouse of Philadelphia, September 1st, 1736.

One hundred fifty one Foreigners from the Palatinate & other Places, who, with their Families, making in all three hundred eighty eight Persons, were imported here in the Ship Harle, of London, Ralph Harle, Master, from Rotterdam, but last from Cowes, as by Clearance thence, were this day qualified as usual." From the Minutes of the Provincial Council, printed in *Colonial Records,* Vol. IV, p. 58 f.

[List 41 B] Palatines imported in the Ship Harle, Ralph Harle, Master, from Rotterdam, but last from Cowes. Qualified September the 1st 1736.

Frans Heckert
Johannes von Laeschet
Johannes Peters von Laschet
Christian von Laaschet

Johannes Krück
Johann Philipp Wick
Johann Philip Wageman
Abraham Tegarden

Johannes (X) Hannavall
Johann Lorentz
Abraham Tiegart
Jacob Gemlich
Johann Valtin Voigt
Johann Mathes Voigt
Johan Da[n]iel Brunn
Johan Michel Graul
Johan Nicolas (X) Sysloof
Johan Baltzar (X) Sysloof
Georg Zeissloff
Wilhelm Hetterling
Daniel (X) Nargar
Johan Peder Nargang
Niclaus Trewer
Michael [Jo]gem
Johan Christoffel Treber
Karl Kern
Nicolas (O) Rebell
Johann Jörg Jöky
Jacob Amandus
Andreas (A) Yokam
Leonhart Cronbach
Vincentz Schacken
Jacob (X) Hofstedler
Jacob Eysen
Johannes (X) Ruppele
Frederick (X) Biegel
Jacob Jayser
Arnd Kurtz
Frederick (O) Memart
Rudolff Hackman
Jacob Follman
Jacob Sontag
Cornelius Weygandt
Adam Seider
Nickel Lang
Adam Bohner
Ludwig (O) Lay
Christian Erb
Peter Rentsch

Hans Melchior (O) Byer
Andreas (N) Nargang
Johannes Bütler
Clemens Stottenbecker
Matheus Speck
Derrick (X) Mart
Hans Jacob (H W) Weyl
Johan Wilhelm Speck
Peter Stotenbecker
Johannes Willems
Hendrich Stotenbecker
Henrich Gerhart
Andreas Grimm
Johan Jacob (O) Towaspeck
Andres Haillman
Johann Mates Bruch
Hans Peter (O) Fegelin
Hans Jerig (X) Mein
Johanns Rothrock
Johan Jacob (X) Paalt
Johan Jacob (O) Zyderman
Niclas Post
Henrich Dubs
Andries Cratz
Jacob Libbert
Vallentin Neu
Johannes Schneider
Johannes Zacharias
Nichlaus Melcher
Balthasar Stupanus
Johann Ludwig Weycker
Johan Henrich Brunner
Eberhart Ebler
Johan Jerig (X) Basel
Ludwig Cämmerer
Johann Michael Weygell
Liworius Merschroth
Christian Schryackh
Conrad (X) Frankberger
Johannes Bosinger
Daniel Meyer

Johannes Rossman

Johannes Hes

Christoph Windmuth

Paulus Brunner

Johann Gorg Wamboldt

Johann Gerg Scheideler

Johan Conradt Grimm

Christian Landes

Andreas (X) Gross

Johann Adam Schauss

Leon^d (X) Yeager

Zacharias Setzler

Johann Vallentin Scherer

Peter (X) Roop

Mich^l (X) Noll

Isach Leboldus Delb

John Jacob Christler

Johannes (X) Meyer

Nickel Anger

Caspar (X) Meyer

Ludwig (X) Meyer

Christian Stöckly

Caspar Stelling

Johann Jacob Nuss

Deowalt Beyer

Hann Conrath Bab

Joh^s (X) Brunt

Mathes Deck

Heinrich Wollgemuht

Abraham Wohlgemudt

Joseph (X) Wulgemacht

Jerg Adam Werner

Christian (O) Suder

Johannes Garber

Jonathan Hager

Mattheus Röser

Jacob Cuntz

Jacob Hollinger

Jacob Lädtermann

Jacob (X) Kochnour

Herman Trott

Johann Philip Müntz

Henrich (X) Wydebach

Caspar (X) Coopersmidt

Johannes Franckeberger

Andreas (X) Frank

Adam Wambold

Hans Georg Handwerch

Johannes Fuchs

Gottfriedt Grüll

Johann Adam Hohenschilt

Johann Peter Wambold

Jerg Migel Fridrich

Johan Albrecht Sigle

Johan Petter Marsteller

Johann Jörg Lohnert

Johann Jörg Windemuth

Michael Linder

Christoph Rudolpf

Peter Hironimus

Tomas (X) Hummell

[List 41 C] At the Courthouse of Philadelphia Septr 1st, 1736.

Present The Honble James Logan Esqr, President, Clement Plumsted, Samuel Hasell, Thomas Laurence, Charles Read, Esq^rs, Councillors, William Allen, Esqr, Mayor of Philadelphia, Derrick Jansen, Esqr, one of the Justices of Philad^ia County.

The Palatines whose names are underwritten, imported in

the Ship Harle, Ralph Harle, from Rotterdam, but last from
Cowes, did this day take & subscribe the Oaths to the Government.

Frans Heckert
Johann von Laschet
Johannes Peters von Laschet
Christian von Laaschet
Johannes Krück
Johann Philipp Wick
Johann Philipp Wageman
Abraham Tegarden
Johans Harnewald
Johann Lorentz
Abraham Tiegarden
Jacob Gemlich
Johann Valtin Voigt
Johann Mathias Voigt
Johann Daniel Brun
Johann Michel Graul
Geo. Niclas (X) Sysloof
Johan Baltzer (X) Zeislof
Jorg Zeisloff
Wilhelm Hetterling
Daniel (X) Nargang
Johan Peter (X) Nargang
Niclaus Trewer
Michael (X) Jochim
Johan Christoffel Treber
Karl Kern
Nicklas (O) Rubel
Johann Jörg Jöky
Jacob Amandus
Andreas (A) Jochim
Leonhardt Cronbach
Vincentz Schacki
Jacob (X) Hoffstädler
Jacob Eysen
Hans (X) Rubel
Friederich (X) Bökel

Jacob Jayser
Arnd Kürtz
Friederich (O) Menhart
Rudolff Hackmann
Jacob Fellman
Jacob Sontag
Cornelius Weygand
Adam Seider
Nickel Lang
Adam Bohner
Ludwig (O) Lay
Christ (M) Erb
Petter Rentsch
Hans Melchior (O) Beier
Andares Mergang
Johannes Bütler
Clemens Stottenbecker
Mathias (O) Beck
Ditrich (X) Mardin
Johan Jacob (H) Weill
Johan Wilhelm Speck
Peter Stotenbecher
Johannes Willems
Hendrich Stotenbecker
Henrich Gerhart
Andreas Grimm
Johan Jacob Daubenspeck
Antres Haillman
Johan Mathais Bruch
Johan Peter (X) Fegly
Johan Jörg (X) Mine
Johannes Rothrock
Johan Jacob (X) Balack
Johan Jacob Seideman
Niclas Post
Henrich Dubs

Andries Cratz
Jacob Libbert
Fallendin Neu
Johannes Schneider
Johannes Zacharias
Nicklaus Melcher
Balthasar Stupanus
Johann Lud. Weycker
Johan Henrich Brunner
Eberhart Ebler
Johan Georg (×) Bassel
Johann Ludwig Cämmerer
Johan Michell Weygel
Liworius Merschrath
Christian Schreyackh
Conrad (×) Franckenberger
Johannes Bosinger
Daniel Mayer
Johanes Ryssmann
Johannes Hes
Joh. Christoph Windmuth
Paulus Brunner
Johann Gorg Wamboldt
Johann Jerg Scheideler
Johan Conradt Grimm
Christian Landes
Andereas (×) Cousse
Johann Adam Schauss
Lenhart (×) Jäger
Zacharias Setzler
Johann Vallentin Scherer
Peter (×) Rup
Johan Michael (×) Noll
Isach Leboldus Delb
John Jacob Christler
Johanes (×) Meyer
Nickel Anger
Caspar (O) Meyer
Ludwig (×) Mauerer
Christian Stöckly

Caspar Stelling
Johann Jacob Nus
Deowalt Beyer
Hann Conrath Bab
Johans (×) Brand
Mathes Deck
Heinrich Wollgemuht
Abraham Wohlgemut
Joseph (×) Wohlgemuth
Jerg Adam Werner
Christian (O) Sutter
Johannes Gerber
Jonathan Heger
Mattheus Röser
Jacob Cuntz
Jacob Holinger
Jacob Lädtermann
Jacob (×) Kochnauer
Herman Trott
Johann Philipp Müntz
Henrich (×) Weidebach
Caspar (O) Kupferschmit
Johannes Franckeberger
Andareas (×) Frank
Adam Wambolt
Hans Georg Handwerch
Johannes Fuchs
Gottfried Grüll
Johann Adam Hohenschilt
Johann Peter Wambold
Jerg Migel Fridrich
Johan Albrecht Sigell
Johann Petter Marsteller
Johan Georg Lohnert
Johann Georg Windemuth
Michael Linder
Christoph Rudolff
Peter Hironimus
Thomas (×) Hummel

[List 42 A] [Palatines imported in the Ship Princess Augusta, Samuel Marchant, Master, from Rotterdam. Qualified September 16, 1736.]

MEN TO BE QUALIFIED	AGES	MEN TO BE QUALIFIED	AGES
Gabril Lamle	26	Adolph Wensel	36
Hance George Bumgartner	26	Hance Jacob Biedert	30
Hance Philip Flexer	31	Christian Sheybly	53
George Meyer	27	Christian Sheibly	17
George Ritter	17	Hance Heckendon	50
Johann Jost Tupps	18	Hance Heckendon	20
Stephen Shust	22	Dannill Heckendon	16
Jacob Meyer	45	Bastian Stoler	42
David Bielman	31	Hance Jacob Grieter	55
Hance Michall Carle	23	Fredrick Grieter	21
Hance Thomas Kurr	19	Martain Grieter	19
Gottfried Loudermilch	28	Tielman Hirnschael	55
Philip Gutchman	29	Durst Thome	57
George Meyer	35	Martain Thome	32
Hance Michall Essich	30	Hance Jacob Thome	29
George Essich	40	Durst Thome	24
Rudolph Essich	70	Jacob Stubes	25
Johan Jacob Bush	26	Joseph Criteer	24
William Huber	29	Jacob Kese	28
Jacob Muller	28	Rudulph Hough	25
Simon Carel	36	Hance Spietteler	45
Jacob Free	28	Hance Spietteler	17
Lorance Free	24	Jacob Domme, sick	39
Nicholos Free	48	Hance George Gerster	26
Hendrick Free	17	Nicholas Tenne	24
Leenhard Styen	46	David Lewesteyn	40
Hance Nicklos Schmitt	28	Jacob Paire	34
Lorance Simon	30	Hance Jacobe	28
Christian Simon	60	Stafen Jacobe	23
Friederick Gartner	35	John Books	23
Hance George Drautman	27	Christian Ruchty	74
George Meyer	63	Abraham Jacke	26
George Mourer, sick	29	Diderich Marschall, sick	29
Hendrick Meyer	26	Sebastian Cackelie	50
Bastian Graff, from Boston	25	Sebastian Cackelie, died	22
George Graff	34	Diderick Cackelie	20

MEN TO BE QUALIFIED	AGES	MEN TO BE QUALIFIED	AGES
Hance Cackelie	17	Nicholas Oree	26
Hance Commer	46	Ennos Newell	36
Dannill Commer	19	Joseph Newell	56
Diederich Werlie	41	Petter Newell	16
Hance Tiseler	23	Jacob Christaman	25
Hance Imber Marty	46	Michall Haling	28
Hance Jacob Keller	30	Marcus Markey	45
Nichlos Jewdie	23	Hance David Markey	17
Hance Joner, died	50	Jacob Altland	28
Jonas Joner	20	Nichlos Mesling	27
Hance Jacob Joner	16	Conerard Gauger	22
Benedictus Jochlie	27	Nichlos Gauger	18
Christian Teppe	30	Petter Weeger	27
Petter Brinhartt	39	Women & Children making in	
Walter Bauman	32	all Three hundᵈ & thirty Per-	
Hance Ebber	31	sons.	
Hance Zwalle	36	Francis Ore, a wife 3 children.	
Hance Stockie	26	Nicolas Ore.	
Hance George Knaap, sick	43	Nicolas Trasbart, a wife and 6	
Hance Rudolph Erb	26	children.	
Jacob Bruderle, sick	42	Pierre Dilon, a wife and 4 chil-	
Petter Pinkley	28	dren.	
Melchior Detwyler	37	Nicolas Gerard, a wife and no	
Christian Schlachter	39	child.	
Petter Delo	40	Jean Francois Chretien, a wife	
Rudolph Bumgartner	55	and one child.	
Francis Christian	40	Eneas Newell, a wife and one	
Nicollas Drasbart	40	child.	
Nichols Gerrard	30	Joseph Newell, a wife and 6	
Petter Pinkelie	32	children, of whom Pierre	
Hance Pinkelie	41	Newell is one.	
Hance Pinkelie	18		
Johannes Keller	65	A true List.	
Johannes Keller	21	Septʳ. 16ᵗʰ 1736.	
Francis Ory	56	Samˡ Marchant.	

"At the Courthouse of Philadⁱᵃ, September 16th, 1736.

One hundred and twelve foreigners from the Palatinate, and other places, who, with their families, making in all three hundred thirty persons, were imported here in the ship Princess

Augusta, Samuel Merchant, from Rotterdam, but last from Cowes, as by Clearance thence, were this day qualified as usual." From the Minutes of the Provincial Council, printed in *Colonial Records,* Vol. IV, p. 72.

[List 42 B] Palatines imported in the Ship Princess Augusta, Samuel Marchant, Master, from Rotterdam, but last from Cowes. Qualified the 16th Day of September 1736.

Johann Gabriel Lämmle
Hans Jorig (X) Bumgartner
Hans Philip Flexser
Jerg Maier
Johann Gorg Ritter
Han Jost Dubs
Stefan Schust
Jacob Meyer
Hanns Davidt Bilmann
Hans Thomas Kurr
Hans Michell Karle
Gottfried Lautermilch
Philip Guttmann
George (X) Meyer
Hanns Michael Essig
Jerg Abraham Essig
Rudolff Essich
Johan Jacob (X) Bush
Wilhelm Huber
Jacob Miller
Simon Carl
Jacob Früh
Lorentz Früh
Niclos (H) Free
Henrich Früh
Leonhardt Stein
Hans Nickel Schmitt
Lorance (LS) Simon
Christian (X) Simon
Frederick (X) Gartner
Hance George (H) Drautman
Hendrick (H) Meyer

Sebastian Graff
Hanns Georg Graff
Han Adolff Wenssel
Hans Jacob Beitratt
Christen Scheublein
Christen Schiblien
Hans Hecken[dorn]
Hans Hegendorn
Daniell (X) Heckendon
Bastian Stoler
Hance Jacob (X) Grieter
Frederick (+) Grieter
Marti Grieder
Thielman Hirnschall
Durst Thommen
Martain (+) Thome
Hans Jacob Domen
Dürst Thomen
Hans Jacob Dups
Joseph Kratzer
Jacob (+) Kese
Rudolff Hauch
Hans Spiteler
Hans Spitler
Hans Jerg Gerster
Niclaes Tomen
David Löuwenstein
Jacob (O) Paire
Hans (O) Jacob
Stephen (O) Jacob
John (+) Books
Christen Ruchty

Abraham (+) Jacke
Sesbastien Caquelin
Didie Caquelin
Jean Caquelin
Jan Comer
Daniel Kommer
Diderick (D) Werlie
Hance (O) Tissler
Hans Imbermord [?]
Hans Jacob Keller
Nichlos (+) Jewdie
Jonas Yoner
II. Jacob Yoner
Bändicht Yuchli
Christen Däppen
Peter (+) Brinhartt
Walthart Bumann
Hans Siber
Hance (+) Zwalle
Hance (+) Stockie
Hance Rudolph (+) Erb
Petter (+) Pinckley
Melchior (+) Detweiler
Christiane Schlächter

Pierre Dulon
Rudolph (+) Bumgartner
Jean François Chrestien
Collas (+) Drasbart
N. Gerard
Petter (+) Pinkelie
Hance (+) Pinkelie
Hance (+) Pinkelie
Johannes Keller
Johannes Keller
François Ory
Nicolas Ory
Enoas (+) Nowell
Joseph Noel
Peter (+) Nowell
Jacob (+) Christaman
Michel Haalling
Marcus (O) Markey
Hance David (+) Markey
Jacob Altlandt
Nichlos (+) Mesling
Johann Conrath Gauger
Georg Nicolaus Gauger
Peter Weger

[List 42 C] At the Courthouse of Philadelphia, Septr 16th 1736. Present The Honble James Logan, Esqr, Presid^t. Thomas Lawrence, Thomas Griffits Ralph Asheton, } Esq^rs. William Allen, Esqr, Mayor of the City of Philad^ia.

The Palatines whose Names are underwritten imported in the Ship Princess Augusta, Samuel Marchant, Master, from Rotterdam, but last from Cowes, did this day take & subscribe the Oaths to the Government.

Johann Gabriel Lämle
Johan George (X) Baumgarden
Hans Philipp Flexser
Jerg Maier
Johann Gorg Ritter
Han Jost Dubs

Stefahn Schust
Jacob Meyer
Hanns Davidt Bilmann
Hans Thomas Kurr
Hans Joseph Carl
Gottfried Lautermilch

Philipp Guttmann
George (X) Meyer
Hans Michael Essich
Jerg Abraham Essich
Rudolff Essich
Johan Jacob (O) Bush
Wilhelm Huber
Jacob Müller
Simon Carl
Jacob Früh
Lohrentz Früh
Nicklas (H) Früh
Henrich Früh
Leonhardt Stein
Hans Nickel Schmidt
Lorentz (S) Simon
Christian (X) Simon
Friederich (X) Gardner
Hans George (H) Drautman
Henrich (H) Meyer
Sebastian Graff
Hanns Georg Graff
Johan Adolph Wenssel
Hans Jacob Beitrat
Christen Scheublein, Senior
Christen Scheublein, Junior
Hans (X) Heckendon, Senior
Hans Hegendorn, Junior
Daniel (X) Heckendon
Bastian Stoller
Hans Jacob (X) Grieter
Friederich (+) Grieter
Marti Grieder
Thielman Hirnschall
Durst Thommen
Martin (+) Thomme
Hans Jacob Domen
Dürst Thomen
Hans Jacob Dups
Joseph Kratzer
Jacob (+) Kissy

Rudolff Hauch
Hans Spiteler
Hans Spitller
Hans Jerg Gerster
Nicklas Tomen
David Löuwenstein
Jacob (O) Barr
Hans (O) Jacob
Stephen (O) Jacob
Hans (+) Bocks
Christen Ruchty
Abraham (X) Jacke
Sebastien Caquelin
Didie Caquelin
Jean Caquelin
Jan Comer
Daniel Kommer
Diterich (D) Werlly
Hans (X) Dissler
Hans Imber Mord
Hans Jacob Keller
Nicklaus Jude
Jonans Yoner
Jacob Yoner
Bändicht Yuchli
Christen Däppen
Peter (O) Brilhartt
Walthar Bumann
Hans Siber
Hans (X) Zwalle
Hans (+) Stockie
Hans Rudolf (O) Erb
Pieter (+) Pinckly
Melchior (+) Dattweyler
Christian Schlästen
Pierre Dulon
Rudolff (+) Baumgarden
Jean François Chrestien
Collas (+) Prasbart
N. Gerard
Peter (+) Bingly

Hans (X) Binckly
Hans Binckly, Junior
Johannes Keller
Johannes Keller
François Ory
Nicolas Ory
Ennos (+) Newell
Joseph Noel
Pieter (X) Newell

Jacob (X) Christman
Michel Haalling
Marcus (O) Markey
Hans Davit (+) Markey
Jacob Altlandt
Nicklaus (+) Mesling
Johann Conrath Gauger
Georg Nicolaus Gauger
Peter Weger

[List 43 B] Palatines imported in the Brig^t John, George Fraiser, Master, from Rotterdam, but last from Dover. Qualified the 19th Day of October 1736.

Abraham Beer
Petter Quattelbaum
Johannes (X) Frans
Johann Georg Wicklein
Johann Ludwig Seib
Ludwig Steadler von Staetler
Johann Philippus Quickel
Johannes (O) Segel
Johan Peter Pritz
Johan Mich^l (O) Quickle
Jacob (O) Keller
Franciscus Josephus Hornig
Johann Caspar Schmidt
Casper Struwel
Casper Lambert
George (O) Keg
Paulus Andoni
Friedrich Bleibtreu
Johannes Geier

Johan Adam Rausch
Johann Jost Mohr
Johan George (+) Quickle
Johannes Schler
Johan Christoffel Heininger
Peter Kohl
Daniel Schroth
Johan Henrich Schmidt
Jacob (X) Plyger
Aberham Dumbaldt
Ernst Fridrich Dumbald
Petter Haas
Johannes Herr
Diebolt Veit
Dirk (O) Schutten
Nicolas (+) Stop
Pieter (O) D'Veau
Godfrid Eberhard

"At the Courthouse of Philad^{ia}, October 19th, 1736.

Thirty seven Foreigners, from the Palatinate, who, with their Families, making in all one hundred and ten persons, were imported here in the Brigantine John, of Perth Amboy, George Frazer, Master, from Rotterdam, but last from Dover, as by Clearance thence, were this day qualified as usual." From the Minutes of the Provincial Council, printed in *Colonial Records,*

Vol. IV, p. 99f. This is the last entry in the minutes of the Provincial Council regarding immigrants.

[List 43 C] At the Courthouse of Philad^ia Octob^r 19th 1736. Present Clement Plumstead, Esqr Mayor of the City of Philad^ia, Thomas Laurence, Esqr, Ralph Asheton, Esqr.

The Palatines whose Names are underwritten imported in the Brig^t John, George Fraiser, Master from Rotterdam, but last from Dover, did this day take & subscribe the Oaths to the Government.

Abraham Beer	Johan Adam Rausch
Petter Quattelbaum	Johann Jost Mohr
Johan (X) Frantz	Johan Georg (+) Quickel
Johann Georg Wicklein	Johannes Schler
Johann Ludwig Seib	Johan Christoffel Heininger
Ludwig Steadler von Stea[tler]	Peter Kohl
Johan Philippus Quickel	Daniel Schroth
Johanes (O) Seger	Johan Henrich Schmidt
Johan Peter Pritz	Jacob (X) Blyger
Johan Michel (O) Quickel	Abraham Dumbald
Jacob (X) Keller	Ernst Friderich Dumbald
Franciscus Josephus Hornig	Peter Haas
Johann Caspar Schmidt	Johannes Herr
Casper Struwel	Diebolt Veit
Casper Lambert	Ditrich (O) Schütz
George (O) Keck	Nicklas (+) Stube
Paulus Andoni	Piter (O) de Wue
Friedrich Bleibtreu	Godfrid Eberhard
Johannes Geier	

[List 44 A] A List of Men Passengers of Sixteen Years of Age & Upwards Imported in the Ship Samuel, Hugh Percy, Master from Rotterdam. [Qualified August 30, 1737.]

NAMES	AGES	NAMES	AGES
Abrah^m Funfurney	64	Jacob Schober	33
Henr^k Wirley	60	Peter Yost	18
Chris^n Miller	27	Nich^s Marret	24
Henr^k Miller	33	Joan^s Scheffler	23
Geo^e Weigel	20	Joan^s Tracksel	47

NAMES	AGES	NAMES	AGES
John Peter Tracksel	19	Lorens Schriber	26
Christⁿ Bringel	20	Simon Minech	35
Andr^s Aulebaker	27	Peter Minech	39
Jacob Counse	23	Joⁿ Jacob Echoltz	25
Bened^t Tomas	27	Joann^s Kashnetz	43
Hans Adam Stout	19	Hans Geo^e Kashnetz	19
Hans Geo^e Huttner	31	Paul Frantz	50
Hans Eppler	39	Hans Ad^m Beidinger	39
Fredr^k Froom	29	Fred^k Eberhardt	40
Hans Mech^l Hetzer	53	Joseph Bishoff	38
Darius Ruff	21	Peter Beidinger	34
Hans Geo^e Zeigler	19	John Ad^m Snider	41
Jno Jacob Kolp	23	Ulerich Rickell	28
Fredr^k Krafft	21	Jno Geo^e Sowerbier	33
Jacob Nuss	36	Lenhard Glazer	46
Fredr^k Stemetts	24	Jno Jacob Maag	30
Philip Backer	54	Conrade Schutz	30
Hans Mich^l Backer	23	Jno Burghart Folck	26
Ludwick Bothner	32	Jno Henr^k Klien	33
Wirich Rutisilia	40	Nichol Finck	33
Thos Kern	36	Nichol^s Meyer	22
Simon Henninger	26	Adam Drum	31
Mich^l Phinstaag	32	Frans^s Fordene	26
Hans Geo^e Lale	34	Mich^l Fordene	22
Jacob Falck	69	Malicha Fordene	19
Joann^s Ries	21	Jacob Baum	45
Jacob Offenbacher	26	Andreas Miller	30
Albert Bier	28	Conrade Miller	50
Joann^s Roohr	20	Joann^s Baum	18
John Geo^e Roth	24	Jacob Lower	50
Henr^k Guthart	37	Mich^l Lower	20
Saml Filbert	27	Mich^l Spangler	26
Wm Strubb	37	Barnard Woomer	29
Chrisⁿ Mickel	27	Christⁿ Doll	25
Ludw^k Kornman	24	Peter Doll	24
Paul Gier	23	Christⁿ Dasher	22
Joann^s Lang	46	Geo^e Weyrigg	34
Joan Valant^e Lang	16	Peter Hugget	35
John Peter Stempel	40	Phil^p Finstermaker	20
Lorens Becker	57	Jacob Lang	27

NAMES	AGES	NAMES	AGES
Jacob Wolf	43	Joannes Stout	30
Jn° Peter Wolf	17	Jn° Jacob Kinser	28
Jn° Willm Welch	25	Jn° Geo^e Gise	30
Jacob Welch	21	Ludw^k Becker	28
Peter Bier	21	Adam Lifner	25
Mich^l Shoemaker	22	Jacob Stout	26
Joann^s Foust	23	Herman Hartman	24
Peter Leight	21	Christ^n Ruth	35
Ludw^k Kein	40		
Wm Rabenholts	35	A true List	
Jn° Henrick Mull	22	Hugh Percy.	

[List 44 B] Palatines imported in the Ship Samuel, Hugh Percy, Master, from Rotterdam, but last from Cowes. Qualified the 30th day of August 1737.

Abraham Farni	Johan Jacob Nuss
Henrich Werer	Friedrich Steinmetz
Christian Müller	Philip (O) Backer
Henerich Müller	Johan Michel [Backer]
Johann Georg Weichel	Ludwig Bothner
Jacob (O) Schober	Weirich Ruti Sieli
Peter (O) Jost	Johann Tomas Kern
Nich^s (+) Marrett	Simon Hönninger
Johannes Schöffler	Michael Pfingstag
Johannes Drachsell	Hans George (X) Lale
Johann Peter Trachsel	Jacob (O) Folke
Christian Brengel	Joannes (X) Ries
Andreas (A) Aulebaker	Jacob Offenbacher
Jacob Kuntz	Albinus Beyer
Benedict (O) Tomas	Johannes Rohr
Hans Adam (l) Stout	Johann Georg Roth
Hans Georg Hüttner	Henrich Guthard
Hans Ebbler	Samuel Filbert
Friederich From	William (W) Strub
Hans Michael Hetzer	Johann Christophel Meckel
Darius Ruff	Ludwig Kornmann
Johann Georg Ziegler	Johann Paul Geiger
Johann Jacob Kollb	Johannes Lang
Johann Friedrich Krafft	Johan Valting Lang

Johann Peter Stembell

Lorens (X) Becker

Lohrentz Schreiber

Simon (O) Minech

Peter (X) Minech

Johann Jacob Eickholtz

Johannes (O) Kashnetz

Hans (H) Castnitz

Paul (O) Frantz

Hans Adam Biediger

Frittrich Eberhart

Joseph Bischoff

Peder Beidinger

Johann Adam Schneider

Ulrich (V) Rickell

Johann Georg Sauerbier

Lenhart Glaser

Johann Jacob Maag

Conrad Schütz

Johan Burkhart Volck

Johann Heinrich Klein

Johann Nickel Finck

Nichel (X) Meyer

Johan Adam Drumm

Francis (F) Fordene

Michel Fortineh

Malicha (M) Fordene

Jacob Baum

Andreas Müller

Johan Cunrath Müller

Johannes Baum

Jacob (L) Lower

Michael (M) Lower

Michael (M) Spangler

Bernard (W) Woomer

John Christian Doll

Johan Peter Doll

Johann Christian Dascher

Jörg Weyrich

Petter Hugett

Philip (X) Finstermaker

Jacob Lang

Jacob Wolff

Peter Wolff

Johann Wilhelm Welsch

Johann Jacob Welsch

Petter Bier

Michel Schumacher

Johannes Faust

Johann Peter Licht

Lodwich (L) Kein

Wilhelm Rabennalt

Johan Henrich Moll

Johannes (X) Stout

Johann Jacob Kintzer

Johan Georg Geiss

Lodwich (O) Becker

Johann Adam Löffler

Johann Jacob Staudt

Christian (KR) Ruth

[List 44 C] At the Courthouse of Philad^ia August 30th 1737. Present The Honble James Logan, Esqr, President, Clement Plumsted, Ralph Assheton, Thomas Laurence, William Allen.

The Palatines whose Names are underwritten, imported in the Ship Samuel, Hugh Percy, Master, from Rotterdam, but last from Cowes, did this day take & subscribe the Oaths to the Government.

Abraham Farni

Heinrich Werlle

Christian Müller

Henrich Müller

Johann Georg Weichel
Jacob (O) Shober
Peter (O) Jost
Mich¹ (+) Marret
Johannes Schöffler
Johannes Drachsell
Johann Peter Trechsell
Christian Brengel
Andreas (A) Aulebaker
Jacob Kuntz
Benedict (O) Tomas
Hans Adam (|) Stout
Hans Jerg Hüttner
Hans Ebbler
Friderich From
Hans Michael Hetzer
Darius Ruff
Johann Georg Ziegler
Johann Jacob Kollb
Johann Friedrich Krafft
Johan Jacob Nuss
Friedrich Steinmetz
Philᵖ (O) Backer
Johan M. Backer
Ludwig (X) Bothner
Weyrich Ruti Sieli
Johann Tomas Kern
Simon Hönninger
Michael Pfingstag
Hans Geo. (H) Lale
Jacob (O) Folck
Joannˢ (X) Ries
Jacob Offenbacher
Albinus Beyer
Johannes Rohr
Johann Georg Roth
Henrich Guthard
Samuel Filbert
Willᵐ (W) Strub
Johann Christophel Meckel

Ludwig Kornmann
Johann Paul Geiger
Johannes Lang
Johann Valting Lang
Johann Peter Stembell
Lorens (X) Becker
Lohrentz Schreiber
Simon (O) Minech
Peter (X) Minech
Johann Jacob Eickholtz
Joannˢ (O) Kashnetz
Hans Jerg Castnitz
Paul (O) Frantz
Hans Adam Biediger
Frittrich Eberhart
Joseph Bischoff
Peder Buidicer
Johann Adam Schneider
Ullerich (V) Ricker
Johann Georg Sauerbier
Leonhart Glasser
Johann Jacob Maag
Conrad Schütz
Johan Burkhart Volk
Johann Heinrich Klein
Johan Nickel Finck
Nichol (X) Meyer
Johan Adam Drumm
Fraᶜ (F) Fordene
Michel Fortineh
Malicha (M) Fordene
Jacob Baum
Andreas Müler
Johann Cunrath Müller
Johannes Baum
Jacob (L) Lower
Mich¹ (M) Lower
Mich¹ (M) Spangler
Barnard (W) Woomer
Johan Christian Doll

John Doll
Johann Christian Dascher
Görg Weyrich
Petter Hugett
Phil^p (X) Finstermaker
Jacob Lang
Jacob Wolff
Peter Wolff
Johann Wilhelm Welsch
Johann Jacob Welsch
Petter Bier
Michel Schum[a]cher

Johannes Faust
Johann Peter Licht
Ludw^k (L) Kein
Wilhelm Rabennalt
Johann Henrich Moll
Joann^s (X) Staut
Johann Jacob Kintzer
Johan Görg Geiss
Ludw^k (O) Becker
Johann Adam Löffler
Johann Jacob Staudt
Christ^n (KR) Ruth

[List 45 A] A List of ye men that are Pallatine Passengers from Sixteen years and upwards on Board the Snow Molly, John Howell, Master, from Dover. [Qualified September 10, 1737.]

Valentine Stober
Valentine Stober, Junr
Jacob Stober
Hans Jonas Ryffel
Frederick Ryffel
Christiper Grooman
John Albert Shaller
John George Albert
George Shaller
John Lenoard Willfort
Nicholas Cochelrise
George Simon Christ
Hans Michael Hartlyn
George Fredarick Wollenweber
Micael Hartlyn
John Winter

Philip Godfriet Munk
Jacob Meyer
John Jacop Kayer
John Philip Kratzer
Valentine Rolevere
Christlper Gommer
Hans Gommer
Philip Adam Endler
John Rytzman
Christiper Shakey
Jacop Shaft
Philip Jacop Shaft
Freadarick Horn
Peter Hane
John Martin Frelich

Sepr 10th 1737.
A true List of the Men of Sixteen years of Age & upwards.
John Howell.

[List 45 B] Palatines imported in the Snow Molly, John Howell, Master. Qualified the 10th day of September 1737.

Weltin Stober
Valentin Stober, Junior
Jacob Stober
Hans Jonas Reiffel
Friederich Reiffel
Johan Christoff Grohmann
Johann Albrecht Schaller
Johann Georg Albert
Georg Albrecht Schaller
Johann Lenhart Wülffart
Nicolaus Kachelriess
Georg Siemon Christ
Hans Mich. Herdlein
Georg Friedrich Wollenweber
Michael Hertlein
John (X) Winder

Philipp Gottfried Müntz
Jacob Meier
Johan Jacob (X) Geyer
Johann Philipp Kratzer
Vallentd. Rohleber
Christ. Christopf Gomer
Johans Adam Gomer
Philip Adam Endler
Johans Reitzmann
Johan Christoffel Schacke
Johann Jacob Schaaf
Philipp Jacob Schaaff
Friederich (X) Horne
Johann Petter Hane
Johan Marti Fröllich

[Endorsed:]
Foreigners by the Snow Molly, John Howell, M^r, from Amsterdam. Qualif^d, Sepr 10th 1737.

[List 45 C] At the Courthouse of Philad^ia, Septem^r 10th, 1737.

Present:

Clement Plumsted, Esqr
Samuel Hasell, Esqr

Ralph Assheton,
Thomas Griffitts.

The Palatines whose Names are underwritten, imported in the Snow Molly, John Howell, Master, from Amsterdam, but last from Dover, did this day take & subscribe the Oaths to the Government.

Veltin Stober
Valetin Stober, Junior
Jacob Stober
Hans Jonas Reiffel
Friederich Reiffel
Johan Christoff Grohmann
Johann Albrecht Schaller
Johann Georg Albrecht
Georg Albrecht Schaller
Johann Lenhart Wülffart

Nicolaus Kahelries
Georg Simeon Christ
Hans Mich. Herdlin
Geörg Friederich Wollenweber
Michael Hartlein
John (X) Winder
Phillipp Gotfried Müntz
Jacob Meier
Jno. Jacob (+) Geyer
Johann Philipp Kratzer

Vallintd. Roh[le]ber

Christstofel Gomer

Johans Adam Gomer

Philipp Adam Endler

Johannes Reitzmann

Johan Christoffel Schade

Johann Jacob Schaaff

Phillipp Jacob Schaaff

Frederick (+) Horne

Johann Petter Hane

Johan Marti Frölich

[List 46 A] A List of Palatine Men Passengers of Sixteen Years of Age & Upwards Imported in the Vertuous Grace, Jn° Bull, Master, from Rotterdam & Cowes. [Qualified September 24, 1737.]

	AGES		AGES
Ant^y Reigel	48	Fredr^k Cromer	21
Ant^y Reigel	24	Jacob Stokie	27
Burg^t Reigel	21	Simon Stokie	18
Jacob Shoub	24	Hans Geo^e Deleman	50
Isaac Koffman	55	Hans Jac^b Deleman	20
Hans Koffman	24	Hans Hich^l Ulerich	30
Isaac Koffman	19	Jerome Smitt	18
Hans Geo^e Remel	53	Christ^n Bullinger	44
Jacob Remel	19	Hans Geo^e Konder	31
Martin Hackadore	45	Peter Konder	26
Chris^n Stoupher	28	Rudolph Duckweela	47
Hans Stoupher	20	Jacob Holinger	40
Wm Miller *	22	Peter Stout	26
Jacob Kooler	50	Andreas Sumwald	39
Hans Jacob Kooler	18	Adam Wize	60
Lenhart Hier	40	Abra^m Wize	26
Rudolph Litzer	60	Geo^e Fredrick	45
Barn^d Houp	45	Fred^k Keefa	33
Barn^d Houp	17	Mich^l Ulerich	37
Hans Geo^e Swartz	24	Henr^h Swaart	41
Jacob Swartz	17	Jacob Wolf	30
Jacob Grove	48	Jac^b Bullinger	38
Albrake Grove	18	Adam Teel	28
Bartel Reimie	54	Wm Fisher	28
Simon Shonk	24	Poltser Hartsoe	24
Jacob Remie	18	Christ^n Toll	24
Ludwick Borne	32	Henr^k Shamberger	35

* Name crossed out.

	AGES		AGES
Henr^k Craseman	44	Joan^s Honsacre	21
Jacob Croiter	38	Mich^l Roush	42
David Brook	22	Joan^s Tasher	39
Hans Jurig Meyer	25	Chris^n Bower	17
Jurigen Haug	28	Jacob Howbelare	26
Jacob Conrade	28	Hans Jac^b Inhoft	18
Henr^k Wideaback	40	Chris^n Piner	38
Hans Eatie	55	Simon Honsacre	18
Joan^s Weiss	22	Henr^k Crim	17
Jac^p Springer	32	Mich^l Carlo	30
Henr^k Engel	53	Albert Leebolt	24

Philad^{ia}, the 24th of Sept^r, 1737. A true List.
John Bull.

[List 46 B] Palatines imported in the Ship Virtuous Grace, John Bull, Master, from Rotterdam, but last from Cowes, as by Clearance thence. Qualified the 24th day of September 1737.

Antoni Rüger	Alber[t] Graf
Antoni Reüger	Bartel (B) Reme
Burckhart Rüger	Simon Schunck
Jacob (O) Shaub	Jacob Remy
Isaac (X) Koffman	Ludwig Born
Hans (H) Koffman	Frederick (O) Cromer
Isaac (I) Koffman, Junr	Jacob (X) Stokie
Hans Görg Reimmel	Simon (X) Stokie
Jacob (H) Remel	Hans Jörg Dillman
Mart. Hegendorn	Henrich Jacob Dillman
Christian Stauffer	Hans Michael Ulbricht
Johannes Stauffer	Jeremi^s (X) Smitt
Hans Jacob Groller	Christ^n (CB) Bullinger
Hans Jacob (X) Kobler	Hans Geo. (H) Konder
Leonhart Heier	Peter (H) Konder
Rutolf Lützler	Rudolph (D) Duckweel
Barnard (BHI) Houp	Jacob (H) Hollinger
Barnard (BHI) Houp	Peter (O) Stout
Hantz Görg Schwartz	Andr^s (H) Sumwold
Jacob (Swar) Swartz	Adam Weiss
Jacob Graff	Abraham (A) Wize

Hans Gerg Fried
Friedrich Kieffer
Michel Ullrich
Henrich Schwerdt
Jacob Wolff
Jacob (O) Bullinger
Adam Dill
Wilhelm Fischer
Poltzer (P) Hartsoe
Christoph (H) Toll
Henrich (HS) Shamberger
Henrich Crössman
Jacob (O) Croyter
David Bruch
Hans Jurig (X) Meyer
Gorg Hack
Johann Jacob Conrad

Henrich (O) Wideaback
Han[s] Ytt
Joannes (A) Wize
Jacob (A) Springer
Henrich (H) Engel
Joannes (X) Honsacre
Michael Rausch
Joan^s (O) Tasker
Christian Bauer
Johan Jacob Hubler
Hans Jacob (A) Inhoft
Christ^n (X) Piner
Simon (X) Honsacre
Henrich Grim
Michel Caller
Albert Leboldt

[List 46 C] At the Courthouse of Philad^{ia}, Sept^h 24th, 1737. Present: The Honble James Logan, Esqr, President, Clement Plumsted, Thomas Griffits, Wm Allen.

The Palatines whose Names are underwritten, imported in the Ship Virtuous Grace, John Bull, Master, from Rotterdam, but last from Cowes, did this day take & subscribe the Oaths to the Government.

Antoni Rüger
Antoni Reüger
Burckhart Rüger
Jacob (O) Shaub
Isaac (X) Koffman
Hans (H) Koffman
Isaac (I) Koffman, Junr
Hans Görg Reimmel
Jacob (X) Remel
Martte Hegendorn
Christian Stauffer
Johannes Stauffer
Hans Jacob Goller
Hans Jacob (X) Kooler
Leonhart Heier

Rutolff Lützler
Barnard (BHI) Houp
Barnard (BHI) Houp
Hans Görg Schwartz
Jacob (X) Swartz
Jacob Graff
Albrecht Graf
Bartel (BR) Reme
Simon Schunck
Jacob Rimy
Ludwig Born
Frederick (O) Cromer
Jacob (O) Stokie
Simon (O) Stokie
Hans Jörg Dillman

Henrich Jacob Dillman
Hans Michäl Ulbricht
James (X) Smitt
Christn (CB) Bullenger
Hans Geo (H) Konder
Peter (H) Konder
Rudolph (O) Duckwell
Jacob (H) Hollinger
Peter (O) Stout
Andrs Sunwold
Adam Weiss
Abraham (A) Wize
Hans Jerg Frid
Friedriech Kieffer
Michell Ullrich
Henrich Schwerdt
Jacob Wolf
Jacob (O) Bullinger
Adamm Dill
Wilhelm Fischer
Baltser (P) Hartsoe
Christopr (H) Toll
Henrich (HS) Shamberger

Henrich Crössman
Jacob (O) Croyter
David Bruch
Hans Jurig (X) Meyer
Gorg Hack
Johann Jacob Conradt
Henrich (O) Wideaback
Hans Ytt
Joannes (A) Wize
Jacob (A) Springer
Henrich (H) Engel
Joannes (X) Honsacre
Michael Rausch
Joannes (O) Tasher
Christian Bauer
Jacob Hubler
Hans Jacob (A) Inhoft
Christn (X) Piner
Simon (X) Honsacre
Henerich Grimm
Michell Caller
Albert Leboldt

[List 47 A] [Palatines imported in the Ship St. Andrew Galley, John Stedman, Master from Rotterdam. Qualified Sept., 26, 1737.]

Joh. Diterich Kelsch
Jacob Keim
Jacob Kintzer
Michel Neihart
Lengart Gerling
Jacob Nis
Philip Hefft
Philip Leibengut
Christian Bürger
Wilhm Schefler
Jacob Frist
Philip Frist
Peter Rab

Michel Kortz
Frist Wambolt
Conrad Jost
Caspar Hüter
Valtin Steinmertz
Joh. Aschemus Geroult
Georg Kern
Georg Schisler
Joh. Jacob Schindeldeker
Joh. Stöer
Henrich Stöer
Philip Stöer
Georg Test, absent

Georg Hefft
Jacob Lintz
Joh. Schnauber
Georg Klupinger
Tobias Pekel
Jacob Kuster
Joh. Meyer, sick
Nicolaus Koch
Andreas Schmidt
Jacob Neyschwanger
Joh. Meyer
Christian Meyer
Joh. Meyer
Martin Amweg
Nicolaus Schyre
Nicolaus Bietel
Conrath Reich
Michel Anders
Michel Braun
Georg Wambolt
Georg Schneider
Elias Rägent
Joh. Spycker
Joh. Peter Spycker
Joh. Spycker
Gerhard Hipschman
Jacob Lingel
David Biler
Joh. Mevius
Philip Wismann
Frederich Heim
Ludowig Kolb
Philip Seger
Georg Rahn
Conrath Rahn
Bernard Dickhoff
Philip Schmid
Balser Beil
Jacob Rosemann
Frederich Neihart
Georg Neihart

Joh. Schotter
Georg Kintz
Christian Tron
Matthys Ledermann
Valtin Baumgarter
Lorentz Keyser
Joh. Altenberger
Joh. Erdmann, absent
Joh. Justus Erdmann
Peter Drast
Conrath Wald
Jacob Werry
Henrich Kreyter
Peter Ling
Adolf Henrich
Nicolaus Scharer
Henrich Schmid
Frederich Schmid
Nicolaus Holler
Wilhm Oller
Paulus Lingel
Henrich Wisler
Christoffel Schaub
Laus Kocher
Martin Kocher
Georg Kocher, sick
Albrech Feid
Joh. Streigeler
Ulrich Horn
Peter Weinland
Joh. Appel
Philip Streiter
Martin Cron
Caspar Zeigener
Ludowig Wildangel
Georg Conrath
Jacob Conrath
Daniel Zab
Georg Gist
Jacob Willer
Daniel Zachery

Christoffel Schwenck
Diterich Helt
Ulrich Zolberger
Matthys Weber
Christian Est
Philip Steffen
Caspar Heyser
Hermann Weber
Henrich Mertz
Valtin Düfel
Caspar Rep
Henrich Schefler
Conrath Delb
Joh. Funck
Peter Knepper
Nicolaus Rägent
Ludwig Demer

Joh. Kelbach
Josep Zolberger
Henrich Frantz
Andreas Heit
Adam Strauch
Philip Edinger
Daniel Reist
Nicolaus Reist
Daniel Hister
Jost Hister
Georg Gernand
Joh. Keler
Frederich Schönfelder
Ernst Seidel
Abraham Wagener
Christoffel Hubener
Christoffel Krausen

Philad^ia, Septr 26th, 1737. A true List.
John Stedman.

[List 47 B] Palatines imported in the Ship St Andrew Gally, John Stedman, Master, from Rotterdam, but last from Cowes, as by clearance thence. Qualified the 26th day of September 1737.

Johann Gorg Kelsch
Jacob Kintzer
Michel Neihart
Jacob Nis
Johan Lenhart Jerling
Philip (H) Hefft
Philip (X) Liebengut
Johann Christian Burger
Wilhelm (W) Scheffler
Jacob (F) Fries
Philipp Fritsch
Petter Rapp
Michael (X) Kurtz
Georg Friedrich Wamboldt
Johann Connrad Jost

Caspar Hüter
Valdin Steinmetz
John Asmus (X) Gerling
Jerg Kern
George (S) Shissler
John Jacob (S) Shindeldecker
Johannes Stöhr
Henrich Stöhr
Fillibs Stöhr
Görg Des
Georg (X) Hefft
Jacob (+) Lentz
Johannes Schnauber
Johann Georg Kläppinger
Dobias Böckell

Jacob (K) Kuster
Johannes Meyer
Nicklaus (K) Koch
Andereas (X) Smith
Jacob (+) Neiswanger
Hans Mei[e]r
Christian (X) Meyer
John (X) Meyer, Junior
Hans Mardin Amwäg
Nicklaus (N) Sheyer
Nicolaus Biettel
Conrath Reich
Michael (XX) Anders
Michael (X) Brown
George (+) Wambold
Johan Georg Schneiter
Elias (+) Ratgen
Johannes Spycker
Joh. (X) Spycker
Joh. Peter Spycker
Gerhardt Hübschman
Johann Jacob Lingel
Johann David Bühler
Johannes Mevius
Johann Philipps Wisman
Johann Friedrich Heim
Johann Ludwig Kolb
Johan Philip Seger
Görg Rahn
Konradt Rahn
Bernt Dyckhoff
Filib Schmit
Balser Beil
Johan Jacob Rosenmann
Jerg Fridrich Neihartt
Georg (H) Neihart
Johannes Schotter
Johann Georg Kuntz
Johann Christian Thron
Mattias (L) Lederman

Vallentin (H) Baumgarden
Lorentz Kayser
Johannes Altenberger
Johann Justus Erdmann
Johann Peter Drass
Conrath Walb
Jacob (X) Werry
Henrich (X) Kreiter
Peter Lin[g]
Johann Adolf Henrich
Nicklaus (X) Shererer
Henrich (X) Smith
Frederick (X) Smith
Nickollas Holler
Wilhelm Ohler
Paulus (+) Lingel
Henrich Wissler
Christoph (X) Shaub
Claus Kocher
Martin (M) Kocher
Görg Kocher
Albrächt Fig
Michel Dreigler
Ullerich (V) Horn
Peter (+) Weyland
Johann Philip Streiter *
Martin Cron
Gorg Caspar Zeigener
Johann Ludwig Wildanger
George (HGK) Conrad
Jacob (O) Conrad
Daniel Zopff
Johann Gorg Gist
Johan Jacob Weller
Daniel Zacharias
Christoff Schwenck
Georg Diedrich Helt
Ullrich Sollberger
Mattheis Weber
Christian (E) Eshe

* A Lutheran Minister.

John Philip (H) Steffen
Caspar (X) Heyser
Johann Herman Weber
Johan Henrich Märtz
Valentin Diebel
Caspar (+) Rabe
Henrich (X) Sheffler
Conrad (O) Delp
John (HF) Funck
Peter (X) Knepper
Nicklaus (R) Rattge
Georg Ludwig Demer
Johannes Geltlach
Joseph (O) Zollberger
Henrich Frantz

Andreas (AH) Heit
Adam (+) Strunch
Johann Philip Edinger
Daniel (X) Reis
Nicklaus (X) Reis
Jost Hüsterr
George Gernandt
Johannes Köhler
Friederich (O) Shenfelder
Ernst Seydel
Abraham Wagner
Christoff Hübner
Christop Krause
Joh. Herm. von Basten *
Candidatus S. Th.

[List 47 C] At the Courthouse of Philad^ia, Septem^r 26th, 1737.

Present

The Honble James Logan, Esqr President,
Clement Plumsted, Ralph Assheton ⎫ Esq^rs
William Allen ⎭

The Palatines whose Names are underwritten, imported in the Ship Saint Andrew Galley, John Stedman, Master, from Rotterdam, but last from Cowes, did this day take & subscribe the Oaths to the Government.

Johann Geörg Kölsch
Jacob Kintzer
Michel Neihart
Jacob Niss
Johan Lenhart Jerling
Philip (H) Hefft
Philip (+) Liebengut
Johann Christian Burger
Wilhelm (W) Scheffler

Jacob (X) Frize
Phillip Fritsch
Petter Rapp
Michael (H) Kortz
Georg Heinrich Wamboldt
Johann Conrad Jost
Casper Hüter
Valdin Steinmetz
John Asmus (+) Gerling

* A Dutch Reformed minister. See Corwin, *Manual of the Reformed Church in America*, 4th ed., 1902, p. 807. Another Reformed minister on this ship, although his name does not occur in the list (probably because he was sick when he landed) was the Rev. Peter Henry Dorsius, who preached in Bucks County, from 1737–1748. See the editor's sketch of Dorsius, in *Papers of Bucks County Historical Society*, Vol. V, pp. 44–67.

Jerg Kern
George (S) Schissler
John Jacob (Sch) Schendeldeker
Johannes Stöhr
Henrich Stöhr
Fillibs Stöhr
Görg Des
George (X) Hefft
Jacob (X) Lentz
Johannes Schnauber
Johann Geör Kläppinger
Dobias Böckell
Jacob (K) Kistler
Johannes Meyer
Nicolaus (K) Koch
Andreas (X) Smitt
Jacob (X) Nysswanger
Hans Meir
Christian (X) Meyer
Johann (+) Meyer
Hans Marden Amwäg
Nicolaus (N) Scheyer
Nicolaus Biettel
Conrath Reich
Michael (XX) Andreas
Michael (X) Brown
George (+) Wambold
Johan Georg Schneiter
Elias (+) Rathen
Johannes Spycker
Joh. (X) Spycker
Joh. Peter Spycker
Gerhardt Hübschman
Joh. Jacob Lingel
Johann David Bühler
Johannes Mevius
Johann Philipps Wisman
Johann Friderich Heim
Johann Ludwig Kolb
Johan Philip Seger
Görg Rahn

Konrad Rahn
Bernt Dyckhoff
Filib Schmidt
Balser Beil
Johan Jacob Rosenmann
Jerg Fridrich Neihartt
George (H) Niehart
Johannes Schotter
Johann Georg Küntz
Johann Christian Thron
Matthias (O) Lederman
Valentine (H) Bumgartner
Lorens Kayser
Johanes Altenberger
Johann Justus Erdmann
Johann Peter Dross
Conraht Walb
Jacob (X) Werry
Henrick (X) Kreyter
Peter Lin
Johann Adolf Henrich
Nicolaus (X) Scharer
Henrich (X) Smitt
Frederick (X) Smitt
Nickollas Holler
Willhelm Ohler
Paulus (+) Lingel
Henrich Wisler
Christopher (X) Schaub
Claus Kocher
Martin (M) Kocher
Jörg Kocher
Albräht Fig
Johanes Dreigler
Ulrick (V) Horn
Peter (+) Weyland
Johann Philipp Streidter
Martin Cron
Görg Casper Zeigner
Johann Ludwig Wildanger
George (HGK) Conrath

Jacob (O) Conrath	Nicolaus (R) Rattge
Daniel Zopff	Georg Ludtwig Demer
Johann Gorg Gist	Johannes Geltlach
Johan Jacob Weller	Joseph (O) Zolberger
Daniel Zacharias	Henrich Frantz
Christoff Schwenck	Andreas (AH) Hiet
Georg Diedrich Helt	Adam (+) Strantch
Ullrich Sollberger	Johann Philip Edinger
Christian (E) Heshe	Daniel (X) Riest
Mattheis Weber	Nicolaus (X) Riest
John Philip (H) Steffen	Jost Hüster
Casper (X) Heyser	George Gernandt
Johann Herman Weber	Johannes Köhler
Johan Hennrich Märtz	Frederick (O) Schenfelder
Velentin Diebel	Ernst Seydel
Casper (X) Rabe	Abraham Wagner
Henrich (+) Schieffler	Christoph Hübner
Conrad (O) Delp	Christoph Krause
Joann (HF) Funck	Joh. Herm. von Basten,
Peter (+) Knepper	Candidatus S. Th.

[List 48 A] Acco^t of Men Passengers on board the Townsend, Thomas Thompson, from Amsterdam. [Qualified October 5, 1737.]

Trission Ewig	Valentin Henneberger
Johan Deterwilt	Simon Ersame
Georg Engel	Anthony Highley
Conraed Holber	Hans Georg Frederik
Conraed Lauterbach	Hans Geo. Kraus
Peter Lauterbach	Jacob Acher
Johan Georg Joh	Balthasar Sies
Johan Casper Nayn	Hans Michel Finter
Joan Georg Hecks	Peter Rausch
Peter Shaad	Vallentin Kieffer
Johan Georg Eyler	George Spengel
Jacob Vogel	Johannes Kistler
Johan Carbo	Andreas Kammener
J. Casper Bremaur	Vincent Kaffer
Eberhart Geswint	Peter Marsteller
Johan Adam Filtzneyer	Hans Georg Eheman

Anthony Himberler
Hans Geo Mayntzer
Andrew Apple
Wendel Zwekseer
Hans Matthias Pheyl
Georg Schutz
Conraed Prys
John Jacob Sower
Leonard Kuyel
Georg Arnold
Georg Frederick Arnold
Johanis Slegel
Christian Asbecke
Martin Phateichen
Conraed Reinhard
Egitias Hoffman
Christian Frederick
Elias Obelhart
Johan Step^n Bernhart
Peter Graaff
Ludwig Frantz
Geo Casper Fensler
Hans Geo. Brey
Casper Wendal, sick

Michael Palmer
Hans Meligor Heneberger
Mattias Gebbert
John Mich. Kirber
Frantz Wilhelm
Johan Barthold
Vallentin Hemmelberger
Peter Wagner
John Peter Bonnet
John Slyger
Johannes Gefeller
Conrad Ripper
Jon Peter Yslow
Peter Gordner
Johan Adam Divanbach
Johannes Lowra
Johan Georg Seyger
Jacob Shantz
Bastian Besh
John Henry Sleyger
Silvester Holvert
George Casper Fernsler
In all 231 persons.

Philad^{ia} October 5th, 1737. A true List,
Thos. Thompson.

[List 48 B] Palatines imported in the Ship Billinder Townshend, Thomas Thompson, Master, from Amsterdam, but last
from Cowes, as by Clearance thence. Qualified the 5th day of
October 1737.

Christian (O) Ewig
Johan Peter (✕) Wild
Geo. Engel
Conrath Holbe
Conrad Lauterbach
Peter Lauderbach
Johan Jerg Joh

Johan Casper Neun
Johann Görg Hyx
Peder Schad
Johan Georg Euler
Jacob Vogel
Jean Corbo
Johann Casber Premauer

Eberhart (X) Geschwind
Johann Adam Filtzmeior
Vallentin (X) Henneberger
Christian (KF) Friedrich
Simon (X) Ersame
Anthon (+) Higler
Hans Georg Friedrich
Hans Georg (X) Kraus
Jacob (XXX) Acoer
Balthasar Süsz
Michel Finter
Peter (HPR) Raush
Vallendin Kieffer
Jerg Spengel
Johannes (X) Kistler
Andreas Cammerer
Vincent (II) Caffer
Petter Mahrsteller
Hans Jerg Ehemann
Anthony (A) Hempele
Han[s] Georg Meintzer
Caspar (KW) Wendle
Andreas Epple
Wendel Zwicker
Hanns Matthes Pfeill
George (G) Shutz
Conrad Preiss
Johan Jacob Sauer
Leonhard (X) Kugel
Georg Arnoldt
Görg Friedrich Arnolt

Johannes Schlegel
Christian Aspeck
Mardin Pfatteicher
Conrad (X) Reinhart
Johann Egidius Hoffman
Elias (X) Obelhart
Johann Stäffen Bernhardt
Pedter Graff
Ludwig Frantz
Hans Georg (H) Brey
Michael Balmer
Hans Melchior (H) Henneberger
Matteis Gilbert
Johann Michael Körber
Johann Frantz Wilhelm
Johann Philip de Bertholt
Peter Wagner
Johan Peter (X) Bonnet
Johan (SH) Shliger
Johannes (X) Gefeller
Conrad (+) Reppert
Johann Peter Yserloh
Petter Gotener
Johann Martin Dieffenbacher
Johannes (X) Lowra
Johan Geo. Seger
Jacob Schantz
Sebastian (BIB) Bish
Silvester Holbe
Georg Casper Fernsler

[List 48 C] At the Courthouse of Philad^ia, October 5th, 1737.

Present
The Honble James Logan, Esqr, President
Ralph Assheton,   Thomas Griffitts
Samuel Hasell

The Palatines whose Names are underwritten, imported in the Billender Townshend, Thomas Thompson, Master, from

Amsterdam, but last from Cowes, did this day take and subscribe the Oaths to the Government.

Christiaen (O) Ewig
Johan Peter (×) Welt
Gorg Engel
Conrat Holbe
Conrade Lauterbach
Peter Lauderbach
Johan Jerg Joh
Johann Casper Neun
Johann Görg Hyx
Peder Schad
Johan Gorg Euler
Jacob Vogel
Jean Corbo
Johann Casbar Bremauer
Eberhart (+) Geswint
Johann Adam Filtzmeior
Valentine (×) Himmelberger
Simon (+) Ersame
Anthony (+) Highler
Hans Georg Friederich
Hans Georg (×) Kraus
Jacob (×××) Acker
Balthasar Süsz
Michel Finter
Peter (HPR) Raush
Valentin Kieffer
Jerg Spengel
Johannes (O) Kistler
Andreas Cammerer
Vincent (V) Kaffer
Petter Mahrsteller
Hans Jerg Ehemann
Anthony (| | |) Hempele
Hans Georg Meitzer
Andreas Epple
Wendel Zwicker
Hans Mattahis Pfeill
Georg (O) Schutz

Conrad Preis
Johann Jacob Sauer
Leonard (×) Kugel
Georg Arnoldt
Georg Friedrich Arnoldt
Johannes Schlegel
Christian Aspeck
Mardin Pfatteicher
Conrad (×) Reinhart
Johann Egidius Hoffman
Elias (×) Obelhart
Johan Stefan Bernhardt
Petter Graff
Ludwig Frantz
Hans George (H) Brey
Michael Balmer
Hans Melchior (H) Henneber
ger
Matteis Gilbert
Johann Michael Kärber
Johann Frantz Wilhelm
Johann Philipp De Berthold
Peter Wagner
Johan Peter (×) Bonnet
Johan (SH) Shliger
Johannes (+) Gefeller
Conrad (+) Reppert
Johann Peter Yserloh
Peter Gottener
Johann Martin Dieffenbacher
Johannes (+) Lowrer
Johann Gorg Seger
Jacob Schantz
Sebastian (B) Bish
Balthasar Holben
George Casper Fernsler
Christian (KF) Friedrich
Caspar (KW) Wendell

[List 49 A] A List of People of the Charming Nancy, Charles Stedman, Com^r from Rotterdam. [Qualified October 8. 1737.]

Hans Georg Getts, sick
Martin Baker
Hans Pieter Schip, sick
Hans Pieter Bergant
Johannes Beltzer
Michael Sommer
Johan Ludwig Heger
Abraham Dannahawer, sick
Hans Georg Dannahawer, sick
Andreas Siegler
Hans Stephen Conradt
Georg Mich^l Wollinger, sick
Leonard Resnor, sick
Hans Georg Hais
Henrich Hais
Hans Georg Hais, Junr
Hans Pieter Conder
Hans Jacob Shoemaker
Jacob Houbely
Hans Martin Risiger
Godlieb Risiger
Hendrick Foltz
Heronimus Eberlie
Hans Jacob Fackler
Georg Mentz
Jacob Sontag
Jacob Sontag, Junr
Johannes Grout
Philip Hertzer
Christian Geyger
Hans Jacob Bowman
Martin Frank
Hans Jacob Kauffman
Hendrick Carlo
Christian Habbecker
Joseph Habbecker
Hans Jacob Habbecker

Jacob Schantz
Hans Schantz
Hans Garber
Hans Garber, Junr
Johannes Holl
Hans Kauffler, sick
Henrich Kauffler
Isaac Holl
Vindle Holl
Hermanus Orendoff
Tielman Wespach
Mathias Hoffman
Christian Lichtie
Hans Wengar
Peter Espacher
Christian Kortz
Hans Mich^l Pointz
Jacob Miller
Abraham Miller
Christian Miller
Valantine Young
Johan Hend^k Grim
Johan Joost Konst
Hans Georg Baker
Benedict Leman
Hans Timmerman
Daniel Zacherias
Jacob Underkauffer
Jacob Biler
Jacob Masht
Michael Zurchen
Ulrigh Spigher
Christian Hersberge
Nicholas Schriver
Elias Schriver
Christian Burkie
Peter Bruiker

Glaus Erbe

Hans Erbe

Glaus Erbe, Jun[r]

Jacob Wilhelm Nice

Herman Younkham

Johan Jacob Wetzel

Valantine Haan

Adam Feller

Fredrick Hoffman

Hans Georg Jieliga Fritz

Jacob Dester

Jacob Dester, Jun[r]

Abraham Haan

Andreas Hagabuck

Mathias Riger

Hans Georg Kiebler

Johan Peter Brander

Peter Lowman

Jacob Rys

Christian Gros

Johan Gross

Lawrentz Nolf

Vindle Henrich

Georg Lodwick Waganer

Titrich Ouler

Fredrick Ouler

Baltzar Huber

Andreas Weber

Christophel Craut

Georg Hendrick Ansparger

Hans Philip Kyser

Johan Mathias Albricht

Georg Fyt Cap

Johannes Keler

Peter Freydinger

Hans Jacob Streckler

Ulrich Streckler

Jacob Philip Forman

Jacob Schop

Christophel Acker

Thomas Peary

Johannes Bowman

Hans Mich[l] Dunts

WOMEN & CHILDRENS NAMES

Maria Magdalena Beltzeer

Catrina Eliza Somer

Urcilla Dannahower

Abraham Dannahower

Anna Maria Dannahower

Maria Dorothea Dannahower

Anna Barbra Shedlerie

Dorothea Hais

Barbara Hais

Catrina Hais

Anna Maria Shoemaker

Paul Shoemaker

Georg Shoemaker

Anna Maria Shoemaker

Catrina Houbely

Eva Houbely

Maria Risiger

Martin Risiger

Magdalena Fackler

Adam Fackler

Barbara Fackler

Eva Margareta Mentz

Maria Margareta Mentz

Eva Margareta Mentz

Catrina Sontag

Johan Lodwig Sontag

Wilhelm Gayger

Barbara Gayger

Magdalena Becker

Catrina Blawami

Barbara Kauffman

Anna Maria Kauffman

Joseph Carlo

Maria Hauserin

Anna Habbecker

Frena Souterin

Catrina Habbecker

Magdalena Habbecker

Maria Habbecker

Catrina Schantz

Barbara Schantz

Catrina Schantz

Elizabetha Schantz

Ferona Schantz

Christian Schantz

Magdalena Schantz

Anna Eliza Kauffler

Barbara Holl

Hans Leeman

Abraham Holl

Anna Marg^a Orondoff

Eliza Bossart

Johanna Wagshiter

Anna Swalla

Joseph Wenger

Eliza Espacher

Christophel Espacher

Barbara Miller

Elizabetha Znydering

Ferona Leman

Barbara Leman

Benedict Leman

Catrina Leman

Barbara Timmerman

Anna Timmerman

Ferona Biler

Barbara Biler

Anna Biler

Christopher Biler

Maria Biler

Elizabeth Biler

Barbara Masht

Catrina Lichtie

Barbara Smel

Maria Spigher

Justina Zurchen

Barbara Hersberge

Anna Hersberge

Peter Hersberge

Maria Eliza Schriver

Heneretta Schriver

Johan Georg Schriver

Philip Schriver

Catrina Burkie

Anna Bruiker

Hans Bruiker

Barbara Bruiker

Anna Bruiker

Catrina Erbe

Anna Erbe

Jacob Erbe

Catrina Erbe

Christian Erbe

Christophel Erbe

Barbara Nice

Anna Barbara Nice

Barbara Feller

Elizabeth Hoffman

Fredrick Hoffman

Appellonia Iliga Fritz

Hans Georg Hilliga Fritz

Magdalena Hagabuck

Barbara Righer

Eva Margareta Righer

Wilhelm Righer

Eva Dorothea Kievler

Maria Eve [Kievler]

Margareta Lorman

Catrina Lorman

Margareta Lorman

Maria Hannah Lorman

Agnes Reys

Anna Maria Nolf

Elizabetha Nolf

Margareta Nolf

Diana Henrich

Margareta Waganer

Maria Magdalena Albricht

Maria Margareta Albricht

Georg Martin Capp
Urdow Leren
Eva Maria Keler
Anna Catrina Strickler
Barbara Strickler
Anna Strickler
Juliana Forman

Catrina Schop
Anna Margareta Bowman
Christina Bowman
Hans Jacob Bowman
Elizabetha Bowman
Anna Mussellmann
132.

Philad^{ia}, Oct. 8th, 1737. A true List.
Charles Stedman.

[List 49 B] Palatines imported in the Ship Charm^g Nancy, of London, Charles Stedman, Master, from Rotterdam, but last from Plymouth, as by Clearance thence. Qualified the 8th day of October, 1737.

Hans Jerg Götz
Johann Martin Becher
Hans Philipp Schilp
Hans Peter Barngardt
Johannes Beitzel
Michael Somer
Johann Ludwig Heger
Andreas Ziegler
Hans Jörg Heiss
Johan Heinrich Heiss
Johan Steffen Konrat
Hans Georg Heiss
Hanns Peter Kuder
Jacob Schuhmacher
Jacob Hubele
Hans Martin (✕) Reisinger
Gottlieb Reisinger
Heinrich Voltz
Hieronymus Eberle
Hans Jacob Fackler
Jacob Sontag
Jacob Sontag
Johannes Krauth
Johann Philip Oetzer
Christian Geiger

Jacob Bauman
Martin Funck
Hans Jacob Kauffman
Hans Karli
Christian Hapeger
Jerg Müntz
Yoseph Habegr
Hans Jacob (✕) Habbecker
Jacob Schantz
Hans Schantz
Hans Gerber
Hans (H) Gerber, Senior
Hanes (H) Holl
Henry (✕) Koffel
Isaac Holl
Wennel Holl
Hermanus (✕) Orendorf
Thielmannus Weschenbach
Matteis (✕) Hoffman
Christian (✕) Lichte
Hans Wenger
Peter (E) Eshbacher
Christian (CK) Kortz
Hans Michael (+) Punch
Jacob (+) Miller

Abraham Müller
Christian Müller
Vallentin Jung
Johann Jost Kuns
Bendict (XX) Lehman
Hans (X) Timmerman
Danniegel Zacharis
Jacob Underkoffler
Jacob Beiler
Jacob (XX) Mast
Michael (O) Zurger
Ullerik (O) Spiker
Christian (+) Hertzberger
Nicolaus Schreiber
Elias Schreiber
Christian Burcki
Peter (P) Bruker
Glaus Erb
Johan Erb
Glaus Erb, Jr.
Jacob Wilhelm Weiss
Johan Herman Junghen
Johann Jacob Wetzel
Johann Vallentin (+) Haan
Adam Gefeller
Frederick (+) Hoffman
Johann Georg Ilgenfritz
Jacob (X) Dester
Johann Jacob Dester, Junior
Abraham Haan

Andreas Hagenbuch
Mattias (X) Richart
Hans Jörg Kübler
Johann Diederich Branner
Peter Lohrman
Jacob Raisch
Christian Gross
George Gross
Lorentz Nolf
Wendel Heinrich
Görg Ludwig Wagner
Dieterich Uhler
Vallentin Uhler
Balthasar Huber
Andreas Weber
Christoph Krauth
Jerg Henrich Ernsperger
Johan Mathias (X) Albrecht
Georg Fyt (X) Cap
Johannes Köhler
Peter Freydinger
Hans Jacob Strickler
Ulrich Strickler
Georg Philipp Fuhrmann
Jacob Schopff
Christophel Ecker
Doms Spieri
Johannes (H) Bowman
Jörg Michel Duntz

[List 49 C] At the Courthouse of Philad^ia, October 8th 1737.
Present
The Honble James Logan, Esqr, President,
Samuel Hasell, Thomas Griffitts, Esqr
William Allen.
The Palatines whose Names are underwritten, imported in
the Ship Charm^g Nancy of London, Charles Stedman, Master,
from Rotterdam, but last from Plymouth, did this day take &
subscribe the Oaths to the Government.

Hans Jerg Götz

Johann Marthin Becher

Hans Petter Schülpp

Hans Peter Berngardts

Johannes Beitzel

Michel Somer

Johann Ludwig Heger

Andres Ziegler

Hans Jörg Heiss

Johan Heinrich Heiss

Johan Steffen Konr[at]

Hans Jerg Heiss

Hannes Peter Kuder

Jacob Schuhmacher

Jacob Hubele

Hans Martin (×) Reisinger

Gottlieb Reisinger

Heinrich Voltz

Hieronymus Eberle

Hans Jacob Fackler

Jacob Sontag

Jacob Sontag

Johannes Krauth

Johon Philib Ortzer

Christian Geger

Jacob Bauman

Martin Funck

Hans Jacob Kauffman

Hans Merckli [?]

Christian Hapeger

Georg Müntz

Joseb Habegr

Hans Jacob (+) Habbecker

Jacob Schantz

Hans Schantz

Hans Gerber

Hans (H) Gerber

Hans (H) Hole

Hans (+) Koffel

Isaac Holl

Wernel Holl

Hermanus (×) Orendoff

Thiellmannus Weschenbach

Mattheis Hoffman

Christian (+) Lichte

Hans Wenger

Peter (O) Eshbacker

Christian (CK) Kortz

Hans Michael (+) Punch

Jacob (×) Miller

Abraham Müller

Christian Müller

Vallendin Jung

Johan Jost Kuns

Benedict (×) Leman

Hans (×) Zimmerman

Danniel Zacharis

Jacob Underkoffler

Jacob Beiler

Jacob (××) Mast

Michael (Z) Zurger

Ulrich (O) Speiker

Christian (+) Hertzberger

Nicolaus Schreiber

Elias Schreiber

Christian Bürcki

Peter (B) Bruker

Claus Erb

Johanes Erb

Clas Erb, Jr. [?]

Jacob Wilhelm Weiss

Johan Herman Junghen

Johann Jacob Wetzel

Johan Valentine (×) Hoan

Adam Gfeller

Frederick (×) Hoffman

Johann Gorg Ilgenfritz

Jacob (×) Dester

Johann Jacob Dester

Abraham Hann

Andreas Hagenbuch

Matthias (×) Richart

Hans Jorg Kubler
Johann Diederich Branner
Peter Lohrmann
Jacob Raisch
Christian Gross
George Gross
Lorentz Nolff
Wendel Heinrich
Georg Lutwich Wagner
Dieterich Uhler
Vallentin Uhler
Balthasar Huber
Andreas Weber
Christoph Krauth

Jerg Henrich Ernsperger
Johannes Matthias (✕) Albrecht
George Fyt (✕) Cap
Johannes Köhler
Peter Freydinger
Hans Jacob Strickler
Ulrich Strickler
Geörg Philipp Fuhrmann
Jacob Schöpff
Christopffel Ecker
Tomas Spiri
Joannes (+) Bowman
Jörg Michel Duntz

[List 50 A] A Least of the men Palentens that is on Board
the Ship William, Joⁿ Carter, Comd^r from Amsterdam.
[Qualified October 31, 1737.]

Mekell Riter
Phill Joel Riter
Jacob Pritell
Hance Adam Citle
Wentell Bon
Johannes Shanz
Johannes Madlong
Petter Sheffer
Casper Sorber
Josent Gett
Hendreck Rode
Hendreck Rodt
Danell Ditto
Dietrick Uhl
Hanees Diedrick Uhl
Mathew Switzer
Johannes Mowrer
Gosper Rigger
Hance George Menzer
Johans Frick Muthart
Hans Michll Hower

Jacob Hower
Johans Michell Hower
Johans Michell Gazell
Johans Kuhle
Han^s Petter Howek
Johans Tebald Shalt
Cresten Miller
Johans Nicklas Fisher
Josp^h Fikus
Petter Ditto
Hance George Becholt
Necklows Muffli
Cresten Yaki
Andrew Casinger
Hance Georg Casing^r
George Fythym
Jocb Crom
Erech Adam Hame,* 15 yrs.
Simen Shetle
Johans Hendrech Sekler,* 15
yrs.

* Name crossed out.

Tho. Pouer
Johans Mekell Pultz
Johans Carol Hefley
Johans Balthaz. Rotgaver
Michell Bower
Johans Michell Spigell
Johans Petter Bumgartner
Johans Freydreck Hainholl
George Hendrech Valinten
  Henke
Johans Gasper Zunft
Hance Jocb Faver
Hance Adam Faver
Conraet Brown
Ereh Jocb Bentz
Joshap Keyler

Jocb Krimus
Miethows Smith
Johans Michell Neyss
Tepolt Long
Johans Petter Willums
Jocb Hendreck Wheetman
Johans Wheetman
Johans Erek Bour
Johans Swing
Johans Miller
Johans Conratt Ernst*
Johans Ventel Renst
Basten Wendell Bower
Johans Gerthart Brener †
In all 180 Passengers.

Philad¹ᵃ, Oct. 31ˢᵗ, 1737. A true List.
  Tho. Petterlo, Mett [Mate].
N. B. The Master is confined to Bed by an Indisposition.

[List 50 B] Palatines imported in the Ship William, John Carter, Master, from Amsterdam but last from Dover, as by Clearance thence. Qualified the 31ˢᵗ of October 1737.

Michel Reuter
Philib Jacob Reuter
Jacob (IB) Vechtel
Hans Adam (+) Kletle
Wendel Bohn
Johannes Schantz
Johannes Madlung
Peter (×) Schäffer
Casper Surber
Johannes (+) Gett
Heinrich (+) Rode, Sr.
Heinrich (+) Rode, Jr.

Daniel Rode
Ditrich Uhle
Johan Ditrich Uhle
Mattias (×) Switzer
Johannes Maurer
Caspar (+) Riger
Hans Gerg Meintzer
Johann Friedrich Muthhart
Hans Michel (H) Hauer, Sr.
Jacob Hauer
Hans Michel Hauer
Johan Michel Gasel

---

* Name written on erasure of Renst. The next name ought also to have been changed to Ernst.

† There is a duplicate captain's list, with slightly different spellings, but just as poor, by the same "mett."

Johannes Küchle
Hans Petter Haukh
Johan Thöbalt Schalk
Christian Miller
Johan Nicklaus Fischer
Jost (H) Ficcus
Hans Jorg Becholtt
Nicklaus Mufli
Christian Jagi
Andres Kessinger
Johann Georg Kessinger
George (JVH) Fitheim
Jacob (H) Krom
Siemon (X) Shedel
Thomas (O) Bauer
Johann Michael Boltz
Johan Carl (JK) Haffele
Johan Balthas. Rath[geber]
Michael (O) Bauer
Johann Michel Spiegel
Johann Peter Baumgartner
Johann Friederich Heinnoldt

Georg Heinrich Valentin Hencke
Johann Caspar (X) Zunfft
Hans Jacob (X) Faber
Hans Adam Faber
Conradt Braun
Gorg Jacob Bentz
Joseph (X) Keller
Jacques Creucas
Matthis Schmidt
Johan Michel Neess
Theobald (X) Lange
Johan Peter Wilms
Jacob Heinrich Weidtmann
Johannes Weydtmann
Johann Georg Beyer
Johannes Schwing
Johannes (X) Miller
Johan Conrath Ernst
Johann Wendel Ernst
Sebastian Winderbauer
Hans Gerhardt Brenner

[List 50 C] At the Courthouse of Philad^{ia}, October 31^t 1737.

Present

Thomas Laurence, Thomas Griffitts, Ralph Assheton,
William Allen, one of the Aldermen of the City.

The Palatines whose Names are underwritten, imported in the Ship William, John Carter, Master, from Amsterdam, but last from Dover, did this day take & subscribe the Oaths to the Government.

Michel Reuter
Philib Jacob Reuder
Jacob (IB) Bechtel
Hans Adam (X) Kletle
Wendel Boh[n]
Johannes Schantz
Johannes Madlung
Peter (X) Schäffer

Casper Surber
Johannes (+) Gett
Heinrich (X) Rode
Heinrich Rode
Daniel Rode
Dietrich Uhle
Johan Ditrich Uhle
Matthias (X) Switzer

Johannes Maurer
Casper (X) Reger
Hans Gerg Meintzer
Johann Friederich Muthhadt
Hans Michel (H) Hauer
Jacob Hauer
Hans Michel Hauer
Johan Michel Gasel
Johannes Küchle
Hans Petter Haukh
Johan Thöbald Schalck
Christiann Miller
Johan Nicklaus Fischer
Jost (H) Ficcus
Hans Jerg Becholtt
Nicklaus Mufli
Christian Jagi
Andres Kessinger
Johann Georg Kessinger
George (IVH) Fitheim
Jacob (H) Krom
Simon (S) Shedel
Thomas (O) Power
Johannes Michael Boltz
John Carl (IK) Haffelee
Johan Balthas. Ratthger

Michael (MB) Power
Johann Michel Spiegel
Johann Friederich Heinoldt
Johann Peter Baumgertner
Georg Heinrich Valentin
  Hencke
John Casper (X) Zunfft
Hans Jacob (XX) Faber
Hans Adam Faber
Conradt Braun
Gorg Jacob Bentz
Joseph (X) Keller
Jacques Creucas
Mattheis Schmidt
Johan Michel Nees
Theobald (X) Longe
Johan Peter Wilms
Jacob Heinrich Weidtmann
Johannes Weydtmann
Johann Georg Beyer
Johanes Schwing
Johannes (X) Miller
Johan Conrath Ernst
Johan Wendel Ernst
Sebastian Winderbauer
Johann Gerhardt Brenner

[List 51 B] Palatines imported in the Brigantine Catharine, Jacob Phillip, Master, from London. Qualified the 27th day of July 1738.

Christian Zuegri
Hans (X) Shnider
Hans (H) Booch
Ulrick (XX) Seiler, Senior

Jacob Zuch
Hans (++) Seiler
Ulerick X) Seilor, Junior

[List 51 C] At the Courthouse of Philadia, July 27th 1738.
Present
The Honble George Thomas, Esqr Lieut Governor,
Ralph Assheton, Thomas Griffitts, Esqrs.
The Palatines whose Names are underwritten, imported in

the Brigantine Catherine, Jacob Phillips Master, from London, did this day take and subscribe the Oaths to the Government.

Christian Zuegri
Hans (X) Schneider
Hans (H) Booch
Ulrich (XX) Seiler
Jacob Zuch
Hans (++) Seiler

Ulrich (X) Seiler, Jun[r]
The underwritten did take the affirmation instead of the oaths prescribed by law.
Hans Lux Falkeysen

[List 52 A] A List of all the mens names and ages from sixteen years and upwards Passengers on b[d] y[e] Winter Gally, Edward Paynter, Commander. [Qualified September 5, 1738.]

	AGES		AGES
Jacob Stall	30	Willm Meyer	16
Nichell Elie	27	Philip Wagener	20
Stofell Heller	50	Johan Wagener	16
Simon Heller	17	Peter Wagener	16
Johanis Peter Miller	49	Sebasting Sedelmeyer	50
Johanis Rore	22	Adam Mager	30
Henrich Weyshart	30	Adam Nesh	60
Frans Ludwig Parrott	39	Johan Philip Seebolt	26
Abraham Kirper	38	Rudolph Shler	31
Andres Beyer	57	Hans Michell Hoglander	32
Martin Beyer	18	Johan Miller	32
Hannis Light	56	Conrade Smith	44
Johan Sauvage	40	Philip Bayer	29
Lorance Henn	56	Philip Waber	20
Albreght Eberard	20	Wilhelm Jans	24
Godlief Eberard	18	Jan Peter Hoffman	27
Hans Adam Schreyner	52	Jurg Hoffman	37
Michell Schreyner	28	Henrich Tiech	29
Henrich Eshbay	32	Jacob Bing	50
John Wintell Losschet	30	Andres Bing	24
John Michell Remer	23	Markes Miller	38
Jacob Deeahuse	18	Jacob Bartelme	40
Wintell Draut	49	Nicholas Walter	41
Johanis Barntz	42	Fredrick Haas	21
Ludwick Meyer	20	Frans Seele	17
Martin Meyer	18	Hans Jurg Gerth	43

	AGES		AGES
Henrich Backer	20	Hans Jacob Doodwiler	28
Samuell Mooke	20	Melchior Weis	20
Michael Knap	20	Hans Adam Kinder	24
Matehys Ulrick	28	Adam Wall	21
Fredrick Kraft	52	Andres Fredrick	21
Henrick Landgraaf	20	Jurig Lockmiller	24
Melchior Stall	21	Nicholas Repel	23
Henrick Fehle	27	Andres Stoop	34
Jan Adam Stupe	21	Jacob Miller	22
Johanis Jager	36	Johan Philip Weiker	20
John Henrick Klinger	50	Jacob Wenigh	19
Hans Michell Rushell	26	Jacob Ronk	22
Jurg Joghim	27	Hans Philip Kochler	21
Simon Deck	35	Jurig Faas	23
Philip Beyer	20	Philip Faas	20
Jacob Han	21	Valentine Stucker	19
Peter Burchart	38	Balthasar Sardorious	27
Martin Shriner	20	Christian Janigh	42
Paul Kurgner	40	Valentine Lemerd	50
Johan Dan¹ Freyligh	39	Lorance Balien	24
Michel Brush	19	Jan Daniel Droonberg	21
Augusteen Brush	14	Jacob Zadler	20
Jacob Debell	26	Jacob Back	20
Cristofell Armbrost	28	Fredrick Farion	36
Philip Harlash	22	Stephen Lang	35
Jnº. Christof¹ Wagner	40	Adam Hofman	23
Andreas Hook	35	Jan Garlegillon	45
Willm Best	26	Chaley Garlegillon	19
Casper Berger	30	Isack Viall	29
Daniell Buterfas	19	Georg Ide	30
Jacob Kraft	38	Johanis Begthold	22
Jan Adam Shefer	24	Jan Jacob Beyer	22
Jurig Ernst Linthell	27	Mathias Gentslen	20
Fredrick Haas	24	Henrick Bullinger	28
Willelm Zacharias Andich	18	Fredrick Thronberg	29
Conrad Dust	38	Conrad Estlinger	21
Conrad Zimmerman	22	Henrick Storff	20
Stoffell Urick	25	Hans Michell Matthys	22
Andres Saim	20	Jurg Mich¹ Hittel	23
Jurig Sibert	25	Johanis Kranister	30

	AGES		AGES
Hans Jurig Smith	21	Johanis Ebert	19
Wilm Kelsendorf	17	Jurg Philip Follinger	20
Johanis Lingeredler	20	Paul Brack	21
Ludwick Fillinger	27		

Sworn to Septem^r 5th 1738.
Edwd Paynter.
Account of Number of Palatines in the Ship Winter Galley.
Those [that] took their qualification 139
Number of women & children 113

In all   252 Passengers.

[List 52 B] Palatines imported in the Ship the Winter Galley, Edward Paynter, Com^r, from Rotterdam, but last from Deal. Qualified 5th Sept^r, 1738.

Johann Jacob Stahl
Nickiel (+) Elie
Christop Heller
Simon Heller
Johann Peter Müller
Johannes Roth
Henrich (H) Weishart
Frantz Lutwig Beroth
Abraham Körper
Andras Beir
Martin Beier
Johann Philipp Bayer
Joanes (H) Light
John (IS) Sauvage
Lorentz Heim
Albrecht Eberhart
Gotlieb Eberhart
Hans Adam Schreiner
Johann Michael Schreiner
Johann Henrich Eschbach
Johan Wendel Laschett
Johann Michael Römer
Johann Friedrich Hase

Wenell Trauth
Johannes Berntz
Lodowick (X) Meyer
Johann Maritin Meyer
Johan Wilhellem Mayer
Johann Filip Wagner
Johannes Wagner
Pheider Wagner
Sebastan (X) Zettlemir
H. Adam Mayer
Adam Nicht [?]
Johann Philipp^s Sebollt
Herudoph (X) Slair
Hans Michael (H) Slotsunder
John (X) Miller
Conrad (XX) Smith
Philip (X) Baier
Phillip Weber
Wilhelm Jans
Johann Petter Hoffman
Jerg Hoffman
Henrich (X) Teich
Jacob Bin

Andereas Bin
Markes (| | |) Miller
Jacob Barthelme
Nicholas (N) Waller
Friederich Has
Frantz Seell
Hansier Girt, dumb
Henrich Becker
Samuel Moch
John Michael (X) Knabe
Mathaus Ullrich
Fridrich Kraft
Henrich (X) Landeraf
Melcher (O) Stall
Hendrich (H) Feelt
Adam (+) Stoop
Johannes (O) Yecher
Henrich (X) Klengler
John Michel (J) Rusher
Jerich (X) Yougham
Simon (+) Deck
Philip (X) Beyer, Junr
Jacob Heen
Peter (B) Bucher
Johann Martin Schreiner
Paul (+) Kenned
Johann Daniel Froelich
Johan Michel Preisch
Haugh (X) Spreis
Jacob (O) Tebolt
Christop Armbruster
Philip (H) Halass
Johann Christoff Wagner
Andreas Hook
William (||) Best
Casper (O) Bercher
Daniel Butterfass
Johann Jacob Krafft
Johann Adam Schäffer
Geo. Erd (O) Shindel
Johann Jacob (O) Huss

Wilhelm Zacharias Andich
Conrad (O) Durst
Conrat Zimmerman
Christoph (X) Urich
Andreas Seum
Georg Seiberth
Hans Jacob (+) Hantwell
Johonn Melcher Weiss
Hans Adam Hinder
Adam Wall, sick
Andres (X) Frederick
Geo. Marti (X) Lochiller
Julius Rübell
Georg Andreas Stupp
Johan Jacob Müller
Johann Philibus Wicker
Jacob Venig
Jacob Runck
Hans Philip Köhler
Johann Görg Faas
Johann Philib Faas
Johann Vallentin Stöcker
Joh. Balthasar Sartorius
Lars Palin
Christian Reinard
Johan Vallentin Lennert
Daniel (D) Drumberg
Jacob (S) Saddler
Jan Jacob Beyer
Jacob Beck
Friderich Fahrion
Stephan Lang
Adam Hoffman
Charles (O) Gillion
Claude Charle
Isaac Vial
Johann Georg Hayde
Johannes Bechtolt
Matthias Gensli
Hendrich (H) Bullinger
Friedrich Ambrosius Tranberg

Conrad (×) Etslingher
Henry (+) Sturf
Johan Mattes
Georg Michael Hyttel
Johannes Cranester
Hans Gerg Schmidt

William (×) Getsindorf
Johannes Lingenfelder
Lutwig Fillinger
Johannes Ewert
Georg Philipp Dollinger
Paul Prack

[List 52 C] At the Court House of Philadelphia, Septem^r
5th 1738.

Present
Anthony Palmer, Clement Plumsted, Ralph Asheton,
William Allen, Esq^rs.

The Palatines whose Names are underwritten, imported in
the Ship the Winter Galley, Edward Paynter, M^r, à Rotterdam,
did this day take and subscribe the Oaths to the Government.

Johan Jacob Stahl
Nichol (+) Elie
Christop Heller
Simon Heller
Johann Peter Müller
Johannes Roth
Henry (×) Weishart
Frantz Luthwig Beroth
Abraham Körper
Andres Beier
Martin Beier
Johann Philipps Bäyer
Johanes (H) Lycht
Johan (IS) Savatsh
Lorentz Heim
Albrecht Ebhart
Gottlieb Eberhart
Hans Adam Schreiner
Johann Michael Schreiner
Johann Heinrich Eschbach
Johann Wendel Laschett
Johann Michael Römer
Johann Friedrich Hase
Wenel Trauth
Johannes Berntz

Ludewig (+) Meyer
Johan Martin Meyer
Johan Wilhellem Mäyer
Johann Filipp Wagner
Johannes Wagner
Petter Wagner
Sebastian (+) Zettelmyer
Adam Mayer
Adam Nicht [?]
Johann Philip Sebolltt
Johan (+) Rudolff Sheler
Hans Michael Hochlander
Johan (×) Miller
Conrad (××) Shmit
Philip (×) Beyer
Phillip Weber
Wilhelm Jans
Johann Petter Hoffman
Jerg Hoffman
Henry (×) Tieshe
Jacob Bin
Anderas Bin
Mathes (|||) Miller
Jacob Barthelme
Nicholas (N) Walter

Fridrich Has
Frantz Seell
Hans George Gerth
Henrich Becker
Samuel Moch
Johan Michael (✕) Knabe
Mathaus Ullrich
Fridrich Kraft
Henrich (✕) Landgraff
Melichor (O) Stall
Henry (H) Fehl
Adam (+) Staub
Johannes (O) Jäger
Henry (O) Klingler
Johan Michael (H) Rischel
George (O) Jochem
Simon (✕) Deck
Philip Beyer, Junior
Jacob Heen
Peter (B) Borchart
Johann Martin Schreiner
Paulus (+) Kirchner
Johann Daniel Frelich
Johann Michel Preisch
August (✕) Preusch
Jacob (D) Debalt
Christoff Armbruster
Philip (H) Harlas
Johann Christof Wagner
Andreas Hook
Willhelm (||) Best
Caspar (O) Berger
Daniel Butterfass
Johann Jacob Krafft
Johann Adam Schäffer
George Ernst (O) Zintel
Johann Jacob (O) Huss
Wilhelm Zacharias Andich
Conrad (O) Turst
Conrat Zimmerman
Christoph (+) Urrich

Andreas Seim
[George] Seiberth
Hans Jacob (+) Tattweiller
Johann Melcher Weiss
Hans Adam (O) Hinder
Adam Wall
Andereas (✕) Frederick
Georg Michael (✕) Lochmiller
Julius Rübell
Jeorg Andreas Stupp
Jacob Müller
Johann Philibus Wicker
Jacob Venig
Jacob Runck
Hans Phipp Köhler
Johann Görg Faas
Johann Philib Faas
Johann Vallendin Stöcker
John Balthaser Sartorius
Christian Jenieg
Johann Vallentin Lennert
Lars Palin
Daniel (D) Trumberg
Jacob (O) Sattler
Jan Jacob Byer
Jacob Beck
Friderich Fahrion
Stephen Lang
Adam Hoffman
Charle (O) Gilliom
Claude Charle
Isaac Vial
Johann Georg Hayde
Johannes Bechtolt
Matthias Gensli
Henrich (H) Bullinger
Fridrich Ambrossius Tranberg
Conrad (✕) Oesslinger
Henry (+) Sturff
Johan Miechell Mattes
Georg Michael Hyttel

Johannes Crauester
Hans Jerg Schmidt
Wilhelm (✕) Götzentorff
Johannes Lingenfelder
Lutwig Fillinger

Johannes Ewert
Gerog Philipp Dollinger
Paul Prack
143 [signers]

[List 53 A] A List containing all the Mens Names from 16 Years and upwards, passengers on bᵈ yᵉ Ship Glasgow, Walter Sterling, Commander. [Qualified September 9, 1738.]

	AGES		AGES
Valentine Grance	32	Gotfriet Serwaes	40
Thoˢ Snyder	52	Johanis Ponteus	20
Leonard Glace	30	Johan Nickell Rouse	35
Thoˢ Snyder	20	Johanis Miller	21
Hans Adam Snyder	30	Philip Hanes	46
Dewalt Yrauf	30	Marks Hanes	19
Johan Philip Reale	28	Daniel Snyder	30
Johanis Zinn	31	Johanis Bartelme	38
Philip Jacobs	42	Joanis Drayer	55
Han Jacob Jacobs	16	Henry Walter	33
Nicholas Mook	33	Johan Nickell Fink	29
Peter Mook	25	Bernherd Roug	24
Mathias Finstermacher	60	Carel Leyman	26
Wm. Finstermacher	25	Henry Lorance	34
Johanis Hippell	40	Johan Jacob Sybert	28
Adam Halbert	35	Philip Gibhert	26
Johan David Diel	32	Peter Koch	36
Nickell Fisher	24	Jacob Man	33
Johan Nickell Klee	30	Wm. Doub	35
Deobald Goet	28	Jacob Groub	40
Philip Drum	36	Peter Joost	55
Daniel Stout	45	Wm. Umboure	32
Peter Stout	17	Joanis Joost	17
Hans Nickell Simon	31	Christofˡ Cauffeld	46
Henry Hall	50	Joanis Coons	45
Deobald Glee	26	Wm. Beil	19
Conrad Wolf	19	Nickell Brower	54
Hans Jacob Bernhard	23	Johan Peter Brower	18
Daniel Corell	27	Joob Mittsler	45
Johan Nichell Wolf	26	Conrad Retman	58

	AGES		AGES
Jurg Klein	21	Johan Nickell Michell	42
Jacob Tiel	21	Frederick Michell	17
Jacob Finstermacher	29	Hans Adam Miller	50
Jurg Mill	35	Fredrick Frey	38
Jacob Anspach	25	Hans Adam Schaer	26
Henry Rodobach	42	Frans Carel Hoeyer	20
Philip Conjus	38	Christofer Neyman	17
Bastian Houd	23	Johan Berrier	29
Henry Baumer	50	Christof' Bernherd	23
Johan Adam Baumer	19	Michal Lutsinger	29
Johan Peter Baumer	16	Michal Miller	40
Gelian Noel	46	Frans Giltner	22
Jacob Fries	25	Peter Doub	20
Philip Bartelme	36	Michal Dewald	20
Peter Engle	20	Tho' Garringer	22
Johan Jacob Seibert	20	Johan Adam Hartman	24
Stephen Braun	37	Abraham Heynes	19
Johan Adam Steyn	38	Henry Gernherd	22
Henry Keller	30	Melcher Klaas	32
Hans Peter Oberkeer	33	Albertus Koch	54
William Garhard	40	Michal Maurer	24
Johan Nickell Kygler	30	Martin Wall	33
Leonard Jurg	30	Deobald Weaver	37
Anthony Erford	40	Mathias Stoler	47
Johan Nickell Pik	27	Yeadie Stoler	18
Johan Bobenhuyzer	46	Jurg Stoler	51
Andres Bobenhuyzer	21	Leonard Stoler	22
Adam Huppart	20	Jurg Stoler	20
Johan Koeks	22	Bernherd Dalheymer	20
Johan Nickell Emerrick	36	120 [men]	
Johan Boos	22		

Sworn that the above is a compleat and true List to the best of my knowledge, Sept' 9th 1738.   Walter Stirling.

The whole number of passengers, of men, women & children: Sworn 120, [women & children] 229, [Total] 349.

[List 53 B] Palatines imported in the Ship Glasgow, Walter Sterling, Commander, from Rotterdam, but last from Cowes in England. Qualified the 9th Day of September 1738.

Vallendin Krantz
Tohmas Schneydter
Melchior Clos
Thomas Schneider
Johan Adam Schneider
Johann Phillips Riehl
Erhardt Kles
Johannis (X) Zinn
Philip (O) Jacobs
Nickel Mock
Mathes Fenstermacher
Johan Willem Fenster[macher]
Johannes Huppel
Adam Albert
Johan Debt Diell
Johan Nichles (X) Fisher
Nickel Kleh
Debalt Guth
Phillips Drum
Daniel (O) Stout
Peter (X) Stout
Hans Nikell (+) Simon
Deobald (K) Glee
Conrad Wolf
Jacob Erenhart
Daniel (C) Corell
Johan Nickel Wolff
Gottfrit Zerfass
Johannes Pontes
Johann Nickel Rausch
Johannes (X) Miller
Johan Philip Heintz
Johann Marx Heintz
Daniel (DS) Snyder
Johanes (+) Dreher
Johan Barttelmi
Johann Henrich Wolter
Johann Nickel Finck
Johann Bernhardt Rauch
Carl Neumann
Henry (X) Lowrence

Johan Jacob Seibert
Phillips Gebhart
Peter (+) Gooch
Jacob (H) Man
William (D) Daub
Jacob Krub
Peter (O) Jost
William (W) Munbour
Johannes Jost
Christopher (O) Confeld
Johannes (O) Kunts
Wilhelm Diel
Johan Nicolas (B) Power
Johan Peter (O) Pour
Jost Metzler
Conrad (X) Rabpman
Jeorg (X) Klein
Jacob (++) Tiel
Jacob Finstermacher
Johan George (M) Mill
Hennrich Jacob Anspach
Henry (H) Rodebaugh
Philips Cunius
Sebastian Haubt
Heinerich Bömmer
Johann Adam Bömmer
Kilian (O) Null
Jacob Fries
Filib Bartelmeh
Peter Engell
Steffan Brun
Johan Adam (+) Steyn
Johann Henrich Keller
Johann Peter Oberkehr
Johann Wilhelm Gerhartt
Leonard (+) Jerich
Anthony (O) Serford
Johan Nickel Pick
Johannes (X) Bobenhuyzen
Andreas Bobenheisser
Johann Adam Hubert

Johannes Guckes
Johann Nickel Emrich
Johannes Boos
Johann Nickel Michel
Johann Friedrich Michel
Hans Adam Miller
Johan Diether Frey
Hans Adam (X) Shade
Frantz Carel Hüget
Johann Christoffel Neumann
Johannes Berger
Christopher (X) Bernherd
Michel (M) Lutsinger
Michael (O) Miller
Frantz Gildner

Peter (X) Daub
Michel Dobalth
Thomas (X) Garinger
Johan Adam (X) Hartman
Abraham (O) Hinds
Hinrich Gernhardt
Albertos Kuch
Michgel Maurer
Martin (H) Wall
Debalt Weber
Mathias (+) Stoler
Görg Stoler
Gerg Stoler
Bernhart Stohler
Bernd Dahlheimer

[List 53 C] At the Courthouse of Philadelphia, September 9th, 1738. Present The Honourable George Thomas, Esqr, Lieutenant Governour, Thomas Griffits, Esqr.

The Palatines whose Names are underwritten, imported in the Ship Glasgow, Walter Sterling, Comr, and the Snow Two Sisters, James Marshall, Comr, but both last from Cowes in England, did this Day take and subscribe the Oaths to the Government, Viz.,

IN THE SHIP GLASGOW

Vallendin Kranz
Tohmas Schneyder
Melchior Closs
Thomas Schneider
Erhardt Kles
Johan Adam Schneider
Johann Philips Riehl
Johannes (X) Zinn
Philip (O) Jacobs
Nickel Mock
Mathes Finstermacher
Wilhelm (F) Fenstermacher
Johannes Huppel

Adam Albert
Joann Debt Diell
Johan Nicklas (X) Fischer
Nickel Kleh
Debalt Guth
Phillips Drum
Daniel (O) Stautt
Peter (X) Stautt
Hans Nicklas (+) Simon
Theobald (X) Klee
Conrad Wolf
Jacob Ehrenhart
Daniel (C) Cuval
Johan Nickel Wolff
Gottfrit Zerfass

Johannes Pontes
Johann Nicklaus Rausch
Johanns (X) Miller
Johan Philip Heintz
Johann Marx Heintz
Daniel (DS) Shnider
Johann Bartelme
Johanes (+) Dreher
Johann Henrich Wolter
Johann Nickel Fink
Johann Bernhardt Rauch
Carl Neumann
Henry (X) Lowrentz
Johan Jacob Seibert
Philip Gebhart
Peter (X) Koch
Jacob (H) Mann
Wilhelm (D) Daub
Jacob Grub
Peter (O) Jost
William (W) Mombauer
Johannes Jost
Christopher (O) Kauffeld
Johannes (O) Kunst
Wilhelm Diel
Johan Nicklas (O) Bauer
Johan Peter (B) Bauer
Jost Metzler
Conrad (+) Rebman
Georg (X) Klein
Jacob (XX) Thiel
Jacob Finstermacher
Johann Georg (M) Mill
Henrich Jacob Anspach
Henrich (H) Radebach
Philips Cunius
Sebastian Haupt
Heinerich Bömmer
Johann Adam Bömmer
Killian (O) Null

Jacob Fries
Fillib Barthelmeh
Peter Engell
Steffe Brun
Johan Adam (+) Stein
Johann Henrich Keller
Johann Peter Oberkehr
Johan Wilhelm Gerhart
Leonhart (X) George
Anthony (O) Erffurt
Johan Nickel Pick
Johanes (X) Bobenheuser
Andreas Bobenheisser
Johann Adam Hubert
Johannes Guckes
Johann Nickel Emrich
Johannes Boos
Johann Nickel Michel
Johan Fridrich Michel
Hans Adam (A) Miller
Johan Dietter Frey
Hans Adam (X) Shade
Frantz Carle Hüget
Johann Christoffel Neuman
Johannes Berger
Christopher (X) Bernhart
Michael (M) Luzinger
Michael (O) Miller
Frantz Gildner
Peter (X) Daub
Mich. (O) Deobalt
Thomas (X) Gerringer
Johann Adam (X) Hartman
Abraham (O) Heintz
Henrich Germertt [?]
Albertus (XX) Koch
Michgel Maurer
Martin (H) Wall
Debalt Weber
Mattias (+) Doller

Gorg Stoler   Bernhart Stohler
Gerg Stoler   Bernernd Dahlheimer*

[List 54 A] A List of all the Palatine Passengers on Board
the Snow Two Sisters, James Marshall, Master, from Rotterdam, last from Cowes in England. [Qualified September 9,
1738.]

	AGES		AGES
Hans Windal Hooft	28	Joh⁵ Hendrick Rydlestack	40
Christⁿ Snyder	32	Hans Wᵐ Wensil	35
Hans Jorick Wagener	34	Philip Smitt	28
Hans Adam Heylman	24	Simon Cruysmeyer	20
Johˢ Tottinger	40	Mathias Keygar	35
Johˢ Wildermoad	20	Baldus Barret	40
Melchior Shertly	55	Hans Jerick Coon	37
Hans Adam Zigler	20	Johanˢ Mirkle	26
Tidrick Benedick	30	Woolf Fangewer	24
Johans Tolder	36	Leonard Revor	32
Woolf Bruyn	45	Johˢ Hendrick Meyer	24
Hans Jerick Graizer	50	Hans Michael Rise	22
Jacob Houser	25		
Hans Marthel Holder	24	WOMEN	
Casparus Holder	26	Catherina Hooften	24
Hans Jerick Ireman	37	Anna Elizabeth Hooften	27
Philip Frederick	40	Anna Maria Hooften	30
Hans Martin Brininger	35	Anna Maria Shertly	40
Johˢ Godlief Brininger	33	Anna Barbara Shertly	32
Michael Easterly	20	Barbara Tolder	34
Bliker Tidrick Zeyler	24	Barbara Brininger	28
Hans Jerick Brandel	28	Anna Shenk	40
Hans Peter Bricker	32	Anna Greiser	37
Andreas Fry	40	Anna Eva Greiser	26
Johˢ Philip Brandel	20	Maria Christina Greiser	33
Leonard Notz	38	Susannah Catharina Greiser	29
Hendrick Funk	36	Maria Margᵗ Ireman	32
Johˢ Joho	37	Maria Herten	39
Christⁿ Everhart	46	Anna Bareble	34

* In the original, List 54 C follows immediately. We have placed it with the
other lists of the Snow Two Sisters, see p. 211.

	AGES		AGES
Elizth Brininger	30	Hans Peter Zeyler	15
Maria Dyer	52	Magdalen Fisher	5
Eliz. Catherina Dyer	32	Catharina Fisher	8
Maria Dorothy Dyer	28	John Hendrick Brandel	11
Barbara Pickering	34	Anna Leonard	5
Catharina Notz	37	Hans Leonard	7
Anna Funk	31	Hans Keygar	7
Marg^t Boamining	26	Barbara Otting	13
Susanna Joho	44	Hans Michael Coon	8
Christian Leonard	50	Andreas Hoover	15 *
Anna Everhart	42	Christⁿ Elizth Swartzen	10
Anna Rydlestack	26	Hans Jacob Holder	12
Anna Keyger	37	France Joseph Ileshever	12
Magdalen Switzen	34	Hans Martha Herten	10
Veronica Coon	47	Jerick Frederick	6
		Eva Knurring	6
CHILDREN—HALF FREIGHTS		Hendrick Fry	12
John William Syman	6	Martha Fry	9
Melchior Rugh	9	Jacob Fry	6
Maria Smitzon	11	Maria Fry	5
John Smitzen	5	Anna Fry	4
Tidrick Shoup	7	Dorothy Notz	4
Ludewick Ileshever	12	Hans Gruve	10
Maria Shoupen	13	Peter Gruve	8
Hans Peterly	15	Anna Greoffin	4
Maria Uliger	9	Veronica Greoffin	9
Anna Margaret Zigler	4	Hannah Rydlestack	10
Christian Shenk	15	41 [men] 30 [women] 39 [chil-	
Jacob Dier	14	dren] [Total] 110	

Sworn that the above is a true and compleat list to the best of my knowledge.
Sepr 9th 1738.

James Marshall.

[List 54 B] Palatines imported in the Snow Two Sisters, James Marshall, Commander, from Rotterdam, but last from Cowes in England. Qualified the 9th Day of September 1738.

* This Andreas Hoover has recently been proved to have been the ancestor of President Herbert C. Hoover. See *National Genealogical Society Quarterly*, Vol. XVIII (1929), p. 7; also pp. 53–56.

Hans Wendel Heft
Christoffel Schneitter
Hans Jörg Wagner
Hans Adam Heylman
Johannes (X) Detinger
Johannes Wildermuth
Melcher Scherdle
Hans Adam (X) Zigler
Titrick (X) Benedict
Johannes (X) Solder
Woolf (X) Braun
Hans Jerich (X) Graiser
Jacob Hauser
Hann Martin Halter
Casper Halter
Hans Jerich (X) Jerman
Philip (X) Fredrick
Johann Gottlieb Breuninger
Hans Martin (X) Brininger
Michael (X) Easterly
Michael Frederick (X) Zeyler

Hans Peter Brücker
Andreas (X) Fry
Johan Phillip Brendel
Lenhart Notz
Heinrich Funk
Johannes (X) Johe
Christian (X) Everhart
Johan Hendrick (X) Hyden-
reich
Johann Willm Wentzel
Philip (X) Smit
Simon (X) Cruysmeyer
Mathias (X) Keyker
Balthas Bahret
Hans Jerick (X) Cran
Johannes Merkhel
Johann Wolfgang Unger[er]
Johann Leonhardt Reber
Johann Henrich Meyer
Hans Michel Reiss

[List 54 C. Passengers imported in the Snow Two Sisters, James Marshall, Master, from Rotterdam. Qualified Sept. 9, 1738.]

Hans Wendel Hefft
Christoffel Schneitter
Hans Jörg Wagner
Hans Adam Heylman
Johanes (X) Duttinger
Johannes Wildermuth
Melcher Scherdle
Hans Adam (X) Zigler
Ditterich (X) Bendict
Wolffgang (X) Brown
Jacob Hauser
Martin Halter
Casper Halter
Philip (X) Friederich
Gottlieb Breuninger

Hanns Martin Breunger
Hans Michael (X) Oesterly
Blenhart Dit. (X) Saillor
Hans Jörg Brendel
Hans Peter Brücker
Anderas (X) Frey
Johan Philip Brändel
Lönhart Notz
Heinrich Funck
Johann Willm Wentzel
Philip (X) Shmit
Simon (X) Crysmeyer
Mattias (X) Geiger
Balthas. Bahret
Hans Georg (X) Gunn

Johannes Merkhel   Johann Henrich Meyer
Johann Wolfgang Ungerer   Hans Michel Reiss
Johann Leonhardt Reber

[List 55 A] A List of Palatines on Board the Ship Robt &
Alice, Walter Goodman, Mas^r, from Rotterdam. [Qualified
Sept 11, 1738.]

Jacob Bransteder   Hans Adam Geizler
Jacob Frans   Theobeld Schelfer, Senr
Mathews Alsback   Theobeld Schelfer, Junr
Peiter Buffell   Andries Meyer
Philip Hertzog   Paul Mosser
Michell Kolp   Johannis Pricker
Peiter Kolp   Jacob Raymon
Johanis Ferch   Michell Miller
Peiter Sybent   Michell Raymon
Jan Adam Snell   Jacob Tomme
Jurick Mich^l Roch   Hans Snyder
Johannis Bener   Andries Bader
Godfry Bener   Christopher Wederigh
Jurich Michell Kolp   Frederick Nicholas Sneuder
Gerit Hedrick   Nicholas Sneuder
Abram Hedrick   Hans Martin
Johannis Honsinger   Joseph Kensell
Hans Michell Torenberger   Jacob Kensell
Oygell Torenberger   Phylip Toffer
Valentine Schults   Jacob Toffer
Luturg Boes   Phylip Weys
Jacob Pricher   Jacob Gorle
David Nagle   Jan Jacob Cophenhever
Daniell Klingesmith   Lundert Nochper
Jan Jurich Hedrick   Hendrick Shingell
Jan Jacob Klunt   Jan Nichol Craft
Nicholas Miller   Hendrick Thomas
Adam Daniell   Conrad Heyt
Casper Weysperger, sick   Abraham Heyt
Peiter Heyl   Pieter Heyt
Casper Dorst   Jan Jacob Shoemaker
Johannis Broan   Johannis Shoemaker
Tobias Stear   Jan Nichol Holl

Jan Abram Holl
Andries Holl
Baltser Renhowser
Christian Groab
Theobel Vink
Jan Jurick Roth
Philip Pehl
Johannis Escogen
Jan Peiter Escogen
Michell Schoemaker
Anthon Bieller
Stephen Jorenboxger
Peter Rubie
Johannis Sleipher
Jacob Peck
Jan Peter Kerch
Jan Adam Granast
Jurich Godfreid
Hans Martin Stersinger
Hendrick Redinhower
Peiter Redinhower

Christian Stadler
Jan Nichol Nagle
Adam Dick
Melchior Jant
Casper Scheilk
Godfried Petzell
Daniell Clingesmith
Lowrans Peirson
Paulus Buliut
Pieter Hedrick
Christopher Hedrick
Michell Clemens
Peiter Keyper
Byle Keyper
Allex^r Schoefert
Jan Paul Kuns
Reynhart Alsback
Hans Trautman
Christian Castle
106 [men], 53 [women], 159 [total].

Sworn that the above List is compleat and true to the best of my knowledge.
Philadelphia, Septr 11th 1738.

Walter Goodman.

[List 55 B] Palatines imported in the Ship Robert and Alice, of Dublin, Walter Goodman, Mas^r, from Rotterdam, but last from Dover in England. Qualified the 11th Day of September 1738.

Caspar Scheck
Gottfriedt Betzel
Daniel Kliengenschmit
Lorentz Birsung
Baullus Balliett
Petter Heydtrich
Christoff Heydrich
Michel Clementz
Petter Kieffer

Johan Peiter (+) Phiel
Alex^d (×) Sheffer
Johan Paullus Kurz
Renhert (R) Alspach
Johannes Trauttmann
Jacob (×) Ransteder
Jacob Frantz
Madeis Alspach
Paul (O) Beifle

Philip (X) Hertzog
Melchior (O) Kolp
Peiter (K) Kolp
Johannes Förch
Petter Seubert
Johan Adam (++) Snell
Jerch Michael Buch
Johannes Röhrer
Johann Gottfried Röhrer
Georg Michel Kolb
Gerard (O) Henry
Jan Abram (+) Hendrick
Johannes Huntzinger
Hans Michel (X) Torenberger
Jan Jacob (X) Torenberger
Valentine (V) Shultz
Lutwick (B) Poes
Jacob (B) Pricker
David (O) Nagle
Frantz Klingenschmitt
Johan Gorg Heitrich
Jan Jacob (O) Klunt
Niklos Miller
Adam (O) Daniel
Petter Heyel
Hans Gaspar Dorst
Johannis (X) Brawn
Tobias Steuer
Hans Adam (+) Gesler
Teobalt Schäffer
Tebelt (D) Skeyler
Andres (N) Meyer
Paul (+) Moser
Johannis (H) Pricker
Hans Jacob (X) Reyman
Michel (+) Miller
Hans Michel (M) Rayman
Jacob Dommen
Johan (A) Sneyder
Andreas Bader
Johann Christoff Wetterich

Johan Nicolaus Schneyder
Johann Friedrich Schneider
Hans (+) Martin
Joseph (H) Kensel
Jacob Kentzel
Philip (O) Tofort
Jacob (O) Tofort
Johann Philipps Weiss
Johann Jacob Kugerle
Jacob (+) Kappenheffr
Leonard (O) Nachber
Hendrick (+) Shingle
Johaniclos Kraft
Heinrich Thommen
Conrad (KH) Hayt
Abram (+) Hayt
Peter (X) Hayt
Johan Jacob Schumacher
Johannes Schumacher
Johan Nicholas (+) Hall
Abraham Holl
Andreas Holl
Beltzer Reydenauer
Christian Grub
Hans Jurick (H) Rath
Thöbalt Finck
Johann Philipp Fehl
Johannes (O) Eskusen
Peter (O) Eskusen
Michal (+) Shumacker
Anthony Biehler
Ulrich (U) Bullher
Peter (X) Ruby
Stephen (+) Durnbercher
Johannes (O) Sleyfard
Jacob Beck
Johan Peter Karch
Johann Adam Groners
Georg Gottfried
Hans Marden Starzman
Hans Henrich Reitenaur

Peter Reittenauer
Christian (X) Stetler
Johan Michel (N) Nagle

Adam (X) Dick
Melcher (MI) Yand
Christian (O) Cassell

[List 55 C] At the Courthouse of Philadelphia, September 11th 1738. Present The Honourable George Thomas, Esqr, Lieutenant Governour,

Clement Plumsted,   Samuel Hassell,
Thomas Lawrence,   Thomas Griffits,   } Esqrs.
Ralph Asheton,

The Palatines whose Names are underwritten, imported in in the Ship Robert and Alice, of Dublin, Walter Goodman, Comr, from Rotterdam, but last from Dover in England, did this day take and subscribe the Oaths to the Government.

Caspar Scheck
Gottfriedt Betzell
Daniel Kliengenschmitt
Lorentz Birsung
Baullus Balliet
Petter Heydtrich
Christoff Heydrich
Michel Clementz
Petter Kieffer
Johan Peter (X) Phiel
Alexander (X) Schäffer
Johan Paullus Kurz
Reinhart (R) Altspach
Johannes Trauttmann
Jacob (X) Ranstäder
Jacob Frantz
Madeis Alspach
Paulus (O) Buffel
Philip (X) Hertzog
Melchior (O) Colb
Peter (X) Colb
Johannes Förch
Petter Seubert
Johan Adam (X) Schnel
Jörch Michel Buch
Johannes Röhrer

Johann Gottfried Röhrer
Georg Michel Kolb
Gerhart (O) Henry
Joh. Abraham (+) Henry
Johannes Huntzinger
Hans Michael (X) Türenberger
Hans Jacob (X) Türenberger
Vallentin (V) Sholtz
Ludwig (B) Bosse
Jacob (B) Brucker
David (O) Negle
Frantz Klingenschmitt
Johan Gerg Heitrich
Johan Jacob (O) Klund
Niklos Miller
Adam (O) Daniel
Petter Heyel
Hans Casper Dorst
Johannes (X) Brown
Tobias Steuer
Hans Adam (+) Gissler
Teobalt Schäffer
Teobalt (D) Schäffer, Junr
Anderas (N) Meyer
Paulus (X) Masser
Johannes (H) Pricker

Hans Jacob (+) Ramman
Michael (+) Miller
Hans Michael (M) Ramon
Jacob Dommen
Johan (A) Shneyder
Andras Bader
Johann Christoph Wetterich
Johann Nicolaus Schneyder
Johan Friederich Schneider
Hans (R) Martin
Joseph (XX) Kentzel
Jacob Kentzel
Philip (O) Thiffort
Jacob (O) Thiffort, Junr
Johan Philipps Weiss
Johann Jacob Kugerle
Jacob (X) Kobenhöffer
Leonhart (O) Nachtbar
Johan Henrich (X) Schänike
Johan Niclos Krafft
Henrich Thommen
Conrad (KH) Hätt
Abraham (+) Hätt
Peter (X) Hätt, Junr
Johann Jacob Schumacher
Johannes Schumacher
Johan Nicklas (H) Holl

Abraham Holl
Andreas Holl
Baltzer Reydenauer
Christian Grub
Hans Georg (H) Roth
Thöbalt Finck
Johann Philipp Fehl
Johannes (O) Eskuchen
Peter (O) Eskugen
Michael (+) Shumacher
Anthony Bieller
Ullerig (U) Burgherr
Peter (X) Ruby
Stephan (X) Törreberger
Johannes (O) Shleiffer
Jacob Beck
Johann Peter Karch
Johann Adam Groner
Georg Gottfried
Hans Mardin Sdartzman
Hans Henrich Reitnauer
Hans Pder Reuner [!]
Christian (X) Stättler
Johann Nicklas (N) Nagel
Adam (X) Dick
Melchior (MI) Jand
Christian (O) Cassel

[List 56 A] A List of all ye Mens Names from 16 years & upwards, Passengers on b^d ye Ship Queen Eliz^a, Alixand^r Hope, Command^r. [Qualified September 16, 1738.]

	AGES		AGES
Ludwick Sible	23	Jn° Georick Sliger	19
Hans Otho Jerselo	45	Andres Felsinger	51
Georick Parkman	33	Jn° Henrick Sides	26
Wm. Brant	50	Andres Lerick	50
Barnet Roat	25	Peter Lerick	20
Hans Otho Sliger	45	Antho. Lerick	18
Georick Sliger	23	Christian Laback	39
Jn° Sliger	21	Rinard Laback	70

	AGES		AGES
Jnº Henrick Silicus	25	Johanes Starr	38
Sigmont Henly	41	Geo. Terr	38
Adam Schislor	30	Martin Weisell	30
Jnº Shimell	26	Christopher Rooss	55
Henrick Weber	41	Jnº Styne	37
Johanis Conkell	30	Henrick Seller	34
Peter Spikt	44	Johanes Lerick	44
Casper Lerick	44	Johanes Shafer	34
Christopher Stroder	32	Johanes Masor	34
Henrick Weber	28	Conrad Stegell	32
Nicholas Tye	24	Henrick Sliger	45
Johanis Letherick	18	Christian Morris	24
Johanes Coch	78	Nicholas Eakers	22
Henrick Coch	23	Henrick Eakers	17
Gabriel Vagell	32	Bernard Lynse	20
Henrick Smith	50	Fredrick Nickton	36
Jnº Smith	20	Georick Sharp	36
Peter Smith	17	Isaac Sharp	26
Charles Rygard	25	Martin Sweednen	51
Ralph Snyder	23	Geo. Konkell	19
Wilhelm Reysner	..	Theobald Smith	50
Conrad Snyder	20	Conrad Lerga	48
Geo. Lorison	26	Henrick Weissell	38
Michell Lorizen	20	Casper Leap	54
Thoˢ Shane	38	Casper Leap	19
Mark Sible	47	Johanes Slegell	32
Jnº Sible	20	Henrick Kyes	29
Henrick Elinger	21	Henrick Nagele	24
Henrick Veis	36	Johanes Alt	40
Nicholas Venholt	48	Henrick Cabill	19
Johanes Snyder	40	Casper Schayber	..
Weinard Weisell	27	Johanis Sulspack	50
Paul Gysell	37	Christian Nighthart	35
Christophel Kirkhofe	43	Henrick William	26
Ernst Sharp	39	Johanes Noman	38
Jnº Georick Sharp	16	Conrad Lepard	58
Ludwick Thomas	34	Johanes Konkell	24
Johanes Straul	37	Wm. Lepard	39
Johanes Peyer	45	Casper Dominick	33
Danˡ Iglebourner	45	Johanes Gotwalts	20

	AGES		AGES
Conrad Miller	23	Nicholas Crack	24
Philip Smith	19	Nicholas Seigler	26
Casper Shafer	25	Johannes Reser	23
Conrad Gable	67	Qualified 104, Women & Child^n	
Jacob Ewald	21	220, Total 324.	

Sworn Sept. 16th that the above is a true and complete list of those above 16 years of Age to the best of my knowledge.

Allex. Hope.

[List 56 B] Palatines imported in the Ship Queen Elizabeth, Alexander Hope, Commander, from Rotterdam, but last from Deal in England. Qualified the 16th Day of September 1738.

Johann Ludwig Seipel
Johan Otto Yserloch
Johan Gorg Bergman
William (B) Brant
Johan Bernart Roth
Hans Otto Schlöcher
Georg Casper Schlöcher
Johann Jost Schlöcher
Johann Georg Schlöcher
Johann Henrich Seitz
Andres (X) Felsinger
Andres (O) Lerich
Peter (X) Lerich
Anthon Lerch
Christian Laubach
Renhard (X) Laubach
Johann Hennrich Silvius
Johann Sigmund Henle
Jon Adam (X) Shisleck
Johannes Schimmel
Johann Henrich Weber
Joannes (C) Kunkel
Johann Peter Specht
Caspar Lörch
Christ. (O) Streter
Johann Henrich Weber

Niclas Feye
Johannes Hetrich
Johann Hennrich Koch
Henrich Koch
Johan Gabriel Vogell
Johan Henrich Schmitt
Johannes Schmidt
Johann Peter Schmidt
John Carel (X) Righart
Johannes Reiffschneyder
Johann Conrad Reiffschneyder
Johan Wilhelm Reiffschneider
Jeorick (X) Loray
Johan Michell (X) Loray
Johan Thomas (X) Schene
Johann Marx Seypell
Johan Ulrich (X) Sibel
Johan Gorge Ellinger
Johan Hennrich Weiss
Nicholas (X) Wenholt
Johannes Schneider
Johann Wernner Weitzel
Paul Geisell
Ernst Schärp
Geo. (X) Sharp
Ludwick (X) Thomas

Johannes Strohl

Johanes (X) Bayer

Daniel (E) Eiglebourner

Johanes (O) Starr

Geörg Deörr

Martin (X) Weitsal

Christophel (X) Ried

Johannes Stein

Hennrich Zeller

Johannes Lörch

Johannes Schäffer

Johannes Möser

Johan Conrath Stichel

Henrich Schleucher

Christian Morietz

Nicolas (X) Yeeks

John Henry (+) Yeeks

Bernard (X) Lynse

Johann Fridrich Nöchtern

Johan (X) Sharpe

Isaac Scharp

Joh. Mardin Schwedener

Johan Geo. (X) Konkell

Teobalt Schmit

Conrad Hergle

Henrich Weützel

Casper (+) Leap, Senr

Casper (X) Leap, Junr

Ernst Schlegel

Johann Henrich Geist

Johannes Alt

Johan Henrich (+) Gabel

Johan Casper (XX) Scriver

Carl Nagel

Johan (O) Sulsback

Christian (X) Nighthart

Henrich Wilhelm

Johan (X) Homan

Conrad Lippert

Johannes Gunckell

Wilhelm Lippert

Casp. David Dumernicht

Johannes Gottwals

Conradt Miller

Philipus Medh

Casper Shever

Casber Scheffer

Conrath Göbel

Jacob (+) Hepwalt

Nicolaus Grack

Nicholas (X) Zigler

Johanes Reser

[List 56 C] At the Courthouse of Philadelphia, Septr 16th 1738. Present The Honourable George Thomas, Esqr, Lieutenant Governour,

Clement Plumsted, Ralph Asheton, ⎫
Thos Lawrence, Thos Griffits, ⎬ Esq^{rs}.

The Palatines whose Names are underwritten, imported in the Ship Queen Elizabeth, Alexander Hope, Master, from Rotterdam, but last from Deal in England, did this day take and subscribe the Oaths to the Government. Viz.,

Johann Ludwig Seipel

Johan Otto Yserloch

Johan Gorg Bergman

Wilhelm (B) Brand

Johan Bernhart Roth

Hans Otto Schlöcher

Georg Caspar Schlöcher

Johann Jost Schlocher

Johann Gorg Schlöcher
Johann Henrich Seitz
Anderas (X) Filtzinger
Anderas (X) Lerge
Peter (X) Lerge
Anthon Lerch
Christian Laubach
Renhart (X) Laubach
Johann Hennrich Silvius
Johan Sigmund Henle
Johan Adam (X) Sheesler
Johannes Schimmel
Johann Henrich Weber
Johanes (O) Gunckel
Johann Peter Specht
Caspar Lörch
Christoph (O) Stredter
Johann Henrich Weber
Niclas Feye
Johannes Hetrich
Johann Henrich Koch
Henrich Koch
Johann Gabriel Vogell
Johan Henrich Schmitt
Johannes Schmidt
Johann Peter Schmidt
Johan Carl (X) Reichart
Johannes Reiffschneyder
Johann Conrat Reiffschneyder
Johann Wilhelm Reiffschneider
Georg (X) Loray
Johan Michel (X) Laray
Johan Thomas (X) Shön
Johann Marx Seypell
Ullerik (XX) Seybel
Johan Gorg Ellinger
Johan Henrich Weiss
Nicklas (X) Winholdt
Johannes Schneidt[er]
Johann Wernner Weitzel
Paul Geissell

Ernst Schärp
George (X) Sharp
Ludwig (X) Thomas
Johannes Strohl
Johannes (XX) Beyer
Daniel (E) Eichelburner
Johannes (X) Större
Geörg Deörr
Martin (X) Weitzel
Christoph (X) Reepe [!]
Johannes Stein
Hennrich Zeller
Johannes Lörch
Johannes Schäffer
Johannes Möser
Johan Conrath Stichel
Heinrich Schleucher
Christian Morietz
Nicklas (X) Hyxes
Johan Henry (X) Hyxes
Bernhart Lintz
Johann Friederich Nöchtern
George (X) Sharp
Isaac Scharp
Joh. Mardin Schwedener
Johan Georg (X) Gunkel
Teobalt Schmit
Conradt Hergl
Henrich Weitzel
Caspar (X) Löbe, Senior
Caspar (X) Löbe, Junior
Ernst Schlegel
Johann Henrich Geist
Johannes Alt
Johan Henry (XX) Göbel
Johann Caspar (++) Shreiber
Carl Nagel
John Jost (O) Sultzbach
Christian (X) Neidhart
Henrich Wilhelm
Johannes (+) Homan

Conrad Lippert
Johannes Gunckel
Wilhelm Lippert
Casp. David Dumernicht
Johannes Gottwals
Conrad Miller
Philipus Medh

Casber (×) Schäffer
Conrath Gobell
Jacob (+) Ibwald
Nicolaus Grack
Nicklas (×) Zigler
Johannes Reser

[List 57 A] [Palatines imported in the Ship The Thistle, John Wilson, Commander, from Rotterdam. Qualified September 19, 1738.]

Daniel Dryghler
Christian Brechbill
Henry Brechbill
William Bishoff
Peter Habaker
Johannes Slighter
Isaac Ommell
Christian Stidler
Valantine His
Jacob Kinar
Abraham Stidler
Elias Abin
Peter Founderburgh
Walter Founderburgh
Jacob Slygh
Thomas Ruygh
Hans Adam Snyder
Jan George Lots
Johannes Gers
Daniel Snyder
Lorenz Gold
Joshep Keller
Johannes Wymuller
Andreas Nayman
Adam Koen
Johannes Keller
Henry Beckholt
Jost Perkerstocks
Carel Witman

George Michl Gras
Johs Leonard Miller
Christian Lutz
Caspar Lutz
Jacob Clodder
Hanus Diedrich
Johannes Kroon
Jacob Kaygar
Hans George Mayer
Jacob Schochman
Conradt Wymuller
Andreas Mints
Elias Siler
Michl Tiel
Caspar Kienar
Michl Vris
Jan Simon Vris
Johannes Vris
Martin Krim
Johannes Krim
Hans Martin·Bilder
Johan Jacob Pfarr
Jost Vryler
Johannes Coen
Hans Adam Lightie
Barent Smith
Melchior Smith
Conradt Kemelie
Michl Underkauffer

Martin Mansberger
Christian Lodder
Johan Herman Schiffer
Johan Henry Riminsnyder
Paulus Schiffer
Bernhard Schiffer
Hend^k Barthol^e Schiffer
Paulus Schiffer
Hend^k Adolph Agenback
Philip Coen
Mich^l Hoeback
Andreas Hanovelt
Valentine Wilt
Lodowick Miller
Conradt Singler
Nicholas Vrydagh
Peter Snyder
Jacob Bender
Elies Nicholas Bender

Jacob Nich^s Bender
Diethrich Six
Johannes Frank
Philip Smelzer
Geo. Kinder
Peter Kinder
Caspar Kinder
Jan Rodolph
Jacob Kalladie
Vindle Lins
Jacob Hoeback
Johannes Mayer
Mich^l Streball
Johannes Westhouse
Geo. Math^s Willer
Johannes Smous
Ulrigh Seger
Mich^l Keysleman
    95 [qualified].

Sworn that the above is a true and complete List of the Males above 16 years of Age imported in the Ship the Thistle. Sept. 19th 1738.

John Wilson.

[List 57 B] Palatines imported in the Ship the Thistle, John Wilson, Commander, from Rotterdam, but last from Plymouth in Old England. Qualified the 19th Day of September 1738.

Daniell Draichle[r]
Christian Brechbull
Willem Bischoff
Johan (+) Slighter
Isaac (V) Ommel
Christian Stettler
Valentine (H) His
Peter (✕) Habacker
Henry (✕) Brightbill
Jacob (✕✕) Kenar
Abraham Stettler

Jerg Elias Ament
Peter (✕) Founderburgh
Walter (✕) Founderburgh
Jacob (H) Sligh
Thos (✕✕) Reigh
Johann Adam Schneider
Johann Görg Lotz
Johan (H) Gers
Daniel Schneider
Joseph (K) Kehler
Lohrentz Gutt

Johannes Weinmüller
Andreas Neuman
Adam Gohn
Joha. (HK) Keller
Hennrich Bechdoldt
Jost Birckenstock
Jacob Carl W. [Witman]
Johan Mich¹ (G) Groets
Johann Leonhart Müller
Christian (×) Lutz
Casper Lutz
Jacob Cloder
Johan (H) Stedright
Johannes Cron
Jacob Geiger
Hans Gerg Moyer
Johann Jacob Schuhmann
Conrade (O) Wegmiller
Andres Mendong
Elias Zöller
Mich¹ (H) Tiel
Casper Kühner
Michel Fris
Simon Fries
Johan (×) Fryts
Johan (×) Krim
Martin Grim
Hans Martin (H) Biller
John Jacob (H) Pfarr
Jost Freüller
Johan (H) John
Hans Adam (A) Lydy
Bernhard (H) Smith
Merchior (M) Smith
Conrad Kühmle
Michäl Underkofler
Marti Mannsperger

Christian Lotter
Johan Herman Schäffer
Johann Henrich Riemenscheider
Paul (B) Schiffer
Bernard (H) Schiffer
Hen^d Barth° (×) Schiffer
Paulus (×) Schiffer
John Rodolph (H) Auchenbaugh
Fielip Gohn
Michael Hubach
Andreas Hannewalt
Valtin Wildt
Johann Ludwig Müller
Johann Conraht Ziegler
Johann Petter Schneider
Nicklaus Freidag
Jacob Bender
Elias Nickel Bender
Jacob Nicolas (××) Bender
Jerich (×) Six
Johan (O) Frank
Johann Phillib Schmelzer
Jörg Günther
Peter Günther
Caspar Günther
Johann Rudolph
Jacob (×) Kalladay
Wendel Lentz
Jacob Hubach
Hans Meyer
Michael Ströbel
Johannes Wiest
Georg Mattys Weller
Hans Zumost [?]
Ulrich (×) Syller
Johann Michael Geisselmann
95 [qualified].

[List 57 C] At the Courthouse of Philadelphia, Septr 19th 1738. Present The Honourable George Thomas, Esqr, Lieutenant Governour,

Clement Plumsted, Sam¹ Hassell,
Thoˢ Lawrence,   } Esqʳˢ.
Ralph Asheton,   Thoˢ Griffits,

The Palatines whose Names are underwritten, imported in
the Ship The Thistle, John Wilson, Commander, from Rotterdam, but last from Plymouth in England, did this Day take
and subscribe the Oaths to the Government, Viz.,

Daniell Dreichler	Casper Lutz
Christian Brechbüll	Jacob Cloder
Willem Bischoff	Johannes (H) Diterich
Johannes (+) Schligter	Johannes Cron
Isaac (V) Ommel	Jacob Geiger
Christian Stettler	Hans Jerg Mayer
Vallentin (H) Heesse	Johann Jacob Schuchmann
Peter (X) Habacker	Conrad (O) Weymiller
Henry (X) Brechbill	Andreas Mendong
Jacob (XX) Kühnert	Elias Zöller
Aberham Stetler	Michael (H) Thiel
Jerg Elias AmEnd	Caspar Kuhner
Peter (V) Von der Borg	Michel Fries
Walter (X) Van der Borg	Johann Simon Fries
Jacob (H) Shleig	Johannes (X) Fries
Thomas (X) Reich	Martin Grim
Johann Adam Schneider	Johannes Grimm
Johann Görg Lutz	Hans Martin (H) Böller
Johannes (H) Gertsch	Hans Jacob (H) Pfarr
Daniel Schneider	Jost Freuller
Lohrentz Gutt	Johannes (H) Gohn
Joseph (K) Keller	Hans Adam (A) Lydy
Johannes Weinmüller	Bernhart (H) Shmit
Andreas Neuman	Melchior (M) Shmit
Adam Gohn	Conradt Kühmle
Johannes (HK) Keller	Michal Underkoffler
Hennrich Becholdt	Marti Mannsperger
Jost Birckenstock	Christian Lotter
Jacob Carl W. [Witman]	Johann Herman Schäffer
George Michiel (O) Krans	Johann Henrich Riemenscheider
Johann Leonhart Müller	Paul (B) Shäffer, Senior
Christian (X) Lutz	Bernhart (H) Shäffer

Henry Bartholome (X) Shäffer
Paulus (X) Shäffer, Junior
John Rudolff (H) Achenbach
Fielip Gohn
Michael Achenbach
Andreas Hannewalt
Valtin Wildt
Johann Ludwig Müller
Johann Conraht Ziegler
Johann Petter Schneidder
Nicklaus Freidag
Jacob Bender
Elias Nickel Bender
Jacob Nicklas Bender
Diterich (X) Sixe
Johannes (O) Franck

Johan Phillib Schmeltzer
Jörg Günther
Pether Günther
Caspar Günther
Johann Rudolph
Jacob (X) Gallete
Wendell Lentz
Jacob Hubach
Hans Meyer
Michael Strobell
Johannes Wiest
Georg Mattäs Weller
Hans Zumost [?]
Uhlerich (X) Sägesin
Johan Michael Geisselmann

[List 58 A] A List of all the men passengers from 16 years & upwards on Board the Ship Friendship, Henry Beech, Commander. [Qualified September 20, 1738.]

	AGES		AGES
Florian Bobinger	22	Hans Peter Rodberger	40
Christian Young	37	Christian Myer	32
Jacob Brust	24	Tobias Ditess	35
Stepha Glaser	48	Dewalt Stenard	31
Valatine Shaller	24	Jacob Zorn	20
Michal Carger	46	Michal Hooverich	25
Hans Jurg Beger	18	Jurg Bueck	30
Joanis Kohn	30	Joanis Swartswalter	50
Dewald Klingler	24	Joanis Sheller	26
Lowrance Dibong	43	Jacob Hoover	25
Joanis Negelie	30	Johan Grenshet	38
Abraham Eker	52	Michal Mesnor	37
Phillip Stover	31	Casper Mesnor	16
Adam Kreps	19	Leopald Jost	36
Henry Syble	27	Jurg Miller	21
Johanis Shryber	32	Bartle Bach	54
Adam Pence	22	Adam Bach	18
Jacob Folmer	40	Jurg Hartman	40
Jacob Folmer	15	Paul Hime	17

NAME	AGES	NAME	AGES
Jacob Hime	16	Wendell Jacobie	29
Joanis Swaner	20	Bernherd Eger	50
Jacob Stamler	18	Jacob Eger	25
Jurg Moler	33	Michall Eger	23
Johanis Stinglie	21	Adam Drollinger	30
Fredrick Pender	33	Fredrick Harle	26
Bernherd Moats	46	Sebastian Neas	55
Hans Michel Brouch	33	Henrich Herner	46
Valatine Pence	48	Danil Kensimer	45
Johan Jordan	26	Vide Bechtle	26
Christoph Wys	17	Jacob Wagner	45
Jacob Derrie	32	Joanis Lenglie	33
Nicholas Strous	25	Lorents Houts	23
John Gofries	36	Joanis Kensimer	17
Valatin Rinesill	17	Joanis Fredrich	17
Abraham Wendell	26	Marks Smith	34
Joanis Fryling	25	Martie Karcher	19
Michal Boret	25	Fredrich Rink	32
Jurg Kaufman	20	Hans Jurg Buck	40
Adam Ritter	27	Fredrich Haylie	20
Peter Louks	32	Martin Speck	35
Phillip Summer	20	Jurg Kenich	30
Jacob Shop	38	Johan Wendel Brown	37
Eberhard Drollinger	32	87 qualified, women & children	
Adam Swartswelder	19	195, whole 282.	
Jurg Kern	38		

[Endorsed:]
Capt. Beech's List, Sepr 28th 1738.

[List 59 A] List of Passengers in the Ship Nancy, Wm.
Wallace, Master, Qualified Sept. 20, 1738.*

NAME	AGES	NAME	AGES
Simon Ideling	27	Lawrence Klyne	22
Jacob Stinebroff	24	Gasper Hoofman	20
Frederick Tryer	26	John Prince	28

* The original is lost. Taken from *Pennsylvania Archives*, 2nd series, Vol.
XVII, p. 164f.

	AGES		AGES
Tobias Hackerman	36	Matthew Reece	17
John Peter	24	John Meyminger	55
Thomas Paulcher	27	Michael Robb	16
Jacob Lassaul	29	Yust Terr	23
Christian Berkman	26	Philip Hiner	20
Michael Jacob	20	Conrod Pletz	28
John Bedsheller	23	Philip Trap	23
Henry Mire	20	Peter Musmer	21
Michael Shole, Sen[r]	63	John Grossnickle	21
Michel Shole, Jun[r]	26	Francis Hackerman	28
Christopher Mire	17	Michael Mire	29
Anthony Englebert	27	Martin Mire	23
Hendrick Kemper	42	Martin Springley	36
Christian Switzer	20	George Shewler	30
John Eyhault	39	Jacob Cloates	22
Hendrick Nikerick	32	William Corst	27
Jacob Mire	27	Philip Bens	27
John Houselbeck	25	Casper Mans	20
Nicholas Robertus	29	Michael Hemperly	26
George Painter	26	Jacob Beck	25
John Mire	24	Philip Kevell	27
George Mackly	37	Jacob Frank	30
Aaron Housneck	43	Thomas Rush	20
Jacob Switzer	23	John Howes	18
Nicholas Onas	38	Jacob Adolph	19
Joseph Mire	25	Martin Snider	31
David Shydeaker	24	Andreas Ringer	17
Ulrick Shydeaker	20	Mellcher Beelman	58
Hans Shydeaker	15	Jacob Easterly	22
Jeremiah Rhode	48	John Kowler	16
Matthias Learer	24	John Kashneate	33
Andrew Kashley	15	Jacob Kavelich	28
George Rowler	39	Martin Mire	15
Jacob Reece	49	John Hesselback	36

[Lists 58–59 B] Palatines imported in the Ship The Nancey, William Wallace, Com[r], and the Friendship, Henry Beach, Com[r], both from Rotterdam, but last from Dover in Old England. Qualified the 20th Day of September 1738.

IN THE SHIP THE FRIENDSHIP

Florian Bübinger
Christian Jung
Stephan (X) Glaser
Jacob (X) Rost
Valentin Schaller
Michel Karcher
Hans Jörg Becher
Johannes Kuhn
Debalt Klingler
Lawrence (D) Debong
Johannes Negele
Abraham (O) Eker
Philip (X) Stover
Adam (A) Greps
Henrich Seibel
Johannes Schrei[ber]
Adam (X) Pence
Jacob Vollmer
Jacob (X) Fulmer
Hans Peter (X) Rousenberger
Christian (X) Meyer
Tobias Dittis
Deobald (O) Stormer
Jacob Zorn
Michael Hubrich
Hans Jerg Bukh
Johanes Schwartzwelder
Johannes Schaller
Hans Jacob (H) Huper
Joan Granget
Michael (XX) Messner
Casper (++) Messner
Leobold Jost
Geörg Müller
Bartl. Bach
Hans Adam Bach
Hans George (X) Hartman
Paul (O) Hime
Jacob (X) Hime

Johannes Schwanner
Jacob Stamler
Hans George (M) Makale
Johannes (X) Stinglie
Fridricht Pfunder
Bernhart Motz
Hans Michal (X) Bronst
Valentin (+) Bence
Jan Jierdan
Christoffel Weis
Jacob (O) Durie
Nicolas (+) Straus
Jean Gauffres
Valetin Reintzel
Abraham Wendel
Johannes (X) Fryling
George Michal (X) Burret
Johan Jerg Kauffmann
Adam Ritter
Peter (X) Laencus
Philip (X) Sowber
Jacob (X) Shup
Eberhard Drollinger
Johann Addam Schwartzwäld
George (IK) Kern
Christoffell Wendell Jacoby
Bernard (O) Eger
Jacob Ege
Johann Michel Ege
Adam Drolling
Fridrig Karle
Sebastian (X) Neas
Henrich Hernner
Geo. Daniel (X) Gesmer [!]
Veit Bechtoldt
Jacob Wagner
Johannes Längle
Lawrence (X) Hauds
Hanrich Gensemer
Johanes (X) Frederick
Marx Schmidt

Johan Martin Karcher

Daniel Friedrich Reinekh

Hans Enger (×) Bough

Dedrich (FH) Hilie

Martin (+) Speck

Hans Georg König

Johan Wendel Braun

IN THE SHIP THE NANCY

Casper (×) Hoofman

Johans Brientz

[Johan Peter] Lauterman

Dhomas Baltzer

Jacob (×) Lassall

Christian (×) Berkman

Michel Jacob

Johannes Betschler

Henry (×) Meyer

Michel Scholl, Senr

Michal (×) Scholl, Junr

Christopher (×) Meyer

Antonius Engelbret

Henrich Kemper

Johannes Ehrhalt

Jacob Meyer

Ernst Hausknecht

Georg Bender

Nicolas (×) Robertus

John (×) Meyer

Nicolas (×) Onas

Joseph (×) Meyer

Ulrich (×) Shydenker

Jost Mich. Roth

Mathias (×) Leazer

Hans Jerg Vallen

Jacob (+) Reece

John (I) Meymenger

Philipp Hainer

Philip (+) Trap

Peter (×) Meesmer

Frantz Ackherman

Michal (×) Mire

Martin (×) Mire

Martin Springenklee

Jacob Klotz

Wilhelm Karst

Johann Philipp Bensch

J. Casper Mantz

Michael Gimperle

Jacob Bookh

Tomas Rosch

Johannes Hass

Melchior (O) Bellman

Jacob Oesterlin

John (×) Kashneats

Jacob (×) Pavilieats

Johan Tetrich Hesselbeck

[Lists 58–59 C] At the Courthouse of Philadelphia, Septem^r 20, 1738.

Present

Clement Plumsted, Andrew Hamilton, ⎫
Saml Hassell, Thomas Griffits, ⎬ Esq^rs.
⎭

The Palatines whose Names are underwritten, imported in the Ships Nancy and the Friendship, Willam Wallace & Henry Beach, Commanders, from Rotterdam, but last from Dover in England, did this Day take and subscribe the Oaths to the Government, Viz.,

[IN THE SHIP THE FRIENDSHIP]

Florian Bubinger
Christian Jung
Jacob (X) Rost
Stephan (X) Glasser
Valentin Schaller
Michel Karcher
Hans Jörg Becher
Johannes Kuh[n]
Debalt Klingler
Lorentz (O) Debong
Johannes Negle
Abraham Ecker
Philip (X) Stouber
Adam (A) Krebs
Henrich Seibel
Johannes Schreiber
Adam (X) Bence
Jacob Vollmer
Jacob (X) Vollmer
Hans Peter Rassenberger
Christian (X) Meyer
Tobias Dettis
Tewald (O) Störnner
Jacob Zorn
Michael Hubrich
Hans Jerg Buch
Johanns Schwartzwelder
Johannes Schaller
Hans Jacob (H) Huber
Joan Granget
Michael (XX) Meesner
Caspar (XX) Meesner
Leobold Jost
Geörg Müller
Bartholme Bach
Hans Adam Bach
Hans George (X) Hartman
Paulus (O) Heime
Jacob (X) Heime

Johannes Schwanner
Jacob Stamler
Hans George (M) Mahler
Johannes (X) Stingly
Fridricht Pfunder
Bernhart Motz
Hans Michael (X) Brants
Vallentin (+) Benz
Jean Jierdon
Christoffel Weiss
Jacob (O) Düry
Nicklas (+) Straus
Jean Gauffres
Valentin Reintzel
Abraham Wendel
Johanes (F) Freyling
Jorge Michael (X) Booret
Johan Jerg Kaufmann
Adam Ritter
Peter (H) Lankus
Philip (X) Sowber
Jacob (X) Shup
Eberhard Drollinger
Johann Adam Schwartzwelder
George (IK) Kernn
Christoffell Wendell Jacoby
Bernhart Egi
Jacob Ege
Johan Michel Ege
Adam Drolling[er]
Fridrig Korle
Sebastian (X) Nesse
Henrich Hernner
Gerge Daniel (X) Gensemer
Veit Bechtoldt
Jacob Wagener
Johannes Längle
Lorentz (X) Hautz
Hannes Gensemer
Johannes (X) Friederik
Marx Schmidt

Johan Martin Karcher
Daniel Friedrich Reinekh
Hans Georg (+) Bauch
Frederik (FH) Heyly
Martin (+) Speck
Hans Georg König
Johan Wendel Braun

IN THE SHIP THE NANCY

Caspar (X) Hoffman
Johans Brientz
Johan Peter Lauterman
Dhomas Baltzer
Jacob (X) Lassall
Christan (X) Bergman
Michel Jacob
Johannes Betschler
Henry (X) Meyer
Michel Scholl, Senior
Michael (+) Sholl, Junior
Christoph (X) Meyer
Antonius Engelbret
Henrich Kemper
Johannes Ehrhalt
Jacob Meyer
Ernst Hausknecht
Georg Bender
Nicklas (X) Robertus
Johan (N) Meyer

Nicklas (X) Lones
Joseph (X) Meyer
Uhllerich (X) Heydecker
Jost Mich. Roth
Matteus (X) Löver
Hans Jerg Vallen
Jacob (X) Ress
Johannes (X) Memminger
Philipp Hainer
Philip (X) Drap
Peter (X) Mesemer
Frantz Ackherman
Hans Michael (X) Meyer
Martin Piter (X) Meyer
Martinn Springenklee
Jacob Klotz
Wilhelm Karst
Johann Philipp Bensch
Casper Mantz
Michael Gimperle
Jacob Boekh
Thomas Rosch
Johannes Hass
Melchior (O) Bellman
Jacob Oesterlin
Johannes (O) Kastnitz
Jacob (X) Paflitz
Johannes Diterich (X) Helsen-
beck

[List 60 A] List of Men Imported in the Snow Fox, Capt Charles Ware, from Holland. [Qualified October 12th 1738.]

	YEARS		YEARS
Michael Kreen	35	Martin Browne	34
Jacob Palmer	26	Michael Kernig	41
Adam Heyser	29	Michael Palmer	45
Godfred Kunig	47	Jockem Stober	45
Adam Ulrich	24	Ulrich Kipsier	40
Philip Hoos	25	Martin Mayer	38
Hans Theobald Throog	41	Martin Reyn	48

	YEARS		YEARS
Hans Martin Reyn	20	Michael Catts, Jun[r]	17
Peter Huterman	45	Mark Claudy	27
Hans Worster	50	Hans Fry	33
Bastian Felti	20	Jacob Hoffman	55
Casper Decker	40	Christian Hoffman	17
Hans Jurig Fout	25	Johannes Ostwald	26
Michael Kryger	53	Sebastian Coleman	32
Michael Kryger, J[r]	20	Philip Jacob Bouha	55
Jacob Kryger	16	Hans Bouha	20
Hans Adam Olmer	55	Chris. Bouha	25
Philip Jacob Baart	19	Melcher Houtmaker	40
Jacob Steyger	33	Philip Jacob Bouha, Jun[r]	30
Garrick Semerly	37	Jacob Hourg	35
Tobias Reesh	34	Christian Caup	24
Learmer Tzink	17	Hans Jurg Felter	26
John Asper	38	47 [men], 23 [women], 6 [chil-
John Goldeberger	23	dren]. [Total] 70 [adults], 6
Michael Catts, Sen[r]	48	[children].

Sworn October 12, 1738, that the above is a true and compleat List of Palatines above the age of fifteen years to the best of my knowledge.

Charles Ware.

[List 60 B] Palatines imported in the Snow Fox, Charles Ware, Commander, from Rotterdam, but last from Plymouth in old England. Qualified Octr 12th 1738.

Michel Grün	Bastian Felte
Jacob Balmer	Hans Jerg Fouth
Adam Heiser	Michel (X) Kreyer
Adam Ullrich	Jacob Stieger
Philip Hos	Adam (H) Ulmer
Hans Diebolt Drog	Hans Geo. (H) Zimerly
Jerg Michel Balmer	Dowies Reusch
Joachim Stober	Johan (HA) Asper
Martin (X) Ryen	Hans (H) Goldeberger
Hans Martin (X) Reyn	Michel Katz
Peter (H) Hesterman	Martin (X) Claudy
Hans Jerg Wüst	Hans Geo. (X) Fry

Jacob (O) Hoofman
Sebastian Kohlmann
Philip Jacob Bueb
Christoph Bub

Christian Kaupp
Ulrich (X) Hupson
Hans Elrich (X) Helger [!]

[List 60 C] At the Courthouse of Philadelphia, October 12th 1738.

Present

The Honourable George Thomas, Esqr, Lieutenant Governour,
Clement Plumsted, Thomas Griffits ⎫
Ralph Asheton,   ⎬ Esq^{rs}.

The Palatines whose Names are underwritten, imported in the Ship Fox, Charles Ware, Commander, from Rotterdam, but last from Plymouth in England, did this Day take and subscribe the Oaths to the Government, Viz.,

Michel Grün
Jacob Balmer
Adam Heiser
Adam Ullrich
Philip Hos
Hans Diebolt Drog
Jerg Michel Balmer
Joachim Stöber
Martin (X) Rein
Hans Martin (X) Rein
Peter (XX) Hesterman
Hans Jerg Wüst
Bastian Felte
Hans Jerg Fauth
Michael (X) Kreeger
Jacob Stieger

Adam (H) Ullmer
Hans Georg (H) Zimmerly
Dowies Resch
Johannes (HA) Asper
Hans (H) Goldeberger
Michel Kotz
Martin (X) Clody
Hans George (X) Frey
Jacob (O) Hoffman
Sebastian Kohlmann
Philip Jacob Bueb
Christoph Bub
Christian Kaupp
Uhlerick (X) Hübser
Hans Georg (X) Velten

[List 61 A] List of People Imported in the Ship Davy, William Patton, from Amsterdam. [Qualified October 25, 1738.]

Martin Fuchs
Nicholas Hebener
Steffen Rous
Johan Nic. Slummer
Andres Born

Peter Domas
Johan Jacob Kuntzler
Johan Jacob Steffen
Theevia Fautzen
Johan Nic. Thys

Christopher Zummer
Melchior Zummer
Johan Dan. Hetzer
Johan Wendel Seyber
Valentin Aut
Johan Frederick Barts
Conrad Lange
Chris. Fueh
Johan Adam Fueh
Jacob Meyer
Johan Adam Schreyer
Johan Nicho. Scherer
Johan Jacob Schluter
Johan Hildesheimer
Johan George Pauly
Johan Matthias Scherer
Johan Casper Stein
Valentin Nichola
Hans Jacob Knecky
Stephanus Klehr
Conrad Kern
Philip Wicker
Johan Henrick Pfleck
Henrick Schneider
Johan. Hen. Abiarius
Christian Stucker
Frederick Schmidt
Christian Schmidt
Sebastian Fehr
Frederick Stempel
Valentin Stempel
Johan Peter Olier
Johan Feldfliegel
Jacob Morgewegg
George Heyer
Jacob Mohr
Nicholas Joost
Johan George Pieck
Jacob Wildschutz
Simon Becherer

Henrick Torner
Abraham Hobler
George Job
Conrad Waldman
Michael Straube
Ulrick Reiger
George Stoltz
Johannes Deck
Jacob Geckan
Philip Gottskind
Gabriel Haller
Baltzaser Lambert
Johannes Deimer
Hans Michael Lange
Hans Mich. Tilzieffer
Jacob Hoffman
Andreas Deck
Andreas Simon
Gottfried Braune
George Sutz
Jacob Frey
Johan Martin Priem
Johan George Weis
Johan Sauter
Johan Feyl
Johan Geo. Beck
Johan Schmuck
Johan Lantzinger
Jacob Schram
Jaques Maronette
Johan Knockell
Philip Wettszell
Paul Weyer
Simon Stoltz
Oswald Winkelman
Hans Lansz
Johan Adam Fux
Johan Ande Kousman
Johan Nic. Kinzer
George Crape

Bernard Seibert
Joh. Jac. Seibert
Hans Ad. Geeik

Geo. Schramp
94 [men] 47 [women]. [Total]
141.

[List 61 B] Palatines imported in the Ship Davy, William Patton, Commander, from Amsterdam, but last from Cowes in England. Qualified the 25ᵗʰ day of October 1738.

Nickel Heffener
Johan Stephen (X) Rauch
Anderas (O) Born
Johan Jacob Kuntz[er]
Johan Nickel Theiss
Johann Wendel Seibertt
Vallentin (O) Alt
Johan Friedrich Bartz
Johann Adam (X) Schreyer
Johannes Holtzner
Johann Mattes Scherer
Johann Casper (X) Stein
Vallentin (S) Nicklaus
Johann Phillips Wickert
Johan Henry (X) Flick
Johann Henrich Schneder
Christian Schmid
Johan Frietrich Stembel
Johan Vallentin (X) Fligel
Johann Georg Bickes

Simon Bogeriss [?]
Conrad (X) Waldman
Uhllerich (UR) Reichart
Georg Stoltz
Hans Adam (J) Jöke
Baltzer Lampert
Hans (X) Timmer
Michael (X) Longe
Hans Michael (X) Tillshöffer
Jacob (X) Hoffman
Gottfriet Braun
George (O) Zutz
Hans Jacob (X) Shmuck
Jacob (JS) Shram
Johan Anderes Kauffmann
Johan Nicklas (+) Keenser
Johann Jerg Krebs
Johann Bernhart Seibert
Johan Jacob (X) Seubert
George (O) Shram

[List 61 C] At the Courthouse of Philadelphia, Octʳ 25ᵗʰ 1738.

Present

Anthᵒ Morris, Clement Plumsted, ⎱
William Allen, Thomas Griffits, ⎰ Esqʳˢ.

The Palatines whose Names are underwritten, imported in the Ship Davy, William Patton, Commander, from Amsterdam, but last from Cowes in England, did this day take & subscribe the Oaths to the Government, Viz.,

Nickel Heffner
Johan Stephen (X) Roush

Andereas (O) Born
Johan Jacob Kuntzer

Johan Nickel Theiss
Johann Wendel Seibertt
Vallentin (O) Alt
Johann Friedrich Bartz
Johan Adam (X) Schreyer
Johannes Holtzmer
Johan Mattes Scherer
Johan Casper (X) Stein
Vallentin (S) Nicklaus
Johann Phillips Wickert
Johan Henry (X) Fleck
Johann Henrich Schneder
Christian Schmied
Johan Frietrich Stembel
Johan Vallentin (X) Fleegel
Johann Georg Bickes
Conrad (X) Waldman
Simon Bogeriss [?]

Uhllerich (UR) Reichart
Georg Stolz
Hans Adam (J) Jök
Baltzer Lampert
Hans (X) Timmer
Michael (X) Longe
Hans Michael (X) Tillshöffer
Jacob (+) Hoffman
Gottfried Braun
George (X) Zutz
Hans Jacob (X) Shmuck
Jacob (JS) Shram
Johann Anderes Kauffmann
Johan Nicklas (+) Keenser
Johann Jerg Krebs
Johann Bernt Seuber
Johan Jacob (X) Seubert
Georg (O) Shram

[List 62 A] A List of the Palatines p^r the S^t. Andrew, John Stedman, M^r. [Qualified October 27, 1738.]

Peter Leight
Han Yerick Keil
Jacob Stintz
Jacob Seam
Johan Hend. Reis
Fran Har. Deal
Manus Sasamandshouse
Johan Soemaker
Hans Ofer
Johannes Kreive
Han Nich. Stoter
Casper Huckaback
Jacob Keiller
Yerick Kreil
Velto Walter
Chris. Wagner
Lewis Vinsent
Johan Conr. Benebender
Victor Speitz

Stephen Akerman
Simon Derrick
Conrad Neigle
And. Sin
Chris. Kinstler
Jacob Cinnerley
Conrad Sryer
Hans Rinerd Bene
Martin Teligin
Jacob Walter
Phed. Buckemier
Chris. Berger
Martin Squartz
Johan Shenkell
Tho. Everhad
William Reiser
Hans Summer
Chris. Hendrick
Jerick Bergener

Anth. Kinter
Nichl. Harman
Hans Wisler
Sam Beem
Hend. Rinewalt
Peter Yosey
Jerick Hylman
Peter Beem
Chris. Souder
Mich^l. Muster
Mich^l. Staylor
Yerick Governor
Jacob Shetzer
Stephen Beninger
Hans Herts
Arn. Sheder
Mich^l Hellibrand
Chris. Trevett
Hendrick Been
Hendrick Sower
Chris. Light
Elias Bald
Martin Fesel
Jacob Odering
Adrius Walker
Mich^l Syder
Hans Hambreet
Hans Michel Witsell
Jurigh Bernard Lowman
Hans Michel Witsell
Viet Hambreght
Hans Wylight Catterman
Hans Jacob Catterman
Hans Michael Sheffer
Hans Mich^l Sheffer
Chris. Stein Claither
Johannes Hootsman
Thomas Everhard
Johannes Groeber
Jacob Beyer
Adam Ambright

Michel Scheyvel
Hans Philip Smit
Jacob Sterne
Hans Casp^r Inderlydner
Jacob Reslaar
Merck Adams Brouns
Hans Adam Brouns
Ulrich Fow
Michel Fraunk
Johan Peter Vonsing
Hans Geo. Webber
Jurig Mich^l Meyer
Christophell Mayer
Hendrick Hoofman
Johan^s Neveling
Chris. Mayer
Mathias Hort
Lorentz Kryger
Johan Christ^n. Handhuize
Jurig Bibighause
Johan Haldhouse
Bestian Bender
Peter Bender
Daniell Bibigause
Wm Haldhouse
Conrad Ambright
Bertho. Mayer
Andreas Grunberger
Hans Martin Welch
Jacob Walsh
Johan Geo. Weber
Tewwis Rezer
Johan Rezer
Joan Hend. Bosveld
Johan Joost Bosveld
Johan Hend. Hoffman
Joost Hooffman
Joost Willm Blecher
Johannes Merker
Johan Jacob Wagner

[Endorsed:]
List of Palatines imported in the St. Andrew, Capt. John
Stedman. Qual. 27th Octr 1738.

[List 62 B] Palatines imported in the Ship St Andrew, John
Stedman, Commander, from Rotterdam, but last from Cowes
in England. Qualified the 27th day of October, 1738.

Peter (L) Light
Hans Jerg (O) Thiel
Johann Henrich Res
Frans Herman (+) Diele
Mainus Sasemanshause
Jost Schumacher
Hans Hoffer
Johann Jacob Kohler
Johann Georg Graüell
Johann Conrath Bittenbender
Johan Victtor Spies
Stephen (++) Ackerman
Conradt Nagel
Anderas Sin
Johann Christoph Kintzel
Hans Jacob Kumerein
Jerg Conrath Schreier
Reynard (H) Rene
Martin Döllinger
Friederich Buckenmeyer
Christoff Berger
Martin Schwartz
Johann Thomas Eberhart
Wilhelm Riser
Hans Gerg Somer
Christian Heinrich
Hans Geörg Behringer
Hans Wissler
Johann Henrich Wald
Peter Böhm
Michael Messer
Johann Nickolas Stähler
Hans Jacob (X) Schertzer

Steffann Beringer
Johannes Hertt
Johan Ar[n]olt Shröter
Michel Hiltenbrantt
Heinrich Saur
Christoffel Leis
Phillip Marti Fissel
Jacob Ottiner
Andreas (X) Walker
Michael (+ +) Syder
Johannes (+) Ambreght
Jerg Bernhart Lauman
Fyt (X) Ambreght
Hans Jacob Katterman
Hans Michael (O) Schyvers
Johanes Utzman
Johannes Gruber
Jacob Beyrer
Adam Hambrecht
Michael Scheiffle
Jacob Stern
Hans Casper Hinderleuthner
Hans Jacob Resler
Hans Adam Braus
Johan Peter Voyzin
Georg Nicolaus Mayer
Henrich Hoffman
Cristian (+) Meyer
Matteus Hirtt
Lorrentz Kriger
Johannes Althaus
Johann Krist Altous
Bastian Benner

Peder ,Benner
Dangel Bibighaus
Johann Gerge Aldhaus
Conrat Hambrecht
Berdolf Meier
Hans Marti Waltz

Johann Georg Weber
Johan Jost (✕) Boffelt
Johannes Hofman
Joost Willem (✕) Blecher
Johanes Mercken
Johann Krafft Röser

[List 62 C] At the Court House of Philadelphia, October 27th 1738.
Present: Antho Morris, Mayor, William Allen, Esqr.

The Palatines whose Names are underwritten, imported in the Ship St Andrew, John Stedman, Commander, from Rotterdam, but last from Cowes in England, did this day take & subscribe the Oaths to the Government, viz.,

Hans Peter (|) Leicht
Johan Georg (N) Kiehl
Johann Heinrich Res
Herman (✕) Thiel
Mannes Sasemanshause
Jost Schumacher
Hans Hoffer
Johann Jacob Kehler
Johann George Grauell
Johann Conrath Bittenbender
Johan Victtor Spies
Stephan (++) Accerman
Conradt Nagel
Andreas Sin
Johann Christoph Kintzel
Hans Jacob Kümrein
Jerg Conrath Schreier
Reinhart (H) Böning
Martin Dollinger
Friederich Buckenmeyer
Christoph Berger
Martin Schwartz
Johann Thomas Eberhart
Wilhelm Riser
Hans Georg Sömer
Christian Heinrich
Hans Geörg Behringer

Hans Wisller
Johann Henrich Wald
Peter Böhm
Michael Messer
Johann Nückolas Stähler
Hans Jacob (✕) Schertzer
Steffann Behringer
Johannes Hertt
Johann Arnoltt Schrödter
Michael Hiltenbrantt
Heinrich Sauer
Christoffel Leis
Phillip Marti Fissel
Jacob Ottiner
Andereas (✕) Wacker
Michael (++) Zider
Johannes (+) Hambrecht
Jerg Bernhart Lauman
Viet (✕) Hambrecht
Hans Jacob Kattermann
Hans Michael (O) Schäffer
Johannes Utzman
Johannes Gruber
Jacob Beyer
Adam Hambrecht
Michael Scheiffle
Jacob Stern

Hans Casper Hinderleuthner
Jacob Resle
Hans Adam Braus
John Peter Voyzin
Georg Nicolaus Mayer
Henrich Hoffman
Christian (+) Meyer
Matteus Hirt
Lorrentz Kriger
Johannes Althaus
Johann Krist Althaus
Bastyan Benner

Peder Benner
Dangel Bibighaus
Johan Gerg Aldhaus
Conrad Hambrecht
Berdolf Meier
Hans Marte Waltz
Johann George Weber
Johan Jost (+) Buschfeld
Johan Hofman
Jost William (×) Blecher
Johanes Mercken
Johann Krafft Röser

[List 63 A] A List of Palatinate Passengers Names Ages on board the Billender Thistle of Philadelphia, George Houston, Commander, from Rotterdam. Philadelphia Nov. 3, 1738.*

MENS NAMES	AGES	MENS NAMES	AGES
Johanan Glyngan	44	Hans Jacob Seiefues	44
Hanse Martin Frets	22	Nicolas Leisser	22
Hanse Nicolas Hansmenger	39	Hanse Adam Feler	20
Samuell Overhard Coup	36	Cristian Fireleigh	17
Godfret Hardlaker	20	Hanse William Busler	23
Hans Petter Lants	30	Hundrick Lillie	22
Uriah Teack	40	Hunderick Tilp	20
Jacob Lants	28	Loadwick Myre	25
Michall Lants	22	Hendrick Young	38
Johanas Gyser	50	Christian Gysler	21
Johanas Petter Gyser	17	Daniele Miller	32
Connered Marcom	23	Loadwick Joseph Bialle	35
Petter Coker	38	Michall Burn	39
Markes Remenger	38	Fredrick Broatsman	42
Gasper Maspeck	29	Petter Stickle	19
Jacob Teack	27	Hendrick Sculps	39
Hans Barrat Steggens	24	Uriah Miller	28
Frederick Miller	26	Hansheria Benss	36
Peter Honshooker	53	Hansheria Hess	31
Abraham Hoonshooker	23	Woldrich Teack	56
Haneriagh Croup	18	Michall Teack	19

* This date does not agree with the other two lists of this ship, 63B and 63C, which are dated October 28, 1738.

MALE CHILDREN UNDER 16	AGES
Petter Teach	14
Michall Stockhalern	12
Daniell Misler	14
William Stockhalern	3
Loadwick Hansminger	7
Philip Cristopher Coup	10
Hanse Nicoll Lants	8
Yoghan Poul Lants	5
Michall Koker	7
Uriagh Carle Klyn	3
Yoghan Cristan Gyser	7
Andrews Hinen Klyn	12
Andreus Seiefues	15
Hanen Cristophele Seiefues	10
Hanen Jacob Seiefues	6
Powell Seiefues	4
Haneriagh Seiefues	3
Fredrick Jacob Young	11
Uriah Jacob Young	10
Cristopher Hendrick Young	9
Gogham Young	4
Daniell Razour	15
Hanse Adam Burn	4
Jacob Hendrick Broatsman	15
Urian Adam Broatsman	10
Yogham Fredrick Broatsman	7
Loadwick Coup	4
Gasper Stickle	11
Daniell Sculpe	7
Hanse Petter Sents	2
Urian Stickle	8
Powell Herbolt	14
Nicolas Herbolt	8
Hans Herbolt	10
Hans Adam Herbolt	4
Jacob Herbolt	8

WOMEN & CHILDREN

	AGES
Elizabath Stockhalern	36

WOMEN & CHILDREN	AGES
Anna Creett Hansminger	35
Cristian Hansminger	13
Kattarina Hansmingar	10
Anna Marrian Hansmingar	3
Anna Timbermon	26
Anna Marelina Timbermon	20
Kattarina Coup	40
Margareta Hardlaker	18
Mareline Coup	8
Charlet Margretta Coup	6
Anneleiss Brightbyle	9
Anna Maria Timbermon	30
Hanah Mariats Timbermon	4
Mariles Pitt Gyser	20
Elizabath Litess	24
Hanah Barbara Porker	53
Meriles Porker	22
Hannah Crett Porker	19
Marelina Kattrin Porker	14
Eveles Koker	29
Hannah Maria Marcom	24
Anna Maria Hefran	24
Elizabath Remeingar	29
Elizabath Resbell	24
Anless Gantson	15
Anless Teack	28
Kattarina Losheart	24
Marelis Tiganer	23
Mariles Sofie Miller	25
Maria Margrat Berian	24
Anna Maria Silks	20
Creetta Honshooker	18
Credle Crighban	13
Anna Lysbet Freligh	13
Anna Margratin Nillen	24
Soffie Klyn	18
Susana Maria Klyn	7
Anelies Seikefues	30
Kattarin Seikefues	12
Anna Maria Seikefus	5

	AGES		AGES
Eveles Byle	18	Creet Olpon	4
Margrat Myre	28	Maria Barbar Broatsman	13
Kattarina Dorte Hoffer	42	Kattarina Felier	22
Rosina Dorte Hoffer	10	Margrat Coup	8
Madlin Young	28	Maria Barball Stickle	13
Kattarina Gysler	20	Anna Barball Sculps	30
Marria Barbara Bushler	60	Anna Maria Sents	20
Kattarina Barball Bushler	10	Kattarina Barbal Sents	8
Hannah Maria Rayzor	3	Anna Kattarina Miller	35
Hannah Sofie Miller	26	Aneria Hess	25
Barball Burn	9	Anna Barball Herbolt	29
Meriat Olpon	39		

[List 63 B] Palatines imported in the Billender Thistle, George Houston, Commander, from Roterdam but last from Cowes in England. Qualified the 28th Octr 1738.

Johannes (X) Kleingenny	Hans Adam Fehler
Hans Martin Fretz	Cristian (X) Frielig
Hans Nickel Ensminger	Johann Wilhelm Bossler
Samuebel Eberhart Kopp	Johann Georg Krob
Godfrett (H) Hardlaker	Hans Jacob (+) Sefues
Hanse (X) Petter Lants	George (X) Lilie
Hanse Georg (H) Teacks	Johan Gorg Delp
Jacob Lantz	Ludwig Meier
Michel Lantz	Henrich Jung
Nickles (O) Gyser	Cristian (O) Gysler
Hans Petter (X) Gyser	Daniel Mueller
Conrath Mehrkam	Ludwig Joseph Bichel
Petter (BK) Coker	Michael (MB) Burn
Markes (MR) Remingar	Fredrick (G) Brotsman
Gasper (X) Maspeck	Joahan Beder Stegel
Johann Jacob Dietz	Hendrick (A) Sculpes
Hanse (O) Barns Ziganer	George (M) Miller
Friederich Miller	Hans Gerig Bintz
Peter Huntzicker	Johan Georg Hess
Abraham Huntzicker	Woldrich (X) Teacks
Nicolas (N) Lesser	Michall (O) Teacks

[List 63 C] At the Courthouse of Philadelphia Octr 28th 1738. Present: Anthony Morris, Esqr, Samuel Hasell Esqr.

The Palatines whose Names are underwritten, imported in the Billender Thistle, George Houston, Commander, from Rotterdam but last from Cowes in England, did this day take & subscribe the Oaths to the Government, viz.,

Johanes (X) Kleinjeny

Hanns Martin Fretz

Hans Nickel Ensminger

Samuel Eberhart Kopp

Gottfried (H) Horrlacher

Hans Peter (X) Lans

Hans Georg (H) Diez

Jacob Lantz

Michel Lantz

Johannes (O) Geisser

Peter (X) Geisser

Conrath Mehrkam

Peter (BK) Cogger

Marcus (MR) Remiger

Caspar (X) Masbeck

Johann Jacob Dietz

Hans Bernhart (O) Steigner

Friedrich Müller

Peter Huntzicker

Abraham Huntzicker

Nicklas (N) Liger

Hans Adam Fehler

Christian (X) Frölich

Johann Wilhelm Bosler

Johann Georg Krob

Hans Jacob (X) Zifus

John George (X) Leelly

Johann Gorg Delpp

Ludwig Meier

Henrich Jung

Christian (O) Geisler

Daniel Müller

Ludwig Joseph Bichel

Michael (MB) Born

Friederich (G) Bratzman

Johan Peter Stegel

Henrich (A) Schultz

Georg (M) Miller

Hans Georg Büntz

Johan Gerg Hess

Uhllerik (X) Dietz

Michel (O) Dietz

[List 64 A] List of Palatines Names pr. the Elizabeth, Capt Hodgson. [Qualified October 30, 1738.]

	AGES		AGES
Lodwick Nicholas	34	Hans Jacob Kesler	25
Jacob Shilkneght	38	Mathias Bartholomew	20
George Arnoldt	34	Conrath Nydagh	19
Johannes Mayer	27	Nicholas Hodele	36
Philip Jacob Leyderberger	34	Johannes Harley	25
Daniel Heyning	30	Hans George Fritz	30
Christian Egan	17	Conradt Kenner	22
Johannes Honether	36	Hans Georg Petery	33
Johannes Mester	43	Laurentz Rous	23
Tobias Swartz	26	Geo. Adam Mayer	19
Bernard Wainmaker	40	Philip Besa	16

	AGES		AGES
John Lodwick Potts	29	Hans Geo. Windlinge	32
Henry Keaghler	28	Mich¹ Deyne	29
Matheas Poriger	39	Martin Dageaback	23
Jacob Frans	34	Ulrich Rodobush	24
Jacob Kern	18	Mathys Deolar	31
Johannes Yeites	21	Christian Creytz	26
Hans Jacob Bener	38	Elias Berniger	24
Conradt Fogleman	35	Lodowick Fansler	..
Andreas Rodenhauser	34	Geo. Adam Yegold	..
Hans Adam Kinsler	25	43 [men] 21 [women] 6 [chil-	
Mathias Chris	50	dren] 64 [persons]	
Christian Lesh	41		

[Endorsed:]
List of Palatines imported in the Elizabeth, Capt Hodgson.
Qual. 30th October, 1738.

[List 64 B] Palatines imported in the Ship Elizabeth,
George Hodgson, from Rotterdam, but last from Cowes in Old
England. Qualified Octr 30th 1738.

Ludwig Nicola	Henrich Kuhler
Jacob Schiltknecht	Mathias (X) Poriger
Johann Görg Arnold	Jacob (J) Frans
Johannes Mähr	Conradt (V) Vogelman
Philib Jacob Leidenberger	Jacob Gern
Daniel Huenig	Joanes (X) Yeites
Christof Egen	Hans Jacob (X) Bener
Johannes Meister	Andereas Rohteneffer
Bernd Wannemacher	John Adam Kintzel
John Jacob (X) Kesler	Matheas (C) Chris
Mathias (X) Bartholomew	Christian (X) Lesh
Conrad (X) Neydagh	Hanns Jerg Windlinger
Nicolas (X) Hodoly	Hans Michael (H) Deinie
Hans Ulrich (X) Fritz	Martin (X) Degenbag
Johannes Carl	Ullrig Raudenbusch
Conrad (X) Kenner	Mattheus Döbler
Hans Geo. (X) Petery	Christophorus Theophilus Creutz
Lawrence (X) Rous	Elias (X) Berneger
Geörg Ernst Mayer	Ludwig Pfantzler
Philip (X) Besa	Geo. Adam (X) Yegold
Lodowich (X) Potts	

[List 64 C] At the Court house of Philadelphia, Octr 30th 1738.

Present

Anthon^i Morris, Mayor, William Allen, } Esq^rs.
Clement Plumsted,

The Palatines whose Names are underwritten, imported in the Ship Elizabeth, George Hodgson, Com^r, from Rotterdam but last from Cowes in England, did this Day take and Subscribe the Oaths to the Government, viz.,

Ludwig Nicola
Jacob Schiltknecht
Johann Görg Arnold
Johannes Mähr
Philib Jacob Leitenberger
Daniel Huenig
Christoff Egen
Johannis Meister
Bernd Wannemacher
John Jacob (✕) Kisler
Mattias (✕) Bartholyme
Conrad (++) Neider
Nicklas (✕) Hodely
Johanes Carl
Hans Uhllerick (✕) Fritz
Conrad (✕) Kenner
Hans George (✕) Petery
Lorentz (✕) Rous
Geörg Ernst Meyer
Philip (++) Bissa
John Ludwig Potts

Henrich Kühler
Mathias (++) Burger
Jacob (J) Frantz
Hans Conrad (V) Vogelman
Jacob Gern
John (++) Yeatz
Hans Jacob (✕) Bönner
Andereas Rotheheffer
John (K) Adam Kintzel
Matteas (C) Cresse
Christian (✕) Leesh
Hanns Jerg Windlinger
Hans Michael (H) Dänny
Martin (✕) Dagenbeck
Ullrig Raudenbusch
Mattheus Döbler
Christophorus Theophilus Creutz
Elias (✕) Beringer
Ludwig Pfantzler
Georg Adam (✕) Egold

[List 65 A] A List of Mens Names imported in the Charming Nancey, Charles Stedman, Com^r, from Rotterdam. November 9th 1738.

	AGES		AGES
Christian Kerwer	46	Mark Folhaver	25
Jacob Didrich	40	Philip Mauer	32
Hans Michael Reyn	24	Jeremie Semer	27
Hans Georg Reyser	26	Hans Jacob Kuntz	42
Hans Adam Didel	30	Hans Jacob Kuntz	21

	AGES		AGES
Jurigh Mich. Kerbel	32	Hans Jacob Broser	36
Hans Jacob Barlin	22	Jurigh David Boos	24
Geo. Fred^k. Barlin	18	Lodowick Loos	18
Abraham Barlin	16	Hendrick Spries	22
Johannes Fayt	22	Hans Georg Bolts	25
Leonard Shust	20	Johan Mich^l Mouse	18
Peter Kreitzer	20	Johannes Sighman	40
Andreas Kreitzer	24	Hans Georg Sighman	20
Everhard Miller	19	Johannes Sighman	18
Christophel Abel	20	Bernhard Sighman	16
Joseph David Dresser	38	Johan Peter Wols	19
Adreas Beyerlie	23	Baltzer Kritzer	37
Michael Klein	22	Johan Hand^k Kippily	22
Jurigh Hatts	38	Johan Ferdinand Dirtzibach	33
Peter Baldsberger	16	Hans Georg Schink	37
Christophel Trenkle	48	Christophel Segman	25
Stephen- Trenkle	20	Christian Miller	26
Jacob Gorgh	26	Hendrick Keesner	40
Conradt Felt	30	Johan Stephen Goodman	27
Johan Adam Semen	22	Hans Jacob Schink	32
Jacob Semen, in sick house	27	Hans Hendrick Woll	23
Abraham Hostwert	24	Hans Jacob Miller	43
Jacob Hostedler	26	Hans Georg Stroball	21
Abraham Kunzigh	24	Jacob Wannamaker	24
Christian Miller	25	Jacob Bour	20
Christian Bullman	20	Peter Potts	20
Hans Fletiker	16	Martin Oadt	24
Nicholas Klaugh	24	65 persons	

Sworn Novem^r 9th 1738, that the above list is all above the age of fifteen Years to the best of my knowledge.

Charles Stedman.

[List 65 B] Palatines imported in the Ship Charming Nancey, Charles Stedman, Com^r, from Rotterdam but last from Cowes in England. Qualified the 9th Day of Novem^r 1738.

Hans Christian Gerber	Hans Adam (+) Didel
Hans Michael (×) Rein	March (+) Fouler
Jacob (×) Ditrek	Philip (×) Moure
Joseph (×) Geisser	Jeremiah (×) Zemier

Hans Jacob (H) Huntz
Hans Jacob (J) Huntz
Geo. Michael (+) Kermer
Jacob (O) Berlin
Geo. Fred^k (X) Berlin
Abraham (A) Berlin
Hans (H) Etimers
Leonard (B) Sheus
Peter (O) Scriver
Andreas (X) Creuser
Johan Jacob Müller
Christophr (X) Creble
Joseph Davidt Trissler
Andres Beyerle
Michael (X) Klein
Jung Geo. (X) Hatz
Peter (O) Bursbeger
Christopher (X) Zingle
David (XX) Zinkle
Jacob (XX Coort
Connrath Fleck
Jeo. Adam (X) Ziman
Jacob (X) Ziman
Abraham Hausswirth
Jacob (X) Howstetter
Hunter (H) Zincie
Christian (X) Miller
Christian (X) Pullman

Christopher (X) Sigman
Hans (X) Fürller
Nicalas (X) Kelaugh
Jurich Geo. (X) Troulst
Ludwig Glotz
Henrich Spies
Hans Geo. (X) Hults
Johan Michael Maurer
Hans (X) Zerichen [?]
Hans (X) Jerick Sigman
John (X) Zigman
Bernard (X) Zigman
Geo. Peter (X) Walts
Johann Baldes Knörtzer
John Hendrich (X) Kepley
Ferdinand Dörtzbach
Hans Jörg Schenck
Christian (X) Miller
Heinrich Kistner
John Stephan Guttman
Hans Jacob (H) Shunk
Hans Henrich (+) Pohl
Hans Jacob Müller
Hans Gorg Strobel
Jacob Wannenmacher
Jacho Bauer
Peter Butz
Marti Tienod

[List 65 C] At the Court House of Philadelphia, November 9th 1738. Present: The Honourable George Thomas, Esqr, Lieutenant Governour.

The Palatines whose Names are underwritten, imported in the Ship the Charming Nancy, Charles Stedman, Com^r, from Rotterdam, but last from Cowes in England, did this day take and Subscribe the Oaths to the Government, viz.,

Hans Christian Gerber
Hans Michael (X) Rehin
Jacob (X) Diterich
Hans Georg (X) Reisser

Hans Adam (X) Dittel
Markus (X) Faulhaffer
Hans Philip (XX) Maurer
Jerimias (|) Zämer

Hans Jacob (H) Kuntz
Hans Jacob (J) Kuntz, Junr
Jork Michel (X) Kerber
Hans Jacob (O) Barling
Georg Frederik (X) Barly
Abraham (X) Barly
Hans (H) Vit
Lenard (B) Just
Peter (S) Greutzer
Andereas (X) Creutzer
Johan Jacob Müller
Christoff (X) Knubel
Joseph Davidt Trissler
Andres Beyerle
Michael (X) Klein
Georg (X) Hatz
Peter (O) Baldesberger
Christoff (X) Drinkel
Stephen (XX) Drinkel
Jacob (XX) Corr
Connrath Fleck
John Adam (X) Simon
Jacob (S) Simon
Abraham Hauswirth
Jacob (X) Hochstadler
Abraham (X) Kuntzy
Christian (X) Miller
Hans (X) Billman

Christoph (X) Sigman
Hans (X) Flidiger
Nicklas Kluge
George Davit (X) Botz
Ludwig Glotz
Henrich Spies
Hans George (X) Holtz
Johan Michael Maurer
Hans (X) Sigman
Hans Georg Sigman
Johnn (X) Sigman
Bernhart (X) Sigman
John Peter (X) Waltz
Johann Baldas Knörtzer
Johan Henry (X) Köply
Ferdinand Dortzbach
Hans Jörg Schenk
Christian (+) Miller
Heinrich Kistner
Johan Stephan Guttman
Hans Jacob (O) Shänk
Hans Henry (X) Pohl
Hans Jacob Müller
Hans Jerg Strobel
Jacob Wannenmacher
Jacho Bauer
Peter Butz
Martin (S) Oats

[List 66 A] A List of Passengers on board ye Snow Enterprise, Lyonell Wood, Commander. [Qualified Dec. 6, 1738.]

Jno Jacob Von der Werdt
Vincent Beiler
Jno Righter
Jacob Hirtzell
Conerat D^o
Jacob Saxer
Jno George Weber
Thos Lang
Jacob Rotherwither

Jacob Mansinger
David D^o
Jno D^o
Frederick Erter, sick
Felix Houser
Jacob Hirtzell
Geo. Nothart
Frederick Recher
Jno D^o

Jacob Restenholtz
Hans Ruth
Hans Burk
Henry D°
Martin Schudy
Martin Griedy
Conradt Weiland

Ralph Meyenhoffer
Jn° Jacob Frolick
Casper Horner
Jacob D°
Casper Keller
Jn° Mich¹ Muller

Sworn Decem^r 6th 1738, that the above is a true & Compleat list of Male Palatines, imported in the Snow Enterprise, above the age of 15 years, to the best of my knowledge.

Lyonell Wood.

[List 66 B] Palatines imported in the Snow Enterprise, Lyonell Wood, Com^r, from London. Qualified Decem^r 6th 1738.

Hanns Jacob Von der Weyt
Vincent (×) Piler
Johannes Richter
Jacob (×) Hirtell
Conradt Hirtell
Jacob (×) Hirtell, Junr
Jacob (×) Saxer
Jn° Geo. (W) Weber
Thomas Lang
Jacob Slothweiler
[Jacob] (×) Mansinger
David (×) Mansinger
Melcher Mantzinger
Felix (×) Hauser
Georg Nodhart

Fritz Recher
[Johann] (HR) Brecher
Jacob Bestenholtz
Hans (×) Ruth
Hans Rudi Bürgi
Henry (×) Berger
Mardin Tschudi
Martin (×) Grider
Rodolph (×) Mayerhousen
Hans Jacob Fröli
Casper (×) Horner
Jacob (×) Horner
Casper (×) Keller
Hans Michel Müller
Matheis Baumgartner

[List 66 C] At the Courthouse of Philadelphia, Decem^r 6th 1738.

Present: Clement Plumsted, Samuel Hassell, } Esq^{rs}.
Ralph Asheton,

The Palatines whose Names are underwritten, imported in the Snow Enterprise, Lyonell Wood, M^r, from London, did this Day take and Subscribe the Oaths to the Government, viz.,

Hans Jacob von der Weyt	Fritz Recher
Vincent (X) Pieller	Johann (H) Recher
Johannes Richter	Jacob Bestenholz
Jacob (X) Hertzel	Hans (X) Ruth
Conrad (X) Hertzel	Hans Rudi Bürgi
Jacob (X) Hertzel, Junr	Henry (X) Burger
Jacob (O) Saxer	Mardin Tschudi
John Georg (W) Weber	Martin (X) Greedy
Thomas Lang	Rudolff (X) Meyerhoffe
Jacob Slothweiler	Hans Jacob Fröli
Jacob (X) Mansinger	Caspar (X) Horner
Davit (X) Mansinger	Jacob (X) Horner
Melcher Mantzinger	Caspar (X) Keller
Felix (O) Houser	Hans Michel Müller
Jerg Nodhardt	Matheis Baumgartner

[List 67 A] A List of Passengers Imported in yᵉ Billinder London, Joshua Pipon, Commander, from London. January 8ᵗʰ 1738/9.

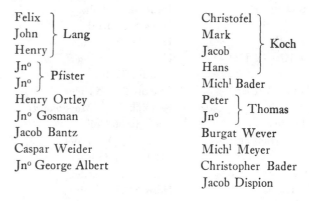

Felix ⎱
John ⎬ Lang
Henry ⎰

Jnᵒ ⎱ Pfister
Jnᵒ ⎰

Henry Ortley
Jnᵒ Gosman
Jacob Bantz
Caspar Weider
Jnᵒ George Albert

Christofel ⎱
Mark ⎬ Koch
Jacob ⎰
Hans ⎰

Michˡ Bader

Peter ⎱ Thomas
Jnᵒ ⎰

Burgat Wever
Michˡ Meyer
Christopher Bader
Jacob Dispion

Sworn January 10ᵗʰ 1738/9, that the above is a true and compleat list of the Male Passengers of Palatines of the Age of Sixteen Years and Upwards to the best of my knowledge.

Joshua Pipon.

[List 67 B] Palatines imported in the Bellinder London, Joshua Pipon, Comʳ, from London. Qualified January 10ᵗʰ 1738/9.

Felix Lang	Mark (×) Koch
John (×) Lang	Jacob (×) Koch
Henry (×) Lang	Hans Koch *
Jerg Hans Pfister	Michel Sautter
Johanis Pfister	Martin (C) Koch
Henry (×) Ortley	Peter Thomas
Hans Gassmann	Johannes Thomas
Jacob (O) Bantz	Burgat (×) Weaver
Caspar Widter	Michael (×) Meyer
John George Albert	Christopher (×) Bader
Christoᵣ (×) Koch	Johann Jacob Dispionit

[List 67 C] At the Court House of Philadelphia, January 10th 1738/9.
Present: Clement Plumsted, Thoˢ Griffitts, Esqʳˢ
　　　　Thomas Lawrence, The Mayor of Philadelphia,
　　　　Samˡ Hassell.
The Palatines whose Names are underwritten, imported in Bellinder London, Joshua Pipon, Comʳ, from London, did take and Subscribe the Oaths to the Government, viz.,

Felix Lang	Marcus (×) Koch
John (×) Long	Jacob Koch
Henry (×) Lang	Martin Koch †
Jurg Hans Pfister	Michel Sautter
Johanis Pfister	Peter Thomas
Henry (×) Ortley	Johannes Thomas
Johannes Gassman	Burgart (×) Weeber
Jacob (×) Bance	Melchior (×) Meyer
Caspar Widter	Christoph (×) Bader
John Georg Albert	Jacob Dispion
Christoph (×) Kock	

[List 68 A] A List of the Mens Names pʳ the Jamaica Galley, Capᵗ. Robᵗ. Harrison, from Rotterdam & Cowes. [Qualified Feb. 7, 1739.]

---

* Name crossed out.
† Martin Koch written over the erasure of Hans Koch.

MENS NAMES	AGES	MENS NAMES	AGES
Hans Conraat Ruseley	41	Christopher Wideman	40
Johannes Wilderson	48	Jacob Hinne	35
Jacobus Muller	38	Jacob Bonger	38
Hans Apely	30	Hendrich Bachman	27
Hendrich User	33	Hendrich Otte	21
Hendrich Hoofman	52	Hendrich Kladney	28
Caspar Mayer	30	Hendrich Kladney	20
Hans Ulrich Angst	25	Ulrich Swarsenbach	33
Felix Hubart	38	Felix Bossart	48
Hans Ulrich Muller	24	Jacob Bossart	20
Leonard Furrer	40	Ulrich Bossart	19
Hendrich Galler	17	Hans Ulrich Hofman	19
Joachim Husley	34	Jacob Boeman	22
Roedolph Bawmer	34	Hans Jacob Boeman	18
Conraat Ackeritt	25	Hendrich Mayer	30
Hendrich Ackeritt	23	Felix Schuts	22
Hans Hendrich Somer	34	Melger Tinker	16
Hendrich Beter	26	Roedolph Schuts	19
Ulrich Smith	29	Ulrich Peninger	20
Jacob Veer	35	Lawrence Riger	34
Jacob Swerber	35	Hans Boogman	27
Hans Moogh	38	Hendrich Stally	25
Caspar Frener	20	Hendrich Roukop	28
Michael Swenk	50	Hendrick Overholds	34
Adam Swenk	18	Barnard Riga	27
Christoffer Muller	24	Hans Friner	25
Jacob Eens	24	Roedolph Ramp	22
Hans Mayer	30	Hans Jacob Peninger	24
Roedolph Decker	40	Hans Ulrich Nef	29
Conraat Bachler	38	Johannes Shibley	21
Jacob Mayer	24	Hans Ulrich Mayer	32
Andrias Nabinger	25	Hans Jacob Shaup	25
Hendrich Brunder	20	Felix Linebaker	56
Roedolph Shuts	22	Hendrich Linebaker	21
Hendrich Shellenberg	22	Hans Sollinger	40
Jacob Hopman	26	Jacob Dunke	38
Hans Jacob Hopman	18	Jacob Mayer	47
Felix Bachman	21	Felix Klatley	36
Jurich Brunder	19	Hans Anner	22
Hans Neusley	45	Hendrich Gans	34

MENS NAMES	AGES	MENS NAMES	AGES
Hendrich Tinkee	30	Hendrich Wert	27
Hans Jacob Kerne	20	Hendrich Shible	20
Hendrich Kramer	24	Felix Franfilder	38
Ulrich Neusley	34	Caspar Wideman	16
Jacob Nergen	28		

Sworn Feb 7th 1738/9, that the above is a true and compleat List of Palatine Males of the Age of Sixteen Years and upwards, to the best of my knowledge.

Robt Harrison.

[List 68 B] Palatines imported in the Ship Jamaica Galley, Robert Harrison, Commander, from Rotterdam, but last from Cowes in England. Qualified February 7th 1738/9.

Hans Künradt Rösli
Johannes Wiltensinn
Jacob Müller
Hans Eppli
Heinrich Hauser
Heinrich Hoffman
Caspar (X) Mayer
Hans Henry (X) Ansgt
Felix Huber
H. Ulrich Müller
Linhart Furer
Henry (X) Galler
Joachim (+) Housley
Roedolph (X) Bawiner
Conraat (X) Askeritt
Heinrich Ackerdt
Hans Heinrich Sommer
Hendrick (X) Better
Ulrick (X) Smith
Jacob Fehr
Jacob (X) Swarber
Hans (X) Moogh
Caspar (X) Freneir
Hans Michael Schweinck

Adam Schweinck
Christofel Müller
Jacob Kuntz
Hans Meier
Rudolf Decker
Conraat (X) Bauchler
Jacob (X) Meyer
Andreas (X) Nabinger
Henrick (X) Brunder
Roedolph (X) Schutz
Heinrich Schellenberg
Jacob (+) Hopman
Hans Jacob (+) Hopman
Felix (X) Bachman
Ulrich (+) Brunder
Hans Nüsli
Christofel Weidman
Jacob (X) Hina
Jacob (+) Boucher
Heinerich Bachman
Henrich (+) Otte
Henrich (+) Glatley, Senr
Henrich (+) Glatley, Junr
Ulrich (+) Swartzenberg

Felix (+) Bossart
Jacob (+) Bossart
Hans Boshart
Hans Ulrich (✕) Hoofman
Jacob B[a]uman
Hans Jacob Bauman
Henrich (✕) Meyer
Felix (✕) Schutz
Melchior [Dün]ki
Roedolph (S) Schutz
Ulrich Bäninger
Lawrense (✕) Riger
Hans (✕) Bochman
Henrich (✕) Stalley
Henrick (✕) Rokoop
Henrick (✕) Overholds
Bernard (✕) Riga
Joannes (✕) Frenner
Roedolph (✕) Ramp
Hans Jacob Bäninger
Hans Ulrich Näff

Johannes (+) Shibley
Hans Ulrick (+) Meyer
Hans Jacob Schaub
Felix (✕) Limbaker
Henrich (✕) Limbaker
Hans (✕) Solinger
Jacob (✕) Dunkel
Jacob (✕) Meyer
Felix (✕) Clatley
Hans (✕✕) Anard
Heinrich Gantz
Heinrich Dümcke
Hans Jacob Kern
Henrich Kremer
Ulrich Nussli
Jacob (✕) Nargen
Henrich (✕) Wert
Henrich (O) Shibly
Caspar (✕) Wideman
Felix (+) Fronfilder

[List 68 C] At the Court House of Philadelphia, February 7th, 1738/9.

Present

The Honble George Thomas, Esqr, Lieutenant Governour,
Clement Plumsted, Thos Griffitts,
Thos Lawrence,   Anthony Morris, Mayor   } Esq[rs].

The Palatines whose Names are underwritten, imported in the Ship Jamaica Galley, Robert Harrison, Com[r], from Rotterdam, but last from Cowes in England, did this Day take and Subscribe the Oaths to the Government, viz.,

Hans Cönradt Rösli *
Johannes Wiltensin
Jacob Müller
Hans Eppli
Heinrich Häuser

Heinrich Hoffman
Caspar (✕) Meyer
Hans Henry Angst
Felix Huber
H. Ulrich Müller

* The original reads: "Ich Hans Cönradt Rösli bekän", which means "I John Conrad Roesli confess", i. e., swear the oath of allegiance.

Linhart Furer
Henry (X) Keller
Jochaim (X) Hensly
Rudolph (X) Baumer
Conrad Ackert
Heinrich Ackert
Hans Heinrich Sommer
Henry (X) Peter
Uhllerich (X) Smith
Jacob Fehr
Jacob (X) Shwarber
Hans (X) Moogh
Caspar (X) Frener
Hans Michael Schweinkh
Adam Schweinckh
Christofel Weller
Jacob Kuntz
Hans Meier
Rudolf Decker
Conrad (X) Barttler
Jacob (X) Meyer
Andereas (X) Navinger
Henry (X) Brunner
Rudolph (X) Shütz
Heinrich Schellenberg
Jacob (XX) Hopman
Hans (O) Jacob Hopman
Felix (X) Bachman
George (X) Bruner
Hans Nüsle
Christofel Weidman
Jacob (X) Hinne
Jacob (X) Bucher
Heinrich Bachman
Henry (+) Otto
Henry (++) Glattly
Henry (+) Glattly, Junr
Uhllerik (X) Shwartzenbach
Felix (X) Bossert
Jacob (X) Bossert

Hans Boshart
Hans Uhllerik (X) Hoffman
Jacob Bauman
Hans Jacob Bauman
Henry (X) Meyer
Felix (X) Shütz
Melichor Dünki
Rudolph (X) Shütz
Ulrich Bäninger
Lorence (X) Riger
Hans (X) Bachman
Henry (X) Ställy
Henry (X) Rohkop
Henry (X) Oberholtz
Bernhart (X) Reege
Johanes (X) Franer
Rudolph (X) Ramp
Hans Jacob Bäninger
Hans Ulrich Näff
Johannes (+) Shibly
Hans Uhllerik (X) Meyer
Hans Jacob Schaub
Felix (X) Leinbacker
Henry (X) Leinbacker
Hans (X) Zollinger
Jacob (+) Duncky
Jacob (+) Meyer
Felix (X) Glattly
Hans (XX) Anner
Heinrich Gantz
Heinrich Düncki
Hans Jacob Kern
Heinrich Kremer
Ulrich Nuesli
Jacob (X) Nargen
Henry (X) Wirth
Henry (X) Sheeply
Caspar (X) Whitman
Felix (+) Fronfelder

[List 69 A] A List of Passingers Names & Ages on board the Samuel, Hugh Percy, Commd^r, from Rotterdam. [Qualified August 27, 1739.]

MENS NAMES	AGES	MENS NAMES	AGES
Danl Buttong	48	Jurig Snyder	18
Johanes Fisher	48	Jacob Lamenich	34
Johanes Broumiller	26	Adam Snyder	35
Mich^l Smeal	34	Danl Cookhart	18
Casper Mead	48	Peter More	36
Johanes Mead	16	Ludwick Gyb	17
Conrade Hartong	29	Jacob Fucks	33
Jurig Snyder	29	Sabastian Doll	40
Juring Bartman	45	Christian Syphert	42
Johan Mich^l Bartman	19	Peter Swink	49
Johan Matthias Bartman	16	Hartman Swink	20
Henrich Dorwart	40	Abraham Hyderick	47
Mich^l Adam	36	Johan Nich^l Hyderick	16
Johan Adam Shaffer	30	Philipus Linsh	57
Jurig Hyer	24	Johan Jurig Nichol	20
Lorince Hentzel	38	Christoffel Timerman	24
Peter Ruhl	45	Johan Henrich Erhard	23
Peter Millhouse	42	Johan David Loudinback	23
Jurig Freman	33	Johanes Byer	19
Matthias Clous	32	Paul Michel	31
Henrich Snirtzel	45	Mich^l Haan	24
Johanes Ermantroud	22	Johanes Haan	18
Philipus Ermantroud	18	Sabastian Koockhart	23
Johan Fredrick Ermantroud	16	Nich^l Simon	63
Peter Stayn	40	Simon Gehres	27
Conrade Housman	26	Peter Shaffer	24
Fredrick Gerhard	25	Adam Becker	25
Willm Gerhard, sick	..	Mich^l Miller	21
Peter Tresler	25	Mich^l Bouer	27
Petter Groub	40	Christ^n Shepffer	52
Danl Groub	17	Christ^n Shepffer	16
Johanes Bischoff	18	Laurince Minech, sick	40
Adam Deihl	52	Philip Schel	23
Danl Deihl	26	Henrich Frais	21
Carl Deihl	22	Peter Brem	39

MENS NAMES	AGES	MENS NAMES	AGES
Philipus Serfas	27	Jacob Reidy	19
Peter Stouber	30	Peter Reidy	16
Abraham Foust	24	Simon Drum	50
Jacob Rice	30	Peter Nickom	24
Philip Hersch	22	Fredrick Nickom	22
Johan Jurig Shous	22	Nichel Helfenstyn	44
Jacob Woolf	20	Daniel Burger	40
Peter Gerhart	22	Paul Samsel	31
Abraham Shryner	20	Philips Klien	55
Christoffel Ruth	37	Johan Adam Klien	30
Johan Jurig Foust	..	Adam Gotwalt	20
Mich^l Miller	42	Nichel Kneesel	26
John Adam Miller	..	Peter Mombour	28
Fredrich Gabel	37	Casper Doll	18
Philip Gabel	41	Abraham Salmon	19
Christ^n Shook	48	Nickel Bach	25
Jacob Cookhart	24	Stoffel Doll	40
Nichel Mombour	50	Philip Doll	27
Johan Nichel Mombour	18	Joseph Beerey	36
Peter Shool	28	Johan Barnard Pedre	16
Johan Otto Reidy	54	111 [persons]	

Sworn that the above is a Compleat and true List of the Male
Palatines of the age of 16 Years and upwards imported in the
Ship Samuel, to the best of my knowledge.
August 27th 1739.

Hugh Percy.

[List 70 A] In the Snow Bettsey from Rotterdam & Deal
[Richard Budden, Com^r. Qualified August 27, 1739.]

Nicholas Leinberger	Christian Prodenbaer
Hans Jacob Geiger	Casper Herde
Johan George Scherer	Hans Martin Barth
Daniel Dalwig	Peter Blaser
Johannes Kiener	Hans Michael Ernste
Bastian Unberhent	Hans Jacob Marum
Melcher Keiner	Gerhard Heinrice Scrutz
Martin Adam	George Wilhelm Hoker
Hans Peter Hoffman	Friedrice Zeitz

Johannes Martin	Andreas Engelhard
John Daniel Osterlin	Friedrich Ehrenfeichter
John Daniel Muller	Jacob Lantz
George Becker	Johannes Bach
Johannes Hasselwanger	Johan Godfried Straube
Hans Jacob Berkel	Jacob Ruff
Coenraad Becker	Peter Oberdice
Velten Becker	Jacob Hess
Valentin Ertel	Henry Streckies
Johan Peter Meyer	Conrad Hakensmith
Joseph Walti	Johan Nicolas Scherer
George David Sockel	Michell Baker
Johannes Reichard	Fredrik Shäfer
Martin Haag	Jacob Unbehendt
Conraad Graaff	Vallentin Unbehendt
Johannes Klein	Conrad Unbehendt
Matthias Hertzell	Hans Martin Bart
Johannes Koch	Johannes Weibel
Frans Wellick	Mathias Hooch
Jacob Goode	Nicolaes Leyenberger
Johan Michael Roth	Jacob Oellen
Johan Henrich Miller	61 [men]

Sworn that the above is a compleat and true list of Male Palatines importe.1 in the Snow Bettsie, of the Age of 16 Years and upwards, to the best of my knowledge. August 27ᵗʰ 1739.

Richard Budden.

[Endorsed:]

List of Palatines imported in the Snow Betsy, Richard Budden, qualifyd August 27ᵗʰ 1739.

[Lists 69–70 B] Palatines imported in the Ship Samuel and Snow Betsie, Hugh Percy and Richᵈ Buden, Comʳˢ from Rotterdam and Deal. Qualified August 27th, 1739.

SHIP SAMUEL	Caspar Meth
	Johan Conrath Hartung
Jan Daniel Bouton	Johannes Schneyder
Joannes (✕) Fisher	Johan Georg Barttman
Joannes (✕) Brownmiller	Johan Michel Bartmann
Michgel Schmöhl	Johan Mathias (+) Bartman

Johannes Meth
Henrich Thorwart
Michel Adam
Johann Adam Schäffer
John Geo. (×✕) Hyer
Johann Lorentz Hänsel
Peter (✕) Rule
Peder Meelhus
George (✕) Freeman
Mathias (✕) Clous
Henrich (✕) Snertzel
Johannes Ermentraudt
Johan Phillip Ermentraudt
Johan Friedrich Ermentraudt
Peter (++) Stein
Conrad (++) Housman
Frederick (✕) Gerhard
William (✕) Gerhard
Johan Peder Dressler
Peter (✕) Grub
Johann Daniel Crub
Johannes Bischof
Hans Adam Diehl
Johann Daniehl Diehl
Carel Adam
George (✕) Snyder
Jacob Lamerck
Johann Adam Schneider
Daniel (IK) Kockhart
Peter (✕) Moor
Lodowich (✕✕) Gybb
Jacob Fucks
Sebastian (DB) Doll
Christian Seyferth
Petter Schwenck
Hartman (✕) Syank
Abraham (✕) Hendrick
Nicholas (+) Hendrick
Philips Lentz
Johann Geörg Nickel
Johann Christofel Zimmerman

John Hendrick (+) Gerhard
John David (✕) Laudenback
Johannes Beyer
Paul (✕) Michael
Michael (✕) Haan
Johannes Hahn
Sebastian Gückert
Michel Simon
Johan Adam (✕) Klein
Simon Geres
Petter Schöffer
Adam Becker
Michael (✕) Miller
Michael (✕) Bour
Christian Schöpfer, Sr.
Christian Schöpfer, Jr.
Lawrence (✕✕) Minich
Philipp Jacob Schell
Johan Henrich Freys
Johan Peter Priem
Johan Philibs Servas
Johan Peter Stuber
Abraham Faust
Jacob Reiss
Philib Hirsch
Johann Jörg Schaus
Jacob Wolf
Peter Gerhard
Abraham Schreyner
Johan Christophel Ruth
Michell Miller
Johann Adam Miller
Joen Fridrich Gabel
Johan Philib Gabel
Christian Schug
Johann Jacob Kockert
Michael (M) Moumbaur
John Nicholas (M) Maumbour
Peter Scholl
Otto Riedy
Johann Jacob Riedy

Johann Peder Rietig
Simon Drom
Peter (X) Nickom
Frederick (X) Nickom
Michael (X) Helfensyng
Daniel Burger
Paul Samsel
John Philip (X) Klein
Johann Adam Gottwals
Nicholas (N) Nysyng
Peter (X) Moumbar
Caspar (X) Doll
Abram (X) Salmond
Johan Michael (X) Baach
Christopher (X) Doll
Philip (+) Doll
Joseph (O) Berie
Johann Bernhardt Bederri

SNOW BETSIE

Nicklaus Leinberger
Hans Jacob Geiger
Daniel Dalwig
Jahns Keiner [?]
Bastian (X) Unberhent
Melcher (X) Keneir
Johan Georg Scherr[er]
Martin Adam
Johann Peter Hoffman
Christian Rodenbach
Casper Herde
Martin Barth
Peter (X) Blaser
Hans Michel Ernst
Hans Jacob Maron
Gerhard Henrich Schütz
Georg Wilhelm Höcker
Frederick (X) Sticky
Johannes (X) Martin
Johann Daniel Oesterlen

Johann Daniel Müller
George (X) Becher
Joanes (++) Haselwanger
Jacob (++) Pertzell
Conradt Becker
Velten Becker
Wallendin Ertel
John Peter (X) Melcher
Andreas (X) Waldi
Geo. David (X) Scholl
Johannes Reichardt
Martin (+) Hock
Conradt Graff
Jonas (X) Klein
Mathias (+) Hartsel
Johannes Koch
Frans (X) Velhell
Jacob (X) Good
Johann Michael Roth
John Henry (I I) Miller
Andreas Engellhard
Jacob (+) Luntz
Friederich Ehrnfeichter
Johannes Bock
Johann Gottfried Straube
Jacob Ruff
Piere Aubertien
Hendrick Strickert
Conrad (+) Hacketsmitt
Johan Nickel Scherer
Michael Becker
Fred. (X) Shaffer
Jacob (X) Unbehen
Valentine (+) Unbehen
Conrad (X) Unbehen
Hans Martin (X) Baar
Johannes Weibell
Mathias (X) Hook
Nicholas (O) Lyberg
Jacob Oellen

[Lists 69–70 C] At the Court House of Philadelphia, August 27th 1739.

Present

The Honourable George Thomas, Esqr, Lieutenant Governour, Samuel Hassel, Thomas Griffitts, Esq^{rs}.

The Palatines whose Names are underwritten, imported in the Ship Samuel and Snow Betsie, Hugh Percy and Richard Buden, Commanders, from Rotterdam, but last from Deal in England, did this Day take and Subscribe the Oaths to the Government, viz.,

SHIP SAMUEL

Jan Daniel Bouton
Johannes (×) Fischer
Johannes (+) Brounmiller
Michael Schmöhl
Casper Meth
Johan Conrath Hartung
Johannes Schneyder
Johan Georg Bartman
Johann Michel Bartman
Johann Matteas Bartman
Johannes Meth
Henrich Thorwart
Michel Aadam
Johann Adam Schöffer
Johan Georg (××) Heyer
Johann Lorentz Hänsel
Peter (×) Ruhl
Peder Meelhus
Gorge (×) Freyman
Matteas (×) Clauser
Henry (×) Schnertzel
Johannes Ermentraudt
Johan Phillip Ermentraudt
Johan Friedrich Ermentraudt
Peter (H) Hein
Conrad (H) Housman

Frederik (×) Gerhart
William Gerhart
Johan Peder Dressler
Peter (×) Grube
Johann Daniel Crub
Johannes Bischoff
Hans Adam Diehl
Johann Daniehl Diehl
Carel Adam
George (×) Schneyder
Jacob Lamerck
Johann Adam Schneider
Daniell (×) Kuckhart
Peter (×) Moor
Ludewig (×) Geibe
Jacob Fucks
Sebastian (DB) Doll
Christian Seyfert *
Petter Schwenck
Hartman (×) Schwenck
Abraham (×) Heiterich
John Nicklas (×) Heitrich
Philips Lentz
Johann Geörg Nickel
Johann Christoffel Zimmerman
Johann Henrich (×) Erhart
Davit (×) Lautenbagh
Johannes Beyer

* A Reformed school-teacher and preacher at Great Swamp, Lehigh County.

Paulus (X) Michael
Michael (X) Hahn
Johanes Hahn
Sebastian Guckert
Michel Simon
Johan Adam (X) Klein
Simon Geeres
Petter Schöffer
Adam Becker
Michael (O) Miller
Michael (X) Bauer
Christian Schöpfer, Sr.
Christian Schöpfer, Jr.
Lorentz (X) Monich
Philips Jacob Schell
Johan Henrich Freys
Johan Peter Friem
Johan Philibs Servas
Johan Peter Stuber
Abraham Faust
Jacob Reiss
Philib Hirsch
Johan Jörg Schaus
J. Jacob Wolf
Peter Gerhard
Abraham Schreiner
Johann Christoffel Ruth
Johan George ( ) Foust, sick *
Meichal Miller
Johann Adam Müller
Jonhan Fridrich Gabel
Johan Pfilib Gabel
Christian Schuy
Johann Jacob Kockert
Michael (M) Mombauer
Johan Nicklas (M) Mombauer
Peter Scholl
Otto Riedy
Johann Jacob Riedi

Johanes Peter Riedig
Simon Drom
Peter (X) Nickum
Friederich (X) Nickum
Nicklas Helffenstein
Daniel Burger
Paul Samsel
Johan Philip (X) Klein
Johan Adam Gottwals
Nicklas (X) Kneeser
Peter (M) Mombouer
Casper (X) Doll
Abraham (X) Salomon
John Nicjlus (X) Bogh
Christoffel (X) Doll
Philip (X) Doll
Joseph Purey
Johann Bern Bederri

SNOW BETSIE

Nickellaus Lenberger
Hans Jacob Geiger
Daniel Dalwig
Jahns Keyner
Sebastian (X) Unbehend
Melichior (X) Küner
Johan Georg Scherer
Martin Adam
Johann Peter Hoffman
Christian Rodenbach
Casper Herde
Marthin Barth
Peter (B) Blasser
Hans Michel Ernst
Hans Jacob (H) Maron
Gerhard Henrich Schütz
Georg Wilhelm Höcker
Friederich (X) Seitz
Johanes (XX) Martin

* A blank space enclosed in parentheses ( ) denotes that the man was absent and that the clerk of court signed the name for him.

Johann Daniel Österlen
Johann Daniel Müller
George (X) Becker
Johanes (++) Hasselwonger
H. Jacob (X) Bergel
Conradt Becker
Velten Becker
Vallendin Ertel
Johan Peter (X) Meyer
Andereas (X) Walte
George Davit Nacke
Johannes Reichardt
Martin (X) Hock
Conradt Graff
Jonas Klein
Matteas (X) Hertzel
Johannes Koch
Frantz (X) Welchel
Jacob (X) Good
Johann Michael Roth
John Henrich (||) Miller

Andreas Engellhard
Friderich Ehrenfeüchter
Jacob (X) Lantz
Johannes Bock
Johann Gottfried Straube
Jacob Ruth
Pierre Aubertien
Hendrich (+) Strickert
Conrath (X) Hackenshmit
Johann Nickel Scherer
Michael Becker
George Friederich (X) Schaffer
Jacob (X) Unbehand
Vallentin (X) Unbehand
Conrath (X) Unbehand
Hans Martin (X) Barr
Johannes Weibell
Mattias (X) Hook
Nicklas (O) Leyberger
Jacob Oellen

[List 71 A] A List of Passengers on board the Robert & Alice, belonging to Dublin, from Rotterdam to Philadelphia, viz. [Qualified September 3, 1739.]

MENS NAMES

MENS NAMES

Christian Hersin
Hans Schans
Hans Jacob Snyder
Peter Risser
Peter Eversool
Joost Eversool
Michel Haan
Nicolas Elenberger
Frans Leyenberger
Joost Steel
Carel Shalle
Hendrik Steinour
Jacob Rieph
Martin Hooffman

Hannis Hooffman
Christopher Bolinger
Hannis Steiner
Jacob Steiner
Hannis Bouman
Casper Scheffer
Hans Miller
Samuel Brandt
Joost Brandt
Peter Biever
David Scheffer
Jacob Stambach
Jacob Smith
David Bielder

MENS NAMES	MENS NAMES
Nicholas Reitenhower	Hans Peter Trett
Hans Mar[n] Bielder	Christiaen Trett
David Scheffer	Matheus Oubolt
Jacob Sirgier	Joseph Oubolt
Johannis Hawecker	Albert Vanderlint
Abram Piethel	Phillip Marstloff
Michel Theobald	Hans Nichel Visser
Hannis Schans	Fredrik Adam Wilhelm
Christophel Ovel	Hans Simon Leenhuys
Jurich Honing	Christiaen Bleym
Nicholas Honing	Lowrens Proau
Johannis Watering	Lowrens Piever
Hannis Bick	Bastian Kleyn
Peter Hooffman	Hans Adam Keere
Daniel Hooffman	Jacob Keere
Peter Fohl	Joseph Welshans
Abram Welshans	Hannis Miller
Samuel Burrier	Leobald Greber
Jacob Burrier	Hans Leobald Karlee
Phillip Burrier	Johan Peter Gamberlen
Hendrik Pamberger, Sen[r]	Conrade Beser
Hendrik Pamberger, Jun[r]	Hans Michall Lesser
Bernard Youtzee	Nicholas Lesser
Christiaen Herart	Johannes Coubersohl
Benedict Lesser	78 [men]
Christiaen Elenberger	218 [Total]

Sworn that the above is a true and compleat list of Male Palatines imported in the Ship Robert and Allice of Dublin, of the Age of 16 Years and upwards, to the best of my knowledge. Philadelphia Septem[r] 3rd 1739.

Walt. Goodman.

[List 72 A] A List of Passengers Names of 16 Years of Age & Upwards, on board the Friendship, W[m] Vitery, Commd[r], from Rotterdam. [Qualified September 3, 1739.]

NAMES	AGES	NAMES	AGES
Hans Myer	40	Johan Philip Illig	36
Johan Riedy Myer	16	Jurig Jacob Borkhart	36
Baltser Hissing	26	Malchi Grous	30

NAMES	AGES	NAMES	AGES
Mich^l Platner, sick	50	Hans Peter Miller	32
Jurig Arnet Leghtner	23	Peter Zimmerman	35
Nickel Swart	20	Jacob Farnee	18
Andreas Haak	20	Fred^k Ulerich	35
Danl Reinhard	23	Francis Prossman	45
Hans Mich^l Laub	22	Fight Miller	25
Jacob Frank	25	Christ^n Ergot	25
Jacob Keiport	20	Henrick Hoyle	40
Jurig Mich^l Paynter	55	Conrade Swartz	32
Peter Attick	33	Lenhard Flowers	29
Conrade Engel	24	Barnh^d Fredel	25
Justin Hofman	25	Hans Jurig Hinkell	32
Steph^n Lash	36	Johan Ludw^k Hebner	22
Johannes Woolfert	44	Henrick Blestre, sick	..
Conrade Floweres	49	Philip Christian Vernor	47
Mich^l Floweres	25	Hans Vernor	20
Martin Bennegar	35	Wm Vernor	17
Anth^y Finshbach	35	Jurig Thos Hoyle	..
Philip Stompach	19	Jurig Thos Hoyle, Junr	35
Jacob Loch	35	Lenh^d Herbott	20
Johanis Loch	16	Johan Henrich Rump	21
Jurig Mich^l Wolf	44	Johan Figt Benner	22
Conrade Wolf	20	Martin Yoak	31
Johan Nickel	25	Johan Adam Housholter	20
Johan Marte Leid	45	Nichol Mourer	23
Gotfrey Christian	36	Conrade Philipien	58

Sworn that the within is a true and compleat List of Male Palatines, imported in the Ship Friendship, of the Age of 16 Years and upwards, to the best of my knowledge.

William Vettery.

Philadelphia, Septem^r 3rd, 1739.

[List 73 A] A List of ye Pallantines Names In ye Loyall Judith, Edwd Paynter, Master. [Qualified September 3, 1739.]

Bartholome Jesran	Jan Jerick Ransier
Jerick Mickell Jesran	Janis Nickell Bullmer
Henrick Kifer	Adam Bullmer
Godfriek Mang	Peter Locke

Phillip Snider
Carle Heyser
Assmes France
Johan Nickell Klaa
Bastian Pluer
William Pluer
France Pluer
Peter Marker
Jahn Nickell Weychell
Hans Adam Phiets
Hans Adam Heuerley
Johan Jerick Shope
Cristophel Shope
Johan Nickell Shield
Johanis Beueriles
Johan Nickell Shield
Johan Jurick Dryer
Peter Wolff
Johan Nickell Dull
David Fordney
Joost Lizer
Jacob Hough
Petter Hough
Casper Leydicker
Vallantine Shey
Petter Rehm
Hans Jurig Burghart
Mathyas Zeberly
Nicholas Schmall
Johan Adam Schmall
Henrick Adam Klyn
Jan Nichol Chateau
Christian Rohrbacher
Johan Henrick Godee
Jacob Rohrbacher
Johan Carle Hey
Barnet Waerth
Johan Adam Rehmer
Mathias Rehmer
Nicholl Rehmer
Petter Bakker

Ludwick Tanyn
Hans Adam Tanyn
Phillip Tanyn
Christian Heither
Henrick Baugh
Phillip Hasselberger
Johan Jacob Thanie
Hans Nichall Kley
Jacob Keuning
Johannis Ruperder
Sabastian Jacobie
Henrick Wolfrom
Hans Adam Wolfrom
Philip Burghart
Petter Bower
Petter Bougher
Batholmye Bougher
Jacob Stuhl
Carel Shoul
Adam Shitterhelm
Carle Keresh
Jan Nikel Kleser
Jurg Loub
Tobias Webber
Ludwick Mous
Hans Nichell Gouw
Stophell Smith
David Weyser
Phillip Risser
Nicholas Rodeberger
Abraham Stout
John Jurig Stout
Mathias Telton
Henrick Handwerke
Nicholas Handwerke
Johanis Tilbouer
Jurig William Thoor
Martin Sinefrin
Hans Jacob Madery
88 [men]

Sworn that the above is a true and compleat list of Male Palatines, imported in the Ship Loyal Judith, of the Age of 16 Years and upwards, to the best of my knowledge.
Philadelphia, Septem^r 3rd 1739.

Edwd Paynter.

[Lists 71–73 B] Palatines imported in the ship Robert & Alice, Capt Goodman, in the ship Friendship, Capt Vettrey, and in the Loyal Judith, Capt Paynter. Qual. 3 Sept. 1739.*

SHIP ROBERT AND ALLICE

Christian Hirschi
Hans (H) Schans
Hans Jacob (+) Snyder
Peter Rüsser
Petter Ebersohl
Jost Ebersohl
Michal Hahn
Frantz Leyenberger
Jost Diehl
Carl Schallin
Henrich Steiner
Hans Jacob (×) Reif
Johann Martin Hoffmann
Johannes Hoffmann
Johan Peter Hoffmann
Christoph Bollinger
Johannes Steiner
Jacob Steiner
Johannes Bauman
Casper (CS) Shever
Hans Müller
Samuel (B) Brant
Jost (B) Brant
Peter Büber
Daviet Schäffer
Jacob (×) Stanback
Jacob (+) Smith
David (H) Miller

Hans Michel Neumauer
Johan Mardin Böhler
David (×) Schiver
Jacob (×) Zerehart
Johannes (HH) Haveker
Abraham Bächtel
Mattis Obolt
Joseph (+) Kubhold
Hanes (++) Schans
Chris. (H) Stovell
Jerg Honi[g]
Johannes Votrin
Johanes Biehn
Michel (×) Shaaff [?]
Daniel Hoffman
Johan Peter Volck
Abraham (W) Welchants
Saml (J) Helburger
Jacob (×) Burgcher
Philip (×) Burgcher
Hendrick (×) Bambergher, Senr
Hendrick (×) Bambergher, Junr
Bernard (H) Yonser
Chris. (CE) Herherard
Benedick (O) Lesseir
Christian Ellenberger
Hans Peter (J) Treit
Christian (H) Treit

* Endorsement used as heading.

Theobald (+) Clewer
Albert von der Lind
Füllibs Martzlof
Nicholas (XX) Fisher
Adam (O) Wilhelm
Simon (M) Mendingham
Christian (P) Klein
Lorentz Brua
Lawrence (X) Bewer
Bastian Klein
Hans Adam Geri
Jacob (X) Gerrhy
Joseph Welschhans
Johanes Miller
Hans Michael (+) Teoomet
Theobald (D) Camore
Johann Peter Genberlin
Benddeck Besser
Hans Michel Diebolt
Nicholas (N) Leiser
Hans Michael (X) Leiser
Johannes Ebersohl

SHIP FRIENDSHIP

Johannes Meyer
Egidi Meyer
Hans Asher (EH) Edans
Johann Phillipp Illig
Georg Jacob Burckhart
Michal (X) Graus
Michael Blatner
Jerg Ernst Bühler
Nicholas (X) Schwarz
Andres Hock
Daniel (X) Reinhart
Johan Michael Laub
Johann Jacob Franck
Jacob Kübortz
Jerich Mich. (X) Paynter
Hans Petter Adich
Johann Conrad Engel

Justinus Hoffman
Steffan Lasch
Johanes Wolfert
Conrad (+) Florans
Martin (B) Pinegar
Anth^s Flincbouch
Fillibs Stambach
Jacob Loch
Johanes (+) Louch
Geo. Mich. (X) Woolf
John Conrad (+) Woolf
Johannes Nicol
Martin (X) Leid
Gottfried Christian
Hans Petter Müller
Better Zimerman
Jacob Farni
Frihrich Ullrich
Frantz Brosman
Michael (X) Frolus
Veit Miller
Chris. (+) Ergot
Henrich Heyl
Conrath Schwartz
Leonard (O) Florer
Bernd Fridtel
Hendrich (X) Vaughner [?]
Lodwich (X) Hevener
Hend. (X) Bleistire
Philipp Christoph Werner
Johannes Werner
Wilhelm Werner
Georg Thomas Heyl
Hans Thos. (X) Hyer
Leonhardt Herboldt
Johann Henrich Rump
John (H) Fybaylor
Martin (O) Joac
John Philip (+) Herberger
Hans Adam ([) Hausholder
Johan Nicolaus Mauer

LOYAL JUDITH

Johon (×) Joup
Bartholme Jeserang
Görg Michal Jeserang
Henrich Kiffer
Gothfrid Mang
Johann Görg Rämsyer
Johan Nickel Ballman
Joh. Adam Bollman
John Peter (O) Lough
Johann Philippus Schneider
Carolo (O) Heiser
Erasmus (HAF) France
Hanes (×) France
Hans Nich. (NK) Cliehn
Bastian Albert
Wm (A) Albert
Johan Frantz Alberd
Peter (M) Martger
Hans Adam (H) Peits
Hans Adamm Haledü
Johan Christ. Fritz [?]
Nicholas (×) Shield
Johan (×) Bevert
John Nich (+) Shield
Geo. (H) Thanner
Johan Peter Wolf
Johan Nickal Doll
David (DF) Fortney
Jost Liesser
David (H) Hooug
Johann Petter Hauch
Casper (+) Letecker
Valentine (O) Shave
Peter Rem
John (×) Burchar
Martin Sebelie
Nicholas (×) Small
John Adam (×) Small
Hend. Adam (×) Klein

Johann Nicklaus (O) Schatto
Christian Rohrbach
Johan Henrich Kohde
Jacob (+) Rorbach
Johan Carl Hey
Bern Warth
Adam (×) Reimor
Mathew (×) Reimer
Nicholas (+) Reimer
Petter Becker
Jacob König
Lodowich (+) Tanneugh
Johan Adam Tanny
Philip (+) Denigh
Christian Hutter
Hendrich (B) Bough
Pillip Hasselberger
Johann Jacob Danny
Johann Nickel Cleh
Johannes Rupperter
Sebast. Jacoby
Henrich Wolfrum
Hans Adam Wolfrum
Joseph (×) Herner
Philip (×) Burchart
Peter Bucher
Bardoll Bucher
John Cabug (O) Stall
Arnald (+) Shouts
Adam Schidenhelm
Johan Karl Geres
Johan Nickel Glaser
Jörg Laub
Tobias Weber
Conrad (O) Turicher [?]
Christoffel Schmidt
Davidt Weiser
Filipp Riss
Nicholas (I) Rodeburger
Abraham Staudt
Johan Jerg Staudt

Mathias (M) Felton
Henry (H) Handwerk
Nieclaus Hantwerck
Hann Dehlbauer

Geo. W^m (+) Thuer
Hans Jacob Madari
Martin Schaffner

[Lists 71–73 C] At the Court House of Philadelphia, September 3rd 1739.

Present

The Honourable George Thomas, Esqr, Lieutenant Governour,
Saml Hasell,   Andrew Hamilton,
Thos Griffitts, William Allen,   } Esq^{rs}.

The Palatines whose Names are underwritten, imported in
the Ships Robert and Allice, Walter Goodman, Com^r, The
Friendship, Wm Vitrey, Com^r & The Loyal Judith, Edward
Paynter, Com^r, from Rotterdam, but last from Deal in England, did this Day take and Subscribe the Oaths to the Government, viz.,

[SHIP ROBERT AND ALICE]

Christian Hirschi
Hans (H) Schantz
Hans Jacob (✕) Shneider
Peter Rüsser
Pedter Ebersohl
Jost Ebersohl
Michal Hahn
Niclaus Ellenberger
Frantz Leyenberger
Jost Diehl
Carl Schallin
Henrich Steiner
Hans Jacob (O) Reiff
Johann Martinn Hoffman
Johannes Hoffmann
Johann Peter Hoffman
Christoph Bollinger
Johannes Steiner
Jacob Steiner
Johannes Baumann
Caspar (CS) Shäffer

Hans Müller
Samuel (B) Brand
Jost (B) Brand
Peter Büber
Daviet Schäffer
Jacob (✕) Stambogh
Jacob (+) Shmit
Davit (O) Bieler
Hans Michel Neumauer
Johann Mardin Böhler
Davit (✕) Shäffer
Jacob (✕) Zurcher
Johannes (HH) Habacker
Abraham Bächtel
Mattis Obolt
Joseph (+) Uphold
Hans (+ +) Shantz
Christoffel (H) Obel
Gerg Honi[g]
Nicklas (N) Honig
Johannes Votrin
Johannes Biehn
Daniel Hoffmann

John Peter Vock
Abraham (W) Welchhans
Samuel (O) Burgher
Jacob (X) Burgher
Philip (X) Burger
Henry (X) Bamberger
Henry (X) Bamberger, Junior
Berhart (B) Jauzy
Christian (CE) Errhart
Benedict (O) Lisser
Christian Ellenberger
Hans Peter (P) Tritt
Christian (H) Thritt
Leobold (+) Gräber
Albert Von der Lind
Fillibs Martzhaf
Nicklas (H) Fisher
Adam (XX) Willhelm
Simon (N) Nenninger
Christian (P) Pleem
Lorentz Brua
Lorentz (X) Beeber
Bastian Klein
Hans Adam Geiri
Jacob (X) Gerry
Joseph Welschhans
Dewald (D) Carel
Johanes Miller
Hans Michel Diebolt
Johann Peter Genberlin
Bendeck Bisser
Hans Michael (X) Lisser
Nicklaus Lisser
Johannes Ebersohl

SHIP FRIENDSHIP

Johannes Meyer
Egidi Meyer
Baltsatzor (B) Hissony
Johann Phillip Illig
Georg Jacob Burckhart

Melchior (M) Kraus
Michael Blatner
Jerg Ernst Bähler
Nicklas (N) Shwartz
Andres Hock
Daniel (X) Reinhart
Johan Michel Laub
Jacob Franck
Jacob Kübortz
Georg Michael (X) Bender
Jorg Petter Adich
Johann Conrad [Engel]
Justinus Hoffman
Steffan Bosch
Johannes Wolfert
Conrad (X) Florans
Martin (B) Beeniger
Anthoni Flinspach
Pillibs Stambach
Jacob Loch
Johannes (X) Loch
Georg Michael (+) Wolff
Johan Conrad (+) Wolff
Johannes Nicol
Martin (X) Leed
Gottfried Christian
Hans Petter Müller
Better Zimerman
Jacob Farnü
Frihrich Ullrich
Frantz Brossman
Michael (X) Floris
Veit Miller
Christian (X) Ergott
Henrich Heyl
Conrath Schwartz
Leonhart (O) Floor
Bernd Fridtel
Georg Henry (X) Henkel
Ludewig (X) Hübner
Henry (X) Pleestery

Philipp Christoph Werner
Johannes Werner
Wilhellem Werner
Georg Thomas Heyl
Hans Thomas (×) Heyl
Leonhardt Herboldt
Johann Henrich Rump
Johan Vit (O) Bähler
Martin (O) Jock
Joehan Conrad (P) Philipom
Hans Adam (×) Householder
Johan Nicolaus Mauer

THE LOYAL JUDITH

John George (S) Shup
Bartholmi Jeserang
Görg Michel Jeserang
Henrich Küfer
Gothfrid Mang
Johann Görg Rämsyer
Johan Nike Ballman
Joh. Adam Bollman
Johan Peter (×) Lough
Johann Philippus Schneider
Carol (×) Heyser
Errasmus (HAF) Frantz
Johannes (×) Frantz
Hans Nicklas (N) Klein
Bastian Albert
William (A) Albert
Johan Frantz Alberd
Peter (PM) Martter
Niclas (×)Weigher
Hans Adam (H) Teelze
Hans Adam Heldi
Johan Christ Fritz [?]
Niclas (×) Sheel
Johanes (×) Bebertz
Johan Nicklas (+) Sheel
Johan Jeorg (H) Threer
Johan Peter Wolf

Johan Nickel Doll
Davit (DF) Fortney
Jost Liesser
Jacob (H) Hough
Johan Petter Hauch
Caspar (+) Leydäcker
Vallentin (O) Shey
Peter Rem
Johan Georg (+) Burghart
Martin Sebelie
Nicklas (×) Shmell
John Adam (+) Shmell
Henry Adam (×) Klein
Johann Nicklaus Schatto [?]
Christian Rohrbach
Johan Henrich Kohde
Jacob (×) Roorbogh
Johan Carl Hey
Bern Warth
Johan Adam (+) Reemer
Matteas (×) Reemer
John Nicklas (×) Remer
Petter Becker
Jacob König
Ludwig (+) Danney
Johan Adam Danny
Philip (+) Danney
Christian Hutter
Henry (B) Bough
Fillip Hasselberger
Johann Jacob Tany
Johann Nickel Cleh
Johannes Rupperter
Sebast. Jacoby
Henrich Wolfrum
Hans Adam Wolfrum
Hans Peter (×) Bouger
Philip (×) Burghart
Peter Bucher
Bardell Bucher
John Jacob (O) Staall

Caral (+) Sholl
Adam Schidenhelm
Johan Carel Geres
Johan Nickel Glaser
Jörg Laub
Tobias Weber
Ludwig (O) Maus
Christoffel Schmidt
Davidt Weiser
Philipp Riss

Nicklas (×) Rodeburger
Abraham Staudt
Johan Jerg Staudt
Mattias (+) Felden
Henry (H) Handwerk
Nieclaus Hantwerck
Han Diehlbauer
Georg William (F) Fuhr
Martin Schaffner
Hans Jacob Madöri

[List 74 A] A List of Men Imported on the Lydia, Ja⁵ Allan, Comʳ. [Qualified December 11, 1739.]

	AGES		AGES
Hans Jacob Houser	23	Hendrick Croop	33
Rodick Frick	30	Caspar Frick	30
Johannes Frick	19	Johanes Hakie	19
Andreas Crook	45	Hans Ulrick Weber	20
Hans Jacob Frie	30	Hans Barr	29
Ulrick Spinder	23	Hendᵏ Barr	20
Hendrick Seeds	28	Hendrick Bone	30
Hendrick Seeds, Junʳ	28	Johannes Reytenaar	40
Hans Jacob Croop	30	Johannes Reytenaar, Junʳ	16
Johannes Laypert	21	Conraadt Frum	36
Barthoˡ Rodolphus Barr	20	Erasmus Hammand, in	
Johannes Weber	20	Nancey	29
Hendᵏ Hober	40		

Philadelphia December 11ᵗʰ 1739.

Sworn that the within is a true and compleat list of the Male Palatines imported in the Ship Lydia, to the best of knowledge, of the Ages of Sixteen Years and upwards.

Ja⁵ Allan.

[List 74 B] List of Palatines imported in the Lydia, Capᵗ. James Allan. Qual. 11ᵗʰ Decʳ, 1739.*

Hans Jacob Houser
Rodick (+) Freck

Johannes (±) Freck
Andreas (×) Crook

* Endorsement used as heading.

Hans Jacob (X) Frie
Ullrich Spinner
Hendrick (±) Seeds
Hendrick (X) Seeds, Junr
Hans Jacob (+) Croop
Johannis Schleipffer
Bart. Rudolp Bär
Joannes (+) Weber
Hendrich (X) Hober
Hend^rk (+) Croop

Caspar (X) Friek
Joannes (S) Hakie
Hans Ulrick (H) Weber
Hans Bär
Henrich Bär
Hendrick (X) Bonie
Joannes (X) Reytenar, Senr
Joannes (X) Reytenar, Junr
Joh. Conradt Fromm

[List 74 C] At the Court House of Philadelphia, December 11th 1739.

Present: The Honourable George Thomas, Esqr, Lieutenant Governour, Edward Roberts, Esqr, Mayor.

The Palatines whose Names are underwritten, imported in the Ship Lydia, James Allen, Com^r, from London, did this day take and subscribe the Oaths to the Government, viz.,

Hans Jacob Houser
Ludwig (+) Frick
Johanes (±) Frick
Andreas (X) Kruk
Hans Jacob (+) Free
Ullrich Spinner
Henry (±) Seetz
Henry (X) Seetz, Junior
Hans Jacob (+) Grop
Johanis Schleipfer
Bart. Rudolf Bär
Johannes (+ +)Weber

Henry (X) Hobert
Henry (X) Grub
Caspar (+)Frick
Johannes (H) Hagy
Hans Ullerik (H) Weber
Hans Bär
Heinrich Bär
Henry ( ) Bony, sick
Johannes (+) Reittenar, Senior
Johannes (X) Reittenar, Junior
Joh. Conradt Fromm

[List 75 A] [Palatines & Switzers imported in the Ship Friendship, William Vettery, Com^r from Rotterdam. Qualified Sept. 23, 1740.]

Fredrick Erash
Hans Cristian
Jacob Mires
Andrew Eshenback
Johanes Cop

Johanes Ryenard
Jacob Kinsley
Ruduf Kinsley
Morris Millhiser
Hermanes Hersling

Sebastian Shoape
Ludiwick Wisinger
Tituas Hardwake
Jacob Lebeck
Mathew Shalk
Henry Rorer
Cloyce Brobeck
Henry Brobeck
Cloyce Spainehower
Jacob Spainehower
Hans Sailer
Godlip Brickner
Henrick Spainehower
Hans George Snider
Hans Fry
Fredrick Fry
Hiney Wagner
Martin Rauft
Joanes Seaes
Lenard Werts

Henry Rickembacker
Jacob Peaterly
Hans Flubacker
Jacob Flubacker
Samuell Rickner
Hiney Geager, Sen[r]
Hiney Geager, Jun[r]
Augustus Spain
Jacob Teager
Theoars Choape
Jacob Rickner
Marting Keller
Jacob Fow
Johannes Fow
Jacob Brooker
Hans Jacob Hansey
Hans Hansey
Marting Halfellfinger
Hans Schofner

The foregoing is a true & compleat List of the Male Palatines of the age of Sixteen years & upwards imported in the Ship Friendship to the best of my knowledge.

Will[m] Vettery.

Sworn Sept[r] 23[d] 1740. Before Tho[s] Lawrence & William Allen, Esq[rs].

[List 75 C] At the Court House of Philadelphia, Sept[r] 23[d] 1740.

Present: Thomas Lawrence, William Allen, Esq[rs].

The Palatines & Switzers whose names are underwritten, imported in the Ship Friendship, William Vettery, Commander, from Rotterdam, but last from Cowes, did this day take & subscribe the Oaths to the Government, viz.,

Friedrich Gerahn
Johan Christy
Jacob Meier

Andreas Eschenbach *
Johannes Kapp
Johans Thomas Reinnhard

* This is the well-known Moravian missionary, Andrew Eschenbach, who was sent to Pennsylvania to work among the German settlers. See L. T. Reichel, *Early History of the Church of the United Brethren*, Nazareth, 1888, p. 81f.

Rudolf Kuenthlein
Moritz (X) Milhaus
Harmanus Hesseling
Bosche Schaub
Ludwig (X) Wissinger
Vitus Hartweg
Jacob Lübeck
Martin (X) Schaug
Heinrich Roh[r]er
Claus Brodtbeck
Hinerich (X) Brobeck
Niglaus (X) Spanhauer
Jacob Spanhuer
Johanes (S) Seiller
Gottlieb Briegner
Heinrich Spehnhauer
Hans Jorg (+) Schneider

Hans (X) Frey
Marthin (X) Raufft
Johannes (S) Süss
Lönert Witz
Heinrich Rickenbacher
Hans Michel Bitterley
Hans (HF) Flebacher
Jacob (X) Flebacher
Heinr. Jeger
Georg Augustus Bern
Jacob Dägen
  Das bekenne ich *
Durs Tschopp
Jacob (H) Hansi
Mard. Häfnenfeger
Heini Grieger

[List 76 A] A List of the mens Names & Ages p^r the Lydia, Capt James Allan, from Rotterdam, but last from Dover. [Qualified Sept. 27, 1740.]

	AGES		AGES
Jacob Knight	36	Johan Wilhelm Peck	18
Johan Jacob Ways	18	Johan Jacob Peck	16
Johan Geo. Chressman	24	Johannes Arnold	25
Johan Geo. Loss	19	Christian Dibos	23
Johan Christian Garnur	19	Christian Mayer	33
Johan Hend^k Ernberger	26	Peter Hendrick Smock	25
Simon Hersh	18	Johan Mich^l Jacks	24
Johannes Hersh	16	Christian Coos	20
Christian Weber	21	Johan Nichol^s Peckoner	36
Johan Herman Leer	21	Johan Nichol^s Peckoner, Junr	15
Christian Holumberger	48	Peter Aldamos	40
Johan Peter Holumberger	16	Fredrick Aldamos	24
Johan Jacob Holumberger	17	Philip Fritz	36
Arnoldus Schnyder	22	Johan Adam Fritz	18
Johan Jost Freesen	26	Jacob Kayzer	40
Johan Wilhelm Folberg	16	Hendrick Kayzer	19
Nicholas Cowalt	18	Michael Rychart	18
John Hendrick Peck	30	Lodwick Hardastein	28

* I. e. "This I confess," referring to the oath he signed.

	AGES		AGES
Jost Lang	25	Johan Diedrick Mart	30
Mathias Kafer	33	Johan Ties Mart	18
Philip Petre	22	Johannes Kieghler	42
Johan Peter Lewi	29	Johan Peter Shoeman	30
Philip Coleman	50	Arnoldus Shoeman	15
Abraham Greenawalt	40	Wilhelm Heldibrandt	20
Georigh Brosius	42	Johannes Couklebergh	45
Daniel Schnyder	19	Wilhelm Couklebergh	15
Daniel Lucas	24	Caspar Wert	32
Christoph¹ Kyst	23	Simon Timor	26
Christoph¹ Fooks	27	Peter Sharpnagh	38
Mathias Fooks	25	Urban Perkhoff	41
Valantine Braght	23	Nicholas Byer	45
Elias Godlif Stein	24	Peter Lorentz	20
Wilhelm Lang	34	Peter Laam	25
Johannes Ties Perkhayser	..	Christopher Rysner	25
Hieart Schnyder	42	Jost Pleher	31
Johan Adam Schnyder	18		

Sworn that the above is a true List. Sept. 27ᵗʰ 1740, Before the Judges of the Supream Court.

Jaˢ Allan.

[List 76 B] [Palatines imported in the Ship Lydia, Capt. James Allan, from Rotterdam. Qualified Sept. 27, 1740.]

Hans Jacob Weiss
Johann Georg Crösmann
Johann George Lohs
Johan Henry Jorenberger
Simon (✕) Hersh
Christian (✕) Weber
Johan Herman (O) Leer
Christian (✕) Holumberger
Johann Jacob Hollenberger
Arnold (✕) Shneider
Johan Jost Fresen
Johan Wilhelm (W) Folberg
Nicholas (✕) Cowalt
Johan Hendᵏ (✕) Peck
Johann Will Beck

Johan Jacob (✕) Peck
Johannes (✕) Arnold
Johan Christ. Diewes
Christian (✕✕) Swegle Mayer
Peter Hendᵏ (✕) Smock
Johan Michˡ (✕) Jacks
Christian (‖) Coos
Johann Nickel Bückener
Peter Althomus
Philip (✕) Fritz
Johan Adam (✕) Fritz
Jacob (H) Kayzer
Hendrick (H) Kayzer
Michael Reichhart
Ludwig Hartenstein

Jost Lang
Mathias (O) Kafer
Philip (XX) Petre
Johan Peter (X) Loie
Philips Culman
Hans Geo. (JB) Brosius
Daniel (D) Schnyder
Daniel (A) Lucas
Christoph Geist
Christoph Fuchs
Matthias Fuchs
Valantine (XX) Braght
Elias Gottlieb Stein
Wilhelm (X) Lang
Johannes Ties (X) Perhawser
Johann Gerhart Schneider

Johan Adam (X) Schnyder
Johan Diedrick (M) Mart
Johan Ties (X) Mart
Johannes Kichler
Johan Peter (+) Shoeman
Arnoldus (O) Shoeman
Wilhelm (X) Hildebrandt
Johannes (X) Cowcklebergh
Casper (X) Wert
Johann Simon Deimer
Urban Kerckhoff
Nicholas (+) Byer
Peter (X) Lorentz
Peter (Peter) Laam
Christoph Reuser
Johan Jost Plöhger

[List 76 C] At the Courthouse Philad^a, Septr 27th 1740.
Present: Jeremia Langhorne, Thomas Graeme }
       Thomas Griffitts,   }Esq^{rs}.

The Palatines whose Names are underwritten, imported in the Ship Lydia, James Allan, Commander, from Rotterdam, but last from Dover, did this day take & subscribe the Oaths to the Government, viz.,

Hans Jacob Weiss
Johann Georg Cräsmann
Johann George Lohs
Johan Henry (X) Jorenberger
Simon (X) Hirsh
Christian (O) Weber
Johan Herman (H) Leer
Christian (X) Hornberger
Johan Jacob Hollenberger
Arnold (X) Shneider
Johan Jost Fresen
Johan Willem (O) Folberg
Nicklas (X) Couwald
Johann Henry (X) Back
Johann Will. Beck
Johan Jacob (+) Back

Johannes (+) Arnold
Johanrich Diewos
Christian Shwaiger (XX)
  Meyer
Peter Henry (O) Shook
Johann Michael (+) Jacks
Christian (||) Coos
Johan Nickel Boeckener
Peter Altomus
Johann Friederich Althomus
Philip (X) Fritz
Johan Adam (X) Fritz
Jacob (H) Keyser
Henry (H) Keyser
Michael Reichhart
Lutwig Hartenstein

Jost Lang
Matteas (C) Kaffer
Philip (XX) Petry
Johan Peter (X) Loee
Philips Culman
Johann Georg (JB) Brosius
Daniel (DS) Shneider
Daniel (H) Lucas
Christoph Geist
Christoph Fuchs
Matthias Fuchs
Vallentin (X) Pracht
Elias Gottlieb Stein
Willhelm (X) Lang
Johanes (X) Berckhyser
Johan Gerhart

Johann Adam (X) Shneyder
Johan Diterig (M) Mark
Johan Deest (M) Mark
Johannes Kichler
Johan Peter (+) Shoemann
Arnold (O) Shoemann
Wilhelm (X) Hildebrand
Johannes (X) Kugelberger
Caspar (X) Wirth
Johan Simon Deimer
Urban Kerckhoff
Nicklas (+) Beyer
Peter (X) Lorentz
Peter Lahm
Christ. Reusser
Johan Jost Plöhger

[List 77 A] [List of the Male passengers imported in the Ship Samuel & Elizabeth, William Chilton, Com^r, from Rotterdam. Qualified Sept. 30, 1740.]

MENS NAMES	AGES	MENS NAMES	AGES
Frist Ebgent	32	Christ. Keerback	30
John Christ. Christfellen	30	Anthony Brandeburger	29
John Tys Fuser	24	Paulus Leenderd	22
John Tys Snoegh	28	John Houbrig Tymoet	31
Peter Berger	50	John Adam Loukenback	24
John Hofman	40	John Henry Loukenback	18
John Christ. Smith	30	Simon Belsener	50
John Christ. Frans	26	John Jurigler	16
Jacob Fisher	20	John Gerradt Loukenback	50
Christ. Peter Scheffer	24	John George Rurigh	21
John Peter Anders	22	John Ernst Rurigh	20
Paulus Dunsman	34	John Adam Hammacher	23
Martinus Smith	25	Hubrig Hammacher	27
Philip Bosart	35	John Peter Dunsman	23
John Tys Fuser	20	John Morris Roh	40
John Adam Meyer	30	John Simon Huler	40
John Adam Schnyder	24	Jacob Wagner	20
John Adam Muller	25	John Henry Miller	50
George Wm Keerback	26	Haman Pessert	36

MENS NAMES	AGES	MENS NAMES	AGES
John Hadorn	30	Conrath Hirst	49
Crymon Schnyder	50	Johan Adam Rurigh	40
John Peter Schnyder	18	John Tys Miller	30
John Adam Benter	36	Henry Reet	34
John Peter Shoemacher	28	John Peter Caspar	16
Joost Craemer	20	Bertrum Clay	50
Tys Schnyder	48	John Wm Clay	29
John Peter Harhouse	30	Christ Shoemacher	37
John Fredrick Schnyder	30	Men in all 56. [women] 28.	
Thomas Schnyder	50	[Total] 84.	

The above is a true List of the Male Passengers of the age of 17 years & upwards imported by me, to the best of my knowledge.

Wm Chilton.

Sworn the 30th day of Septr 1740.
[Endorsed:]
Samuel & Elizabeth, Willm Chilton, from Rotterdam & Deal. List of Palatines. Qualified 30th Septr 1740.

[List 77 B] [Palatines imported in the Ship Samuel & Elizabeth, W^m. Chilton, Com^r, from Rotterdam. Qualified Sept. 30, 1740.]

Fritz Epgert	Martinis Schmitt
Johann Christ Kreisfeller	Philip (II) Oser
Johan^s Ties (X) Fiser	Johan Adam (X) Meyer
Johan Theis Schnug	Johann Adam Schneider
Peter Berger	Johann Adam Müller
Johannes Hoffman	Georg Wilhelm (O) Kirbach
Johan Christ. Schmidt	Christ (X) Kirbach
Johann Christ. Frantz	Johan Friederich Schneider
Johann Jacob Fischer	Johan Andonges Brondenburg
Christ^n Pet^r (X) Fisher	Paulus Löhner
Johan Peder Enders	Johan Aubright (H) Timout
Baulus Dünschman	Johann Adam Luckenbach *

* John Adam Luckenbach was a Reformed schoolmaster; first at Goshenhoppen, then at Muddy Creek, Lancaster County, later at Creutz Creek, York County. Still later he joined the Moravians. He died in 1785 and was buried at Bethlehem. See *History of the Goshenhoppen Charge,* p. 138.

John Henerich Luckenbach
Johan Simon Ertzner
Johannes Gorg Eller
Johan Gerhart Luckenbach
Johannes Görg Rörich
Johan Ernst Rörig
Johann Adam Hammacher
Johann Huberich Hamacher
Johanes Peder Schreiner
Johan Morris (X) Frou
Johann Simon (H) Huller
Carl Jacob Wagner
Hans Henrich (H) Miller
Haman (+) Betzer
Johannes Hadorn
Kreiman Schneider

Johan Peter Schneider
Johan Adam (+) Benter
Johan Peter (X) Shoemaker
Jost Kremer
Thies Schnyder
Johan Peter (X) Harhausen
Thomas Schnider
Conrad (H) Hersh
Johann Adam Rörich
Johan Theis Müller
Johan Peter Kas[per]
Johan Henrich Reth
Johan Berdtram Klein
Johan Willhelm Klein
Crist Schumacher

[Endorsed:]
By the Samuel & Elizabeth, Capt. Chilton, 1740. List of Palatines. Qual. 30th Septr 1740.

[List 77 C] At the Courthouse in Philada, Sept 30th 1740.
Present: Thomas Griffitts, Samuel Hasel
Thos Graeme,   Clemt Plumsted, } Esqrs.
The Palatines whose names are underwritten, imported in the Ship Samuel & Elizabeth, William Chilton, Commander, from Roterdam, but last from Deal, did this day take & subscribe the Oaths to the Government.

Fritz Epgert
Johan Christ Kreisfeller
Johanes Theis (X) Feesser
Johan Dheis Schnug
Peter Berger
Johannes Hoffman
Johan Christ. Schmidt
Johann Christ. Frantz
Johann Jacob Fischer
Christ Peter (X) Fischer
Johan Peder Enders
Baulus Dunschman

Martinis Schmitt
Philip (II) Bosser
Johan Adam (X) Meyer
Johan Adam Schneider
Johan Adam Müller
George Wilhelm (O) Kirbach
Christian (X) Kirbach
Johann Friederich Schneider
Jorge Wilhelm Kerbach
Johan Andonges Brandenburg
Paullus Löhner
Johans Hubrig Dimot

Johann Adam Luckenbach
Johan Henerich Luckenbach
Johan Simon Ertzner [?]
Johannes Joerg Ell[er]
Johan Gerhart Luckenbach
Johannes Görg Rörich
Johann Ernst Rörig
Johann Adam Hammacher
Johann Huberich Hamacher
Johannes Peder Dunschman
Johan Mortiz (✕) Ronh
Johan Simon (H) Hüller
Carl Jacob Wagner
Hans Henry (H) Müller
Haman (✕) Betzer
Johannes Hadorn

Kreiman Schneider
Johan Peter Schneider
Johan Adam (+) Bender
Johan Peter (+) Shoemacher
Jost Kremer
Theis Schneyder
Johan Peter (‖) Harhaussen
Thomas Schnidter
Conrath (Hi) Hirsh
Johan Adam Rörich
Johan Theis Muller
Johan Henrich Reth
Johan Peder Kas[par]
Johan Bardtram Klein
Johan Willem Klein
Crist. Schumacher

[List 78 A] A List of All the Mens Names and [ages] on board The Ship Loyal Judith, Cap^tn Lov[ell Paynter] [Qualified Nov. 25, 1740.] *

	AGES		AGES
Johan Henrich Leshire	31	Willm Ole	60
Willm Harmany	32	Willm Yoast Backer	30
Anthony Keller	30	Johannes Woolfe	23
Christian Princer	32	Balster Hoofeman	36
Willm Sower	50	Goodloop Hermon	36
Henrich Dielboen	16	Henrich Wackenor	48
Andreas Beck	30	Fredrick Backer	19
Joan Willm Oster	36	Nickolas Sell	42
Abraham Hass	27	Peter Shits	60
Jacob Tevalt	44	Justus Lintiman	49
Conrad Snyder	64	Jacob Lintiman	18
Johan^s Ralph Snyder, S^r	54	Henrich Lintiman	16
Andreas Ralph Snyder	16	Henrich Prim	40
Jurg Viant	29	Jacob Prim	18
Joseph Kickiler	24	Hanias Killiand	20
Simon Vear	20	Willm Smith	56
Liniherd Kercherd	43	Willm Smith	24

* Corner of page torn off.

	AGES		AGES
Hanias Smith	17	Andrias Smith	22
Feltie Crim	50	Hanies Diel	27
Jacob Crim	18	Philip Kauff	20
Ulrick Hart	37	Michell Bush	24
Yerick Conrade	50	Peter Diel	25
Jacob Conrade, Junr	16	John^n Peter Moore	19
Feltie Snyder	29	Hemon Hemon	26
Adam Mouere	32	Fredrick Laurance	26
Jacob Cooke	31	Johanes Ley	19
Yerick Snyder	26	Fredr^ck Willm Neagle	24
Conrade Vishang	30	John^n Jurg Gudshell	21
Nickell Breeder	33	Isaac Didrick	16
John Angell	39	Peter Woolfe	25
Peter Becker	22	Jacob Woolfe	20
Willm Beets	38	Johanes Back	25
Carl Crow	44	Yerick Eply	25
Johannes Vervell	33	Yergeorall Meyre	23
Didrick Backer	43	Willm Eseck	25
Bernet Saye	26	Henicall Hoyse	31
Abraham Bulipacker	25	Peter Hanse	40
Michial Fie	24	John^n Yerk Eslin	48
Mathias Smith	28	Hanias Frenk	34
Peter Croll	26	Conrade Douey	50
Conrade Smith	31	Philip Vishang	26
Johanes Adam	27	Henrich Hype	40
Hanas Wackner	20	Peter Miller	25
Nicholas Shire	21	John^n Yurg Seiden	37
Jacob Shatle	24	John^n Candie	28
Johanes Miller	20	Peter Sell	19
France Jhost	22	Jacob Sell	17
Jasper Bonner	20	95 [men]	

Sworn that the foregoing is a true List to the best of his knowledge, before the Honble the Governor, the 25th Nov. 1740.

Lovell Paynter.

[List 78 B] [Palatines imported in the Ship Loyal Judith, Lovell Paynter, Com^r from Rotterdam. Qualified Nov. 25, 1740.]

Johan Henry (×) Logire
Anthony (×) Keller
Christian Brentzer
Willm Sower
Hendrick (×) Dealbone
Andreas Beck
Johann Wilhelm Oster
Johann Abraham Haas
Johann Jacob Theobalth
Conrad Schneider
Andreas Reiffschneider
George (×) Viantt
Joseb Köhler
Simmon Wehr
Linard (H) Carhard
Wilhelm Ohl
Wilhelm Jost Becker
Johannes Wolff
Johann Baltzer Hoffman
Hendrick (×) Wackner
Fred^k Becker
Johan Nickel Zöll
Peter (||) Sheets
Justus Linteman
Jacob Lindeman
Henrich Linteman
Henrich Brem
Jacob (×) Primm
Johannes Kilian
Wilm Schmit
Wilm Schmitt
Johannes [Sch]mitt
Feltin (W) Krimm
Jacob (J) Krimm
Ulrich Harthmann
Yearig (O) Conarad
Vallendin Schneider
Adam (O) Mowrer
Jacob (+) Kock
Johan Georg Schneider
Conrad (O) Wishong

Johann Nickell Bröder
Johann Fridrich Engel
Peter Becker
Johann Wilhelm Betz
Carl Gro
Johanes Werbel
Johan Diterich Becker
Johann Bernhard See
Johann Abraham Bollenbacher
Nicklas (F) F[eit]
Matis (O) Smith
Peter (×) Craul
Conradt Schmidt
Johan (×) Adam
Johanns Wagner
Johannis Nicklaus Scheier
Johan Jacob Schertel
Johannes Miller
Frantz Jost
Andreas Schmidt
Johannes Diehl
Philip (×) Kauff
Johan Michael Busch
Johan Peter Diehl
Johan Peter Mohr
Herman Heyman
Johann Fridrich Lorentz
Johan (×) Ley
Fridrich Wilhelm Nagel
Johan Georg (×) Goodshalk
Isaac Dietrich
Johann Peter Wolff
Johann Jacob Wolff
Johannes Bechk
Johan Jerg Epple
Görg Karle Meier
Johann Willhelm Esig
Johan Niclas Haubt
Johann Peter Hans
Jerig (O) Esling
Johannes Franck

Conradt Thuy
Philip (P) Wishang
Johann Petter Müller
Jon Georg Seyter

Jean Ganty
Peter (X) Sell
Jacob (X) Sell

[List 78 C] At the Court House in Philad[a], Novr 25th 1740. Present: The Honble George Thomas, Esqr, Governor, Samuel Hassell, Esqr, Mayor of Philad[a].

The Palatines whose Names are underwritten, imported in the Ship Loyal Judith, Lovell Paynter, Commander, from Roterdam, but last from Deal—did this day take & subscribe the foregoing Qualifications or Oaths to the Government.

John Henry (X) Logire
Anthony (X) Keller
Christian Brentzer
Wilhelm (X) Sauer
Henry (X) Thielbon
Andreas Beck
Johann Wilhelm Oster
Johan Abraham Haas
Johann Jacob Theobaldt
Conrad Schneder
Andreas Schneider
Jorge (X) Wyant
Joseb Köhler
Simmon Wehr
Lenhart (H) Gerhart
Wilhelm Ohl
Wilhelm Jost Becker
Johannes Wolff
Johann Baltzer Hoffman
Henry (X) Wagner
Friederig (O) Becker
Johann Nickel Zöll
Peter (II) Shütz
Justus Linteman
Jacob Lindemann
Henrich Lindeman
Henrich Brem
Jacob (X) Breem

Johannes Keulian
Wilm Schmit
Wilm Schmit
Johannes Schmitt
Vallentin (O) Greem
Jacob (J) Greem
Ulrich Hartman
George (O) Conradt
Vallendin Schneider
Adam (O) Maurer
Johan Jacob (+) Koch
Johan Georg Schneid[er]
Conradt (O) Wishong
Johann Nickell Bröder
Johann Friehich Engel
Peter Becker
Johann Willhelm Betz
Carli Gro
Johannes Werbel
Johan Dieterich Becker
Johann Bernhard See
Johann Abraham Bollenbacher
Johan Nicklas (F) Vit
Matteas (O) Shmit
Peter (X) Grauel
Conradt Schmidt
Johannes (+) Adam
Johannes Wagner

Johann Klaus Scheier
Johan Jacob Schertel
Johannes Müller
Frantz Jost
Casspar ( ) Boner
Andreas Schmidt
Johannes Diehl
Philip (X) Gauff
Johan Michael Busch
Johann Peter Diehl
Johann Peter Mohr
Herman Heyman
Johann Friedrich Lorentz
Johanes (X) Laye
Friedrich Wilhelm Nagel
Johan George (X) Gottschalck
Isac Dietrich

Johan Peter Wolff
Jacob Wolff
Johannes Bechk
Johann Jerg Eppele
Jörg Karl Meier
Johann Willhelm Essig
Johann Niclas Haubt
Johann Peter Hans
Johan Georg (O) Esley
Johanes Frank
Conradt Thuy
Philip (P) Wishong
Johann Petter Müller
Jan Georg Seyter
Jean Ganty
Peter (X) Sell
Jacob (X) Sell

[List 79 A] A list of Pallatine Passengers on Board the
Robt and Alice, Walter Goodman, Mast^r, from Rotterdam &
Cowes to Philadelphia. [Qualified Dec. 3, 1740.]

Johannis Sidle
Johan Nich^{ll} Sidle
John Hendrick Creytsman, drunk
Philip Balter Chreytsman
Andrices Wint
John Willm Hedelman
John Eader
Wright Sandlyter
John Mich^{ll} Boush
Johannes Rode
Hans Wright Cromer
Andrices Cooler
Andrices Sheib
Christian Redibank
Hans Martin Conrade
Andrices Bence
Hans Mich^{ll} Holtzshoe
Hendrick Hainer
Geo. Wm Nangesser

John Jacob Ratger
John Jacob Timmer
John Hendrick Newman
Peter Eber
Chris^t Magell
John Ulrich Smith
Uldrich Hersman
Dan^{ll} Nort
Blaziers Beer
John Adam Gorsh
Anthony Feltman
Joseph Walter
Joan Peter Scobald
Johan Jost Handzell
John Wm Hullbright
John Frederick Fighthelm
Johannis Beitle
Wright Smith
John Jacob Timmerman

John Philip Heiliger
Wright Lingefelt
Willm Morris Fidle
John Jurich Rough
Johans Gitlick
Hendrick Gitlick
John Milleger Hingering
Chris^t Hellebrant
Robt Reynbrack
Abraham Curts
Hendricus Hanrade
Philip Ishemell
Jacob Becker

Joanis Vogall
Jacob Becker
Jurich Philip Kress
Jacob Kress
Conrade Swettowser
Jacob Bartle
Thos Bruch
Joan Cris^t Bassorer
Peter Granser
John Nick^s Hiple
John Eader
Johannes Crim
Johannes Jacob Crim

[Endorsed:]
A true List sworn to the 3^d Decr. 1740.

Capt. Goodman.

[List 79 B] [Palatines imported in the Ship Robert & Alice, Walter Goodman, Master, from Rotterdam. Qualified Dec. 3, 1740.]

Johann (X) Sidle
Johann Nicolaus Seidel
Philipps Balthaser Crössmann
Johan Henrich Crössman
Johan Willhelm Stadellman
John (X) Eader
Gorg Zahnleyter
Johann Gorg Kromer
Andrias (X) Cooliar
Andrias (X) Sheib
Christian Reidenbach
Hans Michäl Holschuh
Hendrick (O) Stiner
Johann Jacob Radge
Johann Jacob Tiemer
Johann Henrich Neuman
Peter (X) Raper
Cristopher (X) Maghele
John Jurich (X) Smith

Danill (X) Nort
Blatious (O) Bear
Johan Adam Gass
Antoni Feltman
Joseph Walther
Johanis (F) Fogel
Johann Jost Hensel
Johann Wilhelm Volprecht
Antreas Bentz
Johann Friedrich von Fechthelm
Johannes Bückell
John Jurich (X) Schmitt
Johann Jacob Zimerman
John Filip Heiliger
Jurich (L) Lingavelt
Wilhelm Moritz Veitel
Johann Georg Rauch
Johannis (L) Getlick
Hendrick (X) Getlick

Johann Melchior Hengerer	Jacob Barthel
Christoffel Hillebrandt	Hans Martin (X) Conrade
Robert (R) Reynbrack	Thomas Bruch
A. Kurrtz	Johann Christoph Beserer
Hendricus (X) Hanrade	Peiter (+) Grenser
Philip (X) Phunele	Joh. Nicolaus Heppel
Jacob (B) Becker	Johan Casper (X) Eader
Jurich (J) Cress	Johannes Grim
Jacob (H) Cress	Hans Jacob (X) Grim
Conrad (X) Schweighouser	Johann Pöeter Seboldt

[Endorsed:]
List of Palatines imported in Ship Robert & Alice. Qual. 3ᵈ
Decʳ 1740.

[List 79 C] At the Court House in Philadelphia, Dec. 3,
1740.

Present: The Honᵇˡᵉ George Thomas, Esqʳ, Governor,
Clement Plumsted, William Allen ⎫
Abraham Taylor, ⎬ Esqʳˢ
⎭

The Palatines whose Names are under and after written,
imported in the Ships Robert and Alice, Walter Goodman,
Master, and the Samuel, Hugh Peircy, Master, from Roterdam, but last from Cowes and Deal, did this day take & subscribe the Oaths to the Government.

Johanes (X) Seydel	Johannes Grim
Johann Nicolaus Seidel	Johan Henrich Neuman
Philippˢ Balthaser Crösman	Peter (X) Rappert
Johan Henrich Crösman	Christoff (+) Magel
Johan Willhelm Stadellmann	Johann George (X) Shmit
Johann (+) Öther	Daniel (X) North
Gorg Zahnleyter	Blassius (B) Barr
Johann Gorg Kromar	Johan Adam Goss
Andereas (X) Köller	Antoni Feltman
Andereas (X) Sheyb	Joseph Walther
Christian Reidenbach	Johannes (F) Vogel
Hans Michäl Holschuh	Johann Jost Hensel
Henry (X) Steiner	Johann Wilhelm Volprecht
Johann Jacob Radge	Anteras Bentz
Johann Jacob Diemer	Johann Friederich von Fechthelm

Hans Jacob (X) Greem
Johannes Bückell
Johan George (+) Shmit
Johann Jacob Zimmerman
Johann Filip Heiliger
George Michal (X) Längen-
felder
Wilhelm Moritz Veitel
Johann Georg Rauch
Johannes (L) Göttlich
Henrich (X) Göttlich
Johann Melchior Hengerer
Christoffel Hillebrandt
Rubert (O) Reinbracht
A. Kurrtz

Henry (H) Hanrath
Philip (X) Fumel
Jacob (X) Becker
Jeorge Philip (J) Cress
Jacob (H) Cress
Conrad (X) Schveighouser
Jacob Barthel
Hans Martin (X) Conrad
Thomas Bruch
Johann Christoph Besserer
Peter (X) Crentzer
Johann Nicolaus Heppel
Johan Casspar (X) Öther
Johann Pöeter Seboldt

[List 80 A] A List of Mens Names on board the Samuel, Hugh Percy, Commander. [Qualified Dec. 3, 1740.]

	AGES		AGES
Folentine Singrove	32	Jacob Ruperter	40
Nickel Conts	17	Mathias Clain	25
Petter Kenick	18	Jerick Bombock	23
Henrick Wolf	25	Adam Snyder	18
Mickel Burgrett	33	Poolos Hoay	30
Johan Shriber	24	Henrick Frailick	25
Conorod Snus	24	William Bishof	20
John Kenick	21	Godfritt Walther	21
Philip Ruperter	36	Henrick Kaisler	21
Yerick Burn	42	John Fuse	31
Nickel Tayler	30	Jerick Kaiser	26
Petter Spengler	26	Samuel Taner	21
Petter Moay	25	Isack Hancker	18
Lewick Vivel	40	Joseph Neigh	23
Jacob Mower	32	Adam Bushart	28
Adam Stam	25	William Marks	37
Danil Turnah	24	Nickel Crooker	40
Jacob Shuster	22	Nickel Swengel	44
Petter Tsawn	40	Mickel Swengel	20
Gasper Clekner	26	Jerick Swengel	16
Johonos Stol	35	Nickel Smith	40

	AGES		AGES
Philip Laper	25	Gerhartt Timberman	46
Jacob Fox	25	Nickel Hooff	36
Nickel Surfas	20	Hans Nickel Timberman	16
Bartelma Oasterman	36	Jerick Kreger	30
Thomas Torman	20	Petter Hagener	26
Jerick Mous	25	Jerick Rough	45
Jacob Bloy	23	Gasper Tsawn	30
Andrew Miller	24	Jerick Rathaback	22
Petter Verner	20	Johannas Hall	18
Petter Bishof	22	Adam Kettering	27
Orbinos Ashenbrander	37	Fred Geyger	39
Philip Craber	27	Jacob Ammos	66
Henrick Craber	25	Martin Ryzer	..
Past Pheay	25	Mathias Sidler	..
Abraham Shelerbury	21		

Sworn to be a true List of the Males from 16 years old & upwards, Decr 3^d 1740.

[Endorsed:]

Ship Samuel, Capt Hugh Percy. Qual. 3^d Decr 1740.

[List 80 B] [Palatines imported in the Ship Samuel, Hugh Percy, Master, from Rotterdam. Qualified Dec. 3, 1740.] *

Nickell (NK) Conts
Henrich Wolff
Henrich Schreiber
Conrath Schneis
Johann König
Philibus Rupperter
Joerg Born
Nicklis (O) Shelder
Petter (O) Steckell
Petter May
Jacob Maurer
Adam (X) Stump
Dannill (X) Turny
Jacob (X) Shuster
Peter (+) Sane
Casper (O) Clepener
Johannes (+) Stool

Görg Bombach
Adam Schneider
Paulus Huy
Henrich Frölich
Galtheit (X) Walter
Henery (X) Kisnerr
Gürg Keyser
Samuell (S) Daniell
Wilhelm Marx
Nickell (+) Cruper
Johann Nickel Schwingel
Georg Schwingel
Johann Nickel Schmitt
Philip (X) Leaber
Jacob (X) Fucks
Johann Nickel Zerfas
Partellmay (X) Housterman

* Endorsement used as heading.

Thomas Dörner
Georg Maus
Andris (XX) Miller
Peter Werner
Peter Bischof
Urban Aschenbrenner
Philib Kreber
Henrich Kreber
Pastion (O) Phy
Abraham (X) Shelbar
Gerhard Zimerman

Johann Nickel Wüst
Johann Nickel Zimmerman
Peter Hegner
Derick (X) Croub
Jörg Reutenbach
Johannes Heyl
Hans Adam Kettenring
Jacob (+) Hammer
Martin (R) Risell
Matheus (X) Eadler
Fredrich (O) Kikur

[List 80 C] [Palatines imported in the ship Samuel, Hugh Peircy, Master. Qualified Dec. 3, 1740.]

Nicklas (NK) Kuntz
Henrich Wolff
Johannes Schreiber
Conrath Schneiss
Johann König
Philippus Rupperter
Goerg Born
Nicklas (O) Zöller
Peter (X) Spengler
Peter May
Jacob Maurer
Johan Adam (X) Stam
Daniel (X) Durnay
Jacob (X) Shuster
Peter (X) Zahan
Caspar (X) Klöckner
Johannes (+) Staal
Görg Bombach
Adam Schneider
Paulus Huy
Johan Henrich Frölich
Gottfried (X) Walter
Henry (X) Giessler
Gürg Keyser
Samuel (|) Tanner
Wilhelm Marx

Nicklas (+) Gruber
Johann Nickel Schwingel
Georg Schwingel
Johan Nickel Schmitt
Philip (X) Läwer
Jacob (X) Fuchs
Nicol Zerfass
Barthol. (X) Osterman
Thomas Dörner
Gerg Maus
Andreas (XX) Miller
Johann Peter (X) Werner
Peter Bischoff
Urban Aschenbrenner
Philib Kreber
Henrich Kreber
Bastian (O) Vey
Abraham (X) Shelberg
Gerhard Zimmermann
Johan Nick Wüst
Johann Nickel Zimmerman
Peter Hegner
George (X) Raub
Jörg Reutenbach
Johannes Heyl
Hans Adam Kettenring

Jacob (X) Arrnnos   Mattias (X) Siedel
Martin (X) Reisel   Friederich (O) Geiger

[List 81 A] A List of Palatine Men of Age on board Snow
Francis & Ann, Thos Coatam, Master. [Qualified May 30,
1741.]

Jurgh Adam Koch   Winkell Horning
Hans Jurg Koch   Jacob Kiper
Peter Holl   Johanes Do
Johanes Reisler   Johanes Rieser, sick
Conrood Smitt   Martin Bittner
Philip Klem   Michl Biegler
Jurg Adam Ernst   Peter Herpell
Johanes Emmel

[List 81 B] [Palatines imported in the Snow Francis & Ann,
Thomas Coatam, Master. Qualified May 30, 1741.]

George Adam (+) Koch   Johannes Immel
Hans George (+) Koch   Johann Wendel Hornung
Peter Holl   Jacob Keipper
Hans Jerg Rösler   Martin (+) Bittner
Johann Konrad Schmidt   Michel Bigler
Georg Philip (X) Clem   Johann Peter Herbel
Geörg Adam Ernst

[Endorsed:]
Palatines p. Francis & Ann, Capt Coatam, 1741.

[List 81 C] At the Courthouse at Philada, May 30th 1741.
Before Samuel Hasell, Esqr, Mayor.
The Palatines whose names are underwritten, imported in
the Snow Francis & Ann, Thomas Coatam, Master, from Rotterdam, but last from St Christophers, did this day take Oaths
to the Governmt, viz.,

George Adam (X) Koch   Hans Jerg Rössler
Hans George (X) Koch   Johann Konrad Schmidt
Peter Holl   Georg Philip (X) Clem

Georg Adam Ernst
Johannes Immel
Johann Wendel Hornung
Jacob Keipper

Martin (X) Bittner
Michel Bigler
Johann Peter Herbel

[List 82 A] A list of all the mens Names & Ages from 16 Years & upwards on b^d the Ship Malborough, Thomas Bell, Mast^r. [Qualified Sept. 23, 1741.]

	AGES		AGES
Ludwick Caerman	24	Addam Casit	22
Fred^k Frace	24	Han William Enilman	20
William Wolf	22	Michel Sipart	30
Jacob Pert	23	Philip Kuents	29
Andrew Sterp	22	Jacob Arnold	28
Peter Kin	18	Peter Dise	25
Jacob Kin	21	Abraham Haise	20
Johanis Wagner	21	Joanis Kaile	20
Oniri Swider	60	Joanis Welslor	30
Peter Hawes	18	Joanis Tise	30
Michal Pair	55	Nickolas Martine	45
Adam Haile	55	Phillip Slin	40
Michal Welch	65	Jacob Kimper	32
Joanis Latcher	21	Peter Englin	17
Fred^k Mayore	30	Jeare Ruth	26
Jacob Kill	60	Dewaile Poon	30
Garret Plott	36	Michael Hess	24
Simmon Fokle	21	Peter Praiel	22
Nickle Eale	20	Fred^k Rotchmick	24
Fredrick Celnor	40	Fred^k Ratchmon	30
Daniel Crenigor	30	Joanis Cane	22
Michal Creier	20	Ludwick Cole	44
Jacob Loock	40	Mickel Swinte	40
Michel Civer	50	Casper Skaim	40
Peter Stout	42	Peter Partle	25
Jacob Nicholas	17	Tobias Ring	22
Nickolor Clean	27	Nicholas Spurior	20
Parinhorn Trap	20	Milkor Stalmon	25
Daniel Simon	21	Joanis Horn	24
Joanis Toot	40	Han Nickel Smith	17
Joanis Mayor	24	Henrich Filparn	21

	AGES		AGES
Mich¹ Showmaker	23	Lodwick Hanston	22
Gosber Mathias	26	Jacob Pasince	20
Philip Snyder	24	Jacob Gerdhire	19
Antho. Niler	22	Jacob Ditts	19
Adam Carn	26	Carle Frieznor	21

[Endorsed:]
Capt Bells. Qual. 23d Septr 1742. No. 72.

[List 82B] [Palatines imported in the Ship Marlborough, Thomas Bell, Master. Qualified Sept. 23, 1741.]

Johan Ludwig German
Johan Friderrich Freys
Johann Wilhelm Welsch
Johann Jacob Bück
Peter (X) Kühn
Johann Jacob Kühn
Johan Georg Wagner
Ulrich Nafzer
Johan Nicklas (X) Beyer
Johan Michael (X) Welch
Johann Jacob Heyel
Johanes (X) Ladsher
Friederich (F) Meyer
Jacob Hill
Simon Vogelgesang
Johann Nickel Öhl
Friedrich Zöllner
Johan Daniel Kröninger
Michel Kreischer
Jerg Jacob (G) Glug
Michael (X) Seipert
Peter Staudt
Johann Jacob Nicolaus
Lenhard (KL) Klein
Bernhard Rapp
Dangel Simon
Johannes Doll
Johannes (X) Meyer

Jan Adam Kasel
John Wilhelm (X) Engelman
Philipp Kuntz
Jacob Bernhart
Peter (X) Deiss
Abraham Hess
Johannes (H) Kähl
Johannes Worscheler
Johannes (XX) Deiss
Nicklas (NM) Martin
Philipp Linn
Joh. Jacob Kemper
Joh. Peter Engel
George (R) Ruth
Johann Dielbohnn
Nickel Heiss
Peter Breiel
Frederick Baltzar (FBR) Roth-
    smith
Johannes Kuhn
Johann Ludwig Hennrich Kohl
Michael (MS) Shwenck
Aschmes Keim
Peter (BM) Bartholoma
Johann Tobias Rühm
Johan Nicklas (+) Burghart
Melchior Stohlman
Johannes Horn

Johan Nicklas (H) Smith
Henry (HB) Bernhart
Johannes Niclaus Schumacher
Caspar (CM) Modes
Philipus Schneider
Antonius Öhler
Johann Adam Kamp
Johann Ludwich Hanstein

John Jacob (B) Bösentz
Jacob (G) Gartner
Peter (PK) Keeffer
Johann Jacob Dietz
Daniel (DK) Keeffer
Johan Calfrick (X) Eissen
Michael (M) Neuman
Johan (Metz) Carel Metz

[Endorsed:]
The Palatines by the Marlborough, Capt. Thomas Bell.
Qualified Septr 23^d 1741.

[List 82 C] At the Court House at Philad^a, Septr 23^d 1741.
Present: The Honble George Thomas, Esqr, Lieut Govr,
Samuel Hasell, Esqr, Mayor of Philad^a.
The Palatines whose Names are underwritten, imported in
the Ship Marlborough, Thomas Bell, M^r, from Rotterdam,
but the last from Cowes, did this day take Oaths to the Government, viz.,

Johan Ludwig German
Johan Friderrich Freys
Johann Wilhelm Welsch
Peter (X) Kuhn
Johan Jacob Bück
Johan Jacob Kühn
Johan Georg Wagner
Ulrich Naffzer
Johan Nicklas (X) Beyer
Johann Jacob Heyel
Johan Michael (X) Welch
Johanes (X) Ladsher
Friederch (F) Meyer
Jacob Hill
Simon Vogelgesang
Johann Nickel Öhl
Friederich Zöllner
Johan Daniel Kröninger
Michel Kreischer
Jerg Jacob Glug, sick

Michael (X) Seipert
Peter Staudt
Johann Jacob Nicolaus
Lenhart (KL) Klein
Bernhard Rapp
Dangel Simon
Johannes Doll
Johanes (X) Meyer
J. A. Kasel
Joh. Willhelm Engelman
Johann Adam Kasel
Philipp Kuntz
Jacob Bernhartt
Peter (X) Deiss
Abraham Hess
Johannes (H) Kähl
Johannes Worscheler
Johannes (XX) Deiss
Nicklas (NM) Martin
Philip Lang

Joh. Jacob Kemper

Joh. Peter Engel

Georg (R) Ruth

Johann Dielbohnn

Nickel Heis

Peter Breiel

Fredrick Bals. (FBR) Rotsmith

Johannes Kuhn

Johan Ludwig Henrich Kohl

Michael (MS) Swyng

Aschmes Keim

Peter (BM) Bartolemow

Johann Tobias Rühm

John (X) Nicholas

Melchior Stahlman

Johannes Horn

Hans Nicholas (H) Smith

Henry (HB) Bernhart

Johann Nicklaus Schumacher

Casper (CM) Modes

Pilipus Schneider

Anthonius Öhler

Johann Adam Kamp

Johann Ludwich Hanckstein

John Jacob (B) Personz

Jacob (G) Gerdheir

Peter (PK) Keeffer

Johan Jacob Dietz

Daniel (DK) Keeffer

Johan Kall (X) Fishahason

Michael (M) Neumer

Johan (Johan) Carel Metz

[List 83 A] [Palatines imported in the ship St. Mark, Capt. Wilson, from Rotterdam. Qualified Sept. 26, 1741.]

Nicklas Gelbert

Peter Gemling

Hans Philip Ebert

Quard Stelwa

Matteas Foltz

Johanes Von Erde

Jacob Mattey

Wilhelm Muller

John Henry Müller

Peter Bernhart

Matteas Kortt

Conrad Funck

Philip Meess

John Henry Meenker

George Tarrar

John Engel Broun

Lorentz Crone

Nicklas Vogler

Johannes Maetter

Wiepertus Luze

Ullerich Weys

John Herman Ackel

Johannes Hirshner

Christoffel Stump

John Martin Spegt

Johannes Fürst

Johan Adam Von Erde

Christian Von Erde

Peter Jacoby

Michael Fulper

John Frederik Henry

Adam Shmall

Jacob Stambagh

Conrad Michael

John Staarfinger

Philip Shweiger

Jo. Nicklas Mensh

Friederich Reemer

Friederich Hertzog

Martin Becker

Joh. Willhelm Hoffman

Philip Haas

Lorentz Lees

Arrnold Stegh

Joh. Nicklas Stegh

John Michael Gondakker

John Walder Fishbough

George Shmaltz

Michael Rees

Martin Edinbourn

John Caspar Ahlas

John Nicklas Steinert

Hans Adam Renart

Peter Hoffman

John Philip Pinck

John Henry Kost

John George Metz

Jacob Currel

Johannes Currel

Hans Mauerer

Joh. Samuel Mühl

Hans Jacob Metziger

Joh. Philip Maan

Georg Turst

Joh. Henry Mauerer

Conrad Finck

Lenhart Von Berge

Martin Laye

Joh. Nicklas Huber

Johannes Muck

Johanne Bockejus

Joh. Bernhart Denny

Philip Jost

Friederich Klapper

Henry Stoll

J. Jost Shneyder

Johannes Flander

Jost Shneyder, Junior

John Knasterig

Vallentin Stoppelbein

Jacob Stoppelbein

Jacob Gerit

Jacob Beyer

Johannes Weller

Peter Gebhart

Johannes Shoun

Johannes Rewald

Johannes Imhoff

Philip Gallbach

Conrad Stoltz

Christian Orrentorff

Wilhelm Bagos

J. Henry Kroo

Michael Christ

Adam Shreiber

Michael Treytel

John Adam Hebok

Philip Hoffman

Philip Emmert

George Pfaltzgraff

Jacob Kraus

[Endorsed:]
Capt Wilsons List. Ship St Mark, Qual. 26th Septr 1741. 102.

[List 83 B] [Palatines imported in the Ship St. Mark. Capt. Wilson, from Rotterdam. Qualified Sept. 26, 1741.]

Johann Arnoldt Steeg

Johann Nicolaus Steg

Nicklas (X) Gelbert

Peter (X) Greuling

Hans Philip (H) Ebert

Quardt Stellwagen

Matteas (F) Foltz

Johannes Von Erden

Jacob Mattey
Wilhelm Müller
Johann Henrich Müller
Johan Peter Bernhart
Matheus Gorth
Conrad Funck
Philip (✕) Mease
Johann Henrich Müncker
Jorg Darahn
Johannes Engelbert Braun
Lorentz Cron
Nicklas (✕) Vogler
Johannes Meder
Webbertus Lutz
Uhllerich (O) Weys
Johann Herman Ekell
Johannes Herscherrn
Christofel Stumb
Johann Martin Spegt
Johanes (✕) Fürst
Johan Adam Von Erden
Christian Von Erden
Peter Jacobi
Michael (✕) Fulbert
Johann Friederich Henrich
Johan Adam Schmahl
Hans Jacob Stambach
Johann Conrad Michel
Johann Starrfinger
Philip (✕) Shweigert
Johan Nicklas (✕) Mensh
Johann Fridrich Römer
Friederich Hertzog
Martin Becker
Johannes Wilhelm Hoffman
Philip (IAS) Haas
Lorentz Liss
Johan Michel Gundacker
Johann Walther Fischbach
Johan Görg Schmaltz
Michel Riess

Martin (ME) Edenburn
Johann Caspar Ahles
Joh. Nickel Steinert
H. Adam (✕) Renhart
Peter Hoffman
Johann Philibbus Binck
John Henry (✕) Kost
Johan Gerg Metz
Johann Jacob Corell ·
Johannes Correll
Hans (O) Mauerer
Johann Samuel Mühl
Hans Jacob (O) Metziger
Johann Phillip Mann
George (✕) Durst
Johann Henrich Maurer
Conrad Finck
Leonhard Vom Berg
Martin (✕) Laye
John Nicklas (H) Huber
Johanes (✕) Muck
Johannes Bockius
John Bernhart (✕) Denny
Philip (✕) Jost
Friderich Klappert
Henry (✕) Staall
Johann Jost Schneider
Johannes Flander
Jost (O) Shneider
Johannes Knastrich
Johann Valtin Stoppbein
Jacob Stoppelbeinn
Jacob Gerhartt
Jacob Boyer
Johannes Wehler
Peter (+) Gebhart
Johannes Schaun
Johannes Rehwalt
Johannes (✕✕) Immhoff
Filb Kalbach
Conrad Stoltz

Christian Ohrndorf
Wilhelm (XX) Bagos
Henrig Kroh
Michael (X) Christ
Adam Schreiber

Michel Dreydel
Johan (+) Ohrendorf
Johann Jacob Hebach
Fillibs Hoffman

[List 83 C] At Passyunck, the 26th day of September, 1741.
Present: Samuel Hasell, Esq[r], Mayor of Philad[a].
The Palatines whose names are underwritten, imported in
the Ship St Mark, [William] Wilson, M[r], from Rotterdam
but last from Cowes, did this day take the Oaths to the Government, viz.,

Johann Arnold Steeg
Johann Niclaus Steeg
Nickls (X) Gebbard
Peter (X) Criling
Hans Philip (H) Awert
Quardt Stellwagen
Mates (F) Fols
Johannes Von Erden
Jacob Mattey
Wilhelm Müller
Johan Heinrich Müller
Johan Peter Bernhart
Matheus Korth
Conrad Funck
Philip (X) Mees
Johann Henrich Müncker
Jörg Darahn
Johannes Engelbert Braun
Lorentz Cron
Nilas (X) Fogler
Johannes Meder
Wibbertus Lutz
Ueldrick (X) Wise
Johann Hermann Ekell
Johannes Herscherrn
Christoffel Stumb
Johann Martin Spegt
John (X) Harst

Johann Adam Von Erden
Christian Von Erden
Peter Jacobi
Micl. (X) Folber
Johann Friederich Henrich
Johan Adam Schmahl
Hans Stambach
Johann Conrad Michel
Johann Starrfinger
Philip (X) Swiger
Nickel (X) Mench
Johann Fridrich Römer
Friederich Hertzog
Martin Becker
Johannes Wilhelm Hoffman
Philips (PIAS) Hass
Lorentz Liss
Johan Michel Gundacker
Johann Walther Fischbach
Johan Görg Schmaltz
Michel Riess
Martin (ME) Edenborn
Johann Caspar Ahles
Johann Nickel Steinert
Adam (X) Rener
Peter Hoffman
Johann Philib Benck
Hendrich (X) Coist

Johans Gerg Metz
Johann Jacob Corell
Johannes Corell
Hans (O) Moorer
Johann Samuel Mühl
Hans (O) Metsker
Johann Phillip Mann
George (X) Yearst
Johann Henrich Maurer
Conrad Fink
Leonhard Vom [Berg]
Martin (X) Leey
Heinickl (XX) Houer
Conas (X) Mook
Johannes Bookius
Jan Burn (X) Deney
Phillips (X) Just
Friederich Klappert
Henrich Stahl
Johann Jost Schneider
Johannes Flender

Johs (X) Shider
Johannes Knostrich
Johan Valt Stopp[bein]
Jacob Stoppelbein
Jacob Gerhardt
Johannes Wehler
Peter (X) Geberd
Johannes Schaun
Johannes Rehwalt
Johas (X) Jolinloft
Filib Kalbach
Colrad (X) Delcks
Christian Ohrndorff
Willem (XX) Perckes
Henrich Kroh
Michl (X) Geist
Adam Schreiber
Michel Drydel
Johann Christian Orendorff
Johann Jacob Walch [?]
Filibs Hoffman

[List 84 A] A List of Palatine Mens Names p^r the Lydia,
James Allan, Master. [Qualified Sept. 29, 1741.]

MENS NAMES	AGES		AGES
		Hans Adam Many	16
Jacob Brio	30	Jacob Many	24
Abraham Brio	32	Nicholas Kays	36
Hans Nich^l Philips	18	Henry Conradt	40
Casper Philips	35	John Hendrick Like	43
Hans Georg Jacob	27	Hendrick Leer	45
Geo. Sheats	25	Nicholas Lutz	45
Hans Pet^r Wambler	40	Johannes Oger	30
Hans Pet^r Wambler, Junr	18	Abram Knies	24
Hans Mich^l Wambler	16	Jacob Peter	25
Adam Sclap	46	Bernhard Kline	30
Peter Stoutsman	16	Paulus Antonie	22
Jacob Welchhans	25	Hans Geo. Beaver	21
Jacob Many	50	Dieble Beaver	43
Jost Many	19	Hans Jacob Beaver	19

	AGES		AGES
Dieble Beaver	16	Hans Jacob Schnyder	45
Hans Mich¹ Swenk	45	Hans Jost Schnyder	45
Hans Jacob Swenk	16	Hans Peter Schnyder	29
Johannes Schnyder	24	Levit Albright	27
Johannes Matteur	25	Geo. Harter	25
Lorentz Hoshear	17	Peter Ecker	40
Johannes Swartz	24	Christian Ecker	19
Jacob Rudolph Seymour	23	Jacob Leatherman	32
Abram Kessner	21	Peter Tussing	35
John Lodwik Staine	20	Ulrich Roade	45
John Jacob Fleek	36	Christian Hosser	21
Valantine Puff	30	Abram Hosser	18
Peter Clop	30	Jacob Greenawelt	18
Peter Hensell	22	Joseph Peck	16
Conradt Moore	22	Hans Emric Nunmaker	45
Michael Weber	19	Rinhard Nunmaker	20
Mich¹ Grossman	26	Henry Nunmaker	16
John Peter Weys	19	Michael Foultz	20
John Nicholas Laam	35	Philip Karger	20
Charles Miller	25	Peter Ecker	..
Wilhelm Paulus	40	108.	
Jacob Paulus	18		

[List 84 B] [Palatines imported in the Ship Lydia, James Allen, Master. Qualified Sept. 29, 1741.]

Jacob (O) Prio	Hans (×) Adam Many
Abraham (A) Brio	Jacob Mani
Hans Nicklas (H) Philips	Nicklas (×) Geist
Casper Fillipps	Henrich Cunratt
Hans Görg Jacob	Johan Henrich Lück
Jan Gorg Geist	Johanerich Lehr
Hans Peter Wampfler	Johann Nickel Lutz
Hans Peter Wampfler	Johannes (HO) Oger
Hans Michael (×) Wamler	Abraham (O) Knur
Adam (A) Shlappy	Jacob Beutt
Peter (×) Stutzman	Bernhart Klein
Jacob Welschans	Paulus Antoni
Jacob Mani	Debalt (×) Bruaw, Senior
Jost (O) Many	Jacob Brua

Debalt (+) Brua, Junior

Hans (+)Michael Shwenck

Hans Jacob (+) Shwenck

Johannes (+) Shneider

Johannes Mettauer

Lorentz (+) Oshauer

Johannes (X) Shwartz

Jacob Riedesheimer

Hans Abraham (O) Kesseler

Johann Lutwig Steinert

Johann Jacob Flecke

Vallendin Puff

Peter (X) Clap

Petter Hensel

Kunrad Mohr

Michell Weber

Michael (O) Grossman

Johann Nicklaus Lahm

John Peter (H) Weiss

Carel Miller

Willm Paulus

Jacob Paulus

Hans Jacob (+) Shneyder

Hans Jost (+) Shneyder

Hans Peter Schneider

Levy (O) Albrecht

Görg Hürter

Peter (B) Ackert

Christian (+) Ackert

Peter (+) Ackert, Junior

Jacob Lederman

Peter Thussing

Uhllerich (+) Roth

Christian (X) Hosher

Abraham (O) Hasser

Jacob (+) Greenwald

Joseph (++) Pak

Hans Emerich Nonnemacher

Henry (X) Nunmaker

Reinhart (++) Nunmaker

Johann Michel Foltz

Philip (X) Karger

[Endorsed:]
Lydia's 1741. Qualified Sept. 29th 1741. Capt Allan.

[List 84 C] At Wiccacoa, the 29th of September, 1741.
Present: Joshua Maddox, Esqr.

The Palatines whose names are underwritten, imported in the Ship Lydia, James Allan, Master, from Rotterdam, but last from Deal, did this day take Oaths to the Government, viz.,

Jacob (O) Rio

Abram (A) Brio

Hans (H) Nicholas Philips

Chasper Fillipps

Hans Görg Jacob

Jan Gorg Geist

Hans Peter Wampfler

Hans Peter Wampfler

Hans Mich.[1] (X) Wambler

Adam (A) Sclope

Peter (X) Stoutsman

Jacob Welschans

Jacob Mani

Jost (X) Many

Hans Adam (O) Many

Jacob Manie

Nicholas (X) Kayst

Henrich Cunrath

Johan Henrich Lück

Johannerich Lehr

Johann Nickel Lutz
Johannes (HO) Oger
Abram (O) Knees
Jacob (Jacob) Peter
Bernhart Klein
Paulus Antoni
Peter (✕) Beaver
Dieble (✕) Prouva
Jacob Becker
Dieble (✕) Prouva, Junr
Hans Jacob (✕) Swenk
Hans Mich^l (✕) Swenk
Johannes (✕) Schnyder
Johannes Mettauer
Lorentz (✕) Hoshier
Johannes (✕) Swartz
Jacob Riedesheimer
Abram (O) Kessner
Johan Ludwig Steinnert
Johann Jacob Flecke
Vallendin Puff
Peter (O) Clap
Petter Hensel
Cunrad Mohr
Michell Weber
Michael (O) Grosman

Johann Nicklaus Lahn
John Peter (✕) Wise
Carl Miller
Willm Paulus
Jacob Paulus
Hans Jacob (✕) Schnyder
Hans Jost (IOST) Schnyder
Hans Peter Schneider
Levit (O) Albright
Görg Hürter
Peter (B) Ecker
Christian (✕) Ecker
Peter (✕) Ecker, Junr
Jacob Lederman
Peter Thussing
Ulrich (✕) Rode
Christian (✕) Hasser
Abram (O) Hasser
Jacob (✕) Greenawalt
Joseph (✕) Peck
Hans Emerich Nonenmacher
Henry (✕) Nunmacker
Reynard (✕) Nunmaker
Johann Michel Boltz
Philip (✕) Kariger

[List 85 A] List of Mens Names, p^r The St Andrew, Charles Stedman, Com^r. [Qualified October 2, 1741.]

MENS NAMES	AGES	MENS NAMES	AGES
Hendrick Kugley	33	Guilliam Bischon	47
Hendrick Widman	38	Carel Philip Wyles	28
Mich^l Middelercher	40	Jac. Sousberger	20
Paulus Needscher	50	Hend^k Sondagh	31
Johan Nich^s Bouwer	21	Nicolas Youngblood	30
Godfret Wesel	23	Jacob Albright	41
Rudolph Becker	19	Johan Nico^l Hemelright	42
Johannes Peyl	50	Conradt Rifard	33
Peter Keys	17	Jacob Pefer	38

MENS NAMES	AGES	MENS NAMES	AGES
Hans Jacob Miller	22	Jacob Sopen	45
Jacob Humland	25	Johannes Stillcherd	31
Johan Jac. Forster	30	Nicholas Swink	50
Johannes Good	44	Lawrence Swink	18
Maurice Edzebell	24	Johan^s Mich^l Peler	24
Jerich Casp^r Henlen	17	Philip Jacob Remiching	20
Jacob Mayer	29	Daniel Remiching	17
Hans Adam Grahum	26	Hans Peter Miller	22
William Kauf	24	Hans Lodw^k Miller	21
Hans Georg Lochner	33	Jacob Fred^k Seger	21
Bernard Bussard	50	Ulrich Hanbach	34
Carel Crassen	38	Hans Philip Kaufman	21
Valentine Sies	40	Michael Will	22
Hans Georg Miller	40	Hans Peter Miller	20
Christian Supining	22	Johannes Anthony	32
Bernard Reyn	17	Andreas Ruff	36
Hans Soerber	54	Hans Adam Dessler	38
Hans Ulrich Hoober	43	Jur. Fred^k Ubernesser	17
Hans Vileman	16	Hans Adam Stock	40
Diedrich Verner	35	Hans Jurig Wein	26
Hans Mich^l Klyne	25	Rudolph Steinman	27
Johan Philip Ecker	23	Joh^a Nicholas Tringer	31
Conradt Keyse	23	Hans Jacob Alwine	22
Martin Hendrick	32	Frans Kraw	28
Hans Geo. Wileman	24	Mich^l Verner	45
Philip Ullmer	55	Georg Verner	20
Johan Peter Fut	28	Hans Shutes	25
David De Lauder	31	Hans Richman	38
Daniel Kieport	18	Jacob Mayer	37
Geo. Peter Darand	28	Peter Herman	39
Walrad Coumand	50	Jacob Kleyn	20
Hans Philip Coumand	18	Johannes Ernst Oll	19
Jacob Aubel	19	Johannes Schroll	18
Godfret Urbech	22	Richard Bocking	38
Nicholas Niser	20	Carle Young	21
Hans Butterwick	17	Conradt Shereman	44
Nicholas Schabert	21	Jacob Worst	26
Peter Pool	22	Andrew Wisemiller	29
Ulrich Shainy	27	Christian Helbery	24
Hans Kaufman	25	Simon Hend^k Hocker	57

MENS NAMES	AGES	MENS NAMES	AGES
Wilhelmus Hocker	16	Fred^k Christian Becker	18
Johannes Hend^k Walter	23	Danl Hend^k Esch	24
Lod. Willm Becker	27	103 [men]	

[Endorsed:]
St. Andrew. List of Palatines.
Qual. 2^d Octr 1741.
103 [men] 72 [women] 87.6 [children] 262.6 [Total].

[List 85 B] [Palatines imported in the Ship St. Andrew.
Charles Stedman, Com^r. Qualified October 2, 1741.]

Willhelm Ludig Becker
Daniel Henrich Esch
Friedrich Christian Becker
Carl Jung
Johan Mich^l (O) Beler
Johan Gorg Daniel Kubortz
Johan Conrath Rievet [?]
Peter Buhl
Beder Voigt
Nichlaus Jungblud
Johannes (X) Botterweck
Johans Michel Klein
Carl Philipp Witz
Jacob (X) Albright
Ullrich Schömig
Johann Philipp Eckarts
Philib Ulmer
Jacob Seger
Augustus Kauffman
Hans Geo. (X) Legener
Michael Will
Jacob Worst
Paullus Neitzert
David (X) Delader
Nicolaus Bauer
Hans Ulrich (X) Hoebar

Johannes Anthoni
Johannes Pfeil
Conradt (I) Kiesie
Johan Nickel Frenger
Uhlrich Stambach
Jacob (O) Mayer
Hans Philip (|) Hoffman
Reichart Böckney
Johann Peter Geiss
Rodolph (+) Steinman
Johann Philip
Frans Grau
Jacob Pfeiffer
Georg Casper (+) Heiala
Lorentz (X) Swenk
Johan Maurice (X) Double
Jacob Klein
Godfret (+) Urbich
Wilhelm Gauff
Johannes (+) Roll
Johan Nickel Schappert
Bernhartt [Rein]
Nicholas (+) Nieser
Bernhart Bossert
Valantine (X) Sies
Peter (X) Miller

Jacob (X) Auble
Hans Rutschman
Jacob Maier
Jacob (X) Soultzberger

Hans (O) Sourber
Heinrich Weissmüller
Simon Henrick Höcker
Johannes Henrich Walter

[Endorsed:]
St Andrew 1741. Capt. Chas. Stedman. Qualified Octr 2^d 1741.

[List 85 C] At Wiccacoa Octr 2^d 1741.
Present: William Tell, Esqr.

The Palatines whose Names are underwritten, imported in the Ship St Andrew, Charles Stedman, M^r, from Roterdam, but last from . . . did this Day take the Oaths to the Government, viz.,

Wilhelm Ludig Becker
Daniel Henrick Esch
Friedrich Christian Becker
Carl Jung
John Michael (O) Behler
Johann Görg Daniel Kubortz
Johann Conrath Rievet [?]
Peter Buhl
Beder Voigt
Nicklaus Jungblud
Johannes (X) Butterwek
Johannes Michel Klein
Carl Philipp Witz
Jacob (X) Albrecht
Ulrich Schömig
Johann Phillip Eckarts
Philibb Ulmer
Jacob Seger
Augustus Kauffman
Hans Georg (X) Lägner
Michael Will
Jacob Worst
Paullus Neitzert
David (X) Delatter
Nicolaus Bauer

Hans (X) Uhlerich [Huber]
Johannes Anthoni
Johannes Pfeil
Conrad (O) Gissy
Johann Nickel Frenger
Ulrich Stambach
Jacob (X) Meyer
Hans (+) Philip Hoffman
Reichart Böckney
Johan Peter [Geis]
Rudolff (+) Steinman
Johann Philip
Frans Grau
Jacob Pfeiffer
George Caspar (X) Hälle
Lorentz (X) Shwenk
Johan Morritz (X) Dubel
Jacob Klein
Godfried (X) Orbig
Wilhelm Gauff
Johannes (X) Roll
Johan Nickel Schappert
Bernhardt [Rein]
Niclas (X) Neezer
Bernhart Bossart

Vallentin (X) Sees
Peter (X) Müller
Jacob (X) Auby
Hans Rutschman
Jacob Meier

Jacob (+) Sultzberger
Hans (O) Surber
Heinrich Weissmüller
Simon Henrich Höcker
Johannes Henrich Walter

[List 86 A] A List of all the Mens Names & Ages from 16 Years & upwards on board yᵉ Ship Friendship, Alixʳ Thomson Masᵗ. [Qualified October 12, 1741.]

	AGES		AGES
Andreas Huber	20	Joan Jurgen Ems	47
Peter Beer	24	Valentine Ems	19
Paulus Miller	24	Casper Snyder	18
Jurgen Wedleberger	42	Johan Jurgen Koch	22
Peter Brawn	28	Valentine Huberter	31
David Dicker	29	Casmire Weisell	19
Jacob Tiel	21	Johan Nickell Shoster	25
Jurgen Hert	26	Fredrick Helwig	22
Jacob Hert	20	Peter Jung	23
William Erhard	20	Jacob Simon	21
Joanis Erhard	21	Adam Weber	21
Hans Jurg Thebold	30	Jacob Tinges	25
Andreas Cramer	30	William Horster	20
Jacob Sheik	24	Johanes Flohman	40
Adam Eyler	33	Philip Moss	35
Valentine Sheik	44	William Zimer	33
Mathias Shrood	31	Rudolph Zimer	18
Christian Finstermaker	40	Peter Baul	26
Jacob Lieser	25	Peter Turni	30
Jurgen Kaltreuter	33	Simon Croon	48
Philip Kaltreuter	25	Adam Syce	25
Peter Kaltreuter	18	Johannes Melchier	28
Casper Rowland	20	Jurg Ruger	22
Daniel Huber	22	Conrad Lechleter	21
Jurgen Huber	24	Hans Eberdecker	22
Nicholas Bundrigg	25	Daniel Gortman	33
Nickolas Kleyne	19	Hans Jurg Olinger	25
Nickolas Holslenard	25	Philip Olinger	20
Carl Snyder	23	Johan Jacob Shlyfe	33
William Antes	28	Johannes Crist	35

	AGES		AGES
Nicholas Hechler	34	Nichol Shidermandel	26
Jacob Dundier	18	Martin Lamp	36
Henrick Engell	40	Christofel Smukhyd	30
Jacob Klein	40		

[Endorsed:]
Capt Thomsons List, Ship Friendship, Oct. 12. 1741.
No. 67 [Men] 33.6 [women and children] 100.6 [Total].*

[List 86 B] [Palatines imported in the Ship Friendship, Alex^r Thomson, Master from Rotterdam. Qualified October 12, 1741.]

Andrews (H) Hubert
Paullus Müller
Johann Georg Miltenberger
Johann Peter Braun
Davidt Dreher
Jacob Diehl
George (X) Hart
Jacob Herth
William (O) Hear Hart
Johannes Erhardt
Johan Görg Diebalt
Andres Kramer
Jacob Schupp
Adam Euler
Veltin Schick
Matheis Schroth
Jacob Lies
Hans George (O) Kaltriter
Philip (X) Kaltriter
Peter (O)Kaltriter
Casper (O) Crowland
Daniel (H) Hooper

George (HI) Hooper
Nicholas (N) Buntree
Nicholas (X) Clayne
Nicklas Holzbender
Charles (H) Snyder
William (O) Andis
Johan Jörg Embs
Vallentin Vallentin Embs
Johan Casper Schneider
Johann Georg Koch
Valentin Hohwerder
Casmer (O) Wesell
Johann Nickel Schuster
Friederich Helwig †
Peter Jung
Jacob (H) Simmon
Adam Weber
Jacob Dinges
Johann Wilhelm Hoster
Johannes Flichman
William (W) Simmon
Peter (++) Ball

* This may be explained as 67 men, 33 women and 6 children, a total of 100 adults and 6 children.

† Frederick Helwig became later, after 1748, the cantor and "foresinger" of the Reformed Church at Longswamp, Berks County.

Peter (|) Turnee
Simon Jacob Cron
Johann Adam Seysen
Johannes Melchior
Johann Jörg Rigel
Johann Conrad Lechleiter

Daniel Karstmann
Hans Gorg Ollinger
Philip (X) Oligar
Johan Jacob Schleiff
Johann Christoph Schmuckheyde

[Endorsed:]
Palatines of the Friendship, Capt Alex. Thomson, 1741.

[List 86 C] At the Courthouse in Philad^a, Octr 12th 1741.
Present: The Honble George Thomas, Esqr, Lieut. Governor,
Samuel Hasell & Abraham Taylor, Esq^{res}.

The Palatines whose Names are underwritten, imported in
the Ship Friendship, Alex^d Thomson, Master, from Roterdam,
but last from Cowes, did this day take the Oaths to the Government, viz.,

Andereas (H) Hubert
Paulus Müller
Johan George Miltenberger
Johann Peter Braun
Davidt Dreher
Jacob Diehl
Georg (X) Hirt
Jacob Herth
Wilhelm (O) Erhart
Johannes Erhart
Johann George Diebalt
Andres Kramer
Johan Jacob Schupp
Adam Euler
Valtin Schick
Matheis Schroth
Jacob Lies
Hans George (O) Kaldriter
Peter (X) Kaldriter
Caspar (O) Rouland
Daniel (H) Hubert
George (HI) Hubert

Nicklas (N) Bundry
Nicklas (X) Klein
Nicklas Holtzbender
Carel (H) Schneyder
Wilhelm (O) Antes
Johan Jörg Embs
Vallentin Vallentin Embs
Johann Casper Schneider
Johann Georg Koch
Valentin Hohwerder
Cassimir (O) Wessel
Johann Nickel Schuster
Friederich Helwig
Peter Jung
Jacob (H) Simon
Adam Weber
Jacob Dinges
Johann Wilhelm Hoster
Johannes Flichman
Wilhelm (W) Zimmer
Peter (++) Baal
Peter (|) Durrny

Simon Jacob Cron
Johan Adam Seysen
Johannes Melchior
Johan Jörg Rigel
Johann Conrad Lechleiter

Daniel Karstman
Hans Jorg Ollinger
Joh Philip (X) Oliger
Johan Jacob Schleiff
Johann Christoff Schmuckheyde

[List 87 A] A List of all the Men from 16 Years & upwards, On board the Ship Molley, Thomas Olive, Mast^r. [Qualified October 16, 1741.]

	AGES		AGES
Joseph Fabion	41	Christof^l Hine	38
Michael Miller	60	Gooder Dresel	28
George Froke	27	Mical Zeman	38
Adam Scaipe	32	Maties Schilion	44
Martin Greef	29	Philip Esdan	62
Jno Nickel Klyne	40	Andres Unger	50
Jno Jacob Dicker	26	John Jurgen Reitzel	45
Lenerd Bier	27	Herman Sower	47
Conrad Widener	27	Sebast^n Hexleman	28
Michal Broke	28	Andres Miller	18
Jacob Moles	45	Jacob Greef	50
Joanis Stochslegr	40	Jacob Engleman	20
Jacob Rumpea	52	Jacob Engleman, Junr	18
Will ^m Swarm	31	Hans Rudolph Ned	20
Valentine Switzick	49	Jacob Ekron	20
Daniel Gulman	40	Daniel Sink	24
Peter Godfrey	40	Peter Nubergall	22
Jeremia Miller	27	John Yergen Homeney	30
Christ^n Comens	24	Mical Seberlen	40
Bartlemeus Consleymen	45	Martin Regelman	40
Jno Fredelschip	22	Leonard Lemar	30
Peter Muns	28	Hans Mical Swarts	33
Simon Hine	27	Yergen Zemen Waker	45
Joanis Maties	38	Hend^k Smith	38
Daniel Ekron	28	Mical Creman	33
Mical Selman	17	Peter Creaman	34
Nickel Kisar	47	Alexand^r Stocksleger	28
Mical Harps	27	Hend^k Backer	50
Mical Seagle	28	Sam Speagel	33
Jno Yurgen Creaps	23	Mical Herp	30

	AGES		AGES
Hendrick Wedener	18	Jnº Wm. Sauer	17
Hans Mical Waker	17	Jnº Lenerd Sizler	17
Jnº Deder Switzick	24	Jnº Peter Sizler	16
Yournexfiel Roul	22	Maties Maier	32
Conrad Reagleman	20	Bernᵈ Switzick	16
Hans Yergen Reagleman	18	Peter Bendring	24
John Fredᵏ Cline	20	Jnº Casper Greef	22
Christofˡ Rumpea	18	Johanes Greef	16

[Endorsed:]
List of Palatines imported in the Ship Molly, Thomas
Olive. Qual. 16ᵗʰ Octoʳ 1741.
Sir:

In complyance with your order we have carefully examin'd
the State of Health of the Mariners and Passengers on board
the Ship Molly, Capᵗ Ollive, from Roterdam and are of Opinion they have no infectious Disease and may without Danger to
the Inhabitants be immediately landed.
Philadelphia, Octob. 16, 1741.

To his Honour   Lloyd Zachary
The Governour.   Thoˢ Bond.

[List 87 B] [Palatines imported in the Ship Molly, Thomas
Olive, Comʳ, from Rotterdam. Qualified October 17, 1741.]

Joseph Fabion	Peter (P) Godfrey
Michael (✕) Miller	Jeremias Müller
Görg Drück	Christian (✕) Commens
Johann Adam Scheib	Barthlemas (O) Cunsleyman
Martin (✕)Greef	John (✕) Treadelschip
Jnº Nicl. (O) Cline	Peter (✕) Muns
Johann Leonhard Beyer	Simon (✕) Hine ⎤
Philipp Conrath Weydner	Simon Hein ⎦
Mical (✕) Boraka	Johannes Mattheis
Johann Jacob Moltz	Daniel (O) Ekron
Johannes Stockschleger	Johannes Zellman
Jacob Rimbi	Johann Nickel Keyser
Willᵐ (✕) Swarm	Michael Härpster
Valdin Zweisig	Michael Spiegel
Daniel Gillmann	Hans Georg Krebs

Christople (ICH) Hine
Mical (O) Seamen
Matheus Kilian
Filiebus Daum
Andres (O) Unger
Johan Georg Reutzel
Hermen (HS) Sower
Sebastian Herlieman
Johan Jacob Greff
Jacob Engellmann
Jacob Engelman
Johann Ruddiss
Johann Jacob Ekron
Daniel (++) Sink
Johann Peter Niebergall
Michel Seuberlich
Marte Regelman
Lenerd (X) Leamor
Hans Michel Schwartz
Johan Rich. Schmitt
Johann Michel Krämer
Peter (X) Kreamer

Allexander Stock[schläger]
Hennrich Becker
Samuel Spiegel
Johan Michael Herb
Johann Henrich Weyner
Johann Michall Weicker
Jn° Fredrick (X) Switzick
Jerg Philb Ruhl
Conrath [Rigel]man
Hans Vigen (R) Reagelmen
Johann Fridig Klein
Johann Christopfel Rimbi
Johan Willhelm Sauer
Jn° Leanerd (X) Seisler
Jn° Peter (+) Seisler
Maties (X) Maier
Bernard (+) Switzick
Peter Bender
Johann Caspar Gref
Johann Jacob Decker
Jn° Vigen (X) Homeney
Andres (X) Miler

[Endorsed:]
Ship Molly. Qual. 16th Octr 1741. Capt Olive.

[List 87 C] At the Courthouse Philadª, Octr, 17th 1741.
Present: William Allen & Samuel Hasel, Esqrs.

The Palatines whose Names are underwritten, imported in
the Ship Molly, Thomas Olive, Commr from Roterdam, but
last from Deal, did this day take the Oaths to the Government,
viz:

Joseph Fabion
Michael (X) Miller
Johann Görg Drück
Johan Adam Scheib
Martin (X) Greffe
John Nichlas (O) Klein
Johann Lenhard Beyer
Philips Conrad Weydner

Michael (X) Borocker
Johann Jacob Moltz
Johannes Stockschleger
Jacob Rimbi
Wilhelm (X) Shwarm
Valdin Zweisig
Daniel Gillman
Peter (O) Godfried

Jeremias Müller
Christian (X) Commens
Bartollomae (O) Conselman
John Frederik (X) Shipp
Peter (X) Montz
Johan Simon Hein
Johannes Mattheis
Daniel (O) Ecron
Johannes Zellman
Johann Michel Keyser
Michäl Hörpster
Michael Spiegel
Hans Jerg Krebs
Christoffel (JCH) Haine
Michael (O) Simon
Matheus Kilian
Philibs Daum
Andereas (U) Unger
Johan Geörg Reutzel
Herman (HS) Sauer
Sebastian Herlieman
Johan Jacob Greff
Jacob Engellmann
Jacob Engelman
Johann Ruddiss
Johann Jacobb Ekron
Daniel (++) Zinck
Johann Peter Niebergall

Michel Seuberlich
Marte Regelman
Lenhart (L) Lämmer
Hans Michel Schwartz
Johan [Hen]rich Schmitt
Johann Michel Krämer
Peter (O) Krammer
Allexander Stockschleder
Hennrick Becker
Samuel Spiegel
Johan Michael Herb
Johann Henrich Weydner
Johan Michael Weicker
Diterich (X) Shweyzig
Jerg Philb Ruhl
Conrath Riegelman
Hans George (R) Riegelman
Johann Fridig Klein
Johan Christophel Rimbi
Johann Wilhelm Sauer
John Lenhart (X) Seesler
John Peter (X) Seesler
Matteus (X) Meyer
Bernhart (+) Switzig
Joan Peter Bender
Johann Caspar Greff
Johann Jacob Decker
John Georg (X) Hubeny

[List 88 A] A list of all the men from 16 Years of Age &
Upwards from on b^d The Snow Molly, John Cranch, Mas^r.
[Qualified October 26, 1741.]

	AGES		AGES
Peter Smith	36	Henry Pfeil	26
Johan Michal Graff	53	Johan Peter Haas	25
Wilhelm Fey	53	Johanes Haws	18
Johan Yerg Meylander	50	Yerigh Willm Geeseman	23
Jacob Shmith	31	George Funk	27
Peter Horbagh	31	Dewald Braugler	20
Jacob Deys	32	Henry Shneas	17

	AGES		AGES
Stephan Reep	32	Hans Dewald Sewer	16
Frederick Up	30	Godhert Armbreast	18
Valentine Yerkharf	24	Henry Daniel	31
Yerigh Bak	40	Peter Weber	43
Joackim Boorger	32	Henry Zep	19
Peter Meyer	20	Reighart Fawst	22
Michal Young	25	Dewald Weber	17
Peter Simon	20	Johanes Ermel	25
Johan Michal Fey	17	Henry Fawst	26
Antho. Adam	25	George Op	31
Balzasor Hamman	19	Hans Adam Cresman	17
Johan^s Metzler	50	Conrad Pop	26
Johan^s Metzler, Junr	17	Adolph Young	21
Hans Adam Sontagh	27	Sebastian Walder	36
Philip Tash	40	Vitus Shall	30
Peter Metz	18	Christian Hinkell	35
Hans Peter Haws	36		47 [men]

[Endorsed:]
Snow Molly, Capt Cranch.   Qual. 26th Octr 1741. No. 47.
List of Palatines.

$$\begin{aligned} 23.6 \\ \hline 70.6 \end{aligned}$$

[List 88 B] [Palatines imported in the Snow Molly, John Cranch, Master, from Rotterdam. Qualified October 26, 1741.]

Peter Schmitt	George (O) Funk
Johann Michel Gräff	Theobald Brauchler
Johan Wilhelm Fey	Stephan Rüb
Johan George (O) Mylander	Fridrich Opp
Jacob Schmid	Vallendin Gerckhardt
Johann Peter Horbach	Jörig Beck
Jacob Theis	Peter (X) Myar
Henrich Pfeil	Michael Jung
Johann Peter Haas	Peter Simon
Johannes Haas	Johan Michel Fey
Johan George Wilhelm Güsseman	Anthony (O) Adam
	Balzer Hamman

Johannes Metzler
Hann Adamm Sonntag
Johann Philipp Desch
Peter (X) Mez
Hans Peter Has
Hans (X) Deewid Siver

John Godhart (X) Ambreast
Johann Henrich Daniel
Peter (W) Weaver
Johanas (X) Ermel
Theobald Weber
Hans Adam (X) Cresman

[Endorsed:]
Snow Molly, John Cranch, M^r. Qual. Oct. 26, 1741.

[List 88 C] At Philad^a, Octr 26th 1741.
Before William Till, Esqr.

The Palatines whose Names are underwritten, imported in the Snow Molly, John Cranch, Master, from Roterdam, but last from Deal, did this day take the Oaths to the Governm^t, viz.,

Peter Schmitt
Johan Mich. Gräff
Johan Wilhellm Fey
John George (O) Meylander
Jacob Schmid
Johann Peter Herbach
Jacob Theis
Henrich Pfeil
Johann Peter Haas
Johannes Has
Johan Georg Wilhelm Güsseman
George (O) Funk
Johan Theobald Brauchler
Stephan Rüb
Fridrich Opp
Vallendin Gerckhardt
Jörig Beck
Joachim Burger

Peter (X) Meyer
Michel Jung
Peter Simon
Johan Michel Fey
Anthony (A) Adam
Balzer Hamman
Johannes Metzler
Hann Adam Sonntag
Johann Philip Desch
Peter (X) Metz
Hans Peter Has
Hans Dewald (X) Siber
John Godhart (X) Armbreast
Johann Henrich Daniel
Peter (W) Weber
Johannes (X) Ermel
Theobald Weber
Hans Adam (X) Cresman

[List 89 A] A list of all the Mens Names & ages from 16 Years & Upwards, from On b^d the Snow Thane of Fife, Wm Weems, Com^r. [Qualified November 7, 1741.]

	AGES		AGES
Gabriel Young	52	Carell Loutvith	22
Nickle Polander	36	Carell Henrich Pape	30
Jacob Fortiner	20	Anthony Snider	17
Adam Sercher	37	Peter Siner	28
Jerrig Grime	30	Bastian Hoop	37
Carell Grime	22	Henrich Whiteman	37
Adam Grime	25	Hans Adam Whiteman	16
Hans Boos	18	Leonard Arburgher	50
Mathias Scalp	26	Nickle Clase	27
Joler Snesman	19	Jerrie Wightman	25
Valentine Vintersteen	40		

[Endorsed:]
Capt. Weem's List. No. 21. Qual. 7th Novr 1741.

[List 89 B] [Palatines imported in the Snow Thane of Fife, William Weems, Master, from Amsterdam. Qualified Nov. 7, 1741.]

Gabriel Jung
Johann Nikel Bolander
Jacob Fortine
Jno Adam (A) Cheniker
Gerige (HK) Green
Carl Grim
Adam (A) Green
Johanas (X) Boss
Mahias (O) Kolpe
Valtin (O) Neasman

Vallentin Winterstein
Chas Ludewik (+) Essik
John Enrich (+) Bob
Anthony (X) Snyder
Peter (+) Syner
Johann Sebastian Hüb
Lenord (O) Serburger
John Nichol (X) Ketch
John George (X) Whiteman

[Endorsed:]
Palatines of Thane of Fife, Capt Weems. Qual. Nov. 7, 1741. No. 21.

[List 89 C] At the Courthouse Philada, Novr 7, 1741.
Present: The Honble George Thomas, Esqr, Governor, William Till, Esqr.
The Palatines whose Names are underwritten, imported in the Snow Thane of Fife, William Weems, Master, from Am-

sterdam, but last from Aberdeen, did this day cake the Oaths to the Government, viz.,

Gabriel Jung
Johann Nickel Bolander
Jacob Fortine
Johan Adam (A) Kircher
George (HK) Creim
Carl Grim
Adam (A) Grim
Johannes (×) Boss
Mattias (O) Kolb
Vallentin (O) Esman

Vallentin Winterstein
Ludwig (+) Essig
John Henry (+) Bob
Anthony (×) Shneyder
Peter (×) Seinier
Johan Sebastian Hüb
Lenhart (O) Zarburger
John Nicklas (×) Ketch
John Georg (×) Weyman

[List 90 A] A list of Mens Names from Lewes, p^r the Europa. [Qualified November 20, 1741.]

MENS NAMES	AGES	MENS NAMES	AGES
Geo. Biegbie	43	Christian Lezer	32
Henry Ensminger	40	George Righter	27
John Christian Housknight	24	Dieble Shank	25
Christian Beckley	23	Caspar Rupert	29
Daniel Beckly	21	Hans Jost Toby	23
Godfrey Langbane	17	Peter Walmer	21
Andreas Fuyst	24	Henry Kuintz	19
Mich^l Mark	45	Henry Adam	36
Mathias Bower	25	Johan Hendrick	40
John Paul Bower	23	Conradt Laam	22
Michael Bower	20	Jacob Sneck	18
Paulus Fierman	60	Simon Gross	30
Paulus Fierman, Junr	18	Theobald Gross	24
Dewaldt Mayer	27	Fred^k Wolfanger	20
Henry Chrissman	35	Lodwig Bread	21
Christopher Ecker	42	Hans Mich^l Joshower	50
Johan Peter Welhan	40	John Joshower	28
John Christian Welhan	16	Hans Peter Josshower	25
Henry Kauf	25	Johannes Josshower	16
Anthony Naye	21	Andreas Lum	24
Nicholas Wilhelm	30	Daniel Michaeler	20
Jacob Lezer	18	Hans Jurigh Schnyder	40

MENS NAMES	AGES	MENS NAMES	AGES
Jacob Schnyder	16	Christo Waganer	20
Jacob Mawer	33	Philip Swerber	20
Mich¹ Habersack	23	Peter Schryver	27
Anthony Swyn	24	Nicolas Waganer	20
Hans Nichol Horstein	17	Andreas Kryger	22
Philip Critz	26	Godfret Wolloweber	45
Jacob Lunger	25	Philip Naar	26
Conradt Corman	18	Peter Kryger	27
John Nichol Andre	24	Henry Kryger	29
Sebestian Stain	25	Peter Main	30
Johannes Correll	36		

[Endorsed:]
Europa. No. 64. List of Palatines. Qual. 20ᵗʰ Novʳ 1741.
Sir:

Philadelphia, Nov. 17, 1741.

In complyance with your orders we have carefully examined the State of Health of the Passengers on board three Shallops, brought from the Cape from the Europa, Capᵗ Lumsdaine, from Roterdam and found no Disease on board that is infectious.

Thoˢ Graeme

To his Honour
the Governour.

Th. Bond

[List 90 B] [Palatines imported in the Ship Europa. Qualified November 20, 1741.]

Henrich Ensminger
Johan Christian Hausknecht
John Dan¹ (✕) Beyby
Michell Marck
Johan Paul Bauer
Johan Michael Bauer
Paulus Furmann
Pauels Furman, Senʳ
Hans Ehwalt Meyer
Henrich Christmann
Johann Jacob Löser
Johann Christian Löser

Dewalt (W) Shank
Casper (+) Rubert
Johann Jost Thowe
Peter (|) Walmer
Henry (✕) Kuhens
Henrich Adami
Johannes Henrich
Johann Konradt Lahm
Simon Gross
Teobalt Gross
Ludwig Breit
Hans Nicel Eisenhauer

Johan Peder Eisenhauer
Johanis (✕) Isan Hower
Andrias (✕) Lumm
Hans Georg (O) Shnyder
Jacob (O) Shnyder
Michel Haberstüch
Hans Nicholas (✕) Hostain
Philap (+) Crytz
Jacob (+) Plummer
Connrad (✕) Corrman
Johann Nicolaus Andra

Johannes Corell
Johann Christophel Wagner
Philap (✕) Werball
Johann Peter Schreiber
Nicolaus Wagner
Johann Andereas Krieger
Gottfriedt Wolweber
Philap (F) Near
Johann Peter Krieger
Johann Henrich Krieger
Peter (✕) Maim

[Endorsed:]
Palatines of the Europa. 1741, Nov. 20th. No. 64.

[List 90 C] At the Courthouse Philadᵃ, Nov. 20th 1741.
Before Ralph Assheton, Esqʳ.

The Palatines whose Names are underwritten, imported in
the Ship Europa, [Capt. Lumsdaine] * late Master, did this
day take the Oaths to the Government, viz.,

Henrich Ensminger
Johan Christian Hausknecht
John Daniel (✕) Begly
Michell Marck
Johan Paul Bauer
Johann Michael Bauer
Paulus Furman
Paulus Furman, Senior
Hans Ehwalt Meyer
Henrich Christmann
Johann Jacob Löser
Johann Christian Löser
Dewald (W) Shanck
Caspar (✕) Rubert
Johann Jost Thowe
Peter (|) Walmer
Henry (✕) Kuhntz
Henrich Adami
Johannes Henrich

Conradt Lahm
Simon Gross
Teobalt Gross
Ludwig Breit
Hans Nicol Eisenhauer
Johan Peder Eisenhauer
Johan (✕) Eisenhauer
Andreas (✕) Lann
Hans Georg (S) Shneyder
Jacob (S) Shneyder
Michel Haberstüch
Hans Nicklas (✕) Hostein
Philip (+) Creutz
Jacob (+) Lunger
Conrad (+) Cornman
Johann Nicklaus Andra
Johannes Corell
Johann Christophel Wagner
Philip (✕) Wirbel

* For the name of the Captain see the doctor's certificate, p. 318.

Johann Peter Schreiber	Philip (F) Nair
Nicolaus Wagner	Johann Peter Krieger
Johann Andereas Krüger	Johann Henrich Krieger
Gottfriedt Weber	Peter (X) Main

[List 91 A] [Members of the Colony, called by Moravian writers, "The First Sea Congregation," which embarked on the Snow Catharine, Thomas Gladman, Commander, at London, March 15th, and arrived at Philadelphia, June 7th (New Style) 1742.]*

MARRIED MEN	MARRIED WOMEN
Henry Almers	Rosina Almers
David Bischoff	Ann Catherine Bischoff
Peter Boehler	Elizabeth Boehler
John Brandmiller	[Wife not with him]
John Brucker	Mary Barbara Brucker
George Harten	Elizabeth Harten
Robert Hussey	Martha Hussey
Adolph Meyer	[Wife not with him]
Michael Micksch	Anna Johanna Micksch
Samuel Powell	Martha Powell
Joseph Powell	Martha Powell
Paul Daniel Pryzelius	Regina Dorothea Pryzelius
Owen Rice	Elizabeth Rice
Joachim Senseman	Ann Catherine Senseman
Michael Tannenberger	Ann Rosina Tannenberger
John Turner	Elizabeth Turner
David Wahnert	Mary Elizabeth Wahnert
Thomas Yarrell	Ann Yarrell

SINGLE MEN

Andrew, a negro	John Michael Huber
John George Endter	George Kaske
Hector Gambold	Jacob Lischy
John C. Heydecker	John Philip Meurer
John Christopher Heyne	Joseph Moeller

* Original list lost. The above list is taken from Moravian sources. Printed in Abraham Reincke, *A Register of Members of the Moravian Church*, Bethlehem, 1873, pp. 49-54.

John Okely
William Okely
Christopher Frederic Post
Gottlieb Pezold
John Reinhard Ronner
George Schneider

Leonard Schnell
Nathaniel Seidel
Joseph Shaw
Christian Werner
George Wiesner
Matthew Wittke *

[List 91 B] Moravians imported in the Snow Catharine [Thomas Gladman, Master, from London. Qualified May 28, 1742.]

Johann Adolph Meyer
Johann Brandmüller
Paul Daniel Bryzelius
Heinrich Joachim Senseman
Johannes Brucker
Michael Tannenberger
Davidt Bischoff
Michel Micksch
Johann Georg Hardten
Henry Almers
David Wahnert
Nathanael Seidel
Jacob Lischy
Johann Philip Meurer

Johan Leonhardt Schnell
George (×) Wisler
Mathias (×) Wittgee
Christian Werner
George Kaske
George Ender
Joh. Christoph Heyne
Georg Schneider
Johan Georg Heydecker
Joseph Möller
Friedrich Post
Gottlieb Petzold
Johann Reinhard Roner
Johan Michael Huber

[Endorsed:]
Moravians imported in the Snow Catharine. 1742. Fees Rec^d.

[List 91 C] At the Courthouse, Philad^a May 28th 1742.
Present: Clement Plumsted, Esqr, Mayor of Philad^a.

Saml Hasel
William Till   } Esq^rs.
Robert Strettell

The Forreigners whose Names are underwritten, imported in the Snow Catharine, Capt [Thomas] Gladman, Commander, did this day take the usual Oaths or Qualifications to the Government, Viz.,

* The persons who did not sign the oath of allegiance were Englishmen, who were not required to sign, as they were not regarded as foreigners.

Johann Adolph Meyer
Johann Brandmüller
Paul Daniel Bryzelius
Heinrich Joachim Senseman
Johannes Brucker
Michael Tannenberger
Davidt Bischoff
Michel Micksch
Johann Georg Hardten
Henry Almers
David Wahnert
Nathanael Seidel
Jacob Lischy
Johann Philip Meurer

Johan Leonhardt Schnell
George (×) Wiessener
Matheus (×) Wittgie
Christian Werner
George Kaske
Gerge Ender
Joh. Christoph Heyne
Georg Schneider
Johan Georg Heydecker
Joseph Möller
Friedrich Post
Gottlieb Petzold
Johann Reinhard Roner
Johann Michael Huber

[List 92 C] At the Courthouse Philadᵃ, Augᵗ 25ᵗʰ 1742.
Present: Clement Plumsted, Esqʳ. Mayor.

    Robert Strettell,
    William Till,   } Esqʳˢ.
    Abraham Taylor

The Foreigners whose Names are underwritten, imported in the Brigᵗ Mary, John Mason, Master, from Rotterdam, but last from Cowes, did this day take the usual Oaths or Qualifications to the Government, viz.,

Valentin Krafft
Daniel Etter
Johann Phillipp Gertz
Johannes (×) Seivert
Johan Michgel Zeister
John Henry (++) Kookes
Andereas (××) Straub
Martin (×) Arnold
Jacob (O) Reeder
Mardin Schmidt
Constantinus Stilling
Hans George (×) Sneyder
Johann Fridrich Ricker
Christoffer (H) Danner
Jacob Baumann

Jerg Kieffer
Görg Friedrich Gervinus
Johannes Bergerhoff
Peter Burgener
Valentinus Ury
Rupertus Bender
Peter (×) Welch
Gerret Van Kouten
Jan De Mars
Hans Trachsall
Abraham (×) Liettel
Jacob Nägli
Peter (×) Burckner
Christian Bugner

[List 93 A] [Foreigners imported in the Ship Loyal Judith, James Cowie, Master, from Rotterdam. Qualified September 3, 1742.]

MENS NAMES	AGES	MENS NAMES	AGES
Barnard Johnston	45	Andrews Strasburger	25
Kilien Ficcel	43	Simon Jonnas	22
Kilien Ficcel	18	Henrach Woolfscall	30
Hanvinen Ficcel	17	Peter Part	48
Han Yarch Mideier	34	Nicolas Young	24
Godfrit Shiller	24	Andrews Hickman	34
Jacob Towiendicel	28	Peter Richsinger	28
Jacob Winderhamer	40	William Sower	24
Fredrach Carrs	45	Michael Henlang	20
Han Peter Younge	23	Nichlas Hadrach	28
Jacob Shiller	42	Johannas Ficcel	35
Han Yarach Wayman	30	Freats Mingel	48
William Hansbach	24	Jonnas Woolfscall	46
Windel Fadder	29	Philip Henrach Arrwa	45
Jacob Barn Peter	23	Tabald Novenar	28
Danial Longe	19	Henrach Wagener	19
Martin Brand	20	Jacob Crup	25
Johannes Shoutts	35	Jonnas Lowerance	43
Fredrack Shulemburger	40	Hanyarah Yeaher	23
Hannes Martens	20	Philip Crownabarger	27
Peter Hoback	41	Tabald Finck	37
Jacob Share	22	Lanard Fower	28
Roumand Louflimer	34	Jonnas Sallar	19
Johanpol Wisiel	26	Peter Hay	55
Johannes Outenhamer	22	Peter Hay	19
Henerach Tarr	23	Jonnas Misacop	18
Simmon Wishon	41	Pol Wastenburger	17
Fredrach Wineart	22	Ludewich Cline	46
Miccal Starn	30	Peter Cline	18
Johanas Lane	40	Ludewick Shott	29
Hanadan Tereinger	24	Jonnas Kiell	29
Jon Jacob Road	26	Peter Wastenburger	30
Philep Jonnas	22	Zacheres Heller	18
Heneraches Teahoaf	30	Fredrach Pell	50
Fredrack Carmeton	39	Michel Pollas	40

NAMES	AGES	NAMES	AGES
Jon Balster Sheffer	28	Jonnas Reel	38
Jonnas Ficcel	38	Ledwick Midsguer	40
Cristofel Higgher	39	Peter Port	18
Philte Creca	38	Conred Hardman	19
Phalten Clownenghar	17	Jonnas Showmaker	45
Johannas Thomb	40	David Keel	26
Hannas Yearach Sheffer	40	Cristefoal Kelder	17
Sammel Fortenia	17	Simon Crew	34
Lorrance Place	44	Jonnas Fortena	56
Cristefoal Place	32		90 [men]
Cristefoal Barkman	30		

[Endorsed:]
Mr. Callander pray as Soon as the Bearer Comes On board
pray take from the Book Which he has got the Names and
Age of all that is above the Years that I have Meanshined he
being parfetly acqwanted With the thing,

and you ewer oblige
y^rs, James Cowie.

Capt. Cowie.
N° 90:
List of Palatines imported in the Loyal Judith.

[List 93 B] [Foreigners imported in the Ship Loyal Judith,
James Cowie, Master, from Rotterdam. Qualified September
3, 1742.]

Bernhart Janson
Kilian Fischel
Kilian (X) Fischel
Gerg Metzger
Gottfriedt Schüler
Jacob (E) Towbilishell
Johan Jacob Winterehler
Fredrick (X) Kherr
Johan Peter Jung
Jacob Schühler
Johann Jörg Weimann
Wilhelm Anspach
Wendel Vetter

Jacob Berren (+) Petter
Daniel Lang
Martin Brandt
Johannes Schultz
Friedrich Schollenberger
Johannes Martens
Diettrich Hobbach
John Jacob (O) Sheir
Reymound (O) Loufflyn
Johann Paul Weytzel
Johannes Odernheimer
Johann Henrich Dörr
Simon Wischhan

Frin Wingert [?]

Johann Michel Stern

Johannes Lehn

John (O) Adam Turin[ger]

Johann Jacob Roth

Filber Johns

Henricus de Hoff

Friederich Germerdung

Johann Andreas Strassburger *

Simon Jonas

Henrich Wolffskehl

Peter (B) Parth

Nickelas Jung

Andreas Heckman

Peter Rigseger

Welm Sauer

Michael Henlein

Niclaus Hederigh

Johannes Fischell, Senr

Frik (M) Mengal

Johannes Wolffskehl

Philips Henrich Erben

Theobald (O) Nabinger

Johann Henrich Wagener

Johann Jacob Grub

Johannes Lorentz

Johann Görg Jäger

Philippes Cronenberger

Johann Lehart Fuhr

Johannes Alen

Petter Hey

Peter Hey

Johannes Mesenkob

Paulus Westenberger

Peter Klein

Lutwig Schott

Johannes Kühl

Zacharias (X) Heller

Friederich Pfeil

Johann Michel Paulus

Johannes Fissel

Johann Baltzer Schäffer

Christofel Heucher

Vallentin Grün

Johan Vallentin Kloninger

Johannes Domie

Hans George (X) Shaffer

Samuel Fortinneux

Lawrence (LB) Place

Christohf Plantz

Christohf Bergman

Johannes Rühl

Ludwig Metzger

Petter Bortt

Conrad (O) Hartman

Johannes Schumacher

David (||) Kell

Christoffel Geller

Johann Simon Gräff

Jonas (O) Furlly

[Endorsed:]
Palatines by the Loyal Judith. Capt. Cowie, 1742. No. 90.

[List 93 C] At the Courthouse Philad[a], Sept[r] 3[d] 1742.
Present: The Honble George Thomas, Esq[r], Governor,
        Abraham Taylor,   Robert Strettell, Esq[rs].
The Foreigners whose Names are underwritten, imported
in the Ship Loyal Judith, James Cowie, Master, from Roter-

* This is the ancestor of Mr. Ralph Beaver Strassburger. See *The Strassburger Family and Allied Families of Pennslyvania*, 1922, p. 54.

dam but last from Cowes, did this day take the usual Oaths or Qualifications to the Government, viz.,

Bernhart Janson
Kilian Fischel
Johan (✕) Fishel
Gerg Metzger
Gottfriedt Schüler
Jacob (E) Taubefishel
Johan Jacob Winterehler
Friederich (✕) Keher
Johan Peter Jung
Johan Jacob Schühler
Johann Jörg Weiman
Wilhelm Anspach
Wendel Vetter
Jacob Berent (✕) Petter
Daniel Lang
Martin Brandt
Johannes Schultz
Friedrich Schollenberger
Johannes Martens
Diettrich Hobbach
Johann Jacob (✕) Sheer
Reymund (O) Laufflenter
Johann Paul Weytzel
Johannes Odernheimer
Johann Henrich Dörr
Simon Wischhan
Frin Wingert [?]
Johann Michel Sternn
Johannes Lehn
John Adam (✕) Turinger
Johann Jacob Roth
Fillep Johns
Henricus de Hooff
Friederich Germerdung
Johann Andreas Strassburger
Simon Jonas
Henrich Wolffs Kehl
Peter (B) Barth

Nichelas Jung
Andreas Heckman
Peter Rigseger
Welm Sauer
Michael Henlein
Niclaus Hederigh
Johannes Fischell, Senior
Frietz (M) Mengel
Johannes Wolffs Kehl
Philipp Hennrich Erben
Theobald (N) Nabinger
Johann Henrich Wagener
Johann Jacob Grub
Johannes Lorentz
Johann Görg Jäger
Philippes Cronenberger
Johann Lehnhart Führ
Johannes Alen
Petter Hey
Peter Hey
Johannes Mesenkob
Paulus Westenberger
Peter Klein
Lutwig Schott
Johannes Kühl
Zacharias (✕) Heller
Friederich Pfeil
Johann Michel Paulus
Johann Baltzer Schäffer
Johannes (F) Fissel
Christophel Heucher
Valendtin Grün
Johan Vallentin Kloninger
Johannes Domie
Hans George (✕) Schäffer
Samuel Fortineux
Lorentz (LB) Place
Christohf Plantz

Christohf Bergman
Johanes Rühl
Ludwig Metzger
Petter Bortt
Conrath (C) Hartman

Johannes Schumacher
Davit (||) Shäll
Christoffel Geller
Johann Simon Gräff
Jonas (O) Furtuly

[List 94 B] [Foreigners imported in the Ship Francis & Elizabeth, George North, Master, from Rotterdam. Qualified September 21, 1742.]

Johanes Gnäge *
Moritz Zug
Christian Zug
Johannes Gerber
Jacob Kurtz
Johanes Zug
Wilrigh (✕) Staely
Jakob Gut
John Adam (+) Heydrig
John George (✕) Faust
Peter (✕) Faust
Johan Henrick (✕) Cressman
Conrad Bloss
Jacob Hauck
Joh. Peter Geckeler
Johannes Walther
Christof Geiser
Jost (✕) Fox
Henrick (✕) Miller
Hans Jacob Huber
Ludwig Huber
Philap Titter (+) Hoober
Johann Peter Köhler
Gabriel Köhler
Stephan Bopenmeier

Jacob Sarbach
Abraham (A) Koleman
Johann Michael Truckenmüller
Lodwick (+) Smallshafft
Jerg Adam Müller
Hans Michael (HK) Crafft
Christian (✕) Damewald
Johann Henrich Schertz
Jerg Schultz
Carl Philipp Schultz
Mosi Binder
Christian (✕) Eket
Andreas Bachman
Bernhart (+) Kobber
Melcher Schöner
Hans Michael Doll
Johann Michael Bucher
Abraham Groff
Johann Michael Seitz
Johanaus (✕) Kh[oen]
Abraham Schmutz
Matheus Mosiman
Marten (MS) Stover
Davith Rotheheffer
Christian Müller

[Endorsed:]
Francis & Elizabeth,
George Noarth, 1742.

* The first 92 names of the C list are missing on this list.

No. 149   [men]
74½   [women & children]
—————
223½   [Total]

[List 94 C] At the Courthouse Philadelphia, Septᵣ 21ˢᵗ
1742.
Present: William Till & Robert Strettell, Esqʳˢ.

The Foreigners whose names are underwritten, imported in
the Ship Francis & Elizabeth, George North, Master, from
Roterdam, but last from Deal, did this day take the usual
Qualifications to the Governmᵗ, viz.,

Johann Fridrich Jollgo	Johann Peter Waller
Michel Kolb	Christian Gürd
Johan Henrich Stall	Hans Michel Fohl
Christoph Adam Höbel	Thomas Heunmeyr
Michael (‖) Thesser	John Godfried (✕) Rieger
Johann Michel Waidele	Johan Jörg Veith
Johanns (H) Withman	Mich. Koppelger
Johan Jacob Holbein	Johann Peter Köchlein
Uhllerich (O) Halber	Johann Wielhem Werth
Johann Michal Käschster	Jhan Niclaus Cuntz
Johann Henrch Ster	Jacob Binder
Michel Plätscher	Willhelm Ruff
Jacob Geiger	Marti Myer
Johannes Eckert	Peter (✕) Laaber
Peter (R) Rubel	Hans Jerg Binder
Jacob (H) Klein	Melcher Hirtzel
Friderich Kaufman	Jonas Metzger
Hans Adam (✕) Klem	Hans (H) Georg Shenk
Ullrich Neuschwanger	Matthäus Wend Nagel
Nicklaus (H) Walder	Samuel (O) Wholgemuth
Christian (H) Newcomer	Adam Seibert
Christian (H) Newcomer, Junior	Hans Jerg Knödler
Andreas Waltaich	Hans Michel (H) Bouer
Christian Henrich	Johann Mattheis Plantz
Conrad (H) Bassel	Johanes Grob
Henry (K) Cerber	Philip (H) Shleyhouff
Christoph Fruht Schmitt	Rudoff Vallen Weitler
Jacob Schenck	Hans George (✕) Ruthy
Paulus Vater	Andreas Heintz

Ludwig Jacob Friedburg

Hanns Nicl Nort

Johannes Schäfer

Conrat Gerhart

Hennerich Hirt

Johann Adam Stam

Johann Henrich Bengel

Johann Henrich Wolff

Johann Geörg Schüssler

Anton Faust

Niclaus Röhrig

Nicolaus Gottschalk

Martin Kirschner

Peter Lam

Adam (O) Odt, Junior

Adam (X) Ott, Senior

Conrad (X) Ott

Johannes Odt

Johannes Reusswig

Johannes Pedter Odt

Johan Henrich Odt

Johan Henrich Dressler

Christian Rügner

Leonhardt Michael Rügner

Johan Henrich Ohl

Johann Christian Hörner

Johannes Weber

Johanes (X) Bohne

Johan Jacob Bohne

Christian Jotter

Jacob (X) Yoder

Christian Yoder

Fredri (K) Meyer

Christian (+) Miller

Johanes Qnäg *

Moritz Zug

Christian Zug

Johannes Gerber

Jacob Kurtz

Johannes Zug

Uhllerich (+) Ställy

Jakob Guth

John Adam (+) Heydrig

John George (X) Faust

Peter (+) Faust

Johan Henry (+) Creesman

Conrad Bloss

Jacob Hauck

Joh. Peter Geckeler

Johannes Walther

Christof Geiser

Jost (X) Fuchs

Henry (X) Miller

Hans Jacob Huber

Ludwig Huber

Philip Diter (+) Huber

Johann Peter Köhler

Gabriel Köhler

Stephan Bopenmeier

Jacob Sarbach

Abraham (A) Kolman

Johann Michell Truckenmüller

Ludwig (+) Shmaltzhaft

Jorg Adam Müller

Hans Michael (HMK) Krafft

Christian (X) Dannewald

Johann Henrich Schertz

Jerg Schultz

Carl Philipp Schultz

Mose Binder

Christian (X) Ecket

Andreas Bachman

Bernhart (+) Kober

Melcher Schöner

Hans Michael Doll

Johann Michael Bucher

Abraham Groff

Johann Michael Seitz

Johannes (+) Koohn

Abraham Schmutz

* The B list begins with this name.

Mattheus Mosiman   Davits Rotheheffer
Martin (MS) Stouver   Christian Müller

[List 95 C] At the Courthouse Philad^a, Septr 24th 1742.
Present: The Honble George Thomas, Esqr, Governor,
   Samuel Hassel,   William Till,   ⎫
                     ⎬ Esq^rs.
   Abraham Taylor, Robert Strettell, ⎭
   Joseph Turner,
The Foreigners whose names are underwritten, imported in
the Ship Robert & Alice, Martley Cusack, Master, from Roter-
dam, but last from Cowes, did this day take the foregoing
Oaths or Qualifications to the Government, viz.,

Filippus Börgeres	Johann Henrich Werner
Johann Gorg Christ	Peder Geris
Jorg Casper Rausch	Philip (X) Geris
Johan Jacob Metzger	Nicklas (H) Hartt
Johan Nicklas (H) Hyl	Johan Simon Drum
Johan Jacob Benedick	Paulus Hang
Cornelius Miller	Joannehs Runckel
Hans Adam (X) Christ	Adam (A) Gucker
Simon Jacob (O) Theil	Christian (A) Gucker
Fridrich Müller	Michel Weiss
Ludwig (X) Miller	Johann Jacob Schmitt
Johann Georg Schissler	Henry (X) Stawe
Conrad (O) Pooff	Johann Caspar Schell
Philipp Fackenthal *	Dauvit Schmitt
Valtin Paul	Durs Ziegler
Hildebrand (+) Heckeman	Johannes Ziegler
Johann Philip Kercher	Johann Michel Koch
Johan Christoffell Pister	Johan Nicklaus Brosius
Jacob (O) Stübigh	Jacob Weber
Hans Rubi	Jacob Stein
Johan Jacob (X) Bome	Johann Abraham Brosius
Friederig (X) Becker	Johann Georg Riess
Simon Peter Diehl	Lorentz Riess
Johann Friderich Heimer	Johann Jacob Riess
Michel Axer	Johan Jacob Wagner
Michel Wolff	Peter Herber
Heinerich Heydt	Johannes Herber

* This is the ancestor of Dr. B. F. Fackenthal, Jr., of Riegelsville, Pa.

Hans Adam (O) Holdt
Hans Adam (O) Fuctig
Frietderich Schmit
John Jacob (Z) Zervin
Phillips Jacob Eschenfelter
Andres Harter
Adam (F) Furctig
Joanes Forch
Matheas (X) Meyer
David Striel [?]
Davit (O) Mackly

Johannes (O) Krape
Johann Paulus Reuther
Hans Peter (X) Woost
Andres Kessler
Michel Danner
Hans George (X) Katzenstein
Dietrich Danner
Hans Michael (X) Spaar
Peter (X) Maus
Mattheis Heinrich

[List 96 A] A List of all the male passengers, Imported in the ship Francis & Eliz^th, from fourteen years of age upwards. [Qualified August 30, 1743.]

MENS NAMES	AGES	MENS NAMES	AGES
Hannes Burger	32	Henderick Neaff	21
Hannes Cockley	39	Philean Gillok	24
Hannes Cebeley	20	Hans Henderick Neaff	19
Hanes Do ye 2nd	20	Henderick Pomgardiner	48
Hend^k Moor, sick	25	Hannes Meyer	32
Rudolph Merts	20	H^s Jacob Scheurmeyer, absent	30
Johannes Meyer	26	Henderick Groots	34
Hans Henderick Cueser	45	Hans Jacob Neaff	46
Henderick Rutolph	36	Rutolph Miller, dead	44
Henderick Miller	22	Gasper Hinna	32
Hans Henderick Neaff	47	Hans Henderick Hinna	27
Ulderick Neaff	40	Rudolph Smith	21
Henderick Miller, dead	43	Rudey Meyerhover	20
Christophel Bosser	26	Hans Ulderick Bladman	40
Henderick Wideman	20	Christopher Bladman, sick	18
Henderick Eberick	24	Jacob Sorber, dead	20
Hans Jacob Sootter, sick	24	Hennery Sorber, absent	21
Henderick Lear	30	Henderick Linebah	22
Gasper Parrey	22	Hendrick Baltisbarger	28
Hans Hortinger	23	Gasper Gladfelder, sick	33
Henderick Switser	25	Henderick Waltter	30
Hannes Sootter, dead	20	Felix Waltter, sick	26
Gasper Croope	20	Hans Jacob Houser	20
Johanes Hook	20	Joseph Frowenfelder, sick	40

MENS NAMES	AGES	MENS NAMES	AGES
Henderick Bowers	25	Hannes Koor	36
Rudolph Kleynbetter	21	Hannes Toops	24
Jacob Wagman	28	Lenoard Sneabley	24
Hans Jacob Weist	21	Joseph Stelley, sick	28
Fellix Halleman	23	Johannes Parr	23
Henderick Goedt	28	Jacob Parr	20
Johannes Posser	24	Henderick Groop	20
Malichiest Steeley	24	Henderick Hitts	40
Lenoard Aldorff	28	Henderick Sliffer	37
Henderick Seibedorfer	40	Jacob Freek	46
Hans Petter Lee, absent	62	Gasper Sneabley	43
Felex Lee	38	Hannes Hilderbrand	26
Felex Groos	26	Jacob Bookman	23
Hans Conrad Groos	22	Henderick Sutter	23
Hans Jacob Meyer	19	Henderick Sutter, ye 2^d	30
Jacob Odt, sick	24	Daniell Herner	34
Henderick Odt	22	Jacob Fister	25
Johanes Buchey	21	Ulderick Ringer	36
Hans Jacob Rinker, sick	28	Henery Smith	20
Hans Jacob Reidlinger	23	Hans Ulderick Hecetswilder	24
Yacob Brommer	42		

[Endorsed:]
Captn Norths List of Foreigners, imported in the Ship Francis & Elizabeth. Qual. 30th August, 1743.

[List 96 B] [Foreigners imported in the Ship Francis & Elizabeth, George North, Master from Rotterdam. Qualified August 30, 1743.]

Hans Bucher	Ulrick (+) Neaf
Henry (✕) Coughly	Christoph (✕✕) Bosser
Hans Zobeli	Hendrick (✕) Weidman
Hans Zobelin	Henry (+) Hebreight
Rudolf Mertz	Henerick (+) Lear
Hans Meier, Junr	Gaspar (+) Sperry
Hans Heinrich Huber	Hans Gütinger
Hendrick (✕) Rudolph	Henry (✕) Switzer
Heinrich Müller	Gaspar (O) Crop
Hans Henrich Näff	Johannes Hug

Hendrick (+) Naaffe

Kilian (×) Giltt

Hendrich (×) Naaffe

Henry (×) Bumgarner

Hans (×) Moyer

Hendrick (×) Groats

Hans Jacob (Hans) Naafe

Casper Heinen

Hans Henrich Heinen

Rut. Schmidt

Johans Meier

Hans Ulrich (×) Bladman

Henry (+) Lineback

Henry (+) Boltisberger

Ely (×) Walter

Hans Jacob (+) Oozer

Henrich Bauerdt

Rudolph (×) Kleinbeeter

Jacob Wegmann

Hans Jacob Wünst

Felix (×) Hierlyman

Henry (×) Goedt

Johannes Blos

Melcher Steheli

Lenhart Altorfer, Schmid

Henry (×) Diebedorver

Felix (×) Lea

Fellix Gross, Wagener

Hans Kurick (+) Gross

Hans Jacob Meyer

Henrich Ott

Johans Büch

Hans Jacob Rüttlinger

Jacob (×) Brunner

Hans Kuhn

Hans Dubs

Linnhart Schnebeli

Johanns Bär

Jacob Bär

Heinrich Grob

Heinrich Hitz

Heinrich Schleiffer

Jacob Frick

Caspar (×) Sneabeli

Johannes Schild[enrad]

Jacob Buch[man]

Henrich Sut[er]

Henrich Su[ter, Jr.]

Daniel [Herner]

Hans Jacob [Pfister] *

Hans Ullrich Ringer

Henry (×) Smith

Hans Ullrich [Hegensweiller]

[Endorsed:]
30th Augt 1743. Imported by Captn North.

[List 96 C] At the Court House Philad^a August 30th 1743.
Present: The Honourable George Thomas, Esqr, Governor,
Samuel Hassel,   William Allen,   ⎫
Abraham Taylor,   James Hamilton,   ⎬ Esq^rs
Joshua Maddox,   Septimus Robinson ⎭
The Foreigners whose Names are underwritten, imported
in the Ship Francis & Elizabeth, George North, Master, from
Rotterdam, but last from Cowes, did this day take the fore-
going Oaths or Qualifications to the Government, viz.,

* These names are partly effaced.

Hans Bucher
Henry (×) Coughly
Hans Zobeli
Hans Zoblin
Rudolf Mertz
Junghans Meier
Hans Heinrich Huber
Henry (×) Rudolph
Heinrich Müller
Hans Heinrich Näff
Uhllerich (+) Näff
Christopher (×) Bosser
Henry (+) Weidman
Henry (×) Hebrecht
Henry (×) Leer
Casper (×) Spery
Hans Gütinger
Henry (×) Shwitzer
Casper (O) Crop
Johannes Hug
Henry (×) Naff
Killian (×) Gild
Hans Hendry (O) Naff
Hendry (×) Baumgardner
Hans (×) Meyer
Henry (×) Rudsh
Hans Jacob (Hans) Naff
Casper Heinen
Hans Hennerich Heinen
Rut. Schmitch
Johans Meier
Hans Uhllerich (+) Bladman
Henry (×) Leinbach
Henry (×) Poldesberger
Ely (×) Walder
Hans Jacob (×) Usser
Heinrich Bauerdt

Rudolph (×) Kleinpeter
Jacob Wegman
Hans Jacob Wünst
Felix (×) Hierlyman
Henry (×) Good
Johannes Boser
Melcher Steheli
Lenhart Altorfer, Schmid
Henry (×) Diebydorffer
Felix (×) Leea
Fellix Gross, Wagener
Hans (×) Kurekous
Hans Jacob Meyer
Henrich Ott
Johannes Buch
Hans Jacob Rütlinger
Jacob (×) Bruner
Hans (O) Kuhn
Hans Dups
Linnhart Schnebeli
Johannis Bär
Jacob Bär
Heinrich Grob
Heinrich Hitz
Henrich Schleypfer
Jacob Frick
Caspar (×) Snabily
Johannes Schildennrad
Jacob Bachman
Heinrich Suter
Henry (×) Zutter
Daniel Herner
Hans Jacob Pfister
Hans Ullrich Ringer
Henry (+) Shmit
Hans Ullrich Hegenzweiller [?]

[List 97 A] [Foreigners imported in the Ship Loyal Judith, James Cowey, Master from Rotterdam. Qualified September 2, 1743.]

	AGES		AGES
Bardel Zeller	27	Ulrich Freyhofer	30
Bernhard Lauffersweber	22	Rudolf Büchie	19
Hannes Becker	22	Wendel Horst	32
Nicolaus Scharffenberger	43	Philip Wentz	34
Johan Conrad Schütz	26	Valentin Wentz	25
Georg Ebelman	25	Stoffel Weisskopf	27
Jacob Gidelman	22	Stoffel Graffert	22
Wendel Dannefeld	24	Gerhard Fischkus	48
Valedin Hamen	20	Bastian Bomgart	21
Fillip Christian	24	Christian Weiss	37
Wilhelm Becker	35	Johannes Schwind	26
Martin Lind	23	Jacob Wilhelm	22
Asihmes Leber	23	Jacob Huth	25
Michael Steich	15	Jacob Grosskopf	30
Hendrich Maag	15	Hermanus Bott	46
Jacob Maag	42	Antoni Walter	32
Jacob Beyer	27	Nicolaus Keller	28
Adam Moses	33	Lorentz Schmal	32
Georg Müller	19	Adam Schmal	14
Johannes Hönig	18	Gerhardt Scheir	54
Peter Braun	18	Hendrich Scheir	20
Joh. Philip Odenweller	22	Antoni Kapel	35
Johannes Gerst	22	Jacob Hausman	26
Friedrich Fettberger	32	Hans Schreiner	29
Lorentz Lebersweiller	57	Adam Reiss	45
Nicolaus Runckel	27	Johannes Habersoot	35
Jacob Runckel	17	Jacob Petre	21
Adam Brech	21	Mates Hoffert	21
Johannes Jeger	22	Adam Fux	20
Carl Angel	20	Simon Ruffner	56
Johannes Kremer	27	Peter Bott	35
Daniel Mey	20	Georg Fitterer	22
Adam Mor	23	Johannes Brickbaur	25
Philip Peyer	17	Hans Mundschau	30
Johannes Gambach	60	Philip Böhm	18
Philip Gambach	20	Hans Wolf	24
Jacob Närbas	28	Peter Müller	53
Frantz Närbas	23	Andreas Weidbrecht	53
Philip Hoffman	59	Hermanus Höfer	34
Adam Hoffman	16	Jacob Münner	18

	AGES		AGES
Philip Hart	50	Philip Springer	16
Lorentz Hart	21	Hendrich Mey	48
Hans Emrich Bott	42	Hans Bärmas	19
Georg Wolfkil	59	Georg Störich	32
Just Wolfkil	14	Hans Hendrich Maag	20
Adam Schmal	50	Jacob Bantlie	25
Wentz Schmal	15	Baltes Grau	20
Valentin Grosch	36	Georg Friderich Krembeler	24
Friderich Fischkus	36	Jacob Keyser	20
Mates Botterfas	23	Peter Schweigehart	22
Nicolaus Mannebach	26	Hans Hoffman	24
Bernhard Becker	37	Daniel Hoffman	20
Hans Becker	15	Hs. Jacob Fassbender	20
Philip Springer	43	Lorentz Müller *	20

[List 97 B] [Palatines imported in the Ship Loyal Judith, James Cowey, Master, from Rotterdam. Qualified September 2, 1743.]

Bartel Zöller	Johannes Hönig
Bernhard Lauffersweiler	Johann Peter Braun
Nicolaus Scharfenberger	Joen Philipps Odewelder
Hanes Becker	Johanns (×) Kerst
Johann Conrad Schütz	Friederich Feltberger
Johan Georg Eppelman	Lorentz Laffersswiler
Johann Jacob Gittelman	Nickel Runckel
Johan Wendel Danenfelser	Jacob Runckel
John Valentin (O) Hammen	Adam Brech
Philip (O) Christian	Johannes Jäger
Johann Wilhelm Becker	Philips Carl Angel
Marttin Linkh	Johannes Krämer
Jochmus Löhrer	Danniel May
Michel Steitz	Johan Adam Mohr
Hendrick (+) Moag	Johann Philppes Beier
Jacob Maag	Johannes Gambach
Johann Jacob Bayer	Johann Philip Gambach
Johann Adam Moses	Johann Jacob Nehrbass
Georg (O) Muller	Johanns Frantz Nährbass

* This list exists in duplicate form. One in German script, which is followed above, the other in English script, which we omit.

Philips Hoffman
John Adam (O) Hoffman
Ulrich Freyhofer
Rudolph (X) Buchy
Wendell Horst
Johann Phillipps Wentz
Valentin Wentz
Christofel Weisskopf
Gerhart (II) Fishkus
Christoffel Graffert
Bastian Bongart
Christian Weiss
Johannes Schwindt
Johan Jacob Willhelm
Johan Jacob Huth
Jacob (X) Groskopf
Hermanus Bott
Andony Walter
Nickelas Keller
Lorentz Schmahl
Adam (X) Schmahl
Johan Henrich Scheurer
Joh. Georg (H) Scheurer
Andoni Kappel
Jacob Hausman
Johannes Schreyer
Johan Adam (X) Reith
Johannes (X) Habersoot
Johann Jacob Petry
Matthias Hoffer
Johann Adam Fuchs
Simon Ruffener
Peter (X) Boht
George (F) Fitterer
Johannes Brückbauer

Johannes (HM) Mondshauer
Johann Phillipps Böhm, Son
John Phil. (B) Böhm, Father
Hans Wolff (X) Waltz
Peter (X) Miller
Andreas Weybrich
Hermanus Höffer
Jacob Mohner
Johann Philips Hardt
Lorentz Hardh
Johann Emrich Bott
Johann Georg (W) Wolfkehl
Adam (X) Schmahl
Wentz Schmahl
Valentin Grosch
Friederich Fiechgus
Mattheus Butterfass
Nicolas Manenbach
Bernhart Becker
Johannes Becker
Johann Philip Springer
Johann Philip Springer
Johann Henrich May
Johannes Bermes
John George (O) Storich
Hans Heinrich Maag
Jacob Laucks
Balthaser Kroh
George Fred^r (X) Kriebel
Jacob (XX) Keyser
Peter Schweikharth
Johannes Hoffman
Johann Daniel Hoffman
Johann Jacob Fassbendler
Lorentz (+) Muller

[Endorsed:]
Subscriptions of the Palatines imported in the Ship Loyal
Judith. Captn James Cowie. Qual. 2^d 7ber, 1743 .

[List 97 C] At the Court House Philad^a, September 2^d
1743.

Present: William Till,   Abraham Taylor,   ⎱
      Robert Strethill,   Septimus Robinson, ⎰ Esq^{rs}

The Foreigners whose Names are underwritten, imported in the Ship Loyal Judith, Captain James Cowey, Master, from Rotterdam, but last from Cowes, did this day take the foregoing Oaths or Qualifications to the Government, viz.,

Bartel Zöller
Bernhard Lauffersweiler
Hannes Becker
Nicolaus Scharffenberger
Johan Conrad Schütz
Johan Georg Eppelmann
Johann Jacob Gittelman
Johan Wendel Dannenfelser
Johan Vallentin (O) Hammer
Philip (O) Christian
Johann Wilhelm Becker
Marttin Linkh
Jochamus Lörer
Michel Steitz
Heinrich (X) Moag
Jacob Maag
Johan Jacob B[ayer]
Johann Adam Moses
Johan Georg (H) Miller
Johannes Hönig
Jann Peter Braun
Jann Philipps Odewelder
Johannes (X) Kirst
Friederich Feltberger
Lorentz Lafferswiler
Nickel Runckel
Johann Jacob Runckel
Adam Brech
Johannes Jäger
Philip Carl Angel
Johannes Krämer
Daniell Mäy
Johan Adam Mohr
Johann Philppes Beier

Johannes Gambach
Johan Philip Gambach
Johann Jacob Nehrbass
Johannes Frantz Nerbass
Philips Hoffman
Johan Adam (A) Hoffman
Ulrich Freyhofer
Rudolff (X) Buchy
Wendel Horst
Johann Phillipp Wentz
Valentin Wentz
Christoffel Weisskopf
Christoffel Graffert
Gerhart (||) Fishkes
Bastian Bongart
Christian Weiss
Johannes Schwindt
Johan Jacob Wilhelm
Johan Jacob Huth
Jacob (X) Grosskopff
Hermanus Bott
Andony Walter
Nickelas Keller
Lorentz Schmahl
Adam (X) Shmaal
Johan Henrich Scheurer
Hans Georg (H) Sheyer
Andoni Kappel
Jacob Hausman
Johannes Schreyer
Johan Adam (X) Reyd
Johannes (X) Habersod
Johann Jacob Petry
Matthias Hoffer

Johann Adam Fuchs
Simon Ruffener
Peter (✕) Both
George (F) Fitterer
Johannes Brückbauer
Johannes (HM) Mondshauer
Johann Phillips Böhm, Junior
Johann Phillips Böhm
Hans Wolf (✕) Waltz
Peter (✕) Miller
Andreas Weybrich
Hermanus Höffer
Jacob Möhner
Johan Philips Hard
Lorentz Hardh
Johann Emrich Bott
Johann George (W) Wolffskehl
Adam (S) Schmahl
Wentz Schmahl
Valentin Grosch

Friederich Fiechgus
Mattheus Butterfass
Nicolas Manenbach
Bernhart Becker
Johannes Becker
Johann Phillip Springer
Johann Phillip Springer, Junior
Johann Henrich May
Johannes Bermes
Johann George (O) Störy
Frantz. Heinrich Maag
Jacob Bantli
Johann Balthaser Kroh
Georg Frederich (✕) Gribel
Jacob (✕✕) Keyser
Peter Schweickharth
Johannes Hoffman
Johann Daniel Hoffman
Johann Jacob Fassbendler
Lorentz (+) Miller

[List 98 C] At the Court House Philadelphia, 5 Septr 1743.
Present: The Hono^{ble} George Thomas, Esqr, Governor,

Wm Till,   Wm Allen ⎫
                                ⎬ Esq^{rs}
Septimus Robinson,   ⎭

The Foreigners whose Names are underwritten, imported in the Snow Charlotta, John Mason, Master, from Rotterdam, but last from Cowes, did this day take the foregoing Oaths or Qualifications to the Government, viz.,

Adolf Eiler
Hennrich Hant
Johan Nickel Schnell
Johan Peter Schwager
Matteis Bassing
Henry (HS) Shoemacker
Johann Philipp Schnell
Johannes Ickrath
Wilhelm Bretz
Johan Friederich Thor
Jacob Bretz

Johannes (HL) Lees
Johannes Lisch
Johannes Schiffer
Johann Jacob Eyck
Phillippus Mäurer
Jacob Eick
Johannes Gross
Johann Andoni Hellenthal
Anthon Schneider
Johan Georg Miller
David Dauderman

Niclas Wolfart
Henrig Eckenroth
Johan Georg Herman
Johann Daniel Schmitt
Johan Conrath Gutmann
Johannes Koch
Vallentin Lörsch
Johan Balthtes Gir
Johannes Rievet
Johann Jacob (✕) Stamm
Johannes Niemandt
Johan Heinrich Mertz
Henrich (+) Meyer

Friedrich Krämer
Johannes Hermann
Anton Zehner
Hans George (✕) Albrecht
Godlieb Veith
Mattes Heimbach
Jacob (+) Granobel
Johannes Soehn
Johannes Bopp
Johannes Alberächt
Johannes Clossheim
Johannes Umradt
Johannes Nümrich

[List 99 A] A List of The Names & Ages of the Men p^r the Lydia, Capt Ja^s Abercrombie, 19th Septem^r 1743.

MENS NAMES	AGES	MENS NAMES	AGES
Jost Former	43	Johannes Piester	27
Johannes Bender	30	Lodwick Rudolph	27
Johannes Bender, Junr	18	Peter Owl	25
Frans Baker	27	Johannes Platenberger	22
Diedrick Fall	34	Peter Alden	29
Johannes Septer	26	Gerard Wyck	27
Johannes Weeler	27	Wilhelm Apple	29
Johannes Kenke	27	Jurian Willm Eckert	36
Tielman Schutz	42	Willhelm Elzeroot	18
Johannes Ax	25	Hendrick Swartz	19
Heronimus Weber	25	Willhelm Kreiter	20
Christian Walter	23	Hans Adam Cowl	20
Johan Christ^n Reistein	19	Johan Jacob Missenhamer	23
Johan Hend^k Hoffman	35	Rudolph Goodman	47
Johan Jacob Kecker	26	Johan Willm Goodman	16
Hendrick Kecker	19	Johan Geo. Goodman	18
Conradt Weit	31	Mathias Lintz	48
Simon Dreisback	45	Georg Vrie	26
Johan Jost Dreisback	20	Conradt Kool	24
Johan Adam Dreisback	19	Mich^l Reyderback	25
Johannes Young	40	Johan Mich. Reyderback	20
Heronimus Brough	21	Andreas Smith	20
Johannes Konigh	38	Hendrick Leipkiger	30

MENS NAMES	AGES	MENS NAMES	AGES
Jurigh Ament	60	Frans Grayligh	45
Philip Ament	20	Casper Cassner	26
Johannes Ament	18	Johan Christ° Loos	23
Johannes Rood	32	Johannes Sen	36
Conradt Saler	13	Hendrick Vry	40
Christian Neff	25	Johannes Bower	38
Leonard Gesell	31	Johannes Tirn	28
Johan Jacob Ecker	37	Philip Hayer	31
Jurigh Swartz	27	Valentine Kleter	23
Christian Harshe	30	Johann Fredᵏ Hayer	23
Johannes Peltz	26	Johan Valantine Hayer	18
Valantine Smith	26		—
Johan Fredᵏ Ringer	23	Persons in all	73
Valentine Rood	35		32
Johan Nichoˡ Sower	50		—
Jeremias Wytigh	37		105

[Endorsed:]
Captⁿ Abercrombies List of Palatines, 19ᵗʰ Septʳ 1743.

[List of 99 B] [Palatines imported in the Ship Lydia, James Abercombie, Master, from Rotterdam. Qualified September 20, 1743.]

Joost (+) Former
Johannes (+) Bender
Johannes Benner
Frantz Becker
Diedrich Fahl
Johannes (+) Zepter
Johannes (+) Weller
Johannes Hürche
Tilemannus (X) Schutz
Johannes Ax
Hironimus Weber
Johannes Christian Walther
Johann Christ Rischstein
Johannes Henrich Hoffman
Johann Jacob Gücker

Johann Henrich Gücker
Konradt Wirdt
Simmon Dreisbach
Johann Jost Dreisbach
Johann Adam Dreisbach
Johannes Jung
Herrmanus Bruch
Johannes Konig
Johanes Pfister
Johann Ludwig Rudolph
Johann Peter Uhl
Johannes (++) Plattenberger
Peter (X) Althenn
Johann Gerhart Weick
Wilhelm Apbel

George Wilhelm (+) Eckhart
Johann Wilhelm Eckroth
Henrich (||) Schwartz
Johan Wilhelm Kreutter
Johann Jacob Meissener
Johann Adam Gaul
Johann Rudolf Gutman
Matthias Lentz
Georg Frieh
Conrath Kohl
Johan Nickel Reinbech
Johan Michel Reidenbeck
Anreas Schmit
Henrich (O) Lebkucher
Johann Philipp AmEndt
Johannes AmEndt
Johannes (R) Roth
Johan Christian Neff
Johan Leonhard Gesell
Johann Jacob (H) Hecker
Johan Görg Schwartz

Christian (X) Hershee
Johannes (X) Peltz
Valentin Schmidt
Johannes Friedrich Sänger
Valentin (XX) Roht
Johan Nickel Sauer
Jeremias (O) Weydy
Frantz Greulich
Casper Gassner
Johann Christoph (++) Loos
Henrich (X) Frey
Johannes Baur
Johannes Dörr
Philip (||) Hager
Valentin (X) Kletter
Johan Friderich Heyer
Vallandien Heyer
George (X) Ament
Conrad (X) Saller
Joh. Wilh. (X) Goodman
Joh. George (X) Goodman

List of Palatines, imported in the Lydia, Capt. James Abercrombie. Qual. 19th Septr 1743.

[List 99 C] At the Court House Philadelphia, 20th Septr 1743.

Present: The Hon^{oble} George Thomas, Esqr, Governor,

| Saml Hassel, | Wm Till, | |
| Wm Allen, | Septimus Robinson, | Esq^{rs} |

The Foreigners whose Names are underwritten, imported in the Ship Lydia, Captⁿ James Abercrombie, Master, from Rotterdam, but last from Cowes, did this day take the foregoing Qualifications or Oaths to the Government, viz.,

Jost (+) Folmer
Johanns (X) Bender
Johannes Benner
Frantz Becker
Diedrich Fahl
Johannes (+) Zepter

Johannes (+) Weller
Johannes Hürche
Dielman (X) Shütz
Johannes Ax
Hirieonimus Weber
Johannes Christian Walther

Johann Christ Rischstein
Johanns Henrich Hoffman
Johann Jacob Gücker
Johannes Henrich Gücker
Konradt Wirdt
Simmon Dreisbach *
Johann Jost Dreisbach
Johann Adam Dreisbach
Johannes Jung
Herrmanes Bruch
Johannes König
Johannes Pfister
Johann Lutwig Rudolff
Johann Peter Uhl
Johannes (++) Blattenberger
Peter (+) Althen
Johann Gerhardt Weick
Wilhelm Apbel
George Wilhelm (X) Eckhart
Johann Wilhelm Eckroth
Henry (+) Shwartz
Johan Wilhelm Kreutter
Johan Adam Gaul
Johann Rudolff Gutman
Matheas (M) Lentz
Georg Frieh
Conrath Kohl
Johann Nickell Reidenbach
Johann Michel Reidenb[ach]

Anreas Schmit
Henry (O) Lepkücher
Johann Philipp AmEndt
Johannes AmEndt
Johannes (R) Roth
Johan Christian Neff
Johann Leonhard Gesell
Johan Jacob (H) Häker
Johan Gorg Schwartz
Christian (X) Härshy
Johannes (B) Peltz
Valentin Schmidt
Johannes Friedrich Sänger
Vallentin (XX) Roth
Johan Nickel Sauer
Jeremias (X)Weidy
Frantz Greulich
Casper Gassner
Johan Christoffer (XX) Looss
Henry (X) Frey
Johannes Baur
Johannes Dörr
Philip (‖) Heger
Vallentin (X) Kletter
Johan Friderich Heyer
Vallendin Heyer
George (X) Ament
Conrad (X) Sallem
Johan (+) Goodman

[List 100 A] [Foreigners imported in the Ship Rosanna, James Reason, Master, from Rotterdam. Qualified September 26, 1743.]

Christaf Heralde
Hance Yarah Creatsener
William Swishler
David Hufman

Hance Yarah Sturner
Androw Springe
Christaf Shake
Hance Yarak Fox

* Simon Dreisbach, Sr., and Jr., were prominent elders of the Indian Creek Reformed Church in Allen township, Northampton County. See the letter of Simon Dreisbach, Jr., written in January, 1773, published by the Rev. Dr. John B. Stoudt, in the *Reformed Church Review*, vol. XVIII (1914), pp. 206–218.

Marty Markwort
Hance Yarah Markwort
Lenard Fox
Jacob Shevly
Polis Wingart
Johannas Shillman
Hance Marty Miller
Gasper Castler
Hance Felex Wigmore
Casper Miare
Felex Wigmore
Hance Conragh Browner
Jacob Finkey
Roday Kiser
Jacob Kiser
Johanes Youghley
Jacob Surter
Henrack Aldorphia
Hanas Miller
Earak Springer
Henrah Borgart
Corise Miller
Rodlafe Weaste
Conarah Browner
Hance Jacob Hafener
Henrah Miller
Hanas Browner
Marty Vearte
Hance Yarah Heswiler

Hance Melihar Fisher
Johanas Fisher
David Strily
Young Hance Fisher
Jacob Flougar
Jacob Cimbler
David Shats
Fredrick Stall
Hance Michel Droliner
Hanc Jacob Humble
Johanas Cadiman
Jacob Lighiner
Yarah Christaf Herald
Samuel Wolff
Philap Humble
Hance Yarah Cider
Yarah Emmanuel Martine
Lenard Strebel
Heronemos Hennawsh
Johan Earah Herald
Androw Strely
George Elswiler
Christian Hollard
Jacob Hollard
Hans Leonard Wyland
Michael Wyland
Casper Pinchadler
Johannes Roodsman

Captn James [Reason.]
List of foreigners imported from Wittenberg, Turloch [Durlach] & Switzerland. Septr 1743. In the Ship Rosanna.

[List 100 C] At the Court House Philadelphia, 26 Septr 1743.

Present: The Honourable George Thomas, Esqr, Governor,
Wm Till,
Septimus Robinson, } Esq^{rs}

The Foreigners whose names are underwritten, imported in the Ship Rosannah, Captn James Reason, Master, from Rotterdam, but last from Cowes, did this day take the foregoing Qualifications or Oaths to the Government.

Georg Christoph Heroldt
Hans Jerg Gretzinger
Johan Wilhelm Sigler
Jacob Hoffman
Hans Jorg Störner
Andereas (X) Spring
Georg Christophf Schoch
Hans Jeorg Fuchs
Mart. Mycart [?]
Hans George (X) Markwart
Leonhart (X) Fuchs
Jacob Schäuffele
Johannes (X) Shellman
Hans Marten Müller
Casper Kessler
Hans Felix Eckner [?]
  Bekän wie ob steht *
Casper Meier
Hans Conrad (O) Bruner
Jacob (O) Fincky
Rudy (X) Keyser
Jacob (X) Keyser
Johannes (X) Jooghly
Jacob (X) Shootler
Hennrich Bürckart
Hans (X) Miller
George (X) Springer
Gregorius (X) Miller
Hans Brunner

Hans Jacob Haffner
Henry (X) Miller
Hans Uhllerig (X) Huber
Martin (X) Wierd
Hans Melichor (X) Fisher
Johannes (X) Fisher
Jacob Strele
Jurg Johannis Fischer
Leonhardt Pflaugner
Hans Jacob Kemmler
David Schatz
Friederigh (X) Stall
Hannes Jacob Hummel
Johannes (+) Ketteman
Jacob Legler
Joorg Christoff Heroldt
Samuel Wolff
Gorg Philipp Hummel
Hans Jerg Karter
Leonhart Ströbel
Hieronimus Hening
Andreas Strele
Hs. Georg Etzweiller
Christien Haller
Jacob Haller
Hans Leonhart (X) Wyland
Michael (X) Wyland
Casper Bindschädler
Johannes (+) Roodsman

[List 101 C] At the Courthouse at Philadelphia, Septr 30th 1743.

Present: The Honoble George Thomas, Esqr, Lieutenant Govr,

| Samuel Hassel, | Abraham Taylor, | ⎫ Esq^rs |
| Joshua Maddox, | Benjamin Shoemaker, | ⎭ |

The Foreigners whose names are underwritten, imported

---

* I. e., "Confess as above," referring to the oath he signed.

in the Ship Phoenix, William Wilson, Commander, and in the Ship Robert & Alice, Hartley Cusack, Commander, from Rotterdam, but last from Cowes, did this day take the foregoing Oaths or Qualifications to the Government, viz.,

Dewald (H) Hochstäd
Johann Henrich Hans
Willem Adelhyt
Otto Ney
Leonhard Wintergress
Lorentz Protzmann
Johan Adam Wesner [?]
Matheus Truckel
Johannes (XX) Ungar
Christoff (HO) Holwer
Henry (O) Reydmeyer
Jacob (+) Rubly
Michael (+) Bauer
Michael (+) Leavy
Paulus Behringer
Philippus Bayer
Johannes (X) Shnee
Hs. Michael Stumpf
Philip (X) Roesher
Philip Spiegel
Johann Niclos Lohman
J. Ernst (+) Reiffschneider
Johannes Gännslen
Jacob Gänsle
Johan Fridrich Bekh
Joh. Georg Laudenberger
David Seüffert
Friedrich Köhler
Johann Jost Köhler
Jacob (X) Siewer
Jorg Philp Klingkann
Michael (+) Eller
Isaac Wille
Johann Gerg Steinbecker

Johann Valtin Reul
Henry (X) Meyer
Johann Georg Schäffer
Jacob Geiger
Jacob Geiger
Friederich (X) Miller
Matteas (X) Kent
Johann Henrich Wagner
Peter Handwercker
Bendickt (X) Nusbaum
H. Adam (X) Richman
Johannes (H) Baer
Johannes (O) Stam
Peter Göer
Jacob (IK) Keyser
Nicklas (X) Hoffman
Bernhart (X) Makter
H. Jerge (H) Nees
Johann Nickal Gauer
Jacob Böm
Melchior Bär *
Christophel Bär
Melcher Bär
Melchior (X) Seydler
Danel Schwartz
Henry (X) Dornig
Johan Jost Wetter
Michael (X) Steckbek
Anthon Bensinger
Hans Adam (X) Felbaum
Michael (M) Masserley
Conrad (X) Fellbaum
Daniel Maus
Caspar (O) Reithnauer

* The ancestor of the numerous Baer family in Lehigh county. See *Anniversary History of Lehigh County*, Allentown, 1914, vol. II, pp. 34–44.

Johannes Reudnauer
Johan Michael Füchthorn
Peter Bartolmes
Philipus Barthmes
Nicol Fey
Christian (O) Rorbagh
Lorentz (O) Cuntz
Johannes (O) Nusbaum

Jörg Huber
Conrad (O) Wird
Johan Adam Herber
Burckhart Müller
Hans Michael (X) Miller
Johannes Geschwindt
Carols August (X) Erlwein

[List 102 C] The names of those in the Robt & Allice, Martly Cussack, Command^r. [Qualified Septr 30, 1743.]

Johannes Zäner
Simmon Zonger
Nicklas (X) Baker
Jacob (X) Baker
Johannes (+) Good
Joseph (X) Ziebly
Deobald (X) Bauer
Jacob Schock
Johannes Martin
Jacob Marttin
Andreas Lies
Kasber Strom
Johann Philipp Emig
Johan Philip (X) Emig, Senior
Baltzer Schwerdt
Michael Darto
Phillippus Friederich May
Johann Ludwig Schailly
Hans Adam (X) Shally
Johannes (+) Shally
Christian (X) Shally
Johannes (X) Obenheyser
Nicklas (S) Shreiber
John Henry (X) Butz
Johan Kolman Grüner
Jacob Schmith
Hans Jerg Stucki
Matteas (X) Brunn
Johannes (HI) Sheets

Christoff (X) Sheaneman
Karl Schwartz
Samuel Landes
Hans Jacob Käller
Peter Guthman
Conrat Österlen
Johannes (X) Bender
Hans Jerg Österlen
Christoff (X) Oesterlin
Henry (X) Gilbert
Johann Ludwig Truckenmüller
Johann Gorg Frey
Andreas Heuberger
Hans Geörg Endes
Hans Michael Ott
Samuel Bechtel
Hans Hart
Davit Sarbach
Jacob Bucki
Abraham Derst
Christian Müller
Hans Görg Müller
Mattheis Meier
Oswalt Neff
Henrich Stürtzenacker
Philip Heinisch
Hans Jerg (X) Begtel
Johannis (X) Young
Johann Georg Schwartz

Bardel Miller

Felix Zollinger

Henry (X) Fanner

Heinrich Zwick

Felix (X) Fanner

Willhelm (X) Spats

Jacob Gillinger

Baltzer (X) Gilbert

Bernhart Gilbert

Conrad (+) Toll

Ulrich Tresz

Joseph (X) Sheffer

[List 103 A] List of Mens Names p^r the St Andrew, Capt Robt Brown. [Qualified October 7, 1743.]

NAMES	AGES	NAMES	AGES
John Nicholas Reytringer	17	Hans Adam Sommer	27
John Adam Garber	20	John Merkell	25
Hans Jacob Walter	20	Godliph Leweys	26
Geo. Mich^l Weysmiller	19	Jacob Clowser	25
Geo. Andreas Miller	27	Jacob Pringer	25
Fred^k Stall	20	Daniel Mytinger	24
Hans Geo. Mower	23	Jacob Eykhorn	19
Johannes Maak	40	Peter Clowser	18
John Simon Karn	25	John Everhart	24
Hans Peter Kranback	22	Leonard Fooks	22
Andreas Wolinger	19	Heronimus Troutman	34
Ulrich Creble	20	Bernard Veenenger	29
Adam Kaller	20	Andreas Keelham	23
Jacob Strevey	44	Ulrich Bower	21
Mich^l Strevey	17	John Lodwick Krat	18
Joseph Hartman	29	Martian Rood	26
Fredrick Yeiser	20	Jacob Hiss	25
Lorentz Tibber	50	Hans Ulrich Jackelie	20
Philip Korr	33	Hans Ulrich Bakersool	16
Johannes Hauser	22	Hend^k Browner	25
Hans Georg Eter	43	Hans Ulrich Jackle	33
Hans Martin Fisher	25	Jacob Schnyder	32
Georg Gross	30	Hans Weighler	21
Philip Jacob Lodman	23	Hans Ulrich Oatt	18
Mich^l Waganer	25	Hans Hend^k Boshart	21
Sebastian Bych	26	Hans Hend^k Oatt	25
Georg Gardner	24	Fred^k Doughterman	22
Leonard Stain	28	Andreas Doughterman	18
Leonard Dewaldt	28	Ernest Ament	35
Jacob Wayst	28	Fred^k Ziegell	26

NAMES	AGES	NAMES	AGES
Hans Jacob Goldner	33	John Hend^k Knoif	30
Hans Geo. Ament	38	Antony Knoif	20
Melchior Beerlie	30	Daniel Debus	28
Ezekiel Ocher	39	Jacob Debus	26
Johannes Ulrich	38	Lodwick Debus	36
John Fred^k Houbley	25	Johan Hend^k Catenback	17
Hans Geo. Witman	25	Hans Adam Zimmerman	20
Johannes Mayer	30	Nich^l Coblentz	45
Geo. Eler	20	Abram Hobler	27
Peter Warner	35	Phillip Brafshnyder	25
Johannes Wydman	25	Valantine Shutter	45
Mich^l Wolfanger	23	Hend^k Shutter	22
Leonard Kern	24	Godliph Zeigell	22
Hend^k Waganer	28	Phyt Reysner	..
Christ^o Shipert	20	Johan Mar. Say	..
Fred^k Siglar	21		—
Peter Franker	28	Men in all	93
Johannes Righer	33		

[Endorsed:]
List of Palatines imported in the St Andrew, Captn Brown, qualified 7, Octr 1743.

[List 103 B] [Foreigners imported in the Ship St Andrew, Robert Brown, Master, from Rotterdam. Qualified October 7, 1743.]

Han: Nicholas (Z) Zeisinger	Hans Michel Stribey
Johann Adam [Gerber]	Joseph Hartman
Jacob (+) Walter	Friederich Jayser
Gorg Michel Weissmüller	Georg Phillipp Kurr
Friederich Stoll	Johannes Hauser
Hans Jerg Maurer	Hans George (X) Eatter
Johannes (X) Moak	Hans Mardi Fischer
Johan Simon Kern	Philip Jacob Luttman
Hans Peter (C) Grumbach	Johan Michäl Wagner
Andreas (X) Wollinger	Sebastian Busch
Ulrich Krehbühl	Jerg Gärtner
Adam Heyler	Lenhart Stein
Jacob Strieby	Leonard (X) Dewalt

Hans Adam (X) Summer
Jerg Friedrich Zügel
Godlieb (X) Seigel
Johan (+) Merckle
Gottlib Schleeweiss
Jacob (X) Clauser
Johan Jacob (X) Ringer
Daniel Maidinger
Jacob Eichhor[n]
Johannes Eberhardt
Leonard (O) Fuchs
Hyronimus Trauttmann
Bernard (+) Dubinger
Andreas Güllam
Joh. Ludwig Krafft
Marti Roht
Jacob (+) Hesse
Hans Ulrich Jegly
Hans Jerick (H) Backastos
Heinnrich Brunner
Hans Ulrick (X) Yakley
Hans (+) Burgeer
Hans Ullrich Ort
Hans Henry (B) Bossert
Jacob Friederich Dochterman
Andreas Dochterman
Ernest (EA) Amon
Hans Jacob (O) Gouldner

Hans Gerg (X) Amon
Melchior Bührle
Etielle Acker
Johannes (HU) Ulrich
Frederick (X) Hubely
Johann Georg Wittman
Johannes Meyer
Hans Jerg Öhler
Peter Werner
Johanes Widman
Michael (W) Wolfgong
Leonhardt Kern
Heinrich Wagner
Friedrich Ziegler
Hans Peter (X) Frankhousen
Johannes Rieger
Johan Hennrich Knauff
Anthon Knauff
Danniel Debus
Lodowick (+) Dawis
Johann Henrich Gackenbach
Hans Adam Zimmerman
Niclaus Kobelentz
Abraham Hübler
Valentine (H) Shutter
Henry (H) Shutter
Johann Phillipus Raffschneider
Jacob (H) Wist

[Endorsed:]
List of Palatines imported in the St Andrew, Capt Brown. Qual. 7th October, 1743.

[List 103 C] At the Court House at Philadelphia 7th Octr 1743.

Present: The Honourable George Thomas, Esqr, Lieutenant Governor.

James Hamilton,   Septimus Robinson, } Esq^{rs}.
Joshua Maddox,

The Foreigners whose Names are underwritten, imported in Ship St Andrew, Captn Robert Brown, from Rotterdam, but last from Cowes, did this day take the foregoing Oaths or Qualifications, viz.,

Johnn Nicklas (Z) Zeisinger
Joh. Adam Gerber
Jacob (+) Walter
Jorg Michel Weissmüller
Friederich Stoll
Hans Jerg Maurer
Johannes (X) Moak
Johan Simon Kern
Hans Peter (B) Grumbach
Andereas (V) Wollinger
Ulrich Krehbiehl
Adam Heyler
Jacob Striby
Hans Michel Striby
Joseph Hartmann
Friederich Jayser
Georg Phillipp Kurr
Johannes Hauser
Hans George (X) Eatter
Hans Mardi Fischer
Philip Jacob Luttmann
Johan Michael Wagner
Sebastyan Busch
Jerg Gärtner
Lenhart Stein
Leonhart (X) Dewalt
Hans Adam (X) Sommer
Gorg Fridrich Zügel
Gottlieb (X) Zigel
Johan (X) Mergel
Gottlieb Schleew[eis]
Jacob (X) Clausser
Johan Jacob (X) Ringer
Daniel Meidinger
Jacob Eichhorn
Johannes Eberhart
Lenard (O) Fuchs
Hyronimus Trauttmann

Bernhart (X) Dübinger
Andres Güllam
Joh. Ludwig Krafft
Marti Roth
Jacob (X) Hesse
Hans Ulrich Jegly
Hans Jorg (H) Backastos
Heinrich Brunner
Hans Uhllerich (X) Jakly
Hans (++) Burger
Hans Ulerich Ort
Hans Henry (B) Bossart
Jacob Friderich Dochterman
Andreas Dochterman
Ernest (EA) Amon
Hans Jacob (O) Goldner
Hans Jerg (X) Amon
Melchior Bührli
Etzielle Acker
Johannes (HU) Uhllerich
Friderich (X) Hubely
Johann Georg Wittmann
Johannes Meyer
Hanes Jerg Öhler
Peter Werner
Johannes Widmann
Michael (W) Wolfgang
Leonhardt Kern
Heinrich Wagner
Friedrich Ziegler
H. Peter (X) Fronkhousen
Johannes Rieger
Johan Heinrich Knauff
Anthon Knauff
Daniel Debus
Ludewigh (X) Dewys
Johann Henrich Gackenbach
Hanns Adam Zimmerman

Niclaus Kobelentz

Abraham Hübler

Vallentin (H) Shutter

Henry (H) Shutter

Johan Philipp Raffschneider

Jacob (H) Wist

[List 104 C] At the Courthouse at Philadelphia, 10ᵗʰ Novʳ 1743.

Present: Clement Plumsted, Esqʳ, Abraham Taylor, Esqʳ. The Foreigners whose names are underwritten, imported in the Snow Endeavor, Captⁿ Thomas Anderson, from London, did this day take the foregoing Oaths or Qualifications to the Government, viz.,

Matdeis Brauenfelder

Matdeis Brauenfelder

Hans Ulrich Schaub

Adam (X) Shoub

Jacob (+) Frauwalder

[List 105 B] [Foreigners imported in the ship Aurora, Captⁿ Robert Pickeman, from Rotterdam. Qualified October 8, 1744.]

Johan Christ Kell

Johan Adam Hirter

Johan Adam (X) Hirt

Johan Henrich Bock

Johan Adam (X) Shnook

Joh. Christ (W) Wirt

Johann Adam Wagner

Hans Wellem Streder

Johan Görg Müller

Joh. Adam (+) Meyer

Joost (X) Frevel

Johann Hermanus Frevel

Johanes (X) Dornbach

Johannes Peter (X) Sheaf

Johann Wilhelm Gonderman

Johan Henrich Rörich

Conrad (X) Rörich

Joerg Wilhelm Berger

Johan Christian Berger

Johann Thiel Selbach

Joh. Wᵐ (X) Troller

Joh. Philip (X) Fost

Daniel (X) Fost

Johann Wilhelm Sayn

Frantz Willhelm Kulbach

Johann Pauls Krebs

Johan Jacob Henn

Johann Peder Henn

Johan Kunrad Weyer

Joh. Wilhelm (H) Lentz

Joh. Christ (O) Kohl

Joh. Wilh (H) Haugh

Pitter Schäeffer

Johan Peder Weingardt

Joh. Henrich (X) Dornbach

Johann Deis Dornbach

Johan Pether Neytzert

Pierre Aeries

Joh. Peter (F) Feyser

Johannes (X) Becker

Johann Peder Weyer

Joh. Christoph (X) Steegler

Johannes Görg Stiegler
Joh. Bastian (✕) Muller
Johan Besiger Geyer
Johannes Höchstenbach
John Henrich Höffer
Johann Adam Geyer
Johan Henrich Flemer
Joh. George (H) Shooster
Joh. Jorg Heyster
Johannes Vester Cramer
Johan Villm Kall
Joh. Gorg Kall
Matthias (✕) Meyer
Matth. (✕) Meyer, Junr
Nich. (✕) Meyer
Jean Baron
Joh. Jac. (✕) Reyman
Johannes Ludwig Reiman
Johan (✕) Michel
Philibus Fackert

Paulus Winer
Matheis Henn
Gorg Weber
Johan Theis Roler
Johann Marthin Köhler
Godhard (L) Leer
Joh. Wilh^m (M) Meys
Andreas Schuöster
Johann Peter Strunck
Johan Beter Jung
Jacob Scheyer
Anton Noll
Mattias Noll
Johan Atam Schumacher
Bernhart (✕) Neitzer
Joh. Dennis (S) Shmit
Johann Wylhelm Weyer
Marcus (O) Anders
Joh. Matth. (O) Dexter

[Endorsed:]
List of Palatines. 8th Octr 1744. Ship Aurora, Pickeman, Master.

[List 105 C] At the Court House at Philadelphia, 8th Octr 1744.
Present: The Honoble the Governor.
The Foreigners whose Names are underwritten, imported in the Ship Aurora, Captn Robert Pickeman, from Rotterdam, but last from Cowes, did this day take the foregoing Oaths to the Government.

Johann Christ. Kell
Johan Adam Hirter
Johan Adam (✕) Hierte
Johan Henrich Bock
Johan Adam (✕) Shnog
Johan Christ (✕) Wirt
Johann Adam Wagner
Hans Wellem Streder

Johan Jörg Müller
Johan Adam (✕) Meyer
Jost (+) Vrevel
Johannes Hermanus Frevel
Johanes (+) Dornbach
Johan Peter (✕) Sheeff
Johan Wilhelm Gonderman
Johan Henrich Rörich

Conrad (X) Rörig
Jöerg Wilhelm Berger
Johan Christian Berger
Johann Thiel Selbach
Johan Wilhelm (X) Tröller
Johan Philip (X) Fost
Daniel (X) Foost
Johan Wilhelm Sayn
Frantz Wilhelm Kaulbach
Johann Paulls Krebs
Johan Jacob Henn
Johann Peder Henn
Johann Kunrad Weyer
Johan Willhelm (H) Lands
Johan Christ (O) Kohl
Johan Willhelm (H) Hogh
Pitter Schäeffer
Johan Peder Weingart
Johan Henry (X) Dornbach
Johan Deis Dornbach
Johan Peter Neytzert
Pierre Aries
Johan Peter (F) Feyser
Johanes (X) Baker
Johann Peter Weyer
Johan Christoff (X) Stigeler
Johannes Görg Stiegler
Johan Bastian (X) Miller
Johan Besieger [Geyer]
Johannes Höchstenbach
Johan Henrich Häffer
Johann Adam Geyer
Johan Henrich Flemer

Johan George (H) Schuster
Joh. Jorg Heyster
Johannes Peter Cramer
Johan Willm Kall
Joh Gorg Kall
Matteas (+) Meyer
Matteas (+) Meyer, Junior
Nicklas (X) Meyer
Jean Baron
John Jacob (X) Reyman
Johannes Ludwig Reiman
Johanes (X) Michael
Philibus Fackert
Paulus Winer
Matheis Henn
Gorg Weber
Johan Theis Roler
Johann Marthin Köhler
Godhart (L) Löre
Johan Wilhelm (M) Meys
Anderas Schuoster
Johann Peter Strunk
Johan Peder Jung
Jacob Scheyer
Anton Noll
Matthis Noll
Johan Adam Schumacher
Bernhart (X) Neyzart
Johan Dönis (O) Shmit
Johann Wylhelm Weyer
Marcus (O) Anders
Johan Matteus (X.) Dexter
80.

[List 106 C] At the Courthouse at Philadelphia, 20th 8ber 1744.

Present: Edward Shippen, Mayor,
Wm Allen, Recorder,

Ben. Shoemaker.
Septimus Robinson,
Robert Strethill,
} Esqrs.

The Foreigners whose names are underwritten, imported in the Phoenix, William Wilson, Captn, from Rotterdam, & last from Cowes, did this day take the foregoing Oaths to the Government.

Henrich Hartman
Johannes Herberth
George (X) Shön
Johann Wendel Metzler
Johann Adam Megel
Johan Adam Morgen
Lorentz Erbach
Adam Fischborn
Andonius Fischborn
Nicklas Peter
Thiebalt Klein
Casper Schneider
Cunradt Fuchs
Johann Philippes Mauck
Andonius Weyrich
Johan Petter Götz
Christoffel Westerberger
Mattheis Kolb
Johan Jerg Wohnsitler
Friederich Partemer
Philipp Bretz
Mardi Kolb
Johannes Schneider
Dewalt (A) Laub
Jacob Rau
Philips Wendel Klein
Johan Jost (O) Tizler
Johan Henry (X) Mattinger
Jacob Buchman
Johann Hermann Mohr
Gorg Rack
Johannes Klein
Johann Nicolaus Wagner
Johannes Kuhn

Vallentin (X) Winesheim
Fillibs Krebs
Johannes Fluck
Paulus Eberhart
Jorg Wilhem Staudt
Johan Nicolaus Messersschmid
Conrad Elling
Johann Balthasar Fischborn
Paul Schneider
Mardin Clewer
Gerhardt Scheffer
Ip. Fiehl
Peter Tauphäus
Friederich Michael
Conradt Höflich
Henrich Platt
Johann Philipp Andres
Friederich Gresser
Christian Eberhart
Wendel Bröder
Marx Kieffer
Johan George (X) Westberger
Johan Nickel Hun
Andereas (A) Eshbacher
J. Philip (A) Santon
Johan Bach
Friedrich Huber
Joha Pilib Magmer
Johannes (II) Magemer
Johan Reinhart Waltz
Christoffel Dieckenschiet
Johannes Dickert
Johann Jörg Schäffer
Friederich Casimir Müller *

* This name has not been recognized before. It ends the uncertainty as to the arrival of this Reformed preacher. *See History of Goshenhoppen Charge*, p. 151.

Friedrich Stelwag
Johann Valendin Hun
Peter Faust
Gerhardt Fiscus
Jacob (OO) Stephen
Joh. Peter Breyvogel
Jacob ( ) Wagner
Andreas Sörger
Joh. George (X) Meisenheim
John Adam (H) Klein
Conrath Jung
Johan Pfillib Höflich
Friederich (+) Huby
Johan Phillib Kercher
Hans Hennerich Kuntz
Johan Adam Baum
Anthonius Höblich
Andres Grübel
Peter Philipp Hahn
Johann Friederich Sauer
Henry (X) Plad
Johann Dierk Heffner

Phillip Peter Graffert
Bastian Morian
Johan Peter Fuchs
Johan Peter Kolb
Hennrich Lies
Herman (X) Decreiff
Philip (X) Flugh
Christoffel Fiehl
Rudolff Fiehl
Vallentin Huf
Diellman Dieckenschiedt
Johannes (J) Kuntz
Weymar Strunck
Anndon Schneider
Phillip Jacob Bäder
Johan Philip (X) Roth
Hans Dewalt (X) Seltenreich
107 *

110 [men]
55 [women]
———
165 [Total]

[List 107 C] At the Court House at Philadelphia, 2ᵈ Novʳ 1744.
Present: Edward Shippen, Esqʳ, Mayor,
    Wᵐ Allen, Esqʳ, Recorder, Robert Strethill, Esqʳ.
The Foreigners whose names are underwritten, imported in the Friendship, Captⁿ John Mason, from Rotterdam, but last from Cowes, did this day take the foregoing Oaths to the Government.

Herman (H) Weber
Wilhelm Weber
Caspar (H) Weber
Johan Adam (H) Radebush
Gerhart (W) Will
Johann Jacob Ferber
Jacob (H) Fughs
Jacob (E) Engel

Peter Bogert
Valtin Vogt
Anthonius Willar
Johannes Ehrenhardt
Joh. Philip Ehrenhardt
Jürg Bernhart
Johann Heinrich Rädter
Conrath (C) Förster

* The discrepancy in the figures may be due to the death of several passengers.

Niclaus Nich. Kusig
Johan Peter (P) Cusik
John Jacob (S) Summer
John Wilhelm (X) More
Joachim (X) Joan
Theodorus (X) Krahl
Christoph (X) Kolbe
Peter (X) Arensberger
Albrecht Müller
Johannes (O) Gräber
Johannes Moll
Peter Williar
Abraham Mischot
Petter Hann
Adam Schölkopf
Johann (X) Wohlleben
Dewald (A) Speck
Jerg Biewer
Johann Bieber
Dewald (X) Beaber
Casber Zinn
Michel Baumann
Johannes Schmitt
Johann Wilhelm Reuel
Wolfgang Sies
Jeog Emig (+) Haartz
John Adam (+) Haartz
Johannes Weber
Johann Georg Weber
Johann Adam Weber

Andereas Reiffschneyder
Johann (+) Shlögel
Johan Georg Schmidt
Bernhart (X) Roobe
Isack Lobach
Johannes (X) Tieze
Philip (X) Smith
John Peter (X) Noss
John Jacob (X) Bildhous
Johann Jacob Stoltz
Philip (O) Waghmer
Diterigh (+) Shattler
Johan Georg Schädel
Johannis Grob
Johan Adam Grob
Jorg Conrad Krob
Henrich Jacob Krebs
Debalt Werner
Philip (X) Shaffer
Johann Baltzer Köhller
Johann Michael Klein
Johann Ernst Salomon
Peter Gesell
Johannes Wildt
Henrich Schefferr
Henry (X) Feyerbagh
Henrich Koppelberger
Henrich Scheffer

74 [men]

[List 108 C] At the Court House at Philadelphia, 11th Decr 1744.

Present: Edward Shippen, Esqr, Mayor,
Benjm Shoemacker,
Robert Strethill,
Septimus Robinson, } Esqrs

The Foreigners whose Names are underwritten, imported in the Carterel, Captn Stevenson, Commander, from Rotterdam, but last from Cowes, did this day take the foregoing Oaths to the Government.

Philip Stein
Lampertus Schühling
Hans Gerg Doblen
Hans George (X) Klein
Joh. Georg Schaaff
Jacob Krafft
Albrecht Fridrich Binder
Henrik (H) Bullinger
Johann Philipp Binder
Johannes Zörlen
Balsazhar (X) Stamgast
Michäl Hut
Christoffel Weber
Johannes Dewalt
Jacob Lambrecht
Rudolph (X) Meeke
Hans (X) Forster

Christoffel Bittenbender
Fillib Bichler
Jacob Bichler
Waltter (X) Miller
Vallentin (X) Young
Joseph Mayer
Johannes Mayer
Michael (X) Anthon
L. Henry (X) Shwenk
J. Nicolas (X) Herman
Niclas Steinmetz
Johan Christian Rehkopf
Friederic Kop
Fridrich Döbele
Friedrich Döbele
Johannes Clauss
Wilhelm Jungck

This is an imperfect list, sundries being sick. A true list to be made out by —— for Benj. Shoemaker.

[List 109 C] At the Courthouse at Philadelphia, 22^d Decr 1744.

Present: Edward Shippen, Esqr, Mayor, Wm Allen, Esqr, Recorder. Septimus Robinson, Esqr.

The Foreigners whose names are underwritten, imported in the Ship Muscliffe Galley, George Durell, Commander, from Rotterdam & last from Poole in Dorsetshire, did this day take the foregoing Oaths & Qualifications to the Government.

Christian Stauffer
Johannes (X) Staube
Christian Herford
Jacob König
Henry (H) Dochman
Lenhart (K) Klopert
Christian (X) Coats
Hans (X) Lynter
Hans (+) Kurtz
Stephan (++) Kurtz
Hans (X) Eyer

Jacob (X) Engel
Jacob (X) Sharff
Christian (X) König
Samuel (X) König
Daniel German
Christian Krebil
Christian Lang
Abraham Steiner
Hans Liddi
Frantz German
Vallentin (X) Tallebach

John Jacob (X) Meyer
Adam Jacob Maurer
Johann Matthess Gess
Vallentin (O) Heger
Elias Dietrich
Christian (H) Florig
Jacob (H) Höfflig
Leonhard Müller
Conradt Notz
Andreas Heppenheimer
Michael (F) Frohman
Conrat Meckes
Phillib Seible
Johann (V) Meister
Johan Mölcher Bender
Johans Adam Werntz
Philipp Bendt Werntz
Johan Jacob Mertz
Hans Jerg Graff
Hans Georg Schneider
Uhllerich (X) Gotter
Hans Adam (X) Young
Hans Peter Burge[r]
Hans Jerg Dewalt
Henry (X) Thomas
Bernhart (+) Bear
Philip (X) Vetter
Jacob Ebi
Jost (+) Yotter

Johannes (X) Souder
Peter (X) Jutzy
Caspar Schertzer
John (H) Shawalter
Christian (X) Mosser
Reinhard Jung
Jacob Müller
Christian (+) Frätz
Rudolf Hauck
Petter Wittmer
Peter Weiss
Daniel Seiler
Johann Mosiman
Andereas (X) Mosselman
Michael Meyer
Peter (X) Looh
Peter (X) Meyer
Hans David Grün
Jacob Daurschauer
Jacob (+) Jüncker
Johannes (X) Albrecht
Elias (X) Read
Jacob (X) Preegly
Rudolph Herdte
Josua Caspar Herdte
Rudolph Herdte
Jerg Wilhelm Heydelbach
Henrich Schlichter

[List 110 B] [Foreigners imported in the ship Ann Galley, William Wilson, Captain, from Rotterdam. Qualified September 27, 1746.]

Johann Peter German
Wilhelm Schmidt
Johann Henrich Kalbfleisch
John George (XXX) Godshalk
Philip Bohn
Johannes Bohn
Johann Baltzar Bohn

Johannes Dammer
Christopher Tamar
Johann Balthaser Damer
Domas Hahn
Johannes Hahn
Christoph (X) Hoffman
Conrad Räber

Carol (O) Heydrigh
Caspar (X) Heydrigh
George ( ) Heydrigh *
Daniel Zwier
Johann Ludwig Lauman
Michael ( ) Egolff
Johannes ( ) Egolff
Michael ( ) Egolff, Junr
Johannes George (O) Knowdel
Robert ( ) Hartaffel
Simon Wolffer
Martin (X) Lauman
Heinrich Müller
Josef Egenber[ger]
Johannes Kauffman
Hans Jerg Dannenhauer
Martin (X) Blikly
Johanes Ott
Johannes (+) Sheek
Johannes ( ) Sheek, Junr
Johann Gottlieb Wehner
Michael Batz
Jacob Wetzel
Jacob Ziegler
Burckhart Böhner
Andreas Beck
Johannes (X) Krautz
Balthas Nais
Johannes Hummel
Johan Adam Heindel
Matthias Hohl
Hans Jerg Brechle
Johann David Scheyhing
Christian Lentz
John Jacob Lentz
Philip Ziegler
Christoph Lentz
Matheas (X) Bleakly

Conrad Dress
Michael (X) Dieter
Lodowyck (F) Falkenstein
Johannes Sigle
Jacob ( ) Ziegly
George (+) Schneering
Johann Andreas Jetter
Hans George ( ) Trasher
Hans Michael ( ) Newhauser
Johan Baltes Bücher
Christian Strom
Christian Kauffman
Jerg Strom
Abraham Rösch
Friderich Eichholtz
Christian ( ) Wagner
Melger Moll
Johann Wilhelm Horst
Johannes ( ) Shroder
Jacob Freymann
Geörg Ruth
Michael ( ) Sekel
Caspar Schneider
Michael (M) Klawer
Valentine (X) Safftel
Johannes Söfftel
David Küntzel
Georg Bratz
Georg Albrecht Hillegas
George ( ) Hetrigh
Matteis Streichle
Hans Grünenwald
Michel Zimmerman
Abraham ( ) Timmerman
Joseph Alber
Jacob Dauttel
Johannes Michael ( ) Seckel

* This name, as well as several others that follow, was written by the Clerk. But the absence of a mark indicates that the man was absent.

[Endorsed:]
List of Palatines imported in the Ann Gally.

[List 110 C] At the Courthouse at Philadeiphia, 27th 7^{ber} 1746.

Present: The Honourable George Thomas, Esqr, Lieutenant Governor,

James Hamilton   Joseph Turner ⎫ Esq^{rs}.
Abraham Taylor   Septimus Robinson ⎭

The Foreigners whose Names are underwritten, imported in the Ship Ann Galley, William Wilson, Captain, from Rotterdam & last from the Orkneys, did this day take the foregoing Oaths to the Government.

Johann Peter German
Wilhelm Schmidt
Johann Henrich Kalbfleisch
Johan George (×) Godshalk
Philips Bohn
Johannes Bohn
Johann Baltzar Bohn
Johannes Dammer
Johan Balthasar Damer
Christopher (×) Tamer
Domas Hahn
Johannes Hahn
Christoph (×) Hoffman
Conrad Räber
Carol (O) Heyderigh
Caspar (×) Heydrigh
Georg ( ) Heydrigh
Daniel Zwier
Johann Ludwig Lauman
Michael ( ) Egolff
Johanes ( ) Egolffe
Michael ( ) Egolff, Junior
Johan Georg (O) Knatel
Robert Harttaffel
Simon Wolffer
Martin (×) Lauman

Heinrich Müller
Josef Egenberger
Johannes Kauffman
Hans Jerg Danenhauer
Martin (×) Blikly
Johannes Ott
Johannes (×) Sheek
Johannes ( ) Sheek, Junior
Johann Gottlieb Wehner
Michael ( ) Batz
Jacob Wetzel
Jacob Ziegler
Burckhart Böhner
Andereas Beck
Johannes (×) Krauss
Balthas Naus
Johannes Hummel
Johan Adam Heindel
Matthaus Hohl
Hans Jerg Brechle
Johann David Scheyhing
Christian Lentz
John Jacob Lentz
Phillip Ziegler
Christoph Lentz
Matheus (×) Bleakly

Conrad Dress	Johan ( ) Schröter
Michael (×) Dieter	Jacob Freymann
Ludwig (F) Falkenstein	Georg Ruth
Johannes Sigle	Michael Sekel
Jacob ( ) Ziegly	Caspar Schneider
George (×) Shneering	Michael (H) Klawer
Johan Andreas Jetter	Vallentin (×) Safftel
Hans George (×) Trasher	Johannes Söfftel
Hans Michael (×) Newhauser	David Küntzel
Johan Baltes Bücher	Georg Bratz
Christian Strom	Georg Albrecht Hillegas
Peter (I) Reshe	George (×) Hatrich
Christian Kauffman	Mattheis Streichle
Jerg Strom	Hans Grünewald
Abraham Rösch	Michel Zimmerman
Friderich Eichholtz	Abraham ( ) Zimmerman
Christian ( ) Wagner	Joseph Alber
Melger Moll	Jacob Dauttel
Johann Wilhelm Horst	John Michael ( ) Sekel

[List 111 C] At the Court House at Philadelphia, 25: of October 1746.

Present: William Attwood   Thomas Lawrence ⎱
                William Allen   Robert Strettell ⎰ Esquires

The Foreigners whose names are underwritten, imported in the Neptune, Thos Wilkinson, Master, from Rotterdam, but last from England, did this day take the foregoing Oaths to the Government.

Johannes (+) Cawfeld	Peter (×) Sutter
Johannes Heintz	Philip (×) Furet
Johann Frich Winoht	Caspar (×) Sutter
Johann Frich Winoht	Jacob Rauch
Johann Peter Funck	Jacob Bauman
Johan Jacob (+) Pfister	Jacob Bauman, Jr
Etienne Consul	Nicklas (N) Kawffeld
Vallandin Leonhardt	George (H) Kawffeld
Henry (H) Eller	Adam (×) Kewgh
Henry (H) Miller	Johann Christoffel Hausmann
Jacob (H) Shnyder	Daniel (×) Jacob

Franz (X) Reynhart

Andreas Reinhart

Isac Steiner

Nicklas (X) Felle

Jacob Baab

Johann Petter Langenberger

Peter Willem

Willhelm Bausman

Johannes (X) Gabel

Filleb Ginder

Johannes (J) Wald

Johannes Steiner

Johann Philippus Reinhardt

Lorentz Bausman

Henrich Steiner

Jacob Steiner

Christophel Pausch

Georg Weber

Nchl. Lorentz

Conrad (X) Conrath

Jacob Hönntz

Dewalt (X) Angny

Philip Weissner

Caspar (++) Dewalt

Henry (X) Shneyder

Conrad (X) Yotter

Johann Bernhar Fether

Johann Peter Feter

Christian Steiner

Jacob Beiser

Petter Grosnickel

Carl Risch

Michel Fischer

Johannes Breitenbach

Gorge (X) Zimmerman

Jerg Ernst

Johann Christian Leibrock

Friederich (FR) Reinhart

Piero (X) Gerro

Jean (+) Duesto

Paule Huibes [?]

Francoi Convire [?]

Joseph (X) Gerra

Alexander (X) Gibbs

Pärre Raintras [?]

[List 112 C] At the Courthouse at Philadelphia, Augᵗ 1747.
Present: The Honourable Anthony Palmer, Esqʳ, President,
    Thomas Hopkinson, Esquire.

The Foreigners whose names are underwritten, imported in
the Bilander Vernon, from Rotterdam & last from Leith in
Scotland, Thomas Ricks, Master, did this day take the foregoing Oaths to the Government.

Andereas (AB) Bürger

Christofell Bär

Jacob Steinkönig [?]

Henrich Starzman

Christoff (X) Cressel

Dewald (+) Sheyder

Jacob (+) Leesher

Joseph Grünwalt

Hans Michael (K) Kuntz

Hennrich Büttner

Hans Michel Büttner

Samuel (X) Witmer

Marx Egli

Tobias (X) Wagheman

Henry (X) Grub

Abraham (X) Funk

Johannes Meingässner

Hans Caspar (H) Feerer

Johannes (I) Rooghel
Jacob (X) Shappy
Hans Jacob (X) Shappy
Hans Nickell Schmitt
Hans Willhellm Weidner
Felix Weiss
Hans Rudi Wis
Hans Bickell
Hans Bleigestaufer
Jacob Schnebeli
Rudolph (H) Hornecker
Rudolph (H) Hornecker, Junr
Uhllerik (H) Hornecker
Henry (E) Hecker
Peter (X) Bawman
Hans Jacob Wallder
Johannes Walder
Hans Henrich Walder
Hans Casper Wallder

Hans Michel Eysenman
Lutwig Weiter
Rudolf Huber
Jacob Huber
Johann Christian Wampfler
Jörg Wampffler
Christian Wampfler
Johann Lutwich Wampffler
Henrich Huber
Heinrych Huber
Hans Rudolff Bär
Jacob Steinbrüchel
Hans Frick
Hans Gorg Schorr
Killian (O) Indorff
Heinrich Fink
Friederich Wirtz
Willhelm Otz

[List 113 C] At the Courthouse at Philadelphia, 24th 7^ber 1747.

Present: The Honble Anthony Palmer, Esqr, President, Joseph Turner, Esqr.

The Foreigners whose Names are underwritten, imported in the Ship Lydia, Wm Tiffin, Capt, from London, Inhabitants of Switzerland, did this day take the foregoing Oaths to the Government.

Johannes (X) Vogel
John Jacob (XX) Meishter
Hans Martin Wehrner
Michael Vogelfanger Tölly
Jacob (O) Verner
Hans Peiffer
Hans Jacob Grullman

Hans German
Peter (P) Verner
Michael (M) Meyer
Henrick (X) Danner
Daniel Hinrichs
George Jacob Nudell
Thomas Henry Braymoyer

[List 114 C] At the State House at Philadelphia, the 9th 8^ber 1747.

Present: Abraham Taylor   Robert Strittell ⎫
         Thos Hopkinson   Joseph Turner   ⎭ Esq^rs.

The Foreigners whose names are underwritten, imported in

the Ship Restauration, Captn James Hall, from Rotterdam, and last from Leith, Inhabitants of the Palatinate & Places adjacent, did this day take the foregoing Oaths to the Government.

Hieronimus (×) Greber
Dafid Scherkh
Martin Lesch
Johannes Löffler
Johannes Schauch
H. Jerg Stürmer
Nicolaus Miller
Tobias Pflueger
Joh. Georg Kühner
Leonhart (L) Horein
Martin Pfingstag
Johannes Knecht
Johan Peter Beyl
Johan Adam (A) Kauffman
Hans Jerg Jung
Andreas Seitle
Jacob Muller
Jacob Röder
Philip Hinsch
David Ditterich
Johannes Flaum
Mardin Strecker
Johann Lorentz Sträcker
Andreas Riess
Thomas (×) Zigler
Jacob (×) Housht
Joerg Lertschtle
Lucas (LF) Flak
Caspar (×) Ber
Jacob Endi
Geörg Weiss
Ulrich Rohr
Christoph Wagner
Jerg Friderich Klingel
Hans Jerg Klingel
Henrich Rösch

Johan Philip Busch
Johann Daniel Busch
Johann Paulus Misser
Johannes Yetter
Hans Jerg Mebaldt
Baltas (×) Mauerer
Hans George (×) Törr
Joseph Bentzinger
Jacob Hackehr
Joseph (O) Lobwasser
Michael (×) Wagner
Johann Georg Wendel
Petter Moser
Jacob (×) Mosser
Peter Moser
Hans Gutt
Hans George (×) Hoffman
Johann Peter Lutz
Andereas (×) Beyer
Jacob (×) Wetzler
Simon (×) Esbod
Christian (×) Eller
Johannes (×) Fuschs
Jost Kobell
Johannes Schwemmlin
David Kobel
Peter Wittmer
Fridrich (FR) Rohrer
Samuel Rohrer
Jacob (H) Beysely
Michael Funck
Jacob Graff
Adam Tomas
Conrad (ICB) Bisecker
George (WM) Wollmiller
Heinrich Hauptmann

Michael (×) Hoffman
Johann Fräns Lemmlein
Johann Philipp Stock
Hans Michael Weckesser
Philip Hebeisen
Christian Rupp
Johann Jacob Ebener
Johan Konrat Klem
Henry (×) Righer
Christof (×) Thoman
Johann Davidt Klemm
Johann Gottfriedt Bohner
Hans (×) Lay
Michael Keinodt
Hans Jerg Eberhartt
Hans Georg (×) Shnitzer
Michel Föss
Burckhart Beck
George (×) Beyer
Johann Philliph Hopff
Gottfrid Rattenauer
Johan Christoph Siberberg
Johannes Hermann
Mattes Moll
Michel Meyer
Johannes Feldmoyer
Gottfried Laurer

Jacob Seytter
Georg Muckenberger
Hs. Conrad Lutz
Andreas Boshardt
Carl Schill
Hans Michel Schlauch
Chrisopp Mühleisen
Christian Mühleisen
Balthes Zircher
Jacob Rösch
Matheis Maut
Jacob Hebbler
Jacob Schorch
Jerg Friderich Karcher
Philipp Jacob Mayer
Jerg Adam Eppler
Johannes Weissman
Samuel Wendel
Hermanus Neuman
Johann Jacob Schaf
Christian (+) Tragher
Christian Schneider
134 [men]
67 [women]
———
201 [Total]

[List 115 B] [Foreigners imported in the Ship Two Brothers, Thomas Arnott, Captain, from Rotterdam. Qualified October 13, 1747.]

Johannes Fuchs
Johann Henrich Kuntz
Johann Christoffel Müller
Johann Jacob Schmitt
Johan Bernharth Schneider
Johann Jacob Hilgert
Johan Ernst Kurtz
Johan Phillippus Thomas

Johannes (×) Bosse
Johann Peter Bausmann
Johannes Adam
Johannes Buch
Johan Peter Kuntz
Peter (×) Steinmetz
Johannes Opp
Johann Frantz Hammer

Frantz Henrich Gans

Johann Görg Roth

Johann Peter Conradt

Valentine (✕) Buckaker

Johann Adam Kröber

Jacob (✕) Arnold, Senior

Jacob (✕) Arnold, Junr

Mattheis Kern

Johannes Hermann

Johann Philippus Kloninger

Johann Leonhardt Negele

Johann Lorentz Momma

Johann Filb Hermann

Frantz Peter Lorentz

Johan Peter Schweick[hart]

Carl Baumberger

Johann Petter Meissen

Johan Henrich Eberhart

Nicholas (+) Wolf

Henrich Kirch

Görg Kärch

Fransz Bischof

Jost (✕) Fullmer

Johannes Usnr [?]

Johan Wendel Eberhardt

Johann Jacob Bischoff

Christian (✕) Eydam

Adolff May

Johann Dieterich Schmid

Johann Balthaser Hieronymus

Johann Frantz Hieronymus

Henrich Julius

Daniel Sauerwalt

Adam (+) Ingebrand

Johannes Scheffler

Georg Phillippus Groh

Johan Niclaus Frätz

Johannes End

Jacob Hüppel

Johan Christoph Protzman

Johan Filibus Nachtigall

Philipp Fidler

Henry (H) Beyl

Casimör Ortner

Johann Georg Huth

Michel Niederauer

Johann Vallenthin Harth

George (K) Greenemoyer

Sebastian Bauer

George (W) Wendling

Conraet Waagenaer

Anthon (✕) Armrister

Henrich Scharff

Johann Nickel Wust

Herman (✕) Woost

Nicholas (N) Gabhart

Dewald (✕) Knopf

Georgius Borovi

Johannes Scherff

Friedrich Kern

Mathes Bischoff

Frantz Michel Bischoff

Joannes Böhm

Johan Puntzius

Johann Georg Anstatt

Gerg Herman

Johann Christofel Lehr

Johann Conrad Geib

Frantz Willhan

Johannes Sassemanshausen

John Yost (✕) Reese

Franz (✕) Gerligh

Baulus Dilgard

John Yost (J) Bebighausen

Ernestus de Spitzer de et in
  Freyer

Leonhart Müller

Philip (✕) Kolp

Baltzer Mohn

Ullerick (UM) Maan

[Endorsed:]
List of Palatines imported in the Ship Two Brothers, Arnott, Master. Qual. 13th October, 1747.

[List 115 C] The Foreigners whose names are underwritten, imported in the Ship Two Brothers, Thomas Arnett, from Rotterdam & last from Leith, Inhabitants of the Palatinate & places adjacent, did this day take the foregoing Oaths to the Government, 13th 8ber 1747. Present at the Courthouse, the Honble the President, Benjm Shoemaker, Joshua Maddox, Esqrs.

Johannes Fuchs
Johann Henrich Kuntz
Johann Christoffel Müller
Johann Jacob Schmitt
Johann Bernharth Schneider
Johann Jacob Hilgert
Johan Ernst Kurtz
Johan Phillippus Thomas
Johannes (X) Bosse
Johann Peter Bausmann
Johannes Adam
Johannes Buch
Johan Peter Kuntz
Peter (O) Steinmetz
Johannes Opp
Johann Frantz Hammer
Frantz Henrich Gans
Johann Görg Roth
Johann Peter Conradt
Johann Adam Kröber
Jacob (X) Arnold, Senior
Jacob (X) Arnold, Junior
Mattheis Kern
Johannes Hermann
Johann Philippus Kloninger
Johann Leonhart Negele
Johann Lorentz Momma
Johann Filb Hermann
Frantz Peter Lorentz
Johan Peter Schweikharth

Carl Baumberger
Johann Petter Meissen
Johenrich Eberhart
Nickolas (+) Woolfe
Hennrich Kirch
Görg Kärch
Frantz Bischoff
Jost (+) Fullmer
Johannes Usner [?]
Johan Wendel Eberhardt
Johann Jacob Bischoff
Christian (X) Eydam
Johann Dieterich Schmidt
Johann Balthaser Hieronymus
Johann Frantz Hieronymus
Henrich Julius
Daniel Sauerwalt
Adam (X) Ingebrand
Johannes Scheffler
Georg Phillippus Kroh
Johan Niclaus Frätz
Johannes End
Jacob Hüppel
Johann Christoph Protzmann
Johann Pilibus Nachtigall
Philipp Fidler
Henry (H) Beyl
Casimür Ortner
Johann Georg Huth
Michel Niederauer

Johann Vallenthin Harth
George (K) Greenemeyer
Sebastian Bauer
George (W) Wendling
Anthon (A) Armrester
Henrich Scharff
Johann Nickel Wust
Herman (+) Woost
Niclas (N) Gebhart
Dewald (×) Knopff
Georgius Borovi
Johannes Scharf
Friedrich Kern
Matheis Bischof
Frantz Michel Bischof
Joannes Böhm
Johan Puntzius
Johann Georg Anstatt
Jerg Herrman
Johann Christo. Lehr

Johann Conrad Geib
Frantz Wullhan
Johannes Sassenmanshausen
Johan Jost (+) Reesse
Frantz (+) Gerligh
Paulus Dilgard
Johan Jost (+) Bebighausen
Ernestus de Spitzer de et in
   Fryer
Leonhart Müller
Philip (×) Kolp
Baltzer Mohn
Uhllerich (UM) Maan
Vallentin (×) Buchaker
Adolf Mey
Conraet Waagenaer
  96 [men]
  48 [women]
  ───────
 144 [Total]

[List 116 B. Foreigners imported in the Ship . . .] [Qualified October 20, 1747.]

Hans Conrad (HBK) Beck
Johannes Gress
Johann Christian Petersohn
Peter (O) Koch
Henry (O) Bawngwar
Jacob (×) Spring
Jacob Frey
Johannes Frey
Niclaus Lantz
Wilhelm Dauber
Friederich Dauber
Philip Henrich Seng
Jacob Allimang
Jacob Allimang
Adam Birger
Hans (×) Shyer
John Henry (O) Sneyder

Adam Schmitt
Jacob Schwanger
Johanes (O) Meyer
Charles (S) Shmit
Johannes Wenger
Christian Wenger
Jörg Schäffer
Johannes Stumbf
Ludwick (×) Tecker
Christoff (+) Gotchalk
Hans Adam (×) Furny
Jörg Veith
Henrick (×) Frontz
Abraham (F) Frontz
Beder Frantz
Peter (O) Kennel
Hans Jörg Lantz

Christian Griedimer
Durs Kürstner
Hans Philip (O) Baron
Matthias . . .
Simon Conrad Grineus

Johan Wilhelm (+) Yet
Hans (×) Lickwilder
Hans Michael (O) Kline
Hans Dewaldt (H) Leytey
Nicholas (U) Wenger

[Endorsed:]
List of Palatines from Rotterdam. Qual. 20ᵗʰ October 1747.

[List 116 C] At the Courthouse at Philadelphia, 20ᵗʰ Octʳ 1747.

Present: William Attwood, Esqʳ, Mayor, William Allen, Esqʳ, Recorder.

The Foreigners whose Names are underwritten, imported in the . . . Master, from Rotterdam, but last from Leith, did this Day take the foregoing Oaths to the Government.

Hans (HKB) Conrad Beck
Johannes Gress
Johan Christian Petersohn
Peter (O) Koch
Henry (O) Bawngwar
Jacob (×) Spring
Jacob Frey
Johannes Frey
Niclaus Lantz
Wilhelm Dauber
Friedrich Dauber
Philip Henrich Seng
Jacob Allimang
Jacob Allimang
Adam Birger
Hans (×) Sheyer
John Henry (O) Shneyder
Adam Schmitt
Jacob Schwanger
Johannes (O) Meyer
Charles (S) Shmit
Johannes Wenger

Christian Wenger
Jörg Schäffer
Johannes Stumbf
Ludwig (×) Tecker
Christoff (+) Gotshalk
Hans Adam (×) Furny
Jörg Veith
Henry (×) Frontz
Abraham (F) Frontz
Beder Frantz
Peter (O) Kennel
Hans Jörg Lantz
Christian Griedimer
Durs Kürstner
Hans Philip (O) Baron
Matthias . . .
Simon Conrad Grineus
Johan Wilhelm (+) Yet
Henry (×) Likwilder
Hans Mickel (O) Klein
Hans Dewald (H) Leyty
Nicholaus (W) Wenger

[List 117 C] At the Court House at Philad^a, 5th Septr 1748. Present: William Attwood, Esqr, Mayor, William Allen, Esqr, Recorder, Robert Strettell & Benjamin Shoemaker, Esq^rs.

The Foreigners whose Names are underwritten, imported in the Edinburgh, James Russel, Master, from Rotterdam, but last from Portsmouth, did this Day take the foregoing Oaths to the Government.

Johann Valentin Opp
Jacob Schumacher
Andreas Stoudt
Johann Filib Schmitt
Christoph (X) Kunn
Johann Adam Schuster
Johann Stephan Franck
Johann Peter Heyer
Lenert Reyder
Dietrich Strubell
Johann Valentin Klages
Adam (O) Rauch
Jacob Hilsheimer *
Joh. Lorentz
Johann Philip Lorentz
Johan Jacob Gilberth
Johan Velten Lorentz
Thomas Koch
Adam (X) Kirchner
Johann Leonhard May
Frantz Peter May
Johann Wilhelm Gärtner
Johann Peter Von Känne
Johann Jacob Bronner
Johann Jacob Eyler
Johann Nickel Busch
Johann Nickel Mäyer
Johannes Schue [?]

Johann Jacob Schlosser
Johan Herman Clauss
Conrath Clauss
Sebastian Barthelmy
Peter Weingart
Henry (X) Neizart
Peter Wilhelm Caffroth
Philip Haller
Peter (X) Pfiffer
Justus Otto
Johann Wilhelm Fuchs
Friedrich Hubertus Fuchs
Gerhart Peter Döst
Johann Nicolas Döst
Lorentz Werthes
Simon Pilanus
Michael (X) Gugest
Vallentin Husch
Vallentin (V) Hush, Junr.
Vallentin (V) Sherer
Caspar ( ) Franckfurther, sick
John George (H) Kirshner
Philip Reinhart Gossler
Gerg Lenhart Krumrein
Valtin Müller
Johannes Weydenhauer
Felix Sautter
Baltazar (X) Spitznagel

* Jacob Hiltzheimer was a prominent elder of the Reformed Church in Philadelphia. *Extracts from the Diary of Jacob Hiltzheimer* were published at Philadelphia in 1893, by his great-grandson Jacob Cox Parsons.

Johan Adam Bucholtz

Jacob Vierling

Johann Peter Bronner

Lenhard Öhler

Adam Anders

Melchior (X) Brown

Johannes Michgel Hoffman

Jacob Hoffman

Henrich Merkel

Johan Nickel (X) Eberhart

Michel Theiss

Frantz (X) Jantz

Mattias (X) Krammer

Johann David Hamman

Bernhart Diehl

Reinhart Daub

Johannes Diehl

Johannes Diehl

Conrath Grosch

Balthes Erbach

Johan Friederich Antes

Peter Schäffer

Jacob Julius

Vallentin Küwitz

Peter Meitzler

Rufinus Scherer

Henrich Scherer

Hans Jerge Betz

Mattheas (X) Betz

Philip (I) Mark

Baltazar (X) Essig

Peter (X) Kretz

Ludwig (X) Bronholtz

Henrich Schatz

Adam (X) Reem

Martin (X) Klein

Sebastian Stein

Peter Stein

Abraham (X) Stein

Henry (X) Stein

Valtin Reimer

Wilhelm Hanns Mann

Conrad Fritz

Mathias (X) Ebert

Jacob (X) Ebert

Nickel Müller

Johannes Petter Weber

Christoph ( ) Weber, sick

Ludwig Lindenschmitt

Nicolaus Lenhardt

George Jacob (X) Hartman

Michel Hartmann

Filbs Jacob Koch

Friedrich Herget

Johan Daniel Lindenschmitt

Esaias (X) Carl

Dominicus Ridel

Michael (O) Wagner

Paul Ullrich

Johann Peter Michel

Jacob Hermman

Wilhelm (X) Nick

Johannes Rihm

Johann Julius (X) Reehm

Johannes Uhler

Johannes (X) Foltz

George (X) Leuthenger

Conrath Buber

Johan Lorentz Herschfenger

Am Üster [?]

George (X) Erdmayer

127 [men] on List.

[List 118 A] List of the Names & Ages of Men imported in the Hampshire, Capt Thomas Cheesman. [Qualified September 7, 1748.]

AGES		AGES

Name	Age	Name	Age
Hans Adam Willhelm	34	Jacob Rungell	27
Johannes Houst	26	Fred^k Hamer	35
Isaac Stimell	28	Tobias Schall	42
Philip Happ	34	Jacob Holtz	45
Adam Mayer	30	Andreas Hodenar	30
Johannes Bishoff	34	John Yerick Wyl	21
Peter Scheffer	20	Casper Keperling	22
Adam Imenheyser	25	Phillip Wensell	48
Hans Yerrick Smith	18	John Boomgirdle	26
Michael Wydman	24	Michael Baserman	21
Johan Jacob Beck	25	Carles Inglie	25
Hans Yerich Webber	45	Johannes Inglie	22
Peter Ferdigh	46	Phillip Kogh	19
Hans Peter Keller	40	Jacob Schear	28
Yerich Hack	41	John Hend^k Crom	20
Andreas Keyler	24	David Agh	22
Jacob Kool	49	Casper Letherholtz	58
Johan Adam Miller	25	Anthony Ermolt	28
Johannes Myer	53	Johannes Frans Grove	54
John Hend^k Bote	48	Hend^k Crown	17
John Jonas Bote	20	Willhelm Lymester	58
Philip Lodwick Hidige	18	Jacob Smith	20
Hartman Adam	40	John Daniel Ham	20
Johannes Adam	16	Yerick Whytman	34
Lodwick Waganer	20	Yerick Lamley	30
Diedrick Mathias	23	Phillip Carel Biller	22
John Frans Noll	46	Casper Rupy	27
John Hend^k Noll	20	Lorentz Wensell	47
Yerick Styerwald	40	Wolffgang Wolff	36
Fred^k Reets	27	Jacob Hamer	16
John Albertus Wagentbotten	26	Mathias Knip, sick	48
Anth^y Maul	27	Hans Jacob Osterman	28
Conradt Maul	25	Hans Ellmus Schrymer	21
Johannes Duffeydal	23	Johanes Engel	22
Johan Michael Diterich	19	Phillip Hend^k Moore	41
Phillip Vendell Hensell	52	Adam Wys	24
John Tobias	16	Frid^k Blaetz	36
John Phillip Bamm	30	Andreas Miller	35
Nicholas Christ	58	76 [men]	
Michael Orig	35		

[Endorsed:]
List of Foreigners imported in the Hampshire, Captⁿ
Thomas Cheesman. Qualified 7ᵗʰ Septʳ 1748.

[List 118 B] [Foreigners imported in the Hampshire, Captain Thomas Cheesman, from Rotterdam. Qualified September 7, 1748.]

Johann Albert Weygand
Han Adam Wilhelm
Johannes Faust
Isaac Stimmel
Philip (✕) Hap
Adam Mayer
Johannes Bischoff
Johan Päter Schäfer
Adam Immenhauser
Johann Georg Schmid
Michal Widman
Johan Jacob Beckh
Johan Geörg Wäber
Peter (✕) Ferdigh
Hans Petter Köhler
Hans Jerg Hag
Johann Andreas Riegler
Jacob Kuhl
Johan Adam Müller
Johannes Mayer
Johann Henrich Bott
Johann Jonas Bott
Philips Ludwig Hütig
Hartmann Adam
Johannes Adam
Johann Ludwig Wagner
Johann Dieterich Matthy
Johann Frantz Noll
Johann Henrich Noll
George (✕) Styerwald
Johan Friedrich Ruth
Johann Anthon Maul
Conradt Maul

Johannes (+) Duffydal
Philip Swendel (+) Helsel
Johann Tobias Höltzel
Johan Michyel Dietrich
Johann Philippus Baum
Nicholas (✕) Christ
Johan Michel Ohrig
Jacob Runckel
Friederich Hammer
Tobias Schall
Jacob Holtz
Andreas (+) Hoettinger
Johann Georg Weil
Caspar Köberling
Philibus Michel
John Erhart (✕) Baumgirtel
Michael Bassermann
Carl Engel
Phillips Koch
Jacob (✕) Sherr
Johann Henrich Krom
Davith Haag
Johan Caspar Lederholt
Anthony (✕) Armolt
Frantz (++) Grove
Henrich Cron
Johannes Engel
Johann Wilhelm Leymeister
Jacob Schmitt
Johann Daniel Hamm
Johann Georg Weissman
Jerg Lembgen
Phillip Carl Piller

Casper Rubi
Lorentz Wentzel
Wolfgang (X) Wolf
Jacob Hammer
Hans Jacob (XX)Osterman

Anselmus Schreiner
Philip Henrich Mohr
Johann Adam Weiss
Andreas (OOO) Miller
Johann Friederich Plotz

[Endorsed:]
List of Palatines imported in the Hampshire, Capt Thomas
Cheesman & in the Mary Galley, Capt. George Lawson, both
qual^d 7th Septr 1748.

[List 118 C] At the State House at Philad^a, 7th Septr 1748.
Present: Abraham Taylor, Esqr,
Joseph Turner, Esqr.

The Foreigners whose Names are underwritten, imported
in the Hampshire, Captn Thomas Cheesman, from Rotterdam,
but last from Falmouth, did this day take the foregoing Oaths
to the Government.

Johann Albert Weygand
Hans Adam Wilhelm
Johannes Faust
Johann Isaac Stimmel
Philip (X) Hap
Adam Mayer
Johannes Bischoff
Johan Päter Schäfer
Adam Immenhauser
Johann Georg Schmid
Michal Widman
Johan Jacob Beckh
Johann Geörg Wäbber
Peter (X) Ferdig
Hans Petter Kähller
Hans Jerg Hag
Johann Andreas Riegler
Jacob Kuhl
Johan Adam Müller
Johannes Mayer
Johann Hennrich Bott
Johann Jonas Bott

Philip Ludwig Hütig
Hartmann Adam
Johannes Adam
Johann Ludwig Wagner
Johann Diterich Matthy
Johann Frantz Noll
Johann Henrich Noll
Georg (X) Steyerwald
John Fridrich Ruth
Johann Anthon Maul
Conradt Maul
Johannes (+) Diffital
Philip (+) Swendel Helsel
Johann Tobias Höltzel
Johan Michgel Ditrich
Johann Philippus Baum
Nickolaus (X) Christ
Johan Michel Ohrig
Jacob Runckel
Friederich Hammer
Tobias Schall
Jacob Holtz

Andereas (×) Hoettinger	Johann Wilhelm Leymeister
Johann Georg Weil	Jacob Schmitt
Caspar Köberling	Johann Daniel Hamm
Philibs Michel	Johann Georg Weissman
Johan Erhart (×) Baumgirtel	Jerg Lembgen
Michael Bassermann	Phillipp Carl Piller
Carl Engel	Casper Rubi
Phillip Koch	Lorentz Wenzel
Jacob (×) Sherr	Wolffgang (×) Wulff
Johan Henrich Krom	Jacob Hammer
David Hag	Hans Jacob (H) Osterman
Johan Caspar Lederholt	Anselmus Schreiner
Anthony (×) Ermolt	Philip Henrich Mohr
Frants (F) Grove	Johann Adam Weiss
Henrich Cron	Andereas (OOO) Miller
Johannes Enngel	Johann Friederich Plotz

[List 119 A] Men Passengers on board the Mary Galley, George Lawson, Commander. [Qualified Sept. 7, 1748.]

Abia Schneider	Casper Clair
Nicholas Derrick	Jacob Hairs
Michael Konig	John Kippel
Nicholas Dirgris	Peter Barnd
Peter Ederborn	Abraham Giabs
Nicholas Woolfe	Conrad Brunner
Henry Shewhan	William Kohl
Adam Smith	Jacob Back
Georg Keith	Geo. Waber
Godfrey Somerline	David Suder
Peter Raugh	John Wilrick
Jacob Fath	John Adam Weber
Philip Jacob Somerland	25 [men]

And at yᵉ same time & Place yᵉ Foreigners whose Names are also underwritten, being lately imported in yᵉ Mary Galley, Captⁿ Geo. Lawson, Comʳ from London, did also take yᵉ foregoing Oaths to yᵉ Governour.
[Endorsed:]
List of Foreigners imported in the Mary Galley, Captⁿ George Lawson, Qualified 7ᵗʰ 7ᵇᵉʳ, [1748].

[List 119 B] [Foreigners imported in the Mary Galley, Captain George Lawson, Commander, from London. Qualified Sept 7, 1748.]

Abraham Schneider	Philipp Jacob Sommerlad
Nickelas Diedrich	Caspar Klehr
Michael (MK) Konig	Johanes Hüppel
Nickel Thunges	Peter Bern
Peter (IPE) Edeborn	Abraham (X) Geebs
Nickelahs Wollf	Conradt Bruner
Henrich Schuchen	William (X) Khol
Adam (X) Schmith	Jacob Beck
Johann Görg Köth	Jerg Weber
Johann Gottfried Sommerlad	Johan Adam (W) Weber
Johann Peter Rauch	David (X) Sutter
Friedrich Iachof [?]	Johannes (W) Willerick

[List 119 C] And at the same time and place the Foreigners whose Names are also underwritten, being lately Imported in the Mary Galley, Capt. George Lawson, Commander, from London, did also take the foregoing Oaths to the Government.

Abraham Schneider	Philip Jacob Sommerlad
Nickelas Diedrich	Caspar Klehr
Michael (MK) Konig	Johannes Hüppel
Nicklas Thunges	Peter Bern
Peter (IPE) Edeborn	Abraham (+) Geebs
Nickelahs Wollff	Conradt B[r]uner
Henrich Schuchen	William (+) Kohl
Adam (X) Shmith	Jacob Beck
Johann Georg Köth	Jurg Weber
Johann Gottfried Sommerlad	Johan Adam (W) Weber
Johan Peter Rauch	Davit (X) Sudder
Fridrich Iachof [?]	Johannes (W) Willerich

[List 120 A] List of Men Passengers on board the Ship Two Brothers, Thomas Arnot, Master, from Rotterdam. [Qualified September 15, 1748.]

Casper Apfel	Burkhard Braun
Daniel Kreutz	Peter Bier

Peter Bier, Jun[r]
Johannes Hearman
Peter Denick
Simon Basserman
Johannes Knight
Fredrich Hyde
Carl Hyde
Casper Kiefer
Abraham Kiefer
Abraham Kiefer, Jun[r]
Casper Ingle
Johan Sherer
Philip Stevan
Johannes Ebert
Christoffel Hick
Nicholas Clemence
Johan Conrad Fieman
Conrad Rauch
Johannes Werner
Johan Jost Ebert
Baltzer Schriver
Johannes Laubach
Johan Peter Engle
Matthias Ott
Johan Casper Kremer
Henrich Kremer
Johannes Neu
Johannes Holsecker
Hans Jacob Kendell
Johan Jacob Hock
Fritz Weber
Michael Gunter
Conrad Gunter
Paul Junger
Hans Eckkart
Philip Steyn
Michael Raffsnyder
Hans Kellor
Conrad Kehlor
Hans Slegell
Ulrich Wirth

Ewald Gunter
Johan Jurg Messersmith
Johannes Agtung
Johannes Waltz
Peter Anthony
Nicholas Kind
Johannes Kesnar
Matthias Dieder
Johannes Tey
Joost Durrer
Egidius Meffert
Peter Meffert
Johannes Holtz
Jacob Gerrardin
Peter Gerardin
Johannes Slegell
Johannes Slegell, Junr
Peter Ernst
Conrad Kellor
Conrad Kellor, Junr
Jacob Reichart
Johan Jurg Vaas
Michael Hasler
Daniel Snyder
Henrich Frantz
Eitel Engell
Wilhelmus Engell
Johan Engell
Johannes Wyandt
Peter Taubert
Jacob Nyce
Dominicus Presser
Johannes Müller
Ludwig David Ruppell
Daniel Kobir
Nichol[s] Koontz
Peter Velte
Michael Bartjes
Johannes Newhouse
Carl Marth
Philip Grim

Jacob Bretzius
Wilhelmus Müller
Johannes Stöhr
Jacob Schefer
Philip Swaab
Henrich Spicker
Johan Michal Brucker
Jeremias Runkell
Joost Runkell
Peter Leonard

Mathias Hutwohl
Hans Adam Stöher
Mattys Ströher
Daniel Angst
Michal Christman
Mathias Stroher
Johan Fülleps
Johannes Sumerlauter
Johan Jurg Kellor

[Endorsed:]
List of Palatines imported in the Ship Two Brothers, Cap^n
Arnot. Qualified 15th 7^{ber} 1748.

[List 120 B] [Foreigners imported in the Ship Two Brothers, Capt. Arnot. Qualified September 15, 1748.]

Johann Casper Apffel
Johann Daniel Creutz
Burckhard Braun
Peter Bier
Peter Bier
Johannes Herrmann
Johann Peter Denig
Siegmund Bassermann
Johannes Knecht
J. Friedrich Hötz
Görg Carl Hötz
Casper Fünfer
Abraham (O) Kieffer
Abraham Küfer
Johan Kasper Engel
Jacob Scherer
Johann Philip Steffan
Jonas Eberth
Christoffel Heck
Nicklos Clementz
Johann Conradt Viehman
Johan Conradt Rauch
Johannes Wörner

Johann Just Eberth
Johann Balter Schäffer
Johannes Laubach
Jonas Somelade
Johann Peter Engel
Johan Matteus Otto
Johann Caspar Kraümer
Johannes Neun
Johannes (X) Huntzeker
Jacob (O) Kendel
Jacob Höck
Johann Friederich Weber
Michael (+) Gunter
Johan Paul (X) Junger
Johannes Heckart
Philippus Stein
Michael (+) Reiffsneider
Johannes Keller
Conrad Köhler
Johannes Schlegel
Ulrich Wirt
Ewalt Gantter
Johan Gorg Messerschmid

Johannes Achtung
Johannes (X) Waltz
Johans Beter Andoni
Johann Nicklas Kindt
Johannes Gessner
Maddeis Dithart
Johannes Deys
Johann Jöst Dörr
Egidius Meffert
Johann Peter Meffert
Johannes Kloos
Jacob Girardin
Johannes Schlegel
Peter Ernst
Conrad Keller, Junr
Jacob (X) Reiger
Johann Jorg Fass
Michael Hasler
Johann Daniel Schneider
Hennrich Frantz
Lydel Engel
Johann Wilhelm Engel
Johann Henrich Engel
Johannes Weiand
Peter (+) Doubter
Jacob Nies
Magnus Presser

Johannes Müller
Ludwig Davidt Rüpfel
Daniel Kober
Niclaus Kuntz
Peter (X) Fehter
Michel Berges
Johannes (X) Nighouse
Carl Mahrt
Philip Grimm
Jacob (X) Breitius
Johan Wilhelm Miller
Johannes Stehr
Philipps Jacob Schäffer
Johan Philippus Schwab
Johann Henrich Spücker
Johann Michel Brucker
Jeremias Runckel
Johan Jost Runckel
Johann Petter Lenhart
Matthäis Hütwohl
Hans Adam Ströher
Johann Mattes Ströher
Daniel Angst
Michel Christman
Johannes Mathes Ströhr
Johan Jurg (X) Keller

[Endorsed:]
List of Palatines imported in the Ship Two Brothers, Capt.
Thos Arnot.
Qual. 15th September 1748.

[List 120 C] At the Court House at Philadelphia, 15th Sept^r
1749.
Present: William Atwood, Esquire, Mayor, William Allen,
Esquire, Recorder, Robert Strettell, Benj^m Shoemacker, Esqr, Septimus Robinson, Esqr.
The Foreigners whose names are underwritten, imported in
the Ship Two Brothers, Thomas Arnot, Master, from Rotterdam, but last from Portsmouth, did this day take the usual
Oaths to the Government.

Johann Casper Apfel
Johann Daniel Creutz
Johann Burckhard Braun
Peter Bier
Peter Bier
Johannes Herrmann
Johann Peder Denig
Siegmund Bassermann
Johannes Knecht
J. Friedich Hötz
Görg Carl Hötz
Casper Kieffer
Abraham (O) Kieffer
Abraham Küfer
Johan Kasper Engel
Jacob Scherer
Johann Philip Steffan
Johan Eberth
Christoffel Heck
Nickelaus Clementz
Johann Connradt Viehman
Johan Conradt Rauch
Johannes Wörner
Johan Just Eberth
Johann Balter Schäfer
Johannes Laubach
Jones Somerlade
Johann Peter Engel
Johan Matteus Otto
Johann Caspar Krämmer
Johannes Neun
Johann (X) Huntzeker
Jacob Kendel
Jacob Höck
Johann Friederich Reber
Michael (X) Günter
Johan Paul (+) Junger
Johannes Heckart
Philippus Stein
Michael (X) Reiffsnyder
Johanes Koller

Conrad Köhler
Johannes Schlegel
Ulrich Wirt
Ewalt Gantter
Johan Jörg Messerschmid
Johannes Achtung
Johannes (X) Waltz
Johanes Bet. Andoni
Johann Nicklas Kindt
Johannes Gessner
Maddeis Dithart
Johannes Deys
Johann Jost Dörr
Egidius Meffert
Johann Peter Meffert
Johannes Kloos
Jacob Girardin
Johannes Schlegel
Peter Ernst
Conrad Keller, Junior
Jacob Reigher
Johann Jerg Fass
Michael Hasler
Johann Daniel Schneider
Hennrich Frantz
Lydel Engel
Johann Wilhelm Engel
Johan Henrich Engel
Johannes Weiand
Peder (+) Dauber
Jacob Nies
Magnus Presser
Johannes Müller
Ludwig David Rüpfel
Daniel Kober
Nicolaus Kuntz
Peter (X) Felte
Michel Berges
Johannes Neuhaus
Carl Mahrt
Philip Grimm

Jacob (X) Britzius
Johan Wilhelm Müller
Johannes Stohr
Philipps Jacob Schäfer
Johan Philipus Schwob
Johann Henrich Spüker
Johann Michael Brucker
Jermias Runckel
Johann Jost Runckel

Johann Petter Lenhart
Matthäis Hütwohl
Han Adam Ströher
Johann Mattes Ströher
Daniel Angst
Michel (X) Christman
Johannes Mathes Ströher
Johann Jürg (X) Kauller

[List 121 C] And at the same time & place the Foreigners whose Names are also underwritten, being lately Imported in the Judith, Captⁿ James Tait, Commander, from Rotterdam, but last from Cowes, did also take the foregoing Oaths to the Government.   [Qualified Sept. 15, 1748.]

Hans Peter (+) Shäller
Hans Michael Göhr
Johann Adam Leidig
Joh Nicolaus Copia
Johan Peter Peil
Johann Adam Meyer
Conrad (X) Hinkel
Philip Knöbel
Austus Eygenbrod
Henry (X) Althaus
Vallentin Welcker
William (X) Cuntz
Christ. Peter Sauermann
Christian Schmid
Johannes Steffe
Johann Lorentz Weygandt
Caspar (X) Amhyser
Fridrich Gess
Erhart Miller
Johannes Meyer
Ulrich Rathmacher
Conrat Weigand
Feldin Arntt
Johannes Schnall

Michael (+) Ungar
Nickella Ackerman
Johannes Schuy
Jacob Becker
Johann Michael Seefridt
Matdes Bescher
Christian (+) Dapper
Jacob (X) Seyvert
Johan Esaias Weiskob
Johannes Hassinger
Johann Jacob Hassinger
Petter Glück
Johann Michel Bausman
Philipphs Anton Sauerman
Johann Peter Heckman
Conraht Rhein
Johannes Homrighausen
Johan Henrich Beizel
Thebus (X) Spees
Paulus (X) Bender
Georg Michel Warmkessel
Jacob (X) Beltentorffer
Jacob Motz
Hartwig Arnd

Henrich Bub   Johann Heinrich Brosius
Görg Mölchior Stuber   Christofel Sauer

[List 122 A] List of Mens Names & Ages imported in the
Ship Patience, Capt John Brown.   [Qualified Sept. 16, 1748.]

	AGES		AGES
Johan Yerick Enders	38	Johan Adam Diedrick	50
Johan Yerick Rommel	50	Johan Adam Keisacker	20
Valatine Rommel	22	Johan Godfried Hontsman	40
Hend^k Ellaback	17½	Diedrick Rash	19
Adam Cassnar	38	Silvestor Patsman	18
Jacob Beek	35	John Jacob Martin	41
Jacob Heysel	45	Adam Farner	30
Johan Yerick Wack	23	Joseph Martsin	23
Peter Loucks	22	Sebastin Lynenger	50
Bartel Tiesingen	66	Johan Conradt Lyninger	17
Hend^k Tiesingen	18	Johannes Peter Bener	23
Nicholas Mysenar	21	Phillip Herbel	19
Yerick Mich^l Rotderman	20	Lodwick Drager	23
Phillip Carel Haas	47	Johan Nicol Wyker	18
Phillip Peter Keyslinger	26	Carlos Boyer	18
Peter Peterman	25	Johannes Mack	25
Casper Habler	36	Johan Jacob Miller	21
Bartholome Shewbly	19	Michael Miller	24
Conradt Booner	25	Peter Mumma	27
Jan Peter Fols	18	Peter Heysler	27
Valantine Roder	24	Johannes Miller	24
Conradt Reis	43	Phillip Wolf	20
Diederick Sol	37	Hend^k Swap	18
Philip Hefelbower	30	Johannes Gertert	29
Andreas Rudolph	27	Johannes Hinkner	30
Valantine Casper	18	Fredrick Hacknir	29
Yerick Baltus Heifelbower	24	Yerick Baltus Clever	24
Johannes Kungel	44	Phillip Filhawer	24
Johan Kungel	16	Bernhard Kuter	18
Yerick Carl	26	Hans Adam Kungel	66
Yerick Nuts	29	Hans Adam Kungel, Junr	30
Fredrick Hafner	26	Hans Kungel	26
Joseph Piper	26	Hans Somerower	33
Edmund Cobie	29	Anthony Winegat	23
Yerick Adam Nydig	42	Mathias Burger	21

	AGES		AGES
Jacob Haller	17	Barnard Stiglien	18
Adam Bieringer	26	Casper Kaster	37
Andreas Beringer	25	Rudolph Kenil	25
Johannes Smith	36	Johannes Wengar	43
Conradt Lepold	33	Johannes Wengar	16
Hendᵏ Somerower	26	Peter Bartol	24
Johannes Soupinger	29	Samuel Fries	50
Hendᵏ Kuyl	37	Hans Yerick Miller	38
Yerick Sydenspinder	28	Hendᵏ Miller	21
Hendᵏ Pougher	24	Michˡ Crasman	18
Casper Schewbly	23	Jacob Carrel	40
Hans Sibley	30	John Casper Carrel	17
Henry Sibley	18	Lodwᵏ Abling	49
Jacob Laudenberger	19	Hendᵏ Neeter	48
Jacob Orie	46	Hans Jacob Shaffer	19
Peter Seller	32	Andreas Keller	30
Jacob Bleykesoffer	25	Carol Glaser	27
Ulrich Boucher	17	John Nichˢ Knut	24
Jacob Clasley	17	Michˡ Keysler	20
Jacob Markie	45	Phillip Hungel, sore leg	25
Jacob Stizhous	22	John Christopher Sprecker	25
Lawrence Spleman	39	Yerick Adam Carnagal	22
Christopher Beck	26	Yerick Adam Bowman	22
Henry Rickie	22	Johannes Holts	23
Adam Hartman	40	Jacob Miller	23
Nichˡ Wamser	35	122 [men]	
Jacob Webber	32		

A List of Foreigners, imported in the Ship Patience, Captⁿ.
John Brown.
Qualified Sept. 16, 1748.

[List 122 C] At the Courthouse at Philadelphia, 16 September 1748.

Present: Joshua Maddox,   }
        Septimus Robinson, } Esquires

The Foreigners whose Names are underwritten, imported in the Ship Patience, John Browne, Master, from Rotterdam, but last from Cowes, did this day take the usual Oaths to the Government.

Johann Georg Enters
Hans Jerick Romel
Pfielpp Peter Geinser
Vallentin Rummel
Johann Henrich Erlenbach
Adam (H) Kastner
Jacob (X) Beege
Jacob Heisel
Johann Gorg Wack *
Johan Peter Laux
Barthel Deising[er]
Henrich Deissinger
Nicolaus Meisner
Philipp Carl Haas
Georg Michael Rothermel
Peter Peterman
Johann Caspar Höpp[ler]
Bartholomäus Scheibl[y]
Johann Conradt Bohner
Johan Peter Voltz
Valthin Rötter
Conraht Riess
Dietrich Sehl
Philipp Höffelbauer
Andreas Rudolff
Valentin Caspar
Georg Balthas Höffelbauer
Johannes (XX) Cunkel
Johan (XX) Cunkel, Junior
Georg Kast [?]
Georg (++) Nuts
Friederich (++) Hafner
Joseph Peiffer
Erdmann Koppe
Görg Adam Neidig
Johann Adam Dittrich
Johan Ernst Kiesecker
Johann Gottfried Kunstmann
Dietrich Bösch

Silvester Herr [?]
Johan Jacob Marthin
Martin Forner
Johann Jost Mertz
Sebastian Leininger
Johan Conrad (X) Leininger
Johannes Biedenbünder
Johan Philip Herpel
Ludwig Dracker
Johann Nicolaus Weicker
Carollus Peier
Johannes Mackh
Johan Jacob Müller
Michael Müller
Peter (P) Mumma
Peter Heissler
Johannes (X) Miller
Philip (X) Wolfe
Henrich Schwob
Johannes (X) Gerter
Johannes Gintner [?]
Friedrich Hagner
Jerg Balthas Kleber
Jerg Pilipps Wulhauer
Bernhart (X) Kuter
Johann Friederich Forster
Hans Adam Kunckel, Senior
Hans Adam Kunckel, Junior
Hans Kunckel
Johannes Summerauer
Anthoni Weinkoten
Mathäis Burger
Jacob Haller
Adam Böhringer
Andreas Böhringer
Johannes Schmidt
Conradt Leübbel
Heinrich Sumerauer
Johannes Zobinger

* This is the father of the Reformed minister Casper Wack. See Harbaugh, *Fathers of the Reformed Church*, Vol. II, p. 173.

Hendrich (HK) Kuyl
Jörg Seidenspinner
Heinerich Bucher
Casper Schibli zu Niden [. . .]
Hans Zubley
Heinrich Zöbeli
Jacob Laudenberger
Jacob Öry
Pierre Sellier
Jacob Blickenstorfer
Jacob (O) Margel
Jacob Stons
Hans Ullrich Bucher
Jacobin Kleiss
Lorentz Spillman
Christoph Beckh
Heinrich Rüdtschi
Atam Hartman
Nicklas (+) Womser
Jacob Weber
Johan Georg Bernhardt Stiglitz
Caspar Gerster
Johann Rutolf Kenndel

Hans Wanger
Stephan (X) Wenger
Peter (X) Bergtoll
Christian (X) Wenger
Hans (X) Wenger
Samuel Fries
Hans Jerick (X) Miller
Henrich Adam Müller
Michel Christmann
Johann Jacob Carle
Johan Kasber Karle
Ludwig Eberling
Hendry (HN) Nätter
Johann Jacob Schäfer
Andreas Keller
Carl Glaser
Johann Nickel Kind
Michel Kessler
Johann Christoph Speicher
Georg Adam Karnagel
Georg Adam Bauman
Johannes Holl
Jacobus Müller

[List 123 A] List of Persons Names imported in the Patience & Margaret, Capt John Govan, from Rotterdam. [Qualified October 25, 1748.]

	AGES		AGES
John Nicholas Corondorph	22	Fred^k Spoonamer	50
Ludwick Fliger	30	Michael Bayle	28
Baltus Kurne	18	John Peter Nay	25
John Peter Fick	23	Jacob Mathias	30
Hendrick Poole	18	Johannes Keller	32
Hendrick Knoblick	28	John Adam Kebel	31
Diedrick Boynnand	27	Christian Han	19
Phillip Simer	25	Johannes Knep	38
Andreas Speler	48	Johannes Lans	16
Lodwick Seaman	26	Johannes Tiets	50
Hend^k Seymour	23	Michael Tiets	17
Philip Jacob Jacobine	17	Reighart Langer	30

	AGES		AGES
Jacob Liefler	48	Michael Rieghart	27
John Till Wyns	20	Wilhelem Gresher	31
Yerrick Fookes	28	Anthony Brost	33
Peter Strall	34	Baltzer Swop	43
Johannes Myenger	35	Mathias Kebel	34
Johannes Klyn	24	Jacob Oriker	30
John Peter Ham	30	Michael Oriker	27
Fredrick Giger	30	Hendrick Corwar	50
Godfred Zoham	29	John Jasper Brake	40
Adam Shnyder	23	Fred^k Muys	38
John Michel Byerling	33	Hend^k Freeman	30
Hend^k Bretnight	24	Hend^k Bush	26
John Philip Smick	30	Anthony Hampire	24
Yerrick Shade	27	John Bush	21
John Melchior Kritzer	46	John Jacob Hart	24
John Peter Keller	35	Johannes Undersight	40
Godfret Bremhover	27	Wendel Kefer	27
William Waganer	42	Nick^s Young	18
Baltzer Flisher	20	Johannes Lock	24
Hend^k Craft	18	SICK	
Peter Smith	50	Conrat Van Gemita	16
Carel Kahaback	42	Yerrick Rizer	20
Johannes Kahaback	16	71 [men]	
Yerrick Emerick	19	35:6 [women & children]	
John Nicholas Poligh	40		
Jacob Lantz	30	106 [total number]	

[Endorsed:]
List of Palatines imported in the Ship Patience & Marg.,
Captn John Govan.
Qualified 25th 8^{ber} 1748.

[List 123 B] [Foreigners imported in the Ship Patience,
Captain John Govan, Master, from Rotterdam. Qualified
October 25, 1748.]

Johann Nicolas Korndörffer	Johann Henrich Phul
Ludwig Pflüger	Henry (×) Knoblogh
Carl Balthasar Kern	Dieterich Reinharth
Johann Peter Veith	Philip (F) Zimmer

Andreas (A) Spiller
Johann Ludwig Seeman
Henry (X) Seeman
Friedrich Sponheimer
Michel Bihl
John Peter (H) Nay
Johann Jacob Matthias
Johannes Keller
Johan Adam Göbel
Christian Hahn
Johannes Kneist
Johannes Lantz
Jonas Dietz
Johann Michael Dietz
Richard (R) Longer
Jacob (X) Loffner
Johann Diel Wentz
George Henry (O) Fuchs
Peter Strohl
Johanes Meininger
Hannes Klein
Johann Peter Han
Johann Friederich Geiger
Jan Gottfried Soy
Johann Adam Schneider
Johann Michael Deyerling
Johann Henrich Bretheich
Johann Philips Schmäck
Johann Georg Schad

Johann Melchior Kräuter
Johann Peter (X) Galler
Gottfried Premauer
Wilhelm (X) Wagner
Baltzer Fleischer
Henrich Krapf
Peter Schmid
Carlle Gackenbach
Jacob Emrich
Johann Nicol Polch
Jacob (X) Landes
Johann Michael Reichart
Andonius Brust
Baltzer (X) Shwab
Johann Matteas (MG) Gele
Jacob (X) Overkish
Michael (X) Overkish
Henrich Conver
Johann Casper Prach
Friederich Maus
Henrich Busch
Hannes Busch
Johann Jacob Hardt
Johannes Unverzagt
Wendel (X) Keefer
Johann Nickel Jung
Anton Hamscher
Johannes Lotz

[Endorsed:]
Qualifications of Palatines 25th Octr 1748, imported in the Ship Patience, Capt. John Govan.

[List 123 C] At the Courthouse at Philadelphia, 25, 8br. 1748.
Present: The Honoble Benjm Shoemaker, Samuel Hasell, Esqrs.
The Foreigners whose Names are underwritten, imported in the Ship Patience & Margaret, John Govan, Capt, from Rot-

terdam, but last from Leith in Scotland, did this day take the usual Oaths to the Government.

Johann Nicolas Korndörfer *
Ludwig Pflüger
Carl Balthasar Kern
Johann Peter Veith
Johann Henrich Pful
Henry (X) Knobloch
Dietdrich Reinharth
Philip (F) Zimmer
Andreas (A) Spieller
Johann Ludwig Seeman
Henry (H) Seeman
Friedrich Sponheimer
Michel Bihl
Johan Peter (H) Nay
Johann Jacob Matthias
Johannes Keller
Johann Adam Göbel
Christian Hahn
Johannes Kneist
Johannes Lantz
Jonas Dietz
Johannes Michael Dietz
Richart (R) Langer
Jacob (X) Löffner
Johann Diel Wentz
George Henry (O) Fuchs
Peter Strohl
Johannes Meininger
Hannes Klein
Johann Peter Han
Johann Friderich Geiger
Jan Gottfried Soy
Johann Adam Schneider

Johann Michael Deyerling
Johann Henrich Bretheich
Johann Philips Schmäck
Johann Georg Schad
Johann Melchior Kräuter
Johan Peter (X) Galler
Gottfried Premauer
Wilhelm (X) Wagner
Baltzer Fleischer
Henrich Krapff
Petter Schmid
Eckerlle Gackbach
Jacob Emrich
Johan Nicol Polch
Jacob (+) Landes
Johann Michael Reichart
Andonius Brost
Balzar (X) Shwab
Johan Matteas (MG) Gele
Jacob (X) Overkirsh
Michael (X) Overkirsh
Henrich Conver
Johann Casper Prach
Friedrich Maus
Henrich Busch
Hannes Busch
Johann Jacob Hardt
Johannes Unverzagt
Wendal (X) Keeffer
Johann Nickel Jung
Anton Hamscher
Johannes Lotz

---

* John Nicolas Korndörfer was a Reformed schoolmaster. He taught first in the schoolhouse in Marlborough township, Montgomery County, later at Boehm's Church, Blue Bell. He died in the fall of 1800. His account book is still preserved. It is published in the *Perkiomen Region*, vol. I, (1922), pp. 104–108.

[List 124 C] At the Court House at Philadelphia, Thursday the 24th Day of August 1749.

Present: Samuel Hassell,
Robert Strettell } Esquires
Joshua Maddox,

The Foreigners whose Names are underwritten, imported in the Ship Elliot, Captain James Adams, from Rotterdam, but the last from Cowes in England, did this day take the usual Qualifications to the Government. Palatines. By List 87. Souls 240.

Peter (X) Räsh
Gottlieb Schwartz
Friederich Christian
Johan Friedrich Boserman
Johann Görg Wien
Jacob (+) Hoffman
Richart (X) Hoffman
Johan Jost Kreuscher
Anthon Wolff
Johan Vihlib Jantz
Carlen Helwig
Johann Georg Bernhardt
Conrad Henrich Eckhard
Gerg Petter Beisel
Johan Martin Hoffman
Johan Martin Busch
Johan Henrich Breis
Johann (X) Strohshneider
Gottlieb Löfler
Philipp Vorbach
Jacob Arenth
Mattheus Vorbach
Peter (+) Buth
Peter (+) Hop
Conrad (X) Wysner
Johann Georg Kitz
Johannes Jonas
Engel Jonas
Philibs Kreischer
John Nicklas (X) Kreisher

Carl Ludwigh Stumb
Johann Paul Bus
Jacob (X) Kirch
Nicklas (X) Necum
Nickel Nickom, Senr
Peter (X) Nickum
Johannes Jakob
Johann Jacob Jacoby
Johann Philip Biehl
Johannes Staudter
Johan Anthon Simon
Johann Filip Preidenbach
Johann Görg Blume
Michel Jost
John Nicolas (+) Price
Johannes (+) Preice
Nicklas Hasselbach
Johan Jacob Gasser
Christoph Samuel Bildman
Conrat Gebhart
John George (X) Rymisnus
Cunradt Lenner
Hans George (X) Haas
Johann Jacob Mertz
Johannes Degen
Johann Nickel Lang
Jacob (X) Fritz
Jonas Heyl
Peter (X) Kleim
Jacob Baum

Johanes Jerg Schmucker
Henrich Anthon König
Johann Peter Tressler
Joh. Reinhart Shwein
Johann Daniel Miller
Jacob Christian Gleim
Phlippus Wilsenlehr
Herman Beltz
Johannes Philips Peiffer
Georg Adam Gossler
Johann Conradt Gontzler
Johannes Bintzel

Johannes (✕) Heydenreyd
Peter Marckert
Philip (+) Windermeyer
Anthon (+) Windermeyer
Simon (✕) Franckenfelt
Johann Adam Geyer
George Paul (✕) Geyer
Georg Friederich (✕) Küper
Joh. Georg (✕) Foster
Andreas Wolf
Johann Caspar Grasmuck
Johann Martin Berntheusel

[List 125 C] At the Court House at Philadelphia, Wednesday, 30ᵗʰ August, 1749.
Present: The Honourable James Hamilton, Esquire, Govʳ, Joshua Maddox, Esquire.
The Foreigners whose Names are underwritten, imported in the Ship Crown, Michael James, Master, from Rotterdam and last from Cowes in England, did this day take the usual Qualifications to the Government. Switzers p. List 134. Nº 500 or 476.

Hans Jacob (+) Markly
Hans George (✕) Markly
Hans (+) Markly
Claus Berschman
Hans (✕) Erbe
Martin (✕) Weaber
Hans Heinig
Jacob Groff
Hans Peter Groff
Hans Grof
Hans Ullrich Fahr
Henrich Seil
Jacob (✕) Sally
Jacob (✕) Ruber
Johannes Tschudi
Heinrich Buser
Samuel Neueschwander
Friederich (✕) Bruker
Michel Bieler

Nickel Danner
Heinrich Buser
Jacob Sterenfels
Hans Weber, Senior
Hans (✕) Weber, Junior
Heinrich Stahr
Fillib Schmid
Mathis Hubly
Hans Jacob (✕) Ställy
Joh. Emanuel (✕) Pfiffer
Hans (✕) Hawly
Durst (✕) Hawly
Mardin Grun
Mardi Meierhofer
Jacob Giesi
Durst Duren
Martin Tschudi
Jacob Schweitzer
Reinhart Guntzenhauser

Hans Gumler

Hans Jacob (X) Blonk

Martin ( ) Gosh, sick *

Hans ( ) Messnar, sick

Johannes Tschuti

Henry (XX) Garster

Friederick (++) Swonder

Jacob Seiler

Adam ( ) Browbak, Senior

Adam ( ) Browbak, Junior

Jacob (X) Shootin

Heinr. Brobeck

Martin (X) Walleset

Jacob (X) Weisener

Hans Stohler

Baltzar (X) Strowma

Martin (X) Seyler

Jacob Roher

Hans Stohler

Hans Flubecher

Johanes (X) Shitzer

Allexander Danner

Ernst Enders

Yoch. Rudi

Hans Ullrich Ehrensperger

Hans (X) Madery

Adam (X) Weybol

Jacob Weibel

Philip (X) Omme[n]

Durst Ammen

Henry (X) Handshy

Lenhart (X) Booser

Christoffel Seiller

Matheas (X) Seyler

Marte Schneider

Hans (X) Sholtes

George ( ) Sholtes, sick

Hans (X) Busser

Jacob (X) Domme

Heinrich Thomen

Adam Thommen

Hans Jacob (+) Hasler

Hans Jacob Gass

Jacob (X) Wallsener

Daniel (X) Messerly

Hans Jacob (X) Massener

Lorentz (+) Morty

Johannes Marti

Hans Jacob Honegger

Martin Dättwyler

Hans (+) Mesemer

Hans Degen

Henry (+) Leeby

Daniel Lüdin

Jacob Tschopp

Henry (X) Bruner

Hans Jacob (+) Zaller

Heinrich Schneider

Martin (+) Tchop

Johannes Seiler

Hans Ullrich Mösmer

Friter Lytzler

Hans Georg Reininger

Hans Rude Brobeck

Stephen ( ) Spenhover, sick

Hans Lüke

Jacob Hassler

Henry (X) Shaffner

Berhart (X) Romstein

Sepastian (X) Hassler

Hans Jacob (+) Greenblat

Martin (X) Greenblat

Christoff (+) Weeslin

Jacob ( ) Wurtz, sick

Jacob Grimler

Linnert Hey

Matheas (X) Spitler, Senior

Hans Jacob (X) Spitler

Martin (X) Spitler

Matheas (+) Spitler, Junior

* Absent, name signed by Clerk of Court.

Hans (   ) Graver, sick
Hans Greber
Nicklaus Dill
Johannes (✕) Meyer
Johan Lutwig Buda
Jacob (   ) Furman, sick
Conrat Zigler
Peter (✕) Ziegler

Andereas (✕) Donner
Mardin Herbster
Heinerich Buda
Uhllerich (✕) Feeller
Hans Jacob (✕) Frawinger
Johannes Nicolaus Macholt
Abram (✕) Houser
Nicklas (✕) Makhold

[List 126 C] At the Court House in Philadelphia, Saturday the 2ᵈ Septʳ 1749.

Present: The Honourable James Hamilton, Esquire, Governor, Robert Strettell.

The Foreigners whose names are underwritten, imported in the Ship Chesterfield, Thomas Coatam, Master, from Rotterdam, and last from Cowes in England, did this day take the usual Qualifications to the Government. By List 86. Nᵒ Persons 255. Wirtumbergers.

Hans Jacob Albrecht
Gallus Gulden
Balthasar Mäuerle
Johannes Maurer
Jacob Schlotterer
Joseph Speidel
Martin Schauwecker
Hans Cunrad Schauwecker
Martin Schlotterer
Jacob Schlotterer
Pips Gorg Müller
Johannes (HK) Keller
Hans Michael Lätterche
Jaques Moris
Hans Conradt Katz
Johanes (   ) Meyer, sick
Bastian (   ) Meyer, sick
Martin (✕) Waghter
Fridrich Gosner
Maximilianus Speidel
Hans Jorg Speidel
Johann Jacob Kies

Frantz Schwitzer
Nicolaus Reyer
Salomon Gansel
Jacob Reyer
Jacob Gast
Christian Räpple
Jacob Aller
Jacob Deible
Martin (M) Schooler
George (✕) Limbert
Martin (M) Getz
Hanns Uhllerik (   ) Suller, sick
George Jäckel
Losker Meyer
Johann Martin Beck
Balthas Zimmermann
Jacob Scheufler
Jacob Klotz
Jacob (   ) Klotz, sick
Hans Leonhardt Klotz
Gottfriedt Pusch
Elias Steeb

Michael Steb
Hans Nistucher [?]
Calfing [?] Wundend [?]
Werner (✕) Souder
Johannes Henche
Simon Hendche
Josep Seitz
Ludwig König
Ludwig König
Friech Seytter
Adam Wanner
Johannes Klein
Joseph Hiller
Mathies Schlotterer
Johann Conradt Schlotterer
Michael Pfrang
Michel Kirbe
Hans Christ Beuthler
Jacob Metzger
Hans Jerg Closse
Hanns Jerch Haisch
Christoph Gross

Simon Schmidt
Christop Schäffer
Conrad Rattenauer
Hans Eberhard
Johan Marti Hayns
Baltas Mayer
Matthias Lautenschläger
Mich. Tompprätz
Jacob Reinthaler
Elias Eberhardt
Lind Hoch
Joseph Eckert
George Friedrich (✕) Fisher
Hans Jacob Herr
Hans Jerg Hanselmann
Jacob Hauch
Johann Georg Weiss
Johan Michael (M) Christman
Philipp Kübler
Michal Stierlen
Conrad Wolf

[List 127 C] At the Courthouse at Philadelphia, Saturday,
2ᵈ Sept. 1749.

Present: Thomas Graeme ⎫ Esquires.
       Wm. Allen ⎭

The Foreigners whose Names are underwritten, imported
in the Ship Albany, Robert Brown, Master, from Rotterdam,
but last from Cowes in England, did this day take the usual
Oaths to the Government. By the List 108. Number of Souls
285, from Erpacht [Erbach] and Wirtemberg.

Johann Nicolaus Chonrath
Johannes Schimpf
Johannes Garber
John Philip (✕) Beyer
Johan Henrich Mötths
Johan Balthasar Hetzler

Johan Gerg Kraff
Friedrich Götzinger
Johan Michel Kabel
Johan Michael ( ) Kabel, sick
Hans ( ) Cabel, sick *
George (✕) Schwartz

* The signatures with parentheses enclosing blank spaces were written by
the Clerk of Court. They represent absent immigrants.

Hanns Petter Gembler

Hans Michael (×) Gembler

Johann Henrich Blumenschein

Johann Peter Winckler

Nickel Heist

Johann Peter Heist

Johan Philip Heist

George Adam (×) Ewald

Matheas (×) Shoenk

Vallentin (×) Edelman

Hans Peter (×) Edelman

Hans (×) Redman

Georg (×) Truke

Johann Philips Jaxthemer

Wendel Schnorr

Hans Jacob Wagner

Johann Christoph Kintzinger

Michel Beul

Joseph Scholl

Johannes Grauer

Christoph (×) Nutts

Johannes Buchter

Johannes Nibling

Hanns Jerg Fischer

Johann Martin Schuck

Jeorg Michael ( ) Herould, sick

Hans Martin (O) Strein

Hans Georg Dreher

Hans Gerg Edelman

Adam Etelman

Johann Willhelm Volck

Godlib (×) Volcke

Andereas (×) Welker

Johann Jacob Joh

Johann Adam Joh

Johan Petter Hörg

Johann Michel Joh

Hans Petter Jotter

Johanis Jotter

Hans Conradt Rörich

Augustinus Gintner

Johann Jerg Menges

Peter (×) Shäffer

Casper Walser

Matheus Nunnenmacher

Johann Adam Heckman

Frederick (+) Lewy

Hans George (××) Nagel

Hans Baltaser ( ) Shaffer, sick

Johannes Häckman

Peter ( ) Edelman, sick

Johan Willem Süster

Johanes Müller

Adam Lunck

Hans George ( ) Hochzig, sick

J. Nicklas (×) Delp

Johann Zacharias Erdroth [?]

Johann Georg Schäfer

J. Leonhart (×) Meyer

Johann Jerg Dressler

Hans Adam (×) Peetsh

Johann Antoni Walther

Philip Lautenschleger

Phil. Jacob (×) Kreysh

Johanes (×) Graber

Hann Philip Krichbaum

Christoffel (×) Nagel

Johann Adamm Gorm[an]

Peter (×) Brunner

Johann Adam Hotz

Johan Leohnhart German

Adam (×) German

Adam Geissiger

Adam (×) Laudenshlager

Johan Philip Gross

Johanes (O) Klinger

Mardin Rausch

J. Baltasar (×) Jegel

J. George (×) Folck

Valtin Schuck

Georg Michael Frantz

Martin Schäffer
Peter (O) Kill
Philipp Jacob Walther
Alexander Klinger
Nickolaus Beisell
Conrath Menges

Johann Adam Krichbaum
J. Adam (X) Rieffwey
Johan Wilhelm Krichbaum
Johan Adam Rausch
Peter Brunner
Johan Gorg Rettig

[List 128 C] At the Statehouse at Philadelphia, Saturday, the 9th Septr 1749.
Present: The Honourable, the Governor.
The Foreigners whose Names are underwritten, imported in the Ship Saint Andrew, James Abercrombie, Master, from Rotterdam, but last from Plymouth in England, did this day take the usual Qualifications to the Government. By the List 111. Persons 400 Palatines.

Andreas Emmert
Josef Bergtohlt
Arnold (X) Kramer
Johannes Knebel [?]
Johannes (X) Runkel
Henry (X) Hamer
Adam Hinnborger
Jost Streithoff
Jacob (X) Linke
Christian Halte
Peter (+) Bawman
Jacob Rohr
Peter Finger
Christian Graff
Ullrich Ellenberger
Peter Ellenberger
Christian Stauffer
Johann Friedrich Emrich
Isac Schnebeli
Johannes Rohr
Johanes (W) Woosing
Benedick Mellinger
Michael Wagner
Samuehl Kauffman

Christian (X) Hasseler
Hans Rudy Frey
Jacob Hertzler
Jacob Hertzler
Hans Dierstein
Christian Eschbacher
Casber Herschberger
Jacob Herschberger
Johan Georg Vallendin
Hans Michael Vallendin
Johannes (X) Flickesterver
Ullrich Flickstörfer
Jacob Maschberger, Junior
Jacob (J) Mashberger, Senior
Johann Henricus Wenig
Johann Jacob Küblinger
Johann Daniel Küblinger
Johannes Böhmer
Peter (X) Sterneman
Marcus (X) Gruel
Nicholaus Post
Jacob Kern
Johanes (X) Haan
Johann Peter Bach

Jacob Leydig

Christoph Weber

Samuel (✕) Meyer

Leonhart Kessler

Johan Petter Druck

Friederig Neuhoff

Petter Ihrig

Jacob Brandt

Johannes Berr

Ullrich Staufert

Daniel Staufer

Daniel Berr

Johann Friederich Bohr

Andreas Keller

Andreas Keller

Henrich Caspar Racke

Jacob Friedrich Debertshäuser

Johannes Corell

Johann Engelbert Morgenstern

Peter Willhelm

Cunradt Hoffmann

Balser Weinberger

Frans Jans

Christian Hirschberger

Johan Kuns Heisler

Conradt Stichter

Vallentin (✕) Stitter

Johann Wilhelm Franck

Ulerich Hackmann

Henry (✕) Stawffer

Aberham Brübacher

Johannes Walder

Johan Adam Stahler

Johann Conradt Seybel

Jacob Herbig

Hans George (H) Garner

Johan Henrich Gerndt

Valenthein Haag

Johannes Mellinger

Jacob (✕) Eshelman

Johannes Jung

Johannes Funck

Christian Eschbacher

Christian (W) Wenger

Hannes Wenger

Johanes Brubbacher

Peder Eschelmann

Jacob Eimann

Christian (✕) Frisch

Martin Spreng

Adam Helwig

Johannes Eppelmann

Hans Jacob (+) Weyse

Johann Adam Dörr

Hermanus Heger

Johannes Huth

Peter Ahles

Simon Zeherman

Johann Peter Krämer

Christoffel (+) Henzy

Jacob Weiss, Senior

Matheas (✕) Weise

George (✕) Shambach

Johannes Hackman

Ullrich Jordte

Henrich Stauffer

Uhellerich (+) Stover

Hans George (✕) Hobler

[List 129 C] At the Court House at Philadelphia, Monday, the 11th Septr 1749.

Present: Joshua Maddox, Esquire.

The Foreigners whose names are underwritten, imported in the Priscilla, Captn William Muir, from Rotterdam, and last from Cowes in England, did this day take the usual Oaths to the Government. By list 77. Persons 293.

Jacob Baumann
Heinrich Lien
Johannes Kraun
Johannes (O) Miller
Rudolf Bär
Henry (HB) Barr
Heynrich Huber
Johannis Bär
Melchior (O) Leeder
Heinrich Kunst
Heinrich Wollenweider
Jacob Stehli
Hans Merky
Hans (X) Surber
Hans George (X) Isseller
Muller Heinrich
Hans (X) Schneibly
Jacob Gütinger
Jorg [?] Funk
Ullry Hoffecker
Johan Reinhardt Uhl
Johannes Wiss
Rudolf Huber
Jacob Huber
Jacob Bär
Ullrich Hauber
Caspar Pfister
Mades Gallman
Hans Rudolph (X) Gallman
Hans Jacob (M) Meyer
Rudolf Näff
Jacob Näff
Hans Jacob Gubler
Kasper Huber
Henry Huber
Rudy Kuntz
Jacob ( ) Kuntz, sick

Hans Kern
Jacob (X) Mawer
Rudy (X) Mawer
Jacob Hauser
Jacob Folenweider
Hans Hoffecker
Lienhart Scherer
Jacob (X) Shnabely
Jacob (X) Bart
Friederich (F) Shurp
Johanes (X) Shurp
Paulus Schorb
Johann Philiphs Mülhoff
John Peter (X) Mühlhoff
Nickel Peteri
Johann Mich. Boor
Johan Nichl. Lorentz
Michael (+) Franck
Johann Peter Franck
Friederich Stroh
Johann Ludwig Küstner
Johann Philipps Küstner
George Piter (X) Dürr
Johann Jacob Walther
Johan Heinrich Geiger
Johann Friterich Fruschthi
Johann Nickel Göbel
Johannes Michael Malchior
Johann Mattes Borr
Johann Adam Bohr
Johannes Mattes Ströher
Johannes Nicklaus Wedertz
Johannes Mattes Becker
Johan Nickel Neu
Johan Adam Neu
Johan Peter Müller
Henrich Rutschi

Hans (×) Zubler   Henry (×) Meyer
Johan Burkhart Hoffman

[List 130 C] At the Court House at Philadelphia, Wednesday, the 13th 7ber 1749.
                    Present: Joshua Maddox, Esquire.

The Foreigners whose Names are underwritten, imported in the Ship Christian, Captn Thomas Brady, from Rotterdam, but last from Cowes in England, did this day take the usual Oaths to the Government. By List 111. In all 300 [?] [persons] from Wirtemberg, Alsace, Zweybrecht.

Fridrich Gelbach

Frantz (O) Gelbach

Friederich (O) Gelbach

Paulus Brod

Andreas Vogel

Johann Andreas Dresler

Hs. Jacob Schumacher

Hans Jacob Stratz

Hans Adam Hockner

Friederich (O) Erb

Vallentin (O) Kern

Christof Ludtwig

George Ludwig (+) Burg

Ernst Munckel

Heinrich Albrecht

Frantz Ziegler, Senior

Frantz (×) Ziegler, Junior

Beniamin Cuny

Veltin Dellinger

Johannes Mitschler

Martin Bernhart

Julius Christoph Bachman

Hans Jerg Michele

Johann Georg Lang

Johan George (×) Erig

Johannes Schäffer

Johann Caspar Geissinger

Johann Ludwig Bäuerle

Andoni Schneck

Daniel (D) Altik

Johann Philipp Hornn

Willhelm (+) Höltz

Michael (M) Shoemaker

Joseph (+) Ressener

Ludwig Mäintzger

Johan Philb Henrich Sauer

Georg Michel Derr

Georg Lenhardt Braun

Andereas Braun

Georg Michael Braun

Karl Nolden

Philip (×) Kaupt

Johann Anderas Weckesser

Johann Jacob Datisman

George (×) Hummel

Jacob Hieman

David Pfautz

Michael Hauff

Carl Goss

Weybegt Rupp

Martin Schlachenhauff

Michael Hechelman

Johann Michael Mayer

Christian (×) Romich

Hans Jorg Haffer

Hans Jerg Feucht

Hans Jerg Schumacher

Michell Haupt

Johanes (X) Tilly
Matdes Osterdag, Senior
Matheas (X) Osterdag
Johans Michael Sommer
Johan Albrecht (X) Eshelman
Abraham Selman
Michael (X) Rummel
Johan (X) Ehrhart
Hans Georg (+) Unangst
Hans Jacob (X) Uber
Balzazar (Bals) Glisser
Willhelm (X) Heyshe
Mardin Danner
Hans Jerg Merckly
Conradt Bosch
Matheis Weiss
Joseph Schmith
Jacob Risterholtz
Christian Limbacher
Johann Georg Limbacher
Johann Adam Ebert
Johann Jacob Sinn
Johannes Reuter
Jacob Wälckly
Isaac Jung
Christian Osterdag

Balthasar Dock
Peter Goscha
Johannes Schmerber
Samuel Moser
Hans Peter Jung
Hans Beder Ribeled
Jacob Ribelet
Johann Nicolaus Koch
Abraham Ribellet
Thomas (D) Hull
Henrich Dock
Christian Eichart
Johann Jacob Banutz
Christian Glässer
Hans Meck
Peter (X) Hamman
Michael (X) Houswird
Fillib Kugler
Antony Eki
Jacob Rummel
Johan Erhard Knappenberger
Christian (X) Gutknecht
Martin Hirsch
Bernhart (X) Shweighart
Hans Adam Krieger

[List 131 C] At the Court House at Philadelphia, Thursday, the 14th Septr 1749.

Present: Benjm Shoemaker, } Esquires.
Joshua Maddox,

The Foreigners whose Names are underwritten, imported in the Ship Two Brothers, Thomas Arnot, Master, from Rotterdam, & last from Cowes in England, did this day take & subscribe the usual Oaths to the Government. By List 105. 312 Persons, from the Electorate Palatine & Triers.

Johann Gerhard Schneyder
Weigand Schneider
Johann Deis Schneider
Johannes Petter Schneyder

Johan Peter (X) Shneyder
Christian (X) Humbold
Jacob Gruber
Wilhelmus Jacobus Gruber

Johan Konrath Refi
Teys (X) Refy
Adam Hennrich Prentz
Johannes Hermanus
Michael (X) Reyffener
Petter Reiffner
Henry (XX) Wagner
Johan Henry (X) Wagner
Petter Amms [?]
Philibbus Löhr
Hans Peter (X) Lehr
Johannes Oseler
Joh. Jost Blecher
Johan Peter (X) Miller
Johann Herman Niss
Johan Jost Fiessler
Johann Peter Holpasch
Johan Haubrich Löhr
Johan Peter (H) Lay
Johann Christ. Böhmer
Johann Peter Böhmer
Christian (X) Birkingbey
Johan Albert Stecker
Wilhelmus Strickhauschen
Jacob Cambeck
Johan Jost (S) Shäffer
Wilhelm Pfeiffer
Johannes Henrich Hoffman
Johann Henrich Fuchs
Johannes Henrich Schmit
Johan Adam Fucks
Johan (X) Beisbeker
Jeorge Jacob (X) Wird
Christian Matheis Göbeler
Johan Henrich Keuler
Johan Phillippus Sauer
Johan Peter Lupp
Petter Humrich
Simon Höller
Johan Filibus Le[......]
Johannes Ernst Krämer

Johan (X) Venusbaker
Johann Balthasar Schiedt
Henry (X) Weller
Friederich Gottfried Schmidt
Johan Balthasar (X) Shmit
Johann Christ Klein
Johan Peder Schönman
Johan Christoph Ullrich
Johan Martin Schmitgen
Johan Adam Schmitgen
Johann Ludwig Spiess
Johann Wilhelm Mallert
Johann Mardin Gress
Johannes Ernst Greis
Mattheas (X) Trawn
Johannes Cobus Hoffman
Wilhelm Kusche [?]
Johannes Böhmer
Ernst Schäffer
Wilhelmus Dietz
Johannes Petter Jung
Johan Adam (X) Jung
Matheas (O) Baker
Johann Philippus Becker
Johan Adam Becker
Johann Christ Badenhainer
Johann Peter Aller
Johan Petter Braun
Johann Petter Hess
Christian Steltz
Johan Jacob Carl
Johannes Diewes
Johan Georg Schultz
Johanes Petter Du[....]
Bastian Braun
Johan Dheis Dunschman
Johan (X) Säger
Johann Jacob Homer
Willhelm (X) Helt
Johan Deys Rüb
Johan Christ Rüb

Johann Michael Gesel
Ernst Becker
Michel Duenschman
Johann Jullus Schick
Johann Wilhelm Schmidt
Johan Wilhelm Jäger
Johan Peter Rath
Johann Christ Schneyder
Johan Adam (X) Gemmer
Christoff (O) Lenhart

Johannes Petter Seyn
Joachim Henn
Johannes Küm
Henrickes Schmig
Johan Wilm Jung
Johan Deis Bäcker
Christian (Bek) Becker
Johann Peter Schaaff
Johan Peter (X) Miller

[List 132 C] At the Court House at Philadelphia, Friday the 15th 7ber 1749.
Present: Joshua Maddox, Esquire.

The Foreigners whose names are underwritten, imported in the Ship Edinburgh, James Russel, Master, from Rotterdam, but last from Portsmouth in England, did this day take the usual Oaths to the Government. By list 163. 360 whole Freights, from the Palatinate.

Abraham Jung
Peter Lang
Henrich Conrad
George (X) Conrad
Johan Fridrich Dietz
Johannes Schmidt
Philip (P) Mertz
Herman Mauer
John Philip (X) Hanne
Jeremias Bär
Johan Jacob Becker
Philib Peter Becker
Nicklas (X) Biedman
Daniel (DS) Sheimer
Fritrich Scheimer
Michell Scheymer
Johann Daniel Roller
Johann Hennrich Lang
Johann Philip Dick
Johann Friedrich Martin
Vallentin Hembelman

Vallentin Scherrer
Johan Connrad Lutz
Henrich Mindel
Johann Jerg Meundel
Adam (X) Lambe
Christoph Lambert
Philib Diehl
Hannes Spicker
Julius Spicker
Johannes Bauer
Friderich Klärr
Peter (P) Laub
Jacob Hamman
Gorg Fengel
Johann Jacob Schäffer
Peter Küwit
Johannes Rüdinger
Hannes Senffelder
Walter (X) Shmid
Johann Henrich Scheidt
Vallentin Geil

Jacob Wirth
Adam Bauer
Valtin Petry
Andon Scheimer
Johannes Scheimer [?]
Johannes Laudenschlager
Johannes Schneider
Geörg Wacker
Michel Wacker
Johannes Jorg Steiner
Christof Neidlein
Adam (O) Gross
George Henry (R) Rissler
Andreas Stein
Peter Tamerus
Bernhart Scherer
Lorens Scherer
Fridrich Schwob
Stephan (X) Shwerber
Wilhelm (X) Shwerber
Dewalt Schmühl
Samuel Kerch
Jacob Kerch
Nickel Renner
Michel Pens
Stofel Schuhman
John Georg (X) Hindershit
Filip Metzger
Henrich Schmidt
Michael (H) Mauerer
Christian (A) Shmit
Lotharus Pfannenbecker
Nickolas (X) Seltzer
Conrad Knepper
Johan Peter Geis
Johann Adam
Andereas (X) Bieber
Jacob (X) Bieber
Hans Jacob Tamesi
Frantz Nicolaus Faber
Henrich Faber

Johan (X) Buchhamer
Nicklas Rauh
Erasmus Stockius
Christian Axer
Johann Niclas Fellenberger
Madheis Bolland
Stephan Beyer
Christoph Gedeon Myrtetus
Fillipp Dinges
Frantz (O) Hartman
Nicolaus Eisenmänger
Jacob Klein
Johann Jerg Klein
Simon Charmely
Johan Jacob Dästerr
Jorg Michel Mauer
Philip (X) Bucke
Jurg Friederich (S) Siel
Andony Hargesheimer
Michel Hargesheimer
Peter Brauns
Philip (O) Rickhart
Henry (H) Shmit
Jacob (X) Zerel
Johan Wilhelm Schreiner
Johannes Dietz
Jacob Zinn
Jacob Pfannkuchen
Simon Hörch
Conrath Schweitzer
Johannes (H) Althous
Erasmus (+) Althous
Carl Siver
Andon Kirchhart
Bennedictus Dhom
Christophel Klärr
Johannes Von der Lindt
Johann Michel Lawall
Jacob Becker
Jacob Brubacher
Christian Eygr

Johanes (HB) Bender
Henry (+) Bender, Junr
Wendel Essig
Friderich Dick
Johann Jacob Sachs
Johann Michel König
Johanickel Schafer
Conrad (O) Miller
Nicklas (+) Grusius
Jacob Kulman
Johann Walther Schwob
Fritz (F) Shäffer
Johann Wilhelm Pfeil
Johann Gerlach Huhn
Johann Daniel Huhn
Jacob Mohr
Gerlach Strich
Samuel Neitlinger

Friederich Zerfass
Jacob (OO) Goodman
Philip (O) Goodman
Jörg Ranck
Christian Bernhart
Henry (X) Zoll
Henry (X) Marsh
Johann Martin Neubecker
Jacob (+) Hottebach
Joh. Michel Hoffman
Johannes Alder
Bastian (X) Wenig
Johann Jacob Kopp
Johan Peter Weier
Johannes Fritz
John (X) Shermillin
Henry (X) Steinmetz
Friederich Conradt

[List 133 C] At the Court House at Philadelphia, Friday, the 15th Septr 1749.

Present: Joshua Maddox, Esquire.

The Foreigners whose Names are underwritten, imported in the Ship Phoenix, John Mason, Master, from Rotterdam, but last from Cowes in England, did this day take the usual Qualifications to the government. By the List 261. 550 whole Freights, from Zweybrech, Nassau, Wirtemberg, & Palatinate.

Samuel (W) Votring
Georg Caspar Heuss
Hans Ullrich Ott
Caspar (X) Bruner
Jurg Wanenmacher
Johann Ludwig Strauss
Andereas (O) Creiner
Samuel Wannemacher
Joseph Kauffman
Jörg Frantz Philippi
Hans Goerg Weidenauer
Hans Nickel Ott

Hans Adam Baus
Henrich Luta
Hans Petter Roesser
Jerg Adolph Kröber
Georg Härther
Jacob Anthoni
Nicklas (X) Roath
Nicklas (R) Riksaker
Hans Lenart (O) Hinkel
John Georg (X) Shneyder
Andereas (X) Tevental
Simon (X) Walter

J. Rudolph (+) Ginder
Johann Jacob Mestenbach
Johannes Gross
Conrath Jost
Abraham (O) Nonnamacker
Jacob Schneider
Jacob Messerli
Hans Jörg Cleis
Joseph Han
Henrich Ginder
Michael (×) Traxel
George (×) Traxel
Bernard (×) Traxel
Henry (+) Mitshit
John Jacob (×) Mitshit
Dewald (×) Steker
Peter (O) Gerrett
Uhllerik (×) Stoller
Johann Michel Schmidteknecht
Jorg Altman
Anthon Altman
Hans Peter Eichede
Hans Philipus Birson
Salmon (×) Bacher
Theobald Kuntz
Hans Georg (O) Isseman
Ja. Nicklas (×) Isseman
Petder Eisenmann
Petder Eisenmann
Michel Köppel
Johan Nickel Köppel
Jacob (K) Keppel
Niclaus Schnyder
Paulus Köppel
Henrich Köppell
Petter Keppel
Petter Isch
Jacob Altman
Wilhelm Altman
Hans Johann Bonnewitz [?]
Hans Görg Jundt

Cristof Brunner
Daniel (×) Duval
Johan (×) Dugrave
Daniel (×) Darm
Johann Michael Mallo
John Fried^k (×) Hister
Henrich Wilhelm Mählich
Max Myrs [?]
Samuel (×) Dormeyer
Jacob (×) Dormeyer
J. Lutwig
Hans Jacob (×) Witmer
Henry (×) Shaaff
Moritz Klein
Jacob (×) Klein
Frantz Jacob Kühl
Johannes Hort
Andereas (×) Create
Anders Grett
Johanes (×) Creat
Jerg Müller
Philip (+) Miller
John Nicklas (+) Miller
Jeremias Schönbach
Jacob Zollicker
Nicola Dilon
Adam (×) Grantadam
Joseph Chartier
Humber Benoit
Johan George (+) Acker
Joseph Courteuer
Beter Springer
Hans Jerg Springer
Jacob Schneider
Michael (×) Nike
Jacob Nike
Abraham Scherdrong
Mattheus Kersch
Johann Georg Mölig
Johann Reinhart Keller
Herman (++) Latur

Jacob Latur
Marx (O) Springel
Christian (X) Creeste
Conrad Wohlfahrt
Andres Rutsiele
Jacob Laudermilch
Ulerich Seltzer
Johanes (H) Gross
Daniel Groberger
Christoffel Reyer
Frantz (X) Soal
François Grandadam
Felix Kley
Hans (X) Reese
Michael (X) Shaffer
Henrich Lutter
Philip (O) Lance
Bastian Weiss
Nicklas Bab
Johan Adam (W) Walter
Jacob (X) Walter
Martin (X) Walter
Johan Matheas (X) Shoeman
Johan (X) Bender
Willhelm (+) Longhaar
Anthony (+) Nieve
Christian (+) Tathower
Christian Brost
Simon (X) Roorig
Johanes (+) Roorig
Johanes (X) Geeber
Donius (X) Roorig
Anthoni Biber
Jacob Bieber
Hans Nickel Bieber
Jacob (+) Jonger
Samuel (H) Spiger
Hans Adam (+) Herman
Stephan (X) Alman
Samuel (+) Perquy
Hannes Miller

Jacob Schmit
Jacob Widmer
Hans Sälli
Hans Meier
Uhllerick (U) Kindlishberger
Johannes Weller
Johannes Lamot
Johanes (+) Bouchy
Jacob (M) Miller
Christen Fischer
Christian (+) Miller
Peter (+) Miller
Nicolaus (ND) Dartwiller
Daniel Dörtweiler
Martin (X) Dartwiller
Johanes (X) Keeffer
Michael Vüsel
Petter Rott
Hans Strubhar
Christoph (O) Spanler
Jacob (X) Misseler
Josep Mischle
Jacob Seiler
Christian Staufer
Hans George (X) Springer
Michael (Dor) Dormeyer
Jacob Klein
Abraham Drachsel
Durst (O) Deretinger
Benedict (B) Leman
Martin (+) Ritter
Hans Bortz
Hans Jacob Hörnlin
Antoni Stratzer
Davit (O) Miller
Jacob Has
Johan Georg Steinrock
Simon Digler
Jacob Gratze
Jacob Hueber
Anton (+) Beavenan

François Hognon
Johann Michael Steng
Peter Kaufman
Johannes Michal Heller
Friederich Wohlfarth
Hans George (X) Keen
Hann Filb Grünewalt
Johannes Kiehn
Felix (+) Sailor
Sebastian Bissahr
Jörg Bentz
Johann Ludwig Bentz
Jacob (+) Bence
Christian (+) Hartman
Frantz (+) Marshall
Christian Schowalder
Johns Sumer
Christian (+) Summer
Matheis Nafzger
Johanes Farner
Rudolf Nafzger
Christian (O) Kauffman
Jacob Kauffmann
Johannes Lans
Peter (+) Crapy
Jacob Stauch
Hans Jerg Stauch
Abraham Kurtz
Beder von Gumeden
Johannes Rupp
Jacob (X) Rupp
Peter (+) Nafsker
Georg Christian Sim
Christian Kurtz
Jan Hendrik Reckman

Erhart (X) Bom
Theobalt Hoschar
Hans Petter Hoscharr
Henrich Hoschar
Philip (X) Henkel
Johanes (O) Reber
Daniel (X) Rynolle
Andre de Grange
Görg Hertzog
Görg Hertzog, Junior
Kilian Zimmerman
Peter Obersteg
Michael (O) Ridelsberg
Christian (H) Hochstätter
Nicklaus Hochstätter
Johannes Schrandeman
Ulrich Hostetter
Simeon Steckel
Hans Schrantz
Ullrich Ritschart
Ullrich Mischler
Conrad (W) Wagner
Matheas (M) Seygor
Peter (E) Herb
Lutwig Eerlman
Hans Nickel Meyer
Jost Meyer
Jacob (X) Mann
Martin Obersteg
Caspar Frettler
Cunrath Altboter
Frantz Griebel
Johann Michael Walker
Johann Lutwig Gribeler

[List 134 C] At the Court House at Philadelphia, Sunday, Septr 19th 1749.

Present: Joshua Maddox, Esqr.

The Foreigners whose Names are underwritten, imported in the Ship Patience, Captn Hugh Steel, from Rotterdam, but last from Cowes in England, did this day take the usual Qualifications to the Government. By the List 137, Freights 270, from the Palatinate & Duchy of Wirtenberg.

Johannes Steinsieffer
Hermanus Battenberg
Johan Jacob Grisse
Engelbert Jung
Hermanus Schneider
Johannes Michel Stoltz
Johan Jost Zimmerman
Henrich Hartman
Johan Ebert (+) Stein, sick
Dielmanus Grydelbach
Johannes Henrich Güthing
Johan Wilhelm Hart
Hans Henrich Wehler
Johann Friderich Schulte
Johann Georg Heffner
Georg Ludwig Sanner
Johann Jacob Bähr
Hans Adam Gramlich
Hans Adam (✕) Krumbel, Junr
Jacob Creff
Philipp Jacob Creff
Andres Riebman
Johan Marten Hase
J. Henry (✕) Righart
Jacob (+) Richart
Johann Georg Bauman
Johann Bauman
Johann Bauman
Hans Jörg Mieder
Joh. Michel Rittenbach
Andereas (✕) Hecker
Christian (✕) Eslinger
Michael Müller
Johann Adam Zangmeister
Georg Friederich Zangmeister
Hans Georg Bacher
Hans Peter Ciewits [?]

Bernhardt Müller
Jeorg Henerich Unangst
Andres Müller
Georg Peter Glick
Conrath Röger
Johan Christoph Öttinger
Caspar Kilian
Jorg Peter Vogt
Johann Kaspar Senghaas
Adam Hettinger
Jerg Lintz
Georg Lindenmuth
Vallentin (C) Gramly
Carl Kayser
Heinrich Magasch
Johan Bernhard Fehr
Christoph Keylbach
Hans Jörg Kamp
Michael Schlör
Andreas Unangst
Daniel (+) Camp
Davit Kamp
Christian Zimmerman
Hans Jörg Martin
Jorg Petter Uhrig
Hans Philipp Brenner
Philipp Adam Brenner
Philipp Stroh
Petter Spohn
Hans Adam Ludwig
Johann Peter Ludwig
Jacob ( ) Ludewig, sick
Jerck Michel Royer
Maddeus Milling [?]
Hanns Martin Uhler
Hans Görg Hertel
Ludwig Lindenmuth

Hans George (X) Linemuth
Matheus (X) Leeser
Michel Zilling
Willhelm Bosch
Andres Beuschlein
Anderes Feidig
Johann Christoph Walbert
Johannes Endres
Johanes ( ) Ender, Junior, sick
Johannes Eulen
Martin (X) Bawer
Martin Riess
Ferdinand (X) Reed
Josep (+) Beyghart
Johann Adam Gessner
Johann Ludwig Barth
Jerg Koster
Johanes (HE) Eberts
Friderich Dörflinger
Jacob Glaser
Joseph Dummen
Philip (P) Herr
Samuel Ehring
Johanes (X) Wagner
David Keller
Johannes Heillmann
George (O) Smith
Johann Peter Zimmerman
Johann Friedrich Gall

Johann Adam Diem
Johann Adam Hoffman
Jörg Michel Gibler
George (X) Hosner
Hans Georg Schuhman
Matthes Heinlin
Davit Heinlen
Jerg Himelberger
Jakob Kauffman
Michal Okher
Johannes Sauerzapff
Andereas Föhl
Joseph Hauser
Abraham Bauman
Gottlieb Baumann
Daniel Finck
Peter (+) Finck
Lorentz Seyfriedt
Bernhart (X) Pangert
Daniel Kurtz
Johannes Jeyter
Gottlieb Jeyter
Johann Fridrich Strauss
Peter Stetzler
Henrich Häffner
Bernhard Schmid
Andreas Müller
Thomas Kast
Adam (X) Ernst

Memorandum. The Foreigners, in Number 49, Imported in the Ship Francis and Elisabeth, Captn Beal, being sickly, were not permitted to be landed.

———————

Likewise the Foreigners, in Number 53, Imported in the Ship Rachel, Captn Armstrong, were so sickly that it was thought dangerous to suffer them to land all together, whereupon the Sick was ordered to be separated from the well & such as recovered with the well were to be qualified occasionally.

———————

[List 135 C] At the Court House at Philadelphia, Monday, Septr 25th, 1749.

Present: Joshua Maddox, Esquire.

The Foreigners whose Names are underwritten, imported in the Ship Speedwell, Captn James Creagh, from Rotterdam, but last from Cowes in England, did this Day take the usual Qualifications To the Government. By the List 85. 215 Freights, 240 souls, from Wirtembergh, Alsace & Hanau.

Steffen Sadler
Hans Müller
Hans (H) Geradwoll
Joseph (X) Horgher
Christian (X) Hemmler
Johannes Hauser
Christoff Hauser
Hans Georg (X) Pfawty
Dewald (X) Motz
Jacob Grysing
Heinrich Zimer
Joseph (JF) Freymiller
Joseph Freymiller
Johannes Bersch
Hantz Jacob Held
Ludewig (+) Held
Johannes Weiss
Michael (X) Shok
Christoph (X) Meyer
Michel Meyer
Johannes Anstatt
Davit (+) Hamm
Hans (X) Morgedaller
Adam (B) Buchman
Jacob (XX) Wächter
Andereas (+) Gershwiller
Hans Diebolt
Michael (X) Kleim
Joh. Erhardt Müller
Johannes Tuckermann
Jacob (JH) Hann
Andereas (+) Hann

Hans Jacob Schiedt
Johann Friederich Leim
Johann Peter Källner
Johann Michel Müller
Matheas (MS) Onzinger
Ludewig (X) Moser
Gisbertus Ignatius Knipp
Jacob (O) Miller
Adam Layer
Burghart Ertinger
Johan G. (W) Weydner
Johann Egydius Deschner
Johannes (X) Yowch
Michael Kientz
Matheus Schrutt
Fritrich Wentz
Johanes (X) Hell
Philip (X) Seifert
Hans Jerg Achenbacher
Jacob Fenchell
Christoph (X) Stormer
Martin (X) Wurffel
Johann Conradt Giss
Oswald (OH) Haas
Jacob Hecht
Andreas Böhner
Hans Flach
Hans Flach
Andreas Sommer
Andreas Flach
Hans Schlenker
Hans (HA) Armgast

Michael (M) Armgast
Andereas (X) Herster
Georg Schütterlin von Hayl
Georg Ross
Görg Röss
Hans Jacob Röss
Leonhart (+) Ziffe
Isaac (IV) Vetter
Samuel Schneyders

Hans Jacob Hammerle
Hans Jacob Hammerle
Hans Jorg Voll
Josias Grieb
Mathias Lorentz
George (H) Silber
Christian Strahling
Hendrick (X) Workman

[List 136 C] At the Court House at Philadelphia, Tuesday, the 26th Septr 1749.
Present: Benjamin Shoemaker,
　　　　Joshua Maddox, Esqr, Wm Hartley.
The Foreigners whose Names are underwritten, imported in the Ship Ranier, Henry Browning, Master, from Rotterdam, but last from . . . in England, did this day take the Oaths to the Government. By the List 126. Whole Freights 277. [From] Hanau, Wirtemberg, Darmstand, Isenburg.

Martin Katz
Jacob Katz
Johanes (+) Raber
Martin Glas
Johan ( ) Sans, sick
Phillipp Dähn
Johan Alfred Schalter [?]
Johann Christoffel Brust
Johan Conrat Brust
Jacob (+) Clem
Christoph (O) Heyndel
J. Hans Heytzman
Jacob Kartz
Johannes Landmann
Johann Wilhelm Geyer
Johann Conrath Riedel
Johan Jost (II) Reidel
Johanes Shneyder
Hans Jacob Senner
Jacob Boller
Sebastian Weitzel

Friederich (X) Weitzel
Johann Hennrich Weitzel
Thomas (X) Appel
Johann Adam Appel
Johan Philip (X) Wygant
Jacob (X) Grawl
Philip (X) Lawterbach
Conrad (+) Lauterbach
Christian (X) Knipe
Isaac Hess
Johann Nicolaus Hess
Johann Ludwig Hess
Caspar (X) Streader
Johann Henrich Stradter
John Henry (II) Streader
Johannes Ströder, Junior
Dewalt Schudt
Ekhart (X) Keyser
Leonhart (X) Keyser
Jorg Christian Eberhardt
Thomas Erich

Johannes Alberth
Jacob Sauerwein
Johann Henrich Lehr
Johann Friederich Höck
Johan Cunrad Hock
Nicklaus Hess
Hs. Conradt Lutz
Mattheis Graff
Marten Lutz
Hans Jacob Lutz
Hans Melcher Hammer
Johan Jacob Reich
Johann Georg Trippner
Christ Lutz
Christian Gosser
Andreas Meffert
Johannes Meffert
Jacob Förster
Ambrosius Habermehl
Johannes Weber
Johann Henrich Printz
Johann Henrich Faber
Adam Hopff
Johannes Conrad
Johanes (✕) Shertel
Fred. Willem (✕) Geist
John Adam (✕) Fasnackt
Johann Conrath Fassenacht
Johann Henrich Leppich
Johann Philipp Lehmig
Michael (✕) Henckel
John Peter Peppel
Benedicus Weiss
Johann Caspar Schmick
Carl Scharmann
Peter Harting
Johan Conrad Geyer
Johann Henrich Geyer
Peter (✕) Becker
Joachim Nagel

Johann Görg Schultz
Johan Michaell Schmaltz
Andreas Herreder
Johannes Herreder
Johann Petter Schurmann
Jacob Engel
Johannes Falck
Georg Ernst Schmick
Wolf Caspar Geyer
Johann Reinhart Rohrbach
Johann Thomas Schmidt
Johan Henrich Lorey
Johann Melcher Loray
Philips Sultzbach
Johannes Appel
Henrich Eckel
Johan Michel Oberheuser
Melchor (   ) Heppel, sick
Johan Görg Hörpel
John Henry (✕) Heppel
Philip Bebel
Johann Jacob Dänderich
Johannes Dänderich
Georg Ernst Maurer
Joh. Christian Maurer
Michel Reiffschneider
Johannes Jahn
Henrig (+) Hartwich
J. Henry (+) Shreffler
Johannes Gräber
J. Michael (+) Gunkel
Johannes Steygerwalt
Johann Petter Steigerwalt
Johannes Landgraff
Johann Jacob Eckhardt
Melchior (+) Gebhart
Conrad (+) Gebhart
Johann Adam Gräll
Erasmus Rosenberger
Johannes Krebs

Conrad Wagner

Johann Daniel Bauschar

Johan Philippus Jung

Johann Jacob Hettrich

Johanes ( ) Michler, sick

[List 137 C] At the Courthouse at Philadelphia, Tuesday, the 26th Septr 1749.

Present: Joshua Maddox, Esqr.

The Foreigners whose Names are underwritten, imported in the Ship Dragon, George Spencer, Master, from Rotterdam, but last from Deal in England, did this day take the Oaths to the Government. By the List 153. 503 Whole Freights, from the Palatine, & Zweybreckt.

Joh. Nickel Eich

Christoph (X) Eich

Johannes Gödtel

Christian Fuchs

Johan Jorg Fodel

Johann Peter Weyand

Johann Jacob Petermann

Johan Christian Heinrich Beck

Andreas Justus Seyss

Jacob Leber

Johannes Eckel

Gerg Hoffman

Johannes Huff

Bastian Friethrick

Kon. Katzenbacher

Ludewig (O) Haspelhorn

Simon (X) Richter

Hans (X) Gawff

Valentin Weber

Johannes Weber

Jacob Weber

Johann Philips Lauer

John Nicklas (|) Hayn

Johann Nickelaus Reisinger

Johannes Peter Reisinger

Johann Peter Eckert

Anthony (Ost) Oster

Tomas Bohler

Martin (O) Sier

Anthony (O) Moor

Filb Jacob Schmitt

Jacob Many [?]

Johenrich Spengler

Philipp Jacob Eger

Johenrich Sies

Johann Nickel Wentz

Jacob (X) Byshall

Peter Heimbach

Henrich Brill

Jacob (X) Brown

Jacob (M) Miller

Adam Gerber

Henrich Schmitt

Johann Gerg Deller

Matheus (M) Miller

Bernhart (X) Wacker

Friederich (F) Minler

Wilhelm (X) Hoffmann

Peter Sühn

Johannes (J) Wagner

Matteis Wagner

Johannes (O) Zwalle

Melchior (X) Benedict

Casper Zirn

Michael (X) Zyndelbach
Killian (X) Duvinger
Johann Nicolaus Schneider
Tobias Fey
John Diwall
Johann Henrich Weber
Kilian Hager
Johann Peter Schlarbst
Antony Müller
Lenard (X) Wallar
Adam (AE) Egart
Jacob Wendling
Friedrich Schütz
Jacob (J) Bruner
Adam Bronner
Philipp Jacob Schmidt
Jörg Philib Hartung
Vallentin Weber
Johann Mardin Kalter
Dewald (H) Shnyder
Johanes (X) Ross
Friedrich Schweickhart
Ludwig Seitz
Jacob Seitz
Christian (X) Hoffstätter
Jacob Naff
Martin (+) Lorch
Steffan Baur
Jacob (O) Frey
Hans Gorg Hartlieb
Peter (+) Dagen
George (X) Cump

Wilhelm Müller
Weyrich Beck
Michael (X) Lenard
Jacob Roth
Henry (J) Weber
Johan Volandin Weber
Jacob Krauss
Paulus Hartman
Johan Heinrich Harttman
Johann Georg Ludwig
Michael (X) Killian
Phillip Müller
Ambrosius (+) Bender
Frantz Wittman
Jacob Fehr
Johanes (X) Dürr
Joh. Georg Krauss
Tobias (X) Lawer
Martin Föll
Johan Nicklas (X) Shaffer
George Jacob (X) Shaffer
Michal Schneider
Johannes Enders
Johann Fridrich Widmann
Balthaser Von Könne
Martin Von Können
Jacob Weidler
Johan Henrich Egert
Johanes (X) Partts
Anthoni Ohler
Jacob (+) Beck

[List 138 C] At the Court House at Philadelphia, Wednesday, the 27th Septr 1749.

Present: Joshua Maddox, Esquire.

The Foreigners whose Names are underwritten, imported in the Ship Isaac, Captn Robert Mitchell, from Rotterdam, but last from Cowes in England, did this day take the Oaths to the Government. From the Palatinate, by List 79. 206 freights.

Heinerich Grob
Rutolph (+) Haberly
Hans Hug
Johanes Grob
Hans Rutolph (✕) Fisher
Heynry (✕) Grub
Felix Mägli
Peter Becker
Jacob Fliehman
Johan Henrich Grün
Andres Linck
Michael (+) Rudelmos
Johanes (✕) Storm
Hans ( ) Conrath, sick
Ully Kunrath
Hans Kunrad
Johan Jacob Staucki
Hans Jacob Mägli
Rudolf Fries
Heinrich Boshart
Albert (✕) Shutz
Uhllerik (✕) Coppy
Johann Friedrich Cremer
Johann Christian Schiller
Johan Adam (H) Shreiber
Baltus (B) Shreiber
Michael Fischer
Christian Meckel
Johann Vallentin Steinbrech
Johan Jahbler
Matheas (✕) Kehler
Leonhart (✕) Lasher
Conradt Spies
Johannes Klippel
Jurge (✕) Fisher
Andereas (A) Bussart
Jacob Klippel
Hans Adam (A) Maurer
Johannes Henlein
Wendel (+) Becker

Johann Nickel Gerst
Jacob (✕) Wissman
Johan Peter Rit
Johann Nickel Schäffer
Georg Adam Fischer
Johann Caspar Langenberger
Johannes Jungblud
Johann Adam Wolf
Henrich Landes
Rutdolf Landes
Johannes Miller
Mattheus Echternach
Johannes Laudert
Nicklas ( ) Franger, sick
Peter Markhart
Johann Friedterich
Johan Nicolas Senderling
Johann Henrich Heynemann
Johann Görg Schnabel
Johann Nickel Stumpf
Johann Daniel Weber
Frantz Hemmele
Christian (✕) Hemmle
Heiny Huber
Heinrich Burkhart
Jacob Vosseller
Johanes (✕) Bauer
Philip (+) Haber
Lorentz ( ) Haffner, sick
Johann Henrich Beck
Ludewig (✕) Kreps
Ludwig Krebs
Gorg Schlosser
Johann Hennerich Klein
Johannes Wolff
Johann Georg Batz
Herman ( ) Haust, sick
Nicolaus Becker
Johannes Silvius Schreiner

[List 139 C] At the Court house at Philadelphia, Thursday, the 28th Septr 1749.

Present: Edward Shippen, Esquire.

The Foreigners whose Names are underwritten, imported in the Ship Ann, John Spurrier, Master, from Rotterdam & last from Cowes in England, did this day take the usual Qualifications to the Government. By the List 105. Whole Freights 242. From Basil, Wirtemburg, Zweybrecht, Darmstad.

Phillipp Leidyg
Melchior Lüppert
Wilhelm Rübel
Johannes Dansius
Henrich Braun
Johanes (X) Spitler
Jacob (X) Swoob
Johan (X) Shwitzer
Jacob (X) Weeser
Rudolph (X) Viunt
Adam Schaulling
Daniel Scheübly
Henrich Mock
Petter Elser
Hans Adam Hacker
Johan Jacob (X) Sutz
Michel Hengsd
Jean Thoulouzan
Johannes Weber
Johanes Strauwman
Jacob Landgraff
Johann Friedrich Zimmerman
H. Michael Zimmerman
Johanis Zimmerman
Thomas (   ) Lubek, sick
Wendel (WK) Keller
Johannes Mertz
Andräs Scholl
Friederich (M) Meyer
Johann Phillipp Weber

Lorentz Henger
Jacob le Jeunes
Johann Paul Traub
Johann Andon Schwartzbach
Johann Pätter Beisel
Johann Gorg Schreiner
Mardin Eyer
Hans Jerg Schömperlen
Engelhardt Kutrer
Krafft Hünner
Johan Phillipp Falck
Jacob Salathe
Jacob Tschudy
Hans Uhlleryg (X) Bussy
Joseph Gallman
Blasius (BH) Hauck
Bärnhardt Hauck
Melchior Kunter
Gorg Michel Schurtz
Conrad Renninger
Hans Rudolf Kittweiler *
Jacob (X) Sheybethal
Johann Jacob Kreis
Caspar Derffenbecher
Simon (X) Kraus
Hans Jacob Vogt
Adam Heinrich
Johann Ewald Bayer
Hans Jörg Hüber
Christian (X) Schott

* A German Reformed preacher. See *History of the Goshenhoppen Reformed Charge*, pp. 208–211.

Jurg Henrich (X) Shott
Johanes (X) Sucher
Jacob Reichert
Jacob Fucks
Heironimus Brobeck
Mardi Brabeckh
Jost Schümblin Schne [?] *
Michl Breisach
Hans Michel Schuster
Jacob Scheublein
Michel Hassler
Hans Michel Hauck
Jacob (A) Amman
Hans Adam Nees
Hans Nes
Heini Vogt
Johanes (+) Vougt
Jacob Schnell

Adam (S) Sharer
Hans (+) Kuhn
Hans (+) Shutty
Jacob Koller
Niclaus Motherö
Jon Jacob Jetter [?]
Hans Michael Schwab
Johannis Hummel
Jacob Schaffner
Hans Rudi Schafner
Gottlieb Walter
Jor Adam Goranslo
Johann Philipp Henneman
Sebastian (X) Schneidman
Conrat Mayer
Johann Paulus Eyselohr
Johanes (XX) Dummer
Jacob (Jacob) Shupp

[List 140 C] At the State House at Philadelphia, Monday, the 2ᵈ October 1749.

Present: Charles Welling, Esquire, Mayor.

The Foreigners whose Names are underwritten, imported in the Ship Jacob, Captⁿ Adolph De Grove, from Amsterdam, but last from Shields in England, did this day take the usual Oaths to the Government. From Swabia, Wirtemberg & Darmstadt. By the List 107. Persons 249.

Johann Jacob Sinn
Johann Georg Sinn
Friedrich Buckel
Hans Georg (H) Keplinger
Hans Jorg Hoffman
Georg Christian Spängler
Christo. Fürstner
Fredich (   ) Walles, on board
Conradt Lauffer
Philip (H) Storm
Martin Wüst
Michael (++) Miller

Johan Henrich Herget
Gorg Hoffman
Johannes Huber
Johan Christoph Kress
George (O) Bachart
Johann Jerg Steigleder
Joseph Ritter
Johann Conradt Leling
Paul Leling
Georg Michael Laubinger
Hans Georg Krafft
Friedrich Pförsching

* Or is the surname Blinschne?

Jacob Fleischman
Jacob (+) Uhllerich
Johan Hennrich Knöss
Johannes Becker
Daniel (+) Freysinger
Conrad (C) Reese
Johannes Roth
Marttin Bleymeyer
Georg Eberhardt
Friedrich Hoffmann
Jacob (X) Sinder
Joh. Conrad Leithauser
Eberhardt Windmyer
Peter (X) Seyds
Martin Treibel
Christian Fridrich Häberlin
Martin Lerch
Georg Schweyer
Hans Georg Bauer
Johann Georg Stein
Jacob Traudt
Jacob Rupp
Jacob Gilbert
Bernhart Gilbert
Lorentz Hoch
Simon (X) Grassman
Johann Jacob Ber
Johannes Meier
Hans Adam (X) Fakler
Marcus (X) Gönner
Hans Phpp Schöster
Georg Carl (O) Rubert
Henry (X) Rubert
Friderik ( ) Seydler, sick
William (X) Hofman
Matthes Hartmann
Johannes Rahn
Johan Henrich Rohnn

Henry (X) Krahmer
Hans Georg (X) Münig
Johann Georg Huntzinger
Jacob Kautzmann
Gottfried Samuel Walper
Johann Georg Henrich
Johanes Bauman
Johann Adam Hiltenbeittel
Adam Eycholtz
Johann Martin Eichholtz
Velten Villib
Friderich Betzalt
Johann Wendel Kühner
Adam (H) Shneyder
Johanes Zimmerman
Johan Michel (X) Shneyder
Henry (W) Wirdt
Hans Michael Gartner
Johan Jacob Keil
Christoph (X) Herply
Baltaser ( ) Bower, sick
Pillipp Stumpf
Peter (X) Seyler
Johannes Schlatterer
Johanes ( ) Hartman, sick
Jacob (X) Heibly
Johann Adam Roth
Johan Georg Gröther
Mellicher Vogelmann
Melchior (H) Wolfart
Joseph Volck
Johanes (X) Folck
Johann Görg Störner
Hans Michael Gintner
Nicolaus Dötter
Mattis Dötter
Martin Dötter
Claudt Reinaldt

[List 141 C] At the Court House at Philadelphia, Saturday, the Seventh Day of October, 1749.

Present: Thomas Lawrence, Esquire, Mayor.
The Foreigners whose Names are underwritten, imported in the Ship Leslie, Captⁿ J. Ballendine, from Rotterdam, but last from Cowes in England, did this day take the usual Oaths to the Government. By the List 121. 400 Persons from Palatinate, Manheim, Zweybreckt.

Conrad (X) Valentine
Hannes (X) Hanich
Wendel Wahl
Jacob (X) Hamel
Christof (O) Geigenberger
Martin (MA) Andereas
Peter Grünenwalt
Ulrich Jehle
Christopf Etsch
Johanes (J) Hess
Johann Adam Mäuer
Martin Wösener
Johanes (X) Wessener
Matheas ( ) Knaars, sick
Fridrich Schott
Johanes (+) Eckman
Rudolph (X) Hoffman
Henry (O) Mohler
Johann Philipp Kristmann
Peter (PK) Klein
Casper Klein
Johann Herrmann Metz
Johann Jacob Metz
Johann Gerhart Neiman
Friedrich Fuchs
Jost Paul Kuhnroth Gerber
Anthon (X) Koch
Michael (M) Shmeyer
Petter Kraut
Philips Mäuer
Peter Kurtz
Johann Peter Wickert
Johann Paul Wickert
Martin Schwenck

Johann Petter Stimmel
Conrad (C) Wolfe
Johann Jörrig Kind
Martin (X) Kind
Wendell Jung
Christofel Jung
Johann Michael Messener
Johanes (X) Ritcher
Friederich Mey
Balser Schmit
Simon Baumgärttner
Michael (X) Klee
Gottfried Grünzweig
Hans Gerch Scheifflen
Philibs Klein
Johann Diel Klein
Johann Jacob Engler
Wendal (S) Shmeltzer
Johannes Becker
Johann Wilem Arendt
Vallentin Pettry
Jacob Hofman
Peter Imbsweiller
Anthoni Pettersheimer
Jacob Horberger
Michel Huyet
Jacob Womer
Michael (W) Wommer
Christian (M) Melchart
Christian Müller
Phillipp Kärcher
Johannes Pfeil
Johann Jacob Cunius
Johann Adam Correll

Johan Michel Teobalt
Nick. Cuntz
Johann Philip Matheis
Johann Nicolas Müller
Jacob (✕) Straus
Michel Dinges
Peter Weber
Jacob Creitz
Johan Jacob Walter
Gottfried Fenderer
Gottfriedt Rommell
Hans Jerg Fischer
Jerg Marten Hausser
Hs. Stephan Hepp
Bernhardt Hepp
Jerg Hepp
Jacob (✕) Leonhart
Johannes Müller
Johannes Barner
Vallentin (✕) Behler
Conrad Behler
Hans Jerg Brodbeck
Hans Jerg Brodbeck
Georg Müller
Johann Rudolph Espich
Johanes (✕) Lang
Andreas Supper

Johann Phillipp Supper
Johann Adam Dörffling
Jacob (M) Mauerer
Bertholmea ( ) Mertz, sick
Peter (O) Grein
Adam Stum
Philipps Haubt
Jost D. Fissher
Petter Miller
Jacob Jäger
Jerg Imich
Johann Reichardt Böhm
Jost Engeler
Jacob Meyer
Johann Nickklas Mayer
John Atam Bath
Henry (✕) Boce
Friedrich Bender
Christian Schneider
Nicklas (✕) Dienius
Philipps Otto Wagner
Johann Ludwig Sengeysen
Gorge ( ) Shmit, sick
Philip ( ) Adam, sick
Nickolus (+) Diterich
Johann Christoph Fackhler

[List 142 C] At the Court House at Philadelphia, Monday, the 19th 8ber 1749.*

Present: Thos Lawrence, Esquire, Mayor.

The Foreigners whose Names are underwritten, imported in the Ship Lydia, Captn John Randolph, from Rotterdam, but last from Cowes in England, did this day take the usual Qualifications to the Government. By the List 154. Persons . . . Wirtemberg, Dourlach, Zweybrecht, Palatinate.

Jacob (B) Bock
Steffe Maisch
Johannes Beckh

Heinrich Bachman
Michel Kipp
Lonhardt Meyer

* This date is evidently wrong. It should be Oct. 9th. See next ship.

Matheas (O) Oberfeld
Georg Conradt Bloss
Henrich Hübener
Henrich Thomas
Georg Wagner
Bernhart (M) Miller
Andereas Gambler
Henry (X) Heyser
Hans Peder Schmit
Joseb Baliet
Johannes Hantwerk
Konnerat Linss
Davit (O) Bast
Johann Michael Bast
Jabez Beger
Michal Steinborn
George (X) Lambert
Johannes Ohlliger
Johann Peter Clementz
Adam (   ) Wolmer, sick
Reichart Heiss
Henrich Schafer
Jacob (X) Adams
Wilhelm Arnolt
Peter Arnolt
Johannes Arnolt
Jacob Kniess
Jerg Simon Bresler
Nicklas (X) Bresler
George (X) Bresler
Michael Barth
Henrich Koch
Fertinantt Jung
Nickolas (X) Simon
Christian Bentz
Ludwig Herrmann
Michael Bareth
Michel Schack
Jacob (X) Shaak
William (O) Shaak
Georg Jacob Wagner

Johannes Oberle
Johann Peter Oberle
Conrad Glück
Conrad (X) Kohl
Johann Georg Schreiber
Jorg Heinrich Wüst
Peter (X) Rap
Cornelis Van Staveren
Johann Görg Hammer
Johan Jacob (X) Messer
Ambros Remely
Michaelo Pedelo
Michael Mosser
Hans Georg Huff
Johann Henrich Hettich
Matheas (X) Keller
Johannes Schmid
Johannes Scherrer
Philip (O) Häney
Conrad (X) Geidlinger
Ludwig Flach
Jacob Schweinfurth
Hans Jacob (X) Shoemaker
Hans Michael (X) Seitz
Johannes Vogt
Daniel Bock
Johann Jacob Rahn
Andereas (X) Vogler
Baltzer Heyl
Johannes Barth
Hans Gräsch
Jacob Schantz
Carol (X) Shantz
Jacob Bauer
Henry (X) Miller
Michel Bastian
Niclaus Schäffer
Caspar Dorn
Johannes (X) Uhllerich
Görg Kirchner
Gorg Aadam Löble

Wilhelm Löble
Joseph (X) Gebhart
Johannes (O) Himelrigh
Adam Lotz
Johann Jacob Weyden
Johann Philib Öhlweiler
Peter (X) Kratsinger
Johannes Koch
Georg Jacob (X) Shierman
Johan Georg (+) Lutz
Vallendin Schallus
Bastian (X) Shalles
Görg Vogler
Johannes (X) Rau
Hans Jerg Rau
Johannes Weiss
Hendery ( ) Reinhart, sick
Nicklaus Möloth
Johann Philip Haüsman
Jacob Stadler
Michael (X) Weyler
Jacob (X) Tonner
Phillippus Martin Hammell
Matthias Scheiffele
Leonhardt Groninger
Stephan Stieffelmeyer
Jacob Ulmer
Christianus Hentz
David Kehm
Lorentz Weiler
Johannes Gelisen
Nycklaes Gelisen

Wilhelmus Savelkowl
Frieterig Doll
Jerg Breinig
Jacob Brucker
Georg Christoph Müller
Jeorg Crassan
Mich. Brücker
Christian (X) Seyder
George Kaemer
Nicolaus Forshberge
Edmundus Tholl
Georg Ludwig Hoffman
Jörg Rotenburg
Johann Petter Hinckenauer
Valentin Keller
Johann Stephan Dietewig
Vallentin Schweitzer
Johann Nickel Klein
Johan Michael Mintz
Christian Carl Brand, Chirurg *
Johann Monb. Brandt
Johan Christen Brandt
Johannes (+) Storm
Jacob (X) Kantz
Michael (+) Kantz
Jacob Bertsch
Mathias Müller
Philip Bodomer
Andereas (X) Ecker
Johann Davidt Völpert
Ruprecht Haug

[List 143 C] At the Court House at Philadelphia, Tuesday, the 17ᵗʰ 8ᵇᵉʳ 1749.
Present: Thomas Lawrence, Esquire, Mayor.
The Foreigners whose Names are underwritten, imported in the Ship Dragon, Daniel Nicholas, Master, from Rotterdam, but last from Portsmouth in England, did this day take

* I. e., Surgeon.

the usual Qualifications to the Government. Palatines, Wirtembergers, Alsatians. By List 88. Persons 244.

Andereas Mohr
Martin (A) Shrötter
Hans Gerg Wombach
Nicklaus (X) Brikner
Conrad (X) Roth
Wilbert Gambert
Peter (X) Hartman
Johans Gamber
Felix (X) Gartom
Jacob Wolff
Andreas Hertz
Wilhelm Manger
Hans Peder Goltz
Hans (X) Danzel
Michael Schmidt
Christman Duchmann
Peter (X) Tuchman
Hans Michael Cuntz
Henry (X) Jacob
Conrad (X) Engel
Hans Gerg Stambach
Johan Leonhardt Baltser
David Kliednus [?]
Henrich Hubert
Philipp Fischer
Valentin Bender
Davit (H) Shantz
Andres Bircker
Johannes Stiebler
Johann Adam Stiebler
Stephan Furman
Peter (P) Fisher
Jacob Fischer
Hans Georg Burckhard
Andreas Kerchner
Johannes Müller
Johannes Sauter
Johannes Rumppel

Henrich Fischer
Jacob Griess
Peter (Diehl) Thiel
Johan Nicklas (X) Wyner
Johanes (X) Waall
Andres Emmerling
Wilhelm Hoffmann
Johan Jacob Alles
Abraham Alles
Abraham Reiber
Johannes (HSB) Bigler
Adam Sprengel
Jacob Reiber
Simon (M) Metziger
Peter (O) Grow
Johann Simmon Groh
Tohbias Horein
Anthony Zürch
Balthas Schneider
Conrad Vieman
Johann Görg Krummlauf
Conrad (K) Shyd
Georg (X) Shyd
Georg Henry (X) Shyd
Hans Michel Haudenschilt
Henry (X) Heydersh
Hans Michel Haudenschild
Conradt Krumbach
Simon (X) Eshbagh
Jacob Grumbach
Johann Adam Weier
Johann Martin Forster
Caspar Iba
Johann Andreas Wagner
Johanes Schmitt
Johann Henrich Theiss
Hans Michal (X) Kosser
Görg Heinrich Witter

[. . .] Grundell	Wilhelm Zimerle
Johannes Eberle	Johannes Hoffman
Johann Jacob Würth	Johann Gerg Schneider
Johannes Kuhn	Arnold Klehas
Bastian Gernandt	Philipp Lorentz Zimmerle

[List 144 C] At the Court House at Philadelphia, Tuesday, the 17th 8ber 1749.

Present: Thomas Lawrence, Esqr, Mayor

The Foreigners whose names are underwritten, imported in the Ship Fane, Captn Wm Hyndman, from Rotterdam, but last from Cowes in England, did this day take the usual Oaths to the Government. Palatine, Wirtemberg, Rottenstein.* By the List 119. [Persons] 178.6.

Christoffel (X) Graff	Gorg Michel Haas
Christoph Graff, Junior	Johannes Schilling
Christoph Willet	Jacob Stier
Johann Martin Offner	Johan Adam (+) Keilinger
Gottlieb Sohner	Christian Stein
Tobias Maug	Georg Geiger
Samuel Henry (X) Abentshon	Adam (O) Hugly
Reinholt Abendschönn	Ludewig (+) Triber
Christian Abendschön	Johann Christoph Werthwein
Gottfriet Baumgärttner	Mathes Stier
Christoph Altruth	Johann Conradt Häuser
Jacob Schneider	Leonhardt Plantz
Jacob Schneider	Johann Jacob Schneider
Lenhart Lang	Jacob Plantz
Christian Reiner	Georg Jacob Plantz
Georg Reiner	Jost Sasmanshaus
Adam Seifert	Jacob Weyandt
Johann Heinrich Gerlach	Hennerich Benner
Michael Biner	Henrich Mise
Hans Jerg Huber	Arnd Althaus
Johann Georg Huber	Lutwig Benner
Caspar Wagner	Johannes Benner
Paul Geiger	Herman (X) Weber

* There are several villages called Rothenstein in Germany. The fact that it follows the Palatinate and Württemberg makes it probable that it was Rothenstein in Central Franconia, now Bavaria.

Jost (+ +) Weber
Conrad Stenger
Görge Stenger
Conrad Cremer
Konnrath Kremer
Johan Christ Kun
Ernst (+) Klinker
Danniel Marburger
Johann Henrich Rentzel
Jost Wilhelm Rentzel
Johannes Gross
Adam Spies
Wilhelm (X) Shätz
Johann Henrich Scheidt
J. Engel (X) Stokman
Johann Philipps Stockmann
Johann Casber Klein
Jacob (+) Klein
Johanes Klein
Dangel Benner
Johannes (X) Pfeil
Johannes Wahl
Johan Kraft Has
Johann Gerge Zachrias
Jacob Hahn
Jacob Zeller
Conrad Zeuller
Johannis Zeller
Michel Meyer
Martin Schneider
Christoph Schneider
Johann Martin Hauser
Martin Miller
Marti Fägule [?]
Johann Martin Herr
Johann Martin Reiser
Christan Damser

Christoffel (N) Wimer
Martin Pefferle
Johannes Herter
Jacob Kisling
Hans Gerg Meyer
Georg Friedrich Höhn
Hans Jacob Flacher
Samuel (X) Beck
Johannes Fischer
Melcher Heckman
Caspar (X) Zesseler
Johannes Schnitzer
Johannes (+) Algeyer
Hans Jacob Götz
Andreas Schnelle
Hinrich Riess
Hans Norffkoh [?]
Hans George (X) Kern
Jerg Philipp Rieber
Hans Jacob (X) Keller
Melchior (X) Rinhold
Melchior (X) Ram
Nickel Beyer
Johan Dieterich Reiner
Christian Reiner
Wilhelm Claussenius
Paul Müller
Gottfried Tietz
Ullerich Heininger
Jacob Adam Kraut
Johann Conrad Biehn
Johann Friedrich Sting
Leonhart (X) Jung
Lorian (X) Eisely
Johanes (+) Krämer
Johann Leonhard Jung
Conrad (X) Hirsh

[List 145 C] At the Court House at Philadelphia, Thursday, 9th November 1749.
Present: Thomas Lawrence, Esquire, Mayor.

The Foreigners whose names are underwritten, imported in the Snow Good Intent, Benjamin Boswell, Master, from Rotterdam but last from Cowes in England, did this day take the usual Oaths to the Government. 26 p. List. 76 Persons.

Hans Jerg Bösmer	Jacob Mäsner
Johann Christoph Besmer	Hans Jerg Kuntzelman
Johannes Hausman	Christianus Pfingstag
Joseph Hausman	Michael Hug
Paulus Hausman	Georg Heinrich Reinöhl
Johann Adam Kurtz	Georg Meyer
Fridrich Mertz	Jacob Reinholdt
Johannis Greiner	Peter Mattern
Peter Sitzer	Johannes Syrutscheck
Johannes Heininger	Friedrich Bassler
Jacob Heininger	Johannes (X) Kessler
Matheas (P) Plenninger	Ludwig Zwiecrantz [?]
Ludewig (X) Stumb	Henry (X) Seyder

[List 146 C] At the Courthouse at Philadelphia, Saturday, 11th August 1750.

Present: Thomas Lawrence, Esqr, Mayor.

The Foreigners whose Names are underwritten, imported in the ship Patience, Captn Hugh Steel, from Rotterdam, but last from Cowes in England, did this day take & subscribe the usual Qualifications. 124 By List. 266 Freights.

Hans Peter Treger	Johann Jakop Opfertuch
Jacob Heckendorn	Jacob (N) Jacoby
Stephan Bek	Adam Jacobi
Hans Peter Groff	Petter Jacobi
Hans Jacob (X) Groffe	Matheis Jacobi
Peter (O) Groff	Johan Peter Fitz
Henrich Lutz	Jacob Bürckard
Johannes Petter Klein	Johan David Junge
Johann Nickel Müller	Michael (+) Junge
Johann Nickel Cuntz	Peter (+) Junge
Christoff (X) Bener	Jacob (+) Conrath
Johann Wilhelm Fuchs	Jacob (+) Conrath, Junior
Andras Müller	Johan Henrich Leineweber
Georg Schneck	Daniell Miller

Jacob Reichert
Joh. Conradt Wölffle
Christian Ulrich Lentz
Daniel Werner
Johannes (×) Halm
Christoph Kettemann
Johann Georg Kettemann
Peter Wieland
Johann Jacob Rappoldt
Friederich Waltzer
Georg Friedrich Groh
Johan Gerg Bader
Hans Michel Melber
J. Michel Leidich
Johann George Borner
Jacob (×) Shwob
George (+) Loadig
George Adam Eckart
George Adam Eckardt
Johann Christoff Kuntz
Johann Peter Wohner
Johan Wilhelm Wann
Johan Arnolt Reinhart
Johannes Nickel Hennig
Johannes Peter Hennig
Balthasar Vetterman
Johan Peder Schutz
Johannes Adam Lauch [?]
Johann Jacob Weirich
Johann Nickel Bross
Johann Michael (O) Conrad
Johann Nickel Herber
Johan Jacob Lurber
Jeorg Haman
Johannes Peter Diederich
Johan Nickel Jung
Conradt Velten
Phielib Jacob Maurer
Johann Fridrich Pfeil
Hanes Jerg Eslinger
Jacob Mühleysen

Nicklas Mühleysen
Wilhelm Diedrich
Hans Jerg Sing
Johann Conrat Bross
Johannes Baumgärtner
Heinrich Reinhardt
Hans Jerg Nagel
Johanes (××) Roller
Christoff (×××) Fritz
Georg Friederich Haug
Jacob Lendel [?]
Henrich George
Johannes David Görges
Christian Meier
Matheas (A) Oberkirsh
Nicklas (A) Conrad
Jacob Deremot
Aberham Reiland
Andereas (O) Rost
Paulus Reylandt
Johannes Eischly
Dewald (W) Gerst
Friederich (W) Gerst
Davit (×) Smith
Peter (H) Poland
Stephen (H) Poland
Peter Foltz
Jacob (+) Dobeler
Johann Andreas Mühlschlägel
Johan Adam (+) Satson
Hans (×) Hawffman
Johann Philipp Ost
Johan Maties Gerge
Christian (×) Shmith
Philips Hierber
Jacob (×) Kullenthal
Michel Juncker
Johanes (×) Palm
Fritrich Henny
Johann Reihle
Johan Michel Lieb

Casper Greiter
David Stadelmayer
Bartlyme Bentziger
Johann Adam Setzer
Johann Abraham Stiehl
Carel (+) Vollante
Anton Devittus

Joh. Alberth Velten
Jacob Dannckher
Johannes Essewein
Johan Adam Wentzell
Joh. David Limbeck
Johann Jacob Müller

[List 147 C] At the Courthouse at Philadelphia, Monday, the 13th August, 1750.

Present: Thomas Lawrence, Esqr, Mayor.

The Foreigners whose Names are underwritten, imported in the Ship Bennet Gally, John Wadham, Master, from Rotterdam, but last from Portsmouth in England, did this day take and subscribe the usual Qualifications. Jas Shoemaker. 93 p. List. 260 Whole Freights.

Jacob (L) Lange
Adolph Riehl
Isaac (×) Gunst
Hans Michael (+) Beyer
Hans Jacob Holander
Johan Georg Ott
Johanes ( ) Miller, on board
J. Jacob (×) Shnitzlin
Jacob (×) Dencker
Georg Acker
John Frederick (A) Ott
Michael (MS) Gallater
Johann Jakob Rüppel
Carl Gustav
Johann Adam Bayer
Johann David Neuman
Michel Neuman
Johannes (O) Koch
Peter Bücks
Hans George (×) Baldesparge
Jacob Lazrus
Johannes Fillipus Schmit
Jacob (×) Vallentine
Hans Peter (+) Shrantz

Joseph (×) Eck
Christoff (K) Grindler
Adam Steffan
Heinrich Leininger
Wendel Insul
Marttin Binder
Johan Frantz Freis
Johannes Jacob
Peder Merckel
Johann Michel Klass
Gylyan Gunder
Uhlerich (St) Steiner
Casper Stattller
Hans (H) Bergher
D. Carl Gottlieb Diesberger
Frederic ( ) Lawderbrun, on board
Peter Gutman
Bentz (BH) Horny
Balzar (O) Leibrock
H. Nicklas ( ) Blader, on board
H. Jacob (O) Sander
Casper Ledig

Hans Georg Wetzel
Jacob Schäffer
Hans George (+ +) Hallifas
Henry (   ) Peter, on board
Hans Georg Schenckel
Johann Georg Süsz
Hans (+) Rughty
Hans Peter (H) Peters
Nicklaus Mercklin
Hans Georg (H) Horn
George Frederik (H) Horn
George Frederich (X) Heltzel
Hans Michal (X) Hetzel
Peter (X) Funck
Hans Michel Reber
Henrich Jacob Wanderburg
Christoff (X) Ackerman
Hans Michael Roth
Jullius Fridrich Vollandt
Johann Georg Ramster
Benjamin (+) Kelhover
Andreas Müller
Hans Georg (H) Shlagbouer
Hans Jorg Reichert

Michel Kuntz
Hans Düringer
Johanes (X) Bley
Hartman (X) Leibengut
Dewald (H) Wantlin
Christian Friederich Knauss
Friederich (O) Reys
Jacob Reiss
Hans Michel Hell
Johanes (+) Horn
Benedick Peter
Hans Adam (H) Miller
Jörg Jacob Brunsholtz
F. Adam (O) Printzholtz
Hans Thomas Leininger
Adam (A) Fixe
Hans Michal (+) Bonet
Johan Nickle Jost
Johan Fillibs Jacob Scholl
Johann Gorg Hafer
Peter (X) Lazurus
George (N) Lees
Hans Michael (+) Leyby
Diebolt Schwenck

[List 148C] At the Court House at Philadelphia, 13 August, 1750.
Present: Thomas Lawrence, Esquire, Mayor.
The Foreigners whose Names are underwritten, imported in the Ship Edinburgh, Captn James Russel, Master, from Rotterdam, but last from Porthmouth in England, did this day take & subscribe the usual Qualifications. By List 151. 314 Whole Freights. 2 dead.

Johann (+) Corngibel
Johanes (X) Beyer
Johannes Beyer, Junior
Michael Hamburger
J. George (X) Kirshner
Philip Counrath Aumüller
Johann Seyberth Gertz

Valtin Söfftel
Johann Henrich Lotz
Johann Philipps Hock
Stoffel Brüning
Caspar Bröning
Joh. Peter Seyfert
Johan Gorg Rabe

Johan George (X) Flowr
Ludwig Kassler
Jost Schneider
Thomas (X) Kegel
Thomas (X) Klosse
Henrich Klos
Andreas Huck
Johan Jörg Müller
Johan Adam (XX) Stein
Jacob Möler
Jost Schäffer
Johan Casber Rötter
Johann Georg Klein
Johann Philipp Hölsel
Lorentz Bausum
Christophell Mohr
Johannes Wien
Wilhelm Lemer
Daniel Klein
Jacob Schäfer
Philippus Bücksell
Johannis Gertz
Johann Peter Laib
Johannes Feuerstein
Johan (+) Fasnacht
Johanes (X) Telcher
Johannes Delcher
Jacob Wentz
Davit (X) Herbster
Hans Georg (+) Roninger
Johann Hermann Dippel
Johannes Eulert
Wendel (X) Renninger
Jacob Lavasch
George (X) Heyl
Ludwig Protzman
Friederick (X) Brinkman
Daniel (X) Meerbogh
Jacob Koch [?]
Caspar Strohl
Andereas (X) Spielman

Peter Sickenberger
Valentin Keyser
Phillips Begtholt
Caspar Conradi
Friederich Hoffmann
Andreas Ditz
Johan Nickel Ditz
Vallentin Ehntzweith [?]
Fridrich Pilgram
Peter (X) Nees
Caspar Dieffenbacher
Peter Bohrn
Andereas (X) Keanig
Carol (X) Keanig
Philip (X) Shmith
Nicklas (X) Hirt
Johannes Kniss
Christian (X) Haffner
Michael Matinger
Jacob (X) Flug
Nicklas (N) Spring
Johannes Woelschlaeger
Johann Jacob Brang
Simon Peter (+) Fernantz
Johann Ulrich Daumer
Henry (X) Daumer
Conrad Wendel [?]
Johann Gottlieb Rabe
Johan Martin Schäffer
Johann Jörg Höltzer
Johannes (+) Philips
Johan Christophell Scharff
Andreas Barchell
Jacob Daumenlang
Samuel Falckenhahn
Jacob Merckle
Simon Merckle
Nicolaus Wolff
Carl Spedt
Johannes Mohl
Peter (X) Marcus

Conradt Böhm
Johannes Schmitt
Johan Philipp Stang
Godlib (X) Weyda
Caspar (X) Mug
Johann Jorg Dum
Johannes Haffner
Michel Heinle
Peter (X) Collep
Johannes Möller
Christoffel Möller
Diterich Kautz
Conrad Haffner
Johann Leonhardt Christ
Johan Adam (O) Huber
Theobalt Cuntz
Frantz Cuntz
Peter (X) Spengler
Johanes (+) Shmit
Peter (X) Shmit
Severinus (X) Sheffer
Jacob Vorm Walt
Georg Fridrich Heilbruner
Johan Fridrich Heilbruner
Christian Kempf
Jacob Michael
Jacob Schaffner
Anthony (+) Heanz

Jacob (X) Walter
Johan Daniel Bübel
Ludwig Schreiner
Wilhelm Schreiner
Christ Sam. Barchmann
Johann Ludwig Widtmann
Ludwig Baur
Joh. Andreas Seysen
Johan Görg Esch
Nickolas Spiri
Hans Adam Wagner
Gorg Adam Zobel
Nigglaus Bord
Henry (O) Coller
Philliebs Balbirer
Jacob (J) Metziger
Ludwig Spannagel
Thomas (O) Bough
Johan Adam Regel
Johan Henry (X) Sheoman
Johannes Pistor
Andreas Brandner
Georg Sebastian Krauser
Johann Ludwig Eckhart
Matthias Heiss
Nicolaus Gerlach
Johannes (X) Wagner

[List 149 C] At the Court House at Philadelphia, Wednesday, the 15th August, 1750.

Present: Thomas Lawrence, Esquire, Mayor.

The Foreigners whose Names are underwritten, imported in the Ship Royal Union, Clement Nicholson, Commander, from Rotterdam, but last from Portsmouth in England, did this day take & subscribe the usual Qualifications. 156 p. List, 350 Whole Freights, 500 Souls.

Jacob (X) Grob
Johann (O) Brenhauer
Jacob (X) Karner

Hermann Schwamm
Johann Willhelm Lochman
Friederich Schnitzer

Johan Conrad Scheffer
Stephan Märlich
Cristoffel German
J. S. O. Driesch
Adam Strub
Henrich Hauenstein
Casper Schmidt
Philip (X) Prike
Hans (X) Prike
Hans Michel Bauersachs
Andreas Hertzog
Conrad Arnold
Jacob Stehr
Hans (HW) Weertz
Hironymus Schleider
Gustav Friederich Schleider
Heinrich Holtzman
Matheas (X) Rost
Anthoni Emrich
Daniel Braun
Martin (O) Shrenk
Andreas (AH) Haas
Michael Luttman
Hans George (X) Young
Johann Martin Schwartz
Andreas Hoy
Joh. Ulrich Bauer
Adam (X) Long
Gottlieb Utz
Johann Georg Utz
Hans Adam Kautzman
Johann Heinrich Kautzman
Bernhard Oesterle
Michael Eyrich
Matheas (X) Eyrich
Johann Fridrich Glassbrenner
Johann Jacob Eberth
Ludwig von der Schmidt
Philip Jung
Matheis Bernhardt
Johann Jorg

Philipp Eberhart
Jacob (X) Steebly
Hans (   ) Smith, on board
Martin Schmitt
Nickel Faust
Abram (X) Gerhart
Jacob (XX) Shmitt
Peter Zombro
Johann Michel Schül
Nickel Fass
Johann Adam Berger
G. Adam (G) Renecker
Matteas (+) Fesbely
Henry (   ) Wurtz, on board
Johannes Hartman
Peter (+) Mann
Daniel Lüdi
Hans Martin (X) Wurtz
P. Peter (X) Theyl
Johannes Trümper
Jann Gorg Spittler
Friederich Christian Koppe-
    berger
Simon (X) Leyteker
Jacob (X) Beensly
Henrich Müller
Wilhelm Discher
Joachim Wilhelm Stork
Johan Filepes Kirschbaum
Johann Michael Hollich
Jonas Vogt
Johan Peter Presser
Henrich Bauer
Philip (   ) Bauer, on board
Andreas Köth
Fridrich Sieber
Joh Fridrich Beck
Johann Gelberee
Henrick (   ) Hambach, on
    board
Philip Wilhertzbach

Frantz Brunnholtz
Philip Jacob Kümpel
Vallentin (O) Bast
Friedrich Jacob Cunnerad
Jörg Hoffman
Hans (+) Shoub
Martin (+) Shoub
Hans Uhli Statily
Henry Ully (X) Statily
Johann Andreas Fuchs
Phillip Dick
Johann Peter Dick
Wendel Bretz
Henry ( ) Bretz, on board
Ludewig ( ) Bretz, on board
Philips Fuchs
Dielman Fuchs
Nicol Werckhäusser
Johann Friedrich Duy
Johann Christian Duy
Pfilb Baum [?]
Johannes Baum
Wilhelm Müllerr
Johan Miller Schnell
Johann Adam Kern
Vallentin Fidler
Johann Jacob Helwig
Johann Philip Ludwig
Martin Rubbert
Christian Rust
G. Michael (X) Kraus
Jacob (X) Handshy
J. Nickolaus (+) Sanger
Sander ( ) Sanger, on board
Friedrich Paff

Friedrich Meisch
Johannes Miesch
Johann Petter Schneider
Joseph Hug
Joh. Nicolaus Werking
Johannes Schnübli
Marty im Hoff
Johannes Willar
Jacob Wercking
Jacob ( ) Wercking, Junr, on
  board
Valltin (V) Shmeltzer
Johann Adam Schmeltzer
Johannes Christianus Brammerel,
  going through the land.
Anthon Kröber
Johannes Passler
Phillip Wendel Opp
Fridrich Wolff
Peter Wolff
Johannes Gamber
Phipps Welde
Lorentz ( ) Ampel, on board
Mathäus Baffenmayer
Kilian Ganther
Johannes (G) Grimb
Henry ( ) Bousman, on board
Anthony ( ) Samler, on board
Christoff ( ) Eyerman, on
  board
Henrich Wolff
Johan Peter (X) Benner
Isach Widmer
Johannes Rohr
Hans Gerber

[List 150 C] At the Court House at Philadelphia, Saturday, the 18th August 1750.
    Present: Thomas Lawrence, Esquire, Mayor.
    The Foreigners whose Names are underwritten, imported in the Ship St Andrew, Captn Robert Brown, from Rotterdam and

Cowes in England, did this day take & subscribe the usual
Oaths. 102 By List. 279 Persons.

Jacob (+) Crebler
Achior (×) Crebler
Jacob (+) Rorrer
Jacob (×) Rinker
Melchior (M) Keeper
Friederich (F) Keeper
Johanes Zünd
Hans Ullrich Sondergysr [?]
Henry (×) Shmith
Heinrich Fetz
Linhart von Ruff
Linhart Gröli
Rudolf Hemming
Hans Jacob Meyer
Hans George (×) Meyer
Conrad (×) Kuntzly
Ruthy (×) Weyss
Rudolph (O) Sherrer
Henry (H) Frölly
Jacob Bercher
Henry (×) Weys
Heinereich Koch
Hans Jacob Neracher
Hans Rudolff (×) Widmer
Hans Conradt Steinman
Hans Jacob Zöbli
Joseph Lenggenhag
Melcher Winckelman
Jacob (×) Haassler
Abraham (+) Hasseler
Hans Scheurer
Hans George (×) Shaw
Ullreich Wagner
Henry (×) Brinker
Jacob (×) Tshumy
Caspar (×) Waldy
Uhllerich (×) Bitsserker
Hans Caspar Scharer

Johanis Weidmann
Johannes Bimmersdörffer
Philip (O) Bruner
Abraham Im Oberstäch
Heinerich Harniss
Hans Jacob Bär
Jost (+) Funck
Heinrich Weiss
Johannis Swob
Rüdi Maurer
Anthony (×) Suder
Henry (×) Redlinger
Joseph (O) Shomony
Gallus (O) Fricker
Johannes Fricker
Anthoni Fricker
Ludewig (×) Engel
Henry (×) Sifry
Sallomon Kaufman
Jacob Shuredt
Uhllerich (×) Waldmer
Heinerich Bauinger
Gerg Prall
Jacob (×) Waasser
Andereas (×) Shneyder
Johans Zöfner
Tores (×) Pfister
Hans von Huber
Rudolph (×) Guttinger
Conrad (+) Weydman
Christian Flacher
Conrad (+) Buchar
Caspar (+) Buchar
Jacob (H) Lostatter
Nickolas (O) Lostatter
Jacob Lostätter
Conrad (O) Tshakky
Caspar (×) Weber

Henrich Haller
Friedrich Almbach
H. Nickolas (X) Helling
Johanes (X) Turny
Peter (PB) Balsam
Abraham Ab der Halden
Michael (M) Singer
Conrad (X) Kramer
Heinrich Boshart
Christian (XX) Mosser
Hans Jorg Honnold
Johanes (JH) Housser
Felix (+) Housser

Rudi Hauser
Johannes Schneider
Jacob (X) Fisher
Johann Casper Schaff
Johann Adam Mang
Johannes Nickel Jung
Friedrich Specht
Adam Schnefuhes [?]
Jacob Wäspy
Johannes (X) Waspy
Joachim Gehrig
Hans Adam (H) Seydler
Johann Paul Ilges

[List 151 C] At the Courthouse at Philadelphia, Tuesday, yᵉ 21ˢᵗ August, 1750.

Present: Thomas Lawrence, Esqʳ, Mayor.

The Foreigners whose Names are underwritten, imported in the Ship Anderson, Captⁿ Hugh Campbell, from Rotterdam and Cowes in England, did this day take and subscribe yᵉ usual Oaths. 91 p. List, 45.6 [women & children.]

Christian Betz
Ludwig (X) Horst
Johannes Engel Gonderman
Johannes (X) Gunderman
Mardin Weber
Johann Henrich Fick
Johannes Peder Jung
Johann Henrich Cuntz
Peter Heintze
Johann Jörg Schneyder
Gottfriedt Büttner
Johannes Henrich Horn
Johann Jacob Sturm
Johann Christian Sturm
Johannes Henrich Schuster
Jo. Friedrich Mauder
Johannes Lutwig Biel
Johannes Wilhelm Biel
Johann Daniel Rheinert

Henrich Anthon Reinstein
Johann Henrich Schneider
Johann Michel Huber
Johann Jacob Huber
Johann Martinus Reinhart
Samuell (X) Lädtey
Johann Geörg Reichmann
Johann Christ Rick
Johann Baltzer Schmith
Christof Metz
Johanes (+) Shmit
Christian (X) Kawffman
Johannes Kaufman
Jacob Röter
Christian Widman
Hans Jerg Krieger
Michel Wagenmann
Johann Georg Miller
Johannes Jacob Bläser

Oswald (X) Dups
Conrad (X) Housser
Johan Philib Benner
Gerhardt Fuhr
Gerhart (X) Birkenbeyly
Gorg Deobalt Auer [?]
Johannes Marquardt
Conrad Derr
Lorentz Hauck
Jacob Dengler
Vallentin (H) Maitlin
Jonas Mutschler
Johan Phillib Rambach
Hans Jörg Rath
Johannes Hebel
Johan (X) Miller
Johanes Schaurer
Johann Peter Weis
Christoph (M) Miller
Johann Christophel Lentz
Johannes Lentz
Johann Ludwig Ritter
Johann Wilhelm Britzius
Johan (HB) Beck
Johann Peter Batz

Matheas (+) Weymer
John Peter (H) Becker
Jacob (H) Lyme
Henry (X) Reinfeld
Johann Phillips Moll
Melchior (+) Bruner
Jacob (B) Bearrer
Jurg Riebchler [?]
Andereas (X) Shaade
Jacob Ackermahnn
Lenhart (X) Zebolt
Philip (B) Pop
Johann Jacob Bop
Jacob Heillman
Reinhart Hachenburger
Johann Theis Schmidt
Johannes Schwartzhaubt
Johann Gottlieb Naumann
Johan Conrat Ruff
Johann Naumann
Heinrich Leuthold
Christoff Steiner
Conrad Ellscheid
Urban Friebele

[List 152 C] At the Court House at Philadelphia, Friday, the 24th August, 1750.

Present: Thomas Lawrence, Esquire, Mayor.

The Foreigners whose Names are underwritten, imported in the Ship Brothers, Captⁿ Muir, from Rotterdam & last from Cowes, did this day take & subscribe the usual Oaths. By List 90. 198 Whole Freights. 271 Persons.

Adam (X) Shnyder
Johann Jacob Kimmel
John Lenard (X) Miller
Adam (X) Weaber
Johann Leonhard Groh
Erasmus Hess

Johann Peter Seger
Johann Henrich Keller
Jacob (X) Gerdner
Johann Georg Keller
Johannes Koch
Johannes Ohrle

Johann Adam Körner
Philip (×) Kawtzman
Johann Georg Weiss
Johann Philipp Heist
Johannes Blumenschein
Johann Görg Höring
Christian (O) Shott
Johan George (×) Gans
Johan Nickel Gans
Johann Nicolaus Holm
Jacob Klein
Johan Georg Scheurberger
Johannes (W) Walder
Joseph (N) Nagel
Abraham Schneider
Adam (A) Mensch
Johann Mattheis Schäffer
Abraham (×) Glass
Jacob Friedrich Sohn
Christian Fried
Georg Marthin Kühn
Johann Peter Schmuck
Johann George (×) Drear
Johann Adam Wolfart
Johannes Friestner
Friederich (O) Miller
Peter (×) Meyer
Hans Marttin Kurfes
Hans Petter Muller
Benedick Krieger
Johann Daniel Hoffman
Johann Heinrich Hauck
Johann Georg Zerr
Johann Philipp Shüller
Andreas Frey
Hans Jerg Frey
Caspar (+) Caarel
Daniel (+) Cabel
G. Michael (+) Rommigh
Hans George (+) Rommigh

Johann Jacob Schäffer
Nickolas (V) Rome
J. Nickolas (H) Holl
F. Philip (H) Holl
J. Adam (××) Lucas
Joh. Jacob Wagener
Engelhart (××) Wagner
Johann Henrich Gamber
Georg Michael Gamber
Johann Petter Krämer
Johan Jacob Bernauer
Jost Jacoby
Hanns Philip Bender
Johann Georg Koop
Matheihus Miller
J. Jacob (+) Treysh
Johann Adam Franck
Johan Conrad Schultz
Mardin Dreisbach
Martin Treich
Martin (×) Weaber
Johann Georg Müller
Johann Adam Edelman
Johann Peter Laudenschlager
Johan Ludwig Rauhzahn
Otto Daniel Neues
J. Leonhart (+) Reisch
Hans Yerg Stauch
J. Jacob (+) Reybolt
Martin (+) Ulmer
Hans Görg Ganshorn
Johannes Kroll
G. Adam (H) Bartholt
Adam Eberle
Conradt Israel Aberle
Jan Hendrick Leaseman
Johan Peter (+) Fölker
George Adam (×) Young
George Adam (×) Barttel

[List 153 C] At the Court House at Philadelphia, Tuesday, the 28th August, 1750.

Present: Thomas Lawrence, Esquire, Mayor.

The Foreigners whose names are underwritten, imported in the Ship Two Brothers, Capt. Thomas Arnot, from Rotterdam and last from Cowes, did this Day take & subscribe the usual Oaths & By List 98. [Persons] 147.

Philip (+) Peter
Johann Georg Huber
Frederik (++) Prophet
Jacobus Yundt [?]
Johan Matthes Gerner
Hans Jorg Garner
Johannes Kreutzwisser
Johan Adam (X) Holtz
Georg Michel Schupp
Hans Georg (H) Seacrist
David Metzger
Hans Jacob ( ) Metziger, on board
Hans Marti Eche
Hans Adam Pfisterr
Hans Adam (H) Pfesterer
Jacob Stein
Christoph (C) Albrecht
Petter Hergedt
Balsazar (O) Löffler
Stephan (X) Kneisel
Phillip Petter Huff
Johannes Kerlinger
Daniel (+) Sommer
Johannes Battefelt
Philipp Bathenfeld
Hans Adam Battenfeld
Johann Heinrich Leibling
Sebastian (OO) Werner
Leonhart (OO) Heichel
Johann Friedrich Thomas
Johann Jacob Schäffer
Johann Wilhelm Stoll

Johannes Stall
Johannes Böhmer
Johan Peter Böhmer
Johann Willhelm Kölb
Lucas Schäffer
Johann Paullus Müller
Johann Wilhelm Schnyder
Hans Martin Kollmer
Michael Mell
Jacob Roller
Martin Bugh
Bernhart (X) Rothbaus
Hans Christoph Englerth
Christian Matthes
Jacob Rosch
Jacob Adam Nonnemacher
Andreas Wentz
Michael (O) Waltz
Jacob Reble
Hans Balthas Buck
Johan Jacob Klein
Jacob Bloss
Hans Jerg Sauerbrey
Johanes (O) Billheimer
Hans Adam (W) Shmit
Johanes (X) Becker
Anderas ( ) Dürr, on board
Hans George (+) Geltz
Jacob (X) Weis
Martin (X) Weis
Hans Jerg Weiss
Jacob Daniel
Johann David Büchell

Bernhart (+) Berch
Hans Jerg Knodel
Tobias (×) Muller
Tobias Müller, Junior·
Johann Jacob Braun
Matheus Brundle
Christoph Friderich Reutter
Hans Jerg Müller
Matheis Seufried
Hans Wendel (×) Seufrid
Joseph (×) Seufried
Hans Jerg Wüster
Johan Christoph Brentziger
Hans Jerg Madich
Eberhart (×) Bichel
Christoff Buckbeck
Matheis Rössler
Jacob Vottler [?]

Michael (×) Tybly
Peter Martin
Mattheus Marte
Hans Georg Dischler
Johanes (×) Warner
Lorentz Spatz
Johann Friedrich Risch
Balsatzar ( ) Munster, sick
Christoph (+) Meyer
Hans Jerg Saal
Philipp Dellinger
Henry (+) Hillinger
Matheas (×) Berger
Joseph Stumbf
Johannes Jung
J. Daniel (×) Printz
Gotlip ( ) Weniger, on board

[List 154 C] [Foreigners imported in the Ship Phoenix, John Mason, Captain, from Rotterdam, but last from Cowes. August 28, 1750. 339 passengers.] *

Erdman Schultz
Johannes Seltzer
Simon Peter
Christian Bernhardi,
Jacob (×) Saber
Jacob Patz
Johann Georg Leyss
Johan Ludwig Schleber
Johan Nickel Vogelgesang
Johan Conrad Protzman
John Henry (×) Weydigh
Johan Georg Kalteisen
Jean Drapet
Caspar (×) Bruner
Michel Peter

Henrich Gerhart
Hans Wirheimer
Jacob (×) Moog
Ernst Böhm
Conrad (×) Zellner
Georg Betzler
Peter (×) Seigendaller
Ulrich (×) Seigendaller
Johannes Peter
George (×) Hultzler
Jacob (×) Sheel
Jacob (×) Frison
Henry (×) Yeal
George (×) Yure
George (×) Saling

* The first page of this list is lost. Hence we offer from Rupp's *Collection of Thirty Thousand Names*, p. 236 f., the first 100 names that are missing. The list was evidently complete in his day.

George (X) Kop
Jacob (X) Werly
Conrad (X) Hay
Dewald (X) Theil
Jacob Reb
David (X) Frarry
Jacob (X) Muni, Jr.
Jacob (X) Muni, Senr
Debolt Beck
Peter Dinck
Henry (X) Herman
Michael (X) Cuntz
Andreas Hotz
Georg Hauss
Peter Schmitt
Jacob Riffel
Peter (X) Erhart
Dietrich (X) Erhart
Debalt Frantz
Frantz Anton
Georg (X) Gees
Joseph Waltz
Philip (X) Hind
Jacob Anthoni
Solomon Phillips
Johan David Schmitt
Johan Wilhelm Hertzog
Johan Jacob Peter
Michael (X) Forbringer
Heinrich Eberhard
Johann Wilhelm Weiss
Johan Gottfried Rüger
Carl Ernst Rüger
Georg Siegenthahler
Johan Jacob Reich
Philip Jacob Volandt
Hans Michel Nothstein
John George (X) Debald
Henry (X) Haberman

Michael Lehman
Christian (X) Muni
Conrad (X) Muni
Hans Ulrich Schleppi
Andreas (X) Muni
Christopf (X) Durrenberger
Michael (X) Berger
Hans Jacob Seuter
Nicklaus (X) Yeisly
Johann Georg Herman
Andreas Diemer
Johan Friedrich Röhn
Dewald Kuntz
Johan David Ziffel
Johannes Zurbrück
Martin (X) Buchman
Jacob (X) Buchman
Georg Hans Anthoni
Nicklaus Jacob
Georg Friedrich Lintz
Johannes (X) Meyer
Carl Seusterditz
Christoph Fischer
Adam Hiltenbrandt
Abraham (X) Shopffer
Martin Burchhardt
Michael Straub
Henry (X) Meyer
Ulrich (X) Fooks
Dewalt (X) Fooks
George (X) Lohr
Jacob Werner
George (X) Lindeman *
George (H) Hotzinger
Peter Ber
Hans Georg Jung
Nicklas Hegi
Anthoni Grieser
Hans George (O) Eter

* Here begin the signatures that have been preserved. Even here some of the names have been restored in part or in full from Rupp's List.

Görg Henrich Etter
Jacob Friedrich West
Jacob Haber
Johannes Wedel
Johann Friedrich von Rohr
Johann Andreas von Rohr
Gottfried Thiele
Christoph Pfuller
Johan (X) Otmansdorff
Peter Schirmer
Jacob Laubenhauer
Hans Braun
Valentin Mochel
Michael (X) Malleberger
Hennrich Miller
Johann Wilhelm Wigand
Johann Friedrich Wigand
Jacob Grube [?]
Ernst Jacob Dippsberger
Johanes (+) Lips
Abraham (X) Enderly
Christian Gross
Peter Heister
Jacob Heck
Johan (+) Salomon
[Michael] Lederman
[David Dieterich] *
Jacob [Fischer]
Christian Andrae
Adam Weiss
Paul Weber
Johan Jacob Heider
Johann Grim
Johan Heinrich Grimm
Hans (++) Miller
Gottfried Peuckert
Johann Tobias Zimmerman
Friederick (X) Zimmerman
Johan Michael Heuschkehl
Johan Christoph Heuschkell

Beniamin Heuschkel
Godlieb (X) Bobe
George (X) Mattler
Davidt Ensminger
George (H) Reinhart
Hans Heinrich Nägel
Heinrich Presler
Debalt (TF) Farringer
Killian (+) Jaac
Conrad in Hofe [?]
Jerg Voltz
Martin (X) Jost
Philip (+) Finck
Michael Fistler
Gottlieb Thurm
Nickolas (X) Kiffer
Abraham Rith[müller]
Pancratius Reich[held]
Hans Wechterling
Adam (H) Hab[erling]
[Philip Friedrich Winther]
[Johan Georg Malle]
Jacob Schoch
Philipp Ferber
Andreas Wittenmeyer
Andreas Engel
Beder Will
Nicklaus Jost
Johanes (H) Gerber
Joseb Gerber
Johannes Philipi
Johannes Philip, Junr
Andares Philipi
Christian (+) Philipy
Hans Jacob Liebengut
Hans Jacob Liebengutt, Jun.
Beder Liebengut
George (O) Shep
Johan Jacob Leininger
Dewalt Nagel

* Restorations from Rupp's list are enclosed in square brackets.

Adam Seifenbacher	Georg (X) Viet
Ludwig Wohlfahrt	Johann Gottfriedt [Zichelhardt]
Nickel Herman	Jacob Klöti
Caspar (+) Shmit	Willhelm Ehrmann
Georg Claus	Thomas (O) Shlighter
Johannes Claus	Nickolaus (X) Shlighter
Christian (X) Gurdner	Fillib Vock
Johannes Filipipi	Hans Jerg Dieren[berger]
Marx Dahleth	Ullrich Eggler
[Joseph] Peter Bauer	Paulus Bleym[eier]
[Christian] His	Hans Jerg Lutwick
[George Engelhart]	Peter (X) Haberstich
Ludwig Wittenmeyer	Johannes (X) Steckel
Hans (+) Blasser	Sirach Schultz
Heinrich Sterchi	Hans Jerg Foltz
Filipp Walatein	Jacob Guntzerhauser
Hans (D) Diterig	Hans ( ) Wagner, on board

[List 155 C] At the Court House at Philadelphia, Friday,
the 31st August, 1750.
          Present: Thomas Lawrence, Esquire, Mayor.
    The Foreigners whose names are underwritten, imported in
the Ship Nancy, Thomas Coatam, Master, from Rotterdam &
last from Cowes, did this day take the usual Oaths. By List 88.
Persons 270.

Johannes Vollmer	Jeorg Geuling
Balthas Federhaff	Johannis Zweigle
Johan Bernhardt Riede	Friedrich Blankenhorn
Daniel Dosser	Johann Georg Baur
Bernhardt Rockenstihl	Johann Bernhard Wünsch
Daniel Haubensack	Johann Georg Sieger
Johan Conrad Raisch	Johan Georg Musse
Martin Müller	Michael Rieder
Lorentz Schenckel	Andreas Brauer
Joseph Stähle	Michel Jensel
Johan Thobias Rudolph	Johannes Schneider
Hans Jerg Hetler	Georg David Schneider
Martin Jannel	Hans Jerg Kuhner
Fridrich Gann	Christoff Knnodbel
Johannes Gann	Johann Jacob Canz
Thomas (X) Gan	Johannes Glaser

Jonas Raub	Jacob Würtz
Friderich Weiss	Hanns Jerg Gilbert
Wilhelm Gettling	Andres Singele
Hans Jerg Beytenman	Hans Adam Herbolt
Johan Jacob Beitenman	Johann Philipp Haupt
Georg Friederigh Beittenman	Hans Jacob Gilbert
Johan Friedrich Unrath	Johann Michell Bock
Johan Friedrich Unrath	Johan Jacob Batich
Heinrich Behringer	Christian (+) Blosser
Heinrich Behringer	Johannes Löw
Jerg Heinrich Lutz	Christgan Giebeler
Jerg Heinrich Lutz	Jost Henrich Wehler
Georg Wilhelm Marx	Johann Peter Gutelius
Johann Georg Marx	Tilman Creutz
Henderick Willem Stiegel *	Johann Jacob Brumbach
Christian Fauts	Johan Gitting
Johan Jacob Weiss	Daniel (+) Shneyder
Michel Ferster [?]	Dilmanus Weissgerber
Jeremias Horngacher	[Johann]es Reesbach
Johan Ludwig Traber	[Johanes] Jung
Christian Hornberg[er]	Johan Peter (✕) Kleim
Hans Jerg Banner	David Nüss
Matdeis Rahnfelter	Johan Henrich Conrath
H. Bernhart (H) Gilbert	Johann Henrich Klein
Johann Colaus Gilbert	Philip Grabeman
Johann Jacob Gobel	J. Henry (+) Seydenstiker
Christoff Wetzel	Immanuel Boger
Johann Georg Gilbert	Johan Henrich Jung, Jr
Franz Kühlewein	Johann Geörg Braunsberg
Johann Jacob Baum	

[List 156 C] At the Court House at Philadelphia, Wednesday, ye 12ᵗʰ Septʳ 1750.

Present: Thomas Lawrence, Esquire, Mayor.

The Foreigners whose Names are underwritten, imported in the Ship Priscilla, Captⁿ Wm. Wilson, from Rotterdam & Cowes, did this day take and subscribe the usual Oaths, etc. By List 74. Persons 210.

John Henry (✕) Ritzel	Johan Wilhelm Reutzel
Christian Reutzel	Johannes Grack

* The famous glassmaker of Manheim, Lancaster County, Pa.

Conrad Grack
Peter (PH) Hartman
Friederich Steinberger
Nicolaus Weininger
George (✕) Cunkel
Andreas Schuster
Hans Michael Wisner
Johan Gorg Wissner
Vallentin Born
Nicklaus Schäffer
Johannes Guckel
Johann Henrich Rössler
Georg Henrich Rösch
George Ernst (+) Rish
Johannes Tranck
Johannes Meyer
Connradt Hertzog
Johann Georg Keyser
Kasper Oberdorff
Daniel (X) Resseler
Johann Geörg Rössler
Joachim Gottschalck
Eberhard Steygerwalt
Johannes Stang
Johann Adam Börner
Johannes Huth
Wilhelm Adelman
Görg Ernst Becker
Johans Mauss
Hans Andreas Kachel
Andreas Oberdorff
Friederik (✕) Shnyder
John Jacob (✕) Newman
Wendel (✕) Lawmeister
Johannes Ommerth
Johannes Kraushaar
Vallentin (✕) Corngiber

Balsatzer (✕) Simmon
Henrich Lotz
Christian Hartting
Michael (++) Roth
Thomas (✕) Bertholt
Johann Melchior Orth
Johan Adam Roth
Johann Baltzer Stockel
Gerort Philibb Kirscher
J. Peter (+) Günder
Johannes Schlott
Johannes (✕) Heyl
Johannes Hügel
Georg Wachdel
Ludwig (✕✕✕) Shmith
Johannes Schumann
Johann Peter Muth
Baltzer Jäger
Nicklas (+) Berninger
Johannes Föller
Melchior (✕) Kleinfeller
Johannes Möller
Balsatzar (✕✕✕) Filler
Johannes (✕) Lamb
Carl (+) Russ
Andreas Oetzel
John Simon ( ) Oberdorff, on board
Carol ( ) Miller, on board
Johannes Diener
Johan Michael ( ) Stoffel, on board
Johan Henry (+) Rully
Johann Henrich Luft
Simon Schiercher
Conrad Rössler

[List 157 C] At the Court House at Philadelphia, Saturday, the 29th Septr 1750.
Present: The Worshipful Thos Lawrence, Esqr, Mayor.

The Foreigners whose Names are underwritten, imported in the Ship Osgood, Capt William Wilkie, from Rotterdam & Cowes, did this day take & subscribe the foregoing Qualifications. By List 145. Persons 486.

Hendrick (B) Bronk	Hans George (+) Zigler
Jerik (O) Wisht	Johan Martin Neher
Jacob (JW) Wist	Johan Georg Speidel
Laurentius Wüst	Johann Frider Sauter
Jacob Wüst	Ludwig Stotz
Christoph (+) Shmit	Jacob Schneidter
Michael (X) Shmit	[F.] Schweitzer
Hans Jorg Hautzenbieler	Gerg Scheufelen
Johannes Greiner	Christian Schuhler
Conrad (O) Toll	Jacob Scheüfflen
Gerg Becker	Rudolph Christy
Johannes Seyl	Hans Jerg Frietz
Jacob (X) Clauser	Hans Martin Wolffer
Henry (X) Clauser	Jacob (X) Keanigh
Johannes Schwab	Andreas Herther
Andre Baudemont	Jacob Glosser
Nickolas (N) Burg	Johannes Moritz
Heinrich Hörner	Lorentz (O) Dobler
Nicolaus Hörner	Ludwig (LRW) Readwile
Friedrich Hörner	Johann Michel Rietweill
Welten Peterman	Johann Arnolt Kuntz
Michael (X) Peterman	Gerch Uhlrich
Hans Adam (O) Kney	Phillipp Jacob
Wilhelm Humbert	Johannes Dinges
George (HD) Dick	Conrad Mittman
Christian (F) Faas	Gottlieb Mittelberger *
Jacob (H) Krebs	Durst (X) Contick
Gabriel (O) Leydy	Nicolaus Haugendobler
Edar (X) Deghe	Johan Wendel Ackherman
Freiderich Reif	Friderich Ruoss
Jacob Schleich	Michel Bile
Godlib (+) Kauffman	Johann Georg Ackermann
Mathes Schnepp	Ludwig Bitzer
Bartolomeus Eppler	Johannes Bitzer
Hans Baltes Otz	Hans Caspar Eberhard
Petter Stotz	Lorentz Marquedandt

* The author of the "Journey to Pennsylvania," 1750.

Ludwig Eisele
Hans Jerg Marti
Hans Matis Spohn
Lutwig Moritz
Johann Christoph Niedt
Friederich Gauss
Johan George (X) Ludwig
Hans Martin Waltz
Johannis Wolfer
Christian Schmoller
Hans Jacob Binder
Johann Friedrich Binder
Johann Georg Gauss
Anthony (X) Shnyder
Jacob Frasch
Matheas (X) Meyer
Hans Georg (X) Meyer
Hans Martin Kientzein
Hans Martin Kintzein, Junior
Michel Reisinger
Johann Heinrich Lüder
Heinrich Dietmar
Johann Christian Freindel
Johann Gottfried Richter
Christian Iserloh
Johan Gottlob Hoppe
Hans Gorg Koberstein
Johann Martin Kast
Emmanuel Breitscheidt
Jacob Friederich Kümmerlyn
Hans George (X) Fackler
Christian Heusler
Hans Jerg Gnödler
Michael (+) Heinrich
Hans Georg Schweigerth

Hans Jerg Murr
Andereas (X) Knödler
Hans Jerg Kurtz
Christian ( ) Kurtz, on board
Sebastian Kayser
Hans Georg (X) Shnawffer
Hans Michael Dentzer
Johan Daniell Bosch
Johan Jacob Bosch
Johann Michael, Junr
Hans Jerg Gutekunst
Christoph (X) Albrecht
Johan Petter Bender
Johan Beder Benter
Conradt Bender
Johannes Schmoll
Johan Philipp Mosser
Vallentin Heygis
Jerg Heigis
Hans Ludwig Zimmerman
Hans Jerg Mekhel
Hans Ludwieg Stein
Mattheis Miller
Hans Martin Müller
Christian Stotz
Bernhart Wüst
Jacob Epele
Fillip Joseph Schilling
Hs. Gerg Bach
Jacob Liebheim
Jacob (X) Uhllerik
Andereas (A) Kertcher
Hans Jacob (X) Shanker
Louis Grizet

[List 158 C] At the Court House at Philadelphia, Wednesday, the 17th 8ber 1750.

Present: The Worshipful William Plumsted, Esqr, Mayor.

The Foreigners whose names are subscribed, imported in the Brigantine Sally, Captain William Hassleton, from the

City of London, did this day take & subscribe the usual Oaths.
By List 25. Persons ———.

Christoff (   ) Renshaw, sick on board
Joseph (×) Räff
Peter (   ) Millendick, on board
Lutwig Falck
Jacob (W) Winkler
Hans Uhlerik (H) Winsh
Hans (Hans) Stuber
Durst (×) Knor
Nicklas (×) Dick
Hans (   ) Stohl, on board
Hans (×) Ammich
Hans (×) Stuber
Johann Gottfried Diele
Augustin Schepheler
Friderich Schäphler
Johanes (Kuhn) Koon
Hans Jörg Keller
Jacob (   ) Furrer, on board
Christoff (   ) Coblet, on board
Hans George (   ) Frey, on board
Hans (   ) Knerr, on board
Jacob (×) Dick
Christian (×) Stober
Abrahm (   ) Garsing, on board
Jacob (   ) Miller, on board

[List 159 C] At the Courthouse at Philadelphia, Saturday, the 3ᵈ November, 1750.
Present: The Worshipful William Plumsted, Esquire, Mayor.
      Mr. David Martin, Rector of the Academy.
The Foreigners whose Names are subscribed, imported in the Ship Brotherhood, Captain John Thomson, from Rotterdam & last from Cowes, did this day take & subscribe the usual Qualification. By List 119. Persons 300.

Conrat (L) Laubsher
Johan Jacob Laubsher
Johannes Schäffer
Johan Nicolaus Schäffer
Simon Minch
Teobalt Weylland
Johann Elias Willjahr
Johan Adam (H) Heyl
Georg Friedrich Bayer
Matheis Haffner
Johann Peter Binckli
Johann Jacob Maag
Hs. Georg Schaufler
Jacob (×) Stark
Jacob (×) Sicher
Peter (×) Sicher
Johann Nicolaus Meck
Matthäs Brückert
Pierre Paris
Isaac Paris
Isaac Jung
Michael (   ) Shwing, on board
Samuel (×) Shwing
Johannes Schock
Petter Hähn
Jacob (   ) Frey, on board
Michael Fritz
Johannis (+) Albrecht
John Jost (+) Shwalb
Johann Jacob Wolckener

Johanes Knauss
Peter Rotenburger
Johan Henrich Küblinger
Johan Christoffel He[mbel]
Nicolaus Bonn
Johannes (X) Bonn
Nicklas (X) Weisman
Michael (X) Weisman
Paul Jomel
Sebastian Käppler
Christian Däublin
Wilhelm Krum
Hans Zinser
Philieb Leister
Nicklas (X) Leyster
Johanes Lehman
Peter Basler
Joseb Basler
Jacob Basler
Johannes Basler
Jacob Schwalder
Jacob Schowalter
Hannes Schowalter
Joseph Schowalter
Christian Schowalter
Peter Schowalter
Henry (X) Stegel
Peter Lugenbiehl
Simon (X) Wishan
Petter Farne
Joseph Fahrne
Christian Bidmer
Johanes (X) Rub
Christian (X) Rub
Jacob Bürckh
Jacob (O) Lichty
Johannes Holby
[Nicola]us Mihller
Johannes Nast
Christian (X) Furrer
Peter (X) Stuky

Christian Blaich
Hans (X) Konig
Henrich Schwartz
Hans (X) Zorr
Joseph (X) Meyer
Andres Holly
Michel Holly
Christian Kauffman
Beder Dielebach
Peter (X) Fisher
Johannes Rohrer
Johann Anthon Eckell
Johann Philipp Eckel
Johann Jacob Lösch
Johann Adam Stöhr
Jülch Feillein [?]
Michael (X) Wurm
Johannes Schneider
Christian (X) Neucomer
Johann Jorg Beck
Ludwig ( ) Fetzer, on board
Wilhelm (X) Werner
Hans (XX) Gundelfinger
Peter (X) Knabe
Hans Blauch
Jacob Naftziger
Christian (X) Knebel
Hans Knebel
Michael (X) Stuky
Hans Jost Hertzer
Johannes Hertzler
Hans (+) Hertzel
Hans (X) Seegerist
Johan Jost Weigandt
Georg Daniel Orth
Jacob Berg
Andres Berg
Melchior Geissert
Jacob Mösinger
Christgan Nauman
Jerg Rebschleger

Nickolaus Schmidt

Jacob (✕) Reis

Jeorg Weiss

Jacob Graf

Jacob Graf

Jacob Behr

Hanns Funck

Martin Funck

Paul (+) Roth

Jacob Hauser

Johannes Hauser

Johann Georg Bauer

[List 160 C] At the Court House at Philadelphia, Friday, 30th Nov. 1750.

Present: The Worshipful William Plumsted, Esqʳ, Mayor.

The Foreigners whose names are underwritten, imported in the Ship Sandwich, Captain Hazelwood, from Rotterdam and last from Cowes, did this day take & subscribe the usual Qualifications. By List 97. Whole Freights 200.

Michael (✕) Frankhauser

Jacob Simon

Johann Georg Gass

Johan Ludwig

Peter (✕) Sallatin

Christian Fiess

Jacob (R) Rumel

Jörg Fillips Rumel

Johann Phillip Körpert

Leonhard Rupperter

Jacob Fahrner

Joseph Klöpfer

Lorentz Klöpfer

Johannes Willdanger

Jacob Traub

Henrich Schmitt

Johannes (✕) Koch

Matheas (✕) Wiltanger

Martin Weinberger

Johannes Knauss

Johannes Weygel

Adam Weygel

Daniel Debus

Henry (H) Hartzel

Nicklaus (✕) Lorentz

Peter (✕) Huffshmit

Thomas Moll

Johan Petter Schaeffer

Jacob (JB) Böllinger

Hans Jacob Bigler

Johannes Fuchs

Andreas Muntz

Johann Peter Lemberty

Johan (   ) Eastbach, on board

Paulus ( ) Groundler, on board

Hans Adam Biebel

John Christoffel (✕) Lawbach

George (O) Brech

Johann Leonhardt Kessler

Johannes Leutzi

Georg Anthon Deull

Jorg Pilus Teul

Philipp Gassman

Michael (O) Mögan

Henrich Stumpf

Georg ( ) Cooper, on board

Johann Henrich Wäydmann

John Martin ( ) Shouffman

Henry (   ) Haan

Petter Manz

Caspar Vetter

Johann Adam Gross

Jgl. Adam Wagner
Jchoh Georg Wagner
Johannes (×) Reel
Kasper Riffnach
Jacob Langs
Wendel (H) Herman
Friderich Schenckel
Jacob (S) Shmit
Peter (H) Shmit
Martin (O) Nazurus
Johann Jacob Koch
Fillib Becker
Uhllerich (+) Tuxly
Johannes (H) Fleisher
Rolandt May
Geörg Oest
Jacob Bricker
Michel Fünfrock
Nicklaus Schande
Johann Friedrich Eager
Johann Georg Schwartz
Johann Anthon Schwartz

Johann Philipp Schwartz
Johann Anthonius Körner
Moritz Wöber
Jacob Spitler
Martin (O) Birro
Michael Gampler
Jacob (O) Becht
Jerg Habacher
Anthony Hachen
Christian (×) Hagen
Benedicht Im Hoff
Julius Hachen
Lunzy (×) Shmitley
Fried Schor, Senior
Fried (×) Yor, Junior
Hans Weber
Hans Adam Wäber
Michel Schor
Engelhart ( ) Yeiser
Godlieb ( ) Beckly
Caspar Mayer

[List 161 C] At the Court House at Philadelphia, Tuesday,
ye 25th August 1751.
Present: The Worshipful William Plumsted, Esqr, Mayor
of Philadelphia.

The Foreigners whose names are underwritten, imported in
the Ship Anderson, Hugh Campbell, Master from Rotterdam
& last from Cowes, did this day take and subscribe the usual &
foregoing Qualifications. 236 Freights. N° 100. 50 Roman
Catholics. Messrs Stedman.

Lowrance (+) Durst
Hans Jurch Hummerle
Johannes Frick
Mathias (×) Rost
Hans George (O) Hook
Jacob (O) Maud
Joseph (×) Strohle

Michael (×) Chrisback
Hans (O) Martz
Johanes (H) Bower
George (×) Hoozer
Ludwich (×) Werner
Sebastian Greim
Adam Greim

Hans (×) Riter
Johann Friedrich Geyer
Hans George (×) Eisinberg
Peter (O) Breilinger
Peter Klein
Martin (×) Clain
Anthony (×) Yauble
Joseph Voltz
Abraham (+) Rinhart
Hans (O) Adams
Hans (×) Shaver
Georg Vallentin Fehl
Philip (×) Kinder
Andreas (O) Hyder
Petter Wehrner
Ulrich (×) Bernhart
Hans Scheffer
Hans Jacob Bernaht
Michael (H) Moritz
Lorentz Leble
Hans Gorg Schneider
Jost Stroh
Michell Dannerinborgen
Michael Dannerinborgen
Mades Flach
Johannes (O) Zimer
Hans Caspar Strudter
Lorentos (O) Shiney
Joseph Riebell
Hans Michael (×) Koonts
Georg Arbengast
Michael Sommer
Georg Adam Wickersheim
Matthias Sumer
Michael (+) Slauter
Hans Michael (×) Algyer
Hans Yerick (H) Huber
Franciscus (×) Eidier
Johanes (×) House

Philip ( ) House
Michael (×) Bower
Lorents (×) Fisher
Yerick (×) Fisher
Anthony (×) Schydner
Georg Sifridt
Hans Michael (+) Seafredt
Hans Yerick (×) Seafredt
Michael Kintz
Bartholome (BH) Heist
Hans (H) Haysh
Hans (H) Schiff
Joseph Kautz
Michael (+) Reeby
Hans Michael (O) Blanck
Hans Geörg Yundt
Yerick (×) Beck
Yerick (×) Baker
Gerg Bewer
Andres Straub
Jacob Walder
Michael Kürmann
Gorg Kirmann
Marx Kürrmann
Johann Jacob Vogt
Yerick (×) Mertz
Georg Pfotzer
Matthias Kürrmann
Hans Schott
Michael Kann
Johs Rotenberger
Johannes Schüttülerlin *
Hans Jerg Holdeintz
Hans George (×) Bower
Joseph (×) Slater
Martin Schlatter
Hans Görg Ullrich
Johann Georg Aumüller
Hans Yerick (H) Num

* Read Schütterlin.

Jacob (✕) Scheterly   Andreas Schutterlin
Jacob (✕) Miller   Matthias Hess
Petter Descher

[List 162 C] At the State House at Philadelphia, Thursday,
the Fifth Day of September 1751.
Present: The Worshipful William Plumsted, Esqr, Mayor.
The Foreigners whose Names are underwritten, Imported
in the Billander [Elizabeth],* Captain Richgate Castle, from
Rotterdam and last from Cowes in England, did this day take
and subscribe the usual Qualification. No. 91. 130 whole
Freights. 30 Roman Catholics. Messrs. Stedman.

Johannes Götz
Johannes Has
Johan (   ) Ekelman, on board
Mathieu Guery
Georg Römmer
H. Uhllerik (+) Glötzel
Johannes (✕) Stösser
David Ficher
Nicolas Wächnisen
Henrich Pals
Melchior (+) Ruth
Jacob Gangloff
Simon Falck
Dietmar Werner
Nickell Emerich
Christian Willy
Henrich Friderich Degenhart
Jerg Michael Mannbar
Gottfried Paul
Jerg Christian Sert
Jacob Müller
Jacob Züffle
Jacob Schneider
Johanes (✕) Fisher
Georg (   ) Frokman, on board
Andreas (   ) Singly, on board
Johann Carle Bensle

Jacob Lauser
Johann Peter Straube
Jacob Baleur [?]
Johannes Weber
Johannes Lindöhmer
Johann Paulus Kielnecker
Johann Jacob Schue
Johannrich Leischerr
Johanes (✕) Kesseler
Martin (✕) Brown
Hartman Strohpeter
Johann Adam Erben
Johann Jobst Franckh
Michael Barle
Michael Weidt
Barth. Arend
George (✕) Reyser
Adam (+) Storch
Carle Wiederholt
Wilm Loomyer
Joh. Abraham Arbeiter
Otto Haasse
Johann Christian Schour
Wilhelm Hammer
Johan Kilian Feltmann
Johanes Seyfarth
Johann Michael Deininger

* For the name of this ship see the summary of the year 1751, on p. 477.

Hans Gorg Spring
Dominique Fleur
Tomas Füssler
Hendrich Fürstler
Jacob Thüringer
Johann Dietrich Hoffman
Vallentin Claudy
George (+) Miller
H. Michael (H) Metz
Josep ( ) Wittemer, on board
H. Martin (×) Vandalin
Hans Beter Schaub
Christoph Fleur
Hans (O) Straub
Hans ( ) Metz, on board
Christian (+) Rits
Johan Caspar Jungman
Adam Gehrich

Jeremias (×) Taubenheim
Matthias Schwartzwelder
Peter ( ) Weber, on board
Jacob Meier
Jacob (××) Minjan
Hans Jerg Felber
Caspar Vögle
Johannes Geiger
Johannes Hildebrand
Daniel (+) Miller
Johan Georg Reichwein
Hinrig Erhardt
Johann Christoph Uhle
Johannes Michael Gisselbrecht
Joseph Joram
Johan Christian Alter
Augustus Milchsack
Henry (×) Demanche

[List 163 C] At the State House at Philadelphia, Thursday Afternoon, 5th September, 1751.
Present: The Mayor of the City.
The Foreigners whose Names are underwritten, imported in the Ship Shirley, Captn James Allen, from Rotterdam and last from the Orkneys in Scotland, did this day take and subscribe the usual Qualifications. No. 121. 288 whole Freights. 3 Roman Catholics. Messrs Stedman.

Lenard (×) Maas
Johannes Fähr
Johannes Hoff
Hans Jerg Betz
Christof (+) Ludewig
Mattheus Reutter
Jerg Jacob Fäsal
Henry (×) Uhrrer
Joseph Michael ( ) Shottey, on board
Johann Georg Schumacher
Johann Casper Spring
Heinrich Wagner

Johann Martin Kroll
Jacob Huth
Michael Schneider
Godlieb ( ) Rothde, on board
Johannes Heyt
Johann Philipp Wagner
Michael (+) Weiss
Hans George (×) Klobly
Johan Georg ( ) Curr
Johann Lorentz
Hans Mardin Seyfrid
Görg Adam Störr
Hans Adam Gramlich

John Barnhard (×) Shrank
Hans Gerg Schranck
Johann Michael Wagner
Georg Kiebler
Heinrich Krafft
Johann Jacob Braun
Thomas (×) Geiner
Hans Conradt Zilling
Georg Conrad Schweichart
Frieterich Sinn
Gorg Schörkh
Jacob Schweickert
Hans Adam Frank
Jacob (×) Shack
Heinrich Curr
Johan Fredik (×) Teitz
Hans Gorg Kautzman
Jerg Michel Walcker
Martin Leyer
Nickolas (+) Mildeberger
Lorentz (+) Ludewig
Lutwig Schüttler
Friederik (+) Shetz
Frans Stephanus Schweitzer
George (IF) Frantz
Georg Kleeh
Johann (×) Grosskopff
Hans Steffan Marthin
Daniel (O) Pracht
Jörg Balschbach
Jerg Kreidler
Andereas (×) Kuhn
Christoph Grässle
Burckhart Heinrich
Wendel Minch
Jerg Simon Baum
Isa Paris
Johanes (×) Ney
Johan Georg Gassinger
Stephan Schertzer
Hans Samuel (×) Shweyart

Johann David Herbst
Balzar (×) Hening
H. George (×) Ney
Hans Jacob Schoch
Veit Meister
Conrad (×) Sampel
Johannes Gilbert
Johann Henrich Schirm
Frederik ( ) Krafft, on board
Jan Christoff Mook
Johann Martin Sitzer
H. Georg (×) Wurteberger
Christoph Horlacher
Georg Michael Gretter
H. Michael (×) Wurtenberg-
[er]
Johann Georg Rühlin
Johann Conrad Beyrer
Hans Georg Vogelmann
Michael (×) Foegelman
Johann Michael Sommer
Friedrich Wielandt
Christian (×) Sholl
Lenhart (×) Sumer
Michael (+) Arnold
Dietrich Röhm
Peter Mugler
Frederik (×) Shwartz
Johann Georg Blintzinger
Christian (×) Riger
Friderich Gros
Georg Martin Carle
Hans Michel Ott
Davit ( ) Frank
Davit ( ) Edlinger
Francis ( ) Edebberger
Ludwich ( ) Ernst
Jacob Bernard ( ) Danecker
Johannes ( ) Reys
Melchior ( ) Lawall
Hans Georg ( ) Hand

Michael ( ) Foelix
Gabriel ( ) Rössler
Johan George ( ) Epson
Johan Michael ( ) Leytecker
Melchior ( ) Reyval
Andereas ( ) Shmeltzer

Christopher ( ) Ederly
Jacob ( ) Sheyder
Johan Elias ( ) Horrst
Nickolas ( ) Mittelburger
Hans ( ) Shauman
Jacob ( ) Gerringer *

[List 164 C] At the Court House at Philadelphia, Monday, the 9th September 1751.
Present: The Worshipful, the Mayor.

The Foreigners whose Names are underwritten, imported in the Ship Patience, Captain Hugh Steel, from Rotterdam and last from Cowes in England, did this day take and subscribe the usual Qualifications. No. 109. Whole Freights 255. 8 Roman Catholicks.

John ( ) Hendrick
Piere Balmas
Diewald Hig
Andereas (✕) Blechor
Daniel Tien
Jacob (IW) Weingard
Stephan (IW) Deer
Abraham Wild
Isaac Rene
Mathieu Moret
Eberhart Chappelle
Gorg Lutwig Matt
Jean Henri Tien
Johann Andres Bersch
Johannes Strohschneytder
Johannes Strohschneider
Johannes Friderich Strohschney-
ter
Michel Schneider
Daniel Echartt
Christian (✕) Grau
Hans Michael (✕) Mauer
Mich. Borkart
Hans George (M) Worthlin

Hans (✕) Worthlin
Johannes (+) Bock
Jacob Danninger
Michael Mönch
Samuel Pauser
Hanns Petter Enck
Christian ( ) Gally, on board
Christian Carel Conver
H. George (✕) Gerhart
Johan Henrich Hering
Philip Wendel Höring
Johann Henrich Hering
Jacob Wolf
John George (✕) Reely
Johann Georg Gabb
Philipps Freine [?]
Johan Andreos Hütig
Philipps Carl Jüdä
Johann Andreas Becher
Carl Anton Bergman
Jacob Enkisch
Philip (H) Gob
Blasius Isele
Michael Wieder

* All these names were written by the clerk in the absence of the passengers.

Johann Christoph Wieder
Johann Georg Ruoff
Johan Diterich (X) Weitzen
Johan Henrich Weitzel
Johann Frantz Huber
Martin Erdman
Hans Peter (X) Kuber
Philips Conradt Zeiler
Jacob Stöhr
Johan Henrich Stöhr
Lutwig Rimmel
Nicolaus Rimmel
Johann Martin Freitag
Georg Hennrich Joseph
Johann Peter Müller
Johann Henrich Deull
Johan Fillib Haubert
Peter (X) Haubert
J. Peter (A) Andrea
Peter (+) Thomas
Johan Wilhelm Litz
France (FH) Hoff
Hans Peter ( ) Shutz, on board
Peter (O) Hant
Peter Martin
Henry (X) Richart
Johan Diel Schmoll
Johan Nicol Bass
J. Henry Dietzel
J. Adam ( ) Oberkirsh
Johannes (X) Shwarbach
Johann Jacob Weyll

Jacob (X) Martin
Mich. Drarbach
J. Adam (X) Trarbach
Jacob (+) Trarbach
Johan Peter Holderbaum
Johan Adam Barthmes
J. Peter (X) Thomas
Johan Peter Ströher
Conrad (K) Miller
Henry (H) Miller
Johan Georg Scheelmann
Nicola Walter
Joanes Rust
Daniel (H) Hess
Jost (O) Karger
Melchior (S) Spery
Johanes (X) Bloch
Michael (X) Bloch
George (X) Bloch
Hans Adam Didrich
Jacob Leibrock
Nickolas (W) Wolff
Peter (XX) Walcher
Friedrich Möbs
Bernhard Baur
Christian (X) Lindner
Petrus Frauenstadt
Hans Jörg Werner
Lorrentz Voss
Johann Henrich Feger
Hans Michel Hinrich

[List 165 C] At the Court House at Philadelphia, Saturday, the 14th September 1751.

Present: The Worshipful, the Mayor, Joshua Maddox, Esqr.

The Foreigners whose Names are underwritten, imported in the Ship St Andrew, Captn James Abercrombie, from Rotterdam, but last from Cowes in England, did this day take and subscribe the usual Qualification. No. 100. 230 whole Freights.

8 Roman Catholicks. 10 Mennonists. Rem^r Calvinists. Messrs Stedman.

Johanes Lenn
Georg Ludwig Kassenberger
Peter Jacob Weiss
Rudolph Schöppi
Peter (X) Ekman
Wendel Hans
Peter (X) Berringer
Hennrich Seydenbender
Jacob Brandt
Martin (X) Schwob
Jacob Kimmel
Johann Philipp Kimmel
Adam Kimmel
Johann Henrich Lohmann
Georg Henrich Roesch
Hans Peter Henrich
Philipp Ihringer
Christoph Poth
Jacob Stahl
Johans Ehrman
Johann Conrath Baüerle
Hans George (X) Spengler
Michael Spengler
Johann Peter Schmetzer
Thomas Osterstach
Johann Michael Friedle
Valentin Daubenberger
P. Ludwig (X) Dewalt
Johann Jacob Daubenberger
Hans Georg (X) Hitman
Jurg Willhelm Friedrich
J. Philip (X) List
Johanes (X) Frick
Hans Jerg Uhrich
J. Jacob Shumber
Johann Jacob Selig
Augustus Hub
Johann Georg Hub

Valtin Kimmel
Johann Ludwig Ziegler
Georg Adam Allbrecht
Meliger Seib
Johann Görg Threer
Caspar (X) Weighart
Albrecht Reinhardt
Andres Lemel
Johan Georg Kochendörffer
Johann Philipp Teutsch
Hans Petter Strein
Peter (P) Arnold
Johann Frantz Bibler
Albrecht Dederer
Friederich Biebler
Tatcius (X) Geiger
Johann Görg Schäffer
Johann Gorg Feick
Alexander Holder
Martin (X) Benter
Hans Adam Holter
Jerg Peter Hüter
Martin Dietz
Johann Christoph Knirnschildt
Peter (PB) Biniger
H. Matheas (H) Miller
Johann Henrich Eisenmenger
Johann Friedrich Windisch
Görg Siemon Schram
Georg Thomas Heimberger
Kilian Dichtermüller
J. William (X) Volck
Peter Henrich Eysenmenger
Johann Jacob Haffner
Johan Conradt Friedle
Conrad (X) Errich
J. Adam (X) Diersen
Gottlib Ihrich

Abraham Gusman
Johann Adam Bükle
Johann Gottfridt Stückle
Johann Dietrich Sauer
Johann Daniel Betz
Hans (O) Mauerer
J. Wendal (+) Shwob
Johann Georg Neiss
Johanes (J) Frick
J. Balth. Eysenmenger
Michael Caspar Fuchs

Stefan Rigler
Andereas ( ) Krammer, on board
Hans Jorg Sen
Johans Georg (O) Bäck
Johann Georg Lasch
Georg Michael Werber
Joseph Bendter
Josef Ehrmann
J. Adam (X) Kirshbaum
Weybrecht (W) Nushagen

[List 166 C] At the Court House at Philadelphia, Saturday, the 14th Septr 1751.

Present: The Worshipful, the Mayor.

The Foreigners whose Names are underwritten, imported in the Ship Duke of Bedford, Richard Jefferys, Master, from Rotterdam and last from Portsmouth, did this day take the usual Qualifications & subscribe them. No. 129. 260 whole Freights. 9 Roman Catholicks. 120 Calvinists. John Pole.

Johannes Böckel
Friederich (F) Zabory
Friederich (X) Zabory, Junior
Jacob ( ) Zabory, on board
Abraham Beck
Hans Wengert
Hans Michel Schaeffer
Andereas (X) Bek
Johann Jerg Beck
Nicklas (X) Münder
H. Michael (H) Meyer
Joh. Jacob (X) Zigler
Samuel (W) Weiss
Adam (X) Koch
Adam Koch
Michel Koch
J. Michael (X) Koch
Johann Melchior Knor
Andreas Knauer
Hans Knauer

Hans Petter Knauer
Johannes Knorr
Christian Resch
Caspar (X) Weimmer
Görg Balthes Wecker
Casper Scherffig
Andreas Schöffer
Michel Spesserth
Christoph Albert
Matthaus Fetzer
Gerg Fetzer
Michel Gerbrich
Petter Gerbrich
Johann Henrich Krebs
Johan George (X) Ritz
Johann Adam Kolter
Valentin Huth
Michael ( ) Huth, on board
Hendrick ( ) Courpenning
Joseph (X) Fuchs

Frantz (F) Brüner
Jeremias Heriger
Johan Remigius Spiegel
Christian Günther
Erhardt Grimm
Jacob (X) Hobler
Abraham Koll
Christian (X) Gally
Christoph Heller
Heinrich Heller
Johann Gottlieb Zinck
J. Peter (X) Kammer
Friedrich Mutschler
Valletin Mutschler
Johan Christian Lentz
Caspaar Muller
Philip (X) Liebener
Jacob (+) Thürig
Henry (X) Shloder
Caspar (+) Metz
Henry (X) Decker
Johanes (X) Shmuck
Hans Georg Bender
Johan Georg Bender, Junior
Johannes Bender
Johan Marcus Beck
Vallentin (VAS) Shaffer
Peter Weber
Johannes Weber
Johannes Kleinfelter
Hans Peter Spessarth
Martin Matthias Schielin
Georg Davit Krauss
Georg David Reinhard
Hans Michael (X) Knab
Johann Lorentz Stindler
Johann Philips Schmidt
Peter Bluigner
Johann Georg Stotz
Friedrich Lummel
Hans Jacob Gohrmann

Johann Georg Burckhardt
Johann Andreas Heldt
Michael Heyler
Simon Burckhart
Joannes Dewetten
Johann Adam Schick
Jacob Vaser
Jacob Lallemand
Jacob (X) Rewold
Christoph (+) Zieger
Andres Jund
Johan Wendel Weichstier
Peter Herr
J. Joha Fill Diel
Lorentz Kunckel
Hans Petter Kleinfelter
Gerg Kleinfelter
Jacob (X) Grug
Martin Heinrich
Hans George (O) Miller
Nickelaus Schultz
Matthias Rödhele
Hieronymus Römmele
Hans Jacob Kurtz
Hans Jerg Hauser
Rudolph (H) Hoffer
Johannes Schäffer
Peter (X) Grauel
Johan Jacob Fischer
Martin Müller
Mathäs Schöllhorn
Andreas Kolb
Johann Ludwig Einsel
Johan Peter Heygis
Christian Krebs
Peter Ludewig Höyer
Hans Georg ( ) Klein, on board
Jacob Klein
Paulus (X) Sherly
Jacob ( ) Gally, on board
Johannes Stumpp

Jacob Geiger
Friederich Würth
Johann Martin Heügold
Johan Martin Fleischman
Henrich Gerhardt Diener
Carol (✕) Shaffer
Johann Adam Brentzinger
Johan Adam (✕) Pole
Andreas Rück

Hans Jerg Merckle
Johan Adam Stock
Johann Henrich Faber
Hans Gerg (+) Resh
Salomon Heisch
Jacob Hildenbrandt
Nicolas van Münchler
Nicklas (✕) Shmith

[List 167 C] At the Court House at Philadelphia, on Monday, the 16th September 1751.
Present: The Worshipful, the Mayor, Joshua Maddox, Esqr.
The Foreigners whose Names are underwritten, imported in the Edinburgh, James Russell, Master, did this day take the usual Qualifications & subscribed them. 10 Catholicks. Whole Freights 345. No. 160.

Lorence (+) Kuntzman
Jacob Baur
Petter Maurer
Johann Adam Allan
Conrad (+) Zinck
Johannes Göttgen
Philipus Jacob Wagner
Gotlieb Wagman
Willhelm Oerdter
Johan Jacob Huser
Conrad (KB) Bachman
Hans Adam Miller
Hans Mich. Gerber
Henrich Ratz
Casper Wisser
Johann Henrich Guterman
Johann Hentrich Völckner
Johan Jacob Völckner
Johan Peter Zeb
Adam Karl Knes
Frantz Wilhelm Jorholtz
Henrich Stumpf
Joh. Peter Mengen

Johann Henrich Stein
Johann Phieliepps Christ
Johan Henrich Lang
Johan Peter Endt
Johann Heinrich Höltzel
Johann Philipp Senft
Johannes Dorn [?]
Joseph Zombro
Peter (+) Fleck
Willm (+) Saltzman
Heinrich Pfeiffer
Wilhelm Kupferschmid
Hans Adtam Matter
Hans Hendrech Noll
Georg Matter
Jacob Keiser
Jacob Matter
Ands (✕) Keyser
Johann Adam Walthorn
Hans Matter
Johann Petter Schuch
Michel Hardman
Johann Wilhelm Heintz

Philipp Friedrich Meyer

Hans Adam Ferber

Georg Justavus Noll

Balthasar Jung

Wilhelm Adam Wolf

Georg Christophel Brem

Johann Gottfried Kroh

Johan Wilm Ferber

Lorentz Schweissguth

Peter ( ) Prim, sick on b^d

Andreas ( ) Wier, lame on b^d

Henrich Wilhelm Köhler

Johann Nickel Eberth

Johann Philip Eberth

Johann Nicolaus Ebert

Nicolaus Schoppert

Hieronimus (T) Textur

Johann Sigmund Stantze

Johan Goreg Schnell

Abraham (+) Schnell

Nicholas (×) Lindeman

Peter Pfeifer

Heinrich Pfeifer

Christian Luther

Christian Scheib

Michel Weber

Nickel Weber

Johann Michael Stamler

Johann Nickel Weber

Johann Nickel Weber, Senr

Johann Peter Fitting

Johann Abraham Dauber

Johan Friedrich Conrad

Johannes (×) Henrich

Johan Nickel Henrich

Michael (B) Burger

Johannes (O) Ort

Peter Schlosser

Peter Schlosser

Wilhelm Weyerich

Frantz Hihgert

Martin Schuch

Fredrick (×) Grunewald

Johann Jorg Reinheimmer

Johann Friedrich Gräf

Carl (O) Smith

Joh. Nicklaus Weyerbacher

Isaac Weyerbacher

Johannes Weyerbacher

Johann Andreas Wagner

Peter Lang

Carl Schell

Joh. Wilhelm Gräf

Johann Friedterich Fuchs

Henrich Adam Scherer

Peter Rhein

David Rhein

Jacob (×) Zilchart

Johann Henrich Rhein

Adam (KO) Kober

Christian (+) Kober

Hans Adam Kober

Michel Bauerman

Johann Jacob Muller

Johanes Schlater

Johan Nickelas Kern

Christiahn Hahn

Peter Dölpster

Nicholas (×) Mathias

Martin Mateis

Johannes (+) Mathias

Johann Vallentin Benighoff

Johan Philipp Bennighoff

Ehrenfried Bennighoff

Johann Nicklaus Mehl

Friedrich Mehl

Jacob (×) Inder

Johan Willhelm Nagel

Johan Conrad Jost

Simon (HSB) Burchart

Abraham Urjenbacher

Johannes Arbengast

Jacob (HW) Fredrich
Hans Jerg Kast
Johann Phillibes Küster
Jacob (+) Hoover
Frans (+) Hoover
Johann Michell Huber
Philipes Hasselbächer
Thommas Schmid
Johannes Klein
Johannes Schnider
Johann Jacob Bitter
Johanes Scheidt
Jacob Junck
Jacob (X) Schnoudy
Johan Niclaus Marheffen

Anthoni Blum
George (+) Segman
Nicklas (X) Zegler
Christian Steyerwald
Johan (X) Reys
Zachary (X) Reys
Blasius Beckh
Gorg Walker
Daniel Lehmbacher
Henrich Daniel Deill
Christoph Mez
Phillipp Henrich Weis
Johannes Schleich
Johann Nickel Schmidt
Israel (+) Burchart

[List 168 C] At the State House at Philadelphia, On Monday, the 16th September 1751.
Present: The Worshipful, William Plumsted, Esqr. Mayor.
The Foreigners whose Names are underwritten, imported in the Ship Nancy, Capt. Thomas Coatam, from Rotterdam, this Day took the usual Qualifications & subscribed them. One Catholick. Nº 78. Whole Freights 200.

Hans Jacob Klett
Jacob Guth
Johannes Georg Rösch
Hans Georg [?] Genner [?]
A. Conrad Koder
Conrad Koder
Hans Jerg Märle
Davidt Märle
Johann Friderich Rooss
Michael Fries
Johan Friedrich Wurster
Johannes Geckeller
Johann Martin Lang
Johan Georg Gönner
Johannes Hopff
Michael Kapp
Andreas Berenstecher

Hans Jacob Pfeifer
Jacob Kauffman
Hans Michael Schnauffer
Johann Jacob Supper
Hans Fredrich Brendley
Jacob Fredrich Sooper
Hans Jerg Reinthaler
Elias Bär
Jacob (X) Kennely
Johann Ulerich Fischer
Johan Ludwig Nonnenmacher
Hans George (+) Reynthaller
Joh. Jacob Schrenck
Conradt Märle
Jacob Scheible
Johan Michael Rühle
Johann Jacob Neff [?]

Hans Jerg Schnell
Sebastian Schnell
Johann David Weisman
Andreas Messerschmid
Hans Bernhart Messerschmid
Hans Wuchter
Hans Jacob Wizer
Hans Jerg Koder
Andres Bitinger
Christian Nagel
Jacob Kopp
Daniel Kopp
Michel Mauser
Johans Mauser
Johanes ( ) Heydel, on board
William ( ) Swindel
Jacob Hauch
Elias Mayer
Hans Mayer
Hans Martin Kimmerlin
Jacob ( ) Haag, lame

Johannes Kimmerlen
Hans Martin Mohr
Conrad Staiger
Hans Conrad Staiger
Melcher Hammer
Daniel Keuler
Johannes Keuler
Hans Jerg Schnell
Johanes Kohler
Jacob Raub
Hans Georg Reichenächser
Hans Martin Entenmann
Johannes (+) Kircher
Johan Lorenz Wilhelm
J. Philip (+) Gerig
Johann Friderich Billiger
Johann Balthaser Geyer
Michel Schmidt
Hans Hey
Johan ( ) Hay, on board
Baltz ( ) White

[List 169 C] At the Court House at Philadelphia, on Monday, the 16th September 1751.

Present: The Worshipful, the Mayor, Thomas York, Esquire.

The Foreigners whose Names are underwritten, imported in the Ship Brothers, Capt. William Muir, from Rotterdam, did this Day take and subscribe the usual Qualifications. Whole Freights 200. No. 93. Messrs Stedman.

Johannes Leinberger
Johann Jacob Zigenfuss
Johan Philibus Schneck
J. Melchior (X) Swerer
Henry (X) Shneyder
Johannes Bieber
Hans Jacob Farni
Hans Adam Wagner
Joseph (X) Kennel
Friderik (+)' Entzminger

Paul Mercker
Henrich Seytel
Friederich (X) Millefelt
Erhart (X) Millefelt
Michel Bieber
Henrich Bieber
Johan Jacob Schmit
Johannes Schmitt
Christof Weber
Georg Hacker

Peter Abert
Johannes Schmitt
Jeörg Mader
Valtin Matter
Michael (✕) Oberly
Johann Nicolaus Merckel
Görg Conrad Meffert
Philib Frantz
Johan Jacob Ahlem
Andreas Klein
Johan Adam Stein
Johannes Zeiszler
Ludwig (✕) Friedland
Johann Michael Mohr
Peter (✕) Moore
J. Peter (+) Dingis
Peter (+) Heyser
Johann Jacob Blum
J. Jacob (+) Maul
Johannes Seyfarth
J. Peter (✕) Sheesler
Johan Görg Hötzler
J. Jacob (✕) Gerling
Jacob Ludwig
Martin (++) Wolff
Henry (+) Wulff
Adam (+) Adams
Vallentin (✕) Plumenstein
Johann Wendel Beylstein
J. George (✕) Kirchner
Friederich (O) Kirchmer
Christoff Hauer
Christoph Hauer
Jacob (+) Hawer
Bernhart (✕) Hawer
Sebastian Nagel
Martin Maintzer
Johann Michael Haus

Jacob Lehmann
Jacob Heit
Davit Mussgnug
Michael Raub
Johann Georg Stählin
Anthony Hauer
Joachim Nagel
Anthony Nagel
Georg Obermeyer
Anthoni Nagel
Hans Jörg Kappel
Hans Georg Dillman
Michael Weber
Andreas Mor
Johanes (M) Munster
Georg Meintzer
Conrad (+) Menser
Hans Georg (✕) Uhllerik
Anthony (+) Graff
Davit (+) Bietch
Michael (+) Bietch
Johann Adam Heiser
Görg Bastian Eigelberger
Lutwig Schlücker
Jacob (+) Roth
Johanes (✕) Maintzer
Friedrich Danniel Müller
Ludwig Weltner
George (+) Hoffeintz
Jacob Ritter
Ludewig (+) Bender
Daniel Zoller
Jacob Frantz
Joh. Henry ( ) Past, Doct., on
    board
Christian Peter
Heinrich Mag

[List 170 C] At the Court House at Philadelphia, Saturday,
the 21st 7hr 1751.

Present: William Plumsted, Esquire, Mayor.

The Foreigners whose Names are underwritten, imported in the Ship Two Brothers, Thomas Arnot, Master, from Rotterdam and last from Cowes, did this day take the Qualifications to the Government. Freights 239. No. 112. Messrs Shoemaker.

John Christ Fried Wolf
Johannes Bausum
Philippus Bausum
Eytel Gerhart
Johann Henrich Decker *
Johanes Decker
Jeörg Henrich Schmidt
Johannes Rahn
Melchior Jung
Jacob Jung
Abraham Jung
Caspar (O) Steinmetz
Johnn Jacob Steinmetz
John (X) Steinmets
George (X) Ramel
Jacob Pender
Melcher Jung
Christian (X) Rohr
Johannes Stauffer
Simmon Meier
Andreas Brendle
Gerlach Lupp
Johannes Lupp
Johann Christian Lupp
Joh. Wilhelm Stauwer
Joh. Michael Lung
Johan George (X) Setzler
Adam Lung
Casper Augenstein
Ludwig Birckle
Johann Philibus Eyster
Caspar (X) Kalkglaser
Henerrich Kalckglösser

Jorgen Henrich Solinus [?]
Johannes Wilhelm Weynand
Gregorius (X) Richter
Henrich Arndt
Hans Nickel Herzog
Hans Georg (X) Shmit
William (M) Moltzberger
J. Conrad (H) Kreger
Carl Löhr
Johanes (X) König
Daniel Becker
Johannes Becker
Johannes Hein
Johan Görg Henrich
Johannes Heintz
Johannes Henrich
Johan Henrich Hegen
Johann Jost Giersbach
Johannes Orth
Johann Dangel Hoffman
J. Henry (X) Gring
Vallntin (X) Fey
Johannes Kappe
Johann Henrich Hartman
Johann Jörg Decker
Johan Jacob Hoffheintz
Johann Henrich Clos
J. Jost (Frid) Friederich
Andreas Grätz
J. Henry (X) Manerbach
Johann Henrich Nicodemus
Johan Jost Kring
Johann Konnrat Haas

* This is an independent Reformed preacher, who officiated at Hain's church, Berks County, and at Cocalico, Lancaster County, 1752–1762.

Anthonius Seemisch
Philips Henrich Nöll
Johann Martin Kreuder
Johann Michael Wieg
Conrath Pistoir
Johann Daniel Will
Johann Adam Schmidt
Johann Friterich Perlet
Jacob Eberhart
Philipp Thomas
Philippus Hetz
Martin Christofel Röder
Ludwig Kleisinger
Johannes Werbung
Jerg Straub
Jacob Fegert
Johannes Kriestman
Mattheis Hunolt
Wilhelm Hunolt
Jacob (IS) Shawer
Simon (X) Lung

Johannes Molsburger
Johan Jacob Molsbreger
Friedrich Kloppeyn
Johann Christoph Georgy
Friedrich Wilhelm Haman
Johannes Wilhelm Weinandt
Johann Jacob Göbeler
J. Gerhart (X) Zimmerman
Johann Henrich Adam
Johannes (+) Shrout
Johannes Gerhardus Schomacher
Baltz (X) Kentzler
Henry (+) Matheas
Nicolaus Stoltz
Johann Wilhellem Croneberg
Johann Jerg Schück
Johann Wilhelm Badenheimer
Johanes Bentz
Hans Marden Schors
Wolfgang Ruttechell
Jacob (IHB) Heinberger

[List 171 C] Present at the Court House at Philadelphia, Monday, the 23ᵈ September 1751.
Joshua Maddox, Esquire.
The Foreigners whose Names are underwritten, imported in the Ship Neptune, Captⁿ James Wier, from Cowes and Rotterdam, did this day take the usual Qualifications. No. 85. 154 whole Freights. Jno. Pemberton.

Johannes Wilhelm Seyn
Johann Phillippus Böhmer
Johan Adam Böhmer
Johann Wilhelm Glässner
Jacob Hetzel
Anthoni Weimmer
Johannes Gies
Michael (X) Wennert
Adam Weiser
Mattheus Lippoth
Johann Heinrich Vetter

Johann Friedrich Gewinner
Johann Bernhardt Blatt
J. Conrad (X) Koch
Johann Georg Seckel
Johann Allexander Schütz
Johannes Manderbach
Herrmanes Müller
Johann Ludwig Klein
Johann Conrad Wülleweber
Johann Christ Zimmerman
Johann Henrich Röhling

J. Jacob (×) Pool
Johan Henrich Kreis
Johan Bernd Greis
Johan Phillippus Anhorn
J. Henry (×) Tillman
Johann Peter Schaaf
Henrich Gerhart
Johan Engel Weber
Johannes Petter Reusch
Johannes Engelberth Jung
J. Jost (×) Walter
J. Friederich (×) Shreiber
J. Henry (×) Shmit
Johan Philips Krum
Philip Henry (×) Shlotz
Johannes Schlutz
Johan Jakob Gonderman
Nicolas (×) Reybolt
Johannes Busch
Johannes Meyer
Hans Jacob Miller
Michell Lauffer
J. Michael (×) Lauffer
Johannes Vetter
Johannes Öxli
Johannes Beer
Paulus Groninger
Johan Michel Raisch
Johannes Hombert
Johanes (×) Baker
Johann Christbaum

Johan Christ Benner
Johann Christ Lintorff
Johann Philipus Daniel Pfeiffer
Georg Andereas (×) Carle
Balthas Kressmann
Mattheis Lutz
Johan Engl Cuonrad
Johannes Geistweit
Johann Jöerg Christ
Johann Egidius Hecker *
Johann Engel Bücher
Johann Henrich Bücher
Johanes (×) Thomas
Johan Ebert Steyner
Andereas (A) Steyger
Eberhart (||) Thomas
Henry (O) Zimmermann
Johan Philippus Berger
Herman Adolff Schoppenmeyer
Jost (+) Henry, sick
Chrisdian Schmit
Johan Christ Schmitt
Johann Henrich Schmitt
Johan Henry (×) Reinhart
Johannes Henrich Peiffer
Johann Christ Zimmerman
Christhian Hapffer
Johanes Petter Flick
Johan Filibus Flick
Gerlach Paul Flick
Johann Merden Flick

[List 172 C] At the Court House at Philadelphia, Tuesday, the 24th September 1751.

Present: William Peters, Esqr.

The Foreigners whose Names are underwritten, imported in the Ship Neptune, John Mason, Commander, from Rotterdam & last from Cowes, did this day take the usual Qualifications & subscribe them. By List 144. Whole Freights 300. Messrs Shoemaker.

* A German Reformed preacher. See *History of Tohickon Union Church*, pp. 29–38.

Johannes Laurenzius Schmidt,
Med. et Chirg. Doct.
Joh. Pietersz
Christian Armbruster
Matheis Armbruster
Conrad (X) Newmeyer
Henderick Boors
Jacob (X) Sheyer
Fieliepp Klinger
Jean Pierre Arnoul
Abraham Pons
Leonhart Mentzinger
Hans Georg Anstein
Johanes Höring
Johannes (+) Hering
Johann Ludwig Höring
Henrich (+) Lautenschlager
Johan Leonhart Götz
Johannes Adam Winckaus
Johannes Saum
Johanes (+) Redig
Johann Adam Wirdeberger
J. Adam (X) Ewig
Melchior (X) Trautman
Johann Geörg Erhardt
Bernhart (+) Jagel
Adam (X) Pfeiffer
Christoph (X) Cotz
Jurg ( ) Klinbach, sick
Michael (X) Link
George (X) Crope
Johan Philipp Meyer
Johannes Hinsch [?]
Frans Horn
David (X) Maisheller
Johanes Gessner
Elias (X) Emminger
Conradt Schmidt
J. Michael (+) Kurtz
Jacob Walter (X) Wagner
Jacob Tritsch

Jacob ( ) Cnuber, sick on board
Conrad Schepfnit
Johan Wilhelm Grell
Johan Georg Schäfer
Conrad ( ) Rawher, sick on
board
Balsatzar (X) Hess
Georg Kimmel
Johann Peter Schindel
Johanes ( ) Hock, sick
Johann Adam Geis
Johannes Geiss
Martin (MH) Hekenturm
Daniel ( ) Erhart, sick on
board
Peter Klinger
Johann Georg Eisenbeis
Wilhelm Göttman
Andres Drüschel
Andreas Miller
Hans Georg (X) Heysy
Hans Jerg Spohn
Caspar ( ) Spann, sick
Johann Adam Heist
Johann Georg Heist
Tobias Daumiller
Jacob Bogus
Johann Petter Trautmann
Christoph (X) Hollebach
Henry ( ) Deutch, sick on
board
Clementz Frey
Jacob (+) Summer
Ludwig Knoll
Nickelaus Schey
J. Adam (O) Issener
Andreas (O) Reybold
Friederik (X) Zimmerman
Jacob (Z) Zettelmeyer
Georg ( ) Zettelmeyer, on
board

Georg Adam (XX) Weys
Aadam (++) Weys
Caspar (X) Kesseler
Johannes Welte
Jacob Nagel
Johannes Schnüringer
Lorentz Schniringer
Johann Georg Vollert
Henrich Eysenmenger
Christoph Schropp
Johann Michael Hag
Johann Georg Heist
Johannes Vetter
Johan Ludwig Bilger
Steffan Herth
Henrich Hall
Johann Jacob Gottwalt
Antonias Lamprecht
Johann Jacob Arzt
Joh. Daniel Scharmann
Johan Jacob Schneider
Casper Hoffman
Caspar (H) Hoffman, Junior
Christian ( ) Hoffman, sick on
  board
Jacob Bucs
Jacob Buchs
Jacob Horn
Conrat Selhoff
Christoph (X) Vanterbourg
J. Conrad (+) Essy
Johanis Werner
Georg Schöll
Martin Schänkel
Andereas (X) Berlib

Conrad (X) Bower
Josebh Lehmann
Ewald (X) Trummaner
Jacob Höllerman
Jacob (++) Frey
Albrecht (XX) Shleppy
Baltes Laub
Johs Jerg Must
Joseph Zugmeyr
Philip (X) Mallycoat
Jean Couttiez
George (++) Creesh
Johann Lenhard Schäffer
Conrad ( ) Shäffer, on board
Johan Leonhart (++) Traut-
  man
Johan Wilhelm Müller
Johann Peder Klump
Sigmund Copia
Johann Ulrich Dürr
Johan George (+) Hummer
Benedict (+) Ewig
Henry (X) Shröder
Michael Sattler
Uhllerich (+) Shwenckel
Ludewig Klemmer
Frederik (X) Sullinger
David Kulling
Jacob (X) Peterman
Peter (·X) Klases
Hans Jeorg Stehle
Michael Hahn
Martin Kogel
Jacob Appenzeller

[List 173 C] At the Court House at Philadelphia, on Wednesday, the 25th Day of September 1751.
Present: The Worshipful, the Mayor.
The Foreigners whose names are underwritten, imported in the Ship Phoenix, Captn Spurrier, from Rotterdam & Ports-

mouth, were this day Qualified & subscribed the Oaths. No 180.
Whole freights 412. Messʳˢ Shoemaker.

Jörg Matias (+) Weig
Johann Konnratt Bauerr
Johann Adam Bauer
Jacob Bauer
Hans Jörg (✕) Weber
Christian (✕) Laufanor
Martin Maurer
Michael Meyer
John Georg Kappis
Georg Volpp
Hans Michaell (+) Bräunich
Joh Michael Lerchenzeiler
Antoni (+) Stehrn
Georg Stirn
Hans Jacob (✕) Schletzer
Cunrad (O) Höffler
Jacob (✕) Jordan
Andreas (+) Roht
Philipp Ernst Wagner
Jacob Heegy
Johan Melchior (✕) Milh
Johann Fridrich Gärber
Johannes Schilling
Albert (✕) Schneck
Michael Hofman
Christian (✕) Pfeifer
Johan Vallentin (✕) Hofman
Martin (✕) Wagner
Johann Conrad Frech
Johann Balthas Schölhorn
Johann Michael Schuhmacher
Martin Engelbrecht
Johann Georg Kiderer
Balthas Widenmeyer
Martin Ziegler
Michel Lautenschlager
Peter Demler
Johan Conrad Krügele

Johan Tobias Haag
Andreas Hildenbrandt
Hans Jacob (✕) Meyer
Martin (✕) Ludi
Hans Jacob Stambach
David (✕) Denstrell
Martin Herter
Jacob (✕) Kohli
Hans (✕) Kohli
Jörg (✕) Kohli
Hans Jurg Bertsch
Ludwig Teuffel
Jacob (✕) Riger
Gärg Gänsle
Simon Widmayer
Hanns Jerg Hägele
David Herrmann
Carle Hey
Albrecht (✕) Heü
Johann Gottfried Schmelger
Hans Jacob Glas
Matias (✕) Hauser
Jacob (✕) Pfeifer
Jerg Holtzinger
Jacob Wörner
Peter Hofman
Michael (O) Hudere
Johann Gottfried Fuchs
Hans Görg (+) Schloterbeck
Gorg Friederich Baisch
Christoph Küchler
Jacob (O) Reigenbaher
Conrad Hoff
Jacob Linckh
Johannes Gramm
Michael Bossert
Bernhard Brand
Michael Kaucher

Baltzer Bümbel
Matheis Bastian
Antoni (O) Blesinger
Samuel Dirstein
Elias (X) Stocki
Mattheis Hipscher
John Georg Gehringer
Albrecht (+) Hübscher
Kraft (X) Hannold
Gallus Schlichter
Christoph Lick
Jacob Geigle
Martin Ott
Jacob Hauber
Mattheus Kern
Gotlieb (X) Lunenmacher
Jacob Huber
Jacob Kauher
Johannes Ditrich
Jacob Ott
Fridrich Veitzhans
Friedrich Dannwolf
Joseph Böhringer
Johann Siegmundt Ruhle
Christopf Friederich Weyler
Franciscus Auer
Matheus Plocherr
Jacob Bückel
Johannes Albrecht
Samuell (X) Hitzer
Jerg Schiker
Hans Jacob Kiehner
Friedrich (X) Heins
Jacob (O) Seller
Johannes Weltescheidt
Jacob (X) Waltz
Johannes Hammer
Georg Teufell
Christian Bloser

Johannes Rathgeb
Martin Eilting
Bernhardt Schneider
Phillip (Phil) Muller
Hans Cunrad Küchli
Hans Jerg Christein
Christian Christein
Peter Christin
Mattias Diesch
Jacob Harz
Johannes Demuth
Christian Neuffer
Thomas (X) Fisher
Jacob Fischer
Jacob (X) Köhler
Friederig Knechel
Philipp Jacob Geis
Johann Adam Stoltz
Jean Diedier Moret
Michael (X) Laver
Christian Schneider
Dietrich Löffler
Matheus Walter
Jacob Von Könne
Lorentz Schmitt
Heinrich Fritz
Walles Beyer
Gerg Mich. Weimann
Aberham Hausser
Jonas Rupp *
Gorg Ziegler
Jacob (X) Walder
Michaell (X) Muller
Matheis Hanfstein
Fridrich Wolf
Jacob Hermann
Jacob Hermann
Michel Ernst
Andreas Eisenhardt

* This is the paternal grandfather of I. Daniel Rupp, the editor of the *Collection of Thirty Thousand Names.*

Michel Wörnner
Johann Michel Wörnner
Madthes Schieft [?]
Joh. Jacob Wörnner
Christian Schmidt
Johannes Schmitt
Jacob Burckhardt
Michael Mayer
Gabriel Wachter
Johan Georg Fridrich Bayer
Simon Brener
Adam Hettinger
Theoph. Hubbert
Samson Mittelberger

Georg Baumann
Michael Altrith
Friederich Hirsch
Konrad Leuser
Philip Poutmont
Michel Leuttel
Hans Jorg (++) Ehrman
Georg Carle
Christophell Hofman
Hans Jerg Blaser
Hans Jörg (X) Bläser
Phillipp Muller
Balthas Schwickes
John Georg (X) Blatzer

[List 174 C] At the Court House at Philadelphia, Friday, the 4th 8ber 1751.

Present: . . .

The Foreigners whose names are underwritten, imported in the Ship Queen of Denmark, George Parish, Commander, from Rotterdam & Cowes, did this day take & subscribe the usual Qualifications. No. 99. Whole Freights 251. Messrs Stedman.

Christoph (+) Bery
Jerg Wolff
Johann Friederich Hering
Hardtman Fritz
Daniel Meyer
Gorg Jacob Ullrich
Baltzer Martin
Vallentin (X) Brock
Jacob Wolf
Michel Renner
George (X) Licker
Hans Georg (X) Erbolt
Melchior (Z) Zigler
Martin (S) Shewerman
Caspar (O) Wagener
Balzar (BK) Konig
Johanes (J) Wagner
Jacob (X) Kügel

Hans Suter
Friedlie Salade
Jacob Regennas
Johanes (X) Wagner
Jacob Grosjean
Peter Recher
Henrich Stohler
Johanes (XX) Oxeman
Frederik (X) Dickerhoff
Johannes Martin
Hans Gerg Martin
Jacob (G) Geesseler
Johann Michel Hartmann
Andres Fridli
Johannes Andres
Henrich Bachman
Johann Philip Bieg
Stephann Bieg

Johanes (×) Carmane
Jerg Grauss
Andres Roht
J. Nicklas (B) Rippel
George (F) Happes
Conradt Schneider
Johann Henrich Graff
Durs Gruner
Christian Bernhart
Hans Schneberger
Hans Jacob Weis
Hans Uhlerik (×) Hess
Florian Peter Koffler
Marx Oberhänsle
Casper Schneyder
Johann Schaad
Jacob (×) Joder
Hans Schällenberg
Hans Blanck
Hans (H) Reizer
Henry (×) Süss
Michael (×) Meyer
Christian (+) Blanck
Johannes Eydmeyer
Martinus Dreysbach
Johann Friederich Merten
Johann Henrich Hoffmann
Hanns Henrich Wiest
Willhelm Bosch
Hans Henry (H) Shneyder
Johannes Pampus

Antonnius Stutte
Johann Wilhelm Fries
Friederik (+) Ruthy
Jacob (×) Reithlinger
Johanes (×) Shutty
Bastian (+) Mongolt
Hennerich Stehli
Caspar (××) Fisher
Conrad (×) Fuchs
Weinbert Tschudi
Johannes Strub
Johan Fridrich Steiner
Martinus Fries
Andres Lantz
Cunrad Weiss
Friederik (×) Lander
Hans (×) Geisser
Heinerich Seitz
Jacob Steli
Henrich Stehli
Johanes Possert
Johann Fridrich Mentzer
Jacob (   ) Shob, on board
Gorg Schweyler
Hans Melcher an der Egg
Nicklas (×) Weiss
Vallentin Meyer
Henrich Grel
Daniel Wolf
Jörg Wolf
Anthony (×) Carmane

[List 175 C] At the Court House at Philadelphia, Monday, 7th October 1751.
Present: Joshua Maddox, Esqr.
The Foreigners whose Names are underwritten, imported in the Janet, Capt. William Cunningham, from Rotterdam & last from Cowes, were this Day Qualified & subscribed the usual Oaths. By List 99. Whole Freights 220. Messrs Stedman.

Johannes (   ) Waller, sick
Michaell Hollstein

Peter (×) Ganns
Peter (O) Rossburger

Philip (X) Pfiffer
Ehrhardt Thürwächter
Matheas (+) Pfiffer
Adam Jacobi
Marx Breinig
Leonhart (X) Simon
Adam (X) Beckebag
Caspar (XX) Beckebach
Geörg Adam Beckenbach
Johann Georg Beckenbach
Georg Leonhardt Beckenbach
Johan Vallenthin Sommer
Nickolas (X) Eshwyn
Peter Ulmer
Jacob (X) Hauswird
Jacob Kämmerer
Henrich Hetzel
Johann Nickel Stumm
Johannes Kauffman
Johann Adam Bast
Johann Nickel Schmidt
Georg Welter
Michel Finck
Killian (X) Hawsser
Nickolas (X) Steyn
Johan Petter Schang
Henry (+) Carle
Martin (+) Bigler
George (X) Bigler
Jacob (+) Walter
Anderas (O) Altendorff
Johann Lenerdt Gösel
Johannes (H) Lap
Johann Jagob Lapp
Christ Peifer
J. Christoph (X) Weysbach
H. George (HIZ) Zweyer
Stephen (X) Zweyer
Ewerhart Kreiling

H. Adam (X) Diem
H. George (X) Odewalt
Johann Andreas Engelman
Michael (X) Alt
Adam Jordan
Jacob (+) Holtz
Carl Wagner
Georg Jacob Schirmer
Abraham (+) Konig
Philib Enes
Jacob Weimer *
Michael Währlich
Hans Conrad Bauman
Johann Georg Geisler
Jo. Nicklas ( ) Wolff; on board
Johann Valendin Rost
J. Jost (O) Shweiger
Johann Jacob Weltz
Johann Simon Schober
Eberhard Gahnat
Abraham Bitilion
Lönhart Bückel
Johannes Hahn
Wilhelm (X) Ewig
Christian (X) Ewig
Michael (M) Leonhart
Matheas (N) Nass
Henry (H) Haushalter
Heinrich Friedle
Johann Georg Busch
Johann Michael Hoffman
Melcher Krautter
Philipp Jacob Hagenbuch
Matheus König
Jacob König
Enoch (X) Weber
Hans Jacob Hülckert
Christoph Kettman
Jacob Sprecher

* A German Reformed Minister. See Good, *History of the German Reformed Church in the U. S., 1725–1792*, p. 568.

Hans Jorg Sprecher
Philipp Jacob Künlen
Jacob (O) Weimmer
Dewalt (X) Storch
Jacob Diether
Jacob Hahn
H. George (X) Wollhuter
Johann Jorg Reimer
Friedrich Humbert

Philipp Jacob Humbert
Johann Michaell Drion
Diewalt Matter
Jacob (X) Gallman
Philipp Jacob Meder
George (X) Sheud
Jacob (X) Shaffer
Andereas ( ) Kisselberg, on
board

[List 176 C] At the Court House at Philadelphia, Wednesday, the 16ᵗʰ 8ber, 1751.

Present: The Worshipful Robert Strettell, Esquire, Mayor of Philadelphia.

The Foreigners whose Names are underwritten, imported in the Ship Duke of Wirtenberg, Captⁿ Montpelier, Commander, from Rotterdam & Cowes in England, did this day take and subscribe the usual Qualifications. List 169. Whole Freights 406. Messʳˢ Stedman.

Otto Scheuer [?]
Georg Christoph Reichle
Ludwig Heinrich
Theodor Larber
Johann Andreas Mayer
Johann George Mayer
Johann Andreas Mayer
Johann Adam Meckle
Johan Gorg Weiser
Ulrich Braitliger
Johann Georg Maisch
Christian Gretzinger
Johannes Messner
Andreas Schlenckher
Jacob Ludwig Käppele
Conrad (KR) Ram
Johan Leonhard Held
Johannes Brodbeckh
Jacob Umensetter
Michael Umensätter
Christoff Sündel

Mattheus Reich
Michael Wayhinger
Johanes Wayhinger
Johanes Schott
Christian App
Fridrich Zoller
Johanes Gräuttler
Georg Wilhelm Bantlion
Christoph Friederich Bantlion
Hans Georg Schäffer
Friederich Hering
Hans George (H) Dute
David Dütte
Andereas (X) Leaderer
Johanes (O) Doll
Marte Dohl
Johannes Notz
Peter Stückhl
Conradt Eisenhard
George Adam Schlegel
Christoph (X) Shlegel

Martin Ecker
Steffan Wunder
Johanes Meiger
Eberhardt Martin
Johannes Wunderlich
Leonhart (LHD) Behl
Johann Georg Hoch
Matheus Sabernrick
Joseph Brendlinger
Conradt Brendlinger
Georg Adam Greckenberger
Georg Michael Kern
Conrad (X) Klingemeyer
Jo. Conrad Leibbrand
Balthas Götz
Georg Adam Gaal
Hans Jacob Baum
Daniel Baumann
Conrad Gretzinger
Conrad (X) Grietzinger
Martin (+) Brodbeck
Johanes (+) Brodbeck
Dietrich Cämmerer
Peter Kämmerer
Bastian Kämmerer
Jacob Schäfer
Bernhart (XX) Frick
Johan (J) Brodbeck
Krafft (X) Pillab
Johann Georg Sendel
Jacob Greiner
Johann Geörg Englert
Conrad Merckle
Friedrich Kneppert
Jacob Stahlmann
Jacob (XX) Zech
Hans Jerg Wintter
Johanes (X) Wintter
Martin (X) Ebbly
David Ansel
Jacob (X) Beyerly

Fridrich Wibel
Joseph Ahner
Adam Ammon [?]
Hans Jorg Heim
Hans Jorg Wehr
Jacob Jüngling
Christian Gottlieb Schieberle
Hans Peth. Poth
Johan Fridrich Steindorf
Johann Michael Zehntbauer
Johannes Schultheis
Jacob (X) Sherrer
Johann Nadem
Ulrich Hirschman
Matheus ( ) Hirschman, on
  board
Andreas Hirschmann
Johann Adam Hirschman
Johanes (O) Stuky
Hans Michel Moser
Mattheus Dullnick
Johan Georg Säman
Johann Friedrich Stiess
Jacob Schwartz
Johannes Augenstein
Hans Georg Augenstein
Simon (X) Nagel
Phillip Jacob Werner
Fillip Nagel
Michael Deis
Hans Ludwig Roht
Johann Philipp Roth
Johannes Mayer
Johannes Mayer
Johannes Bischoff
Lenhardt Merckle
Hans Martin Bishon [?]
Michel Frikh
Ludwig Frick
Caspar (X) Meyer
Lorentz (X) Wessener

Peter (X) Printly
Christian (O) Fusch
Hans Adam Meyer
Joseph Karg
Jacob Karg
Michael Rosch
Michael Rosch
Hans Martin Fiesten
Michell Hirneisen
Hans Jerg Hirneisen
Hanns Jerg Christi
Jacob Esch
Rudholf Henschler
Johan Georg Dürr
Jacob Wildenmann
Baltas (+) Folck
Christoph (+) Folck
Conradt Stöhr
Michael Katz
Hans Gorg Schneider
Johann Bardel Gottwalt

Filib Mueiller
Hans Bernhardt Frankh
Stephan Katz
Johann Jacob Waltz
Michel Esch [?]
Andereas (A) Wigthorn
Michael Werner
Wilhelm (X) Kooge
Benedick Funck
Aberham Echert
Hans George (+) Eckhart
Johanes (X) Eberhart
Johanes (+) Eberhart
Andreas Lüttich
Hans Jerg Schinckh
Michael Wolf
Conrad (G) Gensly
Hans Jerg Ege
Johann Jacob Ege
Friedrich Heyl
Andereas (X) Kappler

PALATINES IMPORTED IN THE YEAR 1751.*

	[Passengers]	[Signers]
1. The Anderson	236	100
2. The Elizabeth	130	91
3. The Shirley	288	120
4. The Patience	255	109
5. The St Andrew	230	100
6. The Duke of Bedford	260	129
7. The Edinburgh	[345]	[160]
8. The Nancy	200	78
9. The Brothers	200	93
10. The Two Brothers	239	112
11. The Neptune, (Capt. Wier)	154	85
12. The Neptune, (Capt. Mason)	300	144
13. The Phoenix	412	180
14. The Queen of Denmark	259	99

* This summary is found in Exhibit E, p. 40, with the exception of the items bracketed,

[15. The Janet .... 220 .... 99]
[16. The Duke of Wirtenberg .... 406 .... 169]

[4134 .... 1868]

[List 177 C] At the Court House at Philadelphia, Friday, the 15th of September 1752.

Present: Robert Strettell, Esqr, Mayor of Philadelphia.

The Foreigners whose Names are hereunder written, imported in the Ship Two Brothers, Commanded by Thomas Arnot, from Rotterdam but last from Cowes in England, took the Qualifications to the Government in the usual Form.

Georg Eisenmenger
Friederich Mäyer
Kilian Eisenmenger
Jacob Müller
Johann Christoph Friedrich
  Köhler
Christof Arnoldt
Johann Martin Kanz
Johan Peter (X) Lentz
Nölchen Kremmer
Peter (X) Shock
Johan Peter (+) Shock
Leopoldt Valentin Gross
Johannes Henrich Metz
Johann Friedrich Beck
Georch Michael Eberli
F. Conrad (X) Leberling
George Michael (X) Miller
Peter (X) Hommer
Paulus (X) Gross
Philip (X) Bornn
Willhelm (X) Huner
John Peter (X) Rodebagh
Jacob Müller
Conrad (W) Winegarden
Berteram (+) Beum
Paulus (X) Anders
J. Peter (X) Blom

Moritz Hene
Diedrich Wilhelm Dischong
Jacob (X) Anders
Johan Wilhelm Ahlbach
Johannes Gerhart
John Peter (X) Blom, Senior
J. Christian (XX) Ottigen
Peder Dils
Jost Ferschbach
Baulus Böhm
Herbert Schumacher
Johan Deis (X) Wers
Conrad (X) Hanes
Johann Theis Hoffman
Wilhelmus Peter Walles
Johann Wilhelm Meyer
Conradh Schneider
Johan Herber (O) Loer
Caspar Krämer
Johannes Antonius Krämer
Johannes Wilhelmus
Adam Beck
Johan Adam (IAB) Imbotty
Johann Gottfried Krieng
Johanes Jacob
Johann Christ Seyler
Johannes Jacobus Beyer
Johannes Krist Eulenber

Johannes Christianus Liechten-
thäller
Johann Christ Meyer
Anthon (✕) Sheyed
Johan Donis (✕) Starr
Johann Paulus Seehl
Johan Steffen Drybler
Johan Petter Hammer
Johan Christ Albirger
Jacob (+) Oellgarden
Johann Henrich Wirth
Wendel Frey
Hans Henrich Münch
Thomas Gramlich
Jacob Lips
Johann Wilhelm Böttger
Gottfried Kappes
Caspar Lichtenberger
Johann Jerg Metzger
Michael Dieterich
Joseph (K) Konig
Georg Michael Gerhart
Johanes (✕) Metzem
Burckhardt Unangst

Jonas (✕) Pool
Johann Gerlach Meyer
Johann Görg Spies
Jacob Selbach
Johan Peter Schmit
Johann Satt
Simon Ludwig Himroth
Johan Herbert Wingart
Johanes (++) Lutz
Johan Dongshen [?]
Willem Henrich Brandenburger
Johan Thomas Schumacher
Conrat Welder
Johan Seilas (✕✕) Bonn
Johannes Petter Bon
Conrad (++) Linenbergh
Nickolas (O) Linenbergh
Moritz Wilhelm Dils
Jacob Dils
Joh'ann Petter Aller
Johan Petter Putterbach
John Sebastian (S) Onangst
Johan Willm Welter
101.

[List 178 C] At the State House at Philadelphia, Tuesday,
the 19th of September 1752.
Present: Edward Shippen, Esqr.

The Foreigners whose names are underwritten, imported in
the Ship Edinburgh, James Russell, Commander, from Rotterdam but last from Cowes in England, took and subscribed the
usual Qualifications.

Petter Renan
Johan Vallentin Fehrlinger
Johann George Demler
Paulus Hartung
Jacob Bildmann
Frantz Renan
Joh. Samuel Huth
Georg Caspar Lohrmann

Franciscus Dilier
Michell Kümell
Leonhart Claus
Siegfried Billing
Johann Martin Schnepf
Georg Leonhardt Pfeiffer
Martin Harsch
Johann ( ) Kurrlin, on board

Johannes (+) Bernhart
Jacob (+) Hierd
[....] Hibscher
Jacob Beckh
Johann George Bauman
Johannes Reinhart
Paulus Schmidt
Anndreas Gabriel Dietrich
Nicolaus Wager
Johann Wilhelm Trautwein
Jacob Frid
Paulus (O) Mauerer
L. Wilhelm (XX) Keller
Echart ( ) Kurbecker, on board
Christoff (X) Hummel
Baltzar ( ) Turringer, on board
Paulus (X) Waller
Bartholomaeus Lederer
Joseph Antony Schelckhle
Johann Carl Höger
J. Jacob (+) Helm
Jacob ( ) Müller, sick on board
Johannes ( ) Young, sick on
    board
Caspar ( ) Deylinger, sick on
    board
Johan Fridrich Kies
Peter Müh
Jacob (H) Küber
Has Mart. Kirschman
Johannes Roth
Martin (X) Kuntzman
Friedrich Roth
Johanes (+) Bawer
Jacob ( ) Wellen, sick on board
George (+) Shneyder
Jarig Zimmerman
Michael (+) Fetzer
Christian (+) Shneid[er]
Christian Ruger
H. Michael (+) Weismeyer

Christoph Hardtmann
Linhard Lauter
Sebastian Waas
Adam Christoph Lehring
Johannes (+) Shwartz
Michael ( ) Karrg, sick on
    board
Hans Jacob Roth
Johann Christoph Bentz
Johannes Zürn
Stephan ('+) Nerlinger
J. Christian (X) Benish
Johann Christian Göllnitz
Sebastian Dreher
Jacob ( ) Roth, on board sick
Jacob Friedrich Glasser
George ( ) Brown, sick on
    board
George (X) Shilld
Jacob Hauser
Joh. Bernhardt Speth
Johann Jacob Häyd
Michael ( ) Shäffer, sick on
    board
Jacob Rincker
Isaac (X) Buck·
Jacob (X) Meysel
Johannes Zwickel
Hs. Adam Schwartz
J. Friederich (X) Huss
Johannis Gemster
Conrad ( ) Gush, sick on board
Johann Jacob Gretter
Johannes Hutzlern
Heinrich Ottinger
Carl Korn
Friederik (H) Rastlein
Leonhart (X) Roslin
Adam ( ) Stok
Jacob Wierdeman
Andereas (X) Fetzer

Friederich Fees
Michael Dürr
John Adam (+) Rey
Michel Friedrich
Johann Rischerd
Joseph (O) Shennab

Valentin Breitschiett
Jacob Schweller
Frantz Fischer
Christoff ( ) Bower
Hans Jacob Seltzer

[List 179 C] At the State House in Philadelphia, Friday, the 22d, September 1752.
Present: Edward Shippen, Esquire.
The Foreigners whose Names are underwritten, Imported in the Ship Brothers, William Muir, Captain, from Rotterdam and last from Cowes in England, took and subscribed the usual Qualifications. No. 83.

Johannis Rauch
Samuel Herrmann
Carl Funk
Martin (K) Kargh
Andreas Leiser
Peter Hellman
Jacob Seltzer
Johannes (H) Unruh
Daniel Utz
Johann Michael Lindemuth
Stephan Goss
Johann Peter Schwartz
Johannes Eckert
Johannes (XX) Edelman
Hans Adam Heckman
Nicklus Heckman
Johan Conradt Kriechbaum
Johan Jacob Rudisielie
J. Jacob (X) Winter
Peter (X) Bechtel
H. Nicklas (O) Berringer
Johan Jacob Willhelm
J. Peter (X) Gabel
Peter Seip
Johannes (X) Pab
H. Adam (+) Gerig

H. Jacob (H) Miller
H. Peter (H) Edelman
Bastian (XX) Hellman
Andereas (X) Ott
Georg Jacob Ehresmann
G. Henrich (X) Gramlig
George (X) Lentz
Lenhart Hertell
Antonius Müller
J. George (+) Edelman
Jost Edel
Hans Adam (+) Edelman
Johann Georg (X) Schmoltz
Johann George Werner
Johann Georg Esser
H. George (X) Adeler
Johann Erhard Lobstein
H. George (X) Pommer
Jacob Lorentz
Hans Georg Maus
Hans Schütterli
Philip Jacob Gottschalck
Andony Zimmerman
Mathais Geyler
Andereas (XX) Geyler
Hans Gergerich

Michel Lapp
Jacob Ybach
Jacob Ybach
Diebolt Dietrich
Hans Uhlerik (X) Beuttler
Hans Waltz
Abraham Billing
Jacob ( ) Lash, sick on board
Henrich Rachusser
Peter Beisel
Hans Gorg Sommer
Mathis Haas
Jacob Braun
Johannes Sommer
Hans Martin Somer
Hans George (X) Holtz-Shoe

Peter (XX) Hikman
John Nicklas ( ) Shneyder, on
board
Johannes (X) Coelus
Hans Adam Lehr
Philip (X) Seydelman
H. George (X) Markward
Conrad (++) Heylman
Andreas Rotenburger
Killian Führer
Hans Jacob Merckel
Hans Jacob Hage
Hans Adam Schnäbele
Hans Jacob (+) Burgher
Joseph Scheyfle

[List 180 C] At the State House in Philadelphia, Friday
the 22ᵈ September 1752.
Present: Edward Shippen, Esquire.

The Foreigners whose Names are underwritten, Imported in
the Ship Halifax, Captⁿ Thomas Coatam, from Rotterdam and
last from Cowes in England, took this day the usual Qualifications to the Government. No 145.

Johan Melchior Brombach
John Conrad Blecher
Johann Görg Kuntze
Christoffel Witmer
Philib Engel
Nickolas (X) Kohler
Friederik (X) Eberhart
Michael (X) Springer
Martin Dockter
Johan Girg Krybach
J. Johannes Griesse
Joannes Josephus Roth *
Davit (X) Sasmanhausen
Jacob ( ) Roth, on board
Hans Feltz

Anthony (+) Zinck
Christian (+) Gräz
Hans George (X) Doctor
Johanes (X) Paulus
George (X) Paulus
Christian (+) Herman
Johann Jacob Bersy
Johann Ludwig Bersy
Jacob Olenthin
J. Jacob (H) Bruker
Philip (X) Hoffman
Bartholmae (E) Evar
Joachim Schmiet
Petter Reeb
Hans Michall (X) Geyer

* A Lutheran minister.

Friederich (F) Flekstein

Hans Michel Kröner

Hans Philips Etter

Henry (XX) Meyer

Hans Jacob Serber Zimmerman

Felix Dutweiler

Lennert Weidman

Heinrich Maag

Lorentz (++) Durr

Hans Yacob Mülli

Feligi Hirt

Jacob Müller

Conrad Müller

Hadolf Zol [?]

Kunrad Lang

Jacob Müller

Johannis Sürber

Yak. Sürber

Henrich Zobli

Henry (X) Kuntz

Ulrich Kreyser

Hans Jacob Rummen

Hans Heinrich Meir

Caspar (X) Winckur

Hans Conrad (X) Wird

Heinrich Mercki

Hans Casper Schlater

Friedrich Hörsch

Johannes (+) Meyer

Hendrik ( ) Frey, sick on board

Johannes (X) Jordan

Wilhelm Hausamen

Johannes (X) Rudolph

Hans Mickell Müller

Friedrich Kämmer

Jacob Klein

Geörg Hans Diettrich

Jacob Schaaff

Johannes (X) Geer

Johann Phillip Göres

Johan George (++) Weber

Matheas (O) Roth

Otto (X) Pegy

Martin (V) Varinger

Michel Wantz

Anthony (+) Rush

Hans George (X) Gleysler

Jacob (H) Honik

Jacob (IW) Weiseburger

Johannes Müller

Christian ( ) Brokhart, on board

Johannes ( ) Brokhart, on board

Paulus (X) Shäffer

Matheas ( ) Miller, sick on board

Frederik (X) Shaaff

Daniel ( ) Fisher, sick on board

Johann Ludwig Ache

Hermannus Ache

Mathis Kientz

Jacob Dietrich

Jacob Juncker

Petter Wendling

Hans Dewald ( ) Wendlin, on board

Adereas (X) Striber

H. George ( ) Mouser, on board

T. Nicklas ( ) Mouser, on board

Ludwig ( ) Grass, on board

Joseph (++) Weingand

Michel Conradt

Joachi[m] Pury

Johannes Ringeler

Agustus Urban

Johanes ( ) Göthing, on board

Joseph (X) Held

Joseph (X) Reebel

George (X) Riebel
Lorentz (X) Reinhart
Mardin Brungart
Johann David Wildermuth
Georg Wülhelm Müller
Johannes Patt
Johan Jacob (X) Hess
George Ludwig Marburger
Johan (X) Kraffthorn
Peter ( ) Bing, sick on board
Johannes Henrich Gütting
Johannes Jacob Ache
Hieronimues Spies
Johanes Michel
John ( ) Ludewig, sick on board
Johan ( ) Ewers, sick on board
Johannes Schreiber
Martin (+) Stutter
Johann Danniel Steinseiffer
Hans Henrich Kaufer
Hermanus (X) Limper
Hironimus ( ) Shneyder, on board

J. Michael (X) Kuntzer
Georg Adam ( ) Shutz, sick on board
Johann Jacob Brentz
Johan Gorg Hüssung
Uhllerik (X) Glökil
Johannes Meyer
Conrad (X) Ziegler
Joseph Altherr
Hans Jacob ( ) Houser, on bord
Jacob Grass
Michael ( ) Grass, on board
Johann Diedtrich
Johann Jacob Müller
Johan George (X) Lähr
Johann Wienert Blecher
Johannes Michael Bäcker
Hans Nickel Quierin
Johan Nicklas (+) Hoffman
Johan Nicklas (+) Farringer
Joseph (+) Anzemiller

[List 181 C] At the Statehouse in Philadelphia, Saturday, 23 September, 1752.

Present: Edward Shippen, Esquire.

The Foreigners whose Names are underwritten, Imported in the Ship St Andrew, Captain James Abercrombie, from Rotterdam and last from Plymouth in England, did this day take the Oaths to the Government in the usual Form. No 111.

Jacob Baltzer
Christopf [?] Horn
Johann Friedrich Seller
Hans Mardin Zeller
Johann Christoph Rössel
Hans Martin (HMH) Hang
H. Dewalt (XX) Billman
Hans Dommi

Andereas Bartruff
Uhllerich (O) Shergh
Abraham (++) Zety
Johann Philip Keinel
Jacob Orth
Philip (PB) Backer
Philip (K) Kibelinger
Jacob Hiestandt

Christian Bühler

Vallentin (××) Backer

Johannes Arnbühl

Andereas (×) Lintz

Uhllerigh (+) Zurger

Daniel Blim

Ulrich Scherr

Joh. Georg Knoch

Ludwig Spannagel

Gabriel Spannagel

Hans George (+) Holzer [?]

Leonhart (+) Bremer

Wilhelm Reiter

Jacob Reiter

Jacob (×) Blanck

Nickolas (×) Blanck

Matthias Eckh

Johann Jacob Bauer

Jacob (O) Kauffman

Johannes (×) Ruts

Nicolas (×) Booke

Johann Heinrich Kress

Johann Valentin Kräss

Daniel Renold

Christen Schmucker

Hans (H) Blanck

Johann Jacob Boltz

Joseph Kropf

Jacob ( ) Vorney, sick on board

Uhllerik (×) Houser

Dorst (+) Alliman

Leonhart (+) Hedly

Ulriche Fischer

Johan Michell Mauer

Johann Bernhart Eytel

Joseph Gall

Jacob Frid

Philip Wissler

Philipp Ullrich Lauterbach

Michel Lincksweiler

Johannes Mack

Peiter Mack

Dietherich Schmitzer

Eberhart Buttman

Johann Georg Gramlich

Christoph Heinrich Reinhold

John George (+) Küffer

Rudolf Edel [?]

Michael App

Christian Stäbler

Henrich Jacob Hänsler

Bastian Bohrmann

Jorich Bernhart Friedrich

Johann Peter Lang

Steffan Meyer

George Adam Eberth

Hans Jorg Bader

Henrich Schenckh

Johann Görg Kupper

Davit Kattrmann

Heinrich Gebhardt

Johannes Schmitt

Jacob Lutz

Andres Zorn

Jacob Schäffer

Hans Jacob Brener

Marte Steinbrenner

Jacob Steinbrenner

Christopf Carl

Mattheus Breitschwerd

Christian Lutz

Simon Reiht

Johan Leonhart Reuchert

Hans Michel Hottenbach

Johan Georg Hottenbach

Peter Adam

Friederich Planck

David Aller

Hanns Jacob Eberli

Johann Michael Strecker

Jeramias Eberli

Johann Heinrich Riedel

Christoph David Schauer
Philipp Schauer
Fridrich Müller
Johann Geörg Eberle
Hans Jerg Heisch
Ullrich Stauffer
Hans George (X) Piesh

Simon (X) Brand
Johan Petter Kampman
Johann Wilhelm Kampman
Frantz (+) Kamman
Daniel (X) Gerhart
Johan Caspar Ginter

[List 182 C] At the Statehouse in Philadelphia, Saturday, the 23 Septr 1752.
Present: Edward Shippen, Esquire.

The Foreigners whose Names are underwritten, Imported in the Ship Ann Galley, Captain Charles Kenneway, from Rotterdam and last from Portsmouth, did this day take the usual Qualifications to the Government. No. 75.

Bartlome Eibach
Johann Friedrich Fendtner
Andreas Braun
Albrecht Hofmeister
Johann Ludwig Büschler
Philipp Heyd
Sebastian Kiskolt [?]
Johann Jacob Rau
Wilhelm Conrat
Jacob Mettler
Eberhart Christoph Schert
J. Henry (+) Kuntz
Andereas (X) Kissel
Johan George Steiner
Johan Georg Rihm
Michel Obrist
Henry (X) Angeuly
Hans Martinn Stalton [?]
Johann Valentin Seidel
Johann Friederich Springer
Johan Gabriel Springer
Martin (++) Shall
Mart. Waltz
J. Caspar (X) Spoon
Uhllerik (X) Spoon

Balthas Maute
Martin Op [?]
Martin Gerg Wahl
Joseph Mayer
Fridrich Reicheneckher
Rudolph (X) Shoub
Hans Georg Hipp
Simon (+) Zeiner
Nickolas (X) Leyteker
Daniel Nonnenmacher
Ludwig Korrad Schnider
J. Michael (X) Miller
Hans Jerg Schaal
J. George (O) Spengler
Peter (O) Spengler
Benedict Spitzfadem
Henry (X) Vallentin
Peter (X) Compo
Jean (O) Rigony
Rudolph ( ) Shoff, on board
Clemence (++) Ober
George (++) Ludewig
Hans Jerg Meckh
Michael (O) Meck
Michael Muth

Hans Martin Mäck

H. Georg (X) Shley

Thomas Jeidler

Johan Conrad Schuch

Augustin (X) Muor

Peter Inäbnit

Hans Georg (+) Batter

Michael (M) Shwartz

J. Jacob (W) Wintzberger

Jacob (B) Boots

Martin Muller

Johann Geörg Schreiner [?]

Johan Elias

Johann Friederich (++) Braun

Johan Georg Braun

George Jacob (X) Shneyder

Hans Jerg Schwartz

Fillip Bleck

Christian (+) Tomm

Jacob (X) Miller

Willhelm (X) Conrad

[List 183 C] The Foreigners whose Names are underwritten, Imported in the Ship Richard and Mary, John Moore, Master, from Koterdam, and last from Portsmouth, took the usual Qualifications to the Government, Before
Joshua Maddox, Esquire.
The Twenty Sixth Day of September 1752. No. 91.

Jacob Daniel Scherrer

Peter Römer

Henrich Jacob Knerr

Johann Davit Allschbach

Petter Emmer

Caspar (X) Baltzaer

Johanes (+) Weyant

Johann Diehlbeck

John Nicklas (H) Kargher

Michael (X) Beahm

Johann Georg Genheimmer

Nicklas (+) Bernhart

Johan Georg Emmerich

Johann Philb Jäckes [?]

Johann Henrich Kipp

Johann Phillipps Hoffman

Peter (X) Hottebach

Johann Peter Roller

Johan Peter Pfankugen

Andereas (X) Hann

Gabriel Armbrister

Johannes Conrath

Johann Henrich Sponheimer

Johann Phillipp Wentz

Johann Benedictus Müller

George (X) Right

J. Jo. Henrig Scher

Johan Thebald Bauer

Pillib Jacob Kehle

Henrich Heidelbach

George Friederich Emrich

Nicklaus Wüchel

Valentin Schmitt

Johann Jacob Seyfriedt

Johan Heinrich Hummel

Michael Schlayer

Michael (X) Roth

Johann Adam Derting

Jacob Schuckman

Johannes Becker

Dewalt Dannfeltzer

Johann Nickel Hembt

Johannes Stras

Elias Hummel

Johan Gerg Beck
Andereas Jäckle
Martin Holtzhäusser
Johan Thiel (H) Herman
Johanes (H) Herman
Frederik (X) Saamm
Nicolas Samm
Adam Samm
Theobald Becker
Peter (H) Hortt
Petter Bien
Henrich Müssemer
Johannes König
Ludewig (X) Shmit
Jacob Steinbach
Conrad (X) Miller
Henrich Moser
Michael ( ) Graff, on board
Jacob Klar
Henrich Bierbauer
Andres Petri
Jost (X) Shoenwalt
Simon Schumacher

Johann Geörg Haüdt
Adam Bernhardt
Debalt Grub
Johann Wilhelm Stuber
Johann Friederich Stuber
Johann Philibpps Stuber
Hans Jerg Eheller [?]
Daniel Cramer
Michael Lauer
Johann Wilhellem Stricker
Balzasor (X) Dikhans
Georg Peter Eckel
Johannes Küstner
Georg Seider
Simon Hermann
Caspar (X) Lademan
Antonius Walter
Nicolaus Walter
Hans Jacob Gebhardt
Peter Bernhard Henkenius
Johann Henrich Henkenius
Michael (X) Hoffman

[List 184 C] In the Statehouse in Philadelphia, Wednesday, the 27th September, 1752.
Present: . . .
The Foreigners whose Names are underwritten, Imported in the Ship Anderson, Captn Hugh Campbell, from Rotterdam, and last from Portsmouth in England, took and subscribed the usual Qualifications. No. 85.

Leonhardt Bender
Christoph Maurer
Uhlerich (O) Volk
Jerg Riegert
Peter Miller
David Hausmann
Johann Martin Schweitzer
Hans Georg Marquart
Johannes (+) Strätter

Johannes Weill
Jacob Beittel
Daniel Reutter
Michael Heim
Jeremias Ludwig Engelmann
Johann Schneider
Philipp Euler
Peter (+) Piel
Philipp Graf

Mattheis Beugel
Michael Schmid
Nicklaus Renschler
Peter Dückherdt
Fridrich Steinle
Ulrich Stem [?]
Leonhardt Gnärr
Christian (CH) Rapman
Johannes Waltz
Georg Wetzel
Wilhelm Fridrich Schumann
Carl Friedrich Muckenfus
Simm Zimmerman
Jacob Friedrich Fischer
Johann Georg Breymeyer
Wilhelm Chroph Kestbohrer
Christian Dürr
Nicolaus Schuder
David Wegfaller [?]
Joh Friederich Fuchs
Christof Rothacker
Christoph Österle
Michael Schelling
Martin Betz
Andreas Götz
Andreas Eppler
Johanes Kurtz
Pierre Lageau
Johanes (O) Altig
Adam Weissbahrt
Johannes Weber
Andreas Scheibling

Joh. Caspar Windesch
Andras Weg
Peter (✕) Anssel
Joachim Bräuchle
Johan David Horlacher
Johanes (++) Washer
Johann Georg Traub
Johan Jacob Beltz
Georg Michael Beltz
Christoph Gisterer
Johann Jacob Fitzler
Hans Michael (✕) Cretel
Georg Ernst Lindenberger
Moritz Baur
J. George (+) Reest
Thomas Knissel
Johann Jerg Schillger
Johann Friderich Läible
Johan Frid König
Mahteus Kühbauch
Johan Fridrich Spur [?]
Wilhelm Garein
Johann Heinrich Von Rahden
Gottlob Hermann
Thomas ( ) Peel, on board
Michel Ritter
Christian (✕) Peiffly
Jacob (+) Plessing
M. Jacob Friderich Schertlein *
Jacob Reiser
Balthes Friett
Friderich Masser

[List 185 C] At the Court House in Philadelphia, Wednesday, the 27 September, 1752.
    Present: Joshua Maddox, Esquire.
The Foreigners whose names are underwritten, Imported in the Ship President, Captain Dunlop, from Rotterdam and last from . . . in England, did this day take and subscribe the

* A Lutheran Minister. M. = Magister.

Oaths and Affirmations to the Government, in the usual Form.
No. [73.]

Johann Georg Schneider
Johannes Enttiger
Johannes Hauser
Hanns Bauer
Johann Martin Cronmiller
Georg Christop Krüss
Johannes Lutz
Johan Martin Huber
Johann Georg Haas
Johannes Folkner
Hans Marten Schrony
Johan Martin Pfeifer
Philipp Jacob Nass
Georg Albrecht
Johans Albrecht
Michael Pfladdermiller
Ullrich Michael Lauer
Johan Georg Haiteberger
Uhlerick (X) Kraghberger
Michel Ruess
Jacob Nast
Godfried (X) Stough
Michel Fischer
Jerg Friedrich Scherthlen
Wilhelm Schneider
Johan Petter Erman
Carl Klluge
Bernhardt Höhneiss
Wolfgang Lehner
Conradt Huber
Conradt Huber
Hans Jerg Beckh
Christoph Schmid
Johann Georg Weickh
Johann (X) Bruning
Michael (G) Gantner
Jacob Knapper

Salomon Westle
Jacob Müller
Caspar Brintzighofer
Christoph Strobel
Johann Georg Wagner
Johann Heinrich Kostenbader
Adam Sorg
Johanes (X) Faber
Peter (+) Paltzly
Jacob Wild
George (W) Wild
Johan Christoffel Etter [?]
Andreas Plesse
Johannes Schencken
Melcher Belzhuber
Hans Gerg Looser
Johan Jacob Lang
Johann Schwencke
Friederich (X) Shwenck
Adam Angermayer
Jacob Lang
Martin Schillinger
Johann Bernhard Bauer
Andreas Schwartz
Mattheis Boser
Hans Jerg Boser
Johannes Shmit
Jereg Düterle
Jacob ( ) Threr, on board
Johanes Schärthle
Frantz (+) Tulipan
Henry (+) Hossler
Georg Friederich Hengel
Philipp Samuel Püth
Johannis Daichler
Bernhart Allpp

[List 186 C] At the Court House in Philadelphia, Wednesday, yᵉ 27 September, 1752.

Present: Joshua Maddox, Esquire.

The Foreigners whose Names are underwritten, Imported in the Ship Nancy, Captain John Ewing, from Rotterdam and last from Cowes, did this day take and subscribe the usual Qualifications. No. 83.

Jacob Schweude
Jacob Schmidt
Jonas (✕) Bastian
Jerg Hauher
Jacob Friederik (✕) Danninger
Jacob Mussgenug
Carl Frich Siebert
Philipp Jacob Wunder
David Xander
Johann Michael Haas
Samuel Musse
Johan Philipp Bietighoffer
Philipp Mall
Konradt Weiss
Andres Bastian
Adam Friederich Weiss
Johann Georg Friderich Bayer
George (+) Wenig
Jacob Bauerschmid
Jacob Bauerschmidt
Gerg Friderich Jauss
Christoph Rothbaust
Matheas (✕) Dywel
Friderich Baisch
Jacob ( ) Baisch, on board
Johan Andereas (✕) Rothe
Christoff Kreiser
Johann Friderich Uhlandt
Jacob (✕) Armbruster
George Michael (✕) Spatz
Johannes Butz
Jacob Stützmann

Michael (✕) Eyroh
Joseph Steüdel
Johan Ludwig Seiler
Christian Homberg
George (✕) Grass
Jacob Dietrich
Joseph (✕) Bernhart
Joseph (✕) Bernhart, Junior
Hans (N) Kintz
Joseph ( ) Kintz, on board
Johannes (HIM) Herman
Johanis (✕) Shwitzer
Jacob Junchfer [?]
Hans Georg Kautz
Jacob Kautz
Hans Jacob Lersch
Jaque Peirot
Jaque Molac
Frantz (✕) Saltzman
Lutwig Thüringer
Peter (✕) Heatteman
Johann Martin Doser
Michael Doser
Balthas Bauman
Christoph Embich
Christian Mühlheim
Israel Eberlin
Fillib Follen
Joh. Jacob Ernst
Hans Jacob Neusterdt
Vallendin Hagner
Hans Jerg Heudekel [?]

Ludwig Neitz
Jerg Balthas Ernst
Casper Underweg
Mardin Fromm
Andreas Jäger
Johan Max Klopfer
Johann Martin Rädelmeyer
Abraham Birkenber[g]
Henry (+) Shleghter
Herman (+) Matsh
Georg Friederich Schwartz

Christoph ( ) Mast, on board
Paul Waag
Hans Georg ( ) Krebs, on board
Hans Paul Henrich
Rudolph (+) Klarr
Hans Stös
Hans Michael (×) Weller
Johann Georg Braun
Johannes Griess
Jacob (HK) Kautz, Junior

[List 187 C] At the Courthouse in Philadelphia, Wednesday, the 4 October, 1752.
Present: Joshua Maddox, Esquire.
The Foreigners whose Names are underwritten, Imported in the Ship Neptune, Captn John Mason, from Rotterdam and last from Cowes in England, did this day take and subscribe the Oaths and Affirmations to the Government in the usual Form. No. 169.

Johan Ludwig Leib
Hans Michael (×) Goodknecht
Hans Michael (O) Dock
Adam (+) Hardmann
Hans George (×) Hartmann
Valdin Litman
Christoffel Feichtner
Johan Jacob Wolf
Nickolas (×) Barron
Nickel Nählig
Henry (+) Henly
Hans Pett. Hertzog
Goerg Mewes
Johan Valltin Walter
Christian Schmid
Hubert (HB) Baumgarten
Johanes (O) Bernhart
J. Christian (O) Boneblust
Hans Nichelas Nesser
Hans George (×) Kurtz

Stephan (×) Nickans
J. Jacob (+) Becker
Johann Heinrich Yoel
Hans Gerg Kuches
Jorg Lorer [?]
Michael (M) Hoak
Stoffel Hussung
Georg Heinrich König
Daniel (×) Stattler
Daniel (×) Cunrad
Anthony (×) Roth
Philip Jacob (×) Roth
Johanes (×) Cunrad
Caspar (×) Fell
Christian Rohrbacher
Paul Hofman
Jacob (+) Shwartz
Christian Hofman
Adam (+) Pence
Johann Georg Werner

Philipp Christian Weller
Johann Sigmund Hagelgans
Johann Jacob Dietrich
Nicklaus Hoh
Johann Michael Schaeffer
John Adam (++) Wild
Willhelm Trautmann
Michael (O) Busth
Matheas (H) Andrije
Wendal (×) Beessel
Jacob (×) Haberstich
Christian (×) Haberstich
Balsathar (O) Swartz
Hans (×) George Swartz
Paulus (×) Seip
Wilhelm Stauch
Tebalt (O) Shartz
Philip (×) Seip
George (×) Meyer
Jacob (×) Künh
Michael Kutzner
John Adam (×) Tietz
Thomas Straub
Johannes Hortig
Dewalt (+) Witterspor
Johann Peter Assum [?]
Johann Kress
Henry ( ) Kress, on board
Caspar (×) Kress
Carls (×) Kress
Nickolas (H) Shall
Andereas (A) Shall
Nickolas (S) Shall, Junior
Conradt Rösch
Jacob Zieget
Christopher Blumer
Simon (W) Shmith
John George (×) Weber
George (×) Unckel
John Philip (×) Grech
Johan Jacob Tries

George (×) Lawtenshläger
Johanes (×) Feyly
Hans Adam (+) Weber
Johann Michael Heinecke
Johann Adam Heinecke
Matheas (O) Ebener
Nicklaus Schwyer
Joab Dormeyer
Andereas (×) Dormeyer
Jacob ( ) Dormeyer, on board
Johan Christian Gros
Johann Anderes Gros
Johann Heinrich Niess
Peter Schneider
Conrad Schneider
Johann Wilhelm Schneider
Johann Conradt Streuber
Gebhart Bertholt
Samuel Schultz
Ludwig Küster
Jerg Phillips Küster
J. Henry (××) Lohmiller
Johann Görg Rübsaamen
J. George (++) Jung
Philip (××) Wentzel
Johannes Hufnagel
Johann Michael Schmidt
Johannes (××) Geiss
Matteis Haller
Peder Molsbach
Johannes Schäffer
Johann Pilipp Haffner
Henry (×) Lipps
Christoffel Keller
Henrich Schäffer
Johan Philipps Breuning
Johan Adolph Gilman
Johannes Nickellas
J. George (Nick) Nickolas
Joseph (B) Bernart
Christian Baur

Peter (B) Zöngrig
Peter Uhrich
Johann Jacob Baumann
Johann Michael May
Johan Kasper Domen
Johannes Zurflie
Juhans Hirni
Johanes Schwatzer
Johann Henrich Heist
J. Adam (X) Arris
Johannes (+) Arris
Johanes (O) Glass
Johann Jacob Hipge
Heindrich Zurbüchen
Hans Küntzi
George (X) Meyer
Ulrich Sterchi
Hans Weid
Ullrig Sterchi
Christian Sterchy
Michael (++) Spatz
Johan Philip Müller

Johann Peter Muller
Vallentin (X) Lawtenshläger
Michael (X) Hessler
Johannes (X) Blökinger
Uhllerik (X) Feitz
Peter (XX) Shneyder
Johann Georg Kriegenmeyer
Peter (X) Dunter
Johannes Hoffer, Senior
Johanes (+) Hoffer, Junior
Johann Wilhelm Lotz
Johannes Lohmöller
Nicolas (+) Lotz
Christoph Kistling
Johannes Kauz
Christian Kauz
Johann Peter Schmidt
Johann Daniel Becker
Jacob Gross
Johan Bastia[n] Rindt
Johann Jörg Nonyus
Johann Georg Diehl

[List 188 C] At the Court House at Philadelphia, Tuesday, 10th October 1752.

Present: Joshua Maddox, Esquire.

The Foreigners whose Names are underwritten, Imported in the Ship Forest, Captain Patrick Auchterlony, from Rotterdam and last from Portsmouth in England, did this day take the usual Oaths to the Government. No. 106.

Johann Jacob Wiltraut
Johann Georg Englert
Michel Danner
Johannis Scheirer
Jacob Keinadt
Balthas Maute
Matteas ( ) Bader, on board
Hans Gerg Bader
Johannes Andonyus Henner
Johan Peter Schönfelter

Peder Sander
Johannes Peter Schonfelder
Johanes (X) Reebemiller
Johann Geörg Hoffman
Johann Caspar Fitting
Nickolas ( ) Ruth, gone on
    board
Johann Adam Schissler
Peter (+) Pfeill
F. Jacob (+) Kuntz

Jacob (×) Heller
Petter Kirstohber
Johann Adam Wolff
Johanes (×) Wolffe
Johan Carls (×) Wolffe
J. Daniel (×) Jounger
Johan Christian Schwartz
Georg Martin Vött
Hans Jerg Sulger
Conrad Früh
Christian (××) Shnekenburger
Conrad ( ) Luntz, on board
Johann Foglin Schirm [?]
Wallendin Braun
Johann Conradh Wack
Johann Conradh Wack
Johannes Claus
Johan Teys ( ) Claus, on board
J. Henry (××) Herman
Johan Tünges Jung
Johannes Schell
Johannes Peter Clossmeyer
Johann Conrath Fay
Johan Henrich Wiestein
Johann Christ Reis
Johanes (+) Tillman
Conrad Jung
Johann Peter Jung
Christoph Gerhardt
Jacob Notz
Johan Georg Bruder
Johann Jacob Wagner
Johannes Lademacher
Johann Simon Schreyer
Johann Leonhardt Schreyer
Anton Welter [?]
Henry (H) Kaulbach
Johannes Peter Steinenbach
Johannes Henrich Humrich
Johannes Gontert
Johann Jörg Hönner

Johan Deys (×) Reichel
Johann Friederich Schorf
Johan (×) Engel Röder
Caspar Hubert
Johann Filibus Weller
Johannes Schöyrer
Hanes Christ Wykerding
Jung Heinrich Gross
Henry ( ) Gross, on board
Jacob Digel
Hans Martin Neiser
Michael Englert
Johann Lenhard Herriger
Johann Georg Ottenwaldt
Johannes Hagner
Johann Michael Küntzel
Johann Dieterich Riess
Hans Adam (×) Werner
Mattheis Miller
Johan Jacob (×) Miller
Johannes Meyer
Johannes Huss
Henrich Greutz
Wilhelm Creutz
Daniel (×) Light
Johan Jacob (×) Shwartz
Johan Jacob Lorch
Johann Engel Schreter
Johan Peter Scheffer
Johan Henry (×) Shram
Jean Christophel Marekel
Jacob (×) Tilliger
Johann Görg Birck
Christian ( ) Freyly, on board
Emanuel (×) Heynz
Johannes Petter Kirchbischen [?]
Johann Jost Görg
Johan Martin Walter
Christoph Staffel
Lorrentz (×) Pollen
Michel Bitzer

Mattheis Bitzer
Johan Henrich Beil
Johanes (X) Retter
Peter (PK) Crimm

Michael Kegereis
Johannes Adam Adam
Johannes Jacob Donat

[List 189 C] At the Court House at Philadelphia, Monday, the 16th October, 1752.
Present: Joshua Maddox, Esq.

The Foreigners whose Names are underwritten, imported in the Snow Ketty, Theophilus Barnes, Commander, from Rotterdam and last from Portsmouth, did this day take the usual Qualifications to the Government. No. 75.

Friedrich Jacquart
David Welsch
Johann Diether Marckbach
Wilhelm Lenhardt
Christian Closs
Johann Danniel Mutschler
Johan Conrad Oestreich
Johan Conrad Ruth
Johan Christian Burg
Philip (X) Bidelyoung
Johann Christophel Volck
Daniel (X) Klein
John (X) Dewald
Joseph Mey
Johannes Gachon
Leonhardt Seuffert
Geörg Schneyder
Johann Peter Niedenthal
Johann Jacob Neumeyer
Johannes Hen
Johan Phillipp Schneider
Johann Wilhelm Strempel
Jonas Rinderlust [?]
Andreas Heck
Heinrich Müller
Johann Joachim Tölcker
J. George (+) Frey
Christian (X) Wentz

John ( ) Bloat, sick on board
Johann Georg Hartranft
Philip (+) Sheffer
Johann Michel Lind
Johann Jacob Decker
Johann Petter Höll
Johann Jacob Müller
Philip (X) Albrecht
Caspar Bauer
Johan Henrich Heyl
Philipps Jacob Mack
Andereas (X) Mack
Johann Towias Eebele
Christian (X) Sand
Görg Braus
Johann Daniel Weisenberger
Georg Philips Lind
Conrath Thomas Lind
Christoph Süss
Joseph Weber
Henrich Weidner
Philipps Carl Schenckel
Jacob (X) Haen
George Michael (+) Egert
George Michael (+) Hain
Johann Jacob Heintz
Jerg Kopf [?]
Jacob Welde

Martin Grün
Michael (X) Baker
Friedrich Müller
Nickolas (X) Salladin
Henry (X) Hess
Abraham Sontag
George (X) Gass
Johannes Kallenberger
H. George (X) Brenner

Jacob (X) Heyl
Henry (X) Sees
Jacob Schuster
Philipps Schenckel
Geörg Welde
Henrich Schenckel
Nicklaus König
Gottfried König
Peter König

[List 190 C] At the Court House at Philadelphia, Friday, the 20th October, 1752.
Present: Joshua Maddox, Esqr.

The Foreigners whose Names are underwritten, imported in the Ship Duke of Wirtenburg, Daniel Montpelier, Commander, from Rotterdam but last from Cowes, this Day took the usual Qualifications to the Government. No. 143.

Jacob Guth
Michael Stähr
Georg Ziegler
Jacob Bosch
Johan Michael Guth
Johan Georg Guth
Samuel Banher
Johann Martin Both
Conrath Funckbohner
Jacob Bernhardt Schwab
Johan Adam Schwab
Johann Friederich Gross
Michel Meng
Christian (X) Zürn
Immanuel Friderich Weckerlin
Johannis Kleiz
Matthäus Kibler
Tobias Baub
Johann Georg Jayser
John Jacob ( ) Geyser, on
  board
Johanes (X) Blikly
Tobias (-+-+) Mik

Christian Lutz
Matheis Bruder
Johannis Schwartzwälder
Johannes Wehnig
Balthasar Lotz
Jacob Schaiblen
Friederich Stöhr
Friederich Kilgus
Anthony (O) Katterer
Matheas (MD) Zeiger
Georg Berger
Johannis Deschler
Johann Ludwig Uber
Joh. Jacob Fissler
Johann Michael Fissler
Johann Georg Fissler
Hans Henniger
Heinrich Schwab
Christian Adrian
Hans Jereg Keller
Hans Jacob Keller
Sebastian Wagner
Johans Fritilauf [?]

Johann Conrad Hesser
Friederich Dechan
Johann Simon Vogler
Johannes Schwartz
Matheus Stahl
Michel Fahnen
Johanes Lemle
Michel Lömle
Jacob (X) Wessener
Matheas (O) Lang
Johannis Miller
Michel Bach
Jacob Bauman
Christian (||) Brown
Jacob Stiegekhel [?]
Andreas Gering
Matheas (X) Brughly
Joel (X) Waltz
Hans Gerg Heitzmann
Jerg Haber
Johannis Seitz [?]
Michael (X) Hawer
Johanes (X) Facmeyer
Michael (XX) Gardner
Johan Jacob Bauman [?]
Johann Georg Ott
Tomas [?] Simon Lauman
Friderich Mag
Michel Hart [?]
Johannes Zinser
Michael (M) Lyx
Johannes (X) Lyx
Hans Michael Schatz
Johannis Reiblen
Hans Marti Raible
Peter (XX) Haller
Jacob Krauss
Christian (X) Getz
Christian (X) Zigler
Johanes (X) Kughler
Jacob (XX) Shooler

Jacob (X) Weyn
Johan (X) Lockmir
Michael ( ) Frik, sick on board
Albrecht Walter
Marti Haug
Johannes (X) Shoutz
Christian Koch
Joseph Lenz
Jacob Zeitler
Johanes (+) Brown
Johanes (+) Brown, Junior
Johannes Braun
Joseph Bontaux
Jacob Mass
Friederich Schmeltzle
Uhllerich Scheermesser
Hans Max Kugell [?]
Martin (X) Lang
Christian Singer
Mattheis Kress
Friederich Gasser
Johannes Leip
Hans Martin (X) Lang
Hans Jerg Fritz
Andereas Wesener [?]
Friederich Schmidt
Jacob (X) Steely
Jacob (X) Lanck
Jacob Morhardt
Jacob (H) Gündner
Jacob Walter
Augustin Stahl
Johannis Wigold
Matthes Wesner
Christian (X) Hebting
Jacob (X) Beyerly
Jacob (X) Brown
Jacob (X) Brown, Senior
Mick. (X) Matheas
George (X) Haffner
Christian Haas

Johanes (×) Hetzel
Andoni Bürell
Johanes (+) Flait
Johann Jacob Maser
Gottlieb Zinck
Matheus Maser
Hans Georg (+) Haak

Hans Georg Göttle
Jacob (O) Bub
Christian Stahl
Christoff Fridrich Biller
Matheas (×) Van
Hans Jacob ( ) Van, on board
Hans Georg (×) Finkbein

[List 191 C] At the Court House at Philadelphia, Monday, the 23ᵈ of October, 1752.
Present: Edward Shippen, Esqʳ.

The Foreigners whose Names are underwritten, imported in the Ship Rawley, Capt. John Grove, from Rotterdam, but last from Plymouth, this day took the usual Qualifications to the Government. 137.

John George ( ) Bager,* on board
Adam (×) Ship
Henrich Peter Tesch
Adam (×) Tesch
Henrich Klein
Jacob Wann
Philipp Hennrich Grooss
Christoph (×) Reyter
J. Friederich (O) Gakly
G. Michael (×) Breiner
Christian Metzger
Melchior (×) Katyman
Leonhart (×) Bawman
Hans George (××) Shmit
Hans Mickel (××) Shmit
Johannes Heil
Jorg Heil
Engel Wirth Dönges
Conradt Dönges
Peter (××) Shwob
Johanes (×) Pouss

Hans Baus
Johannes (×) Kogh
Johan Fridrig Rubel
Johannis Claus Krausshar
Johanes (×) Krausshar
Jacob Hottenstein
Johanes (×) Shmit
Bernhart Mauer
Morritz (M) Shadigh
Jacob (++) Frey
Daniel Hötzel
Gottfrid Schutz
Johann Wilhelm Engersbach
John Adam (×) Zey
John George (×) Wendel
Johan Gerg Gross
Andreas Haag
Nickolas (×) Miller
Johann Henrich Cress
Michal Rüttger
Johannes Müller
Nickolas (×) Greiffenstein

* This is a Lutheran minister, who preached for many years at Hanover, York County, and in neighboring churches. See T. E. Schmauk, *History of the Lutheran Church*, pp. 388–390.

Andreas Jauch
Martin (XX) Jager
Henry (X) Bouth
Hans Peter (X) Link
Johanes (X) Simmon
Peter (XX) Simmon
Andereas (++) Vey
Johanes (X) Turnn
Daniel Machleit
Michael Kutz
Kilian Bauer
J. Philip (X) Titshler
Johanes (X) Glassler
Wilhelm Gottlieb Jayser
Baltzar (X) Simon
Andreas Berger
Conradt Alster
John Georg (X) Shobig
Valentin Stoll
Johanes (X) Lingker
Heinrich Simon
J. George (X) Eberly
Leonhart (X) Spong
Georg Hartman
F. Peter (++) Bower
John Nicklas (++) Out
Andreas Hötzel
Christian Hugel
Andreas Frischkorn
J. Nicklas (XX) Stous
Nicolaus Böhm
Johannes Rath
Justus Drebbert
Stephannus Lotz
Johannes Lotz
Uhllerich (X) Miller
Jacob (O) Gumeringer
Hans Jerg Steidinger
Johan Philip (X) Frech
George (X) Brown
Johannes Seitz

Lorentz (X) Houshalter
Joseph Burgstahler
Christoph Hacker
Michel Lang
Matheas (X) Miller
Hans Jorg Mock
Hans Jorg Wächter
Johann Gottlieb Frölich
Jacob Nicoll
Mattheus Kron
Conradt Endres
Joerg Heinrich Bentz
Johann Jacob Schuppert
Frederik ( ) Kern, on board
Elias Most
Johann Georg Wunderlich
Hans George (H) Gardner
Philip (XX) Fisher
Daniel Schmidt
Georg Friedrich Klein
Conrad Gohl
Elias Gohl
Davidt Hottenstein
Johannes Stocker
Johan Michel Feger
Georg Eberhart Döring
David Jung
Christian Kress
Michael Wilhelm
Joseph Schweitzer
Leonhard Schweitzer
Jacob (XX) Shweitzer
J. Nickolas (XX) Bender
Andreas Brauss
Carl Bentz
Johannes Ommerth
Jacob (X) Sultzberger
Johannes Fehr
Georg Adam Kern
Johann Heinrich Gattung
Philipp Carges

J. Henry (X) Stowback
Teoboldus Bernhardt
Godfried (XX) Weyland
Johann Tobias Renner
Johann Conradt Trünckhler
Johannes Hebeysen

Christian Hermann
Georg Christoph Steinerth
Jost Henrich Möller
Johannes Möller
Johanes (+) Bone

[List 192 C] At the Court House at Philadelphia, Thursday, the Second of November, 1752.
Present: Edward Shippen, Esqr.

The Foreigners whose Names are underwritten, imported in the Ship called the Phoenix, John Spurrier, Commander, from Rotterdam but last from Portsmouth in England, took the usual Qualifications to the Government.

Bastian (+) Kender
Johann Henrich Schleich
Johan Jacob Wetzal
Johann Baltzar Kleinschmit
Lorentz Michel
Hans Michel Fries
Philipp Jacob Horn
Hagen Horn
Johannes Riess
Matthias Wilhelm Henning
Johan Michael Wissler
Johan Wolf Wissler
Johan Casper Wissler
Peter Dahlmann
Henrich Becker
Jo. Hennrich Katzebach
Conrad (X) Rooss
Joachim Ströver
Thomas (XX) Geisler
Phillip Herdel
J. Jacob (IS) Shellbecher
Jost Phillipp Schnelbacher
J. Henry (X) Sholtes
Jacobus Frütranck
Johann Michael Bäcker
Johanes Borischt

Johannes Stehlert
Johans Michel Bürger
Hans Philip Dosch
Johann Conrad Wassum
Johanes (+) Wassom
Leonhart (+) Wassom
Joh. George (X) Wassom
Adam (X) Heins
Christoff Kuhn
Hans Christoph Schlessmann
Frantz Ihmme
Johann Ludwig Peiffer
Siep Kurz
Abraham Bauman
Johanis Schmid
Johanis Schmit
Johan Christian Heydt
Johannes Götzelman
Hans Michel Ötzel
Andereas (+) Bower
Stephan (+) Bower
Michael (+) Bower
Hans Seubert
J. Jacob (+) Götzelman
Johann Adam Binner
Georg Hörner

Johann Melcher Hörner
Johann Jacob Hörner
Jacob Oberdorf
Andereas Seuberth
Veit Fitterling
Petter Dihm
Jacob Bauer
Andres Drach
Petter Drach
Andereas ( ) Tragh, on board
Hans Dhomas Dihm
Veit Garrecht
Hans Casper Haag
Frederick (×) Hirsh
Ludewigh (×) Haltemeyer
Hans George (×) Haltemeyer
Davit (×) Haltemeyer
Michal Hoffman
Hans Melchior (+) Stieffel
Hans Adam (×) Stieffel
Johann Georg Sauselin
Johanes Bösch
Johann Georg Wimmer
Johann Friedrich Berger
Johan Philip Davidt Spindler
Conrad (×) Kurtz
Johann Heinrich Kiesel
Johann Conradt Duetz
J. ( ) Heyser, sick on board
Hans Peter (+) Meyer
Johann Caspar Reisner
Johann Michael Sahme
John Christoph (×) Weydner
George Adam (×) Frederik
Hans Michael (×) Weaver
Johanes Leonhart ( ) Weaver,
  on board
Adam (++) Rochia
George (×) Bier
Michael Leiberich

Johan Nickles Klein
Johan Petter Weichell
Jeremias Oesterlein
Jodocus Dobler
Niklus Strauss
Johans Hörner
Johan Christoph Büttner
Ludwig Aguntius
Christian Tobias Gaisel
Hans Geörg Egenschneller
Johan Friederich Volck
Johan Heinrich Schlessmann
Hans George (×) Hand
Lorentz Kurtz
Johann Michael Lutz
Andreas Dressler
Peter Ross
Hans Michal Beck
Johann Nickolaus Ott
Andreas Hörauff
Hans Jerg Lang
Gerg Müller
Johannes Fimpel
Hans Jerg Fimpel
Hans Marttin Franck
Johann Peter Reeg
Jacob Wolf
Andreas Eyrich
Andtreas Büttel
Hans Fertig
Nickles Weitzenhöller
Johann Gorg Hoh
George (+) Hopengartner
Conrad (+) Cinkel
Antries Aleberger
Carl Ludwig Mäckelburg
Johann Melch. Peder
Michill Schönlein
Fielieb Jacob Wolf
Johan Nick. Schmal

Johann Peter Schmidt
Andres Lein
Christoph (C) Shawde
Nicolaus Weygant
Casper Beüschleinn
Michael Hunt
Philip (+) Sieur
Sebastian Leybolt
Johanes (+) Kraws
Hans Henry (×) Förster
Nicklas (×) Ingelhoff
Baltzer Lantz
Johannes Scholthes
John Henry ( ) Sholdes, on board
Johannes Weissgerber
Johannes Endres
Hans Adam Schäffer
Jost Peter Stöer
Johanes (M) Miller
August Heinrich Schröter
Jacob Dorner [?]
Christian Schäffer
Valledin Ehrhardt
Johanes (×) Shäffer
Christoph Waltz
Barthel Schätzlein
Johan Henrich Mönch
Hans Adam Hoh
Hans Kranck
Johann Ludwig Bender
And. Ag [?]
Henry ( ) Bed, on board
Johann Georg Strauss
J. Henry ( ) Koch, on board
Christoph Kuhlemann
Adereas (+) Kleim
Johann Conradt Butefisch
Johann Martin Noll
Carl Friedrich Daniel Christian

Johann Adam Härdel
Simon Galvin [?]
Johan Gorg Kallemeyer
Johann Leonhart Karg
David Gottfried Uthe
Lorenz Joseph Dennscherz
Michael ( ) Koghill, sick on board
Michael Dinckel
Carle Schmid
Hans Jürg Englert
Johann Christoph Schaber
Johann Niclaus Schlossman
Johann Stephanus Horn
Johann Phillipp Buch
Hans Gerbrich
Hans Jörg Büttel
Hans Jorg Sell
Hans Tamus Seger
Andres Sell
Jacob Krächman
Johannes Will
Johann Ferdinandus Leis
Henry ( ) Corn, on board, sick
Tobias Retter
Joseph Sommer
Johannes Hartman
Lorentz Heffner
Johan Heffner
Johannes Honnig
Lorrentz (+) Rörrigh
Johann Heinrich Muth
Peter Fleischer
Heinrich Fleischer
Christian Danner
Johann Peter Miler
Peter Müller, Senior
Hermanus Cronenberg
Johann Conrad Strödter
207.

[List 193 C] At the Court House at Philadelphia, Friday, the Third of November, 1752.

Present: Joshua Maddox, Esqr.

The Foreigners whose Names are underwritten, imported in the Ship Queen of Denmark, George Parish, Commander, from Hamburgh, but last from Cowes in England, this day took the usual Qualifications to the Government. 130.

Hinrich Burchard Gabriel Wortmann, P.*

Christopher (×) Pabst

George Thomas (O) Gimpel

Georg Bastian Fischer

Zacharias (+) Bach

Casp. Frederik (×) Lutz

Hans Zacharias (×) Longer

A. Diterich (××) Shell

J. Christian (××) Moronruth

J. Friederich ( ) Hiltsher, on board

G. Leopold (×) Hainig

Georg Gottlieb Paff

Johan Caspar (×) Operman

G. Henry (×) Herholt

Johan Adam Stoltze

J. Nicklas (++) Tränckner

J. Daniel (××) Metzler

P. Matheas (××) Abel

Johan (×) Zwiebeller

Andreas Schott

Jacob (×) Shott

Lambrecht (×) Philip

Jochim Heinrig Detloff

Hans Caspar (×) Batram

Nickolas Daniel (×) Vos

Johann Egen

Magnus Schröder

Peter (×) Bruns

J. Thomas ( ) Kuhn, on board

Johan Henrich Bauer

Johann Schlüter

Godfried Willhelm ( ) Allhelm, on board

Johan ( ) Mink, on board

Simon (+) Marcus

Johann Casper Friederich Grummet

L. Ludewig (×) Winckler

Christophel Ludewig Grummet

J. Gustavus ( ) Kuntz, on board

H. Christian ( ) Willfield, on board

M. Frederik (×) Kippenberg

George Christian ( ) Meyer, on board

Georg Christoffel Günder

Georg Christoph Mück

John Friederik ( ) Günter, on board

H. Zacharias ( ) Hagelberg

J. Jacob (×) Lantzen

Andereas (×) Ultsch

Conradt Schäffer

Johan Ernst ( ) Holland, on board

George (+) Gärtner

Georg Michael (+) Hornisser

Georg Frederik ( ) Zesh, on board

J. Christian (×) Nesselroth

* A Lutheran minister.

Georg Christian Klem
Johan Henry ( ) Klem, on board
Christian Henry ( ) Habight, on board
Christian (×) Naall
Henry Rudolph ( ) Nagel, on board
Heinrich Andreas Nagel
Christoph ( ) Meyer, on board
Michel Ståhl
Hinrich Jacob Struckmeyer
Johan Heinrich Sackman
Joachim Andereas (×) Bräutigam
Hein Von (×) Hoven
Johan Kröther
Joachim (×) Harloff
Jochim Rieck
Davit ( ) Mörsen, on board
Johan George ( ) Klotz, on board
Christoph (×) Meyer
Johan Sebastian Vogt
Johann Joachim Gärttler
Christⁿ Diterich (×) Meyer
J. Friederich (O) Lutzer
Ernest (H) Hornäffer
Christⁿ (×) Wilgenson
J. Henry (×) Shultz
Godfried ( ) Reinknecht, on board
Johann George Göthell
Johann Martin Roettger Ludewig
Heinrich Casper Putscher
Johann Valentin Dantius
Heinrich Magnus
John Ernst (+) Hein
J. Ernst ( ) Simon, on board
Peter (+) Wiese
Johan (+) Ohnshild

J. Friederich ( ) Berghan, on board
Johann Carel Mennecke
H. Michael (+) Mennike
John Adam (×) Gartner
Otto Carol ( ) Brand, on board
J. Andereas (++) Hornäffer
F. Christopher (××) Torson
Frederik Albrecht ( ) Sheller, on board
H. Friederik (×) Lamb
J. Christopher (+) Shletz
Casper Gabriel Miller
John Jogen Berfus
J. Henry ( ) Wendel, on board
Zacharias (×) Straubel
Davit Henry ( ) Heyer, on board
Christian Ludewig Münck
Carl Friederich Grobler
Frans Schütz
Nicklas ( ) Kerel, sick on board
Johan (++) Meyer
Dieterich von Bieren
A. Matheas ( ) Molin, on board
Johan Godfried (O) Zeisiger
John Georg (+) Matheas
Frederik (×) Shreyer
Henry (×) Nothturfft
Christian (×) Henrich
Johann Daniel Eckebret
Hein. Rudolff Stoltze
Hans George ( ) Breyhan, on board
Johan Fritrich Grässler
Johan Ludewig ( ) Stotterman, on board
Johan Bartolt Mühlhahn
Fridrich Salomon Weis
John Adolph ( ) Fluk, on board

Casper Heinrich Grim
Friederich (||) Zimmer
Johann Georg Reinhard
Diterich (+) Volkman

Johan Zacharias Jahn
Johannes Bibr
Johann Henrich Sänger
Johan Christoph Winter

[List 194 C] At the Court House at Philadelphia, Wednesday, the 8th November, 1752.
Present: Edward Shippen, Esquire.
The Foreigners whose Names are underwritten, Imported in the Snow Louisa, Captain John Pittcairne, from Rotterdam and last from Cowes, did this day take the usual Qualifications. No. 71.

Michael Deeg
Franc (+) Carel Von Campe
Matthäus Kepster
Hanns Jerg Hausser
Hans Jerg Reisch
Christoph Kurtz
Jacob Holder
Johan Hermann Rosenblatt
Johann Conradt Kopp
Ulrich Meyer
Johan Christian (F) Friess
Johanes Feiller
Johann Martin Holder
Johannes Meyer
Johannes Ulmer
Johann Michael Geiger
Casper Krieger
Adam (XX) Probst
Hans Gerg Lantzer
Georg Michael Schmidt
Chs. Hofman
Davidt Mellinger
Jacob Hoffman
Albrecht Michelfelder
G. Friedrick (X) Hottenbacher
Willhelm Fordtenbacher
Johannes Geiler
Conradt Schindler

Conradt Schindler
Hans Adam (X) Stahll
Johann Philipp Odenwalt
Johann Georg Koch
Johanes (X) Romig
Frantz Schmid
Johann Petter Schöll
Konradhr Psoh [?]
Johann Georg Sturm
Georg Baltzer Schelling
Balsatzor (X) Sholl
Peter Diem
Georg Gobel
Christoph Gülberth
Johann Georg Gilbert
Johan Jacob Rukhen
Johann Jost Bauer
Johann Georg Laubinger
Andreas Gilbert
Jac. Baltsatzer (++) Volcampe
Joseph Beyrer
Hans Görg Kautz
Johan Philipp Schwartzländer
Tobias (X) Stahl
Christian Ruff
John Philip (XX) Welsh
Johannes Schneider
Johan Georg Meyer

Georg Philipp Bock
Hans Michäll Schmidt
Jacob Hag
Georg Michael Müller
Johan Michael Späth
Johannes Bader
Johannes Has
Jacob Krieg

Jerg Karr
Fridrich Schrade
Johann Martin Hausleither
Johann Jacob Stoll
Georg Christop Nieser
Hans Michael ( ) Carel, on board
Simmon Leitel Huber

[List 195 C] At a Council at the Court House in Philadelphia, Wednesday, the 22ᵈ November, 1752.
Present: Joshua Maddox, Esquire.
The Foreigners whose Names are underwritten, Imported in the Ship Phoenix, Captain Ruben Honor, from Rotterdam and last from Cowes, did this day take the usual Qualifications. No. 149.

Lutwig Hennrich Nussbueckel
Peter (X) Antel
Johan Adam Lotz
Josias Shetzger
Johannes Klos
Joh. Nicklas (+) Althöl
Johann Peter Guttin
Georg Christoph Bauman
Johann Adam Geyer
Jacob Küwit
Johan Joachim [?] Wohand [?]
Johannes Lennenschidt
Johanes ( ) Lenshy, Junior, on board
Johann Henrich Breser
Jean Jaques le Roy
Weinbert Tschudi
Rudolph Hoffmann
Jann Georg Rohrer
Michael Bürgin
Uhllerik (O) Nicoly
Fridrich Steiler
Leonhart Steller
David Zimmermann

Lamberth Smyetch
Johann Henrich Becker
Jacob Friedrich Schneider
Johann Philipp Albert
Frantz Josepf Pfeifer
Johannes Mohr
Andreas Roth
Johannes Roth
Johann Matthes Scheurich
Johan Martin Dostman
Valentin Scheurich
Jacob Scheurich
Christoph Dosch
Hans Michael Adelmann
And. Weiler
Johannes Frölich
Jacob Frölich, my son
Phillib Jacobi
Johanes Haltermeyer
Hans (O) Shneyder, Junior
Bernhard Zendmeyer
J. Jacob (IW) Winter
Johan Jerg Stuber
Guillaumme Sibirit

Johann Adam Speck
Johann Georg Jeck
Jean Botis Nion
Christof Kuhbach
Daniel Gugenhan
Johan Georg Gugenhan
Hans George (✕) Dosh
Johan Jorg Bachhoffen
Hans George ( ) Bakhoffer, on
  board
Jean Michel Lanblenè
Abraham (O) Peter
Michael (✕) Peter
Johann Petter Lehmann
Paul (H) Walleysen
Jacob Egli
Johanes (✕) Statler
Bartolomeus (✕) Hoffman
Thomas ( ) Leyerigh, on board
John Ludwig ( )   Mickel, on
  board
Augustin Fieng
Johann Petter Conver
Abraham Frioth
Hans Michael (✕) Claus
Heinrich Bolleniger
Andereas (O) Koots
Johannes Fischer
John Diterich ( ) Eckly, on
  board
Johan Jacob Schelling
Jacob (✕) Gartman
Johann Georg Meckling
Hans Jörg Zaringer
Jacob Graus
Christian Roth
Johann Michael Ihl
Johann Burckhard [?]
Jacob ( ) Right, sick on board
Rudolf (✕) Döbely
Jacob ( ) Dobely, sick on board

Johanes Schadt
Hans Georg ( ) Bight, sick on
  board
Johan Henrich Schott
Johann Thommas Beck
Henry (✕) Geessler
Joseph Infeld
Uhllerig (✕) Ott
Bernhart Näff
Rudolf Egy
Jacob Haller
Hans George (✕) Meyly
Johanes (✕) Wurtz
Michael Friedrich Buch
Johann Peter Pfannkuchen
Johann Adam Klein
Davit (+) Jougnal
Michael Ullmann
Hans Michael (+) Hoff
Georg (✕) Nebeling
Harolt (W) Weytzel
Peter (✕) Gilliona
Daniel Lawall
Johann Lutwig Lawall
John Davit (✕) Henkel
Henry (✕) Straub
Jacob Guyer
Jörg Michel Lutz
Matheis Krauth
Hans Marthin Scheurich
Adam Le Roy
Johannes Duff
Peter (+) Jonck
Johann Peter Frembes
John Gorg Roth
Wilhelm (✕) Albert
Johann Rudolf Ferrer
Georg Henrich Kop
Georg Henry (O) Koch
Georg Leonthart Kopp
J. Simon Schneider

Johann Michael Christian
Martin Zehenbauer
Christoph (××) Henry
Hans Jacob (B) Back
Johan Melchior Ensly
Johanes Gärber
Jacob Lüpfer
Daniel (×) Kuhn
Piere Guillomons
Wolfgang (×) Winebrener
Hans Jacob (×) Miller
Johann Philipp Straub
Frantz May
Kilian May

Görg May
Michael Schäffer
Johann Rudolff Kraft
George ( ) Huber, sick on
    board
Johann Theobald Closs
Jacob ( ) Lupfer, on board
Anthon ( ) Weinbrener
Jurg (×) Hoffman
Abraham ( ) Freyly, on board
John Godfried ( ) Lifft, on
    board
Jacob ( ) Sheyrish, on board.

[List 196 A] Foreigners imported in the Ship St Michael, Thomas Ellis, Commander from Hamburg, but last from Cowes. Qualified 8th Sept^r, 1753.*

Heinrich Christophel Bartels
John Heinrich Duhin
John Friederich Duhin
Henrich Harman Duhin
Johan Jacob Port
Christian Warner
Johannes Josephus Mayners
John Heinrich Keller
John Heinrich Gross
Peter Gunkel
Andrew Schweishelm
John Heinrich Arnst
John Heinrich Bilsingleben
Hanss Henrich Messersmith
Andreas Bieger
John Friederich Fischer
John Christian Sachse
Johan George Sachse
Johannes Kehr
Friederich Rantenberg
Johan Nichlaus Regkop

Johan Caspar Lading
Wilhelm Lading
Christian Lading
Heinrich Seitling
Lorence Schlieter
Friederich Utter
John Andreas Vougt
Christophel Warnther
Heinrich Krapp
Gourt Heinrich Santher
Peter Muhlberg
Caston Kruger
John Christian Heil
Michael Kind
Daniel Klem
Christoph Wegner
Hironimus Eichler
Conrad Eichler
Ludwig Deberwell
Christoph Gall
Christian Oderhold

* Heading taken from endorsement on back of list,

Eberhard Hansson
Johannes Roesch
Benedik Dues Breitenfeld
Friederich Stern
Ellers Friessen
Andreas Lindner
Herman im Bush
Heinrich Mayer
Franss Arnt Rosse
Heinrich Raertiger

Heinrich Grodion
Gerhard Moger
Heinrich Fetter
John Erich Reither
John Friederich Sachse
John Heinrich Sachse
Willhelm Dill
Johan Kerscher
Mathes Kerscher
George Wilhelm Hookert

[List 196 B] Foreigners imported in the Ship St Michael, Thomas Ellis, Commander, from Hamburgh but last from Cowes. Qual. 8th Septr 1753.

Hendrich (+) Bartols
John Henry (XX) Duhin
John Frederick (X) Duhin
Henry Herman (X) Duhin
Johan Jacob (++) Port
Christian (++) Warner
Johannes Josephus Meinersen
Johan Henry (XX) Keller
Johan Henry (XX) Gross
Peter (XX) Gunkel
Andreas (+) Schweeshelm
Johan Henrich Ahrens
Johan Heinrich Billingesleben
Hans Henry (X) Messersmith
Andreas (+) Bigger
Johan Frederick (X) Fisher
Johan Christian Sachse
Johan George (X) Sachse
Johannes (X) Kehr
Frederick (+) Rontenberg
Johann Nicolaus Rehkopp
Johan Casper (X) Lading
Willhelm (X) Lading
Christian (+) Lading
Henry (+) Seitling
Lawrence (X) Schlieter

Frederick (X) Utter
Johan Andreas (X) Vought
Christopher (+) Wanther
Henry (+) Krapp
Cord Henry (X) Santher
Johan Peter (X) Muhlberg
Caston (X) Krüger
Christian (X) Heil
Michal Künd
Johan Daniehl Klemm
Christo Wegenr
Hieronimus Eichler
Conrad (X) Eichler
Lodwich (LD) Deberwell
Christop (X) Gall
Christian (X) Oderhold
Johan Heinrich Eberhard Hansen
Johannes Resch
Johann Benedicktus Breittenfeldt
Friedrich Heinrich Stern
Ehler Frese
Andreas (X) Lindner
Herman im Buss
Hinrich Meyer
Frantz Arend Rose
Henrich (+) Raertiger

Henrich (+) Grodion
Johan Gerhardt Mayer
George (×) Fetter
Johan Erich Reuter
Johan Friedrich Sachse

Johan Henry (×) Sachse
Christian Wilhelm Töll
Johann Kerscher
Mathias (×) Kersher
George William (+) Hookert

[Endorsed:]
List of Foreigners imported in the Ship S⁺ Michael, Thomas
Ellis, Commander, from Hamburgh last from Cowes.
Qual. 8ᵗʰ Septʳ 1753.

[List 196 C] At a Council at the Court House, Saturday, the
Eighth of September, 1753.
Present: Joshua Maddox, Esquire.
The Foreigners whose Names are underwritten, imported
in the Ship St. Michael, Thomas Ellis, Commander, from Hamburgh but last from Cowes, did this day take the usual Qualifications. No. 62.

Friederich Henrich (+) Bar-
  thals
John Henry (××) Deer
John Friederich (×) Deer
Henry Arent (××) Deer
John Jacob (++) Port
Christian (++) Warner
Johannes Josephus Meinersen
John Henry (++) Keller
John Henry (++) Gross
Peter (××) Gunckel
Andereas (×) Shweishelm
Johann Henrich Ahrens
Johann Heinrich Billingesleben
J. Henry (+) Messershmit
Andereas (+) Böger
J. Friederich (×) Fisher
Johan Christian Sach[se]
J. George (×) Saxe
Johanes (×) Kehr
Friederich (×) Ranberg
Johann Nicolaus Rehkopp

J. Caspar (+) Latink
Willhelm (+) Latink
Christian (+) Latinck
J. Henry (+) Seydling
Lorentz (×) Shlüter
J. Friederich (×) Utter
J. Andereas (+) Vougt
G. Christoph (×) Warinken
J. Henry (×) Krape
Cord Henry (×) Sander
J. Peter (×) Millberg
Clas Casten (×) Kröger
J. Christian (×) Heyl
Michael (×) Kind
Johan Daniel Klemm
Christoph Wegener
Hieronimus Eichler
Conrad (×) Eichler
Ludewig (L) Töpper
H. Christoph (×) Gall
Christian (×) Aterholt
Johan Henrich Eberhart Hansen

Johannes Resch
Johann Benedicktus Breittenfeld
Friedrich Heinrich Stern
Ehler Frese
Andereas ($\times$) Lindner
Herman In Buss
Hinrich Meyer
Frantz Arend Rose
John Henry (+) Ratiker
J. Henry (++) Gootjar

Johann Gerhardt Mayer
Hans Henry (+) Fete
Johann Erich Reuter
Johan Friederich Sachse
Johan Henry ($\times$) Saxe
Christian Wilhelm Töll
Johann Kerscher
Matheas ($\times$) Kersher
George Willhelm (+) Hooker

Philad. Sepr 7, 1753.

Sir :—

In the Morning we visited the Ship St Michael, Capt. Ellis, from Cowes and found twelve of the Passengers on board her with slow Fevers, whom we ordered removed and have again visited her this afternoon and found that our Directions have been complyed with; we therefore think the Ship may now be admitted to come up to the Town and the People to Land without any Risque to the Inhabitants of the City.

To his Honour   Tho. Graeme
The Governour.   Th. Bond
[Endorsed :]

Doctors Report on the Ship St Michael, 7th Septr 1753.

[List 197 A] A list of the Men On board the Ship Beulah, Capt Richey. [Qualified 10th Septr 1753.]

Jacob Bishopberger
Michel Groefestyn
Steph^n Frans Walk
Frederick Walk
Jurg Rap
Johan Michael Baur
Jurg Fred^k Brown
Simon Smick
Frederick Freundt
Vincent Peckary
Mathias Brown
Henrich Hoffman
Johannes Hartman

John Graff Kolp
Frederick Zern
Christian Schick
Jurg Henrich Alter
Jacob Alter
Jurg Fred^k Alter
Albrecht Fisher
Albrecht Fisher, Junr
Anderas Fisher
Stephen Lye
Anderas Lye
Moses Baur
Simon Baur

Peter Hoeber
Conrad Brown
Michael Rap, 14 years old
Thomas Diets
Fredrick Gruber
Stephen Rieler
Jurg Conrad Brown
Michael Krauts
Jurg Brown
Matt^s Mier
Jurg Martin Debily
Jacob Michael
Balthes Schwy
Stophel Schwy
Philip Roleterin
Michael Unger
Philip Bergering
Jurg Fred^k Hiltzebeck
Erhard Schick
Ludwick Schick
Jurg Henrich Schweitzer
Henrich Gebhard
Jurg Ziegeler
John Mich^l Long
Johan Chris^n Niet
Anderas Frey
Jacob Wyn
Fredrick Kast
Jurg Wilett
Albrecht Heckman
Jurg Arnold
Peter Baur

Frederick Baur
William Read
Michael Kuhn
Mich^l Kuhn, Junr
Bastian Hoffman
Johannes Hoffman
Valentin Korn
Martin Burger
Lorentz Hoffner
Henrich Schyfner
Jurg Fred^k Sholl
Adam Walley
Martin Hepinger
Balthes Leonard
Hans Jurg Shaller
Michael Frank
Ludwig Sommer
Jurg Göts
Peter Druckmiller
Jacob Sammett
Christopher Dietz
Andreas Klein
Hans Jurg Kamp
Ludwick Rosemiller
Michael Tiber
Jurg Shimmel
Joackim Kepler
Adam Brenner
Ernst Statteldaller
Anderas Smugg
87.

8 Catholics, the Rest Lutherans.
[Endorsed:]
  List of Foreigners on Ship Beulah.
  Qualified 10 Sept^r, 1753.

[List 197 B] Foreigners imported in the Ship Beulah, Cap^n
Richy, from Rotterdam, were this day Qualified, on the 10th
September, 1753.

Jacob Pishopberger

Johann Michael Greiffenstein

Stephann Fridrich Walch

Jerg Friedrich Volch

Johan Georg Rab

Johan Michael Bauer

Georg Friedrich Braun

Johann Simon Schmieg

Johann Friedrich Freund

Vinsintzius Begari

Johann Matthäus Braun

Johann Heinrich Hoffmann

Johann Graff Kolb

Friederich Zürrn

Christian Schick

Georg Heinrich Alter

Johann Jacob Alter

Georg Friederich Alter

Johan Albrecht Fessler

Johan Albrecht Fessler

Johann Andreas Fessler

Steppfan Lay

Andreas Lay

Moses Baur

Simon Walther

Peter Uber

Georg Conradt Braun

Thomas Dietz

Friedrich Gruber

Johann Stephan Riegler

Jaorch Conrad Braun

Johan Michel Krauss

Johann Georg Braun

Johann Mattheus Mayer

Georg Martin Döbele

Jacob Michel

Balthas (×) Swick

Christoph Zweig

Johan Philipp Rohleder

Johan Michel Ungerer

Johann Philipp Berberich

Fredrick ( ) Hitsberg

Erhardt Schick

Ludwig Schick

Georg Heinrich Schweitzer

Johann Heinrich Gebert

Johann Georg Ziegler

Johann Michel Lang

Johann Christoph Nith

Andres Frey

Jacob Wein

Frederick (+) Kost

Hans Jürg Wilt

Albrecht Heckman

Jörg Arnolt

Johann Petter Bauer

Johann Friederich Bauer

Johann Wilhelm Ruth

Michel Kuhn

Michel Kuhn

Bastian (×) Hoffman

Johannes (×) Hoffman

Veltin Korn

Martin Burger

Lorentz Hoffert

Georg Heinrich Schäffner

Frederick (×) Sholtz

Hans Adam Waly

Mardin Hedinger

Gorig Balthas [Lehner]

Georg Schaller

Joh. Michael Franck

Johann Ludwig Sommer

Johan Georg Dotz

Peter (×) Druckmiller

Jacob (×) Sammet

Georg Christof Dietz

Andereas Klein

Georg (×) Comb

Georg Ludtwig Rosenmüller

Georg Michael Däuber

Jerch Schimmel

Johann Jacob Keppner   Johann Ernst Sattelthaler
Adam Brenner   Johann Andreas Schmieg

[Endorsed:]
List of Foreigners imported in the Ship Beulah, Capt Richy.
Qual. 10th Septr 1753. [No.] 87.   Mr Shoemaker.

[List 197 C] At the Court House at Philadelphia, Monday,
the 10th September, 1753.
                    Present: Joshua Maddox, Esquire.
The Foreigners whose Names are underwritten, Imported
in the Ship Beulah, Captain Richey, from Rotterdam, but last
from Cowes, did this day take the usual Qualifications. No. 86.

Jacob (O) Bishopberger   Georg Conradt Braun
Johann Michael Greiffenstein Thomas Dietz
Stephan Frantz Walch   Friedrich Gruber
Jerg Friedrich Volch   Johann Stephan Riegler
Johann Georg Rab   Georg Conradt Braun
Johann Michael Bauer   Johan Michel Krauss
Georg Friedrich Braun   Johann Georg Braun
Johann Simon Schmieg   Johann Mattheus Mayer
Johann Friedrich Freund   Georg Martin Döbele
Visintzius Beggari   Jacob Michel
Johann Matthäus Braun   Baltus (X) Zweyk
Johann Henrich Hoffman   Christoph Zweig
Johann Graff Kolb   Johan Philipp Rohleder
Friedreich Züern   Johann Michel Ungerer
Christian Schick   Johann Philipp Berberich
Georig Heinrich Alter   J. Friederich (J) Hiltzbeck
Johann Jacob Alter   Erhardt Schick
Georg Friderich Alter   Ludwig Schick
Johan Albrecht Fessler   Georg Heinrich Schweitzer
Johan Albrecht Fessler   Johan Heinrich Gebert
Johann Anderas Fessler   Johann Georg Ziegler
Stephfan Lay   Johann Michael Lang
Andreas Lay   Johann Christoph Nith
Moses Baur   Andreas Frey
Simon Walther   Jacob Wein
Peter Uber   Friederich (+) Cast

Hans Jorg Wilt
Albrecht Heckman
Jörg Arnolt
Johann Petter Bauer
Johann Friederich Bauer
Johann Wilhelm Rüth
Michel (✕) Kuhn
Michel Kuhn
Sebastian (+) Hoffman
Johanes (+) Hoffman
Valtin Korn
Martin Burger
Lorentz Höffert
Georg Heinrich Schäffner
George Friederich (✕) Sholl
Hans Waly
Mardin Hedinger

Georg Balthas Lehner
Georg Schaller
Joh. Michael Franck
Johann Ludwig Sommer
Johann Georg Dietz
Peter Truckin (✕) Miller
Jacob (✕) Sammit
Georg Christof Dietz
Andereas Klein
Hans George (✕) Kamm
Georg Ludtwig Rosenmüller
Georg Michael Däuber
Jerch Schimmel
Johann Jagob Keppner
H. Adam (✕) Brenner
Johann Ernst Sattelthaler
Johann Andreas Schmieg

Sir

Having agreeable to Orders visited the Ship Beulah, Capt Richey, Master, freighted with Palatines from Roterdam and Portsmouth and find them in such good Order, as no objection remains to their entering the port.

Philad^{ia} Septr 10th 1753.   Tho. Graeme
To his Honour the Governor.   Th. Bond

[Endorsed:]

Doctors Certificate on Ship Beulah, Septr 10th 1753.

[List 198 A] A List of Male Names on Board the Ship Queen of Denmark. [Qualified 11th Septr 1753.]

Valentine Etting
Hans Jurger Disseler
Casper Groundberg
Joh. Henr. Valtenberg
Henr. Christ^o Gutige
Ludwig Rashahr
Joh. Ludwig Starke
Henr. Borgfeld
Henr. Ferman
Joh. Geo. Gottschalks

Christ^o Welhausen
Geo. Bottman
Thomas Frochtenicht
Diedrich Dropenstad
Augt Ernest Deliz
John Henr. Besen
Joh. Fred. Junger
Geo. Temme
Ernst Cord
John Evalts

Joh. Andres Rudolph
Joh. Andres Balthaur
Rudolph Goltstad
Joh. Ernst Sommer
Hans Henr. Ahrens
Christⁿ Ahrens
John Henr. Engell
Joh. Augᵗ Spangenberg
Joh. Ludwig Brahl
Joh. Christⁿ Demme
Joh. Jurger Kistner
Valentine Nortmeyre
Ludwig Wilhelm Pockranz
John Henr. Freyre
Andrew Grotheim
Anton von Brunks
Johs. Paul Rauschenbach
Frederick Jordan
Nicholas Shefer
Joh. Jobst Werning
Joh. Taberton
David Albricht
Wilhelm Schele
David Fischer
Joh. Diderich Witte
Jacob Voght
Joh. Augᵗ Frydag
Joh. Frederick De Vehrn
Christian Tolle
Valentine Rausch
Christian Schneyder
Jobst Henrich Kunshe
Hans Hermon Brand
Christⁿ Lanthan
Christᵒ Gabrecht
Christᵒ Ebeche
Peter Weidemer
Joh. Philip Preising
Geo. Wilhelm Reberg
Christⁿ Gobrecht
Joh. Jurgen Geranke

Christian Neice
Frans Henrich Ernst
Lawrence Petere
Geo. Fischer
Joh. Erich Miller
Christⁿ Hippe
Joh. Wilhelm Klencke
Tobias Starke
Christian Lecke
Erhard Reindell
Wilhelm Bromar
John Reichman
Christᵒ Cord, Senior
Christᵒ Cord Junʳ
John Blankart
Geo. Wilhelm von Lude
Joh. Geo. Schefer
John Dingler
Joh. Basen Sanders
Joh. Jurgen Temme
John Beyr
Christᵒ Bechel
Christⁿ Goldstad
Nicholas Christⁿ Otto
Conrad Brandfass
Joh. Fred. Wambeck
Geo. Christⁿ Jordan
Hen. Julius Bohte
Wilhelm Kalls
Daniel Ranberg
Jacob Geber
Nicholas Ulrich
Ernst Ulrich
Christⁿ Ludwig Hardman
Christ Smith
Peter Freder. Nemeir
Christian Goulstet
John Frederich Unger
Johan Bawl Roushenbacht
Christopher Evigher

[Endorsed:]
List of the Hanoverians from Hamburg, imported in the
Queen of Denmark.
Qual. 11th Septr 1753.

[List 198 B] The Foreigners imported in the Queen of Denmark, Captⁿ George Parish, were Qualified 11th September 1753.

Johan Vallendein Ette
Hans (+) Diseler
Casper (X) Grounderberg
Johann Watten[berg]
Chris. (+) Gutige
Ludwig (+) Rashaur
Ludwig (X) Starke
Henery (X) Borgfield
Bothman Bothman *
Thomas (++) Frochtnicht
Deitrick (+) Dropenstod
Ernst Delitz
Jobst Hinrich Behse
Frederick (X) Unger
George ( ) Temme
Ernst (+) Cord
John (+) Evalts
Andreas (++) Rudolph
Andreas (X) Balthaur
Rudolph (X) Golstad
John (+) Engel
Hans (+) Ahrens
Christian (X) Ahrens
[Joh. Aug.] Spangenberg
Ludwig (X) Braul
Johan Christian Temm
John (+) Kistner
Valentine (X) Nortmeyer
Ludewig Wilhelm Bockrantz
John (X) Fryer

Lorentz (X) Pedrie
Andrew (X) Grothein
Anthon   Bartholomäus   von
    Bruncks
Joh. Paul Rauschenbach
Frederick (O) Jordan
Nicolaus Schäffer
Jobst (X) Werning
Johannes Tauber
David (X) Albrecht
Johann Wilhelm Schiele
Johann Daviedt Fischer
Didrick ( ) Wittee
Jacob (X) Voght
John (X) Frydag
John (+) Devehern
Johann Christian Tolle
Johann Vahlentin Rausch
Johann Christian Schneider
Jobst (+) Kuniche
Herman ( ) Brand
Johann Christoph Gobrecht †
Christian (++) Ebechee
Philip ( ) Preising
George (++) Reberg
Johann Christian Gobrecht
John (XX) Gerange
Christian ( ) Nice
Frantz Heinrich Ernst
George (X) Fisher

---

* The other lists give this name more correctly as George Bothman.
† A Reformed minister. See *History of the Tohickon Church*, pp. 38–44.

John (××) Miller

Christian ( ) Hippe

Christian (×) Lecke

Erhard ( ) Reindell

Wilhelm (+) Bremer

Johan Reichman

Christ[n] ( ) Cord

Christ[n] (××) Cord, Junior

Johann Ernst Blankart

Georg Wilhelm von Lüde

Johan Dingler

Johannes Bayer

Christian Gollstadt

Nicolaus Christian Otto

John (++) Wambecht

Hinrich Julius Bohte

Wilhelm Kerls

Peter Friederich Niemeyer *

[Endorsed:]

List of Foreigners imported in the Ship Queen of Denmark, Capt. George Parish.

Qual. 11th Septr 1753.

101.   Mr. Kepler.

[List 198 C] At the Court House at Philadelphia, Tuesday, the 11th September, 1753.

Present: Joshua Maddox, Esquire.

The Foreigners whose Names are here underwritten, Imported in the Ship Queen of Denmark, Captain George Parish, from Hamburgh but last from Cowes, did this day take the usual Qualifications. No. 93.

Johann Vallendein Ette

Hans George (+) Disseler

Caspar (×) Kreenberg

Johann Heinrich Wattenberg

H. Christoffer (×) Shadike

Ludewig (+) Raffgarn

J. Ludewig ( ) Stark, on board

Henry (×) Borgfeld

Georg Bothman

Thomas (++) Forchtnicht

Dieterich (+) Broptenstad

Ernst Delitz

Jobst Hinrich Beh[s]e

J. Johan (+) Friederich Ungar

George ( ) Temmy, on board

J. Ernst (+) Court

Johan (+) Ewald

J. Andereas (+++) Rudolph

J. Anderas (+) Bolthawer

J. Rudolph (+) Bolstead

J. Herman (×) Engel

H. Henry (×) Arrent

Christian (×) Arrent

[Joh. Aug.] Spangenberg

Ludewig (+) Brall

Johann Christian Temme

Johan George (×) Distner

J. Ballentin (×) Normeyer

Ludewig Wilhelm Bockrantz

---

* A Lutheran minister, who preached at the Springfield Union Church, Bucks County, 1774 to 1782.

J. Henry (×) Frey

Lorentz (×) Petry

Andereas (×) Grotheim

Anthon Bartholomaus von Bruncks

Joh. Paul Rauschenbach

J. Friederich ( ) Jordan, on board

Nicolaus Schäffer

Johan Jost (×) Werning

Johannes Taubert

Davit (×) Albrecht

Johann Wilhelm Schiele

Johann Daviedt Fischer

J. Dieterich ( ) Witty, on board

Johan Jacob (+) Voigt

J. August (×) Freytag

J. Friederich (+) Defern

Johann Chrian Tolle

Johann Vallentin Rausch

Johann Christian Schneider

Jost Henry (+) Kinige

Hans Herman ( ) Brand, on board

Johann Christoph Gobrecht

Christoff (++) Endike

Christoffer ( ) Weidemer, on board

Johan Philip ( ) Preising, on board

George Wilhelm (++) Reburg

Johann Christian Gobrecht

J. George (++) Gerang

Christian ( ) Nice, sick on board

Frantz Heinrich Ernst

George (×) Fisher

John Errich ( ) Miller, on board

Christian (++) Hieppe

Christian (×) Luig

Erhart ( ) Reindel, on board

Wilhelm (×) Bremer

Johan Reichman

Christoff ( ) Cort, Senior, on board

Christoff (××) Cort, Junior

Johann Ernst Blankart

Georg Wilhelm von Lüde

Johan Dingler

Johannes Bayer

Christian (×) Gollstäd

Nicolaus Christian Otto

Johan Friederich (++) Wambeck

Hinrich Julius Bohte

Wilhelm Kerls

Peter Friederich Niemeyer

　89 [present]

　11 absent

　——

，100 [total]

Sir

Having visited the Ship Queen of Denmark, Capt. Parish, Master, freighted with Germans from Hanborough and Cowes; and we find to the Number of Eleven under such Indispositions as the Scurvey and slow fevers, as ought to be separated and carryd to the Hospital, after which the Ship and people being well aird, we are of Opinion the remainder may be admitted to enter the port without danger to the Inhabitants.

Philad^ia Septr 10, 1753. Tho. Greeme
To His Ho^r the Govr. Th. Bond
[Endorsed:]
Doctors Report on the Ship Queen of Denmark, 10th Septr 1753.

[List 199 B] Foreigners Imported in the Ship Edinburg, Captn James Russel, were Qualified 14 September, 1753.

Johan Jacob Dindorff
Michal Halberstatt
Julius Brucker
Philip (O) Gabel
Johan Jacob Ham
Samuel Maus
Johan Jacob Wiesinger
Peter (X) Miller
Devalt (X) Criks
Johannes (X) Miller
Abram (X) Miller
Jacob (X) Braun
Philips Lantz
Philips Mülhoff
Conrath Klein
Jacob (X) Dewalt
Conrad Guth
Conrad Guth
Andreas Heffterich
Peter Schuch
Henrich Schupp
Jacob Müller
Bastian (X) Moor
Philipp Jacob Mühlhoff
Michal Lang
Ludwick (++) Bush
Michel Zimmerman
Adam Hamscher
Johann Georg Kuhn
Johan Adam Kreischer
Johann Sebastian Kreischer

Christopher (+) Adam
Josebh Zwirsky
Johan Casber Ross
Conrad (X) Glanter
Johann Peter Bode
Johannes Schwalb
Batzer (X) Pinnele
Johann Jacob Beck
Carl Arnth
Joh. Reinhard Rahmer
John Gerg Jost
Johann Friderich Vogeler
Anderas Schechter
Geörg Marthin
Johannes Limberger
Johan Christof Maurer
Cristopher (X) Frydele
Jacob (X) Kaufman
Peter Diener
Johan Nickel Michel
Wilhelm Stein
Johann Georg Conrad
Jacob (X) Greer
Carrol (X) Bernard
Peter Kuntz
Jacob Schott
Connerad Wagner
Johannes Laffer
Christian (+) Justler
Peter Rödtler
Frederick (X) Mey

Frederick (   ) Creymer
Joh. Herguth
Jacob Threyn
Jacob Zombro
Michael (   ) Dryker
Rudolph (   ) Wootel
Jacob (✕) Knop
Johann Nickel Jacoby
Johann Michel Jacoby
Johann Petter Jacobi
Phillip (✕) Price
Christopher (✕) Reynher
Velthen Hoffman
Jean Pierre DuCorbier
Johan (+) Beym
Johann Adam Böhm
Valentine (✕) Kolman
Theobalt Angene
Jacob Bauer
Friedrich Schwartz
Henery (✕) Lynn
Jacob Bachman
Johan Jacob Bachman
Lorentz Bachman
Johan Jacob Geck
Danniel Heck
Peter Bader
Samuel Brodt
Eberhart Schmitt
David Schmitt
Bastian Lentz
Mardin Geilert
Petter Klein
Ludwig (✕) Young
Johannes (✕) Ensminger
Johanes Büntzel
Henery (✕) Binzel
Johannes (✕) Bindsel
Wilhelm Spira
Johannes Fellentzer
Adolf Meyer

Paulus Schirardin
David Hann
Jacob (B) Bulinger
Johann Kraft Goss
John (✕) Shnoor
Peter (✕) Flickinger
Henery (✕) Rother
Johan Christian Hufnagel
Frantz Henrich Hufnagel
Johann Gorg Weyshaar
Johannes Stötzel
Johann Georg Steinbock
John (✕) Wunderling
Phillip (✕) Weber
Justus Henrich Weber
Conrad (✕) Mintzinger
Johan Willem Wäber
Johan Ullrich Wäber
Johannes Frey
Johannes (   ) Cornhes
Bernhart Beck
Andreas Beckh
Johannes Wohlfahrt
Matthes Ehhalt
Johannes Buchtel
Marteine Braun
Christian (✕) Fisher
Conrad (✕) Fotz
Gregorius Bütsche
Mark (✕) Angst
Frederick (✕✕) Hartman
Wilhelm Hartman
Boulass (++) Harman
Eberhard (++) Harman
Frederick (   ) Hartman
Jerg Gähringer
Frederick (+) Widmeyer
Ludwig (+) Folmer
Andres Hüttenloch
Jeremias Küsterlen
Friderich Jäckler

Johannes (+) Awer
Jacob Knodel
Adam Roser
Johanes Creiner
Johann Christian Dörr
Jacob (X) Polweller
Johannes Schmitt
Henrich Adam Hoffman
Henrich Strack
George Milcher Hiebner
Jacob (X) Miller

Johann Jörg Märcker
Paulus Hochstrasser
Vallentin Fleck
Jacob Ott
Elias Knebler
Johann Michael Hauber
Philipp Lehrer
Sebastian Kabel
Johann Conrad Metz
Jacob (X) Albert
Frieterich Steffan

[Endorsed:]
List of Foreigners imported in the Ship Edinburgh, Capt.
James Russel.
Qual. 14th Septr 1753.

[List 199 C] At the Courthouse at Philadelphia, Friday, the
14th Sept. 1753.
          Present: Joshua Maddox, Esquire.
The Foreigners whose Names are underwritten, Imported
in the Ship Edinburg, Captn James Russell, from Rotterdam,
but last from Portsmouth, were this day qualified on the usual
Qualifications. No. 167. 352 Whole Freights.

Johan Jac. Dindorff
Michal Halberstatt
Julius Bruker
Philip Henry (X) Gäbel
Johann Jacob Ham
Samuel Maus
Johan Jacob Wiesinger
Peter (X) Miller
Dewalt (+) Creutz
Johanes (X) Miller
Abram (X) Miller
Jacob Braun
Philips Lantz
Philips Mülhoff
Conrath Klein

Jacob (J) Dewalt
Conrad Guth
Conrad Guth
Andereas Heffterich
Peter Schuch
Henrich Schupp
Jacob Müller
Bastian (X) More
Philipp Jacob Muhlhoff
Michal Lang
Ludewig (++) Bush
Michel Zimmerman
Adam Hamscher
Johann Georg Kuhn
Johan Adam Kreischer

Johann Sebastian Kreischer
Ernst Christoph (+) Adam
Josebh Zwirsky
Johann Casber Ross
Conrad (X) Klenter
Johann Peter Bode
Johannes Schwalb
Balsazar (+) Pemeller
Johann Jacob Beck
Carl Arnth
Johann Reinhardt Rahmer
Johan Gerg Jost
Johann Friderich Vogeler
Andreas Schter [Schechter]
Joerg Marthin
Johannes Limberger
Johan Christof Maurer
Christoph (XX) Freydel
Jacob (+) Kauffman
Johan Nickel Michel
Peter Diener
Wilhelm Stein
Johann Georg Conrad
Jacob (X) Creear
Carol (X) Bernhart
Peter Kuntz
Jacob Schott
Conrad Wagner
Johannes Laffer
Christian (+) Jutzner
Peter Rödtler
Friederich (X) Mey
Friederich (   ) Kramer, sick on
   board
Johannes Herguth
Jacob Threyn
Jacob Zombro
Michael (   ) Decker, sick on
   board
Rudolph (   ) Woldi, sick on
   board

Jacob (X) Knap
Johannes Nickel Jacoby
Johann Michel Jacoby
Johann Petter Jacobi
Philip (X) Priz
Christoffel (X) Renner
Felthen Hoffman
Jean Pierre Du Corbier
Johan (+) Rauffbem
Johann Adam Böhm
Vallentin (X) Kohlman
Theobalt Angene
Jacob Bauer
Friederich Schwartz
Philip Henry (X) Linn
Jacob Bachman
Johan Jacob Bachman
Lorentz Bachman
Jacob Geck
Daniel Heck
Peter Bader
Samuel Brodt
Eberhart Schmitt
David Schmitt
Bastiann Lentz
Mardin Geilert
Petter Klein
Ludewig (+) Yong
Johan (O) Entzmenger
Johannes Büntzel
J. Henry (X) Pintzel
Johannes (+) Pintzel
Wilhelm Spira
Johannes Fellentzer
Adolf Meyer
Paulus Schirardin
Davit Hann
Jacob (B) Bollinger
Johann Graff Goss
J. Henry (X) Shnoor
Peter (X) Flickinger

Henry ( ) Rodhar, on board
Johan Christian Huffnagel
Frantz Henrich Huffnagel
Johann Georg Weysharr
Johannes Stötzel
Johann Goerg Steinbock
John Henry (X) Wunderling
Philip (X) Weber
Justus Heinrich Weber
Conrad (X) Mentzinger
Andres Barnstein
Johan Willem Wäber
Ullrich Wäber
Johannes Frey
Johannes ( ) Cornhas, sick on b^d
Bernhart Beck
Andreas Beck
Johannes Wohlfahrt
Matthes Ehhalt
Johannes Buchtel
Marteine Braun
Christian (X) Fisher
Conrad (X) Foltz
Gregorius Bütsche
Marcus (X) Angst
Friederich (XX) Hartman
Wilhelm Hartman
Paulus (XX) Hartman
Eberhart (XX) Hartman

Friederik ( ) Hartman, sick
Jorg Gähringer
Friederich (+) Weedmeyer
Ludwig (+) Folmer
Andres Hüttenloch
Jeremias Küsterle
Friedrich Jäckle
Johanes (X) Awer
Jacob Knodel
Adam Roser
Johanes Creiner
Johann Christian Dörr
Jacob (X) Polweller
Johannes Schmitt
Henrich Adam Hoffman
Henrich Strack
Georg Milcher Hiebner
Jacob (X) Miller
Johan Jorg Märcker
Paulus Hochstrasser
Vallentin Fleck
Jacob Ott
Elias Knebler
Johann Michael Hauber
Philipp Lehrer
Seba[st]ian Kabel
Johann Conrad Metz
Johan Jacob (X) Albert
Frieterich Steffan

Sept. 14, 1753.

Sir

We have in obedience to order carefully examin'd the State of health of the seamen and Passengers on board the Ship Edinburgh, Capt. Russel, from Roterdam, and found them without any objection to their being permitted to land in the city.

To his Honour   Tho. Graeme
The Governour.   Th. Bond

[Endorsed:]

Doctors Report on the Ship Edinburg, 14th Septr 1753.

[List 200 A] List of Mens Names and Ages imported in the Ship Patience, Hugh Steel, Commander, September 15th 1753.*

	AGES		AGES
Pierre Armeson	40	Martin Yoss	41
Godfret Giverly	17	Fred^k Rynholt	28
Peter Schibilt	30	Peter Goodier	31
Jacob Bald	35	John Bonnet	22
Paul Caufferel	45	Christopher Hair	21
Mathias Dear	30	Elias Nister	20
Jacob Dear	18	Jacob Baron	28
Jeremias Chappel	25	John Casper Gross	22
Peter Roshon	22	Jacob Synket	23
Hendrick Roshon	20	John Yerr^k Grissinger	32
Adam Siets	30	Johannes Price	30
Jacob Goodier	27	Yerrick Kreytler	22
Jacob Zerway	29	Isaac Gross	20
Lodwick Brime	24	Barnt Hiler	22
Jacob Fisher	22	Daniel Stowfer	20
Michael Ressel	20	Jacob Bickler	21
Yerrick Nodel	37	Michael Alex	27
Jacques Berge	30	Johannes Boatamayer	21
Hans Yerrick Feller	25	Johannes Hensinger	26
John Richardon	25	Johannes Switzer	24
Hans Yerrick Sholter	30	Johannes Hilleir	24
Yerrick Valatine Rynhard	27	Michael Dicker	24
Andrias Minchinar	28	Jacob Oxeryter	40
Joseph Needle	40	Fred^k Verner	27
Johannes Siger	29	Fred^k Oxeryter	28
Jacob Borman	25	Philip Wys	27
Fred^k Ginsel	28	Bernard Young	21
Theodorus Fred^k Honks	30	Ulrick Nodel	27
Johannes Wormley	21	Fred^k Kilie	22
Godliph Hend^k Facundus	27	Yerr^k Sheyligh	24
Hans Yerr^k Bross	21	Casper Simon	29
Michael Schibley	29	Adam Woost	24
Carel Shonick	40	Mathias Alher	22
Ferdinand Wetz	35	John Frederick Foucundus	..
Hans Georg Federhaff	..	Yerr^k Roller	27
Martin Keyser	30	Johannes Kurtz	24

* The other two lists bear the date September 17, 1753.

	AGES		AGES
Philip Riser	27	Leonard Ishenaver	41
Johannes Klintop	22	Peter Buler	27
Christⁿ Klintop	27	Hans Musleman	22
Christⁿ Klykroot	30	Michael Garber	20
Mathias Smith	21	Diedᵏ Stainbrecker	25
Jacob Ackerman	24	Leonard Gerbick	21
Yerrᵏ Shattinger	22	Simon Gerbick	22
Adam Wynhard	24	Christⁿ Smith	21
Christʳ Lorgh	33	Lodwick Smith	22
Christian Bower	27	Stephen Brun	21
Diedᵏ Bower	24	Sebastian Kigts	22
Johannes Brynigh	22	Michael Row	27
Casper Fayster	22	Jacob Gerber	21
John Adleberger	31	Lodwick Priserman	22
Philip Adleberger	27	Gabriel Lus	27
Peter Kible	40	Fredᵏ Oswald	27
Adam Sheffer	41	Michˡ Riem	30
Baltus Irigh	40	Johan Friederich Federhauf	..
Peter Landis	24	108.	
Henry Hackman	22		

[Endorsed:]
List of Foreigners imported in the Patience, Captⁿ Steele.
Qual. 17 Septʳ 1753.
      108.   Mʳ Stedman.

[List 200 B] Foreigners imported in the Patience, Captain
Hugh Steele. Qualified the 17ᵗʰ September, 1753.

Pierre Armingeon	Jaque Goutier
Godfricht (✗) Giverly	Jean Jaques Servai
Jean Pierre Chappelle	Loui Prim
Jaques Balme	Jacob (✗) Fisher
Paul Caffaral	Michael Röszler
Matieu Tier	Johann Georg Knodel
Jacob (✗) Dear	Jaque Berger
Jeremie Chappelle	Hans Jerg Feller
Pierre Rouchon	Jean Richardon
Henri Rochon	Yerrick (✗) Sholter
Adam Seitzs	Georg Valthäin Rienhardt

Andreas Münchinger
Joseph Knittel
Johannes Sieger
Jacob Borman
Friederich Jensel
Theodorus Frid. Haux
Johannes Würmle
Gottlib Heinerich Facundus
Hans Conratt Facundus
Hans Jerg Bross
Michael Scheible
Carol (O) Shoonik
Ferdinandt Würtz
Martin Käyser
Martin Jauss
Friedrich Reinholdt
Pierre Gautier
Jean Bonnet
Christoph Fehr
Elias Nester
Jaque Baron
Johann Casper Gross
Yerrick (X) Crissinger
Johan Gorg Grösinger
Johannes Preyss
Georg Martin Kreidler
Isaak (   ) Spross
Barnt (X) Hiler
Daniel (XX) Stowper
Jacob Büchle
Michael Allex
Johanis Bodanar
Hans (X) Hensinger
Johannes Schweitzer
Johannes Hiller
Georg Michael Decker [?]
Jacob Ochsenreiter
Frederick (+) Verner
Johan Friederich Ochsenreiter
Philip Weiss
Bernhart Jung

Ulrich Knodel
Friedrich Kähle
Hans Gurg Siele [?]
Johann Casper Simon
Jurg Adam Wist
Mathias (XX) Alher
Yerrick (X) Roller
Johannes Kurtz
Phillip (X) Risser
Johannes (+) Klintop
Christopher (+) Klintop
Henrich Christop Bleicherodt
Johan Mathias Smidt
Johann Jacoben
Yerrick (+) Shattinger
Adam (+) Winhard
Christian (   ) Link
Christian (   ) Bower
Deidrick (X) Bower
Johanes Breinig
Casper Fossler
Hans Jerg Adtelberger
Philip Adtelberger
Petter Gröbil
Adam (+) Shafer
Baltas (+) Irigh
Peter (X) Landig
Henrich Hackmann
Leonhard Eschauer
Petter Bühler
Hans Musselmann
Michael (X) Garber
Deidrick (X) Strambruker
Leonard (+) Girbick
Simeon (X) Carver
Christian (X) Smith
Etienne Breun
Sebastian (+) Kigher
Johann Michael Rau
Jacob Gerber
Samuel Bosserman

Gabriel Bausch
Friederich Osswald
Michel Röm

Johan Georg Federhaff
108.

[Endorsed:]
List of Foreigners imported in the Ship Patience, Capt. Steele.
Qual. 17th Septr 1753. 108. Mr Stedman.

[List 200 C] At Philadelphia, Monday, the 17 September, 1753.

Present: Benjamin Franklyn, Esquire.

The Foreigners whose Names are underwritten, Imported in the Ship Patience, Captⁿ Hugh Steel, from Rotterdam and last from Cowes, did this day take the usual Qualifications. No. 108.

Pierre Armingeon
Godfried (+) Haberly
Jean Pierre Chappelle
Jaques Balme
Paul Caffarel
Matieu Tier
Jacob (H) Gerhart
Jeremie Chappelle
Pierre Rouchon
Henri Rochon
Adam Seitzs
Jaques Goutier
Jean Jaques Servai
Loui Prim
Jacob (✕) Fisher
Michael Rössler
Johann Georg Knodel
Jaque Berger
Hans Jerg Feller
Jean Richardon
Hans George (+) Sholter
Georg Valthain Rienhardt
Andreas Münchinger
Joseph Knittel

Johannes Sieger
Jacob Borman
Friedrich Jensel
Theodorus Frid. Haux
Johannes Würmle
Gottlib Heinrich Faxindus
Hans Conratt Fagondus
Hans Jerg Bross
Michael Scheible
Charles (✕) Shonnet
Ferdinandt Würtz
Martin Kayser
Martin Jauss
Friederich Reinholdt
Pierre Gautier
Jean Bonnet
Christoph Fehr
Elias Nester
Jaque Baron
Johan Casper Gross
Jacob (✕) Singquet
Johan Georg Grösinger
Johannes Preyss
Georg Martin Kreidler

Isaac ( ) Grad, on board
Bernhart (×) Heller
Daniel (××) Strawber
Jacob Büchle
Michael Allex
Johanes Bodaner
Hans (×) Hentzinger
Johannes Schweitzer
Johannes Hiller
Georg Michael Deckher
Jacob Ochsenreiter
Johan Friederich (×) Werner
Johan Friderich Ochsenreiter
Philip Weiss
Bernhart Jung
Ulrich Knodel
Johann Fridrich Kähle
Hans Georg Siele [?]
Johann Casper Simon
Jerg Adam Wist
Matheus (××) Alber
Hans George (×) Roller
Johanes Kurtz
G. Willhelm (×) Reeser
Johanes (+) Clantop
Christoffel (×) Clantop
Heinrich Christop Bleicherodt
Johan Madhias Smidt
Johan Jackcobe
Hans George (+) Shättinger
Adam (×) Winhart

Christoph ( ) Lawg, sick on
　board
Christian ( ) Bower, sick on
　board
Diterich (×) Bower
Johannes Breinig
Caspar Faseler
Hans Jerig Adtelberger
Philipp Adtelberger
Petter Gröbil
Hans Adam (×) Shäffer
Bastian (×) Erig
Peter (×) Landig
Henrich Hackmann
Leonhard Eschauer
Petter Bühler
Hans Musselmann
Michael (×) Carber
J. Diterich (×) Steinbrecher
J. Lenhart (×) Gerwig
Simon (×) Carber
Christoph (×) Shmit
Etienne Breun
Sebastian (+) Knartsh
Johann Michael Rau
Jacob Gerber
Samuel Bosserman
Gabril Bausch
Friedrich Oswald
Michel Röm
Johann Georg Federhaff

Septr 15, 1753.

Sir

According to Directions we have carefully examined the
State of Health of the Mariners and Passengers on board the
Ship Patience, Capt Steel, from Roterdam and found no objection to their being admitt'd to land in the City immediately.

To his Honour
The Governour.

Tho. Greeme
Th. Bond

[Endorsed:]
Doctors Report on the Ship Patience, 15th Septr 1753.

[List 201 A] A List of Men on board the Ship Rich^d & Mary, John Moore, Mas^{tr}, September 17, 1753.

Joh. Casper Geyer
Joh. Jacob Geyer
Hans Michael Rou
Joseph Philip Rou
Ulrich Zuyberlig
Carell Zeegele
Joh. Ernst Jonckee
Joh. Hend^k Jonckee
Peter Kicker
Martin Jacob
Fred^k Zern
Johan Knapschnyder
Adam Shober
Johan Eys
Martin Zurer
Anderas Thiem
Joh. Nicholas Schubert
Joh. Michael Schubert
Casper Weyman
Hans Jurg Stump
Johans Zieglin
Joh. Conrad Lampador
Joseph Lampader
Johannes Lampader
Jurg Fred^k Fleger
Joh. Jurg Meys
Joh. Jurg Minder
Hans Martin Minder
Joh. Kimmerly
Joseph Wielt
Hans Adam Hitner
Hans Jurg Gerstemeyer
Casper Wirshon
Jurg Fred^k Sthieff
Adam Stall

Adam Ghruen
Abraham Longer
Jacob Folmer
Fred^k Qua
Charles Sims
Joseph Fredrick
Carl Fred^k Wiedach
Peter Jansem
Christopher Hert
Fred^k Heys
Christⁿ Hotteman
Paul Bruydigham
Joh. Daniel Thys
Joh. Ernst Nagel
Fred^k Souter
William Engelfried
Jurg Paul Langebach
Christopher Mahl
Christⁿ Mailes
Johan Qua
Hans Jacob Adam
Johan Metcher
Peter Ehm
Adam Overdorff
Hans Jurg Gries
Peter Hitsner
Jacob Schlachter
Henry Overlender
Adam Wolf
Johan Schick
Nicholas Strousin
Hans Donner
Philip Steyn
Joh. Christ^r Beck
Conrad Steinmetz

Hendrick Miller
Johans Schriber
Joh. Michael Spannagel
Jacob Witman
Jurg Adam Witman
Paul Hep
Valentine Schoper
Christopher Waltz
Hans Jurg Kley
Christo^r Heykill
Peter Nass
Christopher Grief
Bartol Hick
Peter Seyl
Hans Jurg Schelhammer
Joh. Holscheyt
Casper Aven
William Gafferot
Johan Kerts

Gotfried Knaper
Simon Sack
Johan Swarin
David Rief
Jurg Fred^k Hemminger
Hans Jacob Ostwalt
Philip Hammersmith
Jurg Pick
Peter Richter
Herman Weyshit
Jurg Seytelmier
Philip Grantemier
Michael Kolp
Jurg Ramly
Joh. Jacob Schink
Hans Jurg Hough
Johs. Smith
Matthias Fonner
Joh. Jurg Brown

[Endorsed:]

A List of the men on b^d the Ship Rich^d & Mary, John Moore, mas^r 1753. Qual. 17th Septr. 1753.   108.

Shoemaker.

[List 201 B] Foreigners Imported in the Ship Richard and Mary, Qualified 17th September, 1753. Captⁿ John Moore, Commander.

Johann Caspar Gayer
Johan Jacob Gayer
Hans Michael (✗) Rou
Joseph Schilpp
Ulrich Seuberlich
Johann Carl Siegel
Johann Ernst Juncken
Johann Henrich Juncken
Peter Gucker
Johann Martin Jacob
F. Wilhelm (+) Zern

Johannes Knabschneider
Georg Adam Schober
Johan Christian Kniess
Martin Suhrer
Andreas Dihm
Johann Nicolaus Schubart
Johann Michael Schubart
Joh Casper Wann
Hans George (✗) Stump
Johannes Siglin
Conrad (+) Lampader

Joseph (×) Lampeder

Johannes (+) Lampeder

Georg Friderich Pflieger

Johann Georg Maisch

Johann Georg Gminder

Hans Martin (J) Minder

Jacob Kemmelie

Josias Wild

Johann Adam Körner

Johann Gerstenmeyer

Casper Turschum

Gerg Fridrich Stief

Adam (+) Stall

Adam Grin

Abraham Lang

Michael Vollmer

Fridrich Kuche

Johann Leonhardt Zembsch

Josephus Friederich

Frederick ( ) Wiedach, sick

Peter Janson

Johann Christoff Hirth

Johann Daniel Deuss

C. Frederick (H) Hotteman

Paulus Bräutigam

Johann Friedrich Hess

Johann Ernst Nagel

J. Frederick (×) Souter

Johann Wilhelm Engelfridt

Georg Paul Langenbach

Christopher (+) Mahl

Christ Ludwig Mall

Johannes Kuohn

Hans Jacob (H) Adam

Johan George (×) Metsker

Peter (×) Ehm

Adam Oberdorf

Hans Jerg Kreis

Peter Hitschner

Jacob Schlachter

Johann Henrich Oberlendter

Johann Adam Wolf

Johannes Sack

Nicholas (+) Strouss

Hans Everard (+) Donner

Johann Philipp Stein

Johann Christoph Beck

Johann Conrad Steinmetz

Johann Henrich Müller

Johannes Schreiber

Johan Michel Spannagel

Jacob (×) Witman

Georg Adam Wittman

Paulus Hepp

Vallentin Schobig

Christoff Waltz

Johann Georg Klein

Christoph Heinickel

Peter Nass

Christophel Gref

Hans Barthel Heck

Peter (×) Seyl

Johan Georg Schöllheimer

Johannes Hollscheitt

Johannes Caspar Auen

Ernst Wilhelm Kafferoth

Johannes (++) Kerts

J. Gottfried (++) Knapper

Simon (×) Sack

Johann (××) Swerin

David (++) Reif

Georg Friederich Heiniger

Hans Jacob (×) Ostwald

Philip (×) Hammersmith

Johann Georg Bick

Johann Peter Richter

Herman (×) Weyshit

George (×) Seytelman

Philip (O) Grantemeir

Michael Kolb

George (✕) Ramly   Johann Matheus Pfanner
Jacob Schenck   Johann Georg Braun
Hans Georg Hanf   108.
Johan (✕) Smith

[Endorsed:]
List of Foreigners imported in the Ship Richard & Mary,
John Moore, Commander, from Rotterdam last from Cowes.
Qual. 17th Septr 1753.
       108.   Shoemaker.

[List 201 C] At the Court House at Philadelphia, 17th Septr
1753.
       Present: Thomas Lawrence, Joshua Maddox, Esquires.
The Foreigners whose Names are underwritten, Imported
in the Ship Richard and Mary, John Moore, Commander, from
Rotterdam but last from Cowes, did this day take the usual
Qualification. No. 108.

Johann Casper Gayer   Joseph (✕) Lamparter
Johan Jacob Gayer   Johanes (✕) Lamparter
Hans Michael (+) Raw   Georg Friederich Pflieger
Joseph Schilpp   Johann Georg Maisch
Ulrich Säuberlich   Johann Georg Gminder
Johann Henrich Juncken   Hans Martin (J) Gelinder
Johann Carl Siegel   Hans Jacob Kümmerlie
Johann Ernst Juncken   Josias Wild
Peter Gucker   Johann Adam Körner
Johann Martin Jacob   Johann Gorg Gerstenmayer
F. Wilhelm (+) Zürn   Casper Treschum
Johannes Knabschneider   Gerg Friedrich Stief
Georg Adam Schober   Adam (✕) Stall
Johan Christian Kniess   Adam Grin
Martin Suhrer   Abraham Lang
Andreas Dihm   Michael Vollmer
Johann Nicolaus Schubart   Fridrich Kuche
Johann Michael Schubart   Johann Leonhardt Zembsch
Joh. Casp. Wann   Josephus Friederich
Johan Georg (✕) Stump   Caral Fredig ( ) Weydon, sick
Johannes Siglin   on bd
Conrad (+) Lampater   Peter Janson

Johann Christoph Hirth
Johann Daniel Deuss
C. Friederich (F) Hootman
Paulus Bräutigam
Johann Friedrich Hesse
Johan Frd. (✕) Satler
Johann Ernst Nagel
Johann Wilhelm Engelfridt
Christoff (✕) Mahl
Georg Paul Langenbach
Christ Ludwig Mall
Johannes Kuohn
Hans Jacob (H) Adam
J. George (✕) Metzger
Peter (✕) Rahm
Adam Oberdorff
Hans Jerg Kreis
Petter Hitschner
Jacob Schlachter
Johann Henrich Oberlendter
Johann Adam Wolff
Johannes Sack
George Nicklas (+) Straws
H. Albert (+) Hörner
Johann Philipp Stein
Johann Christoph Beck
Johann Conrad Steinmetz
Johann Henrich Müller
Johannes Schreiber
Johan Michael Spannagel
Jacob (✕) Wittmann
Georg Adam Wittmann
Paulus Hepp

Vallentin Schobig
Christoff Waltz
Johan Georg Klein
Christoph Heinickel
Peter Nass
Christophel Gref
Hans Barthel Heck
Peter (✕) Saillor
Hans Jerg Schöllhammer
Johannes Hollscheitt
Johannes Caspar Auen
Ernst Wilhelm Kafferoth
Johanes (++) Gürtz
J. Godfried (++) Knapper
Simon (✕) Sack
Johanes (✕✕) Perring
Davit (✕✕) Reiff
Georg Fridrich Heiniger
Hans Jacob (✕) Oswald
Philip (✕) Hamershmit
Johann Georg Bick
Johan Peter Richter
Herman (+) Weyshirk
Hans George (✕) Seydelmayer
Philip (O) Grindelmeyr
Michael Kolb
H. George (+) Gramly
Jacob Schenck
Hans Georg Hanf
Johanes (✕) Shmit
Johann Mattheis Pfanner
Johann Georg Braun

Septr 15, 1753.

Sir

According to directions we have carefully examin'd the State of Health of the Mariners & Passengers on board the Ship Richard & Mary, Capt Moore, from Roterdam and found not the least Objection to their being admitted to land in the City immediately.

To his Honour   Tho. Graeme
The Governour.   Th. Bond
[Endorsed:]
    Doctors Report on the Ship Richard & Mary, 15th Sept^r
1753.

[List 202 A] A List of Male Names on Board the Ship
Leathley. 19th Septr 1753.

Joh. Hen. Hening	Philip Furtenbach
And. Full	Ludwig Smith
Peter Coch	Hen. Hinsey
Hen. Wm Foss	Mich^l Uel
Joh. Died. Sheer	Christⁿ Ramberg
Christ^r Slinker	Hen. Schreder
Christ^r Ramblen	Joh. Stas Cock
Joh. Godfrey Colte	Joh. Christ^r Abach
John Wm Slinker	Hermon Alaman
Fred Wilhelm Slinker	Joh^s Heynaman
Christ^r Termell	Nich^s Klein
Christ^r Bremer	Casper Ludwig Seymer
Frans. Hen. Slinker	And^s Busman
Hans Enert Custard	Verner Ruhmont
Casper Elebricht	Joh. Hen. Proby
Christⁿ Neinsted	Hen. Seibas
Rudolph Frechtnicht	Christⁿ Alaman
Daniel Lang	Conrad Schmidt
Ludolph Wethermeir	John Fred. Fischer
And^s Meyer	Joh. Cord Olster
John Justice Miller	Fred. Vecher
Henr. Busman	Valentine Niermeyer
Henning Nemeyr	Casper Hipner
Ernest Still	Fred. Alaman
Kasen Dorman	And. Christ^r Minger
Hen. Bosman	52.
Christⁿ Slemer	

[Endorsed:]
    List of Foreigners imported from Hamburgh in the Ship
Leathley, Captⁿ Lickley & cleared from Cowes.
        Qualified 19th Septr 1753.
        N° 51.

[List 202 B] List Foreigners imported from Hamburgh, in the Ship Leathley, Captain John Lickley, were qualified at the Court House, Wednesday, 19th Septr 1753.

Hener (+) Henning
Andrew (+) Cock
Petter (+) Coch
Johannes (+) Foss
Died (×) Sheer
Christopher (×) Hinker
Christopher (+) Rambler
John Godfry ( ) Colt
Johann Gottfriedt Golde
Christoffel Schlencker
Friederich Wilhelm [Schlen]cker
Hendrick (×) Slinke
Christopher (×) Termel
Christopher (×) Bremer
Hans (|) Custard
Casper (K) Elbricht
Christian Andreas Nierstedt
Rudolph (×) Freechnight
Daniel (×) Lang
Johan Ludolff Wehmeyer
Johann Andreas Meyer
Johann Just Müller
Henery (×) Bussman
Henery (×) Nemeyr
John Henery (×) Busman
Andreas (×) Busman
Ernst Henri Ställy

Casen (+) Dorman
Christian ( ) Sleemer
Johann Phillyps Fordenbach
Ludwich (×) Smith
Henery (×) Hinsey
Miel Uhl
Christian (+) Ramberg
Hendrick (×) Schreeder
John (×) Coch
Johann Christoph Appach
Harm. Alleman
Johannes (×) Heyneman
Johann Nicklaus Klein
Caspar Ludewig Sievert
Vernor (+) Ruchmont
Johan Hen. (×) Proby
Johann Henrich Sievert
Johan Christian Aleman
Conradt (+) Smith
Johann Friedrich Fischer
Cord (+) Olster
Frederick (+) Veeker
Valtin Wehmeyer
Jeorg Casper Höpner
Johan Friedrich Christian Alleman
Andreas (Ch) Minger

[Endorsed:]
Foreigners imported in the Ship Leathley, Captn Lickley.
Qual. 19th Septr 1758.
No. 51.   Kepplee.

[List 202 C] At the Court House at Philadelphia, Wednesday, the 19th September, 1753.
Present: William Plumsted, Esquire.
The Foreigners whose Names are underwritten, Imported

in the Ship Leathley, Captain John Lickley, from Hamburgh and last from Cowes in England, did this day take the usual Qualifications. [No.] 53.

Johan Henry (+) Hening
Anereas (++) Foll
Johan Peter (+) Koch
J. Wilhelm (X) Voss
J. Diterich (X) Sehr
Christian (+) Shlemer
Christoff (X) Amelon
Johann Gottfriedt Golde
Christophel Schlencker
Friedrich Wilhm Schlencker
Frantz Henry (++) Shlencker
Christoffel (X) Termel
J. Christoff (X) Bremer
H. Henry (+) Cöster
Caspar (K) Hillebrecht
Christian Andreas Niestedt
C. Rudolff (+) Rechner
Daniel (+) Lange
Johann Ludolff Wehmeyer
Johann Andreas Meyer
Johan Just Muller
Henry (+) Busman
Henry (X) Neymeyer
Hans Henry (+) Busman
Andereas (+) Busman
Ernst Henri Ställy
J. Carsten (X) Thorman

Christian ( ) Shlemer
Johann Philip Fordenbach
Ludewig (X) Shmit
J. Henry (+) Hinsey
Michael Uhl
J. Christian (+) Ramberg
Henry (X) Shreoder
Johan Stats (+) Koch
Johannes Christoph Appach
Harm. Alleman
Johans (X) Heneman
Johann Nicklaus Klein
Caspar Ludewig Sievert
Henry (+) Werner
J. Henry (+) Probe
Conrad (XX) Shmit
Johann Henrich Sievert
Jan Friedrich Fischer
Johan Christian Ale[man]
J. Cort (X) Holster
Friederich (+) Vecher
Valten Wehmeyer
Georg Casper Höppener
Johan Friedrich Christian Alleman
Ands. Christoff (Ch) Meinken

[List 203 A] A List of Men Passengers Names, Lately Arrived in the Port of Philaia from Rotterdam, in the Ship Neptune, John Mason, Master, in the Year 1753 [24 Septr. 1753.]

Fredrik Millger
Michl Hiltner
Peter Timmick
Michl Schertlin
Pieter Cidele

Jerick Cidele
Nicolas Winegarden
Johan Righter
Jerig Wiger
Sebastian Horn

Laurence Coy
Jerig Swingard
Hans Trump
Peter Clump
Baltzer Rembinger
Nico^{ls} Heblin
Sebastⁿ Werline
Mich^l Weyrlin
Jerig Sweyell
Christo^p Bridleheart
Mich^l Creats
Philip Yirig
Mich^l Enties
Mich^l Heart
Paulus Swart
Andreas Bolk
Adam Theem
Philip Keesecker
Adam Finsick
Adam Soul
Andreas Sniper
Jacob Oberdorff
Jerig Wonder
Peter Reese
Mich^l Dosch
Leonard Rutinger
Sr Bastⁿ Hamerter
Jerig Weal
Johan Rose
Christⁿ Fernaber
Philip Neer
Cono^d Winkler
Jacob Winkler
Thos. Winkler
David Hunsicker *
Casper Dollman
Hans Rees
Jorig Holeback
Mich^l Holeaback
Nico^{ls} Holeaback

Simeon Jost
Jerig Folk
Jerig Lennick
Barnet Pankoce
Milker Hisener
Johan^s Flesher
Chris^{tn} Riseinger
Nico^{ls} Soul
Jerig Founeg
Mich^l Holenback
Peter Foux
Hans Fixer
Johan Weighelt
Ephraim Garbell
Philip Weys
Jurg Baur
Adam Hauk
Jurg Horp
Thos Linnick
Peiter Linnick
Hans Seytz
Casper Foux
Jurg Wolg
Bastⁿ Hinner
Johan Adolphat
Johan Graff
Johan^s Scyner
Welholm Wertz
Jurg Link
Jurg Rap
Barnerd Shop
Casper Sner
Peter Wertz
Johan Saul
Andr^s Triebieg
Seb^s Ries
Mich^l Hoxener
Adam Shrick
Lenord Sower
Jurg Oberdorff

* Name crossed out, perhaps that of a minor.

Casp^r Hinckele

Johan Jurg Beck

Hans Mich^l Keyler

Chirstop Ernst Nieman

Andreas Suybert *

Johannes Vooer

Jurg Philip Moras

Andreas Hammer

Jacob Leyer

Johan Diedich Weyer

Hendrick Oort

Johan Christop^l Keyser

Mich^l Seelig

Joh. Henry Macklin

Hans Macklin

And^s Sybert

Joh. Mich^l Wasom

Adam Nichs Platz

Johan Bolig

Jacob Shaffer

Baltser Oberdorff

Johan Schneh

Johan Watzin

Henrich Schaffer

Jurg Philip Kaggell

Johannes Horn

Baltzer Suyber

Johan Peter Stompff

Nicolas Beringer

Martin Semmel

Baltzer Giegh

Jurg Philip Burger

Peiter Flick

Jacob Wilchart

Hans Leonard Saul

Johannes Borghert

Peiter Hebling

Hans Schatz

Andr^s Zaam

Jurg Wolf

Paulus Blitz

Jacob Schell

Christ^n Bettel

Philip Hoffman

Johan Adam Schantz

Hans Adam Schnepper

Nichol^s Reinheart

Christo^p Horn

Mich^l Suybert

Christop^l Orth

Johan Simon Berger

Johan Paulus Platz

Philip Meyer

Johannes Stickling

Johan Wilhelm Hiltner

Charell Milder

James Schott

N° 146

[List 203 B] A List of Men Passengers Names, Lately arrived in the Port of Philadelphia, from Rotterdam, in the Ship Neptune, John Mason, Master. Anno Domini 1753. Qualified 24th Septr 1753.

Friderich Melcher

Johann Wilhelm Hiltner

Petter Dümmig

Johann Michael Schärthlein

George (G) Keytel

Peter (P) Keytel

Georg Nicolaus Weingätner

Johann Georg Weickert

* Name crossed out.

Hans Michel Rechter

Sebastian Horn

Lorenz Friedrich Croy

Georg Schweikert

Johanes Trump

Better Klümth

Bartel Raumberger

Nicholas (×) Hebling

Sebastian Werlein

Johann Michael Werlein

Johann Gorg Schwab

Johan Christoph Breitenherdt

Michael Kretz

Johann Philip Eyrich

Johann Michel Endres

Johann Michell Heydt

Johann Paul Schwab

Andreas Balch

Hans Adam Diehm

Philip Kieseker

Hans Adam [Finsick]

Johann Adam Sauer

Andreas Schnepper

Jacob Oberdorff

Johann Gorg Wunder

Johann Peter Riess

Johann Michael Dosch

Johan Linhard Rutting[er]

Johann Sebastian Hammeter

Jörg Weiss

Johannes Ross

Johan Christoph Freihaber [?]

Johann Philipp Nern

Conradt Winckler

Hans Jacob Winckler

Hans Domas Winckler

Caspar Dollman

Johans Riess

Johan Georg Hollenbach

Michael (×) Hollerbach

Nicholas (×) Hollerbach

Simmon Jost

Jerg Falck

Jerg Lennich

Johan Bernhard Spahnkuch

Melcher Eisnert

Johannes Fleischer

Christian (O) Reising

Johan Nicklas Saul

Johann Georg Fornnoff

Michael Hollenbach

Georg Peter Fuchs

Johann Nicolaus Feckser

Hans Dries Weickert

Ephrahim Benedigt Garbel

Philip (W) Weiss

Georg Henry (×) Bower

Adam Hauck

George (×) Horn

Better Lennig

Johann Thomas Lennich

Hans Görg Seitz

Hans Casper Fuchs

George Folk

Sebastian Hönner

Johann Heinrich Graf

John Adolph (×××) Ott

Johannes Schriner

Wilhelm (×) Würtz

Wilhelm Würtz, Junr

Johann Georg Conrath Linck

Johan George (×) Roab

Bernard (×) Schop

Johan Casper Schnorr

Johan Adam Saull

Andreas Triebig

Sebastian Riess

Hans Michel Hörner

Johanes Schreck

Johann Leonhard Sauer

Johan Gorg Oberdorff
Casper (C) Hingle
Johann Georg Beck
Hans Michael ( ) Kehler, on
    board
Christian Ernst (X) Nieman
Johannes Fur
George Philip (X) Moras
Andreas (X) Hammer
Jacob Leyer
Johan (X) Leder
Johann Hennerich Ord
Johann Christian Keyser
Johann Michael Seelig
Johan Atam Bolch
Johann Atam Schatz
Jacob Schäffer
Andreas Sam
Baltz Oberdorff
Gerg Wolff
Adam Schreck
Paulus Blitz
Jacob Scholl
Johann Henrich Schäffer
Christoff Büttel
Jörg Fielpp Kahel
Philipp Hoffmann
Johannes Horn
John Michel Schatz
Balsar Seuberth

Hanns Schnepper
John Christopher (O) Stumph
Nicholas (XX) Reinhart
Nicklaus Beringer
Christoph Horn
Martin Semmel
Michael Seubert
Baltzer Gieg
Christian [Orth]
George Philip (X) Burghart
Simon (X) Burghart
Johann Petter Flick
Johann Paulus Platz
Jacob (W) Wilger
Hans Philip (HPM) Meyer
Johan Lenhart Saull
Johannes Stichling
Johannes Burckhart
Peter (X) Hobling
Charles (+) Millday
Hans Schreck
Hans Meckelein
Johan Heinrich Meckelein
Hans Meckelein
Andreas Seuberth
Johann Michael Vassem
Hans Adam (+) Shantz
Valentine (X) Overderf
Adam Nickolas (X) Blatz

[Endorsed:]
List of Foreigners imported in the Ship Neptune, John Mason, Master.
    Qual. 24ᵗʰ Septʳ 1753.
       146.   Shoemaker.

[List 203 C] At the Court House at Philadelphia, Monday, the 24ᵗʰ of September, 1753.
               Present: Thomas Lawrence, Esqʳ.
The Foreigners whose Names are underwritten, imported in

the Ship Neptune, John Mason, Master, from Rotterdam and last from Cowes, did this day take the usual Qualifications. No. 106.

Friederich Melcher
Johann Wilhelm [Hiltner]
Petter Dümmig
Johann Michael Schärthlein
George (G) Keytel
Peter (P) Keytel
Georg Nicolaus Weingätner
Johann Gorg Weickert
Hans Michael Rechter
Sebastian Horn
Lorenz Friedrich Croy
Georg Schweikert
Johannes Trump
Better Klumth
Bartel Raumberger
Nicklas (+) Hebling
Sebastian Werlein
Johann Michael Werlein
Johann Görg Schwab
Johann Christoph Breitenherdt
Michael Kretz
Johan Philip Eyrich
Johan Michel Endres
Johann Michall Heidt
Johann Paul Schwab
Andreas Bolch
Hans Adam Diehm
Philib Kieseker
Hans Adam [Finsick]
Johann Adam Sauer
Andreas Schnepper
Jacob Oberdorff
Johann Gorg Wunder
Johann Peter Riess
Johann Michael Dosch
Johann Linhart Ruttinger
Johann Sebastian Hammeter

Jörg Weiss
Johannes Ross
Johan Christoph Fremhaber
Johann Philipp Nern
Conradt Winckler
Michael (×) Hollebach
Hans Jacob Winckler
Caspar Dollman
Hans Domas Winckler
Johans Riess
Johan Georg Hollenbach
Nicklas Hollebach
Simon Jost
Jerg Falck
Jorg Lennig
Johan Bernhard Spahnkuch
Melchor Eisnert
Johannes Fleischer
Christian (O) Reysing
Johan Nicklas Saul
Johann Georg Fornnoff
Michael Hollenbach
Geörg Peter Fuchs
Johann Nicolaus Feckser
Hans Dries Weikert
Ephrahim Bendigt Garbel
Philip (W) Weyse
George Henry (×) Bower
Adam Hauck
George (×) Horn
Better Lennig
Johann Thomas Lennich
Hans Jörg Seitz
Hans Casper Fuchs
Hans George Carl Volck
Sebastian Hönner
Johann Heinrich Graf

John Adolffe (XXX) Ott
Johannes Schreiner
Willhelm (X) Würtz
Wilhelm ( ) Würtz, Junior, on
    board
Johann Georg Conrath Linck
Johan George (X) Roab
Bernhart (X) Shop
Johann Casper Schnorr
Johan Adam Saull
Andreas Triebig
Sebastian Riess
Hans Michel Hörner
Johannes Schreck
Johann Leonhardt Sauer
Johan Gorg Oberdorff
Caspar (C) Henkel
Johann Georg Beck
Hans Michael ( ) Köller, on
    board
Christian Ernst (X) Nieman
Johannes Fur
George Will (+) Morash
Andereas (+) Hammer
Jacob Leyer
Johan Diedrich Meyer
Johan Heinrich Ord
Johann Christian Keyser
Johann Michael Seelig
Johan Adam Bolch
Johann Atam Schatz
Jacob Schäffer
Andreas Sahm
Baltz Oberdorff
Jörg Wolff
Adam Schreck
Paulus Blitz

Jacob Scholl
Johann Henrich Schäffer
Christoff Büttel
Jörg Fielpp Kahel
Fillpp Hoffman
Johannes Horn
John Michael Schatz
Baltas Seuberth
Hanns Schnepper
Johan Peter (O) Stumff
Nicklas (XX) Reinhart
Nicklaus Beringer
Christoph Horn
Martin Semmel
Michael Seubert
Baltzer Gieg
Christian [Orth]
George Philip (X) Burger
Siemon (+) Bürger
Johann Petter Flick
Johann Paulus Platz
Jacob (W) Willger
Johan Philip (HPM) Meyer
Johan Lenhart Saull
Johannes Stihling
Johannes Burkhart
Peter (+) Höbling
Caral (X) Mildy
Hans Schreck
Hans Meckelein
Johan Heinrich Meckelein
Hans Meckelein
Andreas Seuberth
Johann Michael Vassem
John Adam (+) Shantz
Vallentin (+) Obertorf
Adam Nicolaus (X) Platz

Septr 23, 1753.

Sir
According to direction we have carfully examined the State

of Health of the Mariners and Passengers on board the Ship Neptune, Cap⁺ Mason, from Roterdam and found nothing amongst them which we apprehend can be injurious to the Health of the Inhabitants of the City.

To his Honour   Tho. Graeme

The Governour   Th. Bond

[Endorsed:]

Doctors certificate relating to the ship Neptune, 23ᵈ Septʳ 1753.

[List 204 A] A List of mens Names and ages, Imported in the Ship Peggy, Capᵗ James Abercrombie, from Rotterdam, 24 September, 1753.

Name	AGES	Name	AGES
Martin Bower	44	Jacob Hoor	27
Christian Roth	37	Johan Jerick Blumer	26
Johannis Lintz	19	Johan Michˡ Bohmer	34
Christopher Trouts	27	Johan Fortmayer	26
Christopher Hosp	30	Johannes Steinman	40
Michael Folts	23	Johan Adam Oberwinder	28
Hendrick Holtsman	42	Carle Wagg	21
John Andreas Bock	25	Carle Windmiller	30
Jacob Hendᵏ Herle	35	Jerick Zeigler	24
Christian Fredrick Banser	34	Franciscus Ratity	38
Johan Jacob Kauts	20	Ignatius Voght	20
Fredrick Fetterle	20	Johan Jacob Zucker	25
Johan Casper Nill	33	Ignatius Fiechel	30
Jacob Miller	25	Nicholus Herter	17
Casper Meyly	34	Jerick Anthony Linder	18
Johannes Backman	26	Johan Andreas Shredlin	24
Johan Adam Zwirner	32	Johan Wilhelm Mengel	42
Fretinant Kney	38	Jerick Backer	25
Johannis Rudel	28	Jacob Eberhart	36
Carle Erhart	34	Jacob Steigelman	25
Johan Michael Shoemaker	23	Bernhard Winterman	21
Philip Schwartz	24	Johan Jacob Kleinbub	23
Johan Jacob Aller	30	Johan Michˡ Eberhauf	40
Nicholus Shrack	34	Jacob Streemchild	21
Michael Spann	34	Johan Diedᵏ Opperheimer	24
Casper Schauck	42	Wilhelm Albreght	32

	AGES		AGES
Philip Jacob Brun	24	Adam Sigerist	23
Wilhelm Ganter	30	Nicholus Fyrestein	40
Peter Fies	30	Nicholus Dᵒ, Jun.	21
Jacob Hetrick	17	Hendrick Hashare	26
Jacob Zerbinger	16	Abraham Borell	34
Hans Jerick Lyssey	30	Johan Jerick Sauter	32
Jerick Blanck	28	Conradt Hausman	34
Michael Miller	35	Nicholus Bartholemy	25
Fredrich Dornwind	27	Casper Rometch	24
Johan Sternberger	22	Paulus Dasser	45
Johan Michael Sawrig	24	Agatius Dasser	17
Dewald Sawrig	27	Jerick Shweykert	54
Johan Martin Bedinger	18	Conrad Huber	46
Conradt Jeger	35	Martin Shnyder	26
Michael Bower	17	Philip Jacob Mayer	22
Martin Beck	21	Jerick Rhinholt	30
Jacob Smith	32	Fredrick Engelhart	30
Jerick Matzer	39	Johan Wolfgang Leitzel	30
Johan Jacob Bliecker	26	Casper Phlugfelder	41
Jerick Peter Telp	20	Adam Shack	36
Melchior Kampf	40	Joseph Graff	30
Johan Wolfgang Rhinlen	39	Isaac Miller	23
Peter Musculus	30	Johan Ubel	30
Casper Sheen	38	Anthony Cantzler	27
Hans Walter	35	Jacob Nagel	40
Jacob Walter	25	Johannis Binnighoff	
Jacob Berger	22	Carle Decrafft	
Vallentine Shaffer	30	John Michˡ Jacob	
Philip Kreps	18	John Carle Shakar	
Jacob Kreninger	30	Johan Conrad Kachel	
Jerick Adam Kuys	29	Christian Kreps	
Jacob Harsch	22	Jacob Holler	
Carle Ebersholl	21	Philip Zurg	
Nicholus Dullmayer	32	119	

[Endorsed:]

List of Foreigners imported in the Ship Peggy, Capᵗ James Abercrombie.

Qual. 24ᵗʰ Septʳ 1753.

119.

Stedman.

[List 204 B] Foreigners imported in the Ship Peggy, Capt. James Abercrombie, From Rotterdam. Qual. 25th Septr. 1753.

Martin Baur
Christian Roth
Johannes Lentz
Christoph Trautz
Christoph Hosp
Michael Voltz
Joest Henrich Holtzman
John Andreas (X) Back
Jacob Hendrich (H) Herle
Christian Friedrich Panse
Johann Jacob Kautz
Johanns Nötterle
Johan Caspar Nill
Jacob Miller
Caspar Mäule
Johannes Bachman
Johan Adam Zwirner
Ferdinand (K) Keney
Johannes Bönnighoff
Johannes ( ) Rudel, on board
Joh. Carl Ehrhardt
Johan Michael (++) Shoe-maker
Philipp Leonhard Schwartz
Johan Jacob ( ) Miller, on board
Nicholas (X) Schrach
Michael (M) Spaan
Caspar Schock
Jacob (X) Hoar
J. George (X) Blumer
Michal Böhmer
Johann Forttmeier
Johanes (X) Steinman
Johann Adam Oberwinder
Carl Fridrich Waag
Carl (X) Windmiller
George Philipp Ziegler

Jean Frans Rattez
Ignatius Vogt
Johann Jacob Zucker
Ignathes Fichtl
Nicholas ( ) Herter, on board
Gorg Anton Linder
Johann Andreas Schrödlin
Johan Wilhelm (X) Mengel
George (X) Baker
Jacob (O) Eberhart
Jann Jacob Stigelman
Bernart Wintringer
Johann Jacob Kleinbub
Johan Michael (X) Ehrhof
Jacob (X) Striemshield
Johan Detrick (X) Oppenheiner
Willhelm (X) Albright
Heinrich Philipp Brum
Wilhelm (X) Ganter
Petter Feiss
Jacob Hetrich
Jacob ( ) Serbinger, on board
Hans George (X) Lyssey
George (X) Blank
Michael Müller
Frietrich Dornwind
Johann Theobold Sternberger
Johans Michell Sorg
Diebolt Sorg
Johan Martin Bettinger
Conradt Jäger
Michael Bauer
Marti Beck
Jacob Schmidt
George (X) Matzer
Johann Jacob Bleiker
Gerg Peter Delpp
Hans Melcher Kampf

Johan Peter Musculus
Johan Wolfgang Miller
Peter Casper Schönn
Johanes Walder
Johann Jacob Walther
Jacob Berger
Vallentin Schäffer
Phillip Krebs
Jacob Kreininger
Gerg Adam Geiss
Jacob Hirsch
Carl Ebersohl
Nicholas (X) Dallmeyr
Görg Adam Siegrist
Nickell Füerstein
Nickel Feuer[stein]
Hendrich (X) Hashar
Abraham Borell
Johann Georg Sautter
Joh. Conrad Hausman
Johann Nicolaus Bartholomä
Paul ( ) Dasser, on board
Johan Casper Rumetsch

G. A. Daser
J. G. Schweickhart
Conrad Huober
Martin Schneider
Philipp Jacob Meyer
Georg Christoph Reinhold
Johann Fridrich Engelhart
Johann Wolfgang Leitzel *
Johann Casper Pfugfelder
Johann Adam Schöckh
Joseph Graf
Isaac Müller
Johann Friederich Uebel
Antony Cantzler
Jacob (X) Nagel
Carl (D) De Greiff
Hans Michel Jacob
Johann Carl Jacquart
Johann Conrad Kagel
Johann Christian Krebs
Jacob (X) Holler
Philip (S) Zurg

[Endorsed:]
List of Foreigners imported in the Ship Peggy, Capt. James Abercrombie.
Qual. 24th Septr 1753.

    119 [men]
     21 [women & children]
    ───────
    140 [Total]

Stedman.

[List 204 C] At the Court House at Philadelphia, Monday, the 24 September, 1753.

Present: Thomas Lawrence, Esquire.

The Foreigners whose Names are underwritten, Imported in the Ship Peggy, James Abercrombie, Commander, from

* A Lutheran minister. See *History of Tohickon Union Church*, p. 344.

Rotterdam and last from Plymouth, this Day took the usual Qualifications.

Martin Baur
Christian Roth
Johannes Lentz
Christopf Trautz
Christoph Hosp
Michael Voltz
Joest Hen. Holtzman
John Andereas (×) Bock
Jacob H. (H) Herly
Christian Friedrich Panse
Johann Jacob Kautz
Johannes Nötterle
Johan Caspar Nill
Jacob Miller
Caspar Mäule
Johannes Bachman
Johan Adam Zwirner
Fartinad (F) Geney
Johannes Beinighoff
Johan ( ) Rudel, on board
Johann Carl Ehrhardt
Johan Michael (××) Schumacher
Philipp Leonhard Schwartz
John Jacob ( ) Miller, on board
Nicklas (×) Shreck
George Michael (M) Spoan
Casper Schock
Jacob (×) Hoarr
J. George (×) Pluner
Michael Böm[er]
Johann Forttmeier
Johannes (×) Steinman
Johann Adam Oberwinter
Carl Fridrich Waag
Carol (×) Weinmiller

Georg Philipp Ziegler
Jean Frans Rattez
Ignatius Vogt
Johann Jacob Zucker
Ignathius Fichtl
Nicklas ( ) Harter, on board
Gorg Anton Linder
Johann Andreas Schrödlin
Johan William (W) Engel
George (×) Baker
Jacob (O) Eberhart
Johan Jacob Stigelmann
Bernart Wintringer
Johann Jacob Kleinbub
Jhan Michael (+) Herow
Jacob (+) Stremshild
J. Diterich (×) Openhim
G. Wilhelm (×) Albrecht
Heinrich Philipp Brumm
Wilhelm (×) Gonder
Petter Feiss
Jacob Hetrich
J. Jacob ( ) Selwinger, on board
H. George (H) Leysig
George (×) Lange
Michael Müller
Frietrich Dornwind
Johann Theobold Sternberger
Johannes Michell Sorg
Diebolt Sorg
Johann Martin Bettinger
Conradt Jäger
Michael Baur
Martin Beck
Jacob Schmidt
George (×) Matzon
Johann Jacob Bleiker

Georg Peter Delp	Paulus A. ( ) Dasar, on board
Hans Melcher Kampf	G. A. Daser
Johan Wolfgang Rinlein	J. Georg Schweickhart
Johann Peter Musculus	Conrad Huober
Peter Casper Schönn	Martin Schneider
Johannes Walder	Philipp Jacob Meyer
Johann Jacob Walther	Georg Christoph Reinholdt
Jacob Berger	Johann Friedrich Engelhart
Vallentin Schäffer	Johann Wolfg. Leitzel
Phillipp Krebs	Johann Caspar Pfugfelder
Jacob Kreininger	Johann Adam Schöckh
Georg Adam Geiss	Joseph Graf
Jacob Hirsch	Isaac Müller
Carl Ebersohl	Johann Friederich Übel
Nicklas (X) Turmeyer	Antoni Cantzler
Görg Adam Siegrist	Jacob (O) Nagel
Nickell Füerstein	Carol (D) Degreiff
[Nickell] Feierstein	Hans Michel Jacob
Henry (X) Hasshar	Johann Carl Jacquart
Aberaham Borell	Johann Conrad Kagel
Johann Georg Sautter	Johann Christian Krebs
Jos. Conrad Hausman	Jacob (J) Haller
Johann Nicolaus Bartholomä	Philip (S) Zorge
Johann Casper Rumetsch	

Sir

Having visited the Ship Peggy, Capt. Abercromby, Master, freighted with Palatines from Roterdam and Cowes, and find them in such good Order as no objection arises to their entering the port to the prejudice of the Inhabitants.

Philad^{ia} Septr 24th 1753.

To his Honour the Governor.   Tho. Graeme

Th. Bond

[Endorsed:]

Doctors certificate relating to the ship Peggy, 24th Septr 1753.

[List 205 A] List of mens Names and ages, Imported in the Brothers, Capt William Muir, from Rotterdam and Cowes. Septem^r 26th 1753.

	AGES		AGES
Hans Yerrick Thom	30	George Fredrick Rynhard	27
Peter Isingbrid	27	John Paulus Shut	21
Christian Dim	30	Hans Yerrick Morstall	22
Jacob Funkboner	27	Johannes Strome	21
Mathias Plougher	31	Martin Festerer	27
Michael Shitahell	24	Hans Ulrick Fraenfielder	24
Martin Shitahell	22	Yerrick Andre	30
Michael Wysner	21	David Kunly	27
Jann Ecker	22	Andreas Keyser	24
Casper Khock	27	Philips Jacob Endner	21
Hans Yerrick Ley	21	Paulus Woolen	25
Frans Joseph Boss	21	Yerrick Albright	27
Jacob Honeysen	22	Melchior Flintshback	24
John Simon Jager	27	Jacob Sitzer	21
Ludwick Fisher	22	Stephen Kreyder	25
Hans Yerrick Underwegh	21	Everhard Solomon	27
George Christopher Eberly	24	John Jacob Man	31
Lorentz Kilkere	21	Peter Wilhelm	27
Daniel Wondelrigh	27	Thomas Kogh	21
Melchior Finhold	22	Fredrick Knab	24
Johannes Rooth	28	Johannes Zaberer	22
Ludwick Welts	24	Stephen Reibold	21
Philips Jacob Khreydler	22	Leonard Lukerow	27
John Martin Khreydler	20	Christopher Shenk	29
Burchart Lindaman	35	Nicholas Muller	24
Hans Philips Sprycker	24	Johannes Limback	29
Melchior Rieger	22	Johannes Heleren	30
Johannes Yeater	27	Philip Geyer	31
Fredrick Merkley	28	Hans Yerrick Man	30
Christopher Kirger	30	Jacob Man	41
Philip Hoffman	27	Bernard Snyder	31
Jacob Hester	24	Fredrick Lye	24
Leonard Diedrick	21	Johannes Weyerbacker	21
Christopher Miller	24	Mathias Riesly	27
Jacob Miller	27	Andreas Ackerman	22
Fredrick Miller	24	John Casper Marbook	
Hans Philip Flinsback	22	Martin Snyder	
Lodwick Fritz	27	Michael Snyder	
Hans Windel Gaber	31	Fredrick Limback	
Johannes Meysabacker	21	Fredrick Ken	

Hans Steitly
George Fisher
Johannes Man
Jacob Miller
Hans Wolfsmetser
Hans George Man

Adam Sweigert
John Hartmans
Valentine Rein
George Adam Shreim
Jacob Sweitzer
91

[Endorsed:]
List of Foreigners imported in the Ship Brothers, Capt Muir, from Rotterdam. Qual. 26th Septr 1753.
91.   Stedman.

[List 205 B] List of Foreigners imported in the Brothers, Capt. William Muir, From Rotterdam and last from Cowes. Qual. 26th Septr 1753.

Hans George (X) Hop
Peter (X) Isingbrid
Christian Diem
Hans Jacob Funklohner
Mathies Blocher
Michael Schattenhelm
Martin (X) Shittarell
Michael (M) Wysner
Hans (+) Ecker
Johann Caspar Koch
Hans George (X) Ley
Frantz Joseph Poss
Jacob Hönysen
Johann Simon Jäger
Lodowick (X) Fisher
Hans George (X) Underwegh
Georg Christoph Eberle
Lorentz Külckret
Daniel Wunderlich
Melcher Minolt
Johannes Rust
Johann Ludwig Weltz
Philipp Jacob Kreidler
Johann Marden Kreidler
Burckhardt Linderman

Johann Phipp Sprecher
Melchior Rickher
Johannes (++) Yetter
Frederick (X) Merkley
Christoph Jacob Kärcher
Philib Hoffmann
Jacob Hester
Leonard (X) Tetrich
Christoph Müller
Jacob Müller
Friedrich Müller
Johann Philipp Flinspach
Ludwig Fretz
Hans Wendel Huober
Johans Weisb[acher]
George Frederic Reinhard
Johann Paul Schott
Hans Jerg Marstaller
Johannes Strohm
Martin Pfisterer
Hans Ulrich ( ) Franfelder, on board
Georg Friederich Andrae
Davidt Kienle
Andreas Keyser

Philip Jacob (+) Endner

Paulus Bohler

Gerog Allbrecht Dill

Melchior Flinspach

Jacob (S) Setzer

Steffann Kreidler

Eberhart Sollomon

Jacob Mann

Georg Peter Wilhelm

Thomas Hoch

Friedrich Heinrich Knabe

Johannes Zaberer

Stephen (X) Reipold

Lehardt Leckromme

Christof Schenck

Nicholas (XX) Miller

Johannes (XX) Limbach

Johannes Herlein

Philip Geyer

Hans George (X) Man

Jacob Mann

Bernhardt Schneider

Friderich Lay

Johannes Weyerbacher

Mathais Röstlin

Andreas (E) Ehrman

Johann Caspar Marburg

Michael (   ) Snyder, on board

Friederich Limbach

Friedrich Küntzler

Johannes Steidle

Hanns Jörg Fischer

Johannes Mann

Johann Jacob Müller

Hans Wolf Schmetzer

Hans Jerg Mann

Adam Schweiger

Jean Hartmans

Vallendien Rhein

Jerg Jacob Schramm

Jacob Schweitzer

Frederich Huber

91

[Endorsed:]

List of Foreigners imported in the Ship Brothers, Capt Muir, from Rotterdam.

Qual. 26th Septr 1753.

91.   Stedman.

[List 205 C] At the Court House in Philadelphia, 26th September, 1753.

Present: Joshua Maddox, Esquire.

The Foreigners whose names are Underwritten, Imported in the Ship Brothers, William Muir, Commander, from Rotterdam and last from Cowes in England, this day took the Usual Qualifications. No. 90.

Hans Georg (++) Hop

Peter (XX) Eysenbreit

Christian Diem

Hans Jacob Funcklohner

Mattheis Blocher

Michael Schittenhelm

Martin (X) Shittenhelm

Michael (M) Wäsener

Johanes (+) Caarc
Johan Casper Koch
Hans Gorg Ley
Frantz Joseph Poss
Jacob Honysen
Johann Simon Jäger
Ludewig (×) Fisher
Hans George (×) Baltsonder-
    weg
Georg Christoph Eberle
Lorentz Külckret
Daniel Wunderlich
Melcher Minolt
Johannes Rust
Johann Ludwig Weltz
Philipp Jacob Kreidler
Johann Merden Kreidler
Bruckhard Lindeman
Johann Philipp Sprecher
Melchior Rieckher
Johanes (++) Jödder
Friederich (×) Mergel
Christoph Jacob Kärcher
Phipibb Hoffman
Jacob Hester
Leonhart (×) Diterich
Christoph Müller
Jacob Müller
Friedrich Müller
Johann Philipp Flinspach
Ludwig Fretz
Hans Wendel Huober
Johanes Weisbacher
George Frederic Reinhard
Johann Paul Schott
Hans Jerg Marrstaller
Johannes Strohm
Martin Pfisterer
Hans George (×) Frauenfelder
Georg Friederich Andrae

David Kienle
Anderas Keyser
Isaac (×) Vendner
Paulus Bohler
Georg Allbrecht Dill
Melchior Flinspach
Michael (S) Sitzer
Stäfann Kreidler
Eberhart Sallomon
Jacob Mann
Georg Peter Wilhelm
Thomas Hoch
Friedrich Heinrich Knabe
Johannes Zaberer
Stephan (×) Reybolt
Lenhardt Leckromme
Christof Schenck
Nickolas (++) Miller
Johanes (××) Limbach
Johannes Herlein
Philip Geyer
Hans George (×) Man
Jacob Mann
Bernhardt Schneider
Friderich Lay
Johannes Weyerbacher
Matheis Röstlinn
J. Andereas (E) Ehrman
Johann Caspar Marburg
Martin Schneider
Michael ( ) Snider, on board
Friderich Limbach
Friedrich Küntzler
Johannes Steidle
Hanns Jörg Fischer
Johannes Mann
Johann Jacob Müller
Hans Wolf Schmetzer
Hanns Jerg Mann
Adam Schweiger

Jean Hartmans   Jerg Jacob Schramm
Vallendien Rhein   Jacob Schweitzer

Septr 26, 1753.

Sir

According to directions we have carfully examined the Mariners and Passengers on board the Ship Brothers, Capt Muir, from Roterdam and found nothing amongst them which we apprehend can be injurious to the Citizens from their being admitted to land amongst them immediately.

To his Honour   Tho. Graeme
The Governour.   Th. Bond
[Endorsed:]

Doctors certificate relating to the Ship Brothers, Capt Muir, from Rotterdam.

26th Septr 1753.

[List 206 A] A List of Palatines Arriv^d here in the Ship Windsor, John Goad, Master, from Rotterdam and last from Cowes.   Philadelph^ia 26th Sepr 1753.

Jacob Bowman*, Newlander   John George Smith
Jacob Bushart   Hendrick Bower
Rodolph Phaninger   Christian Wise
Mark Stommer   Daniel Spack
John Rinehard Potts   Jno Willhelm Cromer
John Martin Rackmiller   Michael Breder*, Newlander
John Ludawick Peck   Rinehart Dedrick Kergar
Phalick Snyder   Jno Ferdinand Larer
Martain Failster   Jno Christof Rean
Christian Shobart   Jno George Lutes
Georg Stafon Walhower   Caspar Lutes
John George Man   John Martin Freukamler
Sickmont Bondlieck   Adam Sheatsman
Hendrick Fiestar   Hendrick Shettle
John Craber   Samawiele Settle

---

*Name crossed out. Person called Newlander. He entered Pa. the second time. For "Newlanders" see Diffenderffer, *German Immigration into Pennsylvania*, pp. 189–200.

Hendrick Good Fredmore
John Peter Horn
Christian Koller
John Yoham Yeiser
John Jacob Frice
Peter Groof
John Tomas
Peter Palts
Georg Hauf
Michael Melberchar
George Molsboh
John Kowmer
Casper Deal
Caspar Cobis
Nicholas Linn
Jacob Aswalt
Wilhelm Berksheirs
Fredrick Stillinger
Jacob Streboh

Jacob Martin
Philip Sheap
Philip Rice
Simon Trice
Jacob Rice
Hendrick Aushenech
John Snow,* Newlander
Peter Dean
Jacob Schori
Simon Drop
Adam Labort
William Teasel
George Patts
John Michael Hoober
Andriss Cronowas
Nicholas Mans
George Sommers
Adam Hobach
64

[Endorsed:]
Foreigners imported in the Ship Windsor, Capt John Goad, from Rotterdam.
Qual. 27th Septr 1753.
64.

[List 206 B] Foreigners imported in the Ship Windsor, Capt. John Goad, from Rotterdam. Qual. 27th September 1753.

Joh. Jacob Boshart
Rudolph (×) Phaninger
Mark (×) Stommer
Johann Reinhardt Batz
Johann Martin Riethmüller
Johann Ludwig Beck
Felix Schneider
Martin Fazler
Christian Schober
Georg Stephan Wallhauer
Johann Georg Mann

Sigmund Bondeli
Henrich Pfister
Johannes Gräber
Johann Yorg Schmidt
Henry (×) Bower
Christian Weiss
Daniel Speck
Johann Wilhelm Kromer
Reinhardt Diedtrich Kärcher
Johann Ferdinand Lehrer
Johan Christoph Rein

* Name crossed out.

Hans Jerg Lutz

Caspar Lutz

Johann Martin Truckenmüller

Adam (×) Shatsman

Heinrich Sättele

Samuel Sättle

Heinrich Gottfried Murr

Johann Peter Horn

Christian Keller

Johann Joachim Jayser

Johann Jacob Friess

Johann Peter Grub

Johannes Thomas

Johan Petter Beltz

Georg Haff

Michael Milberger

George (+) Molsbah

Johannes Kaumann

Johann Casper Diehl

Casper (+) Cobis

Johann Nickel Lin

Johan Jacob Ostwald

Wilhelm (×) Berkheiser

Jorg Fridrich Steidgener

Johan Jacob Strieby

Jacob (×) Martin

Johan Philippus Pick

Philip (×) Rice

Simon Reiss

Jacob (×) Rice

Henry (×) Aushenech

Johann Peter Dihm

Jacob (×) Schri

Simon (×) Drop

Adam (×) Labort

Wilhelm (×) Teasel

Johann Georg Betz

Johann Michael Hobbacher

Andreas (×) Cronovar

Nicholas (×) Mans

George (×) Somers

Adam Hoppacher

64

[Endorsed:]
Foreigners imported in the Ship Windsor, Capt. John Goad, from Rotterdam.

Qual. 27th Septr 1753.

64. Okill.

[List 206 C] At the Court House at Philadelphia, Thursday, the 27th September, 1753.

Present: William Peters, Esquire.

The Foreigners whose Names are underwritten, Imported in the Ship Windsor, Capt John Goad, from Rotterdam and last from Cowes in England, did this day take the usual qualifications. No. 64.

Joh. Jacob Boshart

Rudolf (×) Banninger

Marcus (+) Tomer

Johann Reinhart Batz

Johann Martin Riethmüller

Johoham Ludwig Beck

Felix Schneider

Martin Fazler

Christian Schober
Georg Stephanus Wallhauer
Johann Georg Mann
Sigmund Bondeli
Henrich Pfister
Johannes Gräber
Johan Yorch Schmidt
Henry (✕) Bouer
Christian Weiss
Daniel Speck
Johann Wilhelm Kromer
Reinhardt Diedtrich Kercher
Johann Ferdinand Lehrer
Johan Christoph Rein
Hans Jerg Lütz
Caspar Lütz
Johann Martin Truckenmüller
Hans Adam (✕) Shatzman
Heinrich Sättele
Samuel Sättle
Heinrich Gottfrid Murr
Johann Peter Horn
Christian Keller
Johann Joachim Jayser
Johann Jacob Friess
Johann Peter Grub
Johannes Thomas
Johan Petter Beltz

Georg Haff
Michel Milberger
George (✕) Mossbach
Johannes Kaumann
Johann Casper Dihl
Caspar (✕) Cabbas
Johann Nickel Lin
Johan Jacob Ostwald
Wilhelm (✕) Berckhäuser
Jerg Fridrich Steidgener
Johan Jacob Striby
J. Jacob (✕) Martin
Johan Philippus Pick
Philip (✕) Rice
Simon Reiss
Jacob (✕) Reice
Henry (✕✕) Eshrich
Johann Peter Dihm
Jacob (✕) Shrey
Simon Peter (✕) Strauch
Adam (✕) Lepart
J. Wilhelm (✕) Tistel
Johann Georg Betz
Johann Michael Hobba[ch]er
Andereas (✕) Grünau
Nicklas (✕) Mensh
J. George (✕✕) Summer
Adam Hoppacher

Septr 26, 1753.

Sir

According to directions we have carfully examined the State of Health of the Passengers on board the Ship Windsor Capt John Goad from Roterdam and found nothing amongst them which we think can be injurious to the Citizens.

To his Honour   Tho. Graeme
The Governour.   Th. Bond

[Endorsed:]

Doctors' Certificate relating to the Ship Windsor.
26th Septr 1753.

[List 207 A] A List of German Passengers, imported in the Ship Hallifax, Thomas Coatam, Mas^r, from Rotterdam, 28th Septr 1753.

	AGES		AGES
Fredrick Kunner	29	Mathias Zacharies	29
Johannes Kolle	25	Christian Panner	20
Henrick Dhenne	35	Johannes Paulus Wolff	24
Lodwick Luther	31	Johannes Henr^k Stoffle	23
Christopher Fredrick Mache	34	Johannes Harman Gebel	19
Christopher Getzelman	34	Johannes Jacob Rhine	20
Johannes Adam Zhür	33	Johannes Bock	24
Christian Heilman	44	Johannes Jerick Anacker	22
Peter Hann	23	Johannes Mich^l Kock	21
Jerick Mich^l Vaterman	20	Johannes Possart	19
Johannis Mich^l Moeherly	20	Johannes Wagener	20
Jerick Pattus Ungerer	22	Johannes Dan^{ll} Hugo	29
Andreas Seidler	29	Isace Puteman	23
Daniel Prenier	29	Daniel Repert	24
Johannis Adam Schmit	20	Lodwick Ester	27
Hennrick Merke	36	Johannes Casper Weitz	21
Daniel Auman	33	Andreas Heck	42
Andreas Staup	41	Johannes Christopher Schutz	32
Felix Gerber	26	Johannes Ernst Mumbauherr	28
Solomon Hartman	26	Joseph Schmit	23
Johann Schwedinger,*	50	Jacob Streter	30
Christian Henker	34	Ludwick Henrick Karchar	26
Jurs Conrad	37	Johannes Kepner	24
Michael Grosselous	21	Jacob Velter	23
Andreas Engold	21	Johannes Jerick Stecher	23
Johannes Kuntz	20	Johannes Conrad Ketz	18
Rudolph Myer	15	Johannes Henr^k Preasterin	21
Felix Miller	30	Johannes Henr^k Mauritz	38
Johannis Joseph Fishback	20	Godfrey Striete	27
Bernhard Schmitt	20	Conrad Putes	19
Johannis Paulus Veigant	20	Johannes Jacob Kriter	31
Daniel Zacharies	19	Johannes Jerick Kimorth	28
Johannis Ulrich Per	38	Johannes Jerick Prost	27
Graft Verber	32	Johannes Jerick Krauszkeep	25

* Name crossed out. Marked "Newlander."

	AGES		AGES
Johannes Haas	20	Johannes Jerick Bisoph	20
Johannes Jerick Pfhillips	29	Mathias Krambich	20
Johannes Peter Heun	25	Christian Rorhbach	24
Johannes Jerick Roan	28	Jerick Veriting	23
Lodwick Virtz	25	Adam Faeiz	30
Johannes Heinckle	29	Johannes Mich¹ Laup	20
Johannes Arnt Bate	28	Johannes Schwartz	21
Johannes Achenbach	21	Jacob Urban	28
Johannes Jost Schmit	21	Peter Katzenmyerer	26
Johannes Jerich Soneborn	30	Johannes Jerick Staup	18
Johannes Myer	37	Johannes Laup	18
David Deuber	30	Johannes Nicholas Burger	33
Johannes David Pistor	24	Codfery Kaarschnock	32
Jacob Ringolt	24	Casper Kock	32
Johannis Martin Myer	18	Johannes Adam Fersh	22
Johannis Heir	26	Adam Missach	—
Jacob Schaufberk	26	Johannes Theis	—
Nicholas Kriemer	27	Johan George Haney	—

[Endorsed:]
List of Foreigners imported in the Ship Halifax from Rotterdam.
   Qual. 28th Septr 1753.
      103.   Stedman.

[List 207 B] List of Foreigners imported in the Ship Halifax, Capt Thomas Coatam, from Rotterdam. Qualified 28th Septr 1753.

Frederich (O) Keener
Johannes (X) Kolle
Heinrich Thöner
Lodowick (X) Luther
Christopher Frederick (X) Mach
Christopher ( ) Getzelman, on
   board
Johannes Adam (X) Zhur
Christian Heillman
Johann Peter Haenn

Gorg Michael Vettermann
Georg Mächer Berk
Jorg Baldas Ungrer
Andreas (X) Seidler
Daniel (B) Prenier
Joh. Adam Mischt
Heinrich Merki
Daniel (X) Auman
Andreas (X) Staup
Felix Gerber

Salomon Hartman
V. Christen Höngärtner
Jurs (✕) Conrad
Michael (✕) Grosslous
Andreas (+) Engold
Johannes (✕) Kuntz
Rudolph (✕) Myer
Felix ( ) Miller, on board
Johannes Joseph (+) Fishbach
Bernhart Schmidt
Johannes Paul (+) Vigant
Daniel Zacharias
Johannes Ulrick (+) Per
Kraft Weber
Matheis Zacharis
Christian (✕) Panner
Johannes Paulus (✕) Wolf
Henry (✕) Stophel
Herrman Gebel
Jacob Rein
Johannes Buch
Johanes Georg Acker
Michael (✕) Kock
Johannes (H) Passar
Johannes Wagner
Johan Daniel Hugov
Isaac (✕) Pateman
Daniel (✕) Repart
Lodowick (✕) Ester
Johann Caspar Weiss
Andros Hackh
Erns ( ) Mumbauer, on board
Christopher (✕) Schmitt
Joseph Schmitt
Jacob Streder
Ludwig Henrich Karcher
Johannes Heppener
Johann Jacob Welter
Johann Georg Stöcker
Johann Henrich Präster
Johann Conrad Hess

Johann Henrich Moritz
Gottfried Streidtz
Johann Conrad Lies
Jacob ( ) Kriter, on board
Johann Geörg Himroth
Johann Görg Prost
Johann Görg Krausskob
Johannes Haas
Johan Georg Fillibs
Johann Peter Heun
Henrich Rohn
Lutwig Wirtz
Johannes Henckel
Johannes Arnt (✕) Bate
Johannes Achenbach
Johann Jost Schmidt
Johann Görg Sonneborn
Johannes Mayer
Johann David Deuber
David ( ) Piston, on board
Jacob Ringwald
Märten Mayer
Johannes Hoyr
Jacob ( ) Schaufbenk, on board
Nicolaus Kremer
George (✕) Bisoph
Mathias (✕) Kramlich
Christeyan Rohrbach
George (✕) Veriling
Adam Fayst
Michel Laub
Johannes ( ) Schwarz, on board
Jacob (✕) Urban
Peter (✕) Kazenmyrer
John George (✕) Steipe
Johannes Laub
Hans Nicklas Börger
Gottfried Körschnöck
Johan Caspar Koch

Johan Adam Forsch　　　Johann Georg Henney
Adam Milchsack　　　　　103
Johannes Theis

[Endorsed:]
List of Foreigners imported in the Ship Halifax from Rotterdam.
Qual. 28th Septr 1753.
　　103.　　　　　　　　　　　　Stedman.

[List 207 C] At the Court House at Philadelphia, Friday, the 28th of September, 1753.
　　　　Present: William Peters, Esquire.
The Foreigners whose Names are underwritten, Imported in the Ship Halifax, Capt. Thomas Coatam, from Rotterdam and last from Cowes in England, did this Day take and subscribe the usual Qualifications. No. 105.

Friederich (O) Keener
Johanes (X) Colle
Friedrich Thöner
Ludewig (+) Luther
C. Frederich (X) Moage
Christopher ( ) Getzelman, on board
Adam (X) Syrro
Christian Heillman
Jo. Pettder Hann
Gorg Michael Vettermann
Georg Michael Megert
Jerg Baldas Ungerer
Andereas (X) Seydlle
Daniel (B) Brenner
Johan Adam Misch[t]
Heinrich Merki
Daniel (X) Ammon
Anderes (X) Staub
Felix Gerber
Salomon Hartman
Christen Höngärtner
Jost (XX) Conrad

Michael (X) Grossclaus
Andereas (X) Ingan
Johanes (X) Kuhn
Jacob ( ) Meyer, on board
Rudolph (X) Meyer
Felix ( ) Miller, on board
Jost (+) Fishbach
Bernhart Schmid
Paulus (X) Weygant
Daniel Zacharis
Conrad (+) Bornn
Kraft Weber
Matheis Zacharis
Christian (X) Banner
Paulus (X) Wolffe
J. Henry (X) Stoffel
Herrmann Göbel
Jacob Rein
Johannes Buch
Johann Georg Acker
Hans Michael (X) Gock
Johanes (H) Bossert
Johannes Wagner

John Daniel Hugov
Isaac (×) Budeman
Tallyo (×) Repair
J. Ludwig (×) Hester
J. Caspar Weiss
Andros Hakh
Christoph (×) Shütz
Johanes ( ) Monnbouer, on board
Joseph Schmitt
Jacob Streder
Ludwig Henrich Karcher
Johannes Heppener
Johann Jacob Welter
Johann Georg Stöcker
Johanr Counrad Hess
Johann Henrich Moritz
Johann Henrich Präster
Gottfried Streidtz
Johann Konrad Belis
Jacob ( ) Kreyder, on board
Johann Georg Himroth
Johann Görg Prost
Johann Görg Krauskob
Johannes Haas
Johan Georg Füllibs
Johann Peter Heun
Henrich Rohn
Lutwig Wirtz
Johannes Henckel
John Adam (×) Bald

Johannes Achenbach
Johann Jost Schmidt
Johann Görg Sonneborn
Johannes Mayer
Johann David Deüber
Davit ( ) Bistol, on board
Jacob Ringwald
Marten Mayer
Johannis Heyr
Jacob ( ) Shouffbon, on board
Nicolaus Kremer
George (×) Bishoff
Matheas (×) Gromlich
Christeyan Rohrbach
Georg (×) Führling
Adam Fayss
Michel Laub
Johanes ( ) Shwartz, on board
Jacob (×) Urban
Peter (×) Katzenmeyer
J. George (+) Steyb
Johannes Laub
Hans Nicklas Börger
Gottfried Körschnöck
Johan Caspar Koch
Johan Adam Forsch
Adam Milchsack
Johannes Theis
Johann Georg Henny
103

[List 208 A] A List of Men aboard Ship Two Brothers, Thomas Arnot, Mas^r. [Qualified Septr 28th 1753.]

Joh. Fred^k Schie
Johannes Spudt
Matthias Dishon
Wilhelm Dishon
Frans Kleyn
Adolph Zimmerman

Conrad Lessing
Leonard Lessing
Joh. Jacob Hulpes
Joh. Hend^k Lutsch
Joh. Thys Schuts
Joh. Wm Schuts

Joh. Hend^k Heins
Frans Koch
Joh. Philip Heiman
Johan^s Wagoner
Joh. Martin Young
Joh. Peter Young
Joh^s Miller
Teobalt Bossong
Peter Stoube
Joh. Matthias Snyder
Christian Trefenstatt
Johannes Limp
Joh. Philip Kesselar
Joh. William Miller
Joh. Philip Dill
Adolph Kesselar
Johan^s Kuntz
Joh. Peter Soon
Joh. Adam Wirth
Joh. Adam Mier
Joh. Gerhardus Miller
Joh. Thys Seiss
William Dilbraner
Joh. Jurg Kigelar
Joh^s Cram
Joh. Nicho^s Arnholt
Joh. Jurg Folk
Joh. Jacob Severt
Joh. Adam Fatzer
Joh. Lenert Miller
Joh. Adam Colman
Jereminus Brunner
Joh. Adam Babst
Michael Hofman
Joh. Jacob Hering
Joh^s Snyder
Joh. Jurg Backholz
Joh. Peter Kock
Joh. Nicholas Lones
Joh. Jurg Wintter

Johannes Niedig
Stephan Peter
Joh. Adam Long
Joh. Jacob Eysenhimer
Joh. Wm Horstong
Joh. Hand^k Smous
Conrad Smous
Joh^s Smous
Matthias Nied
Joh. Adam Smith
Baltzer Gits
Joh. Adam Gits
Joh. Adam Swartz
Wm Schitz
Johs. Sack
Joh. Ludwick Schrick
Joh. Hend^k Ekil
Joh. Jurg Eckil
Israel Motsfel
Joh^s Peter Helt
Joh^s Wydman
Joh^s Philip Snyder
Joh^s Young
Joh. Jurg Beckholt
Johannes Beck
Conrad Philips
John Wm Shiver
Joh. Paul Scheffer
Frans Smith
Joh. Philip Kleyn
Joh. Chris Lupream
Joh^s Skie
Jacob Haan
Joh^s Riser
Joh^s Paule
Fred^k Croue
Valentine Weaver
Joh. Jacob Coll
Hannes Coll
Joh. Hend^k Hieman

Joh. Hend^k Saeynish John Georg Sivert
Fred^k Haman 96
Elias Conrad Stackman

[Endorsed:]
List of Foreigners imported in the Ship Two Brothers, Capt
Thomas Arnot, from Rotterdam.
Qual. 28th Septr 1753.
96. Shoemaker.

[List 208 B] Foreigners imported in the Ship Two Brothers,
Capt Thomas Arnot, from Rotterdam. Qualified 28th September 1753.

Johan Friedrich Schuy
Johannes Späth
Matthies Dischong
William (O) Dishon
Frantz Klein
Adolph (✕) Zimmerman
Conrad (✕) Lessing
Leonard (✕) Lessing
J. Jacob (✕) Helpes
Johan Henrich Lutsch
Johann Theis Schütz
J. William (+) Schutz
Johan Henrich Heinsman
Johann Frantz Koch
Johan Philipps Heyman
Johannes Wagener
Mardien Jung
Johann Peter Jung
Johannes Müller
Theobald (✕) Bossong
Peter Stauber
Johann Mahteis Schneider
Christian Treffenstätt
Johannes Limp
Johann Philip Kesseler
Johann Wilhelm Müller

Johann Philipp Dill
Johann Adolph Kesseler
Johannes Kurtz
Johann Petter Sohn
Johann Adam Wirth
Johann Adam Meyer
Johannes Gerhardus Müller
Johann Theis Füss
Wilhelm (+) Dilbraner
Johan Gurg Kichler
Johannes Gran
Johan Nichlaus Arnolt
John George (+) Folk
John Job (✕) Sivert
Johan Adam Pfitzer
Johann Leonhard Müller
John Adam (+) Coleman
Jeremiah (✕) Brunele
Johann Adam Pabst
Michael Hofman
Jacob Hering
Johannes Schneider
J. George (+) Backholt
Johan Peter Koch
Johan Nicklaus Lohnes
John George (+) Winther

Johannes (×) Neidig

Johann Stephan Dieter

J. Adam (×) Lang

J. Jacob (×) Eysenhamer

Johann Wilhelm Hardtstang

Henrich Schmaus

Conrad (×) Smous

Johannes Schmaus

Mathias Nied

Johann Adam Schmit

Johann Baltasser Götz

Johan Adam Götz

Johan Adam (+) Swartz

William (×) Schitz

Johannes Seck

John Ladarik (H) Schrack

J. Hendrick (H) Ekell

J. George (×) Ekel

Israel Motzfeld

Jannes Peter Helt

Johannes Weyttman

Johann Philipps Schneider

Johannes Jung

Johann Georg Bechtoldt

Johannes (×) Beck

Connrrath Phillibs

Johan Willem Schäffer

J. Paul (+) Scheffer

Fransiscus Schmidt

Johan Philipus Klein

Johann Christian Luprian

Johanes Schuy

Jacob (×) Haan

Johannes Peuser

Johannes (×) Paule

Friedrich Kroh

Johann Valentin Werber

Jacob Kohl

Hans (×) Coll

Johann Henrich Heyman

Joh. Henri. Saynisch

Frederick (×) Haman

Elias Conrath Stegmann

Johann Georg Sieffert

96

[Endorsed:]

List of Foreigners imported in the Ship Two Brothers, Capt Thomas Arnot, from Rotterdam.

Qual. 28th Septr 1753.

96.   Shoemaker.

[List 208 C] At the Court House at Philadelphia, Friday, the 28th September, 1753.

Present: William Peters, Esquire.

The Foreigners whose Names are underwritten, Imported in the Ship Two Brothers, Capt Thomas Arnot, from Rotterdam and last from Portsmouth in England, did this day take and subscribe the usual Qualifications. No. 96.

Johan Friedrich Schuy

Johannes Späth

Mattis Dischong

Wilhelm (O) Dichong

Frantz Klein

Adolph (×) Zimmerman

Conrad (+) Lützing
Leonhart (+) Lützing
Jo. Jacob (×) Helpfish
Johann Henrich Lütsch
Johann Theis Schütz
J. Wilhelm (+) Shütz
Johan Henrich Heinsman
Johann Frantz Koch
Johan Philipp Heyman
Johannes Wagener
Mardien Jung
Johann Peter Jung
Johannes Muller
Debalt (+) Bosseng
Peter Stauber
Johann Mahtheis Schneider
Christian Treffenstätt
Johannes Limp
Johann Philips Kesseler
Johann Wilhelm Müller
Johannes Philipp Dill
Johann Adolf Kesseler
Johannes Kurtz
Johann Petter Sohn
Johann Adam Wirth
Johann Adam Meyer
Johannes Gerhardus Müller
Johann Theis Füs
William (×) Tillboner
Johann Gurg Kichler
Johannes Gran
Johann Nichelaus Arnolt
J. George (×) Volck
J. Joachim (×) Seebert
Johan Adam Pfötzer
Johann Leonhart Müller
J. Adam (×) Kohlman
Hiroimus (×) Bruner
Johann Adam Pabst
Michael Hofman
Jacob Hering

Johannes Schneider
J. George (×) Bechtol
Johann Petter Koch
Johan Nicklaus Lohnes
J. George (×) Winter
Johanes (×) Neydig
Johann Stephan Dieter
J. Adam (×) Lang
J. Jacob (×) Eysenhawer
Johann Wilhelm Hardtstang
Henrich Schmaus
Conrad (×) Shmaus
Johannes Schmaus
Matthias Nied
Johann Adam Schmit
Johann Baltaser Götz
Johann Adam Götz
J. Adam (+) Shwartz
J. Willhelm (×) Shütz
Johannes Seck
J. Ludewig (++) Shork
J. Henry (H) Jäckel
J. George (×) Jäckel
Israel Motzfeld
Johannes Peter Helt
Johannes Weyttman
Johann Phillipps Schneider
Johannes Jung
Johann Georg Bechtold
Joseph (+) Beck
Conerath Phillibs
Johan Willem Schäffer
J. Paulus (×) Shäffer
Fransiscus Schmidt
Johan Philipus Klein
Johann Christian Luprian
Johannes Schuy
Jacob (+) Hann
Johannes Peuser
Johanes (×) Pauly
Friedrich Kroh

Johann Valentin Werber
Jacob Kohl
Johan (X) Kohl
Johann Henrich Heymann
Joh. Henri Saynisch

Friederich (X) Hamman
Elias Conrath Stegmann
Johann Georg Sieffert
96

Sir

Having in pursuance of Orders visited the Ship Two Brothers, Capt. Arnot, Master, freighted with Palatines from Roterdam and Gosport and find them in such good Order as that they may Enter the port without danger to the Inhabitants. Philad^{ia} Septr 29, 1753.

To his Honour the Governor

[Endorsed:]

Tho. Graeme
Th. Bond

Doctors Report on the Ship Two Brothers. 29th Septr 1753.

[List 209 A] A List of the Names of the Men & Boys above Sixteen Years of Age, Imported in the Ship or Snow, Called the Rowand, Arthur Tran, Master, from Rotterdam. Philad^{ia} Septr 29th 1753.

Philip Smith
George Stark
Christian Winebrenner
Daniel Flinter
Peter Wile
John Steven Gleckner
Christian Krebb
Matthias Krebb
William Young
Peter Myer
Philip Schmid
Philip Bosoner
Peter Baudenheimer
John Kres Kribly
John William Bamell
Peter Kelp
Martin Bugner
John Bugner
Henry Bugner
Christian Mann

Matthias Brand
Jonas Man
Ludowick Lupe
John Saring
Bernard Piper
Martin Hellsinheiser
Philip Folks
John Sailbach
Engle Strunck
Jacob Hass
Francis Zeiler
Conrad Becher
Henry Miller
Philip Seg
Henry Baumer
John Sailbach
Philip Steinbach
George Bare
Peter Shoemaker
George Hutt

David Kisler
Christian Blichenderfer
Jost Blichenstein
Jacob Lingenfeilder
Peter Ruch
Jacob Hass
Peter Miller
John Miller
John Hendrick
John Henry Greitz
Conrad Grau
John Christian Riebsomen
Mathias Hutzgen
John Gerhard Hummell
John Henry Held
Henry Held
John Engle Thomas
Adam Thomas Sterb
John George
George George
John Freind
George Kuertzer
Philip Bool
Jno. Christian Kens
Philip Speat
Henry Speat
Peter Kolb
Christian Kolb
Philip Schenman
Jacob Schuster
Bastian Haine
John Henry Schaffer
John Schaffer
John Bastian Weaver
John Keller

Jacob Behler
Matthias Lauer
Henry Lauer
Francis Cromm
John William Bechker
Henry Wisthafer
John Henry Kuneman
Matthias Kuneman
John Schaffer
John William Schaffer
Matthias Schmidt
John Henry Filger
Matthias Shitz
Martin Diehl
John Henry Stranck
Henry Kempf
John Kempf
John Kregilo
Christian Mann
Peter Lice
John Matthias Rubsan
Paulus Cramm
John Cramm
Christian Stall
Gerlock Stalb
Jno. Bastian Schneider
Andreas Eker
Matthias Zimmerman
Manuel Zimmerman
John Kreitz
John Henry Benix
John Peter Kramer
Engle Brown
John Peter Brown
109

[Endorsed:]
Foreigners imported in the Ship or Snow Rowand, Capt. Arthur Tran, from Rotterdam. Qual. 29th Septr 1753. 109. Mr Danl Benezet & Mic^l Agee.

[List 209 B] Foreigners imported in the Ship or Snow Rowand, Capt. Arthur Tran, from Rotterdam. Qual. 29th September, 1753.

Philippus Schmiedt
Johan Gorg Starck
Johann Christ Weinbrener
Daniel Flender
Johannes Petter Weyel
Johannes Steffan Klöckner
Christ Henrich Greb
Johann Deis Greb
Johannes Wilhelm Jung
Johann Peter Meyer
Johanes Phil. [Schmit]
Johannes Filibes Sommer
Johann Petr Badenhamer
Johan Kres (X) Kribly
Johann Wilhellem Böhmer
Johann Petter Kölb
Martin( ) Bugner, on board
Johann Martin Buchner
Johannes Buchner
Johann Henrich Buchner
Christian Mann
Johann Deis Brandt
Jonas Mann
Ludwig Lupp*
Johannes Zehrung
Bernhart Pfeiffer
Martin (+) Hillsinheiser
Johann Phillippus Foss
Johannes Selbach
Johan Engell Strunck
Johann Jacob Hass
Frantz Zeiller
Conrad Becker
Jost Henrich Möller
Johann Philibus Seyn

Johann Henrich Böhmer
John (X) Stehlbach
Johan Elias Steinbach
George (XX) Bare
Johann Peter Schumacher
George (X) Hutt
Davidt Giessler
Christian Blieckenstörffer
Jost Blickensterffer
Jacob Lingenfelter
Johann Peter Roch
George (X) Hass
Petter Müller
Johannes Müller
Johann Hinrich Creutz
Johan (+) Hendrick
Johann Konrath Gra[u]
Christian Rübsamen
Johann Theis Hüsgen
Gerhard (X) Hummell
J. Henry (X) Held
Johann Henrich Helt
Johann Engel Thomas
Johann Attam [Tho]mas
John (X) George
Johann Jorg Jorg
Johannes Freund
Johan Geörg Knörtzer
Philip (X) Bool
Johann Christ Bentz
Johannes Philippus Späth
Johannrich Späth
Peter Kolb
Christian Kolb
Philibus Schuman

* A Reformed minister. See Good, *History of the Reformed Church in the U. S., 1725–1792*, p. 646.

Jacob (×) Schutz
Johann Bastian Heun
Johan Henrich Schäffer
Johannes Gerlach Schäffer
Bastian (W) Weaver
Johannes Keller
Jacob (B) Bohler
Theis Lauer
Henrich Lauer
Johann Frantz Crum
Wilhelm Becker
Henry (+) Wisthafer
Johan Henrich Kühneman
Johan Theis Kühneman
Johannes Schäffer
Johan Wilhellm Schäffer
Johann Theis Schmit
Johann Henrich Felger
Matthias Schütz
Mardin Diel

Johann Henrich Strunck
Henry (H) Kempf
Johannes Kregeloh
Christian ( ) Mann, on board
Johan Peter Leis
Johann Theis Rübsamen
Paul ( ) Cramm, on board
Johannes Crum
Johann Christ Stahl
Johann Gerlach Stalp
Bastian (×) Schneider
Andreas (×) Eker
Mathias (×) Zimmerman
Hermannus Zimmerman
Johannes Creutz
Henry (×) Benix
Peter (×) Kramer
Johann Engel Braun
Johann Peter Braun
109

[Endorsed:]
Foreigners imported in the Ship or Snow Rowand, Capt.
Arthur Tran, from Rotterdam. Qual. 29th Septr 1753. 109.
Mr Danl Benezet & Michael Agee.

[List 209 C] At the Court House at Philadelphia, Saturday,
the 29 September, 1753.
                    Present: Joshua Maddox, Esquire.
   The Foreigners whose Names are underwritten, imported in
the Ship or Snow called the Rowand, Capt Arthur Tran, from
Rotterdam but last from Cowes in England, did this Day take
the usual Qualification. No. 109.

Philippus Schmiedt
Johan Goerg Starck
Johann Christ Weinbrenner
Daniel Flender
Johannes Petter Weyel
Johannes Steffan Klöckener

Christ Henrich Greb
Johann Deis Greb
Johannes Wilhelm Jung
Johan Peter Meyer
Johanes Fiel[ip]us Schmidt
Johann Philibus Sommer

Johann Peter Badenhaner
Johan Christian (×) Greebel
Johann Wilhellm Böhmer
Johann Petter Kölb
Johann Martin ( ) Buchner, on
    board
Johannes Buchner
Johann Henrich Buchner
Christian Mann
Johann Theis Brand
Jonas Mann
Ludwig Lupp
Johannes Zehring
Bernhart Pfeiffer
Martin (+) Helfeysen
Johann Phillippus Foss
Johannes Selbach
Johan Engell Strunck
Johann Jacob Hass
Frantz Zeiller
Conrad Becker
Jost Henrich Moller
Johann Phililip Seyn
Johann Henrich Böhmer
Johanes (×) Selbach
Johann Elias Steinbach
G. Peter (××) Bear
Johann Peter Schumacher
George (+) Hooter
Davidt Giessler
Christian Blickenstörffer
Jost Blickensterffer
Jost Blickersterffer
Johan Jacob Lingenfelter
Johann Peter Roch
Jacob (+) Heterig
Petter Miller
Johannes Miller
Johann Hinrich Creutz
Johanes (+) Hindert
Johann Konrath Gra[u]

Christian Rübsamen
Johann Theis Hisgen
Johan Gerhart (+) Humbel
Johan Henry (+) Held
Johann Henrich Helt
Johan Engel Thomas
Johan Attam [Tho]mas
Johanes (×) George
Johann Jorg Jorg
Johannes Freund
Johan Georg Knörtzer
Philips (+) Pool
Johann Christ. Bentz
Johannes Philippus Späth
Johan Henrich Späth
Peter Kolb
Johann Christ Kolb
Philibus Schuman
Jacob (×) Shütz
Johann Bastian Heun
Johann Henrich Schäffer
Johannes Gerlach Schäffer
Sebastian (W) Weber
Johannes Keller
Jacob (B) Böller
Theis (×) Lauer
Henrich Lauer
Johann Frantz Crum
Willem Becker
Henry (+) Wästenhaber
Johan Henrich Kühneman
Johan Theis Kühneman
Johannes Schäffer
Johan Wilhellm Schäffer
Johann Theis Schmit
Johann Henrich Filger
Matthias Schütz
Mardin Diel
Johann Henrich Strunck
Henry (H) Kämpffer
Johannes Kregeloh

Christian ( ) Mann, on board

Johan Peter Leis

Johann Theis Rübsamen

Paulus (O) Crum

Johannes Crumm

Johann Christ. Stahl

Johann Gerlach Stalp

Bastian (X) Shneyder

Andereas (XX) Ecker

Matheas (X) Zimmerman

Hermannus Zimmermann

Johannes Creutz

Henry (X) Panix

Johan Peter (X) Krammer

Johan Engel Braun

Johann Peter Braun

Septr 29th 1753.

Sir

According to directions we have carefully examin'd the State of Health of the Mariners and Passengers on board the Snow Rowan, Capt. Alterhand [!] from Roterdam and found nothing amongst them which we apprehend can be injurious to the Healths of the Inhabitants of the City.

To his Honour

The Governour.

Tho. Graeme

Th. Bond

[Endorsed:]

Doctors Report on the Ship Rowan, 29th Septr 1753.

[List 210 A] A List of Males Names Imported in the Snow Good Hope, John Trump, Mas^r, from Hamburg. Sep^t 29th 1753.

Friederick Reling

Henry Christophel Ring

Hans Henry Tutterberg

Jost Henry Seligman

Bearns Stunbear

Peter Knock

Henry Georg Baker

John Henry Klampert

Henry Neetrotock

Andreas Figener

John Peter Tippille

Henry Andreas Wiggman

John Sniber

Christophel Michael

Christoph Homes

Christophel Holborne

Henrich Lowman

Hans Chris. Ingel

John Henrick Naderman

Henry Christoph Diderick

Jacob Nicker

Hans Knieream

Henrick Sigher

Simon Shroader

Jeremiah Flug

Johan Andreas Foster

Christopher Pock

Elias Ouer

Johann Christoph Lemann

John Henderick Worm

Christian Konock

Hans Jockam Mesnar

Gotleap Wacker
John Arban Coulas
John Martin Winberg
Andreas Lowrence Acord
Conrod Hartman
Johan Christopher Momoyr
John Theodore Martine
Jost Carols Martine
Christopher Rineman
Simon Everley
Jacob Reman

Garet Harleman
Johan William River
Johan Christian Backman
Johan Laper
Johan Conrad Klitham
Johann Peter Pickner
Ernest Alborn
Johann Andreas Fredreas
Jorgan Herrich Durgess
53

[Endorsed:]
Foreigners imported in the Snow Good Hope, Capt. John Trump, from Hamburgh. Qual. 9th October 1753. N° 53. Greenway & Rundle.

[List 210 B] Foreigners Imported in the Snow Good Hope, Capt John Trump, from Hamburgh. Qualified the First of October, 1753.

Friederrich Reling
Johan Henrich Christophel Rücke
Hans Henry (+) Tutterberg
Jost Henry (×) Selegman
Joachim Behrnt Steinwehn
Peter (×) Knock
Henry Genger (×) Baker
John Henry (×) Klampert
Henry (+) Nederhood
Andreas Fygner
Johann Petter Dippel
Henry Andreas (+) Wiggman
Johan Erich Schneeberg
Christopher (+) Michael
Gristofel (+) Ohms
Christopher (+) Holborne
Johann Geörg Laumann
Hans Christoph Engel
Henry (×) Neiderman
Henrich Christoff Diedrich

Johann Jacob Niecke
Johannes (×) Knirem
Johan Heinrich Ziegeler
Simon (×) Shre[der]
Jeremiah (×) Flug
Johan Andreas Forster
Christopher (+) Poke
Elias (+) Auer
John Christopher (×) Leman
Henry (+) Worm
Christian (×) Kenich
Hans Joachim Meissner
Johann Gottlieb Wecker
Johann Urbahn Kaulitz
John Martin (+) Winberg
Andrew Lawrence (+) Ackman
Conrad Hartman
Johan Christoffel Mohmeyer
Johann Theodorus Martini
Justus Carl Wilhelm Martini

Christopher (+) Rineman
Christopher ( ) Kniple, on
   board
Simon Eberle
Jacob Rieman
Gerdt Hurrelman
Johann Wilhelm Röber
Johann Christian Bachmann

Jean Jaque Lapierre
Johann Conrad Kleikam
Johann Peter Pügner
Ernest (××) Alborn
Joannes Andreas Friderichs
Jüregen Henrich Dörges
53

Foreigners imported in the Snow Good Hope, Capt. John Trump, from Hamburgh. Qual. 1st October 1753. N° 53. Greenway & Rundle.

[List 210 C] At the State House at Philadelphia, Monday, the First Day of October, 1753.

Present: Septimus Robinson, Esquire.

The Foreigners whose Names are underwritten, imported in the Snow Good Hope, Capt. John Trump, from Hamburgh and last from Cowes in England, did this Day take the usual Qualifications. No 53.

Friederich Reling
Johan Henrich Christoph Rucke
Hans Henry (+) Steedeberger
J. Henry (+) Selligman
Joachim Behrnt Steinwehn
Peter (+) Knobe
H. George (×) Baker
J. Henry (×) Klapper
J. Henry (×) Nederhood
Andreas Fygner
Johann Peter Dippel
H. Adereas (×) Wigman
Johann Erich Schneeberg
Christoff (+) Michael
Christoffel Ohms
Christoffel (+) Ahllborn
Johann Georg Laumann
Hans Christoff Engel
J. Henry (×) Nederman
Henrich Christof Diedrich

Johann Jacob Niecke
Johanes (×) Knierimen
Johan Heinrich Ziegeler
Simon (+) Shröder
Jeremias (×) Pflug
Johann Andreas Forster
Christoffer (×) Pok
Elias (+) Awe
J. Christoff (×) Leman
J. Henry (×) Worm
Christian (×) König
Hans Joachim Meissner
Johann Gottlieb Wecker
Johann Urbahn Kaulitz
J. Martin (+) Weinberg
Andereas (×) Eckhart
Conrad Hartman
Johan Christoffel Mohmeyer
Johann Theodorus Martini
Justus Carl Wilhelm Martini

Christoffel (×) Reinman
Christoffel (   ) Kneply, sick on
    board
Simon Eberle
Jacob Riemann
Gerdt Hurrelman
Johann Wilhelm Röber

Johann Christian Bachman
Jean Jaque Lapierre
Johann Conrad Kleikam
Johan Peter Pügner
Carol (++) Ahlborn
Joannes Andreas Friderichs
Jürgen Henrich Dörges

Septr 29, 1753.

Sir

According to directions we have carefully examined the State of Health of the Mariners and Passengers on board the Snow Good-Hope, Capt Trump, from Hamburgh, and found several of them ill with Scurvies, but no Disease which we apprehend can communicate an Infection to the Inhabitants of the City.

To his Honour   Tho. Graeme
The Governour.   Th. Bond

[Endorsed:]

Doctors Report on the Snow Good Hope, 29th Septr 1753.

[List 211 A] List of People Names & Ages on Board the Ship Edinburgh, Capt John Lion, from Rotterdam. Arrived at Philadelphia, October 2^d 1753.

	AGES		AGES
Christoph Hering	25	Philip Valentin Knefely	16
Conrad Scherrer	18	Philip Wagner	44
Joh. Engel Young	40	John Solomon Finn	24
John Henrich Knoth	32	Gottfried Krum	33
John Henrich Massing	19	John George Miller	37
Henrich Otto	20	Nicolaus Gerlach	26
Friederich Kehler	33	Urban Schettel	30
Johanes Philip Sneiter	22	John Petter Baltof	27
Friederick Behmer	22	Johannes Heith	32
Johanes Wilhelm Haeffer	36	Friederich Loesser	23
John Dennis	48	Andreas Erdman Leynaw	29
Jost Henrich Weyershausen	23	Henrich Kimber	20
Johannes Ruhtrauff	22	Anthon Reish	27
Johannes Friederich Scholl	21	Wilhelm Ehel	20
Gott. Fried. Hehller	20	Christian Detter	49
William Cassel	30	John Wilhelm Stoehr	38

	AGES		AGES
Johannes Henrich Cronraw	37	John Gerlach Mutterspach	24
Conrad Sneiter	25	Anthon Klekner	30
Johannes Preisser	22	Wilhelm Stumpff	28
John George Loss	38	Christoph Hubner	26
Anthonius Haffercam	22	Johannes Heinrich Steinsay-	
Friederich Schnuk	24	fer	28
Jacob Katz	22	John George Reichel	32
John Daniel Rubert	23	Johannes Rein Shmit	25
John Henrich Heinse	19	John Daniel Schlapig	29
Christian Yauch	23	Jerg Scheffer	22
Johannes Henrich Kuntz	19	John Petter Mayer	25
Jacob Loss	24	Conrad Ohrendorff	30
John Philip Kebeel	30	Wilhelm Woolenweber	30
John Petter Laehr	29	Joh. Christ Smit	47
John Jacob Schweitzer	22	John Georg Waller	26
John Joachim Wiesser	23	John Wilhelm Waller	20
Jacob Hoffman	20	Michael Tasch	43
John Georg Sneiter	30	Anthon Krum	40
Adam Nicodemus	30	Hieronimus Sneiter	34
John Adam Krum	19	Ernst Ludwig Krauss	43
Michael Faust	34	Johannes Sneiter	22
John Jost Rostdorff	25	Johannes Petter Stoltz	20
John Ludwig Schweitzer	38	John Heinrich Stoltz	49
John Baltzer Dickert	19	Johannes Kegenlo	35
Joh. Gerlach Bournheker	29	John Petter Kirchhoffer	28
John Anthon Houn	19	John Wilhelm Wiesser	43
Wilhelm Buhll	23	John Georg Sneiter	30
John Georg Stahlsmit	35	John Gerlach Wiesser	24
Joh. Daniel Mauenshagen	30	John Conrad Smit	18
John Friederich Weitzel	18	Johannes Petter Ohrendorff	19
Philip Heinrich Ahrendorff	38	John Heinrich Young	48
Andreas Sneiter	18	John Jost Schlapig	33
Johannes Aurant	28	Johannes Muller	23
John George Schwartz	48	Ernst Christian Miller	21
Hen. Godfried Till	24	Jacob Nickel	30
John Gerlach Klin	35	Johannes Grave	
Johannes Jungst	34		

[Endorsed:]

Foreigners imported in the Ship Edinburgh, Capt. John

Lyon from Rotterdam. Qual. 2ᵈ October, 1753. No. 104.

Keppelee.

[List 211 B] Foreigners imported in the Ship Edinburgh, Capᵗ John Lyon, from Rotterdam. Qual. 2ᵈ October, 1753.

Johann Jörg Christoffel Hering
Johann Conradt Scherer
Johann Engel Jung
Johann Henrich Knodh
Johan Henrich Messing
Johann Henrich Otto
Friedrich Köhler
Johannes Philipp Schneider
Fridrich Böomer
Johannes Wilhelm Höffer
Johannes Denig
Jost Hennrich Weyershaussen
Johannes Rudrauff
Johannes Friedrich Scholl
Johann Gottfried Höhler
Wilhelm Casseler
Philipp Valentin Knefeli
Philip (+) Wagner *
Johann Salomon Fenn
Gottfried (K) Krum
Johan Gorg Müller
Nicklaus Gerlach
Urbann Schäddell
Johan Peter Balduf
Johannes Heyl
Frederick (F) Loesser
Andreas Erdman Leinau
Henry (+) Kimber
Anthon Reusch
Johann Wilhelm Aahl
Christian (✕✕✕) Detter
Johann Wilhelm Sterr

Johannes Henry (   ) Cronraw, on board
Johann Conrad Schneider
Johannes Preuscher
Johan Jorg Loos
Anthon Hafferkam
Freiderich Schnug
Johann Jacob Katz
Johann Daniel Ruppertt
Johannes Henrich Kuntz
Christian Jauch
Johann Hennrich Heintz
Jacob Loos
Johann Philibbus Köbel
John Peter (✕) Laehr
Johannes Jacob Schweitzer
John Joachim (+) Wieser
Johan Jacob Hoffman
Johann Jorg Schneider
Johann Adam Nicodemus
Johann Adam Krum
Michel Faust
John Jost (✕) Rosdorff
Johannes Ludwig Schweitzer
Johann Baltsar Dicker
Johann Gerlach Bornhütter
Johann Anthonius Huhn
Johann Wilhelm Buhl
John George (✕✕) Stahlsmit
John Daniel (+) Mauenshag
Johann Friederich Weitzell
Philip Henrich Arndorff

* The father of the Reformed minister, the Rev. John Daniel Wagner.

Andreas Schneyder
Johannes Aurandt *
George (×) Schwarts
Henrich Gottfried Thiel
Johann Gerlach Klein
Johannes Jüngst
Johann Gerlach Muttersbach
Andon Klöckener
Johannes Wilhelm Stumpf
Christophell Hübener
Johannes Henrich Steinseiffer
Johann Jörg Reichel
Johannes Reinschmit
Danniel Schlappig
George (×××) Scheffer
John Peter (×) Myer
Johann Conrad Orndorff
Johann Wülhelm Wullenweber
Christian (×) Smith
Johann Geörg Wäller
Johann Wilhelm Weller

Michael (×) Tarsh
Anthon Krum
Hieronymus Schneider
Ernst Lutwig Krauss
Johannes (×) Schneider
Johannes Peter Stoltz
Johan Henrich Stoltz
Johannes Kregelo
John Peter (×) Kirchhoffer
John William (×) Wieser
Johan Görg Schneider
John Gerlach (×) Wieser
John Conrad ( ) Smith, on
board
Johannes Peter Orndorff
Johan Henrich Jung
Johann Jost Schlappig
Johannes Müller
Christian Müller
Johann Jacob Nickel
Jòhannes (×) Grave

[Endorsed:]
Foreigners imported in the Ship Edinburgh, Capt John Lyon,
from Rotterdam. Qual. 2d October 1753. No. 104.

Keppelee.

[List 211 C] At the State House at Philadelphia, Tuesday,
the Second Day of October, 1753.
Present: William Peters, Esquire.
The Foreigners whose Names are underwritten, imported
in the Ship Edinburgh, Capt. John Lyon, from Rotterdam but
last from Cowes, did this Day take the usual Qualifications. 104.

Johann Jörg Christoffel Hering
Johann Conradt Scherer
Johann Engl Jung

Johann Henrich Knodt
Johan Henrich Messing
Johann Henrich Otto

* The father of the Reformed minister, the Rev. John Dietrich Aurandt. See
Harbaugh, *Fathers of the Reformed Church*, III, p. 180.

Friederich Köhler
Johannes Philp Schneider
Friderich Böomer
Johannes Wilhelm Höffer
Johannes Denig
Jost Hennrich Weyershaussen
Johannes Rudrauff
Johannes Friedrich Scholl
Johann Gottfried Höhler
Wilhelm Cassler
Philipp Valentin Knefeli
Philip (X) Wagner
Johann Salomon Fenn
Godfried (K) Krum
Johann Gorg Müller
Niclaus Gerlach
Urbann Schäddell
Johan Peter Balduf
Johannes Heyl
J. George Friederich (X) Löser
Andreas Erdman Leinau
Henry (X) Gimper
Anthohn Reusch
Johann Wilhelm Aahl
Christian (XXX) Dötter
Johann Wilhelm Sterr
J. Henry ( ) Cronro, on board
Johann Conrad Schneider
Johannes Preuscher
Johann Jörg Loos
Anthon Haferkam
Friedrich Schnug
Johann Jacob Katz
Johann Daniel Ruppertt
Johannes Henrich Kuntz
Christian Jauch
Johann Hennrich Heintz
Jacob Loos
Johann Philibbus Köbel
J. Peter (X) Lehr
Johannes Jacob Schweitzer

J. Jacob (X) Wiesser
Johan Jacob Hoffman
Johann Jörg Schneider
Johann Adam Nicodemus
Johann Adam Krum
Michel Faust
J. George (X) Rosdorff
Johannes Ludwig Schweitzer
Johann Baltzer Dücker
Johann Gerlach Bornhütter
Johann Anthonius Hun
Johann Wilhelm Buhl
Johan George (++) Staall
J. Daniel (XX) Mauershagen
Johann Friederich Weitzell
Philip Henrich Arndorff
Andres Schneyder
Johannes Aurandt
Johan George (X) Shwartz
Henrich Gottfried Thiel
Johann Gerlach Klein
Johannes Jüngst
Johann Gerlach Muttersbach
Andon Klöckener
Johann Wilhelm Stumpf
Christophel Hubener
Johannes Henrich Steinseiffer
Johann Jörg Reichel
Johannes Reinschmit
Danniel Schlappig
George (XXX) Shäffer
J. Peter (XX) Meyer
Johann Conrad Orndorff
Johan Wilhelm Wullenweber
J. Christian (+) Shmit
Johann Geörg Wäller
Johann Wilhelm Weller
Michael (X) Tasch
Anthon Krum
Hironymus Schneider
Ernst Lutwig Krauss

Johanes (✕) Shneider
Johannes Peter Stoltz
Johan Henrich Stoltz
Johannes Kregelo
J. Peter (✕) Kirchhöffer
J. Wilhelm (✕) Wisser
Johann Görg Schneider
J. Gerlach (✕) Wisser
J. Conrad ( ) Shmit, on board

Johannes Peter Orndorff
Johan Henrich Jung
Johann Jost Schlappig
Johannes Müller
Christgan Müller
Johann Jacob Nickel
Johannes (✕) Gräff
104

Sir

Having in pursuance to Orders Visited the Ship Edinburgh, Capt. Lyon, Master, freighted with Palatines, from Rotterdam and Cowes and find no objection to their entering the port, with any danger to the Inhabitants.

Philad^{ia} Octr 1, 1753.　　　　　　　　Tho. Graeme
To His Honour the Governor.　　　　　　Phineas Bond
[Endorsed:]
Doctors Report on the Ship Edinburgh, 1st October, 1753.

[List 212 A] List of Mens Names and Ages Imported in the Louisa, Capt John Pitcarne, from Rotterdam and Cowes, the 3^d October 1753.

	AGES		AGES
Conradt Riel	40	Wilhelm Hart	18
Benedict Nitlinger	24	John Yerrick Grub	19
Philip Fanel	38	Christian Weber	27
Baltzer Forthback	30	Peter Statil	29
Ernst Jacobie	22	Andreas Kratz	40
Mathias Becker	27	John Philip Zinlaub	32
Adam Datz	21	Carl Phileply	27
Sebastian Datz	19	Johannes Preys	33
Gerrit Bulman	22	John Albright Mowrer	24
Philip See	27	Hans Yerrick Jantz	27
Philip Kleyn	22	Conradt Strot	30
Joh. Yerrick Henners	..	Christian Shew	27
John Peter Speelman	27	Hendrick Smith	29
Johannes Fries	31	Philip Zinlaub	22
Christian Lauer	27	Yerrick Adam Mantel	24
Wilhelm Ruke	24	Christian Mantel	27

	AGES		AGES
Fredrick Heyer	27	Peter Nichol	21
Jacob Neyman	21	Lutherus Righart	27
Conradt Kebling	24	Peter Smith	27
Lodwich Sinser	27	Henrick Fleck	22
Yerrick Brown	22	Philips Fredrick Warth	27
Stephen Riel	27	Yerrick Fredrick Browback	22
Yerrick Wilhelm Baker	24	Carrel Emmerick	27
John Christian Schyber	25	Jacob Neyendorph	22
John Hendrick Weymaer	24	Hendrick Sebergen	21
John Peter Grub	27	Philip Brenly	27
Fredrick Turk	29	Peter Glaucher	
Johannes Muller	27	Andreas Leister	
Philipus Wax	24	Achilles Raugh	
Philipus Haterigh	27	Daniel Zinlaub	
Yerrick Philip Conteron	28	Johannes Glaucher	
Hendrick Smith	24	John Wilhelm Philpel	
Herman Emerick	27	Joseph Guyer	
Johannes Bowman	24	Conrad Speelman	
Diedrick Tran	27	Carl Fehrley	
Johannes Keep	24	Frederick Zinlaub	
Michael Miller	27	Hans George Price	
Hans Casper Biderman	24	Johan George Hoffman	
Peter Mowrer	27	77	
John Yerrick Hasselberger	22		

[Endorsed:]

Foreigners imported on Ship Louisa, Capt. John Pitcarne, from Rotterdam. Qual. 3ᵈ October, 1753. Nº 77.

Stedman.

[List 212 B] Foreigners imported in the Ship Louisa, Capᵗ John Pitcarne, from Rotterdam. Qual. 3ᵈ October, 1753.

Conrad Rühl
Benedictus Neidlinger
Johan Philipp Fahnel
Balthaser Vorbach
Ernst Jakoby
Mathias Becker
Johan Adam Datz

Johan Better Datz
Gerhard Buhlman
Philippus Zeh
Philip (+) Kleyn
Johann Georg Hemmersbach
Johann Peter Spielmann
Johannes Preys

Johann Christian Lauer
Johan Wilhelm Rück
Jeorg Wielelm Hard
Johann Gorg Grub
Christgan Wever
Johan Peter Stadel
Andreas Kratz
Johan Philip [?] Zenlaub
Johan Carle Völbel
Johannes Fuess
Johann Albert Maurer
Hans George (+++) Jantze
Johan Chonrath Strott
Christophel Schöpf
Johann Henrich Schmit
Johan Philp Zumlaube
Georg Adam Mandel
Johann Christian Mandel
Frederick (XX) Heyer
Johann Jacob Neumann
Conradt Köberling
Johann L. Waisser
Johan Georg Braun
Stephen (+) Riel
Heinck Wilhelm Becker
Johann Christian Schreiber
J. Hendrick (+) Weymayer
Johann Peter Grub
Friedrich Dürck
Johannes Müller
Johann Philipus Wachs
Philip Hetrick

Görg Lips Gunderum
Henrich Schmitt
Herman Emrich
Johannes Bauman
Detrich (X) Tran
Johannes Kipp
Hans Michael Muller
Hans Casp. Biderman
Peter Maurer
Johann Görg Hasselbächer
Johan Peter Nickel
Lotharius Richard
Johann Peter Schmitt
Henry (X) Fleck
Philipp Fridrich Warth
Georg Friderich Brodbäck
Carl ( ) Emerick, on board
Jacob Neuendorf
Johann Henrich Seeberger
Philipp Brendtle
Michael Plocher
Andreas Heister
Achilles Rau
Johan Gorg Zenlaub
Johannes (X) Glaucher
Johann Wilhelm Völbel
Joseph (X) Guyger
Conrad (X) Speelman
Carl (X) Fehrley
Frederick (X) Zinlaub
Hans George (X) Price
77

[Endorsed:]
List of Foreigners imported in the Ship Louisa, Capt John Pitcarne, from Rotterdam. Qual. 3^d October, 1753. N° 77.
Stedman.

[List 212 C] At the Court House at Philadelphia, Wednesday, the Third Day of October, 1753.
Present: Joshua Maddox, Esquire.

The Foreigners whose Names are underwritten, imported in the Ship Louisa, Capt. John Pitcarne from Rotterdam and last from Cowes, did this day take the usual Qualification.

Conrad Rühl
Benedictus Neidlinger
Johan Philipp Fehnel
Balthaser Vorbach
Ernst Jacoby
Mathias Becker
Philip (X) Klein
Johan Adam Datz
Johann Beter Datz
Gerhard Buhlman
Philippus Zeh
Johann Georg Hemmersbach
Johann Peter Spielmann
Johannes Pryss
Johann Christian Lauer
Johann Wilhelm Rück
Georg Wielelm Hard
Johan Gorg Grub
Christgan Wever
Johann Peter Stadel
Andreas Kratz
Johann Philip Zenlaub
Johan Carle Völbel
Johannes Fuoss
Johann Albert Maurer
Hans George (X) Jansy
Johan Konrath Strott
Christophel Schöpf
Johann Henrich Schmit
Johan Philb Zumlaub
Georg Adam Ma[n]del
Johann Christian Mandel
Friederick (XX) Heyer
Johann Jacob Neumann
Conradt Köberling
Johann L. Waisser

Johann Georg Braun
Stephan (X) Reel
Henich Wilhelm Becker
Johann Christian Schreiber
J. Henry (X) Wemeyer
Johann Peter Grub
Friedrich Dürck
Johannes Müller
Johann Philippus Wachs
Philip Hetrick
Jörg Lips Gunderum
Henrich Schmitt
Herman Emrich
Johannes Bauman
Peter (X) Tran
Johannes Kipp
Hans Michel Muller
Hans Casp. Biderman
Peter Mauer
Johann Görg Hasselbächer
Johann Peter Nickel
Lotharius Richard
Johan Peter Schmit
Henry (X) Fleck
Philipp Friderich Warth
Georg Friderich Brodbäck
Carol ( ) Emrick, on board
Jacob Neuendorff
Johann Henrich Seeberger
Phillipp Brendtle
Michael Plocher
Andreas Heister
Achilles Rau
Johan Gorg Zenlaub
Johanes (X) Blocher
Johann (X) Wilhelm Völbel

Joseph (×) Geyger
Conrad (×) Spielman
Caral (×) Veny

Frederik (×) Zillow
Hans George (×) Preice

[List 213 A] List of Men Passengers on board the Ship Eastern Branch, James Nevin, Mas^r, from Rotterdam & Portsm^o. [Qualified October 3, 1753.]

Johannes Doet
Step^n Ley
Michael Ruller
Fredrick Bleigh
Joh. Martin Egely
Samuel Bestner
Joh. Martin Fonau
Sebastian Steiger
Andreas Lohrman
Andreas Lohrman, Junr
Christ^n Courfas
Johan David Fees
Johan Martin Keelman
Hans Ulrich Boner
Hans Michal Hitterer
Hans Hitterer
Hans Conrad Fouser
George Willm Slatterer
Christ^n Ney
Henrich Leynart
Chris^t Fredrick Spiegel
Michal Ludwig Keyder
Johan Jacob Smith
Jurg Philip Feyersteyn
Hans Michal Schenick
Hans Jurg Wolff
Sebastian Shaber
Casper Hop
Johannes Hop
Johan Henr. Craus
Ulrich Spierly

Johannes Leeps
Jacob Anthony
Joh. Jurg Firk
Johan Jacob Remp
Johannes Linder
Peter Belfinger
Jacob Snyder
Johan Philip Volgelgesang
Johannes Sherney
Joh. Jurg Christian
Ludwig Christian
Johan Jurg Beck
Johan Philip Kleyn
Jacob Mosletts
Lorentz Zeekrits
Fredrick Faxis
Matthys Stoll
Fredrick Sheefer
Peter Kees
Michal Herreman
Tobias Wandel
Bernard Swaal,* Newlander
Christof^r Wolfell
Michal Brobeck
Jurg Iseman
Wilhelm Decker
Joh. Ludwig Steller
Johan^s Derflinger
Nicholas Seytz
Daniel Parisum
Johan Fred^k Glasser

* Name crossed out.

Johannes Glasser
Adam Dornberger
Jacob Weyninger
Hans Jurg Heyselman
Henry Stultzell
Casper Greyser
Conrad Harr
Michal Basseler
Philip Daniel Gros
Johannes Runner
Andreas Schnabbel
Michal Vogel
Fredrick Teck

Joseph Hannekam
Peter Lorrie
Andreas Teck
Joseph Crispin
Jacob Smotska
Hans Jurg Schenk
Jacob Schenk
Henry Fredrich
Joh. Jurg Michael
Joh. Conrad Gersler
Joh. Conrad Ludwig
Jost Peter
86

[Endorsed:]
Foreigners imported in the Ship Eastern Branch, Capt James Nevin, from Rotterdam and last From Portsmouth. Qual. 3^d October, 1753. N° 86.

Shoemaker.

[List 213 B] Foreigners imported in the Ship Eastern Branch, Capt. James Nevin, from Rotterdam. Qual. 3^d October, 1753.

Johannes Dütt
Stephan Ley
Johan Michael Röller
J. Frederick (×) Bleigh
Joh. Marttin Egle
Samuel Bezner
J. Martin (+) Fonau
Sebastian Staiger
Johann Andreas Lohrman
Johann Andreas Lohrman
Christoph Kurfes
Johan David Fiess
Johann Martin Kielman
Hans Ulrich Stohoner
Hans Michel Ketterer
Johan Carl Ketterer
Hans Conrad (+) Fouser

Georg Wilhelm Schlatterer
Christ Neues, Senr
Henrich Leiner
Christoph Fridrich Spiegel
Michel Ludwig Keitter
Jacob Schmidt
Georg Philipp Feuerstein
Johann Michel Schöneckh
Hans Jorg Wolf
Sebastian Schaber
Johann Caspar Hopf
Johannes Hopf
Johann Henrich Krauss
Ulrich Stierlein
Johannes Löbs
Jacob Anthoni
Johann Georg Förg

Johan Jacob Reineb
Johannes Linte[r]
Peter Bilfinger
Jacob Schneider
Johann Philipp Vogelgesang
Johannes (+) Sherney
Johan Jerg Christian
Lodowick ( ) Christian, on board
Johan Georg Beck
J. Philip (+) Kleyn
Gottfried Muschlitz
Johann Lorentz Siegrist
Georg Friederich Täxis
Mathias (×) Stoll
Fried^er Schäffer
Peter Kees
Michel Hörmann
Tobias Wandel
Christof Wölfle
Johan Michel Brodbeck
Georg Eysemann
Willhelm Decker
Johann Ludwich Heller
Johannes Dörflinger
Johann Nicklaus Zeitz
Daniel Parisien
Friederich Glasser

Johann Johanes Glasser
Adam Dornberger
Jacob Weininger
Hans Jerg Heintzelmann
Henrich Steltzel
Casper (O) Greyser
Conradt Harr
Michael (+) Bosler
Philips Daniell Gross
Johannes (×) Runner
Andreas (×) Schnabel
Michael (++) Vogel
Friedrich Deeg
Joseph (++) Hannekam
Johann Peter Lorie
Andreas Deg
Joseph (××) Crispin
Jacob (××) Smotska
Hans Gorg Schenck
Jacob Fridrich Schenck
Heinrich Fridrich
Hans George ( ) Michael, on board
Johann Conrad Giessler
Johann Conradt Ludwig
Jost Petter
86

[List 213 C] At the Court House at Philadelphia, Wednesday, the Third Day of October, 1753.
      Present: William Peters, Esquire.
   The Foreigners whose names are underwritten imported in the Ship Eastern Branch, Capt. James Nevin, Master, from Rotterdam and last from Portsmouth, did this day take the usual Qualifications to the Government.

Johannes Dütt
Stephan Ley
Johan Michael Röller
Johan Friederich (×) Bleich

Joh. Marttin Egle
Samuel Bezner
J. Martin (+) Fanaw
Sebastian Staiger

Johann Andreas Lohrman
Johann Andreas Lohrman
Christoph Curfes
Johan David Fiess
Johann Martin Kielman
Hans Ullrich Stohoner
Hans Michel Ketterer
Johan Carl Ketterer
Conrad (X) Fausser
Georg Wilhelm Schlatterer
Christ Neues, Senr
Henrich Leiner
Christoph Friedrich Spiegel
Michel Ludwig Keitter
Jacob Schmidt
Georg Philipp Feuerstein
Johann Michal Schöneck
Hans Jerg Wolf
Sebastian Schaber
Johann Caspar Hopf
Johannes Hopf
Johann Henrich Krauss
Ulrich Stierlein
Johannes Löbs
Jacob Anthoni
Johann Georg Förch
Johan Jacob Reinib
Johannes Linte[r]
Peter Bilfinger
Jacob Schneider
Johann Philipp Vogelgesang
Johanes (+) Chirny
Johann Gerg Christian
Ludewig ( ) Christian, on board
Johan Georg Beck
Hans Philip (+) Klein
Gottfrid Muschiltz
Johann Lorentz Siegrist
Georg Friederich Täxis
Matheas (X) Stoll
Fried^r Schäffer

Peter Kees
Michel Hörmann
Tobias Wandel
Christof Wölffle
Johan Michel Brodbeck
Georg Eysemann
Willhelm Decker
Johann Ludwig Heller
Johannes Dörflinger, in Blonnd-
  loch
Johann Nicklaus Zeitz
Daniel Parisien
Friederich Glasser
Johan Johanes Glasser
Adam Dornberger
Jacob Weiniger
Hans Jerg Heintzelman
Henrich Steltzel
Caspar (O) Kreiter
Michael (X) Basseler
Conradt Harr
Philips Daniell Gross
Johanes (++) Ronner
Andereas (+) Shnabel
Michael (++) Vogel
Friedrich Deeg
Joseph (XX) Haanecam
Johann Petter Lorie
Andreas Deg
Joseph (XX) Crissby
Jacob (XX) Shmertzka
Hans Jerg Schenck
Jacob Fridrich Schenck
Heinrich Fridrich
Johann Conrad Giessler
Hans George ( ) Michael, on
  board
Johann Conradt Ludewig
Jost Petter
    86 [men].

[List 214 A] A List of the Passengers Imported in the Ship Friendship, Capt James Seix, from Hambro [Hamburg] into Philadelphia, November 19, 1753.

	AGES		AGES
John Beltz	19	Henr. Jac. Nolte	30
Godfrid Neve	25	Jn° Henry Commellder	32
Jn° Dabel	20	Jn° Died^k Havenshildt	38
Henry Sneider	29	Jn° Henry Bohrmister	44
George Kneiling	30	Henry Chr^s Delcamp	37
Frederick Franciscus Corsenez	17	Conr^d Auhauge	43
Henry Lutterman	25	Adn^s Segenitz	43
Jn. Frederick Langrave	40	Henry Ulr. Rissell	44
Chris^t Wachtler	32	Chr. Mathieson	19
Valentine Rehling	36	Jn° Fred^k Beltz	44
Jn° Folkes	38	Andreas Henry Lange	37
Christⁿ Auhauge	20	Jn° D. Mohle	24
Jn° Hin. Raventlau	20	Hartman Emmell	38
Gotfred Foster	29	John Henry Saman	
Gotfried Leman	34	John Henry Folke	
Fred^k M. Lorensen	21	John Henry Pott	
Conr^d H. Jorns	42	Lawrence Berkley	
Jn° And. Klein	28	Andrew Gerlach	
Jn° Geo. Gantler	35	Adam Stein	
Jn° Chr. Seise	40	Seven sick on board whose Names	
Jacob Bremen	24	are not in this List.	
Jn° Peter Smidt	30	N° 49	
And^s. Blitz	22		

[Endorsed:]
List of Foreigners imported in the Ship Friendship, James Seix, Master, from Hamburgh. Qual. 19th Novr 1753.

C. Willing.

[List 214 B] Foreigners imported in the Ship Friendship, James Seix, Master, from Hamburgh. Qual. 19th November, 1753.

Johann Peltz	George (×) Knaeling
Godfried Nebe	Johann Friedrich Franciscus Cor-
Johan (×) Dabel	sini
Joh. Heinrich Schneider	Christian Hinrich Luttermann

Johan Friederich Landgraff
Christoph Wächtler
Vallendin Reyling
Johan Volcks
Christofel Auhagen
Johann Hinrich Reventlau
Godfridt (++) Forstler
Godfridt (×) Lehman
F. Michael (+) Lorentz
Konradt Heinrich Jorens
Johan Antreas Klein
Johann Jörge Gärtler
Johan Christian Zeise
Jacob Brämer
Johan Peter (++) Shmit
Andreas Blätz
Henry Jacob (++) Noll
Johan Hendrik Comülder
Johan Daniel Haunschilnt

Johan Heinrich Baurmeister
Hinrich Christoph Delckamp
Conrad (+) Ohr
Andreas Siegenitz
Henry Ulrich (×) Rissel
Christopher Matthesen
Johan Friedrich Pelss
Andreas Henrich Langen
Johan (++) Mohl
Johann Hartmann Emmel
Johann Hinrich Sammann
Johann Lorentz Vogel
Johann Heinrich Pott, Cand. Jur.
Lorentz Bürckle
Andreas Gerlach
Adam Stein
Seven sick on board whose Names
are not in the List.
No. 49

[Endorsed:]
List of Foreigners imported in the Ship Friendship, James
Seix, Master, from Hamburgh. Qual. Novr 20th 1753.

[List 214 C] At the Court House at Philadelphia, Monday,
the 19th November, 1753.
Present: Charles Willing ⎱ Esquires
John Mifflin ⎰
The Foreigners whose Names are underwritten, Imported
in the Ship Friendship, James Seix, Master, from Hamburgh
but last from Cowes, did this Day take and subscribe the usual
Qualifications.

Johann Pelz
Gottfried Nebe
Johan (×) Tabel
Joh. Heinrich Schneider
George (+) Kneeling
Johann Friedricus Franciscus
    Corsini
Christian Henrich Luttermann

Johann Friederich Landgraff
Christoph Wächtler
Vallentin Reyling
Johan Volcks
Christofel Auhagen
Johann Henrich Reventlau
Godfried (++) Förster
Godfried (×) Leman

F. Michael (+) Lorentz
Kunradt Heinrich Jörens
Johann Andreas Klein
Johann Jorge Gärttler
Johann Christian Zeise
Jacob Bramer
Johan Peter (++) Shmit
Andtras Blätz
Henry Jacob (++) Noll
Johan Hendrik Comülder
Johan Daniel Haunschilnt
Heinrich Baurmeister
Henrick Christoph Delckamp
Conrad (×) Ohage
Andreas Siegenitz

Henry Uhllerik (×) Russel
Christopher Matthesen
Johan Friederich Pelss
Andreas Hendrich Langen
Joachim Diterich (++) Mohl
Johann Hartmann Emmel
Johann Hinrich Sammann
Johann Lorentz Vogel
Johann Heinrich Pott, Cand. Jur.
Lorentz Bürckhle
Andres Gerlach
Adam Stein
Seven sick on board whose names
are not in the List.
No. 49

[List 215 A] A List of Palentines on board the Ship Nancy, from Rotterdam, John Ewing, Commander. [Qualified September 14, 1754.]

Jacob Bangwalt
Atwan Hoeger
Abraham Hugle
Cha. Hugle
John Jackpie
William Peter Kapp
Han Yerick Stivestan
Johannes Adolph
Mathias Shiet
Nickolas Swartz
Peter Rimble
Simon Kepler
Henry Siset
Jacob Philips
Daniel Miller
Fredrick Rimer
Adam Kenigh
Abraham Zora
Abraham Lurwald
Lodwick Kiner
Abraham Dawdie

Hans Barr
Abraham Gowba
Fredrick Showa
Peter Smith
Albert Uderstal
Johan Peere Beli
Charles Stys
Thomas Bower
Adam Mear
Michael Kock
Johan Hendrick Starks
Stophel George
Christian Tera
Christopher Wolph
Hans Michael Bangwart
Adam Waganer
Michael Klink
Jacob Miller
Peter Wigel
Daniel Zimmer
Conradt Zimmer

Jacob Kuntelman
Hans Yerrick Khumph
Johannes Lap
Berrie Votie
Francis Maer
Berring Green
Johan Piree Monie
John Piree Monie
Hans Jacob Willer
Hans Jacob Brown
Abraham Willer
George Gould
Thomas Penhard
Piree Poushin
Philip Wantler
William Bard
Francis Bard
Jack Burbasa
David Merchan
John Kulma
Johannes Widle
Christian Pase
Casper Rigert

John Mackyo
George Teslo
Alexander Wild
Johannes Ziser
Jacob Lower
Michael Apemaker
John Cato
John Hendrick Heiser
Daniel Fisher
Valatine Hineland
Gabriel Sier
John Christopher Bechin
Godfrid Herick
Alphonso Lewis Wilmer
Philipp Hosinger
Abraham Budinot
Hans Yelonark
Francis Philips Wys
David Budenot
John Peree Dire
John Peree Dire
Johannes Shilling

15 Roman Catholicks, 200 Freights, 87 [Signers].

[List 215 B] Foreigners Imported in the Nancy, Cap^n Ewing, from Rotterdam, took and Subscribed the usual Oaths and Declarations on Saturday, the 14th September, 1754.

Jacob Braunwald
Antoine Hogard
Abram Hugelet
Charles Huguelet
Jean Jaquepie
Wilhelm Biedekopp
Johann Gorg Steubesant
Johannes Adolf
Mattheus Scheidt
Nicholas (+) Swartz
Peter (+) Rimble
Simon Keuppler

Hans Seyser
Johann Jacob Völb
Johann Daniel Meyländer
Friedrich Roemmer
Adam Le Roy
Abraham Joray
Abram Le Roy
Ludwick (+) Shiner
Abraham De Die
Hans (X) Barr
Abraham Gobat
Fredrick (+) Showa

Peter (Peter) Smith
Albert Otto Steg
Johan Peter Wedel
Carl Steiss
Thomas (B) Bower
Adam Maire
Michel Haag
Johann Heinrich Steitz
Stophel (X) George
Christian (X) Tera
Christoffel Wolf
Hans Michall Bonwart
Johann Adam Wagner
Henrich Eisenhuth
Michel Klenck
Jacob Müller
Johanns Weill
Johann Daniel Zimer
Johan Conrath Zümmer
Johann Jacob Cuntzelman
Johann Dietrich Gompf
Johann Jost Lap
Pierre Vautie
Francis (+) Maer
Pierre Griene
Jean Pierre Monnin
Jean Pierre Monnin
Jacob (X) Willer
Johann Nickel Bauer
Abram Vuille
George Got
Pierre Pechin

Peter (+) Poutin
Philip (+) Wanler
Willm (X) Bard
Francis (+) Bard
Jaque Barbezat
David Marchand
Jean Jaque Allemand
Christian Böss
Casper (O) Rigert
Jean Matchait
Jerg Desloch
Alexandre Vuille
Johan Hennrich Häusser
Jacob Lauer
Michel Amacher
J. N. Pechin
Daniel Fischer
Vallendin Hindenlangs
Gabriel Seeger
Jean Christofle Pechin
Godfrid (X) Herick
Alphonse Louis Willemin
Abram Boutherot
Frans Phillip Weis
David (+) Budinot
John (X) Dire
John (X) Dire, Junior
Johannes Schilling
Johann Thomas Bernhard
Hans (+)Shalloback
John (Jean) Belle

[List 215 C] At the Court House at Philadelphia, Saturday, the 14th September, 1754.

Present: Charles Willing, Esquire.

His Excellency, Governor Tinker of Providence, Samuel Wood, Esquire, Cap^n of his Majesties Ship, the Jamaica.

The Foreigners whose Names are underwritten, Imported in the Ship Nancy, from Rotterdam but last from Cowes, did this day take and subscribe the usual Oaths and Declarations to the Government. Captn Ewing. Inhabitants of Lorain. N° 87.

Jacob Braunwald
Antoine Hogard
Abram Huguelet
Charles Huguelet
Jean Jaquepie
Wilhelm Biedekopp
Johann Georg Steubesant
Johannes Adolph
Mattheus Scheidt
Nicklaus (✗) Shwartz
Peter (+) Reammy
Simon Kuppler
Hanns Seyser
Johann Jacob Völb
Johann Daniel Meyländer
Friedrig Roemmer
Adam LeRoy
Abraham Joray
Abram Leroy
Ludewig (+) Keiner
Abraham De Die
Johannes (✗) Baar
Abraham Gobat
Friederik (✗) Showay
Peter (Peter) Smith
Albert Otto Steg
Johan Peter Wedel
Carl Steiss
Thomas (B) Bower
Adam Maire
Michel Haag
Johan Heinrich Steitz
Christoff (✗) Scharlle
Christian (✗) Cälly
Christstoffel Wolf
Hans Michell Bomward
Johann Adam Wagner

Henrich Eisenhuth
Michael Klenck
Jacob Müller
Johnns Weill
Johann Danniel Zimer
Johan Conrath Zümmer
Johann Jacob Cuntzman
Johann Dietrich Gompf
Johann Jost Lap
Pierre Vautie
Franc (✗) La Mera
Pierre Griene
Jean Pierre Monnin
Jean Pierre Monnin
Johan Jacob (✗) Willer
Johann Nickel Bauer
Abram Vuille
George Got
Pierre Pechin
Philip (+) Hoslinger
Philip (+) Spontler
Wilhelm (+) Baar
Franc (+) Baar
Jaque Barbezat
David Marchand
Jean Jaque Allemand
Christian Böss
Caspar (O) Riegel
Jean Mathiat
Jerg Desloch
Alexandre Vuille
Johann Henrich Häusser
Jacob Lauer
Michel Amacher
J. N. Pechin
Daniel Fischer
Wallendin Hindenlangs

Gabriel Seger
Jean Christofle Pechin
John Godfried (✕) Herring
Alphonse Louis Willemin
Abram Boutherot
Frans Philip Weis
Davit (✕) Butner

Joan (✕) Periter
Joan (✕) Periter, Junior
Johannes Schilling
Johann Thomas Bernhard
Johanes (✕) Shallobak
John (Pier Jean) Belly

Sir

Having agreeable to Orders Visited the Ship Nancy, Cap. Ewen, Master, and the Ship Barclay, Capt. Brown, Master, freighted with Palatines from Roterdam and find them in such condition respecting Health, as there is no Objection to their being admitted to enter the Port.

Philadia Septr 14th 1754.

Tho. Graeme.

To His Honour the Governor.

Th. Bond

[Endorsed:]

Doctors Certificate relating to the Ships Nancy and Barclay. 14th Sept. 1754.

[List 216 A] List of Mens Names & Ages imported in the Ship Barclay, Capt. John Brown, from Rotterdam, Philia 14 Septr 1754.

	AGES		AGES
Yerrick Foltz	21	David Eisler	48
Conradt Maack	28	Yerrick Peter Lochey	20
Michl Fauster	18	Abm Felme	18
Abram Dutongen	28	Hans Adam Troup	19
Nichs Bower	20	Yerrick Peter Bock	19
Hans Adam Paus	30	Jacob Troup	18
Hans Growse	32	Christr Pirman	20
Daniel Wyes	30	Gerrard Winter	18
Lodwick Haar	27	Felte Saynhaysen	34
Michael Hoffman	36	Hans Yerrk Eygler	46
Nichs Ash	25	Michl Reif	32
Michael Stayman	40	Samuel Dalabaack	38
Hans Peter Roley	36	Jacob Graver	36
Johann Naffliger *	48	Fredk Shank	46
Yerrick Smith	40	Tobias Risnar	33

* Name crossed out.

	AGES		AGES
Hand Mich[l] Unancks	24	Gotleip Nagle	26
Lorents Shenaw	28	Mathias Shryder	19
Joseph Miller	17	Johannes Basker	19
Hans Peter Inglis	43	Caspar Kaan	19
Lodw[k] Shuster	34	Hans Conradt Barr	20
Hannes Rorick	28	John Shrank	19
Jacob Fred[k] Haller	20	Bernard Rapoon	19
Mathias Renshlar	27	Michael Nill	40
Philip Jacob Fauch	46	Hans Yerr[k] Styel	40
Philip Cotterman	20	Jacob Bukley	35
Andreas Grysil	19	Martin Shrank	26
Martin Heighler	19	Felte Dum	22
Bernard Wirabaack	50	Frank Rudcap	19
Christian Hoffberger	20	Mathias Wagnar	43
Mich[l] Isay	17	Jacob Redacker	30
Bestian Roof	30	John Jacob Strominger	26
Johan Carel Grees	30	Elfreth Nearaman	20
Yerrick Bottsy *		John Mich[l] Seafret	27
Frans Lodw[k] Ely	34	Christ[n] Lykinger	30
Yerrick Wolff Unanks	27	Dewald Branholtz	17
Joseph Britner	33	Yerrick Faucks	20
Johannes Snarenberger	27	Loder[k] Bernard Switzler	23
Johan Adam Toar	44	Johannes Shoman	25
Hans Yerr[k] Haffner	40	Christian Yause	25
Nich[s] Erhard	50	Nich[s] Martin	30
Hans Keeller	24	Johannes Nill	20
Mich[l] Hauk	23	Sebastian Mossleager	40
Hans Yerr[k] Stouck	37	Otto Bigseller	40
Mich[l] Renshlar	34	John Jacob Stow	18
Lodw[k] Stonger	19	Nich[ls] Stow	18
Yerrick Noawys	28	Mich[l] Stow	40
Hans Bernard Axelbaker	40	Philip Shartzer	35
Hans Mich[l] Barr	34	Jacob Eygle	28
Johannis Yenkist	23	Wilhelm Sutzill	38
Yerr[k] Gysler	27	Leonard Meyer	26
Johannes Barr	28	Christopal Kaan	25
Andreas Bowman	19	Philip Jacob Grinler	50
John Martin Unanks	30	Mich[l] Erter	29

* Name crossed out.

	AGES		AGES
Mathias Hauts	20	Otto Purgazer	
Hans Mich. Bleig	24	Johannes Kleynfelt	
Andreas Stow	30	110	
Jacob Sicks	19		

Foreigners imported in the Ship Barclay, Capt. John Brown, from Rotterdam. Qual. 14th Septr 1754. No 110.

Stedman.

[List 216 B] Foreigners Imported in the Ship Barclay, Capn John Brown, from Rotterdam & last from Cowes, took the Oaths and Declarations to the Government, on Saturday, the 14th Septr 1754.

Georg Voltz
Johan Conrat Mock
Michael (X) Fauter
Abram (X) Detinger
Nicholas (O) Bower
Adam (X) Faus
Johanes Kraus
Daniel Weiss
Ludwig Haas
Michael Hofmann
Nicholas (O) Ash
Michal (H) Stayman
Jan Peirre Rollei
Yerrick (O) Smith
David Isller
Peter (O) Lochey
Abraham Felm
Adam (X) Troup
Georg Peter Bock
Jacob (X) Troup
Chris. (M) Perman
Gerhard Winder
Filt (X) Saynhisin
Yerrick (X) Eyler
Michäel Rueb

Samuel (O) De la Bough
Jacob Kräber
Friderich Schenck
Tobias Reissner
Hans (X) Unancks
Lorentz (L) Shinan
Hans (X) Inglis
Joseph (X) Miller
Ludwich Schuster
Johannes (+) Gorrick
Jacob (X) Holler
Mathias (+) Renshlar
Jacob (X) Fauck
Andreas (X) Gresil
Filipp Kattermann
Andreas Kreissel
Bernard (X) Werbach
Christian Hoffbauer
Michell Esge
Bertran (+) Roof
Johann Carl Gries
Frantz Lutwig Uehlein
Yerrick (X) Wolff Unanks
Joseph Büdtner
Johannes Schnurrenberger

Johann Adam Dörr
Yerrick (X) Hoffner
Niclaus Ehrhardt
Johans Köhler
Michael Haukh
Hanns Gerg Stauch
Michael Rentschler
Ludwig Stanger
Yerrick (X) Noaways
Bernard (O) Axebaker
Hans Michell Berr
Johannes Jüngst
Jacob Geissler
Johannes Bahr
Andreas (A) Bowman
Johann Martin Unangst
Gottlieb Nagel
Mathes Scheiner
Johannes Beneset [?]
Caspar Gann
Hans Conrath Ber
John (X) Shrank
Bernard (+) Rapoon
Michl Knihll
Hans Jerg Steyl
Jacob Böckhle
Martin (+) Shrank
Velten Thum
Frans (R) Rudcap
Mathias (X) Wagner
Jacob (+) Redacker

Johann Jacob Strohmenger
Elfreth (X) Nearman
John (X) Seafret
Christoph Laichinger
Dewald (O) Brunhotz
Hans Jerg Fuchs
Ludwig Bernhardt Zwissler
John (X) Shoman
Johann Christian Jauss
Johann Nicolaur Martin
Joans Künhle
Sebastian Muffler
Otto Bürgesser
Johann Jacob Stauch
Michael Stauch
Michel Stauch
Mathias Foutz
Filipp Scherzer
Jacob (X) Eygle
Wilhelm Zotzel
Leonhardt Meyer
Christoph Gan
Philipp Jacob Grindler
Michael Oerther
Hans Michel Bleich
Andreas Stauch
Johann Jacob Seytz
John (+) Klyfelt
Mathias (F) Fretser [?]
110

[List 216 C] At the Courthouse at Philadelphia, on Saturday, the 14th September, 1754.

Present: Charles Willing, Esquire, Mayor.

The Foreigners whose Names are underwritten, Imported in the Ship Barclay, Captn John Brown, from Rotterdam, but last from Cowes, did this day take the usual Oaths and Declarations to the Government. 110 Present. 250 Foreigners from Alsace & Lorrain.

Georg Voltz
Johan Conrat Mock
George Michael (×) Fautzer
Abram (×) Duton
Nicklas (B) Bouer
John Adam (F) Fass
Johannes Kraus
Daniel Weiss
Ludwig Haas
Michael Hoffmann
Nicklas (O) Ash
Mickel (+ +) Steinman
Jan Peirre Rellei
George (O) Shmit
Davit Iseller
G. Peter (O) Loughy
Abrahm Felmi [?]
J. Adam (O) Traub
Georg Peter Bock
Jacob (×) Traub
Christoph (M) Pierman
Gerhard Winder
Vallentin (VZ) Zaneichel
H. George (H) Hechler
Michael Rüeb
Sammuel (O) Tallebaugh
Jacob Kräber
Friederich Schenk
Tobias Reissner
H. Michael (×) Unongst
Lorentz (O) Sheenau[Schönau]
Joseph (×) Miller
H. Peter (+) Engels
Ludwich Schuster
Johanes (×) Kargh
J. Friederich (+) Haller
Matheus (+) Renchler
Wilhelm (×) Jacob Fack
Filipp Kattermann
Andreas Kreissel
Martin (O) Hechler

Bernhart (×) Mirbach
Christian Hoffbaur
Michel Eisge
Bastian (O) Rooff
Johann Carl Griess
Frantz Lutwig Ühlein
George (×) Woff Unong[st]
Joseph Büdtner
Johannes Schnarrenberger
Johann Adam Dörr
H. George (×) Haffner
Niclaus Ehrhardt
Johannes Köhler
Michael Hauch
Hanns Jerg Stauch
Michael Rentschler
Ludwig Stanger
George (×) Naewiss
H. Bernhardt (O) Ochsenbacher
Hans Michell Berr
Johannes Jüngst
Jacob Geissler
Johannes Bahr
Adereas (A) Bauman
Johann Martin Unangst
Gottlieb Nagel
Mathes Scheiner
Johanes Bukoo [?]
Johan (×) Shronck
Caspar Gann
Hans Conratt Ber
J. Bernhart (+) Rebhoon
Michl Kniehl
Hans Jerg Steyl
Jacob Böckhle
Martin (+)Shronck
Velten Thüm
Franc (O) Rotham
Matheas (+) Wagner
Jacob (+) Reatacker
Johann Jacob Strohmenger

Elfrie (+) Kneerimen
J. Michael (XX) Seyfree
Christoph Laichinger
Dewald (O) Brownholtz
Hans Jerg Fuchs
Ludwig Bernhard Zwissler
Johanes (X) Sheoman
Johann Christian Jauss
Johann Niclaus Martin
Janichl Künle
Sebastian Muffler
Otto Bürgesser
Johann Jacob Stauch
Michael Stauch
Michel Stauch

Jacob (XX) Eichely
Filipp Scherzer
Wilhelm Zotzel
Leonhardt Meyer
Christoph Gan
Philipp Jacob Grindler
Matheas ( ) Fautz, sick on
board
Michael Oerther
Hans Michel Bleich
Andreas Stauch
Johann Jacob Seyts
Johanes (X) Kleinfeld
Matheas (XX) Alt
110

Septr 14, 1754.

Sir

According to Directions we have carefully examined the State of Health of the Mariners and Passengers on board the Ship Barclay, Capt Brown, from Roterdam and found Six ill of Fevers which we think ought to be taken out of this Ship, we do [not] apprehend these Fevers to be of an infectious Nature and therefore think the People may be admitted to land in the City without Risque to the Inhabitants.

To his Honour   Tho. Graeme
the Governour   Th. Bond

[Endorsed:]

Doctors Report of the Ship Barclay, Captn Brown, Septr 14, 1754.

[List 217 A] The Ship Adventure from Hamburg, last from Plymouth, Capt. Joseph Jackson. [Qualified September 25, 1754.]

And. Hoffman
Christ^n Shaffer
Johan Ad^m Kohlass
Johan Jurgen Schmidt
Hartman Jager
H^s Peter Rehvey

Johan Geo. Ilgar
Johan Phil. Wagner
And^w Wisse
Johannes Wisse
Johannes Andriola
Johan Jacob Weiman

Jr Gandus
Johan Adm Bulback
Johan Conrd Spangenberg
Christn Liza berbeger
Johan Augt Strauble
Johan Geo. Gottse
Johanes Willd
Johana Christn Demer
Johan Freitzsch
Johan Diedk Eigendenseim
Johan Reim
Baltzer Raab
Johan Christa See
Johan Henrk Neuman
Johan Michl Weise
Johan Henk Rohrman
Johan Ruttger
Jos. Gosser
Johan Geo. Young
Johan Got. Nagel
Phill. Michell
Johan Hachs Steckell
Harman Wagener
Ant. Lemback
Johan Danll Frank
Johan Phill. Danheber
Christn Nerlich
Johan Jacob Reinck
Geo. Kailer
Hans Wm Eckard
Henrk Orich
Johan Jacob Cornelius
Johan Lieberich

Johan Just Heck
Johan Jacob Rathline
Hans Nichls Beck
Johs Diederich
Casper Schryber
Johannes Detmeyer
Phil. Deeringer
Johan Martn Harder
Johan Fredk Ermintrau
Johan Nichs Hunt
Johan Geo. Raush
Johan Geo. Smith
Maths Muller
Henrk Ruple
John Joost Wild
Johannes Mattersteek
Christopher Muller
Michael Huld
Conrad Coot
Frans Peter Evalt
John Hevert
Adolph Ourbach
Frederick Ebernicht
George Steinweg
John Conrad Roerman, Junr
Anthony Reidecker
John Reidecker, Junr
John Jerrick Steinweg, Junior
Martin Matterstack
John Andreas Jusong
Nicholas Gosport
Christian Goser

77

[Endorsed:]
Foreigners imported in the Ship Adventure, Capt Joseph Jackson, from Hamburgh. Qual. 25th Sept 1754. N. 78.

Keppelle.

[List 217 B] Foreigners Imported in the Ship Adventure, Captain Joseph Jackson, from Hamburgh, were qualified the

25th September, 1754, before the Mayor in the Court House.

Christn ( ) Shaffer, sick
Johann Andreas Hoffman
Johann Adam Kohlass
John (+) Schmidt
Johann Hartmann Jäger
Peter (X) Revy
Johann Georg Ilger
Johann Philip Wagner
Andreas Weiss
Johannes Weiss
Johannes Andrioler
Johannes Andrioler
Johan Jacob Weinman
Frantz Gantuss
Johann Adam Bollbach
Johann Conrad Spangenberg
Chrisn (X) Lesberger
Joh. Gottfried Nagel, Mÿnist
  Candid.
Johann August Straube
Johann Gorg Gütsell
Johannes Will
Christ[1] (++) Demer
Johannes Fritz
Johan Dietdrich Balldauf
Johannes Reim
Baltzer (XX) Raab
Johann Christiansen
Johann Henrich Neumann
Johan Michael Weiss
Johann Henrich Rohrmann
Johannes Rüdiger
Jos. (XX) Goser
Johann Görg Jung
Philipp Michael
John (+) Stekel
Herman Wagener
Anthony (+) Lembach
Johann Daniel Franck

John (X) Danheber
Christian Nehrlich
Johan Jacob Reineck
Georg Köhler
Johannes Wilhelm Echert
Henrich (++) Orick
John (++) Corneilus
Johannes Liebrich
Johann Jost Will
Johann Jost Heck
Johann Jacob Räthlein
Johan Nicol Bach
Johannes Didrich
Caspar Schreiber
Johann Dötmar
Philip (+++) Deeringer
Johann Martin Hardert
Johann Friederich Ermetraud
Johann Nicolaus Handt
Johan Jerig Rausch
George (++) Smith
Joh. Mathias Müller
Johann Henrich Ruppel
Johannes Marder Steck
John Christoph Müller
Görch Nicl. Hund
Johan Conrath Gott
Johan Martin Martersteck
Johann Eberth
Johann Andreas Jusang
Adolph (++) Overbeeck
Frederick (+) Ebernicht
Gorg Steinweg
Johann Conrad Rohrmann
Matheus Andonius Rütiger
Johann Rütiger
Nicholas Gosport
Christian (+) Goser

[Endorsed:]

Foreigners imported in the Ship Adventure, Capt Joseph Jackson, from Hamburgh. Qual. 25th Septr 1754. No. 78.

                 Keppelee.

[List 217 C] At the Court House at Philadelphia, Wednesday, the 25th Septr 1754.

    Present: Worshipful Charles Willing, Esquire, Mayor.

The Foreigners whose Names are underwritten, Imported in the Ship Adventure, Captain Joseph Jackson, from Hamborough, but last from Plymouth, Inhabitants of Franconia, did this day take the usual Oaths to the Government & Declarations. 245 Souls. 78 Qualified.

Johann Andreas Hoffman
Christian ( ) Shaffer, sick on
    board
Johann Adam Kohlass
John George (+) Shmit
Johann Hertman Jeger
Hans Peter (X) Rehvay
Johann Georg Ilger
Johann Philip Wagner
Andreas Weiss
Johannes Weiss
Johannes Andrioler
Johannes Andrioler
Johan Jacob Weinman
Frantz Gantus
Johann Adam Bollbach
Johann Conrad Spangenberg
Christian (O) Letzbeyer
Johann August Straube
Johann Gorg Gütsell
Joh. Gottfried Nagel, Mÿnist
    Candid.
Johannes Will
John Christoff (XX) Diemer
Johannes Fritz
Johan Dietdrich Balldauf
Johannes Reim

Balsatzor (++) Raab
Johann Christiansen
Johann Henrich Neumann
Johann Michael Weiss
Johann Heinrich Rohrmann
Johannes Rüdiger
Joseph (XX) Gasser
Johann Görg Jung
Philipp Michäel
J. Zacharias (+) Stökel
Herman Wagener
Anthon (+) Lembach
Johann Daniel Franck
J. Philip (X) Tannhöffer
Christian Nehrlich
Johan Jacob Reinek
Henrich (XX) Urrich
Georg Köhler
Johannes Wilhelm Echert
J. Jacob (++) Cornelius
Johannes Liebrich
Johann Jost Will
Johann Jost Heck
Johann Jacob Räthlein
Johann Nicol Bach
Johannes Didrich
Caspar Schreiber

Johannes Ditmer
Philip (+++) Thiringer
Johann Martin Hardert
Johann Friederich Ermetraud
Johan Martin (M) Matterstek
Johann Nicolaus Handt
Johan Georg Rausch
Johan George (++) Shmit
Joh. Matthias Müller
Johann Heinrich Ruppel
Johannes Mardersteck
Johann Christoph Müller
G. Mich. Hundt

Johan Conradh Cott
Johann Eberth
John Andereas (++) Jusong
Adolph (++) Urbach
J. Friederich (++) Ebnie
Gorg Steinweg
Johann Conrad Rohrman
Matheus Andonius Rütiger
Johannes Rütiger
George Steinweg, Junior
Nicklas (X) Gorshboth
Christian (X) Gasser
78

Sep^t 23, 1754.

Sir

According to Orders we have carefully examined the State of Health of the Mariners and Passengers on board the Ship Adventure, Capt Joseph Jackson, from Hamburgh, and found no objection to their being admitted to land in the City immediately.

To his Honour
the Governour

Tho. Graeme
Th. Bond

[Endorsed:]

23^d Septr 1754. Doctors Certificate relating to the Ship Adventure.

[List 218 A] A List of Men on board the Ship Richard & Mary, John Moore, Mas^r, 1754, from Rotterdam. [Qualified September 30, 1754].

Michael Fisher
Bastian Fisher
Casper Kies
Anderas Zinck
Jacob Zinck
Christophel Zinck
Gottlieb Donte
Jacob Salser
Casper Geyer

David Kohl
Michael Wolf
Jacob Adam
Jacob Wolf
Mich^l Steyger
Ludwig Muse
Johannes Schiesle
Johannes Snurenberger
Jacob Snurenberger

Michael Welte
Jacob Welte
Johannes Guthner
Hans Martin Muller
Michael Leobold
Johan Michael Strubel
Ludwig Strubel
Johannes Brettrere
Jurg Brettrere
Hans Jurg Welki
Adam Knobelick
Hans Jurg Meyer
Jacob Adam Wandell
Jurg Heysel, Sen[r]
Jurg Heysel Jun[r]
Martin Smith
Johan Mich[l] Herman
Ulrich Kost
Christoph Pheifer
Jacob Blesing
Fred[k] Dockwadel
Johannes Mutseler
Fred[k] Theyle
Fred[k] Burr
Jacob Werner
Hans Martin Schoffer
Johannes Wetsell
Casper Hencke
Jacob Steydle
Jacob Busch
Hans Jurg Busch
Wolfgang Ulmer
Han Jacob Volke
David Wolf
Christoph Fetter
Johan Mich[l] Messinger

Daniel Blomeschyn
Ludwig Zimmerman
Anthony Smith
Joseph Fynhaur
Christophel Leyrle
Mathias Susz
Hans Jurg Ramsperger
Jacob Aug
Jacob Ramsperger
Wolfgang Wolf
Christian Zinck
Michael Wolf
Jurg Fred[k] Dietz
Johannes Kow
Casper Dietz
Adam Engel
Jurg Zeb
Hans Jurg Meyer
Johannes Laur
Martin Abbitsch
Hans Jurg Grou
Daniel Stumpf
Hans Jurg Heydle
Hans Jurg Heydle, Jun[r]
Johannes Sloltz
Hans Jurg Kriesel
Jos. Ferd[t] Klinger
Ludwig Kraft
Valentin Leman
Ferd. Fackiundas
Ludwig W[m] Heller
Henry Nagle
Johannes Shutle
Fred[k] Ramminger
Johannes Bloomhart
Christian Kraemer

[Endorsed:] List of Foreigners imported in the Ship Richard & Mary, from Rotterdam. Qual. 30th Septr 1754.

Shoemaker. 91.

[List 218 B] Foreigners imported in the Ship Richard and Mary, from Rotterdam, Capt. Moore. Qual. 30th September, 1754.

Michael (X) Fisher
Remund Fisher
Caspar Kiss
Andreas Zinck
Jacob Zinckh
Christopher (X) Zinck
Gottlieb Tünte
Jacob Saltzer
Hans Casper Geyer
David (XX) Kohl
Michel Wolf
Jacob Adam
Jacob Wolf
Michael Staiger
Ludtwig Musi
Johannes Schiesle
Johannes Schnurenberger
Jacob Schnurnberger
Michel Welte
Jacob Welthe
Johannes Gürthner
Hans Martin Müller
Michel Lebolt
Johan Michael Strobel
Ludwig Strobel
Johannes Bether
Hs. Jerg Bether
Hans Jcrg Welte
Adam (X) Knobelich
Hans George (X) Meyer
Jacob Adam Wandel
George (X) Heysel
Georg Heisel
Martin Schmidt
Michäl Hermann
Ulrich Kost

Christoph Pfeiffer
Jacob (X) Blesing
Georg Friedrich Dockusbadel
Johannes Musseler
Fridrich Deile
Frederick (X) Burr
Jacob Werner
Hans Martin Schöffer
Johannes Wetzel
Casper Hincke
Jacob Steidtle
Hans Georg Busch
Jacob Busch
Wolfgang Ulmer
Jean Jaqe Foulquier
David Wolf
Christof Vetter
Joh. Michael Mössinger
Daniel Blumenschein
Ludwig Zimmerman
Anthonyus Schmidt
Joseph Feinnauer
G. Leyrle
Mathäus Süss
Hans Jerg Ramsperger
Jacob Auch
Jacob Ramsperger
Wolffgang Wolf
Christianus Zinck
Michel Wolf
Georg Friedrich Dietz
Johannes Hohl
Johan Caspar Dietz
Georg Adam Engell
Jerg Zep
Hans Georg (+) Meyer

Johannes (+) Laur
Johan Martin Adisch
Jerg Grau
Daniel Stumpp
Hans Jerg Heidle
Hans Jerg Heidle
Johannes Schlotz
George (×) Kreisel
Joseph Friedrich Klinger

Jerg Ludwig Kraft
Valentine (+) Leman
Ferdinand Faciundus
Ludwig Wilhelm Haller
Johanes Schüttel
Friderick Raminger
Christian Kremer
Johannes Blumhard

[Endorsed:] List of Foreigners imported in the Ship Richard & Mary, from Rotterdam. Qual. 30ᵗʰ Septʳ 1754.
Shoemaker. 91.

[List 218 C] At the Court House at Philadelphia, Monday, the 30ᵗʰ September, 1754.
Present: Joshua Maddox, Esquire.

The Foreigners whose Names are underwritten Imported in the Ship Richard & Mary, John Moore, Master, from Rotterdam and last from Cowes, Inhabitants of the Dukedom of Wirtemberg, did this day take the usual Oaths and Declarations. 6 Roman Catholics. 230 Freights. 91 Qualified.

Michael (×) Fisher
Remund Fisher
Caspar Kiess
Andreas Zinckh
Jacob Zinckh
Christoff (+) Zinck
Gottlieb Tünte
Jacob Saltzer
Hans Casper Geyer
Davit (++) Cohl
Michel Wolf
Jacob Adam
Jacob Wolf
Michael Staiger
Ludwig Musi
Johanns Schiessle
Johannes Schnurrenberger
Jacob Schnurrnberger

Michel Welte
Jacob Welthe
Johannes Gürthner
Hans Martin Müller
Michel Lebolt
Johan Michael Strobel
Ludwig Strobel
Johannes Bether
Hans Jerg Bether
Hans Jerg Welte
Adam (×) Noblig
Hans George (×) Meyer
Jacob Adam Wandel
George (×) Heusel
Georg Heisel, Junior
Martin Schmidt
Michel Hermann
Ulrich Kost

Christoph Pfeiffer
Jacob (XX) Blessing
Georg Friedrich Dockusbadel
Johanes (X) Mutchler
Fridrich Deile
Friederich (X) Burr
Jacob Werner
Hans Martin Schäffer
Johannes Wetzel
Casper Hincke
Jacob Steudtle
Hanns Georg Busch
Jacob Busch
Wolfgang Ulmer
Jean Jaq. Foulquier
David Wolf
Christoph Vetter
Jos. Michael Mössinger
Daniel Blumenschein
Ludwig Zimmerman
Anthonyus Schmidt
J. Joseph Feinauer
Johann Christoph Leyrle
Mathaus Süs
Hans Jerg Ramsperger
Jacob Auch
Jacob Ramsperger
Wolfgang Wolf

Christanes Zinck
Michel Wolf
Georg Friedrich Dietz
Johannes Hohl
Johan Caspar Dietz
Georg Adam Engell
Jerg Zeb
Hans George (+) Meyer
Johanes (X) Lauer
Johan Martin Adisch
Jerg Grau
Daniel Stumpp
Hans Jerg Heidle
Hans Jerg Heidle
Johannes Schlotz
Hans George (+) Rössel
Joseph Friederich Klinger
Jerg Ludwig Kraft
Vallentin (X) Leman
Ferdnand Faciundus
Ludwig Wilhelm Haller
Heinrich Nägele
Johann Schüttel
Friderick Raminger
Christian Kraemer
Johannes Blumhard
91

Sep^t 29, 1754.
Sir

We have carefully examined the State of Health of the Mariners and Passengers on board the Ship Richard & Mary, Capt Moore, from Roterdam, and found them so well that we do not apprehend the least Risque to the Inhabitants of the City from their being admitted to land in it immediately.

To his Honour   Tho. Graeme
The Governour   Th. Bond
[Endorsed:]

    29th September 1754.

Doctors Certificate relating to the Ship Richard & Mary.

[List 219 A] List of Men's Names & Ages, Imported in the Ship Brothers, Capt Wm Muir, from Rotterdam. 30 Septr 1754.

	AGES		AGES
Johannes Bartolome Smith	48	Hannes Hershberger	21
Hans Yerrick Waber	17	Johannes Keeney	23
Jacob Stome	27	Hannes Acker	18
Hannes Miller	20	Michel Sholtz	30
Philip Spoad	42	Johannes Varo	20
Peter Haan	46	Ab^m Haackman	27
Yerrick Chris. Diver	39	Ab^m Browbacker *	21
Hannes Haller	44	Jacob Browbacker	21
Conrad Wagner	29	Jacob Browbacker	29
Daniel Saunder	32	Johannes Spery	26
John Conrad Smith	19	Peter Witsell	18
Conrad Michael	25	Adam Witsell	20
Hend^k Wickman	18	Christopal Weaver	46
Johannes Klayn	23	Frans Burger	44
Johan Klynman	30	Michel Burger	18
Jacob Bernard	34	Jurig Lodw^k Mitinger	33
John Baltzar Smith	42	John Chris Trump	26
William Stout	19	John Jorick Sip	50
Johan Christian Hauh	45	Joseph Sip	18
John Jerrick Licker	30	Casper Waggner	18
Hugh Storleig	30	Fred^k Baker	43
John Deal	45	Agustus Strack	30
John Peter Wert	17	Hend^k Sombroun	36
Hans Jacob Gist	45	Johan Wolfgan Mering	23
Jerrick Kooh	27	Christian Woltz	23
Carel Hend^k Kaufman	36	Johannes Righart	33
Hans Jerrick Spies	28	Hans Milltour	18
Johannes Shodell	33	Jacob Phister	22
Johannes Keemill	20	Baltzar Rimer	40
Mich^l Rich	44	Peter Phister	46
Jacob Hoober	16	Christian Eyeger	46
John Lodw^k Hansetter	38	Daniel Ott	30
Hend^k Graft	19	Valentine Orledig	30
Valentine Moll	27	Ab^m Plystain	26
Ab^m Elinger	22	Yerrick Demer	19
Jacob Sneevly	37	Hans Jerrick Grous	31

* Name crossed out, with note "N. Lander," i. e., Newlander.

	AGES		AGES
Fred^k Andreas	30	Oswald Andreas	30
Valentine Weabel	17	Jacob Baker	27
Hans Jacob Shafner	30	Leonard Crombie	22
David Hungerbalt	23	Jurig Baker	20
Christian Witmer	31	Peter Fry	33
Jacob Witmer	23	Hans Mich^l Kopenhavish	42
Christoffel Folgart	18	Vindle Gilbert	28
Joseph Leaman	21	Ulrich Hessleman	20
Jacob Dedwiller	21	Henry Histant	23
Martin Herman	29	Johannes Seyts	20
Adam Kundell	30	Philip Baas	20
Philip Metskar	31	Joseph Bybykoffer	30
Johannes Frye	34	Casper Knob	29
Christian Hoober	24	Johanes Hans	
Johannis Miller	20		101
Ab^m Strickler	40		

List of Foreigners imported in the Ship Brothers, Capt Muir from Rotterdam. Qual. 30th Septr 1754. 101.

Stedman.

[List 219 B] List of Foreigners, imported in the Ship Brothers, Capt Muir, from Rotterdam. Qual. 30th Septr 1754.

Johannes Smiet	William (X) Stout
Johann Georg Humbert	Johan Christ Hoch
Johann Jacob Stamm	Gerge (X) Licher
Hans (M) Miller	Johann Jost Ulick [?]
Fillippus Jacob Späth	Johann Tiel Werss
Johann Peter Hahn	Johann Petter Petter Werss
Georg Christoph Däuber	Hanns Jacob Geist
Johannes Aller	Johan Kohl
Conrad (X) Wagner	Carl Heinrich Jacob Kauffman
Daniel Sander	Johann Gorg Spies
Johann Conradt Schmidt	Johannes Schadel
Conrad (O) Michael	Johann Nicolaus Kimel
Henry (X) Wickman	Michael (O) Rust
Johannes Klein	Jacob (X) Hoober
Johann Diehl Kleinman	Johann Ludwig Ernst Schiller
Jacob Bernard	Henrig Graf
Johann Balthas Schmidt	Valentin Noldt

Abraham Mellinger
Jacob (×) Sneveley
Johannes Herschberger
Johannes Küny
Johannes Eicher
Georg Michel Schultz
Johannes Forrer
Abraham Hackman
Johann Jacob Prubacher
Jacob Prubacher
Johannes Schori
Peter (+) Witsell
Adam (××) Witsell
Steffan (++) Weber
Michael (××) Burger
Georg Ludwig Meittinger
Johan Christian Trump
Hans Gerg (×) Sip
Joseph Ziepf
Caspar Wagner
Friederich Becher
Augustus Schaad
Heinrich Zum Brun
Johann Wolfgang Möhring
Christian (×) Waltz
Johannes Ritschhart
Hans Müllidaler
Jacob Pfister
Balthasar Reimer
Beter Pfister
Christian Eicher
Daniel Ott
Valentin Urlettig

Abraham Blinstein
Johann Georg Diemer
Hanns Georg Krauss
Valentin Webel
Hans Jacob Schafner
Frederick (+) Andreas
David (×) Hungerbalt
Johann Christian Wittmr
Jacob Wittmer
Christofel Volckerth
Joseph Leman
Jacob Dettweiller
Martin (×) Herman
Adam Kuntel
Philip (×) Metzker
Joannes Frey
Christian Huber
Johannes Müller
Aberham Strickler
Oswald Andreas
Jacob Becker
Leonard (×) Crombie
Johann Görg Becker
Peter Frey
Hanns Michel Koppenhöffer
Wendel (W) Gilbert
Ulrich (O) Heshleman
Henrich Hiestant
Johannes Seiths
Filp As
Joseph Bubikofer
H. Johannes Kantz
101

[Endorsed:]
List of Foreigners imported in the Ship Brothers, Capt Muir, from Rotterdam. Qual. 30th Septr 1754.

101.   Stedman.

Doctors visited Captn Russel at ye same & reported both together on one Paper.

R. B.

[List 219 C] At the State House at Philadelphia, Monday, the 30th September, 1754.

Present: The Worshipful Charles Willing, Esquire, Mayor.

The Foreigners whose Names are underwritten, imported in the Ship Brothers, Captn William Muir, from Rotterdam, and last from Cowes, did this day take the usual Qualifications. 7 Roman Catholicks. 23 Mennonites. 250 Souls. 210 Freights. 101 Qualified. [From the] Palatinate & Mentz.

Johannes Bartelmi Schmi[t]
Johann Georg Humbert
Johann Jacob Stamm
Johannes (M) Miller
Fillippus Jacob Späth
Johann Peter Hahn
Georg Christoph Däuber
Johannes Aller
Conrad (✕) Wagner
Daniel Sander
Johann Conrad Schmidt
Conrad (O) Mercky
Henry (+) Weidman
Johannes Klein
Johann Diehl Kleinman
Jacob Bernard
Johann Balthas Schmidt
Wilhelm (✕) Staut
Johan Christ Hoch [?]
J. George (✕) Lucker
Johan Jost [Ul[ick]
Johann Tiel Werss
Johohnn Petter Wersch
Hanns Jacob Geist
Johann Gerg Kol
Carl Heinrich Jacob Kauffman
Johann Gorg Spies
Johannes Schadel
Johann Nicoclaus Kimmel
Michael (O) Räsh
Jacob (✕) Huber

Johann Ludwig Ernst Schiller
Henrich Graff
Valentin Noldt
Abraham Mellinger
Jacob (✕) Shnable
Johannes Herschberger
Johannes Küny
Johannes Eicher
Gorg Michel Schultz
Johannes Forrer
Abraham Hackmann
Johann Jacob Prubacher
Jacob Prubacher
Johannes Schöri
Peter (✕) Weitzel
Anthony (✕✕) Weitzel
Steffan Weber
Frantz (++) Burghart
Michael (++) Burghart
Georg Ludwig Meittinger
Johan Christian Trump
Hans Gorg (✕) Ziebf
Joseph Ziepf
Caspar Wagner
Friedrich Becher
Augustus Schaad
Henrich Zum Brun
Johann Wolfgang Möhring
Christian (✕) Wolst
Johannes Ritschhart
Hans Mülldaler

Jacob Pfister
Balthaser Reimer
Peter Pfister
Christian Eicher
Daniel Ott
Valentin Urlettig
Abraham Bleistein
Johann Georg Diemer
Hans Georg Krauss
Friederich (X) Andereas
Johann Valentin Webel
Hans Jacob Schaffner
Davit (+) Hungerberer
Johan Christian Wittmer
Joh. Jacob Wittmer
Christofel Volckarth
Joseph Leman
Jacob Dettweiler
Martin (X) Herman
Adam Kuntel

Philip (X) Metzger
Joannes Frey
Christian Huber
Johannes Müller
Aberham Strickler
Oswald Andreas
Jacob Becker
Leonhart (X) Krumbein
Johann Görg Becker
Peter Frey
Hanns Michel Koppenhäffer
Wendal (W) Gilbert
Wilhelm (O) Ashelman
Henrich Hiestant
Johannes Seiths
Filb As
Joseph Bubikofer
Caspar (H) Knag
Johannes Kantz
101

Sepr 30, 1754

S^r

We have carefully examined the State of Health of the Mariners and Passengers on board the Ships Brothers and Edinburgh, Cap^{ts} Muir & Russel and found no objection to their being admitted to land in the City immediately.

To his Honour   Tho. Graeme
The Governour   Th. Bond
[Endorsed:]
30th Septr 1754.
Doctors Certificate relating to the Ships Brothers and Edinburgh.

[List 220 A] List of Names in the Ship Edinburgh, Captn Russel, 30th Septr 1754.

Henry Whiel
Fred^k Wm Frick
Jurg Eberhard Mill

Joh. Henr. Phiefer
Joh. Conrad Shibler
Joh Henry Blecker

Jurg Hilt
Herman Gerlach
Johannes Gerlach
Philip Spitius
Jurg Wilhelm
Christop[l] Kniel
Melchior Strump
Paul Leshorn
Herman Sommer
Philip Sommer
Johan Peter Wolf
Bernhard Mathias
Bernhard Mathias
Johannes Mathias
Jurg Wiesick
Anthony Peter
Andreas Wiel
Jurg Henry Rung
Ludwig Kam
Conrad Neyhart
Johannes Ludwig
Conrad Ludwig
Casper Zorn
Joost Pingman
Fred[k] Shimpf
Anderas Dien
Philip Baster
Daniel Fetsberger
Henry Walter
Johannes Pot
Johannes Linker
Henry Langstorf
Jacob Ludwig
Engelbart Ludwig
Anderas Hebnar
Ludwig Winckler
Jacob Shimpf
Rudolph Troogh
Baltzer Faulsteg
Jurg Lohr
Casper Erb

Samuel Haubt
Johan[s] D[o]
Nich[s] D[o]
Peter Heght
Conrad Lohr
Philip Ludwig
Johannes Huber
Valentin Ulrich
Eberhard Diel
Henry Winckler
Henry Gebhard
Jacob Hammersteyn
Conrad Enters
Peter Wiesman
Conrad Bour
Jacob Slotter
Daniel Grugh
Adam Leobold
Johannes Weaver
Philib Ries
Jurg Kob
Henry Kob
Adam Stram
Henry Stram
Wilhelm Baltzer
Henry Louia
Erhard Weaver
Philib Tauberman
Henry Hock
Anthony Hecht
Jurg Wietzel
Jurg Metzer
Jacob Kern
Math[s] Kern
Michael Wentz
Christoph Essig
Christoph Rable
Jacob D[o]
Henry Hass
Peter Paul
Anthony Morgel

Adam Maurer
Nich^s Hemb
Mich^l Grui
Christophel D^o
Conrad Krim
Johan^s D^o
Jurg D^o
Conrad Philips
Peter Kiel
Conrad Messer
Werner^s Dickel
Peter D^o
Conrad Snyder
Anderas Grauthamel
Bastian Fretz
Daniel Langster
Conrad Langster
Conrad Demand
Fred^k Shimpf
Jacob Gibel
Herman Mathias
Johannes Bender
Conrad Bender
Philip Rorich, on board
Conrad Snyder
Johannes Bup
Jurg Diel
Johannes Cappies, sick
Johannes Kemmer
Henry Loub
Casper Zigler
Jurg Holl
Peter Dorter
Henry Mengin*
Johannes Mengin
Ernst Mengin

Peter Bicher
Rienhard Wies
Henry Rietz
Mathias Ludwig
Lorentz Albon
Gothard D^o
Jacob Hellrich
Christofel D^o
Johannes Sommer
Johannes Sommer
Conrad Kiessel
Herman Kiessel
Johannes Kiessel
Jurg Sorg
Conrad Diel
Jacob Hoffman
Frans Shalter
Jurg Perstler
Johannes Nothymer
Diedrich Fontin
Mich^l Kausler
Johannes Knab
Jacob Renner
Jacob Renner
Jurg D^o
Michael Esber
Gotfried Felker
Christian Meckel
Henry Froder
Johannes Becker
Casper D^o
Henry Stecken
John Smee
George Weitzel
George Kraa

[Endorsed:] Foreigners imported in the Ship Edinburgh, Capt Russel. Qual. 30th Septr 1754.
    160.   Shoemaker

* Name crossed out.

[List 220 B] Foreigners imported in the Ship Edinburgh, James Russel, Master, from Rotterdam, Qual. 30th Septr 1754.

Jacob (J) Schlotter
Henrich Weil
Friedrich Wilhelm Frick
Georg Eberhart Mühl
Johann Henrich Pfeiffer
Johann Conrad Schöppeler
Johann Henrich Blecker
Görg Hilt
Herman (X) Gerlach
Johannes Gerlach
Philippus Spetzius
Christoffel Gihll
Johann Gorg Wilhelm
Melchior Schimpf
Paul (++) Loshoen
Herman (X) Sommer
Philip ( ) Sommer, on board
Johan Peter Wolf
Johannes Mattheus
Bernhart Matthäus
Bernhart Matheus
Jurg (++) Wiesich
Andon Petry
Andräas Weyel
Jurg Henry (++) Rung
Ludwich (++) Kam
Conrad Neuhard
Johannes Ludwig
Conrad (X) Ludwich
Casper (+) Tzorn
J. Jost (X) Bingman
Fridrich Schimpf
Andreas Dein
Philipp Basterer
Daniel Vetzberger
Henrich Walther
Johannes Bott
Johannes Lincker

Henry (+) Langstorf
Jacob Ludwig
Engelwird Ludwig
Andreas Hubner
Ludwig Winckler
Johann Jacob Schimpf
Rudolf Drach
Balthasar Faulstich
George (+) Lohr
Casper (+) Erb
Samuel Haubt
Johannes Haubt
Johann Nickel Haubt
Peter (+) Hecht
Conrad (X) Lohr
Philip (+) Ludwich
Joha^s (X) Huber
Vallentin Ulrich
Eberhard Diehl
Henrich Winckler
Henrich Gebhart
Jacob (+) Hammersteyn
Conrath Enders
Peter Weissmann
Conrad (X) Bour
Johann Daniel Krug
Adam Leopohlt
Johannis (X) Weaver
Philip ( ) Ries, on board
J. Heinrich Kopp
Jerg Heinrich Kopp
Adam Strehm
Johann Henrich Strehm
Wielm Baltzer
Henrich Luy
Philip ( ) Towerman, on board
Erhart Weber
Henrich Hock

Anthoni Hecht
Jurg ( ) Metzer, on board
Johann Georg Weitzel
Jacob Kern
Math^s(+) Kern
Michael Wentz
Christoph (×) Essich
Jacob ( ) Rable, on board
Christoph Reble
Jörg Henrich Haas
Petter Paul
Andon Morckell
Adam Mauerer
Han Jacob Hemb
Michal Gruy
Johann Chruy
Conradt Grim
Johannes Grim
Jeorg Grimm
Conrad (+) Phillips
Peter (×) Kiel
Conrad (×) Messer
Peter (×) Dickell
Werner Dickol
Andrea (×) Krawthamel
Johan Conrad Schneider
Johann Sebastian Fritz
Johann Danigel Langsdorf
Johann Conrath Langsdorf
Conra[d] Deman
Friedrich Hildebrand
Jacob Geibel
Herman (+) Mathias
Johannes Bender
Conrad Bender
Phillip ( ) Rorich, on board
Conrad Schneider
Johannes Rupp
Georg Diel
Johannis ( ) Cappias, on board
Johannes Kemmerer

Henrich Lupp
Casper ( ) Sigler, on board
Jurg ( ) Holl, on board
Henry ( ) Peterson, on board
Petter Derdter
Johannes Menge
Ernst Menge
Peter (+) Bigcher
Reinhard (×) Weys
Mathias ( ) Ludwigh, on board
Henrich Reitz
Lorentz Alwohn
Gotthardt Allwohn
Jacob Hellerich
Christ^n (×) Helrich
Conrad (×) Kiesell
Herman (×) Gysell
Johannes Geisel
Georg (+) Surg
Hans Konrad Diehl
Jacob Hoffmann
Frantz Baltzer Schalter
Jorg Börstler
Johannes Northheimer
Jacob Fondein
Michael Kaussler
Johannes (+) Knob
Jacob Renner
Jacob Renner
Johann Georg Renner
Hans Michael (×) Esper
Gorg Gottfridt Völcker
Christian Meckell
Henrich Fretter
Johannes Becker
Caspar Becker
Henry (××) Steckin
Johannes Schmeh
Hans Iurg Kra
160

[Endorsed:]
Foreigners imported in the Ship Edinburgh, Capt Russel.
Qual. 30th Septr 1754.   Shoemaker.

[List 220 C] At the Court House at Philadelphia, Monday,
the 30th September, 1754.
Present: The Worshipful Charles Willing, Esquire, Mayor.
The Foreigners whose Names are underwritten, imported
in the Ship Edinburgh, James Russel, Master, from Rotterdam and last from Cowes, did this Day take the usual Qualifications. 5 Roman Catholicks. 1 Mennonist. 160 Qualified.
Palatinate & Wirtemberg.

Jacob (J) Slotters	Conrad (+) Ludewig
Henrich Weil	Caspar (X) Zorn
Friedrich Wilhelm Frick	J. Jost Bingman
Georg Eberhart Mühl	Fridrich Schimpf
Johann Henrich Pfeiffer	Andreas Dein
Herman (+) Gerlach	Philipp Basterer
Johann Conrad Schäppeler	Daniel Vetzberger
Johan Henrich Blecker	Henrich Walther
Görg Hilt	Johannes Bott
Johanes Gerlach	Johannes Lincker
Philippus Spetzius	J. Henry (X) Longstorff
Christoffel Gihll	Jacob Ludwig
Johann Jörg Wilhelm	Engelwird Ludwig
Melchior Schimpf	Andräas Huber
Paulus (X) Löshorn	Ludwig Winckler
Herman (X) Summer	Johann Jacob Schimpf
Philip ( ) Summer, on board	Rudolf Drach
Johan Peter Wolf, Senior	Balthasar Faulstich
Johannes Mattheus	George (+) Lohr
Bernhard Matthäus	Caspar (X) Erb
Bernhart Matthäus	Samuel Haubtt
George (XX) Weessig	Johannes Haubt
Anndon Petry	Johann Nickel Haubt
Andräas Weyel	Peter (X) Hecht
George Henry (+++) Rom	Conrad (K) Lohr
Ludewig (++) Kahn	Philip (X) Ludewig
Conrad Neuhart	Johanes (X) Huber
Johannes Ludwig	Jacob (X) Hammerstein

Vallentin Ulrich
Eberhard Diehl
Henrich Winckler
Conrad (+) Bawer
Henrich Gebhart
Conrath Enders
Peter Weissmann
Johann Daniel Krug
Adam Leupholt
Johanes (×) Weber
Philip ( ) Reess, on board
Johann Heinrich Kopp
Jorg Kopp
Adam Strehm
Johann Heinrich Strehm
Wiellm Baltzer
Henrich Luy
Erhart Weber
Philip ( ) Tauberman, on board
Henrich Hock
Anthoni Hecht
Johann Georg Weitzel
George ( ) Metzer, on board
Jacob Kern
Matheas (+) Kern
Michael Wentz
Christoff (+) Essig
Christoph Reble
Jacob ( ) Rehble, on board
Görg Henrich Haas
Petter Paul
Andon Marckell
Adam Mäurer
Han Jacob Hemb
Michael Gruy
Johann Chruy
Conradt Grim
Johannes Grim
Conrad (×××) Philips
Georg Grimm

Peter (+) Keel
Conrad (×) Meuser
Werner Dickel
Peter (+++) Tickel
Johan Conrad Schneider
Andreas (++) Krauthamel
Johann Sebastian Fritz
Johann Danigel Langsdorff
Johann Conrath Langsdorff
Conra[d] Deman
Friedrich Hildebrand
Jacob Geibel
Herman (×) Matheas
Johannes Bender
Johann Conrad Bender
Philip ( ) Roorig, sick
Conrad Schneider
Johannes Rupp
Georg Diel
Johanes ( ) Kopins, sick
Johannes Kemmerer
Henrich Lupp
Henry ( ) Peterson, sick
Caspar ( ) Zigler, on board
Georg ( ) Holl, on board
Petter Derdter
Johannes Menge
Ernst Menge
Peter (×) Pigger
Reinhart (××) Weiss
Henrich Reitz
Matheas ( ) Ludewig, on board
Lorentz Alwohn
Gotthardt Allwohn
Jacob Hellebrich
Christoff (×) Hellerich
Conrad (×) Geysel
Herman (×) Geysel
Johannes Geisel
George (×) Sorge

Hans Conrad Diehl
Jacob Hoffman
Frantz Baltzer Schalter
Jörg Börstler
Johannes (+) Knaab
Johannes Nordhheimer
Jacob Fondein
Michael Kausler
Jacob Renner
Jacob Renner, Junior

Georg Renner
Hans Michael (X) Esper
Gorg Gottfriedt Völcker
Christian Meckell
Henrich Fretter
Johannes Becker
Caspar Becker
Henry (XX) Stecker
Johannes Schmeh
Hans George (+) Krah

Sepr 27, 1754.

Sir

According to Orders we have carefully examined the State of Health of the People on board the Edinburgh, Capt Russel, and found many amongst them in a weak scorbutic State, but do not apprehend their Diseases to be contagious or Infectious.

To his Honour   Tho. Graeme
The Governour   Th. Bond
[Endorsed:]

Doctors Report of the Ship Edinburgh, Capt Russel, 27, Septr 1754. The Secretary was informed that thirty were concealed from the Doctors on this Ship.

[List 221 A] List of Peoples Names on Board the Ship Neptune, Capt. Waire, from Rotterdam, arrived at Philad. Sept 30th 1754.

George Mayer
John Jerg Dechert
Jacob Blassinger
Jerg Michael Fitzcom
Jerg Michael Lehr
Jon. Heinrich Brunbach
Joh. George Cort
Joh. Adam Michael
Andreas Shreiner
Joh. Peter Dachert
Andreas Bengel
Godfrid Gebhard
Johannes Schuhman

Georg Poltz
Jerge Traxel
Thomas Peeshance
Jacob Baussman
Jo. Charl. Harmsdorff
Adam Bakenhaupt
Johannes Reb
Frederich Schneider
Jerge Hoffman
Bernhard More
Jo. Adam Edelman
Nicolaus Hawer
Ph. Fred. Wineyard

Jo. Adam Blyard

Daniel Stegner

Johannes Hoch

Heinrich Klein

Joh. Paul Kemperlin

Nicolas Entzminger

Charls Kemperling

Philip Wild

Jacob Brigel

Jacob Weylands

Friedrich Preis

August Frid. Eichler

Jacob Weyland, Junr

Johannes Shuber

Philip Wild

Christian Reads

Philip Frey

Jerg Kochler

Eberhard Reickman

Philips Jacob Fassig

Benedik Forster

Heinrich Schaffer

Valentin Dalik

Christoph Spak

Philip Dieterick

Johan Peter Ruble

Conrad Wagner

Heinrich Sneyder

John Adam Mangold

Joh. Heinrich Sneyder

Valentin Klemens

Christ^n Hok

John Christian Wissenbach

Jo. George Boundlach

J. Heinrick Capes

Johannes Bekel

Joh. Jost Steverling

Jeremias Hörpell

Johannes Klinbell

Philip Nold

George Weyneman

Jacob Graulich

Heinrich Snyder

Philip Kolb

Conrad Woolf

Christian Bower

Peter Hetzel

Michael Miller

Philip Russell

Frederich Betz

Jacob Wentz

Adam Thomas

Peter Srott

Daniel Hoffman

Johannes Bardenbach

Balzasar Bargman

Jacob Ziemerman

Joh. Michael Shrotte

Jerg Nicolaus Andreas

Christian Andreas

Dieterich Holtzhausser

Abraham Holtzhausser

Heinrich Haufe

Friederich Betz

Adam Hallerman

Conrad Rinn

Jo^s Kaller

Heinrich Houne

Joh^s Smid

Peter Houne

Christ. Houne

John Dance

Friderich Brand

Johan Nicolaus Leidenmiller

Andreas Riegel

Johannes Herman

Johan Baker

Jacob Schoff

Peter Step

Ludwig Haring

Daniel Schreyner

Conrad Weile

Reinhard Bundsstein
Peter Scheyerman
Arnoltz Scherhartz
Conrad Mayer
David Miller
Jo. George Kreebel
Peter Schowmacker
Johannes Keysor
William Grauss
Philips Diehl
John Jacob Dierst
John George Kok
Johannes Philick
Heinrich Hehn
Burchard Sneyder
Valentin Gaspert
Philip Stang
Peter Heliger

Jo. William Curtz
Peter Dinger
Ludwig Kack
Henry Grantz
Martin Leininger
Arnold Baker
Philip Baker
Michael Reap
Georg Reichard
John Kroeller
Frederich Reis
John Jacob Eerzum
John Joost Kack
Conrad Sherfe
Michael Muller
John George Kribell
142

[Endorsed:]
Foreigners imported in the Ship Neptune, Capt Waire, from
Rotterdam. Qual. 30th Septr 1754.
    N° 142.   Keppelee.

[List 221 B] List of Foreigners imported in the Ship Neptune, Capt. Waire, from Rotterdam. Qual. 30th Septr 1754.

Georg Meyer
Johann Georg Decher
Jacob Blessing
Georg Michael Vitzthum
Georg Michel Lehr
Johannes Henrich Brumbach
Johann Jurg Kurcht
John Adam (XX) Michael
Matthias Heiner
Johann Peter Decher
Andreas (X) Bengel
Gottfridt Gebhard
Johannes Schumann
Georg Boltz

Johann Georg Traxel
Johann Thomas Bischantz
Georg Jacob Hausmann
Joan Carl Hermsdorff
Hans Adam Beckenhaub
Johannes Rebb
Frederick (+) Schneider
Göerg Hofmann
Johann Bernhard Mock
John Adam (+) Edelman
Johann Nicklaus Hauer
Philips Friedrich Wünger
Hans Adam Bleier
Daniel (X) Stegner

Johannes (X) Hoch
Henry (+) Klein
Johann Paul Gemberling
Hans Nickel Ensminger
Johan Carl Gemberling
Phillip Wilt
J. J. Brückel
Jacob (HW) Wylands
Fredrick (X) Price
Augustus Siegfried Eychler
Jacob (O) Wyland
Johannes (X) Shober
Philippus Frey
Gristian Rietz
Fillib Wild
Georg (X) Hechler
Eberhard Reichmann
Philipp Jacob Foesig *
Benedict (X) Forster
Henry (X) Shafer
Valentine (X) Dalik
Christoph Speck
Philibs Dietrig
Peter (+) Rubel
Conrad (W) Wagner
Johann Henrich Schneider
J. Adam (+) Mangold
J. Henry (X) Schneider
Valentine Clementz
Christian Hoch
Johann Christian Wiesenbach
Johann Georg Gundlach
Hinrich Cappes
Johannes Böckel
Jost (X) Steveling
Jeremiah (+) Harpel
Johannes Kleinbehl

Johann Philip Nold
George (++) Weyman
Jacob (+) Graulich
Henry (+) Schneider
Johann Philipps Kolb
Johan Conrad Wollf
Christian (+) Bouer
Petter Stätzel
Michael (X) Miller
Johann Philipp Brusel
Frederick (+) Betz
Johann Georg Wentz
Adam (X) Thomas
Peter (X) Srott
Daniel Hoffman
Johannes Bartenbach
Balthasar Bergmann
Johann Michel Schrott
J. Jacob (X) Zimmerman
Gerge Nicholas (X) Andreas
Christian (O) Andreas
Didrich Holtzhauser
Abraham Holtzhauser
Johann Henrich Hauff
Friedrich Betz
Adam Höllerman
Conraht Rim
Johannes Keller
Henrich Haun
Johannes Schmitt
Johann Peter Haun
Johann Christian Haun
Johannes Lentz
Frederick (FB) Brand
Johann Nickolaus Eitenmüller
Anndras Rihl
Johannes Herman

* Philip Jacob Foesig or Faesig (as spelled by some writers) became the Reformed schoolmaster at Reading, Pennsylvania. See Daniel Miller, *History of the Reformed Church in Reading*, Pa., Reading, 1905, p. 32, also Dr. Livingood's *History of the Reformed Church Schools* in the Proceedings of the Pennsylvania German Society, p. 96.

Jacob (+) Baker
Jacob Schoff
Peter (×) Step
Lodowich (×) Haring
Daniel Schroin
Conradt Weiel
Rainhart Puntstein
Johann Petter Scheurman
Arnholt Scheratz
Johann Conraht Meiger
David (×) Miller
J. George Krebel
Peter (×) Shammer
Johanes (×) Kayser
Wilm Grauss
Johann Phylpps Tiel
J. Jacob (+) Durst
Johann Görg Gack

Johannes Völck
Henry (×) Haan
Burgart (×) Schneider
Valentine (×) Gaspert
Philip (+) Stang
Peter (×) Heliger
John William Kurz
Johann Peter Dinger
Lodowich (×) Kack
Johann Henrich Krantz
Mardin Neiniger
Arnolt Becker
Philib Becker
Johan Migel Rapp
Georg Reiger
John (×) Kroelle
Johann Just Gack
Conrad (+) Sherf

[Endorsed:]
Foreigners imported in the Ship Neptune, Capt. Waire, from Rotterdam. Qual. 30th Septr 1754.

N° 142.   Keppelee.

[List 221 C] At the State House at Philadelphia, Monday, the 30th Sept. 1754. P. M.

Present: The Worshipful Charles Willing, Esquire, Mayor.

The Foreigners whose Names are underwritten, Imported in the Ship Neptune, Captain Waire, from Rotterdam and last from Cowes, did this day take the usual Oaths & Declarations. 142 Qualified. 260 Freights. 400 Souls. Palatinate, Darmstad, Zweybrecht. 4 Roman Catholicks.

Goerg Meyer
Johann Georg Decher
Jacob Blessing
Georg Michael Vitzthum
Georg Michel Löhr
Johannes Henrich Brumbach
Johanes Gurg Kurcht
John Adam (××) Michael

Matthias Heiner
Johann Peter Decher
Andereas (×) Bingel
Gottfriedt Gebhard
Johannes Schumann
Georg Boltz
Johann Georg Traxel
Johan Thomas Bischantz

Georg Jacob Hausmann
Joan Carl Hermsdorff
Hans Adam Beckenhaub
Johannes Reb
Friederich (+) Shneyder
Georg Hoffman
Johann Bernhart Mock
John Adam (✕) Edelman
Johann Nicklaus Hauer
Philip Friedrich Wünger
Hans Atem Bleier
Daniel (+) Stegner
Johanes (H) Hogh
Henry (✕) Klein
Johan Paul Gemberling
Hans Nickel Ensminger
Johan Carl Gemberling
Phillip Wilt
J. J. Brückel
Jacob (HW) Wynant
Friederich (+) Preis
Augustus Siegfriedt Eychler
Jacob (+) Weynant, Junior
Johanes (✕) Shober
Philippus Frey
Gristian Rietz
Fillib Wild
Georg Hechler
Eberhardt Reichmann
Philipp Jacob Foesig
Benedictus (✕) Forster
Henry (✕) Shäffer
Vallentin (✕✕) Dalick
Christoph Speck
Phillibs Dietrig
Peter (+) Rubel
Conrad (W) Wagner
Johann Henrich Schneider
J. Adam (+) Angold
J. Henry (+) Shneyder
Vallantin Clementz

Christian Hog
Johannes Christjan Wiesenbach
Johann Geörg Gündlach
Henrich Cappes
Johannes Böckel
J. Jost (✕) Stuberling
Jeremias (+) Herbel
Johannes Kleinbehl
Johann Philip Nold
George (✕✕) Weyman
Jacob (++) Graulich
Henry (+) Shneyder, 2d
Johann Philipps Kolb
Johan Conrat Wolf
Christian (✕) Bauer
Petter Stätzel
Michael (✕) Miller
Johann Philipp Brusel
Friederich (+) Betz
Johann Georg Wentz
J. Adam (+) Thomas
J. Peter (✕) Shrot
Daniel Hoffman
Johannes Bartenbach
Balthasar Bergman
J. Johann Michel Schrott
J. Jacob (+) Zimmerman
G. Michael (A) Andereas
Christian (A) Andereas
Didrich Holtzhauser
Abraham Holtzhauser
Johann Henrich Hauff
Friedrich Betz
Adam Höllerman
Conraht Rim
Johannes Keller
Henrich Haun
Johannes Schmitt
Johann Peter Haun
Johann Christian Haun
Johannes Lentz

Friederich (FB) Brand
Johann Nickolaus Eitenmüller
Anndreas Rihl
Johannes Herman
Jacob (O) Beker
Jacob Schoff
Peter (X) Step
Ludewig (H) Herring
Daniel Schroin
Conradt Weiel
Rainhart Stein
Johann Petter Scheuerman
Arnholt Scherratz
Johann Conrahd Meiger
Davit (M) Miller
Johan George (X) Kribel
Peter (+) Shamar
Johanes (X) Keysar
Wilm Grauss
Johann Phylips Diel
J. Jacob (+) Dorsham

Johann Jörg Gack
Johannes Völck
Henry (X) Hain
Borchart (+) Shneyder
Vallentin ( ) Gösper
Philip (+) Long
Peter (X) Hilliger
John William Kurz
Johan Peter Dinger
Ludewig (X) Gack
Johann Henrich Krantz
Martin Neiniger
Arnolt Becker
Philib Becker
Johann Migel Rapp
Georg Reiger
Johanes (X) Krayly
Johann Just Gak
Conrad (+) Sherrer
142

Septr 30, 1754.

Sir

We this Day carefully examined the State of Health of the Mariners and Passengers on board the Ship Neptune, Capt Waire, from Rotterdam and found no objection to their being admitted to land in the City immediately.

To his Honour   Tho. Graeme
The Governour.   Th. Bond

[Endorsed:]

30th Septr 1754. Doctors Certificate to the Ship Neptune.

[List 222 A] A List of Men on board the Ship Phoenix, John Spurrier, M^r, from Rotterdam 1754. [Qualified October 1, 1754.]

Johannes Young
Jacob Snyder
Ludwig Gotting
Abraham Steyn

Henry Werkyser
Nicholas Gips
Peter Tryer
Johannes Henrig

Peter Henrich
Peter Miller
Joost Shanour
Hannes Riest
Michael Fletter
Lorents Mangel
Burghart Kuch
Marks Widenger
Frans Widenger
Herinimous Greenwald
Ulrich Jesle
Johannes Albert
Johannes Gebhart
Adam Sour
Michael Sour
Johannes Sour
Thomas Endres
Michael Diefel
Jurg Rottenwalder
Leonard Bengel
Bernhard Pop
Jurg Pop
Lorents Albert
Mich¹ Dosh
Hans Kiesecker
Johannes Beck
Anderas Fet
Anderas Fertig
Henry Ungelbach
Christian Shum
Anderas Swartz
Johannes Kilbert
Hannes Schoffer
Philip Wieshar
Abraham Terkonig
Leonard Tort
Henry Ott
Adam Geegh
Herinimous Geegh
Jacob Gragey
Michael Werkey

Peter Nagbarr
Johannes Hartman
Nicholas Bender
Mathias Stumpf
Adam Miller
Jurg Schoffer, Senr
Jurg Schoffer, Junr
Peter Schoffer
Adam Tiem
Peter Berringer
Henry Kam
Casper Joost
Anderas Smith
Casper Oberdorf
Hans Senftleyder
Anderas Bieslin
Thomas Tiem
Adam Tiem
Hans Jurg Liets
Anderas Gerberig
Peter Gerberig
Melchor Webert
Valentine Horner
Martin Sytner
Thomas Bimmer
Jurg Raad
Johan Gabel
Anderas Konkel
Peter Kankel
Henry Muller
Henry Haag
Michael Sietner
Dieter Gerhard
Nich^s Schentelman
Philip Schentelman
Baltzer Goll
Baltzer Hanaus
Baltzer Snyder
Lorents Rouyter
Lorentz Ambtman
Math^s Rhynhart

Conrad Kern

Henry Messersmit

Lorentz Kramer

Nich^s Armsmer

Philip Diel

Johan Helfergramer

Peter Fisher

Johannes Hertz

Martin Schryer

Valentin Keyser

Peter Thomas

Gerhard Thomas

Ludwig Kuntz

Wilhelm Melger

Jacob Helter

Casper Hass

Mich^l Grele

Nicholas Gerhard

Hartman Has

Mathias Bub

Philip Adam Paulus

Jacob Snyder

Johannes Snyder

Philip Shoek

Augustas Krimler

Anderas Fertig

Joseph Rychard

Johannes Hieman

Jacob Burghard

Simon Begler

Peter Bechler

Johannes Beyl

Leonard Zib

Anderas Groh

Philip Wagnor

Jacob Fries

Fred^k Christian

Jacob Angst

Fred^k Schoffer

Gerhard Frankforder

Henry Sax

Nicholas Lemer

Jocham Lemer

Peter Guth

Peter Schott

Ludwig Schott

Peter Neu

Jurg Rouch

Dietrich Wien

Wilhelm Wies

Johannes Kaufman

Johannes Kaufman, Junr

Daniel Diedela

Peter Rohrbacher

Abraham Ettinger

Wilhelm Albert

Adam Hembach

Jurg Gerlach

Anderas Heter

Wendel Krim

Thomas Honsicker

Daniel Honsicker

Daniel Smith

Adam Bretig

Daniel Phiel

Johannes Smith

Albrech Shimel

Peter Shimel

Nicholas Neyman

Michael Dietrich

Richard Wolf

Christoph Miller

Henry Fetter

Fred^k Herman

Jacob Herman

Peter Turnus

Jurg Turnus

Jacob Miller

Adam Smith

Henry Sihttla

Simon Sihttla

Peter Buhl

Daniel Buhl
Jurg Fries
Henry Smith
David Schroder
Philip Zeb
Jacob Bredenbach
Adam Miller
Nicholas Lorentz
Christian Koch
Gerhard Markins
Michael Sommer
Jurg Manus Conrad
Wendel Wendling
Leonard Burger
Johannes Lint
Mathias Miller
Ludwig Wert
Conrad Dibo
Fred^k Miller
Johannes Fiet
Jacob Tissinger
Peter Tick
Christian Brengel
Jacob Brengel
Jacob Bussung
Christian Conrad
Nicholas Paul
Elias Jantus
Henry Kielman
Peter Becker
Wilhelm Becker
Christian Brechbel
Christian Forer
Daniel Forer

Nich^l Shantz
Johannes Eselman
Peter Eselman
Hans Jantz
Isaac Neyswander
Joseph Wenger
Ulrich Engel
Frans Tieler
Ulrick Reist
Ulrich Light
Ulrich Burgholter
Hans Swartz
Hans Shutz
Jacob Moser
Hans Burgholder
Christian Burgholder
Christian Baltzle
Peter Waltzel
Christian Rodrig
Christ. Neyswander
Peter Swartz
Christ. Swartz
Ulrich Neycob
Christ. Keymer, Senr
Christ. Keymer, Junr
Nich^s Moses
Abraham Brechbeller
Jurg Hartway
Christian Neycomer
Christ. Kelghofer
Lorentz Enters
Bartholomew Beringer
239

Capt Spurrier's List 1754, of Foreigners imported from Rotterdam. Qual. 1st Octr 1754.

N° 239.   Shoemaker.

[List 222 B] The Foreigners whose Names are under-written, imported in the Ship Phoenix, Captain John Spurrier, did this first Day of October, 1754, take the usual Qualifications before the Mayor of Philadelphia.

Johannes Jung
Jacob Schneider
Ludwig Göttgen
Abraham Stein
Carl Henrich Werckhäusser
Johann Nickel Gibs
Peter Treier
Johannes Henrichs
Peter Henrichs
Peter Müller
Filib Wetzger
Josh. (+) Shonhour
Hance (+) Rish
Michael Fletter
Lorence (X) Mangal
Burckhardt Kuch
Makos (X) Whithingar
France (X) Whithingar
Jaronames Crinewat
Ulrich Jesel
Johannes Alberth
Johannes (+) Gabhart
Hans Adam Sauer
Hanns Michel Sauer
Johannes Sauer
Thomas Endres
Johan (X) Michal Divel
Jnº Gorge (O) Rotenwaters
Joh. Lenhart Bingel
Bernhart Bob
Johan Georg Bob
Lorentz Alberth
Hance Michal (X) Thosch
Hans Kisecker
Johannes Beck
Andreas Feth
Andreas Fertig

John (+) Henry Angel[bach]
Christoffel Schum
Andreas Schwartz
Johannes Gilbert
Johannes Schäffer
Philip (X) Wyshaar
Lenhardt Ott
Heinrich Ott
Adam Gieg
Heronimus (X) Geegh
Jean Jaque Raiquet
Meisel Bürckie
Jean Pierre Voisin
Johannes Hartman
Nicolaus Bintter
Matheus Stumpf
Adam (+) Miler
Jörg Schäffer
Peter Schäffer
Adam Dihm
Petter Beriger
Henrich Dann
Caspar Jost
Andreas Schmit
Casper Oberdorf
Hans Senfftleber
Andreas Beuschlein
Thomas Dihm
Hans Adam Dihm
Johann Georg List
Andreas Gerbrich
Petter Gerbrich
Melchior Weppert
Valtin Hörner
Martin Seitner
Thomas (X) Baman
Johann Georg Rath

Johannes Gabel
Anderreas Cunckel
Peter Cunckel
Johann Heinrich Müller
Heinrich Haag
Michel Seittner
Titreak (X) Jerhad
Nicolaus Schindtelmann
Johann Philipp Schindelmann
Balthas Goll
Balthasar Rabanus
Abraham Le Roy
Palzer Schneiter
Lorentz Reuter
Lorentz Sandman
Matheis Reinhart
Conrad Kern
Henrich Messerschmidt
Lorentz Cramer
Johann Nicolaus Armsheiner
Georg Philip Diehl
Johann Helffer Cremer
Johann Peter Fisher
Johann (X) Harts
Marten (M) Shriar
Valentin (K) Kiser
Peter Thomas
Gerhardt Thomas
Ludwig Cuntz
Wilhelem (X) Mecker
Johan Jacob Helder
Caspar (X) Haze
Michael Krähl
Nickles (XX) Carhad
Hartman (XX) Haze
Mathas (X) Pape
Filips Adam Paulus
Jacob Schneider
Philipp Schuch
Johannes Schneider

Heinrich Augustus Grimler
Andreas Ferdig
Joseph Reichard
Johann (XX) Gyman
Jakob (X) Workhad
Simon (O) Bechler
Peter (X) Bechler
Johans (O) Bielle
Wilhelam Smit
Andres (X) Cobe
Philip (X) Wagner
Jacob Fries
Fridrack (+) Cristan
Joh. Jacob Angst
Philipp Friedrich Schäfer
Gerhart Franckfurter
Johann Henrich Sacks
Nichlas Lehmer
Jochem Lehmer
Peter Guth
Hanns Petter Schott
Lodweck (+) Chot
Peter (X) Ney
Gorge (+) Row
Johannes Kauffman
Johannes Kauffman, Junior
Dietrich Weinig
Wilhelm Weiss
Danail (X) Deadlo
Peater (X) Rowback
Abraham Edinger
Wilhelm Albert
Adam Heimbach
Hanns Gorg Gerlach
Andreas Hüter
Wendel (W) Kraem
Thomas Hunsicker
Daniel Hunsicker
Danniel Schmit
Johan Adam Britzius

Johan Daniel Pfeil

Johannes Schmidt

Johann Albrecht Stimmel

Johann Peter Stimmel

Nickel Neuman

Michel Diederich

Reichart Wolff

Christoffel Müller

Friedrich Herman

Jacob Herman

Peter (++) Turnas

Johann Gerg Türnies

Jacob (X) Miler

Adam (O) Smit

Henrich Schedler

Simon Schedler

Henery (H) Peater

Petter Biehl

Danil (T) Peater

Jörg Fries

Joh. Henrich Schmitt

David Schröder

Philipp Zepp

Jacob (X) Radaback

Adam Müller

Nicklas (+) Lorence

Christian Koch

Gorge (+) Märtens

Johann Michael Sommer

Georg Magnus Conrad

Wendel Wendeling

Lenart (X) Borghad

Johan (X) Lent

Matthias Müller

Lodewick (X) Whart

Conrea (O) Tevo

Fredreck (O) Miler

Johannes Veith

Jacob Theisinger

Petter Dick

Christian Brengel

Jacob Brengel

Jacob (X) Hosong

Christian (+) Conred

Nickles (X) Powl

Elias (X) Bondas

Henery (X) Kelman

Peter Baker

Wilhelm (X) Begger

Christian Brächtbüll

Christian Führer

Daniel Führer

Niclaus Schantz

Hans Aeschliman

Peter (X) Eslaman

Hance (X) Jonce

Ysach Neuwenschwander

Joseph Wanger

Ulrich Engel

France (X) Caler

Hans Uli Reist

Olerick (X) Light

Ulrich Burchalter

Hance (+) Swarts

Hance (X) Shonts

Hans Jacob Moser

Hance (X) Burghalter

Christian Burckwalder

Christof (X) Bantzler

Petter Balzly

Christof (W) Yetreag

Chrystian Neuwenschwander

Petter Schwartz

Christen Schwartz

Oulreck (X) Neucom

Cristain (XX) Gaymar

Cristian (XX) Gymar, Junior

Niclaus Moser

Abraham Brechbüehler

Georg Hartweg

Christian (✕) Neycomer   Lorentz Enders
Chris^n (✕) Helhoff   Bartholemeus Beringer

[Endorsed:]
List of Foreigners imported in the Ship Phoenix, Capt. Spurrier, from Rotterdam. Qual. 1st October, 1754. No. 239. Shoemaker.

[List 222 C] At the State House at Philadelphia, Tuesday, the 1st October, 1754.
Present: The Worshipful Charles Willing, Esquire, Mayor.
The Foreigners whose Names are underwritten, Imported in the Ship Phoenix, Captn John Spurrier, from Rotterdam & last from Cowes, did this day take the usual Qualifications to the Government. 11 Roman Catholicks. 25 Menonists. Swissers. 300 Souls 554 Freights. [From] Franconia, Palatinate, Zweybreck.

Johannes Jung
Jacob Schneider
Ludwig Göttgen
Abrahamm Stein
Carl Hennrich Werckhäusser
Johann Nickel Gibs
Peter Treier
Johannes Henrichs
Peter Henrichs
Filib Wetzger
Jost (✕) Shoenower
Hans (+) Reish
Michael Fletter
Lorentz (✕) Mangel
Burckhardt Kuch
Marcus (✕) Weidinger
Frantz (✕) Weidinger
Hieronimus (✕) Gereenewald
Ulrich Jesel
Johannes Alberth
Johanes (+) Gebhart
Hans Adam Sauer
Hans Michel Sauer

Johannes Sauer
Thomas Endres
J. Michael (+) Tewbel
J. Georg (O) Ruttenwalder
Joh. Lenhart Bingel
Peter Müller
Johan Bernhartt Bob
Johan Georg Bob
Lorentz Alberth
Hans Mich. [?] Dosch
Hans Kisecker
Johannes Beck
Andreas Feth
Andreas Fertig
J. Henry (✕) Unckelbach
Christoffel Schum
Andreas Schwartz
Johannes Gilbert
Johannes Schäffer
G. Philip (✕) Eysenhaar
Linhardt Ott
Heinrich Ott
Adam Gieg

Hironimus (×) Gieg
Jean Jaque Raiquet
Meischeiel [!] Bürkie
Jean Pierre Voisin
Johannes Hartman
Nicolaus Bindder
Matheus Stumpf
Adam (+) Miller
Jörg Schäffer
Petter Schäffer
Adam Dihm
Petter Beriger
Henrich Dann
Caspar Jost
Andreas Schmit
Carrsper Oberdorf
Hans Senftleber
Andreas Beuschlein
Thomas Dihm
Hans Adam Dihm
Johann Georg List
Thomas (×) Bimmer
Andreas Gerbrich
Petter Gerbrich
Melchior Weppert
Walter Hörner
Martin Seitner
Johann Georg Rath
Johannes Gabel
Andereas Cunckel
Peter Cunckel
Johann Heinrich Müller
Heinrich Haag
Michel Seitner
Diterich (××) Gerhart
Nicolaus Schindtelman
Johann Philipp Schindelmann
Balthas Goll
Balthasar Rabanus
Abraham Le Roy
Palzer Schneiter

Lorentz Reuter
Lorentz Sandman
Matheis Reinhart
Conrad Kern
Henrich Messerschmidt
Lorentz Cramer
Johann Nicolaus Armsheiner
Georg Philip Diehl
Johann Helffer Cramer
Johann Peter Fischer
Johannes (×) Hertz
Martin (M) Shreyer
Vallentin (K) Keyser
Peter Thomas
Gerhardt Thomas
Ludwig Cuntz
Wilhelm (×) Metziger
Caspar (×) Haas
Johann Jacob Helder
Michael Krähl
J. Nicklas (××) Gerhart
Hartman (××) Haas
Matheas (++) Pop
Philip Adam Paulus
Jacob Schneider
Philipp Schuch
Johannes Schneider
Heinrich Augustus Grimler
Andreas Ferdig
Joseph Reichard
Johanes (×××) Geyman
Jacob (×) Burchart
Simon (O) Bechler
Peter (×) Bechler
Johanes (J) Beyl
J. Wilhelm (O) Zwib
Andereas (×) Grub
Philip (×) Wagner
Jacob Fries
Friederich (+) Christian
Johan Jacob Angst

Philipp Fridrich Schääfer
Gerhart Franckfurter
Johan Henrich Sacks
Daniel (+) Ditloh
Nichlos Lehmer
Jochem Lehmer
Peter Guth
Hans Peter Schott
Ludewig (X) Shutt
Peter Ney
George (+) Rau
Johannes Kauffman
Johannes Kauffman, Junr
Dietrich Wenig
Wilhelm Weiss
Peter (X) Rohrbach
Abraham Edinger
Wilhelm Albert
Adam Heimbach
Hanns Görg Gerlach
Andreas Hüter
Wendal (W) Krem
Thomas Hunsicker
Daniel Hunsicker
Daniel Schmit
Johan Adam Britzius
Johann Daniel Pfeil
Johannes Schmidt
Johann Albrecht Stimmel
Johan Peter Stimmel
Nickel Neuman
Michel Diedrich
Reinhart Wolff
Christoffel Müller
Friedrich Herman
Jacob Herman
Peter (++) Dörrnis
Johann Gerg Turnis
Jacob (+) Miller
Adam (+) Shmit
Henrich Schedler

Simon Schedler
Henry (X) Hather
Petter Biehl
Daniel (X) Biehl
Jorg Fries
Joh. Henrich Schmitt
David Schröder
Philipp Zepp
Jacob (X) Rathebach
Adam Müller
J. Nicklas (X)) Lorentz
Christian Koch
Gerhart (X) Martins
Johann Michel Sommer
George Magnus Connrad
Wendel Wendeling
J. Leonhart (X) Burchart
Johanes (X) Linn
Matthias Müller
Ludewig (X) Wird
Conrad (O) Dewo
Friederich (O) Miller
Johannes Veith
Jacob Theissinger
Petter Dick
Christian Brengel
Jacob Brengel
Jacob (+) Hussung
Christian (X) Cunrad
Nicklas (X) Paul
Elias (X) Jentes
Henry (X) Gielman
Peter Becker
Wilhelm Becker
Christian Brächtbül
Christian Fuhrer
Daniel Fuhrer
Nicklaus Schwartz
Hans Aeschlimann
Peter (X) Ashelman
Hans (X) Janz

Ysah Neuwenschwander
Joseph Wanger
Uhlrich Engel
Frantz (X) Teetsler
Hans Üli Reist
Uhlrich (X) Richty
Uhlrich Burghalter
Hans (+) Schwartz
Hans (X) Shütz
Hans Jacob Moser
Hans (X) Burghalter
Christen Burckalder
Christoff (KB) Pantzly
Petter Baltzly
Christoff (CW) Widerich

Christian Neuwenschwander
Petter Schwartz
Christen Schwartz
Uhllerich (+) Newcommer
Christian (XX) Geimmer
Christian (XX) Geimmer,
  Junior
Nicklaus Moser
Abraham Brechbüehler
Georg Hartweg
Christian (X) Newcomer
Christian (X) Helhoff
Lorentz Enders
Bartholomeus Beringer
239

Sepr 30, 1754.

Sir

According to Orders we have carefully examined the State of Health of the Mariners & Passengers on board the Ship Phonix, Capt Spurrier, from Roterdam and found no Disease amongst them which we apprehend can be injurious to the Inhabitants of the City.

To his Honour
The Governour.

Tho. Graeme
Th. Bond

[Endorsed:]
30th Septr 1754. Doctors Certificate relating to the Ship Phoenix.

[List 223 A] Foreigners imported in the Ship Peggy, Capt. James Abercrombie, from Rotterdam. Qual. 16th October, 1754.

John George Krompols
Markus Weckfort
Anthony Redlinger
Fredrick Holst
Francis Stiglin
Baltzar Visserer
Hendrick Fidler
Wendel Warner

Geo. Adam Dorst
Hans Mich^l Smith
Hans Philip Flax
Ferdinand Frank
Jacob Fredrick Meyer
Jacob Vreyberge
Frederick Hinger, N. Lander *
Walledine Meyer

* Name crossed out.

Peter Hobben *, stet
Daniel Hinger
Hans Geo. Rauss
And^w Punchoer
Jacob Schodt
Hans Geo. Schweiger
George Keeler
Michael Shwenkh *, stet
Peter Gubeler *
Hendrick Roeperech
Gaspar Strittenberg *
Bernard Eegel
George Weist
George Weber *, stet
Jacob Frey
Hans Martin Dram
Hans George Dram
Hans George Dram
Ludwick Freysinger
John Gerrit Armbruster
Adam Schnollenberg
Jacob Hickelyoer
Matthias Waterman
Abram Troester
Hans Jurg Rheyn
Jacob Whigel *
Peter Weidener
Fredrick Sluhan
Jno Leopold
Hans Martin Leopold
Johan Caspar Leopold †
Mathias Arnold
Fredrick Kooch
John Hever
George Henrick Bower
John Herman
Mathias Deer
Fredrick Housie
Jno. Frederick Housie †

And^w Hickenluber
Fredrick Lyng
Michael Tierer
Mich^l Koster
John Damer
John Hommel
Conrad Nessel
Jo^s Pouger
John Schuster
Michael Hiptsch
George Brager
Stepen Craws
John Winschum
Henry Lodowick Wenn
Martin Hiss
Michl. Frank, N. Lander *
John Claas
Ludowick Faegler *
Michael Krips
Jno Fredrick Rigger
Hans Jurg Reyster
Jno Schumackker
Jno Pigeler
Michael Wouster
John Walker
Jacob Dom
Hans George Dom
Lawrence Mirgendal
John Speyer
Michael Gleyn
Melchior Jordel †
Hans Schouler
Michael Rosnaegle
Christianus Rick
George Michael Rick
Christianus Rick
Anthony Walhyser †
Jacob Graff †
Jno Adam Fetzer

* Names crossed out, sometimes with the note "Stet."
† Crossed out, with note: "Stet, on board."

George Adam Grottenbenger   Mich¹ Tiets *
John George Frior †   Petʳ Kogendelfer
Mich¹ Kehner †   Wᵐ Reycher
Peter Slim   George Hitler
John Meyer   Jacob Tautz *
Martin Merkel   Jacob Ebbergault *
John Faubel   Joseph Graff, N. Länder *
Hans Jurg Krets   George Lingenfelder *
John Luts   Jacob Spreeker
Stophel Krets   Adam Gront
George Shittinger   Stophel Grosse

[Endorsed:]
List of Mens Names imported on the Ship Peggy, Capt.
James Abercrombie, from Rotterdam. Qual. 16ᵗʰ Octʳ 1754.
Nº 107.

Danⁱ Beneset.

[List 223 B] Foreigners imported in the Ship Peggy, Capᵗ
James Abercrombie, from Rotterdam. Qual. 16ᵗʰ October,
1754.

John Charles (+) Krompols   Andreas Bonjour
Marcus Weckfort   Jacob (J) Schodt
Antony Rettinger   Jurge Schweigr
Friedrich Hust   Jorg Köchel
Francis (✕) Stiglin   Michael Schenkh
Baltzer (+) Visserer   Henry (H) Roeperech
Christian Heinrich Fiedler   Bernard (+) Eegel
Wendel (+) Warner   George (✕) Weist
Georg Adam Dürstler   George (   ) Weber, on board
Hans Michael (H) Smith   Jacob (+) Frey
Hans Philip (H) Flach   Hans Martin Tram
Ferdinand Franckh   Hans Jorg Dram
Jacob Friderich Mayer   Johann George Tram
Jacob Freyberger   Ludwig Friderich Freysinger
Johann Vallentin Meier   Hans Jerg Armbruster
Peter Gobel   Johann Adam Schnellenberger
Danel Hengerer   Jacob (✕) Hickelyfer
Hans George (A) Rauss   Matthias Wassermann

* Name crossed out.
† Crossed out, with note "Stet, on board."

Abraham Trostel
Hans Jerg Reinn
Petter Wund [?]
Jacob Fridrich Zluhan
Johanns Luppoldt
Johans Luppoldt
John Casper (   ) Leopold, on board
Matheus Arnoldt
Frederick (×) Kooch
Johannes Höpfer
George Henry (+) Bower
Johannes Hermann
Matthäs Dir
Friederich Hausihl
John Frederick (   ) Housie, on board
Andreas Heckenleib
Johan Friederich Linck
Hans Michäl Dir
Michael (O) Koster
John (×) Damer
Johannes Hommel
Johann Conrad Möschler
Joseph Boger
John (+) Schuster
Michael (++) Hiptsch
George (××) Brager
Stefan Kraus
Johannes Wirsum
Henrich Ludwig Wörn
Martin Has
Johannes Class
Michael Krebs
Johannes Ricker
Hans Jerg Rätzer
John (×) Shoemaker
Johannes Biecheler

Michael Wurster
Johanes Walckher
Jacob Thum
Georg Thum [?]
Lorentz Mergenschoerler [?]
Johannes Speyer
Michael Klein
Melchior (   ) Jordel, on board
Hans Schuhler
Michael Rossnagel
Christian (+) Rick
Jerg Migel Reck
Christianus Rech
Anthony (   ) Walhyser, on board
Jacob (   ) Graff, on board
Johan Adam Pfisterer
Gorg Adam Grombein
John George (   ) Freir, on board
Michael (   ) Kehner, on board
Johan Peter Schlemb
John (HM) Myer
Martin (HM) Merkel
John (×××) Faurbel
Johan Iörg Kress
Johannes Lutz
Hans Jorg Schiettinger
Michael (   ) Tiets, on board
Jerg Petter Kochendörffer
Wilhelm (O) Reicher
Georg Hörthler
Jacob (   ) Tauts, on board
Jacob (   ) Ebbersault, on board
Jacob Andreas Sprecher
Adam (A) Gront
Stophel (G) Gross
No. 108

[Endorsed:]
List of Foreigners imported in the Ship Peggy, Capt James

Abercrombie, from Rotterdam. Qual. 16ᵗʰ Octʳ 1754. Nº 107.

Danˡ Beneset.

Admitted by the Mayor in the Absence of the Governor.

[List 223 C] At the Court House at Philadelphia, Wednesday, the Sixteenth Day of October, 1754.

Present: The Worshipful Charles Willing, Esquire, Mayor.

The Foreigners whose Names are underwritten, imported in the Ship Peggy, Capᵗ James Abercrombie, from Rotterdam but last from Gosport, did this Day take the usual Qualifications to the Government. 10 Roman Catholicks. [108] Souls. [. . .] Whole Freights. [From] Wirtenberg & the Palatinate.

John Carol (X) Krumholtz
Marcus Weckfort
Antony Rettinger
Friedrich Hust
Frantz (X) Stichling
Balsazar (X) Wisser
Christian Heinrich Fiedler
Wendal (+) Warner
Georg Adam Dürstler
Hans Michael (H) Shmit
Hans Philip (H) Flachs
Ferdinand Franckh
Jacob Friederich Mayer
Jacob Freyberger
Johann Vallentin Meier
Petter Gebel
Danel Hengerer
Hans Georg (A) Kraws
Andreas Bonjour
Jacob (S) Shutt
Jurge Schweigr
Jerg Köchel
Michael Schenk
Henry (H) Rubrecht
Bernhart (+) Eagel
H. Georg (X) West
Georg ( ) Webber, on board
Jacob (+) Frey

Hans Martin Tram
Hans Jorg Dram
Johann Georg Tram
Ludwig Fridrich Freysinger
Hanns Jurg Armbrüster
Johann Adam Schnellenberger
Jacob (+) Hikenleibly
Matthias Wasserman
Abraham Trostel
Hans Jerg Reinn
Petter Wund [?]
Jacob Fridrich Zluhan
Johanes Luppoldt
Johans Luppoldt
John Caspar ( ) Leopold, on board
Matheus Arnoldt
Friederich (XX) Koch
Johannes Höpfer
Jeorg Henrich (+) Bower
Johannes Hermann
Matthäus Dir
John Friederich ( ) Housier, on board
Friederich Hausihl
Andreas Heckenleib
Johan Friederich Linck
Hans Michel Dir

Michael (Mi) Koster
Johan Dammel
Johannes Hommel
Johann Conrad Möschler
Joseph Boger
John (+) Shooster
H. Michal (X) Hüpbish
John George (++) Bragher
Stefan Kraus
Johannes Wersum
Henrich Ludwig Wörn
Martin Has
Johannes Class
Michael Krebs
Johannes Ricker
Hans Jerg Rätzer
Johannes (X) Shoemacher
Johannes Biecheler
Michael Wurster
Johanes Walckher
Jacob Thum
Georg Thum [?]
Lorentz Mergenschonerl
Johannes Speyer
Michael Klein
Melchior ( ) Jordan, on board
Hans Schuhler
Michael Rossnagel

Christian (X) Räck, Senior
Jerg Migel Reck
Christianus Reck, Junior
Anthony ( ) Wallheyer, on board
Jacob ( ) Graaf, sick on board
Johann Adam Pfisterer
Jorg Adam Grombein
Johan Gerge ( ) Kreyer, on board
Michael ( ) Köller, on board
Johan Peter Schlemb
Hans (HM) Meyer
Martin (HM) Marckel
Johanes (XXX) Voubel
Johan Iörg Kress
Johannes Lutz
Hanns Jerg Schiettinger
Michael ( ) Tietz, on board
Jerg Peter Kochendörffer
Wilhelm (O) Reichly
Georg Hörthler
Jacob ( ) Toutz, on board
Jacob ( ) Ebersort, on board
Jacob Andreas Sprecher
Adam (A) Grund
Christoff (C) Graas
108

Octob. 15, 1754.

Sir

According to Directions we have carefully examined the State of Health of the Mariners and Passengers on board the Ship Peggy, Cap.t Aubercrombie, from Roterdam and found a few of them in a low weak condition, but no Disease amongst them which we apprehend infectious.

To his Honour
The Governour.

Tho. Graeme
Th. Bond

[Endorsed:]

15th October 1754. Doctors Certificate relating to the Ship Peggy.

[List 224 A] A List of Foreigners imported in the Ship Friendship, from Amsterdam but last from Gosport. Qual. 21st Oct. 1754.

Adam Neubecker
Gabriel Weeber
Christophel Lang
Johannes Siller
Joseph Wiesent
Albrick Miller
Hans Schoneberger
Philip Do
Hans George Weiffer
Martin Schneider
Johan Jost Berger
Hans Henry Kautz
Jacob Feiner
Hans Wendel Schneider
Reinhard Weckheiser
Peter Rosebach
Gregorius Grem
Han Peter Balbirer
Han Geo. Smith
Matthias Dursch
Andreas Sommer
Han Michel Haak
Johannes Mancker
Henrich Steller
Johannes Koch
Do Smith
Philip Schweager
Jacob Stall
Johannes Young
Gaspar Freyling
Conrad Speller
Reicher Hoffman
Hans Geo. Staall
Hans Michl Staall
Lawrence Althurt
Johannes Zimmel

Christopher Stetler
Mauritz Geable
David Geable
George Steiner
Hans Fredk Korn
Baltzar Harf
Johannes Harf
Johannes Freylang
Johannes Ehrheim
Henrick Do
Henrick Reil
Conrad Schmid
Johan Strole
William More
Jacob More
Johannes Reiber
Baltzar Steltz
Christian Diehl
Henrick Willm Miller
Martin Bender
Geo. Fredrick Anger
Marckus Neyderfer
Carl Wender
William Becker
Philip Schreid
Han Jacob Lautz
Hannes Miller
Jacob Friese
John Seiberg
Daniel Beck * [?]
Nicolas Heyster
Philip Seibolt
Antone Ruse
Philip Bender
Johan Philip Bender
Johannes Orf

* Name crossed out, with note "not 16."

Nicholas Raab
Conrad Freydenberger
Johannes Foch
Henry Ratschlag
Mich¹ Reicher
Wᵐ Henry Leinweber
Conrad Frey
August Kriech
Bernhard Scheffer
Matthias Achabach
Reinhard Schmid
Herman Wetzler
Reinhard Kurtz
Hannes Riehl
Hannes Amand
Conrad Smid
Peter Kleyn
Baltzar Seltzer
Hannes Reck
Conrad Langstaff
Arnold Danhaver
Jnᵒ Peter Bernhard
Peter Steyn
Henrick Eash
Peter Boose

Johannes Boose
Johannes Weeber
Anthony Bickhard
Johannes Schaffstein
Johannes Dauerheim
Hans George Meyerheis
Antone Dauber
Johan Henrick Fusz
Johannes Nult
Henrick Scherer
Johannes Maybus
George Rose
Philipus Leer
Henrick Schmid
George Bott
Henry Peter Killmer
Ludwig Bernhard
Christian Smitt

The following are Lame:
Fredᵏ Steyn
Matthias Diehl
John Miller
Michael Dinges
117

[Endorsed:]
Foreigners imported in the Ship Friendship, Capᵗ Charles Ross, from Amsterdam. Qual. 21ˢᵗ Octʳ 1754. Nᵒ 117.

Beneset.

[List 224 C] At the State House at Philadelphia, Monday, the 21ˢᵗ Day of October, 1754.

Present: The Worshipful Charles Willing, Esquire, Mayor.

The Foreigners whose names are underwritten, imported in the Ship Friendship, Capᵗ Charles Ross, from Amsterdam but last from Gosport, did this day take the usual Qualifications to the Government. 7 Roman Catholicks. Qual. No. 117. Whole Freights 301. From Franconia & Hesse.

Adam Neuberth
Gaberiel Weber

Johann Christophel Lang
Johanes (✕) Zeller

Joseph Wigant
Albrecht Miller
Johanes (+) Shellenberger
Johann Philipp Schöneberger
Johann Jörg Weiffert
Martin (×) Shnyder
Johann Jost Berger
J. Henry (+) Coutz
Jacob (+) Finer
Johan Wedel Schneider
Reinhard Werckheiser
Johann Peter Rossbach
Gregorius Grim
John Ditter Balbierer
John George (×) Shmit
Deys Dersch
Andreas Sommer
John Michael (×) Hock
Johannes Manckell
Hennrich Steller
Johannes Koch
Johannes Schmitt
Philip (×) Sweger
Jacob Stahl
Johannes Junghen
Johan Casbar Fryling
Conrath Spenner
Reichard Hoffman
Johann Görg Stahl
Johann Michael Stahl
Lorentz (×) Althart
Johannes Immell
Chrisofel Stetler
Moritz Göbel
J. Davit (+) Göbel
Georg Steiner
J. Friederich (×) Korn
Johann Balthaser Harff
Johannes Harff
Johannes Freyling
Johannes Eihrrem

Johan Henrich Eehrheim
Henry Henrich Reyel
Johann Konraht Schmidt
Johanes (+) Straull
Johann Wilhelm Mohr
Johann Jacob Mohr
Johannes Reuber
Balthser Steltz
Christian Diehl
Henrich Wilhelm Müller
Martin (×) Bender
Gerg Fridich Anger
Johan Markus Neythöffer
Caral (××) Wender
Johann Wilhelm Becker
Johann Philip Schreidt
Johann Jacob Laux
Johannes Müller
Jacob (++) Friez
Johannes Seyboldt
Nicolaus Heister
Philip (××) Seybolt
Anthon Russ
Johan Filb Bender, Senior
Johann Philib Bender
Nigelas Rab
Konrat Freitenberger
Johannes Vogt
Johann Henrich Rahtschlag
Johann Michel Reichert
Wilhelm Henrich Leinweber
Johan Conrad Frey
August Krieg
Bernhardt Scheffer
Mathaus Achebach
Reinhart Schmit
Herman (×) Wetzlar
Reinhard Kurtz
Johanes (×) Riell
Johanes (×) Amman
Conrad (×) Shmit

Peter Klein
Balser Schaltzer
Johannes Rick
Conrath Langsdorff
Arnolt Dannhöffer
Johann Petter Bernhardt
Peter Stein
Hennrich Esch
Peter Buss
Johannes Buss
Johannes Weber
Johanes (✕) Shaffstall
Johann Daniel Bückhard
Pilip (✕) Leear
Johannes Dauernheim
Johan Geörg Meyreiss

Andon Dauber
Johann Henrich Voss
Johannes Nold
Henrich Scherer
Johannes Mebus
Johann Jorg Ros
Johann Henrich Schmid
George (✕✕) Pott
Henrich Peter Köllmer
Johann Ludwig Bernhardt
Johann Christian Schmit
Frederik Steyn ⎫
Matheas Diehel ⎪
John Miller ⎬ Sick on board
Michael Dinges ⎭

In all 117

Octob. 19, 1754.

S^r

According to Directions we have examined carefully every Mariner and Passenger on board the Ship Friendship, Capt Ross, from Amsterdam, and found but one Person Sick, so that we do not apprehend any Danger to the Inhabitants of the City from admitting the People to land in it immediately.

To his Honour   Tho. Graeme
The Governour   Th. Bond

[Endorsed:]
Doctors Certificate of the Ship Friendship, 15th 8^{br} 1754.

[List 225 A] List of Foreigners imported in the Bannister, Capt John Doyle, from Amsterdam but last from Cowes, qualfyd the 21st October 1754.

Hans Mich^l Miller
Jacob Herman
Johan Peter Adamacher
Bastian Wittmore
George Wittmore
Andreas Eberhart
Johannes Kirsch
Grafft Weeber

Johannes Geistler
Conrad Yough
Matthias Heinlein
Jacob Ludwig Timeling
Dionise Duretch
Joseph Konnet
Johan David Grautz
Christophel Ernfeigter

Matthew Torewort
Johan Fred^k Shiebel
Matthew Torewort, Junr
Alex^r Finck
David Oool
Jacob Tolman
Jacob Barral
Jaques Barral
Johan Christoph Barral
Johan Jacob Barral *
Hans Michael Bildheymer
Hans Geo. Rust
Hans Jacob Rust
Johannes Stirger
Johan Michael Shickel
Simon Ney
Adam Ege
Baltus Miller
Philip Roschon
Johan Valentin Keller
Christophel Bickert
Bastian Geiger
George Wiest
Philip Savius
Peter Putz
Hans Geo. Telicker
Philip Moot
Hannes Weeber
Han Jacob Weeber
Johannes Benner
Johan Peter Kiebler
Matthias Buchman
Valentine Jeger
Jacob Wolf

Peter Wolf
Han George Jeiger
Nicholas Trescher
Abraham Kehr
Conrad Kempf
Adam Mirtorum
Nicholas Basselman
William Leeb
John Henry Ashman
Johan Conrad Jerrick
Han Jacob Mood
Hannes Telb
Han Geo. Hoffman
Peter Meister
Ludwig Lang
Leonard Heisser
Hanicle Mink
Leonard Mink
Christoph Miller
Han Henrick Miller
Johannes Miller
George Wirtman
Wentzel Buderswag
Johan Adam Gebhart
Johan Geo. Gebhart
Elias Hellerman
Johan Peter Weeber
Hanes Weeber
Leonard Weeber
Johan Peter Emerick
Conrad Gildner
Jno Fidler, sick
Jacob Gress, lame
Piere Tolman, D^o

[Endorsed:]
List of Foreigners imported in the Ship Bannister, Capt. John Doyle, from Amsterdam. Qual. 21st October 1754. N°. 84.

D. Beneset.

---

* Name crossed out, with remark "not 16."

[List 225 C] At the State House at Philadelphia, Monday, the 21st Day of October, 1754.

Present: The Worshipful Charles Willing, Esquire, Mayor.

The Foreigners whose Names are underwritten, Imported in the Ship Bannister, Capt John Doyle, from Amsterdam, but last from Cowes, did this Day take the usual Qualifications to the Government. 4 Roman Catholics. No. 84. From Wirtenberg, Westphalia and the Palatinate.

Hans Michael Miller
Jacob Hörmann
Johan Peter Radenmacher
Bastian Wittmer
Geörg Vittmer
Andereas Ebehrth
Johannes Kentsch
Kraft Weber
Johanes (+) Geisler
Johann Conrad Jauch
Matthias Heinlein
Jacob Ludwig Deimling
Dionysius Duretsch
Joseph (X) Connet
Joh. David Krauss
Christoph Ehrnfeuchter
Martin (X) Toorward
Friedrich Schiebel
Martin (X) Toorward, Junr
Alexander (XX) Finck
G. Davit (X) Uhll
Jaques Talmon
Jaque Bara[l]
Jaque Baral
John Christoff Barrall, on bd
Hans Michael Billheimer
Hans Georg Ruoss
Hans Jacob Ruos
Johannes Kärcher
Johann Michael Schickel
Simon (X) Ege
Adam Ege

Balthas Müller
Philippe Rouchon
Johann Vallentin Keller
Christoff (X) Diger
J. Bastian (X) Geyer
Jerg Wiest
Phylype Saryous
Peter Butz
Hans Jerg Döliker
Philip (X) Mode
Johannes Weber
Johann Jacob Weber
Johannes Benner
John Peter (X) Kebler
Matias Buochman
Vallentin (X) Jäger
Johann Jacob Wolff
Johann Peter Wolff
Johann Görg Jäger
Johan Nicolaus Dresser
Abraham Kehr
Adam (X) Mirtorum
Conrad (X) Kemp
Nicolaus Bosermann
William (+) Leeb
J. Henry (+) Ashman
Johann Conrad Georg
Johan Jacob (X) Moode
Johannes Delp
Johan Gorg Hofman
Peter (X) Meister
Lutwig Lang

Johann Lönhardt Häuser
Johann Nickel Minck
Johann Lenhard Münch
Christoffel Müller
Johann Henrich Müller
Johannes Müller
Görg Wärthmann
Wenzel (W) Boteshway
Johann Adam Gebhardt
John George (X) Gebhart

Elias Hellermann
J. Peter (XX) Weber
Johanes (X) Weber
Leonhart (X) Weber
Johann Peter Emrich
Conrad (X) Gildner
John ( ) Fietler ⎫
Jacob ( ) Greess ⎬ sick, on b^d
Piere ( ) Tolman ⎭
In all 84

Octob. 21, 1754

S^r

According to Directions we have carefully examined the State of Health of the Mariners and Passengers on board the Ship Bannister, Capt Doyle, from Amsterdam, and found them generally well, so that we are of Opinion the Ship may be permitted to come into Port & the People to land in the City without Risque to the Inhabitants.

To his Honour   Tho. Graeme
The Governour.   Th. Bond

[Endorsed:]

21st October, 1754. Doctors Certificate of the Ship Bannister, Capt Doyle.

[Note]

The vessel was admitted, when the Governor was at Newcastle.

[List 226 A] Foreigners imported in the Ship Hennrietta, Capt John Ross, from Rotterdam, but last from Cowes. Qual. 22^d October, 1754.

Johannes Nieb
Everhard Metchar, board
Christ^n Swartzwild
Jacob Liebolt
Chris^n Spring
Jacob Koltman
Peter Dieterich
George Stor
Jacob Knibler
Joh. Adam Lintz, b^d

Leo. Ritlinger, b^d
Bernhard Russe
Louis Hagel
Rynhard Saur
John Danl Pier
Johannes Pier
Peter Henry Pier
Philip Bladdell
Johann Geo. Reed
Jacob Shifferdecker

Jacob Folmer
John Hartman Raus
Hans Geo. Erbst
Jn° Eberhard Bintz, b^d
George Adam Glee
John Mich^l Sner
Fred^k Keyser
Jacob Etsner
Peter Stro
Heny Swalbach
Simon Heidell
Philip Gross
Johann Styntryser
Johann Starts, dead *
Conrad Bole
Conrad Pope
Jn° Geo. Pater
David Firlinge
Anth° Graff
Hans Geo. Neuman
Jacob Kurtz, b^d
Simon Lible
Hen^y Buck
Michael Jeder
Johan Roteburger
Andreas Haller, b^d
Jn° Geo. Snyder
Johannes Karg
George Frank
Baltes Tieringer
Conrad Slimmer
Christoph Syder
Christoph Hysler
Jn° Adam Roeland

George Fetter
George Frank
Johannes Heysler, dead *
Albertus Swynfurth
Elias Thom
Michael Thom
Andreas Kryner, b^d
Mich^l Rieb, dead *
Albertus Rose
Peter Franck
Johann Keynert
Jeremiah Eckert
Jean Wolf Kryer
George Hygas
Geo. Fred^k Stuger
Fred^k Stuger, Jr. under age
Fred^k Shallin, b^d
Ludwig Zieger
Andreas Turolf
Jn° Henry Kinder
Mich^l Kun
Jos. Smith
Philip Eygle, b^d, under 16
Henry Smith, under 16
Johannes Koch
Bernhard Speck
Jacob Eyler
Philip Beyerly
Joh. Jacob Meyer
Christoph Philip Smith, b^d *
Joh. Geo. Reit
Jacob Sner
George Eyle
Godfrey Lodwig

[Endorsed:]

List of Foreigners imported in the Ship Henrietta, Capt. John Rose, from Rotterdam. Qual. 22^d Octr 1754. N° 80.

Hillegas.

This vessel was admitted when the Governour was at Newcastle.

* Name crossed out.

[List 226 C] At the State House at Philadelphia, Tuesday, the Twenty Second Day of October, 1754.

Present: Joshua Maddox, Esquire.

The Foreigners whose names are underwritten, Imported in the Ship Henrietta, Capt. John Ross, from Rotterdam but last from Cowes, did this Day take the usual Qualifications to the Government. 3 Roman Catholicks. From Franconia, Wirtenberg, Hesse etc.

Johannes Neipp
Christian Schwartzwelder
Jacob Leyboldt
Johan Christoph Spring
Jacob (X) Kaltmiller
Peter Dietrich
Görg Stohr
Jacob Knödler
Johann Bernhardt Rusing
Noah (+++) Hagy
Johan Reinhard Sauer
Johann Daniel Pier
Johanes (B) Beer
Peter Henry (H) Beer
Filibus Ladert
Johann Göerg Reith
Jacob (O) Shiefferdecker
Jacob (X) Volmer
Hartman (X) Raush
Johann Georg Herbst
Georg Adam Klee
Hans Michel Schnerr
Friedrich Kayser
Jacob (++) Itschner
Peter Stroh
Johan Henrich Schwalbach
Pilipus Gruss
Simonn Hydel
Jonas Steinheuser
Conrad Bohl
Johann Caspar Bopp
Johann Georg Bader

David Festinger
Johan Anthon Graff
Johan George (O) Newman
Simon Laible
Georg Heinrich Beckh
Johann Michael Jetter
Johannes Rothenburger
Johann Georg Schneider
Johannes Karch
Johann Geörg Franck
Balthas Thüringer
Conradt Schlemmer
Christoph Sauther
Christoph Häusler
Johan Adam Rohlandt
Jörg (X) Vetter
Georg Franck
Allbrecht Schweinforth
Elias (O) Tomm
Michael (O) Tomm
Albertus Roosen
Peter Franck
Johannes Keinarth
Jerimias Eckert
Johan Wolraht Krüger
Johan Gerg Heiges
Georg Friedreich Stuber
Lüdwig Zucker
Andereas (++) Duron
Johann Heinrich Günther
Mächel Kohn
Joseph Schmidt

Johannes Koch	Jacob Schner
Bernhard Speck	Johann Jorrg Ihle
Jacob Öhler	Godfried (G) Ludewig
Johann Phillip Beuerle	In all 80
Hans Jacob Mayer	

Philad. Oct. 19, 1754.

S^r

According to Directions we have carefully examined the State of Health of every Mariner & Passenger on board the Ship Hennrietta, Capt Ross, from Roterdam, and found the Chief Mate, Carpenter, Johnson, & Clawson, Mariners, ill of Fevers. Henry Stawip, Margret Oldmany, Martin Fraily, his wife and childⁿ in N. 81, likewise 6 women 4 children and one man in Numb. 5, 12, 13, 33 & 39 ill of the same kind of Fevers. Many of the other People appear to be in a convalescent State. We were informed most of them had been indisposed. The Capt. says he had lost 14 Freights in the Voyage, and that he had not concealed any Person nor landed more than one Sailor. The Fever with which these People are affected is of the putrid Kind, arising from corrupted Air and bad Dyet, but is not accompanyed with the usual Symptoms of a high Degree of Virulence, and we are of opinion if the sick were taken out of the Vessel and put into separate Lodgings, there would be little Danger of their communicating any infection and that the Ship might afterwards with Safety to the Inhabitants of the City be permitted to come up to it.

To his Honour   Tho. Graeme
The Governour.   Th. Bond
[Endorsed:]

Drs. Certificate of the Ship Henrietta. 19th 8^{br} 1754.

[Note] 19th 8^{br} [1754].

The Doctors and Mr. Hillegass, one of the Attorneys, were examined by the Govr in the presence of the Chief Justice & Recorder, and the Trustees of the Pest House were sent for, and afterwards an order given to them to receive the sick and Prohibit them to come up till further orders.

This was the first ship from which any danger was suspected.

[List 227 A] List of Mens Names Imported in the Halifax, Thomas Coatam, Master, from Rotterdam & Plymouth. October 20th 1754.

Johan Haas
Yerrick Merlin
Johan Frerick
Hans Yerrick Best
John Michael Clenshrod
Hans Wolph Minebower
Michael Swink
Hans Yerrick Overseler
Hans Philip Hofman
Yerrick Leonard Smith
Bengrad Snitzer
John Wolpgan Diedrick
John Michael Dreser
Bestian Garenger
Hendrick Hinish
Johan Michael Kaufman
Albright Obestain
Anthony Sulster
Andreas Shover
Michael Obelman
Adam Smith
Hans Michael Bush
Johan Righart
Johan Conradt Biler
John Yerrick Sous
Bernhard Krite
Hans Overseler
Hans Fredrick Smith
Anthony Grover
Casper Wall
Martin Folkamayer, b[d]
John Michael Fiel
Lorentz Dinnlar
Michael Klyne
Johannes Kigar
Mathias Staire
Elias Jordan
John Yerrick Rees
Paul Dusing
John Michael Funberg
Godfret Nicholas Lomberger, b[d]

Jacob Dorn
Yerrick Righter
Hans Thomas Sliser
Hans Yerrick Ele
John Jacob Road
John Nichol Weterhold
Jacob Weterhold
Gustavus Rief
Jacob Strow
Johannes Eafi
Jacob Gresel
Hans Adam Sewer
Adam Beck
Nicholas Dusin
John Michael Kogh
Martin Dorheimer
Johan Hendrick Amering
Andreas Shorpe, b[d]
Jacob Wolphinger
John Fredrick Albrigtberger
Simon Shilaberger
Hans Leonard Fritz
Nicholas Garinger, on b[d]
Hendrick Geyst
Nicholas Feelix
Jacob Free
Andreas Free
Hans Adam Eva
Anthony Tuner
Valatine Ungehand
Lorentz Casper
Peter Engle
Daniel Hick
Hans Fight Livigood
Jacob Wys
David Plank
John Albright Hendrick Berkit,
    on board
Jacob Sigman
Martin Rear
Johan Diedrick Bread

Hans Michael Swink
Henry Varni
Anthony Brown
Michael Buback
Johannes Kock
Christopher Kiell
Johannes Bachman
Johan Jost Kock
Martin Briel
Hendrich Briel
Herman Briel
Hans Martin Shirk
Peter Mathias Gansh
Johan Hendrick Haas
Jacob Turner

John George Maul
George Ritter *
Johannes Swope
John Israel Rhode *
Bernard Miller
Conrad Beter *
Jacob Hannegraft
Philip Gesel
Nicholas Dusing
Leonard Kokenderfer
Jacob Long
Martin Fifer
Hans George Shuss
106

[Endorsed:]
List of Foreigners imported in the Ship Halifax, Capt Thomas Coatam, from Rotterdam. Qual. 22^d October, 1754. N° 106.

Stedman.

[List 227 C] At the State House at Philadelphia, Tuesday, Twenty Second Day of October, 1754.
Present: Joshua Maddox, Esquire.
The Foreigners whose names are underwritten, imported in the Ship Halifax, Capt Thomas Coatam, from Rotterdam but last from Plymouth, did this Day take the usual Qualifications to the Government. 10 Roman Catholicks. No. 102. Souls 370. Whole Freight 280. From Wirtenberg, Hesse, Franconia, & the Palatinate.

Johan Haas
Hans George (+) Merling
Johann Förch
Johann Georg Best
Johann Michael Kleinschroth
Peter Mathes Ganshor
Johann Wolfgang Gmeinbauch
Michal Schnekh
Hans George (H) Overzeller

Johann Philipp Hofmann
Leonhard Schmith
Bongrad (++) Nietzel
Johann Wolfgang Dieterich
Johan Michal Trösters
Bastian (×) Gerringer
Henry (××) Heinnish
Johann Michel Obelmann
Albrecht Rabenstein

* Name crossed out.

Anthoni Sulzer
Andreas Schober
Johann Michel Kaufman
Hanns Adam Schmidt
Johan Gunder (O) Bush
Johann Rickert
Conrad Bühler
Hans (++) Overzeller
Bernhardt Kreith
H. Friederich (XX) Shmit
Anthony (X) Gruber
Johan Caspar Wahl
Martin Volkemeyer, on board
Lorentz (XX) Sencler
Michel Klein
Johan Michael ( ) Fiel, on board
Johannis Geiger
Matheas ( ) Tarr, on board
Elias Jordan
Johann Geörg Riess
Paullus Tussing
Nicklas Romburger, on board
Johann Michael von Berg
Jacob Dornn
Georg (X) Richter
H. Thomas (X) Shlösser
Hans Jorg Ihle
Johan Jacob Rot
Johan Nickel Wetterhold
J. Jacob (W) Wertherholt
Gustavus Reeb
Jacob Stroh
Johannes Ihle
Hans Adam (X) Waner
Jacob (G) Grassel
Adam Beeck
Johann Michael Koch
Martin Dorschheimer
John Henry (X) Amrein
Andereas ( ) Shop, on board

Hans Jacob Frey
Johann Friederich Albrecht Birckert
Johan Simon Schelberger
Johann Leonhard Ilgenfritz
Nicklas ( ) Gerringer, on board
Henrich Geiss
Nicolaus Felix
Andras Frey
Johann Adam Eva
Anthony (X) Dirner
Velten Unbehendt
Lorentz Coster
Peter Engels
Jacob Wolfinger
Johann Daniel Heck
Hanes Frit Livenguth
Jacob Wis
Davit (X) Blanck
John Albrecht Henry ( ) Birkel, on b^d
Jacob (XX) Stegman
Martin (MR) Rorr
Johan Tieterich Brecht
Hans Michael (+) Shwenk
Heinerich Werni
Anthoni Braun
Michael (+) Poobagh
Johannes Koch
Christofel Cheil
Johannes Bachman
Johan Jost (++) Koch
Marttin Briel
Johann Henrich Briehll
Johann Herman Briell
Hans Martin Schierg
John Henry ( ) Haas, on board
Hans Jacob (X) Dirner
Johan George (X) Maull
Johanes (+) Shwab

Johann Bernhart Miller
Jacob Hanengrath
Fillib Gresel
Johan Le[n]hart Kochendöffer
Jacob (+) Long

Martin Pfeiffer
Hans George (+) Shütz
Hans Michel Dussing
In all 106

October 21, 1754.

S^r

According to Directions we have carefully examined the State of Health of the Mariners and Passengers on Board the Ship Halifax, Capt. Coatam, from Rotterdam and found the following Persons indisposed. A Woman in Numb 8. A Man and Woman in Numb 9. A Child in 25. A Girl in 33. A Boy in 35. A Woman in 42. Another in 44. A Boy in 43. A Girl in 41. A Woman in 55. Another in 45. John Kestner and Ann Oversell on Deck. Three or four of these with Fevers, the others only weak. The Fever has not the least Appearance of Malignity or Virulency but appears to us to be of the Calenture kind, which we are of opinion is not infectious and that therefore the Ship may be admitted.

[Endorsed:]

21st October 1754. Doctors Certificate relating to the Ship Halifax, Capt. Coatam.

[List 228 A] List of Foreigners imported in the Snow Good Intent, John Lasly, Commander, from Amsterdam and last from Gosport, qualified the 23rd October, 1754.

Anthony Schultz
Mark Anthony Shultz
Nicholas Hoffmanin
Fredrick Holtzapple
Johannes Link
Conrad Heisser
Hannes Heisser
Jost Martin
Bernhard Lickhart
Johannes Urt
Gaspar Swing
Hannes Bolander
Johan Gaspar Farber

Ludwig Kenrick Kreider
Hans Philip Lick
Johan Geo. Kaes
Johan Christophel Lang
Johan Leonard Rust
Johan Baltzar Rust
Francis Jacobus Miller
Andreas Zwansiger
Fredrick Kleyn
Hans William Niese
Jacobus Scheffer
Andreas Scheffer
William Lieber

Peter Staub
Matthias Staub
Johan Felt Hinckle
Peter Solt
Hans Geo. Hoff
Christian Meyer
Hans Jost Meyer
Johan Peter Bleygenbacher
Conrad Omiller
Johannes Omiller
George Fredrick Wolfer
Johannes Buck
Johannes Lorey
Johan Gaspar Lorey
Johannes Vogel
Geo. Henrick Vogel
Johan William Christian
Conrad Lorey
Johan William Becker
Anthony Solman
Johan Adam Solman
Henry Schwertzel
Johan Teis Schwertzel
Johan Jost Schwertzel
Johannes Glick
Philip Glick
Christophel Gaab
Johan Geo. Hinckle

Fredrick Teysinger
Michael Inneberger
Johan Adam Hollander
Andreas Mich¹ Reaboch
Nicholas Tielman
Adam Blickly
Johan Nicholas Rischie
John Christopher Hentz
Jacob Kieler
Fredrick Sinzel
Fredrick Betler
Lawrence Arnold
Hannes Haut
William Arnold
Johannes Breiderbach
Johan Philip Gleitz
Johannes Steffhannes
Fredrick Niebel
Sam¹ Fredrick Rieger
Gaspar Buch
Fredrick Reinhard Fischer
Philip Schread
Baltzar Fritz
Peter Rosber
Christian Schied
Johan Willm Niese, sick
Michael Sommer, lame

[Endorsed:]
Foreigners imported on the Snow Good Intent, Capt John Lasly, from Amsterdam. Qual. 23^d October, 1754. N° 81.

L. Beneset.

[List 228 B] Foreigners imported in the Snow Good Intent, Capt John Lasly, from Amsterdam. Qual. 23^d October, 1754.

Frantz Peter Schultz
Mark Anthony (X) Schultz

Johann Nicolaus Hoffmann
Frederick (++) Holtzapple

Johannes (++) Link
Conrad (++) Heisser
Johannes (XX) Heisser
Jost Marthin
Johann Bernhard Lickhardt
Johannes (XX) Urt
Caspar Schwing
Johannes Bohlander
Jan Casber Faber
Ludwig Henrich Kreutter
Johann Filib Lich
Johann Gorg Göch
Johann Christoph Lang
Johann Leonhart Rost
Balthaser Rost
Francis Jacob ( ) Miller, on
    board
Andreas Zwanzger
Frederick (X) Klein
Johan Willem Niess
Johann Jacob Schöffer
Andreas Schöffer
Johann Wilhlem Lieber
Peter (+) Staub
Matthias (+) Staub
Johan Felt (+) Hincle
Johann Peter Zoll
Johann Görg Hoff
Christian (+) Meyer
John Jost (+) Meyer
Johan Peter Bleickenbacher
Canrath Aumiller
Johannes Aumiller
Gerg Friederich Wolfer
Johannes (X) Buck
Johannes Loray
Johann Caspar Loray
Johannes Vogel
Geörg Henrich Vogell
John William (XX) Christian

Conrad (X) Lorey
Johan Wilelm Becker
Anthon Zollman
Johan Adam Zollman
Johan Henrich Schwörtzel
John Ties (S) Schwertzel
John Jost (S) Schwertzel
Johannes Glück
Johann Philips Glück
Christopher (++) Gaab
John George (XX) Hincle
Fried. Deüssinger
Michael (XX) Inneberger
Johan Adam Bohlender
Andreas Michael (A) Reaboch
Nicholas (T) Tilman
Adam Blichle
John Nicholas (++) Risch
Joh. Christoph Heintz
Jacob (X) Kieler
Friedrich Süntzel
Frederick (FB) Betler
Lorentz Arnold
Hans (+) Haut
William (+) Arnold
Johannes Breidenbach
Johann Philips Kleiss
Johannes (X) Stevanus
John Frederick (N) Nebel
Samuehl Friederich Rügerr
Caspar (++) Buch
Frederick Reinhart (X) Fisher
Philip (X) Schrea
Baltzer (X) Fritz
Petter Rosper
Christian Scheidt
John William ( ) Niese, on
    board
Michael ( ) Sommer, on board
81

[List 228 C] At the State House at Philadelphia, Wednesday the Twenty Third day of October, 1754.
Present: Robert Strettell, Esquire.

The Foreigners whose names are underwritten, imported in the Snow Good Intent, Cap.ᵗ John Lasly, from Amsterdam but last from Gosport, did this day take and subscribe to the Qualifications. 7 Roman Catholicks. 81 Qual. From Hesse, Hanau, Palatinate & a few from Switzerland.

Frantz Peter Schultz
Marcus Anthony (✕) Shultz
Johann Nicolaus Hoffmann
Friederich (++) Holtzappel
Johanes (✕✕) Linck
Conrad (✕✕) Heyser
Johannes (++) Heyser
Jost Marthin
Johann Bernhard Linckardt
Johanes (✕✕✕) Ortt
Caspar Schwing
Johannes Bohlander
Jan Casber Faber
Ludwig Henrich Krutter
Johann Filib Lich
Johann Gorg Göss
Johan Christoph Lang
Johann Leonhart Rost
Balthaser Rost
Frances Jacob ( ) Miller, on
   board
Andreas Zwanzger
G. Friederich (✕) Klein
Johan Willem Nies
Johann Jacob Schöffer
Andreas Schöffer
Johann Wilhelm Lieber
Peter (✕) Staub
Mathias (S) Staub
John Vallentin (+) Henkel
Johann Peter Zoll
Christian (✕) Meyer

Johann Gurg Hoff
John Jost (+) Meyer
Johan Peter Bleickenbacher
Conrath Aumiller
Johannes Aumüller
Georg Friederich Wolfer
Johannes (✕) Bock
Johannes Lory
Johann Caspa[r] Loray
Johannes Vogel
Geörg Henrich Vogel
John Wilhelm (✕✕) Christian
Conrad (✕) Lorra
Johan Wilelm Becker
Anthon Zollman
Johann Adam Zollmann
Johan Henrich Schwörtzel
Johann (✕) Teitz
Johan (++) Teitzwortzel, Jr.
Johannes Glück
Johann Philibs Glück
Christoph (++) Koap
Johan George (✕✕) Hinckel
Fried. Deussinger
Michael (++) Lineberger
Johann Bohlender
Michael (✕✕) Rehbock
Nickolas (✕) Tillman
H. Adam Blichle
Nicklas (✕) Reesh
Joh. Christoph Heintz
Jacob (✕) Köller

Friedrich Süntzel
Friederich (++) Pepler
Lorentz Arnold
Johannes (✕) Hauk
Wilhelm (AA) Arnolt
Johannes (+) Breidenbach
Johann Philips Kleiss
Johannes (✕) Stephanus
J. Friederich (N) Nebel
Samuehl Heinerich Rügerr

John Caspar (✕✕) Buk
F. Reinhart (✕) Fisher
Philip (+) Read
Balsatzar (+) Frietz
Petter Rosper
Christian Scheidt
John Will ( ) Niesse ⎱ sick on
Michael ( ) Sommer ⎰ board
In all 81

Octob. 21, 1754.

Sir

According to Orders we have carefully examined the State of Health of the Mariners and Passengers on board the Snow Good Intent, Capt John Lesley, from Amsterdam and found amongst them Six Persons ill of Fevers, but without any Symptoms of a malignant or contagious Nature, the Rest of the People are uncommonly Healthy, we therefore do not apprehend there is any Infectious Disease amongst them.

To his Honour   Tho. Graeme
The Governour.   Th. Bond

[Endorsed:]

Doctors Report of the Snow Good Intent, Capt Lesley. 31, Octr 1754. Admitted by the Mayor in the absence of the Governor.

[List 229 A] A List of Names of all the Palatine Male Passengers from Sixteen to Sixty years of age, Imported in the Ship Recovery, Amos Jones, Mast^r, From Rotterdam & Cowes at Wilmington. Humbly presented to the Honble Govr Morris. Octr 23, 1754.

Daniell Hanes
Gerick Timmer
Gerick Millar
Johannes Gaber
Ludwick Stiley
Daniell Serk
Johannes Lents
Jacob Hober

Johannes Hober
Peter Hober
Peter Helfenstine
George Freck
David Fethercoile
Jacob Millar
Ludwick Bochman
Nicholas Dycker

Martin Shiller
Daniell Schuster
Heronomus Wise
Lenard Gerick
Gerick Goodnight
Jacob Jaquey
Henry Rick
Paltser Sheafer
Peter Stiley
Jacob Stiley
Jacob Stiley, Junr
Jacob Croff
Fredrick Au
Gerick Au
Christafur Au
Nicholas Buskey
Gerick Droutner
Martin Croll
Andreas Bushon
Michell Swarts
David Rambahar
Jacob Harman
Samuell Shanks
Isaac Horniger
Johanes Mercher
Paul Stern
Albert Gerick
Michell Swarts
Peter Herolt
Johannes Leiher
Casper Byerley
Peter Kealer
Ge° Simon Melhorn
Wolf Hidebruner
Michell Singhawse

Fredrick Stamcast, a Roman
  Cath.
  Gone ashore:
Christian Shaneck
Christian Denar
Ludwick Crow
Gerick Marquart
Michael Metseir
Gerrick Holander
Gerrick Young
Hagen Waltd
Jacobus Heller
Daniell Hotts
Phillip Slypher
Fredrick Sypert
Joseph Moll
Phillip Sheafer
Gerhard Moire
Charlos Fonron
Peter Sypert
Jacob Earp
Henry Sowder
Abram Snowfer
Hanse Lenard
Peter Longjear
Phillip Vagoner
Martin Ungra
Simon Carle
Michell Hitter
Johannes Carle
Charles Wise
Simon Melhorne
George Melhorne
Michell Parvent

[Endorsed:]
List of Palatinates on board the Recovery, at Wilmington.
[23] 8^{ber} 1754.

[List 230 A] List of Foreigners imported in the Mary and

Sarah, Captn Thomas Brodrick, from Amsterdam but last from Portsmouth. Qual. 26th October, 1754.

Jacob Fisel
Mich^l Lane
Jno Chris Hess
Johan Wilhelm Schneider
Mich^l Winhard
Adam Breitinger
Carl Menges
Peter Folk
Nicholas Ilesleger
Jacob Sterner
Jacob Schumbert
Jno Adam Scheffer
Han Adam Schwebel
Jacob Haller
Joseph Roarer
Anthony Roarer
Leonard Kesler
Conrad Menges
Hans Geo. Brincker
Hans Peter Karl
Hans Geo. Eigel
Hanicle Eher
Mich^l Slough
Nicholas Seabrod
Han Titer Sieler
Anthony Cling
Hannes Brunner
Han Jacob Helm
Adam Reibolt
Nicholas Carl
Hanicle Ausleberman
Hannes Role
Peter Edleman
Harm Nimand
Lawrence Maurer
Peter Menges
Jacob Karl
Hannes Edelman

Adam Bartman
Jacob Smith
Geo. Adam Reiser
Philip Somer
Peter Menges
Han Geo. Menges
Adam Menges
Johan Geo. Kraws
Matthias Kraws
Johan Peter Kraws
Mich^l Hubert
Han Leonard Neidich
Han Adam Meister
Fredrick Weigan
Mich^l Wirt
Fredrick Folk
Johan Adam Weeber
Johan Philip Hartman
Han Philip Kool
Han Leonard Drumheller
Conrad Geyer
Peter Schnur
Johannes Erig
Adam Neidig
Hans Peter Yorigh
Jost Beichel
Philip Schurch
Samuel Lefeu
David Lefeu
Philip Naab
Kief Hartz
Johan Adam Hickman
Ludwig Nunnenmacher
Johannes Pfeiffer
Bastian Schreder
Daniel Neidich
Han Mich^l Scholl
Martin Kister

Bernhard Meyer
Leonard Kister
Johannes Risht
Geo. Schaffer
Johan Jost Lets
Peter Yough
Geo. Michel

Han Jacob Helm
Johan Geo. Edelman, sick
Hans Edelman, D°
Jost Will, D°
Hans Schnellenberger, D°
Geo. Kauffman, D°
Johannes Bresslauer, D°

[Endorsed:]
Foreigners imported in the Brigantine Mary & Sarah, Capt
Thomas Brodrich, from Amsterdam. Qual. 26. Octr 1754. N°
90.   Benezet.

[List 230 B] Foreigners imported in the Brigantine Mary &
Sarah, from Amsterdam, Capt. Thomas Brodrich. Qual. 26th
October, 1754.

Jacob Visser
Michael (✕) Lane
Johann Christofel Heiss
Johan Wilhelm Schneider
Michael (✕) Vinhard
Adam (✕✕) Breitinger
Carl (+) Menges
Peter (+) Folk
Nicolaus Oellenschläger
Jacob Störner
Jacob (✕✕) Schubert
Adam Schäffer
Hans Adam (✕✕) Schwebel
Jacob (+) Haller
Joseph Rohrer
Anthony (+) Roarer
Johann Leonhardt Kessler
Conrad (+) Menges
Johann Georg Brincker
Hans Peter (+) Karl
Hans Jerg Aüchele
Johann Nickel Lehr
Michael (+) Slough

Nicholas (✕) Seabrod
Johan Titrick (+) Sieler
Andhon Kling
Johannes Brunner
Jn° Jacob (+) Helm
Adam (+) Reibolt
Nicolaus Carl
Nicholas (O) Leberman
Johannes Roll
Peter Edelman
Hermen Neyman
Lawrence (O) Maurer
Peter Menges
Jacob (OO) Karl
Johannes Edelmann
Johannes Adam Bartman
Jacob (✕) Smith
Gorg Adam Rayser
Philip (+) Summer
Hans Peter Menges
Johann Gerg Menges
Adam Menges
J. Geo. (+) Kraws

Matthias (X) Kraws
John Peter (X) Kraws
Michael ( ) Hubert
J. Leonard ( ) Neidick
J. Adam ( ) Meister
Fredrick (W) Weigan
Michael (+) Wirt
Fredrick (X) Folk
J. Adam (W) Weeber
J. Philip (H) Hartman
Johan Philipp [Kuhl]
J. Leonard (X) Drumheller
Conrad (+) Geyer
Peter (+) Schnur
Johannes (+) Erig
Adam Neidig
J. Peter (O) Yorigh
Jost (X) Beichel
Filip Jacob Schorck

Saml (L) Levy
Dafit Löwe
Philipp Naab
Hartz (X) Kief
J. Adam (+) Hickman
Georg Ludwig Nonnenmacher
Johannes Pfeiffer
Bastian Schröder
Daniel Neydig
Johann Michel Scholl
Martin Kistner
Johann Bernhardt Mayer
Johann Lenhart Kistner
Johannes (X) Risht
Georg Schöffer
J. Jost (X) Lets
Peter Joh
Johann Georg Michel
Johan Jacob (H) Helm

[Endorsed:]
Foreigners imported in the Brigantine Mary & Sarah, Capt
Thos Brodrich, from Amsterdam. Qual. 26th October, 1754.
No 90.   Benezet.

[List 230 C] At the Court House at Philadelphia, Saturday, the Twenty Sixth Day of October, 1754.
                Present: William Peters, Esquire.
The Foreigners whose Names are underwritten, imported
in the Brigantine Mary and Sarah, Capt Thomas Brodrich,
from Amsterdam but last from Portsmouth, did this Day take
and subscribe to the usual Qualifications. Six Roman Catholicks. No 90. From Franconia, Wirtenberg and the Palatinate.

Jacob Visser
Michael (X) Lehn
Johann Christof Heiss
Johan Wilhelm Schneider
Michael (+) Wenhart
Adam (++) Breydinger

Carol (X) Menges
Peter (X) Volck
Nicolaus Oellenschläger
Jacob Störner
Jacob (XX) Shumbert
Adam Schäffer

J. Adam (XX) Shwäbel

Jacob (X) Haller

Joseph Rohrer

Anthony (+) Rohr

Johann Leonhardt Kessler

J. Conrad (+) Menges

Johann Georg Brincker

H. Peter (+) Carel

Hans Jerg Aüchele

Johann Nikl Lehr

J. Michael (X) Shlaugh

Nickolas (X) Seewald

J. Diterich (+) Zieller

Andhon Kling

Johannes Brunner

J. Jacob (X) Helm

H. Adam (+) Reybolt

Nicolaus Carl

Nickolas (O) Leberman

Johannes Roll

Peter Edelman

Herman Neyman

Lorentz (O) Mauerer

Peter Menges

Jacob (OO) Carel

Johannes Edelmann

Johann Bartman

Jacob (X) Shmit

Gorg Adam Räuser

Philip (+) Summer

Hans Peter Menges

Johann Georg Menges

Adam Menges

J. George (+) Kraus

Matheas (X) Kraus

J. Peter (X) Kraus

Michael (O) Hubert

J. Leonhart (+) Neidig

Hans Adam (+) Meister

Peter (W) Weygand

Michael (++) Wirth

Friederich (X) Volck

J. Adam (W) Weber

H. Philip (H) Hartman

Johann Philipp Kuhl

J. Leonhart (+) Trumheller

Conrad (+) Geyer

Peter (+) Shnurr

Johanes (X) Jhrig

Adam Neidig

Hans Peter (X) Yowh

Jost (X) Beichgel

Philip Jacob Schorck

Samuell (W) Levy

Davit Löwe

Pihhipp [!] Naab

Hertz (O) Kiest

J. Adam (+) Heckman

Georg Ludwig Nonnenmacher

Johannes Pfeiffer

Bastian Schröder

Daniel Neydig

Johann Michel Scholl

Martin Kistner

Johann Bernhardt Mayer

Johann Leohaart Kistner

Johanes (X) Reest

Jeorg Schöff[er]

Johan Jost (+) Shlitz

Petter Joh

Johann Georg Michel

Johan Jacob (H) Helm

Johan George ( ) Edel-⎫
man

Hans ( ) Edelman

Jost ( ) Witt   ⎬ sick on

Hans ( ) Shnellen-   ⎰ board
berger

George ( ) Kauffman

Johanes ( ) Breslauer ⎭

In all 90

Octob. 24, 1754.

Sir

According to Directions we have carefully examined the State of Health of the Mariners and Passengers on Board the Brig Mary & Sarah, Capt Brothric, from Amsterdam, and did not find one Person ill amongst them, so that we do not apprehend any Danger from their being admitted to land in the City.

To his Honour   Tho. Graeme
                                            Th. Bond

[Endorsed:]

Doctors Report of the Brigantine Mary & Sarah, 24 Oct° 1754. Admitted by the Mayor in the absence of the Governor.

[List 231 A] List of Foreigners imported in the Jn° & Elizabeth, from Amsterdam & Portsmouth, Captain Ham. Qualifyed the Seventh Novem^r 1754. [From] Hanau, Palatinate, Wirtemberg. 330 whole freights.

N° 1 *	11
Nicholas Lang	Hannes Winholt
Conrad Herman	12
Bartle Hendrick	Philip Render
3	Melchior Meichler
Wendel Britzuse	Hannes Poley
5	Fred^k Dersch
Han Geo. Burgemeyer	13
Geo. Preiter	Martin Reinhard
Hans Fred^k Schultz	14
Henry Willflingen	Gebhard Leitheiser
6	16
Martin Kreps	Han Geo. Runer
Fred^k Theobald	17
Henrick Eyler	Leonard Peatrie
Nicholas Desch	Jacob Amand
7	19
Hannes Nees	Han Geo. Feack
9 & 10	Danl Decksheimer
Henrick Schmid	21
	Jurg Meisner

* These numbers seem to refer to the cabins on the Ship.

23
Johannes Kleyn
Barthold Millioneau
24
Herman Senger
25
Theobald Peyn
26
Johannes Hahn
Jost Siess
Christian Kramer
27
Jacob Wagener
28
Johannes Eltman
Paul Hoffman
Johannes Meister
Henrick Smid
29
Jacob Endt
Grafft Fronheiser
30
Hannes Schumacker
Dan¹ Leickel
Henrick Troestbach
Philip Achaback
31
Willm Schneider
33
Johan Jacob Kifie
34
Henrich Frank
Johannes Roht
Hannes Blecher
Wilhelm Blecher
35
Johan Henrick Tehr
36
Jurg Oder
Johannes Greiffestand

37
Jurg Wm Schneider
38
Christophel Mengel
Martin Caller
40
Hannes Weigand
Michel Schek
Burget Hense
Johannes Schuster
41
Johan Adam Minse
42
Gaspar Diener
Mich¹ Staub
Mich¹ Neiff
Johan Adam Zehner
43
Jacob Wirtmiller
Nicholas Kleyn
44
Fred^k Mortel
45
Johannes Flinder
46
Johannes Menich
Johanes Loras
Henrick Sneigel
47
Mich¹ Homan
48
Mich¹ Krug
49
Johan Martin Lesch
50
Johan Geo. Riehlman
51 & 52
Jacob Schlesser
Jacob Schlesser, Junr
53
Peter Fischer

54
Wendel Laux
Henrich Bach
55
Albert Klung
Han Geo. Feit
57
Johan Peter Hauf
58
Hans Geo. Miller
Adol Flor
59
Stephel Aubel
60
Hans Geo. Aabel
Hans Mich¹ Uting
Johan Kempff
61 & 62
Jacob Bernhard
Nicholas Thea
David Andreas Gebhard
63
Han Geo. Florin
Hannes Florin
65
Mich¹ Smid
68
Hans Geo. Kleynpeter
69
Jacob Gander
Johannes Deringer
70
Han Henrich Schuster
Henrich Swartabach
71
Johannes Deringer, Junr
72
Philip Buger
Andreas Schwartz

73
Christian Hauswert
74
Jacob Togend
Adam Bartleman
75
Joseph Dubier
76 & 77
Johan Wendel Kenigsfeldt
Jacob Eincap
78
Hanicle Seydel
Han Philip Kleyn
79
Philip Christian Gross
Johan Jacob Gross
80
Andreas Getz
Christophel Mey
81
Carl Kleym
82
Christian Keller
Daniel Baat
82
Hans Geo. Schitz
84
Peter Herman
Valentine Brickman
Jacob Miller
85
Conrad Keyl
Gaspar Fanstick
Burgard Brown
88
Peter Panoch
Sick
Jn° Adam Nees
Reichard D°
Hannes Minich

131

[Endorsed:]
Foreigners imported in the Ship John & Elizabeth, Capt.
Peter Ham, from Amsterdam. Qual. 7th Novr 1754. N° 130.

Benezet.

[List 231 B] Foreigners imported in the Ship John & Elizabeth, Capt Ham from Rotterdam. Qual. 7th November, 1754.

Nicklauus Lang
Conradt Hermann
Bartle Hendrick (X) Bott
Wendal Pritzius
Hans George (X) Burgemeyer
George (+) Preiter
Carl Friedrich Schultz
Henry (X) Wilflinger
Martin Krebs
Friederich Theobald
Henry (X) Eyler
Nicolaus Desch
Johannes Neess
Johan Henrich Schmid
Hans (W) Winholt
Johann Phillipp Renner
Melchior (XX) Meichler
Johannes Polay
Friederich Adam Derst
Martin Reinharth
Johann Gebhart Leitheuser
Hans George (X) Runer
Leonhart Peteri
Jacob (X) Amand
Johann Gorg Feeck
Daniel Dexheimer
Georg Meissner
Johannes Klein
Barthelemi La Gneau
Hermann Senger
Theobald Pein
Johannes Han
Johann Jost Süsse

Christian Krämer
Jacob Wagener
Johannes Heldmann
Paul Hoffman
Johannes Meister
Johann Henrich S[chmid]
Jacob End
Johann Craft Fronheüser
Johannes Schumacher
Daniel Leukel
Henrich Dresbach
Philib Achebach
Wilhelm (X) Schneider
Jean Jaque Kifie
Johann Henrich Franck
Joanes Roth
Johannes Blecher
Wilhelm Blecher
Johann Henrich Dörr
Jürgen Uder
Johannes (++) Greiffestand
Jörge Wilhelm Schneider
Christopher (++) Mengel
Martin Cacheller
Johannes Weygandt
Michael Scheck
Burget (O) Hense
Johannes (X) Schuster
Johan Adam Männig
Casber Diener
Michel Staub
Michael (+) Neiff
Johann Adam Zahner

Jacob Werthmüller
Nicglaus Klein
Fridrich Mergel
Johannes Flimer
Johannes Männig
Johannes Larosch
Henry (+) Sneigel
Michael Homan
Michel Krug
Johann Martin Lösch
Johann Georg Rällman
Johann Jacob Schlötzer
Jacob (++) Schlesser, Senr
Peder Fischer
Johann Wendel Laux
Henry (+) Bach
Alberdt Klunck
Johann Görg Fey
Johan Petter Hauff
George (+) Miller
Adolph Flohri
Steffan Abel
Hans George Abel
Johann Michael Uhting
Johan (++) Kempf
Jacob Bernhardt
Johann Nicolaus Deh
Andreas Gebhardt
George (×) Florin
Hans (×) Florin
Michael (×) Smith
Hans Geörg Kleinpetter
Jacob (×) Gander

Johannes Därendinger
Johann Henrich Schuster
Henry (×) Swartzenbagh
Johannes Därendinger
Philip (PB) Buger
Andreas Schwartz
Christoph Hauswirth
Jacob (××) Togend
Adam (×) Bartleman
Joseph (+) Dubier
Johann Wendel Königsfeldt
Jacob Weingart
Johann Nicolaus Seidel
Johann Philips Klein
Philip Christian (×) Gross
John Jacob (+) Gross
Johann Andreas Götz
Christopher (+) Mey
Carl Gleim
Christian Keller
Daneil Pfadt
Johan Jorg Schütz
Johann Peter Hermann
Johann Valentin Brukmann
Jacob Müller
Johann Conrad Keil
Johann Peter Bannot
Caspers Fonstock
John Adam Nees ⎫
Richard Nees ⎬ on board
Hans Minich ⎭

130

[Endorsed:]
Foreigners imported in the Ship John & Elizabeth, Capt. Peter Ham, from Amsterdam. Qual. 7th Novr 1754. No 130.
Benezet.

[List 231 C] At the Court House at Philadelphia, Thursday, the 7th November, 1754.

Present: The Worshipful Charles Willing, Esquire, Mayor of
  Philadelphia.

The Foreigners whose Names are underwritten, Imported
in the Ship John and Elizabeth, from Amsterdam & Portsmouth, from Hanau, the Palatinate & Wirtemberg, Captn
Ham, did this day take the usual Oaths and Qualifications. 330
Whole Freights. 11 Roman Catholicks. 120 Protestants.

Nicklauus Lang	Johann Jost Süsse
Conradt Hermann	Jacob Wagener
Bartholt Henry (X) Pott	Johannes Heldmann
Wendel Pritzius	Paul Hoffman
J. George (X) Birckenmeyer	Johannes Meister
George (X) Hochrytter	Johann Henrich Schmidt
Carl Friedrich Schultz	Jacob Ende
Henry (X) Welfling	Johann Craft Fronheuser
Martin Krebs	Johannes Schumacher
Johann Friedrich Thebald	Daniel Leuckel
Henry (X) Eyler	Henrich Dresbach
Nicolaus Desch	Philib Achebach
Johannes Nees	Wilhelm (X) Shneyder
Johanes (W) Winholt	Jean Jaque Kifie
Johan Heinrich Schmid	Johann Henrich Franck
Johan Philleps Rener	Johannes Roth
Melchior (++) Meichler	Johannes Blecher
Johannes Boley	Johan Henrich Dörr
Friederich Adam Derst	Wilhelm Blecher
Martin Reinharth	Jürgen Uder
Johann Gebhart Leitheuser	Johannes (XX) Greyffenstein
J. George (G) Gruner	Görge Wilhelm Schneider
Leonhart Peteri	Christoffel (++) Mengel
Jacob (X) Amman	Martin Cacheller
Johann Georg Feeck	Johannes Weygandt
Daniel Dexheimer	Michael Scheck
Georg Meissner	Burchart (O) Hence
Johannes Klein	Johanes (+) Shuster
Barthelemi La Gneau	Johan Adam Männig
Hermann Senger	Casber Diener
Theobald Pein	Michel Staub
Joannes Hahn	Michael (+) Neyff
Christian Kramer	Johann Adam Zehner

Jacob Werthmüller
Niglaus Klein
Fridrich Margel
Johannes Flimer
Johannes Männig
Johannes Lorasch
Henry (×) Schneyder
Michael Homan
Michel Krug
Johann Martin Lösch
Johann Georg Rüllmann
Johann Jacob Schlotzer, Junior
J. Jacob (++) Schlötzer, Senior
Peder Fischer
Johann Wendel Laux
Henry (×) Bachy
Alberth Klunck
Johann Gorg Fey
Johan Petter Hauff
H. Georg (+) Miller
Adolff Flohri
Steffan Abel
Hans George Abel
Johan Michael Uhting
Johann (++) Rentz
Jacob Bernhardt
Joan Nicolaus Deh
Andres Gebhardt
George (×) Flory
Johanes (×) Flory
Michael (×) Shmit
Hans Geörg Kleinpetter
Jacob (++) Gander

Johannes Därendinger
Johann Henrich Schuster
Henry (×) Shwartzenbach
Johannes Därendinger
Philip (PB) Boger
Andreas Schwartz
Christian Hauswirth
Jacob (×) Dogent
Adam (××) Bartholoma
Joseph (+) Debeer
Johan Wendel Königsfeldt
Jacob Weingart
Johann Nicolaus Seidel
Johann Philips Klein
P. Christian (+) Gross
J. Jacob (×) Gross
Johann Andreas Götz
Christoph (+) Mey
Carl Gleim
Christian Keller
Daneil Pfadt
Johann Jorg Schütz
Johann Peter Hermann
Johann Valentin Bruckman
Jacob Müller
Johann Conrad Keil
Johann Peter Bannot
Caspers Fonstock ⎫
Johan Adam Nees ⎬ sick on
Richard Nees   ⎭ board
Hans Minik

In all 130

[List 232 A] List of the Peoples, age and name, on Board the Ship Neptune, William Mallane, Commander, from Hamburgh, arrived at Philadᵃ Decemʳ 12ᵗʰ 1754.

	AGES		AGES
John George Schindler	44	Christoph Rindelman	36
Godfrid Fakey	23	Johan Andreas Knochen	20

	AGES		AGES
Nicolaus Olberts	28	John Heinrich Pleasing	16
Heinrich Schaffer	32	John Peter Usbeak	28
John Simon Kehler	22	John Christoph Uhrig	30
Heinrich von Bestenbost	38	Johannis Offenheisser	24
John Martin Martine	36	Antus Glass	27
Hans George Bohlig	36	Michael Filler	34
John Godlep Boosser	38	Johannes Liebendraut	28
Anthon Gunther	38	Conrad Junkhan	36
John Christoph Zachrias	32	John Argus Koenig	25
Julius Caspar Strebig	24	Jacob Fredrick Shroter	16
William Antheis	27	John Christian Krager	19
John Christian Werlick	19	Alexander Withman	38
Philip Ludwig Limp	28	John Caspar Roehrig	19
And^r Jacob Eichenmoyer	32	Christian Kenneman	16
John Heinrich Welthner	19	Christian Kolkbrener	42
Hironimus Dieterich Sol-		Heinrich Frederick Staman	43
though	20	Frederick Withesale	32
Adam Miller	28	Christian Henry Jacoby	28
George Christoph Muscote	40	Henrich Heller	28
John Christian Schrater	30	John Julius Sorge	30
John Godlop Kensselman	36	John Godfred Reither	46
Conrad Zorn	36	John Holther	17
Helias Israel	24	John Philip Albertin	32
John Abraham Klimph	28	John Adam Berger	28
Joseph David	18	John Peter Keneydrok	20
Bathelo^m Christ^n Berg	19	Philip Rickstein	29
John Ernst Zigler	30	John Holther	23
Christoph Godhard Zigler	16		

[Endorsed:]
Foreigners imported in the Ship Neptune, Capt Wm Maclane, from Hamburg. Qual. 13th Decr 1754. N° 58.

Kepler.

[List 232 B] The Foreigners whose Names are underwritten, Imported in the Neptune, Captain William Malane, from Hamburg, did on the 13th December 1754, take the usual Qualifications to the Government before William Plumsted Esquire, Mayor of the City of Philadelphia.

Andreas Schindler
Gottfried Ficke
Christoffer Rintelman
John Andereas (X) Knochen
Johann Heinrich Schäffer
Johann Simon Kähler
Nicolaus Olbers
Hinrich Graven [?] von Besten
  Bostel
John Martin (+) Martin
Johan Geörg Bohlich
J. Godlop (X) Basler
Anthon Günther
Johan Christoph Zachriss
Julius Caspar (X) Strebig
Wilhelm (X) Antheis
Johann Christian Werlisch
Filib Lutwig Limb
Andreas Jacob Emeyer
Johann Heinrich Weidner
Jerome Diederrick Soltang
Adam Müller
Georg Christoph Muschcat
Johann Christian Schrader
Johann Gottlob Küntzelmann
Conrad (X) Zorn
Elias (OO) Israel
Joh. Abraham Glimpf *
B. Christ^r (X) Beckel

Johann Ernst Ziegler
Christoph Gotthart Ziegler
Johann Hinrich Plesse
Johann Beter Usbeck
John Christoff (X) Uhrry
Johannes Offenhäuser
Winantus (+) Claar
Michael (X) Filler
Johanes ( ) Libentraut, on
  board
Conrad Junghenn
Johann August König
Jacob Fri. Schröder
J. Christian (X) Kroger
Alicksantter Wittmann
Caspar (+) Orig
Christian (+) Küneman
Christian Kalckbrenner
Henrich Friedrich Stamman
Fridrich Wiedensahl
Christ. Hinr. Jacobi
Georg Heinrich Heller
Johann Julius Sorge
Johann Gottfried Ritter
Johann Holter
Johann Arnt Berger
Peter (+) Hendrytrok
John Phillib Ruchstein
John (+) Rotter

[Endorsed:]
Foreigners imported in the Ship Neptune, Capt Maclane, from Hamburg. Qual. 13th Decr 1754. No 58.

Kepler.

[List 232 C] At the Court House at Philadelphia, Friday, the 13 December, 1754.
Present: The Worshipful William Plumsted, Esq., Mayor of Philadelphia.
The Foreigners whose Names are underwritten, Imported

* Name also in cursive Hebrew script.

in the Ship Neptune, Captain William Malane, from Hamburg and last from Cowes, did this day take the usual Qualifications to the Government. 58 Qualified. 147½ whole Freights. From Hamburg, Hanover & Saxony.

Andreas Schindler
Gottfriedt Ficke
Christoffer Rintelman
John Andereas (X) Knochen
Johann Heinrich Schäffer
Johann Simon Kähler
Nicolaus Olbers
Hinrich Graven [?] Von Besten
    Bostel
Johan Martin (X) Martine
Johan Geörg Bohlich
J. Godlop (X) Basler
Anthon Günther
Johan Christoff Zachriss
Julius Caspar (X) Strebig
Wilhelm (X) Antheis
Johann Christian Werlisch
Filb Ludwig Limb
Andreas Jacob Emeyer
Johann Heinrich Weidner
Jerome Diederich Soltan
Adam Müller
George Christoph Muschcat
Johann Christian Schrader
Johan Gottlob Küntzelmann
Conrad (X) Zorn
Elias (O) Israel
Johann Abraham Glimpf *
B. Christian (X) Barkel
Johann Ernst Ziegler

Christoph Gotthart Ziegler
Johan Hinrich Plesse
Johann Beter Usbeck
John Christoff (X) Urry
Johannes Offenhäuser
Winantus (+) Claar
Michael (X) Filler
Johanes ( ) Libentraut, on
    board
Conrad Junghem
Johann August König
Jacob Fridrich Schröder
Johan Christ (+) Kroger
Alecksantter Wittmann
J. Caspar (X) Örrig
J. Christian (X) Kühnman
Christian Kalckbrenner
Heinrich Friedrich Stammann
Friedrich Wiedensahl
Christ. Hinr. Jacobi
Georg Heinrich Heller
Johann Julius Sorge
Johann Gottfried Ritter
Johan (X) Holter
Johann Philipp Alberti
Johan Arnt Berger
Peter (+) Hendrytrok
Johan Philib Ruchstein
John (+) Rotter

Decemb. 12, 1754.

Sir

We have this Day carefully examined every Person we could find on Board the Ship Neptune, Capt Mellum, fom Hamburg,

* Name is also written in cursive Hebrew script.

and saw only one Man ill. He has a Fever, but no Symptoms that show it to be malignant or contagious. The Ship is large and has not above 150 Freights on Board. The Capt. says the People have been healthy in the Voyage that he has lost only three Freights and three Children. Mr Trotter after examining the different Parts of the Ship informed us that no sick Person on Board had been concealed in any Part of her from us, we therefore do not apprehend there is any contagious Fever aamongst either the Marines or Passengers of this Vessel, nor any other Disease we have discovered that can infect the Inhabitants of the City.

To his Honour   Tho. Graeme

The Governour.   Th. Bond

Doctors Report of the Ship Neptune, Cap^n Meclum, 12th Decr 1754.

The Captn waited on the Governor & made oath before him that he had not concealed from the Doctors any sickly persons nor imported any sickly persons to be landed before they came to visit the ship after which the ship was permitted to come up & the passengers to be qualified.

R. Peters.

[List 233 A] A List of men Passengers on board the Two Brothers, Thomas Arnot, Mas^r, from Rotterdam, from the Electorate Palatine & Triers, Hapsburg.*

Johan Gerhard Snyder	Hendrick Wagenaar
Wyant Snyder	Johan Henrich Wagenaar
Johan Chris^n Snyder	Peiter Amoes
Johan Peter Snyder	Philip Leür
Johan Chris^n Humbel	Johan Peter Leur
Jacob Grubert	Johannes Asseloer
Wilhelm Grubert	Johan Jost Bleiker
Johan Conrad Reffie	Johan Peter Müller
Tys Reffie	Jost Fisser
Henrich Preins	Johan Herman Nies
Herman Hutier	Peter Hulbus
Michael Reifenaar	Hobrick Luer
Peiter Reifenaar	Peter Lies

* This list is omitted by Rupp. It is printed in *Pennsylvania Archives*, 2nd series, XVII, p. 377 f.

Christ[n] Bemer
Peter Bemer
Christian Bierkenbeyl
Albertus Herk
Wilhelm Strikhausen
Jacob Kambeck
Jost Schefer
Wilhelm Peifer
Henrich Hofman
Henrich Fox
Johannes Smith
Adam Fox
Teys Baeker
Jerrig Werth
Chris[n] Mathias Gubler
Henrich Kueler
Henrich Jong
Philipus Souer
Peter Lup
Peter Homerick
Simon Hueller
Philipus Liest
Ernst Kraemer
Tonis Baeker
Henrich Willer
Baltzer Smith
Fredrick Smith
Chris[n] Klein
Peter Schiuman
Christ[l] Hulbues
Ludwig Spies
Martin Smitten
Adam Smitten
Wilhelm Maeler
Martyn Grys
Johannes Grys
Mathias Traen
Jacobus Hofman
Wilhelm Koets
Johannes Bemer
Arnold Schiefer

Wilhelm Dieds
Peter Jong
Adam Jong
Teys Baeker
Philip Baeker
Chris[n] Badenheimer
Peter Allen
Peter Broun
Peter Haes
Christian Stels
Jacob Barb
Johan Tevis
Jerg Schultz
Peter Dick
Bast[n] Broun
Theis Dinsman
Theis Seier
Jacob Humer
Wilhelm Helm
Theis Rueb
Christ Rueb
Michal Gessel
Arnst Baeker
Michael Dinsman
Philipus Smith
Wilhelm Smith
Johan Wilhelm Jaeger
Peter Hats
Christ[n] Sneyder
Adam Geimer
Stoffel Leonard
Peter Sein
Hendrick Bemer
Peter Gimbel
Christ[n] Jong
Wilhelm Jong
Andreas Jong
Theis Baeker
Chris[n] Baeker

105

[List 234 A] A List of Men on board the Ship Neptune, George Smith, M[r], from Rotterdam. [Qualified Oct. 7,] 1755.

Christian Acker
Philip Krey
Peter Haff
Jurg Peter Höffner
Stophel Kaufman
Henry Metz
Potto Otta
Joh. Adam Deutchenbach
Thomas Tanzenbecker
Ludwig Tanzenbecker
Joseph Kleyman
Casper Petorf
Conrad Wirhime
Fred[k] Dielman
Christian Reyter
Jacob Perch
Nicholas Reem
Jacob Wertz
Fred[k] Ditz
Peter Finck
Johan Henry Finck
Thomas Lutz
Henrich Hinckle
Gotfried Zwigebul
Sebastian Smith
Carl Houser
Casper Henderstief
Albrecht Shappert
Hans Mich[l] Krous
Jacob Stierle
Adam Wenig
Hans Kenor
Christoph Kenor
Mich[l] Claus
Mich[l] Schintel
Jacob Schock
Johan Casper Zincker
Christian Ludwig Konig

Joh. Henrik Messer
Johannes Keyser
Hans Jurg Snyder
Wilhelm Walter
Casper Ulrick
Christian Stohr
Hans Jurg Scheffer
Hans Buck
Christian Bachman
Conrad Bachman
Jacob Buck
Johannes Herbsheyser
Michael Werner
Mich[l] Werner, Jun[r]
Andereas Hofter
Christoph Mier
Fred[k] Aegie
Math[s] Oberfehl
Johan Peter Rietel
Joh. Nick[l] Kast
Joh. Christ. Kast
Philip Jacob Behr
Joh. Peter Heckman
Joh. Adam Helmsteter
Joh. Mich[l] Spitz
Math[s] Preys
Anderas Mesner
Wilhelm Kerner
Melchor Hirt
Johannes Steynll
Joh. Philip Fisher
Sebastian Sunleyder
Conrad Miller
Johannes Maltthaner
Adam Vogel
Christ[n] Bantor
Christoph Weybrich
Joh. Mich[l] Weys

Adam Lorentz Dietrich
Johann^s Smierer
Jacob Ulrich Hass
Bernhard Eygelsheymer
Mathias Weys
Jurg Mich^l Swab
Hans Jurg Kellor
Hans Jurg Volk
Henrich Emmert

Peter Frutche
Jurg Klingensmith
Jurg Blankenbuller
Hannes Kran
Samuel Backrack
Israel Manhim
Isaac Levy
Reymer Lant
93

[Endorsed:]
Foreigners imported in the Ship Neptune, Capt Geo. Smith, from Rotterdam. Qual. 7th Octr 1755. N° 93.

Shoemaker.

[List 234 B] Foreigners imported in the Ship Neptune, George Smith, Master, from Rotterdam. [Qualified October 7, 1755].

Reimer Landt
Bodo Otto
Christian Acker
Philips Krieg
Peter Haaf
George Peter (+) Haffman
Christopher (✕) Kaufman
Isaac Levy *
Israel Josep
Henrich Metz
Johann Adam Teütschenbach
Thomas (✕) Tansenbecher
Johann Ludwig Dantzebecher
Joseph Kleinman
Johann Caspar Bittorff
Johan Conradt Birheim
Gerg Friedich Dillman
Christian Reutter
Jacob Bertsch
Nicklaus Reim
Jacob Würtz

Friedrich Dietz
Peter (F) Fink
Johann Henrich Finck
Thomas Lutz
Heinrich Henkell
Gottfried Zergiebel
Sebastian Schmid
Carl Hausser
Caspar Hindersteiff
Albrecht (✕) Shepherd
Hans Michael Krauss
Jacob Stierle
Atam Weniger
Hans Keingar
Johan Christoph Kinger
Michael Claas
Michhel Schindel
Johann Jacob Schock
Johann Caspar Zincke
Christian Ludwig König
Johann Heinrich Möser

* Written also in cursive Hebrew script.

Johanes Kaiser
Hans Jerg Schneider
Wilhelm Walter
Casper (++) Ulrich
Christian Stöhr
Hans Görg Scheffer
Hans Buch
Christian Baumann
Conrad Bauman
Jacob Buch
Johannes Erbsfuser
Michael Warr[ner]
Michael Wörner
Andreas (×) Heflinger
Christoph Mayer
Friederich Ege
Matthäus Obergsäll
Johann Peder [Rietel]
Johann Nickl Gast
Johan Christijan Gast
Philipp Jacob Bär
Johan Peter (+) Hickman
Johann Adam Helmstätter
Johannes Spitz
Anders Mässner
Mathias Preisgärtner

Johann Wilhelm Körner
Johann Melchior Hirth
Johannes (×) Steilich
J. Philip (×) Fisher
Sebastian Sonleider
Conrath Müller
Johannes Malther
Fridrich Adam [Vogel]
Christian Bannadurer
Georg Christoff Wibrecht
Johan (+) Michael Weiss
Adam Lorentz Dieterich
Johannes Schmierer
Jacob Ullrich Haas
Bernahad (×) Eilsamer
Mathias (O) Weiss
G. Michael (×) Swabb
Hans Jörg Keller
Joh. Gorg Volck
Heinrich Emert
Johann Petter Frutzuy
Georg Klingenschmidt
Johann Georg Blanckenbiller
Jean Grentier
Samuel Bachrach

[Endorsed:]
Foreigners imported in the Ship Neptune, Capt Geo. Smith, from Rotterdam. Qual. 7th Octr 1755. N° 93.

Shoemaker.

[List 234 C] At the Court House at Philadelphia, Tuesday, the Seventh Day of October, 1755.

Present: Septimus Robinson, Esquire.

The Foreigners whose Names are underwritten, imported in the Ship Neptune, George Smith, Master, from Rotterdam but last from Gosport, did this Day take and subscribe the usual Qualifications. 226 Whole Freights. Shoemaker.

Reimer Landt
Bodo Otto

Christian Acker
Philips Krieg

Peter Haaf
Georg Peter (+) Häffner
Christoff (×) Kauffman
Isaac Levy *
Israel Josep
Henrich Metz
Johann Adam Teütschenbach
Thomas (×) Tantzebeker
Johann Ludwig Dantzebecher
Joseph Kleinman
Johann Caspar Bittorff
Johan Conradt Birheim
Gerg Fridrich Dillman
Christian Reütter
Jacob Bertsch
Niclaus Reim
Jacob Würtz
Fridrich Dietz
Peter (F) Finck
Johan Henrich Finck
Thomas Lutz
Heinrich Henkell
Gottfried Zergiebel
Sebastian Schmid
Carl Hausser
Caspar Hindersteiff
Albrecht (×) Shabert
Hans Michael Krauss
Jacob Stierle
Adam Weniger
Hans Keingar
Johannes Kincker
Michael Claas
Michgel Schindel
Johann Jacob Schock
Johann Caspar Zinke
Christian Ludewig König
Johann Heinrich Möser
Johanis Kaiser
Hans Jerg Schneider

Wilhelm Walder
Caspar (++) Uhllerik
Christian Stöhr
Hans Görg Scheffer
Hans Buckh
Christian Bauman
Conrad Bauman
Jacob Buck
Johannes Erbshuser
Michael Wer[ner]
Michael Wörner
Andereas (×) Höftlinger
Christopf Mayer
Friderich Ege
Matthäus Obergsäll
Johan Peder [Rietel]
Johannickl Gast
Johan Christijan Gast
Philipp Jacob Bär
Johan Peter (×) Hickman
Johann Adam Helmstätlerr
Johannes Spitz
Mathias Preisgärtner
Andres Mössner
Johann Wilhel Körner
Johann Melchior Hirth
Johanes (×) Steiney
J. Philip (×) Fisher
Sebastian Sonleider
Conrath Müller
Johannes Malther
Fridrich Adam [Vogel]
Christen Bannadurer
Georg Christoff Weibrecht
Johan Michael (+) Weise
Adam Lorentz Dieterich
Johannes Schmierer
Jacob Ullrich Haas
Bernhart (×) Eilsheimer
Mathias (W) Weis

* Written in cursive Hebrew script.

G. Michael (✕) Shwab   Georg Klingen Schmidt
Hans Jörg Keller   Johan Georg Blanckenbiller
Johann Gerg Volck   Jean Grentier
Henrich Emert   Samuel Bachrach
Johann Petter Frutzuy   93

Sr

Agreeable to Orders we have Visited the Ship Neptune,
Capt. Smyth, Master, freighted with Palatines from Rotterdam
and find the Passengers all in good health, except one Man and
Woman, and that but very slightly ailing, so that we can not
report any Infectious distemper being aboard the sᵈ Vessel,
therefore there can be no objection to her being admitted to
Enter the Port.   Tho. Graeme
To his Honour the Governor   Phineas Bond
Philadⁱᵃ Octr 9ᵗʰ 1755.
[Endorsed:]
Doctors Certificate of the Ship Neptune, 7, 8 1755.

[List 235 A] List of Palatine Passengers on Board the Ship
Pennsylvania, Charles Lyon, Comʳ, from London. Philadⁱᵃ
Novʳ 1, 1755.

Philip Libeck *   Hendrick Fisher
Fred Libeck   Johannes Young
Falten Ryder   Melchior Hornan
Law. Sites   Uste Hopeman
And. Riddle   Fred. Hopeman
Lodowick Oakima   Philip Fisher
Geo. Cook   Conrad Timber
Fredrick Waber   Hendrick Allbes
Dan. Bridegam   And. Nicholas Allen

[Endorsed:]
Foreigners imported in the Ship Pennsylvania, Capᵗ Charles
Lyon, from London. Qual. 1ˢᵗ November, 1755. N° 17.
                                        Abel James.

[List 235 B] Foreigners Imported in the Ship Pennsylvania,
Capᵗ Charles Lyon, from London. Qual. 1ˢᵗ November 1755.

* Name crossed out.

Frederick (+) Libeck
Johan Valtin Reuter
Lorentz Seitz
Andreas Riedel
Georg Ludwig Hochheimer
Johann Iurgen Koch
Georg Friderich Weber
Johann Daniel Bräutigam
Johan Heinrich Fischer

Johannes Jung
Johnn Milchior Hornung
Johan Just Hopman
Johann Friederich Hopman
Johann Philip Fischer
Conraht Timpe
Johann Heinrich Albers
Andreas Nicolaus Halling

[Endorsed:]

Foreigners imported in the Ship Pennsylvania, Capt Charles Lyon, from London. Qual. 1st November, 1755. No 17.

Abel James.

[List 235 C] At the Court House at Philadelphia, Saturday, the First day of November, 1755.

Present: Septimus Robinson, Esqr.

The Foreigners whose Names are underwritten, Imported in the Ship Pennsylvania, Capt. Charles Lyon, from London, did this Day take and subscribe the usual Qualifications. 34 Whole Freights. Jer. Warder & Abel James.

Friederich (+) Leydig
Johan Valtin Reüter
Lorentz Seitz
Andreas Rietel
Georg Ludwig Hochheimer
Johan Jurgen Koch
Georg Friederich Weber
Johann Daniel Bräutigam
Johan Heinrich Fischer

Johannes Jung
Johann Milchior Hornung
Johan Just Hopman
Johann Friederich Hopmann
Johann Philip Fischer
Conraht Timpe
Johann Henrich Albers
Andreas Nicolaus Halling

[List 236 C] At the State House at Philadelphia, Wednesday, the Tenth of November, 1756.

Present: Atwood Shute, Esquire.

The Foreigners whose Names are underwritten, [imported] in the Snow Chance, Capt Lawrence, last from London, did this day take and subscribe the usual Qualifications. 109½ whole Freights.

Abel James.

Georg Ludwig Eberle
Bernhard Ühlein
Casper Burckhart
Paulus (+++) Kamb
Joha. Andreas Klunck
Johann Peter Klunck
Johann Nickel Kuhn
Erhardt Conradt
Georg Ludwig Crusius
Gorg Doll
Leonard Dürr
Simon Hengel
Hans Wolff Gundel
Nicklaus Hahn
Wolfgang Nicolaus Heymann
Johann Peter Körner
Johann Heinrich Klöpper
Michle Muller
Nicklas Pauly
Johann Valentin Panzer
Johanes (×) Sombero
Balte Sching

Adam Schmidt
Johann Sack
Johann Wilhelm Stiernkorb
Friedrich Schöff
Johan Georg Schmidt
Franz Waner
Johann Görg Weinig
Caspar Biener
Johannes Weytzel
Johan Peter Weber
Johann Nickel Wagner
Friederich Walther
Christian Segnitz
Johan Nickellas Zimerman
Johanes (××) Haas
Christian Pauli
Johan Magnus Pauli
Valentin Dürr
Johann Nickel Wagner
Rudolff (++) Fullewiler.
Hans Opplinger

[List 237 C] At the Courthouse of Philadelphia, October 21st, 1761.

Present:

Jacob Duché, Mayor ⎫
Henry Harrison ⎬Esq^{rs}
William Peters ⎭

The Palatines whose Names are underwritten, imported in the Snow Squirrel, John Benn, Master from Rotterdam, but last from Portsmouth, did this day take & subscribe the Oaths to the Government. Viz.

Caspar Knoblauch
Peter Mischler
Eberhart Disinger
Christofel Lomberg
Johannes Beyerle
Fallendhin Annewallt
Johann Simon Meyer

Andreas Krafft
Stephan Danner
Johann Wilhelm Seeger
Johan Conrath Seeger
John Nickl Hertzog
Johan Nickel Becker
Georg Friderich Rohrer

Daniel (X) Schaub
John Henry (X) Diessinger
Johann Jacob Hackman
Johann Friederich Diehl
Frederick (+) Lieberknecht
Nicolaus Schweitzer
Johann Nicolaus Diehl
John Jacob (+) Vogelgesang

Georg Vogelgesang
Wilhelm Becker
Frantz Eckhardt
Heinrich Holtzapffel
Johan Lutwig Probst
Johann Jacob Probst
Frederick (X) Probst
Johann Dietherich Taub

[List 238 C] At the State House at Philadelphia, Wednesday, the 5ᵗʰ day of October, 1763.

Present:

Jacob Duche
Daniel Benezet } Esquires.

The Foreigners whose Names are underwritten, imported in the Ship Richmond, Capt. Charles Young Husband, from Rotterdam, but last from Portsmouth, did this Day take and subscribe the usual Qualifications. 162 whole Freights. Benjᵃ & Samuel Shoemaker.

Johan Jacob Peiffer
Johannes Zimmerman
Johann Jacob Hoffman
Johan Theis Cromm
Johannes Schuntz
Johann Herman Klappert
Johannes Klappert
Johann Engell Bäcker
Johann Michel Bäcker
Johannes Henrich Schneider
Johann Schütz
Rudolph Hehr
Peter Katz
Jacob Katz
Georg Daum
D. Dieterich Burchardt
Andreas Holtzmann
Johan Thomas Scholl
Ludwig Agricola
Friederich Schoenleber
Johannes Schneider

Johann Daniel Körschner
Joseph Fischer
Frantz Multz
Görg Bender
Conrad (+) Betis
P. Paule
Joseph (+) Bonn
August (X) Hemerlin
Johann Georg Hibler
Johann Henrich Niess
Johannes Peter Schneider
Jans Pieliep Mehrenholtz
Johan Jost Hänner
Johannes Häner
Johan Jost Dietz
Johann Christigann Scheidt
J. Hnrich Läck
Paul Grin
Henrich Dietz
Peter Götz
Johannes Claus

Daniel Paulus
Johan Henrich Baulus
Johannes Henrich Paulus
Johann Friederich Stüll
Johann Michael Motz
Peter Hauberd
Jacob Otho
Jost Heintz
Johannes Busel
Hermanus Ganber
Casper Müller
Andres Dress
Willhelm Völlmar
Wilhelm Lick
Johann Georg Ginsberg
Johannes Peter Ginsberg
Johannes Engel Ginsberg
Herman Donat
Johann Engel Jud
Andreas Mertz
Henry (X) Wagoner
Mathias (+) Lockner
Jacob Gläsener

Johann Henrich Gläsener
Lorentz Knöri
Henrich Bernöller
Martin (X) Schaffner
August (X) Isinger
Dilmanis Bäcker
Johann Daub
Phillipp Werner
John (X) Sollberg
Martin Forsch
Jacob Bergman
Friedrich Bergmann
Johannes Jüd
John Marbes
Gerg Friedrich Huber
Johannes Schott
Henry Bonnart
Joh. Henrich Wensell
Geo. (+) Bastian
Conratt Wolff
Johannes Wickel *
86 persons

[List 239 C] At the State House at Philadelphia, Tuesday, the 1st November, 1763.
Present: Isaac Jones, Esquire.

The Foreigners whose Names are underwritten, imported in the Ship Chance, Captain Charles Smith, from Rotterdam, but last from Cowes, did this Day take and subscribe the Usual Qualifications. 193 whole Freights. 97 Persons. (Benjamin & Samuel Shoemaker.)

Johannes (X) Schellenberger
Joseph Seyferdt
Henrich Debertshäuser
Vallentin Gänsel

Philip (X) Casner
Jean Henri Gaydon
David Golter
Johannes Ludy

* Judging by the neat handwriting this seems to be the Reformed preacher, John H. Wickel, who preached at Boehm's Church, in Montgomery County. Harbaugh, *Fathers*, II, p. 400, gives his name as Weikel, but documents preserved by the church show that his name was Wickel. He preached at Boehm's Church from March 1776 to August 1777.

Johann Georg Vetter
Georg Ebert
Filb Schabbert
Nicolaus Schapperdt
Joh. Jacob Schnorss
Johannes (X) Shnors
Johann Peter Kesler
Henrich (X) Alsbach
Phillip Schmit
Jacob (+) Spielman
Johann Christian Schwab
Phillip Zumstain
Johann Jerg Dornech
Georg Ludwig Kesselrinck
Casper (X) Huber
Bernhardt Raichert
Georg Günther
Jacob Jantz
Johannes Gern
Johannes Rotter
Andrew (ANT) Teyer
Johann Georg Mühlheim
Johann Gorg Henninger
Jacob Baltzel
Carl Baltzel
Georg Jacob Baltzel
Johan Petter Hauck
Adam (X) Sampel
Hans Peter Studi
Görg Gantz
Geo. (F) Fisher
Michael (X) Becker
Hans George (X) Zeiner
Michael (X) Zeiner
Jacob Schädt
Johann Henry (X) Shuntz
Johannes Dorst
Jacob Schlick
Johann Michael Altz
Jacob Behr

Jacob Ebersoll
Peterus Wolf
Christian Mangolt
Frietrig Arnolt
Johann Jacob Sonntag
Johann Jakob [?] Hoffman
Johann Valatin Hauck
Peter Krafft
Georg Heinrich Planckenhorn
Johannes Doerbaum
Friedrich Wilhelm Stahl
Johann Benedictus Grieben
Adam Schmid
Michel Schmidt
Daniel Zutter
Balthaser Zutter
Henry (H) Schwarts
Johannes Weller
Johann Wendell Fackler
Johannes Engelberth
Jnº Henry (X) Miller
Anthon Hausam
Martin Braun
Samuel Müller
Jacob Bernhart
Johann Thomas Gil
Johannes Jacob Jud
Johannes Peter Münner
Johannes Engel Örder
Johann Eckart Oerter
Michel Stoffel
Jost Henrich Schmidt
Johann Henrich Keil
Johannes Peter Becker
Henrich Menges
Johann Ernst Thiel
Samuel Cyriaci
Balthasar Christ
Valentin Nicodemus
Johannes Krätzer

Michael (+) Spielman   Nicolaus Wistadius

Emanuel (×) Miesterrer   Philipp Georg Kneicht

[List 240 C] At the State House at Philadelphia, Friday, the 25th November, 1763.

Present: Isaac Jones, Esquire.

The Foreigners whose names are underwritten, imported in the Brigantine Success, Captain William Marshall, from Rotterdam, did this day take and subscribe the usual Qualifications. 36 Whole Freights. Gilbert Barclay, Owner.

Johann Henrich Hedrich   Hanns Mates Steffan

Abraham Neu   Johann Heinrich Fetzer

Johann Jacob Müller   Johann Marthin Schuster

Jacob (+) Helm   John George (×) Bauman

Leonhart Wass   Anthon Naeryes

Charles (O) Christman   Johanes Kayser

Mathias (×) Chrisman   13 persons

[List 241 C] At the State House at Philadelphia, Friday, the 25th Novemr, 1763.

Present: Isaac Jones, Esquire.

The Foreigners whose names are underwritten, imported in the Ship Pallas, Richard Milner, Master, from Rotterdam but last from Portsmouth, did this day take & subscribe the usual Qualifications. 196½ Whole Freights. 65 Persons. (Benjamin & Samuel Shoemaker.)

Henrich Just Röhrig   Jorg Wilhelm Janson

Isaac Droquet   Gottlieb Roll

Georg Kühnle   Peter Opp

Conradt Meyer   Michel Opp

Georg Friederich Hammer   Johann Wendel

Georg Mayer   Johann Henrich Strauch

Johannes Schmit   Frederick (×) Holtzhausser

David Jansohn   Michael Braun

Jacob Weissert   Conradt Scherrer

Johannes Schaaff   Johann Joerg Höchst

Ludwig Amaus   Martin Schneider

Ullrich Brukholder   Johann Christ Reiff

Martin Scholder
Jacob Häuser
Lewis (✕) Stutz
Jost Vahll
Willhelm Bleiniger
Jnᵒ Henry (✕) Miller
Johann Mertin Merck
Jnᵒ Henry (+) Freind
Johann Conradt Keyser
Johann Jacob Schweitzer
Johannes Joerg
Jacob Heintz
Henrich Flick
Henrich Kraft
Johannes Blum
Peter (✕) Schultz
Jereg Miller
Johann Adam Hoffheintz
Johann Danngel Hoffheintz
Wilhelm Ritter
Casper Reyde

Anderas Obmann
Lorentz Obmann
Mardin Steffen
Jorg Thomas Gerhardt
Valentine (✕) Seipel
Peter (✕) Werckin
Abraham Senner
Henry (+) Pfeiffer
Baltzer Schock
Jean Andree Stokinger
Jean Louis Seiz
Friederich Hüttner
Philips Faust
Johann Georg Prechtel
Leonhart Frischkorn
Phillipp Miller
Johannis Schittenhelm
Johan Christian Schreiber
Christopher (✕) Pfeiffer
Gerlach (✕) Witterstein
65 persons

[List 242 C] At the State House at Philadᵃ, Wednesday, 8ᵗʰ Augᵗ 1764.

Present: William Peters, Esquire.

The Foreigners whose names are underwritten, imported in the Ship Chance, Capt. Charles Smith, from Rotterdam, did this day take and subscribe the usual Qualifications. Consigned to Mr. Robᵗ Ruecastle, Merchᵗ. 208 Whole Freights. 93 Persons. Paid for 107 à 1/6—£8. 0. 6. Sepᵗ 13, 1764.

Daniel Dexheymer
Johann Ludwig Dexheymer
Sebastian (✕) Bender
Johann Peter Schmidt
Henry Christⁿ (+) Shiel
Peter (✕) Riger
Johann Phillipp Toma
Johanes Schneider
Philip (✕) Shifferer

Johann Adam Schiffer
Balds Kappes
Valetin Metzger
Johann Martin Hess
Johan Michael Habtügel
Bernhard Geiger
Johann Friederich Müller
Johanes Strenger
Johan Friderich Weeger

Johan Georg Haas
Geörg Peter Beck
Michel (+) Bandel
Ferdend [?] Wanner [?]
Johann Wilhelm Weiss
Johann Jacob Sties
Geo. (O) Sleig
Mattheus Roth
Johann Nickel Mayer
Johann Herman Meyer
Johan Peder Durst
Fridrich Altherr
Georg Leonhart Stutz
Fiteli Brogli
Johannes Gehard
Johannes Tondt
Peter (+) Grosh
Geo. (✕) Haag
Peder Meier [?]
Stefan Freundt
Ludwig Schad
Joh. Geörg Gebhardt
Johannes Wench
Joh. Jacob Grob
Johannes Rittesheim
Antoni Vogt
Andreas Scholl
Johann Jacob Schifferer
Peter Arendt
Jacobus (O) Arendt
Matheus Premich
Johann Steffan Saam
Peter Krapff
Mich¹ (✕) Bremig
Johann Adam Bremich
Johanes Keller
Johan Georg Haudt
Jacob Eckfeldt

Hennrich Schäffer
Philip Abrahamm Hoenich
Johann Görg Strein
Peter Zürn
Friderich Wahl
Philip (+) Blum
Johan Henrich Somern [?]
Simon Discher
Johann Christian Tischer
Anderas Bartel
Johanes Wyll [?]
Antreas Meisch
Johanes Freund
Ludwig Feter [?]
Joseph (++) Chaser
Peter Rücker
Johannes Späth
Johannes Rick
Peter (✕) Haas
Johan Goerg Theiss
Johannes Theisen
Fred. (✕) Hoffman
Daniel Weniger
Philib Will
Geo. (+) Sherer
Andʷ (And) Martin
Frantz Schwartz
Mathias (M) Kemp
Andreas Druckenbrodt
Ludwig (+) Huber
Johannes Wernberger
Sebastian Seyberth
Jörg Gielbert
Fred. (✕) Ringer
Michel Wilhelm
Geo. Wendel (✕) Zimmerman
Valentin Bauer

[List 243 C] At the Courthouse, Wednesday, Septemʳ 19ᵗʰ 1764.

Present:

Isaac Jones } Esquires.
Daniel Benezet }

The Foreigners whose names are underwritten, imported in the Ship Polly, Captⁿ Robert Porter, from Rotterdam, but last from Cowes, did this day take and subscribe the usual Qualifications. 184 whole Freights. 81 persons in the List. Robert Ruecastle, Merch^t (6 Roman Catholicks, 55 Protestants.) p^{d.} 13, Octr. 1764.

Johann Christophel Schmidt
Johans Schadt
Johann Jost Schreckengast
Johann Jacob Graff
John Melchior (×) Hollebach
Bernhard Beck
Johannes Riff
Nich^l (+) Schluhter
Johann Görg Schmit
Johann Peter Trein
Friederich Galle
Johann Jacob Reudt
Johan Hefa [?]
Johann Georg Eller
Hans Grimm
Johann Çasbar Guttenburg
Johann Michael Bergman
Jacob (×) Berckel
Johann Jacob Mann
Christian (×) Bergman
Cashper Wenger
Jacob Wenger
Nicklaus Lugebüel
Johann Friedrich Strass
Johann Conradt Strass
Johan Carl Laubach
Johann Henrich Els
Johan Georgen Wyckel
Johann Nicklas Franck
Johan Adam Franck

Joh. Daniel König
Johann Heinrich Schell
John George (+) Schwaab
Geo. Adam (×) Graff
John Martin (×) Stoll
Johannes Leiser
Johannes Culman
Johan Nickol Herbst
Peter (+) Stigelman
Frantz Petter Hackert
Johann Valtin Dumm
Johan Friedrich Zimmerman
Christian (+) Long
Peter (+) Marks
Andres Grebiel
Pedder Grebiell
Linhard B[a]ur
Conrad (×) Bauer
Beter Thormyer
Antoni Jutz
Anthon Noschang
Peter (+) Dieterick
Adam (O) Michell
Johannes Mattias Hoffmann
Christian Ernst Beschler
Jacob Neblinger
Carl Schmidt
Wilhelmus Moser
Anthoni Welte

61 in all

[List 244 C] At the Court House at Philadelphia, September, the 20th 1764.

Present: Samuel Mifflin, Esquire.

The Foreigners whose names are underwritten, imported in the Ship Sarah, Capt. Francis Stanfell, from Rotterdam, but last from Portsmouth, did this day take & subscribe the usual Qualifications. 230 Freights. 108 persons in ye List. Robt Ruecastle. p^d. 13, Oct^r, 1764.

Mardin Hoffman
Paul (+) Hoffman
Godfrey (+) Keyser
Conrad Bischoff
Geo. (O) Scherer
Georg Jacob Scherer
Johann Ludwig Betz
Johann Urbahn Betz
Johann Adam Schäffle
Michell Laüth
Adam Göttell
Peter Göttell
Friedrich Brandstetter
Henrich Eich
Theobald (+) Lehman
Jacob (+) Hoy
Henrich Cortern
Theobald (X) Itzberger
Jno Henry (X) Kisauer
Israel Grob
Christian Frömbdling
Benjamin Frömbdling
Peter Schwaab
Jacob (A) Altvatter
Beter Hub
Theobald (HD) Weber
Adam Ludy
Johann Jacob Kaufman
Frans (X) Kettering
Christian (H) Meyer
Simon Friederich Schober

Johannes (X) Spielman
Jno Theob^d Spielman
Johann Daniel Fuhrman
Jacob Allspach
Daniel Frick
Konrad Frick
Daniel (X) Dausman
Filib Hoffecker
John George (H) Hubacker
Johan Migel Thran
Michel Hoffecker
John George (X) Drachsel
Jacob Kieffer
Henrich Ochsenbecher
Hans Georg Schyre
Johannes Henrich [?] Hoff
John Peter (X) Weber
Leonhard Benckner
Johann Lichtenfeldt
Hann Dider Hoff
Johan Geörg Grossglass
Johan Mattes Dibel
Andreas Vollprecht
Johann Friederich Kücherer
Johannes Welte
Johan Philipp Welde
Michael Funck
Jacob (H) Schantz
Jacob (X) Feiock
Joha Henrich Schaub
John (HS) Schissler

Mich. (M) Metzger
Johann Georg Specht
Jacob (+) Gensel
Geo. (HF) Fisher
Conrad (×) Fisher
Jacob (+) Trein
Henrich Schreiner
Martin Rauch
Johanes Eininger
Johan Henrich Fashaus
Johannes Dörr
Johan Herman
Johann Wilhelm Weber *
Johan Jost Strack
Johann Petter Ottersholt
Carl Eckhart
Johannis Hegenstill [?]
Petter Kuhn
Arent (×) Kriesing
Frantz Thomas Hartmann

Johan Christoffel Bintz
Geo. Henry (+) Hartman
Wendel (+) Sheets
Christel König
Georg Schurg
Gerg Kuhn
Johann Georg Wetzel
Johannes Hitz
Johan Philip Kuhn
Johannes Gast
Johannes Blitz
Henrich Nickel Raque
Hans Chris^n (×) Raque
Oswald (W) Rap
Johann Daniel Löhr
Peter (×) Göttel
Moritz (MM) Master
Johann Michel (×) Jung
Johan Petter Steiler
Conrad Schäffer

[List 245 C] At the Court House at Philadelphia, September 26th 1764.

Present: Isaac Jones, Esquire.

The Foreigners whose names are underwritten, imported [in] the Ship Brittania, Capt. Thomas Arnot, from Rotterdam, did this day take and subscribe the usual Qualifications. 112 persons in the List. 250 Whole Freights. (Benjamin & Samuel Shoemaker).

Gottfried Lampard
Christoph Heger
Johannes Sim. Zepp
Johann Paullus Kapffenbrener
John (×) Weber
Andrew (×) Ketteman
Augustus Weiss
Nich^s (×) Smith

Georg Michel Schmitt
Johan Henrich Völcker
Daniel Ring
Georg Sauter
Friedrich Bäntzler
Theobald Roth
Johann Carl Schmidt
Georg Philipp Karwin

* This is the Reformed schoolmaster and minister, the Rev. John Wm. Weber. See Good, *History of the Reformed Church, 1725–1792*, p. 574.

Martin Jetter
Georg Adam Zepp
Henrich Morschheimer
Jacob Tusching
Andreas Vogt
Johann Wilhelm Etsperger
Henrich Gick
Jacob Gich
Adam ($\times$) Fink
Filips Gerschheimer
Jn° Geo. ($+$) Reiff
Georg Michael Oettinger
Johan Baum
Adolph Carl Schneider
Casber Erhardt
Philipp Lautenschlager
Thomas Wagner
Johan Bernhart Oth
Johann Andreas Schmitt
Christian Haushalter
Georg Heinrich Schmitt
Christian Schellman
Johannes Waibel
Stephⁿ ($\times$) Weibel
Adam ($\times$) Miller
Andreas Freyberger
Johannes Freyberger
Justus Lechleider
Johann Martin Ott
Carl Garaus
Vallentin Stettler
Jacob Masohlder
Johann Friederich Vogel
Georg Wilhelm Schmitt
David Schneider
Christian ($+$) Fleckstein
Peter Wiser
Johannes Crombach
Johan Conrath Crombach
Johann Philipp Von Nieda
Johann Friedrich Mopps

Gerhart Steinbrecker
Gorg Fridrich Heldt
Jacob Schäfer
Johann Görg Greff
Johann Adam Greff
Johannes Höchst
Johann Görg Creutz
Ewerhardus Leicht
Georg Vallentin Deegen
Johann Andres Welck
Johann Philip Seidenstricker
Johann Valtin Horter
Johann Adam Rau
Erhard (B) Rodenstein
Johann Jacob Schmidt
Johann Friederich Koch
Philip Henrich Engel
Johann Phillipp Racke
Philipp Henerich Miller
Johann Henrich Spitzer
Johan Anderas Spitzer
Jacob Brückert
Christoph Brückert
Johannes Kalbfleisch
Johann Friedrich Beyermeister
Johann Dietrich Hauck
Abraham Messer
Fred. (O) Jochim
Christian (O) Eberhard
Andreas Jäger
Hans Gerg Schieferdecker
Georg Lehner
Johann Philipp Schäffer
Henry (O) Seidenstreicher
Jerg Lombarth
Hans Michal Lampart
Christian Ludwig Schäffer
Georg Kuntz
Henrich Wegner
Johann Henrich Fabricius
Jacob Bäyerlein

John George (✕) Menges
Christian (++) Rupp
Johann Michell Michell
Nichˢ (✕) Staller
Fridrich Sachsman
Christian (+) Sachsman
Hans Atam Taxler

Jacob Bart Scherrer
Hans Nickel Resser
Fritrich Gerhart
Ott Philipp Seidensticker
Martin Bühler
Christoph Keller

[List 246 C] At the State House at Philadelphia, Octʳ 3ʳᵈ 1764.

Present: William Peters, Esquire.

The Foreigners whose names are underwritten, imported in the Ship King of Prussia, Captain James Robinson, from London, did this day take and subscribe the usual Qualifications. In the List 53. 94 whole Freights. Messʳˢ James & Drinker. pᵈ. 13ᵗʰ Octʳ 1764.

Johan Peter Vadel
Johann Georg Ther
Jacob Stadel
Henrich Schell
Georg Peter Deisert
Johan Ligtmüller
Philip (✕) Resher
Jocip Weber
Christian Weber
Gerlach Grau
Johannes Ott
Mathias (✕) Hendrick
Lutwig Schell
Johann Philip Rauschkobb
Johann Nicolaus Dippel
Philip Jacob (✕) Breszler
Johan Philip Steinmetz
Johann Filp Mattes
Ernst Ludwig Reinbold
Johann Georg Ernst
Georg Schwerdt
Johann Nicolaus Schwerdt
Johannes Salade

Johann Peter Fischer
Philip Jacob (O) Suder
Johannes Kolb
Migel Salate
Geo. Michˡ (✕) Hart
Sem. Wickert
Frantz Schweitzer
Joh. Nickel Horst
Andʷ (✕) Finck
Johannes Stutz
Wendel Apfel
Johann Martin Hierdt
Geo. (+) Schlemb
Henrich Strohm
Geo. (✕) Appel
Geo. (✕) Ridle
Paul Schreck
Niclas Scherrer
Johann Georg Gantz
Johann Nicol Wagner
Christian Wickert
Albertus Häffner
Geo. (✕) Kenttner

Elleias Apel
Jacob Specht
Johann Philip Mühlmichel

Christian (+) Appel
Geo. (+) Doll
Johannes Köster

[List 247 C] At the Court House at Philad^a, Saturday, 20th Octr 1764.

Present: Jacob Duche, Esquire.

The Foreigners whose names are underwritten, imported in the Ship Richmond, Capt. Charles Younghusband, from Rotterdam, did this day take and subscribe the usual Qualifications. 110 persons in ye List. 224 whole Freights. (Benj. & Samuel Shoemaker.) 1766, 29 Nov^r, p^d £8.5.

Johann Christian Thiel
Jacob Noll
Johann Peter Gerhard
Johann Georg Diebert
Eberhard (✗) Kirsheyer
Jn° Geo. (✗) Fullman
Friederich Gelberdt
Johan Conrath Kaufman
Jacob (+) Kerber
Christoffel Weber
Christoffel Wöber
Carl Weber
Bernhart Schneider
John (IA) Allman
Jn° Adam (✗) Sebeinger
Hannes Starck
Johannes Rupert
Johann Martin Rupert
Johann Wendel Barthelmey
Jn° Adam (✗) Heckman
Johann Peter Schell
Dan¹ (✗) Weichel
Johan Fridrich Henrich
Michel Halm

Conrad Jacoby
Jacob Harbach
Wendel Runckel *
Dewalt Gülcher
Michel Keiser
Friederich Hirschfeldt
Mattheis Koch Weber
Frantz Kuhn
Joseph Breisch
Baldt Sennar
Sebastian Stier
Johannes Glück
Samuel Stauffer
Christoph Martin Gemandt
Heinrich Kurtz
Hans Jerg Kurtz
Johann Jacob Bühler
John Geo. (✗) Geiger
Hans Jerg Hagenbach
Jn° Martin (✗) Knobloch
Georg Taub
Mathes Löchner
Michael Reiner
Gottfried Schott

* The father of the Reformed minister, the Rev. John Wm. **Runckel.** See *Fathers of the Reformed Church,* II, p. 284.

Johann Andreas Kolb
Daniel Sätzler
Mich¹ (×) Reidebach
Johann Philip Müller
Johannes Seitz
Johann Adam Schütz
Wendell Gutdänder
Michael May
Johannes Mensch
Paul Kober
Peter Müller
Jacob Metz
Johan Michel Stoffl
Henrich Allman
Abraham Jacob
Johann Jacob Engelhardt
Jnᵒ Geo. (+) Ord
Wolfarth Reinhard Edinger
Jnᵒ Geo. (×) Haffner
Jnᵒ Peter (×) Beckel
Conrad Minger
Johannes Jacob Quandel
Johannes Henrich Horn
Johannes Erlenheiser
Jnᵒ (×) Erlenheiser
Frederick (×) Kühlman
Jörg Leonhard Pfeiffer
Jacob Kleh
Hans Michael Welss

Jacob Schneyder
Johann Winkelgriet
Michel Becker
Peter Reidenbach
Jacob Breisch
Christian Jung
Jacob Bardon
Hans Michael Herwig
Conrat Dieffenbacher
Wilhelm Feickert
Nickel Kammerer
Peter Hardtmann
Walter Fromm [?]
Adam Rieth
Nickel Götz
Michael Mayer
Gottlieb Böckle
Georg Stattler
Johann Dieterich Heiss
Wendel (O) Heiss
Philipp Friedrich Müller
Wilhelm Spengler
Johann Petter Chrypfeius [?]
Johann Adam Weber
Johan Balthaser Häuser
Johannes Spengler
Johann Christoph Ulrich Kreuzer
Johann Nickel Reidenbach
Melchior Edinger

[List 248 C] At the State House at Philadelphia, Saturday, 27ᵗʰ October, 1764.

Present: Thomas Willing, Esquire.

The Foreigners whose names are underwritten, imported in the Ship Hero, Ralph Forster, from Rotterdam, but last from Cowes, did this day take and subscribe the usual Qualifications. 500 whole Freights. 200 in the List (Messʳˢ Willing & Morris.) 21ˢᵗ Nov. pᵈ· £15.

Johannes (✕) Hufer
Johann Georg Weymer
Jacob (✕) Karg
Johannes (W) Wise
Johannes (+) Welsh
Johann Andreas Schad
John (✕) Berg
Andrew (✕) Wolff
Jacob (✕) Hass
Johann Christian Gernet
Petter Müller
Jerg Fiol
Lenhard Büchler
Wilhelm Henrich Biegel
Johan Loretz Beck
Johann Adam Rudolph
Jost Meyer
Görg Adam Weickel
Jerg Etter
John Reinhard (+) Cauffman
Jacob Lässle
Henrich Schwerdt
Jacob Sauerheber
Mattes Petter
Jacob (✕) Hauck
Johannes (IH) Hauck
Petter Schauer
John (S) Schuman
Rudolph (O) Schuman
Peter Scheide
Christopher (✕) Radebach
Martin Seewald
Johannes Fuhrmann
Johann Ludwig Sewalt
Gustavus (✕) Schlosser
Martin Heylemann
Petter Wedel
Johann Jörg Wetzel
Johann Adam Bausch
Gottfried Eppling

Friederich Eppling
Johanes Wage
Johannes Will
Johann Ernst Dreniel [?]
Johann Adam Seyberth
Hans Geo. (✕) Goetz
Daniel Strickler
Mich¹ (✕) Schub
Lazarus Herby
Johan Michel Walter
Jacob (+) Hönick
Johannes Ludwig
Johan Pilip Rummerth [?]
Johannes (✕) Gress
Jacob Schibb
Conrath Dörr
Abraham Petter
Johann Dürr
Jacob Düffordt
Lorrentz Dürr
Dieterick (✕) Jäger
Johann Michael Klein
Hans Nickel Bierr
Phillipp Ecker
Michael (✕) Philipi
Adam Pilepi
Johannes Trehr
Adam Fögle
Joh. Hoffmann
Johannes (O) Feltman
Johannes Ring
Johann Georg Weydenmeyer
Urban Weidenmeier
Eberhardt Weydenmyer
Nicholas (✕) Anthony
Adam (　) Nass
Ullrich Eymann
Peter Nicklas
Johannes Gernet
Lutwick Freiburger

Adam Meyer
Johann Jacob Gross
Conrad Bingmann
Valentin Simon Korn [?]
Jerg Altschuh
Paulus Pauli
Henrich Fucks
Johannes Fritsch
Johann Georg Adam
Michael (×) Reff
Görg Wentz
David (+) Konig
Conrad König
Johann Nickelaus Knab
Johann Adam Bruckhausen
Johan Henrich Lutz
Friederich Haffner
Abraham (×) Schantz
Georg Wilhelm
Egidius Jung
Henrich Kohl
Conrad (+) Haffentrager
Hans Jaeblin [?]
Jacob Kauffmann
Nicholas (K) Ott
Johannes Sellheim
Johann Henrich Heyl
Johann Georg Heyl
Johann Conrad Heyl
Johann Jacob Heyl
Johan Petter Hoffstatt
Johann Jacob Leiman
Josebh Hertel
Johan Henrich Bausch
Geo. (×) Heyman
Johann Velten Becker
Martin Schupp
Antreas Keck
Simon (+) Fisher
Bernard (+) Steiner
Lorenz Andony

Christian Schowalder
Jost Dettweiller
Johann Michael Bridebach
Jacob Richardt
Joseph Renan
Henry (×) Baum
Johannes Wittig
Gorg Philb Pettry
Carl Ludwig Baum
Johann Egeman
Melchior Weydemeyer
Friedrich Roth
Johann Danniel Franck
Michel Nieth
John Geo. (+) Reser
Gottlieb Nith
Georg Sachs
Geörg Deg
Albrecht Schuhmacher
Benedictus Gälle
Johann Philipp Göttmann
Johann Gottfried Weiss
Michael Walter
Johann Ludwig Weber
Samuel Schober
Andreas Michel
Johannes Michel Hirschlag
Johannes Kugellwerth
Johan Martin Klein
Mich^l (×) Schaffer
Martin (×) Heit
Nicolaus Breidbach
Daniel Brenneman
Christian Brubacher
Johannes Riesser
Johannes Kunkelmann
Jacob Seitz
Daniel Joder
[. . . .] Breuninger
Rudolph Kägy
Peter Krebil

Christian Stauffer
Henrich Schneider
Valentin Volck
Jnº Henry (+) Lannert
Adam German
Peter (×) Harris
Nickolaus Überroth
Johann Jacob Nagel
Gorg Bortz
John Adam (+) Beach
Friedrich Lofinck
Hans Geo. (+) Baumonk
Herrman Wittscher
Nickel Gerisch
Adam (×) Ruth
Georg Petter Zentler
Peter (×) Ambrose
Peter (+) Ziefus

Johann Michael Nagel
Johann Andreas Unangst
Michel Rossmoyer
Peter Jung
Christopher (×) Hess
Simon Klas
Jacob Klamm
Abraham Petter
Gerg Michal Klamm
Jorg Simon Rieger
Johann Davidt Schaadt
Friederich Wurtzbacher
Johann Glaser
Johann Henrich Schöneberger
Johann Mardin Mäder
Michel Büttner
Nickl Ba . . .
Conr. Hüldenbrand

[List 249 C] At the Court House Philadelphia, 5ᵗʰ November, 1764.

Present: Isaac Jones, Esquire.

The Foreigners whose names are underwritten, imported in the Jeneffer, Captain George Kerr, from Rotterdam, but last from Cowes, did this day take and subscribe the usual Qualifications. 247 Whole Freights. 102 contained in the List. (Consigned to Mʳ Robert Ruecastle.) 1764, Novʳ 29, pᵈ. £7.13.

Johann Ludwig Degen
Johann Philips Enders
John (×) Fuhrman
Hans Jergen
John George (×) Leininger
Jost Reuter
Johan Gottfrit Meyer
Frantz Krämer
Frantz Rübsamen
John (×) Jager
Johann Martin Neb
Johan Tönges Crämm

Antonias Cromm
Henrich Krom
Simon Görg
Johann Christ Lindorff
Johann Best Weber
Görg Schön
Johann Gerlach Traut
Johann Gerlach Finck
Johan Peder Weber
Johann Wilhelm Strunck
Johann Jacob Jung
Johannes Gerlach Strunck

Johannes Henrich Au
Peter Hürstman
Johannes Peter Petery
Johann Gürg Reyman
Andreas (X) Brown
Johanes Ochsa
John George (+) Maur
John Con^d (+) Stiebel
Johann Jacob Schaefer
Jn° Geo. (X) Upper
Jn° Dieterich (X) Schmidt
Jn° Diet. (X) Fehring
John Christ (X) Fuhrsbach
Jost Henrich Frantz
Johann Wilhelm Frantz
Johann Jacob Frantz
Thomas Weller
Johannes Rübelandt
Fred. (+) Decker
Jn° Chas (+) Hetrig
Johann Christ Heuser
Johannes Görg Reusch
Martin (X) Keller
Johann Andreas Wentzell
Johann Davidt Mahn
Johann Frantz Busch
Christian Roth
Johannes Volck
Anthon Stock
Gottfried Stock
Philip (+) Stock
Conrad (+) Braun
Christian Zimmer
Jacob Landes

Johannes Landes
Ulrick (+) Bieber
John Adam (+) Steinweis
Jn° (XX) Miller
Johann Henrich Gihl
Heinrich Stöckel
Vallentin Schuster
Nicklaus Meissel
Jacob (+) Meissel
Hans Georg Suter
Philipp Schmidt
Hans Gorg Schmit
Johann Michael Braun
Henrich Wilhelm Gruck
Jn° Ad^m (X) Miller
Jn° (X) Schwab
Johann Henrich Felenkeuser
Johann Adam Bingel
Christ Jan Hautzel
Johann Jacob Bate
B. (O) Diefenbach
Peter Schick
Abram (O) Kapler
Johannes Gerhard Klein
Jacob (O) Werns
Johann Wilhelm Reyman
Stephan Petri
Wilhelm Petri
Jacob Brenneman
Petter Krebihl
Joh. Peter Hachenberg
John Engel (X) Stoehr
Johnnes Wilhelm Klein

[List 250 C] At the Court House, Philad^a 5th Novem^r 1764.
Present: Isaac Jones, Esquire.
The Foreigners whose names are underwritten, imported in
the Ship Prince of Wales, James Edgar, Mast^r, from Rotter-

dam, but last from Cowes, did this day take and subscribe the usual Qualifications. 79 Qualified. 131 Whole Freights. Consigned to Mr Jas Searle. (pd. 29th Novr £5.18.6).

Peter Römer
Johanes Muth
Philip (×) Becher
Christopfel Schmit
Casber Fries
Ludwig Mader
Johannes Schoritzer
Johannes Starck
Adem Zenberge [?]
Peter Julien
Philip (×) Golb
Johann Philipp Bittman
Carl Uhl
Jacob Schanckweiler
Conrath Korfmann
Nicolaus Boos
Georg Wilhelm Keseler
Hennrich Happel
Jacob Dorscheimer
Johannes Manderfelth
Peter Dörr
Johannes Eckel
Peter (×) Rasbach
Willhelm Kircher
Petter Herrberrger
Paul Biehler
Gorg Peter Kessler
Wilhelm Kuntz
Johannes Kuntz
Jörg Jäger
Henrich Jäger
Charles (×) Norheimer
Wilhelm Henrich Rupp
Johann Nicklas Schneider
Johann Valtin Schneider

Adam Kaiser
Phillip Mittmann
Johannes Schnell
Martin Seybert
Carrelle Stoltz
Johann Conrad Stoltz
Johann Jacob Mattheis
Johann Christoffel Rauch
Johannes Orth
Peter Laubenstein
Johann Peter Laubenstein
Johann Philipp Thuy
Gottlieb Becker
Philipp Barth
Jacob Espenschied
Georg Schäffer
Peter Wann
Adam (×) Gless
Henrich Reihm
Peter Umstatt
Peter Cärius
Jacob Petri
Georg Schmit
Georg Adam Dückel
Sebastian (+) Kehl
Tohmas Polhans
Petter Hesler
George (×) Forster
Christopher (×) Heidrich
Henrich Berninger
Carl Starck
John (J) Schneider
Johan Burckhardt Culman
Johannes Weissgerber

[List 251 C] At the State House at Philad[a], the 10th Nov[r] 1764.

Present: John Lawrence, Esq[r].

The foreigners whose names are underwritten, imported in the Ship Boston, from Rotterdam, but last from Cowes, Mathew Carr, Master, did this day take & subscribe the usual Qualifications. 203 Whole Freights. 69 in the List. Consign'd to M[r] Rundel. p[d] 29. Nov. £5.3.6.

Johann Andreas Fuchs
Henry (O) Spor
Johannes Schwarm
Henrich Bachman
Anthony Boley
Johann Casper Keipper
Johannes Wentz
Johan Peder Schohl
Johannes Walther
Johann Georg Muth
Phillib Glass
Johannes Kessler
Johann Vallenthin Dickes
Peter (X) Wentz
Hans Gorg Büttner
Johann Carl Boley
Görig Dannefeltzer
Hans Adam Hartmann
Peter Reidenar
Jerg Reidenauer
Nickelaus Reitenauer
Johannes Pflaum
Dibolt Lertz
Andröas Köppel
Lorentz Jung
Andres Schneider
Simon Peter Baidemann
Ludwig (X) Scheffer
Michel Geörg
Christian Jacob
Johan Teobald Klein

Johan (X) Schepfling
Diebolt Beitz
Lewis (X) Shimfassel
Jacque Dépré
Issac Bertschi
Johann Philipps Weytzel
Henrich Herwagen
Adam (X) Lampart
John (+) Lampart
Jacob (X) Buss
Frantz Lambert
Christ[t] (CM) Muhlseisen
Henry (+) Bauer
Peter Westerman
Johan Nichol Weck
Mich[l] (O) Weck
Petter Halm
Jacob Conrath
Andreas Bausmann
Rubertus Waller
Bernhart Döss
Philipps Jacob Bausman
Justus Eckhard
Henry (X) Scheffer
Henrich Fuchs
Caspar Bernhard
Wilhelm Bernhardt
Peter Geiss
Johann Dieter Blodel
Conradh Friederich Bientelheimer
Peter Fuchs

Henrich (+) Fuchs	Johannes Sponknöbel
Johann Geörg Stättler	Peter Steffan
Nickellas Hittel	Philip (+) Gerber

[List 252 C] At the State House at Philad^a, the 4th Decem^r 1764.

Present: William Coxe, Esquire.

The foreigners whose names are underwritten, imported in the Snow Tryall, John Clapp, Mas^r. from Amsterdam, but last from Tingmouth, did this day take and subscribe the usual Qualifications. 23 in the List. 47½ Whole Freights. Consign'd to Mr. Ja^s Searls. rec^d 34/6—12 Febr. 1765.

Johann Daniel Gros *	Johannes Roscher
Jacob (K) Kessel	Filibus Stein
Georg Bender	Johannes Jung
Andreas Emrich	Bastian Bender
Johannes Graus	Nickellas Alberthal
Henrich Lautzenheiser	Anthony Opp
Peter Lautzenhäuser	Johann Jacob Enck
Jacob Lautzenhäuser	Johannes Gaull
Johannes Bender	Jasper (×) Schönbruck
Henrich Stroher	Valenthin Braun
Abraham Schäffer	Carel Johst
Christopher (×) Mathias	

[List 253 C] At the State House at Philadelphia, the 24th Aug^t, 1765.

Present: William Coxe, Esquire.

The Foreigners whose names are underwritten, imported in the Ship Polly, Robert Porter, Master, from Rotterdam, but last from Cowes, did this day take and subscribe the usual Qualifications. 85 in the List. 169 Whole Freights. 45 half Freights. (Consign'd to Mr. Robt Ruecastle.) p^d. 26, Sepr 1765.

* A German Reformed Minister. See Good, *History of the Reformed Church in the U. S. 1725-1792*, p. 563.

Johann Adam Fried. Ottwalt

Jacob Nägele

Andreas Heintz

Jacob (✕) Huntzicker

Jacob Gay

Joseph Stecher

Christoph Ehret

Jacob Gemberling

Jacob Gemberling

Christian (W) Wunder

Conrad (✕) Hauenstein

Geo. Jacob (+) Hauenstein

Elias Werner

Christoph Strigel

Johann Leon^d (++) Devil

Andres Ehresmann

Andreas Buchhecker

John Mich^l (✕) Gronninger

Johann Bernhard Dietrich

Peter Sigfrit

Conrad Münch

Gottfried Münch

Jacob (M) Meyer

Peter Zeiler

Lawrence (+) Gronninger

Georg Aadam Bresler

Johan Michael Dühmer

Michael (✕) Widerick

Valentin Kauffman

Jacob Wunder

Elias Wigandt

Jacob (O) Faut

Georg Simon Haushalter

Geo. Adam (✕) Teis

Peter Gram

Jacob Treuttle

Jacob (+) Schultz

Johann Martin Obermüller

Jacob (+) Behr

Samuel (✕) Behr

Christoph Dietterich

Friederich Wilhelm Meyer

Jacob Thorwarth

Heinrich Bothgiss

Jacob Hetzel

Christian Häffner

Jacob Schneck

Johann Phillipp Harttung

Jacob Blanck

Wendel Emmert

Paulus Sturm

Johannes Rothacker

Geo. (✕) Stadler

Christoph Ginähle

Hans Georg Schneck

Hans Georg Schneck

Heinrich Hopf

Fridrich Hippel

Jorg Urffer

Christian Maurer

Christoph Hanmüller

Johann Jacob Hanmüller

Johann Berndt Mannbekh

Rudolph Mannbeckh

Johannes Voltz

Johann Jacob Hofelen

Johann Georg Hoff

Johann Jacob Schreffel

Johannes Müller

Johannes Schmidt

Johann Nickel Fischer

Johann Wilhelm Bender

Frantz Arnold Lyhn

Magel (✕) Hoff

Jo. Mich. (+) Bishop

Martin (✕) Claubough

Johannes May

Jacob Müller

Johann Jacob Mohr

Anthony (A) Rein

Johan Georg Kachler   Peter (+) Rudolph
Mich¹ (+) Mensebach   Peter (×) Gress

[List 254 C] At the State House at Philadelphia, the 9 September, 1765.

Present: John Lawrence, Esqʳ.

The Foreigners whose Names are underwritten, imported in the Ship Chance, Charles Smith, Master, from Rotterdam, but last from Cowes, did this day take and subscribe the usual Qualifications. 96 in the List. 216 Whole Freights. Consigned to Mʳ Rᵗ Ruecastle; pᵈ. 26 Sepʳ.

Peter (×) Kebler	Jacob Guth *
Geo. (×) Krebs	Johann Gottfried Gampffer
Matthes Lora	Valentine (×) Metzger
Chaˢ (×) Grim	John (×) Klein
Jacob Müller	Jacob (×) Kendel
Jacob Krieger	Georg Wilhelm Müller
Johannes Schüslerr	Jacob (×) Kehl
Casber Roth	Joes Orendorff
Henrich Lambert	Christ Köhl
Peter Schmidt	Johan Philib Melter
Balthas Breitenbücher	Eberhard (×) Lüttig
Johann Georg Bauer	Michael Heyl
Tobias Hafferstock	Martin (×) Weber
Jnᵒ Philip (+) Hafferstock	Michael Kettenring
Jacob Deinius	Johann Jacob Kettenring
Jacob (+) George	John Jorg Paulus Christman
Christopher (×) Kessler	Israel Bockreiker
Michael Müller	Frederick (+) Keller
Wiegand Fecher	Johann Wilhelm Neytzer
Danˡ (MD) Meyer	Peter (+) Beiritsch
Jonᵒ (O) Danehauer	Nicklaus Ludi
Jacob (×) Krafft	Philipp Henrich Mayer
Heinrich Kägel	Johann Christophel Kurtz
Johan Georg Phillip Lessig	John (×) Dinius
Johann Christian Lässig	Johannes Wilhelm Schäffer

* A Reformed schoolmaster, the great-grandfather of the Rev. James I. Good, D.D.

Johann Conrad Escher
Johann Wendel Kübeller
John Henry (++) Reichard
Jonas Dill
Maths (+) Hartmeyer
Johann Adam Graim
Christoff Ketering
Wendel Schanck
Andreas Franck
Joh Ernst Kaps, Apoticaire
Johannes Fries
Rudolph (X) Brengel
Johann Friderich Beyrer
Johan Burck Krebs

Jacob (X) Kebel
Johannrich Gernerdt
Johann Michael Seitzer
John (+) Russ
Valentine (+) Roeback
Abraham Breitenbächer
Johann Pfillip Müller
Joh. Daniel Müller
Johannes Giedelmann
Isaac Frantz
Johan Michael Höger
Jnº Gerg (+) Ferer
Michael Ritter
Christian Brützius

[List 255 C] At the State House at Philadª, the 19th September, 1765.

Before Samuel Mifflin, Esquire.

The Foreigners whose Names are underwritten imported in the Ship Betsey, John Osman, Commander, from Rotterdam, but last from Cowes, did this Day take and subscribe the usual Qualifications. 75 in the List. (Consign'd to Samˡ Howell). pᵈ, 31 Octʳ. 1765.

Ludwich Bener
Heinrich Herrmann
Johann Mattheus Dollmann
Jacob Printz
Daniel Cobbel
Michel Löwenstein
Henrich Pfeiffer
Jacob Idler
Hans Michael Brattler
Johann Jacob Brattler
Isaac (X) Cartman
Abram (A) Schming
Philip Godfried (X) Mathias
Benjamin Gassman
Martin (+) Becker
Godfrey (K) Grumbach
Jacob Zehner

Johann Carl Gabriel
Wilhelm Schäfer
Hans George (+) Ochs
Jacob Friederich Schäffer
Gottlob Jacob Löffler
Johann Jacob Thiel
Johann Georg Pletz
Petter Schneider
Willhelm Freund
Johan Görg Schneider
Johan Ebert Oerter
Johann Jost Linck
Johannes Henrich Ohrndorff
Johann Adam Schneyder
Johann Christjan Betz
Daniel Zwigart
Johan Adam Arnsterger

George (✕) Shiff
Peter Garthner
Michael Zehner
Stephan Höpffer
John (+) Heins
Martin Gegner
Philip Jacob (+) Stockel
Jacob Gauss
Benedich (+) Smith
Laurence (✕) Rinkle
Hans Geörg Printz
Hans (✕) Merckle
Johannes Wolff
Abraham Glading
Johann Phillipus Müller
Jacob (O) Clow
David Straus
Jacob Hiller
Johannes Riem
Martin (+) Ostertag
Jörg Deschner

Johannes Peter Zepperfeld
Johann Jacob Bircki
Friedrich Heckel
Christjan Wehr
Andreas Häckel
Johan Ruben Weller
Jacob Licht
Johann Nickel Licht
Johann Jacob Licht
Johan Conrath Lang
Johann Henrich Clement
Johann Philip Schneider
Josua Metzger
Davit Gottschall
Conrad Schuller
Johannes Braun
Philipp Peter Laplace
John Frederic Ernst
Jacob Rockenbäuch
Johann Henrich

[List 256 C] At the Court House at Philadelphia, Saturday, the 21st day of September, 1765.
Present: Jacob Duché, Esquire.

The Foreigners whose Names are underwritten, imported in the Ship Myrtilla, Capt James Caton, from London, did this day take and subscribe the usual Qualifications. In the List 40 persons. Whole Freights about 70. Number of Souls in all 81. (Consigned to Samuel Howell.) pd. 31 Oct. 1765.

Mertin Schmidt
Christian Haus
Jacob Rapp
Sammuel Funck
Martin Frey
Martin Behr
Philipp Behr
Anderas Heyderich
Jacob Ditrich

Stoffel Ditrich
Johannes Burgholder
Christian Burgholter
Jacob Burgholter
Heinrich Keller
Adam Eckel
Sebastian Nill
Lutwig Schehlman
Jacob Meyer

Jo. Christian
Josue Dedie ⎤
Jean Dedie   ⎥ French
Jean Pier Dedie ⎥ Swiss
Abraham de Roche ⎟ Prot-
Jean Jaque Etienne ⎥ estants
Jean Richard Rivisard ⎦
Johannes Müchel Meyer

Heinerich Frey
Ludwig Ischler
Jacob Räumann
Johannes Krebiell
Ulrich Wissler
Jacob Wissler
Henrich Küny

[List 257 C] At the Court House at Philadelphia, Monday, 7th Octr 1765.

Present: Thomas Lawrence, Esquire.

The foreigners whose names are underwritten, imported in the Ship Countess of Sussex, Captn Thomas Gray, from Rotterdam, did this day take and subscribe the usual Qualifications. In the List 24. Whole Freights 41. Number of Souls 50. 28 Octr 1765, pd by Capt Gray.

William (X) Hagher
Jno Christopher (X) Schonfelder
David Wohl
Rudolf Küpfer
Frantz Carl Beaujacque
Johan Leonhardt Hirsch
Henry (+) Sevon
Joh. Theodor Hofius *
Johann Jacob Scheppach
Jorg Michael Hertle
Johann Thomas Metzler
Melchior (O) Metzler

Jacob Standemeyer
Christian Schneider
Johan Gotlip Ponce
Johannes Gotlip Ponce
Conrad Brombach
Johannes Brombach
Johan Henrich Bender
Johann Henrich Heyde
Johan Henrich Moll
Antres Hubertz
Johan Christoph Schultz

[List 258 C] At the Court House, Philadelphia, Tuesday, the 23d day of September, 1766.

Present: Samuel Mifflin, Esquire.

The Foreigners whose Names are underwritten, imported in the Ship Chance, Charles Smith, Master, from Rotterdam but last from Cowes, did this day take and subscribe the usual Qualifications. 200 Freights in the whole Number of Souls.

---

* Hofius settled in Schaefferstown, Lebanon County, and was there the first schoolmaster of the Reformed church school of the Schaefferstown Reformed Church. See A. S. Brendle, *Brief History of Schaefferstown*, York, 1901, p. 15.

112 In the List. (Consigned to Messrs Willing & Morris.)
p^d October, 1766.

Johann Georg Freytag
Johannes Gröll
Johan Friederich Altvatter
Conradt Störckell
John (✗) Hoy
Peter Bloss
Johann Henrich Ullrich
Johanns Müller
Johannes Lipp
Wilhelm Seelheimer
Johannes Conradi
Johann Georg Ermold
Conrath Eurich
Johann Görg Eurich
Johann Petter Mehrling
Jacob Weitzel
Jno Henry (✗) Kerg
Johann Peter Faust
Johann Franciscus Faust
Johannes Meister
Nicholas (+) Arnold
Henrich Gross
Johannes Vogt
Johann Christian Kunckel
Johann Jacob Vögler
Migel Grünewald
Phillipp Blitz
Johann Peter Hör
Johann Friederich Helm
Johann Adam Ohl
Johannes Emrich
Martin Lantz
Johannes Graul
Johann Georg May
Johannes Leis
Friderick Lüderitz
Johann Georg Seib
Johann Adam (✗) Flick

John (O) Hasler
Johan Bortlehr
Johann Benedick Schneider
Johan Lutwig Waltmaier
Johann Nicolaus Seitz
Johann Wilhelm Klöpper
Johann Valenthin Klepper
Johann Gabriel Kröber
Gabriel Becker
Johann Michael Weingärtner
Henerich Frey
Johanes Mates
Johann Henrich Dentzel
Johan Dietrich Köster
Zacharias Endres
Heinrich Bossel
Paul Conrad
Andreas Weiss
Fridrich Locher
Hennrich Locher
Henrich Dewalt
Hannes Waldtmann
Johann Daniel Frischmuth
Johann Nickel Martin
Gorg Gramlich
Henrich Jüngst
Johannes Miesemer
Johann Jacob Reinhardt
Johan Peter Löw
Sebastian (✗) Heckman
Johan Friederich Müller
Johan Jacob Matzenbacher
Andon Schäffer
Hans Jerg Schnepp
Georg Conrad Seip
Johann Wilhelm Seip
Johann Georg Weber
John Adam (+) Sand

Heinrich Ehrhart
Johann Christoph Simon
Peter Burging
Johan Peter Trump
Georg Trump
Johann Hirschlag
Johannes Kehl
Johann Georg Zimmerman
Simon Peter Deobad
Peter Weber
Christopher (+) Unger
Simmon Bichler
Phillipp Colman Rämlander
Joseph Schmidt
Johannes Reb

Christof Luger
Johannes Luger
Johann Michael Kuch
Johannes Weber
Johann Christoph Kämpf
Johann Michael Lauer
Johann Georg Olt
Johann Nicolaus Viebel
Anton Meidorf
Johannes Schnabel
Johannes Georg Allspach
Joh. Henrich Leuthäuser
Francis (×) Beler
Simon Guckert

[List 259 C] At the Court House, Philadelphia, October 13ᵗʰ 1766.

Present: Jnᵒ Lawrence, Esqʳ, Mayor,
George Bryan, Esquire.

The Foreigners whose names are underwritten, imported in the Ship Betsy, John Osmond, Master, from Rotterdam, but last from Cowes, did this day take and subscribe the usual Qualifications. In the List 95. Whole Freights 154. (Consigned to Samˡ Howell) pᵈ January 1767.

Daniel Zimmerman
Johannes Brenckert
Nicolaus Böhler
Johannes Schmid
Johan Helman Karle
John Jacob (+) Karl
Johann Gorg Benfer
Mannes Gelessener
Jacob (×) Kenckel
Michel Raht
Dangel Benner
Jost Henry (×) Volmer
Gerg Schiltwächter
Johann Gerge Volmer
Johan Rotger Miller

Johann Jost Miller
Johan Daniel Afflerbach
Johann Gorg Fischer
Joseph Stauch
Johannes Benner
Jacob Schäffer
Jacob Kaufman
Johann Melcher Endlich
Johann Heinrich Bär
Johan Henrich Schraag
Joseph Singer
Gottlieb Geyher
Fredrick (×) Hoffman
Joh. Philipp Lambach
J. G. E. Hirschmann

Johannes Meyer
Friderich Schittenhelm
Jacob (+) Shittenhelm
Johans Lahm [?]
Georg Michael Schährer
Johann Jacob Hausmann
Jonas Baromo
Johann Bernhard Borst
Lawrence (×) Boris
Egieties Lochner
Jost Kern
Jacob Günther
Johann Heinrich Fessler
Johann Jacob Fessler
Georg Friederich Immich
Friedrich Frantz Feck
Johann Philipp Götz
Louis Robert
Johan Georg Lichtenberger
Hans Marti Ziegler
Johann Gorg Snell [?]
Johann Höckert
Johan Nickel Keyser
Jacob (×) Hähn
Jacob (×) Wagner
Johannes (O) Link
Johann Michael Schäffer

Valentin Schürling
Petter Lutter
Andreas Lutter
Michel Weiss
Johannes Gottfried Hage
Peter (+) Reyt
Johann Filbert Glach [?]
Christoph Willemann
Jacob Greuther
Christian (×) Wolff
Johannes Hayser
Johannes Moser
Valentin Hamm
Johannes Wüst
Lenhardt Eckert
Christian Frey
Johann Bernhardt Körth
John (+) Keller
Philip (×) Buchman
Peter (×) Guité
Lorens Ladenberger
Joseph Salter
Jerg Bub
Joost (×) Kuntz
Christopher (+) Becher
David Waltman
Joh. Georg Schneyder

[List 260 C] At the dwelling House of John Lawrence, Esqr, Mayor, Philad^a October, the 15th 1766.

Present the s^d John Lawrence, Esqr, Mayor.

The Foreigners whose names are under written, imported in the Ship Cullodian, Richd Hunter, Master, from Lisbon, did this Day take and subscribe the usual Qualifications. (Consigned to Cunigham & Nesbit.) 12 p^d Octr 1766.

Pedro Oberländer
Ignacio Onder
Francis (+) Frey
Peter (+) Schotter

Paul (×) Abzieger
Carl Geissinger
Erhard Schlagel
Niclaus Schnoller

John (+) Meyer   Francis (×) Fisher
Johann Reck   Peter (+) Polo

[List 261 C] At the Court House at Philadelphia, on Saturday, the 18th day of October, 1766.
Present: Thomes Willing, Esquire.
The Foreigners whose Names are underwritten, imported in the Ship Polly, Robert Porter, Master, from Rotterdam, but last from Cowes, did this day take & subscribe the usual Qualifications. In the List 55. Whole Freights 112. Half D° 33. Children 36. 181 Souls. (Consigned to Messrs Willing & Morris). pd Octr 1766.

Michel Schättel
Christian Reiss
Görg Schättel
Johann Nickel Lauer [?]
Nickel Stoltzfus
Christian Staltzfus
Hans Geörg Horn
Jacob (H) Holler
Frantz Herman
John George (×) Herman
Jacob (×) Helfer
Philipps Heinrich Fuchs
Hans Görg Cuntz
John (B) Proednier
Johann Fillib Jacob
Jacob Diemer
Johan Jacob Lentz
Hans Adam Duhmann
Johannes Reuther
Johann Jacob Schreiner
Johann Henrich Müller
Johannes Peter Stockmann
Ernst Wilhelm Christ
Johannes Geitling
Johann Adam Widerstein
John Henry (×) Issenburger
Johann Philipps Gielberth

John Conrad (×) Sheippen
Johan Tünges Lupp
Johann Eberth Michael
Gorg Friedig Steiner
John (×) Edelman
Johann Jörg Schryber
Johan Philib Weltzheimmer
Hans Görg Petry
Johannes Schiren
Johan Philipus Schreiner
Johannes Bloch
Philipp Walter
Georg Valt Steiner
Johann Henrich Herdel
John Conrad (+) Crick
Peter Müller
Jno Wm (O) Herman
Hans Jacob Motz
Andres Stetzel
Johann Jacob Heinninger
Hanes Schrag
Abraham Danner
Johann Caspar Trump
Valentine (O) Wild
Michael Friederich Gutekunst
Ernst Schmidt

[List 262 C] At the Hoñble the Mayor's house, in Philadelphia, Novr 4th 1766.

Present: John Lawrence, Esquire, Mayor.

The Foreigners whose names are underwritten, imported in the Ship Sally, . . . [?] John Davidson, Master, from Rotterdam, but last from Portsmouth, did this day take and subscribe the usual Qualifications. Consigned to Jn° Ross, Merch^t. p^d.

Georg Jacob Elsass	Georg Friedrich Gröbs
Paul Amecker	Johann Georg Sturmfels
Christoph Heinerich Augustinus	Jacob Brandenburger
Johannes Lemp	

[List 263 C] At the Office of Thomas Willing, Esqr, Philadelphia, 13 January 1767.

Present: Thomas Willing, Esqr.

The Foreigners whose names are underwritten, imported in the Ship Juno, John Robertson, Master, from Rotterdam, but last from Berwick on Tweed, did this day take and subscribe the usual Qualifications. In the List 11. Souls on board 36. Consigned to Messrs Willing & Morris. 16/6 p^d. 11. March 1767. J. K.

Johann Michael Götz *	Johannes Clemens Gulich [?]
Johan Georg Seuberth	Johann Peter Böll
Johan Georg Huber	Johannes Mass
John Henry (×) Hirsh	Georg Michael Rittelmeyer
Johann Heinrich Kühn	Johan Henrich Sebo
Johann Henrich Holdinghausen	

[List 264 C] At the Court House, Philadelphia, Octo^r 5th, 1767.

Present: Saml Mifflin, Esquire.

The Foreigners whose names are underwritten, imported in the Ship Sally, John Osman, Master, from Rotterdam but last from Cowes, did this day take and subscribe the usual Qualifications. In the List 116. Consigned to Saml Howell. p^d 23 Octr 1767, to J. K. £8.14.—

* Introduced by the phrase "bekenne ich," i. e., "I confess," namely, the oath or affirmation that was required.

Adam (X) Knoblauch
Henrich Kleiber
Georg Kleiber
Georg Henrich Focht
Jurg (+) Leidich
Jacob Dukany
Frieterich Ramppendahl
Martin Bornträger
Johannes Sommer
Peter (W) Wilrich
Jacob (X) Weber
Johann Theodor Hartmann
Hans Jurg (+) Matthies
Stephan Tuchman
Christoph Didrich Dottweiler
Hans Atam Baur
Johan Jorg Würtzer
Philibus Krimmel
Joan Emmerich Adam
Leonhard Eglin
Michel Gutchrel
Johannes Andreas Seuling
Petter Anchementer [?]
Wendel Bernhartt
Georg Bernhardt
Adolph Dill
Theobald Fisher
Adam Dörr
Gorg Henrich Reitz
Johann Philipp Reitz
Johann Philipp Huff
Wilhelm Doudnet
Johann Petrygandt
Chr^r (CM) Müller
Andreas Sperling
Johan Cunrad (++) Bertsh
Johan Nicolaus Weygandt
Jureg Kilian Werth
Johan Henrich Kraft
Leonhardt Beyer
Joh. Nicolaus Ludwig

Johann Michel Bast
Johann Hironimus Augustin
Hanns Jerg Graberth
Johannes Kemperling
Johann Adam Lechler
Gabriel Leon
Johannes Muller
Johann Phillipp Lutz
Joh. Jacob Heiser
Johann Simon Höh
Frantz (O) Höh
Simon Höh
Jacob (+) Eckenberger
Jacob (X) Berndt
Johann Bernhardt Hoffman
Jacob (+) Berndt, Junr
Henrich (X) Weber
Hans (HSB) Schonenberger
Nickel Huber
Caspar (A) Acker
Adam Huber
Philip (+) Frölich
Johann Jeorg Miller
Danniell Lauth
Jacob Lauth
Michel Miller
Adam Müller
Valenthin Höh
Phillipp Huber
Johann Adam Reb
Jerg Adam Keffer
Johan Henrich Fücks
Jacob Linn
Jacob (+) Küffer
Hans Adam (X) Palm
Wilhelm Reuter
Jacob (JK) Kirt
Peter (X) Diel
Kunrad Heuer
Peter (+) Miller
Frantz Willhelm

Adam (+) Reyter

Leonard (O) Albrecht

Michel Klein

Philip (+) Dietz

Dewald (+) Ziegler

Hannes Zieler

Mich. Jürg

Gerg Hembelmann

Adam Schummary

Frederick Reinel

Johann Nickel Alberthal

Jacob (+) Reyter

Jacob Lamberdt

Peter (+) Schweitzer

Walter (H) Heyl

Jacob (+) Zebalt

Frederick (X) Kass

Hans Jurg (X) Buchman

Johann Fridrich Schlemb

Adam (+) Eckenberger

Johan Carl August Kiess

Henrich (X) Kiess

Johann Jacob Appel

Phillipp Rottmann

Jacob Görtler

Caspar Spies

Jacob (+) Reder

Jacob Rummel

Johann Wilhelm Boyneburg

Jacob Stellwagen

Johan Casber Schneider

Philipp Leonhart Hardtman

Baltaser Heinrich

Nicolaus Cabbell

[List 265 C] At Mʳ Willing's Office, October 6ᵗʰ 1767.
Present: Thomas Willing, Esquire.

The Foreigners whose names are underwritten, imported in the Ship Hamilton, Commanded by Charles Smith, from Rotterdam, did this day take and subscribe the usual Qualifications. Consigned to Messʳˢ Willing & Morris. In the List 152. Whole Freights 302. pᵈ 9ᵗʰ Novemʳ 1767.

Johann Nickelas Frick

Johan Henrich Baydemann

Johann Hennrich Grosshard

Johann Friederich Anspach

Christoffel Henritzy

Johann Phillips Loniger

Geo. Leonᵈ (X) Zoller

Johann Peter Krumm

Phil. (X) Smith

Peter Rothrock

Mathis Cuntz

Hans Michˡ (+) Dreer

Andreas Dreher

Friedrich Sattler

Nicklaus Schäffer

Michehl Wannebach

Michael Morlock

Johan Christian Kirschenmann

Jacob Hochstrasser

Georg Jacob Bauman

Christ (W) Wineman

Henry (+) Felton

Henrich Nickel Heydrich

Geo. Michˡ (+) Rhoade

Georg Michael Nuss

Johann Nickel Pick

Joha. Johan Joh

Johan Nickel Kulman

Heinrich Ketterer

Peter (K) Krassle

Peter Neuschwenter

Peter Neuschwender

Peter Diether

Christoph Seiler

Caspar Silvius

Heinrich Seyler

Conrad Böhmer

Friedrich Böhmer

Johann Gorg Butz

Johannes Weiss

Conrad Wagner

Jacob Eicher

Michael Haintz

Gorg Jacob Süss

Jacob (×) Nuss

Christ^l (+) Shitertz

Leonhart Knor

Wendel Heintz

Johannes Huber

Heinrich Walther

Conrath Rau

Diebolt Kelchoffner

Conrad Mahler

Jacob Veiock

Niclaus Mattern

Henrich Der [?]

Philip Baltzer

Philipp Christian Schrader

Johann Conrad Schlupp

Johann Gottlieb Blümler

Friderich Möllinger

Jn° Nich^s (+) Smith

Johann Peter Heess

Johann Melchior Reuschling

Johann Friederich Heintz

Michel Endres

Johan Lienhart Hoch

Conrad (×) Henrick

Fridrich Willhelm Rauhman

P. E. Leonie

Peter von Huben

Gerg Cuntz

Daniell Stollberger

Caspar Walter

Christian Steiner

Johann Jacob Benckler

Christoph Hartman

Jn° Phil. (×) Monick

Jacob Schneider

Jn° Adam (×) Beck

Johannes Hedinga

Johannes Schneider

Johans Burckert

Peetter Sekatz

Johan Jacob Frick

Adam Lotz

Christgan Winscher

Johann Gerg Biss

Henry (×) Vagner

Geo. (×) Hoock

Hartmann Schneider

Peter Michael Klein

Frantz Hopp

Lodwick (+) Hort

Martin (+) Kalchaufer

Joseph Blesch

Johann Conradt Reyss

Leonard Gramm

John (W) Vistermyer

Jorg Peter Kassel

Johan Zacharias Donselt

Henrich Medtart

Joseph Schloser

Frid. (+) Hart

John (×) Ewig

Friderich Stimmel

Philipp Jacob Cuntzmann

Danl (+) Barch

Friderich Conrath Hoff

Casimir Bernhard Alberti

Jorg Friederich Knobelloch

Adam Humbert

Heinrich Horn
Francis Wm. (+) Schwig
Sebastian Ettel
Frid. (+) Fogle
Lorrentz Schmidt
Michel Kieffer
Gottlieb Geist
Jacob (+) Bodel
Jacob (×) Albright
Mich¹ (+) Erhart
Joh. Lieb Hauck

Stephanus Fütter
Philipp Cullman
Jacob Schell
Hans Philipp Bodt
Peter (B) Pollinger
Querinus (+) Michael
Johann Peter Klatz
Matthis Grässel
Joseph Dubernock
Johan Schultz
Andreas (×) Neiman

[List 266 C] At the Court House at Philadelphia, the 26ᵗʰ of October, 1767.
Present: Isaac Jones, Esquire, Mayor.

The Foreigners, whose names are underwritten, imported in the Ship Brittania, Alexander Hardy, Master, from Rotterdam, but last from Portsmouth, did this day take and subscribe the usual Qualifications. 39 in the List. Consign'd to Samˡ Shoemaker, Esqʳ. pᵈ 23 Novʳ 1767.

Johannes Horn
Casper (×) Dieterich
Henrich Georgi
Michael (+) Köhler
Johanes Kleinfelter
Friederich Steygerwalt
Johann Petter Hoch
Johanns Georg
Henrich (×) Heiser
Johannes Bauer
Johannes Steigerwald
Johannes Staub
Johanes Kunckel
Henrich Kunkel
Friedrich Stegel
Adam Ditterich
Johannes Kistner
Friedrich Fliehmann
Michael Jacob Bach
Johann Phillip Falck

Johannes Keyser
Leonhart Krömer
Johannes Kunckel
Carl Rörig
Lorentz Schuster
Johan Michal Schlot
Migel Küntzler
Johannes Breitenbach
Velentin Breitebach
Jacob (+) Plat
Johann Henrich Lorey
Johannes Christian
Johannes Kohler
Johannes Bach
Peter Schuster
Johann Peter Uhl
Johannes Glück
Matteus Köhler
Johannes (×) Hem

[List 267 C] At the Office of Thomas Willing, Esqʳ, Octoʳ 29ᵗʰ 1767.

Present: Thomas Willing, Esquire.

The Foreigners whose names are underwritten, imported in the Ship Minerva, John Spurrier, Master, from Rotterdam & but last from Cowes, did this day take and subscribe the usual Qualifications. In the List 99. 182 Frᵗˢ. 194 Souls. Consign'd to Messʳˢ Willing & Morris. pᵈ 9 Novʳ 1767.

Johannes Nauman
Johannes Nauman
Jeremiah (✕) Neuman
Nicholas (✕) Blacher
Johann Tetmolder
Hans Jerg Mayer
Hs. Barnhardt Mayer
John (✕) Miller
Peter (+) Schumaker
Johannes Peter Schumacher
Johannes Simeon Schurz [?]
John (✕) Fisher
Mattheis Fischer
Johann Diterich Hachenberg
Johan Wil Enders
Johannes Jerg Opfer
Johannes Herr
Johan Jacob Zechiel
Jnᵒ (✕) Miller
Johann Valentin Batteiger
Geörg Adam Teutsch
Jacob Hellman
Christian Kauffman
Friedrich Höy
H. Hanebach
Jan Matthys Sleemann
Vallendien Faber
Christian Faber *
Valledien Faber
Jacob Faber

Jacob Gorsch
Peter Fuchs
Görg Wittenmeyer
Gorg Adam Winterbauer
Anthony Schoch
John (✕) Massholder
Johann Martin Motzer
Johann Martin Motzer
Gottfried Haager
Valentin Kamper
Jacob Weiss
Michal Buch
Jacob Drill
Henrich Laux
Johann David Bordili
Hans Jork Haage
Conrad Schneider
Johann Görg Schäffer
Nicolaus Albrecht
Deterick (+) Rydemeyer
Nicodemus Ungerer
Johann Wolfgang Bolschner
Eberhard Leitenberger
Bastian Dauberr
John Melchior (✕) Blancken-
  berg
Christian Balmstrom
Johann Georg Schade
George (+) Kessel
Johann Ernst Dauber

* In October, 1767, arrived the Reformed minister, John Christopher Faber. He was perhaps sick and for that reason does not appear among these signers.

Johan Adam Kaltbeker

Johann Iacop Neitzert

Johannes Mengen

Phillippus Jacob Gäntzler

John William (✕) Jasper

Jno. Wm. (O) Beam

Jnº Lud. (✕) Bausher

Johannes Breuer

Francis (+) Flamer

Johann Andreas Kirchner

Friederich Maximilian Hahn

Jacob Wackenhut

Johann Michael Holber

Michˡ (+) Kraus

Wᵐ (+) Zills

Joseph Kund

Johann Threibos [?]

Jeremiah (+) Algeir

Sip Hitzler

Johann Daniel Wilhelm

Müchael Seitz

Petter Muller

Valtin Stahl

[. . . .] Hertter

Johann Jacob Lang

Johann Adam Pfeiffer

Johannes Schmit

Johann Daniel Schmolze

Johann Lutwig Dieterich

Johannes Füsser

Jacob Kohlwein

[List 268 C] At the Worshipful, the Mayor's house, 4 Novʳ 1767.

Present: Isaac Jones, Esquire, Mayor.

The Foreigners whose are underwritten, imported in the Brigantine Grampus, from Rotterdam, Commanded by Henry Robinson, did this day take and subscribe the usual Qualifications. In the List 8, pᵈ. Consigned to Messʳˢ Shervel and Salter.

Adrian Granget

Johan Peter Glökler

Christian Schlumber

Michael Unseld

Johann Bernharth Welte

Nicolaus Müller

Peter (+) Dertwa

[List 269 C] At the Court House, Novemʳ 10, 1767.

Present: John Gibson, Esquire.

The Foreigners whose names are underwritten, imported in the Ship Sally, Patrick Brown, Master, from Rotterdam, but last from Cowes, did this day take and subscribe the usual Qualifications. 62 whole Freights. 36 in the List. Consign'd to Mʳ Jnº Ross, Merchᵗ. pᵈ 23 Novem. 1767.

Adam Hersperger

Johannes Egel

Daniel Ernst Sirach

Lawrence (+) Huber

Hans Tschopp
Jacob Ertzberger
Marten Möller
Johannes Hänner
Marty Stohler
Simon Stein
Christian (+) Aldhouse
Friederich Bäntz
Conrad (X) Hering
Johan Gänssli
Hans Michael (X) Bony
Simon Boni
Georg Friederich Wiedmayer
Johannes Burman
Adam Michael Bützel
Michael Länhart
Johan Rudolf Bapp

Martin Nicolaus Tschudy
Georg Carl Mändel
Georg Wachter, from Mem-
    mingen
Christoff Lochner
Valentin (XXX) Neissel
Henrich Dölle
Philipp Jacob Fuchs
Johannes Glotz
Johann Christian Roth
Johannes Tschudy
Jacob Bobell
Mardi Tschudi
Johannes Rudi
Martin Muller
Henry (+) Schaub

[List 270 C] At the Worshipful, the Mayor's Office, the 3ᵈ October, 1768.

Present: Isaac Jones, Esquire, Mayor.

The Foreigners whose names are underwritten, imported in the Ship Pennsylvᵃ Packet, Robert Gill, Master, from London, did this day take and subscribe the usual Qualifications & cᵃ. 33½ whole Freights. 28 in the List. pᵈ 12 Novʳ 1768, 42/. Consigned to Samˡ Howell.

Mart. Pontzius
Frantz Petter Brenner
Ludwig Brenner
Reichart Schell
Jacob Linder
David Figenel
Johannes Schumacher
Wilhelm Pynne
J. Frantz Helm
Jacob Koch

Nicklas Kulman
Jacob Kulman
Frantz Jacob Hoffman
David Pontzius
Jonas Appel
Johann Geörg Würts
Jacob Maus
Johann Georg Jung
Johan Peter Müller
        9 absent

[List 271 C] At the Court House, Philadelphia, Octoʳ 10, 1768.

Present ᵣ Samuel Shoemaker, Esqʳ.
Isaac, Jones Esqʳ, Mayor.

The Foreigners whose names are underwritten, imported in the Ship Minerva, Thomas Arnott, Master, from Rotterdam, but last from Portsmouth, did this day take and subscribe the usual Qualifications. 247 whole Freights. 108 in the List. p^d 12 Decr 1768. Consign'd to S. Shoemaker, Esqr.

Johannes Mohr
Johann Christian Holland
Johannes Kunkel
Friederich Stapf
Rudolff Dresch
Willhelm Schildknecht
Wendel Engel
Pfellib Höhl
John Jacob (IH) Hell
Jacob Hell
Wendel Decker
John (+) Strobanck
Hans Jacob Rippass
Heinerich Strauman
Johannes Busser
Nich^s (+) Latch
Ludwig Orth
Johannes Schroth
Daniel Weber
Cassmir Hembd
Frederick (X) Brand
Conrad Braun
Conradt Lückhaub
Michael Wolf
Valentin Sandel
Johann Petter Kranz [?]
Peter (+) Karp
Michael Ehrman
Johannes Söffner
Johann Wolfgang Seyboth
Johan Leonhard Wagner
Christian Wilhelm Frutz
Johan Andreas Wiest
Philipp Gruntzge

Johann Georg Michael Strecker
Johannes Stuckerdt
Johan Georg Eisenman
Johann Christoph Weil
Christian Phul
Henrich Müller
Georg Mühl
Johann Peter Graff
Johann Balthaser Graff
Jacob (J) Frauenfelder
Johann Christiann Steymann
Johann Balthaser Kroh
Johann Anton Stephan
Johann Leonhardt Horr [?]
Michel Villgentz
Johannes Schmidt
Johann Conrad Rau
Georg Adam Rau
Christian Koch
Paul (+) Weichenbacher
Jacob (+) Zimmelman
Michael (X) Scheussler
Johann Adam Meyer
Jacob Clautsch
Jeremiah Cline
Jeorg Henrich Seyberth
Thomas Seyberth
Jost (X) Goetz
Matheus Rockenbauch
Philip Peter Hautz *
Johannes Theis Müller
Phillipp Jacob Ohler
Johann Peter Merckel
Maximilian Neitzert

* The father of the Rev. Anthony Hautz, a Reformed minister.

Johann Mathias Müller
Jacob Neu
Christian Echternach
Johann Wilhelm Klemann
Frantz Samant
Georg Heinrich Haug
Erhard Giebelhaus
Mich¹ (O) Levy
Johann Jacob Walther
Johann Jacob Dieterich
Paul Büchert
Johan Jacob Hörrman
Johan Peter Maier
Johann Wilhelm Paulus
Johann Peter Sieffert
John (✕) Klemmer
John Peter (✕) Meyer
Philipp Scheckler
Michael Hieber
Josephus Hybler

Johann Mates Best
Johann Georg Scheuerman
Philip Sahl
Wilhelm Fuchs
Michael (✕) Maurer
Johann Tobias Mohr
John (+) Hasselberger
Johann Valentin Krauss
Melchior Schmidt
Johan Peter Schmitt
Peter Obersheimer
John Mich⁵ (✕) Huber
John Philip (✕) Schleicher
Johan Henrich Haubt
Johan Jacob Schaffner
Jacob Zoll
Johann Daniel Kauff
Peter (+) Fisher
Johannes Schuster
Görg Eminger

[List 272 C] At the Office of Thomas Willing, Esqʳ, October 26ᵗʰ 1768.

Present: Thomas Willing, Esqʳ.

The Foreigners whose Names hereunder written, imported in the Ship Crawford, Charles Smith, Master, from Rotterdam but last from Cowes, did this day take and subscribe the usual Qualifications. Whole Freights 200 & odd. In the List 198. pᵈ 30ᵗʰ Decʳ 1768. Consigned to Messʳˢ Willing & Morris.

John (✕) Gerst
Franˢ (✕) Goucher
Jacob Schmitt
Gottfried Schlang
Johann Samuel Amweg
Johan Jacob Escher
Johann Georg Scher
Christian Aescher
Gabriel (G) Esher
Joh. Jacob Kümmel
Jacob (✕) Seltzer

Johannes Schäffer
Johanes Eschman
Peter Farny
Geo. (+) Erlinger
Johan Vanltin Priehl
Johann Christophel Keller
Andʷ (✕) Ussener
Carll Ludwig Staudehauer
Jerg Wilhelm Beck
Johann Philipp Haas
Conrad (✕) Scheffer

Johann Schütz
Johann Andönius Frölig
Jacob Welcker
Johannes Welcker
Fridrich Hoffman
Michael Welcker
Friderich Samuel Heller
Johannes Kreiter
Jn⁰ Geo. (+) Green
Henrich Blum
Abraham Saurain
Isacque de Die
Samuel Saldret
Jean Pierre Welle
Abram Voisin
Marti Rahm, Schuhst. [?]
Jacob Rahm
Carl Gottlob Schwartz
Johan Samuel Güdtner
Jacob Ulrich Siltzel
Jan Dronah [?]
Johann Henrich Fahrman
Johan Philipp Michell
Henrich Herschberger
Michel von Huber
Phillipp Götz
Hannes Weickert
Georg Hofmann
Ignatzius Zengerle
Martin Schnabel
Jo. Henrich Schnabel
Johann Conrad Schnabel

Daniel (11) Spies
Conrad Kreyl [?]
Martin Paff
Jn⁰ Philip (✕) Fries
Johann Matthias Hartman
Georg Henrich Fisher
Emanuel Waltman
Görg Jacob Waltman
Johann Isac Cochet
Jn⁰ Geo. (✕) Beilstein
Caspar Lütschy
Peter Galloe
Johann Wilhelm Diehl
Johan Jacob Dietz
Johann Nickelaus Heckmann
Johannes Henrich Walterschee
Jn⁰ Herman (✕) Obermeyer
Jn⁰ Henry (✕) Lys
Jost Henrich Schneider
Johann Erhart Scheidel
Ludwig (✕) Kiehl
Johann Adam Staud
Johann Henrich Strom
Jost Henrich Müller
Johann Wilhelm Hartmann
Johan Nickel Hartmann
Philip (✕) Huff
Johann Wilhelm Waltman
Isaac Cochet
Georg Dietrich Cochet
Andreas Gotthard Loebel
Sebastian Hinderle

[List 273 C] At the Court House, Philadelphia, 26ᵗʰ October 1768.

Present: Samuel Mifflin, Esquire.

The Foreigners whose Names are hereunder written, imported in the Ship Betsy, Captain Sˡ Hawk, from Rotterdam, but last from Portsmouth, did this day take and subscribe the usual Qualifications. Consigned to Samˡ Howell. In the List 116. pᵈ £8.14.— the 12. Novʳ 1768.

Johann Gerhart Thiel
Johann Philip Naas
Jacob Anthony
Tomas Manwiller
Johann Matheus Mannwiller
Jacob Andoni
Frantz (X) Christman
Salomon Stenger
Peter Kämmer
Jacob Brentz
Nicol Bieber
Abraham Modweil
Jacob Stenger
Jacob Naschi
Johannes Niess
Christian Seyffert
Johannes Peter Gerhard
Nicklaus Rauscher
Philliphs Munsch
Adam Anthoni
Felden Bieber
Johan Gorgs
Jacob (X) Bever
Theobalt Pfaff
Gerhard (X) Krug
Peter Reisdorff
Jacob Schultheiss
Johann Philipp Opp
Feder Armenbeter
Johannes Schluheis
Jacob Motz
Adam Stenger
Andreas Hauck
Johann Friederich Lich
Adam Horn
Henrich Jockel
Johann Henrich Marx
Johann Niclas Müller
Johannes Schweyer
Frantz Schnell
Martin Weisshardt

Jos Emrich
Jacob Stenger
Daniel Stenger
Christian (+) Conse
Wendel Günther
Gorg Dupont
Friedrich Wilhelm Hoffman
Mathias Müller
Stefanus Felix
Johannes Felix
Martin Felix
Michell Lang
Karll Schlütt
Christoph (X) Kirchsetten
Hans Görg Kacher
Johan Jacob Loorentz
Johann Gorg Threin
Johan Nickel Lintz
Johan Nickel Lintz, Jr.
Philip (X) Micher
Johann Nicel Scholl
Philipp Schanno
Martin Bauer
Nicolas (X) Shirra
Petter Müller
Hans Adam Müller
Johannes (X) Tedweiler
Friederich Bracklohr
Johan Peter (X) Frick
Daniel [?] Hadner
Hannes (X) Greissell
Jacob (X) Mayer
Frentz Licher [?]
Peter Sieber
Henry (X) Benter
Peter (+) Mennel
Friederich Mahler
Georg (X) Mutz
Hans Ludwick (+) Herman
Peter Driessler
Jacob (+) Götz

Mich¹ (++) Wilhelm

Daniel (+) Gerhard

Hans Adam (+) Shory

Michall Zimer

Nicoles (+) Gläzer

Joh. (+) Mathies

Jacob Scholl

Johannes Pfau

Hans Jörg Ber

Andreas (+) Schmidt

Görg Wendling

Daniel Kämmer

Johannes Hess

Johann Petter Jacquart

Johan Heinrich Herrmann

Georg Huber

Andreas Bach

Jacob (H) Hausknecht

Nichol (O) Hardt

Johann Henrich Krähmer

Adam Bernhardt

Johann Adam Stenger, Sr.

Mich¹ (+) Raum

Henrich Zibig

Nickel Ber

Georg Etelwein

Dangel Kämmer

Philipp Rippel

Adam Klein

Christian Stenger

Memorandum : Philadelphia, the 14ᵗʰ day of February 1769.

John Cottringer of the City of Philadelphia, Taylor, being a Foreigner, and not having taken the usual Qualifications on his first coming to reside in this Province, did this day, of his own free Will & Accord, appear before me, and take and subscribe the legal Oaths of Allegiance Fidelity & abjuration. Taken and Subscribed before me,

  John Penn   John Cottringer

[List 274 C] Philadelphia, yᵉ 1ˢᵗ of Septemʳ 1769.

At the Mayor's Office

Present: Isaac Jones, Esquire, Mayor.

The Foreigners whose Names are hereunder written, imported in the ship Nancy & Sucky, Captain William Keys, from London, did this Day take & Subscribe the usual Qualifications. Consign'd to Gibs & West. 18½ freights; 12 in the List; paid the 28ᵗʰ of October, 1769, £0.18.0.

Joannes Guilielmus Pythan *

Johann Balthasar Odernheimer

Friedrich Roth

Johann Henrich Stophel Roth

Wilhelm Usener

Jacob Grob

Johann Georg Wunder [?]

Johannes Gabriel

* A German Reformed minister, from Heidelberg, Germany. See Good, *History of the Reformed Church in the United States, 1725–1792*, Reading, 1899, p. 587.

Uli Schrack   Nicolaus Ernst
Joseph Tschantz   Christian (X) Roth

[List 275 C] At the Mayors Office, Philadelphia, the 29th of Septem^r 1769.

Present: Isaac Jones, Esquire, Mayor.

The Foreigners whose Names are hereunder written, imported in the Ship London Pacquet, Captain James Cook, from Lisbon, did this Day take & Subscribe the usual Qualifications. Consign'd to Jeremiah Warder & Richard Parker. 15 Whole Freights. paid the 14th of October 1769 £1.2.6.

Wentzel Serb   Joseph Schmeüll
Martin (+) Long   Frantz Gomb
Johannes Miller   Fred. (X) Diess
Thomas Brust   Adrian (X) Brust
Hermanus (+) Cazo   Joēs Franciscus Todt
Martin Gält   Jn° Herman Frid. (X) Lippen-
Jn° Henry (+) Block   kan
Hinrich Michael Dhämer   Pitre Inclev

[List 276 C] At the Court House, Philadelphia, ye 13th of October 1769.

Present: Samuel Shoemaker, Esquire, Mayor.

Isaac Jones, Esquire.

The Foreigners whose Names are hereunder written, imported in the Ship Minerva, Captain Thomas Arnott, from Rotterdam, but last from Portsmouth, did this day take & subscribe the usual Qualifications. Consigned to Mr Samuel Shoemaker. in the List 95. paid £7.2.6.

Johann Philipp Becker   Conrad Bock
Johann Georg Göllman   Johann Mattheis Katzenbach
Andreas Heyer   Johann Jacob Lentz
Lorentz Heier   Johann Nicklas Schaffer
Michael Häyer   Johann Theobald Emrich
Friedrich Grommè   Johann Adam Klein
Hans Geörg Bopp   Johann Adam Weller
Johan Christoffel Ferdig   Johannes Theis Arnd
Philips Henrich Bohlender   Johann Hennrich Manderbach

Johann Hennrich Mannderbach

Johann Henrich Dischardt

Johann Wilhelm Schu

Georg Friedrich Rück

Michel Baur

Friederich Kesseler

Johann Georg Zundel

Abraham Mellinger

Johann Nicolaus Döbler

Peter Ullrich

Phillip Moses

Leonhard Karg

Phillip Seyfrit

Hans Georg Jacob

Georg Henrich Jacob

Joseph Farni

Jacob Farny

Jacob Müller

Jacob Musselman

Jacob Sulger

Michael Hertz, a Jew *

Conrad Hofman

Michael Neff

Michael Dosch

Johann Mattheus Dock

Daniel Scheffer

Johann Jacob Walter

Theobald Schramm

Jacob Berg

Henrich Klein

Nickelas Weber

Nichs (×) Bernet

Jacob Friedrich Arnold

Philipp Conrad Häusler

Jacob Diehl

Christoph Pasch

Henrich Carl Stumpf

Philip Peter Rothenheuser

Jacob (×) Fryer

Johannes Rothenheuser

John (×) Bollick

Georg Heinrich Ziegler

Heinrich Fentz

Daniel Nauman

Johannes Schneider

Johann Leohnhard Printzel

Johann Philipp Frey

Johann Jacob Walther

Johann Henrich Pfeiffer

Johannes Herr

Christian Jung

Johann Caspar Pauli

Johann Ludwig Wasser

Anthon Fuchs

Joh. Christoffel Scherrer

Johann Adam Stock

Johan Andreas Strassburger †

Andreas Heger

Johannes Weber

Johann Adam Steuer

Johannes Vallentinus Klein

Joh. Jacob Kifer

George (O) Sermatt

Joh. Michael Radmacher

Joh. Jacob Fritz

Johann Filb Honnetz

Theobald (+) Hess

Hans Vogt

Peter Saubel

Marcell Eberth

Antoni Drexel

Stanislaus Matter

Johann Hemrier [?]

Gorg Martin Jentz

Henrich Priester

---

* Name written also in cursive Hebrew.
† The second entry of Mr. Strassburger's ancestor.

[List 277 C] At Messrs Willing & Morris's Store, Philadelphia, the 24th of October, 1769.

Present: Thomas Willing, Esquire.

The Foreigners whose Names are hereunder written, imported in the Ship Crawford, Charles Smith, Commander, from Rotterdam, did this day take & subscribe the usual Qualifications. Consign'd to Willing & Morris. 20 in the List. 38 Freights. paid £1.10.0, the 26 Decemb^r 1769.

Georg Rinecker	Peter Thorn
Johann Adam Barnitel	Willm Muller
Michael Batt	Johann Wilhelm Flick
Johanes Hinckel	Jost Henrich Thiel
Johann·Wilhelm Stoll	Christoffel Schmidt
Friedrich Kneip	Johann Theis Kempff
Dieter Beyerle	Johann Gerhart Kempff
C. Guttman	Anthon Mueller
Johenrich Hoff	Johan Deissmiller
Vallentin Hoffman	

[List 278 C] At the Office of Isaac Jones, Esquire, Philadelphia 27 July, 1770.

Present: Isaac Jones, Esquire.

The Foreigners whose Names are hereunder written, imported in the Snow Neptune, Thomas Edward Wallis, Commander, from Lisbon, did this day take and subscribe the usual Qualifications. Consigned to Mr John Wilcocks. 8 in the List. 10 Freights.

Gorg Henrich Bremer	Philip Jacob (+) Michael
John (X) Nuttles	Johann Georg Bradtfisch
Mich^l (X) Nuttles	Johann Paul Kurz
Francico Weyzer	John (+) Baptisto

[List 279 C] At the office of and before Isaac Jones, Esquire, Philadelphia, August 29th 1770.

The Foreigners whose Names are hereunder written, imported in the Brig Dolphin, Captain George Stephanson, from London, arrived at the Port of Philadelphia and consigned to James Pemberton and Company. 16 Freights. 9 in the List.

Johann Jost Klein   Peter (×) Miller
Joseph Solomon   Jaque Monie
Jean Seirieux   Pierre Parit
George Alizon   George Pary
Nicola Pary

[List 280 C] At the Office of Samuel Shoemaker, Esquire, Philadelphia, September the 10th 1770.
          Present: Samuel Shoemaker, Esquire, Mayor.
                    Isaac Jones, Esquire.
The Foreigners whose Names are hereunder written, imported in the Snow Rose, George Ord, Master, from Lisbon, did this Day take & subscribe the usual Qualifications.

Johan Enes   Pitro Claude
Peter (×) Moore   Gille (+) Sarier
Johann (×) Kreusser   Lewis (×) Patier
Antoine Doré

[List 281 C] At Messieurs Willing and Morris's Store, Philadelphia the 1st of October, 1770.
          Present: Thomas Willing, Esquire.
The Foreigners whose Names are hereunder written, imported in the Ship Minerva, Thomas Arnott, Master, from Rotterdam but last from Cowes, did this day take and subscribe the usual Qualifications. Consigned to Messieurs Willing & Morris.

Gerg Mengs   Philip (+) Fritz
Michel Schmitt   Anderas Eyrich
Georg Jacob Sturm   Lorentz Vix
Hans Gerg Schill   David Ott
Johan Gorg Kammerer   Geo. (+) Gilli
Johannes Schell   Caspar Fetsch
Georg Müller   Mathias Weber
Michäel Nonnenmacher   Johann Peter Bösinger
Johann Georg Schnepp   Adam Lieber
Jacob Kuntz   Adam Wolf
Jacob Marx   Fridrich Hehlhoffer
Vallendien Hetsch   Theob^d (O) Bish

Friderich (+) Greiner
Jacob Greiner
John Geörg Pfüll
Georg Heinrich Maurer
Sebastian Hitz [?]
Johannes Scheib
Johan Gorg Müller
Jacob Lück
Jacob (J) Schmit
Jno (H) Leiffer
Georg Luck
Mathias Scheuermann
Jacob (X) Luck
Mardin Wager [?]
Christian Wiest
Peter Schmit
Johannes Becker
Martin (+) Kerner
Philip (+) Preisseman
Jno (H) Weyer
Johann Georg Bastian
Jo. Heinrich Bastian
Johannes Spröth
Jerg Rickel
Johannes Zumbott
Conrad Holsten
Georg Paul Freyer
Heinrich Freyer
Jacob Paulus
Petter Miller
Mathias Widmer
Phi. Jacob (B) Bessinger

Willhelm Schlemilch
Hans Jerg Herrman
Stäffan Fünfrock
Mich. (H) 5 Rock
Michel Fünfrock, Jr.
Hanns Geörg Mallo
Philip (X) Simon
Jacob Heintz
Johan Heinrich Hornberger
Jno Geo. (X) Zimmerman
Geo. (W) Weir
Hans Jerg Weidman
Michel Kammer
Johan Schantz
Christian (+) Schutz
Georg Heinrich Braunig
Michel Gerst
Jacob Coblentz
Danl (+) Hirshberger
Michael (+) Schaffer
Jacob Ferber
Heinrich Gärthner
Jacob Doll
Conrad Sebastian Röller
Johan Philips Hoorn
Jacob Offenbach
Anderras Offenbach
Joh. Theobalt Gaul
Michael (X) Pessinger
Andres Kiefer
Martzolf Heintz
Johann Heinrich Völlkle [?]

[List 282 C] At the Office of Isaac Jones, Esquire, Philadelphia, October 3d 1770.
Present: Isaac Jones, Esquire.
The Foreigners whose Names are hereunto subscribed, imported in the Snow Britannia, Richard, Eyres, Master, from Lisbon, did this Day take and subscribe the usual Qualifications. Capt Robert White, Owner. 6 Freights.

J. Didier   Jean (+) Vinettier
J. De Labeaume   Jean (+) Hissard
Guillaume Mommaton   Marys Kreys

[List 283 C] At the Court House, Philadelphia, October the 29th 1770.

Present: Samuel Mifflin, Esq[r].

The Foreigners whose Names are hereunder subscribed, imported in the Ship Sally—— John Osmond, Master, from Rotterdam but last from Cowes, did this Day take and subscribe the usual Qualifications to the Government. 143 Freights. 89 in the List of which 9 absent. Mr Samuel Howell, Merchant, Owner.

Georg Christian Völcker
Jn⁰ Anton (+) Trager
Dieterich Wilhelm Bücking
Christoph Müller
Francis (X) Stein
Jn⁰ Geo. (X) Altefried
Thomas Engelhardt
Peter (X) Joseph
Paul (X) Mingel
Johan Friedrich Heffein
Johann Jost Sasmanshausen
Johann Kraft Achebach
Jn⁰ Henry (X) Denner
Bernhart Seipp
Daniel (X) Volmer
Johan Henrich Ceil
Johannes Schmit
Johann Jost Birckelbach
Johannes Ditman
Johan Henrich Afflerbach
Johan Henrich Weyand
Johann Jost Weyand
Johann Christopher (X) Dietz
Johann Teobaldt Franck
Henrich Wietterstein

Johannes Nechti [?]
Alexander (AL) Lighty
Johannes Cries
Jacob Schneyder
Jacob Schnell
Ludwig Daniel Staudt
Johannes Reichel
Johann Nickolaus Walter
Johann Georg Schleicher
Johann Balthas Klein
Johan Henrich Kliebensteinn
Martin Hebeysen
Johann Georg Denzel
Johann Adam Haar
Georg Andreas Wagner
Johann Chris[n] (X) Brechner
Christian Sürbi
Paulus Kolbe
Henry (H) Wernley
Johannes Bibighaus *
Johan Nickel Haas
Johannes Vollmer
Johann Nickel Bach
Johannes Pick
Johannes Franck

* The father of the Rev. Henry Bibighaus. See *Fathers of the Reformed Church,* III, p. 333.

Johanes Weyandt

Johann Jost Weyandt

Johann Christ vom Hoff

Justus Schmidt

C. G. Hauck

Henricus Horn

Johan Peter Gräb

Jacob Bühler

Georg Ludwig Fischer

Johaneis Lahrwind [?]

Joh. Marthin Gaul

Johann Martin Bauman

Friederich Wilhelm Bauman

Peter Vogt

Jacob Hubacker

Paridon Petersen

Friedrich Borsch

Rudolph (×) Miller

Matteis Merckell

Hans Christner

Christian Aeschliman

Johan Jacob Hennrigl

Baltzer (+) Henrichel

Christian Ludwig Henrigel

Daniel Mise

George (+++) Emmert

Christoph Beck

Johannes Hothem

Johann Koch

Johann Valentin Franck

[List 284 C] At Messrs Willing & Morris's Store, Philad^a, November 23^d 1770.

Present: Samuel Mifflin, Esquire.

The Foreigners whose Names are hereunto subscribed, imported in the Ship Crawford, Charles Smith, Master, from Rotterdam but last from Cowes, did this day take and subscribe the usual Qualifications to the Government. Messrs Willing & Morris owners. 60 Freights including Newlanders. 26 Qualified.

Daniel Stauffer

Johannes Hiestandt

Jacob Rohrer

Cornelius Gramm

Wilhelm Gramm

Tobias Hartmann

Carl Wilhelm Keck

Peter (+) Mueller

Johannes Luft

Jacob Utt

Francis (+) Coolman

Johannes Ginther

Ernst (+) Berg

Johannis Jaus

Johannes Diehl

Carl Adolph Seitz

Andreas Surerus

Henrich Schaub

Geörg Kleiderlein

Andres (O) Gutting

Johannes Gummy

P. F. Droz

Andreas Brand

Jacob Geiger

Henrich Geiger

Cornelius Braun

[List 285 C] At the Office of Isaac Jones, Esquire, Philadelphia 17 June, 1771.

Present: Isaac Jones, Esquire.

The Foreigners whose Names are hereunto subscribed, imported in the Ship Pennsylvania Packet, Peter Osborne, Master, from London, did this day take & subscribe the usual Qualifications. Consign'd to Joshua Fisher & Sons.

Conrad Bachmann	Ludwig Rohrer
Abraham Mayret	Joh. Georg Fried. Bechtel
Philipp Jacob Weiss	Johann Adam Lauth
Abram David Reymond	Johannes Heyler

[List 286 C] At the Office of Isaac Jones, Esquire, Philadelphia 27ᵗʰ July, 1771.

Present: Isaac Jones, Esquire.

The Foreigners whose Names are hereunto subscribed, imported in the Brig America, William Copeland Lattimore, Commander, from London, did this Day take & subscribe the usual Qualifications.

Johannes Beckman	Johann Georg von Nieder
Johannes Hepp	Jnᵒ Martin (+) Van Nieder
Justus Kornscheuer	Jnᵒ Jacob (+) Van Nieder
Lorens Pfahl	Georg Jacob Köller
Johann Geörg Hals	Jacob Ruff
Johan Dietrich Heppe	Valtin Krieg

[List 287 C] Before the Honourable Thomas Willing, Esquire, Philadelphia 17ᵗʰ Day of September 1771.

The Foreigners whose Names are hereunto subscribed, imported in the Minerva, Thomas Arnot, Master, from Rotterdam, but last from Cowes, did this day subscribe the usual Qualification. Consigned to Willing & Morris. 204 Freights. 99 in the List.

Jacob (✕) Wentz	Johann Henrich Schmaltz
Henrich Spiess	Geo. Jacob (+) Stoltzel
George (✕) Miller	Johan Georg Jordy
Joh. Barth. Roehm	Johannes Peter Lütsch
Johann Daniel Schrödter	Philip Müller
Wihl. Fried. Seeger	Christian Knobel
Carl Philipp Ebert	Johann Peter Kuntz
Gabriel (✕) Gasha	Johann Peter Grissler

Jacob Beier
Peter (+) Hertel
Henrich Schäffer
Henrich Matterkuns
Johann Georg Christman
Henry (X) Dieterich
Jacob (X) Weiss
Casper Osser [?]
Johan Henrich Sche
Conrath Oster
Johannes Günttert
Jacob (X) Young
Johannes Leynoldt
Michael Pilrege
John (X) Werger
Alexander Osram [?]
Johan Michael Schmidt
Johan Jacob Moder
John Geo. (+) Roth
Andereas Hettmansperger
Jacob Wentz
Adam Wagner
Johan Georg Stierle
Johann Michael Hölz
Nichs (+)-Waldman
Willhelm Heist
Michael Trussler
Friedrich Seigmuller
Fred. (+) Hirsh
Valentin Linn
Jacob Grünenwalt
Carl Welcker
Jacob Welcker
Phillipp Helick *
Henrich Kurtz
Uhlrich Käyser
Johann Adam Mallo
Johann Georg Süss
Matheis (+) Engel

Johan Friederich Dörsch
Johann Conrad Roth
Andres Gratziger
Friederich Dewaldt
Johannes Best
Jacob (+) Reiff
Christian Gaul
Nickel Schmidt
Johann Conrad Schneider
Hans Baltzer (+) Peterman
Jno Henry (+) Peterman
Johann Philipp Schenckel
Jacob Harzer [?]
Anton (X) Glantz
Valentin Sasla Pfostadecker [?]
Theobalt Leibrock
Philipp Jacob May
Lutwig Stegner
Peter Kurtz
Sebastian Marcker
Jacob Laux
Jacob Culman
Adam Molitor
Johann Michael Traub
Jacob Huthmacher
Johannes Gerhardt Kaltschmidt
Johan Stefan Guck
Johan Jost Otterbach
Johann Erhard Geyer
David Drexler
Peter Meyer
Jno Peter (X) Leer
Erasmus (X) Purtsch
Dionisius Busch
Philipp Henrich Knapp
Philipps Conradt Christ
Hinrich Windlandt
George Christophel Helmbold
Johann Georg Friederich Scheller

---

* A Reformed schoolmaster at Easton and Dryland. See Livingood, *Eighteenth Century Reformed Church Schools,* pp. 135, 141.

[List 288 C] Philadelphia, September 19th 1771. At the Court House, Present, Samuel Mifflin, Esquire.

The Foreigners whose Names are hereunto subscribed, imported in the Ship London Packet, Captain Cook, from Lisabon, did this day take and subscribe the usual Qualifications. Consigned to Jeremiah Warder & Son. 9 Whole Freights.

Carolus Gottlob Griell
Hendrick Borger
Gerardus Westens
Peter (X) Schmuke
Etienne Teissier

Jean Baptiste
Michel Esteue
Pier (+) Gabory
Michelle (+) de Vignair

[List 289 C] Philadelphia Octo^r the 31st 1771. Before James Humphreys, Esqr, the Foreigners whose Names are here unto subscribed, imported in the Brigantine Recovery, . . . Bull, Master, from Rotterdam, but last from Cowes, did this day take & subscribe the Usual Qualifications. Consigned to Messrs Willing & Morris. At the Store of Messrs Willing & Morris. 52.

John (X) Hauel
Gottfried Lebrecht Schmidt
Johan Georg Reiss
Warner Fel [?]
Jacob Schupp
Michel Gundry
Johannes Ortmann
Johann Henrich Ortmann
Chrisⁿ (+) Furman
Gottfried Heinrich Diethoff
Johannes Hirschman
Paul (X) Ackerman
Philipp Burbach
Johannes Nicolaus Neu
Daniel Niederhaus
Johann Michael Lahm
Nicholas (X) Becker
Christoffel Lärtges
Peter (+) Schneider
Johann Peter Schneiter

Albert Deliss
Johannes Peter Schneider
Christian Weber
Johannes Christian Horster
Albertus Kratz
Johann Jacob Odenkirchen
Jacob Henrich Willhelm
Ludwig Schneider
Allecsander Schumacher
Johannes Benner
Andres Schneider
Philipp Gräff
John (+) Martin
Jacob Welsch
Johann Nickel Welsch
Jacob Welsch
Johann Jost Schnéyder
Willhellm Oertter
Fallentin Thomas
Johann Adam Leonhardt

Hans Jacob Schäffer
Jacob Schäffer
Michel Schäffer
Johan Conrad Spangenberg
Johannes Eckstein
Wilhelm Ernst Felbach

Johannes Schnell
Johannes Schnell, Jr.
Johan Martin Hisgen
Johann Henrich Filger
Johann Jacob Becker
Peter Becker

[List 290 C] At Messrs Willing & Morris's Store, at Philadelphia, the 19th of November 1771.
Present: George Bryan, Esquire.

The Foreigners whose Names are underwritten, imported in the Ship Tyger, George Johnson, Master, from Rotterdam but last from Cowes, did this day take and subscribe the foregoing Oaths & Qualifications. Consigned to Messrs Willing & Morris. 130 in the List.

John (X) Freble
Hans Gerg Benner
Peter (XXX) Trumpheller
Peter (XXX) Waggoner
Nicholas (+) Shireman
Jacob (+) Waggoner
Ludwig Schneider
Johannes Müller
Peter Wasser
Adam Steiner
Johann Jacob Beyerle
Henry (+++) Apple
Sebastian Wille
Dominicus (+++) Heyrom
Niclaus Grünwald
Johann Lautenschläger
Henry (+) Wilber
Anthony (+) Cline
Nicholas (X) Yost
Johannes Sigel
Jerg Michael Weiss
Johann Daniel Schwanfelder
Jacob Samuell Golde
Valthin Fauth
Caspar Beyer

Johann Nicol Fuchs
Johann Michael Beltz
John (X) Le Port
Georg Niclas Kaffenberger
Johannes Motte
Nichlaus Köhller
Hans Georg Ackerman
Johan Wilhelm Fleck
Friedrich Foltz
Jacob Burg
Georg Simon Grün
Jacob Hoffman
Henrich Jacob Raubenheimer
George (X) Hann
Johannes Wucherer
Johann Henrich Lautenschläger
Nicholas (X) Hoffman
Johannes Willman
Jonas Blesch
Georg Heinrich Riedle
Jacob (X) Erick
Niclaus Samuel Golde
Johannes Waltmann
Georg Friedrich Rühle
Gustavus Müller

Johannes Lupp
Peter Odern
Johann Christ Jäger
Willem Schmit
Johann Petter Weill
Johan Georg (×) Scheüermann
Johan Daniel Cleiss
Johann Michel Ihrig
Christoph Störner
Wilhelm Kumpf
Henrich Muilberger
Johann Friederich Dörr
Johannes Ihrig
Martin Grahn
Henrich Rickos
Johannes Muller
Johannes Mitzel
George (+) Isenring
Johann Peter Ihrig
John Gotlip (+) Steinbecker
Leonard (×) Kessler
Georg (+) Foulke
Johann Georg Horn
Johannes Schneider
Johann Adam Löw
John Bernard (+) Leyer
Peter (×) Kessler
Johann Casper Lorentz
Hann Heinnrich Zimmermann
Carl Benner
Johannes Benner
Marten Benner
Johann Wilhelm Schneider
Gottfried Kihner
Jacob (×) Marks

Adam (×) Grosshart
Johan Nicol Martin
Johannes Burckhardt Henn
Peter (+) Trexler
Michael (×) Trexler
Jacob (×) Keesler
Conrad Haasse
Johann Ludwig Starck
Johann Adam Dracker
Johan Konrath Germann
Johann Leonhard Nagel
Conrad (+++) Meyer
Johannes Schott
Johannes Peter Rausch
Christ Jacobus Schmidt
Johannes Reusch
Conrad (+) Radman
Lewis (+) Noy
John (×) Noy
Sebastian Schürch
Johannes Schletzer
Martin (×) Evert
John (+) Yorts
Jacob (+) Schibeley
Johan Jacob Menges
Jacob (×) Sanner
Johannes Niebel
Philip (+) Egle
Johann Geörg Laudenschläger
Johann Hennrich Lautenschläger
Andres Ehman
Cunrath Vonholt
Adam Als
Andon Eberhardt

[List 291 C] At Messieurs Willing & Morris's Store, Philadelphia, 25th November, 1771.
Present: George Bryan, Esquire.
The Foreigners whose Names are underwritten, imported
in the Ship Crawford, Charles Smith, Commander, from Rot-

terdam but last from Cowes, did this Day take and subscribe the foregoing Oaths & Qualifications to the Government in the usual Form. Consigned to Messrs Willing & Morris. 8 in the List.

Michäl Mohrlock	Daniel (W) Wolf
Jacob Friderich Höckhlen	Matthias (X) Kraus
Johann Peter Kuch	Godfrey (X) Stoll
Johann Stephan Sulger	Christoff Gottlieb Thielemann

[List 292 C] At the State House in the City of Philadelphia, the 4th Day of December, 1771.
Present: John Gibson, Esquire, Mayor.
The Foreigners whose Names are under written, imported in the Brig Betsey, Andrew Bryson, Commander, from London, did this Day take and subscribe the foregoing Oaths and Qualifications to the Government in the usual Form. Consigned to Mr James Christie. 46 in the List. 78 Freights.

Jacob (+) Fry	Jean Gaspard Horthe
Jacob Schneider	Sebastian (+) Strauman
Johan Flumbacher	Conrad Schwesterümller
Jacob Flubacher	Peter Flin
Heinrich Meier	Wilhelm Schuhmacher
Heinrich Bussler	Jacob Heer
Heinrich Bärley	Henrich Dicke
Marthin Thommen	Hermanus Dicke
Jacob Bäy	Johannes Klappert
Jacob Rügger	Johann Martin Frey
Christophel Winder	Sebastian Harth
Matheis Fuselbach	Rudy Funck
Johannes Schmidt	Daniel Volck
Johannes Straub	Martin Funck
Jacob Kugler	Jno (+) Cook
Paulus Bauersachs	Wm (+) Becker
Heinrich Fichter	Jacob Schuhmacher
Has. Heinrich Hesler	Michael Frey
Jacob Zimmerman	Johannes Feinst

[List 293 C] At the Office of Isaac Jones, Esquire, at Philadelphia, 10th December, 1771.

Present: Isaac Jones, Esquire.

The Foreigners whose Names are underwritten, imported in the Ship General Wolfe, Richard Hunter, Commander, from Lisbon, did this day take & subscribe the foregoing Oaths and Qualifications to the Government in the usual form. Consigned to the above named Richard Hunter. [10] in the List. paid 15/—

Charles (+) Smith	Nich^s (+) Biss
Kasper Berger	Jn° Fajon
Anton (+) Ernst	Joannes Baptista
Franc^s Pros	Jo. (×) Carl
Casper (×) Trible	Johannes Schmitt

[List 294 C] At Messrs Willing & Morris's Store Philadelphia, 24th February, 1772.

Present: Peter Miller, Esquire.

The Foreigners whose Names are underwritten, imported in the Ship Hope, Captain John Robertson, from London, did this day take and subscribe the foregoing Oaths & Qualifications to the Government in the usual Form. Consigned to Messrs Willing & Morris. 23 in the List. 26 Freights.

Johann Friederich Hönninger	Johann Andreas Fritze
Johann Ernst Ziegler	Johann Ulrich Bayr
Henrich Meisner	Deitrick (×) Munger
Hyronimus Henrici	Friderick (×) Hector
Christian Schmidt	Johann Georg Truchäuser
George (+) Adam Jacob	Theobaldt Klein
Johan Jacob Schwentzer	Lemmill Loser
Christoph Wohler	Johann Georg Meyer
Johan Heinrich Steitz	Theobalt Bastian
Johann Heinrich Voigt	Marti Sudtne
Philip Wilh. May	Johann Melchior Vass
Johann Jacob Hartman	

[List 295 C] At the Province Island, Wednesday, the 30th of September, 1772.

Present: Peter Miller, Esquire.

The Foreigners whose Names are underwritten, imported in the Ship Minerva, James Johnston, Commander, from Rot-

terdam (but last from Cowes), did this day take & subscribe
the foregoing Oaths & Qualifications to the Government in the
usual Form. Consigned to Messrs Willing & Morris. 48 in the
List. Freights 97. (Rec^d £3.12.0, the 29th Decem^r 1772).

Johannes Meyer	Hans Casper Heier
Caspar Vintz	Jacob (+) Ballmer
Hans Plattner	Thomas Moll
Heinrich Schäublin	Jacob Schwele
Ullrech Heiberger	Jerg Henrich Dehn
Johannes Hauck	Hans Jacob (X) Molle
Jacob (+) Hoffacker	Frantz Beckh
Hans Schuy	Johan Gorg Kessler
Jno Christ^n (+) Flick	Johann Davyd Bennz
Ludwig (+) Mill	Johannes Schwerdle
Gottlob Hempel	Jno (X) Arnoldus
Hans Baltzer Büry	Hans Jacob Meier
Henri Perret	Gottfried Zepernick
Hans Peter Römmer	Jno Geo. (B) Bander
Johan Martin Zimmer	Jacob (X) Uberer
Jacob Schaub	Johann George Kuhr
Johann Fridrich Ulmer	Martin (X) Rudy
Christian Apffel	Wm. Nycius (X) Meyer
Johannes Wasling	Heini Wissich
Henrich Schweitzer	

[List 296 C] At Messrs Willing & Morris's Store at Philadelphia, the 16 of October, 1772.

Present: Thomas Willing, Esquire.

The Foreigners whose Names are underwritten, imported
in the Ship Crawford, Charles Smith, Master, from Rotterdam
but last from Cowes, did this day take & subscribe the foregoing Oaths & Qualifications in the usual Form. Consigned to
Messrs Willing & Morris. (Rec^d £10.17.6, the 29th Decemb
1772) 145 in the List.

Andrew (+++) Hoffman	Johann Christian Gerber
Martin Hauck	Johann Theobald Merckel
Jacob Demmel	Jacob Schwartz
Johannes Fischer	Henrich Franckforther
Johann Philipp Fitting	Vallenthin Welcker

Johann Peter Ochsner

Hans Martin Meyer

Godfrey (+++) Whitman

Friedrich Beyer

Johann Heinri[ch] Wagenhorst

Johann Carl Wagenhorst

Hans Jerg Preis

Johannes Hörers

John George (XXX) Wertman

Jacob Scherer

Godfrey (XXX) Feckely

Christian Schlauch

Johann Marsch

L. Smith

John Henry (+++) Zimerman

Johannes Sauter

Mattheus Lindermeyr

Jacob Abbriter

Friederich Vogel

Michael Warthman

Samuel Fridrich Winter

Phillipp Hammann

Andreas Weissert

Georg Martin Füchtner

Michael Sautter

Jonathan Treuttle

Peter Hammann

Friederich Linck

Jonathan Linek

Johann Georg Baum

Frederick (+++) Fightmyer

Christoph Mohr

Marte Wieland

Bernhard Wieland

Andreas Holtzwarth

Johannes Schmidt

Johannes Kintzi

Marx Schneider

Jacob Rupp

Samuel Schoch

Gerg Franck

Johannes Buchmüller

Heinrich Weissmüller

Christan Pettry

Willem Baltzer

Johann Christoph Scheibe

Jacob Freiderich Laufer

Joh. David Ziegler

Jn° Jacob (X) Aberly

Joh. Georg Einwächter

Johann Conrad Discher

Martin Möllinger

Jacob Möllinger

Henrich Zercher

Johann Leonhard Fichter

Andreas Müller

Albrecht Kümmerle

Jacob (+) Lautermilk

Georg Heinrich Maurer

Johan Polmieser [?]

Johannes Beer

Peter Galte

Friederich Wilhelm Hess

Stephan Pless

Franz Carl Widmann

Peter Lambert

Andreas Lambert

Johannes Peter Harbach

Jerg Friedrich Betz

Johan Friedrich Betz

Gerg David Herm

Philipp Jacob Sartorius

Joseph Stumpp

Michael Müll

Rudolph Sultzer

Geo. Mich. (X) Miller

Geo. (X) Shuman

Isaac (X) Bergdoll

Jn° (X) Gramer

Martin Fischer

Friederich Linck

Abraham Köhler
Balthas Bertsch
Peter Weymer
Petter Weymer
Christoph (+) Fandrich
Jonas Nothstein
Johan Wendel Weigele

Georg Adam Gahraus
Johann Gram
Stephan Foght
Joseph (X) Graff
Jacob Schmit
Johannes Quast
Frantz Petter Drexler

[List 297 C] At the Office of John Gibson, Esquire, Philadelphia the 19ᵗʰ of October, 1772.
Present: John Gibson, Esquire, Mayor.

The Foreigners whose Names are hereunder written, imported in the Ship Catharine, [James] Sutton, Master, from Rotterdam but last from London, did this day take the foregoing Oaths & Qualifications in the usual Form. Consigned to Messʳˢ Keppele & Steinmetz. 20 in the List. (Recᵈ £1.10.0, 28 Decembʳ 1772)

Charles Frederic Knoery
Francis Stephany
Joh. Caspar Koch
Christaan Lindemaan
Leonhard Müller
Gotthard David Flickwir
Ulrich Otto
Henrich Rihmer
Georg Keller
George Bardeck

Mardin (X) Schude
Francis Geisse
Frantz Fidelis Schneckenburger
Joh. Christoph Lotspeich
Frantz· Frickh
Peter Paul
Frantz Wertz
Peter Mohrmann
Henrich Gerding

[List 298 C] At the Office of John Gibson Esquire, Mayor of the City, Philadelphia the 19ᵗʰ October, 1772.
Present: The sᵈ George Gibson, Esqʳ.

The Foreigners whose Names are hereunder written, imported in the Ship Phebe, Captain Castle, from London, did this day take the foregoing Oaths and Qualifications in the usual Form. (7 in the List). Consigned to Messʳˢ Bringhurst and Mifflin. (pᵈ Mʳ Shippen 10/6 Fees, the 19ᵗʰ of October, 1772)

Nicholas (X) Jacobson
Johann Reinhardt Schäbeller
Johann Friederich Bahlsdorf

Friederich Schröder
Friederich Klette
Georg Rehfeld

[List 299 C] At the Court House at Philadelphia, the 3ᵈ of November, 1772.

Present: The Worshipful John Gibson, Esquire, Mayor.

The Foreigners whose Names are hereunder written, imported in the Sally, John Osmond, Master, from Rotterdam but last from Portsmouth, did this Day take the foregoing Oaths and Qualifications in the usual Form. Consigned to Samuel Howell. 65 in the List. (Mr. Howell for 64 à 1/6 is £4.16.0, yᵉ 31 Decemʳ 1772)

Johann Theis Schnell	Johannes Kram
Jnᵒ (✕) Miller	Johannes Peter Schneider
Gerlach Hass	Johann Henrich Jörg
Nicolaus Trautwein	Peter (+) Rothenberg
Jnᵒ Geo. (✕) Osterdag	Johann Georg Knabeloch
Danniel Rust	Philip Peter (+) Schneider
Johan Jacob Eller	Johannes Fritzinger
Samˡ Peter (✕) Reiss	Jacob Michel
Wilhelm Henrich Ritter	Wilhelm Reiss
Carl Meier	Heinrich Dieterich
Johann Adam Matzenbacher	Burchard (+) Heir
Johann Freymuht	Nickel Paulus
Ernst Heinrich Fritzinger	Hans Georg Schiedörfer
Johann Matheus Böttger	Jnᵒ Philip (+) Bauer
John Jost (✕) Langebach	Godlieb (+) Schlichter
Johann Henrich Hartmann	Conrad Röder
Johannes Schieberstein	Johann Jost Betz
Jnᵒ (✕) Holtz	Joh. Jacob Eull
Johann Gerlach Lupffer	Jan Halewyn
Johann Dangel Lopffer	Johan Wilhelm Meyer
Karl Geissler	J.W. Lopffer
Johann Georg Rübbel	Jacob Theis
Wilhelm Lehman	Christian Schmid
Christian Trautmann	Matthias Paul
Wynant (+) Rohr	Christian Reusse
Henrich Rolandt	Johann Nicolaus Schuhriem
Jacob Albrecht	

[List 300 C] At Messrs Willing & Morris's Store at Philadelphia, 3^d December, 1772.

Present: Peter Miller, Esquire.

The Foreigners whose Names are underwritten, imported in the Ship Hope, George Johnston, Master, from Rotterdam but last from Cowes, did this day take and subscribe the foregoing Oaths and Qualifications in the usual Form. (Consigned to Messrs Willing & Morris.) Recd £3.9.0, the 29th Decem-1772. List 40.

Johannes Zacharias Langbein	Jacob Cacho
Johan Georg Pfleiderer	Paulus Huwer
Philipp Wilhelm Schmidt	Anthon Rausch
Henrich Lehr	Anthony (+) Auer
Philips Hardmann	Phillib Martin Keilhauer
Johannes Ohlwein	Jorg Kirchner
Jacob (×) Frick	Henrich Schuler
Johann Philib Müller	Johan Adam Funck
Johannes Bentz	Fridrich Steinhauer
Johannes Lösch	Jacob Moser
Peter Keller	Christian Stucky
Johannes Elgerth	Justus Battenfeld
Wilhelm Becker	Christian Sahm
Jacob Bincklie	Johann Jacob Pfautz
Jn° (×) Frickheffer	Jerg Tilwits
Jn° Jacob (×) Gieb	Jn° Jost (×) Frickheffer
Friedrich Jacob Laux	Isaac (O) Heyman*
Wilhelm Friedterich Dampf	Herman Roosen
Görg Wilhelm Ber	Johann Jost Dahmer
Arnold Peters	Carle Ohlweinny

[List 301 C] At the Court House at Philadelphia, 24th day of December, 1772.

Present: The Worshipful John Gibson, Esquire, Mayor.

The Foreigners whose Names are underwritten, imported in the Brig Morning Star, George Demster, Master, from Rotterdam, but last from Cowes, did this Day take and subscribe the foregoing Oaths Declarations & Qualifications in the usual Form. 106 whole Freights. In the List 62 Men. 15 half

* Written also in cursive Hebrew.

Freights, making 113½ Freights in all. 131 Souls, including Men Women & Children. Consigned to Mᵣ James Christie, Merchant in Baltimore.

Johannes Ludwig Maxseiner	William Francis Turner
Henrich Adam Maxseiner	Johann Georg Kessler
Gottfried Fisterer	Andonny Schäffer
Jacob Weltner	Petter Nauätter
John (+++) Wychel	Johann Adam Esch
Andrew (XXX) Stelting	Johann Hennrich Meffert
Johannes Hamscher	Johann Gottfried Grasmeher
Niclaus Lüderacher	Johann Adam Stoll
Jacob Kuster [?]	Johan Lemer [?]
Johan Feierabend	Ludwig Reineck
Jnᵒ Jacob (+) Naneiker	Bernard (+) Nickel
Conrad (X) Langebach	Philip (X) Suppert
Ludwig Henrich Deisman	Johann Jacob Pfeiffer
Willᵐ (++) Kemp	Friedrich Winder
Johann Henrich Küntz	Johann Carl Miller
Jnᵒ Jacob (X) Genems	Frantz Honorius Heger
Conrad Underseel	Christian Wenger
Jacob Nusser	Johan Jacob Kelcher
Abraham (X) Richard	Johann Peter Ullrich
Jnᵒ (X) Runkel	Jeorg Schwartz
Jacob (X) Hess	Jacob Niebergall
Friederich Hoffman	Frans Mentger

Memorandum: Philadelphia, the 2ᵈ of February, 1773.

Francis Casper Hasenclever, of the City of Philadelphia, Merchant, being a Foreigner, has Petitioned the House of Assembly for a Law to Naturalize him, and, not having taken the usual Qualifications on his first coming to reside in this province, did this day, of his own free Will and Accord, appear before me, and take the Oaths of Allegiance and Abjuration, and make, repeat and subscribe the Declaration directed to be taken and subscribed by Act of Parliament.

Francis Caspar Hasenclever

Taken and Subscribed
  before me, Richᵈ. Penn.

[List 302 C] At the Mayors Office at Philadelphia, the 30ᵗʰ day of April, 1773.

Present: The Worshipful John Gibson, Esquire, Mayor.

The Foreigners whose Names are underwritten, imported in the Ship Pennsylvania Packet, Peter Osborne, Commander, from London, did this day take and Subscribe the foregoing Declarations and Qualifications in the usual Form. Consigned to Joshua Fisher & Sons. 24 in the List.* 32 Freights.

Edeme Halbon	Johan Christoph Hebigt
Pier Carle Pouponnot	Philip (B) Bone
Gerhard Meyer	Andreas Kleinschmiedt
Johann Friederich Rintelman	Johann Philipp Rieffenach
Arnold Bödeker	Christop Reincke
Johannis Miller	Adolph Strohl
Johann Hartman	Johann Daniel Lehmann
Cond (C) Gabel	Sebastian Kleinschmidt
Anton (+) Le Roy	Josep Bourghell
Charles Glukner	Gottfried Gebauer
Heinrich Kese	Friederich Basermann

[List 303 C] At the Mayor's Office at Philadelphia, the 30th day of April, 1773.

Present: The Worshipful John Gibson, Esquire, Mayor.

The Foreigners whose Names are underwritten, imported in the Ship Catharine, [James] Sutton, Commander, from London, did this day take and subscribe the foregoing Declarations and Qualifications in the usual form. Consigned to Messrs Keppeler & Steinmetz. 23 in the List.† 42 Freights.

Henry Mollwitz	Johan Schmit
Ch. Friedrich Oberlaender	Henry Javet
Johan Christoph Schweigerts	Georg Baumann
Henrich Conrad Boger	Robert Hall
Etienne Moret	Jean Daniel Pouriot
Pierre Faetzet	Siméon Meyland
Philippe Vunbert	Etienne Marlier
Uldrig Bossig	Augusten Gage
Jno Bapdhiste Doudemand	. . . . Mercier
Jean (X) Gourdain	

* The list has only 22 names.
† The list has only 19 names.

[List 304 C] At the Court House at Philadelphia, the 31ˢᵗ day of May, 1773.

Present: The Worshipful John Gibson, Esquire, Mayor.

The foreigners whose Names are underwritten, imported in the Brigantine Dolphin, Arthur Hill, Commander, from London, did this day take and subscribe the foregoing Declarations and Qualifications in the usual Form. Consigned to Mr Richard Neave, Junʳ; 38 in the List. 58 Freights.

Friederich Heyn	Johann Ahlemann
Georg Pfotzer	Jochem Birstädt
Jacob Mosck	Nich. (+) Hyer
Johan Martin Weber	Michˡ (+) Flyder
Johann Georg Kuntz	Friederich Schleiff
Christian (X) Bashidoch	Zachrias Lohret
Henry (O) Course	Andreas Franck
Henrich Weitzler	Peter Kappus
Jacob Grübe	Nicholas (X) Gottman
Michael Horn	Christopher (XX) Keeger
Andreas Reinhardt	Jacob (X) Leshong
Nichˢ (+) Bordon	Fred. (X) Fey
Mathaus Borelle	Johann Georg Vogeley
Henrich Arcularius	Christopher (+) Riegel
Philip Jacob Arcularius	Balthasar Faulstich
Jacob Rinpfenthall	John (XX) Wiseman
Ludwig Reinhart	Evart (X) Vareffen
Johannes Engel	Christian Pfeiffer
Andʷ (+) Heimlich	

[List 305 C] At the Mayors Office at Philadelphia, the 4ᵗʰ of June, 1773.

Present: The Worshipful John Gibson, Esquire, Mayor.

The foreigners whose Names are underwritten, imported in the Ship Carolina, Benjamin Loxley, Junʳ, Master, from London, did this day make & subscribe the foregoing Declarations and Qualifications in the usual Form. Consigned to Messʳˢ Jeremiah Warder & Son. 8 in the List. 29 Freights.

Gab. Valier	Johann Georg Egert
Louis Demarer	Johann Andreas Schmidt

Hennricus Marten
Joachim (+) Hartkopff

John (X) Eller
Gilli Doutremer

[List 306 C] At Messrs Willing and Morris's Store at Philadelphia, the twenty third Day of August, 1773.
Present: George Bryan, one of the Justices &c.

The Foreigners whose Names are underwritten, imported in the Ship Sally, John Osmon, Commander, from Rotterdam in Holland, but last from Portsmouth in England, did this Day take and subscribe the foregoing Oaths and Qualifications in the usual Form. Consigned to Samuel Howell & Son. 153 in the List. 193 Freights.

Mathias Friderich Däubler
Christian Ludwig Bussel
Carl Gottlob Fiedler
Johann Matthias Hinck
Christopher (+) Mingel
Johann Henrich Philibahr
Johann Georg Van Berg
Johann Frantz Fuchs
Mathias (+) Ham
John W^m (+) Petri
Johann Gottfridt Fischer
Daniel Mesore
Johann Peter Köbrich
Johann Heinrich Thiele
Ernst Mengerling
Jno Henry (+) Bartram
Joseph (+) Remmler
Johann Carl Büttner
Christian Leuthe
Friderich Beüser
Herman (+) Feldich
Frietrich Brieff
John Lorentz (X) Temple
Johan Conrad Nasemann
Henry (+) Beck
Georg Wolf
Johan Henrich Dreyman

Adolph Gottfried Carl Rose
Johann Fridrich Rukuck
. . . . Regters
Christopher (+) Schlockmann
Philip (+) Keyser
Gerhard Henry (+) Nobel
Isaac (+) Levi
Georg Reyninger
Leonhard Hornung
William (+) Ubung
Johannes Gädecke
Hendrick Hilgerd
Johannes Brücher
Johann Jacob Engel
Johann Jacob Müller
Johan Jacob Bastian
Mathieu Falliéz
Johann Jacob Becker
Carl Van Nuwenhuys
Albertus Schilack
Jan Peietrs
Bartel (X) Metilmolske
Johann Emanuel Kloss
Friedrich Marcus Montelius
John Henry (X) Hupper
Jno Henry (+) Schwitgen
Johann David Mandeler

Jnº Chrisʳ (+++) Schultz

Godfrey Werner (+) Grimmel

John Nichˢ (+) Harms

John Bernᵈ (+) Hubner

Bruchardt Jung

Andreas Jung

Better Lösch

Heinrich Conrat Hyronimus Schultze

Antonius Henricus Ritter

Johann Christoffel Bosse

John Daniel (+) Weissmuth

Johann Gottfried Strietzel

Johann Gottfried Nestler

Wᵐ (+) Dollendorp

Jnº Henry (✕) Fratcher

Ernst Paul (+) Petri

Johann Carl Rosenkrantz

John (✕) Daman

John (+) Vanderhuyst

Jnº Henry (+) Kelman

Johan Peter Walter

Carl Enoch Schildbach

Jnº Tobias (+) Hess

Johann Friderich Beck

Johann Gottfried Neimrich

Martin Krohnmeyer

Jnº Christopher (✕) Baut

Mark (✕) Rolff

Francis (+) Van Bauke

Pieter Denye

Adolph (+) Unfug

Gottfried Vogel

Jnº (✕) Feig

Johan Conrad Brackmann

Theobald (+) Stephan

John Conrad (✕) Arnd

John Aug. (✕) Just

Frantz Mutschler

Valtin Christian Lehnig

Johannes (✕) Brown

Andrew (+) Waggoner

Johann Adam Schmidt

John Herman (+) Rodolph

Johann Jodocus Merck

Johann Christian Merck

Andreas Hampe

Casimir Leitz

Frantz Freischtze

Johann Christop Fasel

Tobias Böhnet

Ignatius Graffenperger

Johann Joachim Welsnack

Conrad Maurer

John Valentine (✕) Kinberg

Henry Fred. (✕) Riestner

Jnº Henry Christian (✕) Bremmer

Heinrich Wilhelm Busse

John (✕) Kirshner

Geo. (+) Shenk

Geo. Jnº (✕) Rauch

Andʷ (✕) Fahrencorn

[List 307 C] At Joshua Fisher & Son's Store, Philadelphia, the 18ᵗʰ of September, 1773.

Present: James Young, Esquire.

The Foreigners whose Names are underwritten, imported in the Ship Britannia, James Peter, Master, from Rotterdam, but last from Cowes, did this day take and subscribe the foregoing Oaths and Declarations in the usual Form. Consigned to Joshua Fisher & Sons. 150 in the List. 250 Freights.

Christof Ludi [?]

Daniel Gentes

Simon Schnuck

Geo. Adam (X) Vogelgesang

Gerg Miller

John (+) Grein

Johann Henrich Löhr

Paul (X) Motz

Johann Gerg Ehrendfried

Hennrich Somer

Johann Dieterrich Bönig

Hans Jörg Klein

Hans Joreg Weyl

Andrew (X) Löb

Jacob Ludi

Johannes Michael [?]

Peter (X) Eckel

Johann Fridrich Cammerlich

Johann Henrich Herbst

Johann Nickolaus Bastian

Christian Becker

Johannes Mertz

Johann Jacob Waiblinger

Anthony (+) Weaver

Philipp Oberthüer

Jacob Schauffler

Pether Conrath

Augusdin Hes

Hans Guckes [?]

Johann Peter Schott

Lorentz Schultz

Ludwig (X) Gerlinger

Traugott Leberecht Buhzer

Christian Leytich

Johan Georg Kramer

Jacob (ID) Degen

Johann Nickel Reuthnauer

Johann Philip Pflieger

Johan Jacob Beheling

Johann Martin Krammer

Johann Georg Kramer

Christian Schütz

Adam Ränninger

Johann Philippus Lück

Christoffell Orth

Johan Conrath Emich

Johann Adam Engert

Johann Conrad Netscher

Carl Andon Maas

Mich. (X) Runkel

Andreas Ott

Johan Daniel Roth

Joh. Georg Wenner

Johann Jeremias Bönnig

Johanes Aal

Herrmanus Schoeler

Danl Spies

Danl (Dan) Young

Michel Jung

Jacob Schott

Johannes Daub

Michael Ruff

Christian Noll

Johann Georg Gunckel

Johann Carl Wentzell

Martin Kramer

Ludwig Kramer

Johan Georg Huss

Georg Martin Eberhardt

Johann Baldasar Kramer

Johann Adam Kramer

Joseph (X) Schaak

Christoph Henckel

Johann Simon Linck

Johann Gorg Linck

Thomas Bauman

Johann Nickel Staudt

Johann Friederich Becker

Bernard (+) Weber

Philip (+) Runckel

Bernhardt Schmidt

Jacob Wenner

Jacob Wenner
Phillipp Bönnig
Jacob Neu
Stofel Neu
Johan Christian Fabritzius
William (X) Rockenbrod
Johann Wilh. Mertz [?]
Johann Michael Kirschbaum
Gottlieb Mayer
Hans Adam (X) Weiss
Michel (X) Haas
Peter (X) Haas
Johan Michel Franck
Hans Geo. (X) Stettelbauer
John Mich. (X) Ellig
Michel Jung
Jacob Schneider
Wilhelm Voltz
Johann Georg Herschler

Jacob Heintz
Jacob (X) Degen
Andres Furch
Jacob Schweitzer
Conrad Voltz
Georg Henrich Geck
Frans (+) Smith
Henry (+) Erb
Adam Schmel
Johan Michel Füscher
Andreas Gröner
Daniel Schütz
Johann Gerg Reiner
Adam Schneider
Jacob (X) Schneider
Johann Michael Thome
Michel Kieffer
Michael Poth

[List 308 C] At the Mayor's Office at Philadelphia, the 21ˢᵗ September, 1773.

Present: John Gibson, Mayor of the sᵈ City.

The Foreigners whose Names are hereunto subscribed, imported in the Ship Catharine, James Sutton, Commander, from London, did this day take & subscribe the foregoing Oaths and Declarations in the usual Form. In yᵉ List 20. Consigned to Messʳˢ Keppele & Steinmetz.

Johann Schrecka
Jac. Lud. Videbant
Georg Lufft
Conrad Trippel
Hinrich Andreas Meyer
Johann Heinrich Becker
Johannes Sander

Phillipp Wild
Casimir Delbig
Christian Kühn
Michael Hobach
Johannes Klein
Görg Lauerr
Martin Eberhard

[List 309 C] At Mʳ Robert Ritchies Store at Philadelphia, September 27ᵗʰ 1773.

Present: James Young, Esquire.

The Foreigners whose Names are underwritten, imported in the Ship Union, [Andrew] Bryson, Master, from Rotterdam but last from Portsmouth, did this day take & subscribe the foregoing Oaths and Declarations in the usual Form. Consigned to Mr Robert Ritchie (paid). 107 in the List. 247 Freights.

Christophel Beinn
Balthasar Hammen
Johannes Brannd
Johann Peter Schiaurer
Johannes Wickel
Jn° (+++) Gennett
Jno Philb. (+) Dieffebach
Jn° Peter (F) Fuchs
Jn° Henry (X) Dambeller
Johannes Nickel Lenhart
Ludwig Bachmann
Georg Philip Gruber
Dangel Bernhard
Vallenthin Götz
Christgan Götz
Johann Jacob Hörner
Geo. Adam (X) Wendel
Geo. (X) Shrier
Jn° Geo (X) Stoertzemeyer
Jn° Adam (X) Zeits
Jacob (+) Smith
Jn° Mich^s (X) Clements
Johannes Roscher
Adolph Schutz
Johann Zacharias Rexrodt [?]
Johinrich Bauch
Johann Lenhardt Ihrig
Johannes Baus
Philips Andes Schadt
Johan Madäs Flach
Joh. Jacob Aurandt
Johann Philipp Dönges
Johann Valtin Stegmüller
Johannes Kiffer

Jn° (X) Zimmerman
Johannes Adler
Jn° Adam (K) Krausser
Johannes Spammann
Jacob Arnoldt
Niclaus Stier
Henrich Valten Storger
Johan Peter Schmid
Johann Filib Hauck
Ludwig Schenckel
Johann Adam Reichert
Jn° Geo. (+) Holtzshooe
Hannes Schmidt
Philipps Daniel Gräff
Jn° Geo. (X) Sheffer
Jacob Nicolaus Firnhaber
Johannes Firnhaber
Andres Friederich Schwentzel
Johan Georg Leonhardt
Christian Beck
Friedrich Grames
Johann Leonhard Göllman
Johan Peter Stöhr
Nicklaus Bachrodt
Jacob von Lahnen
Johann Gottlieb Mezger
Andreas Fischer
Wilhelm Spies
Johann Henrich Weber
Johann Philipp Gräber
Johannes Pfeiffer
Herrman Spies
Johann Henrich Bräusser
Philipp Peter Gruber

Johann Georg Keilhauer
Johann Joachim Gruber
Johann Adam Hartman
Willhelm Busch
Jn° Leon^d (×) Roedel
Jn° Geo (×) Erig
Johan Migel Horrn
J. Bourquin
Johannes Batz
Conrad Mardorf
Johann Nickel Schmaus
C. Varlet
Jn° (×) Egel
Jn° Geo. (×) Egel

Jn° (+) Hartman
Johannes Herstein
Geo. (×) Hartman
Jacob Garte
Adam Rosmeissel
Willhelm Nickel
Jn° Conrad (×) Riebel
Jn° Jost (×) Leydecker
Johann Jacob Hoof
Johann Jost Lenhard
Georg Adam Bückel
Johannes Schäffer
Johann Willhelm Krüger
Johannes Wilheiser

[List 310 C] At Wicacoa, this 1st of October, 1773.
Present: Thomas Willing, Esquire.

The Foreigners whose Names are underwritten, imported in the Ship Hope, George Johnston, Master, from Rotterdam but last from Cowes, did this day take and subscribe the foregoing Oaths and Declarations in the usual Form. Consigned to Messrs Willing & Morris, 94 in the List. paid £7.1.0.

Andreas Dengler
Johann Peter Weber
Matthias (×) Wall
Johann Jost Busch
Johann Henrich Busch
Matthias (+) Wexler
Jonas Dottinger
Jn. Chris^n (+) Good
Nicolaus Henrich Stephan
Johannes Wilhelm Carle
Johann Jost Bruch
Johan Carl Mattis
Henry (+) Steinbrink
Michel Stumpf
Carl Ferdinand Conrad
Johann Michael Conrad
David Niess
Petter (+++) Soast

Jn° (+) Carr
Christian (+) Kebelring
Johan Bernhardt Rau
Mich^l (+) Bauman
Johann Michel Oberdorff
Andterreas Oberdorff
Johann Friederich Sasmanshausen
Yost (×) Oldhouse
Krafft Weyand
Conrad (+) Gerhard
Johann Wilhelm Semann
Fred. (+) Völckel
Henry (+) Meyer
Johannes Hess
Johann Jeremias Ballenberger
Johann Wilhelm Eckhart
Görg Wunderlich
Johannes Hesse

Johann Christoph Thiel

Filib Adam (×) Schuck

Johan Lorentz Dihm

Johann Michael Frisch

Johan Henrich Dörn

Johan Conrad Jung

Frann Schmit

Johann Ludwig Santz

Andreas Adam Lutz

Jost Velckel

Johan Friedrich Velckel

Philipp Isemann

Johann Michel Seydel

Johann Georg Seidel

Johann Henrich Sasmanshaus

Friederich Röser

Johan Henrich Klein

Henry (×) Miller

Johann Ludwig Affleber

Johannes Strackbein

Leonhadt Schmidt

Jacob Schlatter

[List 311 C] At Dowers & Yorkes Rigging Loft, Philad[a] 22[d] October, 1773.

Present: James Humphreys, Esquire.

The Foreigners whose Names are underwritten, imported in the Ship Charming Molly, Robert Gill, Master, from Rotterdam but last from Portsmouth, did this day take and subscribe the foregoing Oaths & Declarations in the usual Form. Consigned to Messrs Sam[l] Howell & Sons (paid). 96 in the List.

Johan Martin Päff

Johan Hentery Hensse

Christian (+) Ernst

Nicola (+) Chaillot

Han Adam (+) Weitzel

Johan Michael Fuchs

Joh. Conrad Leonhard

Johann Filli[b] Berg

Valentine (×) Chorist

Johannes Dietz

Thomas Krebs

Casimir May

Johann Henrich Freytag

Johannes (×) Stekkel

Frierich Wilh[el]m

Johannes Lechleitner

Johan Ludwig Schwens

Pierre Milo

Johan Christen Letten

Johann Eberhart Ohl

Johan Jost Blecher

Johan Henrich Wentzel

Matthias (+) Astimer

Joseph Friedrich Honstein

Engelbert (×) Classen

Antreas Emmrich

Johann Pfatteich

Johann Daniel Bonn

Jacob (×) Elgart

Henry (+) Daybener

. . . . Baltzel

Feliep Scherer

Christian (+) Schonefield

Nicholas (+) Zutheimer

Daniel Weibel

Eberhard (×) Meyer

J. B. DuBret

Joseph (+) Cauffman

Johann Friedrich Prauel

Johann Fridrich Vogel

Caspar (+) Gysinger
Johan David Steinmann
Fred. (+) Dietrich
Johann Georg Vogel
Hendrich Kleyn
Frid. Müller
Georg (✕) Reichart
Caspar Adam
Johann Petter Geyer
Johannes (✕) Hartman

Johann Adam Lang
Johannes Koch
Joh. Pet. (✕) Ermolt
Carl Heinrich Hartig
Christian Lambert
Bernhard Baur
Jacob Graff
Johann Georg Müller
Johann Georg Theys
Arns (+) Shullicus

[List 312 C] At John Appowen's Sail Loft at Philadᵃ 25ᵗʰ October, 1773.

Present: James Young, Esquire.

The Foreigners whose Names are underwritten, imported in the Ship Crawford, Charles Smith, Master, from Rotterdam but last from Cowes, did this day take and subscribe the foregoing Oaths and Declarations in the usual Form. Consigned to Messʳˢ Willing & Morris. 99 in the List. paid £7.8.6.

Johann Heinrich Dittman
Johann Jost Strackbein
Johannes Buch
Christian Mertel
Johann Conrath Triewitz
Jacob Trewitz
Johann Jost Mätz
Johan (✕) Schlichter
Johannes Peter Stahl
Jnᵒ Mathˢ (✕) Weber
Johannes Henrich Kiel
Johann Friedrig Mannalther
Johan Henrich Achen
Wilhelm Schneyder
Jnᵒ Bap. (✕) Nonn
Johann Carl Rentzheimer
Andreas Zahnle
Jnᵒ Geo. (✕) Steiner
Carl Christian Friedrich List
Johannes Kleppert
Johan Müller

Hennrich Ober
Johannes Geistweit
Johann Henrich Graff
Johann Geörg Birkelbach
Johann George Berckelbach
Jacob Henrich Bast
Johann Daniel Hesz
Johann Nickel Thomas
Johann Georg Rauhman
Johann Fillip Kress
Johann Henrich Schumacher
John Siegesmund Stedtekorn
Killian Heller
Jnᵒ Wᵐ (✕) Humer
Gorg Philib Zissler
Johann Fürst [?]
David (✕) Reich
Daniel Meyer
Johannes Diebler
Christⁿ (✕) Meyer
Adam Michel

Ludwig Güthing

Matthias Höffer

Jnº Lud. (✕) Becker

Johann Theis Sieffner

Jan Peter Rostweiler

Wilhelm Schöler

Michel Müller

Johannes Pedermand

Johann Henrich Dörner

Johann Jorg Schneider

Johann Heinrich Looss

Henry (✕) Brunt

Geo. (+) Lebank

Jnº (✕) Fisher

Hans Henrich Scheirer

Johan Jacob Schweissfurth

Wilhelm Walther

Johan Henrich Hoffman

Johannes Demandt

Johann Daniel Schweitzer

Jnº Geo. (✕) Hartman

Adam Kamm

Andereas Hild

Joachim Stremmel

[List 313 C] At the Mayor's Office at Philadelphia, the 23ᵈ of November, 1773.

Present: William Fisher, Esquire, Mayor.

The Foreigners whose Names are underwritten, imported in the Snow Neptune, Thomas Edward Wallace, Master, did this day take and subscribe the foregoing Oaths and Declarations (except the Oath of Abjuration) in the usual Form. Consigned to John Wilcocks (paid)

Joseph Lefran

Charles (✕) Capell

Wᵐ (✕) Black

Anthony (+) Sinclair

Joseph Martin

[List 314 C] At the Mayor's Office at Philadelphia, the 24ᵗʰ of November, 1773.

Present: William Fisher, Esquire, Mayor.

The Foreigners whose Names are underwritten, imported in the Ship Fame, James Duncan, Master, from Lisbon, did this day take and shbscribe the foregoing Oaths and declarations in the usual Form. Consigned to Mʳˢ Coxe & Furman (paid).

Geo. (✕) Ravere

John (+) Martine

Danˡ (+) Shapue

[List 315 C] At the Mayor's Office at Philadelphia, the 7ᵗʰ of December, 1773.

Present: William Fisher, Esquire, Mayor.

The Foreigners whose Names are underwritten, imported

in the Clementina, Patrick Brown, Master, from Lisbon, did this day take and subscribe the foregoing Oaths & declarations in the usual form. Consigned to M^r Jn° Ross & W^m McMutrie (paid).

Francis (+) Villeneave	Francis (×) Duchand
François Pechenet	Maro Seroni
John (+) Pesser	Joseph Louvat
Charles Zemmer	

[List 316 C] At the House of Peter Miller, Esquire, in the City of Philadelphia, the eighth Day of December, 1773.
Present: Peter Miller, Esqr.
The Foreigners whose Names are under written, imported in the Ship Montague, Wm. Pickels, Commander, from London, did this day take and subscribe the usual Qualifications. Consigned to Joshua Fisher & Sons. In the List 27.

John Henry (+) Lau	Traugott Gottfried Mäyen
Johann Friederich Pieckert	Georg Ludwig Helmold
Christian Hallitschke	Mathias Conrad
Joh. Wendel Andreas	Anthon Henrich Gnäscheler
Jacob Fürst	Friederich Oberle
Friedrig Waltz	Johann Adam Schanckweiler
Peter Arendt	Joachim Neubauer
Joh. Ludewig	Joseph Walcker
Phillippe Engerost	Joseph Wagner
Jacob Kissner	Johan Jeorg Speiser
Johan Adam Handel	Joh. Matthey
Johan Heinrich Krauel	Johannes Finseler
Joachim Friederich Zinckwintz	Johann Christian Duncker

[List 317 C] At the House of Peter Miller, Esqr, at Philadelphia, the 21st June, 1774.
Present: The said Peter Miller, Esqr.
The Foreigners whose Names are underwritten, imported in the Brigantine Nancy, Thomas Armstrong, Master, from Hamburgh, did this day take and subscribe the foregoing Oaths & Declarations in the usual Form. Consigned to John Jones &c. (paid 10/6)

Christopher (X) Fure   Carl Friederich Müller
Joseph Lorentz Herrmann   Cornelis Fues
Herman (X) Shoeman   Johann Fred. (+) Matz
Joh. Math. Bauer

[List 318 C] Snow Sally, Cap^n Stephan Jones, arrived at Philad^a the 15th August 1774. Consigned to Messrs Mease & Callents, the foll^g Foreigners arrived, viz. (paid 12/)

Conrad (+) Bernard   John (+) Dickel
Conrad (+) Seifert   John Geor[g] ( ) Gesel
Mich^l (+) Liligenthal   Jno W^m ( ) Sauter
John (+) Ulrich   John ( ) Sauter

[List 319 C] At the Office of Peter Miller, Esqr, at Philadelphia, the 29th September, 1774.
Present: The said Peter Miller, Esqr.

The Foreigners whose Names are underwritten, imported in the Ship Charming Molly, Robert Gill, Master, from London, did this day take and Subscribe the foregoing Oaths and Declarations in the Usual Form. Consigned to Saml Howell. (paid £1.2.6) 15 in the List.

Henrich Küntzel   Peter Stephan
Georg Jacob Weiss   Georg Fridrich Frick
Laurens Frost   Johann Georg Schneegantz
Georg Paulus Merckle   Johannes Schwenck
Christian Langspech   Johann Georg Fritzlen
Christianus Heyll   Johann Heinrich Moser
Carl Christoph Nicht   Johann Ludwig Bethmann

[List 320 C] At the Store of Mr Henry Neill, at Philadelphia, the 30th Sept. 1774.
Present: Peter Miller, Esqr.

The foreigners whose Names are underwritten, Imported in the Ship Union, Andrew Bryson, Master, from Rotterdam but last from Portsmouth, in England, did this Day take and Subscribe the foregoing Oaths and Declarations in the Usual Form. In the List 156. Consigned to Mr Robert Ritchie. (paid £11.14.0.)

Casper (×) Nuyne

Andrew (+) Schneynow

Johann Wilhelm Müller

George (+) Rummell

Johann Martin Schweickart

Hennrich Dörr

Matthias Wild

Carl Purpur

Johannes Fuchs

Johann Anthon Rühl

Johannes Heimbach

Henrich Frick

Adam Seibert

Nicklas Grauss

Hartman (×) Wink

Bernard (×) Schwing

Phillipp Jung

Abraham Stoffel Jacoby

Philipp Klein

Michael Klein

Jost Leibinger

Caspar Steinmetz

Henrich Steinmetz

Carl Steinmetz

Johannes Hock

Jacob Boss

Carl Böhringer

Michael Müller

Adam (+) Stam

Friedrich Kölhoffer

Adam Koeningsfeld

Philipp Thiebaut

Laux Kochges

Jean Bartholmeus Ney

Johan Georg Gottfriedt

Johann Adam Specht

Philipp Müller

Jacob Eyler

Christian Rossen

Jost Spengler

Alexander Otto

Peter Spruchmann

Nicklas Fitincher

Johann Zimerman

Peter Kuner

Niclaus Schweppenhaüser

Leonhart Opp

Philips Jacob Wagner

Friedrich Gantz

Nicholas (×) Boyer

Vallenthin Beyer

Henrich Adam Waltman

Samuell Schenck

Johan Detweiller

Gotthold Frid. Enslin

Fabian Kurtz

Beter Schimmel

Johannes Schaum

. . . . Rüttiger

Johann Friedrich Strauch

Jacob Voltz

Chri[st]ian Wittmer

Johan Adam Schlott

Johannes Stofflet

Friederich Bergman

Friedrich Weyler

Johann Carl Rentzheimer

Peter (×) Schwabeland

Matheis Feiring

Johann Adam Friederich

Johann Gottfr. Paul Zimmerman

Friederich Bayer

Dangel Frickert

Martin Weimer

Michael David Esch

Chris. Wilh. Ruthardt

Johannes Becker

Christob Staufer

Melchior Wickert

Nicol Sutor

Peter (×) Wallman

Johann Georg Bauer

Valentin Göttert
Petter Sintz
Johann Stadtler
Johann Nicolahr
Henrich Schwing
Johann Adam Steinbach
Johann Adam Müller
Johann Nicolaus Quast
Jacob Leibenzeter
Johann Adam Leber
Friedrich Hehl
Carl Christian Louis
Nicholas (+) Guit
Joseph Fötsch
Albreck (✕) Webher
Ludwich (O) Schwabeland
Christian (✕) Schwabeland
Jacob (✕) Leher
Ludwick (✕) Axe
Johann Petter Kurtz
Daniel (✕) Wolff
John Georg (+) Baltz
Johann Conrad Eiselen
George(++) Eckhart
John George (+) Rutter

Johann Jacob Roth
Michael (+) Shilling
Johann Jacob Medart
Jacob Gucker
Christoph Herbster
Heinrich Engelfried
Friderich Freytag
Fridrich Schaumenkessel
Johann Daniel Nieler
Martin Schwartz
Johan Christian Wilms *
Johann Jacob Dieterle
Casper (+) Uhl
Johann Adam Stock
Frederick (✕) Beyerle
Georg Jacob Häussler
Johans Carolus
Georg Adam Marggrander
Christian Glaufliegel
Erhardt Freytag
Leon^d Croneman
Johannes Foltz
Johann Georg Müller
Israel Leypole
Michäll Miller

[List 321 C] At the Mayor's Office, Philadelphia 29th October, 1774.

Present: Samuel Rhoads, Esquire, Mayor.

The Foreigners whose Names are underwritten, imported in the Snow Patty & Peggy, Robert Hardie, Master, from Lisbon, did this day take & Subscribe the foregoing Oaths & Declarations in the usual Form. Consigned to Duncan & Co. (paid 21/) 14 in the List.

Joas (+) Moraubley
Jons (✕) Contono
Jabryel Hequedas
Manuel (✕) Rodrigue

Franco Barnexa
Fransisco Pabane
Joas (+) Cameli
Franc^s (✕) Cloter

* A Reformed minister, who preached in Lancaster County.

Hipolito (+) Poncelly   Juan (+) Domingo
Franco Poz   Juan Kinanso

[List 322 C] At the Court House, Philadelphia, 31ˢᵗ October, 1774.
Present: Peter Miller, Esquire.

The Foreigners whose Names are underwritten, imported in the Ship Sally, John Osmond, Master, from Rotterdam but last from Cowes, did this day take and subscribe the foregoing Oaths and Declarations in the usual form. Consigned to Samuel Howell. 52 in the List (paid £3.18.0)

Christian Müller   Peter Löwenberg
Christian Ehmig   Philipp Löwenberg
Johann Maximilian Hahn   Friederich Löwenberg
Hans Keller   Dieboldt Klein
Ludwig Seltz   Willhelm Bromer
Andreas Bühler   Peter Bartholomi
Johann Jacob Welcker   Carl Bartholomae
Johann Jacob Welcker   Michael Barth[ol]omä
Casber Miller   Georg Schmaltzridt
Friedrich Mayer   Joh. Paul Thomas Teichgräber
Peter Köhler   Lutwig Fichter
Joseph (×) Kem   Johann Conrad Scheidt
Jacob Stoff   Johannes Künsinger
Johann Peter Cronenberger   Johannes Schäffer
Georg Katz   Friederich Cronenberger
Baltasar Eberharth   Daniel Zittel
Geo. (×) Habel   Wilhelm Wenner
Jnᵒ Henry (×) Klein   Joel Klein
Johann Philip Weber   Anthony (×) Weaver
Johann Jacob Sunckel   Johan Georg Burckhardt
Christoph Friebele   Christian Laros
Christian Schwenck   Conrad Bindenberger
Henrich Oberkircher   Jacob Mussgenug
Christianus Rommel   Pr. Maison
Adam Siegel

[List 323 C] At the Store of Mʳ Henry Keppele, Junʳ, in the City of Philadelphia, the 16ᵗʰ Day of January, 1775.
Present: Peter Miller, Esquire.

The Foreigners whose Names are here underwritten, imported in the Ship Catherine, commanded by John Baron, from London, have this Day taken and subscribed the forgoing Oaths and Declarations. Consigned to Messrs Keppele & Stonemetz. In the List Seven.

Johann Georg Friederich Wagner   Johan Adam
Gaspar Beaufort   Thomas Klenée
Johan Jacob Holtzer   David Zabern
Joachim Jacob Brandt

[List 324 C] At the Court House Philadelphia, the 9th of October, 1775.

Present: Samuel Powel, Esquire, Mayor.

The Foreigners whose Names are underwritten, imported in the Ship King of Prussia, William Potts, Master, from Rotterdam but last from Falmouth, did this Day take and subscribe the foregoing Oaths and Declarations in the usual Form. (Consigned to Jacob Viney) (paid by Jacob Viney £5.8.0, the 17th October 1775). (In the List 72).

Johann Fridrich Huy   Johann Paul Blin
Ludwig Eller   Thomas Rentzheimer
Georg Conrad Busch   Johannes Rentzheimer
Conradt Tresenreuther   Johannes Eckenberger
Gerge Eberhardt   Johann Nickel Wendeling
Jacob Müller   Johann Nickel Meyer
Nicolaus Sandmeier   Johann Friedrich Meyer
Johann Gorg Weyell   Vallentin Höh
Johannes Oberscheimer   Nicholas (X) Rudy
Johann Wilhelm Schilack   Niclaus Groll
Johann Georg Linns   Henricus Denner
Johan Kilian Boos   Joh. Jacob Schmidt
Johann Michael Trumpf   Johannes Kriedelbach
Jacob Kohlman   Matthäs Köhler
Johann Phillip Kohlman   Leonhard Götz
Johann David Weber   Carl Ritter
Phillip Weber   Johannes Fanth
Johann Michael Hans   Johan Valdin Mündel
Johann Peter Geissheiner   Stephanus Spach
Johann Sigwalt   Michel Kromer

Carl Eller
John (+) Seiss
Jost Alstatt
Nickollaus Zimmer
Nicolaus Borman
Casper Nickel
Philliebs Peter Müller
Johann Ernst Kessler
Johann Herrman
Johann Jacob Knabenschu
Christian Weissbach
Xtian Vätter
Jacob Vätter
Jacob Bintzel

Friederich Schönholtz
Conrad Becker
Jacob Jost
Thiels (×) Zerfas
Georg Friderich Gravan
Johann Jacob Grawan
Johan Simon Schlarp
Nicol Neufang
Johannes Sähler
Peter Horbach
Paul Sturmfels
Ludwig (×) Weiss
Jacob Friedrich Grammer
Christian Gottlieb Willert

APPENDIX I

[List 30 A] [Captain's List of the passengers imported in the Ship Elizabeth, Captain Edward Lee. Qualified Aug. 27, 1733].*

MENS NAMES	AGES	MENS NAMES	AGES
Johanes Kesnoser, farmer	40	Simon Lindor	53
Philip Sever, tailor	23	Simon Lindor, Jr.	16
Johanes Moon, farmer	33	Friedrich Oneself, weaver	24
Mical Cowell, farmer	32	Michael Fabor, fiddler	35
Johan Josep Fuler,	23	Andrew Pogener, fiddler	34
Johan Jereck Petery,		Steven Lowman, bone	
weaver	27	maker	31
Johan Henrick Shirt,		Hance Jerech Porger,	
farmer	22	cooper	25
Conrat Shott, farmer	50	Jacob Bunett, farmer	32
Philip Foust, weaver	30	Wolf Con. Milor	41
Micoll Rut, weaver	56	Simon Sherman, sadler	49
John Henrich Tinick,		Johanes Knoll, farmer	29
joiner	33	Jacob Hubler, farmer	30
Coblin Hetrick, farmer	40	France Wice, smith	27
Henrich Stance, shoemaker	39	Tabell Troud, smith	27
Hance Peter Hofman,		Hance Martin Troud,	
farmer	28	farmer	56
Johanes Jong, shoemaker	20	Johan Henrich Ley, miller	28
Johan Peter Foust, farmer	40	Jerrick Oare, farmer	51
Philip Foust, farmer	20	Johanes Henrich Oare	19
Jacob Gibe, farmer	34	Jacob Sorver, carpenter	56
Olrich Shugh, farmer	48	Jacob Sorver, carpenter	26
John Jacob Shugh	20	Rodelph Sorver, carpenter	21
Johanes Lutts, weaver	55	Jacob Houswet, weaver	34
Mathias Whitman, farmer	56	Jacob Hendrich, farmer	28
Mathew Whiteman, farmer	34	Johan Henrich Tabas,	
Henrich Still	60	farmer	27

* This list came to light after list 30 A was in print. As it was undated, it was not identified until the index of names had been prepared,

MENS NAMES	AGES
Nicklos Slay, farmer	24
Jacob Shittel	22
Philip Smith, wagoner	33
Hance Jerick Nort	45
Jacob Tillingor, farmer	33
Andries Clipsadell, butcher	22
Jerick Hendrick March, shoemaker	20
Johan Olrich Cooll, joiner	30
John Fagley, weaver	28
Hinrich Stiner, weaver	23
Michell Rinehed, farmer	23
Mickell Mikt, farmer	54
Hance Jacob Mikt	20

WOMENS NAMES	AGES
Kertroudt Kesnoser	50
Marilos Honing	20
Margret Moon	44
Ann Eliza Cowell	23
Savena Cowell	24
Anna Catrina Shott	49
Anna Clara Shott	16
Anna Catrina Foust	21
Anna Margret Rut	56
Anna Margret Tinick	36
Elizabeth Hetrick	35
Maria Stance	31
Anna Eliza Foust	40
Catrina Gibe	34
Ann Eliza Shugh	48
Ever Eliza Shugh	17
Margret Luts	38
Maria Catrina Whitman	38
Margret Whiteman	30
Margret Lindor	39
Catrina Lindor	17
Sarah Fabor	33
Catrina Pogener	37
Mary Bunett	32

WOMENS NAMES	AGES
Margret Milor	53
Susanna Stoning	27
Catrina Sherman	40
Marilis Sherman	22
Maria Sherman	19
Ann Mary Knoll	26
Eliza Bovern	22
Anna Barbara Hubler	25
Barbara Wice	20
Anna Crate Troud	27
Cughlick Troud	52
Marg. Apell. Troud	24
Eliza Lee	18
Eliza Oare	46
Fronegh Sorver	54
Barbara Sorver	23
Maria Houswett	34
Elizabeth Shittell	21
Dorothy Smith	30
Maria Barbara Nort	43
Maria Kret Nort	18
Maria Barbra Tillingor	28
Solmey Cooll	30
Anna Barbara Fagly	26
Catrina Rinehed	22
Anna Mikt	46

CHILDRENS NAMES	AGES
Conreet Kesnoser	14
Johan Yerck Kesnoser	12
Anna Catrina Honing, dead	5
Maria Moon	10
Matiles Moon	8
Vernor Moon	6
Conen Lutwick Moon	3½
Anna Catrina Cowell, dead	3½
Conreet Cowell, dead	3½
Conhenas Shott	9
John Jacob Foust	4
John Adam Foust	2

CHILDRENS NAMES	AGES	CHILDRENS NAMES	AGES
John Hendrick Foust	0½	Hance Jerck Lindor	3¾
Anna Barbara Tinick	8	Babor Fabor	4½
Michel Tinick, dead	5	Michal Fabor	2
Anna Margaret Tinick,		Johan Tobias Pogener	3
dead	1½	Susanna Bunett, dead	4
John Onst Hetrick	17	Christina Bunett, dead	2
William Hetrick	10	Margret Bunett	8
Catrina Hetrick	8½	Johan Simon Bunett	0¾
Johan Henrick Hetrick	2	Jacob Milor	17
Anna Margret Hetrick,		Jerick Sherman	17
dead	3	Catrine Sherman	13
Anna Maria Stance	11	Philip Sherman	6½
Maria Catrina Stance	7	Daniel Sherman, dead	3
Maria Dorotea Stance	4	Elizabeth Knoll	3¾
Hance Jacob Stance	1½	Margaret Knoll	1½
Micol Foust	13	Anna Hubler	3½
Johanes Foust	11	Anna Maria Hubler	2¼
Johan Peter Foust	9	Frances Hubler	0¼
Ann Eliz. Foust	5	Johanes Troud	1½
Matelina Foust, dead	3	Johan Henrick Ley	13
Johan Hendrick Foust	2	Barbara Houswett	13⅓
Andries Gibe	12	Cradell Houswett	10
Micoll Gibe	9	Maria Houswett	8
Marlina Gibe	4½	Anna Maria Houswett,	
Elizabeth Gibe	2	dead,	4½
Anna Eliz. Shugh	13	Caspar Houswett, dead	2
Hance Martin Luts	11	Jacob Houswett, dead	0¼
Catrina Luts	9	Anna Lies Houswett	8½
Elizabeth Luts, dead	2	Philip Smith, dead	0¾
Mariradell Luts	4	Tobias Nort	11
Johanes Whitman	15	Lavanna Nort	10
Eliza Whitman	13¾	Johan Fredrick Tillingor	8
Christoffer Whiteman	8	Mathies Cooll	9
Mathias Whiteman	6	Maria Cooll	7
Wendell Whiteman	3½	[Totals: 61 men, 50 women, 81	
Elizabeth Whiteman, dead	2	children, of whom 16 dead, 192	
Elizabeth Lindor	11	names, 176 living passengers]	
Larance Lindor	8		

APPENDIX II

SUMMARY OF SHIPS AND PASSENGERS

DATES	SHIPS	A	B	C	TOTALS
		LISTS			
1. 1727, Sep. 18,	William & Sarah	109	51	..	400
2. 1727, Sep. 27,	James Goodwill	54	50	..	200
3. 1727, Sep. 30,	Molly	72	61	..	300
4. 1727, Oct. 2,	Adventure	55	31	..	140
5. 1727, Oct. 16,	Friendship	52	38	..	200
6. 1728, Aug. 23,	Mortonhouse	80	69	..	205
7. 1728, Sep. 4,	Albany	31	29	..	100
8. 1728, Sep. 11,	James Goodwill	42	41	..	90
9. 1729, Aug. 19,	Mortonhouse	122	62	62	180
10. 1729, Sep. 15,	Allen	127	53	53	126
11. 1730, Aug. 29,	Thistle	76	74	73	260
12. 1730, Sep. 5,	Alexander & Ann	46	46	46	130
13. 1730, Nov. 30,	Joyce	57	24	24	57
14. 1731, Aug. 16,	Samuel	109	39	39	109
15. 1731, Sep. 10,	Pennsyl. Merchant	172	57	57	175
16. 1731, Sep. 21,	Britannia	269	104	104	269
17. 1731, Oct. 14,	Lowther	78	33	33	78
18. 1732, May 15,	Norris	..	13	13	..
19. 1732, Aug. 11,	Samuel	270	106	106	270
20. 1732, Sep. 11,	Pennsyl. Merchant	171	69	70	171
21. 1732, Sep. 19,	Johnson	306	111	111	306
22. 1732, Sep. 21,	Plaisance	190	72	72	190
23. 1732, Sep. 23,	Adventure	147	58	57	147
24. 1732, Sep. 25,	Loyal Judith	120	115	115	...
25. 1732, Sep. 26,	Mary	69	61	61	191
26. 1732, Sep. 30,	Dragon	70	55	55	185
27. 1732, Oct. 11,	Pleasant	57	42	42	...
28. 1732, Oct. 17,	John & William	169	60	60	169
29. 1733, Aug. 17,	Samuel	292	89	89	292
30. 1733, Aug. 27,	Elizabeth	62	58	58	172
31. 1733, Aug. 28,	Hope	230	84	84	230

DATES	SHIPS	LISTS			TOTALS
		A	B	C	
32. 1733, Sep. 18,	Pennsyl. Merchant	192	67	67	192
33. 1733, Sep. 28,	Richard & Elizabeth	138	43	43	138
34. 1733, Sep. 29,	Mary	171	54	54	171
35. 1733, Oct. 11,	Charming Betty	63	15	15	63
36. 1734, Sep. 12,	St. Andrew	261	83	83	261
37. 1734, Sep. 23,	Hope	150	49	49	150
38. 1735, May 29,	Mercury	185	54	54	185
39. 1735, June 28,	Mary	39	13	13	39
40. 1735, Aug. 26,	Oliver	44	18	18	44
41. 1736, Sep. 1,	Harle	207	151	151	388
42. 1736, Sep. 16,	Princess Augusta	120	112	112	330
43. 1736, Oct. 19,	John	...	37	37	...
44. 1737, Aug. 30,	Samuel	109	108	108	...
45. 1737, Sep. 10,	Molly	31	31	31	...
46. 1737, Sep. 24,	Virtuous Grace	76	75	75	...
47. 1737, Sep. 26,	St. Andrew	142	139	139	...
48. 1737, Oct. 5,	Townshend	78	75	75	231
49. 1737, Oct. 8,	Charming Nancy	249	109	109	249
50. 1737, Oct. 31,	William	70	67	67	180
51. 1738, July 27,	Catharine	..	7	8	..
52. 1738. Sep. 5,	Winter Galley	139	140	140	252
53. 1738, Sep. 9,	Glasgow	120	112	112	349
54. 1738, Sep. 9,	Two Sisters	110	40	35	110
55. 1738, Sep. 11,	Robert & Alice	106	106	106	159
56. 1738, Sep. 16,	Queen Elizabeth	104	104	103	324
57. 1738, Sep. 19,	Thistle	95	95	95	...
58. 1738, Sep. 20,	Friendship	87	87	87	282
59. 1738, Sep. 20,	Nancy	74	48	48	...
60. 1738, Oct. 12,	Fox	47	31	31	76
61. 1738, Oct. 25,	Davy	94	40	40	141
62. 1738, Oct. 27,	St. Andrew	119	78	78	...
63. 1738, Oct. 28,	Thistle	141	42	42	141
64. 1738, Oct. 30,	Elizabeth	43	41	41	70
65. 1738, Nov. 9,	Charming Nancy	65	64	64	...
66. 1738, Dec. 6,	Enterprise	31	30	30	...
67. 1739, Jan. 8,	London	21	22	21	...
68. 1739, Feb. 7,	Jamaica	89	89	89	...
69. 1739, Aug. 27,	Samuel	111	110	111	...
70. 1739, Aug. 27,	Betsie	61	60	60	...

DATES	SHIPS	LISTS			TOTALS
		A	B	C	
71. 1739, Sep. 3,	Robert & Alice	78	78	78	218
72. 1739, Sep. 3,	Friendship	58	58	58	...
73. 1739, Sep. 3,	Loyal Judith	88	87	88	...
74. 1739, Dec. 11,	Lydia	24	23	23	...
75. 1740, Sep. 23,	Friendship	49	..	38	...
76. 1740, Sep. 27,	Lydia	71	62	63	...
77. 1740, Sep. 30,	Samuel & Elizabeth	56	55	56	84
78. 1740, Nov. 25,	Loyal Judith	95	89	90	...
79. 1740, Dec. 3,	Robert & Alice	64	58	58	...
80. 1740, Dec. 3,	Samuel	71	56	56	...
81. 1741, May 30,	Francis & Ann	15	13	13	...
82. 1741, Sep. 23,	Marlborough	72	71	72	...
83. 1741, Sep. 26,	St. Mark	101	99	98	...
84. 1741, Sep. 29,	Lydia	71	70	71	108
85. 1741, Oct. 2,	St. Andrew	103	60	60	262
86. 1741, Oct. 12,	Friendship	67	55	54	106
87. 1741, Oct. 16,	Molly	76	74	72	...
88. 1741, Oct. 26,	Snow Molly	47	35	36	76
89. 1741, Nov. 7,	Thane of Fife	21	19	19	...
90. 1741, Nov. 20,	Europa	65	46	46	...
91. 1742, May 28,	Catharine	56	28	28	...
92. 1742, Aug. 25,	Mary	..	..	29	...
93. 1742, Sep. 3,	Loyal Judith	90	86	86	...
94. 1742, Sep. 21,	Francis & Elizabeth	..	50	142	223½
95. 1742, Sep. 24,	Robert & Alice	..	..	75	...
96. 1743, Aug. 30,	Francis & Elizabeth	89	73	73	...
97. 1743, Sep. 2,	Loyal Judith	108	108	108	...
98. 1743, Sep. 5,	Charlotta	..	..	48	...
99. 1743, Sep. 19,	Lydia	73	72	70	105
100. 1743, Sep. 26,	Rosanna	65	..	57	...
101. 1743, Sep. 30,	Phoenix	..	..	83	...
102. 1743, Sep. 30,	Robert & Alice	..	..	70	...
103. 1743, Oct. 7,	St. Andrew	93	82	82	...
104. 1743, Nov. 10,	Endeavor	..	..	5	...
105. 1744, Oct. 8,	Aurora	..	81	81	...
106. 1744, Oct. 20,	Phoenix	..	..	107	165
107. 1744, Nov. 2,	Friendship	..	..	74	...
108. 1744, Dec. 11,	Carterel	..	..	34	...
109. 1744, Dec. 22,	Muscliffe	..	..	79	...

DATES	SHIPS	LISTS			TOTALS
		A	B	C	
110. 1746, Sep. 27, Ann		..	89	90	...
111. 1746, Oct. 25, Neptune		..	..	67	...
112. 1747, Aug. — Vernon		..	..	55	...
113. 1747, Sep. 24, Lydia		..	..	14	...
114. 1747, Oct. 9, Restauration		..	..	121	...
115. 1747, Oct. 13, Two Brothers		..	95	95	144
116. 1747, Oct. 20, —————		..	44	44	...
117. 1748, Sep. 5, Edinburgh		..	..	127	...
118. 1748, Sep. 7, Hampshire		78	76	76	...
119. 1748, Sep. 7, Mary		25	24	24	...
120. 1748, Sep. 15, Two Brothers		105	99	99	...
121. 1748, Sep. 15, Judith		..	..	52	...
122. 1748, Sep. 16, Patience		122	...	124	...
123. 1748, Oct. 25, Patience & Margaret		71	65	65	106
124. 1749, Aug. 24, Elliot		..	..	84	240
125. 1749, Aug. 30, Crown		...	...	134	476
126. 1749, Sep. 2, Chesterfield		..	..	87	255
127. 1749, Sep. 2, Albany		..	..	105	285
128. 1749, Sep. 9, St. Andrew		..	..	116	400
129. 1749, Sep. 11, Priscilla		..	..	77	293
130. 1749, Sep. 13, Christian		..	..	109	300
131. 1749, Sep. 14, Two Brothers		..	..	109	312
132. 1749, Sep. 15, Edinburgh		..	..	160	360
133. 1749, Sep. 15, Phoenix		..	..	257	550
134. 1749, Sep. 19, Patience		..	..	132	270
135. 1749, Sep. 25, Speedwell		..	..	81	240
136. 1749, Sep. 26, Ranier		..	..	127	277
137. 1749, Sep. 26, Dragon		..	..	117	503
138. 1749, Sep. 27, Isaac		..	..	79	206
139. 1749, Sep. 28, Ann		..	..	96	242
140. 1749, Oct. 2, Jacob		..	..	100	249
141. 1749, Oct. 7, Leslie		..	..	121	400
142. 1749, Oct. 9, Lydia		..	..	151	...
143. 1749, Oct. 17, Dragon		..	..	86	244
144. 1749, Oct. 17, Fane		..	..	120	184
145. 1749, Nov. 9, Good Intent		..	..	26	76
146. 1750, Aug. 11, Patience		..	..	123	266
147. 1750, Aug. 13, Bennet		..	..	94	260
148. 1750, Aug. 13, Edinburgh		..	..	151	314

DATES	SHIPS	LISTS			TOTALS
		A	B	C	
149. 1750, Aug. 15,	Royal Union	..	..	153	500
150. 1750, Aug. 18,	St. Andrew	..	..	102	279
151. 1750, Aug. 21,	Anderson	..	..	87	142
152. 1750, Aug. 24,	Brothers	..	..	91	271
153. 1750, Aug. 28,	Two Brothers	..	..	100	147
154. 1750, Aug. 28,	Phoenix	..	..	222	339
155. 1750, Aug. 31,	Nancy	..	..	91	270
156. 1750, Sep. 12,	Priscilla	..	..	75	210
157. 1750, Sep. 29,	Osgood	..	..	141	486
158. 1750, Oct. 17,	Sally	..	..	25	...
159. 1750, Nov. 3,	Brotherhood	..	..	124	300
160. 1750, Nov. 30,	Sandwich	..	..	95	200
161. 1751, Aug. 25,	Anderson	..	..	97	236
162. 1751, Sep. 5,	Elizabeth	..	..	90	130
163. 1751, Sep. 5,	Shirley	..	..	118	288
164. 1751, Sep. 9,	Patience	..	..	110	255
165. 1751, Sep. 14,	St. Andrew	..	..	97	230
166. 1751, Sep. 14,	Duke of Bedford	..	..	139	260
167. 1751, Sep. 16,	Edinburgh	..	..	158	345
168. 1751, Sep. 16,	Nancy	..	..	76	200
169. 1751, Sep. 16,	Brothers	..	..	94	200
170. 1751, Sep. 21,	Two Brothers	..	..	108	239
171. 1751, Sep. 23,	Neptune (Capt. Wier)	..	..	84	154
172. 1751, Sep. 24,	Neptune (Capt. Mason)	..	..	144	300
173. 1751, Sep. 25,	Phoenix	..	..	182	412
174. 1751, Oct. 4,	Queen of Denmark	..	..	98	251
175. 1751, Oct. 7,	Janet	..	..	99	220
176. 1751, Oct. 16,	Duke of Wirtenberg	..	..	165	406
177. 1752, Sep. 15,	Two Brothers	..	..	101	...
178. 1752, Sep. 19,	Edinburgh	..	..	104	...
179. 1752, Sep. 22,	Brothers	..	..	82	...
180. 1752, Sep. 22,	Halifax	..	..	147	...
181. 1752, Sep. 23,	St. Andrew	..	..	111	...
182. 1752, Sep. 23,	Ann	..	..	71	...
183. 1752, Sep. 26,	Richard & Mary	..	..	89	...
184. 1752, Sep. 27,	Anderson	..	..	82	...
185. 1752, Sep. 27,	President	..	..	73	...
186. 1752, Sep. 27,	Nancy	..	..	85	...
187. 1752, Oct. 4,	Neptune	..	..	166	...

	DATES	SHIPS	LISTS			TOTALS
			A	B	C	
188.	1752, Oct. 10,	Forest	..	..	108	...
189.	1752, Oct. 16,	Ketty	..	..	74	...
190.	1752, Oct. 20,	Duke of Wirtenberg	..	..	141	...
191.	1752, Oct. 23,	Rawley	..	..	136	...
192.	1752, Nov. 2,	Phoenix	..	..	208	...
193.	1752, Nov. 3,	Queen of Denmark	..	..	131	...
194.	1752, Nov. 8,	Louisa	..	..	71	...
195.	1752, Nov. 22,	Phoenix	..	..	150	...
196.	1753, Sep. 8,	St. Michael	62	62	62	...
197.	1753, Sep. 10,	Beulah	88	86	86	...
198.	1753, Sep. 11,	Queen of Denmark	101	77	78	...
199.	1753, Sep. 14,	Edinburgh	...	166	167	...
200.	1753, Sep. 17,	Patience	110	108	108	...
201.	1753, Sep. 17,	Richard & Mary	108	108	108	...
202.	1753, Sep. 19,	Leathley	52	53	52	...
203.	1753, Sep. 24,	Neptune	147	146	146	...
204.	1753, Sep. 24,	Peggy	119	119	119	140
205.	1753, Sep. 26,	Brothers	91	91	91	...
206.	1753, Sep. 26,	Windsor	67	64	64	...
207.	1753, Sep. 28,	Halifax	104	103	104	...
208.	1753, Sep. 28,	Two Brothers	96	96	96	...
209.	1753, Sep. 29,	Rowand	109	109	109	...
210.	1753, Sep. 29,	Good Hope	52	53	53	...
211.	1753, Oct. 2,	Edinburgh	104	104	104	...
212.	1753, Oct. 3,	Louisa	78	77	77	...
213.	1753, Oct. 3,	Eastern Branch	87	86	86	...
214.	1753, Nov. 19,	Friendship	49	49	49	...
215.	1754, Sep. 14,	Nancy	87	87	87	200
216.	1754, Sep. 14,	Barclay	112	110	110	250
217.	1754, Sep. 25,	Adventure	77	76	77	245
218.	1754, Sep. 30,	Richard & Mary	90	89	90	230
219.	1754, Sep. 30,	Brothers	102	99	101	250
220.	1754, Sep. 30,	Edinburgh	159	156	156	...
221.	1754, Sep. 30,	Neptune	142	138	138	400
222.	1754, Oct. 1,	Phoenix	238	238	238	554
223.	1754, Oct. 16,	Peggy	116	107	107	...
224.	1754, Oct. 21,	Friendship	119	...	117	301
225.	1754, Oct. 21,	Bannister	84	...	83	...
226.	1754, Oct. 22,	Henrietta	88	...	72	...

DATES	SHIPS	LISTS			TOTALS
		A	B	C	
227. 1754, Oct. 22,	Halifax	109	...	104	...
228. 1754, Oct. 23,	Good Intent	81	81	81	...
229. 1754, Oct. 23,	Recovery	83	..	..	...
230. 1754, Oct. 26,	Mary & Sarah	90	84	90	...
231. 1754, Nov. 7,	John & Elizabeth	131	130	130	330
232. 1754, Dec. 12,	Neptune	58	56	57	147½
233. 1754, —,	Two Brothers	106	..	..	...
234. 1755, Oct. 7,	Neptune	93	93	93	226
235. 1755, Nov. 1,	Pennsylvania	18	17	17	34
236. 1756, Nov. 10,	Chance	..	..	43	109½
237. 1761, Oct. 21,	Squirrel	..	..	30	...
238. 1763, Oct. 5,	Richmond	..	..	86	162
239. 1763, Nov. 1,	Chance	..	..	92	193
240. 1763, Nov. 25,	Success	..	..	13	36
241. 1763, Nov. 25,	Pallas	..	..	65	196½
242. 1764, Aug. 8,	Chance	..	..	93	208
243. 1764, Sep. 19,	Polly	..	..	59	184
244. 1764, Sep. 20,	Sarah	..	..	102	230
245. 1764, Sep. 26,	Britannia	..	..	111	250
246. 1764, Oct. 3,	King of Prussia	..	..	52	94
247. 1764, Oct. 20,	Richmond	..	..	106	224
248. 1764, Oct. 27,	Hero	..	..	198	500
249. 1764, Nov. 5,	Jeneffer	..	..	91	247
250. 1764, Nov. 5,	Prince of Wales	..	..	69	131
251. 1764, Nov. 10,	Boston	..	..	68	203
252. 1764, Dec. 4,	Tryall	..	..	23	47½
253. 1765, Aug. 24,	Polly	..	..	84	214
254. 1765, Sep. 9,	Chance	..	..	78	216
255. 1765, Sep. 19,	Betsey	..	..	75	...
256. 1765, Sep. 21,	Myrtilla	..	..	33	81
257. 1765, Oct. 7,	Countess of Sussex	..	..	23	50
258. 1766, Sep. 23,	Chance	..	..	105	200
259. 1766, Oct. 13,	Betsey	..	..	84	154
260. 1766, Oct. 15,	Cullodian	..	..	12	...
261. 1766, Oct. 18,	Polly	..	..	53	181
262. 1766, Nov. 4,	Sally	..	..	7	...
263. 1767, Jan. 13,	Juno	..	..	11	36
264. 1767, Oct. 5,	Sally	..	..	116	...
265. 1767, Oct. 6,	Hamilton	..	..	134	302

	DATES	SHIPS	A	B	C	TOTALS
266.	1767, Oct. 26,	Britannia	..	..	39	...
267.	1767, Oct. 29,	Minerva	..	..	90	194
268.	1767, Nov. 4,	Grampus	..	..	7	...
269.	1767, Nov. 10,	Sally	..	..	36	62
270.	1768, Oct. 3,	Pennsylvania Packet	..	..	19	33½
271.	1768, Oct. 10,	Minerva	..	..	108	247
272.	1768, Oct. 26,	Crawford	..	..	86	200
273.	1768, Oct. 26,	Betsey	..	..	112	...
274.	1769, Sep. 1,	Nancy & Sucky	..	..	12	18½
275.	1769, Sep. 29,	London Packet	..	..	15	15
276.	1769, Oct. 13,	Minerva	..	..	93	...
277.	1769, Oct. 24,	Crawford	..	..	19	38
278.	1770, July 27,	Neptune	..	..	8	10
279.	1770, Aug. 29,	Dolphin	..	..	9	16
280.	1770, Sep. 10,	Rose	..	..	7	...
281.	1770, Oct. 1,	Minerva	..	..	88	...
282.	1770, Oct. 3,	Britannia	..	..	6	6
283.	1770, Oct. 29,	Sally	..	..	80	143
284.	1770, Nov. 23,	Crawford	..	..	26	60
285.	1771, June 17,	Pennsylvania Packet	..	..	8	...
286.	1771, July 27,	America	..	..	12	...
287.	1771, Sep. 17,	Minerva	..	..	94	204
288.	1771, Sep. 19,	London Packet	..	..	9	9
289.	1771, Oct. 31,	Recovery	..	..	52	...
290.	1771, Nov. 19,	Tyger	..	..	119	...
291.	1771, Nov. 25,	Crawford	..	..	8	...
292.	1771, Dec. 4,	Betsey	..	..	38	78
293.	1771, Dec. 10,	General Wolfe	..	..	10	...
294.	1772, Feb. 24,	Hope	..	..	23	26
295.	1772, Sep. 30,	Minerva	..	..	39	97
296.	1772, Oct. 16,	Crawford	..	..	105	...
297.	1772, Oct. 19,	Catharine	..	..	18	...
298.	1772, Oct. 19,	Phoebe	..	..	6	...
299.	1772, Nov. 3,	Sally	..	..	53	...
300.	1772, Dec. 3,	Hope	..	..	40	...
301.	1772, Dec. 24,	Morning Star	..	..	44	131
302.	1773, Apr. 30,	Pennsylvania Packet	..	..	22	32
303.	1773, Apr. 30,	Catharine	..	..	19	42
304.	1773, May 31,	Dolphin	..	..	37	58

DATES	SHIPS	LISTS			TOTALS
		A	B	C	
305. 1773, June 4, Carolina		..	..	8	29
306. 1773, Aug. 23, Sally		..	..	115	193
307. 1773, Sep. 18, Britannia		..	..	119	250
308. 1773, Sep. 21, Catharine		..	..	14	...
309. 1773, Sep. 27, Union		..	..	96	247
310. 1773, Oct. 1, Hope		..	..	58	...
311. 1773, Oct. 22, Charming Molly		..	..	60	...
312. 1773, Oct. 25, Crawford		..	..	66	...
313. 1773, Nov. 23, Neptune		..	..	5	...
314. 1773, Nov. 24, Fame		..	..	3	...
315. 1773, Dec. 7, Clementina		..	..	7	...
316. 1773, Dec. 8, Montague		..	..	26	...
317. 1774, June 21, Nancy		..	..	7	...
318. 1774, Aug. 15, Sally		..	..	8	...
319. 1774, Sep. 29, Charming Molly		..	..	14	...
320. 1774, Sep. 30, Union		..	..	132	...
321. 1774, Oct. 29, Patty & Peggy		..	..	12	...
322. 1774, Oct. 31, Sally		..	..	49	...
323. 1775, Jan. 16, Catharine		..	..	7	...
324. 1775, Oct. 9, King of Prussia		..	..	68	...

TOTALS OF SUMMARIES

KINDS OF LISTS	NO. OF SHIPS	PASSENGERS	SIGNERS
Captains' Lists	138	13,760	
Allegiance Lists	138		9,999
Abjuration Lists	314		25,646
Grand totals:	324	65,040*	29,902†

* Estimated on the basis of 5 passengers for every 2 signers. The number of signers was: 26,016.

† This figure is made up of the following items: 25,646 in C lists, 730 in first eight B lists, 3742 additional names in captains' lists, not in B or C lists, 129 additional names in list, printed in appendix I, 15 additional names in B lists, not in C lists, making a grand total of 29,902 different names on the lists.